e-Business & e-Commerce

HOW TO PROGRAM

Deitel & Deitel
Books and Cyber Classrooms
published by
Prentice Hall

Visual Studio® Series
Getting Started with Microsoft® Visual C++™ 6 with an Introduction to MFC
Visual Basic® 6 How to Program
Getting Started with Microsoft® Visual J++® 1.1

How to Program Series
e-Business and e-Commerce How to Program
Internet and World Wide Web How to Program
Java™ How to Program, 3/E
C How to Program, 3/E
C++ How to Program, 3/E
Visual Basic® 6 How to Program

Multimedia Cyber Classroom Series
e-Business and e-Commerce Multimedia Cyber Classroom
Internet and World Wide Web Multimedia Cyber Classroom
Java™ Multimedia Cyber Classroom, 3/E
C & C++ Multimedia Cyber Classroom, 3/E
Visual Basic® 6 Multimedia Cyber Classroom

The Complete Training Course Series
The Complete e-Business and e-Commerce Programming Training Course
The Complete Internet and World Wide Web Programming Training Course
The Complete Java™ Training Course, 3/E
The Complete C++ Training Course, 3/E
The Complete Visual Basic® 6 Training Course

For continuing updates on Prentice Hall and Deitel & Associates, Inc. publications visit the Prentice Hall web site

`http//www.prenhall.com/deitel`

To communicate with the authors, send email to:

`deitel@deitel.com`

For information on corporate on-site seminars and public seminars offered by Deitel & Associates, Inc. worldwide, visit:

`http://www.deitel.com`

e-Business &
e-Commerce
HOW TO PROGRAM

H. M. Deitel
Deitel & Associates, Inc.

P. J. Deitel
Deitel & Associates, Inc.

T. R. Nieto
Deitel & Associates, Inc.

PRENTICE HALL, Upper Saddle River, New Jersey 07458

Library of Congress Cataloging-in-Publication Data
on File

Vice President and Editorial Director: *Marcia Horton*
Acquisitions Editor: *Petra J. Recter*
Assistant Editor: *Sarah Burrows*
Project Manager: *Crissy Statuto*
Editorial Assistant: *Karen Schultz*
Production Editor: *Camille Trentacoste*
Managing Editor: *David A. George*
Executive Managing Editor: *Vince O'Brien*
Chapter Opener and Cover Designer: *Tamara Newnam Cavallo*
Art Director: *Heather Scott*
Marketing Manager: *Jennie Burger*
Manufacturing Buyer: *Pat Brown*
Manufacturing Manager: *Trudy Pisciotti*
Assistant Vice President of Production and Manufacturing: *David W. Riccardi*

 © 2001 by Prentice-Hall, Inc.
Upper Saddle River, New Jersey 07458

Printed in the United States of America

10 9 8 7 6 5 4 3 2 1

ISBN 0-13-028419-X

Prentice-Hall International (UK) Limited, *London*
Prentice-Hall of Australia Pty. Limited, *Sydney*
Prentice-Hall Canada Inc., *Toronto*
Prentice-Hall Hispanoamericana, S.A., *Mexico*
Prentice-Hall of India Private Limited, *New Delhi*
Prentice-Hall of Japan, Inc., *Tokyo*
Pearson Education Asia Pte. Ltd., *Singapore*
Editora Prentice-Hall do Brasil, Ltda., *Rio de Janeiro*

In loving memory of Miriam Zigman.
  Barbara, Harvey, Paul and Abbey Deitel

To Chester Ng
  "Nothing or double."
  Tem R. Nieto

1   1 2 3
2   8 9 10
3   13 - 18
4
5
6
7
8
9
10 Projects

Contents

9 Introduction to HyperText Markup Language 4 (HTML 4)

Illustrations

11   Ultimate Paint

12   Microsoft FrontPage Express

13   JavaScript/JScript: Introduction to Scripting

14   JavaScript/JScript: Control Structures I

26   ASP Case Studies

27   XML (Extensible Markup Language)

28   Case Study: An Online Bookstore

29   Perl 5 and CGI (Common Gateway Interface)

30   Dynamic HTML: Structured Graphics ActiveX Control

31   Dynamic HTML: Path, Sequencer and Sprite ActiveX Controls

32   Multimedia: Audio, Video, Speech Synthesis and Recognition

34   Accessibility

A   HTML Special Characters

B   HTML Colors

C   ASCII Character Set

D   Operator Precedence Charts

Preface

Live in fragments no longer. Only connect.
Edward Morgan Forster

Welcome to the exciting world of e-business and e-commerce. This book is by an old guy and two young guys. The old guy (HMD; Massachusetts Institute of Technology 1967) has been programming and/or teaching programming for 40 years. The two young guys (PJD; MIT 1991 and TRN; MIT 1992) have each been programming and/or teaching programming for 19 years. The old guy programs and teaches from experience; the young guys do so from an inexhaustible reserve of energy. The old guy wants clarity; the young guys want performance. The old guy seeks elegance and beauty; the young guys want results. We got together to produce a book we hope you will find informative, challenging and entertaining.

E-business and e-commerce are evolving rapidly, if not explosively. This creates tremendous challenges for us as authors, for our publisher—Prentice Hall, for instructors, and for students and professional people.

Why We Wrote e-Business and e-Commerce: How to Program

Dr. Harvey M. Deitel taught introductory programming courses in universities for 20 years with an emphasis on developing clearly written, well-designed programs. Much of what is taught in these courses is the basic principles of programming with an emphasis on the effective use of data types, control structures, arrays and functionalization. Our experience has been that students handle the material in this book in about the same manner as they handle it in introductory Pascal or C courses. There is one noticeable difference though: students are highly motivated by the fact that they are learning three leading-edge scripting languages (JavaScript, VBScript and Perl) and a leading-edge programming paradigm (object-based programming) that will be immediately useful to them as they leave the university environment and head into a world of e-business and e-commerce in which the Internet and the World Wide Web have a massive new prominence.

Our goal was clear: produce a textbook for introductory university-level courses in programming and business for students with little or no programming experience, yet offer the depth and the rigorous treatment of theory and practice demanded by traditional, upper-level programming and business courses in order to satisfy professionals' needs. To meet this goal, we produced a comprehensive book that patiently teaches the concepts behind a successful e-business as well as the principles of control structures, object-based programming and various markup languages (HTML, Dynamic HTML and XML) and scripting languages (JavaScript, VBScript and Perl). After mastering the material in this book, students will be well prepared to take advantage of the Internet and the Web as they take upper-level courses and venture into the rapidly changing business world.

e-Business and e-Commerce How to Program is the seventh book in the Deitel/Prentice Hall *How to Program* series. *It is distinguished by its focus on Web-based application development (emphasized in our server-side treatment) and using it to create effective online businesses.*

We have emphasized color throughout the book. The World Wide Web is a colorful, multimedia-intensive medium. It appeals to our visual and audio senses. Someday it may even appeal to our senses of touch, taste and smell as well! We suggested to our publisher, Prentice Hall, that they should publish this book in color. The use of color in this book is crucial to understanding and appreciating scores of the book's programs. From the start, the Web has been a color-intensive medium. We hope it helps you develop more appealing Web-based applications.

Many books about the Web concentrate on developing attractive Web pages. We certainly discuss that subject intensely. But more important, the key focus of this book is really Web-based applications development focussed on building e-businesses. Our audiences want to build real-world, industrial-strength, Web-based e-businesses. These audiences care about good looking Web pages. But they also care about client/server systems, databases, distributed computing, etc. In the world of business, success depends on both marketing and reliability.

Many books about the Web are reference manuals with exhaustive listings of features. That is not our style. We concentrate on creating real applications. We provide the live-code examples on the CD accompanying this book so that you can run the applications and see and hear for yourself the multimedia outputs. One of the most exciting features of this text is an introduction to Macromedia's Flash—a cutting-edge multimedia technology for developing Web-based applications. It allows the user to develop interactive animated movies at a fraction of the size of traditional media file types. A Flash movie can be embedded into a Web site or run as a stand-alone program. You will learn how to make Flash movies with sound and interactive features that can be incorporated into your e-business Web sites.

The Web is an artist's paradise. Your creativity is your only limitation, but the Web contains so many tools and mechanisms to leverage your abilities that even if you are not artistically inclined, you can still create stunning outputs. Our goal is to help you master these tools and mechanisms so that you can maximize your creativity and development capabilities.

We are excited about the enormous range of possibilities the Internet and the Web offer. We performed extensive research for this book and located hundreds of Internet and Web resources (which we provide as live links on the CD-ROM that accompanies this book) to help you learn about building e-businesses. These links include general information, tutorials and demonstrations. Many of the demos are fun to try such as the E*TRADE investing game in which you can win cash prizes for participating in the demo. The resources also point you to lots of free stuff on the Internet.

This book is appropriate for students and professional people who wish to start their own e-businesses. Many of the Internet and Web resources we include point you to turnkey solutions (some for a fee and some free) for creating e-businesses. You will also be able to use the programming technologies presented here to create e-businesses yourself (you will also need to connect with a bank and use an industrial-strength database system). Please read the tour of the book in Chapter 1 to familiarize yourself with the technologies we present for building real e-business and e-commerce applications.

We have worked hard to create hundreds of useful live-code examples to help you master Internet and Web programming quickly and effectively. All of the code examples are on the accompanying disk and are available for free download from our Web sites:

```
www.deitel.com
www.prenhall.com/deitel
```

We cover in depth Microsoft's Dynamic HTML as a means of adding "dynamic content" to World-Wide-Web pages. Instead of creating Web pages with only text and static graphics, we use Dynamic HTML to make Web pages "come alive" with audios, videos, animations, interactivity and three-dimensional imaging. Dynamic HTML's features are precisely what businesses and organizations need to meet today's information processing requirements.

Teaching Approach

E-Business and e-Commerce How to Program contains a rich collection of examples, exercises, and projects drawn from many fields to provide the student with a chance to solve interesting real-world problems. The book concentrates on the principles of good software engineering and stresses program clarity. We avoid arcane terminology and syntax specifications in favor of teaching by example. The book is written by educators who spend most of their time writing about, and teaching, edge-of-the-practice programming topics in industry classrooms worldwide for Deitel & Associates, Inc. The text emphasizes good pedagogy.

Live-Code Teaching Approach

The book is loaded with hundreds of live-code examples. This is the focus of the way we teach and write about programming, and the focus of each of our multimedia *Cyber Classrooms* as well. Each new concept is presented in the context of a complete, working program immediately followed by one or more windows showing the program's input/output dialog. We call this style of teaching and writing our *live-code approach*. *We use programming languages to teach programming languages.* Reading these programs is much like entering and running them on a computer.

E-Business and e-Commerce How to Program first explains cutting-edge technologies and business models that are changing the way commerce is conducted, then shows how to create e-business Web sites starting with HTML programming, then rapidly proceeding to programming in JavaScript, Microsoft's Dynamic HTML, VBScript, Perl and XML. Students really want to "cut to the chase." There is great stuff to be done in all these languages, so let's get right to it! Web programming is not trivial by any means, but it's fun and students can see immediate results. Students can get graphical, animated, multimedia-based, audio-intensive, database-intensive, network-based programs running quickly through "reusable components." They can implement impressive projects. They can be much more creative and productive in a one- or two-semester course than is possible in introductory courses taught in conventional programming languages such as C, C++, and even Visual Basic or Java.

World Wide Web Access
All of the code for *e-Business and e-Commerce How to Program* (and our other publications) is on the Internet free for download at the Deitel & Associates, Inc. Web site

www.deitel.com

Please download all the code then run each program as you read the text. Make changes to the code examples and immediately see the effects of those changes. It's a great way to learn programming. [*Note:* You must respect the fact that this is copyrighted material. Feel free to use it as you study, but you may not republish any portion of it in any form without explicit permission from Prentice Hall and the authors.]

Objectives
Each chapter begins with a statement of *Objectives.* This tells students what to expect and gives them an opportunity, after reading the chapter, to determine if they have met these objectives. It is a confidence builder and a source of positive reinforcement.

Quotations
The learning objectives are followed by quotations. Some are humorous, some are philosophical, and some offer interesting insights. Our students enjoy relating the quotations to the chapter material. Many of the quotations are worth a "second look" *after* you read each chapter.

Outline
The chapter *Outline* helps students approach the material in top-down fashion. This, too, helps students anticipate what is to come and set a comfortable and effective learning pace.

14120 Lines of Code in 258 Example Web Pages (with Program Outputs)
We present features in the context of complete, working Web pages. This is the focus of our teaching and our writing. We call it our "live-code" approach. Each Web document is followed by the outputs produced when the document is rendered in a Web browser (We use Microsoft's Internet Explorer 5) and its scripts are executed. This enables students to confirm that the Web pages are rendered as expected. Reading the book carefully is much like entering and running these programs on a computer. The programs range from just a few lines of code to substantial examples with several hundred lines of code. Students should download all the code for the book from our Web site, and run each program while studying that program in the text. The Web documents are available on the CD accompanying this book and at **www.deitel.com**.

554 Illustrations/Figures
An abundance of charts, line drawings and program outputs is included. The discussion of control structures, for example, features carefully drawn flowcharts. [Note: We do not teach flowcharting as a program development tool, but we do use a brief, flowchart-oriented presentation to specify the precise operation of JavaScript's control structures.]

355 Programming Tips

We have included programming tips to help students focus on important aspects of program development. We highlight hundreds of these tips in the form of *Good Programming Practices*, *Common Programming Errors*, *Testing and Debugging Tips*, *Performance Tips*, *Portability Tips*, *Software Engineering Observations* and *Look-and-Feel Observations*. These tips and practices represent the best we have gleaned from a total of almost eight decades of programming and teaching experience. One of our students—a mathematics major—told us that she feels this approach is like the highlighting of axioms, theorems and corollaries in mathematics books; it provides a foundation on which to build good software.

83 Good Programming Practices

Good Programming Practices are highlighted in the text. They call the students attention to techniques that help produce better programs. When we teach introductory courses to non-programmers, we state that the "buzzword" of each course is "clarity," and we tell the students that we will highlight (in these Good Programming Practices) techniques for writing programs that are clearer, more understandable and more maintainable.

95 Common Programming Errors

Students learning a language—especially in their first programming course—tend to make certain kinds of errors frequently. Focusing on these Common Programming Errors helps students avoid making the same errors. It also helps reduce long lines outside instructors' offices during office hours!

28 Performance Tips

In our experience, teaching students to write clear and understandable programs is by far the most important goal for a first programming course. But students want to write the programs that run the fastest, use the least memory, require the smallest number of keystrokes, or dazzle in other nifty ways. Students really care about performance. They want to know what they can do to "turbo charge" their programs. So we have include Performance Tips to highlight opportunities for improving program performance.

23 Portability Tips

Software development is a complex and expensive activity. Organizations that develop software must often produce versions customized to a variety of computers and operating systems. So there is a strong emphasis today on portability, i.e., on producing software that will run on a variety of computer systems with few, if any, changes. Achieving portability requires careful and cautious design. There are many pitfalls. We include numerous Portability Tips to help students write portable code.

79 Software Engineering Observations

The Software Engineering Observations highlight techniques, architectural issues and design issues, etc. that affect the architecture and construction of software systems, especially large-scale systems. Much of what the student learns here will be useful in upper-level courses and in industry as the student begins to work with large, complex real-world systems.

29 Testing and Debugging Tips

This "tip type" may be misnamed. When we first decided to incorporate Testing and Debugging Tips, we thought these tips would be suggestions for testing programs to expose bugs and suggestions for removing those bugs. In fact, most of these tips tend to be observations about capabilities and features that prevent bugs from getting into programs in the first place.

18 Look-and-Feel Observations

We provide Look-and-Feel Observations to highlight graphical user interface (GUI) conventions. These observations help students design their own graphical user interfaces to conform with industry norms.

Summary (1420 Summary bullets)

Each chapter ends with additional pedagogical devices. We present a thorough, bullet-list-style *Summary* of the chapter. On average, there are 42 summary bullets per chapter. This helps the students review and reinforce key concepts.

Terminology (2751 Terms)

We include in a *Terminology* section an alphabetized list of the important terms defined in the chapter—again, further reinforcement. On average, there are 81 terms per chapter.

607 Self-Review Exercises and Answers (Count Includes Separate Parts)

Extensive self-review exercises and answers are included for self-study. This gives the student a chance to build confidence with the material and prepare for the regular exercises. Students should attempt all the self-review exercises and check their answers.

658 Exercises (Solutions in Instructor's Manual; Count Includes Separate Parts)

Each chapter concludes with a substantial set of exercises including simple recall of important terminology and concepts; writing individual statements; writing small portions of Web pages and scripts; writing complete Web pages and Web-based e-businesses; and writing major term projects. The large number of exercises across a wide variety of areas enables instructors to tailor their courses to the unique needs of their audiences and to vary course assignments each semester. Instructors can use these exercises to form homework assignments, short quizzes and major examinations. The solutions for most of the exercises are included in the *Instructor's Manual* and on the disks **available only to instructors** through their Prentice-Hall representatives. **[NOTE: Please do not write to us requesting the instructor's manual. Distribution of this publication is strictly limited to college professors teaching from the book. Instructors may obtain the solutions manual only from their regular Prentice Hall representatives**. **We regret that we cannot provide the solutions to professionals**.] Solutions to approximately half of the exercises are included on the *e-Business and e-Commerce Programming Multimedia Cyber Classroom* CD (available in bookstores and computer stores; please see the last few pages of this book or visit our Web site at **www.deitel.com** for ordering instructions).

Approximately 6000 Index Entries (with approximately 8100 Page References)

We have included an extensive *Index* at the back of the book. This helps the student find any term or concept by keyword. The *Index* is useful to people reading the book for the first time and is especially useful to practicing programmers who use the book as a reference. The terms in the *Terminology* sections generally appear in the *Index* (along with many more index items from each chapter). Students can use the *Index* in conjunction with the *Terminology* sections to be sure they have covered the key material of each chapter.

"Double Indexing" of All Live-Code Examples and Exercises

e-Business and e-Commerce How to Program has 258 live-code examples and 658 exercises (including parts). Many of the exercises are challenging problems or projects requiring substantial effort. We have "double indexed" each of the live-code examples and most of the more challenging projects. For every source-code program in the book, we took the figure caption and indexed it both alphabetically and as a subindex item under "Examples." This makes it easier to find examples using particular features. The more substantial exercises are indexed both alphabetically and as subindex items under "Exercises."

Bibliography
An extensive bibliography of books, articles and online documentation is included to encourage further reading.

Software Included with e-Business and e-Commerce How to Program

The CD-ROM at the end of this book contains a variety of software, including Microsoft Internet Explorer 5, Ultimate Paint, the W3C Amaya 3.1 Web browser, AspTear 1.0, Microsoft Agent, CUESoft EXml Editor and Jumbo Browser v0.1. The CD also contains the book's code examples and an HTML Web page with links to the Deitel & Associates, Inc. Web site, the Prentice Hall Web site and the many Web sites listed in the Web resources sections of the chapters. If you have access to the Internet, the Web page on the CD can be loaded into your World Wide Web browser to give you quick access to all the resources.

If you have any questions about using this software, please read the introductory documentation on the CD-ROM. Additional information is available at our Web site: **www.deitel.com**. We do not provide technical support for the software application programs. However, if you have any technical questions about the installation of the CD, please email **media.support@pearsoned.com**. They will respond promptly.

e-Business and e-Commerce Programming Multimedia Cyber Classroom and The Complete e-Business and e-Commerce Programming Training Course

We have prepared an optional interactive, CD-ROM-based, software version of *e-Business and e-Commerce How to Program* called the *e-Business and e-Commerce Programming Multimedia Cyber Classroom*. It is loaded with features for learning and reference. The *Cyber Classroom* is wrapped with the textbook at a discount in *The Complete e-Business and e-Commerce Programming Training Course*. If you already have the book and would like to purchase the *e-Business and e-Commerce Programming Multimedia Cyber Classroom* separately, please call 1-800-811-0912 and ask for ISBN# 0130895407.

The CD has an introduction with the authors overviewing the *Cyber Classroom*'s features. The 258 live-code example Web documents in the textbook truly "come alive" in the *Cyber Classroom*. If you are viewing a document and want to execute it, simply click on the lightning bolt icon and the document will be loaded into a Web browser and rendered. You will immediately see—and hear for the audio-based multimedia Web pages—the program's outputs. If you want to modify a document and see and hear the effects of your changes, simply click the floppy-disk icon that causes the source code to be "lifted off" the CD and "dropped into" one of your own directories so that you can edit the document and try out your new version. Click the speaker icon for an audio that talks about the document and "walks you through" the code.

The *Cyber Classroom* also provides navigational aids including extensive hyperlinking. The *Cyber Classroom* remembers in a "history list" recent sections you have visited and allows you to move forward or backward in that history list. The thousands of index entries are hyperlinked to their text occurrences. You can key in a term using the "find" feature and the *Cyber Classroom* will locate occurrences of that term throughout the text. The *Table of Contents* entries are "hot," so clicking a chapter name takes you to that chapter.

Students like the hundreds of solved problems from the textbook that are included with the *Cyber Classroom*. Studying and running these extra programs is a nice way for students to enhance their learning experience.

Students and professional users of our *Cyber Classrooms* tell us they like the interactivity and that the *Cyber Classroom* is an effective reference because of the extensive hyperlinking and other navigational features. We recently had an e-mail from a person who said that he lives "in the boonies" and cannot take a live course at a university, so the *Cyber Classroom* was a good solution to his educational needs.

Professors tell us that their students enjoy using the *Cyber Classroom*, spend more time on the course and master more of the material than in textbook-only courses. Also, the *Cyber Classroom* helps shrink lines outside professors' offices during office hours. We have also published the *C++ Multimedia Cyber Classroom (3/e)*, the *Visual Basic 6 Multimedia Cyber Classroom, the Java 2 Multimedia Cyber Classroom 3/e* and *the Internet and World Wide Web Programming Multimedia Cyber Classroom.*

Acknowledgments

One of the great pleasures of writing a textbook is acknowledging the efforts of the many people whose names may not appear on the cover, but whose hard work, cooperation, friendship and understanding were crucial to the production of the book.

Many other people at Deitel & Associates, Inc. devoted long hours to this book.

- Barbara Deitel managed the preparation of the manuscript, coordinated the production of the book with Prentice Hall and spent long hours researching the quotations at the beginning of each chapter. She did all this in parallel with handling her extensive financial and administrative responsibilities at Deitel & Associates, Inc., including servicing as Chief Financial Officer.

- Abbey Deitel, a graduate of Carnegie Mellon University's industrial management program, and President of Deitel & Associates, Inc., co-authored Chapter 7, "Computer Security."

- Kate Steinbuhler, a graduate of Boston College with a major in English and Communications, and Editorial Director of Deitel & Associates, Inc., wrote Chapter 6, co-authored Chapter 5 and edited Chapters 3, 4, 7 and 8. She would like to acknowledge Dale Herbeck, Chair and Associate Professor of Communication at Boston College, who provided input for Chapter 6.

- Peter Brandano, a graduate of Boston College with a major in computer science, wrote Chapters 33, 34 and the streaming media portion of Chapter 32. Peter is our Director of Multimedia Development.

- Paul Brandano, a graduate of Boston College with a major in marketing, and Director of Marketing and Corporate Training Programs at Deitel & Associates, Inc., wrote Chapter 3 and contributed to Chapters 4–8.

- Sean Santry, a computer science and philosophy graduate of Boston College, and Director of Software Development at Deitel & Associates, Inc., co-authored Chapter 8. Sean is a lead developer with Paul Deitel on our forthcoming book, *Advanced Java How to Program.*

- Christine Connolley, a graduate of the Boston College School of Management with concentrations in finance and marketing, wrote Chapter 4 and contributed to Chapters 3 and 5–8. Christy is now Director of Public Relations for Deitel & Associates, Inc.

- Matt Kowalewski, a graduate of Bentley college, co-authored Chapters 8 and 33, verified Chapter 34 and contributed to Chapters 3 through 7.

The Deitel & Associates, Inc. *College Internship Program* offers a limited number of salaried positions to Boston-area college students majoring in Computer Science, Information Technology, Marketing or English. Students work at our corporate headquarters in Sudbury, Massachusetts full-time in the summers and/or part-time during the academic year. Full-time positions are available to college graduates. For more information about this competitive program, please contact Abbey Deitel at **deitel@deitel.com** and check our Web site, **www.deitel.com**. Deitel & Associates, Inc. student interns who worked on this book include:

- Neil Agarwal, a Harvard student majoring in Mathematics, co-authored Chapter 7.

- Rudolf Faust, a freshman at Stanford University, edited all the chapters and the Preface, and wrote features for Chapters 1, 5 and 6.

- Carlo Garcia, a senior majoring in computer science at Boston University, helped develop Chapters 11, 25 and 26. He also wrote a section for Chapter 34.

- Justin Gordon, a junior majoring in economics and computer science at Brandeis University, helped develop Ch. 29; edited "Web Server Installation" and edited "ActiveState Perl Installation."

- Joshua Gould, a senior majoring in computer science at Clark University, verified Chapters 9 and 10 for technical accuracy.

- Hani Hamandi, a second-year graduate student in computer science at Boston University, helped develop Chapters 25 and 26, and implemented the case studies in Chapter 26.

- Jaimee Lederman, an economics graduate of Brown University, co-authored Chapter 5.

- Andrew Jones, a senior majoring in Engineering at Dartmouth College, edited Chapter 29.

- Melissa Jordan, a senior majoring in graphic design at Boston University, helped develop Chapter 11 and created artwork throughout the book.

- Audrey Lee, a junior majoring in mathematics and computer science at Wellesley College, wrote a section of Chapter 27, contributed to Chapter 32 and verified Chapter 2 for technical accuracy.

- Ted Lin, a computer science major at Carnegie Mellon University, helped develop, edit, and refine Chapters 25 through 28. He implemented the online bookstore case study in Chapter 28. He also verified Chapters 13 through 23, 30 and 31 for technical accuracy.

- Jeff Listfield, a junior majoring in computer science at Harvard University, helped develop Chapter 29 in which he implemented the shopping-cart application. He also edited the appendix, "Setting up an ODBC Data Source Name."

- David McPhie, a physics graduate of Harvard College and a first-year student at Harvard Law School, co-authored Chapter 29.

- Blake Perdue, a junior majoring in computer science at Vanderbilt University, extensively edited Chapters 25 through 27.

- Jason Rosenfeld, a junior majoring in computer science at Northwestern University, extensively edited Chapters 33 and 34.

- Praveen Sadhu, a first-year graduate student in computer systems engineering at Northeastern University, helped develop Chapter 27.

- Jeremy Shelpler, while a senior at Bentley College, did initial development work on the Chapter 26 shopping-cart application.

- Lauren Trees, a senior majoring in English at Brown University, edited Chapters 3 through 8.

- Ben Wiedermann, a senior majoring in computer science at Boston University, edited Chapters 25 through 27.

We would also like to thank our high-school interns. Fletcher Bowland, a senior at Lincoln-Sudbury Regional High School, wrote exercises and questions for Chapter 33 and verified Chapter 24. Gary Grinev, a senior at Framingham High School, wrote exercises for Chapters 33 and 34.

We are fortunate to have been able to work on this project with the talented and dedicated team of publishing professionals at Prentice Hall. We especially appreciate the extraordinary efforts of our computer science editor, Petra Recter, our project manager, Crissy Statuto, our assistant editor, Sarah Burrows, and their boss—our mentor in publishing—Marcia Horton, Editor-in-Chief of Prentice-Hall's Engineering and Computer Science Division. Vince O'Brien and Camille Trentacoste did a marvelous job managing production.

The *e-Business and e-Commerce Programming Multimedia Cyber Classroom* was developed in parallel with *e-Business and e-Commerce How to Program*. We sincerely appreciate the "new media" insight, savvy and technical expertise of our multimedia, computer-based training and Web-based training editors, Mark Taub and Karen McLean. They did a remarkable job bringing the *e-Business and e-Commerce Programming Multimedia Cyber Classroom* to publication under a tight schedule.

We owe special thanks to the creativity of Tamara Newnam Cavallo (**smart_art@earthlink.net**) who did the art work for our programming tips icons and the cover. She created the delightful bug creature who shares with you the book's programming tips.

We wish to acknowledge the efforts of our reviewers and to give a special note of thanks to Crissy Statuto of Prentice Hall who managed this extraordinary review effort:

Adam Miller (CEO, Kore)
Carl Burnham (Web Director, Southpoint.com)

Carmen Schwarting (DePaul University)

Dan Lynch (Lynch Enterprises, LLC)

Dan McCracken (CUNY)

Daniel Dardailler (WAI team, W3C)

Devan Shepherd (St. Paul Technical College)

Doron Haendle (E-Commerce Manager, First Data Merchant Services)

Greg Wood (Canisius College)

Ian Jacobs (WAI team, W3C)

Ian Stallings (Software Engineer, Olympus Group)

Jasmine Merced (Tintagel Net Solutions Group)

Jennifer Baker (Pyramid Research)

Jeremy Kurtz (Stark Technical Institute)

Jim Condon (CEO, Cybercash)

John Varghese (University of Rochester)

Jonathan Hazelwood (Send.com)

Joseph Ladanyi (Megalux LTD)

Judy Brewer (Director, Web Accessibility Initiative, W3C)

Julie Mehan (Information and Infrastructure Technologies, Inc.)

Ken Cox (Senior Technical Advisor, Nortel Networks)

Lynn Kyle (author, "Essential Flash 4 for Web Professionals")

Martin Bryan (The SGML Centre)

Michel Biezunski (Infoloom)

Mike Brown (XML and SGML Services)

Mike Shaffer (VP Development SportsStandings, Inc.)

Mohan Menon (Director of e-Commerce, University of South Alabama)

Orest Saj (Okina Consulting)

Rachel Collett (Peregrine Publishers)

Richard Yalch (University of Washington)

Rick Larowe (Baltimore Technologies)

Rob Kolstad (Program Manager, SANS Institute)

Shenzao Fu (University of San Francisco)

Simon Johnson, SecuritySearch.net

Simon North (Synopsys)

Steve Burnett (RSA Security)

Steve Mendoca (Compaq)

Steve Potter (Information Control Corporation)

Steve Smith (Senior Consultant, Software Architects)

Wendy Chisholm (WAI team, W3C)

William Conroy (Bank of America)

Under a tight time schedule, these reviewers scrutinized the text and made countless suggestions for improving the accuracy and completeness of the presentation.

We would sincerely appreciate your comments, criticisms, corrections and suggestions for improving the text. Please address all correspondence to our email address:

`deitel@deitel.com`

We will respond immediately. Well, that's it for now. Welcome to the exciting world of e-business and e-commerce programming. We hope you enjoy this look at leading-edge computer applications development. Our best wishes to you.

Dr. Harvey M. Deitel
Paul J. Deitel
Tem R. Nieto

About the Authors

Dr. Harvey M. Deitel, CEO of Deitel & Associates, Inc., has 40 years experience in the computing field including extensive industry and academic experience. He is one of the world's leading computer science instructors and seminar presenters. Dr. Deitel earned B.S. and M.S. degrees from the Massachusetts Institute of Technology and a Ph.D. from Boston University. He worked on the pioneering virtual memory operating systems projects at IBM and MIT that developed techniques widely implemented today in systems like UNIX, Linux and Windows NT. He has 20 years of college teaching experience including earning tenure and serving as the Chairman of the Computer Science Department at Boston College before founding Deitel & Associates, Inc. with Paul J. Deitel. He is author or co-author of several dozen books and multimedia packages and is currently writing many more. With translations published in Japanese, Russian, Spanish, Elementary Chinese, Advanced Chinese, Korean, French, Polish and Portuguese, Dr. Deitel's texts have earned international recognition. Dr. Deitel has delivered professional seminars internationally to major corporations, government organizations and various branches of the military.

Paul J. Deitel, Executive Vice President of Deitel & Associates, Inc., is a graduate of the Massachusetts Institute of Technology's Sloan School of Management where he studied Information Technology. Through Deitel & Associates, Inc. he has delivered Java, C, C++, Internet and World Wide Web courses for industry clients including Compaq, Sun Microsystems, White Sands Missile Range, Rogue Wave Software, Computervision, Stratus, Fidelity, Cambridge Technology Partners, Open Environment Corporation, One Wave, Hyperion Software, Lucent Technologies, Adra Systems, Entergy, CableData Systems, NASA at the Kennedy Space Center, the National Severe Storm Laboratory, IBM and many other organizations. He has lectured on C++ and Java for the Boston Chapter of the Association for Computing Machinery, and has taught satellite-based Java courses through a cooperative venture of Deitel & Associates, Inc., Prentice Hall and the Technology Education Network. He and his father, Dr. Harvey M. Deitel, are the world's best-selling Computer Science textbook authors.

Tem R. Nieto, Director of Product Development with Deitel & Associates, Inc., is a graduate of the Massachusetts Institute of Technology where he studied engineering and computing. Through Deitel & Associates, Inc. he has delivered courses for industry clients including Sun Microsystems, Digital, Compaq, EMC, Stratus, Fidelity, Art Technology, Progress Software, Toys "R" Us, Operational Support Facility of the National Oceanographic and Atmospheric Administration, Jet Propulsion Laboratory, Nynex, Motorola, Federal Reserve Bank of Chicago, Banyan, Schlumberger, University of Notre Dame, NASA, various military installations and many others. He has co-authored several books and multimedia packages with the Deitels and has contributed to virtually every Deitel & Associates, Inc. publication.

The Deitels are co-authors of the best-selling introductory college computer-science programming language textbooks, *C How to Program: Third Edition*, *C++ How to Program: Third Edition* and *Java How to Program: Third Edition*. With Tem R. Nieto, they have co-authored *Visual Basic 6 How to Program*, *Internet and World Wide Web How to Program* and *e-Business and e-Commerce How to Program*. The Deitels are also co-authors of the *C & C++ Multimedia Cyber Classroom: Third Edition*—Prentice Hall's first multimedia-based textbook and the *Java 2 Multimedia Cyber Classroom: Third Edition*. Tem Nieto joined them as a co-author on the *Visual Basic 6 Multimedia Cyber Classroom* (with Tem R. Nieto), the *Internet and World Wide Web Programming Multimedia Cyber Classroom* and the *e-Business and e-Commerce Programming Multimedia Cyber Classroom*. The Deitels are also co-authors of *The Complete C++ Training Course: Third Edition*, The *Complete Visual Basic 6 Training Course* (with Tem R. Nieto), *The Complete Java 2 Training Course: Third Edition*, *The Complete Internet and World Wide Web Programming Training Course* and *The Complete e-Business and e-Commerce Programming Training Course* (with Tem R. Nieto)—these products each contain the corresponding *How to Program Series* textbook and the corresponding *Multimedia Cyber Classroom*.

About Deitel & Associates, Inc.

Deitel & Associates, Inc. is an internationally recognized corporate training and publishing organization specializing in programming languages, Internet/World Wide Web technology and object technology education. Deitel & Associates, Inc. is a member of the World Wide Web Consortium. The company provides courses on Java, C++, Visual Basic, C, Perl, Python, XML, Internet and World Wide Web programming, e-business and e-commerce programming and Object Technology. The principals of Deitel & Associates, Inc. are Dr. Harvey M. Deitel and Paul J. Deitel. The company's clients include many of the world's largest computer companies, government agencies, branches of the military and business organizations. Through its publishing partnership with Prentice Hall, Deitel & Associates, Inc. publishes leading-edge programming textbooks, professional books, interactive CD-ROM-based multimedia *Cyber Classrooms*, satellite courses and Web-based training courses. Deitel & Associates, Inc. and the authors can be reached via email at

`deitel@deitel.com`

To learn more about Deitel & Associates, Inc., its publications, and its worldwide corporate on-site curriculum, see the last few pages of this book and visit:

`www.deitel.com`

Deitel & Associates, Inc. has competitive opportunities in its College Internship Program for students in the Boston area. For information, please contact Abbey Deitel at `deitel@deitel.com`.

Individuals wishing to purchase Deitel books, Cyber Classrooms and Web-based training courses can do so through

`www.deitel.com`

Bulk orders by corporations and academic institutions should be placed directly with Prentice Hall—see the last few pages of this book for worldwide ordering details.

Introduction to Computers, the Internet and the Web

Objectives

- To understand basic computer science concepts.
- To become familiar with different types of programming languages.
- To understand the evolution of the Internet and Web.
- To become familiar with the paradigms of e-business and e-commerce
- To understand JavaScript, VBScript and Perl's roles in developing distributed client/server applications.
- To preview the remaining chapters of the book.

Our life is frittered away by detail … Simplify, simplify.
Henry Thoreau

High thoughts must have high language.
Aristophanes

The chief merit of language is clearness.
Galen

My object all sublime
I shall achieve in time.
W. S. Gilbert

He had a wonderful talent for packing thought close, and rendering it portable.
Thomas Babington Macaulay

Egad, I think the interpreter is the hardest to be understood of the two!
Richard Brinsley Sheridan

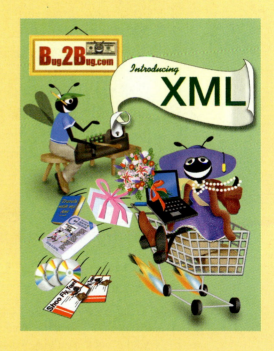

Outline

1.1 Introduction

Welcome to the world of e-business and e-commerce! We have worked hard to create what we hope will be an informative, entertaining and challenging learning experience for you. As you read this book, you may want to refer to our Web site

`www.deitel.com`

for updates and additional information on each subject.

The technologies you will learn in this book are fun to use for novices while simultaneously being appropriate for experienced professionals building substantial information systems. *e-Business and e-Commerce How to Program* is designed to be an effective learning tool for each of these audiences. How can one book appeal to both groups? The answer is that the common core of the book emphasizes achieving program *clarity* through the proven techniques of *structured programming* and *object-based programming*. Nonprogrammers will learn programming the right way from the beginning. We have attempted to write in a clear and straightforward manner. The book is abundantly illustrated.

This book will challenge you for several reasons. Your peers over the last few years probably learned C, C++ or Java™ as their first computer programming language. Indeed, the Advanced Placement Examination that is administered to high-school students wishing to earn college credit in computer programming is now based on C++ (switched recently from Pascal, a programming language widely used at the college level for two decades). Until recently, students in introductory programming courses learned only the programming methodology called *structured programming*. You will learn *both* structured programming and the exciting newer methodology called *object-based programming*. After this you will be well-prepared to study the C++ and Java programming languages and learn the even more powerful programming methodology of *object-oriented programming*. We believe that object orientation is the key programming methodology as we begin the new millennium. You will work with many *objects* in this course.

Perhaps most important, the book presents hundreds of working programs and shows the outputs produced when those programs are run on a computer. We present all programming concepts in the context of complete working programs. We call this the *live-code approach*. These examples are available from three locations—they are on the CD-ROM inside the back cover of this book, they may be downloaded from our Web site **www.deitel.com** and they are available on our interactive CD-ROM product, the *e-Business and e-Commerce Programming Multimedia Cyber Classroom*. The *Cyber Classroom*'s features and ordering information appear in the last few pages of this book. The *Cyber Classroom* also contains answers to approximately half the exercises in this book, including short answers, small programs and many full projects. If you purchased our boxed product *The Complete e-Business and e-Commerce Programming Training Course*, you already have the *Cyber Classroom*.

1.2 The Future of Computing

Most people are familiar with the exciting things computers do. Using this textbook, you will learn how to command computers to do those things. It is *software* (i.e., the instructions you write to command the computer to perform *actions* and make *decisions*) that controls computers (often referred to as *hardware*). Computer use is increasing in almost every field of endeavor. In an era of steadily rising costs, computing costs have been decreasing dramatically because of the rapid developments in both hardware and software technology. Computers that might have filled large rooms and cost millions of dollars just two decades ago can now be inscribed on the surfaces of silicon chips smaller than a fingernail, costing perhaps a few dollars each. Ironically, silicon is one of the most abundant materials on earth—it is an ingredient in common sand. Silicon chip technology has made computing so economical that hundreds of millions of general-purpose computers are in use worldwide, helping people in business, industry, government, and in their personal lives. That number could easily double in a few years.

Advances in hardware and software have led to the explosion of the Internet and World Wide Web. Propelling the wave of innovation is a constant demand for new and improved technology. People want to transmit pictures and they want those pictures to be in color. They want to transmit voices, sounds and audio clips. They want to transmit full-motion color video. And at some point, they will insist on three-dimensional, moving-image transmission. Our current flat, two-dimensional televisions will eventually be replaced with three-dimensional versions that turn our living rooms into "theaters-in-the-round" or sports stadiums. Our business offices will enable video conferencing among colleagues half a world apart as if they were sitting around one conference table. Consumers who want to buy products from electronic storefronts will be able to see perfect 3D images of them beforehand. The possibilities are intriguing and the Internet is sure to play a key role in making many of these possibilities become reality.

There have been predictions that the Internet will eventually replace the telephone system. Why stop there? It could also replace radio and television as we know them today. It's not hard to imagine the Internet and the World Wide Web replacing newspapers with completely electronic news media. Many newspapers and magazines already offer Web-based versions, some fee based and some free. Over 95 percent of printed material is currently not online, but in the future it may be. The e-book, an electronic text that is encryption-protected by the publisher, is on the rise and could well supplant the paper book. With a chemistry e-book, students could watch animations of chemical reactions, and a history e-book could be updated to include current events. Increased bandwidth is making it possible to stream audio and video over the Web. Companies and even individuals already run their own Web-based radio and television stations. Just a few decades ago, there were only a few television stations. Today, standard cable boxes accommodate about 100 stations. In a few more years, we will have access to thousands of stations broadcasting over the Web worldwide. This textbook you are reading may someday appear in a museum alongside radios, TVs and newspapers in an "early media of ancient civilization" exhibit.

The Internet has enabled people worldwide to communicate easily with one another. Online communities have been, are being and will be formed to bring together people of similar backgrounds, lifestyles, professions and interests. These communities provide resources for their members as well as forums in which their members can meet and chat. Professionals such as lawyers, doctors and scientists have online communities that offer a wealth of readily accessible information and an ideal environment for exchanging ideas. The number of online communities is proliferating and will continue to do so.

People with disabilities form one of the largest online communities, as the Internet and Web have enabled them to take advantage of computing and communication to perform tasks of which they were not previously able. Things that were once difficult for people with disabilities, such as buying goods at a store, will be made easy by e-commerce technologies. However, at the time of this writing, 95 to 99 percent of all Web sites are inaccessible to the visually, hearing or mobility impaired. In this regard, the World Wide Web Consortium (W3C) is pursuing its *Web Accessibility Initiative*. Information about the Web Accessibility Initiative is available at **www.w3.org/WAI**.

To enable people with disabilities to author their own Web sites, the WAI is instituting the *ATAG (Authoring Tools Accessibility Guidelines)*, which contains specifications for software developers to follow. The goal of the WAI is to transform the Web into a medium in which all people are able to access and use the technology and information available. In the future, their aim will undoubtedly be achieved.

1.3 e-Business and e-Commerce

The Internet and World Wide Web are revolutionizing conventional business models and in some cases producing new ones. For instance, before the World Wide Web, most people did not participate in auctions. With the advent of eBay and other online auction sites, however, people are auctioning off everything from computer games to gardening tools. Another groundbreaking innovator is Priceline.com, which has enjoyed enormous success with a model that lets the customer name their price for a certain item.

To figure out just how fast the Internet economy is growing, the Center for Research in Electronic Commerce at the University of Texas at Austin conducted a study of over 2000 Internet companies. It found explosive growth from $322 billion in 1998 to $524 billion in 1999, a 68 percent increase. The fastest growing sector was e-commerce, which skyrocketed by 72 percent from $99.8 billion to $171.5 billion. According to researchers' estimates, over 50,000 companies make some or all of their money online. By 2002, over a trillion dollars in revenue will be generated through the Internet.

E-business has become standard operating procedure for the vast majority of companies. Setting up and running an e-business, especially one that processes a large number of transactions, requires technical, marketing and advertising expertise. Customers want access to products and services on a 24-by-7 basis, and the easiest way to provide that is to move operations online. The businesses that provide the most reliable, most functional, most user-friendly and fastest services will be the ones that succeed.

Banks are moving all of their operations online, as it becomes clear that the Web, unconstrained by geographic boundaries, is a more efficient vehicle for their services and allows them to work on a truly global scale. Real-time trading in foreign markets has been made possible, as has instantaneous currency conversion. Soon, global data on financial activity will be available online in real time and global transactions through the Internet will become the norm.

People are currently able to pay their bills, write and cash checks, trade stocks, take out loans, mortgage their homes and manage their assets online. Money as we know it may cease to exist, replaced by more convenient technologies such as smart cards and digital cash. Intelligent programs will take care of the financial and logistical aspects of the interactions between both the individuals and the corporations who populate the Internet. All that a person will need to go shopping is a connection, a computer, and a digital form of payment.

Traditional "brick and mortar" stores are already being replaced by a multitude of electronic storefronts populating the World Wide Web. No single brick-and-mortar store can offer 50,000 products, but an online store has the capability to offer a limitless number of them. Services exist that will comparison shop for a consumer, finding the best deal on items from cooking equipment to cars. An increasing amount of consumer information is being made available, leading to better deals for customers. For instance, Web sites that post car invoice prices have made it possible for auto buyers to circumvent the sticker price. Internet shopping is already beginning to eclipse more traditional modes, according to research done during the Christmas season of 1999, which found higher satisfaction rates for shopping online than it did for shopping at a brick-and-mortar store or through a catalog.

In addition to business-to-consumer operations such as electronic stores, business-to-business marketplaces and services are also taking their place on the Internet. A business which orders products from a supplier online not only completes the transaction with greater speed and convenience, but also can keep track of the shipment constantly. Business-to-business e-commerce Web sites are also channels that permit close cooperation between different business as well as the outsourcing services that are and will continue to be so crucial to the Internet economy.

The transition from brick-and-mortar businesses to "clicks" businesses is happening in all sectors of the economy. It is now possible for a business to work without an office, because the employees can conduct all communication via phone, voice mail, fax, e-mail and the emerging capabilities of the Internet. There are already Internet services that integrate phone, fax, voice and e-mail, and in the future, new technologies will further facilitate the virtual office. Some businesses have already divested themselves of all their bricks-and-mortar and gone completely online. Despite the shift online, the brick-and-mortar segments of many businesses will not become obsolete. They will still have their uses and purposes, but in order to work effectively, they must be integrated with their online counterparts, as the Internet economy requires integration to facilitate the transfer of information.

Many e-businesses can personalize the user's experience, tailoring Web pages to their individual preferences and letting them bypass irrelevant content. This is done by tracking the consumer's movement through the Internet and combining that data with information provided by the consumer, which could include billing information, interests and hobbies, among other things. Personalization is making it easier and more pleasant for many people to surf the Internet and find what they want.

Hand in hand with the promise of personalization, however, comes the problem of privacy invasion. What if the e-business to whom you give your personal data sells or gives that data to another organization without your knowledge? What if you do not want your movements on the Internet to be tracked by unknown parties? What if an unauthorized party gains access to your private data, such as credit card numbers? These are some of the many questions that must be addressed by consumers, e-businesses and lawmakers alike.

Personalization is just the tip of the privacy iceberg, as there are many other ways that privacy can be compromised on the Internet. However, there are many organizations and companies which crusade for privacy and provide privacy software. Pretty Good Privacy (PGP), an encryption program written in 1991, was so strong that the U.S. government could not crack it.

The unprecedented information-transfer capabilities, unregulated nature, and breakneck growth of the Internet have fostered rampant copyright infringement and piracy of intellectual property. Innovative new technologies such as MP3 have been used in an illicit manner to transfer music over the Internet—touching off litigation by the recording industry against companies whose technologies can be used to facilitate the transfer of illegal copies of recordings. Electronic piracy of books and printed material is also common, yet it does not concern the publishing industry as much, as sales of paper books have not yet been noticeably affected. The demand for the security of intellectual property is helping drive the development of new technologies including digital signatures, digital certificates and digital steganography. These technologies, which are constantly advancing to higher degrees of security, are becoming standard for online transactions and communications.

Today's users want multimedia and e-commerce in a package that is both powerful and user-friendly. Programmers want all these benefits in a truly portable manner so that applications will run without modification on a variety of *platforms* (i.e., different types of computers running different operating systems). In this book we present a number of powerful software technologies that enable readers to build substantial Web-based, client/server, database-intensive, "multi-tier" applications suited to an e-business. We begin with a discussion of computer hardware and software fundamentals.

1.4 What is a Computer?

A *computer* is a device capable of performing computations and making logical decisions at speeds millions, and even billions, of times faster than human beings can. For example, many of today's personal computers can perform hundreds of millions of additions per second. A person operating a desk calculator might require a lifetime to complete the same number of calculations a powerful personal computer can perform in one second. (Points to ponder: How would you know whether the person added the numbers correctly? How would you know whether the computer added the numbers correctly?) Today, the world's fastest *supercomputers* can perform hundreds of billions of additions per second, and computers that perform a trillion instructions per second are already functioning in research laboratories!

Computers process *data* under the control of sets of instructions called *computer programs*. These computer programs guide the computer through orderly sets of actions specified by people called *computer programmers*.

The various devices (such as the keyboard, screen, disks, memory and processing units) that comprise a computer system are referred to as *hardware*. Regardless of differences in physical appearance, virtually every computer may be envisioned as being divided into six *logical units* or sections. These are:

1. *Input unit.* This is the "receiving" section of the computer. It obtains information (data and computer programs) from various *input devices* and places this information at the disposal of the other units so that the information may be processed. Most information is entered into computers today through typewriter-like keyboards, "mouse" devices and disks. In the future, most information will be entered by speaking to computers, by electronically scanning images and by video recording.

2. *Output unit.* This is the "shipping" section of the computer. It takes information processed by the computer and places it on various *output devices* to make the information available for use outside the computer. Information output from computers is displayed on screens, printed on paper, played through audio speakers, magnetically recorded on disks and tapes or used to control other devices.

3. *Memory unit.* This is the rapid access, relatively low-capacity "warehouse" section of the computer. It retains information that has been entered through the input unit so that the information may be made immediately available for processing when it is needed. The memory unit also retains information that has already been processed until that information can be placed on output devices by the output unit. The memory unit is often called either *memory, primary memory* or *random access memory (RAM)*.

4. *Arithmetic and logic unit (ALU).* This is the "manufacturing" section of the computer. It is responsible for performing calculations such as addition, subtraction, multiplication and division. It contains the decision mechanisms that allow the computer, for example, to compare two items from the memory unit to determine whether or not they are equal.

5. *Central processing unit (CPU).* This is the "administrative" section of the computer. It is the computer's coordinator and is responsible for supervising the operation of the other sections. The CPU tells the input unit when information should

be read into the memory unit, tells the ALU when information from the memory unit should be utilized in calculations and tells the output unit when to send information from the memory unit to certain output devices.

6. *Secondary storage unit.* This is the long-term, high-capacity "warehousing" section of the computer. Programs or data not being used by the other units are normally placed on secondary storage devices (such as disks) until they are needed, possibly hours, days, months or even years later. Information in secondary storage takes longer to access than information in primary memory. The cost per unit of secondary storage is much less than the cost per unit of primary memory.

1.5 Types of Programming Languages

The computer programs that run on a computer are referred to as *software*. Programmers write the instructions that comprise software in various programming languages, some directly understandable by the computer and others that require intermediate translation steps. Hundreds of computer languages are in use today. These may be divided into three general types:

1. Machine languages

2. Assembly languages

3. High-level languages

Any computer can directly understand only its own *machine language.* Machine language is the "natural language" of a particular computer. It is defined by the hardware design of that computer. Machine languages generally consist of strings of numbers (ultimately reduced to 1s and 0s) that instruct computers to perform their most elementary operations one at a time. Machine languages are *machine dependent* (i.e., a particular machine language can be used on only one type of computer). Machine languages are cumbersome for humans, as can be seen by the following section of a machine-language program that adds overtime pay to base pay and stores the result in gross pay.

```
+1300042774
+1400593419
+1200274027
```

As computers became more popular, it became apparent that machine-language programming was simply too slow and tedious for most programmers. Instead of using the strings of numbers that computers could directly understand, programmers began using English-like abbreviations to represent the elementary operations of the computer. These English-like abbreviations formed the basis of *assembly languages. Translator programs* called *assemblers* were developed to convert assembly-language programs to machine language at computer speeds. The following section of an assembly-language program also adds overtime pay to base pay and stores the result in gross pay, but more clearly than its machine-language equivalent.

```
LOAD        BASEPAY
ADD         OVERPAY
STORE       GROSSPAY
```

Although such code is clearer to humans, it is incomprehensible to computers until translated to machine language.

Computer usage increased rapidly with the advent of assembly languages, but programming in these still required many instructions to accomplish even the simplest tasks. To speed the programming process, *high-level languages* were developed in which single statements could be written to accomplish substantial tasks. The translator programs that convert high-level language programs into machine language are called *compilers.* High-level languages allow programmers to write instructions that look almost like everyday English and contain commonly used mathematical notations. A payroll program written in a high-level language might contain a statement such as:

```
grossPay = basePay + overTimePay
```

Obviously, high-level languages are more desirable from the programmer's standpoint than either machine languages or assembly languages. C, C++, Visual Basic® and Java are among the most powerful and most widely used high-level programming languages.

The process of compiling a high-level language program into machine language can take a considerable amount of computer time. *Interpreter* programs were developed to execute high-level language programs directly without the need for compiling those programs into machine language. Although compiled programs execute much faster than interpreted programs, interpreters are popular in program-development environments in which programs are recompiled frequently as new features are added and errors are corrected. Once a program is developed, a compiled version can be produced to run most efficiently. In this book we study three key programming languages, namely JavaScript, VBScript and Perl. Each of these so-called *scripting languages* is processed by interpreters. You will see that interpreters have played an especially important part in helping scripting languages achieve their goal of portability across a great variety of platforms.

1.6 Other High-Level Languages

Hundreds of high-level languages have been developed, but only a few have achieved broad acceptance. *Fortran* (FORmula TRANslator) was developed by IBM Corporation between 1954 and 1957 to be used for scientific and engineering applications that require complex mathematical computations. Fortran is still widely used.

COBOL (COmmon Business Oriented Language) was developed in 1959 by a group of computer manufacturers and government and industrial computer users. COBOL is used primarily for commercial applications that require precise and efficient manipulation of large amounts of data. Today, about half of all business software is still programmed in COBOL. Approximately one million people are actively writing COBOL programs.

Pascal was designed at about the same time as C. It was created by Professor Nicklaus Wirth and was intended for academic use. We say more about Pascal in the next section.

Basic was developed in 1965 at Dartmouth University as a simple language to help novices become comfortable with programming. *Bill Gates* implemented Basic on several early personal computers. Today, *Microsoft*—the company Bill Gates created—is the world's leading software development organization, Gates has become—by far—the world's richest person and Microsoft has been included in the list of prestigious stocks that form the Dow Jones Industrials–from which the Dow Jones Industrial Average is calculated.

1.7 Structured Programming

During the 1960s, many large software development efforts encountered severe difficulties. Software schedules were typically late, costs greatly exceeded budgets, and the finished products were unreliable. People began to realize that software development was a far more complex activity than they had imagined. Research activity in the 1960s resulted in the evolution of *structured programming*—a disciplined approach to writing programs that are clearer than unstructured programs, easier to test and debug, and easier to modify.

One of the more tangible results of this research was the development of the Pascal programming language by Nicklaus Wirth in 1971. Pascal, named after the seventeenth-century mathematician and philosopher Blaise Pascal, was designed for teaching structured programming in academic environments and rapidly became the preferred programming language in most universities.

The Ada programming language was developed under the sponsorship of the United States Department of Defense (DOD) during the 1970s and early 1980s. Hundreds of separate languages were being used to produce DOD's massive command-and-control software systems. DOD wanted a single language that would fulfill most of its needs. Pascal was chosen as a base, but the final Ada language is quite different from Pascal. The language was named after Lady Ada Lovelace, daughter of the poet Lord Byron. Lady Lovelace is generally credited with writing the world's first computer program in the early 1800s (for the Analytical Engine mechanical computing device designed by Charles Babbage). One important capability of Ada is called *multitasking;* this allows programmers to specify that many activities are to occur in parallel. Other widely used high-level languages such as C and C++ generally allow programs to perform only one activity at a time. Java, through a technique called *multithreading*, also enables programmers to write programs with parallel activities.

1.8 History of the Internet

In the late 1960s, one of the authors (HMD) was a graduate student at MIT. His research at MIT's Project Mac (now the Laboratory for Computer Science—the home of the World Wide Web Consortium) was funded by ARPA—the Advanced Research Projects Agency of the Department of Defense. ARPA sponsored a conference at which several dozen ARPA-funded graduate students were brought together at the University of Illinois at Urbana-Champaign to meet and share ideas. During this conference, ARPA rolled out the blueprints for networking the main computer systems of about a dozen ARPA-funded universities and research institutions. They were to be connected with communications lines operating at a then-stunning 56KB (i.e., 56,000 bits per second), at a time when most people (of the few who could be) were connecting over telephone lines to computers at a rate of 110 bits per second. HMD vividly recalls the excitement at that conference. Researchers at Harvard talked about communication with the Univac 1108 "supercomputer" across the country at the University of Utah to handle calculations related to their computer graphics research. Many other intriguing possibilities were raised. Academic research was about to take a giant leap forward. Shortly after this conference, ARPA proceeded to implement what quickly became called the *ARPAnet*, the grandparent of today's *Internet*.

Things worked out differently than originally planned. Although the ARPAnet did enable researchers to share each others' computers, its chief benefit proved to be the capability of quick and easy communication via what came to be known as *electronic mail (e-mail)*. This is true even today on the Internet, with e-mail facilitating communications of all kinds among millions of people worldwide.

One of ARPA's primary goals for the network was to allow multiple users to send and receive information at the same time over the same communications paths (such as phone lines). The network operated with a technique called *packet switching* in which digital data was sent in small packages called *packets*. The packets contained data, address information, error-control information and sequencing information. The address information was used to route the packets of data to their destination, and the sequencing information was used to help reassemble the packets (which—because of complex routing mechanisms—could actually arrive out of order) into their original order for presentation to the recipient. This packet-switching technique greatly reduced transmission costs from those of dedicated communications lines.

The network was designed to operate without centralized control. This meant that if a portion of the network should fail, the remaining working portions would still be able to route packets from senders to receivers over alternate paths.

The protocols for communicating over the ARPAnet became known as *TCP—the Transmission Control Protocol*. TCP ensured that messages were properly routed from sender to receiver and that those messages arrived intact.

In parallel with the early evolution of the Internet, organizations worldwide were implementing their own networks for both intra-organization (i.e., within the organization) and inter-organization (i.e., between organizations) communication. A huge variety of networking hardware and software appeared. One challenge was to get these to intercommunicate. ARPA accomplished this with the development of *IP—the Internetworking Protocol*), truly creating a "network of networks," the current architecture of the Internet. The combined set of protocols is now commonly called *TCP/IP*.

Initially, use of the Internet was limited to universities and research institutions; then the military became a big user. Eventually, the government decided to allow access to the Internet for commercial purposes. Initially there was resentment among the research and military communities—it was felt that response times would become poor as "the net" became saturated with so many users.

In fact, the exact opposite has occurred. Businesses rapidly realized that, by making effective use of the Internet they could tune their operations and offer new and better services to their clients, so they started spending vast amounts of money to develop and enhance the Internet. This generated fierce competition among the communications carriers and hardware and software suppliers to meet this demand. The result is that *bandwidth* (i.e., the information carrying capacity of communications lines) on the Internet has increased tremendously and costs have plummeted. It is widely believed that the Internet has played a significant role in the economic prosperity that the United States and many other industrialized nations have enjoyed over the last decade and are likely to continue enjoying for many years.

1.9 Personal Computing, Distributed Computing and Client/Server Computing

In 1977, Apple Computer popularized the phenomenon of *personal computing*. Initially, it was a hobbyist's dream. Computers became economical enough for people to buy them for their own personal or business use. In 1981, IBM, the world's largest computer vendor, introduced the IBM Personal Computer. Literally overnight, personal computing became legitimate in business, industry and government organizations.

But these computers were "standalone" units—people did their work on their own machines and then transported disks back and forth to share information (this is often called "sneakernet"). Although early personal computers were not powerful enough to timeshare several users, these machines could be linked together in computer networks, sometimes over telephone lines and sometimes in *local area networks (LANs)* within an organization. This led to the phenomenon of *distributed computing,* in which an organization's computing, instead of being performed strictly at some central computer installation, is distributed over networks to the sites at which the work of the organization is performed. Personal computers were powerful enough to handle the computing requirements of individual users and the basic communications tasks of passing information back and forth electronically.

Today's most powerful personal computers are as powerful as the million dollar machines of just a decade ago. The most powerful desktop machines—called *workstations*—provide individual users with enormous capabilities. Information is easily shared across computer networks, where computers called *file servers* offer a common store of programs and data that may be used by *client* computers distributed throughout the network, hence the term *client/server computing.* C and C++ have become the programming languages of choice for writing software for operating systems, computer networking and distributed client/server applications.

1.10 History of the World Wide Web

The *World Wide Web* allows computer users to locate and view multimedia-based documents (i.e., documents with text, graphics, animations, audios and/or videos) on almost any subject. Even though the Internet was developed more than three decades ago, the introduction of the *World Wide Web* was a relatively recent event. In 1990, *Tim Berners-Lee* of CERN (the European Laboratory for Particle Physics) developed the World Wide Web and several communication protocols that form the backbone of the World Wide Web.

The Internet and the World Wide Web will surely be listed among the most important and profound creations of humankind. In the past, most computer applications ran on "stand-alone" computers, i.e., computers that were not connected to one another. Today's applications can be written to communicate among the world's hundreds of millions of computers. The Internet mixes computing and communications technologies. It makes our work easier. It makes information instantly and conveniently accessible worldwide. It makes it possible for individuals and small businesses to get worldwide exposure. It is changing the nature of the way business is done. People can search for the best prices on virtually any product or service. Special-interest communities can stay in touch with one another. Researchers can be made instantly aware of the latest breakthroughs worldwide.

e-Business and e-Commerce How to Program presents programming techniques that allow applications to use the Internet and the World Wide Web to interact with other applications and with databases. These capabilities allow programmers to develop the kinds of distributed applications so popular in modern e-business and e-commerce. If you have been hearing a great deal about e-business and e-commerce lately, and if you are interested in developing e-business and e-commerce applications, then learning the software-development techniques discussed in this book may be the key to challenging and rewarding career opportunities for you.

1.11 Hardware Trends

The Internet community thrives on the continuing stream of dramatic improvements in hardware, software and communications technologies. Every year, people generally expect to pay at least a little more for most products and services. The exact opposite has been the case in the computer and communications fields, especially with regard to the hardware costs of supporting these technologies. For many decades, and with no change in the fore-seeable future, hardware costs have fallen rapidly, if not precipitously. This is a phenome-non of technology, another driving force powering the current economic boom. Every year or two, the capacities of computers, especially the amount of *memory* they have in which to execute programs, *secondary memory* (such as disk storage) they have to hold programs and data over the longer term, and processor speeds—the speed at which computers exe-cute their programs (i.e., do their work)—each tend to approximately double. The same has been true in the communications field, with costs plummeting, especially in recent years as the enormous demand for communications bandwidth has attracted tremendous competi-tion. We know of no other fields in which technology moves so quickly and costs fall so rapidly.

When computer use exploded in the sixties and seventies, there was talk of huge improvements in human productivity that computing and communications would bring about. But these improvements did not materialize. Organizations were spending vast sums on computers and certainly employing them effectively, but without the productivity gains that had been expected. It was the invention of microprocessor chip technology and its wide deployment in the late 1970s and 1980s that laid the groundwork for the productivity improvements of the 1990s that have been so crucial to economic prosperity.

1.12 The Key Software Trend: Object Technology

One of the authors, HMD, remembers the great frustration that was felt in the 1960s by soft-ware development organizations, especially those developing large-scale projects. During his undergraduate years, HMD had the privilege of working summers at a leading computer vendor on the teams developing time-sharing, virtual memory operating systems. This was a great experience for a college student. But in the summer of 1967, reality set in when the company "decommitted" from producing as a commercial product the particular system that hundreds of people had been working on for many years. It was difficult to get this soft-ware right. Software is "complex stuff."

Hardware costs have been declining dramatically in recent years, to the point that per-sonal computers have become a commodity. Unfortunately, software development costs have been rising steadily as programmers develop ever more powerful and complex appli-cations without being able to significantly improve the underlying technologies of software development. In this book you will learn proven software development methods that can reduce software development costs—top-down stepwise refinement, functionalization and especially object-based programming.

There is a revolution brewing in the software community. Building software quickly, correctly and economically remains an elusive goal, and this at a time when demands for new and more powerful software are soaring. *Objects* are essentially reusable software *components* that model items in the real world. Software developers are discovering that using a modular, object-oriented design and implementation approach can make software development groups much more productive than is possible with **previous** popular programming techniques such as structured programming. Object-oriented programs are often easier to understand, correct and modify.

Improvements to software technology did start to appear with the benefits of so-called *structured programming* (and the related disciplines of *structured systems analysis and design*) being realized in the 1970s. But it was not until the technology of object-oriented programming became widely used in the 1980s, and especially widely used in the 1990s, that software developers finally felt they had the tools they needed to make major strides in the software development process.

Actually, object technology dates back at least to the mid 1960s. The C++ programming language developed at AT&T by Bjarne Stroustrup in the early 1980s is based on two languages: C, which was initially developed at AT&T to implement the Unix operating system in the early 1970s; and Simula 67, a simulation programming language developed in Europe and released in 1967. C++ absorbed the capabilities of C and added Simula's capabilities for creating and manipulating objects. Neither C nor C++ was ever intended for wide use beyond the research laboratories at AT&T. But grass-roots support rapidly developed for each.

What are objects and why are they "magic"? Actually, object technology is a packaging scheme that helps us create meaningful software units. These are large and highly focused on particular applications areas. There are date objects, time objects, paycheck objects, invoice objects, audio objects, video objects, file objects, record objects and so on. In fact, any noun can be represented as an object.

We live in a world of objects. Just look around you. There are cars, and planes, and people, and animals, and buildings, and traffic lights, and elevators, and so on. Before object-oriented languages appeared, programming languages (such as Fortran, Pascal, Basic and C) were focussed on actions (verbs) rather than things or objects (nouns). Programmers living in a world of objects would get to the computer and have to program primarily with verbs. This paradigm shift made it a bit awkward to write programs. Now, with the availability of popular object-oriented languages such as Java and C++ and many others, programmers can program in a manner similar to the way in which they perceive the world. This is a more natural process than procedural programming and has resulted in significant productivity enhancements.

One of the key problems with procedural programming is that the program units programmers created do not easily mirror real-world entities effectively. So they are not particularly reusable. It is not unusual for programmers to "start fresh" on each new project and wind up writing very similar software "from scratch." This wastes precious time and money resources as people repeatedly "reinvent the wheel." With object technology, the software entities created (called *objects*), if properly designed, tend to be much more reusable on future projects. Using libraries of reusable componentry such as *MFC (Microsoft Foundation Classes)* and those produced by Rogue Wave and many other software development organizations can greatly reduce the amount of effort it takes to implement certain kinds of systems (compared to the effort that would be required to reinvent these capabilities on new projects).

Some organizations report that software reuse is not, in fact, the key benefit they get from object-oriented programming. Rather, they indicate that object-oriented programming tends to produce software that is more understandable, better organized and easier to maintain. This can be significant because it has been estimated that as much as 80% of software costs are not associated with the original efforts to develop the software, but are in fact associated with the continued evolution and maintenance of that software throughout its lifetime.

Whatever the perceived benefits of object-orientation are, it is clear that object-oriented programming will be the key programming methodology for at least the next several decades.

Software Engineering Observation 1.1

Use a building block approach to creating programs. Avoid reinventing the wheel. Use existing pieces—this is called software reuse *and it is central to object-oriented programming.*

[*Note*: We will include many of these *Software Engineering Observations* throughout the text to explain concepts that affect and improve the overall architecture and quality of a software system, and particularly, of large software systems. We will also highlight *Good Programming Practices* (practices that can help you write programs that are clearer, more understandable, more maintainable, and easier to test and debug), *Common Programming Errors* (problems to watch out for so you do not make these same errors in your programs), *Performance Tips* (techniques that will help you write programs that run faster and use less memory), *Portability Tips* (techniques that will help you write programs that can run, with little or no modification, on a variety of computers), *Testing and Debugging Tips* (techniques that will help you remove bugs from your programs, and more important, techniques that will help you write bug-free programs in the first place) and *Look and Feel Observations* (techniques that will help you design the "look" and "feel" of your graphical user interfaces for appearance and ease of use). Many of these techniques and practices are only guidelines; you will, no doubt, develop your own preferred programming style.]

The advantage of creating your own code is that you will know exactly how it works. You will be able to examine the code. The disadvantage is the time-consuming and complex effort that goes into designing and developing new code.

Performance Tip 1.1

Reusing proven code components instead of writing your own versions can improve program performance because these components are normally written to perform efficiently.

Software Engineering Observation 1.2

Extensive class libraries of reusable software components are available over the Internet and the World Wide Web. Many of these libraries are available at no charge.

1.13 JavaScript: Object-Based Scripting for the Web

JavaScript provides an attractive package for advancing the state of programming language education, especially at the introductory and intermediate levels. JavaScript makes World Wide Web pages "come alive."

JavaScript is an object-based language with strong support for proper software engineering techniques. You create and manipulate objects. For universities, these features are powerfully appealing. Students will learn *object-based* programming from the start. They will simply think in an object-based manner.

The fact that JavaScript is included as a part of today's most popular Web browsers is appealing to colleges facing tight budgets and lengthy budget-planning cycles. Also, as bug fixes and new versions of JavaScript become available, these become available immediately over the Internet, so colleges can keep their JavaScript software current.

Does JavaScript provide the solid foundation of programming principles typically taught in first programming courses—the intended audience for this book? We think so.

The JavaScript chapters of this book are much more than just an introduction to Java-Script. They also present an introduction to the fundamentals of computer programming including control structures, functions, arrays, strings, objects, etc. Experienced programmers will be able to read Chapters 13 through 18 quickly and master JavaScript mostly by reading our live-code examples and examining the corresponding input/output screens. Nonprogrammers will learn computer programming in these carefully paced chapters with a large number of exercises. We cannot provide answers to all these exercises because this book is a textbook—college professors use the examples for homeworks, labs, short quizzes, major examinations and even term projects. We do, however, provide answers to many of the exercises in the companion product to this book called *The e-Business and e-Commerce Programming Multimedia Cyber Classroom*. If you purchased our boxed product, *The Complete e-Business and e-Commerce Programming Training Course*, you already have the *Cyber Classroom* CD. If you have the book and would like to order the CD separately please see the advertorial at the end of this book for ordering instructions.

JavaScript is a powerful scripting language. Experienced programmers sometimes take pride in being able to create some weird, contorted, convoluted usage of the language. This is a poor programming practice. It makes programs difficult to read, more likely to behave strangely, more difficult to test and debug, and more difficult to adapt to changing requirements. This book is also geared for novice programmers, so we stress program *clarity*. The following is our first *Good Programming Practice*.

Good Programming Practice 1.1

Write your programs in a simple and straightforward manner. This is sometimes referred to as KIS *("keep it simple"). Do not "stretch" the language by trying bizarre usages.*

You will hear that JavaScript is a portable scripting language, and that programs written in JavaScript can run on many different computers. Actually, *portability is an elusive goal.* Here is our first *Portability Tip* and our first *Testing and Debugging Tip*.

Portability Tip 1.1

Although it is easier to write portable programs in JavaScript than in most other programming languages, there are differences among interpreters and computers that can make portability difficult to achieve. Simply writing programs in JavaScript does not guarantee portability. The programmer will occasionally need to deal directly with platform variations.

Testing and Debugging Tip 1.1

Always test your JavaScript programs on all platforms on which you intend to run those programs.

We have done a careful walkthrough of the JavaScript documentation and audited our presentation against it for completeness and accuracy. However, JavaScript is a rich language, and there are some subtleties in the language and some topics we have not covered. The *Bibliography* at the back of this book lists additional books and papers on Java-Script.

Good Programming Practice 1.2

Read the documentation for the version of JavaScript you are using to be sure you are aware of the rich collection of JavaScript features and that you are using these features correctly.

Testing and Debugging Tip 1.2

Your computer and compiler are good teachers. If, after carefully reading your documentation, you are not sure how a feature works, experiment and see what happens. Study each error or warning message you get when you browse pages containing JavaScript programs (referred to simply as scripts) and correct the programs to eliminate these messages.

In this book we explain how JavaScript works in its current implementations. JavaScript programs execute interpretively on the client's machine. Interpreters execute slowly compared to fully compiled machine code.

Performance Tip 1.2

Interpreters have an advantage over compilers for the JavaScript world, namely that an interpreted program can begin execution immediately as soon as it is downloaded to the client's machine, whereas a source program to be compiled must first suffer a potentially long delay as the program is compiled before it can be executed.

For organizations wanting to do heavy-duty information systems development, software packages called *Integrated Development Environments (IDEs)* are available from the major software suppliers. IDEs provide many tools for supporting the software-development process.

1.14 Browser Portability

One of the great challenges of developing Web-based applications is the great diversity of client-side browsers in use. Not only is the browser world divided into *Netscape Navigator*, *Microsoft Internet Explorer*, and many other Web browsers, but for any particular browser, many versions (1.0, 2.0, etc.) for many different platforms (Unix, Microsoft Windows, Apple Macintosh, IBM OS/2, Linux, etc.) are in use. There is great value to knowing the details of all these browsers when developing Web-based applications, but this is confusing to students learning this subject for the first time. We had to make a judgement call on this. We chose to include as many portable topics as possible (such as HTML, JavaScript, Cascading Style Sheets, e-Commerce, database/SQL, Perl/CGI and XML, among others). But we also chose many Microsoft-Windows-specific topics such as the Internet Explorer 5 browser, the Ultimate Paint graphics package for Windows, Dynamic HTML, multimedia, VBScript, Personal Web Server, database access via ADO and Active Server Pages (ASP). For many of our readers, this amount of Microsoft-specific technology will not be appropriate.

Portability Tip 1.2

The Web world is highly fragmented and this makes it difficult for authors and Web developers to create universal solutions. The World Wide Web Consortium (W3C) is working towards the goal of creating a universal client-side platform.

Deitel & Associates, Inc. is a member of the World Wide Web Consortium.

1.15 Evolution of the *How to Program* Series: C and C++

For many years, the Pascal programming language was preferred for use in introductory and intermediate programming courses. The C language was evolved from a language called B by Dennis Ritchie at Bell Laboratories and was implemented in 1972—making C a contemporary of Pascal. C initially became widely known as the development language of the UNIX operating system. Today, virtually all new major operating systems are written in C and/or C++. Over the past two decades, C has become available for most computers. C is hardware independent. With careful design, it is possible to write C programs that are *portable* to most computers.

Many people said that C was too difficult a language for the courses in which Pascal was being used. In 1992, we published the first edition of *C How to Program* to encourage universities to try C instead of Pascal in these courses. In the book we urged instructors to please "trust us" that Pascal should be replaced in the introductory courses with C and that they would be using C for the next 10 years or so in these courses. We used the same pedagogic approach we had used in our college courses for a dozen years, but wrapped the concepts in C rather than Pascal. We found that students were able to handle C at about the same level as Pascal. But there was one noticeable difference. Students appreciated that they were learning a language (C) likely to be valuable to them in industry. Our industry clients appreciated the availability of C-literate graduates who could work immediately on substantial projects rather than first having to go through costly and time-consuming training programs.

C++, an extension of C, was developed by Bjarne Stroustrup in the early 1980s at Bell Laboratories. C++ provides a number of features that "spruce up" the C language, but more importantly, it provides capabilities for *object-oriented programming*.

C++ is a hybrid language—it is possible to program in either a C-like style (called procedural programming, in which the focus is on actions), an object-oriented style (in which the focus is on things) or both. [*Note:* Java, as we will see, is essentially a pure object-oriented language.]

One reason that C++ use has grown so quickly is that it extends C programming into the area of object orientation. For the huge community of C programmers, this has been a powerful advantage. An enormous amount of C code has been written in industry over the last several decades. Because C++ is a superset of C, many organizations find it to be an ideal next step. Programmers can take their C code, compile it, often with nominal changes, in a C++ compiler and continue writing C-like code while mastering the object paradigm. Then the programmers can gradually migrate portions of the legacy C code into C++ as time permits. New systems can be written entirely in object-oriented C++. Such strategies have been appealing to many organizations. The downside is that even after adopting this strategy, companies tend to continue producing C-like code for many years. This, of course, means that they do not quickly realize the full benefits of object-oriented programming and they produce programs that are confusing and hard to maintain due to their hybrid design.

While we were writing *C How to Program*, we had already begun teaching C++ courses. Feeling that C++ would be of great interest to our C readers, we included a brief introduction to C++ at the back of the C book. We then went to work on *C++ How to Program*. Late in 1993 Prentice Hall urged us to write the second edition of *C How to Program*, explaining that the introductory market was still primarily using C with only incidental need for C++. We felt strongly about C++ based on the feedback we were getting in our industry courses, so we insisted on completing the C++ book first. We worked out a compromise solution. We would do the second edition of *C How to Program* first, as long as we could include a much enhanced, several-hundred-page section on C++. Prentice Hall agreed and *C How to Program: Second Edition* was published in January, 1994. In May 1994 we published the first edition of *C++ How to Program,* a 950-page book devoted to the premise that C++ and OOP were now ready for prime time in introductory college courses for many schools that wanted to be at the leading edge of programming languages education.

Once again, we asked college instructors to please "trust us," that it was now time to shift from C and procedural programming in the introductory courses to C++ and object-oriented programming and that this would likely be stable for the next decade—and this only two years after we suggested to college instructors that they were likely to use C for a decade! Our credibility was in question.

1.16 Java and *Java How to Program*

Many people believe that the next major area in which microprocessors will have a profound impact is intelligent consumer electronic devices. Recognizing this, Sun Microsystems funded an internal corporate research project code-named Green in 1991. The project resulted in the development of a C and C++ based language which its creator, James Gosling, called Oak after an oak tree outside his window at Sun. It was later discovered that there already was a computer language called Oak. When a group of Sun people visited a local coffee shop, the name *Java* was suggested and it stuck.

But the Green project ran into some difficulties. The marketplace for intelligent consumer electronic devices was not developing as quickly as Sun had anticipated. Worse yet, a major contract for which Sun competed was awarded to another company. So the project was in danger of being canceled. By sheer good fortune, the World Wide Web exploded in popularity in 1993 and Sun software engineers saw the immediate potential of using Java to create Web pages with so-called *dynamic content* (a subject we investigate in great detail in this book). This breathed new life into the project.

Sun formally announced Java at a trade show in May 1995. Ordinarily, an event like this would not have generated much attention. However, Java generated immediate interest in the business community because of the phenomenal interest in the World Wide Web. Java is now used to create Web pages with dynamic and interactive content, to develop large-scale enterprise applications, to enhance the functionality of Web servers (the computers that provide the content we see in our Web browsers), to provide applications for consumer devices (such as cell phones, pagers and personal digital assistants), and much more.

In 1995, we were carefully following the development of Java by Sun Microsystems. In November 1995 we attended an Internet conference in Boston. A representative from Sun Microsystems gave a rousing presentation on Java. As the talk proceeded, it became clear to us that Java would play a significant part in the development of interactive, multimedia Web pages. But we immediately saw a much greater potential for the language.

We saw Java as the proper language for teaching first-year programming language students the essentials of graphics, images, animation, audio, video, database, networking, multithreading and collaborative computing. We went to work on the first edition of *Java How to Program* which was published in time for fall 1996 classes. We once again asked instructors to please "trust us" that it was now time to shift from C++ in the introductory courses to Java and that instructors should now teach object-oriented programming as they were doing with C++, but with the addition of discussing Java's extensive class libraries of reusable software components that do graphics, graphical user interfaces, networking, multimedia, and the like. Once again, we suggested that Java would likely remain the key language in the introductory courses for a decade!

At this point it was not clear why anyone should believe us. It seemed as if, every two years, we were urging instructors to shift their courses to a different programming language while asking that they please "trust us" and use the new language for a decade! Over the exciting decade of the 1990s, several things have become clear to us:

1. Programming language technology is moving so quickly that any attempt to forecast the direction of the technology for long periods is doomed to failure.

2. The developments in programming language technology are so exciting and so valuable that instructors responsible for introductory, college-level courses have to be prepared to reevaluate the content of those courses much more frequently than in the past.

3. We as authors, and Prentice Hall as our publisher, need to produce new editions of our books and new books on emerging programming languages much more rapidly than in the past.

4. Capabilities such as graphics, graphical user interfaces, networking, client/server computing, Internet and World Wide Web technologies, multimedia, database and many more, that used to be accessible through technologies ancillary to programming languages are now intimately associated with the programming languages themselves. It is now important to talk about these technologies extensively in the programming language textbooks we publish. The era of 500-page programming language textbooks is gone!

After establishing this pattern of recommending a new programming language every two years, we looked for the next major shift in 1998, but we did not see one clearly defined. So we took a diversion and worked on our *Visual Basic 6 How to Program* book, which was meant not to replace *Java How to Program*, but to be an appropriate introductory textbook more for the information technology curriculum than for the computer science curriculum. Sun kept us on our toes, though, by so enhancing Java in the Java 2 platform that we were forced to write *Java How to Program: Third Edition* which was published in 1999.

In addition to its prominence in developing Internet and intranet-based applications, Java is certain to become the language of choice for implementing software for devices that communicate over a network (such as cellular phones, pagers and personal digital assistants). Do not be surprised when your new stereo and other devices in your home will be networked together using Java technology!

1.17 *Internet and World Wide Web How to Program*

Throughout 1998 we saw an explosion of interest in the Internet and the World Wide Web. We immersed ourselves in these technologies and a clear picture started to emerge in our minds of the next direction to take in introductory programming courses. Our recent books on Java and Visual Basic included significant treatments of Internet and World Wide Web Programming. *Electronic commerce*, or *e-Commerce*, as it is typically called, began to dominate business, financial and computer industry news. We saw this as a total reconceptualization of the way organizations operate and transact their business. Should we be writing programming language principles textbooks, or was a new picture beginning to emerge where we should be writing textbooks focused more on the enhanced capabilities that organizations want to incorporate into their information systems? We still had to provide a solid treatment of programming principles, but we felt compelled to do it in the context of the technologies that businesses and organizations need to create Internet-based and Web-based applications. With this realization, *Internet and World Wide Web How to Program* was born, and was published in December of 1999.

1.18 e-Business and e-Commerce How to Program

The continuing growth of e-commerce and its increasing importance caused us to go a step further than we did with *Internet and World Wide Web How to Program* and create a book that explicitly taught programming for the purposes of e-business and e-commerce.

   This book provides a comprehensive introduction to the world of e-commerce for anybody interested in starting an e-business or understanding the principles behind one. Chapters 3 through 8 provide a firm grounding in all the essential aspects of conducting business online, including business models, marketing, security and payment methods. There are numerous case studies to illustrate the many innovations that have come with doing business online.

   You will learn computer programming and basic principles of computer science and information technology. Since the material we discuss must still be presented in typical college courses, we cannot use programming languages as rich as C++ or Java as these would take the entire course to present. Instead, we chose as our primary programming language JavaScript, a condensed programming language that is especially designed for developing Internet and Web-based applications. Chapters 13 through 18 present a rich discussion of JavaScript and its capabilities, including dozens of working, live-code examples followed by screen images showing typical inputs and outputs of these programs.

   After you have learned programming principles from the detailed JavaScript discussions, we present condensed treatments of the two other most popular Internet/Web scripting languages. In Chapter 24 we discuss Microsoft's VBScript, a language based on Microsoft's enormously popular Visual Basic. In Chapter 29 we discuss Perl (and CGI) programming; throughout the 1990s, Perl was the most widely used scripting language for building the server side of Internet-based and Web-based client/server applications. Perl/CGI programming is continuously being improved and is certain to remain popular for many years.

   e-Business and e-Commerce How to Program teaches not only programming languages and programming language principles, but also models, concepts and issues that apply to e-businesses. We focus on a range of important e-commerce technologies that will help you build real-world Internet-based and Web-based business applications.

1.19 Dynamic HTML

What is Dynamic HTML? This is an interesting question because if you walk into a computer store or scan some online software stores, you will not find a product by this name offered for sale. Rather Dynamic HTML, which has at least two versions—Microsoft's and Netscape's—consists of a number of technologies that are available for download and known by other names. Microsoft Dynamic HTML includes: HTML, JavaScript/JScript, Cascading Style Sheets, the Dynamic HTML Object Model and Event Model, ActiveX controls and other related technologies. It is geared to a world of developing high-performance, Web-based applications in which much of the application's work is performed directly on the client rather than placing burdens on servers and the Internet. Dynamic HTML is the key subject of most of Chapters 9 through 23 and 30 through 32 of this book that cover client-side programming.

In our Dynamic HTML presentation, we use *Microsoft's Dynamic HTML Object Model* rather than the more generic *Document Object Model*. Each of these models is accessible through Microsoft Internet Explorer 5, the browser included on the CD with this book.

Chapters 2, 9 through 24 and 30 through 32 form the client-side programming portion of the book. They discuss Internet Explorer 5, HTML 4, JavaScript/JScript (ECMA common standard), Cascading Style Sheets (CSS), Microsoft's Dynamic HTML and VBScript. The server-side programming portion of the book covers the two most popular paradigms for building the server side of Web-based applications development: Microsoft's Active Server Pages (ASP) and Perl/CGI. The server side portion of the book also includes unique chapters on Servers, Databases and XML.

This book is intended for several academic markets, namely introductory course sequences for students who wish to gain both a theoretical understanding of the concepts and models governing e-commerce and the technical programming skills necessary to implement Web-based business applications; upper-level elective courses for students who already know programming; and as a supplement in introductory courses where students are first becoming familiar with computers, the Internet, the Web, e-business and e-commerce. The book offers a solid one- or two-semester introductory programming experience or a solid one semester upper-level elective. The book is also intended for professional programmers in corporate training programs or doing self-study.

We will publish fresh editions of this book promptly in response to rapidly evolving Internet and Web technologies. [*Note:* Our publishing plans are updated regularly at our Web site **www.deitel.com**. The contents and publication dates of our forthcoming publications are always subject to change. If you need more specific information, please email us at **deitel@deitel.com**.]

1.20 A Tour of the Book

In this section, we take a tour of the subjects you will study in *e-Business and e-Commerce How to Program*. Many of the chapters end with an Internet and World Wide Web Resources section that provides a listing of resources through which you can enhance your knowledge of e-business and e-commerce programming. Many chapters also include a recommended readings section. In addition, you may want to visit our Web site to stay informed of the latest information and corrections.

Chapter 1—Introduction to Computers, the Internet and the Web
In Chapter 1, we present some historical information about computers and computer programming and introductory information about the Internet, the World Wide Web, e-business and e-commerce. We also present an overview of the concepts you will learn in the remaining chapters in the book.

Chapter 2—Introduction to Internet Explorer 5 and the World Wide Web
Prior to the explosion of interest in the Internet and the World Wide Web, if you heard the term *browser,* you probably would have thought about browsing at a bookstore. Today

"browser" has a whole new meaning. Now a browser is an important piece of software that enables you to browse the Internet ("surf" the Web). You have a world of information, services and products to browse. The two most popular browsers are *Microsoft's Internet Explorer* and *Netscape's Communicator*.

Using tools that are part of the Internet Explorer 5 software package (enclosed on the CD included with this book), we discuss how to use the Web to its fullest potential. These tools include the Internet browser, email, newsgroups and chat.

This chapter shows readers who are not familiar with the Internet and the World Wide Web how to begin browsing the Web with Internet Explorer. We demonstrate several commonly used features of Internet Explorer for searching the Web, keeping track of the sites you visit and transferring files between computers. We also discuss several programs that accompany Internet Explorer. We demonstrate sending email, receiving email and using Internet newsgroups with *Microsoft Outlook Express* and using Microsoft *NetMeeting* and *Microsoft Chat* to have live meetings and discussions with other people on the Internet. The chapter ends with a discussion of *plug-ins* that provide browser users access to the ever increasing number of programs and features that make your browsing experience more enjoyable and interactive.

Chapter 3—e-Business Models and Case Studies
The Web has caused a complete rethinking of the way systems should most effectively be designed and implemented. e-commerce has been a major topic over the last few years in business publications, but it has been equally prominent in the computing literature. The Internet, and especially the Web, are causing profound rethinking and restructuring of the way in which the world's business is conducted. Every major organization and most smaller groups are working hard to incorporate Internet and Web technology into existing systems and new information systems designs. In this chapter we discuss the fundamentals of conducting business on the Internet and the Web. We present a number of case studies, with the key goal of highlighting the common core of technologies needed to implement e-commerce systems. We emphasize the importance of Internet and Web technology, database technology, security technology and others. Then in the server-side programming chapters, we put many of these technologies to work in constructing actual multitiered, client/server, database-intensive Web-based systems. The Internet and the Web "level the playing field" making it possible even for small companies to quickly establish a business presence in worldwide markets, something that was extraordinarily difficult to do just a few years ago.

Chapter 4—Internet Marketing
In business, marketing and advertising often mean the difference between success and failure. Chapter 4 covers the many options that an e-business has for promoting itself online. It discusses the effectiveness and costs of different types of advertising and marketing, examining methods of targeting advertisements, strategic partnerships with other e-businesses and ways to analyze market trends. There are many different ways to spread your banners and links throughout the Internet, including buying ad space, strategic partnerships and affiliate programs. Your marketing strategy can only be effective if you know how to target your market. Various techniques and technologies that help e-businesses accomplish this, such as customer tracking and data mining, are described, as are their common applications. The Internet opens many new marketing opportunities, which, when correctly employed, can lead to success.

Chapter 5—Online Monetary Transactions
Chapter 5 describes the techniques and technologies used to process online payments. Some of them, such as e-wallets, bill paying and online banking, are Internet extensions of conventional methods of payment. New paradigms for financial transactions are also emerging in the form of smart cards, digital cash and micropayments. Many, if not all, of these payment models will be important to e-business in the future, especially since some of them are in a position to supplant traditional transactions.

Some companies focus on specific aspects of online monetary transactions, and others, such as CyberCash, attempt to function as comprehensive platforms for electronic payment. Each approach to handling money online has its own advantages and disadvantages, as well as uses for which it is particularly well-suited. Leaders in each area of online financial services are presented as case studies for the reader. Trends toward standards for online payment processing are also examined.

Chapter 6—Legal, Ethical, and Social Issues; Internet Taxation
The explosive growth of the Internet, the increasing access that it provides to all types of information and its nature as an unregulated medium have raised many legal, ethical and social issues. What happens when things that can be found and bought on the Internet are legal in one region or country and illegal in another? Where should the line be drawn between personalization and consumer privacy? With e-business and e-commerce undergoing explosive growth, taxation of goods and services provided via the Internet has also become a complex dilemma. These issues are examined in Chapter 6, which contains information on laws, landmark cases and what consumers and companies are attempting to do to ensure that their rights are protected when they interact online.

Chapter 7—e-Business Security
To have a successful online business, it is essential to protect consumer information and ensure secure transactions. Four things are required for a secure transaction or communication: authentication of the parties involved, verification of the information's integrity, privacy of the information and proof that the information was sent and received. Chapter 7 examines the systems and technologies–including Public Key Cryptography, SSL, SET, digital signatures, digital certificates, digital steganography and the cutting-edge technology of biometrics—used to meet these requirements. Other types of network security such as firewalls and anti-virus programs are also covered in detail, and common security threats such as cryptanalytic attacks, DoS attacks, viruses, worms and Trojan Horses are discussed. Successful security breaches and network attacks can cause immense damage, loss of productivity and loss of credibility to the affected individuals or organizations, making it essential for e-businesses to protect their customers and for customers to watch out for themselves.

Chapter 8—Internet Hardware, Software and Communications Technologies
Chapter 8 describes the technologies on which the Internet and the World Wide Web are built and how these technologies work together to transfer information. The chapter also provides an understanding of the hardware, software and communications technologies used by businesses in the world of e-commerce. Among the technologies discussed are routers, servers, operating systems, browsers and internet connections.

Wireless Internet is already available on some cellular phones, personal digital assistants and special modems. The advantages and limitations of this promising new technology are discussed. In addition to technology, many types of services and solutions for creating e-businesses are explored.

Chapter 9—Introduction to Hypertext Markup Language 4 (HTML 4)

In this chapter, we begin unlocking the power of the Web with *HTML*—the *Hypertext Markup Language*. HTML is a *markup language* for identifying the elements of an HTML document (Web page) so that a browser, such as Microsoft's Internet Explorer or Netscape's Communicator, can render (i.e., display) that page on your computer screen.

We introduce the basics of creating Web pages in HTML using a technique we call the *live-code approach.* Every concept is presented in the context of a complete working HTML document (or Web page) that is immediately followed by the screen output produced when that HTML document is rendered by Internet Explorer. We write many simple Web pages. Later chapters introduce more sophisticated HTML techniques, such as tables, which are particularly useful for presenting and manipulating information from databases.

We introduce basic HTML *tags* and *attributes*. A key issue when using HTML is the separation of the *presentation of a document* (i.e., how the document is rendered on the screen by a browser) from the *structure of that document*. This chapter begins our in-depth discussion of this issue. As the book proceeds, you will be able to create increasingly appealing and powerful Web pages.

Some key topics covered in this chapter include: incorporating text and images in an HTML document, linking to other HTML documents on the Web, formatting text (including fonts, font sizes, colors and alignment), incorporating special characters (such as copyright and trademark symbols) into an HTML document and separating parts of an HTML document with horizontal lines (called *horizontal rules*).

Chapter 10—Intermediate HTML 4

In this chapter, we discuss more substantial HTML elements and features. We demonstrate how to present information in *lists* and *tables*. We discuss how to collect information from people browsing a site. We explain how to use *internal linking* and *image maps* to make Web pages easier to navigate. We also discuss how to use *frames* to make attractive interactive Web sites. By the end of this chapter, you will be familiar with most commonly used HTML tags and features. You will then be able to create more complex and visually appealing Web sites.

Chapter 11—Using a Graphics Package: Ultimate Paint

Knowledge of HTML alone is not quite enough to make attractive, successful Web sites. Great Web pages often burst with rich graphics and multimedia that make them "come alive." You can tap into an extensible pool of free graphics available at many popular Web sites. If you would like to create your own unique graphics, the enclosed CD includes Ultimate Paint. This easy-to-use, inexpensive graphics package offers the functionality of more expensive packages. Chapter 11 explains how to use many of Ultimate Paint's graphics capabilities. We use Ultimate Paint to create a few images that can add flair to your Web pages.

Chapter 12—Microsoft FrontPage Express

In Chapters 9 and 10 we showed how to create Web pages working directly in HTML—the underlying "language of the Web." We will continue to work directly in HTML and Dynamic HTML throughout the book. Working at this level is appropriate for "heavy-duty"

Web developers (i.e., the kind of people this book is intended to produce) who push the limits of the Web's capabilities. However, there is also a lightweight level at which to develop Web pages. There are many products generically referred to as *HTML editors*. These include products like *Microsoft's FrontPage* and *FrontPage Express* (the latter of which is included on the CD as part of the complete Internet Explorer 5 installation).

In this chapter, we walk through the process of creating Web pages quickly and conveniently with FrontPage Express. We repeat several of the examples from Chapters 9 and 10 to show how easy it is to work with FrontPage Express. This product is one of a class of products referred to as *WYSIWYG ("What You See Is What You Get") editors*. FrontPage Express presents an interface like that of Microsoft Word where you use point-and-click, drag-and-drop functionality to lay out and create professional-looking Web pages. You can find free demo versions of other HTML editors on the Web.

Chapter 13—JavaScript: Introduction to Client-Side Scripting

Chapter 13 presents our first JavaScript *programs* (also called *scripts*). Scripting helps Web-pages "come alive" by allowing a Web page developer to manipulate elements of a Web page dynamically as the client browses that page. Chapters 13 through 18 present the features of the JavaScript scripting language which are then used in Chapters 19 through 23, 27, 28 and 30 through 32 to demonstrate how to dynamically manipulate the contents of Web pages. JavaScript enables us to present fundamental computer-science concepts at the same depth as other programming languages (such as C, C++, Java and Visual Basic) but in the exciting context of the Internet and World Wide Web.

[*Note:* JavaScript was created by Netscape. Microsoft's version is called *JScript*. The languages are close. Netscape, Microsoft and other companies are cooperating with the European Computer Manufacturer's Association (ECMA) to produce a universal, client-side scripting language, the current version of which is referred to as ECMA-262. JavaScript and JScript each conform to this standard. We tested the JavaScript programs in Chapters 13 through 18. Each of these programs works in the latest Netscape and Microsoft browsers.]

Using our live-code approach, every concept is presented in the context of a complete working JavaScript program that is immediately followed by the screen output produced when the HTML document containing the program is loaded into a Web browser. The chapter introduces nonprogrammers to basic programming concepts and constructs. The scripts in this chapter illustrate how to write (*output*) text into a Web page for display to the user and how to obtain (*input*) data from the user at the keyboard. Some of the input and output is performed using the browser's ability to display predefined *graphical user interface (GUI)* windows (called *dialog boxes*) for input and output. This allows a nonprogrammer to concentrate on fundamental programming concepts and constructs rather than developing HTML forms containing GUI components and using the more complex GUI *event handling* in which a JavaScript program responds to the user interactions with an HTML form. Chapter 13 also provides detailed treatments of *decision making* and *arithmetic operations*. After studying this chapter, the student will understand how to write simple, but complete, JavaScript programs.

Chapter 14—JavaScript: Control Structures I

Chapter 14 focuses on the program-development process. The chapter discusses how to take a *problem statement* (i.e., a *requirements document*) and from it develop a working JavaScript program, including performing intermediate steps in a program development tool called *pseudocode*. The chapter introduces some simple control structures used for decision making (**if** and **if/else**) and repetition (**while**). We examine counter-controlled repetition, sentinel-controlled repetition and introduce JavaScript's increment, decrement and assignment operators. The chapter uses simple flowcharts to graphically show the flow of control through each of the control structures. This chapter helps the student develop good programming habits in preparation for dealing with the more substantial programming tasks in the remainder of the text.

Chapter 15—JavaScript: Control Structures II
Chapter 15 discusses much of the material JavaScript has in common with the C programming language, especially the *sequence*, *selection* and *repetition* control structures. Here we introduce one additional control structure for decision making (**switch**) and two additional control structures for repetition (**for** and **do/while**). This chapter also introduces several more operators that allow programmers to define complex conditions in their decision making and repetition structures. The chapter uses flowcharts to show the flow of control through each of the control structures and concludes with a summary that enumerates each of the control structures. The techniques discussed in Chapters 14 and 15 constitute a large part of what traditionally has been taught in the universities under the topic of structured programming.

Chapter 16—JavaScript: Functions
Chapter 16 takes a deeper look inside scripts. Scripts contain data called *global* (or *script-level*) *variables* and executable units called *functions*. We discuss predefined JavaScript functions and programmer-defined functions. The techniques presented in Chapter 16 are essential to the production of properly structured programs, especially the kinds of larger programs that Web programmers are likely to develop in real-world, Web-based applications. The *divide and conquer* strategy is presented as an effective means for solving complex problems by dividing them into simpler interacting components. In this chapter, we also introduce *events* and *event handling*—elements required for programming graphical user interfaces (GUIs) in HTML forms. Events are notifications of state change such as button clicks, mouse clicks, pressing a keyboard key, etc. JavaScript allows programmers to respond to various events by coding functions called *event handlers*. This begins our discussions of *event-driven programming*—the user drives the program by interacting with GUI components (causing *events such as mouse clicks*) and the scripts respond to the events by performing appropriate tasks (*event handling*). The event-driven programming techniques introduced here are used in scripts throughout the book. Dynamic HTML event handling is discussed in detail in Chapter 21.

Chapter 17—JavaScript: Arrays
Chapter 17 explores the processing of data in lists and tables of values. We discuss the structuring of data into *arrays*, or groups, of related data items. The chapter presents several examples of both single-subscripted arrays and double-subscripted arrays. It is widely recognized that structuring data properly is just as important as using control structures effectively in the development of properly structured programs. Examples in the chapter investigate various common array manipulations, sorting data and passing arrays to functions. This chapter also introduces JavaScript's **for/in** control structure that is specifically designed to work with collections of data stored in arrays.

Chapter 18—JavaScript: Objects

This chapter begins our discussion of *object-based programming* with JavaScript's built-in objects. The chapter discusses the terminology of *objects*. The chapter overviews the Java-Script **Math** object's methods and provides several examples of JavaScript's string, date and time processing capabilities with the **String** and **Date** objects. An interesting feature of the **String** object demonstrated here is a set of methods (functions associated with particular objects) that help a script programmer output HTML from a script by wrapping strings in HTML elements. The chapter also discusses JavaScript's **Number** and **Boolean** objects. Many of the features discussed in this chapter are used throughout the Dynamic HTML chapters (19 through 23 and 30 through 32) and the XML chapters (27 and 28) as we illustrate that every element of an HTML document is an object that can be manipulated by JavaScript statements.

Chapter 19—Dynamic HTML: Cascading Style Sheets (CSS)

In earlier versions of HTML, Web browsers controlled the appearance (i.e., the rendering) of every Web page. [If you placed an **H1** (i.e., a large heading) element in your document, the browser rendered the element in its own manner. With the advent of *Cascading Style Sheets*, you can now take control of the way the browser renders your page.] Applying Cascading Style Sheets to Web pages can give major portions of your Web site (or the whole Web site for that matter) their own distinctive look. Cascading Style Sheets technology allows you to specify the style of your page elements (spacing, margins, etc.) separately from the structure of your document (section headers, body text, links, etc.). This *separation of structure from content* allows greater manageability and makes changing the style of your document easier and faster.

Chapter 20—Dynamic HTML: Objects Model and Collections

There is a massive switch occurring in the computer industry. The procedural programming style used since the inception of the industry is being replaced by the object-oriented style of programming. Object orientation has demonstrated its worth to the extent that the vast majority of major new software efforts use object technology in one form or another. Some languages make it easy for you to create your own objects by various means, either "from scratch" or by inheritance from object "blueprints" called classes. The scripting languages we discuss in this book are most commonly used to manipulate existing objects by sending them messages that either inquire about the objects' attributes or that ask the objects to perform certain supportable methods. In this Chapter we continue the discussion of object technology we began in Chapter 18, presenting Microsoft's Dynamic HTML object model. Working with this object model is a key to the power of Dynamic HTML in Chapters 19 through 23, 27, 28 and 30 through 32. As IE5 downloads your page from a server, it converts each of the elements on the page into an object. Objects store data (their *attributes*) and can perform functions (their methods). Through scripting languages (such as JavaScript), you can write commands that will *get* or *set* (i.e., read or write) an object's attributes. You can also write commands that call an object's methods to cause that object to perform its various functions.

Chapter 21—Dynamic HTML: Event Model

We have seen that HTML pages can be controlled via scripting. The HTML 4 specification includes HTML's *event model* that enables scripts to respond to user actions and change the Web page accordingly without having to download another Web page from the World

Wide Web. This makes Web applications more responsive and user-friendly, and can reduce server load—a performance concern we discuss in Chapters 25 through 29.

With the event model, scripts can respond to a user moving and/or clicking the mouse, scrolling up or down the screen or entering keystrokes. Content becomes more dynamic while interfaces become more intuitive. We discuss how to use the event model to respond to user actions. We give examples of event handling for many of the most common and useful events, which range from mouse capture, to error handling to form processing. For example, we use the **onreset** event to prompt a user to confirm that he or she really wants to reset a form. Included at the end of the chapter is a table of all DHTML events.

Chapter 22—Dynamic HTML: Filters and Transitions

Internet Explorer includes a set of filters that let the author perform complex image transformations completely in the Web browser without the need for further downloads from a Web server. Especially important is that the filters are scriptable, so the author can create stunning animations with a few lines of client-side JavaScript. We introduce the **fliph** and **flipv** filters, which can mirror text and images horizontally and vertically. The **chroma** filter applies transparency to an image, and the **mask** filter applies an image mask. The **gray**, **xray** and **invert** filters all apply simple transformations to images. The **shadow** and **dropShadow** filters both apply shadowing effects to text and images, and the **light** filter allows you to simulate light sources illuminating your document. The **alpha** filter allows you to create transparency gradients, and the **glow** filter allows you to create dynamic, glowing text. The **blur** filter applies a directional motion blur, and the **wave** filter applies a sine-wave distortion to your elements.

Internet Explorer also provides *transitions* that are similar to those in professional PowerPoint-like presentation packages, in which transitions between slides are marked with visual effects such as Box in, Circle out, Wipe left, Vertical blinds, Checkerboard across, Random dissolve, Split horizontal in, Strips right up and Random bars horizontal. Besides these transitions which are applied with the **revealTrans** filter, there is a **blendTrans** filter, which allows you to gradually fade in or fade out an HTML element over a set period of time.

Chapter 23—Dynamic HTML: Data Binding

This is one of the most important chapters in the book for people who will build substantial, real-world, Web-based applications. Businesses thrive on data. Dynamic HTML helps Web application developers produce more responsive data-intensive applications.

With *data binding*, data need no longer reside exclusively on the server. The data can be maintained on the client and in a manner that distinguishes that data from the HTML code on the page. Typically, the data is sent from the server to the client and then all subsequent manipulations take place on that data directly on the client thus improving performance and responsiveness by eliminating server activity and network delays. Once the data is available on the client, the data can then be *sorted* (i.e., arranged into ascending or descending order) and *filtered* (i.e., only the portion of the data relevant to the user's needs is selected) in various ways. We present examples of each of these operations.

To bind external data to HTML elements, Internet Explorer employs software capable of connecting the browser to live data sources. These are known as *Data Source Objects (DSOs)*. There are several DSOs available in IE5—in this chapter we discuss the most popular DSO—the *Tabular Data Control (TDC)*.

Chapter 24—VBScript

In Chapter 24, we assume the reader is now familiar with the principles of programming, so we present Microsoft's *VBScript* condensed into a single chapter (exactly as we do with Perl scripting in Chapter 29). *JavaScript/JScript* has become the language of choice for *client-side scripting*. All major browsers support this language, which has been standardized through the *European Computer Manufacturers Association* as *ECMA-262*. VBScript is a subset of Visual Basic. It can certainly be used for client-side scripting, but it is a Microsoft-specific technology and is not supported by many leading browsers (although so-called *plug-ins* are available to help some of those browsers understand and process VBScript). So many people browsing Web pages containing VBScript will not experience the full functionality intended by the page designers. VBScript, however, has become the preferred language for writing server side *Active Server Pages (ASP), a Microsoft-specific technology* which we discuss in detail in Chapter 25. Because we need to discuss VBScript before ASP, we have chosen to include this chapter as the last in our discussion of client-side scripting before we begin our discussion of server-side topics. This will prepare you to use VBScript on the client-side in Microsoft communities and in Microsoft-based *intranets* (i.e., internal networks that use the same communications protocols as the Internet). It will also prepare you to use VBScript with Active Server Pages.

Chapter 25—Active Server Pages (ASP)

In this chapter we discuss Microsoft's Active Server Pages (ASP), the first of the two server-side software development paradigms the book presents. Active Server Pages can be programmed in a variety of languages—by far the most popular of these is Microsoft's VBScript (which is discussed in Chapter 24). In a typical *multitiered Web-based application*, there is a *top-tier* containing the code that interacts directly with the user. This tier, called the *client*, is usually the browser (such as IE5) rendering a Web-page and executing scripting commands. These commands can be implemented in a variety of languages, but JavaScript has almost become the universal de facto standard *client-side scripting language*. Microsoft offers its version of JavaScript which it called *JScript*. We have tried to use the common portions only of these languages for most of the client-side scripting code in the book. The *bottom tier* is the database containing the organization's information. The *middle tier*, called the *server*, contains the *business logic*. It receives client requests from the top-tier, references the data stored in the database in the bottom tier, and responds to the client by creating a new HTML/Dynamic HTML page and sending the page to the client to be rendered by the browser. The HTML/Dynamic HTML sent to the client can be anything the programmer wishes—especially information retrieved from databases. Active Server Pages is Microsoft's technology for implementing middle-tier business logic. Key business implementations of ASP, such as in the use of session tracking and cookies, are covered thoroughly.

The chapter also discusses the *structured query language (SQL)* for manipulating database data. ActiveX Data Objects (ADO)—a high-level programming interface used by Microsoft languages such as Visual Basic, Visual C++, VBScript, etc. to access databases—is also introduced.

We have worked hard to create a book that will help you construct complete Web-based multitiered, client/server, database-intensive systems. From Chapters 9 through 24, we have focussed on the client side. Chapters 25 through 29 focus on the server side, discussing many technologies crucial to implementing successful Web-based systems. One of the crucial decisions you will make in building Web-based systems is what server(s) to use.

The two most popular are *Apache* in the UNIX world and *Internet Information Server (IIS)* in the Microsoft world. Each of these is a "heavy-duty," "industrial strength" server designed to handle the high volumes of transactions that occur in active, real-world systems. These require considerable system resources and administrative support, as is typical of real systems. To help people enter the world of server programming, Microsoft provides *Personal Web Server (PWS)*—a lightweight version of IIS. PWS is easy to install and run on Windows-based systems, a large part of the intended audience for this book. We focus on PWS in our case studies so that students and professional readers with Windows 95 and Windows 98 systems will be able to run our server-side programs easily. This a crucial chapter for those readers who will want to implement Web-based applications. [*Note:* For Windows 2000 users, we also discuss Microsoft Internet Information Services Web Server which is similar to PWS.]

Chapter 26—e-Business Implementations with ASP
Chapter 26 presents three case studies that show how to combine HTML, VBScript, ASP and database manipulation to form e-business solutions. Each of the case studies is a three-tiered application with HTML as the client-side tier, ASP as the middle tier and a database that stores customer information and tracks inventory as the third tier. The first case study implements a shopping cart using cookies; the second is an online auction site which allows registered users to bid on and sell items; and the third is a comparison pricing bot that searches the Web for the lowest price of a book.

Chapter 27—XML (Extensible Markup Language)
In this chapter we provide an introduction to XML (Extensible Markup Language). XML is a technology that allows programmers to create portable documents that contain structured data. XML is a language for creating new markup languages that precisely describe data. XML could be used, for example, to create HTML. The key to XML is that it is not limited to a fixed set of tags as is HTML. Rather, XML allows the document author to create new elements and tags specific to their applications areas.

This chapter introduces many different XML-related technologies including custom markup languages derived from XML, document type definition (DTD) files for specifying an XML document's structure, XSL (Extensible Stylesheet Language) documents for specifying how an XML document is rendered and schema for specifying an XML document's structure. Schema is an emerging technology that is designed to replace DTDs.

The chapter provides an introduction to the XHTML™ (Extensible Hypertext Markup Language)—the proposed successor to HTML. XHTML is combines XML technology with HTML 4. XHTML is seen by many in industry as the technology that will provide a smooth transition from HTML to XML. We also provide a brief discussion of two emerging Microsoft technologies BizTalk™ and SOAP which define ways businesses can transfer data and conduct transactions. Both of these technologies heavily use XML.

The possible uses for XML are endless. Baseball fans might want to develop a language that lets them transmit structured information about games. Chess fans might want to transmit marked-up chess moves. Businesses might want to transmit marked-up information about their financial transactions. Stock brokerage houses might want to transmit marked-up transaction information for buying and selling stocks and bonds. Clients might want to transmit marked-up purchase-order information to vendors. Actually all of this information can be transmitted in simple files without XML. But with XML, the information is described precisely, so applications, such as browsers, can work with the information more intelligently.

Chapter 28—Case Study: An Online Bookstore

This chapter presents a large case study that combines many of the technologies introduced earlier in the book. In particular, the case study heavily uses DHTML, JavaScript and Active Server Pages. This fully functional case study uses a shopping cart—implemented with XML. Business-to-consumer (B2C)—where the user is interacting with the bookstore—and business-to-business (B2B)—where the bookstore is interacting with a warehouse—models are implemented in the case study.

This case study is divided into two pieces: Chapter 28 in the book and a PDF file on the CD-ROM that accompanies this book. Chapter 28 contains the architecture and text description for the case study. The PDF file "Chapter 28 Code Listings" contains the source code listing for each document with line numbers. The source code for the entire case-study is in the Chapter 28 examples directory.

Chapter 29—Perl 5 and CGI (Common Gateway Interface)

There are a variety of popular server-side technologies for developing Web-based applications. Historically, the most widely used (and the second such technology we cover in this book) has been Perl/CGI. Despite the onrush of the newer technologies from Microsoft and Sun—Active Server Pages (ASP) and Java Server Pages, respectively—the Perl/CGI community is well entrenched and will remain popular for the foreseeable future. Chapter 29 presents a nice introduction to CGI and Perl, including many real-world, live-code examples and discussions, including demonstrations of some of the most recent features of each of these technologies. A shopping cart implementation is also included as a case study.

Chapter 30—Dynamic HTML: Structured Graphics ActiveX Control

Although high-quality content is what visitors to your site are usually looking for, it may not be enough to hold their attention and keep them coming back. Eye-catching, animated graphics may help. This chapter explores the Structured Graphics ActiveX Control included with Internet Explorer 5. The Structured Graphics Control is a Web interface for the widely used DirectAnimation subset of Microsoft's DirectX software, used in many popular video games and graphical applications. This control allows you to create complex graphics containing lines, shapes, textures and fills. As with other elements of a Web page, the control is accessible through scripting which allows the graphics to be manipulated dynamically.

Chapter 31—Dynamic HTML: Path, Sequencer and Sprite ActiveX Controls

In this chapter we discuss three additional DirectAnimation ActiveX controls available for use with Internet Explorer 5: the *Path Control*, the *Sequencer Control* and the *Sprite Control*. Each of these controls allows Web-page designers to add animated multimedia effects to Web pages. The Path control allows you to control the positioning of elements on the screen. This is more elaborate than CSS absolute positioning, as you can define lines, ovals and other shapes as paths along which objects move. Every aspect of motion is controllable through scripting. The Sequencer Control allows you to perform tasks at specified time intervals. This is useful for presentation-like effects, especially when used with the transitions we covered in Chapter 22. The Sprite Control is a mechanism for creating animations for use on the Web. We also discuss, for comparison purposes, animated GIFs—another technique for producing web-based animations.

Chapter 32—Multimedia: Audio, Video, Speech Synthesis and Recognition

HTML is not just for text. Our focus in this chapter is on the explosion of audio, video and speech technology appearing on the Web. We discuss adding sound, video and animated characters to your Web pages (primarily using existing audio and video clips). Your first reaction may be a sense of caution, because these are complex technologies about which most readers have had little education. Yet, you will quickly see how easy it is to incorporate multimedia into your Web pages and control it with Dynamic HTML. This is one of the beauties of today's programming languages. They give the programmer easy access to complex technologies.

Multimedia files can be quite large. Some multimedia technologies require that the complete multimedia file be downloaded to the client before the audio or video begins playing. With *streaming audio* and *streaming video* technologies, the audios and videos can begin playing while the files are downloading, thus reducing delays. Streaming technologies are quite popular on the Web. This chapter demonstrates how to incorporate streaming media into Web sites and features the technologies of several important streaming media companies.

The chapter also includes an extensive set of Internet and Web resources such as Web sites that show interesting ways in which designers use multimedia enhanced Web pages.

Chapter 33—Macromedia Flash

Macromedia's Flash is a cutting-edge multimedia technology for applications on the Web. It allows the user to develop interactive animated movies at a fraction of the size of traditional media file types. A Flash movie can be embedded into a Web site or run as a stand-alone program. Advanced features such as *tweening*, where the frames in between two key points in an animation are drawn automatically, enable even those who are not artistically talented to make respectable movies. In this chapter, you will learn how to make Flash movies with sound and interactive features. With this knowledge, we show how to create applications including an online storefront and a product demonstration. When you finish this chapter, you will have a solid understanding of developing Flash movies—opening a world of advanced Flash multimedia development to you.

Chapter 34—Accessibility

Currently, the World Wide Web presents a challenge to those who are physically impaired. Multimedia-rich Web sites often present difficulty to text readers and other programs designed to help the vision impaired, and the increasing amount of audio on the Web is inaccessible to the deaf. To rectify this situation, the World Wide Web Consortium started the Web Accessibility Initiative, which provides guidelines on how to make Web sites accessible to people with disabilities. This chapter provides a description of these methods, such as use of the **<HEADERS>** tag to make tables more accessible to page readers, use of the **ALT** attribute of the **<IMG>** tag to describe images, and proper use of HTML and CSS to ensure that a page can be viewed on any type of display or reader.

VoiceXML, can also be used to increase accessibility with speech synthesis and speech recognition. In the future, easy navigation of Web sites by all users with all types of hardware and software will be mandated.

Other accessibility technologies are covered as well. We walk through the setup for the Windows 2000 accessibility tools and examine accessibility features of Internet Explorer. Two of the most popular text readers, Microsoft Narrator and Henter-Joyce JAWS, are discussed as well.

Appendix A—HTML Special Characters
A table shows many commonly used HTML special characters, called *character entity references* by the World Wide Web Consortium (W3C).

Appendix B—HTML Colors
An explanation of how to create any color using either color names or hexadecimal RGB value is provided, along with a table that matches colors to values.

Appendix C—ASCII Character Set
This appendix contains a table of the 128 alphanumeric symbols and their ASCII numbers.

Appendix D—Operator Precedence Chart
A series of tables show the precedence of the operators in JavaScript/JScript/ECMAScript, VBScript and Perl.

Appendices on the CD-ROM that Accompanies this Book
There are also four appendices on the CD-ROM that accompanies this book. *Number Systems* discusses the binary, octal, decimal and hexadecimal number systems. It considers how to convert numbers between bases and explains the one's complement and two's complement binary representations. *Setting Up an ODBC Data Source Name (DSN)* walks the user through the creation of a DSN, which is used by some of the examples in Chapters 25, 26, 28 and 29 that access databases. *Installing a Web Server* walks the reader through the installation of Microsoft's Personal Web Server (PWS), which is used in Chapters 25, 26, 28 and 29 to serve Web documents to client Web browsers. *ActiveState Perl Installation* walks the reader through the installation of ActiveState's implementation of Perl for Windows (used in Chapter 29).

Well, there you have it! We have worked hard to create this book and its optional interactive multimedia *Cyber Classroom* version. The book is loaded with hundreds of working, live-code examples, programming tips, self-review exercises and answers, challenging exercises and projects and numerous study aids to help you master the material. The technologies we introduce will help you write Web-based applications quickly and effectively. As you read the book, if something is not clear, or if you find an error, please write to us at `deitel@deitel.com`. We will respond promptly, and we will post corrections and clarifications on our Web site

`www.deitel.com`

Prentice Hall maintains `www.prenhall.com/deitel`—a Web site dedicated to our Prentice Hall textbooks, multimedia packages and Web-based training products. The site contains "Companion Web Sites" for each of our books that include frequently asked questions (FAQs), example downloads, errata, updates, additional self-test questions and other resources.

You are about to start on a challenging and rewarding path. We hope you enjoy learning with *e-Business and e-Commerce How to Program* as much as we enjoyed writing it!

1.21 Internet and World Wide Web Resources

www.deitel.com
Please check this site for daily updates, corrections and additional resources for all Deitel & Associates, Inc. publications.

www.learnthenet.com/english/index.html
Learn the Net is a Web site containing a complete overview of the Internet, the World Wide Web and the underlying technologies. The site contains information that can help people Internet and Web get novices started.

www.w3.org
The W3C homepage is a comprehensive description of the Web and where it is headed. The World Wide Web Consortium is an international joint effort with the goal of overseeing the development of the World Wide Web. The goals of the W3C are divided into categories: User Interface Domain, Technology and Society Domain, Architecture Domain and Web Accessibility Initiatives. For each Internet technology with which the W3C is involved, the site provides a description of the technology and its benefits to Web designers, the history of the technology and the future goals of the W3C in developing the technology. Topics discussed on the site include Hypertext Markup Language (HTML), Cascading Style Sheets (CSS), Document Object Model (DOM), multimedia, graphics, Hypertext Transfer Protocol (HTTP), Extensible Markup Language (XML) and Extensible Stylesheet Language (XSL). This site is of great benefit for understanding the standards of the World Wide Web. Each of these topics is discussed (at various levels of depth) in this book.

SUMMARY

[Note: Because this chapter is primarily a summary of the rest of the book we have not provided a summary section. In each of the remaining 33 chapters we provide a detailed summary of the points covered in that chapter.]

TERMINOLOGY

Active Server pages (ASP)	computer
Ada	computer program
ALU (arithmetic and logic unit)	computer programmer
arithmetic and logic unit (ALU)	CPU (central processing unit)
array	data binding
assembly language	database
bandwidth	disk
Basic	divide and conquer strategy
bottom tier	dynamic content
browser	Dynamic HTML
C	e-business
C++	ECMA-262
Cascading Style Sheets (CSS)	e-commerce
central processing unit (CPU)	editor
client	electronic commerce
client/server computing	event-driven programming
COBOL	execute phase
compiler	extensible markup language (XML)

filters
Fortran
FrontPage Express
function
hardware
high-level language
HTML (Hypertext Markup Language)
IDE (Integrated Development Environment)
input device
input unit
input/output (I/O)
Internet
Internet Explorer 5
interpreter
intranet
IP (Internet Protocol)
Java
JavaScript
JScript
KIS (keep it simple)
live-code approach
machine language
memory unit
method
Microsoft
Microsoft's Internet Explorer Web browser
middle tier
multimedia
multitasking
multithreading
Netscape's Communicator Web browser
object
object-based programming (OBP)
object-oriented programming (OOP)
output device
output unit
Pascal

Path Control
Perl
personal computing
platforms
portability
presentation of a document
primary memory
problem statement
procedural programming
programming language
reusable componentry
secondary storage unit
Sequencer Control
server
servlets
software
software reuse
sorting data
speech
Sprite Control
streaming audio and video
structure of a document
Structured Graphics Control
structured programming
Sun Microsystems
syntax error
TCP (Transmission Control protocol)
TCP/IP
transitions
translator programs
Ultimate Paint
VBScript
Web Accessibility Initiative (WAI)
Web server
World Wide Web (WWW)
World Wide Web Consortium (W3C)
WYSIWYG

SELF-REVIEW EXERCISES

1.1   Fill in the blanks in each of the following:
   a) The company that popularized personal computing was _____.
   b) The computer that made personal computing legitimate in business and industry was the _____.
   c) Computers process data under the control of sets of instructions called _____.
   d) The six key logical units of the computer are the _____, _____, _____, _____, _____ and _____.
   e) The three classes of languages discussed in the chapter are _____, _____ and _____.
   f) The programs that translate high-level language programs into machine language are called _____.

1.2   Fill in the blanks in each of the following sentences.

    a) The _____ programming language was created by Professor Nicklaus Wirth and was intended for academic use.

    b) One important capability of Ada is called _____ this allows programmers to specify that many activities are to occur in parallel.

    c) The _____ is the grandparent of what is today called the Internet.

    d) The information carrying capacity of a communications medium like the Internet is called _____.

    e) The acronym TCP/IP stands for _____.

1.3   Fill in the blanks in each of the following statements.

    a) The _____ allows computer users to locate and view multimedia-based documents on almost any subject over the Internet.

    b) _____ of CERN developed the World Wide Web and several of the communications protocols that form the backbone of the Web.

    c) _____ are essentially reusable software components that model items in the real world.

    d) C initially became widely known as the development language of the _____ operating system.

    e) In a client/server relationship, the _____ requests that some action be performed and the _____ performs the action and responds.

ANSWERS TO SELF-REVIEW EXERCISES

1.1   a) Apple. b) IBM Personal Computer. c) programs (or scripts). d) input unit, output unit, memory unit, arithmetic and logic unit, central processing unit, secondary storage unit. e) machine languages, assembly languages, high-level languages. f) compilers.

1.2   a) Pascal. b) multitasking. c) ARPAnet. d) bandwidth. e) Transmission Control Protocol/ Internet Protocol.

1.3   a) World Wide Web. b) Tim Berners-Lee. c) Objects. d) UNIX. e) client, server.

EXERCISES

1.4   Categorize each of the following items as either hardware or software:

    a) CPU

    b) compiler

    c) ALU

    d) interpreter

    e) input unit

    f) an editor program

    g) XML

    h) CD-ROM drive

    i) mouse

    j) COBOL

1.5   Why might you want to write a program in a machine-independent language instead of a machine-dependent language? Why might a machine-dependent language be more appropriate for writing certain types of programs?

1.6   Fill in the blanks in each of the following statements:

    a) Which logical unit of the computer receives information from outside the computer for use by the computer? _____.

    b) The process of instructing the computer to solve specific problems is called _____.

      c) What type of computer language uses English-like abbreviations for machine language instructions? _____.

      d) Which logical unit of the computer sends information that has already been processed by the computer to various devices so that the information may be used outside the computer? _____.

      e) Which logical unit of the computer retains information? _____.

      f) Which logical unit of the computer performs calculations? _____.

      g) Which logical unit of the computer makes logical decisions? _____.

      h) The level of computer language most convenient to the programmer for writing programs quickly and easily is _____.

      i) The only language that a computer can directly understand is called that computer's _____.

      j) Which logical unit of the computer coordinates the activities of all the other logical units? _____.

1.7   Fill in the blanks in each of the following statements.

      a) The two most popular World Wide Web browsers are Netscape Communicator and Microsoft _____.

      b) A key issue when using HTML is the separation of the presentation of a document from the _____ of that document.

      c) A function associated with a particular object is called a _____.

      d) With the advent of _____ Style Sheets you can now take control of the way the browsers render your pages.

      e) The data of an object is also referred to as that object's _____.

      f) Visual effects such as Box in, Circle out, Wipe left, Vertical blinds, Checkerboard across, Random dissolve, Split horizontal in, Strips right up and Random bars horizontal are all examples of Internet Explorer 5 _____.

      g) The process of arranging data into ascending or descending order is called _____.

      h) The _____ Control allows you to perform tasks at specified time intervals.

      i) With _____ audio and video technologies, audios and videos can begin playing while the files are downloading, thus reducing delays.

      j) The _____ scripting language has become the de facto standard for writing server-side Active Server Pages.

      k) The acronym XML stands for the _____ Markup Language.

      l) The two most popular Web Servers are _____ in the UNIX world and in the Microsoft world.

      m) In a multitiered Web-based application, the middle tier is called the server and contains the _____.

      n) MathML and CML are markup languages created from _____.

Introduction to Internet Explorer 5 and the World Wide Web

Objectives

- To become familiar with the Microsoft Internet Explorer 5 (IE5) Web browser's capabilities.
- To be able to use IE5 to search the "world of information" available on the World Wide Web.
- To be able to use Microsoft Outlook Express to send and receive email.
- To be able to use Microsoft NetMeeting to have online conferences with friends and colleagues.
- To feel comfortable using the Internet as an information tool.

Give us the tools, and we will finish the job.
Sir Winston Spencer Churchill

We must learn to explore all the options and possibilities that confront us in a complex and rapidly changing world.
James William Fulbright

Outline

2.1 Introduction

Prior to the explosion of interest in the Internet and the World Wide Web, if you heard the term *browser,* you probably would have thought about browsing at a bookstore. Today "browser" has a whole new meaning. Now a browser is an important piece of software that enables you to browse the Internet ("surf" the Web). You have a world of information, services and products to browse. The two most popular browsers are Microsoft's Internet Explorer and Netscape's Communicator—we will study Internet Explorer in depth.

You sit down at a computer and literally search the world in seconds with special Internet sites called *search engines*. Through your browser, you request your favorite search engine, then you type in your request, and the search engine responds in seconds, listing many Web sites that have information on the subject you requested. What a wonderful way to learn about the world in which we live—what a marvelous way to improve our productivity!

The Internet is also a wonderful medium for exchanging information. Using tools that are part of the Internet Explorer 5 software package (enclosed on the CD included with this book), we discuss how to use the Web to its fullest potential. These tools include the Internet browser, email, newsgroups, chat, and much more.

2.2 Connecting to the Internet

To connect to the Internet, you need a computer, a modem or network card, Internet software, and knowledge of how to install and run programs.

The first step to getting on the Internet, which we cannot cover here (because the method differs widely depending on your situation), is registering with an *Internet Service Provider* (ISP). An ISP connects your computer to the Internet through a modem or a network connection. If you are living on a college campus, you may have a free network connection available; contact your college computer support staff for more information on getting a network hookup. If you do not have a network connection available, then you will have to connect through a commercial ISP such as America Online, CompuServe, or many others.

Once you have signed up for your account (with your ISP), you should start the **Internet Connection Wizard** (ICW). This program should be located in your **Start** menu under **Programs**-**Accessories**-**Communications**. The screen that appears upon starting this program should look like Fig. 2.1.

Simply follow the instructions in **Internet Connection Wizard** to make the appropriate settings for your Internet connection with your computer. Making these settings will help things run more smoothly and will also help you reconnect to the Internet if you are ever disconnected accidentally.

If you are interested in learning more about the Internet and its features, click on the button labeled **Tutorial**, located in the first ICW screen.

Once your connection has been set up, you are ready to communicate over the Internet.

Performance Tip 2.1

You will get the best browsing performance when viewing the Web if you have as few programs as possible open on your system. This precaution will maximize the amount of memory available for your browser and its extensions to use.

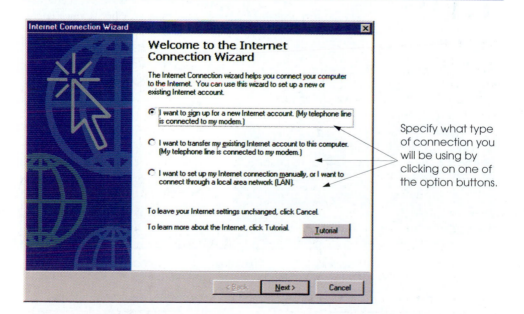

Specify what type of connection you will be using by clicking on one of the option buttons.

Fig. 2.1   Using **Internet Connection Wizard** to get on the Internet.

2.3 Features of Internet Explorer 5

The browser is a program that showcases certain files on the Internet in an accessible, visually pleasing way. Figure 2.2 shows the main browser window in Microsoft's Internet Explorer 5 (IE5).

A *URL (Uniform Resource Locator and Universal Resource Locator are both common usage)* is displayed in the **Address** bar, toward the top of the browser window. The URL describes the location of the file your browser is displaying or loading. If you are viewing a page on the Web, then the URL will usually begin with **`http://`**. The acronym **`http`** stands for *HyperText Transfer Protocol*. This is the format of most URLs you will be viewing. We discuss additional types of URLs later in this chapter.

To go to a new URL, click anywhere inside the address bar. Once the current URL text is highlighted, type in the URL for the site you would like to visit (this overwrites the highlighted URL) and hit the *Enter* key.

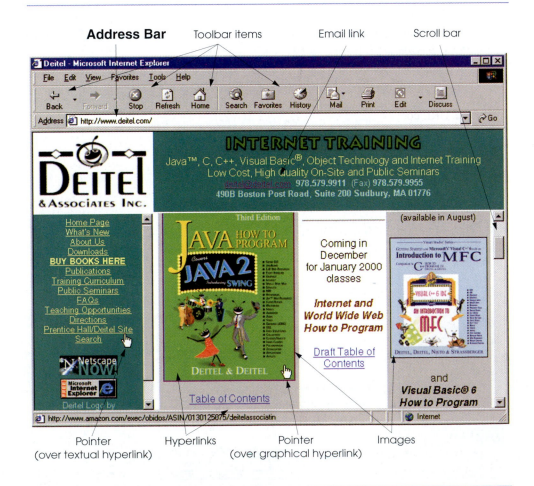

Fig. 2.2   Deitel & Associates, Inc. home page.

A *hyperlink* is a visual element on a Web page that, when clicked, loads a specified URL into the browser window. By clicking on this hyperlink (also known as an *anchor*), you will make your browser automatically load the new URL. Your mouse appears as a pointer by default. When it is passed over a hyperlink, it is transformed into a hand with the index finger pointing upward (to indicate that this is indeed a link). Originally used as a publishing tool for scientific texts, hyperlinking has been crucial to making the Internet a more interesting and dynamic environment for sharing information.

IE5 has built-in controls that record the URLs sites your browser has loaded. This record is called your *history* and is stored in chronological order by date. We discuss several ways to use this history. The simplest is to use the **Forward** and **Back** buttons located at the top of your browser window (Fig. 2.2). If you click on **Back**, then your browser will reload the last page you viewed in the browser. The **Forward** button loads the next page in your history (you can use the **Forward** button only after you have gone backward in your history). On pages that are frequently updated, you may want to click the **Refresh** button. This will cause your browser to reload an up-to-the-minute version of the current URL.

You can skip forward or backward several entries in your history at a time by clicking on the small arrow pointing down, located directly to the right of both the **Forward** and **Back** buttons. This will display a list of your last/next five sites in your history. You can go directly to one of these sites by highlighting and clicking its entry in this list.

As mentioned earlier, hyperlinks are used to direct your browser towards a specified URL. This URL could be another Web page, or it could lead to an email address or a file. If the hyperlink is targeted to an email address, clicking it will not load a new Web page. Instead, it will load your default email program and open a message addressed to the specified recipient email address. We will discuss emailing in greater detail later on in this chapter.

If a URL is targeted towards a file that the browser is incapable of displaying, then you will be given the option to *download* the file. When you download a file, you are making a copy of it on your computer. Examples of downloadable files are programs, documents and sound files.

The browser interface also enables you to download all elements of a Web page, including its code and any graphical elements that appear on the page. You save images on the page by right-clicking, choosing **Save Picture As...** from the options box that pops up, then specifying a location on your hard drive to save the image (Fig. 2.3). You can have the browser save the image as your background wallpaper by clicking **Set as Wallpaper** in the right-click menu (*wallpaper* is the background for your main operating system screen). To save the code of the page, click **Save As...** in the file menu and specify a location.

A new feature of IE5 that is related to the history function is the address bar *AutoComplete*. AutoComplete remembers all the URLs you have visited for a set time span (30 days by default). When you start typing a URL stored in the history, a scrollable drop-down menu like the one in Fig. 2.4 appears beneath your address bar, listing all URLs in the history that are potential matches for the URL you are entering. To go to one of these URLs, highlight your desired address in the AutoComplete bar (with your mouse or arrow keys), and either click on it or press *Enter*. Your browser will then load the file at the selected URL as if you had clicked a hyperlink targeting that URL.

Fig. 2.3   Capturing a picture from a Web site.

Partial address

AutoComplete address options

Fig. 2.4   AutoComplete address options. (Courtesy of United States Senate.)

There is an extension of the AutoComplete feature for dealing with *forms* (areas on Web sites where you can enter information). While browsing the WWW, you will often encounter forms for entering and dispatching information. Examples of forms you might use are a username and password form to enter a site, or an address and credit card form for buying a book online. AutoComplete gives you the option (which you can decline if you like) to remember some of your common entries to forms. It will then provide an AutoComplete drop-down menu when you go to a place in a form where these commonly typed terms might be placed, thus saving you time.

The interactive history bar (Fig. 2.5) can be activated by clicking the button marked **History** in the row of buttons at the top of your browser window. The interactive history bar will show you your history over the past 30 days (or whatever length of time you specify). It has heading levels ordered chronologically by week, by day, alphabetically by site directory name and by individual URL. You can choose directories and URLs to visit with your mouse. This tool is useful for returning to a recently visited site for which you have forgotten the URL.

Fig. 2.5   **History** options.

2.4 Searching the Internet

The most commonly used method of finding a Web site related to a specific topic is to search the Internet by using sites called *search engines*. Search engines constantly explore Web pages throughout the Internet and keep searchable records of the sites they encounter. You can search through their catalogs by going to a search engine site such as *Yahoo* (**www.yahoo.com**), *AltaVista* (**www.altavista.com**), *Excite* (**www.excite.com**) and *InfoSeek* (**www.infoseek.com**), and then entering your desired topic. The search engine returns a list of hyperlinks to sites containing information on your topic.

IE5 has a nice feature that saves you time in querying the major search engines for a site that you want. This feature is accessible by clicking the **Search** button on the toolbar at the top of your browser window (Fig. 2.6). The window that appears after you click the **Search** button is easy to use. First, click the button next to the type of information for which you would like to search (you can select only one of these so-called *radio buttons*). Options include Web sites, addresses, businesses and online maps. After your specified search options load in the window, fill in the required fields in the search form and click the **Search** button. After a few seconds (the actual time depends significantly on the speed of your Internet connection and how busy the site is), the search results appear as hyperlinks in the search window. Click a link that interests you and let the surfing begin!

Fig. 2.6   Searching the Internet with IE5.

If you are not satisfied with the results of the search you can click on the button at the top of the search window labeled **Next,** and IE5 will automatically send your search string to another search engine.

2.5 Online Help and Tutorials

Solutions for most problems you may encounter while using Internet Explorer have been included with the software. IE5 includes an online **Tour** and a built-in **Help** feature. These can be accessed through the **Help** menu (Fig. 2.7).

When you click on **Tour**, your Web browser is directed to a site run by Microsoft, the developer of IE5. This site, which features an expanded version of the **Tour** available through the **Internet Connection Wizard**, presents a basic overview of the Internet, browsers and IE5, along with more specific information on IE5's features. This tour is navigated via hyperlinks.

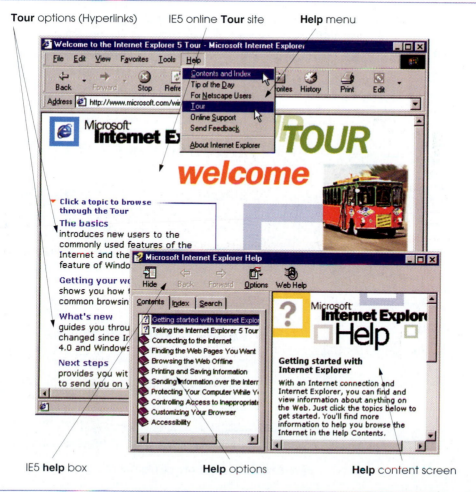

Fig. 2.7   Microsoft IE5 Online **Tour** and **Help** window.

If there is a menu item or a function that you do not understand in IE5, your best bet for finding assistance is the **Contents and Index** feature, accessible through the **Help** menu. There are three **Help** tabs here: **Contents**, which provides a summary of the major **Help** topics available; **Index**, which provides an alphabetical list of all **Help** topics available; and **Search**, which provides you with a mechanism to search the **Help** index for a topic that gives answers to your question.

2.6 Keeping Track of Your Favorite Sites

As you browse the Web, you may identify sites that contain useful information, games and activities to which you would like to return. IE5 provides a mechanism called **Favorites** that allows you to save the URLs of sites you frequently visit, so you can easily return to those sites in the future (Fig. 2.8).

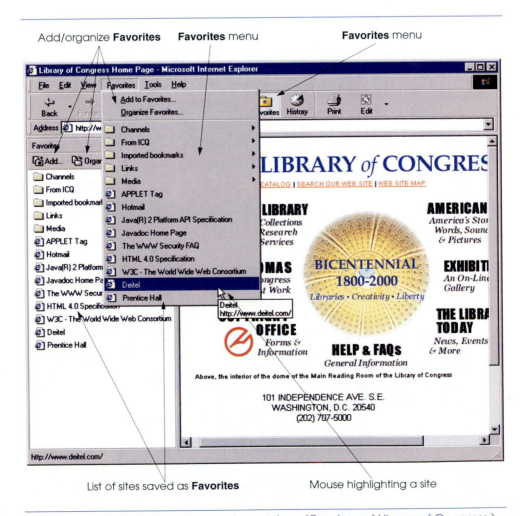

Add/organize **Favorites**   **Favorites** menu   **Favorites** menu

List of sites saved as **Favorites**   Mouse highlighting a site

Fig. 2.8   The **Favorites** button and menu bar. (Courtesy of Library of Congress.)

Chapter 2　　Introduction to Internet Explorer 5 and the World Wide Web　　49

When you visit a site that you would like to save as a favorite, select the **Add to Favorites...** option in the **Favorites** menu. The site will now be listed in the **Favorites** menu, identified by the page's title (the title is shown on the colored bar at the top of the browser window). You can later go to any site saved as a favorite by opening the **Favorites** menu and clicking the site.

Favorites functions are also accessible via clicking the **Favorites** button on the toolbar at the top of your browser window. IE5 also allows you to customize your favorites (Fig. 2.9).

Through the **Organize Favorites** dialog box, which is accessible by clicking **Organize Favorites...** in the **Favorites** menu, you can rename favorites, create folders to organize favorites, place favorites into and remove favorites from these folders, and delete favorites. All these options are available by clicking their buttons on the left of the **Organize Favorites** dialog box. The **Organize Favorites** box indicates how many times you have visited that site. You can have IE5 save the pages branching from a specific favorites site, so that you can view the info when not online. This option can be accessed by clicking the **Make available offline** checkbox.

2.7 FTP (File Transfer Protocol)

Earlier in this chapter, we touched upon downloading—the process of copying a file from the Internet to your hard drive. You will normally be downloading programs, or compressed versions of programs (i.e., programs that have been reformatted to take up less space), to install on your computer. Downloading is typically initiated on a Web page by clicking a hyperlink targeted at file on a Web site or *FTP* site. FTP stands for *File Transfer Protocol*, an old but still popular method for making data available over the internet. An FTP site URL begins with **ftp://** rather than **http://** (used with Web page addresses).

You typically access FTP sites via hyperlinks. You can also access FTP sites through the IE5 Web browser interface (see Fig. 2.10).

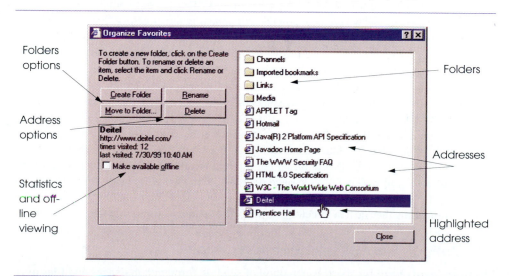

Fig. 2.9　**Organize Favorites** dialog.

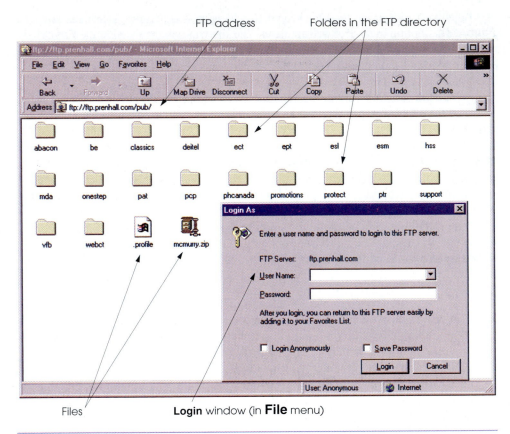

Fig. 2.10   Using IE5 to access FTP sites.

When you point your browser to the URL of an FTP site, you see the contents of the specified site directory. Two types of objects will appear in the directory: files available for download, and other directories to open. You can download a file by right-clicking on its icon, choosing **Save target as...** and specifying the location to which you would like to download the file. To enter another directory, double-click on its folder icon.

When you log on to an FTP site, IE5 automatically sends your email address and your name (which is set by default to **anonymous**). This occurs on FTP sites with *public access*. Many FTP sites on the Internet have *restricted access*—only people with specific usernames and passwords are allowed to access such sites. If you try to enter a restricted-access FTP site, a dialog box like the one in Fig. 2.10 appears for entering your information.

Sending a file to another location on the Internet is called *uploading* and can be done through the FTP protocol. To place a page on a Web site, you will usually have to upload it to a specific restricted-access FTP server (this is dependent on your ISP). This process involves uploading the file to a directory on the FTP site that is accessible through the Web.

2.8 Outlook Express and Electronic Mail

Electronic *mail* (email for short) is a method of sending formatted messages and files over the Internet to other people. Depending on Internet traffic, an email message can go anywhere in the world in as little as a few seconds. Email is one of the most heavily used Internet services.

Your Internet Service Provider will give you an email address in the form *username@domainname* (e.g., **deitel@deitel.com**). The domain name is normally a combination of your ISP's name (e.g., **aol**, **msn**, **prodigy**, etc.) and an extension specifying the email address type. Common domain types are **.com** (commercial), **.net** (network), **.org** (non-profit organization), **.edu** (educational), **.mil** (military) and **.gov** (government). Many domain name suffixes are reserved for country addresses such as **.uk** for Great Britain. With the number of available domain names decreasing, ICANN (Internet Corporation for Assigned Names and Numbers) approved a recommendation to add at least one new suffix to the top-level domains that currently include **.com**, **.net** and **.org** extensions.

Popular email programs such as Outlook, Netscape Messenger and Eudora are available on the Internet for free download or for sale. Microsoft *Outlook Express* installs with IE5 (included on the CD). The opening screen of Outlook Express is shown in Fig. 2.11. The figure also shows the **Internet Accounts** dialog for adding email and news accounts to Outlook Express.

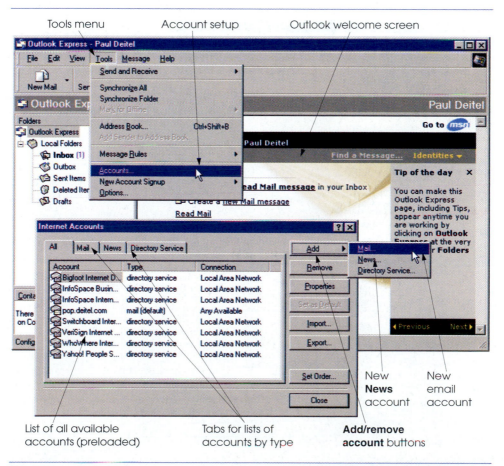

Fig. 2.11   Outlook Express opening screen and the **Internet Accounts** dialog.

When you start Outlook Express for the first time, you will have to enter information about your connection to the Internet and about your email account. You will do this in the dialog box that appears the first time the program is run. You will be asked for the names of your incoming and outgoing *email servers*. These are addresses of servers located at your ISP that administer your incoming and outgoing email. You should obtain the server addresses from your network administrator.

You can manage more than one email account with Outlook Express. You can add new accounts by clicking the **Accounts** option in the **Tools** menu; this will bring up a box listing all your accounts (there are a number of built-in accounts, as you will see). To add a new account, click the **Add** button in the upper-right corner of the box and select either a **Mail** or a **News** account. Figure 2.12 shows the account sign-up dialog box at various points in the sign-up process. We will discuss **News** accounts later in the chapter, but the sign-up process is nearly the same.

Outlook Express provides a straightforward interface for managing your accounts and messages. When you receive messages, you can save them on your hard drive for later access. Outlook Express allows you to create folders for saving messages.

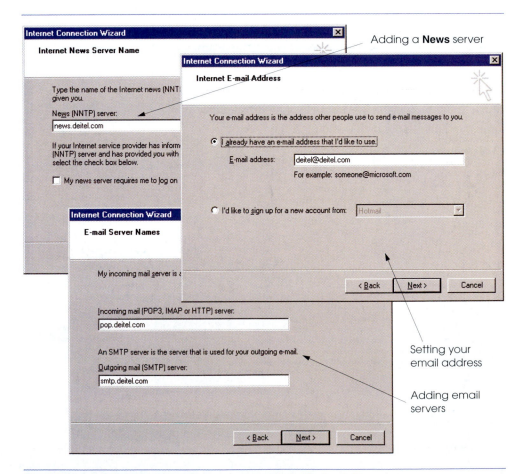

Fig. 2.12   Adding email and news accounts in Outlook Express.

Outlook Express automatically checks for new messages several times per hour (this frequency can be changed). When a new message arrives it is placed in your **Inbox**. The **Inbox** setup is shown in Fig. 2.13.

The layout of the **Inbox** screen is fairly simple. Across the top of the window are buttons you can use to start **New Mail** messages and to **Reply** to, **Forward**, **Print**, **Delete** and **Send/Recv** messages. The right side of the window contains a list of messages in your inbox (listed by date and time received), the message subjects and the senders. Below this is a content preview of the selected message. To view the message in its entirety, double-click its entry in the **Inbox**. To do other things with the message (such as reply to its sender or print the message), highlight the message and click the appropriate button at the top of the screen. To move the message from the **Inbox** to another message box, highlight and drag the email entry to the left side of the screen and drop it into the selected message box.

The left side of the screen contains your folder structure and your *address book*. To add a new message box, right-click on **Local Folders** and select the **New Folder** option. In your address book, you can store the names and email addresses of people with whom you communicate frequently.

To set new entries for the address book, click on the **Addresses** button at the top of the window or click on the **Address Book...** entry in the **Tools** menu. The **Address Book** is shown in Fig. 2.14.

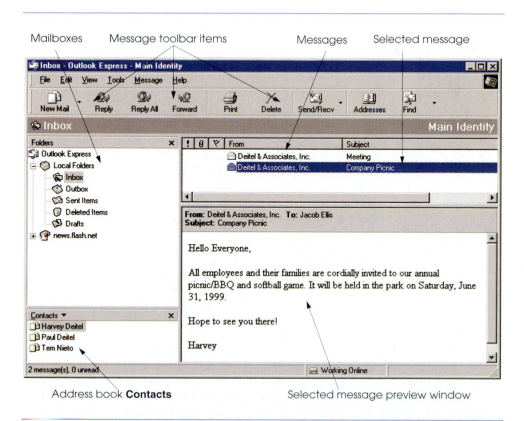

Fig. 2.13   The Outlook Express email main screen.

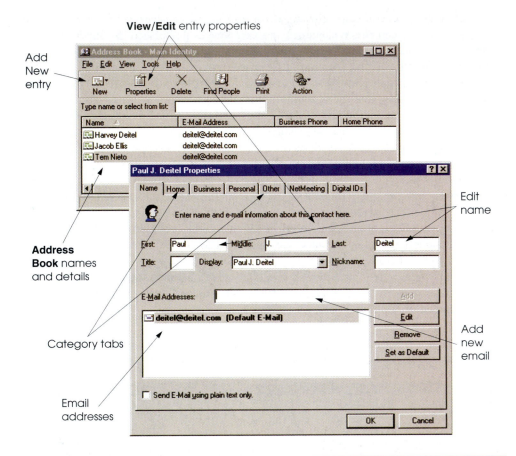

View/Edit entry properties

Add
New
entry

Edit
name

**Address
Book** names
and details

Category tabs

Add
new
email

Email
addresses

Fig. 2.14 Adding and modifying names in your **Address Book**.

All entries in the **Address Book** are listed in the main dialog box. You can send a message to anyone in your list by highlighting that person's entry, clicking the **Action** button, then clicking **Send Mail**. This sequence will open a blank message addressed to the selected recipient. To add an entry to the list, click the **New** button, then click **Contact**. This sequence will open a dialog box like the one in Fig. 2.14 and will give you a place to insert information on that person. You can also enter personal information, such as addresses and phone numbers, for reference outside Outlook Express.

When you initiate a new message through any source, a message box like the one in Fig. 2.15 opens.

There are several properties that can be associated with a message. The only mandatory property is the email address of the recipient, which should be put in the form described earlier in this chapter and placed in the field labeled **To:**. To send your message to more than one recipient, you can type in multiple email addresses in the **To:** field, separated by commas. You should always enter a subject in the **Subject** field. The **Subject** should give the recipient an idea of the message's contents before it is opened. The **CC:** (Carbon Copy) field is for sending messages to people who, although the message is not addressed to them directly, may be interested in the message. If you want to change the *pri-*

ority of the message, click the **Priority** button on the toolbar. High priority messages will be flagged to get the attention of the message recipient.

Finally, your message gets entered in the main window of the message box. You can format the text (font size, colors, styling) with the buttons above the message area. After you have entered your message, click **Send** and your message will be on its way to the designated recipient(s).

2.9 Outlook Express and Newsgroups

With a *newsgroup*, a person can post messages to a shared online viewing area. Other people can then view these messages, reply to them and post new messages. Imagine it as a way of sending email not to anyone in particular, but to a place where people interested in the email's subject can read it. Tens of thousands of newsgroups are available, on virtually any topic, and new groups are created daily.

Outlook Express has a built-in capability to view newsgroups. An Outlook Express newsgroup screen is shown in Fig. 2.16.

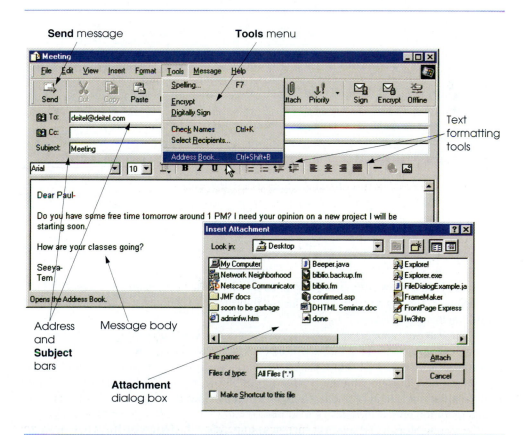

Fig. 2.15   An email message in **Outlook Express**.

Current Newsgroup   Messages in Newsgroup   View Newsgroups

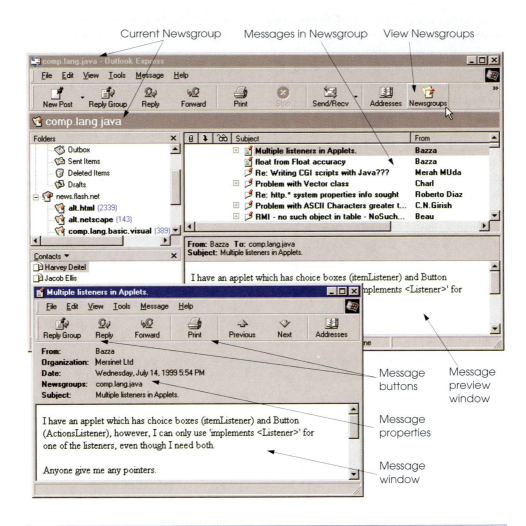

Fig. 2.16   Using **Outlook Express** to browse newsgroups.

To be able to view Newsgroups, you must first register your server settings with Outlook Express. Use the same process illustrated in Fig. 2.11, but select **News...** instead of **Mail...** on the popup menu.

After entering your server information, you can access newsgroups by clicking the **Newsgroups** button on the toolbar, or by clicking on the **Read News** hyperlink on the main Outlook screen. This action brings you to the main newsgroups screen, which ordinarily lists the groups to which you have subscribed. A subscribed newsgroup is comparable to a favorite site in IE5. The program will remember its location and give you easy access to its contents at the click of a button.

To search through and subscribe to newsgroups, click the **Newsgroups** button on the top of the main screen. Outlook Express will then download a list of all the available newsgroups (this search can take several minutes, as there are often tens of thousands of new-groups available on a server). Use the search bar to search the list by typing in keywords. When you find a group you like, double-click its entry and you will be "subscribed" to it. All groups you have subscribed to are listed underneath the mail folders on the left side of the screen and on the main newsgroups screen. To view the contents of a newsgroup, double-click its entry.

The look and functionality of the individual **Newsgroup** view is similar to that of the email message box. You will find message lists and previews in the same places. Posting a message to the group is done the same way you write a new email message. Likewise with replying to a message, printing and reading messages.

You can use a newsgroup to find information, to correspond with a group, to exchange news or to learn new subjects. Be cautious about entering too much personal information about yourself, because newsgroups are public forums.

2.10 Using FrontPage Express to Create Web Pages

Every World Wide Web site you view on the Internet was created by someone. At one time, someone sat down and used a program or a coding language to define the text, formats and layouts of every page on the Internet. Many of these Web pages are designed with special programs that make the Web page authoring and editing process as simple as possible.

Included on your CD is a Web page authoring program called *FrontPage Express*. Chapter 6 explains FrontPage Express in detail. Here is a brief sampling of its uses and features, in case you want to get a head start on Web page production. Figure 2.17 shows a sample FrontPage Express window.

FrontPage Express has a straightforward interface. Most functions you can use to create and format textual and graphical elements are located on the buttons toolbar directly above the main editing area. These controls include buttons for changing text size, color, style, font and justification; for inserting images; and for creating hyperlinks. Experiment with these capabilities.

The pages you create using FrontPage Express are viewable with any Web browser (as long as you are careful to use browser-independent features). The files you create are then typically uploaded via FTP to a Web server.

2.11 NetMeeting and Chat

Internet Explorer 5 is packaged with two programs for communicating with people over the Internet via live written text and other media such as audio and video. The first of these programs is *NetMeeting* (see Fig. 2.18). NetMeeting is designed for business and for work-related collaborations.

You can use NetMeeting to communicate with groups of people via textual and visual aids. These include sound (you can use a microphone to speak with people) and video (you can use video cameras to transmit live video). You can also use NetMeeting to share files (there are built-in mechanisms for the group editing of files and for the sharing of diagrams via the *whiteboard*, a drawing application that allows you to share visual effects with other people in the meeting).

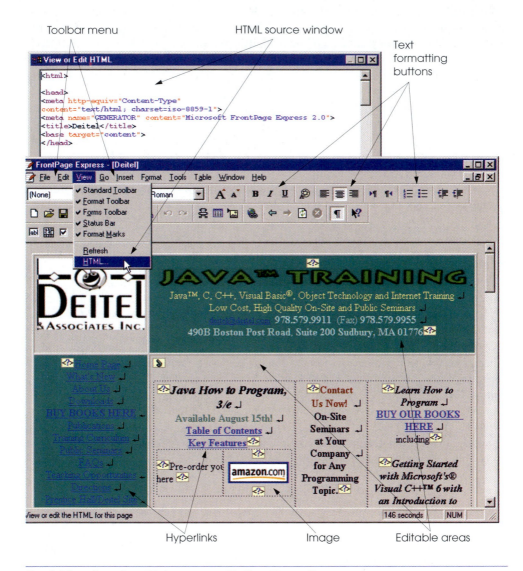

Fig. 2.17   Creating Web pages with FrontPage Express.

NetMeeting opens with a setup screen in which you set your initial options. Next, a screen appears that displays a list of the people who are available to chat using NetMeeting. You can also initiate a one-on-one meeting with an individual by using the **Call** button on the top toolbar. You can use the **Address Book** feature in NetMeeting to save commonly used addresses.

Once you begin a meeting, buttons appear on your screen and options become available on the toolbar for using the various communication media. You should experiment with these tools to determine how to use NetMeeting to its fullest potential.

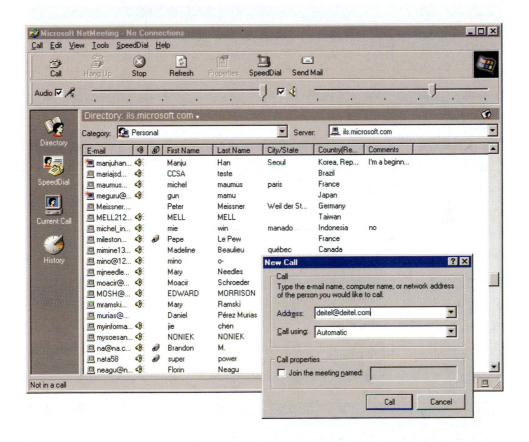

Fig. 2.18   Using NetMeeting to "speak" with people on the Internet.

Microsoft Chat is similar to NetMeeting, though its operation is simpler. Chat also offers a more casual atmosphere than NetMeeting. You start by choosing a "nickname" with which you would like to be referred to in the chat groups. Then connect with the server and you will be presented with a list of chat groups. Find one you like by scrolling down or searching, then join the chat by double-clicking on the group's entry.

Chat then displays a screen much like the one in Fig. 2.19. A list of people in the chat group appears on the right. You can start a private conversation with a person in this list by right-clicking on that person's name and selecting the appropriate option. You type text into the chat by typing it into the text bar at the bottom of the screen.

The group's conversation appears in the main screen. This is in plain text format (which can be styled using the toolbars above the conversation window) or in a delightful cartoon format. These two styles of chat can be toggled using the buttons in the middle of the toolbar above the conversation window. Have fun chatting with and meeting new people, but be cautious about revealing your true identity and contact information.

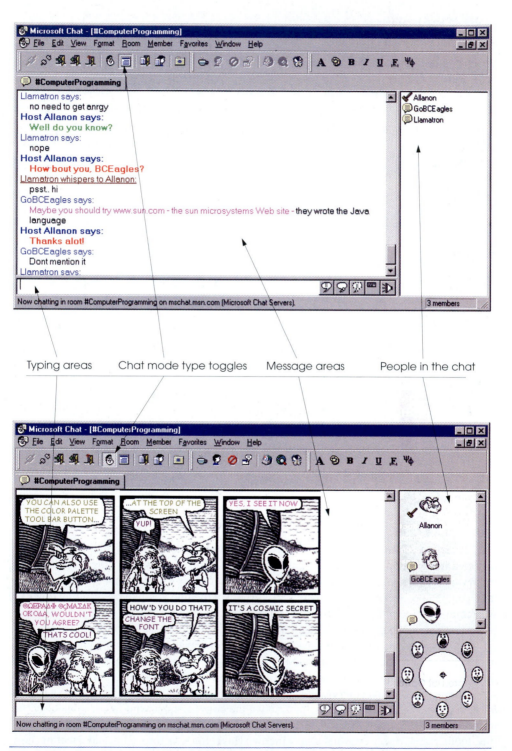

Fig. 2.19   Chatting with Microsoft Chat.

2.12 Controlling the Details

IE5 is installed with a myriad of default settings that affect the way sites are displayed, the security measures browsers take and the way browser outputs appear. Most of these settings are modifiable in the **Internet Options** dialog (Fig. 2.20).

Let us consider some of the more significant options that affect your browsing experience. If you have a slow connection and you do not mind less colorful pages being displayed in your browser, you might want to consider toggling off the **Load Pictures** setting, located under the **Advanced** tab. This stops the browser from loading images on a Web page. Images can require long load times, so this toggle can save precious minutes during every browsing session. Under the **Programs** tab, you can specify the default programs you want IE5 to use for such common Internet procedures as viewing newsgroups and sending email. Specifying these causes the designated programs to be accessed when there is a need for their respective technologies in your browsing. For example, if you designate **Outlook Express** as your default email program, then, when you click on an email hyperlink, **Outlook Express** will open a new email message for you to compose.

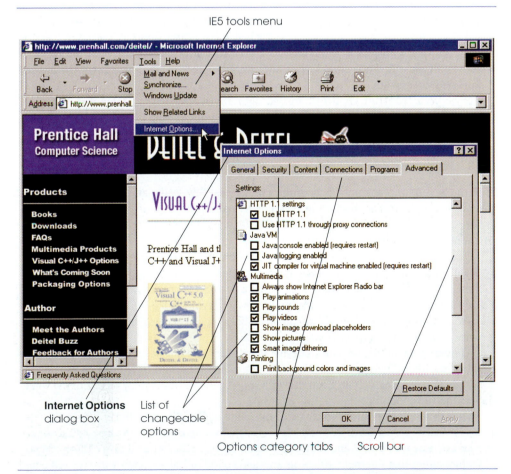

Fig. 2.20   Changing your **Internet Options** in IE5.

Under the **Security** tab, you can specify the level of caution IE5 should exercise when browsing sites in general and also for specific sites. There are four levels of security, the most lenient will not bother you much about downloading and *cookies* (files that are placed on your computer by Web sites to retain or gather information between sessions); the most secure will provide a constant flow of alerts and alarms about the security of your browsing. You should find a setting that balances your comfort level with the Internet against your tolerance for interruptions while browsing.

Finally, in the **General** options tab, you can specify a home page, which is the World Wide Web site that is loaded when the browser starts and also appears when you click the **Home** button on top of the browser window. You can designate here the length of time for which you would like to keep a history of URLs visited. By clicking on the **Settings...** button, you can set the amount of disk space you would like to reserve for your Web page *cache*. The cache is an area on your hard drive that a browser designates for automatically saving Web pages and their elements for rapid, future access. When you view a page that you have visited previously, IE5 checks the cache to see if it already has some elements on that page saved in the cache and so can save some download time. Having a large cache can considerably speed up Web browsing, whereas having a small cache can save disk space. However, caching can be a problem, as Internet Explorer does not always check to make sure that the cached page is the same as the latest version residing on the Web server. Clicking the **Refresh** button near the top of the browser window will remedy this by making Internet Explorer get the latest version of the desired Web page from the site.

Once your **Internet Options** are set, click the **Apply** button, then click **OK**. This sequence will apply your changes and will once again display the main browser window.

2.13 Plug-ins

With the advent of many new technologies in the past few years, an increasing number of programs and features are becoming available to make your browsing experience more enjoyable and interactive. Programs called *plug-ins* have been developed that work in conjunction with your browsers.

One of the most versatile plug-ins available on the Internet is *RealPlayer*, developed by Real Networks (Fig. 2.21). Download the most recent version of **RealPlayer** by clicking on the **Download Now** link on `http://www.real.com`. It is capable of playing live or prerecorded sound file, and even of playing video (with a fast enough connection). There are also a number of *channels* that you can access, including news, sports, comedy, talk shows and live events.

Another plug-in that provides Internet sound services but has a lesser following than RealAudio is the *Windows Media Player,* which is included with IE5. You can use this the same way you use RealPlayer. Each site with sound capabilities displays icons of the sound players the site supports.

Many Internet sites allow you to take advantage of **RealPlayer**. For example, the sites `http://www.broadcast.com/`, `http://www.npr.org/`, `http://internetradio.about.com/` and `http://wmbr.mit.edu/stations/list.html`. all feature either live Internet radio programs and sound or links to sites with live radio and sound events.

Progress bar

Playback controls

RealAudio
Channels

Current channel

Volume control

Status

Fig. 2.21   RealPlayer dialog.

As useful as HTML is for transferring information, it is still a rather primitive markup language. The *Adobe Acrobat Reader* plug-in reads documents with advanced formatting. Figure 2.22 shows a file displayed with the *Adobe Acrobat Reader* plug-in.

The Acrobat reader is a multiplatform software plug-in (i.e., it works on many operating systems) that is capable of showing documents online without changing the original format of the document. Many manuals and forms are available for download in the Acrobat format (**.pdf**, or *Portable Data Format*). When you visit a site that requires the Acrobat reader, there will normally be a link to download the plug-in.

Macromedia *Shockwave* is a plug-in that, when installed and run with a site designed to take advantage of its capabilities, can produce breath-taking dynamic effects. You will be given an option to download this plug-in when you first encounter a Web site using its functions, or you can download the plug-in directly at **http://www.shockwave.com**. Figure 2.23 displays one of the thousands of Shockwave enabled sites on the Internet. Shockwave is used mostly for displaying motion on a Web page, so it is impossible to do it justice with a static screen capture.

In most cases, you are given an option or a link to download a plug-in whenever you visit a site that requires you to use the plug-in for the most effective browsing experience. If you cannot find a place to download a desired plug-in, you can probably find it at **http://www.download.com** or **http://www.shareware.com**. These sites have large searchable indexes and databases of almost every program available for download on the Internet.

2.14 Internet and World Wide Web Resources

There is a host of information on the Internet that no one could list in any book, let alone in one chapter; however, here are some useful Web sites that can get you started.

Adobe Acrobat controls   Browser area   Document area

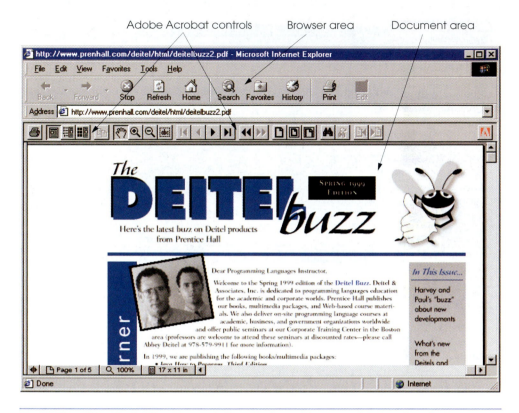

Fig. 2.22   "The Deitel Buzz" newsletter displayed from an Adobe Acrobat formatted file.

http://www.altavista.com/
Altavista is one of the oldest search engines on the Internet. Developed by Digital several years ago, it is a very useful and comprehensive site.

http://www.yahoo.com/
Yahoo is one of the most popular sites on the Web. It serves both as a search engine and a site catalog.

http://www.excite.com/
Excite is a newer search engine which is often useful when neither Yahoo or Altavista provide useful search results.

http://www.askjeeves.com/)
AskJeeves is a search engine which allows users to type their requests in plain English and searches other search engines for the answer. It also catalogs commonly asked questions for faster response times.

http://www.broadcast.com/
broadcast.com is a comprehensive site for streaming audio and video. Hundreds of live events are available daily for listening with RealPlayer.

http://internetradio.about.com/
Internet Radio is another site that offers many live broadcasts from radio stations throughout the country, covering a broad range of topics.

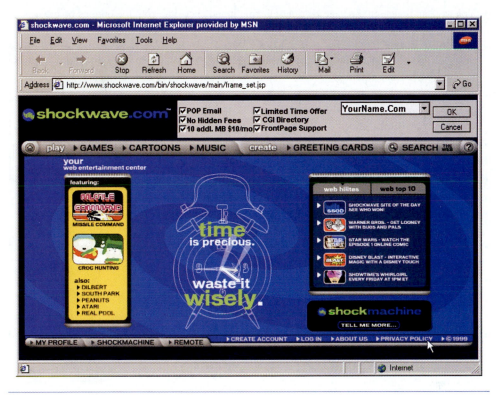

Fig. 2.23   An example of the Shockwave plug-in in use.
(Courtesy of **shockwave.com**.)

SUMMARY

- A browser is an important piece of software that enables you to view pages on the Internet.
- The two most popular browsers are Microsoft's Internet Explorer and Netscape's Communicator.
- To connect to the Internet, you will need a computer, a modem and Internet software.
- The first step to getting onto the Internet is registering with an Internet Service Provider (ISP). Once you have signed up for your account, you should start the **Internet Connection Wizard**.
- If you are interested in learning more about the Internet and its features, click on the button labeled **Tutorial**, located in the first Internet Connection Wizard screen.
- The URL describes the location of the file your browser is displaying or loading.
- The URLs of files viewed on the Web normally begin with **http://**.
- When a hyperlink is clicked, the browser loads a specified URL into the browser window.
- IE5 has built-in controls that record the sites that your browser has loaded, called the history.
- If you click on **Back**, then your browser will automatically switch the URL to (and load) the previous page in your history. The **Forward** button loads the next page in your history.
- On pages that are frequently updated, you may want to click the **Refresh** button. This action will cause your browser to reload the current URL.

- You save an image on the page by right-clicking it and choosing from the options box that pops up **Save Picture As...**.

- A nice new feature of IE5 is the address bar AutoComplete: when you start entering a URL stored in the history, a scrollable menu appears listing all URLs in the history that are potential matches for the URL you are entering.

- The interactive history bar can be activated by clicking the button marked **History** in the row of buttons at the top of your browser window. This shows you your history over the past month chronologically and alphabetically.

- Searching the Internet is usually done through search engines. Search engines constantly explore the Internet through hyperlinks, recording characteristics of the sites they encounter.

- Solutions for many problems you might encounter while using Internet Explorer are accessible through an online **Tour** and a built-in **Help** feature, each accessible through the **Help** menu.

- IE5 provides a mechanism called **Favorites** that allows you to save the URLs of sites, to give you easy access to those sites in the future.

- When you visit a site that you would like to save as a favorite, select the **Add Favorites...** option in the **Favorites** menu. The site will be listed in the **Favorites** menu, identified its title.

- Through the **Organize Favorites** dialog box, you can rename favorites, create folders to organize favorites, place and remove favorites from these folders and delete favorites.

- Downloading is initiated on a Web page by clicking a hyperlink to a file on a Web or FTP site.

- FTP stands for File Transfer Protocol, a popular method for sending files over the Internet. The address of an FTP site begins with `ftp://`.

- When you point your browser to the URL of an FTP site, you will be presented with the contents of the specified directory.

- Many FTP sites on the Web have restricted access. This means that only people with specific usernames and passwords will be allowed to access the FTP site.

- Sending a file to another location on the Internet is called uploading.

- Electronic mail, or email for short, is a method of sending formatted messages and files over the Internet to other people.

- When you sign up with an Internet Service Provider, you are given an email address in the form of *username@domainname*.

- Popular email programs include Microsoft Outlook, Netscape Messenger, and Eudora.

- Outlook Express allows you to manage more than one email account. You can add new accounts by clicking the **Accounts** option in the **Tools** menu.

- Outlook Express provides an easy interface for managing your accounts and messages. When you receive messages you have the option of saving them on your hard drive for later access.

- Outlook Express checks for new messages several times per hour. When a new message arrives it is placed in your **Inbox**.

- To set new entries for the address book, click on the **Addresses** button at the top of the window, or click on the **Address Book...** entry in the **Tools** menu.

- You can send a message to anyone in your **Address Book** by highlighting that person's entry, clicking the **Action** button, then clicking **Send Mail**.

- The only mandatory property is the email address of the recipient, which is put into the **To:** field.

- When you have entered your message, click **Send**, and your message will be on its way to the designated recipient.

- Using newsgroups, a person can post messages to online viewing areas. Other people can then view these messages, reply to them and post new messages.
- Outlook Express has a built-in capability to view Newsgroups. You must first register your newsgroup server settings with Outlook Express.
- A subscribed newsgroup is comparable to a favorite site in IE5. The program will remember its location and give you easy access to its contents at the click of a button.
- To search through and subscribe to newsgroups, click the **Newsgroups** button on the top of the main screen. Outlook Express will then download a list of all available newsgroups.
- To view the contents of a newsgroup, double-click on its entry.
- IE5 provides NetMeeting and Chat for communicating with people over the Internet via live written text and other media.
- You can use NetMeeting to communicate with groups of people via textual and visual aids.
- Microsoft Chat is similar to NetMeeting in its basic layout and procedures, though it is simpler and offers a more casual atmosphere than NetMeeting.
- Be cautious about revealing your true identity and contact information in NetMeeting and in Chat.
- IE5 is installed with a myriad of default settings, called **Internet Options**, that affect the way sites are displayed.
- Toggling off the **Load Pictures** setting will stop the browser from loading images from a Web page and so save time.
- Under the **Programs** tab, you can specify the default programs you want IE5 to use for such common Internet procedures as viewing newsgroups and sending email.
- Under the **Security** tab, you can specify the level of caution IE5 should exercise when browsing sites in general and also for specific sites.
- In the **General** options tab, you can specify a home page, which is the Web site that is loaded when IE5 starts.
- The most recent version of **RealPlayer** plays live or prerecorded sound files and videos.
- The Adobe Acrobat reader is a multiplatform software plug-in that is capable of showing documents online without changing the original format of the document.
- Macromedia Shockwave is a plug-in that when installed and run with a site designed to take advantage of its capabilities, can produce breath-taking dynamic effects.

TERMINOLOGY

`.com`	America OnLine
`.edu`	anchor
`.gov`	applets
`.mil`	Ask Jeeves (`http://www.askjeeves.com`)
`.net`	attachments to email
`.org`	audio clip
`.pdf` (Portable Data Format)	audio conferencing
Acrobat Portable Data Format (**.pdf**)	AutoComplete
Active Desktop	**Back** button
Address bar	background wallpaper
Address Book in Outlook Express	bookmark
Adobe Acrobat reader	browser
AltaVista (`http://www.altavista.com`)	browsing the Web

cache
capturing an image
cartoon format in Microsoft Chat
channel
Chat (software from Microsoft)
chat group
chat room
collaboration
CompuServe
Connecting to the Internet
Content Advisor and ratings
cookies
copying graphics from a Web site
copying text from a Web site
download file with FTP
electronic mail
email attachments
email server
Enter key
Excite (**http://www.excite.com**)
Favorites button and Menu Bar
Forward button
FrontPage Express
FTP (File Transfer Protocol)
FTP site
General tab of **Internet Options**
graphics
Help
history list
home page
http:// (Hypertext Transfer Protocol)
http://www.altavista.com
http://www.excite.com
http://www.infoseek.com
http://www.yahoo.com
hyperlink
images
Inbox in Outlook Express
InfoSeek (**http://www.infoseek.com/**)
interactive history bar
Internet Connection Wizard
Internet Explorer 5 (IE5)
Internet options dialog box
Internet Service Provider (ISP)
ISP (Internet Service Provider)
links bar
Macromedia Shockwave
Menu
Microsoft
Microsoft Chat

multimedia
navigating the Web
"netiquette"
NetMeeting conferences
Netscape
News Server
newsgroups
online help
online Web tutorial
Organize Favorites dialog
Outlook Express (from Microsoft)
plug-ins
Programs tab of **Internet Options**
public-access FTP site
radio buttons
ratings and the **Content Advisor**
Real Networks
RealAudio **Channels**
RealPlayer plug-in
restricted-access FTP site
Save as background...
Save As...
Save Picture As...
search engine
searching the Internet
Security tab of **Internet Options**
Shockwave (from Macromedia)
shopping
subscribe to a newsgroup
surfing the Web
tables
toolbar
Tour
upload a file with FTP
URL (Uniform Resource Locator)
Usenet newsgroups
video clip
video conferencing
wallpaper
Web
Web browser
Web page
Web server
Web site
WebCrawler
whiteboard in NetMeeting
Windows Media Player
wizards
World Wide Web
Yahoo (**http://www.yahoo.com**)

SELF-REVIEW EXERCISES

2.1   Answer each of the following:
a) The two most popular browsers are _____ and _____.
b) A browser is used to view files on the _____.
c) The location of a file on the Internet is called its _____.
d) The element in a Web page that, when clicked, causes a new Web page to load is called a _____; when your mouse passes over this element, the mouse pointer changes into a _____ in IE5.
e) The record IE5 keeps of your Web travels is called the _____.
f) You can save an image from a Web page by right-clicking it and selecting _____.
g) The feature of IE5 that provides options for completing URLs is called _____.
h) The feature of IE5 that lets you save URLs of sites you visit often is called _____.

2.2   Expand the following acronyms:
a) HTTP
b) FTP
c) URL
d) WWW
e) email

2.3   State whether each of the following is *true* or *false*. If the statement is *false*, explain why.
a) There are about 1,000 newsgroups on the Internet.
b) You will have to download and install most plug-ins in order to use them.
c) NetMeeting and Chat are identical programs that do the same thing but look different.
d) FTP is a popular Internet mechanism by which files are uploaded and downloaded.
e) You can probably find a site on a topic you are looking for through a search engine.
f) You can access any FTP site by logging in as **anonymous**.

ANSWERS TO SELF-REVIEW EXERCISES

2.1   a) Internet Explorer, Netscape Navigator. b) Internet and the Web. c) URL. d) hyperlink, hand. e) history. f) **Save Picture as...** g) AutoComplete. h) **Favorites**.

2.2   a) HyperText Transfer Protocol. b) File Transfer Protocol. c) Universal/Uniform Resource Locator. d) World Wide Web. e) Electronic mail.

2.3   a) False. There are tens of thousands of newsgroups, and more are added every day. b) True. c) False. NetMeeting is geared more for business use, and includes many features that can help the sharing of information. Chat is intended for more casual use on Chat servers. d) True. e) True. f) False. Many FTP sites are private, and do not admit the general public.

EXERCISES

2.4   Search for the same terms on HotBot (**http://www.hotbot.com**), AltaVista (**http://www.altavista.com**) and Lycos (**http://www.lycos.com**). List the top three results from each search engine.

2.5   Use Internet Explorer's FTP capability to access both **ftp.cdrom.com** and **sunsite.unc.edu**. List the directory output for both sites.

2.6   Log on to a NetMeeting server and initiate a conversation with a friend.

2.7   Use Outlook Express to subscribe to the newsgroup **alt.html**

2.8   Find a radio station on **http://www.broadcast.com** and listen to it with RealPlayer.

3

e-Business Models

Objectives

- To understand the different business models being implemented on the Internet.
- To explore the transition of brick-and-mortar businesses to e-Businesses.
- To understand Internet business models as they are used among the leading online industries.
- To learn the terminology and basic principles behind e-commerce.
- To learn about the many options open to Web entrepreneurs.

The Road to the City of Emeralds is paved with yellow brick.
Lyman Frank Baum

Ye shall no more give the people straw to make brick.
The Old Testament

All intelligent thoughts have already been thought; what is necessary is to try and think them again.
Johann Wolfgang von Goethe

And the portal opens to receive me...
Ann Radcliffe

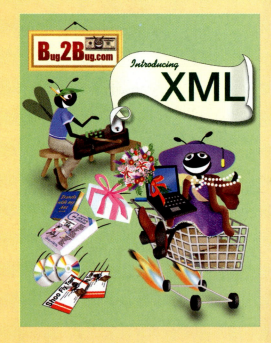

Outline

3.1 Introduction

There are many benefits of bringing your business to the Web. An e-business can offer personalized service, high-quality customer service, and improved supply chain management. In this chapter we explore the different types of businesses operating on the Web, as well as the technologies needed to build and run an e-commerce Web site.

Amazon.com, eBay, Yahoo! and others have helped to define industry categories and business models on the Web. Entrepreneurs starting e-businesses need to be aware of these models and how to implement them effectively. In this chapter, we review the storefront model, the auction model, dynamic pricing models, the portal model and other Web business models. *An e-business* is defined as a company that has an online presence. E-businesses that have the ability to sell, trade, barter and transact over the Web can be considered *e-commerce* businesses. The combination of a company's policy, operations, technology and ideology define its business model. In this chapter, we define a number of models and the technologies that make them possible. Businesses within a particular model can leverage these fundamental technologies to differentiate themselves from the competition.

3.2 Storefront Model

Shopping online is an increasingly popular activity. At the close of 1999, nearly 55 million people, 60 percent of Internet users, were shopping online.[1] The move toward e-commerce presents many benefits, as well as a host of new considerations. The storefront model is what many people think of when they hear the word e-business. The storefront combines transaction processing, security, online payment and information storage to enable merchants to sell their products on the Web. This is a basic form of e-commerce where the buyer and the seller interact directly.

To conduct storefront e-commerce, merchants need to organize an online catalog of products, take orders through their Web sites, accept payments in a secure environment, send merchandise to customers and manage customer data (such as customer profiles). They must also market their sites to potential customers—a topic further explored in Chapter 4, "Internet Marketing".

Although the term e-commerce is fairly new, large corporations have been conducting e-commerce for decades by networking their systems with those of business partners and clients. For example, the banking industry uses *Electronic Funds Transfer (EFT)* to transfer money between accounts. Many companies also use *Electronic Data Interchange (EDI),* in which business forms, such as purchase orders and invoices, are standardized so that companies can share information with customers, vendors and business partners electronically.

Until recently, e-commerce was feasible only for large companies. However, the Internet and the World Wide Web make it possible for small businesses to compete with large companies. E-commerce also allows companies to conduct business *24-by-7*, all day, everyday, worldwide.

Some of the most successful e-businesses are using the storefront model. Many of the leading storefront model companies are *B2C* (business-to-consumer) companies. For example, **More.com** (**www.more.com**) is a health and beauty e-commerce site that uses a shopping cart to allow customers to shop, buy and arrange shipment. Products include skin care, eye care, pharmaceuticals and many other products associated with health and wellness.

Ticketmaster.com (**www.ticketmaster.com**) uses the Internet to sell tickets improve its customer service. Customers have access to seating plans, show listings and price discounts. Ticketmaster uses shopping-cart technology, an advanced database system and a strong supporting infrastructure to make this possible.

Although both companies use a shopping cart and supporting technologies to offer their products and services to customers, each has chosen a different approach to e-commerce.

3.2.1 Shopping-cart Technology

One of the most commonly used e-commerce enablers is the *shopping cart*. This order-processing technology allows customers to accumulate items they wish to buy as they continue to shop. Supporting the shopping cart is a product catalog, which is hosted on the *merchant server* in the form of a *database*. The merchant server is the data storage and management system employed by the merchant. A database is a part of the merchant server designed to store and report on large amounts of information. For example, a database for an online clothing retailer would typically include such product specifications as item description, size, availability, shipping information, stock levels and on-order information. Databases also store customer information, such as names, addresses, credit-card information and past purchases. The **Amazon.com** feature explains the these technologies and how they are implemented.

Amazon.com

Perhaps the most widely recognized example of an e-business that uses shopping-cart technology is **Amazon.com**.[2, 3] Opened in 1994, the company has rapidly grown to become one of the world's largest online retailer. Amazon offers millions of products to more than 17 million customers in 160 countries. For customers who prefer choice, **Amazon.com** also offers online auctions.

In its first few years, **Amazon.com** served as a mail-order book retailer. Their line of products has since expanded to include music, videos, DVDs, electronic cards, consumer electronics, hardware, tools, beauty items and toys. The Amazon catalog is constantly growing, and the site allows you to navigate quickly among millions of products.

Amazon.com uses a database on the server side that allows customers on the client side to search for products in a variety of ways. This is an example of a *client/server application*. The Amazon database consists of product specifications, availability, shipping information, stock levels, on-order information and other data. Book titles, authors, prices, sales histories, publishers, reviews and in-depth descriptions are also stored in the database. This extensive database makes it possible to cross-reference products. For example, a novel may be listed under various categories, including fiction, best-sellers and recommended titles.

Amazon.com personalizes its site to service returning customers; a database keeps a record of all previous transactions, including items purchased, shipping and credit-card information. Upon returning to the site, customers are greeted by name, and lists of recommended titles presented, based on customer's previous purchases. Amazon searches the customer database for patterns and trends among its clientele. By monitoring such customer data, the company provides personalized service that would otherwise need to be handled by sales representatives. Amazon's computer system drives sales of additional items without human interaction.

Buying a product at Amazon is simple. You begin at the **Amazon.com** home page and decide the type of product you would like to purchase. For example, if you are looking for *C++ How to Program: Third Edition*, you can find the book by using the **Search Box** in the top-left corner of the home page. Select **Books** in the **Search Box**, then type the title of the book into the window. This takes you directly to the product page for the book. To purchase the item, select **Add to Shopping Cart** on the top-right corner of the page. The shopping-cart technology processes the information and displays a list of the products you have placed in the shopping cart. You then have the option to change the quantity of each item, remove an item from the shopping cart, check out or continue shopping.

Amazon.com (Cont.)

When you are ready to place your order, you proceed to checkout. As a first-time visitor, you will be prompted to fill out a personal identification form including name, billing address, shipping address, shipping preference and credit-card information. You are also asked to enter a password that you will use to access your account data for all future transactions. Once you confirm your information, you can place your order.

Customers returning to Amazon can use its *1-Click*[SM] *system*. This allows the customer to reuse previously entered payment and shipping information to place an order with just one click of the mouse. This is an excellent example of how an intelligently designed database application can make online business transactions faster and easier.

When your order is placed, Amazon sends a confirmation to you by e-mail. A second e-mail is sent when the order is shipped. A database monitors the status of all shipments. You can track the status of your purchase until it leaves the **Amazon.com** shipping center by selecting the **Your Account** link at the bottom of the page and entering your password. This will bring you to an **Account Maintenance** page. You can cancel your order at any time before the product is shipped, which usually occurs within 24 to 48 hours of purchase.

Amazon.com operates on secure servers that protect your personal information. If you feel uncomfortable using your credit card on the Web, you can place your order through their Web site using the last five digits of your credit card and later complete your order by calling Amazon's Customer Service Department to provide the remaining numbers. We discuss Web security in Chapter 7.

Although the shopping cart is only one method of conducting transactions online, it is an effective way of buying and selling products on the Internet. Many companies combine a number of purchasing methods to give their customers a wide array of options. In Chapter 26, you will learn to build your own storefront using key technologies such as the shopping cart, online auction technology and price-comparison technology.

While shopping-cart technology offers consumers the convenience of quick and easy transactions, it creates problems regarding consumer privacy and online security. These issues will be discussed at length in Chapter 6 and Chapter 7. For more examples of e-businesses who have found success using this technology visit **www.etoys.com**, **www.webvan.com**, and **www.cdnow.com**.

3.2.2 Online Shopping Malls

Online shopping malls present consumers with a wide selection of products and services. They are often considered to be more convenient than searching and shopping at independent online storefronts for several reasons. Consumers can search and shop for a variety of products, and rather than making several separate purchases, they can use the mall's shopping-cart technology to purchase items from many stores in a single transaction. Often these sites act as shopping portals, directing traffic to the leading shopping retailers for a specific product.

Leading online malls include **Mall.com** (**www.mall.com**), which features many of the same vendors you will find in your local brick-and-mortar mall—offline retailers such as JCrew, Harrods, and the Sharper Image. **Shopnow.com, www.shopnow.com** and **www.DealShop.com** are other online malls offering a wide variety of shopping options.

3.3 Auction Model

Forrester Research reveals that an estimated $3.8 billion will be spent on online person-to-person auctions in the year 2000 alone. This number is dwarfed by the $52 billion that is projected to be spent on business-to-business auctions in 2002.[4] The Web offers many different kinds of auction sites, in addition to sites designed to search existing auction sites in order to pinpoint the lowest prices on an available item.

Usually, auction sites act as forums through which Internet users can log-on and assume the role of either bidder or seller. As a seller, you are able to post an item you wish to sell, the minimum price you require to sell your item and a deadline to close the auction. Some sites allow you to add features, such as a photograph or a description of the item's condition. As a bidder, you may search the site for availability of the item you are seeking, view the current bidding activity and place a bid (bids are usually in designated increments). Some sites allow you to submit a maximum bidding price and will continue bidding for you. Auction technology will be explained inn depth in the eBay feature.

The *reverse auction model* allows the buyer to set a price as sellers compete to match or even beat it. One example of a reverse auction site is **Liquidprice.com** which processes your auction within two days. A faster option is available when the buyer sets a *reserve price.* A reserve price is the lowest price that the seller will accept in any type of auction. Sellers can set the reserve price higher than the minimum bid. If no bid meets the reserve price, the auction is unsuccessful. If a seller sets a reserve price at **Liquidprice.com**, the seller will receive a series of bids within six hours of their initial post. However, if a successful bid is made, the buyer and seller must commit.

Although auction sites usually require a commission on sales, these sites are only a forum for online buying and selling. They do not involve themselves in payment or delivery. After the auction has been completed, both the seller and the bidder are notified, and the method of payment and the cost of delivery is then worked out between the two parties.

---

eBay™

Online auctions have become an enormously successful method of e-commerce. The leading company in this business is eBay (Fig 3.1).[5, 6] At the time of publication, eBay was one of the most profitable e-businesses. The successful online auction house has its roots in a 50-year-old novelty item—Pez® candy dispensers. Linda Omidyar, an avid collector of Pez® dispensers, came up with the idea of trading them over the Internet. When she expressed this idea to her boyfriend, Pierre Omidyar (now her husband), he was instantly struck with the soon-to-be-famous e-business auction concept. In 1995, the Omidyars created a company called AuctionWeb. The company was renamed eBay and has since become the premier online auction house, with as many as 4 million unique auctions in progress and 450,000 new items added each day.

eBay™ (Cont.)

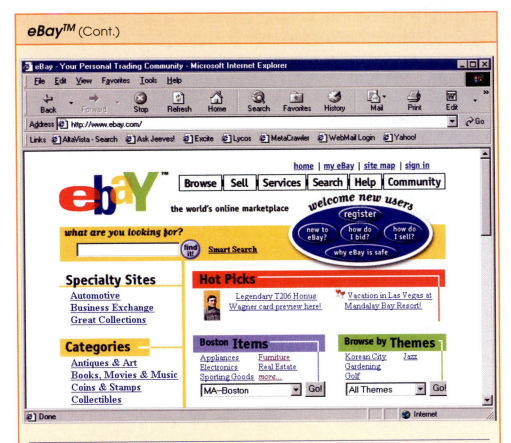

Fig. 3.1   The eBay home page. (These materials have been reproduced by Prentice Hall with the permission of eBay, Inc. COPYRIGHT © EBAY, INC. ALL RIGHTS RESERVED.)

On eBay, people can buy and sell just about anything. The company collects a submission fee plus a percentage of the sale amount. The submission fee is based on the amount of exposure you want your item to receive, with a higher fee required if you would like to be among the "featured auctions" in your specific product category, and an even higher fee if you want your item to be listed on the eBay home page under **Featured Items**. This listing will not appear every time you go to the home page, but it will be shown on the site periodically. Another attention-attracting option is to publish the product listing in a bold-face font; this requires a small additional charge.

eBay uses a database to manage the millions of auctions that it offers. This database evolves dynamically as sellers and buyers enter personal identification and product information. When a seller enters a product to be auctioned, the seller provides a description of the product, keywords, initial price, date and personal information. This data is used to produce the product profile seen by potential buyers. (Fig. 3.2).

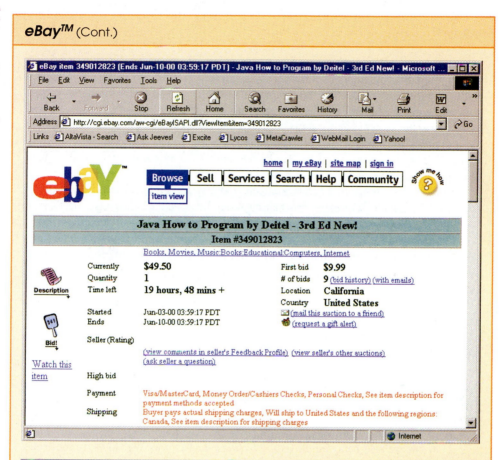

eBay™ (Cont.)

The auction process begins when the seller posts a description of the item for sale and fills in the appropriate registration information. The seller must specify a minimum opening bid. If potential buyers feel this price is too high, the item may not receive any bids. In many cases, a reserve price is also set. Sellers might set the opening bid lower than the reserve price to generate bidding activity.

If a successful bid is made, the seller and the buyer negotiate the shipping details, warranty and other particulars. eBay serves as a liaison between the parties—it is the interface through which sellers and buyers can conduct business. eBay does not maintain a costly physical inventory or deal with shipping, handling or other services that businesses such as Amazon and other retailers must provide. eBay has spawned a number of new businesses that use the site as their means of selling products. These businesses depend on eBay to remain up and running. Because downtime can be costly to an online business, companies like eBay make investments in *high-availability computing* and *continuous-availability computing*.

eBay™ (Cont.)

High-availability computing attempts to minimize down time; continuous-availability computing attempts to eliminate it completely. One key to such technologies is *fault-tolerant systems* that use *redundancy*. Every crucial piece of hardware—processors, disks and communications channels—has one or more levels of backup, so that, in a failure, the system simply shifts from a failed component to a backup component. This enables the system to keep running while the failed component is fixed or replaced. The same is true of data. Because companies cannot afford to lose their business data, it is also maintained redundantly.

Tandem and Stratus build continuous-availability and high-availability computing systems, respectively. For more information about these technologies, visit the Tandem Web site at `www.tandem.com` and the Stratus Web site at `www.stratus.com`.

The impact of eBay on e-business has been profound. The founders took a fairly restrictive offline business model and, by using the Internet, were able to bring it to the desktops of consumers worldwide. This business model consistently generates a profit on the World Wide Web. A recent article in *Business Week* states, "The bidding and close interaction between buyers and sellers promotes a sense of community—a near addiction that keeps them coming back".[7] By implementing traditional marketing strategies and keeping the process simple, eBay has offered a successful alternative to storefront-style e-commerce.

There are several other online auction sites. A few of the largest auctions sites are Yahoo! Auctions (`auctions.yahoo.com`), Amazon Auctions (`www.amazon.com`). FairMarket, Inc. (`www.fairmarket.com`) and Sotheby's (`www.sothebys.com`). If you prefer to see the auction as it happens visit `www.ibidlive.com`. There is a demo available on this site.

Auctions are also being employed by *business-to-business* Web sites. In these auctions the buyer and the seller are companies. Auctions are a good way for a company to sell excess inventory and gain access to new, price-sensitive customers. Three examples of B2B auction sites are DoveBid, Inc. (`www.dovebid.com`), WorldCall Exchange (`www.worldcallexchange.com`) and U-Bid-It.com (`www.u-bid-it.com`).

3.4 Portal Model

Portal sites give visitors the chance to find almost everything they are looking for in one place. They often offer news, sports and weather, as well as the ability to search the Web. When most people hear the word portal they think of search engines. *Search engines* are *horizontal portals*, or portals that aggregate information on a broad range of topics. Other portals are more specific, offering a great deal of information pertaining to a single area of interest.—these are called *vertical portals*.

Online shopping is a popular addition to the major portals. Sites such as `Hotbot.com`, `About.com`, `altavista.com` and `Yahoo.com` provide users with a shopping page that links them to thousands of sites carrying a variety of products.

Portals linking consumers to online merchants, online shopping malls and auction sites provide several advantages. See the feature on Yahoo! for a better example of a shopping portal. Portals help users collect information on the item for which they are looking and allow users to browse independently owned storefronts, unlike some online shopping malls. Yahoo! permits users to browse a variety of sites while maintaining the convenience of paying through their Yahoo! account.

About.com offers its users an individualized experience through *GuideSite*, a service that acts as a personal shopper for the user. **About.com**'s "guides", each specializing in a particular product type, continually update the Web site and are accessible via e-mail for consumer comments and questions.[8]

Consumers must be savvy when using portals to do their online shopping. Each portal structures its online shopping experience a little differently. Some portals charge merchants for a link, others do not. For example, **GoTo.com** bills merchants per consumer "click-through." The more a business is willing to pay for each consumer "click," the higher that business will appear in **GoTo.com**'s ranks. Because charging merchants may limit the options available to customers, this may not be the best method.[8] Other sites, **About.com** and **altavista.com** for example, do not charge merchants to appear in some locations on their sites (**About.com**'s *GuideSite* and **Altavista.com**'s *Shopping and Services Categories*) but reserve the best areas of the site for paying customers.[9, 10]

Yahoo!

Yahoo! is a horizontal portal with an enormous number of site links and categories.(Fig. 3.3) It also provides consumers with shopping cart capabilities. Through Yahoo!, consumers can link to a variety of online stores adding items to their Yahoo! shopping cart. When they are ready to check out, consumers can purchase all their items through Yahoo! rather than moving from store to store. By limiting the number of registration and billing forms, this use of shopping-cart technology greatly reduces the time needed to make an online purchase.

To participate, a consumer clicks on the **Shopping** link at the top of Yahoo!'s home page. From there, a consumer can search for a product by selecting a category, conducting a keyword search or visiting one of the **Featured Stores**. Other features included on this page are gift registration, **Hot Products**, **What's Selling Now** and the Yahoo! Points reward system. In order to purchase through Yahoo!, you must register with the site. This is a simple process completed by clicking the **Sign-In** link and creating a username and password.

Once you are registered, you may begin searching for products within many Yahoo! Stores. After selecting a product and merchant, users have the option of adding the item to their shopping cart or putting it on their wish list.

Yahoo! Shopping is just one of the many sections within Yahoo! A visitor to the site can search the Web for any product. In order to improve the quality of their Web-searching capabilities, Yahoo! recently partnered with **Google.com**. When Web surfers enter a keyword into a search engine using Google search technology, they receive a list of links based on the popularity of each site. More specifically, the Web links are returned in descending order based on the number of people who link to that particular site.[11]

Yahoo! (Cont.)

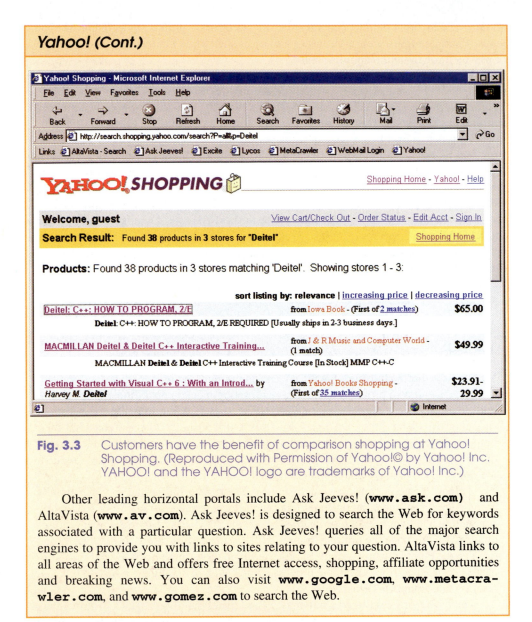

Fig. 3.3   Customers have the benefit of comparison shopping at Yahoo! Shopping. (Reproduced with Permission of Yahoo!© by Yahoo! Inc. YAHOO! and the YAHOO! logo are trademarks of Yahoo! Inc.)

Other leading horizontal portals include Ask Jeeves! (**www.ask.com**) and AltaVista (**www.av.com**). Ask Jeeves! is designed to search the Web for keywords associated with a particular question. Ask Jeeves! queries all of the major search engines to provide you with links to sites relating to your question. AltaVista links to all areas of the Web and offers free Internet access, shopping, affiliate opportunities and breaking news. You can also visit **www.google.com**, **www.metacrawler.com**, and **www.gomez.com** to search the Web.

Vertical Portals and Community Sites

Vertical portals offer a large amount of information in one subject area and are often described as community sites (see AOL feature). Community sites for an enormous number of special interest groups can be found online. Community sites create customer loyalty by allowing visitors to contribute to the sites, chat with friends and find information specifically targeted to them. Vertical portals tend to attract repeat visitors.

Many portal sites provide information pertaining to professional fields such as medicine and law. As a medical community site, Healtheon WebMD (**www.webmd.com**) offers a repository of documentation relating to the medical field. WebMD can also help you find doctors and medical professionals. Physicians can become members of WebMD; joining the specialized practice portal allows them to keep up-to-date with medical announcements, read the latest medical journals and communicate with other members of the medical community. Medscape (**www.medscape.com**) and Dr. Koop (**www.drkoop.com**) also offer medical-portal sites.

There are many legal portals on the Web. The services provided by LEXIS (**www.lexis.com**) and its partner site NEXIS (**www.nexis.com**) are fee-based and usually purchased on a licence basis by law firms. LEXIS provides access to case and other legal data, as well as relevant news articles. Lexis speeds up the research process for people within the legal profession.

Other types of online communities center themselves around a particular demographic. **Bolt.com** is an online teen community that offers chat forums, message boards, polls and shopping. Bolt promotes longer visits by giving visitors free access to content targeted to teens and a chance to communicate with others in the same age group.

IVillage.com is a portal site for women. News and information on women's health, hobbies and general interest are available for free. Message boards are available for women who need questions answered or who would like to speak out on a given issue. **iEmily.com** (**www.iemily.com**) is a similar site designed for teenage women.

Internet.com is a portal site for the Internet and e-commerce. The latest news is offered along with links and a search option. **Internet.com** is loaded with content. All of the news articles are available free.

Epinions (**www.epinions.com**) gives visitors a chance to speak out on their hobbies, politics, favorite media, etc. Members are paid a few cents for each opinion they post. Epinions is a good place to find out real opinions on products and services you are considering. Some members have written hundreds of reviews on everything from film to automobiles.

3.5 Dynamic Pricing Models

The Web has changed the way business is done and the way products are priced. Companies such as Priceline (**www.priceline.com**) and Imandi (**www.imandi.com**) have enabled customers to name their prices for travel, homes, automobiles and consumer goods.

In the past, bargain hunters had to search out deals by visiting numerous local retailers and wholesalers. Today, a few mouse clicks is all you need to find the lowest price available.

America Online

America Online (Fig. 3.4) began this century with its highly publicized merger with Time Warner Entertainment.[12] Just 16 years after Steve Case started the company in his dorm room, AOL has become the leading media organization on the Web. The network of AOL companies includes Compuserve, Netscape, Digital City, ICQ and AOL Movie Phone.

On the Web, AOL has succeeded by offering a user-friendly and powerful community that allows the world to interact. According to the Web Site, AOL's 22 million users are able to conduct all of their browsing, email, chatting and downloading within the AOL format.

America Online (Cont.)

Fig. 3.4   The America Online home page. (Courtesy of America Online, Inc.)

Buying in bulk has always driven prices down, and there are now Web sites that allow you to lower the price by joining with other buyers to purchase products in large quantities. Another pricing strategy used by many e-businesses is to offer products and services for free. By forming strategic partnerships and selling advertising (Chapter 4, "Internet Marketing") many companies are able to offer their products at a greatly reduced rate and often for free. Bartering and offering rebates are other ways companies are keeping prices down on the Internet.

3.5.1 Name-Your-Price Model

The *name-your-price* business model empowers customers by allowing them to choose their price for products and services (See the Priceline.com feature). Many of the business- es that offer this service have formed partnerships with leaders of industries such a travel, lending, retail etc. These industry leaders receive the customer's desired price from the in- termediary and decide whether or not to sell the product or service. If the customer's price is not reasonable then that customer will be asked to choose another price.

Priceline.com

Employing the name-your-price business model has catapulted **Priceline.com** into the spotlighT. You can name your price for airline tickets, hotel rooms, rental cars and mortgages. Its patented business mechanism, called the *demand-collection system*, is a *shopping bot* that takes customers' bids to the Priceline partners to see whether they will accept the prices for the requested products and services. Many e-businesses are using intelligent agents such as shopping bots to enhance their Web sites. Shopping bots are often used to scour data contained within a single database or across the Web to find answers to specific questions.

The buying process is easy at **Priceline.com**. Purchasing an airline ticket will be used as an example. When looking for a domestic flight, you first enter your departure location, destination, bid price and the number of tickets you would like to purchase. You then select the travel dates and airports in or near the departure or arrival cities. The more flexible you are with your travel arrangements, the greater your chance of getting the airline ticket for your stated price.

The **Priceline.com** bot presents the bid to the airlines and attempts to negotiate a fare below the customer's bid price. If the bid is accepted, **Priceline.com** retains the difference between the customer's bid and the actual fare price. The markup percentage varies with the price that is accepted by the airline. For domestic flights, the whole process takes about an hour.

Priceline.com is another example of how the Internet and Web are profoundly changing the way business is conducted. In the case of airlines, hundreds of thousands of airline seats go empty each day. **Priceline.com** helps airlines sell these seats. By facilitating the sale of excess inventory at a discount, **Priceline.com** allows airlines to realize increased revenue and helps passengers save money.

3.5.2 Comparison Pricing Model

The *comparison pricing model* allows customers to poll a variety of merchants and find a desired product or service at the lowest price (See the **Bottomdollar.com** feature). These sites often get their revenue from partnerships with particular merchants. Thus, you need to be careful when using these services, because you may not necessarily be getting the best price available on the entire Web. Other similar sites search the most popular stores on the Internet, trying to appeal to the largest audience.

3.5.3 Demand-Sensitive Pricing Model

The Web has enabled customers to demand better, faster service at cheaper prices. It has also empowered buyers to shop in large groups to achieve a group rate.

The concept behind the demand-sensitive-pricing business model is that the more people who buy a product in a single purchase, the lower the cost-per-person becomes. Selling products individually can be expensive because the vendor must price a product so that it covers selling and overhead cost while still generating a profit. When customers buy in bulk, this cost is shared and the profit margin is increased. Mercata (**www.mercata.com**) sells products using this business model for the home, electronics, computers and peripherals among many other things. Customers become loyal to Mercata for helping them save money. MobShop (**www.mobshop.com**) offers comparable services. Because pricing and products do vary between these and other similar sites, so you may want to visit several such sites before making a purchase.

BottomDollar.com

BottomDollar.com uses *intelligent-agent* technology to search the Web and find the products you want at the best available prices. Intelligent agents are program that search and arrange large amounts of data, and report answers based on that data. A customer can use **BottomDollar.com** to search for a product or to browse the various categories on the site (Fig. 3.5). The service searches the catalogs of over 1,000 online retailers to find the products you want at the best available prices. The search usually takes less than a minute. Imagine trying to visit 1,000 different stores one-by-one to find the best price!

Fig. 3.5   The **bottomdollar.com** home page. (Courtesy of Network Commerce Inc.)

BottomDollar.com (Cont.)

Shopping bots and intelligent agents are changing the way people shop. Rather than going directly to the stores with established brand names, customers are using services like **BottomDollar.com** to get the best available prices. This forces online retailers to keep their prices competitive.

Similar comparison pricing sites include **Dealtime.com**, **Deja.com**, and **MySimon.com**. Unlike other comparison shopping sites, DealTime (**www.dealtime.com**) selects merchants based on customer popularity, reliability and reviews.

Deja.com (**www.deja.com**) is a multi-faceted Web site offering shopping, discussion groups, customer ratings and comparison shopping. Users of the service can then write opinions in the discussions and review sections. MySimon (**www.mysimon.com**) offers a comparison pricing search from a small number of better-known retailers.

3.5.4 Bartering Model

Another popular method of conducting e-business is *bartering*, or offering one item in exchange for another. **Ubarter.com** (**www.ubarter.com**) is a site that allows individuals and companies wishing to sell a product to post their listings. The seller makes an initial offer with the intention of bartering to reach a final agreement with the buyer. A broad range of products and services is available for barter.

If a business is looking to get rid of an overstocked product, iSolve (**www.isolve.com**) can help sell it. Products can be sold directly or on a barter basis. Potential customers send their pricing preferences to the merchant who evaluates the offer. Deals are often part barter and part cash. Examples of items typically bartered are overstocked inventory items, factory surplus and unneeded assets.

3.5.5 Rebates

Rebates can help attract customers to your site. Many companies offer "everyday low prices" and specials to keep customers coming back. eBates is a shopping site where customers receive a rebate on every purchase. eBates has formed partnerships with wholesalers and retailers who will offer discounts—the company passes these discounts to customers in the form of rebates. By adding value to a customers visit, eBates builds customer satisfaction and loyalty. What eBates retains a portion of the savings.

3.5.6 Offering Free Products and Services

Many entrepreneurs are forming their business models around advertising-driven revenue streams. Television networks, radio stations, magazines and print media use advertising to fund their operations and make a profit. The following sites offer their products for free on the Web. Many of these sites also form partnerships with companies to exchange products and services for advertising space and vise versa.

The Hollywood Stock Exchange (**www.hsx.com**) is a free gaming site where visitors become traders of entertainment stocks and star bonds. Traders are able to track the value of their movie and music stocks and bonds as they fluctuate. The strongest portfolios are rewarded with prizes. The company is able to offer its services free by selling advertising to sponsors.

iWon.com (**www.iWon.com**) is a portal site that rewards users with raffle points as they browse the site's content. iWon has the appearance of a traditional search engine, offering links to news, sports, weather, and other topics. However, users registering and surfing the site become eligible for daily, weekly, monthly and annual prizes. Every advertisement and link has a point value and, as your points accrue, so do your chances of winning. **iWon.com** is able to support its free contests through advertising revenue and partnerships.

Freelotto.com (**www.freelotto.com**) also offers free contests supported by advertising revenue. After registering with **Freelotto.com**, you can enter a free lottery. FreeLotto awards tens of millions in cash and prizes through its online lottery system. However, you must visit sponsoring Web sites in exchange for your visit. **Freelotto.com** generates its income from these sponsors.

Freemerchant.com offers free hosting, a free store builder, a free shopping cart, free traffic logs, free auction tools and all necessary elements for running an e-commerce storefront. Freemerchant makes money from its strategic partnerships and referrals. Freemerchant partners are companies who can help small businesses establish a presence on the Web. These partners offer their services free of charge in exchange for advertising.

At **Startsampling.com** (**www.startsampling.com**) you can earn prizes for trying and reviewing products. This site allows you to request free samples from companies across the country.

Other Web sites that offer free resources are **free-programs.com**, **freestuff-center.com** and **emazing.com**.

3.6 B2B Exchanges

B2B e-commerce is defined as buying, selling, partnering, bartering or trading conducted between two or more businesses. Goldman Sachs has estimated that B2B e-commerce will generate as much as 1.5 trillion dollars in revenues by 2004, with some estimates running even higher.[13] The B2B marketplace is one of the fastest growing segments of e-commerce. Industry leaders have begun using B2B marketplaces and exchanges to improve their business methods on the Web. B2B exchanges allow businesses to buy, sell, auction, barter and distribute products and services. This cuts costs while improving efficiency.

Procurement (acquiring goods or services) and effective supply chain management can be difficult and costly aspects of running businesses. ICG Commerce Systems (**www.icgcommerce.com**) is a site that enables businesses, customers, suppliers, purchasers and any combination of these to interact and conduct transactions over the Internet. The system supports B2B, B2C and all variations of these models.

TradeAccess (**www.tradeaccess.com**) helps businesses form relationships and facilitate negotiations. The site aggregates all of the documentation and materials appropriate for a specific contract and negotiates the terms over the Web.

ItoI stands for Industry to Industry. This site, located at **www.itoi.com**, is designed for inter-industry trading and offers services in the chemical, retail, construction and energy industries. Visitors have the option of buying through traditional methods, auctioning or conducting exchanges. In an exchange, customers make requests and merchants attempt to fill their request at the best price. The business provides a marketplace for raw materials, chemicals, equipment and services.

Another kind of B2B exchange is available online at **eWork.com,** which allows businesses to exchange employees to complete short-term projects. cWork can search its databases and find qualified professionals to help you complete all of your projects. eWork is just one of many online companies that can help a business exchange human resources.

Other B2B exchanges include **www.cynomix.com** and **www.biz2biz.com**.

3.7 B2B Service Providers

B2B service providers make B2B transactions on the Internet easier. These e-businesses help other businesses improve policies, procedures, customer service and general operations.

Ariba (**www.ariba.com**) is a B2B service provider. Solutions include supply chain management, procurement, logistics, customer service features and many others.

Freemarkets.com is a B2B marketplace connecting buyers and sellers. Companies with surplus inventory can use Freemarkets to sell extra assets. Freemarkets specializes in hard-to-sell raw materials, property and equipment.

Because of the intense competition among Web sites for customers, the Web makes it more important than ever to keep your customers happy. Customer service and troubleshooting are important. **Liveperson.com** has found a way to improve customer service on the Internet, by offering a product that connects visitors to your help center through a live text-based chat. By clicking an Icon on the site the visitor can speak directly with a company representative. Try the system at **www.liveperson.com**.

Business travelers who wish to do work often have to pay for time on a computer within a hotel's business center. PCRoomLink (**www.pcroomlink.com**) provides computers and secure Internet access to business travelers by putting computers in their hotel rooms. Membership is free and required when using the service.

B2B services are also available from **www.ceverything.com** and **www.magnifi.com**.

3.8 Online Trading and Lending Models

Another fast-growing area of e-commerce is online securities trading.[14, 15] According to U.S. Bancorp Piper Jaffray, Company and Industry Sources (**www.piperjaffray.com/re/re_ne2.asp?id=188**), "online trading volumes accounted for 37 percent of all retail trades for the first half of 1999, up from 30 percent in the second half of 1998."[14, 15]

Stock trades used to be handled only through brokers who were paid commissions for their services. However, due to the popularity of online trading, many brokerage houses have established a presence on the Web. Trading sites allow you to research securities, buy, sell and manage all of your investments from your desktop. Online trading often costs less than conventional brokerage.

Charles Schwab (**www.schwab.com**) is becoming one of the leading online trading providers. DLJ Direct (**www.dljdirect.com**) and Fidelity Investments (**www.fidelity.com**) offer similar services.

For more information about e-commerce and online trading, check out the latest news reports or review back issues of *Business Week* at **www.businessweek.com** and of *The Industry Standard* at **www.thestandard.com**. The Motley Fool (**www.fool.com**) is another good resource for online trading information.

E*TRADE

One of the leaders in online trading is E*TRADE (Fig. 3.6). The company was founded in 1982 to offer online stock quotes to the nation's major investment firms. With the development of the Web, E*TRADE created a Web site (**www.etrade.com**) where individual investors could manage their own investments, eliminating the need for brokers.

At E*TRADE, you can buy, sell and research stocks, bonds and other securities. If you have little knowledge about buying and selling stocks, E*TRADE offers two games in which you use fake "game money" to carry out stock trades or stock and options trades. Each player starts with $100,000 in virtual trading dollars and is given access to charts, graphs and recent news articles to help the player choose their investments. There is no risk of losing real money, so the players can feel free to experiment with different trading strategies. Each trade takes approximately one minute to process. The goal of each game is, of course, to increase the value of your portfolio. The E*TRADE games are a friendly way for beginners to experiment with online trading. Each game lasts a month and, at the end of each game, thirty-two players with the highest-valued portfolios receive prizes. To play the E*TRADE games and to learn more about online trading, visit **www.etrade.com**. An exercise at the end of the chapter encourages the reader to play the E*TRADE game. If you win a prize, please let us know!

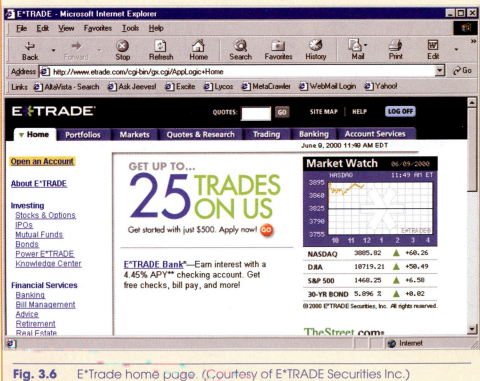

Fig. 3.6   E*Trade home page. (Courtesy of E*TRADE Securities Inc.)

3.9 Getting a Loan Online

Online lending is a growing segment of e-commerce. You might find a loan with a lower rate online than through traditional lending channels. The following companies make loans to customers over the Web.

E-LOAN (`www.eloan.com`) offers credit-card services, home equity loans and the tools and calculators to help you make educated borrowing decisions.

Rated the number-one mortgage e-commerce site by `Gomez.com`, Mortgagebot (`www.mortgagebot.com`.) offers a five-vendor rate search. This allows customers to find a bank in their neighborhood that is willing to offer them the lowest possible interest rate.

E-businesses can seek loans at eCredit (`www.ecredit.com`). This company has formed partnerships with leading lenders to speed the financing process. Once a business has received funding, eCredit will also help the business manage their new assets. eCredit customers include Hewlett-Packard, Intel and many other Fortune 1000 companies. Loans-Direct (`www.loansdirect.com`) offers a comparable service. It is important to investigate a variety of options when getting a loan. A difference of a few interest points can significantly increase bills.

3.10 Recruiting on the Web

Recruiting and job searching can be done effectively on the Web (See the `monster.com` feature) Whether you are an employer or a job seeker, the Internet can improve your ability to recruit or find a job. Job seekers can learn how to write a resume and cover letter, post it online and search through job listings to find the jobs that best suit their needs. Employers can post jobs that can be searched by an enormous pool of applicants. In this section we will examine some of the recruiting options available on the Web.

`Dice.c. om` (`www.dice.com`) is a recruiting Web site that focuses on the computer industry. Fees are based on the number of jobs a company wishes to post and the frequency with which the postings are updated. Job seekers can post their resumes and search the job database for free.

`Guru.com` (`www.guru.com`) is a recruiting site for contract employees. Independent contractors, private consultants and trainers can use `guru.com` to find short-term and long-term work. Tips, articles and advice are available for contractors who wish to learn more about their industry and the best way to contract their work. Other sections of the site teach you how to run your business, buy the best equipment and manage legal issues. `Guru.com` includes an online store where you can buy products associated with small business management. Companies wishing to hire contractors need to register.

SixFigureJobs (`www.sixfigurejobs.com`) is a recruitment site designed for experienced executives. Executive positions are often hard to fill due to the high demands and experience required for the jobs. This site is designed to help fill these executive positions. Resume posting and job searching is free to job seekers.

`Refer.com` (`www.refer.com`.) rewards visitors for successful job referrals. Highly sought-after positions can earn thousands of dollars. If you refer a friend or family member and they are hired, you receive a commission.

These are just a few of the many recruiting-related sites on the Web. Some sites are targeted at specific groups of people such as computer programmers or electrical engineers, while others offer their services to anyone. It is worthwhile to search and post on many of the sites at one time.

monster.com

Super Bowl ads and effective marketing have made **monster.com** one of the most recognizable online brands (Fig. 3.7). **monster.com** allows people looking for jobs to post their resumes, search job listings, read advice and information about the job-search process and take proactive steps to improve their career. These services are free to job seekers. Employers can post job listings, search resume databases and become featured employers.

Posting your resume at **monster.com** is simple and free. **monster.com** has a resume builder that allows you to post a resume to its site in 15-30 minutes; you can store up to 5 resumes and cover letters on the **monster.com** server. Some companies offer their applications directly on the **monster.com** site. **monster.com** has job postings in every state and all major categories. Furthermore, you can decide who gets to see your personal identification information. As one of the leading recruiting sites on the Web, **monster.com** is a good place to start your job search or to find out more about the search process.

Fig. 3.7   The **monster.com** home page. (Courtesy of **monster.com**.)

3.11 Online News Services

As we move into the information age, there is no question that the Web will play a major role in the publishing and news industries. Well-known news organizations such as CNN (see feature), The Wall Street Journal and Newsweek have all found the Web to be a dynamic environment on which to feature their content.

The Wall Street Journal (**www.wsj.com**), is one of the most widely read newspapers in the world, is offered in an online edition which includes full text and 24-hour updates. You can start by trying the online version on a free-trial basis, and, if you choose to subscribe, you will receive full access to the Barrons (**www.barrons.com**.) database—an online database of commentary and articles by leading investment analysts.

ESPN.com provides the latest sporting news and allows users to get in-depth information on their favorite players, teams, etc. **ESPN.com** offers live text, audio and video of games and highlights. Visitors can also enroll in fantasy sporting games, such as football, baseball and golf.

Quality writers with reliable sources can begin publishing their content on the Web. Traditional barriers of entry such as printing and distribution costs do not exist on the Web. This allows independent Web news organizations to compete with traditional news leaders. Matt Drudge has become a celebrity due to the success of his online news site, The Drudge Report (**www.drudgereport.com**).

3.12 Online Travel Services

Web surfers can search for and arrange all of their travel and accommodations online, and can often save money doing so. The Web gives people access to much of the same information previously accessible only by travel agents. (See the **Travelocity.com** feature) You will find the lowest prices, best times and the best accommodations available to you.

CNN Interactive

CNN Interactive is one of the most visited and most interactive sites on the Web. CNN has a network of sites designed to give current, highly targeted news and information to their visitors. Each of these sites offers streaming audio and video (Chapter 32) taken from broadcasts on the television network.

CNNallpolitics is a site offering more in-depth articles about politicians and their campaigns, public policy and global politics. CNNSI is the all-sports section of the CNN network. You can follow teams in every league or just catch up on the latest scores and highlights. CNNFN allows you to track financial news and securities data from your Web browser. MyCNN allows you to personalize the news and information that appears on your browser. You can choose text, audio and video in any category. You can then customize the way CNN appears when you visit the site.

CNN has also built sitLes offering information in foreign languages. They include news and information specific to each country and region. The network of sites that make up CNN Interactive uses the highest quality multimedia and content to add value to customers' experiences.

Microsoft offers travel services through **www.expedia.com**. Microsoft Expedia allows you to book all of your travel arrangements, including transportation and lodging. Membership is free, and members are given access to a database of information offering them the best available options.

Cheaptickets (**www.cheaptickets.com**) is a similar site that helps customers find discount fares for airline tickets, hotel rooms, cruise vacations and rental cars. Users are given access to a database of up-to-the-minute flight schedule data.

Many travel sites are targeting business travelers specifically. **BizTravel.com** will reimburse customers in the event of a late or cancelled flight, lost luggage, or poor in-flight service. The rate of reimbursement is based on the severity of the problem. All flights that are cancelled or arrive more than two hours later than scheduled are reimbursed in full. Lost luggage is also paid for in full. This system is designed for business travelers.

Another site designed for business travelers, **GetThere.com** (**www.getthere.com**), helps corporate clients cut travel costs by connecting them directly to airlines, hotels and rental cars through its site. GetThere also outsources its technology, allowing portal sites to offer similar services.

3.13 Online Entertainment

The Web is based on the communication of high-quality information developed with high-quality multimedia. The entertainment industry has recognized this and has leveraged its power to sell movie tickets, albums and any other entertainment-related content they can fit on a Web page. Some of the Web's greatest controversies surround the online entertainment industry. Internet copyright cases are becoming the norm as individuals begin to use the Internet to trade their media such as music and videos. These problems are discussed in Chapter 6, "Legal, Ethical and Social Issues: Internet Taxation".

Travelocity.com

The travel service industry has achieved tremendous success on the Web in the past few years. Consumers are booking their travel itineraries online, often at lower prices than those available through travel agents. **Travelocity.com** (**www.travelocity.com**) is an online travel service that enables you to make your travel arrangements with a single visit to their Web site. You can book flights, rental cars, hotel rooms and vacation packages without involving a travel agent.

Travelocity.com uses shopping-bot technology. For example, a customer who wishes to fly from New York to Los Angeles enters a time frame for the trip and airport codes to receive up-to-date fare information. The shopping bot scans airline rates and scheduling databases for matches. The site then displays a list of flights that fit the submitted criteria, rate information and a ticket-purchase option. Travelocity is just one of many sites offering this service.

iCast.com (**www.icast.com**) is a multimedia-rich entertainment site. Audio and Video downloads of popular music and films are available for free. Each news article is accompanied by a supporting multimedia file. For instance, news regarding a particular actress may include the trailer of her latest feature film. Visitors to the site will benefit from a high-speed connection. The iCast media player is a free product that allows visitors to play audio and video from the site.

The Internet Movie Database (**www.imdb.com**) combines a huge database, a well-designed and easily maneuverable site and interesting content to create a highly entertaining site. IMDB helps you to locate and learn more about your favorite films, actors, executives, production companies and news relating to filmed entertainment. A search for any given film will give information pertaining to that film's cast and crew and their personal history. IMDB is part of the **Amazon.com** network of Web sites.

3.14 Online Automotive Sites

Various sites allow users to research and purchase new and used cars. Whether or not you actually make your final arrangements for the purchase of a new vehicle online, many of the preliminary steps can be completed. Online auto sites provide users with the ability to explore options more efficiently than traveling among dealerships. Online automobile appraisers also offer users leverage in negotiating a price on a new car by giving them access to instant value estimates.

Autobytel (**www.autobytel.com**) is a one-stop shop where users buy, sell, maintain and learn more about automobiles. You can search classified ads for used cars or find the best price on a new car. Additionally, If you are looking to service your car, you can contact your local service station and request an estimate. You can also find out where to get the best value on car insurance.

Autoparts.com is an online auction site for people buying and selling auto parts. Once you register, you can begin searching through the database of auto parts. You can search for parts by year, make and model.

Auto.com is an online version of the Detroit Free Press. The site offers news and information regarding the automotive industry. The site is a good place to learn about the automobile industry as well as the car you drive.

Scour.net

Scour.net (**www.scour.net**) uses intelligent-agent technology to locate multimedia files on the Web. Users can find video clips, audio, images, live radio broadcasts and breaking news. The bot "scours" the Web in search of the multimedia that the user specifies. **Scour.net** uses its SmartMatch intelligent agent to respond to customer queries, even if only partial names are entered and words are misspelled. It searches for specific file types, such as **.mpg** files for video and **.au** files for audio (Chapter 32, "Multimedia"). Such searches would be difficult to conduct offline.

Currently, **Scour.net** is the most comprehensive multimedia search site available. Lycos offers a search for sounds and images within their search engine at **www.lycos.com**. AltaVista also offers a multimedia search capability at **www.altavista.com**.

3.15 Energy Online

A number of companies have set up energy exchanges where buyers and sellers come to communicate, buy, sell, and distribute energy. These companies sell crude oil, electricity and the products and systems for distributing them.

HoustonStreet (**www.houstonstreet.com**.) is an online market for traders looking to buy energy commodities. Traders can buy and sell crude oil, refined products and electricity from the HoustonStreet Web site.

Altranet (**www.altranet.com**.) also sells energy commodities. Utility companies can buy natural gas, electricity and heating oil directly from the site. Altranet also facilitates the distribution of products with the help of its subsidiaries.

Retail Energy (**www.retailenergy.com**) is a directory for the energy industry. This site was designed by the Power Marketing Association and offers a comprehensive listing of energy providers. Current energy prices for both electricity and natural gas are available.

3.16 Selling Brainpower

Companies can buy patents and other intellectual property online. It is often difficult for small businesses to invest time and money in research and development. Other companies have trouble finding the talent to create such property.

Companies who do not have the human resources to complete complex projects can find help at **HelloBrain.com**. When merchants post the projects they need completed and the compensation they are willing to pay, proposed answers will be sent from companies and contractors that can help. HelloBrain acts as the middleman offering free postings to merchants.

The Question Exchange (**www.questionexchange.com**) allows businesses and individuals to access programming-specific troubleshooting as well as customer service. Companies pay a subscription fee to gain access to the system—in exchange, users are able to ask programming-related development questions and access a database of 10,000 archived questions.

Yet2 (**www.yet2.com**) is an e-business designed to help companies raise capital by selling intellectual property such as patents and trademarks. Yet2 is backed by industry-leading companies who wish to sell intellectual property assets. You must register to get a full view of the properties, but Yet2 does offer a sample listing.

3.17 Online Art Dealers

The Web offers a new outlet for your favorite supplies and artwork which you can often find at a discount on the Web. shopping-cart technology and express shipping allow you to have your art and supplies within a few days of your order.

Art.com allows you to choose between fine art, photography, posters and prints, animations and many other media. You can search the **art.com** database by artist, medium, decor, size, subject, and genre. Artists also list their favorites, for you to peruse.

Guild.com is another art dealer offering pieces in a wide variety of media. The products are well documented, easy to find and range from a few hundred dollars to thousands of dollars. There are more than 7,000 products available to your shopping cart.

Atom Films (**www.atomfilms.com**) is one of the leading film sites on the Web and has frequently turned down offers to bring their content to the big screen. Members of Atom Films have access to award-winning short films and animations delivered via streaming video.

Art.net (**www.art.net**) offers links to many art resources on the Web, including artists' home pages, suppliers and supporting services.

3.18 E-Learning

The e-learning industry is growing rapidly as the number of individuals with access to computers and hand-held-devices increases.[16] Universities and corporate-training companies offer high-quality distance education directly over the Web. There are companies on the Web that aggregate e-learning products and services from content creators and publishers worldwide, and offer them on a subscription basis to individuals and corporations. As technology increases and audio and video quality on the Web improve, so will the quality and availability of e-learning programs.

Click2Learn (**www.click2learn.com**) has created a database of products and services to help individuals and companies find the education they need. Click2Learn also has a skills assessment feature that helps customers evaluate their e-learning needs. Companies wishing to develop their own training can use the Click2Learn *Toolbook* product in order to develop and sell courses on the Click2Learn site. Once a customer has developed courseware for the Web, the course can be included within the Click2learn Web site.

Saba (**www.saba.com**) also aggregates e-learning materials and courses. Companies can create Saba learning e-stores—customized storefronts—to sell their e-learning products. Saba helps their customers turn traditional instructor-led courses into Web-based training courses. Additionally, customers can use Saba as an e-learning portal where they can find training products for themselves and their employees.

Blackboard.com (**www.blackboard.com**) allows teachers and educational organizations to post their courses on the Web. Once a company has bought a license for the **Blackboard.com** *CourseInfo*™ course-development product, they can begin posting and offering their training materials and courses over the Web. For an additional fee, **Blackboard.com** offers trainers e-commerce capabilities, special marketing opportunities, more server space, and access to customer support.

WebCT (**www.webct.com**) helps educators and students leverage the power of the Web to improve their educational experience. WebCT sells a course development tool that enables educators to quickly build supplementary course materials or full courses to be offered through the WebCT learning hub. The company has offered courses to more than one million students.

Deitel & Associates, Inc. (**www.deitel.com**) teaches instructor-led training courses for many of the world's largest organizations. Deitel publications are used in each of its training courses, and in thousands of colleges and universities worldwide.

The Version 1 Deitel Web-based training courses are similar to the Deitel interactive multimedia *Cyber Classroom* products. The courses include the full content of the textbooks as well as complete audio walkthroughs, "live-code" examples and hundreds of solved problems. The products also include course management, scheduling and assessment features. The Version 2 Web-based training courses emulate the instructor-led training experience with more extensive lecture and lab features.

Colleges and universities have also begun integrating e-learning into their curricula. Jones International University (**www.getmymba.com**), the University of Illinois (**www.online.uillinois.edu**) and the University of Phoenix (**www.universi-tyofphoenix.com**) are among the first schools to offer complete degree programs online. Students are able to apply online and take courses at home using the Internet.

Many publishers are beginning to add electronic publishing departments to meet the demand for electronic books.[16] Electronic books, or *e-books* are publications that can be downloaded onto your computer or to a hand-held device and read at your convenience. Xlibris (**www.xlibris.com**) specializes in publishing books in electronic form. Other electronic publishing companies include **iPublish.com** (**www.ipublish.com**) and **netLibrary.com** (**www.netlibrary.com**).

3.19 Click-and-Mortar Businesses

Brick-and-mortar companies who wish to bring their businesses to the Web must determine the level of cooperation and integration the two separate entities will share. A company that can offer its services both online and offline can add value to the customers' experience. One of the major issues in e-commerce today is how to integrate the Internet into offline businesses. The following companies have all worked out successful answers to this question.

Barnes & Noble (**www.bn.com**) has established itself as a leader in the booksellers market both online and offline. Customers have access to the same inventory online as they do in the actual stores. In the event that a customer is dissatisfied with a purchase made online, they can return it to their local brick-and-mortar B&N store.

1-800-Flowers (**www.1800flowers.com**) has established a presence on the Web. Their customers can now view pictures of floral arrangements before making a purchase.

CircuitCity (**www.curcuitcity.com**), a store specializing in consumer electronics, appliances, audio and video, has effectively integrated its online and offline entities. CircuitCity has tied its offline stores to its online store, allowing customers to order online and pick up at their local stores, though shipping is still available.

The Web has created such great opportunities for some companies that they have abandoned their bricks all-together. **Egghead.com** (**www.egghead.com**) started out as a company that sold computers and peripherals through small brick-and-mortar stores. Many of their competitors were catalog businesses that often underpriced them. The Web gave Egghead the opportunity to abandon unnecessary property overhead and access a global market.

SUMMARY

- An e-business can offer personalized service, high-quality customer service, and improved supply chain management.

- An e-business is defined as a company that has an online presence. e-Businesses that have the ability to sell, trade, barter and transact over the Web can be considered e-commerce businesses.

- A combination of a company's policy, operations, technology and ideology define its business model.

- The storefront combines transaction processing, security and information storage to allow merchants to sell their products on the Web.

- The banking industry uses Electronic Funds Transfer (EFT) to transfer money between accounts.

- Many companies also use Electronic Data Interchange (EDI), in which business forms, such as purchase orders and invoices, are standardized so that companies can share information with customers, vendors and business partners electronically.

- E-commerce allows companies to conduct business 24-by-7 worldwide.
- B2C stands for business-to-consumer.
- The merchant server is the data storage and management system employed by the merchant.
- A database is a part of the merchant server designed to store and report on large amounts of information. Databases also store customer information, such as names, addresses, credit-card information and past purchases.
- Online shopping malls present consumers with a wide selection of products and services. Consumers can search and shop for a variety of products, and, rather than making several separate purchases, they can use the mall's shopping-cart technology to purchase items from many stores in a single transaction.
- Forrester Research reveals that an estimated $3.8 billion will be spent on online person-to-person auctions this year alone. This number is dwarfed by the $52 billion that is projected to be spent on business-to-business auctions in 2002.[4]
- Reverse auctions, or auctions that allow the buyer to set a price as sellers compete to match or even beat it, are becoming more popular.
- An faster option is available when the buyer sets a reserve price. A reserve price is the lowest price that the seller will accept in any type of auction.
- eBay uses a database to manage the millions of auctions that it offers. This database evolves dynamically as sellers and buyers enter personal identification and product information.
- High-availability computing attempts to minimize down time; continuous-availability computing attempts to eliminate it completely.
- For example, every crucial piece of hardware—processors, disks and communications channels—has one or more levels of backup, so, in a failure, the system simply shifts from a failed component to a backup component. The system keeps running while the failed component is fixed or replaced.
- Portal sites give visitors the chance to find everything they are looking for in one place. They often offer news, sports and weather, as well as the ability to search the Web.
- Search engines are horizontal portals, or portals that aggregate information on a broad range of topics and help the user find what they are looking for.
- Vertical portals offer a large amount of information in one subject area.
- Community sites create customer loyalty by allowing visitors to contribute to the sites, chat with friends and find information specifically targeted to them. Vertical portals tend to find repeat visitors.
- In the past, bargain hunters had to search out deals by visiting numerous local retailers and wholesalers. Today, a few mouse clicks is all you need to find the lowest price available.
- Buying in bulk has always driven prices down, and there are now sites on the Web that allow you to lower the price by waiting for others to purchase the product at the same time.
- Another pricing strategy used by many e-businesses is to offer products and services for free.
- Bartering and offering rebates are other ways companies are keeping prices down on the Internet.
- The name-your-price business model empowers customers by allowing them to choose their price for products and services.
- Shopping bots are often used to scour data contained within a single database or across the Web to find answers to specific questions.
- The comparison pricing model allows customers to poll merchants and find a desired product or service at the lowest price. These sites often take their revenue from partnerships with merchants.
- The Web has allowed customers to demand better, faster service at cheaper prices. It has also empowered buyers to shop in large groups to achieve a group rate.

- The concept behind the demand-sensitive pricing business model is that, the more people who buy a product in a single purchase, the lower the cost-per-person becomes.

- Selling products individually can be expensive because the vendor must price a product so that it covers the selling and overhead cost while still generating a small profit.

- Another popular method of conducting e-business is Bartering, or offering an item you do not want or need in exchange for something for which you have a need.

- Rebates are a good way to attract customers to your site. Many companies offer everyday low prices and specials to keep customers coming back.

- B2B e-commerce is defined as buying, selling, partnering, bartering or trading conducted between two or more businesses. Goldman Sachs has estimated that B2B e-commerce will generate as much as 1.5 trillion dollars in revenues by 2004, with some estimates running even higher.[13]

- The B2B marketplace is one of the fastest growing segments of e-commerce. Industry leaders have begun using B2B marketplaces and exchanges to improve their business methods on the Web.

- Procurement, or acquiring goods or services, and effective supply chain management can be a difficult and costly aspect of running a business.

- ItoI stands for Industry to Industry.

- B2B service providers make business-to-business transactions on the Internet easier. These e-businesses help other businesses improve policy and procedure, customer service and general operations.

- Due to the popularity of online trading, many brokerages have established a presence on the Web.

- Online lending is a growing segment of e-commerce. You might find a loan with a lower rate online than through traditional lending channels.

- Recruiting and job searching can be done effectively on the Web. Whether you are an employer or a job seeker, the Internet can improve your ability to recruit or find a job.

- As we move into the information age, there is no question that the Web will play a major role in the publishing and news industries.

- Web surfers can search for and arrange all of their travel and accommodations online. The Web gives people access to much of the same information previously accessible only by travel agents.

- Whether or not you actually make your final arrangements for the purchase of a new vehicle online, many of the preliminary steps can be completed.

- Online auto sites provide users with the ability to explore options more efficiently than traveling among dealerships.

- A number of companies have set up energy exchanges where buyers and sellers come to communicate, buy, sell, and distribute energy. These companies sell crude oil, electricity and the products and systems that help to distribute them.

- Companies who wish to buy patents and other intellectual property can now do so online.

- Artwork and supplies can be expensive. However, you can often find discounts on the Web. Shopping-cart technology and shipping allow you to have your supplies within a few days of your order.

- The e-learning industry is growing rapidly as the number of individuals with access to a computers and hand-held devices increases.

- There are companies on the Web that aggregate information on the e-learning products and services available from companies around the World. As technology increases and audio and video quality on the Web improves, so will the quality and frequency of e-learning programs

- Many of the leading corporate training organizations use the Web to train their customers.

- Brick-and-mortar companies who wish to bring their businesses to the Web must determine the level of cooperation and integration the two separate entities will share.

- A company that can offer its services both online and offline can add value to the customer's experience.
- One of the major issues in e-commerce today is how to integrate the Internet into offline businesses.

TERMINOLOGY

1-Click^{SM} system	fault-tolerant systems
24-by-7 basis	high-availability computing
B2B	horizontal portal
B2C	intelligent agent
bartering	ItoI
brick-and-mortar business	merchant server
business-to-business	name-your-price model
client/server application	Pez®
comparison pricing model	procurement
continuous-availability computing	redundancy
database	reserve price
demand collection system	reverse-auction model
e-books	search engine
e-business	shopping bot
e-commerce	shopping cart
Electronic Funds Transfer (EFT)	Toolbook
Electronic Data Interchange (EDI)	vertical portal

SELF-REVIEW EXERCISES

3.1 State whether the following are true or false. If the answer is false, explain why.
a) A shopping cart allows customers to continue to browse after selecting each item they wish to purchase.
b) In a reverse auction the seller sets a price and customers make individual bids to buy the item.
c) A reserve price is the highest bid a customer is willing to make.
d) In the demand-sensitive pricing model, the price decreases as more people buy.
e) The name-your-price model is an auction-based model.
f) Brick-and-mortar companies are businesses that build the infrastructure of an e-commerce Web site.
g) Web-based training is not yet possible, but will be when streaming audio and video technology improve.
h) **Priceline.com** employs the name-your-price model.
i) B2B exchanges are e-businesses that facilitate the sale, purchase and exchange of goods and services between one or more companies.
j) High-availability computing refers to the minimization of downtime for a company.

3.2 Fill in the blanks in each of the following:
a) A business that has a presence off but, not on the Web is described as a _____ company.
b) The _____ model is designed to bring prices down by increasing the number of customers who buy a particular product at once.
c) Customers can shop for products and store them for later purchase using a _____.
d) Reserve prices are set by a buyer in an _____.
e) The two types of portals are called _____ and _____.

f) iVillage, WebMD and **Bolt.com** can be described as horizontal portals or _____ sites.

g) Auctions that allow the buyer to set a price and have the merchants compete for the best deal are called _____.

h) _____ are designed to help businesses buy, sell and barter their products and services to other businesses over the Internet.

i) E*trade and Charles Schwab are companies that offer _____.

j) The e-businesses that allows customers to find the lowest price on a particular item are called _____ pricing sites.

ANSWERS TO SELF-REVIEW EXERCISES

3.1   a) True b) False. This is the concept of a true auction. c) False. A reserve price is the lowest price a seller will accept in an auction. d) True e) False. The name-your price model allows customers to get a lower price by clearing the price with a number of vendors. This does not involve an auction. f) False. Brick-and-mortar business are offline businesses. This term is often associated with companies who have both and online and offline presence. g) False. Web-based training is currently used by organizations around the world. h) True i) True j) True

3.2   a) Brick-and-mortar b) Demand sensitive pricing model c) shopping cart d) auction e) vertical, horizontal f) community g) reverse auctions h) B2B exchanges i) online trading j) comparison shopping

EXERCISES

3.3   Categorize each of the following items as it best relates to the storefront model, the auction model or dynamic pricing models:
  a) reserve price
  b) liquidprice
  c) shopping cart
  d) catalog
  e) mercata
  f) bottomdollar

3.4   Define each of the following terms:
  a) Web-based training
  b) name-your-price model
  c) shopping cart
  d) reverse auction
  e) redundancy
  f) high-availability computing
  g) merchant server

3.5   Have a brainstorming session to discuss potential e-business concepts. List the technologies that would be necessary in order to implement these concepts. Which business model would you implement? Why?

3.6   E*Trade offers a stock and options trading simulation at **www.etrade.com**. Each player is allocated an initial $100,000 in order to make his or her trades. As the round progresses, a player's stocks will gain or lose value, reflecting the actual stock market activity. Players compete to earn the greatest return on their investment (i.e., profits) for the round. Each new round begins on the first day of each month. At the end of the month, all portfolios are compared, and the thirty-two highest finishers each receive a prize! The E*TRADE game is free for your use and gives potential investors a chance to see how their stock picks would perform without actually putting their money at risk.

For this exercise, the class will be divided into teams. Each team should decide on a name and use it to register for the "stock trading only" version of the game. This exercise will let the teams compete over a period of three days to see which can create the most valuable stock portfolio. Each team should begin the game on the same day. Teams should be aware that investing all of the available funds will not necessarily give you a more profitable portfolio. A market downturn could spell disaster for a fully invested team! (Note: E*TRADE automatically resets the game at the end of each month. Be sure to start this exercise at least three days prior to the end of the month, so that you do not lose your data.)

In order to begin trading, you should complete the following tasks. Good luck! Please let us know if you win a prize!

   a) Create a written log of your stock choices.
   b) Record the initial purchase value of each stock.
   c) If a stock is sold, make a note of its sale in the log. How much was it sold for?
   d) Record the value of your portfolio at least twice a day. Include the time it was recorded.
   e) Record the final value of each stock and of the overall portfolio at the end of three days.
   f) How did your stocks perform?
   g) What rank did your portfolio achieve in the competition?

3.7   If you were to start your own e-business, which models would you employ and why? Discuss the pros and cons of each approach you choose.

WORKS CITED

The notation <*www.domain-name.com*> indicates that the citation is for information found on that Web site.

1.   J. Dodd, "Avoid the Hustle and Bustle," *PC Novice* 11 May 2000: 4.

2.   F. Hayes, "Amazoned!" *Computerworld* 17 May 1999: 116.

3.   L. Himelstein, and R. Hof, "eBay vs. Amazon.com," *Business Week* May 1999: 128.

4.   Iconocast, "Where the Auction is—The B2B market hits $52 billion in 2002," <**www.icono-cast.com**> 23 March 2000.

5.   F. Hayes, "Amazoned!" *Computerworld* May 17, 1999, p. 116.L.

6.   L. Himelstein, and R. Hof, "eBay vs. Amazon.com," *Business Week* May 1999: 128.

7.   L. Himelstein, and R. Hof, "eBay vs. Amazon.com," *Business Week* May 1999: 128.

8.   M. Nelson, "Portals to the Products You Need," *PC Novice* 11 May 2000: 24.

9.   <**www.about.com**>.

10.   <**www.av.com**>.

11.   T. Foremski, "Google Spins Web of Success," *Financial Times* 6 July 2000: 12.

12.   S. Burke, " AOL Time Warner Merger: A New Model For Partnerships," *Computer Reseller News*, <**www.techweb.com/wire/finance/story/INV20000110S0008**>.

13.   Iconocast, "Where the Money is: B2B -- Money is in the profiling B2B buyers" <**www.iconocast.com/issue/2000010603.html**> 6 January 2000.

14.   T. Hoffman, "Merrill Lynch Bows to Low-Cost Net Trading," *Computerworld*, Online News, 1 June 1999.

15.   J. Weber, "World Wide Web Economy," *The Industry Standard* 21 June 1999: 2.

16.   Carvahal D. "4 Giants Set to Embrace Electronic Publishing" *The New York Times* 23 May 2000: C1.

RECOMMENDED READINGS

Batcheldor, B. "Auction Site Offers New Consumer Electronics." *InformationWeek* 31 January 2000: 82.

Dragan, R. "Microsoft Site Server 3.0 Commerce Edition." *PC Magazine* 14 December 1998: `<www.zdnet.com/filters/printerfriendly/0,6061,374713-3,00.html>`.

Copage, E. "Web Sites Clamor for Teens Attention." *The New York Times* 13 April 2000: E10.

Fletcher, J. "The Great E-Mortgage Bake-Off." *The Wall Street Journal* 2 June 2000: 12.

Goncalves, M. "Consortium Aims for Standards for E-Business." *Mass High Tech* 28 August 1999: 17.

Goodison, D. "Kozmo.com Wraps up Food deal, and Faces Redlining Rap." *Boston Business Journal* 28 April 2000: 27.

Guglielmo, C. "Don't Write Off Barnes & Noble." *Upside*: 132-137.

Guthrie, B. "When Trouble Strikes." PC Novice 11 May 2000: 17.

King, J. "How to B2B." *ComputerWorld* 28 February 2000.

Kosiur, D. *Understanding Electronic Commerce*. Redmond, WA: Microsoft Press, 1997.

Kwon, R. Delivering Medical Records, Securely." *Internet World* 10 August 1998: 23.

McNamara, P. "Emerging Electronic Commerce Standard Passes First Big Test." *Network World* 6 October 1997: 55.

Methvin, D. W. "How to Succeed in E-Business." *Windows Magazine* August 1999: 98–108.

Nemzow, M. *Building CyberStores*. New York: McGraw-Hill, 1997.

Price, D.L. *Online Auctions at* eBay*: Bid with Confidence, Sell with Success.* Rocklin, CA: PRIMA TECH a Division of PRIMA Publishing 1999.

Ranjay G. and Garino J. "Bricks to Clicks." *Siliconindia* June 2000: 75-78.

Symoens, J. "Site Server is a fine set of tools for Web site building." *InfoWorld* 26 January 1998: `<www.infoworld.com>`.

Wagner, M. "Google Bets Farm on Linux." *InternetWeek* 5 June 2000: 1, 84.

Walker, R. "Get Big Fast." *PC Novice* 11 May: 210-212.

Weber, J. "Clicks and Mortar." *The Industry Standard* 2 August 1999: 5.

Wilson, T. "Up Next: An Exchange Of Exchanges." *Internet Week* 10 April 2000: 25.

Internet Marketing

Objectives

- To explore various Internet marketing strategies.
- To discuss the importance of effective Web design.
- To discuss how to increase Web-site traffic.
- To understand Internet advertising.
- To realize the importance of e-business public relations.
- To discuss the use of tracking devices and the benefits of personalization.
- To understand search engines and how to increase rankings on search-engine result lists.
- To discuss partner and affiliate programs.
- To understand the implications of running a global e-business.

The new electronic independence recreates the world in the image of a global village.
Marshall McLuhan

If we value the pursuit of knowledge, we must be free to follow wherever that search may lead us.
Adlai E. Stevenson

"Will you walk into my parlor?" said the Spider to the Fly; "Tis the prettiest little parlor that ever did you spy."
Mary Howitt

You can tell the ideals of a nation by its advertisements.
Norman Douglas

4.1 Introduction

In the early stages of electronic commerce, having the most efficient and creative site was enough for your e-business to prosper. Today, competition is intense, and a solid Internet marketing strategy can give your company an advantage.

The Internet and World Wide Web provide marketers with new tools and added convenience that can increase the success of marketing efforts. In this chapter we explore various aspects of an *Internet marketing campaign* such as advertising, promotions, public relations, partnering and Customer Relationship Management (CRM) systems. We also discuss creating and joining affiliate programs and using search engines to increase traffic to your Web site.

We will see that keeping user profiles, recording visits and analyzing promotional and advertising results are key to measuring the effectiveness of your marketing campaign. By discovering your *target market*—the group of people toward whom it is most profitable to aim your marketing campaign—you can focus your campaign and increase visits, responses and repeat purchases. Internet marketing should complement traditional marketing to attract new customers to your site.

4.2 Choosing a Domain Name

How many advertisements for various Web sites have you heard or seen recently? From television commercials to the sides of buses, Internet domain names are everywhere. Do the people who see your advertisements remember your name? Do these people return to your site regularly? If your advertisements do not register in the minds of your target market, your campaign may not be the problem. It may be the result of a poorly chosen domain name.[1] Choose a name that people will be able to recognize and type easily. Because your Web site will be accessible worldwide, it is important to consider how different groups of people from different countries and cultures will interpret your domain name.

As domain names with the dot-com (**.com**) extension are becoming rare, people are beginning to use dot-net (**.net**) and dot-org (**.org**). Dot-net is usually used for network-related sites, while dot-org is used to denote an organization.[2] With the number of available domain names decreasing, ICANN (Internet Corporation for Assigned Names and Numbers) approved a recommendation to add at least one new suffix to the top-level set of domains that currently includes **.com**, **.net** and **.org** extensions.[3] The following sites assist you in searching, registering and buying domain names: **www.domainit.com**, **www.register.com** and **www.networksolutions.com**.

4.3 Internet Marketing Research

Marketing research has traditionally consisted of focus groups, interviews, paper and telephone surveys, questionnaires and *secondary research*—findings based on previously conducted investigations. Research can now be performed over the Internet, giving marketers a faster option for finding and analyzing industry, customer and competitor information. The Internet also provides a relaxed and anonymous setting to hold focus group discussions and distribute questionnaires.

Many marketing research firms provide e-commerce research results online. Forrester Research (**www.forrester.com**) gives you access to research findings on Internet and e-commerce activities. It also offers a free e-research demonstration and free research reports.

Adknowledge is a company that has total research solutions and offers free marketing research information about the online advertising industry. The free reports can be downloaded at **www.adknowledge.com**. Other popular research companies are Jupiter Communications (**www.jup.com**) and Media Metrix (**www.mediametrix.com**).

Data collected from your own Web site can also provide you with valuable marketing research. Technologies exist that can reveal consumer preferences. @Plan (**www.atplan.net**) provides Internet marketing research tools as well as support for the utilization of these instruments. GoGlobal Technologies (**www.goglobal.com**) creates online surveys for corporations and marketing research firms. KVO (**www.kvo.com**), provides research for companies involved in the e-commerce and Web advertising industries, and Macro Consulting Inc. (**www.macroinc.com**) offers traditional and Internet marketing research and consultations.

4.4 Web Design

When on the Web, the ability to locate and purchase goods and services differs from the same task in real space. Low *switching costs*, or the ability to choose one competitor over another quickly and easily, makes e-commerce fiercely competitive.[4] There are many features that should be included on your Web site to attract new and repeat consumers.

Site navigational tools that help users find and price products, services and information should be included. A *frequently asked questions (FAQ)* section and conveniently located contact information also contribute to a user-friendly site.

Multimedia, such as streaming video and audio, can be appealing, but not all users have computer systems and Internet connections with the capabilities to download this kind of information efficiently. When building your site, be aware of the time each element takes to load. Would you stay long in the local convenience store if all the products were slowly placed on the shelves while you waited? Your site should provide the users with simpler but equally effective Web pages.

A *privacy policy* detailing the intended uses of consumers' personal information should be made available to the consumer as well. Links to this information are an important element to include on your site. Privacy is discussed in detail in Chapter 6.

4.5 E-Mail Marketing

E-mail marketing campaigns can provide a cheap and effective way to target potential customers. Before beginning an e-mail marketing campaign, a company must first decide on the goals of the campaign. These include defining the *reach*, or span of people you would like to target, including geographic locations and demographic profiles; and determining the level of personalization. Personalized *direct e-mail* targets consumers with specific information. By using customer names, offering the right products at the right time and sending special promotions targeted to consumers' interests, the marketer makes a stronger connection with the people receiving the e-mails.

If companies plan to enter the global market, personalization methods should include sending e-mails translated into the proper languages, for the convenience of international consumers. The Italian translation company Logos® (**www.logos.it**) offers free access to its online dictionary of more than twenty languages and will translate e-mails for a fee.[5] AltaVista offers a free text and Web-site translation service that can be accessed through the translate link at **www.altavista.com**.

Personalization technology also allows the marketer to target campaigns to a specific market, which can improve the *response rate*—the percentage of responses generated from the target market. Products and services are available to help you personalize your e-mails and manage your e-mail campaigns. One option is to *outsource* e-mail marketing. Outsourcing means that parts of your company's operations are performed by other companies. Some service providers allow the marketer to maintain control of content, mailing lists and campaign timing. Outsourcing services should be used when direct e-mailing becomes too difficult to manage because of e-mail volume and inadequate staff or technical support. **Boldfish.com** provides a tutorial on how its e-mail marketing campaign system works. Other electronic mail software and service sites are **www.messagemedia.com**, **www.digitalimpact.com**, **www.ilux.com**, **www.247media.com** and **www.econtacts.com**.

E-mails can also be used to improve your customer service. For example, adding an e-mail link to your Web site provides a convenient way for customers to voice their opinions and ask questions. Although placing a link on your Web site to enable people browsing the site to send you e-mails is a good idea, you should make certain that your business has the ability to handle the anticipated volume of e-mails. E-mail systems can be set up so that incoming e-mails will be automatically sorted and directed to the most knowledgeable people.[6] E-mails can also assist customers by helping them track the location of their orders, informing them of when to expect delivery and possible delays and providing information such as the carrier's name.

Internet mailing lists are available to assist in the targeting of personalized e-mails. *Opt-in e-mail* is sent to people who explicitly choose to receive offers, information and promotions.[7] NetCreations' Web site **PostMasterDirect.com** will send your e-mail campaign to those on a NetCreations list who have expressed interest in your business category. **Yesmail.com** and **Xactmail.com** are other companies that create lists of people who want to receive information about certain subjects.

It is important to avoid sending e-mail to people who have not shown interest in your products and services. *Spamming*—mass e-mailing to customers who have not expressed interest—can give your company a poor reputation. Spamming and its ramifications are discussed in Chapter 6, "Legal, Ethical and Social Issues; Internet Taxation."

E-mail can be combined with *traditional direct marketing*—including sending information by mail and using telemarketers to contact prospective customers—to allow marketers to reach a large number of possible customers. Although direct mailing can be more expensive, more difficult to analyze and can have a lower response rate than direct e-mailing, some companies such as **www.eletter.com** and **www.mbsmm.com** can provide efficient direct-mailing services. Telemarketing can offer the benefit of live interaction between customers and service representatives. Also, people may find it more difficult to ignore phone calls than e-mails. However, e-mail messages can arrive if the recipients are busy or away from their computers, and receivers can deal with the e-mails at their own convenience. By using these both forms of marketing, you can experience the benefits of each.

4.6 Promotions

E-business *promotions* can attract visitors to your site and can influence purchasing. These can be conducted both online and offline and may include frequent-flyer miles, point-based rewards, discounts, sweepstakes, free trials, free shipping and coupons.

Offering frequent-flyer miles, to be used for flights on participating airlines, provide an incentive for consumers to shop at your site. This method of promotion can also serve as a means to attract repeat visitors by allowing them to access their accumulated miles; this can be made available through a username and password system. **Netcentives.com**, a company that can provide your business with customer reward programs, offers *ClickRewards*. This program allows your customers to accumulate frequent-flyer miles, called *ClickMiles*. *ClickRewards* requires that both your customer and your company are signed up with the program.

A *points-based promotion* is similar to a frequent-flyer-miles-based promotion. Every time a customer performs a pre-specified action, they can receive points redeemable for products, services, rebates, discounts, etc. Giving away items that display your company logo for redeemed points increases brand exposure. **Branders.com** allows you to upload your company's designs and logos to the site to view how these designs will look on t-shirts, mugs and other promotional items.

Offering discounts on products or on shipping and handling is a good way to attract consumers. Placing discount advertisements in magazines, newspapers and direct e-mails can bring new and repeat customers to your Web site. Discount advertisements should also be placed on other Web sites, allowing customers to click through to your Web page.

Another way to help consumers feel comfortable about using your site is to offer free trials. At **www.travelocity.com**, customers can sign up for free or can try the service as guests. This business helps customers plan their travel and purchase travel services; and it frequently updates its site with discount offers and special promotions.

Some Web sites offer *online coupons* for online shopping. Your company can place coupons on these sites in order to target consumers and bring them to your site. Some sites that advertise coupons are **www.directcoupons.com**, **www.coolsavings.com** and **www.valupage.com**. To offer free promotional items, visit and register with portals such as **free.com**, **free2try.com** and **freeshop.com**. You can also visit **www.promotionworld.com/tutorial/000.html** to view an online promotional outline containing information on ways to promote your site.

4.7 E-Business Advertising

Today, a great deal of e-business advertising is conducted through traditional channels such as television, movies, newspapers and magazines. Many e-businesses advertise in prime-time television slots, which are the most expensive times to air commercials. E-businesses should establish and continually strengthen branding. Your brand should be unique, recognizable and easy to remember.[8] Publicizing your URL on all direct mailings, business cards and print advertisements are other ways to increase brand awareness and bring more visitors to your site.

While newspapers, magazines, television and films all provide effective advertising channels, online advertising is quickly becoming a significant part of the promotional world. By 2005, online advertisers are expected to spend $45.5 billion, compared to the $5.3 billion spent worldwide this year.[9] Online advertising can include placing your links and banners on other companies' Web sites and registering your site with search engines and directories. You can also charge other companies for placing their advertisements on your site, providing you with additional income.

4.7.1 Banner Advertising

Web page *banner ads*, which act like small billboards containing graphics and an advertising message. The benefits of banner advertising include increased brand recognition, exposure and possible revenue gained through purchases by consumers. Banners can be created in different sizes and placed in various positions on your Web site. Some banner advertisements are designed just for viewing, while others provide a link to the home page of the product or service being advertised.

When designing a banner advertisement, determining how you would like your company to be recognized plays an important role. For example, Deitel & Associates, Inc. could use its signature bug logo on every banner, enhancing brand recognition. Inventive color schemes and movement will also grab a viewer's attention. Movement can include flashing, scrolling text, pop-up boxes and color changes. A *pop-up box* is a screen containing an advertisement that appears separate from the screen the user is viewing. The box pops up randomly or as a result of user actions.

Before placing banner ads on Web sites, note how many ads these sites already carry. Many consumers are annoyed by Web sites cluttered with ads. Try different positions on Web pages and analyze the results to determine what position gets the greatest number of click-throughs.

After selecting where to place your banners, you will have to choose a method of payment. Some sites will post your banner advertisement during specific times. Advertising space is normally more expensive during peak traffic times. Exchanging banners with another site is also an option. Some sites will carry your banner ads for free.[10]

Although recent studies have indicated that banner advertisements are losing their effectiveness,[11] these ads still lead to recognition and possible purchases and should be a part of your marketing strategy. A few of the many sites dedicated to banner advertising are **www.adbility.com** and **www.bannertips.com**.

4.7.2 Buying and Selling Advertising on the Web

Buying advertising space on sites that receive a large number of hits and that target a market similar to yours can increase the number of hits on your site and lead to higher revenues. Selling advertising space on your own site can also provide you with additional income.

For buying and selling advertising purposes, it can be important to distinguish a site's *unique visitors* from the total number of *hits* it receives. Visiting any site registers one unique visit. Hits are recorded for each object that is downloaded and there could be many such objects per unique visit. For instance, if you were to visit a Web site with three images and background music, five hits would be recorded: one for each image, one for the audio and one for the page itself. This visit would still count as only one unique visit.

Companies have adopted different advertising payment systems for advertising on their sites. Monthly charges for online advertising are rarely used today. Some sites may require you to pay a designated fee for every one thousand people who view the site on which your banner is located—this is called the *CPM* (*cost per thousand*). If the company hosting your ad has 50,000 visitors per month, your advertisement will cost 50 times the CPM. The problem with this form of payment is that many people may be at the site but may not see the advertisement. This means that the advertiser would be paying for an advertisement based on a number of people who are viewing the site, but not the advertisement.

With some advertising payment schemes, you will be charged only if the customer performs an action predetermined by you and the Web site managers. *Pay-per-performance* fees include *pay-per-click, pay-per-lead* and *pay-per-sale*.[12] When using the pay-per-click method, you pay the host according to the number of click-throughs to your site. Pay-per-lead means that you pay the host for every lead generated from the advertisement, and pay-per-sale means that you pay the host for every sale resulting from a click-through.

Another advertising option involves exchanging advertising space on your site for advertising space on another's site. This structure is effective for businesses that complement one another, and is usually free.

If you wish to sell advertising space, provide the appropriate contact information on your Web site. You can also register with organizations that will sell your space for you. These companies typically charge a percentage of the revenue you receive from the advertisements placed on your site (see ValueClick feature). Some advertising companies that offer banner advertising options include ValueClick (`www.valueclick.com`), Double-Click (`www.doubleclick.com`), AdSmart (`www.adsmart.net`) and LinkExchange (`www.linkexchange.com`).

ValueClick[13]

ValueClick (`www.valueclick.com`) manages advertising campaigns. The company acts as a broker for people who want to buy and sell advertising space (Fig 4.1). ValueClick has access to advertising space on thousands of Web sites and gives you the option of targeting specific markets.

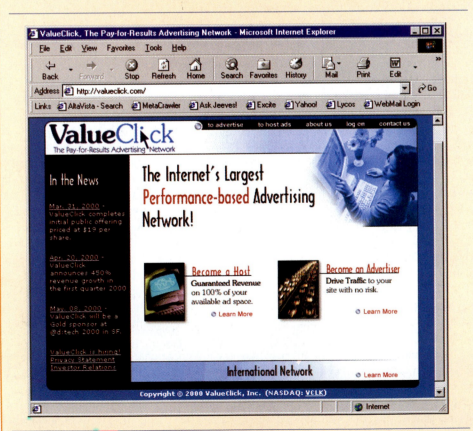

Fig. 4.1   ValueClick home Page. (Courtesy of ValueClick, Inc.)

ValueClick[13] (Cont.)

In order to buy advertising through ValueClick, you must first design a banner. A representative of ValueClick can then help you determine what program best fits your advertising needs. Payment is made in advance and is based on the number of click-throughs you want to receive.

ValueClick offers many *segmented markets* for advertising. Segmented markets are people or companies with similar characteristics. You can select a particular segment or advertise on a variety of sites. ValueClick does not offer services to companies hosting illegal or questionable content.

When hosting advertisements on your site through ValueClick, your earnings will depend on the number of click-throughs resulting from the advertisements. ValueClick pays the host monthly as long as revenues are greater than a certain amount. If you do not meet that amount in one month, the balance rolls over to the next month.

ValueClick offers four options for hosting advertisements on your site: the Value-Click Affiliate, Premium, AdVantage and AdVantage Plus programs. Each program requires a certain minimum number of clicks before ValueClick will pay higher prices per click. Payments per click increase progressively as you move from the Affiliate program to the Premium program to the AdVantage programs. The AdVantage Plus program is for the largest Web sites on the Internet.

4.8 Webcasting and Interactive Advertising

Webcasting uses streaming media to broadcast an event over the Web. *Streaming video* simulates television. Marketers must consider, however, that many people still have relatively slow Internet access—the slower the connection, the more disconnected the video appears.[14]

Victoria's Secret's Webcast was the most popular ever held on the Web.[15] The first time Victoria's Secret, a lingerie store for women, tried to Webcast a fashion show, the servers could not handle the volume of traffic to the site and the show was unavailable to many individuals. The store found success in a more recent fashion-show Webcast.[16] Visit **www.victoriassecret.com** to view the 2000 Victoria's Secret fashion show. We discuss streaming media in Chapter 32, "Multimedia."

Some streaming media experts include Resource Marketing (**www.resource.com**), a company offering a variety of services for Internet marketing, and Clear Digital (**www.cleardigital.com**), a company that develops Web commercials and extensive Web sites. Navisite (**www.navisite.com**) offers consulting, development and implementation of a variety of streaming events. Cyber-Logics (**www.cyber-logics.com**) designs Web sites and e-commerce sites and develops streaming media. To find out about streaming media conferences, news, company directories and many other streaming media details, visit **www.streamingmedia.com**. Macromedia (**www.macromedia.com**) offers many media software products, employing audio and visual technologies.

Burst.com offers *Burstware®*, a client-server software package that delivers video and audio content through *bursting* (rather than streaming). Streaming delivers a flow of data in real time. By contrast, bursting delivers content faster so that it builds up substantially at the receiving end, potentially enabling a smoother appearance. Visit the site

www.burst.com for an explanation of the difference between streaming and bursting and to view some examples of bursting.

Interactive advertising involves using a combination of rich media (such as audio, video, images and animations) and traditional advertising forms (such as print, television and radio advertisements) to execute an advertising campaign. Involving consumers in the advertising process makes them more likely to remember your company. Nike developed a campaign that included interactions between the consumer, television and its Web site. Nike aired television commercials with an ending that directed viewers to **www.nike.com**. This site also offers a link to a Nike digital video. The consumer has the option to select various action pictures of an athlete and music to be played in the background. The consumer can then view the constructed video and send it to other people via e-mail, providing free advertising for Nike.

Another example of interactive advertising is *WebRIOT*, a game show on MTV™. The game is aired on television, and viewers can join in the game at the same time by playing online. The top online players' screen names are then featured on TV. To try WebRIOT, visit **www.mtv.com** and download the game. Visit H$_2$O Design (**www.h20design.com**) and Lot21 (**www.lot21.com**)—additional companies that specialize in interactive advertising.

4.9 E-Business Public Relations

Public relations (PR) keeps your customers and your company's employees current on the latest information about products, services and internal and external issues such as company promotions and consumer reactions. It includes communicating with your consumers and employees through press releases, speeches, special events, presentations and e-mails.

Chat sessions are one method of learning what people think about your company or products. A bulletin board on your Web site will enable people to post comments, and you can also involve consumers by organizing a special event or function on your Web site. *Brand awareness* and increased exposure can result from attending and participating in trade shows and exhibitions at which you can speak with prospective customers.

Press releases, which announce current events and other significant news to the press, can be delivered over the Web. Your Web site should contain a link that connects to your company's press releases. PR Web (**www.prweb.com**) allows you to submit a press release for free which will be distributed to the contacts in its database. This site also gives you access to public relations firms, current press releases and newsletters. Another site that offers public relations information and helps visitors find jobs in the field is **www.thePRnetwork.com**.

Video clips of news appearances, speeches, commercials and advertisements can be effective publicity for your company. Visit **www.prnewswire.com** and **www.businesswire.com** to view recent press releases that include audio and video news.

PR specialists must be able to contact companies who will distribute and print press releases. MediaMap is a company that provides PR contacts and software designed for PR. Visit **www.mediamaponline.com** to sign up for a free trial of MediaMap. The trial provides access to the company's database of contacts and allows users to create their own concentrated sample lists of media contacts. MediaMap also offers white papers on its product and how to use it.

Crisis management, another responsibility of PR, is conducted in response to problems the company is having. For example, many investors and consumers follow the financial news about Internet companies closely. When your company is doing well financially, this should be made public. However, if the company is doing poorly, your public relations department must be ready to issue information about what is causing the problem and what will be done to correct it.

4.10 Customer Relationship Management (CRM)

The sum of a company's customer service solutions makes up its *Customer Relationship Management (CRM)* system. The complexity and depth of an e-business' CRM system will depend on its levels of traffic and available resources. CRM systems can include call handling (the maintenance of out-bound and in-bound calls from customers and service representatives), sales tracking (the tracing and recording of all sales made) and transaction support (the technology and personnel used for conducting transactions), as well as many other functions. The Internet has created new ways to understand customers, which in turn can improve customer service. Tools used to improve these solutions include log-file analysis, data mining and cookies.

Data mining is one way to analyze information collected from visitors. Data mining uses algorithms and statistical tools to find patterns in data gathered from customer visits. These patterns can improve your CRM and marketing campaigns by helping you better understand your customers. Data Distilleries (**www.datadistilleries.com**) offers Customer Relationship Management services and products including its data mining software called *DD/Marketer*. This site also offers white papers about data mining. Other sites offering data mining services are **www.appliedmetrix.com**, **www.datain-stincts.com** and **www.smartdrill.com**.

A CRM system keeps records of customers' behavior to provide fast and effective service and, when necessary, to implement corrective measures. Customers should feel confident that their transactions are secure and that products are reliable and will be received on time. Customers should also be able to conduct transactions and get answers to their questions through a *call center*. Call centers house customer-service representatives who can be reached by an 800 number or through e-mail, online text chatting or real-time voice communications.

eGain (**www.eGain.com**), a leader in the Customer Relationship Management software market,[17] offers an extensive program that implements a CRM system for a client. The *eGain Commerce*™ platform incorporates all of your company's customer communication services. eGain calls this implementation the *eGain Jumpstart*™. After the system is "jump-started," the eGain professionals adjust the system to meet your company's specific needs. eGain's customer service operates 24-by-7 and gives you access to a variety of support plans. Companies offering similar services are Kana Communications (**www.kana.com**), Oracle Systems (**www.oracle.com**) and Siebel Systems (**www.siebel.com**).

E.piphany (**www.epiphany.com**) has evolved as a well-recognized Customer Relationship Management solutions provider.[18] Its E.piphany™ E.4 product offers a suite of Web-based CRM solutions. E.piphany™ E.4 allows you to collect data from your present software systems and third-parties. This data can be information on customers, visitors to the Web site, partners, affiliates and product revenues. E.piphany™ E.4 analyzes this data to determine the profitability of specific campaigns, return-on-investment, purchase patterns of your consumers, etc. The data analyses can be used to personalize a customer's visit. E.piphany™ E.4 can also provide recommendations in real time for a customer service representative's course of action during an employee-to-customer interaction.

4.10.1 Keeping Track of Your Visitors

On the Internet, millions of visitors can access an advertisement in a single day. By using *tracking devices*, Web masters can determine the number of Internet users exposed to an advertisement and the percentage of those viewers who actually click on the ad. This kind of instant feedback helps marketing sales teams analyze ad campaigns, determine demographics and create more effective online publicity.

Log-file analysis is a useful way to keep track of your visitors. *Log files* consist of data generated by site visits, including each visitor's location, IP address, time of visit, frequency of visits and many other indicators. See the WebTrends feature for information on log-file analysis products.

Companies may want to develop tracking technologies themselves. One example is a *cookie*, a technology that keeps a profile on each visitor. Cookies are discussed in Chapter 6, "Legal, Ethical and Social Issues; Internet Taxation." Programming with cookies is discussed in Chapter 25, "Active Server Pages" and Chapter 26, "ASP Case Studies." Data gathered through log-file analysis, cookies and other tracking devices can be used to personalize each visitor's experience, find trends in customer use and demonstrate the effectiveness of a Web site over time.

4.10.2 Customer Registration

Customer registration—requiring visitors to fill out a form with personal information that is then used to create a profile— is recommended when it will provide a benefit to the consumer. By obtaining information from registration, companies will be able to determine who their consumers are and what they want. This information will allow businesses to customize their Web sites, customer service and marketing strategies more effectively.

Getting customers to register can be difficult. People are often reluctant to fill out a form requiring personal information. The best way to start building a consumer profile is to require minimal information, such as a username, password and possibly an e-mail address. You should give potential customers an incentive to register. If the site offers an online service, offer a free-trial or a free demonstration to familiarize the user with the service. Businesses selling products can offer promotions such as free gift certificates, free calling cards or discounts on online purchases to entice consumers to register. The registration process should be quick and easy so that the consumer does not go elsewhere.

After consumers have registered, you should send an e-mail including their usernames and welcoming them to your Web site. Consumers can check the e-mail if they have forgotten their usernames. Some sites ask each user to provide a specific question to which only the user will know the answer— if users forget their passwords, they will be asked the questions. Upon receipt of the correct answers, the site e-mails users their passwords.

4.10.3 Personalization

Personalization technology can help a company understand its customers' needs and the effectiveness of its Web site. *Personalization* customizes a person's interactions with a company's products, services, Web site and employees. Consumers can benefit from the unique treatment that results from personalization. **HomePage.com** offers outsourced home-page development. **Epage.com**, a solution from **HomePage.com**, works with a company's customers to personalize their Web-interaction experiences. Involving customers in the personalization process makes them feel more comfortable with, and more in control of, their Web-site visits. Other sites that provide personalization products include **www.allaire.com**, **www.blazesoft.com**, **www.netgen.com** and **www.personify.com**.

WebTrends[19]

WebTrends® (**www.webtrends.com**) provides solutions for tracking visitors (Fig. 4.2). It offers products that allow you to profile site visitors and measure the effectiveness of each of your Web pages. After downloading a WebTrends product, the user must specify the source of the log files, types of reports and location where data is stored. Then the analysis is conducted automatically. The program can be scheduled to analyze data during non-business hours in order to maximize its efficiency. The collected information can be used to evaluate e-commerce methods, customer service and Web-site design.

WebTrends offers free trial versions of many of its products. Once you have downloaded and installed a WebTrends product, it will use your log files to show you the effectiveness of your site. Fig. 4.3 shows a graphical example of the analysis from a WebTrends product.

If your log files are not available, you can access and manipulate sample log files provided by WebTrends. You can choose to view the report in one of many applications including Microsoft Word, Excel, HTML and text format.

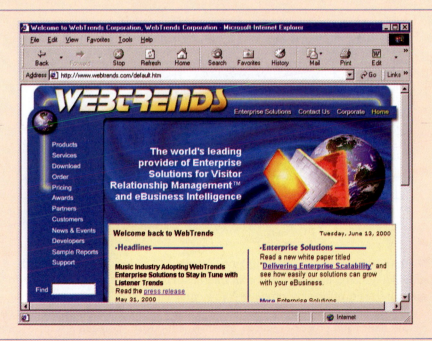

Fig. 4.2   WebTrends home page. © 2000 WebTrends Corporation. All rights reserved. WebTrends is a registered trademark of WebTrends Corporation. (Courtesy of WebTrends Corporation.)

WebTrends[19] (Cont.)

The WebTrends program will report its progress as it analyzes the data. Depending on the output format you have chosen, you will be presented with a graphical interpretation of the log files. You can view demographic and geographic data, technical analysis of the Web site's effectiveness, top-referring sites—sites that most frequently refer visitors to your site—and many other analyses that can help you improve your site.

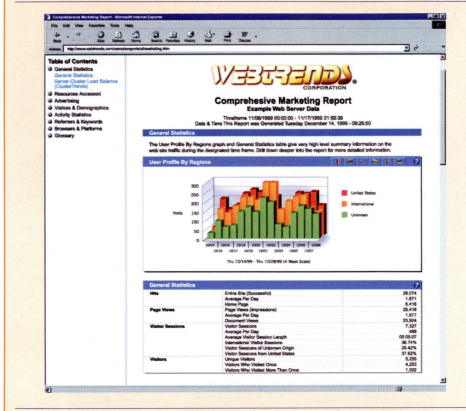

Fig. 4.3   Example analysis from a WebTrends product. (Courtesy of WebTrends Corporation.)

One-to-one marketing, or marketing that attempts to address the unique needs of each customer individually, is important for an Internet marketing campaign. E-mails that confirm purchases and offer new products show your customers that you appreciate their patronage. Calling your customers personally to see if everything went well in the purchasing and delivering processes can be effective but costly. You can also provide a link on your site to a live customer service representative. *RealCall® Alert™* is a service that allows customers to connect to your customer service representatives from your Web site.[20] To offer this kind of connection, you place a RealCall button on your Web site. When the user wants to speak to a person, the user clicks on the button. The request is sent through the Web to a RealCall server which then sends the request to the Web-site owner's phone. From here, the owner can call the customer to assist them. Visit `www.real-call.com` to experience a live demonstration of RealCall Alert. Also visit `www.click-ichat.com` and `www.liveperson.com` to try demonstrations of human-to-human communication using online text chatting over the Web.

As more people start using the Web, the issue of personalization versus privacy is becoming important. Some people feel that personalization represents an invasion of their privacy, whereas others may not even be aware that personalization is occurring at a site. At the heart of this debate is the ethical implication of the technology allowing personalization. For example, cookies allow e-commerce sites to record visitor behavior and identify more valuable customers. Many customers are not aware that customer profiles called "cookies" are being stored on their computers as these customers browse particular sites. Marketers must be careful how they use the personal information gained from data research. Cookies and the issue of privacy are discussed in depth in Chapter 6, "Legal, Ethical and Social Issues; Internet Taxation."

4.11 Business-to-Business Marketing on the Web

The emerging key to *business-to-business (B2B) e-commerce* is effective Customer Relationship Management (CRM). In the context of business-to-business commerce, CRM includes integrating systems to combine selling, buying, marketing and front-end and back-end operations performed within the company.

B2B marketing can be different from *business-to-consumer (B2C) marketing*. When you sell your product to another business, you may be selling to someone who is not the direct user of your product. Because the user of the product might have an opinion or comment different from what you are hearing from your business contact, ask your contact to speak with the end users. You may find that end users have suggestions that could improve your product or service.[21]

Industry *marketplaces* are good resources for those who want to sell to other businesses. Searching marketplaces for possible clients can help you define a target market and generate customer leads more effectively. Business-to-business marketplaces for a variety of industries are available on the Internet. For example, construction companies can find appropriate B2B marketplaces at `www.construction.com`, `www.e-cement.com` and `www.redladder.com`, while retailers can visit `www.globalnetxchange.com` or `www.worldwideretailexchange.com`.

Commerce One is a company that offers solutions for e-businesses. Its portal, `www.marketsite.net`, helps buyers and sellers find each other and relevant business-to-business exchange sites worldwide. Commerce One also helps companies build industry-specific marketplaces. Connect Inc. (`www.connectinc.com`), Concur Technologies (`www.concur.com`) and Ariba (`www.ariba.com`) also provide technology and consulting for creating marketplaces for buyers and sellers.

4.12 Search Engines

Search engines allow people to find information relative to a subject of interest amidst the large amounts of information available on the Internet and World Wide Web. Finding information on the Web would be difficult without the use of search engines. A search engine is a program that scans Web sites and forms a list of relevant sites based on keywords or other search-engine ranking criteria. *Search-engine ranking* is important to bring consumers to your site. The method used by search engines to rank your Web site will determine how "high" your site appears in search results. You can customize and register your site so that it can make appearances on many search-engine result lists.

4.12.1 META Tags

A *META tag* is an HTML tag that contains information about a Web page. We study HTML and META tags in depth in Chapters 9 and 10 and then use HTML throughout the remainder of the book. This tag does not change how a Web page is displayed, but can contain a description of the page, keywords and the page's title. Search engines often use this information when ranking a site.

Most search engines rank your site by sending out a program, called a *spider*, to inspect the site. The spider reads the META tags, determines the relevance of the Web page's information and keywords, and then ranks the site according to that visit's findings. You should examine your competitors' sites to see what META tags they are using. Ask yourself, if I wanted to search for products or services that my company offers, what keywords would I type when using a search engine? You want your site to appear in the top ten results because often people will not look further. For valuable information about keyword selection, visit `www.keywordcount.com` and `www.websearch.about.com/internet/websearch/insub2-m02.htm`.

4.12.2 Search-Engine Registration

Registering with search engines is crucial. When you register your site with a search engine, you submit keywords and a description of your business to the engine. The search engine will add your information to its database of Web sites. This essentially adds your site to an index of sites similar to your own. Consequently, when someone uses that search engine, your Web site may appear in the list of results. However, not all search engines use databases; some search the entire Internet every time. Many search engines are constantly scouring the Web, visiting and ranking Web pages. Even if you do not register, the search engines may still find your page. By registering, you eliminate this uncertainty.

Various companies will register your Web site with many search engines for a fee. To view information about some of the major search engines' requirements for registering, as well as general tips about search engine registration and META-tag development, visit `www.searchenginewatch.com/Webmasters/index.html`.

Many search engines do not charge a fee for registering, although some require payment to use other services they provide. Excite[SM] is a search engine that allows people to register their sites for free, although you are given an option to apply to be added to the *Best of the Web Directory*. Upon acceptance, you are charged a one-time fee and your site is placed in categories across the LookSmart[TM] network.[22] Popular search engines include `www.yahoo.com`, `www.lycos.com`, `www.altavista.com`, `www.google.com` and `www.askjeeves.com`. Ask Jeeves[SM] uses *natural-language technology* that allows people to enter their search subjects in the form of full sentences rather than keywords. This works well because the engine maintains a database of question templates that it uses to match questions with possible answers.[23]

4.13 Partnerships

Partnering is forming a strategic union with another company. When two e-businesses decide to be partners, legal contracts are usually written to define the relationship precisely and to protect the interests of each company.

Partnering can help your company provide consumers with complementary services and products. Suppose that your site sells computer science textbooks. It may benefit you to have a site that sells computers linked to your site and vice versa. You and your partners may also be able to exchange technical research or customer information.

Providing a link to the site of a partner that offers a product or service complementary to your own is a good way to give your site a competitive advantage. Consumers will appreciate the option of being "a click away" from their next desired purchase.

Forming partnerships can also benefit a company when its partner has a service that the company could use to improve its management or operations. Outsourcing part of your product or service operations to your partner can help your company operate more efficiently.

4.13.1 Affiliate Programs

An *affiliate program* is an agreement between two parties that one will pay the other a commission based on a designated consumer action. Affiliate programs establish new income streams for companies and individuals that host the advertising of affiliate Web sites. If a merchant sells computer science text books on its Web site and a company's site hosts content related to computer science, it might benefit the merchant to have the company as an affiliate. The merchant can place a banner advertisement on the affiliate's Web site. When a person clicks through the merchant's site via the link on the affiliate's site and makes a purchase, a commission on the sale is typically awarded to the affiliate. Some programs pay commissions to affiliates for recruiting new affiliates.

4.13.2 Creating an Affiliate Program

When creating an affiliate program, you will need to decide on a reward structure. There are a number of different affiliate program models. One is the *pay-per-click model*, which rewards an affiliate for each click-through generated by a banner hosted by the affiliate. A problem with this approach is that click-throughs can be falsified. Other affiliate programs use the *pay-per-lead model*, which rewards affiliates based on the number of qualified leads generated. The most effective method is the *pay-per-sale model*, which compensates affiliates for each sale resulting from affiliate-hosted advertisements. Since a sale is more valuable than a lead or click-through, the reward to the affiliate is usually larger—typically a percentage of the sale price.

To start an affiliate program, you must be able to track the effectiveness of each affiliate, payment systems must be put in place, and you must be sure that the system is correct and able to be auditable.

LinkShare (**www.linkshare.com**) develops affiliate programs for business-to-business and business-to-consumer companies. QuickClick (**www.quickclick.com**), Commission Junction (**www.cj.com**) and Be Free (**www.befree.com**) also develop affiliate programs. See the Be Free, Inc. feature for more information on its affiliate program process.

Be Free, Inc.[24]

One of the leading providers of affiliate program management solutions is Be Free, Inc. (Fig. 4.4). The company was formed when two companies combined to create the *BFAST*™ product line. Be Free landed its first client, **barnesandnoble.com**, in 1996. The BFAST product is an affiliate-program enabler. The system is designed to build performance-based, highly targeted sales channels. Be Free allows its merchant customers to retain the look and feel of their brand on the interface that affiliates use to manage their programs. Rewards and compensation are determined by the merchant and can be implemented quickly and easily.

Be Free has developed a comprehensive performance marketing solution. The company acts as an intermediary, tracking impressions, click-throughs and sales for both the merchant and its affiliate partners. Be Free provides its merchant customers and their affiliate partners with the knowledge and services to improve their performance results continuously. Merchants place promotions on affiliated Web sites that are relevant to their industry. Payment is collected when a lead is generated or a sale is completed. In Figs. 4.5-4.8, you can view a step-by-step process that Be Free uses to demonstrate how performance marketing works.

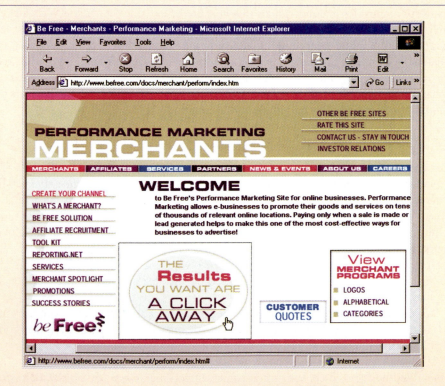

Fig. 4.4   Be Free's performance marketing merchant's page. (Courtesy of Be Free, Inc.)

Be Free, Inc.[24] (Cont.)

Fig. 4.5   Be Free demonstration: How promotions work, step 1. (Courtesy of Be Free, Inc.)

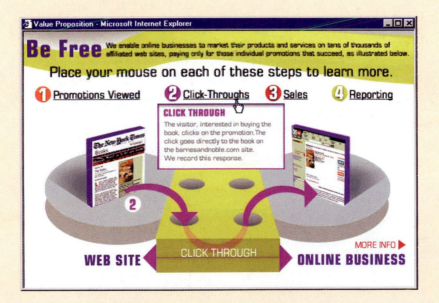

Fig. 4.6   Be Free Demonstration: How the click-through process works, step 2. (Courtesy of Be Free, Inc.)

Be Free, Inc.[24] (Cont.)

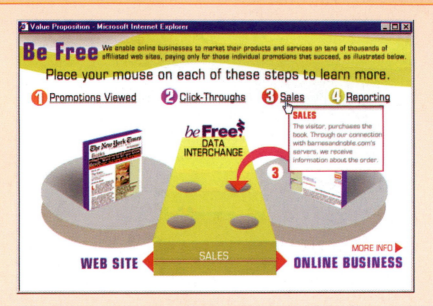

Fig. 4.7   Be Free Demonstration: How sales are completed, step 3. (Courtesy of Be Free, Inc.)

Fig. 4.8   Be Free demonstration: How the reporting feature works, step 4. (Courtesy of Be Free, Inc.)

4.14 Marketing to the World

Global marketing has always presented unique challenges. If marketers are not sensitive to linguistic, legal and cultural differences, failures in product or service marketing can result. With the global reach of the World Wide Web, online marketers must pay particularly close attention to how their international consumers interact with their Web sites. Web design must provide content in various languages, and provide prices in various currencies. A customer should be able to access currency exchange rate information from your site.

Businesses should consider what markets will be most profitable to enter. Conducting international business successfully is often contingent on effective distribution methods. Does the country have the infrastructure in place to support your e-business on a broad scale? What kind of distribution channels reach your consumers? Shipping costs vary greatly in different parts of the world.

Services and software exist that are designed to translate e-mails and Web sites to help your marketing effort expand to a global reach. Although this technology can be helpful, you must be aware that translations will not be perfect, and mistakes could cause misunderstandings. Transparent Language (**www.transparentlanguage.com**) provides translations for Internet companies and users. Its *Enterprise Translation Server*™ allows your customers to click on a link from your Web site and view your site translated into different languages. Transparent Language's Web site offers a free demonstration that allows you to view any Web site in the language you specify. Alis Technologies (**www.alis.com**) offers a solution called Gist-In-Time™ that converts Web pages into various languages, depending upon the users' preferences. Netscape Navigator 6 uses this solution to offer *AutoTranslate*; users can go to the **View Menu** and select **Translate**, allowing them to view any Web site in another language. See the Logos Group, Italy feature for another translation solution.

By understanding each culture to the best of your ability, and by testing your site and marketing campaign on a smaller scale with focus groups and trials, you can reduce the possibility of misconceptions and misunderstandings before you launch your site for the whole world to see.

4.15 Internet and World Wide Web Resources

Domain Name Registration

www.catalog.com
Catalog.com allows you to search and register domain names. This site also provides Web hosting.

www.domainbank.net
Domain Bank, Inc. gives you the option of finding domain names and registering them.

www.icann.org/registrars/accredited-list.html
The Internet Corporation for Assigned Names and Numbers lists accredited and accreditation-qualified registrars.

Direct E-mailing

www.radicalmail.com
Radicalmail.com is a company that performs streaming multimedia e-mails. Visit the site for demonstrations of its latest e-mail capabilities.

Logos Group, Italy[25]

Logos, an Italian translation company, provides assistance for those who are in need of translations, as well as an online language translation dictionary. This "multi-lingual e-translation portal" will instantly translate any typed word or phrase into many different languages. See Figs. 4.9 and 4.10 for a sample translation using the Logos dictionary. You can also click on a button to hear how the word is pronounced. If you are not sure how one of the translated words is used, *Logos' Wordtheque* demonstrates the use of the word in context. From here you can click on the *Word Exchange Forum*, where professionals around the world are willing to help you with a word or phrase that may be troubling you. For further information or to try a translation, visit `www.logos.it`.

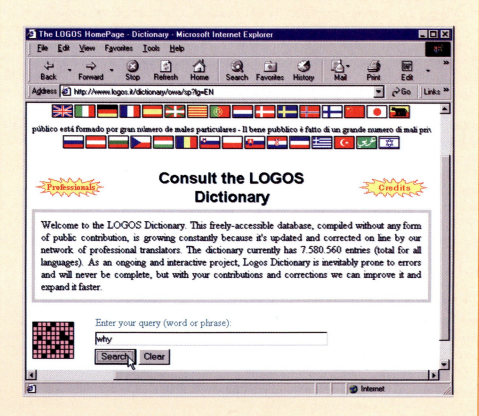

Fig. 4.9   Logos Dictionary query page with sample query. (Courtesy of Logos Group, Italy.)

Fig. 4.10   Logos query results page with sample query result. (Courtesy of Logos Group, Italy.)

www.flonetwork.com
FloNetwork, Inc. manages direct e-mail campaigns. The company provides real-time tracking and analysis of e-mail campaigns.

www.clickaction.com
ClickAction offers e-mail campaign management.

Online Promotions

www.webpromote.com
WebPromote.com offers information on Internet marketing, including Web site promotion.

newapps.internet.com/appstopics/
Win_95_Web_Site_Promotion_Tools.html
This site is a resource listing tools to help a business conduct effective promotional campaigns. These include Web-tracking software and search-engine effectiveness software, some of which is free.

www.promotionworld.com/tutorial/000.html
Promotion World has an online promotional outline containing information on site promotion.

Internet Marketing Research

www.iconocast.com
ICONOCAST is a source providing marketing information, including access to a newsletter.

www.zonaresearch.com
Zona Research offers marketing research reports.

www.idc.com
International Data Corporation offers specialized marketing research on the Internet, e-commerce and information technology.

Online Advertising

www.engage.com
Engage Media offers a variety of Internet marketing products and services.

www.adresource.com
Ad Resource offers Internet advertising resources, including software information, events and articles.

www.burst.com
Burst.com uses bursting to deliver video content. Visit the site for a demonstration of the difference between bursting and streaming.

Webcasting and Interactive Advertising

www.streamingmedia.com
Streamingmedia.com is a site where you can learn about current streaming media conferences, industry news, company directories and information on streaming media.

www.digiknow.com
Digiknow.com offers interactive advertising, including online, on-disk and on-paper advertising. Visit the site to see demonstrations.

www.bluestreak.com
Bluestreak offers interactive banners. Visit the site to see demonstrations.

Business-to-Business Marketing on the Web

www.verticalnet.com
VerticalNet, Inc. provides a list of industry communities. It also has a variety of e-business solutions that help bring buyers and sellers together. This gives marketers options for B2B marketing.

www.commerceone.com
Commerce One offers a portal (**www.marketsite.net**) for businesses to exchange products around the world. *Commerce One* also assists companies in building industry marketplaces.

www.linkshare.com
Linkshare is one of the few companies offering business-to-business affiliate programs for companies in addition to business-to-consumer affiliate programs.

Public Relations

www.mediarelations.com
Media Relations provides publicity, marketing and event management.

www1.internetwire.com/iwire/home
Internet Wire offers a free PR newsletter.

www.newsiq.com
NewsIQ offers a service that tracks its clients' appearances in the news.

Customer Relationship Management on the Internet

www.crm-forum.com
CRM forum contains articles, tutorials, presentations, and white papers on improving the quality of customer relationship management on the Internet.

www.isky.com
iSky provides assistance for companies who need customer care systems. A company can outsource Customer Relationship Management to *iSky*.

www.sychrony.net
Synchrony offers a product that integrates all forms of communication to provide one single profile of a customer's history.

Personalization

www.andromedia.com
Andromedia provides a personalization solution, LikeMinds, which allows you to personalize your customers' experiences on your Web site based on their previous visits.

www.bluemartini.com
BlueMartini has created a product, The Customer Interaction Server, that allows a business to manage the needs of individual customers by tracking and mining customer visits.

www.broadbase.com
Broadbase Software, Inc. provides solutions for all aspects of e-commerce. The E-Marketing product assists the marketer in planning, executing and analyzing personalized marketing campaigns.

Search Engine Information

www.submiturl.com/metatags.htm
This site has a brief tutorial on META tags.

www.webdeveloper.com/html/html_metatags.html
The *Webdeveloper* provides a tutorial on META tags.

www.tiac.net/users/seeker/searchenginesub.html
This site offers direct links to the registration portions of many search engines.

Affiliate Programs

www.quickclick.com
Quickclick.com reviews many of the top-paying and most-effective affiliate and pay-per-action advertising programs online.

www.cashpile.com
This site aggregates information on a large number of affiliate programs. They offer tutorials, news and links to top sites.

www.atWebsites.com/startaffiliate/index.html
This site is a step-by-step walkthrough explaining how to set up an affiliate program.

General Internet Marketing Information

www.asknetrageous.com/AskNetrageous.html
Asknetrageous offers answers to Internet marketing questions. You can subscribe to any of the e-mail newsletters for free.

www.eMarketer.com
eMarketer aggregates Internet marketing content, including news, statistics, profiles and reviews.

www.channelseven.com
Channelseven is a news and information site that helps marketing and advertising professionals keep up to date with the Web.

www.roibotlibrary.com/index.htm
ROIbotlibrary is a listing of free Internet marketing resources. These resources include a free 5-day marketing course sent to you over the Internet. The Web site also provides free marketing software.

Total Internet Marketing Solutions and Services

www.wheelhouse.com
Wheelhouse provides consulting and implementation assistance for various marketing strategies. This company implements marketing systems.

www.hyperlink.com

Hyperlink is a full-service company that offers customer acquisition management tools and relationship marketing consultancy.

www.ilux.com
Ilux develops and sells software for Internet marketing solutions and also provides services including evaluation of Web sites, outsourcing and *Ilux* software utilization assistance.

SUMMARY

- A solid Internet marketing strategy can include e-mailing, advertising, promotions, public relations, partnering, affiliate programs and Customer Relationship Management (CRM) systems.

- Keeping user profiles, recording visits and analyzing promotional and advertising results are key to measuring the effectiveness of your marketing campaign.

- By discovering your target market you can increase visits, responses and possible purchases.

- Internet marketing should be used with traditional marketing to attract new customers and bring them back to your site repeatedly.

- Choose a domain name that people will be able to recognize and type easily.

- Marketing research can now be performed over the Internet.

- Your Web site should include a privacy policy detailing intended uses of consumer information.

- Web sites should be designed with the consumers' preferences in mind.

- Organizations that plan to enter the global market must have the ability to send e-mails translated into the proper languages.

- Personalization technology allows the marketer to target campaigns to a specific market.

- Determining a goal for your campaign involves defining the reach, or the span of people you would like to target, including geographic locations and demographic profiles.

- Good Internet mailing lists include the contact information for people who have opted-in to receive information by e-mail.

- Traditional direct marketing should be used with e-mailing in order to reach more people.

- E-mails can be used to improve customer service.

- Spamming is mass e-mailing customers who have not expressed interest in receiving such e-mail.

- Promoting products and services can attract visitors to a site and may influence their purchasing.

- Offering something extra, such as frequent-flyer miles for participating airlines, to consumers when they purchase products or services online can increase brand loyalty.

- In a points-based promotion, points are awarded to customers every time they perform a pre-designated action. These points can be accumulated and redeemed for products or services.

- You can help consumers feel comfortable about using your site by offering a free trial.

- Your company can place your coupons on sites that offer online coupons in order to target consumers and bring them to your site.

- E-businesses should establish and continually strengthen branding. Your brand should be unique, recognizable and easy to remember.

- Publicizing your URL on all direct mailings, business cards and advertisements will bring people to your site. Placing your links on other companies' Web sites and registering your site with search engines and directories are other means of increasing traffic to your site.

- Web-page banner ads, which act like small billboards, usually contain graphics and an advertising message. The benefits of banner advertising include increased brand recognition, exposure and possible revenue gained through purchases by consumers.

- A pop-up box is a screen containing an advertisement that appears separate from the screen the user is viewing. The box pops up randomly or as a result of user actions.

- By placing ads in different positions on Web pages and analyzing the results, you can determine what position gets the greatest number of click-throughs.

- Buying advertising space on sites that receive a large number of visitors and that target a market similar to yours can increase the number of hits on your site and lead to higher revenues. Selling advertising space on your own site can provide you with additional income.

- The fee for every one thousand people who view the site on which your banner is located is called the CPM (cost per thousand).

- One unique visit registers when you visit a site. Hits are recorded for each object that is downloaded. To determine the value of a Web site for advertising purposes, one should use the number of unique visitors, not total hits.

- Pay-per-click means that you pay the host for people's click-throughs to your site. Pay-per-lead means that you pay the host for every lead generated from the advertisement, and pay-per-sale means that you pay the host for every sale resulting from a click-through.

- Another advertising option involves exchanging advertising space on your site for advertising space on another's site. This structure is effective for complementary businesses.

- You can register with companies that sell your advertising space for you. These companies typically charge a percentage of the revenue you receive from the advertisements placed on your site.

- Webcasting involves using streaming media to broadcast an event over the Web.

- Bursting delivers content faster than streaming; bursting causes a substantial build up of content at the receiving end, potentially allowing the video to appear smoother.

- Interactive advertising includes using many forms of rich media (such as audio, video, images and animations) and traditional advertising forms (such as print, television and radio advertisements).

- Public Relations (PR) includes communicating with your consumers and company through press releases, speeches, special events, presentations and e-mails.

- To learn what people think about your company or products, try hosting chat sessions. Consider using a bulletin board on your Web site to enable people to post comments. You can also involve consumers by organizing a special event or function on your Web site.

- Press releases can be delivered over the Web.

- Your Web site should contain a link that connects to all of your company's press releases.

- Video clips of news appearances, speeches, commercials and advertisements can be effective publicity for your company.

- A Public relations department should use crisis management to respond to company problems.

- The sum of your company's customer service solutions makes up its Customer Relationship Management (CRM) system.

- One-to-one Internet tools include log-file analysis, cookies and the use of infomediaries.

- A CRM system will keep records of your customers' behavior to provide fast and effective service and, when necessary, to implement corrective measures.

- People should be able to conduct transactions and get answers to questions through call centers.

- Data mining uses algorithms and statistical tools to find patterns in data gathered from customer visits. These patterns can help you implement proper customer relationship management and marketing campaigns by providing information about your customers.

- By using tracking devices to determine the number of Internet users exposed to an advertisement and the percentage of those viewers who actually click on the ad, marketing sales teams can analyze ad campaigns, determine demographics and create more effective online publicity.

- Log files consist of data generated by site visits, including each visitor's location, IP address, time of visit, frequency of visits and many other indicators that can be used to track visitors.

- Registration—requiring visitors to fill out a form with personal information that is used to create a profile—is recommended when it will provide a benefit to the consumer. By obtaining information from registration, companies will be able to evaluate who their consumers are and what they want.

- People are often reluctant to fill out a form requiring personal information. To start building a consumer profile, you can require only the minimum information, such as a username, password and possibly an e-mail address. You may also want to give customers an incentive to register such as a free-trial run or a free demonstration of your site's service.

- Human-to-human contact with your consumers is important and can be provided by a link on your site to a live customer representative.

- Some people feel that personalization represents an invasion of their privacy, whereas others may not even be aware that personalization is occurring.

- B2B marketing can be different from B2C marketing because when you sell your product to another business, you may be selling to someone who is not the direct user of your product.

- Searching marketplaces for possible clients can help you generate customers and find your target market.

- Search-engine ranking methods will determine how "high" your site appears in search results.

- Most search engines rank your site by sending out a spider to inspect the site. The spider reads the META tags, determines the relevance of the Web page's information and keywords, and then ranks the site according to that visit's findings.

- When you register your site with a search engine, you submit keywords and a description of your business to the engine. The search engine will add your information to its database of Web sites.

- Submitting a site to search engines increases the chance that the site will appear in result listings.

- Various companies will register your Web site with many search engines for a fee.

- Partnering can help your company provide consumers with complementary services and products.

- The success of international businesses is often contingent on distribution methods.

- Language translation services and software are available to help you to translate your Web site and e-mails into various foreign languages.

- By understanding different cultures to the best of your ability and by testing your site and marketing campaign on a smaller scale with focus groups and trials, you can reduce the possibility of misconceptions and misunderstandings before you launch your site for the whole world to see.

TERMINOLOGY

affiliate program
AutoTranslate
banner ad
BFAST™
brand awareness
bursting
Burstware®
business-to-business (B2B) e-commerce
business-to-consumer (B2C) marketing
call center
cookie
(CPM) cost per thousand
crisis management
Customer Relationship Management (CRM)
customer registration
data mining
DD/Marketer
direct e-mail
eGain Commerce™
Enterprise Translation Server™
frequently asked questions (FAQ)
hits
interactive advertising
Internet mailing list
Internet marketing campaign
log file
log-file analysis
Logos® Wordtheque
marketplace
META tag
natural-language technology
one-to-one marketing
online coupons
opt-in e-mail

outsource
partnering
pay-per-performance
pay-per-click
pay-per-click model
pay-per-lead
pay-per-lead model
pay-per-sale
pay-per-sale model
personalization
points-based promotion
pop-up box
press release
privacy policy
promotions
public relations (PR)
reach
RealCall® Alert™
response rate
search-engine ranking
secondary research
segmented markets
spamming
spider
streaming video
switching costs
target market
tracking device
traditional direct marketing
unique visitor
Webcasting
WebRIOT
Word Exchange Forum

SELF-REVIEW EXERCISES

4.1 State whether each of the following is true or false; if false, explain why.
a) Spam is soliciting consumers with unwanted e-mail.
b) Pay-per-click affiliate programs reward affiliates for every sale made.
c) CPM stands for Consumer Product Management.
d) Storing data in a database is called data mining.
e) An affiliate program is a form of public relations.
f) Switching costs are higher when shopping online than shopping offline.
g) A target market is the group of people toward whom you direct a marketing campaign.
h) Using Webcasting for your online advertising can simulate television commercials.
i) Search engine-registration is important to increase traffic to your site.
j) A banner ad can include motion, scrolling text and color changes.

4.2 Fill in the blanks in each of the following.
a) A _____ announces current events and other significant news to the press.

b) Keeping the public and your company's employees current on company news is called _____.

c) A _____ is what a search engine sends out to rank a Web site.

d) The group of people to whom you tailor your marketing campaign is your _____.

e) _____ is used to make Webcasts appear like television.

f) Allowing a company to advertise on your Web site in return for receiving money for users who click-through the advertisement to that company's site is called an _____ .

g) _____ occurs when the data collected is studied and programs are run to find hidden patterns.

h) Keywords, a title for your Web page and descriptions can all be found in _____ tags.

i) Providing one-to-one marketing and a call center in addition to assisting customers with their problems is having good _____.

j) Online focus groups, surveys and interviews are all part of _____.

ANSWERS TO SELF-REVIEW EXERCISES

4.1   a) True b) False, Pay-per-click affiliate programs reward affiliates for every click-through made. c) False, CPM stands for cost-per-thousand and is used in reference to advertising costs. d) False, data mining is using already gathered information to find patterns in the data. e) False, an affiliate program is a form of Internet marketing. It is a partnership where one company provides traffic to another site in return for some form of compensation. f) False, switching costs are higher when shopping offline than shopping online. g) True h) True i) True j) True

4.2   a) press release b) public relations c) spider d) target market e) streaming video f) affiliate program g) data mining h) META i) Customer Relationship Management j) Internet marketing research

EXERCISES

4.1   Research and compare three different Internet advertising agencies.

4.2   Define each of the following terms:
   a) Reach
   b) Response rates
   c) Switching costs
   d) Spamming
   e) Opt-in e-mail
   f) Internet mailing lists

4.3   Explain the three common types of pay-per-performance advertising campaigns.

4.4   Write an e-mail in English and then run it through the various translation services of AltaVista. If you speak another language, compare the translation with the original and comment on the effectiveness of the translation service.

4.5   Choose a traditionally marketed product or service and create an Internet marketing strategy. Discuss the following:
   a) Direct e-mail
   b) Interactive advertising
   c) Banner advertising
   d) Target market
   e) Affiliate or partnering program
   f) Public relations
   g) Promotions
   h) Internet marketing research

    i)   Search engine registration

    j)   International issues

WORKS CITED

The notation <*www.domain-name.com*> indicates that the citation is for information found on that Web site.

1.   D. Tynan, "What to Name the Baby," *The Industry Standard* 24 April 2000: 158+.

2.   K. Kaplan, "New Competitors for Dot-com," <`Latimes.com`> 10 July 2000.

3.   T. Bridis, "ICANN Approves Creations of More Web Addresses," *The Wall Street Journal* 17 July 2000: B5.

4.   J. Nielsen and D. Norman, "Usability On The Web Isn't A Luxury," *Information Week* 14 February 2000: 65.

5.   T. Siebel and P. House, *Cyber Rules: Strategies for Excelling At E-Business* (New York: Random House, Inc., 1999) 78.

6.   P. Seybold and R. Marshak, *Customers.com* (New York: Random House, Inc., 1998) 92-93.

7.   D. Greening, "When Push Comes To Shove," *Webtechniques* April 2000: 23.

8.   B. Warner and L. Shuchman, "Getting Heard Above the Noise," *The Industry Standard* 27 December 1999-3 January 2000: 53.

9.   S. Nathan, "Moneyline: Internet Ads," *USA Today* 28 March 2000: B1.

10.   L. Cunningham, "Marketing: Only Performance Counts," *Inter@ctive Week* 1 May 2000: 116.

11.   D. Lehman, "Privacy Policies Missing on 77% of Web Sites," *Computer World* 17 April 2000: 103.

12.   L. Cunningham, "Marketing: Only Performance Counts," *Inter@ctive Week* 1 May 2000: 116.

13.   K. Weisul, "ValueClick Could Live Up To Its Name," *Inter@ctive Week* 27 March 2000: 92. and <`www.valueclick.com`>.

14.   M. Smetannikov, "Perchance To Dream Of Bannerless Ads," *Inter@ctive Week* 17 April 2000: 22.

15.   M. McCarthy, "Webcast Show Fashions Success," *USA Today* 22 May 2000: 8B.

16.   McCarthy, 8B.

17.   E. Cone, "EGain Reaches Two Markets," *Inter@ctive Week* 29 May 2000: 38.

18.   <`www.epiphany.com`>.

19.   <`www.webtrends.com`>.

20.   <`www.realcall.com`>.

21.   D. Peppers, M. Rogers, Ph.D., and B. Dorf, *The One To One Field Book: The Complete Toolkit for Implementing a 1 to 1 Marketing Program* (New York: Bantam Doubleday Dell Publishing Group, Inc., 1999) 42-46.

22.   <`www.excite.com`>

23.   <`www.askjeeves.com`>.

24.   <`www.befree.com`>.

25.   <`www.logos.it`>.

RECOMMENDED READINGS

Amor, D. *The E-business (R)Evolution.* New Jersey: Prentice Hall, 2000.

Bond, J. "Marketers, Your Stock Has Never Been Higher." *Revolution* March 2000: 55-59.

Cunningham, L. "Marketing: Only Performance Counts." *Inter@ctive Week* 1 May 2000: 116.

Estabrook, A. "Drive Customers To Your Web Site." *e-Business Advisor* November 1999: 22-25.

Girishankar, S. "Customer Service For Business Partners." *Informationweek* 17 April 2000: 65+.

Gray, D. *The Complete Guide To Associate and Affiliate Programs on the Net: Turning Clicks into Cash.* New York: McGraw-Hill, 2000.

Kuehl, C. "E-mail Marketing, Spam's Good Twin." *Internet World* 1 May 2000: 31-38.

Mann-Craik, F. "The Power of Advertising Your Internet Firm." *Tornado-Insider* February 2000: 92-94, 96.

Peppers, D., et al. *The One To One Field Book: The Complete Toolkit for Implementing a 1 to 1 Marketing Program.* New York: Bantam Doubleday Dell Publishing Group, Inc., 1999.

Seybold, P. and R. Marshak. *Customers.com: How To Create A Profitable Business Strategy For The Internet and Beyond.* New York: Random House, Inc., 1998.

Siebel, T. and P. House. *Cyber Rules: Strategies for Excelling At E-Business.* New York: Random House, Inc., 1999.

"Special Report: CRM e-volves." *Global Technology Business* May 2000: 48+.

"Special Report: Online Marketing: Customer Conundrum." *Upside* April 2000: 145+.

Tiernan, B. *E-tailing.* Chicago: Dearborn Financial Publishing, Inc., 2000.

Walsh, B. "Building A Business Plan For An E-Commerce Project." *Network Computing* 15 September 1998: 69-71+.

Waters, J. "Getting Personal On The Web." *Application Development Trends* May 2000: 25-32.

Online Monetary Transactions

Objectives

- To explore various methods of conducting online monetary transactions.
- To review the application of traditional payment models to the Internet.
- To discuss the role of security in support of online monetary transactions.
- To understand Internet-based monetary transaction models: e-billing, micropayments, peer-to-peer payments and digital currency.
- To explore the development of online banking.

Alas, how deeply painful is all payment.
Lord Bryon

Cash payment is not the sole nexus of man with man.
Thomas Carlyle

Ah, take the Cash, and let the Credit go...
Edward Fitzgerald

So far as my coin would stretch; and where it would not, I have used my credit.
William Shakespeare

Beautiful credit! The foundation of modern society.
Mark Twain

I cried all the way to the bank.
Liberace

Outline

5.1 Introduction

The electronic transfer of funds is a growing aspect of e-commerce, and one that is key to conducting e-business successfully. In this chapter we examine how individuals and organizations perform monetary transactions on the Internet. We discuss online monetary transactions including payments by credit card, cash, and check; payments to businesses; peer-to-peer payments; banking and bill paying.

Also in this chapter, we list many of the companies who are developing online payment technology. We explain the products, software, and services that these companies produce, and direct you to their Web sites for further information. Many of these Web sites include animated demonstrations.

Internet security, a major issue surrounding the operation and trustworthiness of monetary payment systems, is discussed in depth in Chapter 7.

5.2 Credit-Card Transactions

Although credit cards are a popular form of payment for online purchases, many people resist their appeal and simplicity due to security concerns. Customers fear credit-card fraud by merchants and other parties. Credit cards, such as the Prodigy Internet® Mastercard®, for example, have been developed to accommodate online and offline payments. The Prodigy card also guarantees online fraud protection as well as a point-based reward program that allows card holders to redeem points for free Prodigy Internet access.[1]

In order to accept credit-card payments, a merchant must have a *merchant account* with a bank. Traditional merchant accounts accept only *POS (point-of-sale) transactions*, or those that occur when you present your credit card at a store. With the growth in e-commerce, specialized Internet merchant accounts have been established to handle online credit-card transactions. These transactions are processed by banks or third-party services.

Companies like CyberCash (**www.cybercash.com**) and iCat (**www.icat.com**) enable merchants to accept credit-card payments online. These companies have established business relationships with financial institutions that will accept online credit-card payments for merchant clients. iCat acts as a third party that receives consumer credit information and securely interacts with both the consumer and merchant bank accounts to verify the sale and make monetary transfers.[2]

Trintech, another company offering online credit-card transaction capabilities, has created the *Payware®* product suite that enables companies to process electronic transactions. The suite includes the *eMerchant* program, which enables merchants to accept online payments; *eHost*, which can accommodate transactions from multiple stores; and *eIssuer,* which issues the consumer a *virtual credit card* that is stored on the user's computer, providing one-click shopping at participating merchants. Trintech is also developing a *mobile payments* option that can be used from mobile phones. A demo[3] of the process can be found at

```
www.trintech.com/products/payware_eissuer/
payware_eissuer_flash.html
```

CyberCash[4]

CyberCash enables businesses to receive payments through the Internet. *CashRegister*, an online service created by CyberCash, makes it possible for merchants to receive credit-card numbers, offer the numbers to the appropriate financial institution for validation and accept credit-card payments in a secure environment over the Web. All major credit cards, such as Visa, Mastercard, Discover/Novus, and some debit cards can be processed by CashRegister. In addition to their CashRegister technology, Cyber-Cash also offers affiliate-marketing services (see Chapter 4, "Internet Marketing") and payment solutions for offline businesses.

The CashRegister system works by establishing a direct connection between its own servers and the Web sites of its e-business customers. A software application called the *Merchant Connection Kit (MCK)* is used to make this connection; the kit also includes HTML files and sample scripts to use when adding CashRegister to an existing e-commerce site (technical discussions of HTML and scripting are presented throughout the book). In most cases, CashRegister can be built into generic shopping carts and storefronts, eliminating the need for customized software (shopping-cart technology is discussed in Chapter 3).

The CashRegister process begins once a customer is finished shopping on a merchant's Web site. The customer completes a form, entering credit-card and shipping information, and is presented with a screen containing items selected, prices and billing information. This information is then sent to CyberCash for validation. Once validation is received, the purchase can be completed, and funds are transferred electronically from the customer's account to the merchant's account.

CyberCash Instabuy is another product available to merchants; it allows customers to store their purchasing information in an Instabuy *e-wallet*. An e-wallet electronically stores purchasing information. When customers are ready to check out, they can use the wallet to transfer payment information quickly and securely.

CyberCash[4] (Cont.)

Through efficient use of technology, CashRegister offers both convenience and security to its users. Using a complete set of *redundant servers*, or identical servers for back up if one server fails, CyberCash is able to maintain continuous service and minimize downtime. CashRegister also keeps track of all transactions completed through a merchant's Web site and produces reports to assist the merchant with record keeping and customer tracking. To protect users' private information, all financial information transmitted via the Internet is encrypted and digitally signed.

CyberCash also offers fraud detection to protect merchants. *Standard Fraud Detection* is designated for merchants who want to use a standardized set of requirements for determining fraudulent activity. The merchant selects the appropriate fraud detection rules; the same rules are then used for every purchase. *Advanced Fraud Detection* is offered for merchants who wish to use different fraud detection rules for different types of purchases.

Visit the CyberCash Web site at **cybercash.com/cashregister/ solutions_software.html**. This site has an extensive list of e-commerce software products that have incorporated CashRegister into their solutions.

5.3 E-Wallets

To facilitate the credit-card order process, many companies are introducing electronic wallet services. E-wallets allow you to keep track of your billing and shipping information so that it can be entered with one click at participating merchants' sites. They also store e-checks, e-cash and your credit-card information for multiple cards.

Credit-card companies, such as Visa, offer a variety of e-wallets (**www.visa.com/ pd/ewallet/main.html**). Some Visa e-wallets are co-sponsored by specific banks; for example, the *bankonewallet[SM]* is available to Bank One customers for use only with a Visa/Mastercard credit or check card. MBNA offers an e-wallet that allows the consumer to perform one-click shopping at member sites. Its e-wallet automatically fills in transfer, shipping and payment information on the forms of non-member merchants.[5]

Entrypoint.com offers a free, personalized desktop toolbar that includes an e-wallet to facilitate one-click shopping at its affiliate stores (Fig. 5.1). The toolbar's features include news reports, sports scores and a stock ticker. Similar to MNBA, the Entrypoint e-wallet facilitates automatic form completion at non-member stores. For a product demonstration, visit **www.entrypoint.com** and follow the links.[6]

Fig. 5.1   The EntryPoint Internet Toolbar. (Courtesy of EntryPoint Incorporated.)

There are many digital wallets on the market that are not accepted by all vendors. In order to standardize e-wallet technology and gain a wider acceptance among vendors, Visa, Mastercard and a group of e-wallet vendors have standardized the technology with the *Electronic Commerce Modeling Language (ECML)*. Since the standard was unveiled in June, 1999, many of the leading online vendors have adopted the standard.[7]

5.4 Alternate Consumer Payment Options

Although *electronic payment* is more convenient, Internet merchants that do not accept credit cards can accept payments such as checks or money orders through the mail. Cash on delivery (COD) is another possible, but rarely used, option for those hesitant to pay electronically.

Debit cards offer an alternative for card-holders to access their savings, checking and other accounts. These cards are used like credit cards, but, instead of paying a monthly bill, the funds are instantly deducted from the customer's checking account. Customers are also able to withdraw cash from their accounts through *Automatic Teller Machines (ATMs)*.

Banks and businesses are also creating options for online payment that do not involve credit cards. Companies such as AmeriNet (`www.debit-it.com`) allow merchants to accept a customer's checking-account number as a valid form of payment. AmeriNet provides authorization and account settlement, handles distribution and shipping (known as *fulfillment*) and manages customer service inquiries (Fig. 5.2).[8]

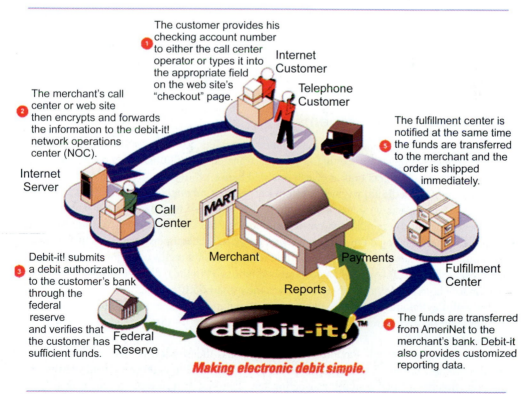

Fig. 5.2   Amerinet debit-it process flow. (Courtesy of www.debit-it.com.)

5.5 Digital Currency

There are many forms of digital currency; *digital cash* is one example. It is stored electronically and can be used to make online electronic payments. Digital cash accounts are similar to traditional bank accounts; consumers deposit money into their digital cash accounts to be used in their digital transactions. Digital cash is often used with other payment technologies, such as digital wallets.

Aside from alleviating some of the security fears that many people have about online credit-card transactions, digital cash allows people who do not have credit cards to shop online, and merchants accepting digital-cash payments avoid credit-card transaction fees.

eCash Technologies, Inc. (**www.ecash.com**) is a secure digital-cash provider that allows you to withdraw funds from your traditional bank account. A demo of the purchasing process can be found at **www.ecash.net/Consumers/ConsDemo.asp**.

Gift cash, often sold as points, is another form of digital currency that can be redeemed at leading shopping sites. It is an effective way of giving teen shoppers, or those without credit cards, the ability to make purchases on the Web. Flooz (**www.flooz.com**) is an example of gift currency. Flooz can be used at over 60 online stores including **toysrus.com** and **barnesandnoble.com**.[9]

Some companies offer points-based rewards paid for collected for completing specified tasks. These tasks may include visiting Web sites, registering or buying products. One such reward scheme, beenz (**www.beenz.com**), is an international, points-based currency system. Through a partnership with beenz, vendors can offer promotional systems. For instance, a retail site on the Web could offer beenz for registering with the Web site. As beenz are accumulated the customer can earn prizes, discounts or other rewards.[10]

Internetcash.com is a digital-cash model aimed exclusively at teenagers. It sells cards in various monetary denominations at convenience stores and gas stations. These cards are activated over the Internet and can be used to shop at teen-oriented member stores.[11]

5.6 Peer-To-Peer Payments

Peer-to-peer transactions allow online monetary transfers between consumers. eCash runs a peer-to-peer payment service that allows the transfer of digital cash via e-mail between two people who have accounts at eCash-enabled banks.

PayPal offers a digital payment system known as *X payments*. PayPal allows a user to send money to anyone with an e-mail address, regardless of what bank either person uses, or whether or not the recipient is pre-registered with the service. People wishing to send money to others can log on to PayPal at **www.paypal.com**, open an account and register the amount to be sent. That amount is billed to the person's credit card. Payment notification is sent to the recipient, and an account is established in the recipient's name. When the person to whom the payment is sent receives the e-mail notification, he or she simply registers with PayPal and has access to an account containing the payment. The funds in this account can be transferred to the recipient's bank account by direct deposit or mailed by check from PayPal.

Transactions through PayPal are instantaneous, the service is free for individuals sending money to one another and the payee is not required to enter any credit-card information. Businesses pay a small transaction fee. The system is simple to use and the site offers a demo at **www.paypal.com/cgi-bin/webscr?cmd=home/works**.

The X Payment system can also be used to enable credit-card payment for auction items in *real time*. This means that the transaction begins processing immediately after it is initiated, reducing the risk of fraud or overdrawn accounts. Credit-card information is checked before a transaction is initiated. The buyer or the seller can initiate the service. If you refer someone to PayPal, you will receive a small monetary reward.[12]

eBay and Wells Fargo offer another form of peer-to-peer payment called BillPoint. It allows buyers to submit electronic payments to sellers' checking accounts.[13] Prior to this technology, buyers were required to send checks or money orders. Sellers can choose to include BillPoint as a payment option on their auction pages, so anyone can use the service without registering. Sellers pay a flat fee for the transaction and a percentage fee on the sale price above a given amount. In the future, eBay and Wells Fargo plan to sell this technology for use on other sites. Visit **www.billpoint.com/help/tutorial.html**[14] to view a tutorial on the Billpoint system.

Another peer-to-peer payment company, **Tradesafe.com**, accommodates the larger amounts typically involved in B2B transactions. Tradesafe offers peer-to-peer credit-card transactions and also provides its services to electronic merchants. If a purchase exceeds a certain amount, Tradesafe acts as an intermediary and withholds payment to the seller until the goods arrive in acceptable condition. Tradesafe also accepts personal checks, money orders and wire transfers.[15]

5.7 Smart Cards

A *smart card,* a card with a computer chip embedded on its face, is able to hold more information than an ordinary credit card with a magnetic strip. Smart-card technology can be used with pay phones, health care, transportation, identification, retail, loyalty programs and banking, to name a few. The same smart card can store information about your health-care plan and your frequent-flyer loyalty program.

There are *contact* and *contactless* smart cards. In order to read the information on the smart card and update information on the computer chip, contact smart cards need to be placed in a *smart card reader.* A contactless smart card has both a coiled antenna and a computer chip inside, enabling the card to transmit information. The contactless card enables faster information exchange than is possible using a contact smart card. For example, contactless cards are convenient for transportation services such as an automatic toll payment. A contactless smart card can be placed in a device in your car to charge your account as you drive through toll booths.[16]

Smart cards can require the user to have a password, giving the smart card a security advantage over credit cards. Information can be designated as "read only" or as "no access." Security measures such as encryption, which is discussed in Chapter 7, can also be used. For additional security, the card can have a picture on its face to identify the user. However, some argue that there is too much personal information stored on the card, creating the possibility of personal identity theft.

Similar to the smart card, eConnect provides solutions to make Internet transactions more secure through hardware devices. The company has technology that allows customers to use ATM cards to make purchases over the Internet. eConnect also has technology for securing credit-card payments. eConnect's product, *eCashPad,* is a device that connects to your computer and scrambles financial data, making it secure to send that data over the Internet. *ePocketPay* is another product developed by eConnect that allows a consumer to make secure purchases from the ePocketPay portable device. This device acts as a cell phone with a card reader built into it. It will allow you to make secure purchases anywhere.[17]

Financial institutions employ smart cards to provide benefits for their members. Visa has created *Visa Cash*, a smart card used to store money and make purchases. When you need to make purchases, you can place your Visa Cash card into the smart-card reader and view the balance before and after the purchase. Visa makes both disposable Visa Cash cards, which can be thrown out after their value has been used up, and reloadable cards, to which money can be added. Additional information can be found at **www.visa.com/nt/chip/info.html**.

For more information about smart-card technology and smart-card companies, visit the Smart Card Industry Association at **www.scia.org**.

5.8 Micropayments

Merchants must pay a fee for each credit-card transaction that they process; this can become costly when customers purchase inexpensive items. The cost of some items could actually be lower than the standard transaction fees, causing merchants to incur losses. *Micropayments,* or payments that generally do not exceed $10, offer a way for companies offering nominally priced products and services (music, pictures, text or video) to generate a profit; they offer consumers a cost-efficient means of acquiring this material. Millicent (see Millicent feature in this section) is a micropayment technology provider.

To offer the option of micropayments, some companies have formed strategic partnerships with utility companies. For instance, a phone bill is essentially an aggregation of micropayments that are charged at the end of a particular period of time in order to justify the transaction fees. Many e-businesses have formed partnerships with utility companies, allowing customers to charge their small purchases to their monthly bills. eCharge gives companies the ability to offer this option to their customers.

eCharge uses *ANI (Automatic Number Identification)* to verify the identity of the customer and the purchases they make. The eCharge software can only be used with a dial-up connection. In order for your payments to be charged to your phone bill, a 1-900-number must be called. eCharge temporarily disconnects the user from the Internet to do this. Once the payment is complete, the user is reconnected. This process is completed quickly, with little inconvenience to the user. iPin (**www.ipin.com**) offers a similar service, billing payments through your ISP.[18]

A number of companies will allow you to outsource your payment-management systems. Many of these systems can handle multiple payment methods including micropayments. Qpass is an example of a company that can manage micropayments for pay-per-download, subscription-based and pay-per-click systems. Qpass enables periodicals such as *The New York Times* and *The Wall Street Journal* to offer subscriptions over the Web. Customers that buy products and services through a Qpass-enabled company receive monthly bills that include descriptions of all purchases made during that month. For a graphical example of the Qpass transaction process, see Fig. 5.3.

Additional services offered by Qpass include: the Qpass *PowerWallet*, which registers passwords, credit-card information and other preferences necessary to make online transactions more efficient; customer service; marketing and sales assistance. Visit Qpass at **www.qpass.com**.[19]

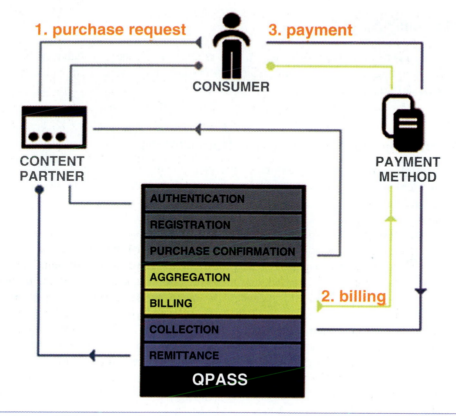

Fig. 5.3   QPass Transaction Process. (Courtesy of QPass Inc.)

Millicent™

Millicent[20] is a micropayment technology provider. Companies that use Millicent payment technology allow their customers to make micropayments using credit or debit cards, prepaid purchasing cards or by adding purchases to a monthly Internet Service Provider bill or phone bill. The customer uses any one of these payment methods to prepay a sum of money that can then be used to make micropayments.

Millicent handles all of the payment processing needed for the operation of an e-business, customer support and distribution services. Vendors can direct the transactions to Millicent, or the vendors can install the Millicent processing software on their own systems.

Millicent's services are especially useful to companies that offer subscription fees and small pay-per-download fees for digital content. This content may include text, audio, video, software applications or Web-based training products. Millicent payment technology can also be used with affiliate programs; the Millicent system will generate a payment to the affiliate once earnings exceed a pre-determined minimum. Affiliate programs are discussed in Chapter 4, "Internet Marketing."

Millicent™ (Cont.)

Millicent is a product of Compaq. The product is currently available in Japan; North American and European service will be available soon. Visit Millicent at `www.millicent.com`.

5.9 Business-to-Business (B2B) Transactions

The fastest growing sector of e-commerce payments is *business-to-business (B2B) transactions*. These payments are often much larger than B2C transactions and involve complex business accounting systems.[21]

Paymentech™ (`www.paymentech.com`) is one of the largest payment solutions providers for point-of-sale transactions on the Internet. It has taken its credit-card processing expertise into the world of e-commerce. Its systems are used by companies such as CyberCash, CyberSource® and AT&T SecureBuy. Brick-and-mortar and electronic merchants can choose from many transaction-processing options, including debit cards, credit cards, bank cards, checks and EBT authorization and settlement; reporting and processing tools and services to help manage a merchant account; and electronic check processing. *EBT (Electronic Benefits Transfer)* is defined by the USDA as the electronic transfer of government funds to retailers for the benefit of the needy.[22] Paymentech supports all types of credit and debit cards and conducts all transactions in a secure environment. Paymentech's online authorization systems, available on a 24-by-7 basis, enable merchants to initiate, transmit and receive authorizations in one phone call. Address verification can also be performed online.

Merchants using Paymentech can customize their payment-processing plans to fit their needs. For corporate use, Paymentech offers a Mastercard/Visa credit card, which, in addition to allowing charges, enables electronic checking and billing, and access to its *PaymentNet* online reporting service. PaymentNet allows merchants to track their expenses in a secure environment on a 24-by-7 basis. Its features include custom reporting, e-billing and cross-compatibility with other third-party expense reporting tools.[23]

eCredit (`www.ecredit.com`) provides real-time, credit-transaction capabilities of B2B size. Using its *Global Financing Network* ™, eCredit customers can have access to automated credit approval and financing. eCredit's linked system of financing agencies and information networks makes large-scale commercial transactions convenient. eCredit establishes a relationship with a business and integrates automated systems at all levels of business transactions.

eCredit services such as *InfoLink* and *BusinessVerify* allow businesses to access information databases that check the credit and validity of new customers. More comprehensive `ecredit.com` services, such as *DecisionDesktop,* integrate financial information with the customer's credit policy to approve or deny transactions. eCredit also provides services that integrate the company's existing financial systems and that automate the collections process.[24]

Clareon also facilitates B2B transactions by providing digital payment and settlement services (Fig. 5.4). Payment is digitally signed, secured and authenticated via *digital payment authentication (DPA)*. Unlike traditional EDI, Clareon is compatible with all *enter-*

prise resource planning (ERP) systems and can adapt electronic records for companies, banks and each member of a given transaction. Clareon software downloads the DPA and remittance data and converts it into an XML format. We discuss XML in detail in Chapter 27. From there, the information is again converted; the remittance data is sent to the seller and the DPA is forwarded to the bank. Both the buyer and the seller have access to the payment status. [25]

Aside from enabling electronic payment, many business-oriented services are aimed at electronic consolidation and reconciliation of the business transaction process. By consolidating information from all entities involved in a trade transaction and by accessing this information from a central portal, companies can keep track of an entire transaction from "order-to-cash"—ordering, invoicing and settlement—while reducing administrative costs, errors, waste and complexity in the supply chain. eTime Capital (**www.etimecapital.com**) offers software applications to track payment and delivery systems with a simple Web-based interface. By supplying all parties with details of both the financial and logistical aspects of the transaction, eTime Capital facilitates smooth coordination of shipping and payments. The service also provides a forum for all parties to settle disputes that may arise over obligation fulfillment, thereby shortening delivery time and reducing costs.[26]

Other firms are *order-fulfillment providers*. Now that it has become so easy to open an electronic storefront, many companies suddenly find themselves dealing with *logistics*, or management details, and distribution. **SubmitOrder.com** attempts to bring its supply chain expertise and logistical services to small Internet businesses, providing a distribution network for smaller merchants. **SubmitOrder.com** can receive shipments at its warehouses directly from the merchant's manufacturers; the service then keeps track of the inventory and communicates electronically with the merchant. Orders are received directly at its shipping centers, where products are then packaged and shipped.[27]

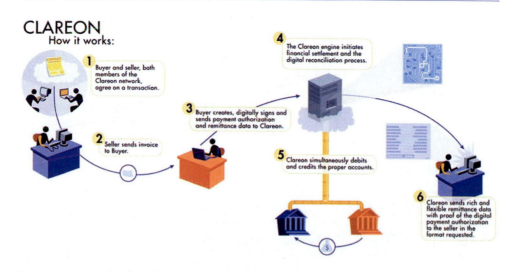

Fig. 5.4   Diagram of Clareon service. (All Rights Reserved, Clareon Corporation 2000.)

TradeCard[28]

The TradeCard network provides a global B2B e-commerce infrastructure, expanding current e-commerce capabilities to the international level. Particular attention is paid to the complexity of cross-border data management and payment. TradeCard attempts to provide an inexpensive and comprehensive solution to expedite all phases of global commerce.

Before using the TradeCard system, buyers and sellers must become TradeCard members. Coface, Thomas Cook and TradeCard evaluate potential members to determine a credit score and perform anti-money laundering and *Office of Foreign Assets Control (OFAC)* checks to name a few. OFAC is responsible for enforcing international trade sanctions.[29] The buyer creates a pre-formatted electronic purchase order on the TradeCard system and presents the document to the seller for negotiation and agreement. The purchase order data is stored electronically in the TradeCard database, and electronic invoices and packing slips are produced from this data. All of these documents are available online to the relevant parties involved in the transaction. Furthermore, TradeCard uses a patented "data compliance engine" to check the information on the documents against the original purchase order (Fig. 5.5). If any discrepancies are found, concerned parties are notified immediately and can negotiate to resolve the conflict.

TradeCard then awaits delivery confirmation from a *third-party logistics services provider* (3PL), the industry terminology for a shipping company. When confirmation is received and compliance is met, TradeCard completes the financial transaction by sending a request for payment to the buyer's financial institution. The actual monetary transfer to the seller's account is performed by Thomas Cook, a travel and financial services firm that is an alliance of TradeCard. Thus, TradeCard enables large-scale and large-dollar commerce without credit-card payment through direct interaction with existing financial institutions. For a demonstration of the process, visit **www.tradecard.com**. As a value-added service, TradeCard provides customers with access to a wide variety of integral trade service providers such as logistics and international inspection companies.

Overall, many see Internet-based electronic B2B transactions as a convenience that will augment, but not replace, traditional *Electronic Data Interchange (EDI)* systems. EDI remains a useful technology for standard orders and business transactions between firms with established business relationships. Internet-based B2B seems to be gaining popularity in auction-type marketplaces and for sharing of transaction documents over the Internet.

5.10 E-Billing

E-billing technologies are finding success in the B2C market, where transactions are less complicated than B2B transactions. *Electronic Bill Presentment and Payment (EBPP)* was estimated to be a $30 million market in 1999, with 5% of high-volume billers offering such services and an additional 25% planning to do so within a year.[29] EBPP offers the ability to present a company's bill on multiple platforms online, and it offers actual payment processes. Payments are generally electronic transfers from consumer checking accounts. This is conducted through the ACH (*Automated Clearing House*), the current method for processing electronic monetary transfers.

TradeCard[28] (Cont.)

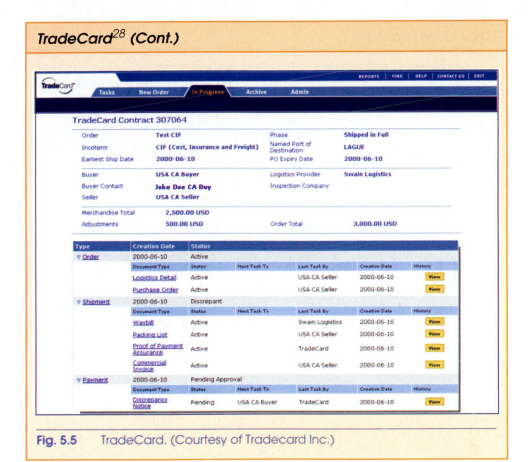

Fig. 5.5   TradeCard. (Courtesy of Tradecard Inc.)

CheckFree [30]

CheckFree is a *consolidation service* that can service any biller and present consumers with all their bills in one interactive online environment. Many financial institutions that offer EBPP use Checkfree technology, including Yahoo! and most major U.S. banks.[31] If a biller has a partnership with CheckFree, the bill will arrive electronically in the recipient's CheckFree inbox.

If the company or person you wish to pay does not offer electronic billing, you can still set up payment to them from any bank account using the *pay everyone* service. All that is necessary is the recipient's address. CheckFree will print out a hardcopy check against your account and send it to anyone you wish to pay.

For billers, the e-billing option can add convenience and lower costs. While it costs anywhere between 50 cents and $2 to process a paper bill, e-bills cost 35 to 50 cents each.[32] For financial institutions, CheckFree offers its technology and services to enable a bank's site to become a comprehensive bill-payment portal.

CheckFree *(Cont.)* [30]

All payments and outstanding bills can be tracked online and consumers have interactive access to their entire payment histories. Users can postdate payments as with paper checks and set up automatic recurring payments for such things as mortgage payments and insurance premiums. CheckFree will alert you if there is a problem with any of your payments. Records of transactions can be exported to financial software such as Quicken. A Flash demo of the user experience can be found at **www.check-free.com**. We discuss Flash in detail in Chapter 33—Macromedia Flash makes Web sites "come alive" with graphics, animations, audios and even videos.

Paytrust (**www.paytrust.com**) has a consumer-focused approach to e-billing. Users send their bills directly to Paytrust, which then scans them and places them online for the consumer to view. Paytrust e-mails to the customer announcements of newly arrived bills and impending payment-due dates, and it will make automatic payments on any bill up to a threshold amount. It offers users the option to pay their bills anywhere using the Palm VII hand-held computer. Paytrust also offers *SmartBalance*, which enables secure integration of users' Paytrust activity with their online bank account balances.[33] For a demo visit **demo.paytrust.com/server/BillCenter.asp**.

Other companies accommodate billers, presenting them with services to enable EBPP. One such company is Derivion (**www.derivion.com**), which entered a partnership with Paytrust to accelerate consumer adoption of EBPP. Derivion provides billers with electronic capabilities in conjunction with Paytrust's service. Derivion offers billing companies the technology and expertise needed to transfer from paper to electronic billing through a product known as *iNetBiller*[SM]. iNetBiller also allows the billing company to maintain control over its e-bills. Billers can continue to use customized bills including their logo and style to maintain continuity. This increases cross-marketing possibilities and individual access to consumers. For example, a credit-card bill could include a link to upgrade the card level if the bill exceeds a predetermined threshold. Another example is a phone bill including a link to wireless services offered by the same provider. A demo can be found linked at **www.derivion.com**.[34]

Encirq (**www.encirq.com**) partners with banks that issue credit cards, presenting the consumer with what Encirq calls an *illuminated statement.* The illuminated statement is interactive, placing special offers from retail merchants to correspond with the itemized charges on a credit-card statement. Encirq's product offers even more cross-marketing possibilities than those previously mentioned in that both the financial institution and the merchant are able to target customers with promotions.

Encirq does this by building and updating a highly specific consumer profile each time a new set of charges is received. Then the consumer is categorized and matched with advertisers and specific advertisements. All of this is done in a secure environment where neither the merchant nor Encirq itself is privy to the consumer's statement. The Encirq program is loaded onto the consumer's desktop and advertisements are matched to the consumer's purchasing profile.[35]

Encirq receives revenue from merchant ads and splits the profits with the financial institutions that host the illuminated statements.[36] This allows financial institutions to put to use the valuable marketing information they have about their customers without violating the consumer's privacy. This service is optional. If consumers are happy with the service and take advantage of the merchant's offers, the result is greater use of the financial institution's credit cards, increasing profits and customer loyalty. Overall, this will provide financial institutions with a further reason to offer direct online billing services.[37]

5.11 Online Banking

One of the fastest growing online service industries is online banking, either as an extension of services from a traditional bank or as a purely online entity.[38] Banks such as Wells Fargo and Bank of America offer online banking and services such as e-wallets. *Internet-only banks* offer convenience and lower rates to their customers by forgoing traditional services provided by banks, such as interest rates and fees.[39]

Despite the number of Internet-only banks, the desire for physical banks among consumers is apparent. Customers still like to know that there is a physical branch to visit in case they need to speak with a representative when they are having banking problems.[40]

Nevertheless, the convenience of online banking appeals to many, especially those who have had a hard time keeping track of their finances and who appreciate having access to an instantly updated account history. Internet-only banks are looking into techniques for establishing a physical presence, such as partnering with existing bank ATM networks. For example, **E*Trade.com**'s new online banking service has placed interactive kiosks that can accept deposits in stores.[41]

The hybrid bank model has found much success, with nine of the nation's ten leading commercial banks offering online services.[42] In addition, going online has become important for the survival and growth of small local banks—those that have traditionally relied on customer relations skills to attract customers. By going online, small banks can offer competitive services and attract national customers. An example is the Busey Bank, based in the college town of Urbana, Illinois. Busey went online in an effort to retain college customers who were away for the summer months. In a year it doubled its online customers, citing the customer-service opportunities available through e-mail as a major factor in its success.[43]

Smaller banks will usually partner with third-party service providers to make the transition to the Internet. Overall, this is cheaper than larger banks' attempts to implement electronic banking from scratch.[44]

This is the major trend affecting online banking institutions of all sizes. Since the repeal of the *Glass-Steagle Act*—which prohibited financial institutions from engaging in multiple financial operations—banks, brokerages and insurance companies are permitted to offer a wide range of financial services. **Excite.com** has partnered with Bank One to add various financial services to its general Web portal, while **E*Trade.com** has developed online banking in addition to its brokerage services. Most online financial services offer EBPP as well, and the vast majority use CheckFree's technology through partnership.[45]

Claritybank.com is an Internet-only bank that specializes in loans to new-economy firms.[48] Claritybank's marketing and Web site stress the high-speed abilities of online banking as a selling point to technology firms. Claritybank offers a customized portal service and a B2B center. Free Internet access is also available in exchange for keeping a navigation bar with Claritybank's logo on your screen, is also available. After only two weeks in operation, the bank has collected $6 million in deposits and has enjoyed strong loan-application volume.[49]

Wells Fargo[46]

Wells Fargo (`www.wellsfargo.com`) is a leading provider of online banking services. The bank has achieved a large online clientele based on the strength of its traditional banking services. Its online services are geared towards accounts of all sizes.

Services are broken into three main sectors; personal finance, small business and commercial banking. The bank's strategy is to promote itself as a financial resource center, offering personal banking customers free bill-paying and checking-account comparisons, as well as a help center for paying taxes.

Wells Fargo also plans to unveil a portal site that will offer financial services, such as stock trading, as well as news, weather and other services.[47] The site will send e-mail alerts of price changes in customers' stocks. It is also planning to use its portal site as a *financial aggregator*, which would allow people to view information from all of their financial accounts, regardless of holding institution.

In addition to the portal service, Wells Fargo is establishing highly specialized resource centers for students, retirees and those looking to purchase cars or homes. Such centers offer financial information and other links. The retirement center, for example, offers education and interactive tools on retirement planning, featuring special reports from outside sources. Customers can also open IRAs online and seek financial counseling. The student center features information on student checking and credit, and links to outside loan and scholarship information.

The Wells Fargo site cross-markets the products and services of other companies as well, such as Internet-access from Pacific Bell.

Another online bank that has enjoyed success in a specific market is `OneCore.com`, which targets small businesses.[50] The bank offers packages to businesses at different stages of growth. Packages include interest rates on loans and customized services. They offer financial-overview services that are compatible with leading financial software packages. Payroll and 401K services, enabling of credit-card processing for would-be merchants, and payables streamlining services are also offered. Additionally, an "electronic financial officer" is available who will answer business financial questions via e-mail.[51]

5.12 Internet and World Wide Web Resources

General

`www.thestandard.net`
`thestandard.net` is an online magazine devoted to the Internet economy. E-commerce is among the subject headings and it provides a list of links to various electronic-payment systems.

`ganges.cs.tcd.ie/mepeirce/Project/oninternet.html`
A list of links to various electronic payment systems is provided at this site.

`www.internetindicators.com`
This site provides Internet economic data. It is intended for people interested in learning about the Internet economy.

NetBank[52]

Netbank began offering lending, investing and high-interest checking services on the Web in 1996. NetBank is the largest bank operating solely on the Internet. Customers have the ability to open checking, savings and credit accounts which can be managed from their desktop. Customers can also plan for retirement using IRAs and other types of investment accounts as well as conduct online trading through NetBank.

NetBank customers can obtain mortgage, car and business loans by applying directly on the Web. All details of this process are outlined on the NetBank Web site along with the rates and calculators to help you make a qualified decision.

Customers have the choice of using money-market funds, buying certificates of deposit (CD), trading stocks and bonds and investing in their retirement. Each of these options is available at competitive rates.

Customers also receive a line of credit, free online bill payment and presentment, an ATM card and a Visa credit card. For a demonstration on online bill payment and presentment visit **www.netbank.com/demo/demo_index.htm**.

Credit–Card Payment

www.cybercash.com
CyberCash provides e-merchants with the ability to accept credit-card payments online. They also offer an e-wallet technology and an online bill-paying service.

www.icat.com
iCat enables merchants to accept credit cards online. It will host your Web site and aid in site design.

www.trintech.com
Trintech offers a secure credit-card payment system that enables simultaneous purchases from multiple stores. This is used in virtual shopping malls.

shopping.altavista.com/home.sdc
This is the site of AltaVista's shopping mall. It uses the Payware eIssuer technology.

www.intelicharge.com
Intelicharge specializes in merchant-account management. It settles merchant accounts on the same day of the request.

www.onlineorders.net
Onlineorders.net provides links and factual information regarding online payments and the methods of implementing payment systems.

E-Wallets

www.visa.com/pd/ewallet/main.html
Visa offers various e-wallets for use with Visa credit cards. These wallets are backed by a specific financial institution that issues a Visa card.

www.entrypoint.com
Entrypoint's product is a personalized desktop toolbar that offers easy access to news, sports, finance, travel and shopping. It includes an e-wallet feature for use at affiliate Internet stores.

www.MBNAwallet.com
MBNA allows you to make all of your online purchases quickly and easily.

`www.brodia.com`
Brodia promises e-wallet services which allow users to store their credit-card numbers and other purchasing information for shopping online.

Checking Account Payment
`www.debit-it.com`
`debit-it.com` allows merchants to draw against the balance in their checking account number as a valid form of payment over the Internet.

`www.netchex.com`
`Netchex.com` allows customers to set up an online debit-card system where all purchases are deducted from a single Netchex account. This enables people to shop without using a credit card.

Digital Cash
`www.ecash.net`
eCash offers digital cash services for both online purchases and peer-to-peer payment.

`www.flooz.com`
Flooz is a form of digital cash that is used as a gift currency. Customers buy Flooz currency with their credit cards and then establish accounts as gifts. The recipient can then spend the Flooz account at participating stores.

`www.beenz.com`
beenz is an international, points-based currency system. It allows vendors to offer a promotional system on their Web site.

`www.giftcertificates.com`
`Giftcertificates.com` allows Internet users to purchase gift certificates online.

`www.internetcash.com`
Internetcash is a digital currency that is aimed at teenagers. The currency is purchased through prepaid cards at convenience stores. Affiliated merchants are targeted to a young demographic.

`abracad.users.netlink.co.uk/emoney.html`
This is a link to a general resource page on digital cash technology.

Peer-To-Peer Payment
`www.paypal.com/cgi-bin/webscr?cmd=index`
PayPal offers a peer-to-peer payment system that enables anyone to receive payment from anyone else via e-mail. The payment can be made by credit card or checking account.

`www.billpoint.com`
This site offers a peer-to-peer credit-card payment system designed by eBay and Wells Fargo and used on the eBay auction site.

`www.tradesafe.com`
Tradesafe is a credit-card peer-to-peer payment system that is aimed at business-to-business transactions. They provide B2B services and special security for large transactions.

Smart Cards
`www.scia.com`
The Smart Card Industry Association Web site provides information of smart-card technology and services.

`www.visa.com/nt/chip/info.html`
This page contains information on the forthcoming smart card being offered by Visa, which will contain a digital cash application and e-wallet services.

www.smart-card.com
A monthly e-magazine that contains comprehensive information on smart-card technology, as well as links to other sites.

www.nextcard.com
Nextcard has developed a credit card specifically designed for the Web. Online payments can be made with a built-in digital wallet.

Micropayments

www.hut.fi/~jkytojok/micropayments
This is a paper on electronic-payment systems with a focus on micropayments.

www.echarge.com
eCharge partners with AT&T to provide micropayment services billed to the user's phone bill.

www.ipin.com
iPin allows charges from micropayment purchases to appear on the customer's ISP bill.

www.trivnet.com
Trivnet's technology bills micropayment purchases to the customer's ISP bill.

www.qpass.com
Qpass is an e-commerce enabler. It allows companies to sell products and conduct secure transactions over the Web. It can provide the infrastructure needed to run your e-business.

www.millicent.digital.com
Millicent allows customers and e-businesses to conduct transactions using micropayments.

www.hut.fi/~jkytojok/micropayments/index.html
This is a tutorial on micropayments written by Jari Kytöjoki, Vesa Kärpijoki for the Department of Computer Science at Helsinki University of Technology.

www.w3.mag.keio.ac.jp/ECommerce/Micropayments/Overview.html#What
This overview of micropayments was created by the World Wide Web Consortium (W3C).

B2B

www.ecredit.com
eCredit helps entrepreneurs and established businesses find credit to support their online operations. eCredit will also help you manage your money once it has been earned.

www.clareon.com
Clareon provides full cycle e-commerce solutions connecting buyers and sellers with a secure payment system.

www.etimecapital.com
eTimeCapital provides a solution for accounts receivable and cash-flow management on the Web.

www.tradecard.com
Tradecard handles international trade and e-commerce over the Web. Tradecard provides secure online payments.

EBPP

www.checkfree.com
Checkfree allows you to receive and pay your bills online.

www.paytrust.com
Paytrust is a an online bill-payment system. Paytrust allows you to access and pay your bills with the *Palm VII* organizer.

www.derivion.com
Derivion gives bill-payment capabilities to companies like **CheckFree.com**

www.encirq.com
Encirq allows bill payment sites to add targeted advertising to online customer statements.

Online Banking

www.netbank.com
NetBank is the leading Internet-only bank.

www.etrade.com
E*TRADE is an online brokerage firm that is preparing to become a financial portal site.

www.clarity.com
This is an online bank that specializes in helping technology firms.

www.onecore.com
This is an online bank that specializes in helping small businesses.

www.wellsfargo.com
Wells Fargo is an online branch of California-based commercial bank.

SUMMARY

- The electronic transfer of funds is a growing aspect of e-commerce, and one that is key to conducting e-business successfully.
- The major online payment schemes currently in use include payments by credit card, cash, and check, payments to businesses, peer-to-peer payments, banking and bill paying.
- Customers fear credit-card fraud by merchants or other parties.
- In order to accept credit-card payments, a merchant must have a merchant account with a bank.
- E-wallets allow you to keep track of your billing and shipping information so that it can be entered with one click at participating merchants' sites. They also store e-checks, e-cash and your credit-card information for multiple cards.
- In order to standardize e-wallet technology and gain a wider acceptance among vendors, Visa, MasterCard, American Express and a group of e-wallet vendors have developed the Electronic Commerce Modeling Language (ECML).
- Although electronic payment is more convenient, Internet merchants that do not accept credit cards can accept payments such as checks or money orders through the mail.
- Debit cards offer an alternative for card-holders to access their savings, checking and other accounts. These cards can be used in the same way as a credit card, but, instead of paying a monthly bill, the charge is automatically deducted from the customer's checking account.
- Banks and businesses are also creating options for online payment that do not involve credit cards.
- There are many forms of digital currency; digital cash is one example. It is stored electronically and can be used to make online electronic payments.
- Digital-cash accounts are similar to traditional bank accounts; consumers deposit money into their digital-cash accounts to be used in their digital transactions.
- Aside from alleviating some of the security fears that many people have about online credit-card transactions, digital cash allows people who do not have credit cards to shop online, and merchants who accept digital cash payments avoid credit-card transaction fees.
- Gift cash, often sold as points, is another form of digital currency that can be redeemed at leading shopping sites. It is an effective way of giving teen shoppers, or those without credit cards, the ability to make purchases on the Web.

- Some companies offer points-based rewards offered in exchange for completing specified tasks. These tasks may include visiting Web sites, registering or buying products.

- Peer-to-peer transactions allow the online transfer of money between consumers.

- PayPal allows a user to send money to anyone with an e-mail address, regardless of what bank either person uses or whether or not the recipient is pre-registered with the service.

- The X Payment system can be used to enable credit-card payment for auction items in real time. This means that the transaction begins processing immediately after it is initiated, reducing the risk of fraud or overdrawn accounts.

- eBay and Wells Fargo offer another form of peer-to-peer payment called BillPoint. It allows buyers to submit electronic payments to sellers' checking accounts.[13]

- Another peer-to-peer payment company, **Tradesafe.com**, accommodates the larger amounts typically involved in B2B transactions.

- A smart card, a card with a computer chip embedded on its face, is able to hold more information than an ordinary credit card with a magnetic strip.

- Smart-card technology has many applications. Smart cards can be used to store health care, transportation, identification, purchasing, loyalty programs and banking information, to name a few.

- There are contact and contactless smart cards.

- eConnect's product, eCashPad is a device that connects to your computer and scrambles financial data, making it secure to send over the Internet.

- Visa has created Visa Cash, a smart card used to store money and make purchases.

- Micropayments, which generally do not exceed $10, offer a way for companies offering nominally priced products and services (music, pictures, text or video) to generate a profit; they offer consumers a cost-efficient means of acquiring this material.

- The fastest growing sector of e-commerce payments is business-to-business (B2B) transactions. These payments are often much larger in size than B2C transactions and involve complex business accounting systems.

- EBT (Electronic Benefits Transfer) is defined by the USDA as the electronic transfer of government funds to retailers for the benefit of the needy.

- eCredit provides real-time, credit-transaction capabilities of B2B size.

- Aside from enabling electronic payment, many business-oriented services are aimed at electronic consolidation and reconciliation of the business transaction process.

- **SubmitOrder.com** can receive shipments at its warehouses directly from the merchant's manufacturers; the service then keeps track of the inventory and communicates electronically with the merchant.

- E-billing technologies are finding success in the B2C market, where transactions are less complicated than B2B transactions.

- Paytrust has a consumer-focused approach to e-billing. Users send their bills directly to Paytrust, which then scans them and places them online for the consumer to view.

- Encirq's illuminated statement is interactive and includes special offers from retail merchants that correspond with the itemized charges on a credit-card statement.

- One of the fastest growing online services is online banking, either as an extension of services from a traditional bank or as a purely online entity.

- Despite the number of Internet-only banks, the desire for physical banks among consumers is apparent. Customers still like to know that there is a physical branch to visit in case they need to speak with a representative when they are having banking problems.

- Internet-only banks are looking into techniques for establishing a physical presence, such as partnering with existing bank ATM networks.

TERMINOLOGY

ACH (Automated Clearing House)	Glass-Steagle Act
Advanced Fraud Detection	Global Financing Network
Amerinet	InfoLink
ANI (Automatic Number Identification)	illuminated statement
AutoBuy	iNetBiller
Automatic Teller Machines (ATMs)	Internet-only banking
business-to-business (B2B)	logistics
bankonewallet	merchant account
BusinessVerify	Merchant Connection Kit (MCK)
consolidation service	micropayment
contact smart card	mobile payment
contactless smart card	Office of Foreign Assets Control (OFAC)
CyberCash CashRegister	order-fulfillment provider
CyberCash Instabuy	pay-everyone services
debit card	PaymentNet
DecisionDesktop	peer-to-peer payment
digital cash	point-of-sale (POS) transactions
digital payment authentication (DPA)	PowerWallet
eCashPad	real time
Electronic Benefits Transfer (EBT)	redundant servers
Electronic Bill Presentment and Payment (EBPP)	smart card
Electronic Commerce Modeling Language (ECML)	smart card reader
	SmartBalance
Electronic Data Exchange (EDI)	Standard Fraud Detection
eMerchant	third-party logistics service provider
e-PocketPay	Trintech eHost
enterprise resource planning (ERP)	Trintech eIssuer
e-wallet	virtual credit card
electronic payment	Visa Cash
fulfillment	X Payments

SELF-REVIEW EXERCISES

5.1 State whether the following are true or false. If the answer is false, explain why.
a) An e-commerce site must establish a merchant account with a bank before credit-card orders can be processed online.
b) `E*Trade.com` has developed online banking in addition to its brokerage services.
c) The MBNA digital wallet allows the user to store their purchasing information in a universal wallet, that can be used when making purchases at different sites.
d) eCash is accepted by all e-commerce Web sites as a form of payment.
e) Peer-to-peer payment can only be conducted using a credit card.
f) eCharge is a micropayments system that is billed through your e-mail account.
g) Micropayments are small sums of money that can be charged to a user for products and services bought online.
h) INetBiller is a peer-to-peer payment system.
i) Smart cards can only be used to make online purchases.
j) A contactless smart card has both a coiled antenna and a computer chip inside.

k) EBPP stands for electronic bill presentment and payment.

5.2   Fill in the blanks in each of the following:
   a) Millicent offers a cost effective system of collecting small sums of money over the Internet. These small sums are called _____.
   b) Credit cards offering a higher level of security and interactivity over the Internet are called _____.
   c) One-click payments are made possible through the use of a(n) _____.
   d) A(n)_____ allows a business to accept a credit card online.
   e) The e-wallet solution available from CyberCash is called _____.
   f) The _____ payment system allows for monetary transactions over the Internet between two consumers.
   g) iPin offers micropayments that are billed to the client within their _____ bill.
   h) A _____ stores information on the user's computer, providing one-click shopping at participating merchants.
   i) _____, an online service created by CyberCash, makes it possible for merchants to receive credit-card numbers, offer the numbers to the appropriate financial institution for validation and accept them as a form of payment in a secure environment over the Web.
   j) Visa, Mastercard and a group of e-wallet vendors have standardized e-wallet technology with the _____.
   k) The _____, now repealed, prohibited financial institutions from engaging in multiple financial operations.

ANSWERS TO SELF-REVIEW EXERCISES

5.1   a) True. b) True. c) True. d) False. Only participating stores accept eCash. The customer, merchant and bank must all be able to use the eCash system e) False. Payment options vary by vendor. Some options include e-mail, and through account held within a secure Web site. f) False. eCharge is a micropayments system that automatically places charges on your home phone bill. g) True. h) False. INetBiller is a online billing provider offering custom products. i) False. Smart cards are traditional bank cards with added security and interactivity. j) True. k) True.

5.2   a) Micropayments. b) Smart cards. c) E-wallet. d) Merchant account. e) Instabuy. f)Peer-to-peer. g) ISP. h) virtual credit card. i) CashRegister. j) Electronic Commerce Modeling Language (ECML). k) Glass-Steagle Act.

EXERCISES

5.3   Categorize each of the following items as either e-billing or peer-to-peer payment:
   a) PayPal
   b) Consumer-to-consumer
   c) CheckFree
   d) Encirq
   e) BillPoint
   f) TradeSafe

5.4   Take the BillPoint test drive at **www.billpoint.com/help/tutorial.html**. What do you think of the BillPoint system? What are its strengths? What are its weaknesses?

5.5   Take a few minutes and surf the Web. Make a top ten list of the companies providing electronic banking services. Make a note of significant differences or points of interest you come across.

5.6   Define each of the following terms:
   a) digital cash
   b) peer-to-peer payment

c) Wells Fargo
d) e-wallet
e) micropayments
f) EBPP
g) merchant account
h) smart card

5.7   Search the Web for e-money. Find ten different forms of e-currency (e-cash, beenz, etc.). How do these systems differ? List each of the ten forms of currency and include a description. Rank each one against the others. Which do you think is the best form of online currency and why?

5.8   Draw a diagram illustrating the relationship between the customer, the customer's bank, the merchant and the merchant's bank in a typical offline cash transaction. Then draw a diagram using an electronic cash payment system to illustrate these relationships.

5.9   Categorize each of the following items as either a peer-to-peer company, an online payment system or a Micropayment company.

a) Qpass
b) Millicent
c) PayPal
d) TradeSafe
e) iPin
f) smart card
g) e-wallet
h) BillPoint

5.10   In the chapter we discuss online payment systems. What is your preferred transaction method? Discuss the methods we covered:

a) Smart cards
b) E-billing
c) Peer-to-peer billing
d) E-cash
e) Others

5.11   This exercise will have to be done in groups. Each member of the group will play a role. One member will play the role of a merchant. The next will play a customer. The rest of the group should become the banks for both parties. Remove three pieces of paper. On the first, write payment. On the second write product. On the third write smart card. Conduct the transaction for the following scenarios.Did you run into problems? What conclusions can you draw from the exercise? Is the Internet more efficient for conducting transactions?

a) A traditional purchase and sale
b) Cash on delivery
c) Smart card
d) Peer-to-peer payment

WORKS CITED

The notation *<www.domain-name.com>* indicates that the citation is for information found at that Web site.

1.   `<www.prodigycard.com/About.html>`.
2.   `<www.icat.com>`.
3.   `<www.trintech.com>`.
4.   `<www.cybercash.com>`.

5.   `<www.visa.com/pd/ewallet/main.html>`.

6.   `<www.entrypoint.com>`.

7.   M. Barnett, "Credit-Card Heavies Unveil E-wallet Standard," **`<Thestandard.com>`** 14 June 1999.

8.   `<www.debit-it.com>`.

9.   `<www.flooz.com>`.

10. `<www.beenz.com>`.

11. `<www.internetcash.com>`.

12. `<www.paypal.com>`.

13. G. Anders, "EBay, Wells Team Up on Web Payments," *The Wall Street Journal* 1 March 2000.,

14. `<www.billpoint.com>`.

15. `<www.tradesafe.com>`.

16. `<www.gemplus.com/basics/what.htm>`.

17. `<www.econnectholdings.com/econ_intro.html>`.

18. `<www.echarge.com>`.

19. `<www.qpass.com.>`.

20. `<www.millicent.com>`.

21. J. Vijayan, "Business-to-Business Billing No easy Task," *Computerworld* 13 March 2000: 20.

22. `<www.usda.gov>`.

23. `<www.paymentech.com>`.

24. `<www.ecredit.com>` and customer service representative.

25. `<www.clareon.com>`.

26. `<www.etimecapital.com>`.

27. `<www.submitorder.com>`.

28. `<www.tradecard.com>`.

29. `<www.treas.gov/ofac>`.

30. `<www.checkfree.com >` and customer service representative.

31. M. Richey, "A Checklist for CheckFree," **`MotleyFool.com`** 23 May 2000.

32. Le Beau, C. "The Big Payoff," **`TheStandard.com`** 8 May 2000.

33. `<www.paytrust.com>`.

34. `<www.derivion.com>`.

35. `<www.encirq.com>`.

36. M. Charski, "Extending Credit-Card Bills," *Inter@ctive Week* 22 May 2000: 63.

37. `<www.encirq.com>`.

38. G. Gottlieg, "Big Changes Coming in the Banking Industry," *Net Commerce Magazine* March 2000: 16.

39. S. Rose, "The Truth About Online Banking," *Money* April 2000: 119.

40. J. Labate and G. Silverman, "World Wide Web Is Not Wide Enough," *Financial Times* 6 April 2000: 20.

41. P. Patsuris, "Veterans From First USA, Wingspan Form New Net Bank," **Forbes.com** 25 May 2000.

42. S. Junnakar, "Web Banks Look to Branch Out," <**news.cnet.com/news/0-1007-200-1551999.html**>16 February 2000.

43. L. Berlin, "Small Change," **TheStandard.com** 8 May 2000.

44. J. Sapsford, "Smaller Institutions Make Web Inroads Via Outsourcing," *The Wall Street Journal* 21 January 2000: C1.

45. E. Buckley, "Green Revolution," **TheStandard.com** 8 May 2000.

46. <**www.wellsfargo.com**>.

47. D. Levine, "Wells' Next Stage," **TheStandard.com** 8 May 2000.

48. K. Weisul, "Wingspan Causes Online Banking Flap," *Inter@ctive Week* 27 March 2000: 24.

49. B. Menninger, "Small or Not at All," **TheStandard.com** 8 May 2000.

50. Menninger, "Small or Not at All."

51. <**www.onecore.com**>.

52. <**www.netbank.com**>.

Legal, Ethical and Social Issues; Internet Taxation

Objectives

- To explore the issues of online privacy.
- To review the current applications of traditional law to the Internet: defamation, intellectual property, unsolicited e-mail and sexually explicit speech.
- To understand the impact of traditional law on e-commerce.
- To understand the limitations of traditional law with regard to the Internet.
- To explore the issues of Internet regulation.
- To examine the creation of online communities.
- To understand the Internet's global challenges.
- To review issues regarding Internet taxation.

We deal with the right of privacy older than the Bill of Rights – older than our political parties, older than our school system.
William O. Douglas

He plants trees to benefit another generation.
Caecilius Statius

Truth is generally the best vindication against slander.
Abraham Lincoln

Taxes, after all, are the dues we pay for the privilege of membership in an organized society.
Franklin D. Roosevelt

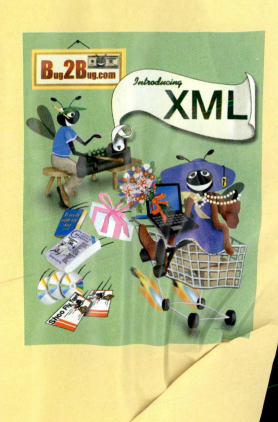

Outline

Introduction

chapter we explore the ways in which the Internet has presented us with legal, ethical
challenges. We will investigate the differences between "*real space*," our phys-
content consisting of temporal and geographic boundaries, and "*cyberspace*," the
in which transmission not limited by geography. In real space, we operate under a
ethics. In cyberspace, this is not necessarily the case. It is a unique forum
languages of programming, govern.[1]

6.2 Legal Issues: Privacy on the Internet

The application of traditional law to the Internet is not always a smooth process. In this section we will explore technologies that present new challenges to the maintenance of privacy.

6.2.1 Right to Privacy

An individual's right to privacy is not explicitly guaranteed by the Constitution, but it is implicitly guaranteed through the First, Fourth, Ninth and Fourteenth Amendments.[2] Of those listed, the Fourth Amendment provides U.S. citizens with the greatest assurance of privacy in that it protects them from search and seizure.

> The right of the people to be secure in their persons, houses, papers, and effects, against unreasonable searches and seizures, shall not be violated, and no Warrant shall issue, but upon probable cause, supported by Oath or affirmation, and particularly describing the place to be searched, and the person or things to be seized.

When the Fourth Amendment was drafted, trespassing was the privacy issue of greatest concern. Problems with applying the Fourth Amendment began to appear when the right to individual privacy moved beyond private property. In the landmark case, *Olmstead v. United States*, which involved the telecommunication of illegal alcohol sales during the Prohibition era, the Supreme Court ruled that information obtained through the tapping of telephone wires fell outside the protection of the Fourth Amendment.

This example demonstrates the need for *translation*,[3] or interpreting the Constitution to protect the greater good. At the time, trespassing was the violation in question. The invention of the telephone required the regulation against trespassing to be interpreted to meet the needs of the majority of the population.

6.2.2 Internet and the Right to Privacy

The Internet is currently a *self-regulated medium*, which means the Internet industry essentially governs itself. This enables the Internet to flourish without the constraints of legislation, but it also creates problems because there are no specific guidelines to follow.

Privacy is one of the driving forces behind potential federal regulation. The FTC found that 97 percent of Web sites studied collected personal information, but only 62 percent of those sites gave any indication to the consumer that information was being collected and 57 percent of studied sites contained third-party tracking devices.[4] In another survey, conducted by **Enonymous.com**, a Web company that provides privacy-sensitive marketing services and technologies, only 3.5 percent of the 30,000 Web sites studied earned a four-star rating (out of four stars) on their privacy policies. Four stars signify internal-use-only of user information and request-only solicitation.[5]

Recent studies show that 90 percent of consumers say online security is a major concern, and 50 percent are hesitant to use their credit-card number for online transactions. These statistics are particularly significant given the many advantages of conducting sales versus doing business through traditional *brick-and-mortar establishments*.

Many Internet companies collect users' personal information as they browse a site. While privacy advocates argue that these efforts violate individuals' rights, online marketers and advertisers disagree—they suggest that, by recording likes and dislikes of online consumers, online companies can better serve their customers.

The U.S. is establishing commissions to study online privacy. The *Financial Services Modernization Act of 1999* establishes a set of regulations concerning the management of consumer information. For example, businesses must provide consumers with an opportunity to *opt out* of having their information shared with third parties.[7]

6.2.3 Tracking Devices

Some of the methods used by online advertisers, online communities and online businesses to keep track of their visitors' behavior are called *tracking devices*. Online tracking identifies what activities and products are most popular among consumers. While having the Web experience tailored to them may appeal to some users, others consider having their actions recorded to be a violation of their privacy.

The *Personalization Consortium* is a newly formed alliance of major Web sites. Its goal is to accommodate those individuals who prefer to have their Web experiences tailored. In June, 2000, the Consortium released a study suggesting that most users actually prefer to have their information stored and actions tracked. The results of the study can be viewed at **www.personalization.org**.[7]

Several tracking devices are used online. In addition to cookies, which will be discussed later in this section, advertisers and Web-site owners also use *ID cards, click-through banner advertisements* and *Web bugs.*

An ID card enables information to be sent to your computer from a Web site. Your name and e-mail address are not included. Only the numerical address of your PC on the Internet, your browser and your operating system are necessary for your computer to retrieve information.[9]

Click-through advertisements are similar to the billboards you see along the side of the highway. Consumers can view the service or product by "clicking" on the advertisement. This also serves as a tracking device, as advertisers can learn what sites generate the most click-through sales.[10]

Web Bugs, or *clear GIFs,* are embedded in an image on the screen. Site owners allow their partners to hide these information-collecting programs on various parts of their sites. This method of tracking allows affiliates to gather consumer information.[11]

6.2.4 Cookies

A *cookie* is a text file stored by a Web site on an individual's personal computer that allows a site to track the actions of its visitors. The first time a computer visits a Web site it may receive a cookie. This cookie is reactivated each time the computer revisits that site or an affiliate site. The information collected is intended to be an anonymous account of log-on [times], the length of stay at the site, purchases made on the site, the site previously visited [and the] site visited next. Although the cookie resides on an individual's hard drive, it does [not interact] with other information stored on the system.

[Cookies] can be beneficial to the consumer. They record passwords for returning visitors, [keep track] of shopping-cart materials and register preferences. Cookies also help businesses [by enabling] them to address their target market with greater accuracy. However, [these advantages ma]y be gained at the price of consumer privacy. The use of cookies for [online advertising] advertising was discussed in Chapter 4.

Suppose you are browsing the Web for the lowest price on a digital camera. You might register for a contest or make a purchase, leaving your mailing address and some other personal information. As you travel from site to site, you might notice the advertisements are for companies that sell digital cameras. If you return to a former site you might be welcomed by name. Potentially, the sites you have visited belong to a direct advertising network, and, rather than one site gathering this information about you and using it for future sale, information from several sites will be used to create a *consumer profile*.

This type of tracking can be beneficial to the consumer. After you complete your first purchase at **Amazon.com**, all subsequent purchases can be made without having to re-enter your mailing address and contact information. If you are looking for a specific item, advertisements that appear along the way can lead you in the right direction.

Now consider a different scenario. Let us suppose you are planning your first trip to Washington, D.C. You would like to visit the White House Web site, so you type in **www.whitehouse.com**. Actually, the White House is a government establishment, so the domain extension you need is "**.gov**" (**www.whitehouse.gov**). Before you realize this, you enter the address ending in **.com** and, to your surprise, you are now browsing a pornography site. At the time you may consider this a small inconvenience. You go and enjoy your trip.

Six months later, you are bidding on an apartment in a respectable neighborhood. The landlord is reviewing the applications, comes across a documentation of your Internet activity, discovers you have recently visited a pornography site (**www.white-house.com**) and decides that you are not eligible to rent the apartment. This is only one of many problems privacy advocates fear.

Many people are unaware that they can disable cookies. However, it must be noted that disabling a cookie may exclude the user from some Web sites. Cookie files can be viewed by searching the hard drive for the appropriate directory containing the "cookie" file. To locate this file on your PC, go to **Search** on your **Start** menu and search for the cookie directory.

DoubleClick: Marketing with Personal Information

While privacy advocate groups argue that the Web will not survive without some form of regulation, advertising organizations disagree. DoubleClick, an Internet advertising firm, suggests advertising must be effective to minimize Internet-related costs. Regulation of the Internet could limit a company's efforts to buy and sell advertising. As with television and radio advertising, the money generated by Internet advertising can allow people of all economic means to use the medium.[12]

Web sites use a variety of tracking methods to record where visitors come fr... where they go and what catches their interest along the way. This information i...ant your computer's IP address (i.e., the numerical address of your comp... over Internet), Web browser and operating system; it is used by marketers to...[13] This advertisements at specific computers. DoubleClick has an advertis...ally target 1,500 sites where banner advertisements for 11,000 of their... enables DoubleClick to combine data from many sites t... advertisements for particular computers.

DoubleClick: Marketing with Personal Information (Continued)

However, targeting a specific IP address, browser and operating system is less effective than targeting a specific consumer. In 1999, DoubleClick acquired Abacus Direct Corp., a direct-marketing organization. Abacus stores names, addresses, telephone numbers, age, gender, income levels and a history of purchases at retail, catalog and online stores. This acquisition enabled DoubleClick to attach personal information to the activities of what were once "nameless" personal computers.

One concern with this method of collecting and utilizing data is termed *digital redlining*.[14] Digital redlining suggests that a company could skew an individual's knowledge of available products by basing the advertisements the user sees on past behavior. This could allow advertisers to influence consumers' habits by limiting information they see to what the advertisers determine the consumers want to see.[15]

Direct marketing in the traditional sense affords a time lapse between an individual's purchases, the processing of that information and the use of that information to target that customer. However, users can be targeted instantly, as they browse the Internet.[16]

Perhaps of greater concern is the recording of personal activities. The Internet is valued as a medium in which users can search for information and express opinions anonymously. Privacy advocates are concerned that such data could be used against individuals attempting to obtain housing, get a loan, apply for insurance coverage or even deal with spousal disagreement and divorce.[17] For example, a user visiting a Web site to learn more about an illness might not want that information to be made available to insurance companies. DoubleClick promises to uphold its privacy policy, which assures users that the company will not collect financial, sexually oriented or medical information.

In response to privacy concerns, DoubleClick has postponed the merger of the information that it acquired from Abacus Direct with the data it gathered previously from online advertisements until an agreement among consumers, privacy advocates and the Internet industry is reached to determine the proper use of such consumer information.[18]

6.2.5 Employer and Employee

Many businesses monitor employee activities on corporate equipment. One of the newest surveillance technologies, *keystroke cops*, is creating tension between employers and employees.[19]

Keystroke software provides an inexpensive, easy-to-use method of monitoring productivity and the abuse of company equipment.[20] Products such as *Computer Usage Compliance Survey* from Codex Data Systems (**www.codexdatasystems.com**) allow business owners to create a custom user's policy to define how the company will monitor surfing, e-mailing, visits to restricted sites, downloading of inappropriate images and encryption. Another company, **www.surfsecurity.com**, offers a variety of surfware that is available at a fee for download from their site (**www.softse-**). The KCap TSR Keystroke Capture Utility 1.0, Stealthlogger ProBot v1.0 and 0 are available as free-trial downloads from **www.hotfiles.com**. loaded onto the hard drive of an employee's computer, or it can be sent as an e-mail attachment. Once activated, the software registers each keystroke before it appears on the screen. Many products also have scanning capabilities that enable them to search through documents for keywords such as "boss" and "union."[21]

The issue is most often one of company time and company equipment versus the First Amendment rights of employees. Situations may involve employees who neglect responsibilities to write personal e-mails, surf the Web or conduct online tirades against management in chat rooms.

In order to determine the outcome of court cases on those issues, the courts propose two criteria: 1) did the employee have a *reasonable expectation of privacy* and 2) does the business have *legitimate business interests* that would reasonably justify the intrusion of employee privacy?

Companies do have legitimate reasons for monitoring their employees' activities on the Internet. Employees that use company time for irrelevant Web surfing not only waste time, but also attract unsolicited e-mail. Increased traffic to the server means slower access for those employees using the Web for legitimate purposes.[22]

E-mails can reach large groups of people quickly and easily, creating the possibility of harassment suits. For example, e-mails of a questionable nature could be used to argue that the workplace is an unfriendly environment. To see how this works, read *Michael A. Smyth v. The Pillsbury Company*: Viewing Expectations of Privacy and Reasonable Business Interests.

Letting your employees know what is expected of them will, in many cases, cut back on the amount of time wasted surfing the Internet and sending e-mail to family and friends. When implementing a surveillance mechanism, make it known. This way, surveillance takes on a preventative role, saving both parties time and energy.

Michael A. Smyth v. The Pillsbury Company: Viewing Expectations of Privacy and Reasonable Business Interests

Based upon a series of unprofessional e-mail messages transmitted to his supervisor in October of 1994, Michael A. Smyth was dismissed as regional operations manager at The Pillsbury Company in February of 1995. After receiving his notification of termination, Mr. Smyth sued the company.

Mr. Smyth claimed that the Pillsbury Company had assured its employees that e-mail would not result in reprimand. However, under Pennsylvania law "an employer may discharge an employee with or without cause, at pleasure, unless restrained by some contract."[23]

Having to give up his claim of wrongful termination, Mr. Smyth then restructured his argument. Mr. Smyth suggested that the use of his personal e-mail against him was a violation of public policy. Examples of public policy violations condemned by the court include reprimanding an employee called for jury duty and denial of employment as a result of previous convictions.

However, the court did not find in favor of Mr. Smyth. It determined there was no reasonable expectation of privacy, nor was Mr. Smyth made to share personal information. Rather, the court determined that the Pillsbury Company had legitimate business purposes for its actions against Mr. Smyth.

6.2.6 Protecting Yourself as a User

Users are able to take on falsified identities or use software to maintain anonymity on the Web. For example, **PrivacyX.com**, a free Internet service, allows users to surf the Web unidentified (Fig. 6.1). To do this, **PrivacyX.com** creates a digital certificate for new users when they register. We discuss digital certificates and encryption in Chapter 7. What is unique to **PrivacyX.com**'s service is that anonymity can be maintained even in the digital certificate, which holds no personal information the user does not wish to include. **PrivacyX.com** then uses the digital certificate to return the requested information to the user, encrypted.

The World Wide Web Consortium is introducing the *Platform for Privacy Preferences Project (P3P)*. The Consortium will release a questionnaire to those users who have downloaded a newer version of the more popular browsers (e.g., Netscape Navigator and Internet Explorer) asking individual users about the level of privacy they desire. Then the browser will comply in accordance with users' answers by allowing them to interact in specific ways.[24] This method has been endorsed by the federal government as a means of avoiding legislation. Many Web sites, including AOL, AT&T, Microsoft and IBM, have begun to meet the P3P protocol.[25]

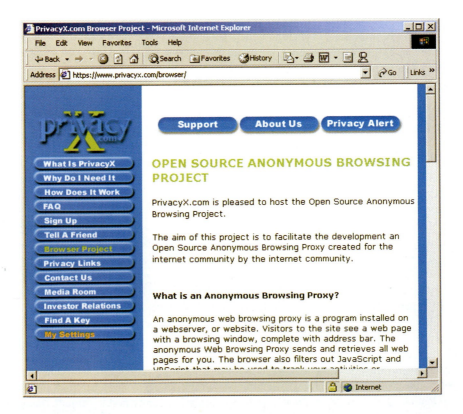

Fig. 6.1   PrivacyX.com (Courtesy of PrivacyX.com Solutions.)

Sites such as **www.junkbusters.com** and **www.privacychoices.org**, run by DoubleClick, instruct visitors how to avoid receiving direct mail and how to disable cookies. To find more information on privacy issues visit **www.cdt.org**, **www.eff.org**, **www.epic.org** and **www.privacyrights.org**.

6.2.7 Protecting Your Business: Privacy Issues

It is important to include a *privacy policy* on your Web site, respect the stated policy and treat your visitor's information with care. This means conducting regular audits to know exactly what information is being collected through your site. In the programming chapters of this book, we show you how to design, program and display forms on your clients' systems. We also show how to capture that information at your servers and use that information to update databases.

There are several services available over the Web that can generate a privacy policy according to your needs. For example, **PrivacyBot.com** features a questionnaire regarding your interest in collecting consumer information and how you plan to use the information you collect (Fig 6.2). For a fee, **PrivacyBot.com** issues an XML version of your privacy policy, authorizes the use of the official Trustmark seal to ensure users that you have an approved privacy policy and offers a mediation service should problems arise.[26] We discuss XML thoroughly and present case studies in Chapters 27 and 28.

Fig. 6.2   PrivacyBot.com. (Courtesy of Invisible Hand Software, LLC.)

PriceWaterhouseCoopers offers a similar service through its *BetterWeb*[SM] Program. Based on the study of businesses, consumer input, current industry standards and the arguments of privacy rights advocates, PriceWaterhouseCoopers created this program to assist developing and preexisting Web sites with their customer service programs. *The BetterWeb Standards*, as PWC has termed them, work for the benefit of both the consumer and the business by providing the consumer with "what they can expect from an online business regarding sales terms, security and privacy policies and consumer complaint procedures."[27] For more information, visit **www.pwcbetterweb.com/betterweb/index.cfm**.

Not all sites carrying the mark of a security company make the effort to follow their privacy guidelines. **TRUSTe.com**, one of the most recognized auditing organizations, grants businesses its seal to signify a trustworthy privacy protection plan. When users visit a **TRUSTe.com** site, they can be reasonably sure their information is being properly protected. However, it is still up to the organization to honor its stated privacy policies.

The Federal Trade Commission (FTC) has established five *Core Fair Information Practices* regarding online marketing tactics that involve gathering and using consumer information. They include: 1) Consumers should be made aware that personal information will be collected, 2) The consumer should have a say in how this information will be used, 3) The consumer should have the ability to check the information collected to ensure that it is complete and accurate, 4) The information collected should be secured, and 5) The Web site should be responsible for seeing that these practices are followed.[28]

6.3 Legal Issues: Other Areas of Concern

In this section, we will explore defamation, sexually explicit speech, copyrights and patents, trademarks, unsolicited e-mail and online auctions and how these issues are affected by the Internet and the First Amendment of the Constitution.

The First Amendment of the Constitution is designed to protect freedom of expression.

"Congress shall make no law respecting an establishment of religion, or prohibiting the free exercise thereof; or abridging the freedom of speech, or of the press; or the right of the people peaceably to assemble and to petition the Government for a redress of grievances."

6.3.1 Defamation

Defamation is the act of injuring another's reputation, honor or good name through false written or oral communication.[29] Because the First Amendment strongly protects the freedom of anonymous speech, it is often difficult to win a defamation suit.

Defamation consists of two parts, *libel* and *slander*. Slander is spoken defamation, whereas libelous statements are written or are spoken in a context in which they have longevity and pervasiveness that exceed slander. For example, broadcasting is considered libelous even though it is spoken.

To prove defamation, a plaintiff must meet five requirements: 1) The statement must have been published, spoken or broadcast, 2) there must be identification of the individual(s) through name or reasonable association, 3) the statement must, in fact, be defamatory 4) there must be fault (for public persons the statement must have been made in *actual malice*, for private persons the statement needs only to have been *negligent,* or published, spoken or broadcast when known to be false), and 5) there must be evidence of injury or *actual loss*.[30]

The responsibility of defamatory statements is addressed in the cases, *Cubby v. Compuserve* and *Stratton Oakmont v. Prodigy* (see *Cubby v. Compuserve and Stratton Oakmont v. Prodigy*).

Congress passed the *Good Samaritan* provision, *Section 230 of the Telecommunications Act*. This protects ISPs from defamation lawsuits in the ISPs' attempts to control potentially damaging postings, including those that are: "obscene, lewd, lascivious, filthy, excessively violent, harassing or otherwise objectionable." The Telecommunications Act further protects ISPs by excusing them from publisher status even after they have been informed of defamatory material posted on their site. This premise relieves ISPs of the time-consuming activity of exploring all defamation claims, and it protects the freedom of expression by allowing unpopular opinions to appear. Without the added protection, an ISP, concerned about being charged with defamation, would simply remove all questionable material.

Because a plaintiff in a defamation suit cannot seek reward from the ISP, they must then seek out the author of the content. Most often, the speakers are anonymous and can remain so through bogus e-mail accounts and *anonymity indexes* (e.g., `PrivacyX.com` and `www.anonymizer.com`) in which they (the users) can claim an alternate identity. When plaintiffs pursue such cases, they create what is called a *John Doe suit*.[31] In an attempt to resolve the situation, the ISP will receive a request to provide the user's information. In the meantime, John Doe, whoever he or she might be, is being sued for what may or may not be a defamation case. In order to bring the case to court, John Doe's identity must be revealed, which is arguably a violation of John Doe's First Amendment right to anonymous free speech.[32]

Cubby v. Compuserve and Stratton Oakmont v. Prodigy

In the case *Cubby v. Compuserve*, an anonymous individual used a news service hosted by Compuserve to post an allegedly defamatory statement. As the provider of the bulletin board, Compuserve claimed that it could not be held liable for the defamatory statements because Compuserve was not the publisher of the statement.

The deciding factor in this case rested on the distinction between *distributor* and *publisher*. In the court's opinion, a distributor cannot be held liable for a defamatory statement unless the distributor has knowledge of the content.

As a result, Compuserve and other providers cannot be held responsible for their users' statements. However, as we will discover when addressing the case *Stratton Oakmont v. Prodigy*, there was a fine line between claiming responsibility as a publisher of users' content and maintaining the "distance" of a distributor.

Prodigy differed from Compuserve in that it, as an ISP, claimed responsibility to remove potentially defamatory or otherwise questionable material when brought to its attention. Prodigy further claimed that it had an automatic scanning device that screens bulletin board postings before they are posted.

As a result, Prodigy assumed the role of a publisher by claiming control over specific statements made by its users. As a publisher, Prodigy was held liable for the posted statements. This decision later spurred Congress to pass Section 230 of the Telecommunications Act, which protects ISPs actively seeking to control the content of their sites.[33]

6.3.2 Sexually Explicit Speech

As determined in *Miller v. California (1973)*, the *Miller Test* identifies the criteria used to distinguish between obscenity and pornography. Pornography is protected by the First Amendment. In order to be determined by the Miller Test to be obscene, material has to: 1) appeal to the prurient interest, according to contemporary community standards, and 2) when taken as a whole, lack serious literary, artistic, political or scientific value.[34]

The Internet, with its lack of geographic boundaries, challenges the Miller Test. As we have discussed, the Test is dependent on contemporary community standards. In cyberspace, communities exist independent of geographic boundaries.

Cyberspace complicates jurisdiction by making it possible, for example, for a person in Tennessee, where the tolerance for pornography is relatively low, to view a site in California, where there is a higher tolerance for pornography (*United States v. Thomas*: Reviewing the Question of Jurisdiction).

United States v. Thomas: Reviewing the Question of Jurisdiction

Thomas, an Internet business owner in California, had established a pornographic Web site from which merchandise could be ordered. The Web site was membership based, and a review of all applications was conducted before passwords were distributed to users. By California community standards, the Web site was legitimate.

In court, Thomas was found guilty of distributing obscenity, even though his site was established in California, where the actions were considered legitimate. The determining factor, and Thomas' critical mistake, was in the application process. The court argued that Thomas knew that the applicant was from Tennessee. The address and phone number appeared on the application. It suggested that, having this knowledge, Thomas should have denied any individual from an area of less tolerant community standards access to his Web site.

How then should the Internet be regulated to protect individuals like Thomas? The site, however disagreeable, was legal as far as his resident state was concerned. To answer this question, the courts have looked at the regulation of broadcasting and print.

The Internet has characteristics similar to those of broadcast media and print media, yet there are problems with applying traditional regulations to communications on the Web. Broadcasting is considered highly pervasive. The Internet resembles broadcasting because of its ability to reach a broad audience with little or no warning.[35] Print, however, focuses more on the regulation of the audience and less on the content of the material. Defined as *non-content-related means*, print restrictions allow adults to view pornographic material while limiting an adolescent's ability to obtain that material. This is distinctly different from regulating the material itself. Non-content related means is an effort to control the audience rather than controlling the material. The Internet mimics this method by requiring users to provide identification before entering specific sites.

6.3.3 Children and the Internet

Elementary and junior high schools implement Web-based learning in much the same way as high schools and universities. Most public libraries provide visitors with Internet access. Often, younger Internet audiences are able to gain access to the same information as adults without the constraints that might be found in real space. The Internet is not subject to the same zoning laws that would prohibit a pornography store from locating near an elementary school.

Let us revisit a previous example. Suppose you are a parent whose fourth grader has been assigned a report on the White House. The teacher has requested that the students conduct their research on the Internet. While working on the project, your fourth grader stumbles across **www.whitehouse.com**, a pornography site, and other undesirable sites targeted toward unsuspecting viewers.

This presents a complicated issue. Parents are concerned with protecting the well-being of their children. Yet, by limiting speech in an effort to protect younger audiences, we run the risk of infringing upon the constitutional right to the freedom of expression. For example, **www.whitehouse.com**, however distasteful, is protected under the First Amendment. It is the right of an adult to construct, own and visit a site of this nature.

The *Communications Decency Act of 1996* (CDA) and the *Child Online Protection Act of 1998* (COPA) were designed to restrict pornography on the Internet, particularly in the interest of children. Both CDA and COPA, however, have several flaws that have been pointed out by free-speech advocates.

Both the CDA and COPA were accused of being *overbroad*, reaching beyond the group they intended to protect. They attempted to enforce regulation when sites offered information that was "patently offensive," "indecent" and "harmful to minors." Arguments rested on the ambiguity of these defining terms. Opponents of CDA and COPA argue that decisions become arbitrary when the actual crime is too hard to define.[36] Thus, individuals may not have violated the guidelines intentionally; or, of equal concern, they will limit their speech to avoid a lawsuit. This is commonly referred to as the *chilling effect*.[37]

Children's privacy is also a concern. The *Children's Online Privacy Protection Act of 2000* (COPPA) prohibits Web sites from collecting personal information from children under the age of 13 without parental consent. While COPPA may be effective in protecting younger children, studies have indicated that teenagers are more likely than children to divulge information and are, therefore, at greater risk.[38] Web sites will often target this group by running promotions and contests.

6.3.4 Alternate Methods of Regulation

Software companies have developed *blocking and filtering* technologies to help parents and teachers protect children from questionable material. This software allows users to select what kinds of information can and cannot be received through their browsers. This technology is available at Web sites such as **www.surfwatch.com**, **www.cybersitter.com** and **www.netnanny.com** (Fig. 6.3).

Although blocking software is an effective way of keeping children away from sites that may not be suitable for them, the software may also be considered a violation of First Amendment rights in that the user is never in control of what can and cannot be viewed. Once users turn that responsibility over to the software, they have limited their knowledge of what information is available to them.

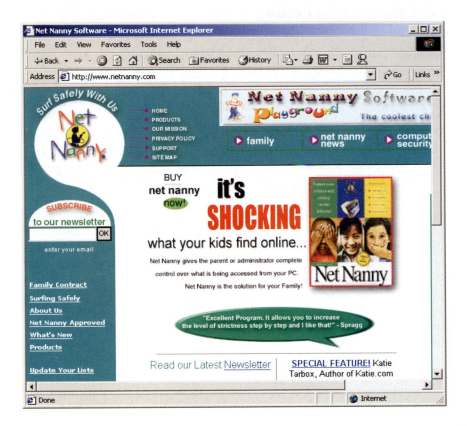

Fig. 6.3   Net Nanny home page. (Courtesy of Net Nanny Software International Inc.)

Blocking technology often exceeds its purpose by blocking out sites which can be thought of as educational. The Electronic Privacy Information Center (EPIC), a privacy-rights group in Washington DC, found that "family friendly" filtering technology blocked access to well over 90 percent of "decent material on the Internet." EPIC loaded up the family software, then used powerful Internet searching systems to locate information about schools; charitable and political organizations; educational, artistic and cultural institutions; using search terms including "American Red Cross," the "San Diego Zoo," and the "Smithsonian Institution," as well as such concepts as "Christianity," the "Bill of Rights" and "eating disorders."[39]

As an alternative to filtering software, Web sites are available to counsel parents on supervising their children on the Internet. Visit **www.cyberangels.com**, **www.get-netwise.com** and **www.parentsoup.com** for more information.

6.3.5 Intellectual Property: Patents and Copyright

Copyright, according to the U.S. Copyright Office, is the protection given to the author of an original piece, including "literary, dramatic, musical, artistic and certain other intellectual works," whether the work has been published or not. For example, copyright protection is provided for literature, music, sculpture and architecture. Copyright protects only the expression or form of an idea and not the idea itself.

Copyright protection provides incentive to the creators of original material by guaranteeing them credit for their work for a given amount of time. Currently, copyright protection is guaranteed for the life of the author plus seventy years.

Because of the ease with which material can be reproduced on the Internet and because *digital copies* are perfect duplicates of the original, concerns have been raised regarding the level of protection offered through traditional law (see **MP3.com** and **Napster.com**: Determining Copyright Infringement).

The music industry is currently in debate with these Web sites and others like them over the effects of unauthorized reproduction on record sales. In a study released by the Digital Media Association, 66 percent of users suggest they are prompted to buy the album after downloading the MP3.[44] This is something to think about seriously.

MP3 : Raising Copyright Issues

MPEG-1 Audio Layer 3, or *MP3*, is a compression method used to substantially reduce the size of audio files with no significant reduction in sound quality.[40] This compression method facilitates the exchange of audio files over the Internet. Recently, this technology has been used by Web sites such as **Napster.com** and **MP3.com** to help listeners access MP3-compressed recordings of their favorite music. MP3 compression also enables up-and-coming musicians to circulate their music quickly and easily worldwide. Much of the music available in MP3 format is copyrighted so this exchange, implemented differently by each of these companies (and others), has raised copyright issues. Similar copyright issues were raised with the advent of photocopying, audio-tape and video-tape technologies.

Napster uses central servers to help users locate MP3 files stored on other Napster users' hard drives. After locating the files, Napster members are then able to download these files to their own hard drives; the files are not stored on Napster's servers. Consequently, **Napster.com** suggests it cannot control the use (or misuse) of those files, and therefore it is not violating copyright laws. As we learned earlier in the chapter, this argument relies on the distinction between a distributor and a publisher.[41]

MP3.com *Instant Listening*[TM] service allows users to immediately begin listening to music from CDs they have purchased online. When a user purchases a CD from a select online retailer, all of the songs from the purchased CDs are added to the user's account on **MyMP3.com** The user can then listen to that music from any computer on the Internet. *Beam-It*[TM], another service from **MP3.com**, allows users to upload songs from CDs they already own to **My.MP3.com** enabling those users to access their music anywhere over the Internet. To prevent long uploads, **MP3.com** stores thousands of MP3s on its servers, so that if a user attempts to upload a song that is already on the servers, **MP3.com** simply gives the user access to that version.[42] This raised copyright concerns with the music industry, which was also concerned that borrowed CDs could be used to establish **MyMP3.com** accounts.

Recently, **MP3.com** has worked out agreements with several music companies to license their music and to house the MP3 versions of that music on **MyMP3.com**.[43]

The software industry is also experiencing a loss in sales due to online copyright infringement. Microsoft cites a 1998 study which indicates an $11 billion loss in desktop application sales was the result of software piracy.[45] Losses can be the result of license sharing, differing cultural perspectives on copyright and ownership of information and counterfeit reproductions.

In a landmark case, *United States v. LaMacchia*, Congress recognized the inability of traditional copyright law in the U.S. to regulate the Internet. As a result, several attempts were made to ensure that creators (i.e., software developers, writers, artists, etc.) and resource providers could maintain the same protection for digitally transmitted material as is afforded for other material under traditional law.

The *Digital Millennium Copyright Act of 1998* (DMCA) represents the rights of creative bodies to protect their work as well as the rights of educators and resource providers to receive access to this work. The DMCA makes it illegal to delete or otherwise alter the identifying information of the copyright owner. It prevents the circumvention of protection mechanisms and/or the sale of such circumvention mechanisms, but limits this to activity outside research, encryption, technological development and the testing of security measures. The DMCA protects the rights of the ISP by providing a *safe-harbor* provision in which the Webcasting of such property can be permitted by the purchase of license. Finally, the DMCA protects the *fair use* of copyrighted material.[47]

Fair use is defined as the use of a copyrighted work for education, research, criticism, etc. Four criteria have been established in order to determine whether fair use can be applied to the reproduction of a copyrighted work.

First, the purpose of the copyrighted work is examined. For example, was the reproduction of the copyrighted material for commercial use?

Second, the nature of the copyrighted work is taken into account. When determining the nature of a reproduction, the court looks at whether the original material was factual or fictitious. It is the expression of ideas that receives protection—not the ideas themselves.

Third, the amount of the material that has been reproduced is reviewed. This creates a gray area in which it is impossible to determine whether the amount of material reproduced is guaranteed copyright protection. Rather, it is the significance of the material. How crucial was the piece of information to the whole?

United States v. Lamacchia: Copyright Infringement and the "Commercial Gain" Loophole

In 1994, the U.S. Court made a landmark decision that changed the face of copyright protection. The case involved an M.I.T. student who had posted computer software on his Web site. Users could then access his site and download the copyrighted material for free, costing computer software companies lost sales.

Although the material posted was not original, the courts could not find LaMacchia guilty of copyright infringement according to the *Copyright Act of 1976*. In order to be guilty of copyright infringement under the Act, the violation must have been conducted "willfully and for purposes of commercial advantage or private financial gain."[46]

In this particular case, LaMachhia did not profit from the copyright violations and could not be tried as such. Consequently, LaMacchia was not convicted for his actions.

Fourth, the effect is taken into consideration. How does the reproduction of the copyrighted material affect the potential market?

However, the DMCA does not address all the concerns facing copyright protection. For example, issues such as first sale, which allows an owner to sell a used item and permits the reproduction of material used in distance-learning programs, still need to be addressed.[48] Opponents of the legislation also feel that it is too restrictive, limiting the progression of *open source code,* or code that is able to be accessed and modified by anyone.

Patents, which grant the creator sole rights to the use of a new discovery, present another issue. There are opponents to the length of patents. Given the growth rate of the Internet, some argue that the 20-year duration of patents discourages continuous software development and improvement.

In 1998, the federal regulations governing the distribution of patents increased the scope of patented discoveries to include "methods of doing business."[49] In order to be granted a patent for a method of doing business, the idea must be new and not obvious to a skilled person.[50]

To some, the inability to share information freely appears to be in opposition to the founding principles of the Internet, and the ability to restrict competition would hinder the growth of e-commerce (see: **Amazon.com** and the 1-Click Patent).

6.3.6 Trademark and Domain Name Registration

There are several methods by which an alleged trademark infringement can occur in cyberspace. One method is to become a *parasite*. A parasite selects a domain name based on common typos made when entering a popular domain name.

Amazon.com and the 1-Click[SM] Patent

At the time of publication, **Amazon.com** was at the forefront of the dispute over patent grants. Innovator of the 1-Click[SM] system, **Amazon.com** received a patent on the new method of online purchasing in September, 1999.[51] The 1-Click system allowed **Amazon.com** users to make purchases on the site without having to go through the checkout process.

This technology is significant, as studies show that approximately 65 percent of online shopping carts are abandoned before a purchase is complete. While there are several variables that may cause a user to leave a shopping cart with unmade purchases, the dominant theory suggests that the long and complicated checkout process is at the top of the list.[52]

The 1-Click patent gave **Amazon.com** an advantage over its competitors, enabling Amazon.com to provide faster, more efficient service to its customers than was legally available at any other site. **Barnesandnoble.com** quickly discovered this after losing a legal dispute involving its check-out technology, *Express Lane.*[53]

According to the criteria for a method-of-doing-business patent, the 1-Click system was correctly protected by a patent. The system was unlike any checkout system on the Internet, and the patent's usefulness was adequately demonstrated by the similar version created by **Barnesandnoble.com**.

Another way trademark infringement can occur is called *cybersquatting*. A cyber-squatter buys an assortment of domain names that are obvious representations of a brick-and-mortar company. When these previously established companies make the transition to the Internet, they are forced to buy the domain name from the cybersquatter.

Congress enacted the *Anticybersquatting Consumer Protection Act of 1999* (ACPA) in an effort to protect traditional trademarking in cyberspace. Consumer fraud, decreased revenue for the trademark holder and the hindrance of e-commerce are among the reasons for ACPA.

Trademarks belonging to a person or entity other than the person or entity registering or using the domain name are protected. Registering a domain name that is similar to an established trademark to cause confusion, intentionally deceive or to dilute the established trademark is illegal. However, persons registering domain names are protected from prosecution if they have a legitimate claim to the domain name, such as if it is their first or last name, or if the domain name was registered prior to the first use of the registered trademark.[54] In addition, domain names cannot be registered with the intention of resale to the rightful trademark owner.

6.3.7 Unsolicited Commercial e-mail (SPAM)

E-mail is an exceedingly popular form of online communication. In 1996, an estimated 20,000,000 e-mail users in the United States were sending an estimated 500,000,000 messages per day. By 2002 those numbers are expected to reach 105,000,000 users sending 1,500,000,000 messages per day.[55] AOL estimates that nearly one-third of the messages sent daily can be categorized as unsolicited commercial e-mail (UCE), most commonly referred to as *SPAM*.[56]

Electronic mail is different from the direct mail you might receive via the U.S. Postal Service. With direct mail, printing, packaging and postage fees are absorbed by the advertiser. In the case of e-mail, the ISP and the receiver bear the cost through maintenance and monthly subscription fees, similar to receiving junk faxes or telemarketing calls on a cellular phone.

Often, organizations responsible for distributing large quantities of unwanted messages will either maintain anonymity or present themselves as a legitimate company. In the former case, receivers cannot request to be taken off the organization's mailing list. Consequently, they will continue to receive the unwanted messages. In the second case, legitimate companies' reputations could be damaged, or they might have to waste valuable resources responding to the receivers' often angry replies.

The arguments in support of government regulation of e-mail transactions focus minimizing the cost and protecting integrity of legitimate electronic communication. At the time of publication, the Federal government is reviewing the *Unsolicited Electronic Mail Act*.[57] This would mandate that the nature of the e-mail be made clear. For example, advertisements must be labeled as such. This would, in effect, require online marketers to know the policy of every ISP they encounter on the Web, as different ISPs will have different rules governing the transmission of e-mail.[58]

There are alternate ways to protect your time and business against unwanted e-mail. Web sites such as **unitedmessaging.com** offer services that allow subscribers to control the information they receive. The service, *Message Control*, reduces the amount of SPAM received, and it also protects users against viruses and specified content. Other similar services include **www.spambouncer.org** and **www.scambusters.org**.

6.3.8 Online Auctions

Sites such as eBay and Bidland allow Internet users to post and search a wide variety of items. Auctions are regulated by government on several levels.

North Carolina, for example, has had a law in effect for several years requiring an auctioneer's license to conduct an auction. The state has decided to enforce the regulation on the Internet as well. This means that, in order to sell an item on an auction site, an individual must take a state certification exam and pay a series of fees. Anyone posting an item without a license is subject to a fine.[59]

Many countries, including Germany, France, Italy and the Netherlands, also restrict auctions to individuals certified to conduct them. At the time of publication, France had issued a fine to be paid to anti-racist groups by Yahoo! for allowing Neo-Nazi merchandise to appear in online auctions. The site was given two months to discontinue access in France due to violations of French laws against racism.[60]

Copyright infringement is another pressing issue for online auction sites. eBay, the most popular auction site, earns commissions from transactions completed at its site. Comprehensive auction sites that use *intelligent agents*, or programs designed to search for information designated by the user and to compare auctions on a variety of auction sites, continually search the Web for this information. As a result, the livelihood of one site depends on taking information from others. The same is true for a variety of other Web sites. AOL and **Amazon.com** also depend heavily on access to previously acquired information. In a recent court decision, the courts awarded eBay an injunction to protect the site against copyright infringement.[61]

Designed to protect the compiled lists of organizations like eBay, *The Collections of Information Antipiracy Act* (CIAA) makes it easier to prosecute any group which takes listings from one organization and, in doing so, harms the original business. A lack of protection of this sort, proponents argue, would cause sites like eBay to create restrictions for accessing their site. Opponents argue that CIAA would limit the growth potential of the Internet.[62] They suggest that CIAA would limit access to public information, making it more difficult to conduct comparison shopping.

Fraudulent activity is another problem for online auction sites. This can consist of bogus bidding, bids that are unsubstantiated and *shill bidding*, when sellers bid for their own items in order to increase the bid price.

6.3.9 Online Contracts

The *Electronic Signatures in Global and National Commerce Act of 2000*, otherwise known as the E-Sign bill, was recently passed into law. The legislation is designed to promote online commerce by legitimizing online contractual agreements. Under the bill, digital agreements will receive the same level of validity as their hard-copy counterparts. The bill also allows cooperating parties to establish their own contracts, as opposed to a government-mandated format, thereby maintaining industry control. This is expected to reduce the time and expense of paperwork.

Security features, which are discussed in greater detail in Chapter 7, can be used to validate online contracts. Digital signatures, the electronic equivalent of handwritten signatures, are used to authenticate the participating parties and ensure the integrity of the message.

6.4 Social Issues: Online Communities

The Internet is redefining our definition of communities. By enabling people to form communities outside of a geographic setting and the limits it imposes, the Web allows larger and more diverse groups to communicate, share information and exchange opinions.

Web sites are being created to accommodate a variety of individuals with different backgrounds, interests and ideas. In this section, we will explore how the Internet is developing to meet people's needs and desires by creating communities and facilitating access to large stores of information.

6.4.1 Online Communities: Defining the Difference

The Internet alters the ways people meet and interact; it has changed first impressions. In cyberspace we do not notice a person's appearance first, unless they have posted a picture or are communicating through a video camera. In cyberspace, it is not our appearance that draws people to us; rather, we learn about each other through conversation.[63]

Virtual communities also allow an individual with many different likes, dislikes, ambitions and hobbies to focus on one particular defining characteristic and nurture that characteristic. For example, a visitor of any demographic make-up can visit an online cooking portal. During this time, the visitor is not identified as anything other than a user who is interested in cooking. Gender, race, creed, age and sexual orientation play no role in the user's experience. This is not necessarily the experience that the same individual would have with a brick-and-mortar establishment.

Sites such as **www.oxygen.com**, **www.pleiades-net.com**, **www.planetout.com**, **www.youthpride.com**, **www.match.com** and **www.singles.com** are examples of popular online communities.

6.4.2 Online Activism

Some communities organize around political and social action. For example, **www.youthactivism.com** (Fig. 6.4) has created a forum for individuals under the age of 18 to discuss and debate issues that concern them. The site provides young adults with information on picking a cause, team organization and decision-making in order to implement change. The site also features success stories, advice to adults who want to participate and resources for getting publicity and financial support.

www.igc.org is a portal of a progressively political nature, hosting sites concerned with human rights, racism and sexism.[65] The site is divided into four categories – WomenNet, EcoNet, PeaceNet and Anti-RacismNet and is home to such groups as the National Organization for Women and the Hunger Project.

Other organizations that promote causes on the Internet include: The Student Environmental Action Coalition (**www.seac.org**), Amnesty International (**www.amnestyusa.org**) and the Peace Corps (**www.peacecorps.gov**).

6.4.3 Disabilities and the Web

WeMedia.com (Fig. 6.5) is a Web site dedicated to providing disabled individuals with the same opportunities as the general population. The site serves 54 million disabled consumers with an estimated one trillion dollars in buying power.[64]

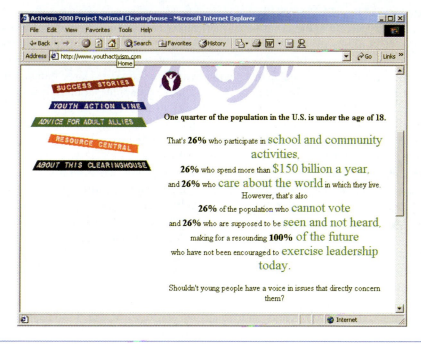

Fig. 6.4   Youthactivism.com (Courtesy of Activism 2000 Project.)

Fig. 6.5   WeMedia.com's home page. (Courtesy of We Media, Inc.)

The Internet has also enabled disabled individuals to work in a vast array of new fields. Prior to this, 25 percent of the 15 million Americans with disabilities found employment as a result of the *Americans with Disabilities Act* (ADA), but this did not include the number of people who wanted to be working.[66] Technologies such as voice activation, visual enhancers and auditory aids enable disabled individuals to work in a large number of positions. For example, visually impaired people might use computer monitors with enlarged text or electronic equipment with braille operating controls.

Within the next year, information provided through technology will have to be equally accessible to individuals with disabilities.[66] For example, federal regulations similar to the disability ramp mandates will be applied to the Internet for those who have impaired hearing, sight and speech. In the future, sites that are heavily laden with graphic images might have to simplify their appearance. Highly graphic sites are difficult to read through visual-to-audio technology and consequently limit the access of visually impaired users.[67]

The company CitXCorp is developing new technology that translates information over the Web through the telephone. Information on a specific topic will be accessed by dialing the designated number. The new software is expected to be made available to users for $10 per month.[68] For more information on regulations governing the design of Web sites to accommodate the disabled, visit **www.access-board.gov**.[69]

In alliance with Microsoft, GW Micro and Henter-Joyce, Adobe Systems Inc. is also working on software to aid disabled individuals. Adobe Acrobat and Adobe's PDF will be manufactured to comply with Microsoft's application programming interface (API), allowing businesses to reach a disabled audience. JetForm Corp is also meeting the needs of disabled audiences with the development of their server-based XML software. The new software will allow users to download a format modified to best meet their needs.[70] We will discuss XML in depth in Chapter 27 and we will discuss how to make software and Web sites accessible in Chapter 34, "Accessibility."

6.5 Global Issues

The Internet poses challenges to a world comprised of different cultures, attitudes, languages, codes of conduct and government authorities. For example, in Europe, bringing your business to the Web is less of a priority than it is for a business owner in the United States.[71]

In addition to different attitudes toward the potential of e-commerce, the question of government regulation also affects the growth rate of the Internet. For example, Americans are extremely protective of copyright. Intellectual property in the U.S. cannot be used, with few exceptions, without gaining the creator's permission or citing the source of the information.

The United States also has a different reaction to the use of personal information than many other countries. In Europe, respect for privacy is much greater. This difference of opinion points to an important issue arising in relation to the Internet. How do we create a global communication forum maintaining respect for one another's different cultures and codes of conduct?

The issue of privacy has come under attack and has presented the world with some difficult questions. How are standards to be developed, and who will develop them? Under whose jurisdiction will violations of legal, ethical and social code be reviewed? Who should be held responsible? (Felix Somm and the International Perspective on Privacy discusses this last issue).

Felix Somm and International Perspective on Privacy

Felix Somm, an overseas agent for the American ISP Compuserve, was held accountable under German law for providing German subscribers access to sexually explicit material. Because Compuserve was an internationally operating ISP, material posted in the United States was also accessible to Compuserve's international members.

Germany is among the nations that exhibit a lower tolerance for pornography than the United States. The content found on Compuserve was, according to German mandates, bestial and obscene, and, because of his role as an international representative, Felix Somm was found guilty in the German courts.

The courts determined that Compuserve had knowledge of the material available through the server and, disregarding the sensitivity of its subscribers, failed to remove the material or effectively block its accessibility. They further determined that Compuserve was acting in favor of commercial gain. Due to his position within the company, Felix Somm was held personally responsible.

The case went to the court of appeals in Germany, and the decision was overturned in favor of Somm. Recognizing the distinction between a distributor and a publisher and Felix Somm's technical inability to block German access to specific content on the site, the court reasoned that Somm could not be held accountable. The case, however, raised important issues regarding the global aspects of the Internet and international jurisdiction.

The United States is negotiating with the European Union to promote the growth of international e-commerce. The *European Union Directive on Data Protection* is an agreement among its members on the regulations that apply to information exchange. The Directive mandates that personal information be kept current and used in a lawful manner for its designated purpose. Because of the different treatment of privacy in the United States, many U.S. sites could be in violation of this ordinance.

In order to address the issue of international differences, the U.S. and the European Union have a pending agreement in which the U.S. will compile a list of American Web sites that meet the criteria designated by the Directive. In the case of a violation of the directive, the case will be tried in the United States.

6.6 Internet Taxation

Internet taxation is a monumentally controversial topic. In 1999, lobbying efforts for both sides of the issue were estimated at $14 million. By April, that figure had already reached $2.7 million for the year 2000.[72] While one side argues for a permanent ban on Internet taxation, the other maintains the necessity of fairly taxing Internet sales.

The geographic location of the vendor, consumer, ISP, server and other participating parties present a major issue. If both a vendor and a consumer are located in the same state, a sales tax can be imposed. If the vendor and the consumer are not located in the same state, then the sale is subject to a *use tax*. The state in which the purchased property or service is used directly imposes this tax upon the consumer. If the vendor has a physical presence, or *nexus*, in that state, then it is required to collect the tax; otherwise the vendor must assess the tax and pay it directly to the state. This assessment is a voluntary responsibility, and, although compliance often occurs in business-to-business transactions, it is far less common in business-to-consumer sales.

There are other problems with interstate taxation. Physical presence is proving to be a difficult term to define. Should it be determined by the location of the ISP, the location of the server or the location of the home page? States also vary according to what transactions are subject to taxation. What is considered a taxable item in one state may be considered a necessity, and consequently non-taxable, in another.

Many state and local governments support remote taxation of the consumer based on the location of the vendor's physical presence. Sales tax revenues are the largest single source of a state's revenue and are used to fund government-subsidized programs, including the fire department, the police and the public education systems. Figures from 1999 suggest that the amount of uncollected sales taxes due to online shopping was $525 million.[73] State and local governments further argue that removing taxation methods from their jurisdiction infringes upon state sovereignty, an element of the checks-and-balances system maintained by the United States Constitution.

Opponents to Internet taxation claim that it will inhibit the growth of the Internet. There are an estimated 7,500 different taxation methods.[74] To appropriately meet the taxation requirements of all parties in online transactions, e-businesses would be required to know and understand all these methods. Opponents also suggest that the real revenue for state and local governments will come as a result of the high-paying technical positions created by Internet growth. They further argue that brick-and-mortar businesses will continue to survive, despite the growth of online purchasing, because a brick-and-mortar purchase provides instant gratification and sales personnel offer human-to-human communication.

The *Internet Tax Commission*, created by the *Internet Tax Freedom Act*, was developed to review the issue of Internet taxation and return a recommendation to Congress in April 2000.[75] Issues to be addressed by the commission included a revision of state and local taxes to make taxing a feasible process for Internet businesses, clearer definitions on the meaning of "physical presence" and universal taxation exemptions.

The panel included members of federal, state and local government, industry leaders and trade organization officials. Despite the lack of unanimity, the commission agreed on several recommendations. These included an extension to the moratorium on Internet taxation and international e-commerce taxation and the elimination of taxes on digital content (i.e. music and software). The commission further recommended that a clear definition of "physical presence" be determined, taxation methods be simplified by each state and welfare money be allocated for Internet access. Consumer privacy and Internet access for the poor were also among the issues presented by the Commission to Congress.[76]

Taxation problems with regard to the Internet are as abundant internationally as they are in the U.S. Each country in the European Union imposes a *value-added tax* (VAT) ranging from 15–25 percent on goods sold to consumers within the E.U. All E.U. companies are VAT registered, while non-E.U. companies are not. Under the current system, when a non-E.U. business sells to an E.U. business, the buyer is required to self-assess the VAT. However, when a non-E.U. business sells online to an individual consumer in the E.U. the VAT is not paid. This gives non-E.U. businesses an advantage, as their products are ultimately less expensive for the consumer.[77]

6.7 Internet and World Wide Web Resources

Legal References

`www2.bc.edu/~herbeck/cyberreadings.html`

Prof. D. Herbeck of Boston College has established this site to provide students with readings and court cases relevant to the development of cyberlaw. The site includes several landmark cases in the development of the freedom of expression in the U.S. as well as more current debates over speech and the Internet.

`www.fcc.gov`

The Federal Communications Commission is the government body responsible for regulating interstate and international communications, including radio, television, satellite, etc. The FCC plays an active role in determining the need for government regulation of the Internet.

`www.findlaw.com`

This site provides users with state and federal court decisions as well as current law.

`www.legalengine.com`

This comprehensive Web site has links to Federal, state, county and local laws. It includes world law, Supreme Court decisions and cyberlaw.

`europa.eu.int`

Links to information regarding the European Data Protection Act and U.S. agreements for the management of international Web sites.

Online Privacy

`www.privaseek.com`

Now called Persona, this company provides users with the tools to protect their privacy online.

`www.enonymous.com`

Developer of privacy-oriented marketing strategies and service, **Enonymous.com** provides privacy ratings of various Web sites and presents them to users on a scale of 0-to-4 stars (0 being the lowest, 4 being the highest).

`www.doubleclick.com`

Doubleclick is an online advertising agency. The site was recently in the headlines for its consumer-tracking techniques.

`www.codexdatasystems.com`

Codex Data Systems manufactures tracking and surveillance software.

`www.softsecurity.com`

This private organization develops security software.

`www.cdt.org`

The Center for Democracy and Technology has expertise in the legal and technological development of the Web. Its mission is centered around the protection of privacy and free speech.

`www.eff.org`

The Electronic Frontier Foundation is a non-profit organization concerned with privacy and the freedom of expression in the digital age.

`www.privacyrights.org`

The *Privacy Rights Clearinghouse* is a non-profit organization designed to help consumers better understand and protect their privacy.

`www.truste.com`

This site is the leading provider of online privacy protection. **Truste.com** audits member organization to ensure consumers that the sites are upholding the particulars of their privacy policies.

www.privacybot.com
This site generates privacy policies for your Web site. For a fee, users can enter information, that is incorporated into the policy. The service is supported by Trustmark.

www.privacyx.com
This free Internet service allows users to surf the Internet anonymously. New users create a digital certificate under a username, which enables the server to intercept messages and send them, encrypted, to the user.

www.privacychoices.org
This site, operated by DoubleClick, aids users in understanding privacy policies, how to avoid receiving junk mail and how to disable cookies.

www.epic.org
The Electronic Privacy Information Center (EPIC) is concerned with the use of consumer information by online companies. The Web site allows users to register for regular e-mails that discuss updates on the current issues surrounding privacy and First Amendment rights.

www.junkbusters.com
Junkbusters is a privacy advocacy and consulting group that aids consumers and businesses in reducing the amount of junk mail they receive. Although not a supplier of legal advice, the organization offers products designed to protect users from unsolicited e-mail.

www.getagriponit.com
WQuinn offers a software solution to monitor the material that is being stored on your server. The collection of outdated mail, sexually explicit images and otherwise sensitive material on your hard drive can lead to slow service or legal complications. The site offers a free 30-day trial of the software.

www.privaseek.com
Persona, formerly known as *Privaseek*, enables consumers to control their personal information through *MyPersona*. It provides material to alert users to privacy issues and provides a list of resources where users can continue researching these issues.

www.netcoalition.com
A consortium of major Web sites including, **Amazon.com**, Yahoo!, Lycos, etc. **Netcoalition.com** attempts to meet the needs of e-business while matching the demands of the consumer regarding online privacy.

www.ftc.gov/kidzprivacy
The Federal Trade Commission's site details the treatment of children's personal information on the Internet. The site includes the Child's Online Privacy Protection Act (COPPA) enacted in April of 2000.

Regulation Methods
www.surfwatch.com
The first to enter the Internet filtering market in 1995, Surfwatch advertises a 90–95 percent success rate in filtering questionable content.

www.cybersitter.com
Cybersitter filtering software is available for free trial, or to buy as a download.

www.getnetwise.com
GetNetWise is an organization that provides and promotes a valuable Web experience. The site provides information on safe surfing.

www.unitedmessaging.com
This site aids users in managing incoming e-mail messages. Message Control, a service provided, protects users from unwanted mail and viruses.

`www.pwcbetterweb.com`
PriceWaterhouseCoopers' auditing and privacy policy development program.

Social Issues

`www4.nscu.edu/unity/users/j/jherkert/index.html`
The Society on Social Implications of Technology (SSIT) provides information regarding the effects of technology on society. The environment, health, safety, ethics and responsibility are the foundational topics. The SSIT is a division of the Institute of Electrical and Electronic Engineers (IEEE).

`www.cpsr.org`
Computer Professionals for Social Responsibility (CPSR) is an organization concerned with the development and use of computers and the effects they have on society. The group has addressed issues including the national information infrastructure, civil liberties and privacy, computers in the workplace and technology policy and human needs. CPSR serves as an advisory board to policy makers and the public.

`www.igc.com`
The Institute for Global Communications is a progressively political portal acting as home to Web sites dedicated toward addressing racism, gender, the environment, human rights and international disputes.

`www.ekidnetwork.com`
This portal operates with many of the same features available to adults on the Internet today, yet safeguards children from accessing questionable material on the Internet or conducting an unsupervised conversation through e-mail or in a chat room.

`www.youthactivism.com`
This site is targeted towards political activists under the age of 18. It provides younger audiences with information and advice for the initiation of political change.

`www.planetout.com`
The leading Web site for the gay population, PlanetOut provides users with headline news and other relevant information.

`www.gay.com`
This is a popular Web site targeted to the gay population.

`www.match.com`
This site, one of the leaders in online dating services, provides users with access to hundreds of potentially significant others. For a fee the site will pair members according to their areas of interest.

`www.wemedia.com`
This site is a portal for individuals with disabilities. It provides information and services making the Web more accessible.

`www.oxygen.com`
This site is targeted toward female audiences, providing information on health, motherhood, relationships, entertainment and fashion.

`www.pleiades-net.com`
This site is designed for women. It provides information on Internet usage, activism, relationships of various orientations and feminist issues.

SUMMARY

- In real space, we operate under a code of laws and ethics. In cyberspace, this is not necessarily the case. It is a unique forum in which code, or the languages of programming, govern.
- The application of traditional law to the Internet is not always a smooth process.

- An individual's right to privacy is not explicitly guaranteed by the Constitution, but it is implicitly guaranteed through the First, Fourth, Ninth and Fourteenth Amendments.
- Translation is the interpretation of the Constitution to protect the greater good.
- The Internet is currently a self-regulated medium.
- The Financial Services Modernization Act of 1999 establishes a set of regulations concerning the management of consumer information.
- While having the Web experience tailored to their individual patterns appeals to some users, others consider having their every action recorded to be a violation of their privacy.
- Several tracking devices are used online including; cookies, ID cards, click-through banner advertisements and Web bugs.
- A cookie is a text file stored by a Web site on an individual's personal computer that allows a site owner to track the site's visitors.
- Keystroke software provides an inexpensive, easy-to-use method of monitoring productivity and the abuse of company equipment.
- The courts propose two criteria to determine an employee's right to privacy: 1) did the employee have a reasonable expectation of privacy and 2) does the business have legitimate business interests that would reasonably justify the intrusion of employee privacy?
- Users are able to take on falsified identities to maintain anonymity on the Web.
- The World Wide Web Consortium has introduced the Platform for Privacy Preferences Project (P3P). This enables a user to select the type of information to be accepted by the browser.
- It is important to include a privacy policy on your Web site, respect the stated policy and treat your visitor's information with care.
- Not all sites carrying a certified security trademark make the effort to follow their privacy guidelines. It is still up to the organization to honor its stated privacy policies.
- The Federal Trade Commission has established five Core Fair Information Practices regarding the use of online marketing tactics for gathering and using consumer information.
- Defamation is the act of injuring another's reputation or good name through written or oral communication.
- Slander is spoken defamation, whereas libelous statements are written or are spoken in a context in which they have longevity and pervasiveness exceeding that of slander.
- Without the added protection of Section 230 of the Telecommunications Decency Act, an ISP, concerned about being charged with defamation, would simply remove all questionable material.
- Pornography is protected by the First Amendment.
- In order to be determined by the Miller Test to be obscene, material has to: 1) appeal to the prurient interest, according to contemporary community standards, and 2) when taken as a whole, lack serious literary, artistic, political or scientific value.
- Broadcasting is considered highly pervasive. The Internet resembles broadcasting in its ability to reach a broad audience with little or no warning.
- Print focuses more on the regulation of the audience and less on the content of the material. Defined as non-content-related means, print restrictions allow adults to view pornographic material while limiting an adolescent's ability to obtain that material.
- The Communications Decency Act of 1996 (CDA) and the Child Online Protection Act of 1998 (COPA) were designed to restrict pornography on the Internet, particularly in the interest of children.
- Both the CDA and COPA were accused of being overbroad, reaching beyond the group they intended to protect.

- The Children's Online Privacy Protection Act of 2000 (COPPA) prohibits Web sites from collecting personal information from children under the age of 13 without parental consent.

- Software companies have developed blocking and filtering technologies to help parents and teachers protect children from questionable material.

- Blocking technology often exceeds its purpose by blocking out educational sites.

- Copyright, according to the U.S. Copyright Office, is the protection given to the author of an original piece, including "literary, dramatic, musical, artistic and certain other intellectual works," whether the work has been published or not.

- Copyright protection provides incentive to the creators of original material by guaranteeing them credit for their work for a given amount of time. Currently, copyright protection is guaranteed for the life of the author plus seventy years.

- In a landmark case, United States v. LaMacchia, Congress recognized the inability of traditional copyright law in the U.S. to regulate the Internet.

- The Digital Millennium Copyright Act of 1998 (DMCA) represents the rights of creative bodies to protect their work as well as the rights of educators and resource providers to access this work.

- The DMCA protects the rights of the ISP by providing a safe-harbor provision in which the Webcasting of such property can be permitted by the purchase of license.

- Fair use is defined as the use of a copyrighted work for education, research, criticism, etc.

- Patents grant the creator sole rights to the use of a new discovery.

- In 1998, the federal regulations governing the distribution of patents increased the scope of patented discoveries to include "methods of doing business."

- A parasite selects a domain name based on typos made when entering a popular domain name.

- A cybersquatter buys an assortment of domain names that are obvious representations of a brick-and-mortar company.

- Congress enacted the Anticybersquatting Consumer Protection Act of 1999 (ACPA) in an effort to protect traditional trademarking in cyberspace.

- Persons registering domain names are protected from prosecution if they have a legitimate claim to the domain name, such as if it is their first or last name, or if the domain name was registered prior to the first use of the registered trademark.

- Domain names cannot be registered with the intention of resale to the rightful trademark owner.

- AOL estimates that nearly one-third of the messages sent daily can be categorized as unsolicited commercial e-mail (UCE), most commonly referred to as SPAM.

- Often, organizations responsible for distributing large quantities of unwanted messages will either maintain anonymity or falsely present themselves as a legitimate company.

- The Federal government is reviewing the Unsolicited Electronic Mail Act. This would mandate that the nature of the e-mail be made clear.

- Many states have laws that require an auctioneer's license to conduct an auction.

- The Collections of Information Antipiracy Act (CIAA) makes it easier to prosecute any group which takes listings from one organization and, in doing so, harms the original business.

- Fraudulent activity is another problem for online auction sites. This can consist of bogus bidding, bids that are unsubstantiated and shill bidding—sellers bidding for their own items in order to increase the bid price.

- The E-Sign bill is designed to promote online commerce by legitimizing online contractual agreements.

- Web sites are being created in order to accommodate a variety of individuals with different backgrounds, interests and ideas.
- The Internet alters the ways in which people meet and interact.
- Virtual communities also allow an individual with many different likes, dislikes, ambitions and hobbies to focus on one particular defining characteristic and nurture that characteristic.
- Technologies such as voice activation, visual enhancers and auditory aids increase the number of job opportunities available to disabled individuals.
- Within the next year, information provided through technology will have to be equally accessible to individuals with disabilities.
- We must examine how to create a global communication forum to maintain respect for one another's cultures and codes of conduct.
- The European Union Directive on Data Protection is an agreement among its members on the regulations that apply to information exchange.
- Many state and local governments support remote taxation of the consumer based on the location of the vendor's physical presence.
- Sales tax revenues are the largest single source of state revenue and are used to fund government subsidized programs, including the fire department, the police and the public education systems.
- State and local governments argue: to remove taxation methods from their jurisdiction infringes upon state sovereignty, an element of the checks and balances system maintained by the Constitution.
- Opponents to Internet taxation claim that it will inhibit the growth of the Internet.
- The Internet Tax Commission, created by the Internet Tax Freedom Act, was developed in order to review the issue of Internet taxation and return a recommendation to Congress in April, 2000.
- Taxation problems with regard to the Internet are as abundant internationally as they are in the U.S.

TERMINOLOGY

actual
malice
actual loss
Americans with Disabilities Act
anonymity indexes
Anticybersquatting Consumer Protection Act of
 1999
Audio Home Recording Act
Beam-it
BetterWeb
blocking and filtering methods
brick-and-mortar
Child Online Protection Act of 1998
Child Online Privacy Protection Act of 1999
chilling effect
clear GIFs
click-through banner advertisements
client-server networking model
Collections of Information Antipiracy Act
Communications Decency Act of 1996
Computer Usage Compliance Survey
consumer profile

cookie
copyright
Copyright Act of 1976
Core Fair Information Practices
cybersquatting
cyberspace
defamation
Digital Millennium Copyright Act of 1998
digital copies
digital redlining
distributor vs. publisher
Electronic Signatures in Global and National
 Commerce Act of 2000
European Union Directive on Data Protection
fair use of copyrighted material
Financial Services Modernization Act of 1999
Good Samaritan provision
ID cards
Instant Listening
Internet Tax Commission
Internet Tax Freedom Act
intelligent agents

John Doe suit
keystroke cops
legitimate business interests
libel
Message Control
MPEG-1 Audio Layer 3
MP3
Miller Test
negligent
nexus
non-content-related means
open source code
opt out
overbroad
parasite
Personalization Consortium
Platform for Privacy Preferences Project (P3P)

privacy policy
publisher
real space
reasonable expectation of privacy
Section 230 of the Telecommunications Decency
    Act
self-regulated medium
shill bidding
slander
SPAM
tracking devices
translation
Unsolicited Electronic Mail Act
use tax
value-added tax
Web Bugs

SELF-REVIEW EXERCISES

6.1   State whether the following are true or false. If the answer is false, explain why.
  a) The Internet is currently regulated by an international committee.
  b) If a Web site has a posted privacy policy, it is reasonable to assume that the policy is be-
     ing upheld.
  c) Web bugs or clear GIFs are tiny programs hidden in images that return user activity to a
     partner site.
  d) An Internet Service Provider (ISP) can be held accountable for a statement posted on a
     bulletin board by an anonymous user.
  e) Non-content related means suggests that the medium by which the material is distributed
     receives regulation rather than the content of the material itself.
  f) Copyright protection is extended to protect an idea.
  g) In order to receive legitimate copyright protection an artist must have registered the ma-
     terial with the U.S. Copyright Office.
  h) An individual's right to privacy is guaranteed explicitly by the Constitution.
  i) Registering a domain name that is similar to an established trademark to cause confusion,
     intentionally deceive or to dilute the established trademark is considered illegal.
  j) Many state and local governments support remote taxation of the consumer by the loca-
     tion of the vendor's physical presence.

6.2   Fill in the blanks in each of the following:
  a) The five criteria that must be met in order to bring forth a defamation suit are
     _____, _____, _____, _____ and _____.
  b) The two types of defamation are _____ and _____.
  c) The two criteria used to determine whether the intrusion into an employee's e-mail ac-
     count by an employer was justifiable are _____ and _____.
  d) The three criteria that distinguish obscenity from pornography are _____,
     _____ and _____, and the name of the U.S. Supreme Court case that deter-
     mined this definition was _____.
  e) Copyright protection is guaranteed for the life of the author plus _____.
  f) Limiting speech to avoid a lawsuit is commonly referred to as the _____.
  g) _____, _____, _____ and _____ are four examples of a tracking
     device.

h) _____ and _____ were the cases that helped to define the difference between a distributor and a publisher on the Internet.

i) The five _____ provide guidelines for the use of online marketing tactics for gathering and using customer information.

j) The _____ provision of Section 230 of the Telecommunications Act protects ISPs from defamation lawsuits in their attempts to control potentially damaging postings, including those that are lewd, lascivious, filthy, excessively violent, harassing or otherwise objectionable.

ANSWERS TO SELF-REVIEW EXERCISES

6.1   a) False. The Internet is an industry (or self) regulated medium. b) False. There are no regulatory bodies to guarantee that a Web site is upholding its privacy policy. c) True. d) False. Under the "Good Samaritan" provision of the Telecommunications Decency Act, ISPs are recognized as a distributor and are consequently protected. e) True. f) False. Copyright protection guarantees protection to the expression of an idea, but not the idea itself. g) False. Copyright is guaranteed upon the creation of the material. However, material registered with the U.S. Copyright Office perhaps receives a higher level of protection because it is easier to defend proof of ownership. h) False. The right to privacy is guaranteed implicitly through the Fourth, Fifth, Ninth and Fourteenth Amendments. i) True. j) True.

6.2   a) The statement must be defamatory, identify the plaintiff (this can be through allusions and descriptions), have been published or broadcast, have been done in negligence or actual malice, and there must be evidence of injury or actual loss. b) Libel and slander. c) Reasonable expectation of privacy and legitimate business interests. d) The material in question must appeal to the prurient interest according to contemporary community standards and, when taken as a whole, lack serious literary, artistic, political or scientific value. e) Seventy years. f) The chilling effect. g) Web bugs, ID cards, cookies and click-through banner advertisements. h) Cubby vs. Compuserve and Stratton Oakmont vs. Prodigy. i) Core Fair Information Practices. j) Good Samaritan.

EXERCISES

6.3   The chapter discussed defamation and how it is applied. Surf the Internet and find a defamation case (preferably one that has been decided) and write a brief summary detailing how the five criteria were applied to determine defamation.

6.4   The chapter discusses the use of cookies in order to track consumer activity and provide targeted advertising. Spend an hour surfing the Web, and record what sites you visit and the pattern of advertising that you find as you go along. Do the ads reflect the sites you have previously visited? Record any advertising agencies that sponsor the ad (this information will be available in the navigation bar located at the bottom of your screen). Then, try to find the cookie file on your hard drive. Did it keep an accurate recording of your travels? Write a brief summary describing your findings.

6.5   This chapter discusses the issue of online privacy. According to the Personalization Consortium, there are a number of people who are in favor of targeted advertising. After reviewing the different sides of the argument, survey your friends and family to evaluate their stance on online privacy.

WORKS CITED

The notation <*www.domain-name.com*> indicates that the citation is for information found at that Web site.

1.   L. Lessig, *Code and Other Laws of Cyberspace* (New York: Basic Books, 1999) 6.

2.   D. Herbeck, Chair and Associate Professor of Communication, Boston College, 29 February 2000, lecture notes.

3. L. Lessig, *Code and Other Laws of Cyberspace* (New York: Basic Books, 1999) 114.

4. D. Hendrickson, "FTC Proposal for Web Privacy Guidelines Meets with Mixed Reception," *Mass High Tech* 5 June -11 June 2000: 11.

5. M. Nelson, "Majority of Web Sites Lack Privacy Policies," *Information Week* 17 April 2000: 173.

6. R. Wright, "Can the Internet Ever Be Tamed," *Toronto Star News* 24 February 2000.

7. **<www.personalization.com>**.

8. **<www.crimetime.com/S900.html>**.

9. T.E. Weber, "Tricks of the Web Snoop's Trade," *The Wall Street Journal* 23 February 2000: B1.

10. Weber, B1.

11. Weber, B1.

12. "DoubleClick Advertisement: "Committed to Privacy," *The New York Times* 14 February 2000: C19.

13. B. Tedeschi, "In a Shift, DoubleClick Cuts Off Plan for Wider Use of Personal Data of Internet Consumers," *The New York Times* 3 March 2000: C5.

14. R. Tomkins, "Cookies Leave a Nasty Taste: Marketing Internet Privacy," *Financial Times* 3 March 2000: 16.

15. Tomkins, 16.

16. "The DoubleClick Dilemma," *The Boston Globe* 2 March 2000: A16.

17. J. Beauprez, "Giant Online Database Dropped DoubleClick, Yields to Privacy Concerns," *The Denver Post* 6 March 2000: C1.

18. J. Buskin, "Our Data, Ourselves," *The Wall Street Journal* 17 April 2000: R34.

19. M.J. McCarthy, "Thinking Out Loud: You Assumed 'Erase' Wiped Out That Rant Against the Boss? Nope," *The Wall Street Journal* 7 March 2000.

20. McCarthy, "Thinking Out Loud: You Assumed 'Erase' Wiped Out That Rant Against the Boss? Nope."

21. McCarthy, "Thinking Out Loud: You Assumed 'Erase' Wiped Out That Rant Against the Boss? Nope."

22. R. Beck, "Cyber Liability Updates Old Risks," *Mass High Tech* 31 January–6 February 2000: 27.

23. Michael A. Smyth v. The Pillsbury Company, C.A. No. 95-5712 (1996).

24. "The DoubleClick Dilemma," *The Boston Globe* 2 March 2000.

25. "White House backs initiative for Net privacy," *The Boston Globe* 22 June 2000.

26. B. Machrone, "The Web Solves the Same Problem It Creates," *PC Week* 17 January 2000: 55.

27. **<www.pcwbetterweb.com>**.

28. "Generic Code of Fair Information Practices," **<www.cdt.org/privacy/guide/basic/generic.html>**

29. *Webster's New World College Dictionary*, (USA: MacMillan, 1999).

30. **<www.abbotlaw.com/defamation.html#I>**.

31. M. France and D. Carney, "Free Speech on the Web? Not Quite," *Business Week* 28 February 2000: 93–94.

32. R. Kerber, "Free Speech of Cyber-slander?" *The Boston Globe* 29 February 2000.

33. Cubby vs. Compuserve, 776 F. Supp. 135 at _ (1991) and Stratton Oakmont vs. Prodigy, 23 Media L. Rep. 1794 at _ (1995).

34. Miller vs. California, 413 U.S. 15 at 24-25 (1973)

35. FCC v. the Pacifica Foundation 438 U.S. 726 (1978)

36. D. Herbeck, Chair and Associate Professor of Communication, Boston College, 1 February 2000, lecture notes.

37. Herbeck, 1 February 2000, lecture notes.

38. K. Thomas, "For a Net 'Gift,' Teens Will Share Wealth of Family Info," *USA Today* 15 March 2000: 7D.

39. S. Davies, "Make It Safe, But Keep It Free," *The Independent (London)* 4 September 1998: 5.

40. RIAA v. Diamond Multimedia Systems, 180 F 3d. 1072 at _ (9th Cir. 1999).

41. "Napster Closes 300,000 Music Accounts," *The New York Times* 12 May 2000: C6.

42. D. Clark and M. Peers, "MP3 Chief Rocks and Roils Music," *The Wall Street Journal*: B1

43. `<pr.mp3.com/pr/110.html>` and `<pr.mp3.com/pr/111.html>`

44. A. Mathews, "Music Samplers On Web Buy CDs in Stores," *The Wall Street Journal* 15 June 2000: A3.

45. "2000 Policy Issue Fact Sheet," `<www/microsoft.com/freedomtoinnovate/policyissues.htm>`.

46. U.S. vs. LaMachiaa, 871 F. Supp. 535 at _ (D. Mass. 1994).

47. D. Young, "Congress Modifies Copyright Protection for the Digital Age," *Legal Backgrounder* Vol. 14, No. 6.

48. Young, Vol. 14, No. 6.

49. L. Lessig, "Patent Problems," *The Industry Standard* 31 January 2000: 47.

50. R. Libshon, "Madness in the Method: Will 'Method of Doing Business' Patents Undermine the Web?" *Net Commerce Magazine* March 2000: 8.

51. Libshon, 8.

52. Libshon, 8.

53. Libshon, 8.

54. Section 4, Anti-cybersquatting Consumer Protection Act.

55. D. Herbeck, Chair and Associate Professor of Communication, Boston College, 2 March 2000, lecture notes.

56. D. Herbeck, Chair and Associate Professor of Communication, Boston College, 28 March 2000, lecture notes.

57. P. Thibodeau, "Defining 'Spam' Technically Isn't Easy," *Computerworld* 8 May 2000: 12.

58. Thibodeau, 12.

59. S. Collett, "States to Require Licenses for Online Auctioneers," *Computerworld* 6 December 1999: 4.

60. "French Court Says Yahoo Broke Racial Law," *The New York Times* 23 May 2000: C27.

61. B. Gruley and G. Simpson, "eBay Battles Yahoo! and Other Web Giants Over Privacy Protections," *The Wall Street Journal* 10 April 2000: B1.

62. B. Gruley and G. Simpson, B1.

63. L. Lessig, *Code and Other Laws of Cyberspace* (New York: Basic Books, 1999) 65.

64. `<www.wemedia.com>`.

65. M. Richtcl, "Promoting Peace Through Portals," *Yahoo! Internet Life* March 2000: 86, 88.

66. M. Conlin, "The New Workforce," *Business Week* 20 March 2000: 65.

67. S. Tillet, "E-Commerce for the Blind," *Internet Week* 8 May 2000: 31.

68. Tillet, 31.

69. "Web Disability," *Inter@ctive Week* 10 April 2000: 92.

70. S. Lais, "Coming Soon: Easier-to-Use Software For the Disabled," *Computerworld* 1 May 2000: 70.

71. "Cautious Embrace," *Global Technology Business* January 2000: 36–39.

72. K. Murphy, "Costly Tax Showdown," *Internet World* 15 April 2000: 41–42.

73. "States Lose Millions in Tax Dollars to Internet," *Computerworld* 6 March 2000: 62.

74. D. Brown, "Will E-Commerce Stay a Tax Free Haven," Inter@ctive Week 27 March 2000: 14.

75. D. Brown, "Gilmore's Commisssion Issues E-Tax Report," *Inter@ctive Week* 17 April 2000: 20.

76. Brown, 20.

77. `<www.ecommercetax.com` and `www.eurovat.com>`.

RECOMMENDED READINGS

"Adobe Enhances Accessibility of Adobe Acrobat Software for the Disability Community." 18 April 2000<http://www.adobe.com/aboutadobe/pressroom/pressreleases/200004/20000418acr.html>ACLU v. Reno, 929 F. Supp. 824, 849 (Ed. Pa. 1996).

Legislation and Legal Cases

American Civil Liberties Union of Georgia vs. Miller, 1:96-cv-2475-MHS (N.D. Ga. 1997).

Basic Books, Inc. vs. Kinko's Graphics Corp., 758 F. Supp. 1522 (S.D.N.Y. 1991).

Blumenthal vs. Drudge, 992 F. Supp. 44 at _ (1998).

Child Online Protection Act of 1998 (COPA).

Children's Online Privacy Protection Act of 2000 (COPPA).

Communications Decency Act of 1996 (CDA).

Compuserve vs. Cyber Promotions, 962 F. Supp. 1015 at _ (S.D. Ohio 1997).

Cubby vs. Compuserve, 776 F. Supp. 135 at _ (1991).

Cyber Promotions Inc. vs. America Online, 948 F. Supp. 436 at _ (Ed. Pa. 1996).

Digital Millenium Copyright Act (DMCA).

Encyclopedia Britannica Educational Corp. vs. Crooks, 542 F. Supp. 1156 (W.D.N.Y. 1982).

FCC vs. Pacifica Foundation, 438 U.S. 726 at 748-751 (1978).

"German Compuserve Judgment," `<www.qlinks.net/comdocs/somm.html>`.

Ginsberg vs. New York, 390 U.S. 629 at _ (1968).

Harper and Row Publishers, Inc. v. Nation Enterprises, 471 U.S. 539 (1985).

Intermatic vs. Toeppen (N.D. Ill. 1996).

Internet Tax Freedom Act.

Miller vs. California, 413 U.S. 15 at 24-25 (1973).

MTV vs. Curry (S.D. N.Y. 1994).

Playboy Enterprises, Inc. vs. Frena, 839 F. Supp. 1552 at _ (1993).

Reno vs. American Civil Liberties Union, 117 S Ct. 2329 at _ (1997).

RTC vs. Netcom, 907 F. Supp. 1361 at _ (N.D. Cal. 1995).

Sable Communications vs. FCC, 492 U.S. 115 at _ (1989).

Section 230 of the Telecommunications Act.

Sega Enterprises Ltd. vs. MAPHIA, 857 F. Supp. 679 at _ (N.D. Cal. 1994).

Smyth v. Pillsbury Co., 914 F. Supp. 97 at _ (Ed. Pa. 1996).

Steve Jackson Games, Inc. v. U.S. Secret Service (5th Cir. 1994).

Stratton Oakmont vs. Prodigy, 23 Media L. Rep. 1794 at _ (1995).

United States Constitution.

U.S. vs. LaMachiaa, 871 F. Supp. 535 at _ (D. Mass. 1994).

United States v. Thomas, 74 F3d 701 at _, cert.denied, 117 S Ct. 74 (1996).

Zeran vs. America Online, Inc., 129 F. 3d 327 at _ (1997).

Zippo Mfg. Co. vs. Zippo Dot Com, Inc. (W. Pa. 1997).

7

Computer and Network Security

Objectives

- To understand basic security concepts.
- To understand public-key/private-key cryptography.
- To learn about popular security protocols such as SSL and SET.
- To understand digital signatures, digital certificates and certification authorities.
- To become aware of various threats to secure systems such as viruses and denial-of-service attacks.
- To understand emerging security techniques such as biometrics and steganography.

Three may keep a secret, if two of them are dead.
Benjamin Franklin

Attack—Repeat—Attack.
William Frederick Halsey, Jr.

Private information is practically the source of every large modern fortune.
Oscar Wilde

There must be security for all—or not one is safe.
The day the Earth Stood Still, screenplay by Edmund H. North

No government can be long secure without formidable opposition.
Benjamin Disraeli

Outline

7.1 Introduction

The explosion of e-business and e-commerce is forcing businesses and consumers to focus on Internet security. Consumers are buying products, trading stocks and banking online. They are entering their credit-card numbers, social-security numbers and other highly confidential information through Web sites. Businesses are sending confidential information to clients and vendors over the Internet. At the same time, we are experiencing increasing numbers of security attacks. Individuals and organizations are vulnerable to data theft and hacker attacks that can corrupt files and even shut down e-businesses. Security is fundamental to e-business. According to a study by International Data Corporation, organizations spent $6.2 billion on security consulting in 1999, and they expect the market to reach $14.8 billion by 2003.[1]

Modern computer security addresses the various problems and concerns of protecting electronic communications and maintaining network security. There are four fundamental requirements of a successful, secure transaction: *privacy*, *integrity*, *authentication* and *non-repudiation*. *The privacy issue*: How do you ensure that the information you transmit over the Internet has not be captured or passed on to a third party without your knowledge? *The integrity issue*: How do you ensure the information you send or receive has not been compromised or altered? *The authentication issue*: How do the sender and receiver of a message prove their identities to each other? *The non-repudiation issue*: How do you legally prove that a message was sent or received?

In addition to these requirements, network security addresses the issue of *availability*: How do we ensure that the network and the computer systems it connects will stay in operation continuously?

In this chapter, we will explore Internet security from secure electronic transactions to secure networks, and the fundamentals of secure business—known as *s-business*. We will discuss how e-commerce security is achieved using current technologies. We encourage you to visit the Web resources provided in section 7.14 to learn more about the latest developments in e-commerce security. These resources include many demos you will find to be informative and entertaining.

7.2 Ancient Ciphers to Modern Cryptosystems

The channels through which data passes over the Internet are not secure; therefore, any private information that is being passed through these channels must be protected. To secure information, data can be encrypted. *Cryptography* transforms data by using a *key*—a string of digits that acts as a password—to make the data incomprehensible to all but the sender and the intended receivers. Unencrypted data is called *plaintext*; encrypted data is called *ciphertext*. Only the intended receivers should have the corresponding key to decrypt the ciphertext into plaintext. A *cipher* or *cryptosystem* is a technique or algorithm for encrypting messages.

Cryptographic ciphers were used as far back as the ancient Egyptians. In ancient cryptography, messages were encrypted by hand with a method usually based on the alphabetic letters of the message. The two main types of ciphers were *substitution ciphers* and *transposition ciphers*. In a substitution cipher, every occurrence of a given letter is replaced by a different letter—for example, if every "a" is replaced by a "b," every "b" by a "c," etc., the word "security" would encrypt to "tfdvsjuz." In a transposition cipher, the ordering of the letters is shifted—for example, if every-other letter starting with "s" in the word "security" creates the first word in the ciphertext and the remaining letters create the second word in the ciphertext, the word "security" would encrypt to "scrt euiy." Complicated ciphers were created by combining substitution and transposition ciphers. The problem with many historical ciphers is that their security relied on the sender and receiver to remember the encryption algorithm and keep it secret. Such algorithms ("algorithm" is a computer science term for "procedure") are called *restricted algorithms*. Restricted algorithms are not feasible to implement among a large group of people. Imagine if the security of U.S. government communications relied on every U.S. government employee to keep a secret.

Modern cryptosystems are digital. Their algorithms are based on the individual *bits* of a message rather than letters of the alphabet. A computer stores data as a *binary string*, which is a sequence of ones and zeros. Each digit in the sequence is called a bit. Encryption and decryption keys are binary strings with a given *key length*. For example, 128-bit encryption systems have a key length of 128 bits. Longer keys have stronger encryption; it takes more time and computing power to "break the code."

Until January 2000, the U.S. government placed restrictions on the strength of cryptosystems that could be exported from the United States. The government limited the key length of the encryption algorithms. Today, the regulations on exporting cryptosystems are less stringent. Any cryptosystem may be exported as long as the end-user is not a foreign government or from a country with embargo restrictions.[2]

7.3 Secret-key Cryptography

In the past, organizations wishing to maintain a secure computing environment used *symmetric cryptography*, also known as *secret-key cryptography*. Secret-key cryptography uses the same symmetric secret key to encrypt and decrypt a message (Fig. 7.1). In this case, the sender encrypts a message using the symmetric secret key, then sends the encrypted message and the symmetric secret key to the intended recipient. A fundamental problem with secret-key cryptography is that before two people can communicate securely, they must find a way to exchange the symmetric secret key securely. One approach is to have the key delivered by a courier, such as a mail service or Federal Express. While this may be feasible when two individuals communicate, it is not efficient for securing communication in a large network, nor can it be considered completely secure. The privacy and the integrity of the message could be compromised if the key is intercepted as it is passed between the sender and the receiver over insecure channels. Also, since both parties in the transaction use the same key to encipher and decipher a message, you cannot authenticate which party created the message. Finally, to keep communications private with each receiver, a different key is required for each receiver, so organizations could have huge numbers of symmetric secret keys to maintain.

An alternative approach to the key exchange problem is to have a central authority, called a *key distribution center (KDC)*. The key distribution center shares a (different) symmetric secret key with every user in the network. In this system, the key distribution center generates a *session key* to be used for a transaction (Fig. 7.2). For example, say a merchant and a customer want to conduct a secure transaction. The merchant and the customer each have unique symmetric secret keys they share with the key distribution center. The key distribution center generates a session key for the merchant and customer to use in the transaction. The key distribution center then sends the session key for the transaction to the merchant encrypted using the symmetric secret key the merchant already shares with the center. The key distribution center sends the same session key for the transaction to the customer, encrypted using the symmetric secret key the customer already shares with the key distribution center. Once the merchant and the customer have the session key for the transaction, they can communicate with each other, encrypting their messages using the shared session key.

Using a key distribution center reduces the number of courier deliveries (again, by means such as mail or Federal Express) of symmetric secret keys to each user in the network. In addition, users can have a new symmetric secret key for each communication with other users in the network, which greatly increases the overall security of the network. However, if the security of the key distribution center is compromised, then the security of the entire network is compromised.

One of the most commonly used symmetric encryption algorithms is the *Data Encryption Standard* (*DES*) which was developed by the National Security Agency (NSA) and IBM in the 1950s. DES has a key length of 56 bits. For many years, DES has been the standard set by the U.S. government and ANSI (American National Standards Institute). However, cryptanalysts today believe that DES is not completely secure because the key length is too short. As a result, the current standard of symmetric encryption is *Triple DES*, a variant of DES that is essentially three DES systems in a row, each having its own secret key. The United States government is in the process of selecting a new, more secure standard for symmetric encryption. The new standard will be called the

Advanced Encryption Standard (AES). The *National Institute of Standards and Technology (NIST)*, which sets the cryptographic standards for the U.S. government, is currently evaluating algorithms from five finalists based on strength, efficiency, speed and a few other characteristics.[3]

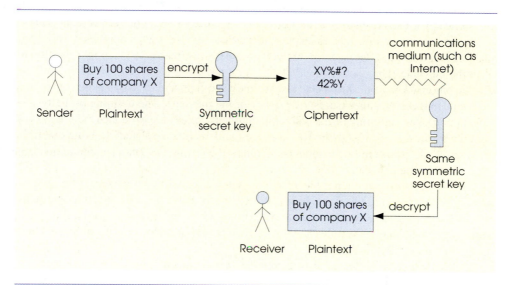

Fig. 7.1   Encrypting and decrypting a message using a symmetric secret key.

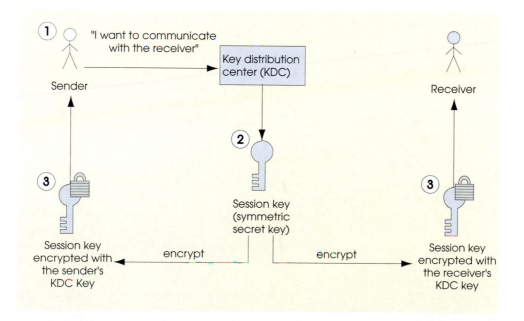

Fig. 7.2   Distributing a session key with a key distribution center.

7.4 Public Key Cryptography

In 1976, *Whitfield Diffie* and *Martin Hellman*, two researchers at Stanford University, developed *public-key cryptography* to solve the problem of exchanging keys securely. Public-key cryptography is asymmetric. It uses two inversely-related keys—a *public key* and a *private key*. The private key is kept secret by its owner. The public key is freely distributed. If the public key is used to encrypt a message, only the corresponding private key can decrypt it, and vice versa (see Fig. 7.3). Each party in a transaction has both a public key and a private key. To transmit a message securely, the sender uses the receiver's public key to encrypt the message. The receiver decrypts the message using the receiver's unique private key. No one else knows the private key, so the message cannot be read by anyone other than the intended receiver; this ensures the privacy of the message. The defining property of a secure public-key algorithm is that it is computationally infeasible to deduce the private key from the public key. Although the two keys are mathematically related, deriving one from the other would take enormous amounts of computing power and time, enough to discourage attempts to deduce the private key.

An outside party cannot participate in communication without the correct keys. Thus, the security of the entire process is based on the secrecy of the private keys. If a third party obtains the decryption key, then the security of the whole system is compromised. If the integrity of a system is compromised, you can change the key instead of changing the whole encryption or decryption algorithm.

Either the public key or the private key can be used to encrypt or decrypt a message. For example, if a customer uses a merchant's public key to encrypt a message, only the merchant can decrypt the message using the merchant's private key. Thus, the merchant's identity can be authenticated since only the merchant knows the private key. However, the merchant has no way of validating the customer's identity since the encryption key the customer used is publicly available.

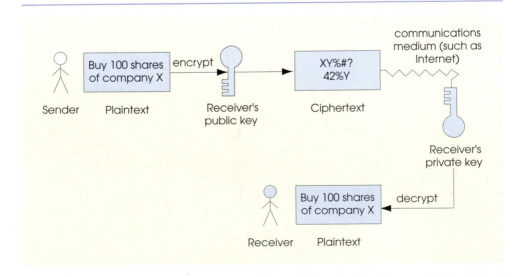

Fig. 7.3   Encrypting and decrypting a message using public-key cryptography.

If the decryption key is the sender's public key and the encryption key is the sender's private key, the sender of the message can be authenticated. For example, suppose a customer sends a merchant a message encrypted using the customer's private key. The merchant decrypts the message using the customer's public key. Since the customer encrypted the message using her private key, the merchant can be confident of the customer's identity. This all holds true if the merchant can be sure that the public key with which the merchant decrypted the message belongs to the customer and not a third party posing as the customer. The problem of proving ownership of a public key is discussed in section 7.8.

These two methods of public-key encryption can actually be used together to authenticate both participants in a communication (Fig. 7.4). Suppose that a merchant wants to send a message securely to a customer so that only the customer can read it, and suppose also that the merchant wants to provide proof to the customer that the merchant (not an unknown third party) actually sent the message. First the merchant encrypts the message using the customer's public key. This guarantees that only the customer can read it. Then the merchant encrypts the result using the merchant's private key, which proves the identity of the merchant. The customer decrypts the message in reverse order. First, the customer uses the merchant's public key. Since only the merchant could have encrypted the message with the inversely-related private key, this authenticates the merchant. Then the customer uses the customer's private key to decrypt the next level. This insures the content of the message was kept private in the transmission since only the customer has the key to decrypt the message.

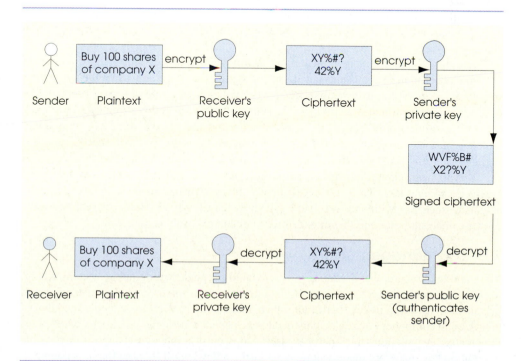

Fig. 7.4   Authentication with a public-key algorithm

The most commonly used public-key algorithm is *RSA*, an encryption system developed by Ron Rivest, Adi Shamir and Leonard Adleman in 1977. These three MIT professors founded *RSA Security Inc.* in 1982. Today, their encryption and authentication technologies are used by most Fortune 1000 companies and leading e-commerce businesses. With the emergence of the Internet and the World Wide Web, their security work has become even more significant and plays a crucial role in e-commerce transactions. Their encryption products are built into hundreds of millions of copies of the most popular Internet applications, including Web browsers, commerce servers and e-mail systems. Most secure e-commerce transactions and communications on the Internet use RSA products. For more information about RSA, cryptography and security, visit **www.rsasecurity.com**.

PGP (Pretty Good Privacy) is a public-key encryption system used to encrypt e-mail messages and files. It is freely available for non-commercial use. PGP is based on a "web of trust;" each client in a network can vouch for another client's identity to prove ownership of a public key. The "web of trust" is used to authenticate each client. To learn more about PGP and to download a free copy of the software, go to the MIT Distribution Center for PGP at **web.mit.edu/network/pgp.html**.

7.5 Key Agreement Protocols

A drawback of public-key algorithms is that they are not efficient for sending large amounts of data. They require large amounts of computer power which slows down communication. Thus, public-key algorithms should not be thought of as a replacement for symmetric secret key algorithms. Instead, public-key algorithms can be used to allow two parties to agree upon a key to be used for symmetric secret key encryption over an insecure medium. The process by which two parties can exchange keys over an insecure medium is called a *key agreement protocol*. A *protocol* sets the rules for communication. Exactly what encryption algorithm(s) are going to be used?

The most common key agreement protocol is a *digital envelope* (Fig. 7.5). Using a digital envelope, the message is encrypted using a symmetric secret key, then the symmetric secret key is encrypted using public-key encryption. For example, a sender encrypts the message using a symmetric secret key. The sender then encrypts that symmetric secret key using the receiver's public key. The sender attaches the encrypted symmetric secret key to the encrypted message, and sends the receiver the entire package. The sender could also digitally sign this package before sending it to prove the sender's identity to the receiver. To decrypt the package, the receiver first decrypts the symmetric secret key using the receiver's private key. Then, the receiver uses the symmetric secret key to decrypt the actual message. Since only the receiver can decrypt the encrypted symmetric secret key, the sender can be sure that only the intended receiver can read the message.

7.6 Key Management

Maintaining the secrecy of private keys is crucial to keeping cryptographic systems secure. Most compromises in security result from poor *key management* (e.g., the mishandling of private keys resulting in key theft) rather than attacks that attempt to decypher the keys.[4]

A main component of key management is *key generation*—the process by which keys are created. A malicious third-party could try to decrypt a message using every possible decryption key. Keys are made secure by choosing a key length so large that it is computationally infeasible to try all such combinations.

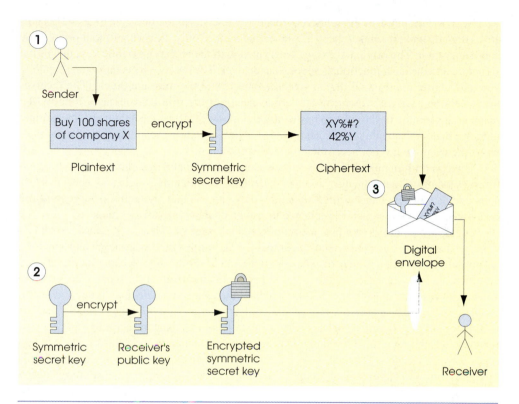

Fig. 7.5　　Creating a digital envelope.

Key generation algorithms are sometimes unintentionally constructed to choose only from a small subset of possible keys. If this subset is small enough, then it may be possible for a malicious third party to try every possible key to crack the encryption (see section 7.9 on cryptanalysis). Therefore, it is important to have a key-generation program which is truly random.

7.7 Digital Signatures

Digital signatures, the electronic equivalent of written signatures, were developed to be used in public-key cryptography to solve the problems of authentication and integrity. A digital signature authenticates the sender's identity, and, like a written signature, it is difficult to forge. To create a digital signature, a sender first takes the original plaintext message and runs it through a *hash function*, which is a mathematical calculation that gives the message a *hash value*. For example, you could take the plaintext message "Buy 100 shares of company X," run it through a hash function and get a hash value of 42. The hash function could be as simple as adding up all the 1s in a message, though it is usually more complex. The hash value is also known as a *message digest*. The chance that two different messages will have the same message digest is statistically insignificant. *Collision* occurs when multiple messages have the same hash value. It is computationally infeasible to compute a message from its hash value, or to find two messages with the same hash value.

Next, the sender uses the sender's private key to encrypt the message digest. This creates a digital signature and authenticates the sender since only the owner of that private key could encrypt it. The original message, encrypted with the receiver's public key, the digital signature and the hash function, is sent to the receiver. The receiver uses the sender's public key to decipher the original digital signature and reveal the message digest. The receiver then uses the receiver's own private key to decipher the original message. Finally, the receiver applies the hash function to the original message. If the hash value of the original message matches the message digest included in the signature, then there is *message integrity*—the message has not been altered in transmission.

There is a fundamental difference between digital signatures and hand-written signatures. A hand-written signature is independent of the document being signed. Thus, if someone can forge a hand-written signature, they can use that signature to forge multiple documents. A digital signature is created using the contents of the document.

Digital signatures do not provide proof that a message has been sent. Consider the following situation: a contractor sends a company a digitally signed contract, which the contractor later would like to revoke. The contractor could do this by releasing its private key and then claiming that the digitally signed contract came from an intruder who stole the contractor's private key. *Timestamping*, which binds a time and date to a digital document, can help solve the problem of non-repudiation. For example, suppose the company and the contractor are negotiating a contract. The company requires the contractor to digitally sign the contract and then have the document digitally timestamped by a third party called a *timestamping agency*. The contractor sends the digitally signed contract to the timestamping agency. The privacy of the message is maintained since the timestamping agency sees only the encrypted, digitally signed message (as opposed to the original plaintext message). The timestamping agency affixes the time and date of receipt to the encrypted, signed message and digitally signs the whole package with the timestamping agency's private key. This timestamp cannot be altered by anyone except the timestamping agency, as no one else possesses the timestamping agency's private key. Unless the contractor reports its private key to be compromised before the document is timestamped, the contractor cannot legally prove the document was signed by a third party. The sender could also require the receiver to digitally sign and timestamp the message as proof of receipt. To learn more about timestamping, visit **AuthentiDate.com** (**www.authentidate.com**).

The U.S. government's digital-authentication standard is called the *Digital Signature Algorithm* (*DSA*). The U.S. government recently passed digital-signature legislation that makes digital signatures as legally binding as hand-written signatures. This will result in an increase in e-business. For the latest news about U.S. government legislation in information security, visit **www.itaa.org/infosec**. For more information about the bills, visit the following government sites:

```
thomas.loc.gov/cgi-bin/bdquery/z?d106:hr.01714:
thomas.loc.gov/cgi-bin/bdquery/z?d106:s.00761:.
```

7.8 Public Key Infrastructure, Certificates and Certification Authorities

One problem with public-key cryptography is that anyone with a set of keys could potentially assume another party's identity. For example, say a customer wants to place an order with an online merchant. How does the customer know that the Web site being accessed indeed belongs to that merchant and not to a third party that posted a site and is masquerading as that merchant to steal credit-card information? *Public Key Infrastructure* (*PKI*) integrates public-key cryptography with *digital certificates* and *certification authorities* to authenticate parties in a transaction.

A digital certificate is a digital document issued by a *certification authority (CA)*. A digital certificate includes the name of the subject (the company or individual being certified), the subject's public key, a serial number, an expiration date, the signature of the trusted certification authority and any other relevant information (Fig. 7.6). A CA is a financial institution or other trusted third party, such as *VeriSign*. The CA takes responsibility for authentication, so it must carefully check information before issuing a digital certificate. Digital certificates are publicly available and are held by the certification authority in *certificate repositories*.

The CA signs the certificate by encrypting either the public key or a hash value of the public key using the CA's own private key. The CA has to verify every individual's public key. Thus, users must trust the public key of a CA. Usually, each CA is part of a *certificate authority hierarchy*. A certificate authority hierarchy is a chain of certificates, starting with the *root certification authority*, which is the Internet Policy Registration Authority (IPRA). The IPRA signs certificates using the *root key*. The root only signs certificates for *policy creation authorities*, which are organizations that set policies for obtaining digital certificates. In turn, policy creation authorities sign the digital certificates for CAs. CAs sign digital certificates for individuals and organizations.

VeriSign, Inc. is a leading certificate authority. For more information about VeriSign, visit **www.verisign.com**. For a listing of other digital-certificate vendors, please see the Internet and World Wide Web Resources section at the end of this chapter.

Periodically changing key pairs is helpful in maintaining a secure system in case your private key is compromised without your knowledge. The longer you use a given key pair, the more vulnerable the keys are to attack. As a result, digital certificates are created with an expiration date to force users to switch key pairs. If your private key is compromised before the expiration date, you can cancel your digital certificate and get a new key pair and certificate. Canceled and revoked certificates are placed on a *certificate revocation list* (*CRL*). CRLs are stored with the certification authority that issued the certificates.

Many people still perceive e-commerce to be insecure. In fact, transactions using PKI and digital certificates are more secure than exchanging private information over phone lines, through the mail or even paying by credit card in person. After all, when you go to a restaurant and the waiter takes your credit card in back to process your bill, how do you know the waiter did not write down your credit-card information? In contrast, the key algorithms used in most secure online transactions are nearly impossible to compromise. By some estimates, the key algorithms used in public-key cryptography are so secure that even millions of computers working in parallel could not possibly break the code in a century.

To obtain a digital certificate to digitally sign your personal e-mail messages, visit **www.verisign.com** or **www.tawte.com**. VeriSign offers a free 60-day trial, or you can purchase the service for a yearly fee. Thawte offers free digital certificates for personal e-mail. Web server certificates may also be purchased through Verisign and Thawte, however they are more expensive.

Fig. 7.6   A portion of the VeriSign digital certificate. (Courtesy of VeriSign.)

Digital-certificate capabilities are built into many e-mail packages. For example, in Microsoft Outlook, you can go to the **Tools** menu and select **Options**. Then click on the **Security** tag. At the bottom of the dialog box you will see the option to obtain a digital ID. This will take you to a Microsoft Web site with links to several worldwide certification authorities. Once you have a digital certificate, you can digitally sign your e-mail messages.

7.9 Cryptanalysis

Even if keys are kept secret, it may be possible to compromise the security of a system. Trying to decrypt ciphertext without knowledge of the decryption key is known as *cryptanalysis*. Commercial encryption systems are constantly being researched by cryptologists to ensure that these systems are not vulnerable to a cryptanalytic attack. The most common form of cryptanalytic attacks are those in which the encryption algorithm is analyzed to find relations between bits of the encryption key and bits of the ciphertext. Often, these relations are only statistical in nature and incorporate outside knowledge about the plaintext. The goal of such an attack is to determine the key from the ciphertext.

Weak statistical trends between ciphertext and keys can be exploited to gain knowledge about the key if enough ciphertext is known. Proper key management and expiration dates on keys help prevent cryptanalytic attacks. Also, using public-key cryptography to securely exchange symmetric secret keys allows you to use a new symmetric secret key to encrypt every message.

7.10 Security Protocols

Everyone using the Web for e-business and e-commerce needs to be concerned about the security of their personal information. There are several protocols that provide transaction security, such as *Secure Sockets Layer (SSL)* and *Secure Electronic Transaction™ (SET™)*. We discuss these security protocols in the next several sections.

7.10.1 Secure Sockets Layer (SSL)

The *Secure Sockets Layer (SSL) protocol,* developed by Netscape Communications, is a non-proprietary protocol commonly used to secure communication on the Internet and the Web.[5, 6] SSL is built into many Web browsers, including Netscape Communicator, Microsoft Internet Explorer and numerous other software products. It operates between the Internet's TCP/IP communications protocol and the application software.

In a standard correspondence over the Internet, a sender's message is passed to a socket that interprets the message in *TCP/IP* (Transmission Control Protocol/Internet Protocol). TCP/IP is the standard set of protocols used for communication between computers on the Internet. Most Internet transmissions are sent as (possibly large) sets of individual message pieces, called *packets*. At the sending side, the packets of one (possibly long) message are numbered sequentially, and error-control information is attached to each packet. TCP routes packets to avoid traffic jams, so each packet might travel a different route over the Internet. At the receiving end, TCP makes sure that all of the packets have arrived, puts them in sequential order and determines if the packets have arrived without alteration. If the packets have been altered, TCP/IP will re-transmit them. TCP/IP then passes the message to the socket at the receiver end. The socket translates the message back into a form that can be read by the receiver's application. In a transaction using SSL, the sockets are secured using public-key cryptography.

SSL uses public-key technology and digital certificates to authenticate the server in a transaction and to protect private information as it passes from one party to another over the Internet. SSL transactions do not require client authentication. To begin, a client sends a message to a server. The server responds and sends its digital certificate to the client for authentication. Using public-key cryptography to communicate securely, the client and server negotiate *session keys* to continue the transaction. Session keys are symmetric secret keys that are used for the duration of that transaction. Once the keys are established, the communication proceeds between the client and the server by using the session keys and digital certificates.

Although SSL protects information as it is passed over the Internet, it does not protect private information, such as credit-card numbers, once stored on the merchant's server. When a merchant receives credit-card information with an order, the information is often decrypted and stored on the merchant's server until the order is placed. If the server is not secure and the data is not encrypted, an unauthorized party can access that information. Hardware devices called *PCI (peripheral component interconnect) cards* can be installed on Web servers to secure data for an entire SSL transaction from the client to the Web server.[7] The PCI card processes the SSL transactions, freeing the Web server to perform other tasks. Visit **www.phobos.com/Products/infamily.htm** for more information about these devices.

For more information about the SSL protocol, check out the Netscape SSL tutorial at `developer.netscape.com/tech/security/ssl/protocol.html` and the Netscape Security Center site at `www.netscape.com/security/index.html`.

7.10.2 Secure Electronic Transaction™ (SET™)

The *Secure Electronic Transaction (SET) protocol*, developed by Visa International and MasterCard, was designed specifically to protect e-commerce payment transactions.[8, 9] SET uses digital certificates to authenticate each party in an e-commerce transaction, including the customer, the merchant and the merchant's bank. Public-key cryptography is used to secure information as it is passed over the Web.

Merchants must have a digital certificate and special SET software to process transactions. Customers must have a digital certificate and *digital wallet* software. A digital wallet is similar to a real wallet; it stores credit (or debit) card information for multiple cards as well as a digital certificate verifying the cardholder's identity. Digital wallets add convenience to online shopping; customers no longer need to re-enter their credit-card information at each shopping site.[10]

When a customer is ready to place an order, the merchant's SET software sends the order information and the merchant's digital certificate to the customer's digital wallet, thus activating the wallet software. The customer selects the credit card to be used for the transaction. The credit card and order information are encrypted by using the merchant's bank's public key and sent to the merchant along with the customer's digital certificate. The merchant then forwards the information to the merchant's bank to process the payment. Only the merchant's bank can decrypt the message since the message was encrypted using the bank's public key. The merchant's bank then sends the amount of the purchase and its own digital certificate to the customer's bank to get approval to process the transaction. If the customer's charge is approved, the customer's bank sends an authorization back to the merchant's bank. The merchant's bank then sends a credit-card authorization to the merchant. Finally, the merchant sends a confirmation of the order to the customer.

In the SET protocol, the merchant never sees the client's proprietary information. Therefore, the client's credit-card number is not stored on the merchant's server, considerably reducing the risk of fraud.

Although SET is designed specifically for e-commerce transactions and provides a high level of security, it has yet to become the standard protocol used in the majority of transactions. Part of the problem is that SET requires special software on both the client and server side; that requirement increases transaction costs. Also, the transactions are more time-consuming than transactions using other protocols, such as SSL. Both Visa and MasterCard have taken steps to reduce the financial burden to merchants in an effort to encourage more merchants to use SET. However, with higher transaction fees and little pressure from customers, many businesses are still reluctant to switch.[11]

SET Secure Electronic Transaction LLC is an organization formed by Visa and MasterCard to manage and promote the SET protocol. For more information about SET, visit `www.setco.org`, `www.visa.com` and `www.mastercard.com`. Visa has a demonstration of an online shopping transaction using SET at `www.visa.com/nt/ecomm/security/main.html`. GlobeSet, a digital-wallet software vendor, also offers a tutorial of an SET transaction that uses a digital wallet at `www.globeset.com`.

Microsoft Authenticode

How do you know the software you ordered online is safe and has not been altered? How can you be sure that you are not downloading a computer virus that could wipe out your computer? Do you trust the source of the software? With the emergence of e-commerce, software companies are offering their products online so that customers can download software directly onto their computers. Security technology is used to ensure that the downloaded software is trustworthy and has not been altered. *Microsoft Authenticode*, combined with VeriSign digital certificates (or *digital IDs*), authenticates the publisher of the software and detects whether the software has been altered. Authenticode is a security feature built into Microsoft Internet Explorer.

To use Microsoft Authenticode technology, each software publisher must obtain a digital certificate specifically designed for the purpose of publishing software—such certificates may be obtained through certification authorities, such as VeriSign (Section 7.8). To obtain a certificate, a software publisher must provide its public key and identifying information and sign an agreement that it will not distribute harmful software. This gives customers legal recourse if any downloaded software from certified publishers causes harm.

Microsoft Authenticode uses digital signature technology to sign software (Section 7.5). The signed software and the publisher's digital certificate provide proof that the software is safe and has not been altered.

When a customer attempts to download a file, a dialog box appears on the screen displaying the digital certificate and the name of the certificate authority. Links to the publisher and the certificate authority are provided so that customers can learn more about each party before they agree to download the software. If Microsoft Authenticode determines that the software has been compromised, the transaction is terminated.

To learn more about Microsoft Authenticode, visit the following sites:

```
msdn.microsoft.com/workshop/security/authcode/signfaq.asp
msdn.microsoft.com/workshop/security/authcode/authwp.asp
```

7.11 Security Attacks

Recent cyber attacks on e-businesses have made the front pages of newspapers worldwide. *Denial-of-service attacks*, *viruses* and *worms* have cost companies billions of dollars. Denial-of-service attacks usually require the power of a network of computers working simultaneously—the attacks cause networked computers to crash or disconnect from the network, making services unavailable. Denial-of-service attacks can disrupt service on a Web site and even shut down critical systems such as telecommunications or flight-control centers.

Viruses are computer programs—usually sent as an attachment or hidden in audio clips, video clips and games—that attach to, or overwrite, other programs to replicate themselves. Viruses can corrupt your files or even wipe out your hard drive. Before the Internet, viruses spread through files and programs (such as video games) transferred to computers by removable disks. Today, viruses are spread over a network simply by sharing infected files embedded in e-mail attachments, documents or programs. A worm is similar to a virus except that it can spread and infect files on its own over a network; worms do not need to be attached to another program to spread. Once a virus or worm is released, it can spread rapidly often "infecting" millions of computers worldwide within minutes or hours.

A denial-of-service attack occurs when a network's resources are taken up by an unauthorized individual, leaving the network unavailable for legitimate users; typically the attack is performed by flooding servers with data packets. This greatly increases the traffic on the network, overwhelming the servers and making it impossible for legitimate users to download information.

Another type of denial-of-service attack targets the *routing tables* of a network. Routing tables are essentially the road map of a network, providing directions for data to get from one computer to another. This type of attack is accomplished by modifying the routing tables, thus disabling network activity. For example, the routing tables can be changed to send all data to one address in the network. In a *distributed denial-of-service attack*, the packet flooding does not come from a single source, but from many separate computers. Actually, such an attack is rarely the concerted work of many individuals. Instead, it is an individual who has installed viruses on various computers, gaining illegitimate use of the computers to carry out the attack. Distributed denial-of-service attacks can be difficult to stop since it is not clear which requests on a network are from legitimate users and which are part of the attack. In addition, it is particularly difficult to catch the culprit of such attacks since the attacks are not carried out directly from the attacker's computer.

Who is responsible for viruses and denial-of-service attacks? Most often these people are referred to as *hackers*. Hackers are usually skilled programmers. Some hackers break into systems just for the thrill of it without causing any harm to the compromised systems (except, perhaps, humbling and humiliating their owners); others have malicious intent. Either way, hackers are breaking the law by accessing or damaging private information and computers. In February, 2000, distributed denial-of-service attacks shut down high-traffic Web sites including Yahoo!, eBay, CNN Interactive and Amazon. In this case, a hacker used a network of computers to flood the Web sites with traffic that overwhelmed the sites' computers.

Viruses, one of the most dangerous threats to network security, are typically malicious programs. There are many classes of computer viruses. A *transient virus* attaches itself to a specific computer program. The virus is activated when the program is run and deactivated when the program is terminated. A more powerful type of virus is a *resident virus*, which, once loaded into the memory of a computer, operates for the duration of the computer's use. Another type of virus is the *logic bomb*, which triggers when a given condition is met, such as a *time bomb* that is triggered when the clock on the computer matches a certain time or date.

A *Trojan horse* is a malicious program that hides within a friendly program or simulates the identity of a legitimate program or feature, while actually causing damage to the computer or network in the background. The Trojan horse gets its name from Greek history and the story of the Trojan war. Greek warriors hid inside a wooden horse which the Trojans took within the walls of the city of Troy. When night fell and the Trojans were asleep, the Greek warriors came out of the horse and opened the gates to the city, letting the Greek army enter the gates and destroy the city of Troy. Trojan horses can be particularly difficult to detect since they appear to be legitimate, useful programs. In June, 2000, news spread of a Trojan horse disguised as a video clip sent as an e-mail attachment. The Trojan horse was designed to give the attacker access to the infected computers, potentially to launch a denial-of-service attack against Web sites.[15]

Two of the most famous viruses to date were *Melissa*, which struck in March, 1999, and the *ILOVEYOU virus* that hit in May, 2000. Both viruses cost organizations and individuals billions of dollars. The Melissa virus spread in Microsoft Word documents sent via e-mail. When the document was opened, the virus was triggered. Melissa accessed the Microsoft Outlook address book on that computer and automatically sent the infected Word attachment by e-mail to the first 50 people in the address book. Each time another person opened the attachment, the virus would send out another 50 messages. Once into a system, the virus infected any subsequently saved files.

The ILOVEYOU virus was sent as an attachment to an e-mail posing as a love letter. The message in the e-mail said "Kindly check the attached love letter coming from me." Once opened, the virus accessed the Microsoft Outlook address book and sent out messages to the addresses listed, helping to spread the virus rapidly worldwide. The virus corrupted all types of files, including system files. Networks at companies and government organizations worldwide were shut down for days trying to remedy the problem and contain the virus. Estimates for damage caused by the virus were as high as $10 billion to $15 billion, with the majority of the damage done in just a few hours.

Viruses and worms are not just limited to your computer. In June, 2000, a worm named *Timofonica* that was propagated through e-mail quickly made its way into the cellular phone network in Spain, sending prank calls and leaving text messages on the phones. No serious damage was done, nor did the worm infect the cell phones, but experts predict that we will see many more viruses and worms spread to cell phones in the future.[16]

Why do these viruses spread so quickly? One reason is that many people are too willing to open executable files from unknown sources. Have you ever opened an audio clip or video clip from a friend? Have you ever forwarded that clip to other friends? Do you know who created the clip and if any viruses are embedded in it? Did you open the ILOVE YOU file to see what the love letter said?

Most antivirus software is reactive, going after viruses once they are discovered rather than protecting against unknown viruses. New antivirus software, such as Finjan Software's SurfinGuard® (**www.finjan.com**), looks for executable files attached to e-mail and runs the executables in a secure area to test if they attempt to access and harm files. For more information about antivirus software, see the feature on **McAfee.com** anti-virus utilities.

Web defacing is another popular form of attack by hackers wherein the hackers illegally enter an organization's Web site and change the contents. CNN Interactive has a special report titled "Insurgency on the Internet," with news stories about hackers and their online attacks. Included is a gallery of hacked sites. One notable case of Web defacing occurred in 1996 when Swedish hackers changed the Central Intelligence Agency Web site (**www.odci.gov/cia**) to read "Central Stupidity Agency." The hackers put obscenities, messages and links to adult-content sites on the page. Many other popular and large Web sites have been defaced.

The rise in cyber crimes has prompted the United States government to take action. Under the National Information Infrastructure Protection Act of 1996, denial-of-service attacks and distributing viruses are a federal crimes punishable by fines and jail time. For more information about the United States government's efforts against cyber crime or to read about recently prosecuted cases, visit the U.S. Department of Justice Web site at **www.usdoj.gov/criminal/cybercrime/compcrime.html**. Also check out

www.cybercrime.gov, a site maintained by the Criminal Division of the United States Department of Justice.

The *CERT® Coordination Center* (*Computer Emergency Response Team*) at Carnegie Mellon University's Software Engineering Institute responds to reports of viruses and denial-of-service attacks and provides information on network security, including how to determine if your system has been compromised. The site provides detailed incident reports of viruses and denial-of-service attacks with descriptions of the incidents, their impact and the solutions. The site also includes reports of vulnerabilities in popular operating systems and software packages. The *CERT Security Improvement Modules* are excellent tutorials on network security. These modules describe the issues and technologies used to solve network security problems. For more information, visit the CERT Web site at **www.cert.org**.

To learn more about how you can protect yourself or your network from hacker attacks, visit AntiOnline™ at **www.antionline.com**. This site has security-related news and information, a tutorial titled "Fight-back! Against Hackers," information about hackers and an archive of hacked sites. You can find additional information about denial-of-service attacks and how to protect your site at

> **www.irchelp.org/irchelp/nuke**

McAfee.com Anti-Virus Utilities

McAfee.com provides a variety of anti-virus utilities (and other utilities) for users whose computers are not continuously connected to a network, for users whose computers are continuously connected to a network (such as the Internet) and for users connected to a network via wireless devices such as personal digital assistants and pagers.

For computers that are not continuously connected to a network, McAfee provides their anti-virus software *VirusScan®*. This software is configurable to scan files for viruses on demand or to scan continuously in the background as the user does their work.

For computers that are network and Internet accessible, McAfee provides their online **McAfee.com** Clinic. Users with a subscription to McAfee Clinic can use the online virus software from any computer they happen to be using. As with VirusScan software on standalone computers, users can scan their files on demand. A major benefit of the Clinic is its *ActiveShield* software. Once installed, ActiveShield can be configured to scan every file that is used on the computer or just the program files. It can also be configured to check automatically for virus definition updates and notify the user when such updates become available. The user simply clicks the supplied hyperlink in an update notification to connect to the Clinic site and clicks another hyperlink to download the update. Thus, users can keep their computers protected with the most up-to-date virus definitions at all times. For more information about McAfee, visit **www.mcafee.com**. Also check out Norton security products from Symantec at **www.symantec.com**. Symantec is a leading security software vendor. Their product Norton™ Internet Security 2000 provides protection against hackers, viruses and threats to privacy to both small businesses and individuals.

7.12 Network Security

The goal of network security is to allow authorized users access to information and services, while preventing unauthorized users from gaining access to, and possibly corrupting, the network. There is a trade-off between network security and network performance—increased security often decreases the efficiency of the network.

7.12.1 Firewalls

A basic tool in network security is the *firewall*. The purpose of a firewall is to protect a *local area network* (*LAN*) from intruders outside the network. For example, most companies have internal networks that allow employees to share files and access company information. Each LAN is connected to the Internet through a gateway which usually includes a firewall. For years, one of the biggest threats to security came from employees inside the firewall. Now that businesses rely heavily on access to the Internet, an increasing number of security threats are originating outside the firewall—from the hundreds of millions of people connected to the company network by the Internet.[12] A firewall acts as a safety barrier for data flowing into and out of the LAN. Firewalls can prohibit all data flow not expressly allowed, or can allow all data which is not expressly prohibited. Choosing between these two models is up to the network security administrator and should be based on the need for security versus the need for functionality.

There are two main types of firewalls: *packet-filtering firewalls* and *application-level gateways*. A packet-filtering firewall examines all data sent from outside the LAN and automatically rejects any data packets that have local network addresses. For example, if a hacker from outside the network obtains the address of a computer inside the network and tries to sneak a harmful data packet through the firewall, the packet-filtering firewall will reject the data packet since it has an internal address but originated from outside the network. A problem with packet-filtering firewalls is that they consider only the source of data packets. They do not examine the actual data itself. As a result, malicious viruses can be installed on a user's computer, giving the hacker access to the network without the user's knowledge. The goal of a application-level gateway is to screen the actual data. If the message is deemed safe, then the message is sent through to the intended receiver.

Using a firewall is probably the single most effective and easiest way to add security to a small network.[13] Often, small companies or home users who are connected to the Internet through permanent connections, such as DSL lines, do not employ strong security measures. As a result, their computers are prime targets for hackers to use in denial-of-service attacks or to steal information. It is important for all computers connected to the Internet to have some degree of security on their systems. There are numerous firewall software products available. Several products are listed in the Web resources in section 7.13.

7.12.2 Kerberos

Firewalls do not protect you from internal security threats to your local area network. Internal attacks are common and can be extremely damaging. For example, disgruntled employees with network access can wreak havoc on an organization's network or steal valuable, proprietary information. It is estimated that 70% to 90% of attacks on corporate networks are internal.[14] *Kerberos* is a freely available, open-source protocol developed at

MIT. It employs symmetric secret-key cryptography to authenticate users in a network, and to maintain integrity and privacy of network communications.

Authentication in a Kerberos system is handled by a main Kerberos system and secondary *Ticket Granting Service* (TGS). This system is similar to key distribution centers as described in Section 7.3. The main Kerberos system authenticates a client's identity to the TGS; the TGS authenticates client's rights to access specific network services.

Each client in the network shares a symmetric secret key with the Kerberos system. This symmetric secret key may be used by multiple TGSs in the Kerberos system. The client starts by entering a login and password into the Kerberos authentication server. The authentication server maintains a database of all clients in the network. The authentication server returns a *Ticket-Granting Ticket* (*TGT*) encrypted with the client's symmetric secret key that it shares with the authentication server. Since the symmetric secret key is only known by the authentication server and the client, only the client can decrypt the TGT, thus authenticating the client's identity. Next, the client sends the decrypted TGT to the Ticket Granting Service to request a *service ticket*. The service ticket authorizes the client access to specific network services. Service tickets have a set expiration time. Tickets may be renewed by the TGS.

7.12.3 Biometrics

An innovation in security is likely to be *biometrics*. Biometrics uses unique personal information such as fingerprints, eyeball iris scans or face scans to identify a user. This eliminates the need for passwords, which are much easier to steal. Have you ever written down your passwords on a piece of paper and put it in your desk drawer or wallet? These days, people have passwords and PIN code for everything—Web sites, networks, e-mail, ATM machines and even for their cars. Managing all those codes can become a burden. Recently, the cost of biometric devices has dropped significantly. Keyboard-mounted fingerprint scanning devices are being used in place of passwords to log into systems, check e-mail or access secure information over a network. Each user's iris scan, face scan or fingerprint is stored in a secure database. Each time a user logs in, their scan is compared to the database. If a match is made, the login is successful. Two companies that specialize in biometric devices are IriScan (**www.iriscan.com**) and Keytronic (**www.keytronic.com**). For additional resources, see Section 7.14.

7.13 Steganography

Steganography is the practice of hiding information within other information. The term literally means "covered writing." Like cryptography, steganography has been used since ancient times. Steganography allows you to take a piece of information such as a message or image, and hide it within another image, message or even an audio clip. Steganography takes advantage of insignificant space in digital files, in images or on removable disks.[17] Consider a simple example: if you have a message that you want to send secretly, you can hide the information within another message so no one but the intended receiver can read it. For example, if you want to tell your stock broker to buy vs. sell a stock and your message must be transmitted over an insecure channel, you could send the message "BURIED UNDER YARD." If you have agreed in advance that your message is hidden in the first letters of each word, the stock broker picks these letters off and sees "BUY."

An increasingly popular application of steganography is *digital watermarks*. An example of a conventional watermark is shown in Fig. 7.7. A digital watermark can be either visible or invisible. It is usually a company logo, copyright notification or other mark or message that indicates the owner of the document. The owner of a document could show the hidden watermark in a court of law, for example, to prove that the watermarked item was stolen.

Digital watermarking could have a substantial impact on e-commerce. Consider the music industry. Music publishers are concerned that MP3 technology is allowing people to distribute illegal copies of songs and albums. As a result, many publishers are hesitant to put content online as digital content is easy to copy. Also, since CD-ROMs are digital, people are able upload their music and share it over the Web. Using digital watermarks, music publishers can make indistinguishable changes to a part of a song at a frequency that is not audible to humans, to show that the song was, in fact, copied.

Blue Spike's Giovanni™ digital watermarking software uses cryptographic keys to generate and embed steganographic digital watermarks into digital music and images (Fig. 7.8). The watermarks can be used as proof of ownership to help digital publishers protect their copyrighted material. The watermarks are undetectable by anyone who is not privy to the embedding scheme, and thus the watermarks cannot be located and removed. The watermarks are placed randomly.

Giovanni incorporates cryptography and steganography. It generates a symmetric secret-key based on an encryption algorithm and the contents of the audio or image file that will carry the watermark. The key is then used to place (and eventually decode) the watermark. The software identifies the perceptually insignificant areas of the image or audio file, enabling a digital watermark to be embedded inaudibly, invisibly and in such a way that if removed, the content is likely to be damaged.

Digital watermarking capabilities are built into some image-editing software applications such as Adobe PhotoShop 5.5 (**www.adobe.com**). Companies that offer digital watermarking solutions include Digimarc (**www.digimark.com**) and Cognicity (**www.cognicity.com**).

7.14 Internet and World Wide Web Resources

Security Resource Sites

www.securitysearch.net
SecuritySearch.net is a comprehensive resource for computer security. The site has thousands of links to products, security companies, tools and more. The site also offers a free weekly newsletter with information about vulnerabilities.

www.esecurityonline.com
eSecurityOnline.com is a great resource for online security. The site has links to news, tools, events, training and other valuable security information and resources.

www.epic.org
The *Electronic Privacy Information Center* deals with protecting privacy and civil liberties. Visit this site to learn more about the organization and their latest initiatives.

theory.lcs.mit.edu/~rivest/crypto-security.html
The *Ronald L. Rivest: Cryptography and Security* site has an extensive list of links to security resources including newsgroups, government agencies, FAQs, tutorials and more.

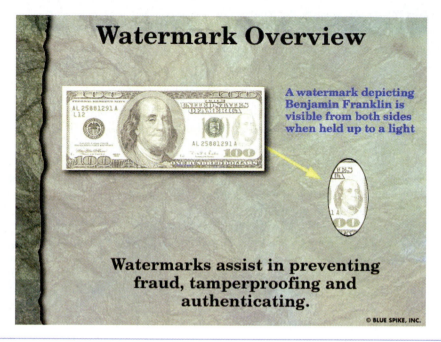

Fig. 7.7   Example of a conventional watermark. (Courtesy of Blue Spike, Inc.)

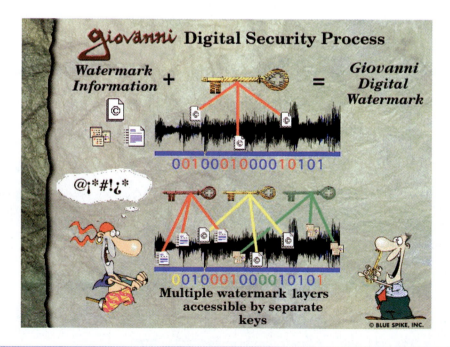

Fig. 7.8   An example of steganography: Blue Spike's Giovanni digital watermarking process. (Courtesy of Blue Spike, Inc.)

`www.w3.org/Security/Overview.html`
The *W3C Security Resources* site has a FAQ, information about the W3C security and e-commerce initiatives and links to other security related Web sites.

`web.mit.edu/network/ietf/sa`
The Internet Engineering Task Force (IETF), which is an organization concerned with the architecture of the Internet, has working groups dedicated to Internet Security. Visit the *IETF Security Area* to learn about the working groups, join the mailing list or check out the latest drafts of their work.

`dir.yahoo.com/Computers_and_Internet/Security_and_Encryption`
The *Yahoo Security and Encryption* page is a great resource for links to security and encryption Web sites.

`www.counterpane.com/hotlist.html`
The Counterpane Internet Security, Inc. site includes links to downloads, source code, FAQs, tutorials, alert groups, news and more.

`www.rsasecurity.com/rsalabs/faq`
This is an excellent FAQ about cryptography from RSA Laboratories, one of the leading makers of public key cryptosystems.

`www.nsi.org/compsec.html`
Visit the National Security Institute's *Security Resource Net* for the latest security alerts, government standards, legislation, plus a security FAQ links and other helpful resources.

`www.itaa.org/infosec`
The Information Technology Association of America (ITAA) *InfoSec* site has information about the latest U.S. government legislation related to information security.

`staff.washington.edu/dittrich/misc/ddos`
The *Distributed Denial of Service Attacks* site has links to news articles, tools, advisory organizations and even a section on humor.

`www.infoworld.com/cgi-bin/displayNew.pl?/security/links/security_corner.htm`
The Security Watch site on **Infoword.com** has loads of links to security resources.

`www.antionline.com`
AntiOnline has security related news and information, a tutorial titled "Fight-back! Against Hackers," information about hackers and an archive of hacked sites.

`www.microsoft.com/security/default.asp`
The Microsoft security site has links to downloads, security bulletins and tutorials.

Magazines, Newsletters and News sites

`www.networkcomputing.com/consensus`
The *Security Alert Consensus* is a free weekly newsletter with information about security threats, holes, solutions and more.

`www.infosecuritymag.com`
Information Security Magazine has the latest Web security news and vendor information.

`www.issl.org/cipher.html`
Cipher is an electronic newsletter on security and privacy from the IEEE (Institute of Electrical and Electronics Engineers). You can view current and past issues online.

`securityportal.com`
The *Security Portal* has news and information about security, cryptography and the latest viruses.

`www.scmagazine.com`
SC Magazine has news, product reviews and a conference schedule for security events.

`www.cnn.com/TECH/specials/hackers`
Insurgency on the Internet from CNN Interactive has news stores on hacking, plus a gallery of hacked sites.

`rootshell.com/beta/news.html`
Visit Rootshell for security news and white papers.

Government Sites for Computer Security
`www.cit.nih.gov/security.html`
This site has links to security organizations, security resources, plus tutorials on PKI, SSL and others.

`cs-www.ncsl.nist.gov`
The *Computer Security Resource Clearing House* is a resource for network administrators and others concerned with security. This site has links to incident reporting centers, information about security standards, events, publications and other resources.

`www.cdt.org/crypto`
Visit the *Center for Democracy and Technology* for United States legislation and policy news regarding cryptography.

`www.epm.ornl.gov/~dunigan/security.html`
This site has links to loads of security related sites. The links are organized by subject and include resources for digital signatures, PKI, smart cards, viruses, commercial providers, intrusion detection and several other topics.

`www.alw.nih.gov/Security`
The *Computer Security Information* page is an excellent resource with links to news, newsgroups, organizations, software, FAQs and extensive WWW links.

`www.fedcirc.gov`
The *Federal Computer Incident Response Capability* deals with security of government and civilian agencies. This site has information about incident statistics, advisories, tools and patches and more.

`axion.physics.ubc.ca/pgp.html`
This site has a list of freely available cryptosystems with discussion of each and links to FAQs and tutorials.

`www.ifccfbi.gov`
The *Internet Fraud Complaint Center*, founded by the Justice Department and the FBI, fields reports of Internet fraud.

`www.disa.mil/infosec/iaweb/default.html`
The Defense Information Systems Agency's *Information Assurance* page includes vulnerability warnings, virus information, incident reporting instructions and other helpful links.

Internet Security Vendors
`www.rsa.com`
RSA is one of the leaders in electronic security. Visit their site for more information about their current products and tools which are used by companies worldwide.

`www.ca.com/protection`
Computer Associates is a vendor of Internet security software. They have various software packages to help companies set up a firewall, scan files for viruses and protect against viruses.

`www.checkpoint.com`
Check Point™ Software Technologies Ltd. is a leading provider of Internet Security products and services.

www.mycio.com
MyCIO provides Internet security software and services.

www.opsec.com
The Open Platform for Security (OPSEC) has over 200 partners that develop security products and solutions using the OPSEC to allow interoperability and increased security over a network.

www.baltimore.com
Baltimore is an e-commerce security solutions provider. Their most popular product is UniCERT, a digital certificate product that is used in PKI. They also offer SET, public-key cryptography and digital certificate solutions.

www.ncipher.com
nCipher is a vendor of hardware and software security products. Their products include an SSL accelerator that speeds up transaction of SSL Web servers and a secure key management system.

www.entrust.com
Entrust Technologies provides e-security products and services.

www.tenfour.co.uk
TenFour® provides software for secure e-mail.

www.antivirus.com
ScanMail® is an e-mail virus detection program for Microsoft Exchange.

www.contenttechnologies.com/ads
Content Technologies is a security software provider. Their products include firewall and secure e-mail programs.

www.zixmail.com
Zixmail™ is a secure e-mail product that allows you to encrypt and digitally sign your messages using different e-mail programs.

www.pgp.com/scan
PGP Security software protects your site from denial-of-service attacks.

web.mit.edu/network/pgp.html
Download *Pretty Good Privacy*® freeware which allows you to send messages, files, etc. securely.

www.radguard.com
Radguard provides large-scale security solutions for e-businesses.

www.certicom.com
Certicom provides security solutions for the wireless Internet.

www.raytheon.com
Raytheon Corporation recently launched *SilentRunner*, a product that monitors activity on a network—such as Web browsing and file transfers—to find internal threats such as data theft or fraud.

SSL and SET
developer.netscape.com/tech/security/ssl/protocol.html
This Netscape page has a brief description of SSL, plus links to an SSL tutorial and FAQ.

www.netscape.com/security/index.html
The Netscape Security Center is an extensive resource for Internet and Web security. You will find news, tutorials, products and services.

psych.psy.uq.oz.au/~ftp/Crypto
This FAQ has an extensive list of questions and answers about SSL technology.

www.setco.org
The Secure Electronic Transaction LLC was formed through Visa and MasterCard to work on the SET specification. Visit this Web site to learn more about SET and the companies using SET in their products, and check out the brief FAQ and glossary.

www.visa.com/nt/ecomm/security/main.html
The *Visa International* security page includes information on SSL and SET. There is a demonstration of an online shopping transaction, which explains how SET works.

www.mastercard.com/shoponline/set
The *MasterCard SET* Web site includes information about the SET protocol, a glossary of SET-related terms, the latest developments and a demonstration walking you through the steps of a purchase using SET technology.

www.openssl.org
The *Open SSL Project* provides a free, open source toolkit for SSL.

Public-Key Cryptography

www.rsa.com/ie.html
RSA Data Security is a company that specializes in cryptography. Check out their detailed FAQ about cryptography.

www.entrust.com
Entrust produces effective security software products using Public Key Infrastructure (PKI).

www.cse.dnd.ca
The Communication Security Establishment has a short tutorial on Public Key Infrastructure (PKI) that defines PKI, public-key cryptography and digital signatures.

www.magnet.state.ma.us/itd/legal/pki.htm
The Commonwealth of Massachusetts Information Technology page has loads of links to sites related to PKI that contain information about standards, vendors, trade groups and government organizations.

www.ftech.net/~monark/crypto/index.htm
The Beginner's Guide to Cryptography is an online tutorial with links to other privacy and cryptography sites.

www.faqs.org/faqs/cryptography-faq
The *Cryptography FAQ* has an extensive list of questions and answers.

www.pkiforum.org
The *PKI Forum* promotes the use of PKI.

www.counterpane.com/pki-risks.html
Visit the Counterpane Internet Security, Inc.'s site to read the article "Ten Risks of PKI: What You're Not Being Told About Public Key Infrastructure."

Digital Signatures

www.ietf.org/html.charters/xmldsig-charter.html
The *XML Digital Signatures* site was created by a group working to develop digital signatures using XML. You can view the group's goals and drafts of their work.

www.elock.com
E-Lock Technologies is a vendor of digital signature products used in Public Key Infrastructure. This site has a FAQ covering cryptography, keys, certificates and signatures.

www.digsigtrust.com
The Digital Signature Trust Co. is a vendor of Digital Signature and Public Key Infrastructure products. They have a tutorial titled "Digital Signatures and Public Key Infrastructure (PKI) 101."

Digital Certificates

www.verisign.com
VeriSign creates digital IDs for individuals, small businesses and large corporations. Check out their Web site for product information, news and downloads.

www.thawte.com
Thawte Digital Certificate Services offers SSL, developer and personal certificates.

www.silanis.com/index.htm
Silanis Technology is a vendor of digital certificate software.

www.belsign.be
Belsign issues digital certificates in Europe. They are the European authority for digital certificates.

www.certco.com
Certco issues digital certificates to financial institutions.

www.openca.org
Set up your own CA using open source software from The OpenCA Project.

Digital Wallets

www.globeset.com
GlobeSet is a vendor of digital-wallet software. They have an animated tutorial demonstrating the use of an electronic wallet in an SET transaction.

www.trintech.com
Trintech digital wallets handle SSL and SET transactions.

wallet.yahoo.com
The *Yahoo! Wallet* is a digital wallet that can be used at thousands of Yahoo! Stores worldwide.

Firewalls

www.interhack.net/pubs/fwfaq
This is an extensive Firewall FAQ.

www.spirit.com/cgi-bin/report.pl
Visit this site to compare firewall software from a variety of vendors.

www.zeuros.co.uk/generic/resource/firewall
Zeuros is a complete resource for information about firewalls. You will find FAQs, books, articles, training and magazines.

www.thegild.com/firewall
The *Firewall Product Overview* site has an extensive list of firewall products with links to each vendor's site.

csrc.ncsl.nist.gov/nistpubs/800-10
Check out this firewall tutorial from the U.S. Department of Commerce.

www.watchguard.com
WatchGuard® Technologies, Inc. provides firewalls and other security solutions for medium to large organizations.

www.networkice.com
BlackICE Defender from Network ICE combines a firewall with intrusion detection.

Kerberos

www.nrl.navy.mil/CCS/people/kenh/kerberos-faq.html
This is an extensive Kerberos FAQ from the Naval Research Laboratory.

web.mit.edu/kerberos/www
Kerberos: The Network Authentication Protocol is a FAQ by MIT.

www.contrib.andrew.cmu.edu/~shadow/kerberos.html
The Kerberos Reference Page has links to several informational sites, technical sites and other helpful resources.

www.pdc.kth.se/kth-krb
Visit this site to download various Kerberos white papers and documentation.

Biometrics

www.iosoftware.com/products/integration/fiu500/index.htm
This security device scans a user's fingerprint to verify identity.

www.identix.com/flash_index.html
Identix specializes in fingerprinting systems for law enforcement, access control and network security. Using their fingerprint scanners, you can log on to your system, encrypt and decrypt files and lock applications.

www.iriscan.com
Iriscan's *PR Iris*™ can be used for e-commerce, network and information security. The scanner takes an image of the user's eye for authentication.

www.keytronic.com
Key Tronic manufactures keyboards with fingerprint recognition systems.

Steganography and digital watermarking

www.bluespike.com/giovanni/giovmain.html
Blue Spike's *Giovanni* watermarks help publishers of digital content protect their copyrighted material and track their content that is distributed electronically.

www.outguess.org
Outguess is a freely available steganographic tool.

www.cl.cam.ac.uk/~fapp2/steganography/index.html
The Information Hiding Homepage has technical information, news and links related to digital watermarking and steganography.

www.demcom.com
DemCom's *Steganos Security Suite* software allows you to encrypt and hide files within audio, video, text or HTML files.

www.digimarc.com
Digimarc is a leading provider of digital watermarking software solutions.

www.cognicity.com
Cognicity specializes in digital watermarking solutions for the music and entertainment industries.

Newsgroups

news:comp.security.firewalls

news:comp.security.unix

news:comp.security.misc

news:comp.protocols.kerberos

SUMMARY

- There are four fundamental requirements of a successful, secure transaction: privacy, integrity, authentication and non-repudiation.

- The privacy issue: How do you ensure that the information you transmit over the Internet has not be captured or passed on to a third party without your knowledge?

- The integrity issue: How do you ensure the information you send or receive has not been compromised or altered?

- The authentication issue: How do the sender and receiver of a message prove their identities to each other?

- The non-repudiation issue: How do you legally prove that a message was sent or received?

- The issue of availability: How can we allow authorized users in a network to access information and services while keeping unauthorized users out?

- The channels through which data passes over the Internet are not secure; therefore, any private information that is being passed through these channels must be protected.

- To secure information, data can be encrypted.

- Cryptography transforms data by using a key—a string of digits that acts as a password—to make the data incomprehensible to all but the sender and the intended receivers.

- Unencrypted data is called plaintext; encrypted data is called ciphertext.

- A cipher or cryptosystem is a technique or algorithm for encrypting messages.

- Longer keys have stronger encryption; it takes more time and computing power to "break the encryption code."

- Secret-key cryptography uses the same symmetric secret key to encrypt and decrypt a message.

- A fundamental problem with secret-key cryptography is that before two people can communicate securely, they must find a way to exchange the symmetric secret key securely.

- In a network with a key distribution center, each user shares one symmetric secret key with the key distribution center.

- Users can have a new symmetric secret key for each communication with other users in the network, which greatly increases the overall security of the network.

- One of the most commonly used symmetric encryption algorithms is the Data Encryption Standard (DES) which was developed by the National Security Agency (NSA) and IBM in the 1950s.

- The current standard of symmetric encryption is Triple DES, a variant of DES that is essentially three DES systems in a row, each having its own secret key.

- The United States government is in the process of selecting a new, more secure standard for symmetric encryption. The new standard will become the Advanced Encryption Standard (AES).

- In 1976, Whitfield Diffie and Martin Hellman, two researchers at Stanford University, developed public key cryptography to solve the problem of exchanging keys securely.

- Public-key cryptography is asymmetric. It uses two inversely-related keys—a public key and a private key. The private key is kept secret by its owner. The public key is freely distributed.

- If the public key is used to encrypt a message, only the corresponding private key can decrypt it, and vice versa.

- Although the two keys are mathematically related, deriving one from the other would take enormous amounts of computing power and time.

- Using public key algorithms, each person in a network needs only two keys—one encryption key and one decryption key.

- Since each user is responsible for the user's own private key, key management in public-key cryptography is less of a burden than in secret-key cryptography.
- If the user's decryption key is the public key and their encryption key is private, the sender of the message can be authenticated.
- The most commonly used public-key algorithm is RSA, an encryption system developed by Ron Rivest, Adi Shamir and Leonard Adleman in 1977.
- Public key algorithms can be used to allow two parties to agree upon a key to be used for symmetric encryption over an insecure medium.
- The process by which two parties can exchange keys over an insecure medium is called a key agreement protocol.
- The most common key agreement protocol is a digital envelope.
- Digital signatures, the electronic equivalent of written signatures, were developed to be used in public-key cryptography to solve the problems of authentication and integrity.
- A digital signature authenticates the sender's identity, and, like a written signature, it is difficult to forge.
- Digital signatures do not provide proof that a message has been sent.
- Timestamping, which binds a time and date to a digital document, can help solve the problem of non-repudiation.
- The timestamping agency affixes the time and date of receipt to the encrypted, signed message and digitally signs the whole package with the timestamping agency's private key.
- The digital authentication standard of the U.S. government is called the Digital Signature Algorithm (DSA).
- Public Key Infrastructure (PKI) adds digital certificates to the process of authentication.
- A digital certificate includes the name of the subject (the company or individual being certified), the subject's public key, a serial number, an expiration date, the authorization of the trusted certification authority and any other relevant information.
- A certification authority (CA) is a financial institution or other trusted third party, such as VeriSign.
- The CA takes responsibility for authentication, so it must carefully check information before issuing a digital certificate.
- Digital certificates are publicly available and are held by the certification authority in certificate repositories.
- Periodically changing key pairs is helpful in maintaining a secure system in case your private key is compromised without your knowledge.
- By some estimates, the key algorithms used in public-key cryptography are so secure that even millions of computers working in parallel could not possibly break the code in a century.
- Trying to decrypt ciphertext without knowledge of the decryption key is known as cryptanalysis.
- SSL uses public-key technology and digital certificates to authenticate the server in a transaction and to protect private information as it passes from one party to another over the Internet.
- SSL transactions do not require client authentication.
- Session keys are symmetric secret keys that are used for the duration of that transaction.
- The Secure Electronic Transaction (SET) protocol, developed by Visa International and MasterCard, was designed specifically to protect e-commerce payment transactions.
- SET uses digital certificates to authenticate each party in an e-commerce transaction, including the customer, the merchant and the merchant's bank.

- A digital wallet is similar to a real wallet; it stores credit (or debit) card information for multiple cards as well as a digital certificate verifying the cardholder's identity.

- In the SET protocol, the merchant never actually sees the client's proprietary information. Therefore, the client's credit-card number is not stored on the merchant's server—this considerably reduces the risk of fraud.

- Microsoft Authenticode uses digital signature technology to sign software. The signed software and the publisher's digital certificate provide proof that the software is safe and has not been altered.

- Denial-of-service attacks usually require the power of a network of computers working simultaneously.

- Viruses are computer programs—usually sent as an attachment or hidden in audio clips, video clips and games—that attach to or overwrite other programs to replicate themselves.

- A worm is similar to a virus except that it can spread and infect files on its own over a network; worms do not need to be attached to another program to spread.

- A denial-of-service attack occurs when a network's resources are taken up by an unauthorized individual, leaving the network unavailable for legitimate users; typically the attack is performed by flooding servers with data packets.

- Another type of denial-of-service attack targets the routing tables of a network. This type of attack is accomplished by modifying the routing tables, thus disabling network activity.

- A resident virus, once loaded into the memory of a computer, operates for the duration of the computer's use.

- Another type of virus is the logic bomb, which triggers when a given condition is met, such as a time bomb that is triggered when the clock on the computer matches a certain time or date.

- A Trojan horse is a malicious program that hides within a friendly program or simulates the identity of a legitimate program or feature, while actually causing damage to the computer or network in the background.

- Most antivirus software is reactive, going after viruses once they are discovered rather than protecting against unknown viruses.

- Web defacing is another popular form of attack by hackers wherein the hackers illegally enter an organization's Web site and change the contents.

- A firewall protects a local area network (LAN) from intruders outside the network.

- There are two main types of firewalls: packet-filtering firewalls and application-level gateways.

- A packet-filtering firewall examines all data sent from outside the LAN and automatically rejects any data packets that have local network addresses.

- The goal of a application-level gateway is to screen the actual data. If the message is deemed safe, then the message is sent through to the intended receiver.

- Firewalls do not protect you from internal security threats to your local area network.

- Kerberos is a freely available, open-source protocol developed at MIT. It employs symmetric secret-key cryptography to authenticate users in a network, and to maintain integrity and privacy of network communications.

- Authentication in a Kerberos system is handled by a main Kerberos system and a secondary Ticket Granting Service (TGS).

- The main Kerberos system authenticates a client's identity to the TGS; the TGS authenticates client's rights to access specific network services.

- Biometrics uses unique personal information such as fingerprints, eyeball iris scans or face scans to identify a user. This eliminates the need for passwords, which are much easier to steal.

- Steganography is the practice of hiding information. The term literally means "covered writing."
- Steganography allows you to take a piece of information such as a message or image, and hide it within another image, message or even an audio clip.

TERMINOLOGY

ActiveShield
Advanced Encryption Standard (AES)
application-level gateway
asymmetric algorithms
authentication
Authenticode (from Microsoft)
availability
binary string
biometrics
bit
CERT (Computer Emergency Response Team)
CERT Security Improvement Modules
certification authority (CA)
certificate authority hierarchy
certificate repository
certificate revocation list (CRL)
cipher
ciphertext
collision
cryptanalysis
cryptography
cryptosystem
Data Encryption Standard (DES)
data packets
decryption
denial-of-service attack
Diffie-Hellman Key Agreement Protocol
digital certificate
digital envelope
digital IDs
Digital Signature Algorithm (DSA)
digital signature
digital wallet
digital watermarking
distributed denial-of-service attack
encryption
firewall
hacker
hash function
hash value
ILOVEYOU Virus
integrity
Internet Policy Registration Authority (IPRA)
Kerberos
key

key agreement protocol
key distribution center
key generation
key length
key management
local area network (LAN)
logic bombs
Melissa Virus
message digest
message integrity
Microsoft Authenticode
National Institute of Standards and Technology
network security
non-repudiation
one-way hash functions
packet-filtering firewall
packets
PCI (peripheral component interconnect) cards
plaintext
policy creation authorities
privacy
private key
protocol
public key
public-key algorithms
public-key cryptography
Public Key Infrastructure (PKI)
resident virus
restricted algorithms
root certification authority
root key
routing tables
RSA Security, Inc.
s-business
secret key
Secure Electronic Transactions (SET)
Secure Sockets Layer (SSL)
service ticket
session keys
SET Secure Electronic Transaction LLC
steganography
substitution cipher
symmetric encryption algorithms
TCP/IP (Transmission Control Protocol/Internet
    Protocol)

Ticket Granting Ticket (TGT)   Triple DES
time bombs   Trojan horse
timestamping   VeriSign
timestamping agency   virus
timofonica   Web defacing
transient virus   worm
transposition cipher

SELF-REVIEW EXERCISES

7.1   State whether the following are true or false. If the answer is false, explain why.
   a) In a public key algorithm, one key is used for both encryption and decryption.
   b) Digital certificates are intended to be used indefinitely.
   c) Secure Sockets Layer protects data stored on the merchant server.
   d) Secure Electronic Transaction is another name for Secure Sockets Layer.
   e) Digital signatures can be used to provide undeniable proof of the author of a document.
   f) In a network of 10 users communicating using public key cryptography, only 10 keys are needed in total.
   g) The security of modern cryptosystems lies in the secrecy of the algorithm.
   h) Users should avoid changing keys as much as possible, unless they have reason to believe the security of the key has been compromised.
   i) Increasing the security of a network often decreases its functionality and efficiency.
   j) Firewalls are the single most effective way to add security to a small computer network.
   k) Kerberos is an authentication protocol that is used over TCP/IP networks.

7.2   Answer each of the following questions.
   a) Cryptographic algorithms in which the message sender and receiver both hold an identical key are called _____.
   b) A _____ is used to authenticate the sender of a document.
   c) In a _____, a document is encrypted using a symmetric secret key and sent with that symmetric secret key, encrypted using a public key algorithm.
   d) A certificate that needs to be revoked before its expiration date is placed on a _____.
   e) The recent wave of network attacks that have hit companies such as eBay, Yahoo, etc. are known as _____.
   f) A digital fingerprint of a document can be created using a _____.
   g) The four main issues addressed by cryptography are _____, _____, _____ and _____.
   h) A customer can store purchase information and multiple credit cards in an electronic purchasing and storage device called a _____.
   i) Trying to decrypt ciphertext without knowing the decryption key is known as _____.
   j) A barrier between a small network and the outside world is called a _____.

ANSWERS TO SELF-REVIEW EXERCISES

7.1   a) False. The encryption key is different from the decryption key. One is made public, and the other kept private. b) False. Digital certificates are created with an expiration date to encourage users to periodically change their public/private key pair. c) False. Secure Sockets Layer is an Internet security protocol, which secures the transfer of information in electronic communication. It does not protect data stored on a merchant server. d) False. Secure Electronic Transaction is a security protocol designed by Visa and MasterCard as a more secure alternative to Secure Sockets Layer. e) False. A user who digitally signed a document could later intentionally give up his private key, and then claim that the document was written by an imposter. Thus, timestamping a document is necessary so that users cannot repudiate documents written before the pubic/private key pair is reported invalidated. f) False. Each user needs a public key and a private key. Thus, in a network of 10 users, 20 keys are needed in total. g) False. The security of modern cryptosystems lies in the secrecy of the encryption and decryption keys. h) False. Changing keys often is a good way to maintain the security of a communication system. i) True. j) True. k) True.

7.2   a) Symmetric key algorithms. b) Digital signature. c) Digital envelope. d) Certificate Revocation List. e) Distributed Denial of Service Attacks. f) Hash function. g) Privacy, authentication, integrity, non-repudiation. h) Electronic wallet. i) Cryptanalysis. j) Firewall.

EXERCISES

7.3   What can online businesses do to prevent hacker attacks such as Denial of Service or virus attacks?

7.4   Define the following security terms.
    a) digital signature
    b) hash function
    c) symmetric key encryption
    d) digital certificate
    e) Denial of Service attack
    f) worm
    g) message digest
    h) collision
    i) triple DES
    j) session keys

7.5   Define each of the following security terms and give an example of how it is used.
    a) secret key cryptography
    b) public key cryptography
    c) digital signature
    d) digital certificate
    e) hash function
    f) SSL
    g) Kerberos
    h) firewall

7.6   Identify and describe each of the following acronyms.
    a) PKI
    i) RSA
    j) CRL
    k) AES
    l) SET

7.7   List the four problems dealt with by cryptography and give a real world example of each one.

7.8   Compare symmetric key algorithms with public key algorithms. What are the benefits/drawbacks of each type of algorithm? How are these differences manifested in the real world uses of these two types of algorithms?

7.9   The Visa International Web Site includes an interactive demonstration of the Secure Electronic Transaction (SET) protocol that uses animation to explain this complicated protocol in a way that most people will understand. Visit Visa at **www.visa.com/nt/sec/no_shock/**

`intro_L.html` to view the demo. Write a short summary of SET. How does SET differ from SSL? Why are digital wallets important? How are they used? If you were asked to choose between the two protocols, which would you choose and why?

7.10　Explain how, in a network using symmetric key encryption, a Key Distribution Center can play the role of an authenticator of parties.

7.11　Go to the VeriSign Web site at `www.verisign.com`. Write an analysis of the features and security of VeriSign's digital certificates. Then go to five other certification authorities and compare the features and security of their digital certificates to VeriSign.

7.12　Research the Secure Digital Music Initiative (`www.sdmi.org`). Describe how security technologies such as digital watermarks can help music publishers protect their copyrighted work.

7.13　Distinguish between packet-filtering firewalls and application-level gateways.

7.14　Using steganography, hide the message "MERGER IS A GO" inside a seemingly unrelated paragraph of text. Insert your secret message as the second character of each word in the paragraph.

WORKS CITED

1.　A. Harrison, "Xerox Unit Farms Out Security in $20M Deal," *Computerworld* 5 June 2000: 24.

2.　RSA Laboratories, "RSA Laboratories' Frequently Asked Questions About Today's Cryptography, Version 4.1," <`www.rsasecurity.com/rsalabs/faq`>, RSA Security, Inc., 2000.

3.　A. Harrison, "Advanced Encryption Standard," *Computerworld* 29 May 2000: 57.

4.　RSA Laboratories, "RSA Laboratories' Frequently Asked Questions About Today's Cryptography, Version 4.1," <`www.rsasecurity.com/rsalabs/faq`>, RSA Security, Inc., 2000.

5.　S. Abbot, "The Debate for Secure E-Commerce," *Performance Computing* February 1999" 37-42.

6.　T. Wilson, "E-Biz Bucks Lost Under the SSL Train," *Internet Week* 24 May 1999: 1,3.

7.　M. Bull, "Ensuring End-to-End Security with SSL," *Network World* 15 May 2000: 63.

8.　S. Machlis, "IBM Hedges its Bets on SET," *Computerworld* 20 July 1998: 4.

9.　J. McKendrick, "Is Anyone SET for Secure Electronic Transactions," *ENT* 4 March 1998: 44, 46.

10.　W. Andrews, "The Digital Wallet: A concept revolutionizing e-commerce," *Internet World* 15 October 1999: 34-35.

11.　S. Machlis, "MasterCard Makes SET More Attractive," *Computerworld* 12 January 1998: 3.

12.　R. Marshland, "Hidden Cost of Technology," *Financial Times* 2 June 2000: 5.

13.　T. Spangler, "Home Is Where the Hack Is," *Inter@ctive Week* 10 April 2000: 28-34.

14.　S. Gaudin, "The Enemy Within," *Network World* 8 May 2000: 122-126.

15.　H. Bray, "Trojan Horse Attacks Computers, Disguised as a Video Chip," *The Boston Globe* 10 June 2000: C1+.

16.　A. Eisenberg, "Viruses Could Have Your Number," *The New York Times* 8 June 2000: E7.

17.　S. Katzenbeisser and F. Petitcolas, Ed., *Information Hiding: Techniques for Steganography and Digital Watermarking* (Norwood, MA: Artech House, Inc., 2000) 1-2.

RECOMMENDED READINGS

Berinato, S. "Feds Sign Off on e-Signatures." *eWeek* 29 May 2000: 20-21.

Deitel, H. *An Introduction to Operating Systems.* Second Edition, Reading, MA: Addison Wesley, 1990.

DiDio, L. "Private-key Nets Unlock e-Commerce." *Computerworld* 16 March 1998: 49-50.

Ford, W., and M. Baum. *Secure Electronic Commerce: Building the Infrastructure for Digital Signatures and Encryption.* Upper Saddle River, NJ: Prentice Hall, 1997.

Garfinkel, S. and Spafford, G. *Web Security and Commerce.* Cambridge, MA: O'Reilly, 1997.

Ghosh, A. *E-Commerce Security: Weak Links, Best Defenses.* New York, NY: Wiley Computer Publishing, 1998.

Goncalves, M. *Firewalls: A Complete Guide.* New York, NY: McGraw-Hill, 2000.

Kippenhahn, R. *Code Breaking.* New York, NY: The Overlook Press, 1999.

Kosiur, D. *Understanding Electronic Commerce.* Redmond, WA: Microsoft Press, 1997.

Marsland, R. "Hidden Cost of Technology." *Financial Times* 2 June 2 2000: 5.

Pfleeger, C. *Security in Computing: Second Edition.* Upper Saddle River, NJ: Prentice Hall, 1997.

RSA Laboratories. "*RSA Laboratories' Frequently Asked Questions About Today's Cryptography, Version 4.1.*" <**www.rsasecurity.com/rsalabs/faq**> RSA Security Inc., 2000.

Sager, I. "Cyber Crime." *Business Week* 21 February 2000: 37-42.

Schneier, B. *Applied Cryptography: Protocols, Algorithms and Source Code in C.* New York, NY: John Wiley & Sons, Inc., 1996.

Sherif, M. *Protocols for Secure Electronic Commerce.* New York, NY: CRC Press, 2000.

Smith, R. *Internet Cryptography.* Reading, MA: Addison Wesley, 1997.

Spangler, T. "Home Is Where The Hack Is." *Inter@ctive Week* 10 April 2000: 28-34.

Wrixon, F. *Codes, Ciphers & Other Cryptic & Clandestine Communication* New York, NY: Black Dog & Leventhal Publishers, 1998.

Hardware, Software and Communications

Objectives

- To introduce some of the communications media and hardware used to connect computers on the Internet.
- To introduce many of the technologies used for high-speed Internet connections, such as fiber optics, DSL and broadband.
- To discover the uses, advantages and limitations of the wireless Internet for PDAs, digital cellular phones and mobile computers.
- To explore new services offered on the Internet for building e-commerce Web sites.
- To introduce consulting companies and turnkey solutions for creating complete e-businesses.

The road to business success is paved by those who continually strive to produce better products or services.
G. Kingsley Ward

Sometimes give your services for nothing...
Hippocrates

Outline

8.1 Introduction

In Chapters 1 and 2, we introduced the basic concepts of computer hardware, software and the Internet. In this chapter we explore the advances currently being made in all these areas. We discuss fiber-optic technology, which, as a high-speed communications medium, accelerates data transfers over the Internet. We introduce digital subscriber lines (DSL) and broadband Internet media, new technologies that provide relatively inexpensive, high-speed Internet service to homes and businesses. We also discuss wireless connectivity, which will eventually allow users to access the Internet from anywhere in the world. We discuss turnkey solutions provided over the Internet for helping you set up your own complete e-business quickly and economically.

Years ago, application development was expensive due to high hardware, software and communications costs. Computers and communications were much slower than they are today. With advancements in technology, these costs are rapidly decreasing. Power is increasing and, with fiber optics, the speed of data transfers over the Internet is becoming virtually unlimited. Today, the only limitations on you as an application developer are the limits of your own imagination. In this book you will learn how to build the software for Web-based applications in a world of powerful and economical hardware and communications resources.

8.2 Structure of the Internet

The Internet is a network of interconnected *host computers,* or *hosts.* Each host is assigned a unique address called an *IP address.* An IP address is much like the street address of a house. Just as people use street addresses to locate houses or businesses in a city, computers use IP addresses to locate other computers on the Internet.

Computers on the Internet communicate with each other by sending *packets* of data across the network. A packet is much like a letter sent through the post office. A letter has an envelope with a return address that indicates the address of the person who sent the letter, a delivery address that indicates the house or business to which the letter should be delivered and the letter's contents. Packets sent across the Internet contain a *source address*, a *destination address, sequencing information, error-control information* and the *data* to be delivered to the destination address. The source address is the IP address of the computer that sent the packet and the destination address is the IP address of the computer to which the data was sent. When a computer sends data across the Internet, the data is usually divided into multiple packets. These packets may arrive at the destination host out of order. The host that receives the packets uses the sequencing information to rearrange the data into its proper order.

Packets are generally not sent directly to the destination address. The Internet is a large, complex network; each host could not possibly know the best route by which a packet should be sent to another host on the Internet. Therefore, a special kind of host called a *router* is used to move packets across the Internet in an efficient way. A packet may pass through many routers before it reaches its destination. Sending a packet through many computers may seem inefficient, but the Internet was designed so that if one part of the network failed, the remaining parts could still function. Routers are responsible for redirecting packets around any areas of the network that may have failed and ensuring that packets are delivered to the proper destination hosts.

8.3 Hardware

The physical structure of the Internet employs many advanced hardware technologies. In this section, we discuss the various communications media used to connect hosts together as well as the different roles hosts may play on the Internet.

8.3.1 Servers

A *server* is a host on the Internet that manages network resources and fulfills requests from *clients.* There are many types of servers, including *Web servers, e-mail servers, database servers* and *file servers.* A single server may provide multiple services. For example, one server may act as both a Web server and a file server.

A Web server stores Web pages and delivers those pages to clients upon request. As we saw in Chapter 2, a Web browser uses the *hypertext transfer protocol (HTTP)* to request and transfer pages from a Web server. We examine HTTP closely and use it to build working Web-based applications later in the book. A *protocol* defines the steps necessary for computers to communicate over the Internet. Other common protocols include the *file transfer protocol (FTP)*, the *post office protocol (POP)* for receiving e-mail and the *simple mail transfer protocol (SMTP)* for sending e-mail.

Most requests to a Web server from a browser are requests for HTML documents. We present a thorough introduction to HTML in Chapters 9 and 10 and then use it extensively throughout the remainder of the book.

8.3.2 Communications Media

A *communications medium* is the hardware that connects computers and other digital equipment together. The most important measure for a communications medium is its *bandwidth*, which indicates how much data can be transferred through the medium in a fixed amount of time. If we were plumbers, we might measure the number of gallons of water that could flow through a pipe in one second. A wide pipe allows more water to flow through in one second than a narrow pipe. Likewise, a high-bandwidth communications medium allows more data to flow through in one second than a low-bandwidth communications medium. Bandwidth is usually measured in *bits per second (bps), kilobits per second (Kbps)* or *megabits per second (Mbps)*. A medium that can transmit data at a rate of 1.5 Mbps is able to transfer approximately 1,500,000 bits of data in one second.

For many years, *copper wire* has been the primary communications medium for communications. The *plain old telephone system (POTS)*, used for voice-telephone calls around the world, was built with copper wire. There are many advantages to using copper wire, including wide availability, reliability, and ease of installation. However, copper wire has proven inadequate for handling high-speed data transmission between computers.

Fiber-optic cable, which is composed of flexible glass fiber, is thinner and lighter than traditional copper wire, yet it has much wider bandwidth. Traditional copper wire carries electronic signals that are interpreted by the computer as bits (i.e., "binary digits"—pieces of data that can have the value 0 or 1). Fiber-optic cable uses short bursts of light to represent bits. An *optical modem*, which stands for *optical modulator* and *demodulator*, translates digital signals from a computer into light through a process called *modulation*. The light is transmitted over the fiber-optic cable to the receiver's optical modem, which converts the light back into an electrical signal through a process called *demodulation*.

Recently, an advanced optical technology called the *opto-chip* was developed. The opto-chip is able to convert the most basic particle of light, the photon, into an electric current. This allows tremendously increased amounts of data to be sent over fiber-optic networks using a particle 100 times smaller than the diameter of a human hair.[1] Further enhancements to fiber-optic technology allow multiple wavelengths of light to be transmitted over a single fiber. Each additional wavelength greatly increases the data-carrying capacity of fiber-optic technology.

The strength of a signal transmitted over a communications medium such as copper wire or fiber-optic cable is reduced as the signal travels farther and farther. Copper wire and fiber-optic cable are therefore limited by the distances over which they can transmit signals reliably. *Repeaters* can be used to alleviate this problem by amplifying and retransmitting the signal across segments of copper wire or fiber-optic cable. Fiber-optic cable is able to maintain a stronger signal than copper wire over longer distances and therefore requires fewer repeaters.

For many applications, fiber-optic technology is prohibitively expensive. Fiber-optic cable is more expensive than copper wire and installation of fiber-optic cable is more complicated than the installation of copper wire. Because fiber-optic cable transmits light, it must be carefully cut and polished to ensure proper signal transmission.[2] Additionally, copper wire is already widely used, so switching to fiber-optic cable requires rewiring and purchasing new hardware.

8.3.3 Storage Area Networks (SANs)

Companies produce large volumes of data to support sales analysis tools, enterprise resource planning (ERP), multimedia Web sites and e-commerce. The complexities of maintaining these data in a reliable and fault-tolerant way becomes increasingly difficult as the volume of data increases. A *storage area network (SAN)* provides high-capacity, reliable data storage and delivery on a network. Using a SAN allows network administrators to collect data in logical groups on data servers distributed throughout the network. *SAN devices* store large volumes of data and may also provide backup and recovery services. Using *mirroring* technology, a SAN device stores *redundant* copies of data so that if one copy is lost or damaged, a mirrored copy can be used to recover the lost data. SANs use *fibre-channel* technology to connect computers on the network to SAN devices. Fibre channel is a high-speed communications medium based on fiber-optic technology that provides transfer rates of 100 Mbps.

Companies such as EMC (**www.emc.com**), Compaq (**www.compaq.com**), IBM (**www.ibm.com**) and Hewlett-Packard (**www.hp.com**) all provide high-capacity *network storage devices* for use in SANs. StorageNetworks (**www.storagenetworks.com**) also provides SANs as a service to companies. For a fee, StorageNetworks will store multiple *terabytes* (one terabyte equals one trillion bytes) of your company's data in its data centers worldwide. StorageNetworks provides access to the data through a high-speed fiber-optic line connected directly between the StorageNetworks data center and your company.

8.4 Connecting to the Internet

There are many ways for computers to connect to the Internet. A summary of the common types of Internet connections and their comparative speeds and availability can be found in Fig. 8.1. Most home users subscribe to an *Internet Service Provider (ISP)* in order to connect to the Internet. Typical ISPs allow customers to connect to the Internet using normal telephone lines. Using an *analog modem*, a user connects to an ISP, which then connects the user to the Internet. A modem takes *digital* signals from the computer and turns them into sound. The sound, which is an *analog signal*, can be transmitted over a telephone line just like a human voice. A modem at the ISP then converts the sound back into a digital signal that can be transmitted over the Internet.

Most ISPs charge monthly fees for Internet access. However, some Internet providers offer free Internet access (Fig. 8.2) in return for personal demographic data, such as your age, address, interests and income level. These ISPs then display advertisements on the Web pages you view.

Method	Speed (Kbps)	Send Speed = Receive Speed	Cost	Number of Users	Availability for Businesses
Modem	33 - 53	No	Very Low	1-2	Universal
Cable Modem	384 - 1,500	No	Medium	10-20	Very Limited
ISDN	56 - 128	Yes	High	5	Widely Available
xDSL	384 - 55,000	No	Low	10-50	Limited Availability
Frame Relay/ T1	64 - 1,544	Yes	Very High	50+	Widely Available

Fig. 8.1   Connection comparison chart. (Data courtesy of eXchangeBridge.)

Company	URL
NetZero	`www.netzero.com`
Alta Vista	`www.zdnet.com/downloads/altavista/index.html`
ISfree.com	`www.isfree.com`
DialFree	`www.dialfree.net`
Address.com	`www.address.com`
Free Internet	`www.freeinternet.com`
FreeLane	`freelane.excite.com`
iFreedom.com	`www.ifreedom.com`

Fig. 8.2   Internet Service Providers that provide free Internet access.

8.4.1 Digital Subscriber Lines (DSL)

A *Digital Subscriber Line (DSL)* offers high-bandwidth Internet access over existing copper telephone lines. The abbreviation xDSL is used to describe the many types of DSL that are available, such as *asymmetric DSL (ADSL), symmetric DSL (SDSL), high-speed DSL (HDSL)* and *very high-speed DSL (VDSL).*

DSL transforms standard copper telephone wires into high-speed digital connections. Since this wiring is already in place in most homes and offices, millions of users can start using DSL service without any additional rewiring, which helps lower the cost of DSL services. DSL takes advantage of the portion of the bandwidth not used for voice calls and splits your phone line into three information-carrying channels. One carries data from the Internet to your home computer. Another transports data from your home computer to the Internet. The third handles regular phone calls and faxes.

In terms of bandwidth, DSL connections offer transfer speeds of up to 55 Mbps. These speeds are much faster than those possible using a modem over regular telephone lines. However, DSL connections require special hardware at the local telephone company's *central office* and at the user's location. Also, because of limitations on DSL technology, the speed of a DSL connection decreases over distance. Therefore the fastest DSL connections are available only to homes and businesses located within a few thousand feet of a central office. Lower-speed DSL connections are available up to 20,000 feet from a central office.

ADSL connections are *asymmetric* because the connection speed for sending data to the Internet *(upstream)* is slower than the connection speed for receiving data from the Internet *(downstream)*. ADSL is popular with home users since the data these users send upstream consists mostly of e-mail messages and requests for Web pages, whereas the data they receive downstream often includes Web pages, download files, graphics and multi-media content that can be of considerable size.

Unlike ADSL, SDSL is *symmetric* in that it transfers data at the same speed both upstream and downstream. SDSL can transmit data at rates of up to 3 Mbps. HDSL also provides equal bandwidth for upstream and downstream transfers at rates of up to 1.544 Mbps. For users within 4,500 feet of a central office, VDSL offers symmetric transfer rates of between 13 Mbps and 55 Mbps.[3]

The high-bandwidth capabilities of DSL allow DSL providers to offer enhanced services to their customers. For example, *voice-over-DSL (VoDSL)* promises to be a cost-efficient technology for managing data and voice services for small businesses and home offices. VoDSL takes advantage of the high bandwidth of a DSL connection to provide voice telephone services and high-speed data access over a single standard telephone line. An *integrated access device (IAD)* installed at the customer's location provides network connections for high-speed Internet access as well as connections for multiple voice telephone lines. The IAD transmits voice data over DSL to a *gateway* device at the DSL provider. The gateway takes the voice data transmitted by the IAD and sends it across the standard telephone system. Both voice data and high-speed network data can be transmitted over DSL simultaneously. Since these technologies use a single standard telephone line, the cost of providing the services is dramatically reduced. Packaging voice and data services over a single telephone line will help DSL providers reduce the cost of these services for consumers and businesses. To find out what DSL services are available in your area, visit **www.getspeed.com**.

8.4.2 Broadband

Broadband is a category of high-bandwidth Internet service provided mainly by cable television and telephone companies to home users. Broadband communication can handle voice, data and video information. Adding broadband capabilities to a network enables videoconferencing, real-time-voice and streaming-media applications. Like DSL, broadband service is always connected, eliminating the need to dial into an ISP to use the Internet.

A *cable modem* translates digital signals for transmission over the same cables that already bring cable television to homes and businesses. Unlike DSL, the bandwidth delivered to cable modem connections is shared among many users. This can reduce the bandwidth available to each user when there are many people in one neighborhood or building using the system at once. Cable modems typically offer downstream transfer speeds of between 384 Kbps and 1.5 Mbps and upstream speeds of 128 Kbps. Using a cable modem in your home eliminates the need for an extra phone line for your computer.

8.4.3 Integrated Services Digital Network (ISDN)

Integrated Services Digital Network (ISDN) provides high-speed connections to the Internet over both digital and standard telephone lines with transfer speeds of up to 128

Kbps. A specialized piece of hardware called a *terminal adaptor (TA)* and an ISP that provides ISDN service are needed. Because of these restrictions, ISDN availability is limited and costly.

ISDN bandwidth is divided into three channels that each perform different tasks using *Basic Rate Interface* (BRI). Two *bearer (B)* channels each support data transfers at 64 Kbps, while the *data (D)* channel is used to transmit routing information. Each B channel can be used for either voice or data communications. The B channels may also be combined to provide the maximum ISDN transfer rate of 128 Kbps.

8.4.4 Wireless

With the proliferation of consumer devices such as *personal digital assistants (PDAs)* and *digital cellular phones*, the possibility of connecting these devices to the Internet has become attractive for many reasons. Wireless Internet access allows users manage their information while away from their desktop computers. Through PDAs such as the Palm handheld computer and the Pocket PC, and through cellular phones and laptop computers, users are able to buy airline tickets and groceries, surf the Web, trade stocks and check the weather and their e-mail from remote locations.[4] These examples represent only a small fraction of the conveniences provided by wireless communication.

Feature: Sprint PCS

Sprint PCS (`www.sprintpcs.com`) is a nationwide network that offers an array of wireless solutions for both business and personal applications. The main technology driving the PCS network is called *Code-Division Multiple Access* (CDMA).

CDMA is a technology used for digital, wireless communications. With CDMA, each transmission is assigned a specific channel, giving the transmission the benefit of the entire bandwidth within that channel and reducing the possibility that a connection will be broken. To ensure security, CDMA technology is able to assign each transmission on the PCS network a unique code.

Sprint's Wireless Web Browser, Wireless Web Connection and Wireless Web Messaging allow users to access information on the Internet from remote locations. Sprint's Wireless Web Browser, called the *UP.Browser*, acts like the browsers used on a connected desktop. Through the UP.Browser, users are able to view Web sites designed specifically for wireless Web browsers. These sites include: Yahoo!, `Amazon.com`, Ameritrade, `MapQuest.com`, AOL, `CNN.com`, eBay and many others. Users with Shockwave software can view a demonstration of the Wireless Web Browser by visiting `www.sprint.com/wireless/wwbrowsing.html` and following the links.

Through the Sprint Wireless Web Connection kit, customers can use their PCS phone to connect to the Internet as they would with a regular modem and telephone line. Users can browse the Web, send and receive e-mail and access electronic schedules.

Through Sprint Wireless Web Updates and Yahoo!, users can request to have weather information, stock quotes, current news and forwarded e-mail messages delivered directly to their PCS phone.

Wireless communication offers a way to meet the needs of busy consumers. Banks and brokerage houses are developing wireless access to allow consumers to monitor their portfolios. Wireless navigation systems help travelers find directions using the *global positioning system (GPS)*. Handheld devices with GPS capabilities are able to pinpoint the latitude and longitude of a user's location. Web sites like **Go2.com** use this location information to provide a list of nearby restaurants, hotels, coffee shops.[5]

Wireless capabilities are also being expanded to meet the needs of the *business-to-business (B2B)* community. Currently, wireless devices have a limited ability to access word processor files and spreadsheets.[6] Company databases and billing systems will enable ordering and billing to be conducted from a remote location. More advanced applications, such as adding video capabilities to wireless devices, are under development.

One of the most important approaches to wireless communication is standard accessibility. In 1997, the *Wireless Application Protocol* (WAP) was developed by Nokia, Ericsson, Motorola and others to foster the emergence of the wireless Internet.[7] The *Wireless Markup Language* (WML) is a language for designing Web content for delivery to wireless handheld devices. WML removes unnecessary items from Web pages, such as graphics and animations. *Microbrowsers*, designed with limited bandwidth and memory requirements, access the Web via the wireless Internet. Without graphics and animations, the transmission consumes less bandwidth and becomes easier to view on the small screens of wireless devices.

Personal Digital Assistants: The Palm Handheld and Microsoft Pocket PC software

With the Palm VII wireless handheld computer, Palm Computing introduced *Web-Clipping*, which is a technology for displaying Web content. Using the *Query Application Builder (QAB)*, Web designers build *Palm Query Applications (PQAs)* to be installed on users' Palm handheld computers. With a PQA for a particular Web site installed on a Palm VII handheld, a user can view the tailored content for that Web site. A tutorial covering PQA can be found at **www.palm.com/devzone/palmvii/tutorials/tutorial_palm.html**.[8] Also, a demonstration of the Palm handheld can be found at **www.palm.com/products/palmvii**.

The *Internet Kit*, supplied by Palm, provides wireless capabilities to Palm III and Palm V series handheld computers through the use of a snap-on modem or wireless phone. *Multimail* (by ActualSoft), allows users to access any standard e-mail account from their Palm handheld computer. The Internet Kit also provides Palm devices with the ability to view Web pages.

OmniSky (**www.omnisky.com**) adds wireless capabilities to the Palm V and Vx handhelds with the *Wireless Minstrel V* modem, which allows users to check e-mail and browse the Web wirelessly. Unlimited Internet service is available for a monthly fee.

Microsoft's PocketPC platform takes a different approach to displaying Web content on handheld devices. PocketPCs include Pocket Internet Explorer, which reformats complete Web pages as they are downloaded from the Internet for display on the PocketPC. This allows PocketPC users to access most of the content currently available on the Web and alleviates the need to tailor Web content for delivery to handheld devices (S. Alexander, "Wireless Web Access," Computerworld 5 June 2000: 84.).

Wireless devices have several limitations, including occasionally unreliable connections and slow connection speeds. For example, a cellular connection could easily be interrupted before the completion of a transaction. Wireless-device bandwidth ranges from 9.6 Kbps to 14.4 Kbps, about one-fifth of the capabilities of a standard dial-up connection. (T. Hughes, "The Web unwired," Global Technology Business December 1999: 32). As a result, businesses will have to tailor their content to meet the capabilities of wireless devices and decide which services and products offered might best be suited for wireless access.

In the future, *general packet radio services (GPRS)* will enable wireless devices to transmit data at speeds of up to 114 Kbps. This will be closely followed by the launch of the *universal mobile telecommunications standard (UMTS)*, which will offer transfer speeds up to 2 Mbps for wireless devices.[9] Other developments for wireless Internet access include the use of smart phones for secure, mobile transactions.

Bluetooth is a wireless technology that provides short-range, high-speed communication between devices. Bluetooth provides up to 1 Mbps of data transfer capability between devices up to 100 feet apart. Many types of devices such as PCS phones, PDAs and laptop computers can incorporate Bluetooth technology and use it to communicate with one another.[10]

8.4.5 WebTV

WebTV is a low-cost technology for connecting to the Internet through the user's television instead of a PC. WebTV users can dial into an ISP through a modem to surf the Web, send and receive e-mail and chat with other people on the Internet. When sending e-mail, the user can add pictures and audio clips using a video camera, digital camera and VCR. WebTV also enhances television programming by allowing the user to pause, fast forward and replay both live and recorded programs as they watch.

The basic WebTV system includes a wireless keyboard, 8.6-GB (i.e., "gigabytes"— one gigabyte of storage can hold one billion characters of data) hard drive, a 56-Kbps modem, and the capability to record up to 6 hours of television programming. A more expensive version of the WebTV system allows users to record up to 12 hours of television programming by adding a larger, 17-GB hard drive.

8.5 Software

In this section we discuss the types of software available for developing and maintaining a business on the Internet. We will explore *application service providers (ASPs)*, *operating systems* and *databases*. Marketing software, another key resource for developing a successful Web site, is discussed in Chapter 4.

8.5.1 Application Service Providers (ASPs)

Traditionally, large companies needing software to manage business processes such as project management, order processing, and sales calculations would develop these applications in their own *information technology (IT)* departments. Alternatively, some companies would hire outside consulting firms to build these applications for them. ASPs provide customized business software applications over the Internet. ASPs develop a single set of commonly used applications and then provide customizations of those applications to each of their customers. The ASP has the responsibility of maintaining the applications and updating them as necessary. By using an ASP for business applications, companies can eliminate the costs associated with developing and maintaining business applications themselves. Instead, each company pays a fee that allows its users to access the applications over the Internet. Applications provided by ASPs are also available for use more immediately than applications developed by an IT department or outside consulting firm because the ASP has already built and tested the applications. Companies such as Corio (**www.corio.com**), Breakaway Solutions (**www.breakaway.com**), Adgrafix (**www.adgrafix.com**), Fair Isaac (**www.fairisaac.com**) and Verio (**home.verio.com**) are among the companies that provide application services.

Security is a major concern for companies that outsource their business applications to ASPs. The data managed by these applications is stored on servers owned by the ASP and then transferred over the Internet. Consequently, ASPs provide *virtual private networks (VPNs)* that allow customers to connect to their applications securely over the Internet. VPNs use the *point-to-point tunneling protocol (PPTP)* to create a secure channel of communication between the customer and the ASP.

ASPs also provide customization services for the applications they provide. While many companies need the same applications to manage projects, individual companies may manage projects differently from one another. As part of the services they provide, many ASPs will enhance their applications to take into account the needs of individual customers. ASPs will also provide customized appearances for applications. For example, an ASP might use a customer's company logo in an inventory management application.

8.5.2 Operating Systems

An *operating system* (OS) is software that manages the resources on a computer, such as the *central processing unit (CPU)*, *random access memory (RAM)* and *input/output devices (I/O)*.

Akamai[11]

Akamai (**www.akamai.com**) provides an enhanced *content delivery service* for Web sites. Typical Web pages are composed of many different types of data, including text, images and multimedia objects. When a user visits a Web site, all of these images and multimedia objects must be downloaded from a Web server. If a company's Web server is located in Australia and a user in the United States visits the Web site, the images and multimedia content of the site have to be transmitted half-way around the globe. Akamai's *FreeFlow* technology speeds the delivery of images, multimedia and other Web content by placing that content on servers worldwide. Using the FreeFlow Launcher, Web site designers "Akamaize" their site by marking content to be delivered using the Akamai network. FreeFlow takes this content and stores it on Akamai Web servers around the world. When a user visits a Web site that has been "Akamaized," the images and multimedia content are downloaded from an Akamai server near the user for faster content delivery. Akamai also provides *FreeFlow Streaming,* which employs similar content-delivery techniques for streaming video and audio over the Internet.

There are several different types of operating systems including *multi-user, multi-processing, multi-tasking* and *multi-threading*. A multi-user operating system allows more than one user to run a program at the same time. A multi-processing OS controls a computer that has many hardware CPUs. A multi-tasking OS allows multiple applications to run simultaneously. For example, a user may have both a spreadsheet application and a word processor open at the same time. A multi-threading OS allows an individual program to specify that several activities should be performed in parallel.

A *software platform* provides the basic services that *applications* need to run. Applications are programs such as spreadsheets, word processors and Web browsers. The major operating systems used in desktop computers are Unix, Linux, Macintosh and Windows.

One of the most popular software platforms for hosting Web sites and applications is *Linux*. Linux is a Unix-like operating system that has been developed by volunteers worldwide. Linux is one of many *open-source software* projects in development. Open-source software is a class of software for which source code is made freely available so that anyone can use and make updates to the software. All of the source code for the Linux *kernel*, which is the core of the operating system, and for most of the applications that run on Linux is freely available over the Internet and on many CD-ROM distributions. Although the source code for open-source software is made public, most open-source software products have licensing agreements that govern the use of the source code. One of the most widely used open-source licenses is the *GNU General Public License (GPL)*. The GPL requires, among other things, that the source code for GPL-licensed software, as well as the source code for any modifications or improvements to that software, is made freely available to the public. Details about the GPL are available at **www.fsf.org/copyleft/gpl.html**. One of the most popular Web servers on the Internet, Apache (**www.apache.org**), is also open-source software.

Even though open-source software is freely available to the public, many companies are able to profit from products and services based on open-source software. A number of companies, including Red Hat (**www.redhat.com**) and Caldera (**www.caldera.com**) sell complete Linux software packages on CD-ROM as well as customer service and support. Other companies, including VA Linux (**www.valinux.com**) and Dell (**www.dell.com**), sell computer hardware with the Linux operating system pre-installed. Application software companies are also beginning to sell commercial software that is compatible with Linux. Corel has made a free downloadable (but not open-source) version of the popular WordPerfect word processor available for the Linux platform in addition to a commercial version available for purchase. Oracle has also made its database products available for purchase on the Linux platform.

8.5.3 Databases

Most computerized information is stored in databases. A *database* is an integrated collection of data. A *database management system (DBMS)* involves the data itself and the software that controls the storage and retrieval of data. Database management systems provide mechanisms for storing and organizing data in a manner that facilitates satisfying sophisticated queries and data manipulations.

The most popular database systems in use today are *relational databases*. A language called *Structured Query Language* (*SQL*—pronounced "sequel") is almost universally used with relational database systems to make *queries* (i.e., to request information that satisfies given criteria) and manipulate data. Some popular enterprise-level relational database systems include Microsoft SQL Server (**www.microsoft.com/sql**), Oracle (**www.oracle.com**), Sybase (**www.sybase.com**), DB2 (**www.ibm.com/db2**) and Informix (**www.informix.com**). A popular personal relational database is Microsoft Access (which we use for simplicity in our examples later in the text).

The *relational database model* is a logical representation of the data that allows the relationships between the data to be considered independently of the physical implementation of the data structures.

A relational database is composed of tables. Figure 8.3 illustrates a sample table that might be used in a personnel system. The name of the table is **Employee**; its primary purpose is to illustrate the attributes of an employee and how they are related to a specific employee. Any particular row of the table is called a *record* (or *row*). This table consists of six records. The **Employee** table's **Number** field of each record in this table is used as the *primary key* for referencing data in the table. The records of Fig. 8.3 are ordered by primary key. Tables in a database normally have primary keys. Primary key fields in a table cannot contain duplicate values.

Each column of the table represents a different *field* (or *column* or *attribute*). Records are normally unique (by primary key) within a table, but particular field values may be duplicated between records. For example, three different records in the **Employee** table's **Department** field contain number 413. A primary key may also be composed of more than one field in the database.

8.6 Building a Web Site

The appearance, usability and functionality of a Web site are integral to its success. Visual appeal and ease of navigation encourage users to return to a site. If a site makes it difficult for users to find the information they need, they are likely to become frustrated and leave the site. Although a Web site with many graphics and multimedia effects can be visually appealing, it can also take a long time to download, which may cause users to become frustrated and leave.

Table: **Employee**

	Number	Name	Department	Salary	Location
	23603	JONES, A.	413	1100	NEW JERSEY
	24568	KERWIN, R.	413	2000	NEW JERSEY
A record	34589	LARSON, P.	642	1800	LOS ANGELES
	35761	MYERS, B.	611	1400	ORLANDO
	47132	NEUMANN, C.	413	9000	NEW JERSEY
	78321	STEPHENS, T.	611	8500	ORLANDO

Primary key   A column

Fig. 8.3   Relational database table.

Microsoft Site Server Commerce Edition

Large companies that need custom e-commerce solutions may choose to build and maintain their own e-commerce sites. *Microsoft Site Server Commerce Edition* is a popular software package that allows companies to manage transactions, offer secure payment services using both the SSL and SET security protocols (which we discussed in Chapter 7), support a large catalog of products, keep records of online transactions and even design Web sites.[12, 13, 14] Site Server Commerce Edition, which can be installed on a company's own servers, offers more options for an online business than pre-packaged e-commerce solutions such as Yahoo! Store or iCat Web Store.

Site Server Commerce Edition is designed for use with Microsoft Windows NT and Microsoft SQL Server. Microsoft Windows NT is an operating system that allows companies to build secure computer networks. Microsoft SQL Server is a powerful, commercial-quality database application that allows large organizations to store massive amounts of information, such as consumer profiles. Microsoft Site Server Commerce Edition also includes Visual InterDev, which is Microsoft's high-end Web application development software.

Microsoft Site Server Commerce Edition is more powerful than most prepackaged store-builder solutions, but it is also more costly to license, manage, develop and support. To run successful online stores, merchants must maintain their own 24-by-7 support.

8.6.1 Web-Site Construction Services

Several companies offer services and software that facilitate the creation of Web sites. **Freemerchant.com** offers a free *turnkey solution* for building an online store. The site offers hosting, store-building capabilities and a shopping cart model at no cost to the user. Once the user gets the store up and running, Freemerchant supplies other tools to enhance the business. These include online auction tools, package tracking and free technical support. Merchants are, however, required to pay for a *merchant account*, which allows them to accept credit-card payments. Visit **Freemerchant.com** to explore these benefits.[15]

BigStep.com takes a user step-by-step through the process of building an online store. The topics that it covers include building a homepage, registering with search engines and accepting credit-card transactions. **Bigstep.com** also provides status and activity reports. A demonstration of the process can be viewed at **www.bigstep.com/foyer/examples.jhtml** and examples of sites constructed through BigStep can be found at **www.bigstep.com/foyer/examples.jhtml**. Most services offered through Big-Step are free; however, in order to accept online credit-card payments, merchants must pay to set-up a merchant account. BigStep also charges a small transaction fee for each purchase made through the Web site.[16]

eCongo.com offers a free e-commerce site builder that helps a user build and maintain an online store. **eCongo.com** also provides marketing support for a small fee. With **eCongo.com**, store owners can set up e-mail links that will forward e-mail to their personal e-mail accounts. A return policy can be defined and published on the site as well. eCongo will also help e-businesses create effective advertising and register their store catalogs with search engines to increase traffic.[17]

`tripod.com` offers *SiteBuilder*—a tool for creating and building Web sites. Tripod provides several preset page layouts. Once the layout is chosen, Tripod provides another page with sample text and graphics. The user can change text, insert graphics and create new links. Tripod also supports the construction of a product catalog. Within this catalog, a user can display photos of products, assign product numbers, list prices and provide product descriptions. Tripod merchants are paid for advertising, but are required to purchase a merchant account and register a domain name.[18]

Commerce One (`www.commerceone.com`) offers *business-to-business (B2B)* e-commerce solutions. *BuySite* is a commercial solution that allows companies to set up their own B2B exchanges. Users are able to offer full procurement services to their customers, including supply-chain management and other supplementary services associated with B2B e-commerce.[19]

Virtual Spin (`www.virtualspin.com`) offers a full range of e-commerce services. The company designs and implements all of the infrastructure necessary to run an e-business. It will soon introduce an online mall where Virtual Spin members can sell their products. Virtual Spin can also help you build and manage an affiliate program (see Chapter 4). Virtual Spin merchants are charged by the number of items in their store as well as for the support services they use.[20].

Using Yahoo! Store to Set up an Online Store

There are many online *store-builder* solutions that allow merchants to set up online storefronts, complete with catalogs, shopping carts and order-processing capabilities. These fixed-price options are available to businesses of all sizes, but they are ideal for small businesses that cannot afford custom solutions or do not have secure merchant servers. *Yahoo! Store* is one of the most popular e-commerce store-builder solutions.[21] Yahoo! Store is available at `store.Yahoo.com`

Yahoo! Store charges a monthly fee based on the number of items you want to sell. This prepackaged product is designed to simplify the process of creating an online store. All of the features you need to set up a complete e-commerce site are included.

To set up your own demo store, go to `store.yahoo.com` and click the **Create a Store** link. Under **I'm a New User**, click **Sign me up!** You will need to enter the address and name for your site. Then click **Create**. You will be presented with the Yahoo! Store Merchant Service Agreement which you must accept before you can proceed to build your demo store. Setting up a demo store is free, but you cannot accept orders through a demo store. After accepting the agreement, Yahoo! Store provides detailed directions to help merchants set up active online storefronts.

You can change the style of your Web site by clicking on the **Look** button. There are several style templates. If you do not like the templates, you can select **Random** to change the colors and fonts. Yahoo! Store automatically sets up the shopping cart and secure order forms so customers can purchase products through your new Web store.

To set up a working storefront where you can accept orders, you must sign on with Yahoo! Store and set up a merchant account with a bank, enabling your site to accept credit-card payments. Generally, merchant banks and/or credit-card companies collect a small percentage of each transaction as their fee.

Using Yahoo! Store to Set up an Online Store (Cont.)

Yahoo! Store e-commerce sites are hosted on Yahoo! secure servers. Yahoo! maintains the servers on a *24-by-7 basis*—they keep your store up and running 24 hours a day and seven days a week. Yahoo! backs up all the information needed to run your store and provides SSL technology to encrypt all credit-card transactions.

Yahoo! Store merchants can track sales, see how customers are getting to their site, and use the Yahoo! wallet—e-wallets are discussed in Chapter 5. Also, each Yahoo! Store is included in Yahoo! Shopping, allowing customers to access your store through a link at the Yahoo! Web site.

8.6.2 Web-Site Hosting

W*eb-hosting* companies provide customers with a variety of services related to building and maintaining Web sites. Many Web-hosting companies offer customers space on a Web server where the they can build a Web site. Often these are Web sites created by individuals.

For businesses, Web-hosting companies offer more advanced services including *dedicated servers* and *co-location*. A dedicated server is used by a Web-hosting company to serve only one customer's Web site. Co-location services provide a secure physical location for a business' server hardware. Typical co-location services include dedicated Internet connections and protection from power outages and fire.

Each level of service provided by a Web host offers different amounts of storage space and data transfers. Basic plans allot small amounts of each, providing sufficient resources for a small content site to operate. Larger e-commerce sites require more resources to handle the intense activity they receive each day.

DellHost[22]

Dell is a leader in the computer hardware industry. Dell's Web-hosting service, *DellHost*, is able to accommodate everything from small Web sites to large e-commerce sites.

DellHost provides its customers with basic, enhanced and premium e-commerce options. The basic package offers 100 MB of storage capacity, 5 GB of transfers a month, 10 e-mail accounts and a shopping cart using *Mercantec Softcart*—DellHost's shopping technology. This package is sufficient for a small e-commerce site with up to 50 products in its catalog. The premium package provides 300 MB of storage, 25 GB of transfers per month, 100 e-mail accounts and Mercantec Softcart. The premium package has the ability to handle an e-commerce site with unlimited products in its catalog.

Users are given 24-hour access so they can update their site at any time. DellHost guarantees 99.9% uptime for all of the Web sites it hosts. For marketing purposes, Dell-Host reports on all site traffic and performance. The service also includes Secure Socket Layer (SSL) support for secure online transactions. SSL is discussed in Chapter 7. Unlimited e-mail forwarding and e-mail auto responders are also provided. Users can make use of *Common Gateway Interface (CGI)* programs for processing data from forms submitted on the Web, and up to 5 streams of audio or video (we discuss "CGI programming with Perl" in Chapter 29 and streaming audio and video in Chapter 32, "Multimedia").

> ### DellHost[22] (Cont.)
>
> DellHost also provides site-designing and site-promotion services. By making use of a control panel, the merchant can make changes to the site once it is built. Another option available to the merchant is the use of *Trellix Web*. Trellix Web is software that the merchant can use to build a site. This resource is made available to the customer for free and requires no HTML or graphics experience.
>
> DellHost offers a range of services that help merchants reach a wide customer base and attract visitors to their Web sites. DellHost can help the merchant register with search engines to increase the chance of customers visiting the site through Internet searches. The product can also assist in the creation of press releases. Using existing *opt-in e-mail lists*, DellHost can send standard e-mails to potential customers. DellHost also provides services to build advertising banners and place them on Web sites to encourage customers to visit your site.

8.6.3 Domain Names

People in the real estate business often say that the three most important attributes of a piece of real estate are "location, location, location." The same is true of *domain names*, which are the real estate of the Internet. A domain name represents a group of hosts on the Internet; it combines with a *host name* and *top-level domain (TLD)* to form a *fully qualified host name*, which provides a user-friendly way to uniquely identify a site on the Internet. The *domain name system (DNS)* translates fully-qualified host names into IP addresses. For example, the Deitel Web site can be reached by typing `www.deitel.com` into a Web browser. The DNS translates `www.deitel.com` into the IP address of the Deitel Web server (i.e., `207.60.134.230`). Alternatively, you could type the IP address of the Deitel Web server to be brought to the same site.

Finding an unused domain name can be difficult. According to a 1999 survey of 25,000 standard English-language dictionary words, 93% are registered as domain names.[23]

The fully qualified host name of a computer on the Internet has three major parts: the host name, the domain name and the TLD. The host name is the name of the particular host on the internet. Most Web servers use `www` as a host name. A domain name is often the name of the company that owns a site or a word or phrase that otherwise describes the site. The TLD usually describes the type of organization that owns the domain name. For example, the `com` TLD usually refers to a commercial business, whereas the `org` TLD usually refers to a non-profit organization. Each country also has its own TLD, such as `us` for the United States, `ca` for Canada, and `uk` for the United Kingdom.

The *Internet Corporation for Assigned Names and Numbers (ICANN)* is the organization that regulates domain names and IP addresses. Network Solutions (`www.networksolutions.com`) and `register.com` are domain name *registrars*. Registrars are responsible for managing the registration of domain names with individuals and businesses.

8.7 E-Commerce Consulting

Many organizations do not have the resources to build e-commerce sites, so they hire consulting firms to create and maintain these sites. The remainder of the text is devoted to the software technologies that are used to build Web-based applications. Figure 8.4 lists some of the top e-commerce consulting companies.

8.8 Internet and World Wide Web Resources

DSL

www.bellatlantic.com/infospeed
This is Bell Atlantic's DSL information site.

www.dsl.net
DSL.net provides the small to mid-sized company with DSL solutions from Internet access to Web hosting and e-commerce capabilities.

dsl.gte.net
This site explains the advantages of DSL, its uses and how it works. It also offers pricing information and comparisons to other similar technologies.

www.sorenson-usa.com/dsl-mac.html
This site offers information about DSL Internet access for MacIntosh users.

www.nwfusion.com/dsl
NetworkWorldFusion provides resources such as tutorials and information on the different types of DSL for both DSL users and those interested in acquiring DSL. This site also distributes newsletters and provides news groups on various DSL topics.

www.alliancedatacom.com/paradyne-dsl-tutorial.asp
This tutorial helps users become more familiar with DSL service. It starts with the basics and moves on to more in-depth subjects including DSL networks. This tutorial also includes a DSL glossary.

www.2wire.com/dsl/dsl_tutorial.html
2Wire provides a low-level DSL tutorial that discusses how to find a provider. This site also discusses the applications of DSL for telecommuters and businesses.

www.dslprime.com
DSL Prime is a DSL information site.

www.dslreports.com
This is another DSL information site.

Company Name	URL
Akamai	`akamai.com`
Andersen Consulting	`andersen.com/ecommerce`
iPlanet	`iplanet.com`
KPMG Consulting	`www.kpmgconsulting.com`
my SAP.com	`mysap.com`
PriceWaterhouseCoopers	`www.e-business.pwcglobal.com`
Sun Microsystems	`www.sun.com/service/sunps/jdc/intovw.html`

Fig. 8.4   List of e-commerce consulting firms.

Free Internet Access

`dslforfree.homepage.com`

This site provides free Internet access along with free DSL services. Also on this page are links to other free services related to the Internet.

`www.freedsl.com`

In exchange for "nameless" demographic information about your use of their service, FreeDSL provides the user with free DSL services at speeds as high as 144-Kbps.

`www.dialfree.net`

DialFree provides its subscribers with free Internet access. DialFree is able to do so by requiring its subscribers to fill out a monthly survey. This information is passed on to DialFree's partners to help them better understand the views and behavior of Internet users.

`download.freeinternet.com`

By placing banner ads on the viewing window of the browser, Freeinternet is able to provide free Internet access through advertising revenue.

`freelane.excite.com`

Freelane provides free Internet access through a navigation bar that is downloaded from the Internet using any browser.

`www.isfree.com`

ISfree offers Internet access for a flat month fee. Why then do they call themselves free? Through a referral program, your monthly fees may become free, or you may even end up getting paid to be a subscriber. For every person that signs up for the service and uses you as a referral, you get a credit against your fees. After four referrals, you get a free month of service.

Broadband

`www.alliedriser.com`

Allied Riser offers a range of broadband services on their fiber-optic networks inside office buildings.

`www.cidera.com`

Cidera provides satellite-based broadband services as an alternative to land lines for content providers and distributors on the Internet.

`www.globix.com`

This company provides broadband services via its nationwide fiber-optic network and offers many e-business solutions including Web hosting and security.

`www.qwest.com`

Qwest is a leading provider of broadband Internet connections for home users as well as small and large businesses.

Hosting

`www.digex.com/freeflow`

Digex provides Web and application-hosting services for e-businesses.

`www.gettheconnection.com`

This site is run by Cable and Wireless, which offers a wide range of e-business solutions including Web hosting, intranets, Web-page setup and integrating with third-party services.

`www.rackspace.com`

A leader in outsourced Web servers, Rackspace provides reliable hosting, data facilities and customer service to all types of businesses.

`www.intermedia.net`

This company provides NT or IIS-based virtual Web hosting and a variety of related services including unlimited e-mail, database, CyberCash, chat and many more.

home.verio.net/services
Verio Internet services offers solutions for Internet access, e-business, Web-site hosting and security.

www.aismedia.com
AIS Media Corporations provides several different solutions for an e-commerce business including web hosting, credit-card merchant services and consulting.

Consulting
www.excalib.com
Excalibur Communications offers e-business and e-commerce solutions for searching and manipulating data online.

www.3com.com
3Com provides many Internet solutions including mobile connectivity and LAN integration.

www.interconnect.com
This is a research and development consulting firm that provides software and services that help businesses go online.

www.webdiner.com/commerce
This tutorial compares the different solutions that exist in the online small business market. The solutions provided range from inexpensive to costly and from simple to elaborate. Along with a short description of the solution, the authors list the pros and cons of each solution.

www.bignosebird.com/ssl.shtml
The topic of this basic overview tutorial is secure servers.

www.ibm.com/e-business/what/how
According to this tutorial, online entrepreneurs should establish what they want to do, target customers, plan their finances and then get expert help to get started.

Wireless
www.nextel.com
Nextel provides wireless Web services in some parts of its cellular and digital network.

www.sprint.com
Sprint provides a variety of Internet services for all types of users. They offer wireless Web services, Web hosting, security, connectivity and e-business solutions among many others.

www.skytel.com
An MCI WorldCom company, Skytel offers many wireless services, including Web surfing, e-mail, and interactive messaging. It is the leading provider of such wireless technology.

www.aethersystems.com
Aether systems is a provider of wireless and mobile computer services and technologies.

www.blackberry.net
Blackberry provides wireless e-mail access using a pager-like handheld device.

Fiber Optics
www.sff.net/people/Jeff.Hecht/history.html
This site provides a short history of fiber optics and references a more in-depth explanation that is included in the author's book.

www.commspecial.com/fiberguide.htm
Communications Specialties, Inc., provides a detailed introduction to fiber optic-technology and concepts.

www.fiberopticsonline.com
Fiber Optics Online is an industry portal with information about fiber-optic products and technology.

SUMMARY

- The Internet is a network of interconnected host computers, or hosts.
- Computers on the Internet communicate by sending packets of data across the network.
- Packets contain a source address, a destination address, sequencing information, error-control information and the data to be delivered to the destination address.
- A router moves packets across the Internet in an efficient way.
- A server is a host on the Internet that manages network resources and fulfills requests from clients.
- A Web server stores Web pages and delivers those pages to clients upon request.
- A protocol defines the steps necessary for computers to communicate over the Internet.
- A communications medium is the hardware that connects computers and other digital equipment.
- Bandwidth is a measure of how much data can be transferred through a communications medium in a fixed amount of time.
- Bandwidth is usually measured in bits per second (bps), kilobits per second (Kbps) or megabits per second (Mbps).
- Fiber-optic cable is composed of flexible glass fibers that transmit light.
- An optical modem, which stands for optical modulator and demodulator, translates digital signals from a computer into light through a process called modulation.
- Repeaters amplify and retransmit signals across segments of copper wire or fiber-optic cable.
- A storage area network (SAN) provides high-capacity, reliable data storage and delivery on a network.
- Most home users subscribe to an Internet Service Provider (ISP) in order to connect to the Internet.
- Some Internet providers offer free Internet access in exchange for personal demographic data, such as age, address, interests and income level.
- A Digital Subscriber Line (DSL) offers high-bandwidth Internet access over existing copper telephone lines.
- ADSL connections are asymmetric because the connection speed for sending data to the Internet (upstream) is slower than the connection speed for receiving data from the Internet (downstream).
- Symmetric DSL transfers data at the same speed both upstream and downstream.
- Broadband is a category of high-bandwidth Internet service provided mainly by cable television companies to home users over existing cable television wiring.
- Integrated Services Digital Network (ISDN) provides high-speed connections to the Internet over both digital and standard telephone lines with transfer speeds of up to 128 Kbps.
- The Wireless Markup Language (WML) is a language for designing Web content for delivery to wireless handheld devices.
- Wireless devices have several limitations, including occasionally unreliable connections and slow connection speeds.
- Bluetooth is a wireless technology that provides short-range, high-speed communication between devices.
- WebTV is a low-cost technology for connecting to the Internet through the user's television instead of a PC.
- Application service providers (ASPs) deliver customized business software applications over the Internet.
- A virtual private network (VPN) uses the point-to-point tunneling protocol (PPTP) to effectively create a secure channel of communication over the Internet.

- An operating system (OS) is software that manages the resources on a computer such as the central processing unit (CPU), random access memory (RAM) and input/output devices (I/O).
- A software platform provides the basic services that applications need to run.
- Linux is an open-source, Unix-like operating system that has been developed by volunteers worldwide.
- Open-source software is a class of software for which source code is made freely available so that anyone can use and make updates to the software.
- One of the most widely used open-source licenses is the GNU General Public License (GPL).
- A database is an integrated collection of data.
- The relational database model is a logical representation of data that allows the relationships between the data to be considered without concerning oneself with the physical implementation of the data structures.
- The appearance, usability and functionality of a Web site are integral to its success.
- Web hosting companies provide customers with a variety of services related to building and maintaining Web sites.
- Co-location services provide a secure physical location for a business' server hardware, including dedicated Internet connections as well as protection from power outages and fire.
- A domain name represents a group of hosts on the Internet.
- A domain name is combined with a host name to form a fully-qualified host name, which provides a user-friendly way to uniquely identify a site on the Internet.
- The domain name system (DNS) translates fully-qualified host names into IP addresses.
- The fully-qualified host name of a computer on the Internet has three major parts: the host name, the domain name and the top-level domain (TLD).
- Many organizations do not have the resources to build e-commerce sites, so they hire consulting firms to create and maintain these sites.

TERMINOLOGY

24-by-7	column
analog modem	Common Gateway Interface (CGI)
analog signal	communications medium
Application Service Provider (ASP)	content delivery service
asymmetric	copper wire
Asymmetric Digital Subscriber Line (ADSL)	data channel
attribute	database
bandwidth	Database Management System (DBMS)
Basic Rate Interface (BRI)	database server
bearer channel	dedicated connection
bits per second (bps)	dedicated server
Bluetooth	demodulator
broadband	destination address
Business-to-Business (B2B)	digital cellular phone
cable modem	Digital Subscriber Line (DSL)
central office	domain name
Central Processing Unit (CPU)	Domain Name System (DNS)
Code Division Multiple Access (CDMA)	downstream
co-location	e-mail server

error control information
fiber optics
fiber-optic cable
fibre channel
file server
File Transfer Protocol (FTP)
fully qualified host name
gateway
General Packet Radio Services (GPRS)
global positioning system (GPS)
GNU Public License (GPL)
High-speed Digital Subscriber Line (HDSL)
host computer
hosting
Hypertext Transfer Protocol (HTTP)
Information Technology (IT)
input/output devices
Integrated Access Device (IAD)
Integrated Services Digital Network (ISDN)
Internet Corporation for Assigned Names and
    Numbers (ICANN)
Internet Service Provider (ISP)
IP address
kernel
Kilobits per second (Kbps)
Linux
MB
Megabits per second (Mbps)
merchant account
microbrowser
modem
modulator
multi-processing
multi-tasking
multi-threading
multi-user
network storage device
open-source software
Operating System (OS)
optical modem
opto-chip
outsource
packet
Personal Digital Assistant (PDA)
Plain Old Telephone System (POTS)

platform
Point-to-Point Tunneling Protocol (PPTP)
Post Office Protocol (POP)
primary key
processor speed
protocol
Random Access Memory (RAM)
record
redundant
registrar
relational database
repeater
router
row
sequencing information
server
Simple Mail Transfer Protocol (SMTP)
software platform
source address
Sprint PCS
Storage Area Network (SAN)
storage devices
store-builder
Structured Query Language (SQL)
symmetric
Symmetric Digital Subscriber Line (SDSL)
TCP/IP
terabyte
Terminal Adapter (TA)
Top-Level Domain (TLD)
turnkey solution
Universal Mobile Telecommunications Standard
    (UMTS)
Unix
upstream
uptime
Very high-speed Digital Subscriber Line VDSL
Virtual Private Network (VPN)
Voice over Digital Subscriber Line (VoDSL)
Web hosting
Web server
Wireless Application Protocol (WAP)
Wireless Markup Language (WML)
xDSL

SELF-REVIEW EXERCISES

8.1   Fill in the blanks in each of the following:
       a) A _____ is a computer that is connected to the Internet.
       b) Every computer on the Internet is assigned a unique _____ address.

c) _____ is a high-bandwidth communications medium made of flexible strands of glass.

d) _____ is a measure of the amount of data that can flow through a communications medium in a fixed amount of time.

e) DSL is an acronym for _____.

f) _____ allows handheld devices like cellular phones to connect to the Internet.

g) _____ is a language used to create Web content for wireless devices.

h) An _____ provides business applications for use over the Internet.

i) A _____ provides a user-friendly address for a company's computers on the Internet.

j) Open source software makes the _____ for programs freely available to the public.

8.2   State whether the following are *true* or *false*. If the answer is *false*, explain why.

a) *DSL* offers a lower bandwidth connection to the Internet than an analog modem.

b) The connection speed of DSL is limited by the distance from the telephone company's *central office*.

c) A *cable modem* allows a user to watch television programming on a computer.

d) The bandwidth delivered over cable television systems is shared among users in a neighborhood or apartment building.

e) The *Wireless Application Protocol (WAP)* provides a way to access Internet content using a wireless device.

f) Three technologies for viewing Internet content on a wireless device are *WAP*, *Web clipping*, and *Pocket Internet Explorer*.

g) A *database* is an integrated collection of data.

ANSWERS TO SELF-REVIEW EXERCISES

8.1   a) host. b) IP. c) Fiber-optic cable. d) bandwidth. e) digital subscriber line. f) WAP. g) WML. h) ASP. i) domain name. j) source code.

8.2   a) False. DSL offers much higher bandwidth than is available using an analog modem. b) True. c) False. Cable modems are used to connect a computer to the Internet. d) True. e) True. f) True. g) True.

EXERCISES

8.3   Using the Internet, learn about two or three different e-commerce site-building solutions available for a small business to establish an e-commerce site. Look at available features and capabilities for each and evaluate which provides the best service.

8.4   Use the Internet to locate emerging communication technologies that will be important to e-commerce. Prepare a short list of these technologies then choose one. Describe the technology and how it relates to e-commerce.

WORKS CITED

The notation <*www.domainname.com*> indicates that the citation is from information found at that web site.

1.   A. Boyle, "Opto-chip breaks records," `<www.zdnet.com/zdnn/stories/news/0,4586,2523487,00.html>` 6 April 2000: 2.

2.   S. Strange, "Transition Networks—Fibre White Paper," `<www.transition.com/products/fiber_wp.html>`.

3.   `<www.vectris.com/reference>`.

4. B. Issberner, "How 'context switch radios' will streamline with the personal area network," *Wireless Integration* `<wi.pennwellnet.com/home/articles>` 1 March 2000.

5. L. Vaas, "Going2 the wireless world," *PC Week* 20 March 2000: 68.

6. S. Neil, "Walking the Wireless Web," *PC Week* 20 March 2000: 80.

7. T. Hughes, "The Web unwired," *Global Technology Business* Dec 1999: 33.

8. T. Powell and J. Lima, "The Challenges of a Wireless Web," *Network World* 20 March 2000: 81.

9. T. Hughes, "The Web unwired," *Global Technology Business December* 1999: 32.

10. T. Hughes, "The Web unwired," *Global Technology Business December* 1999: 32.

11. `<www.akamai.com>`.

12. Bethoney, H., and Repoza, J., "Microsoft Beta Bundles Basics for E-commerce," *PCWeek Online* `<www.zdnet.com/pcweek/reviews/0126/26site.html>` 26 Jan 1998.

13. Dragan, R., "Microsoft Site Server 3.0 Commerce Edition," *PC Magazine* `<www.zdnet.com/products/stories/reviews/0,4161,374713,00.html>` 14 Dec 1998.

14. Symoens, J., "Site Server is a fine set of tools for Web site building," *InfoWorld* `<www.info-world.com>` 26 Jan 1998.

15. `<www.freemerchant.com>`.

16. `<www.bigstep.com>`.

17. `<www.econgo.com>`.

18. `<www.tripod.com>`. Tripod is owned by Lycos, Inc., and is a part of the Lycos Network of sites.

19. `<www.commerceone.com>`.

20. `<www.virtualspin.com>`.

21. Nemzow, M., *Building Cyberstores*, New York, NY: McGraw-Hill, 1997.

22. `<www.dellhost.com>`.

23. D. Tyron, "What to Name the Baby," *The Industry Standard* 24 April 2000: 160.

RECOMMENDED READING

Alexander, S. "Wireless Web Access." *ComputerWorld* 5 June 2000: 84.

Armstrong, L. "Changing the Cyber House Rules, No-fee access is making the old profit models obsolete." *Business Week* 7 Feb 2000: 46.

Booker, E. "Webcams Help Sites Provide Real-time Views of Inventory." *Internet Week* 10 Jan 2000: 15.

Borella, M. "Protocol helps stretch IPv4 addresses." *Network World* 17 Jan 2000: 43.

Cauley, L. "A Speed Bump to the Wire Web." *The Wall Street Journal* 17 Feb 2000: B1+.

Cole-Gomolosky, B. "E-commerce education brings IT, Business Together in Classroom." *ComputerWorld* 2 Aug 1999: 32.

Deckmyn, D. "Wireless Web Access will be Vital." *ComputerWorld* 10 Jan 2000: 81.

Duvall, M. "E-Marketplaces Getting Connected" *Inter@ctive Week* 10 Jan 2000: 40-46.

"Everything you always wanted to know about connecting to the Internet but were afraid to ask." *The Boston Globe* 20 Jan 2000: D5.

Furchgott, R. "Web to go—Sort of. Today's Net phones are OK for email, but surfing is a chore." *Business Week* 14 Feb 2000: 144.

Greene, T. "Voice-Over-DSL turns heads at ComNet." *Network World* 31 Jan 2000: 8.

Hendrickson, D. "All aboard the e-commerce express" *Mass Tech High* 7-13 Feb 2000: 15.

Howe, P.J. "Setting Net on its ear. Analysts: Wireless Web is the next big thing, and speech recognition is key." *Boston Globe* 14 Feb 2000:

Keen, P.G. "E-commerce: Chapter 2." *ComputerWorld* 13 Sep 1999: 48.

McGarvey, J. "E-Commerce Drives Bandwidth Needs." *Inter@ctive Week* 8 Nov 1999: 16.

Mossberg, W. "A simple little gadget lets you go online without using a PC." *The Wall Street Journal* 27 Jan 2000: B1.

Rewick, J.L. "OnlineAds Turn to Hand-held Devices." *The Wall Street Journal* 4 Feb 2000: B6.

Riggs, B. "Convergence Culture Shock." *Information Week* 13 Dec 1999: 143.

Spangler, T. "Wireless Web: Wait a Second." *Inter@ctive Week* 24 Jan 2000: 66.

Stedman, C. "Moving to Web Applications? Don't Forget Bandwidth." *ComputerWorld* 31 Jan 2000: 59.

Viajayan, J. "Wireless Markup Language." *ComputerWorld* 24 Jan 2000: 62.

Wallace, B. "The Internet Unplugged, Wireless Net Access is Creating New Opportunities." *InformationWeek* 13 Dec 1999: 22.

"Wireless Emerges as Remote Access Option." *InternetWeek* 1/10/2000, pg 12, author: C. Moozakis.

Whyman, B. "Crossing the Fault Line." *The Industry Standard* 21 Feb 2000: 129.

Zimmerman, C. "Akamai's Intervu Deal Bolsters Content-Delivery Capabilities" *Internet Week* 14 Feb. 2000: 8.

Introduction to HyperText Markup Language 4 (HTML 4)

Objectives

- To understand the key components of an HTML document.
- To be able to use basic HTML tags to write World Wide Web pages.
- To be able to use HTML to format text.
- To be able to add images to your Web pages.
- To understand how to create and use hyperlinks to transit between Web pages.

To read between the lines was easier than to follow the text.
Henry James

Mere colour, unspoiled by meaning, and annulled with definite form, can speak to the soul in a thousand different ways.
Oscar Wide

High thoughts must have high language.
Aristophanes

I've gradually risen from lower-class background to lower-class foreground.
Marvin Cohen

9.1 Introduction

Welcome to the wonderful world of opportunities being created by the World Wide Web. The Internet is now three decades old, but it was not until the World Wide Web became popular in the 1990s that this current explosion of opportunities began. It seems that exciting new developments occur almost daily—a pace of innovation unlike what we have seen with any other technology. In this chapter, you will begin developing your own Web pages. As the book proceeds, you will be able to create increasingly appealing and powerful Web pages. In the last portion of the book you will learn how to create complete Web-based applications.

We begin unlocking the power of the Web in this chapter with *HTML*—the *Hypertext Markup Language*. HTML is not a procedural programming language like C, Fortran, Cobol or Pascal. Rather it is a *markup language* for identifying the elements of a page so that a browser, such as Microsoft's Internet Explorer or Netscape's Communicator, can render that page on your computer screen.

In this chapter we introduce the basics of creating Web pages in HTML. We write many simple Web pages. In later chapters we introduce more sophisticated HTML techniques, such as *tables*, which are particularly useful for presenting and manipulating information from databases.

In this chapter we introduce basic HTML *tags* and *attributes*. A key issue when using HTML is the separation of the *presentation of a document* (i.e., how the document is rendered on the screen by a browser) from the *structure of that document*. Over the next several chapters, we discuss this issue in depth.

9.2 Markup Languages

HTML is a *markup language*. It is used to format text and information. This "marking up" of information is different from the intent of traditional programming languages, which is to perform actions in a designated order. In the next several chapters, we discuss HTML markup in detail. (Note that we are specifically not doing action-oriented programming.) Then we introduce JavaScript and Dynamic HTML and show how you can introduce action-oriented programming into your HTML-based Web pages to make those pages "come alive" for the viewer.

In HTML, text is marked up with *elements*, delineated by *tags* that are keywords contained in pairs of angle brackets. For example, the HTML *element* itself, which indicates that we are writing a Web page to be rendered by a browser, begins with a start tag of **<HTML>** and terminates with an end tag of **</HTML>**, as shown in Fig 9.1.

Good Programming Practice 9.1

HTML tags are not case sensitive. However, keeping all the letters in one case improves program readability. We choose uppercase, which we believe helps make the tags stand out from the surrounding code.

Common Programming Error 9.1

Forgetting to include closing tags for elements that require them is a syntax error and can grossly affect the formatting and look of your page. However, unlike in conventional programming languages, a syntax error in HTML does not usually cause page display in browsers to fail completely.

These elements format your page in a specified way. Over the course of the next two chapters, we introduce many of the commonly used tags and how to use them.

9.3 Editing HTML

In this chapter we show how to write HTML in its *source-code form*. We create *HTML files*—also called *HTML documents*—using a text editor. In Chapter 12, we explain how to use a software package called *FrontPage Express* to create Web pages visually, without the need for the page developer to code with HTML directly.

A text editor called **Notepad** is built into Windows. It can be found inside the **Accessories** panel of your **Program** list, inside the **Start** menu.

You can also download a free HTML source-code editor called HTML-Kit at **www.chami.com/html-kit**. Programs like this can perform useful tasks, such as validating your code and speeding up some repetitive tasks.

All HTML files typically have either the **.htm** or the **.html** file name extension (this is dependent on the server software). When HTML was first developed, most personal computers were running the Windows 3.1/DOS operating system, which allowed only three-character file name extensions. Current versions of Windows allow more characters in the extension, so the common usage has switched to **.html**. We recommend that you name all of your HTML files with the **.html** extension.

Good Programming Practice 9.2

Assign names to your files that describe their functionality. This practice can help you identify pages faster. It also helps people who want to link to your page, by giving them an easier-to-remember name for the file. For example, if you are writing an HTML document that will display your products, you might want to call it **products.html**.

As mentioned previously, making errors while coding in conventional programming languages like C, C++ and Java often produces a fatal error, preventing the program from running. Errors in HTML code are usually not fatal. The browser will make its best effort at rendering the page, but will probably not display the page as you intended. In our *Common Programming Errors* and *Testing and Debugging Tips,* we highlight common HTML errors and how to detect and correct them.

The file name of your *home page* (the first of your HTML pages that a user sees when browsing your Web site) should be **index.html**, because when a browser does not request a specific file in a directory, the normal default Web server response is to return **index.html** (this may be different for your server) if it exists in that directory. For example, if you direct your browser to **www.deitel.com**, the server actually sends the file **www.deitel.com/index.html** to your browser.

9.4 Common Tags

Fig. 9.1 shows an HTML file that displays one line of text. Line 1

```
<HTML>
```

tells the browser that everything contained between the opening **<HTML>** tag and the closing **</HTML>** tag (line 15) is HTML. The **<HTML>** and **</HTML>** tags should always be the first and last lines of code in your HTML file, respectively.

```
1    <HTML>
2
3    <!-- Fig. 9.1: main.html -->
4    <!-- Our first Web page   -->
5
6    <HEAD>
7    <TITLE>Internet and WWW How to Program - Welcome</TITLE>
8    </HEAD>
9
10   <BODY>
11
12   <P>Welcome to Our Web Site!</P>
13
14   </BODY>
15   </HTML>
```

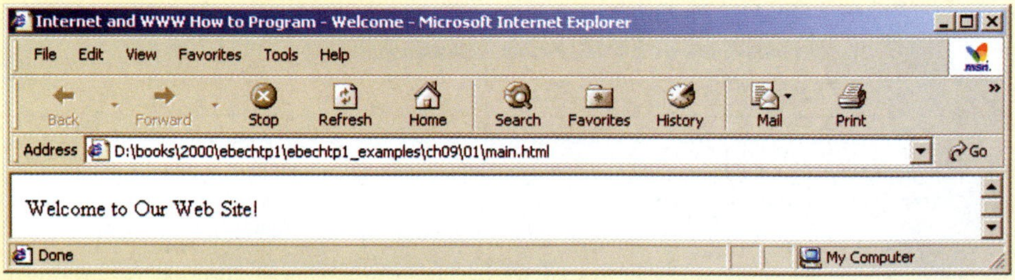

Fig. 9.1   Basic HTML file.

Good Programming Practice 9.3

Always include the **<HTML>...</HTML>** *tags in the beginning and end of your HTML document. Place comments throughout your code. Comments in HTML are placed inside the* **<!--...-->** *tags. Comments help other programmers understand the code, assist in debugging and list other useful information that you do not want the browser to render. Comments also help you understand your own code, especially if you have not looked at it for a while.*

We see our first comments on lines 3 and 4:

```
<!-- Fig. 9.1: main.html -->
<!-- Our first Web page   -->
```

Comments in HTML always begin with **<!--** and end with **-->**. The browser ignores any text and/or tags inside a comment. We place comments at the top of each HTML document file giving the figure number, the file name and a brief description of the file being coded. We also include abundant comments in the code, especially when we introduce new features.

Every HTML file is separated into a header element, which generally contains information about the document, and a body, which contains the page content. Information in the header element is not generally rendered in the display window but may be made available to the user through other means.

Lines 6 through 8,

```
<HEAD>
<TITLE>Internet and WWW How to Program - Welcome</TITLE>
</HEAD>
```

show the header section of our Web page. Including a title is mandatory for every HTML document. To include a title in your Web page, enclose your chosen title between the pair of tags **<TITLE>...</TITLE>**, which are placed inside the header.

Good Programming Practice 9.4

Use a consistent title naming convention for all pages on your site. For example, if your site is called "Al's Web Site," then the title of your links page might best be "Al's Web Site - Links," etc. This practice presents a clearer picture to those browsing your site.

The **TITLE** element names your Web page. The title usually appears on the colored bar at the top of the browser window, and will also appear as the text identifying your page if a user adds your page to his or her list of **Favorites**. The title is also used by search engines for cataloging purposes, so picking a meaningful title can help the search engines direct a more focused group of people to your site.

Line 10

```
<BODY>
```

opens the **BODY** element. The body of an HTML document is the area where you place all content you would like browsers to display. This includes text, images, links, forms, etc. We discuss many elements that can be inserted in the **BODY** element later in this chapter. These include backgrounds, link colors and font faces. For now, we will use **<BODY>...</BODY>** in its simplest form. Remember to include the closing **</BODY>** tag at the end of the document right before the closing **</HTML>** tag.

Various elements enable you to place text in your HTML document. We see the *paragraph element* on line 12:

```
<P>Welcome to Our Web Site!</P>
```

All text placed between the **<P>**...**</P>** tags forms one paragraph. This paragraph will be set apart from all other material on the page by a line of vertical space both before and after the paragraph. The HTML in line 12 causes the browser to render the enclosed text as shown in Fig. 9.1.

Our code example ends on lines 14 and 15 with

```
</BODY>
</HTML>
```

These two tags close the body and HTML sections of the document, respectively. As discussed earlier, the last tag in any HTML document should be **</HTML>**, which tells the browser that all HTML coding is complete. The closing **</BODY>** tag is placed before the **</HTML>** tag because the body section of the document is entirely enclosed by the HTML section. Therefore, the body section must be closed before the HTML section.

9.5 Headers

Headers are a simple form of text formatting that vary text size based on the header's "level." The six header elements (**H1** through **H6**) are often used to delineate new sections and subsections of a page. Figure 9.2 shows how they are used and their relative display sizes. Note that the actual size of the text of each header element is selected by the browser and can in fact vary significantly between browsers. Later in the book we discuss how you can "take control" of specifying these text sizes and other text attributes as well.

```
1    <HTML>
2
3    <!-- Fig. 9.2: header.html -->
4    <!-- HTML headers        -->
5
6    <HEAD>
7    <TITLE>Internet and WWW How to Program - Headers</TITLE>
8    </HEAD>
9
10   <BODY>
11
12   <!-- Centers everything in the CENTER element -->
13   <CENTER>
14   <H1>Level 1 Header</H1>    <!-- Level 1 header -->
15   <H2>Level 2 header</H2>    <!-- Level 2 header -->
16   <H3>Level 3 header</H3>    <!-- Level 3 header -->
17   <H4>Level 4 header</H4>    <!-- Level 4 header -->
18   <H5>Level 5 header</H5>    <!-- Level 5 header -->
19   <H6>Level 6 header</H6>    <!-- Level 6 header -->
20   </CENTER>
21
22   </BODY>
23   </HTML>
```

Fig. 9.2   Header elements **H1** through **H6** (part 1 of 2).

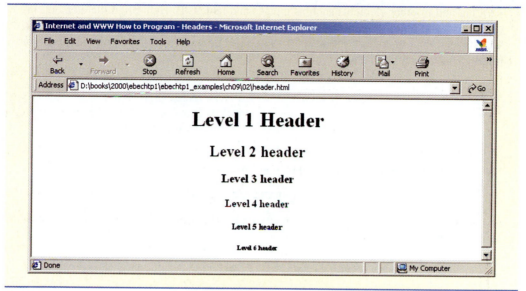

Fig. 9.2   Header elements **H1** through **H6** (part 2 of 2).

 Good Programming Practice 9.5

Adding comments to the right of short HTML lines is a clean-looking way to comment code.

Line 13

```
<CENTER>
```

introduces element **CENTER** which centers horizontally in the browser window all the material between its **<CENTER>** and **</CENTER>** tags. Most elements of an HTML page are left adjusted on the screen by default. Later, we discuss how to align individual elements.

Line 14

```
<H1>Level 1 Header</H1>
```

introduces the **H1** header element, with its opening tag **<H1>** and its closing tag **</H1>**. Any text to be displayed is placed between the two tags. All six header elements, **H1** through **H6**, follow the same patterns but in successively smaller type font sizes.

 Look-and-Feel Observation 9.1

Putting a header at the top of every Web page helps those viewing your pages understand what the purpose of each page is.

9.6 Text Styling

In HTML, text can be highlighted with bold, underlined and/or italicized styles (Fig. 9.3). Our first style, the *underline*, appears on line 11

```
<H1 ALIGN = "center"><U>Welcome to Our Web Site!</U></H1>
```

Notice the statement **ALIGN = "center"** inside the **<H1>** tag. This is the method by which any single element of the page can be aligned. This same attribute can be used in the

<P> tag and in other elements such as images and tables. To right-align the element, include the statement **ALIGN = "right"** inside the opening tag of the element. The HTML 4.0 convention is to enclose the **ALIGN** value (**left**, **center**, or **right**) in quotation marks. This convention applies to most attribute values.

Good Programming Practice 9.6

When you have nested tags, always close them in the reverse order from that in which they were started. For example, if you have a word both italicized and underlined: **<EM><U>**Hello!**</U></EM>**, *then close the* **U** *element before the* **EM** *element.*

As you can see, all text enclosed in the **<U>**...**</U>** tags is displayed underlined. A second style, the *emphasis* or *italic* style, is shown on line 14

```
about the wonders of <EM>HTML</EM>. We have been using
```

and is used in the same manner as the underline tag. The last style, the *strong* or *bold* style is shown on line 15:

```
<EM>HTML</EM> ever since <U>version<STRONG> 2.0</STRONG></U>,
```

<STRONG> and **<EM>** are used instead of the tags **<B>** and **<I>** (the old standard usages for *bold* and *italic*). This is because the purpose of HTML is simply to mark up text, while the question of how it is presented is left to the browser itself. Therefore, the tags **<B>** and **<I>** are *deprecated* (i.e., their use in valid HTML is discouraged and their support in browsers will eventually disappear), because they overstep this boundary between content and presentation.

```
1    <HTML>
2
3    <!-- Fig. 9.3: main.html -->
4    <!-- Stylizing your text -->
5
6    <HEAD>
7    <TITLE>Internet and WWW How to Program - Welcome</TITLE>
8    </HEAD>
9
10   <BODY>
11   <H1 ALIGN = "center"><U>Welcome to Our Web Site!</U></H1>
12
13   <P>We have designed this site to teach
14   about the wonders of <EM>HTML</EM>. We have been using
15   <EM>HTML</EM> since <U>version<STRONG> 2.0</STRONG></U>,
16   and we enjoy the features that have been added recently. It
17   seems only a short time ago that we read our first <EM>HTML</EM>
18   book. Soon you will know about many of the great new features
19   of HTML 4.0.</P>
20
21   <H2 ALIGN = "center">Have Fun With the Site!</H2>
22
23   </BODY>
24   </HTML>
```

Fig. 9.3   Stylizing text on Web pages (part 1 of 2).

Fig. 9.3   Stylizing text on Web pages (part 2 of 2).

For example, people who have difficulty seeing can use special browsers that read aloud the text on the screen. These *text-based browsers* (which do not show images, colors or graphics) might read **STRONG** and **EM** with different inflections to convey the impact of the styled text to the user.

Look-and-Feel Observation 9.2

Be cautious when underlining text on your site, because hyperlinks are underlined by default in most browsers. Underlining plain text can be confusing to people browsing your site.

Look-and-Feel Observation 9.3

Use the **<STRONG>** *and* **<EM>** *tags instead of the* **<B>** *and* **<I>** *tags to ensure that your page is rendered properly by all browsers.*

You should also notice inside line 15

```
<U>version <STRONG>2.0</STRONG></U>
```

Here, the **U** and **STRONG** elements overlap each other. This causes the text included in both elements ("**2.0**") to have both styles applied.

You should also observe the order of the closing tags in the above example from line 15. Because the **STRONG** element started after the **U** element, the **STRONG** element's closing tag appears before that of **U**. Although the order of the closing tags does not always matter to the browser, it is good practice to close them in the reverse order from the order in which they were started.

9.7 Linking

The most important capability of HTML is its ability to create hyperlinks to documents elsewhere on the server and on different servers and thereby make possible a world-wide network of linked documents and information. In HTML, both text and images can act as *anchors* to *link* to other pages on the Web. We introduce anchors and links in Fig. 9.4.

```html
1    <HTML>
2
3    <!-- Fig. 9.4: links.html        -->
4    <!-- Introduction to hyperlinks -->
5
6    <HEAD>
7    <TITLE>Internet and WWW How to Program - Links</TITLE>
8    </HEAD>
9
10   <BODY>
11
12   <CENTER>
13   <H2>Here are my favorite Internet Search Engines</H2>
14   <P><STRONG>Click on the Search Engine address to go to that
15   page.</STRONG></P>
16
17   <!-- Hyperlink form: <A HREF = "address"> -->
18   <P>Yahoo: <A HREF = "http://www.yahoo.com">
19   http://www.yahoo.com</A></P>
20
21   <P>AltaVista: <A HREF = "http://www.altavista.com">
22   http://www.altavista.com</A></P>
23
24   <P>Ask Jeeves: <A HREF = "http://www.askjeeves.com">
25   http://www.askjeeves.com</A></P>
26
27   <P>WebCrawler: <A HREF = "http://www.webcrawler.com">
28   http://www.webcrawler.com</A></P>
29   </CENTER>
30
31   </BODY>
32   </HTML>
```

Fig. 9.4   Linking to other Web pages.

The first link can be found on lines 18 and 19:

```
<P>Yahoo: <A HREF = "http://www.yahoo.com">
http://www.yahoo.com</A></P>
```

Links are inserted using the **A** *(anchor) element*. The anchor element is unlike the elements we have seen thus far in that it requires certain attributes inside its opening tag in order to activate the hyperlink. The most important attribute is the location to which you would like the anchoring object to be linked. This location can be any accessible page, file or email URL. To specify the address you would like to link to, insert the **HREF** *attribute* into the anchor tag as follows: **<A HREF = "***address***">**. In this case, the address we are linking to is **http://www.yahoo.com**. The hyperlink created on line 18 activates the text on line 19, **http://www.yahoo.com** as an anchor to link to the indicated address.

Anyone who loads your page and clicks on the hyperlinked word(s) will have their browser go to that page. Figure 9.4 contains several other examples of anchor tags.

Figure 9.4 also further demonstrates element **P**. Recall that the paragraph element adds vertical space around the paragraph area. On lines 18 through 28, there are four complete paragraph tags. Each one is a new paragraph and therefore has vertical space around it.

Anchors can also link to email addresses. When someone clicks on this type of anchored link, their default email program initiates an email message to the linked address. This type of anchor is demonstrated in Fig. 9.5.

Email links use a syntax almost identical to that for links to other Web pages. We see an email link on lines 14 and 15:

```
<P>My email address is <A HREF = "mailto:deitel@deitel.com">
deitel@deitel.com</A>.
```

The form of an email anchor is **<A HREF = "mailto:***emailaddress***">...</A>**. It is important that this whole attribute, including the **mailto:**, be placed in quotation marks.

```
1   <HTML>
2
3   <!-- Fig. 9.5: contact.html  -->
4   <!-- Adding email hyperlinks -->
5
6   <HEAD>
7   <TITLE>Internet and WWW How to Program - Contact Page</TITLE>
8   </HEAD>
9
10  <BODY>
11
12  <!-- The correct form for hyperlinking to an email address -->
13  <!-- is <A HREF = "mailto:address"></A>                     -->
14  <P>My email address is <A HREF = "mailto:deitel@deitel.com">
15  deitel@deitel.com</A>. Click on the address and your browser
16  will open an email message and address it to me.
17  </P>
18
19  </BODY>
20  </HTML>
```

Fig. 9.5   Linking to an email address (part 1 of 2).

Fig. 9.5   Linking to an email address (part 2 of 2).

9.8 Images

We have been dealing exclusively with text. We now show how to incorporate images into
Web pages (Fig 9.6).

```
1    <HTML>
2
3    <!-- Fig. 9.6: picture.html   -->
4    <!-- Adding images with HTML -->
5
6    <HEAD>
7    <TITLE>Internet and WWW How to Program - Welcome</TITLE>
8    </HEAD>
9
10   <BODY BACKGROUND = "bckgrnd.gif">
11
12   <CENTER>
13   <!-- Format for entering images: <IMG SRC = "name"> -->
14   <IMG SRC = "deitel.gif" BORDER = "1" HEIGHT = "144"
15        WIDTH = "200" ALT = "Harvey and Paul Deitel">
16   </CENTER>
17
18   </BODY>
19   </HTML>
```

Fig. 9.6   Placing images in HTML files.

For this page, an image background has been inserted in line 10:

```
<BODY BACKGROUND = "bckgrnd.gif">
```

As mentioned earlier, attributes can be added to the **BODY** tag to set certain characteristics of the page, one of which is ***BACKGROUND***. A background can consist of an image or a color. In this case, we are using an image. To use an image as a background, include the attribute **BACKGROUND** = *"filename"* inside the opening **<BODY>** tag. The filename of the image in this case is **bckgrnd.gif**.

An image used as a background does not need to be large In fact, large background images greatly increase the time it takes for a page to load. The image used for the background in Fig. 9.6 is only 325 *pixels* wide and 85 *pixels* high—the browser *tiles* the image across and down the screen. The term pixel stands for "picture element". Each pixel represents one addressable dot of color on the screen.

Look-and-Feel Observation 9.4

Using an image for your background can be visually appealing. Make sure, however, that the image does not have any sharp color changes, as they can be disorienting to the user, making the text on top hard to read. Also try to use an image that tiles, that is, blends smoothly with the surrounding repetitions of itself.

The image in this code example is inserted in lines 14 and 15:

```
<IMG SRC = "deitel.gif" BORDER = "1" HEIGHT = "144"
     WIDTH = "200" ALT = "Harvey and Paul Deitel">
```

You specify the location of the image file in the ***<IMG>*** tag. This is done by adding the **SRC** = *"location"* attribute. You can specify the ***HEIGHT*** and ***WIDTH*** of an image, measured in pixels. This image is 200 pixels wide and 144 pixels high.

Good Programming Practice 9.7

*Always include the **HEIGHT** and **WIDTH** of an image in the **IMG** tag. When the browser loads the HTML file, it will know immediately how much screen space to give the image and will therefore lay out the page properly, even before it downloads the image.*

Common Programming Error 9.2

Entering new dimensions for an image that change its inherent width-to-height ratio distorts the appearance of the image. For example, if your image is 200 pixels wide and 100 pixels high, you should always make sure that any new dimensions have a 2:1 width-to-height ratio.

You can add a border (black by default) to images with attribute ***BORDER*** = *x*. If *x* is a number larger than 0, the width of the border will be that number of pixels. The image in this example has a border of 1 pixel, as indicated by the image attribute **BORDER** = **1**.

An important image attribute is ***ALT***. In Fig. 9.6, the value of this attribute is

```
ALT = "Harvey and Paul Deitel"
```

ALT is provided for browsers that have images turned off, or that cannot view images (i.e., text-based browsers). The value of the **ALT** attribute will appear on-screen in place of the image, giving the user an idea of what was in the image.

Good Programming Practice 9.8

*Include a description of every image using the **ALT** attribute in the **IMG** tag.*

Now that we have discussed placing images on your Web page, we will show you how to transform images into anchors to link your site to other sites on the Internet (Fig. 9.7).

We add a background on line 10 with

```
<BODY BGCOLOR = "#CDCDCD">
```

This is similar to the method we used in Fig. 9.6. The difference is that instead of using a background image, we use a solid background color. Because of this, the attribute name is *BGCOLOR* instead of **BACKGROUND**.

```
1   <HTML>
2
3   <!-- Fig. 9.7: navigationbar.html -->
4   <!-- Using images as link anchors -->
5
6   <HEAD>
7   <TITLE>Internet and WWW How to Program - Nav Bar</TITLE>
8   </HEAD>
9
10  <BODY BGCOLOR = "#CDCDCD">
11  <CENTER>
12
13  <A HREF = "main.html">
14  <IMG SRC = "buttons/about.jpg" WIDTH = "65" HEIGHT = "50"
15     BORDER = "0" ALT = "Main Page"></A><BR>
16
17  <A HREF = "links.html">
18  <IMG SRC = "buttons/links.jpg" WIDTH = "65" HEIGHT = "50"
19     BORDER = "0" ALT = "Links Page"></A><BR>
20
21  <A HREF = "list.html">
22  <IMG SRC = "buttons/list.jpg" WIDTH = "65" HEIGHT = "50"
23     BORDER = "0" ALT = "List Example Page"></A><BR>
24
25  <A HREF = "contact.html">
26  <IMG SRC = "buttons/contact.jpg" WIDTH = "65" HEIGHT = "50"
27     BORDER = "0" ALT = "Contact Page"></A><BR>
28
29  <A HREF = "header.html">
30  <IMG SRC = "buttons/header.jpg" WIDTH = "65" HEIGHT = "50"
31     BORDER = "0" ALT = "Header Page"></A><BR>
32
33  <A HREF = "table.html">
34  <IMG SRC = "buttons/table.jpg" WIDTH = "65" HEIGHT = "50"
35     BORDER = "0" ALT = "Table Page"></A><BR>
36
37  <A HREF = "form.html">
38  <IMG SRC = "buttons/form.jpg" WIDTH = "65" HEIGHT = "50"
39     BORDER = "0" ALT = "Feedback Form"></A><BR>
40  </CENTER>
41
42  </BODY>
43  </HTML>
```

Fig. 9.7   Using images as link anchors (part 1 of 2).

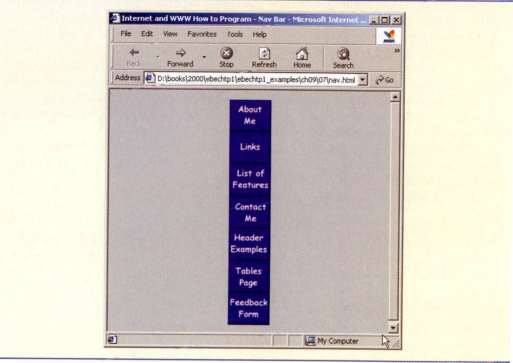

Fig. 9.7   Using images as link anchors (part 2 of 2).

To indicate the color for your background, you can use either a preset color name, of which there are more than 100 (see the index of colors in Appendix B), or you can use a *hexadecimal* code to tell the browser what color you want to use (see the code **#CDCDCD** above). This method is also used to change your font color, as we show you in the next section. All colors are composed of varying shades of red, green and blue (so-called *RGB* colors). The first two characters in the "hex" color code represent the amount of red in the color, the second two represent the amount of green and the last two represent the blue. **00** is the weakest a color can get and **FF** is the strongest a color can get. Therefore, **"#FF0000"** is red, **"#00FF00"** is green, **"#0000FF"** is blue, **"#000000"** is black and **"#FFFFFF"** is white. For now, you can just use the preset colors in Appendix B. Later in the book, we explain how to find the hex code of any color you may want to use.

We see an image hyperlink in lines 13 through 15:

```
<A HREF = "main.html">
<IMG SRC = "buttons/about.jpg" WIDTH = "65" HEIGHT = "50"
   BORDER = "0" ALT = "Main Page"></A>
```

Here we use the **A** element and the **IMG** element. The anchor works the same way as when it surrounds text; the image becomes an active hyperlink to a location somewhere on the Internet, indicated by the **HREF** attribute inside the **<A>** tag. Remember to close the anchor element when you want the hyperlink to end.

If you direct your attention to the **SRC** attribute of the **IMG** element,

```
SRC = "buttons/about.jpg"
```

you will see that it is not in the same form as that of the image in the previous example. This is because the image we are using here, **about.jpg**, resides in a subdirectory called **buttons**, which is in our main directory for the site. We have done this so that we can keep all our button graphics in the same place, making them easier to find and edit.

You can always refer to files in different directories simply by putting the directory name in the correct format in the **SRC** attribute. If, for example, there was a directory inside the **buttons** directory called **images**, and we wanted to put a graphic from that directory onto our page, we would just have to make the source attribute reflect the location of the image: **SRC = "buttons/images/filename"**.

You can even insert an image from a different Web site into your site (after obtaining permission from the site's owner, of course). Just make the **SRC** attribute reflect the location and name of the image file.

We introduce the *line break* element in line 15:

```
BORDER = "0" ALT = "Main Page"></A><BR>
```

The **BR** element causes a line break to occur. If the **BR** element is placed inside a text area, the text begins a new line at the place of the **
** tag. We are using **
** here so that we can skip to the line below the image.

9.9 Formatting Text With **<FONT>**

We have seen how to make pages visually richer using backgrounds and images. Figure 9.8 shows how to add color and formatting to text.

We demonstrate the common methods of formatting in lines 15 through 17:

```
<P><FONT COLOR = "red" SIZE = "+1" FACE = "Arial">We have
designed this site to teach about the wonders of
<EM>HTML</EM>.</FONT>
```

Here, several attributes of the **FONT** element are demonstrated. The first attribute is **COLOR**, which indicates the color of the formatted text in the same manner in which you indicate a background color: You enter either a preset color name or a hex color code. Remember to include the quotation marks around the color name.

Note that you can set the font color for the whole document by putting a **TEXT** attribute into the **BODY** element and indicating the color in the same manner as above.

```
1   <HTML>
2
3   <!-- Fig. 9.8: main.html            -->
4   <!-- Formatting text size and color -->
5
6   <HEAD>
7   <TITLE>Internet and WWW How to Program - Welcome</TITLE>
8   </HEAD>
9
10  <BODY>
11
12  <H1 ALIGN = "center"><U>Welcome to Our Web Site!</U></H1>
13
```

Fig. 9.8   Using the **FONT** element to format text (part 1 of 2).

```
14    <!-- Font tags change the formatting of text they enclose -->
15    <P><FONT COLOR = "red" SIZE = "+1" FACE = "Arial">We have
16    designed this site to teach about the wonders of
17    <EM>HTML</EM>.</FONT>
18
19    <FONT COLOR = "purple" SIZE = "+2" FACE = "Verdana">We have been
20    using <EM>HTML</EM> since <U>version<STRONG> 2.0</STRONG></U>,
21    and we enjoy the features that have been added recently.</FONT>
22
23    <FONT COLOR = "blue" SIZE = "+1" FACE = "Helvetica">It
24    seems only a short time ago that we read our first <EM>HTML</EM>
25    book.</FONT>
26
27    <FONT COLOR = "green" SIZE = "+2" FACE = "Times">Soon you will
28    know about many of the great new features of HTML 4.0.</FONT></P>
29
30    <H2 ALIGN = "center">Have Fun With the Site!</H2>
31
32    </BODY>
33    </HTML>
```

Fig. 9.8   Using the **FONT** element to format text (part 2 of 2).

The second attribute in the example is **SIZE**, which is used to change the size of the text being formatted. To make the text larger, set **SIZE="+*x*"**. To make the text smaller, set **SIZE="-*x*"**. In each case, *x* is the number of font point sizes by which you want to enlarge or diminish the text.

The last font attribute shown in our example is **FACE**. This attribute is used to change the font of the text you are formatting. Enter a font name in quotation marks, and the text will be changed to that font.

Common Programming Error 9.3

When using the font face attribute, be careful to only use common fonts like Times, Arial, Courier and Helvetica (just to name a few). Avoid more obscure fonts, because the browser default will be displayed instead (usually Times New Roman).

9.10 Special Characters, Horizontal Rules and More Line Breaks

In HTML, the old QWERTY typewriter setup no longer suffices for all our textual needs. HTML 4.0 has a provision for inserting special characters and symbols (Fig. 9.9).

There are some *special characters* inserted into the text of lines 18 and 19:

```
<P>All information on this site is <STRONG>&copy;</STRONG>
Deitel <STRONG>&amp;</STRONG> Associates, 1999.</P>
```

All special characters are inserted in their code form. The format of the code is always *&code;*. An example of this is **&**, which inserts an ampersand. Codes are often abbreviated forms of the character (like **amp** for ampersand and **copy** for copyright) and can also be in the form of *hex codes*. (For example, the hex code for an ampersand is 38, so another method of inserting an ampersand is to use **&**.) Please refer to the chart in Appendix A for a listing of special characters and their respective codes.

```
1   <HTML>
2
3   <!-- Fig. 9.9: contact.html       -->
4   <!-- Inserting special characters -->
5
6   <HEAD>
7   <TITLE>Internet and WWW How to Program - Contact Page</TITLE>
8   </HEAD>
9
10  <BODY>
11
12  <!-- Special characters are entered using the form &code; -->
13  <P>My email address is <A HREF = "mailto:deitel@deitel.com">
14  deitel@deitel.com</A>. Click on the address and your browser
15  will automatically open an email message and address it to my
16  address.</P>
17
18  <P>All information on this site is <STRONG>&copy;</STRONG>
19  Deitel <STRONG>&amp;</STRONG> Associates, 1999.</P>
20
21  <!-- Text can be struck out with a set of <DEL>...</DEL>    -->
22  <!-- tags, it can be set in subscript with <SUB>...</SUB>, -->
23  <!-- and it can be set into superscript with <SUP...</SUP> -->
24  <DEL><P>You may copy up to 3.14 x 10<SUP>2</SUP> characters
25  worth of information from this site.</DEL><BR> Just make sure
26  you <SUB>do not copy more information</SUB> than is allowable.
27
28  <P>No permission is needed if you only need to use <STRONG>
29  &lt; &frac14;</STRONG> of the information presented here.</P>
30
```

Fig. 9.9   Inserting special characters into HTML (part 1 of 2).

```
31    </BODY>
32    </HTML>
```

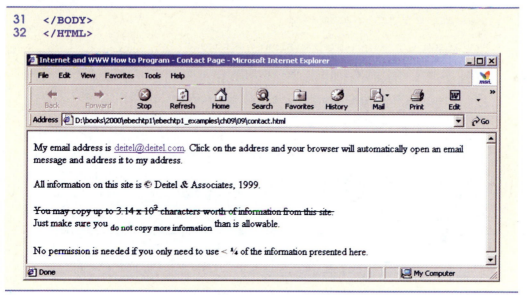

Fig. 9.9   Inserting special characters into HTML (part 2 of 2).

In lines 24 through 26, we introduce three new styles.

```
<DEL><P>You may copy up to 3.14 x 10<SUP>2</SUP> characters
worth of information from this site.</DEL><BR> Just make sure
you <SUB>do not copy more information</SUB> than is allowable.
```

You can strike-through text with a horizontal line by including it in a **DEL** element. This could be used as an easy way to communicate revisions of an online document. To turn text into *superscript* (i.e., raised vertically to the top of the line and made smaller) or to turn text into *subscript* (the opposite of superscript, lowers text on a line and makes it smaller), use the **SUP** and **SUB** elements, respectively.

We touched on line breaks in Fig. 9.7. We now provide an example of a textual line break with a horizontal rule (Fig. 9.10).

```
1    <HTML>
2
3    <!-- Fig. 9.10: header.html          -->
4    <!-- Line breaks and horizontal rules -->
5
6    <HEAD>
7    <TITLE>Internet and WWW How to Program - Horizontal Rule</TITLE>
8    </HEAD>
9
10   <BODY>
11   <!-- Horizontal rules as inserted using the format: -->
12   <!-- <HR WIDTH = ".." SIZE = ".." ALIGN = "..">      -->
13   <HR WIDTH = "25%" SIZE = 1>
14   <HR WIDTH = "25%" SIZE = 2>
```

Fig. 9.10   Using horizontal rules (part 1 of 2).

```
15    <HR WIDTH = "25%" SIZE = 3>
16
17    <P ALIGN = "left"><STRONG>Size:</STRONG>4
18    <STRONG>Width:</STRONG>75%
19    <HR WIDTH = "75%" SIZE = "4" ALIGN = "left">
20
21    <P ALIGN = "right"><STRONG>Size:</STRONG>12
22    <STRONG>Width:</STRONG>25%
23    <HR WIDTH = "25%" SIZE = "12" ALIGN = "right">
24
25    <P ALIGN = "center"><STRONG>Size:</STRONG>8
26    <STRONG>Width:</STRONG>50%
27    <STRONG><EM>No shade...</EM></STRONG>
28    <HR NOSHADE WIDTH = "50%" SIZE = "8" ALIGN = "center">
29
30    </BODY>
31    </HTML>
```

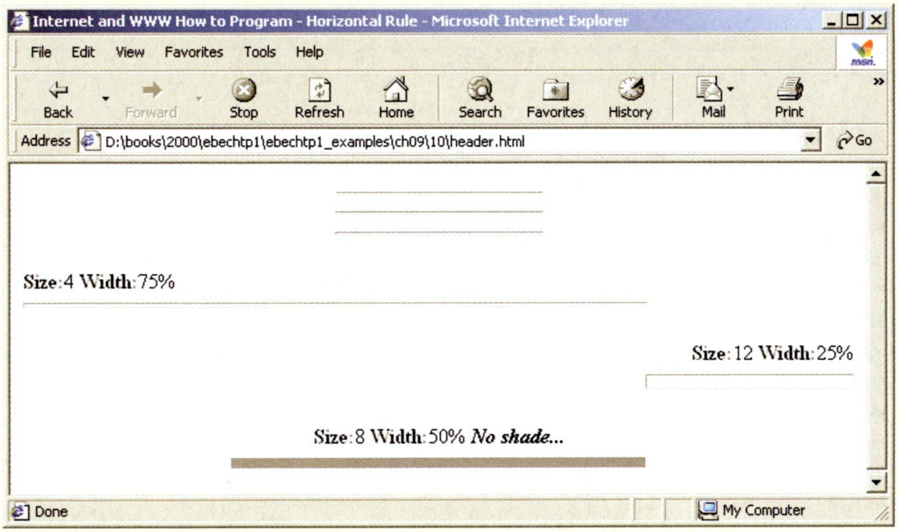

Fig. 9.10   Using horizontal rules (part 2 of 2).

Line 13

    <HR WIDTH = "25%" SIZE = 1>

inserts a horizontal rule, indicated by the **<HR>** tag. A horizontal rule is a straight line going across the screen horizontally. The **HR** element also inserts a line break directly below it.

You can adjust the width of the horizontal rule by including the **WIDTH** attribute in the **HR** tag. You can set the width either by entering a number, which will indicate the width in pixels, or by entering a percentage, which indicates that the horizontal rule will occupy that percent of the screen width. For example, if you enter **WIDTH = "50%"**, and your screen resolution is 640 pixels, then the **HR** will measure 320 pixels across.

Look-and-Feel Observation 9.5

Inserting horizontal rules into your document can help break text up into meaningful units and so make the text easier to read.

This method of entering the width of an element is used with other elements in HTML 4, the most common being the **TABLE** element, which we discuss in the next chapter.

The **SIZE** attribute determines the height of the horizontal rule, in pixels. The **ALIGN** attribute, as we used with the **IMG** element, aligns the **HR** element horizontally on the page. The value of **ALIGN** can be either left, center or right. One final attribute of the **HR** element is *NOSHADE*. This eliminates the default shading effect and instead displays the horizontal rule as a solid-color bar.

9.11 Internet and WWW Resources

There are many resources available on the World Wide Web that go into more depth on the topics we cover. Visit the following sites for additional information on this chapter's topics.

www.w3.org/
The *World Wide Web Consortium* (W3C), is the group that makes HTML recommendations. This Web site holds a variety of information about HTML—both its history and its present status.

www.w3.org/TR/REC-html40/
The *HTML 4.0 Specification* contains all the nuances and fine points in HTML 4.0.

www.freewebpromotion.com/harvillo/index.htm
Harvillo's Finest HTML Help. This site contains step-by-step instructions for beginners on building a Web page.

www2.utep.edu/~kross/tutorial
This University of Texas at El Paso site contains another guide for simple HTML programming. The site is helpful for beginners, because it focuses on teaching and gives specific examples.

SUMMARY

- HTML is not a procedural programming language like C, Fortran, Cobol or Pascal. It is a markup language that identifies the elements of a page so a browser can render that page on the screen.

- HTML is used to format text and information. This "marking up" of information is different from the intent of traditional programming languages, which is to perform actions in a designated order.

- In HTML, text is marked up with elements, delineated by tags that are keywords contained in pairs of angle brackets.

- Create HTML files—also called HTML documents—using a text editor. A text editor called Notepad is built into Windows. You can also download an HTML shareware source-code editor or use Microsoft's Visual InterDev.

- All HTML files require either the **.htm** or the **.html** file name extension.

- Making errors while coding in conventional programming languages like C, C++ and Java often produces a fatal error, preventing the program from running. Errors in HTML code are usually not fatal. The browser will make its best effort at rendering the page but will probably not display the page as you intended. In our Common Programming Errors and Testing and Debugging Tips we highlight common HTML errors and how to detect and correct them.

- The filename of your home page should be **index.html**. When a browser requests a directory, the default Web server response is to return **index.html**, if it exists in that directory.

- **`<HTML>`** tells the browser that everything contained between the opening **`<HTML>`** tag and the closing **`</HTML>`** tag is HTML.

- Comments in HTML always begin with **`<!--`** and end with **`-->`** and can span across several source lines. The browser ignores any text and/or tags placed inside a comment.

- Every HTML file is separated into a header section and a body.

- Including a title is mandatory for every HTML document. Use the **`<TITLE>`...`</TITLE>`** tags to do so. They are placed inside the header.

- **`<BODY>`** opens the **`BODY`** element. The body of an HTML document is the area where you place all content you would like browsers to display.

- All text between the **`<P>`...`</P>`** tags forms one paragraph. This paragraph will be set apart from all other material on the page by a line of vertical space both before and after the paragraph.

- Headers are a simple form of text formatting that typically increase text size based on the header's "level" (**`H1`** through **`H6`**). They are often used to delineate new sections and subsections of a page.

- The **`CENTER`** element causes all material between its **`<CENTER>`** and **`</CENTER>`** tags to be centered horizontally in the browser window.

- The attribute **`ALIGN`** is the method by which any single element of the page can be aligned. The HTML 4.0 convention is to enclose the **`ALIGN`** value (**`left`**, **`center`** or **`right`**) in quotation marks. This convention applies to most attribute values.

- The purpose of HTML is simply to mark up text; the question of how it is presented is left to the browser itself.

- People who have difficulty seeing can use special browsers that read the text on the screen aloud. These browsers (which are text based and do not show images, colors or graphics) might read **`STRONG`** and **`EM`** with different inflections to convey the impact of the styled text to the user.

- You should close tags in the reverse order from that in which they were started.

- The most important capability of HTML is creating hyperlinks to documents on any server to form a world-wide network of linked documents and information.

- Links are inserted using the `A` (anchor) element. To specify the address you would like to link to, insert the **`HREF`** attribute into the anchor tag, with the address as the value of **`HREF`**.

- Anchors can link to email addresses. When someone clicks on this type of anchored link, their default email program initiates an email message to the linked address.

- Attributes can be added to the **`BODY`** tag to set certain characteristics of the page. To use an image as a background, include the attribute **`BACKGROUND = `** `"file.ext"` inside the opening **`<BODY>`** tag.

- Large background images greatly increase the time it takes for a page to load. The browser tiles the image across and down the screen.

- The term pixel stands for "picture element". Each pixel represents one dot of color on the screen.

- You specify the location of the image file with the **`SRC = `** `"location"` attribute in the **`<IMG>`** tag. You can specify the **`HEIGHT`** and **`WIDTH`** of an image, measured in pixels. You can add a border by using the **`BORDER = `** `"x"` attribute.

- **`ALT`** is provided for browsers that cannot view pictures or that have images turned off (text-based browsers, for example). The value of the **`ALT`** attribute will appear on-screen in place of the image, giving the user an idea of what was in the image.

- **`<BODY BGCOLOR = "#CDCDCD">`** adds a solid background color. To indicate the color to use specify either a preset color name (Appendix B) or a hexadecimal code.

- All colors are composed of varying shades of red, green and blue (i.e., so-called RGB colors). The first two characters in the "hex" color code represent the amount of red in the color, the second two represent the amount of green and the last two represent the blue. **00** is the weakest a color can get, and **FF** is the strongest a color can get.

- You can refer to files in different directories by including the directory name in the correct format in the **SRC** attribute. You can insert an image from a different Web site onto your site (after obtaining permission from the site's owner). Just make the **SRC** attribute reflects the location and name of the image file.

- The BR element forces a line break. If the **BR** element is placed inside a text area, the text begins a new line at the place of the **
** tag. Attribute **COLOR** indicates the color of the formatted text in the same manner in which you indicate a background color; you enter either a preset color name or a hex color code. Remember to include the quotation marks around the color name.

- Use **SIZE** to change the size of the text being formatted with **<FONT>**. To make the text larger, set the **SIZE = "+x"**. To make the text smaller set **SIZE = "-x"**. Use **FACE** to change the font of the text you are formatting.

- HTML 4.0 has a provision for inserting special characters and symbols. All special characters are inserted in the format of the code, always &code;. An example of this is **&**, which inserts an ampersand. Codes are often abbreviated forms of the character (like amp for ampersand and **copy** for copyright) and can also be in the form of hex codes. (For example, the hex code for an ampersand is 38, so another method of inserting an ampersand is to use **&**.) Please refer to the chart in Appendix A for a listing of special characters and their respective codes.

- You can strike-through text with a horizontal line by including it in a **DEL** element. To turn text into superscript or subscript, use the **SUP** and **SUB** elements respectively.

- **<HR>** inserts a horizontal rule, a straight line going across the screen. You can adjust the width of it by including the **WIDTH** attribute, using a number of pixels or a percentage of screen width. **NOSHADE** will remove the 3D shading, rendering the **HR** as a solid-color bar. This method of entering the width of an element is used with other elements in HTML 4, for example the **TABLE** element.

TERMINOLOGY

<!--...--> (comment)
<BODY>...</BODY>
<HR> element (horizontal rule)
A element (anchor; **<A>...</A>**)
ALIGN = "center"
ALIGN = "left"
ALIGN = "right"
ALT
&
anchor
attributes of an HTML tag
BACKGROUND attribute of **BODY** element
BGCOLOR attribute of **BODY** element
bold
border of an image
CENTER element (**<CENTER>...</CENTER>**)
CLEAR = "all" in **
**
closing tag
color
COLOR in **<BODY>**
comments

content of an HTML element
DEL element
EM element (**<EM>...</EM>**)
emphasis
FACE = in **<FONT>**
FONT element (**<FONT>...</FONT>**)
FORM element (**<FORM>...</FORM>**)
FrontPage Express
H1 element (**<H1>...</H1>**)
H2 element (**<H2>...</H2>**)
H3 element (**<H3>...</H3>**)
H4 element (**<H4>...</H4>**)
H5 element (**<H5>...</H5>**)
H6 element (**<H6>...</H6>**)
HEAD element (**<HEAD>...</HEAD>**)
height
hexadecimal color codes
horizontal rule
HREF attribute of **<A>** element
.htm
.html

HTML (HyperText Markup Language)
HTML document
HTML element (**<HTML>**…**</HTML>**)
HTML file
HTML tags
HTML-Kit
hyperlink
hypertext
image
IMG element
index.html
italic
line break element (**
…</BR>**)
link
link attribute of **BODY** element…
mailto:
Markup Language
Name attribute of FRAME element
opening tag
P element (paragraph; **<P>**…**</P>**)
paragraph element (**<P>**…**</P>**)
presentation of a Web Page

RGB colors
SIZE = in **<FONT>**
source-code form
special characters
SRC attribute in **IMG** element
STRONG element (**<STRONG>**…**</STRONG>**)
structure of a Web page
SUB (subscript)
SUP (superscript)
tags in HTML
TEXT in **BODY**
text-based browser
tiling an image across the screen
TITLE element (**<TITLE>**…**</TITLE>**)
U element
unordered list (**<UL>**…**</UL>**)
Web site
WIDTH attribute
width by percentage
width by pixel
World Wide Web

SELF-REVIEW EXERCISES

9.1 State whether the following are *true* or *false*. If the answer is *false*, explain why.
  a) You can specify the background of the page as an attribute in the **<HTML>** tag.
  b) The use of the **EM** and **STRONG** elements is deprecated.
  c) The name of your site home page should always be **homepage.html**.
  d) It is a good programming practice to insert comments into your HTML document that explain what you are doing.
  e) A hyperlink is inserted around text with the **LINK** element.

9.2 Fill in the blanks in each of the following:
  a) The _____ element is used to insert a horizontal rule.
  b) Superscript is formatted with the _____ element and subscript is formatted with the _____ element.
  c) The _____ element is located within the **<HEAD>**…**</HEAD>** tags.
  d) The smallest text header is the _____ element and the largest text header is _____.
  e) The _____ element is used to format the size and color of text.
  f) You can center a section of your page by enclosing it between _____ tags.

9.3 Identify each of the following as either an element or attribute.
  a) **HTML**
  b) **WIDTH**
  c) **ALIGN**
  d) **BR**
  e) **SIZE**
  f) **H3**
  g) **A**
  h) **SRC**

ANSWERS TO SELF-REVIEW EXERCISES

9.1   a) False. You specify the background with either the **BACKGROUND** or the **BGCOLOR** attribute in the **BODY** element. b) False. The use of the **I** and **B** elements is deprecated. **EM** and **STRONG** should be used instead. c) False. The name of your homepage should always be **index.html**. d) True. e) False. A hyperlink is inserted around text with the **A** (anchor) element.

9.2   a) **HR**. b) **SUP, SUB** c) **TITLE** d) **H6, H1** e) **FONT** f) **<CENTER>...</CENTER>**

9.3   a) Tag. b) Attribute. c) Attribute. d) Tag. e) Attribute. f) Tag. g) Tag. h) Attribute.

EXERCISES

9.4   Mark up the first paragraph of this chapter. Use **H1** for the section header, **P** for text, **STRONG** for the first word of every sentence, and **EM** for all capital letters.

9.5   Mark up the first paragraph again, this time using left-aligned horizontal rules to separate sentences. The size of each horizontal rule should be the same as the number of words in the preceding sentence. Every alternate horizontal rule should have the **NOSHADE** attribute applied.

9.6   Why is this code valid? (*Hint*: you can find the W3C specification for the **P** element at **www.w3.org/TR/REC-html40/struct/text.html**.)

```
<P>Here's some text...
<HR>
<P>And some more text...</P>
```

9.7   Why is this code invalid? (*Hint*: you can find the W3C specification for the **BR** element at the same URL given in Exercise 9.6.)

```
<P>Here's some text...<BR></BR>
And some more text...</P>
```

9.8   Given: We have an image named **deitel.gif** that is 200 pixels wide and 150 pixels high. Use the **WIDTH** and **HEIGHT** attributes of the **IMG** tag to a) increase image size by 100%; b) increase image size by 50%; c) change the width-to-height ratio to 2:1, keeping the width attained in a).

9.9   Create a link to each of the following: a) **index.html**, located in the **files** directory; b) index.html, located in the **text** subdirectory of the **files** directory; c) **index.html**, located in the **other** directory in your *parent directory* (*Hint*: **..** signifies parent directory.); d) A link to the President's email address (**president@whitehouse.gov**); e) An **FTP** link to the file named **README** in the **pub** directory of **ftp.cdrom.com** (*Hint*: remember to use **ftp://**).

Intermediate HTML 4

Objectives

- To be able to create lists of information.
- To be able to create tables with rows and columns of data.
- To be able to control the display and formatting of tables.
- To be able to create and use forms.
- To be able to create and use image maps to aid hyperlinking.
- To be able to make Web pages accessible to search engines.
- To be able to use the `<FRAMESET>` tag to create more interesting Web pages.

Yea, from the table of my memory
I'll wipe away all trivial fond records.
William Shakespeare

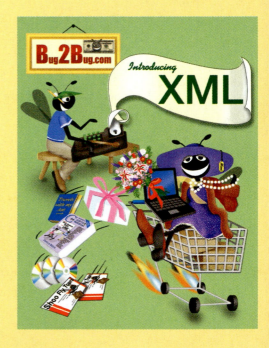

Outline

10.1 Introduction

In the previous chapter, we discussed some basic HTML features. We built several complete Web pages featuring text, hyperlinks, images, backgrounds, colors and such formatting tools as horizontal rules and line breaks.

In this chapter, we discuss more substantial HTML elements and features. We will see how to present information in *lists* and *tables*. We discuss how to use forms to collect information from people browsing a site. We explain how to use *internal linking* and *image maps* to make pages more navigable. We also discuss how to use *frames* to make attractive interactive Web sites.

By the end of this chapter, you will be familiar with most commonly used HTML tags and features. You will then be able to create more complex and visually appealing Web sites. Throughout the remainder of the book we introduce many more advanced HTML capabilities such as *scripting*, *Dynamic HTML*, *Perl/CGI*, *ASP* (*Active Server Pages*) and *XML* (*Extensible Markup Language*).

10.2 Unordered Lists

Figure 10.1 demonstrates displaying text in an *unordered list*. Here we reuse an HTML file from Chapter 9, adding an unordered list to enhance the look of the page. The *unordered list element* creates a list in which every line begins with a bullet mark. All entries in an unordered list must be enclosed within **<UL>**...**</UL>** tags, which open and close the unordered list element. We also removed the centering from the list of sites.

```
 1    <HTML>
 2
 3    <!-- Fig. 10.1: links.html -->
 4    <!-- Unordered Lists        -->
 5
 6    <HEAD>
 7    <TITLE>Internet and WWW How to Program - Links</TITLE>
 8    </HEAD>
 9
10    <BODY>
11
12    <CENTER>
13    <H2>Here are my favorite Internet Search Engines</H2>
14    <P><STRONG>Click on the Search Engine address to go to that
15    page.</STRONG></P>
16    </CENTER>
17
18    <!-- <UL> creates a new unordered (bullet) list -->
19    <!-- <LI> inserts a new entry into the list     -->
20    <UL>
21    <LI>Yahoo: <A HREF = "http://www.yahoo.com">
22    http://www.yahoo.com</A></LI>
23
24    <LI>Alta Vista: <A HREF = "http://www.altavista.com">
25    http://www.altavista.com</A></LI>
26
27    <LI>Ask Jeeves: <A HREF = "http://www.askjeeves.com">
28    http://www.askjeeves.com</A></LI>
29
30    <LI>WebCrawler: <A HREF = "http://www.webcrawler.com">
31    http://www.webcrawler.com</A></LI>
32    </UL>
33
34    </BODY>
35    </HTML>
```

Fig. 10.1   Unordered lists with HTML.

The first list item appears on lines 21 and 22

```
<LI>Yahoo: <A HREF = "http://www.yahoo.com">
http://www.yahoo.com</A></LI>
```

Each entry in an unordered list is inserted with the **<LI>** (*list item*) tag, which creates a line break and inserts a bullet mark at the beginning of the line. You then insert and format any text. The closing tag of the list element (**</LI>**) is optional; we prefer to include it to maintain the clarity of the code. At the end of the list, close the **UL** element with the **</UL>** tag.

10.3 Nested and Ordered Lists

Figure 10.2 demonstrates *nested lists*. This feature is useful for displaying information in outline form.

```
1   <HTML>
2
3   <!-- Fig. 10.2: list.html              -->
4   <!-- Advanced Lists: nested and ordered -->
5
6   <HEAD>
7   <TITLE>Internet and WWW How to Program - List</TITLE>
8   </HEAD>
9
10  <BODY>
11
12  <CENTER>
13  <H2><U>The Best Features of the Internet</U></H2>
14  </CENTER>
15
16  <UL>
17  <LI>You can meet new people from countries around
18     the world.</LI>
19  <LI>You have access to new media as it becomes public:</LI>
20
21     <!-- This starts a nested list, which uses a modified  -->
22     <!-- bullet. The list ends when you close the <UL> tag -->
23     <UL>
24     <LI>New games</LI>
25     <LI>New applications </LI>
26
27        <!-- Another nested list, there is no nesting limit -->
28        <UL>
29        <LI>For business</LI>
30        <LI>For pleasure</LI>
31        </UL> <!-- This ends the double nested list -->
32     <LI>Around the clock news</LI>
33     <LI>Search engines</LI>
34     <LI>Shopping</LI>
35     <LI>Programming</LI>
36        <UL>
37        <LI>HTML</LI>
```

Fig. 10.2   Nested and ordered lists in HTML (part 1 of 2).

```
38         <LI>Java</LI>
39         <LI>Dynamic HTML</LI>
40         <LI>Scripts</LI>
41         <LI>New languages</LI>
42         </UL>
43      </UL>    <!-- This ends the first level nested list -->
44   <LI>Links</LI>
45   <LI>Keeping in touch with old friends</LI>
46   <LI>It is the technology of the future!</LI>
47   </UL>    <!-- This ends the primary unordered list -->
48
49   <BR><CENTER><H2>My 3 Favorite <EM>CEO's</EM></H2></CENTER>
50
51   <!-- Ordered lists are constructed in the same way as    -->
52   <!-- unordered lists, except their starting tag is <OL> -->
53   <OL>
54   <LI>Bill Gates</LI>
55   <LI>Steve Jobs</LI>
56   <LI>Michael Dell</LI>
57   </OL>
58
59   </BODY>
60   </HTML>
```

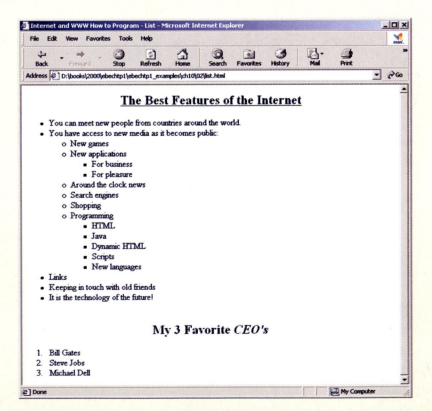

Fig. 10.2   Nested and ordered lists in HTML (part 2 of 2).

Our first nested list begins in lines 23 and 24

```
<UL>
<LI>New games</LI>
```

A nested list is written in the same way as the list we showed you in Fig. 3.2, except that the nested list is contained in another list element. Nesting the new list inside the original will indent the list one level and will change the bullet type to reflect the nesting.

Note the line of space that occurs when you close the unordered list element, for example between "For pleasure" and "Around the clock news" (Fig 10.2). Browsers insert a line of whitespace after every closed list.

Good Programming Practice 10.1

Indenting each level of a nested list in your code makes the code easier to edit and debug.

In Fig. 10.2, lines 16 through 47 show a list with three levels of nesting. When nesting lists, be sure to insert the closing **</UL>** tags in the appropriate places. Lines 53 through 57

```
<OL>
<LI>Bill Gates</LI>
<LI>Steve Jobs</LI>
<LI>Michael Dell</LI>
</OL>
```

define an *ordered list* element with the tags **<OL>**...**</OL>**. Every item in an ordered list begins with a sequence number. By default, ordered lists use decimal sequence numbers (1, 2, 3, …). Figure 10.3 demonstrates alternate labeling schemes for list items.

```
1   <HTML>
2
3   <!-- Fig. 10.3: list.html              -->
4   <!-- Different Types of Ordered Lists -->
5
6   <HEAD>
7   <TITLE>Internet and WWW How to Program - List</TITLE>
8   </HEAD>
9
10  <BODY>
11
12  <CENTER>
13  <H2>Web Site Outline</H2>
14  </CENTER>
15
16  <!-- Change the character style by specifying it in  -->
17  <!-- <OL TYPE = "style"> OR <LI TYPE = "style"> as    -->
18  <!-- decimal=1, uppercase Roman=I, lowercase Roman=i -->
19  <!-- uppercase Latin=A, lowercase Latin=a            -->
20  <OL>
21  <LI>Home page</LI>
22  <LI>Links page</LI>
23     <OL TYPE = "I">
```

Fig. 10.3　Different types of ordered lists (part 1 of 2).

```
24      <LI>Links to search engines</LI>
25      <LI>Links to information sites</LI>
26         <OL TYPE = "A">
27         <LI>News sites</LI>
28            <OL>
29            <LI TYPE = "i">TV based</LI>
30               <OL TYPE = "a">
31               <LI>CNN</LI>
32               <LI>Headline News</LI>
33               </OL>
34            <LI TYPE = "i">Text based</LI>
35               <OL TYPE = "a">
36               <LI>New York Times</LI>
37               <LI>Washington Post</LI>
38               </OL>
39            </OL>
40         <LI>Stock sites</LI>
41         </OL>
42      <LI>Links to "fun" sites</LI>
43      </OL>
44   <LI>Feedback page</LI>
45   <LI>Contact page</LI>
46   <LI>HTML Example Pages</LI>
47   </OL>
48
49   </BODY>
50   </HTML>
```

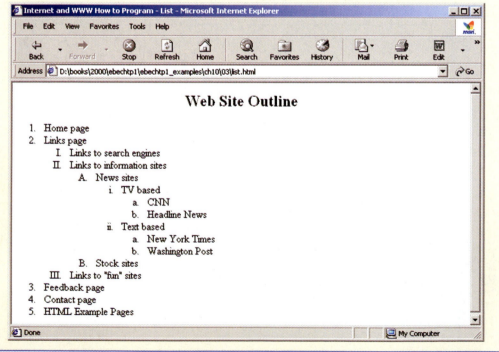

Fig. 10.3   Different types of ordered lists (part 2 of 2).

The four types of list item labeling appear in lines 23 and 24

```
<OL TYPE = "I">
<LI>Links to search engines</LI>
```

lines 26 and 27

```
<OL TYPE = "A">
<LI>News Sites</LI>
```

line 29

```
<LI TYPE = "i">TV based</LI>
```

and lines 30 and 31

```
<OL TYPE = "a">
<LI>CNN</LI>
```

To change the sequence type, use attribute **TYPE** in the **<OL>** opening tag. You can insert the **TYPE** attribute into an individual **<LI>** tag if you would like the change to affect just that list entry. The default type is **TYPE = "1"**, which uses the 1, 2, 3, … sequence. The second type, **TYPE = "I"**, makes an uppercase Roman numeral sequence (I, II, III, …). A variant of this second type is **TYPE = "i"**, which creates the lowercase Roman numeral sequence (i, ii, iii, …). The last two types are **TYPE = "A"** and **TYPE = "a"**, which produce uppercase and lowercase alphabetic sequences, respectively.

 Look-and-Feel Observation 10.1

Using different types of ordered lists can add a well-organized look to your site and can help you categorize and outline information effectively.

10.4 Basic HTML Tables

Another way to format information using HTML 4.0 is to use *tables*. The table in Fig. 10.4 organizes data into rows and columns.

```
1   <HTML>
2
3   <!-- Fig. 10.4: table.html -->
4   <!-- Basic table design    -->
5
6   <HEAD>
7   <TITLE>Internet and WWW How to Program - Tables</TITLE>
8   </HEAD>
9
10  <BODY>
11
12  <CENTER><H2>Table Example Page</H2></CENTER>
13
14  <!-- The <TABLE> tag opens a new table and lets you put in -->
15  <!-- design options and instructions                       -->
16  <TABLE BORDER = "1" ALIGN = "center" WIDTH = "40%">
```

Fig. 10.4   HTML table (part 1 of 2).

```
17
18    <!-- Use the <CAPTION> tag to summarize the table's contents -->
19    <!-- (this helps the visually impaired)                       -->
20    <CAPTION>Here is a small sample table.</CAPTION>
21
22    <!-- The <THEAD> is the first (non-scrolling) horizontal      -->
23    <!-- section. Use it to format the table header area.         -->
24    <!-- <TH> inserts a header cell and displays bold text        -->
25    <THEAD>
26    <TR><TH>This is the head.</TH></TR>
27    </THEAD>
28
29    <!-- All of your important content goes in the <TBODY>. -->
30    <!-- Use this tag to format the entire section          -->
31    <!-- <TD> inserts a data cell, with regular text        -->
32    <TBODY>
33    <TR><TD ALIGN = "center">This is the body.</TD></TR>
34    </TBODY>
35
36    </TABLE>
37
38    </BODY>
39    </HTML>
```

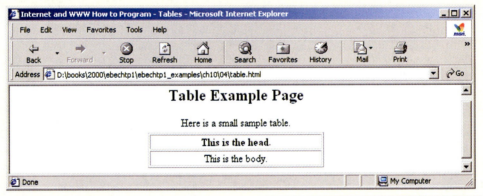

Fig. 10.4   HTML table (part 2 of 2).

All tags and text that apply to the table go inside the **<TABLE>**...**</TABLE>** tags, which begin on line 16

```
<TABLE BORDER = "1" ALIGN = "center" WIDTH = "40%">
```

There are a number of attributes that can be applied to the **TABLE** element. The *BORDER attribute* lets you set the width of the table's border in pixels. If you want all lines to be invisible, you can specify **BORDER = "0"**. You should experiment to find the best "look" for each table. In the table shown in Fig. 10.4, the value of the border attribute is set to **1**.

The horizontal alignment we saw before also applies to tables (**ALIGN = "left"**, **"center"** or **"right"**). The *WIDTH* attribute sets the width of the table, and is used exactly as in the **HR** element— you specify either a number of pixels or a percentage of the screen width.

Line 20

```
<CAPTION>Here is a small sample table.</CAPTION>
```

inserts a *caption* element into the table. The text inside the **<CAPTION>…</CAPTION>** tags is inserted directly above the table in the browser window. The caption text is also used to help *text-based browsers* interpret the table data.

Tables can be split into distinct horizontal and vertical sections. The first of these sections, the head area, appears in lines 25 through 27

```
<THEAD>
<TR><TH>This is the head.</TH></TR>
</THEAD>
```

Put all header information (for example, the titles of the table and column headers) inside the **<THEAD>…</THEAD>** tags.

The **TR**, or *table row element*, is used for formatting the cells of individual rows. All of the cells in a row belong within the **<TR>…</TR>** tags of that row. In the next section we discuss how to use **TR** for row formatting.

The smallest area of the table we are able to format is the *data cell*. There are two types of data cells, located in the header (**<TH>…</TH>**) or in the table body (**<TD>…</TD>**). The code example above inserts a header cell. Header cells, which are usually placed in the **<THEAD>** area, are suitable for titles and column headings.

The second grouping section, the **TBODY** element, appears in lines 32 through 34

```
<TBODY>
<TR><TD ALIGN = "center">This is the body.</TD></TR>
</TBODY>
```

Like the **THEAD**, the **TBODY** is used for formatting and grouping purposes. Although there is only one row and one cell in the above example, most tables will use **TBODY** to house the majority of their content. In this code example, **TBODY** includes only one row and one data cell. The cell is marked by the **<TD>…</TD>** tags.

Regular data cells are left aligned by default. In the above example, notice that there is an **ALIGN** attribute included inside the opening **<TD>** tag. This attribute affects the horizontal alignment (we will see how to set vertical alignment in the next code example). The **ALIGN** attribute is used here in the same way as it is used to align other HTML tags.

Look-and-Feel Observation 10.2

Use tables in your HTML pages to organize data attractively and effectively.

Common Programming Error 10.1

Forgetting to close any of the area formatting tags inside the table area can distort the table format. Be sure to check that every element is opened and closed in its proper place to make sure that the table appears as intended.

10.5 Intermediate HTML Tables and Formatting

In the previous section and code example, we explored the structure of a basic table. In Fig. 10.5, we extend our table example with more formatting attributes.

```
1   <HTML>
2
3   <!-- Fig. 10.5: table.html      -->
4   <!-- Intermediate table design -->
5
6   <HEAD>
7   <TITLE>Internet and WWW How to Program - Tables</TITLE>
8   </HEAD>
9   <BODY>
10
11  <H2 ALIGN = "center">Table Example Page</H2>
12
13  <TABLE BORDER = "1" ALIGN = "center" WIDTH = "40%">
14     <CAPTION>Here is a small sample table.</CAPTION>
15
16     <THEAD>
17     <TR>
18        <TH>This is the Head.</TH>
19     </TR>
20     </THEAD>
21
22     <TBODY>
23     <TR>
24        <TD ALIGN = "center">This is the Body.</TD>
25     </TR>
26     </TBODY>
27
28  </TABLE>
29
30  <BR><BR>
31
32  <TABLE BORDER = "1" ALIGN = "center">
33
34     <CAPTION>Here is a more complex sample table.</CAPTION>
35
36     <!-- <COLGROUP> and <COL> are used to format entire   -->
37     <!-- columns at once. SPAN determines how many columns -->
38     <!-- the COL tag effects.                              -->
39     <COLGROUP>
40        <COL ALIGN = "right">
41        <COL SPAN = "4" ALIGN = "center">
42     </COLGROUP>
43
44     <THEAD>
45
46     <!-- ROWSPANs and COLSPANs combine the indicated number -->
47     <!-- of cells vertically or horizontally                -->
48     <TR BGCOLOR = "#8888FF">
49        <TH ROWSPAN = "2">
50           <IMG SRC = "deitel.gif" WIDTH = "200" HEIGHT = "144"
51              ALT = "Harvey and Paul Deitel">
52        </TH>
```

Fig. 10.5   A complex table with formatting and color (part 1 of 3).

```
53              <TH COLSPAN = "4" VALIGN = "top">
54                  <H1>Camelid comparison</H1><BR>
55                  <P>Approximate as of 8/99</P>
56              </TH>
57          </TR>
58
59          <TR BGCOLOR = "khaki" VALIGN = "bottom">
60              <TH># of Humps</TH>
61              <TH>Indigenous region</TH>
62              <TH>Spits?</TH>
63              <TH>Produces Wool?</TH>
64          </TR>
65
66          </THEAD>
67
68          <TBODY>
69
70          <TR>
71              <TH>Camels (bactrian)</TH>
72              <TD>2</TD>
73              <TD>Africa/Asia</TD>
74              <TD ROWSPAN = "2">Llama</TD>
75              <TD ROWSPAN = "2">Llama</TD>
76          </TR>
77
78          <TR>
79              <TH>Llamas</TH>
80              <TD>1</TD>
81              <TD>Andes Mountains</TD>
82          </TR>
83
84      </TBODY>
85      </TABLE>
86
87      </BODY>
88      </HMTL>
```

Fig. 10.5   A complex table with formatting and color (part 2 of 3).

The new table begins on line 32. The **COLGROUP** element, used for formatting groups of columns, is shown on lines 39 through 42

```
<COLGROUP>
   <COL ALIGN = "right">
   <COL SPAN = "4" ALIGN = "center">
</COLGROUP>
```

The *COLGROUP* element can be used to group and format columns. Each *COL* element in the **<COLGROUP>...</COLGROUP>** tags can format any number of columns (specified with the **SPAN** attribute). Any formatting to be applied to a column or group of columns can be specified in both the **COLGROUP** and **COL** tags. In this case, we align the text inside the leftmost column to the right and center the text in the remaining four columns. Another useful attribute to use here is **WIDTH**, which specifies the width of the column.

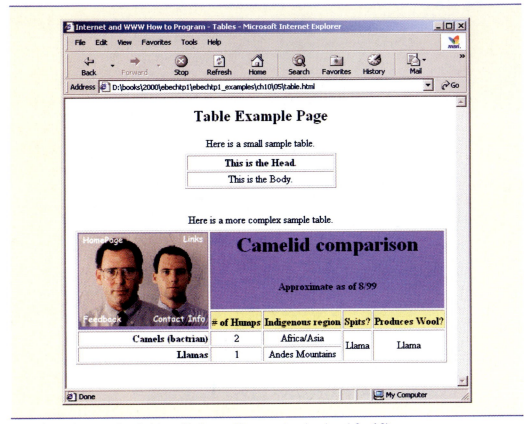

Fig. 10.5   A complex table with formatting and color (part 3 of 3).

Lines 48 and 49

```
<TR BGCOLOR = "#8888FF">
   <TH ROWSPAN = "2">
```

introduce several more table formatting capabilities. You can add a background color or image to any row or cell with the **BGCOLOR** and **BACKGROUND** attributes, which are used in the same way as in the **BODY** element.

It is possible to make some data cells larger than others. This effect is accomplished with the *ROWSPAN* and *COLSPAN* attributes, which can be placed inside any data cell opening tag. The attribute value extends the data cell to span the specified number of cells. Using our line of code, for example, **ROWSPAN = "2"** tells the browser that this data cell will span the area of two vertically adjacent cells. These cells will be joined vertically (and will thus span over two rows). An example of **COLSPAN** appears in line 53:

```
<TH COLSPAN = "4" VALIGN = "top">
```

where the header cell is widened to span four cells.

We also see here an example of vertical alignment formatting. The *VALIGN* attribute accepts the following values: **"top"**, **"middle"**, **"bottom"** and **"baseline"**. All cells in a row whose **VALIGN** attribute is set to **"baseline"** will have the first text line

occur on a common baseline. The default vertical alignment in all data and header cells is
VALIGN = "middle".

The remaining code in Fig. 10.5 demonstrates other uses of the table attributes and elements outlined above.

Look-and-Feel Observation 10.3

*Using the **COLSPAN** and **ROWSPAN** attributes in your tables adds a nice look and can help you format the data cells to contain your information more effectively.*

Common Programming Error 10.2

*When using **COLSPAN** and **ROWSPAN** in table data cells, consider that the modified cells will cover the areas of other cells. Compensate for this in your code by reducing the number of cells in that row or column. If you do not, the formatting of your table will be distorted, and you may inadvertently create more columns and/or rows than you originally intended.*

10.6 Basic HTML Forms

HTML provides several mechanisms to collect information from people viewing your site; one is the *form* (Fig. 10.6).

```
1    <HTML>
2
3    <!-- Fig. 10.6: form.html     -->
4    <!-- Introducing Form Design -->
5
6    <HEAD>
7    <TITLE>Internet and WWW How to Program - Forms</TITLE>
8    </HEAD>
9
10   <BODY>
11   <H2>Feedback Form</H2>
12
13   <P>Please fill out this form to help us improve our site.</P>
14
15   <!-- This tag starts the form, gives the method of sending -->
16   <!-- information and the location of form scripts.         -->
17   <!-- Hidden inputs give the server non-visual information   -->
18   <FORM METHOD = "POST" ACTION = "/cgi-bin/formmail">
19
20   <INPUT TYPE = "hidden" NAME = "recipient"
21      VALUE = "deitel@deitel.com">
22   <INPUT TYPE = "hidden" NAME = "subject"
23      VALUE = "Feedback Form">
24   <INPUT TYPE = "hidden" NAME = "redirect"
25      VALUE = "main.html">
26
27   <!-- <INPUT type = "text"> inserts a text box -->
28   <P><STRONG>Name:</STRONG>
29   <INPUT NAME = "name" TYPE = "text" SIZE = "25"></P>
30
```

Fig. 10.6   Simple form with basic fields and a text box (part 1 of 2).

```
31   <!-- Input types "submit" and "reset" insert buttons -->
32   <!-- for submitting or clearing the form's contents  -->
33   <INPUT TYPE = "submit" VALUE = "Submit Your Entries">
34   <INPUT TYPE = "reset" VALUE = "Clear Your Entries">
35   </FORM>
36
37   </BODY>
38   </HTML>
```

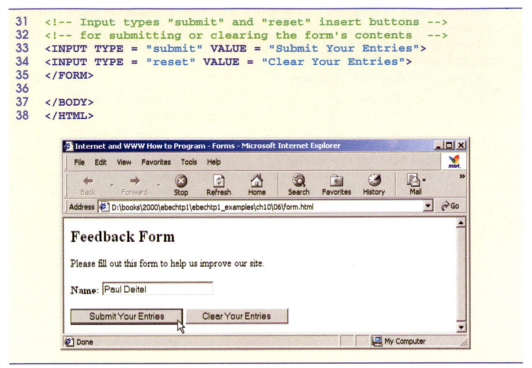

Fig. 10.6   Simple form with basic fields and a text box (part 2 of 2).

The form begins on line 18

```
<FORM METHOD = "POST" ACTION = "/cgi-bin/formmail">
```

with the **FORM** element. The **METHOD** attribute indicates the way the *Web server* will organize and send you the form output. Use **METHOD = "post"** in a form that causes changes to server data, for example when updating a database. The form data will be sent to the server as an *environment variable,* which scripts are able to access (you will learn how to do this in Chapter 29 when we cover Perl). The other possible value, **METHOD = "get"**, should be used when your form does not cause any changes in server-side data, for example when making a database request. The form data from **METHOD = "get"** is appended to the end of the URL (for example, **/cgi-bin/formmail?name=bob&order=5**). Because of this, the amount of data submitted using this **METHOD** is limited to 4K. Also be aware that **METHOD = "get"** is limited to standard characters, and can not submit any special characters, as discussed in Section 9.10.

A *Web server* is a machine that runs a software package such as Microsoft's PWS (Personal Web Server), Microsoft's IIS (Internet Information Server), Apache or Jigsaw. Personal Web Server is described later in the book in Chapter 25 on "Active Server Pages." Web servers handle browser requests. When a browser requests a page or file somewhere on a server, the server processes the request and returns an answer to the browser. In this example, the data from the form goes to a CGI (Common Gateway Interface) script, which is a means of interfacing an HTML page with a script (i.e., a program) written in Perl, C, Tcl or other languages. The script then handles the data fed to it by the server and typically returns some information for the user. The **ACTION** attribute in the **FORM** tag is the path to this script; in this case, it is a common script which emails form data to an address. Most Internet Service Providers will have a script like this on their site, so you can ask your system administrator how to set up your HTML to use the script correctly.

There are several pieces of information (not seen by the user) that you need to insert in the form. Lines 20 through 25

```
<INPUT TYPE = "hidden" NAME = "recipient"
   VALUE = "deitel@deitel.com">
<INPUT TYPE = "hidden" NAME = "subject"
   VALUE = "Feedback Form">
<INPUT TYPE = "hidden" NAME = "redirect"
   VALUE = "main.html">
```

obtain this information by the use of *hidden input elements*. The **INPUT** element is common in forms and always requires the **TYPE** attribute. Two other attributes are **NAME**, which provides a unique identification for the **INPUT** element, and **VALUE**, which indicates the value that the **INPUT** element sends to the server upon submission.

As shown above, hidden inputs always have the attribute **TYPE = "hidden"**. The three hidden inputs shown are typical for this kind of CGI script: An email address to which to send the data, the subject line of the email and a URL to which the user is redirected after submitting the form.

Good Programming Practice 10.2

*Place hidden **INPUT** elements in the beginning of a form, right after the opening **<FORM>** tag. This makes these elements easier to find and identify.*

The usage of an **<INPUT>** element is defined by the value of its **TYPE** attribute. We introduce another of these options in lines 28 and 29:

```
<P><STRONG>Name: </STRONG>
<INPUT NAME = "name" TYPE = "text" SIZE = "25"></P>
```

The input **TYPE = "text"** inserts a one-line text box into the form. The value of this **INPUT** element and the information that the server sends to you from this **INPUT** is the text that the user types into the bar. A good use of the textual input element is for names or other one-line pieces of information.

We also use the **SIZE** attribute, whose value determines the width of the text input, measured in characters. You can also set a maximum number of characters that the text input will accept by inserting the **MAXLENGTH = "***length***"** attribute.

Good Programming Practice 10.3

*When using **INPUT** elements in forms, be sure to leave enough space for users to input the pertinent information.*

It is important to note here the placement of text relative to the **INPUT** element. You must make sure to include a textual identifier (in this case, **Name:**) adjacent to the **INPUT** element, to indicate the purpose of the element.

Common Programming Error 10.3

Forgetting to include textual labels for a form element is a design error. Without these labels, users will have no way of knowing what the function of individual form elements is.

There are two types of **INPUT** elements in lines 33 and 34

```
<INPUT TYPE = "submit" VALUE = "Submit Your Entries">
<INPUT TYPE = "reset" VALUE = "Clear Your Entries">
```

that should be inserted into every form. The *TYPE = "submit"* **INPUT** element places a button in the form that submits data to the server when clicked. The **VALUE** attribute changes the text displayed on the button (the default value is *"submit"*). The input element *TYPE = "reset"* inserts a button onto the form that, when clicked, clears all entries the user entered into the form. This can help the user correct mistakes or simply start over. As with the **submit** input, the **VALUE** attribute of the **RESET** input affects the text of the button on the screen, but does not affect functionality at all.

Good Programming Practice 10.4

Be sure to close your form code with the **</FORM>** *tag. Neglecting to include this can affect the actions of other forms on the same page.*

10.7 More Complex HTML Forms

We introduce additional form input options in Fig. 10.7.

```
1   <HTML>
2
3   <!-- Fig. 10.7: form.html    -->
4   <!-- Form Design Example 2 -->
5
6   <HEAD>
7   <TITLE>Internet and WWW How to Program - Forms</TITLE>
8   </HEAD>
9
10  <BODY>
11  <H2>Feedback Form</H2>
12
13  <P>Please fill out this form to help us improve our site.</P>
14
15  <FORM METHOD = "POST" ACTION = "/cgi-bin/formmail">
16
17  <INPUT TYPE = "hidden" NAME = "recipient"
18     VALUE = "deitel@deitel.com">
19  <INPUT TYPE = "hidden" NAME = "subject"
20     VALUE = "Feedback Form">
21  <INPUT TYPE = "hidden" NAME = "redirect"
22     VALUE = "main.html">
23
24  <P><STRONG>Name: </STRONG>
25  <INPUT NAME = "name" TYPE = "text" SIZE = "25"></P>
26
27  <!-- <TEXTAREA> creates a textbox of the size given -->
28  <P><STRONG>Comments:</STRONG>
29  <TEXTAREA NAME = "comments" ROWS = "4" COLS = "36"></TEXTAREA>
30  </P>
```

Fig. 10.7   Form including textareas, password boxes and checkboxes (part 1 of 2).

```
31
32   <!-- <INPUT TYPE = "password"> inserts a textbox whose    -->
33   <!-- readout will be in *** instead of regular characters -->
34   <P><STRONG>Email Address:</STRONG>
35   <INPUT NAME = "email" TYPE = "password" SIZE = "25"></P>
36
37   <!-- <INPUT TYPE = "checkbox"> creates a checkbox -->
38   <P><STRONG>Things you liked:</STRONG><BR>
39
40   Site design
41   <INPUT NAME = "things" TYPE = "checkbox" VALUE = "Design">
42   Links
43   <INPUT NAME = "things" TYPE = "checkbox" VALUE = "Links">
44   Ease of use
45   <INPUT NAME = "things" TYPE = "checkbox" VALUE = "Ease">
46   Images
47   <INPUT NAME = "things" TYPE = "checkbox" VALUE = "Images">
48   Source code
49   <INPUT NAME = "things" TYPE = "checkbox" VALUE = "Code">
50   </P>
51
52   <INPUT TYPE = "submit" VALUE = "Submit Your Entries">
53   <INPUT TYPE = "reset" VALUE = "Clear Your Entries">
54   </FORM>
55
56   </BODY>
57   </HTML>
```

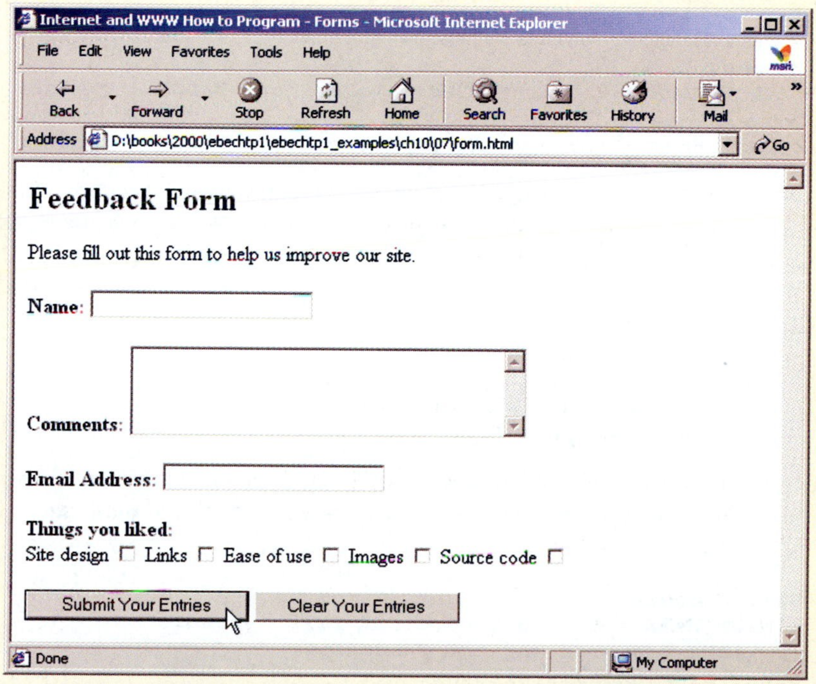

Fig. 10.7   Form including textareas, password boxes and checkboxes (part 2 of 2).

Line 29

```
<TEXTAREA NAME = "comments" ROWS = "4" COLS = "36"></TEXTAREA>
```

introduces the **TEXTAREA** element. This type of form component has its own element name. The **TEXTAREA** element inserts a box into the form. You specify the size of the box (which is scrollable) inside the opening **<TEXTAREA>** tag with the **ROWS** attribute, which sets the number of rows appearing in the **TEXTAREA**. With the **COLS** attribute, you specify how wide the **TEXTAREA** should be. This **TEXTAREA** is four rows of characters tall and 36 characters wide. Any default text that you want to place inside the **TEXTAREA** should be contained within the **<TEXTAREA>**...**</TEXTAREA>** tags.

The input **TYPE = "password"** in line 35

```
<INPUT NAME = "email" TYPE = "password" SIZE = "25"></P>
```

inserts a text box with the indicated size. The only difference between a password input and a text input is that, when data is entered into a password area, it appears on the screen as asterisks. The password is used for submitting sensitive information which the user would not want others to be able to read. It is just the browser that displays asterisks—the real form data is still submitted to the server.

Lines 40 through 49 introduce another form input **TYPE**.

```
Site design
<INPUT NAME = "things" TYPE = "checkbox" VALUE = "Design">
Links
<INPUT NAME = "things" TYPE = "checkbox" VALUE = "Links">
Ease of use
<INPUT NAME = "things" TYPE = "checkbox" VALUE = "Ease">
Images
<INPUT NAME = "things" TYPE = "checkbox" VALUE = "Images">
Source code
<INPUT NAME = "things" TYPE = "checkbox" VALUE = "Code">
```

Every **INPUT** element with **TYPE = "checkbox"** creates a new checkbox in the form. Checkboxes can be used individually or in groups. Each checkbox in a group should have the same **NAME** (in this case, **NAME = "things"**). This notifies the script handling the form that all of the checkboxes are related to one another, and are typically listed in the same output line in the email generated by the form.

Common Programming Error 10.4

*When your form has several checkboxes with the same **NAME**, you must make sure that they have different **VALUE**s, or else the script will have no way of distinguishing between them.*

Yet more form elements are introduced in Fig. 10.8. In our final form code example, we introduce two new types of input options. The first of these is the *radio buttons*, introduced in lines 53 through 67

```
Search engine
<INPUT NAME = "how get to site" TYPE = "radio"
    VALUE ="search engine" CHECKED>
Links from another site
<INPUT NAME = "how get to site" TYPE = "radio"
    VALUE = "link">
```

```
Deitel.com Web site
<INPUT NAME = "how get to site" TYPE = "radio"
   VALUE = "deitel.com">
Reference in a book
<INPUT NAME = "how get to site" TYPE = "radio"
   VALUE = "book">
Other
<INPUT NAME = "how get to site" TYPE = "radio"
   VALUE = "other">
```

Inserted into forms with the **INPUT** attribute *TYPE = "radio"*, radio buttons are similar in function and usage to checkboxes. Radio buttons are different in that only one in the group may be selected at any time. All of the **NAME** attributes of a group of radio inputs must be the same and all of the **VALUE** attributes different. Insert the attribute *CHECKED* to indicate which radio button you would like selected initially. The **CHECKED** attribute can also be applied to checkboxes.

Common Programming Error 10.5

*When you are using a group of radio inputs in a form, forgetting to set the **NAME** values to the same name will let the user select all the radio buttons at the same time: an undesired result.*

```
1   <HTML>
2
3   <!-- Fig. 10.8: form.html     -->
4   <!-- Form Design Example 3 -->
5
6   <HEAD>
7   <TITLE>Internet and WWW How to Program - Forms</TITLE>
8   </HEAD>
9
10  <BODY>
11  <H2>Feedback Form</H2>
12
13  <P>Please fill out this form to help us improve our site.</P>
14
15  <FORM METHOD = "POST" ACTION = "/cgi-bin/formmail">
16
17  <INPUT TYPE = "hidden" NAME = "recipient"
18     VALUE = "deitel@deitel.com">
19  <INPUT TYPE = "hidden" NAME = "subject"
20     VALUE = "Feedback Form">
21  <INPUT TYPE = "hidden" NAME = "redirect"
22     VALUE = "main.html">
23
24  <P><STRONG>Name: </STRONG>
25  <INPUT NAME = "name" TYPE = "text" SIZE = "25"></P>
26
27  <P><STRONG>Comments:</STRONG>
28  <TEXTAREA NAME = "comments" ROWS = "4" COLS = "36"></TEXTAREA>
29  </P>
30
```

Fig. 10.8   HTML form including radio buttons and pulldown lists (part 1 of 3).

```
31   <P><STRONG>Email Address:</STRONG>
32   <INPUT NAME = "email" TYPE = "password" SIZE = "25"></P>
33
34   <P><STRONG>Things you liked:</STRONG><BR>
35
36   Site design
37   <INPUT NAME = "things" TYPE = "checkbox" VALUE = "Design">
38   Links
39   <INPUT NAME = "things" TYPE = "checkbox" VALUE = "Links">
40   Ease of use
41   <INPUT NAME = "things" TYPE = "checkbox" VALUE = "Ease">
42   Images
43   <INPUT NAME = "things" TYPE = "checkbox" VALUE = "Images">
44   Source code
45   <INPUT NAME = "things" TYPE = "checkbox" VALUE = "Code">
46   </P>
47
48   <!-- <INPUT TYPE="radio"> creates a radio button. The      -->
49   <!-- difference between radio buttons and checkboxes is     -->
50   <!-- that only one radio button in a group can be selected -->
51   <P><STRONG>How did you get to our site?:</STRONG><BR>
52
53   Search engine
54   <INPUT NAME = "how get to site" TYPE = "radio"
55      VALUE = "search engine" CHECKED>
56   Links from another site
57   <INPUT NAME = "how get to site" TYPE = "radio"
58      VALUE = "link">
59   Deitel.com Web site
60   <INPUT NAME = "how get to site" TYPE = "radio"
61      VALUE = "deitel.com">
62   Reference in a book
63   <INPUT NAME = "how get to site" TYPE = "radio"
64      VALUE = "book">
65   Other
66   <INPUT NAME = "how get to site" TYPE = "radio"
67      VALUE = "other">
68   </P>
69
70   <!-- The <select> tag presents a drop down menu with -->
71   <!-- choices indicated by the <option> tags          -->
72   <P><STRONG>Rate our site (1-10):</STRONG>
73   <SELECT NAME = "rating">
74   <OPTION SELECTED>Amazing:-)
75   <OPTION>10
76   <OPTION>9
77   <OPTION>8
78   <OPTION>7
79   <OPTION>6
80   <OPTION>5
81   <OPTION>4
82   <OPTION>3
83   <OPTION>2
```

Fig. 10.8   HTML form including radio buttons and pulldown lists (part 2 of 3).

```
84    <OPTION>1
85    <OPTION>The Pits:-(
86    </SELECT></P>
87
88    <INPUT TYPE = "submit" VALUE = "Submit Your Entries">
89    <INPUT TYPE = "reset" VALUE = "Clear Your Entries">
90    </FORM>
91
92    </BODY>
93    </HTML>
```

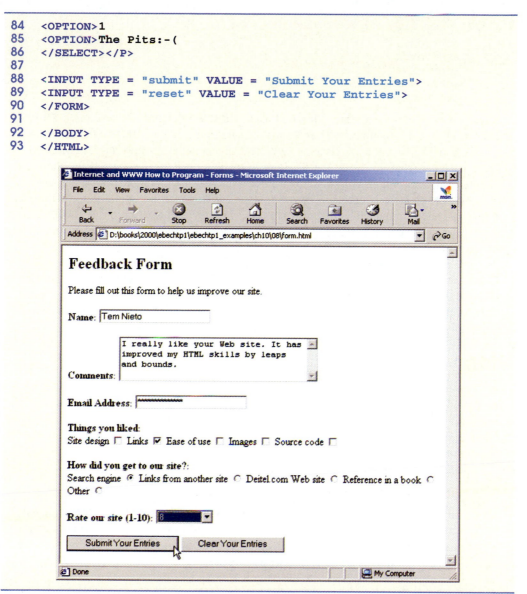

Fig. 10.8   HTML form including radio buttons and pulldown lists (part 3 of 3).

The last type of form input that we introduce here is the ***SELECT*** element, on lines 73 through 86 of our code. This will place a selectable list of items inside your form.

```
<SELECT NAME = "rating">
<OPTION SELECTED>Amazing:-)
<OPTION>10
<OPTION>9
<OPTION>8
<OPTION>7
<OPTION>6
```

```
<OPTION>5
<OPTION>4
<OPTION>3
<OPTION>2
<OPTION>1
<OPTION>The Pits:-(
</SELECT>
```

This type of type of form input is inserted using a **SELECT** element instead of an **INPUT** element. Inside the opening ***<SELECT>*** tag, be sure to include the **NAME** attribute.

To add an item to the list, insert an ***OPTION*** element in the ***<SELECT>…</SELECT>*** area, and type what you want the list item to display on the same line. If an option is selected, this text will be sent to you in the form output email. Although a closing tag for the **OPTION** element is optional, its use is deprecated, and it is generally not included. When you have completed the list of **OPTION**s, close the **SELECT** area. The **SELECTED** attribute, like the **CHECKED** attribute for radio buttons and checkboxes, applies a default selection to your list.

The preceding code will generate a pull-down list of options, as shown in Fig. 10.8. There is another attribute that can be included in the opening **<SELECT>** tag which changes the appearance of the list: You can change the number of list options visible at one time by including the ***SIZE = "x"*** attribute inside the **<SELECT>** tag. Use this attribute if you prefer an expanded version of the list to the one-line expandable list.

10.8 Internal Linking

In Chapter 9, we discussed how to link one Web page to another by using textual and image anchors. Figure 10.9 introduces *internal linking*, which lets you assign a location name to any individual point in an HTML file. This location name can then be added to the page's URL, enabling you to link to that specific point on the page instead of being limited to linking to the top of the page.

Line 14

```
<A NAME = "features"></A>m
```

shows an internal hyperlink. A location on a page is marked by including a **NAME** attribute in an **A** element. Our line of code specifies its location on the page as having **NAME = "features"**. Since the name of the page is **list.html**, the URL of this point in the Web page is referred to as **list.html#features**.

```
1   <HTML>
2
3   <!-- Fig. 10.9: list.html  -->
4   <!-- Internal Linking      -->
5
6   <HEAD>
7   <TITLE>Internet and WWW How to Program - List</TITLE>
8   </HEAD>
9
10  <BODY>
```

Fig. 10.9   Using internal hyperlinks to make your pages more navigable (part 1 of 3).

```
11
12   <CENTER>
13   <!-- <A NAME = "..."></A> makes an internal hyperlink -->
14   <A NAME = "features"></A>
15   <H2><U>The Best Features of the Internet</U></H2>
16
17   <!-- An internal link's address is "xx.html#linkname" -->
18   <H3><A HREF = "#ceos">Go to <EM>Favorite CEO's</EM></A></H3>
19   </CENTER>
20
21   <UL>
22   <LI>You can meet new people from countries around the world.
23   <LI>You have access to new media as it becomes public:
24      <UL>
25      <LI>New games
26      <LI>New applications
27         <UL>
28         <LI>For Business
29         <LI>For Pleasure
30         </UL>
31      <LI>Around the Clock news
32      <LI>Search Engines
33      <LI>Shopping
34      <LI>Programming
35         <UL>
36         <LI>HTML
37         <LI>Java
38         <LI>Dynamic HTML
39         <LI>Scripts
40         <LI>New languages
41         </UL>
42      </UL>
43   <LI>Links
44   <LI>Keeping In touch with old friends
45   <LI>It is the technology of the future!
46   </UL><BR><BR>
47
48   <A NAME = "ceos"></A>
49   <CENTER><H2>My 3 Favorite <EM>CEO's</EM></H2>
50   <H3><A HREF = "#features">Go to <EM>Favorite Features</EM></A>
51   </H3></CENTER>
52
53   <OL>
54      <LI>Bill Gates
55      <LI>Steve Jobs
56      <LI>Michael Dell
57   </OL>
58
59   </BODY>
60
61   </HTML>
```

Fig. 10.9 Using internal hyperlinks to make your pages more navigable (part 2 of 3).

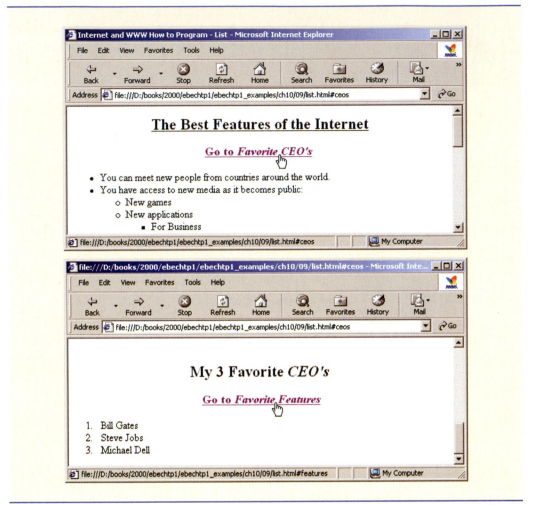

Fig. 10.9   Using internal hyperlinks to make your pages more navigable (part 3 of 3).

Line 50

```
<H3><A HREF = "#features">Go to <EM>Favorite Features</EM></A>
```

shows the insertion of a regular hyperlink, the target destination being the internal hyper-link location **#features**. Clicking on this hyperlink in a browser would scroll the browser window to that point on the page. Examples of this occur in Fig 10.9, which shows two different screen captures from the same page, each at a different internal location. You can also link to an internal location on another page by using the URL of that location (using the format **HREF = "page.html#name"**).

Look-and-Feel Observation 10.4

Internal hyperlinks are most useful in large HTML files with lots of information. You can link to various points on the page to save the user from having to scroll down and find a specific location.

10.9 Creating and Using Image Maps

We have seen that images can be used as anchors to link to other places on your site or elsewhere on the Internet. We now discuss how to create *image maps* (Fig. 10.10), which allow you to designate certain sections of the image as *hotspots* and then use these hotspots as anchors for linking.

```
1   <HTML>
2
3   <!-- Fig. 10.10: picture.html        -->
4   <!-- Creating and Using Imape Maps -->
5
6   <HEAD>
7   <TITLE>Internet and WWW How to Program - List</TITLE>
8   </HEAD>
9
10  <BODY BACKGROUND = "bckgrnd.gif">
11
12  <CENTER>
13  <!-- <MAP> opens and names an image map formatting area -->
14  <!-- and to be referenced later -->
15  <MAP NAME = "picture">
16
17  <!-- The "SHAPE = rect indicates a rectangular area, with   -->
18  <!-- coordinates of the upper-left and lower-right corners -->
19  <AREA HREF = "form.html" SHAPE = "rect"
20     COORDS = "3, 122, 73, 143" ALT = "Go to the form">
21  <AREA HREF = "contact.html" SHAPE = "rect"
22     COORDS = "109, 123, 199, 142" ALT = "Go to the contact page">
23  <AREA HREF = "main.html" SHAPE = "rect"
24     COORDS = "1, 2, 72, 17" ALT = "Go to the homepage">
25  <AREA HREF = "links.html" SHAPE = "rect"
26     COORDS = "155, 0, 199, 18" ALT = "Go to the links page">
27
28  <!-- The "SHAPE = polygon" indicates an area of cusotmizable -->
29  <!-- shape, with the coordinates of every vertex listed      -->
30  <AREA HREF = "mailto:deitel@deitel.com" SHAPE = "poly"
31     COORDS = "28, 22, 24, 68, 46, 114, 84, 111, 99, 56, 86, 13"
32     ALT = "Email the Deitels">
33
34  <!-- The "SHAPE = circle" indicates a circular area with -->
35  <!-- center and radius listed                            -->
36  <AREA HREF = "mailto:deitel@deitel.com" SHAPE = "circle"
37     COORDS = "146, 66, 42" ALT = "Email the Deitels">
38  </MAP>
39
40  <!-- <IMG SRC=... USEMAP = "#name"> says that the indicated -->
41  <!-- image map will be used with this image                 -->
42  <IMG SRC = "deitel.gif" WIDTH = "200" HEIGHT = "144" BORDER = "1"
43     ALT = "Harvey and Paul Deitel" USEMAP = "#picture">
44  </CENTER>
45
```

Fig. 10.10 A picture with links anchored to an image map (part 1 of 2).

```
46   </BODY>
47   </HTML>
```

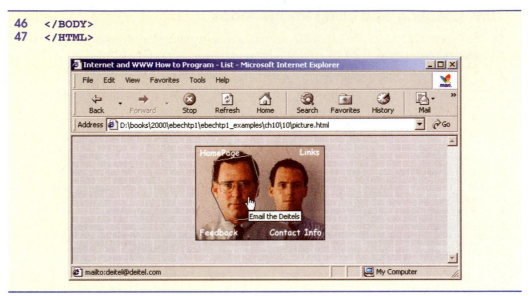

Fig. 10.10   A picture with links anchored to an image map (part 2 of 2).

All elements of an image map are contained inside the **<MAP>...</MAP>** tags. The required attribute for the **MAP** element is **NAME** (line 15)

```
<MAP NAME = "picture">
```

As we will see, this attribute is needed for referencing purposes. A hotspot on the image is designated with the **AREA** element. Every **<AREA>** tag has the following attributes: **HREF** sets the target for the link on that spot, **SHAPE** and **COORDS** set the characteristics of the area and **ALT** functions just as it does in **<IMG>** tags.

The first occurrence of the **SHAPE = "rect"** is on lines 19 and 20:

```
<AREA HREF = "form.html" SHAPE = "rect"
    COORDS = "3, 122, 73, 143" ALT = "Go to the form">
```

This statement causes a *rectangular hotspot* to be drawn around the *coordinates* given in the **COORDS** element. A coordinate pair consists of two numbers, which are the locations of the point on the *x* and *y* axes. The *x* axis extends horizontally from the upper-left corner and the *y* axis vertically. Every point on an image has a unique *x–y* coordinate. In the case of a rectangular hotspot, the required coordinates are those of the upper-left and lower-right corners of the rectangle. In this case, the upper-left corner of the rectangle is located at 3 on the *x* axis and 122 on the *y* axis, annotated as (3, 122). The lower-right corner of the rectangle is at (73, 143).

Another map area is in lines 30 through 32:

```
<AREA HREF = "mailto:deitel@deitel.com" SHAPE = "poly"
    COORDS = "28, 22, 24, 68, 46, 114, 84, 111, 99, 56, 86, 13"
    ALT = "Email the Deitels">
```

In this case, we use the **SHAPE = "poly" AREA** attribute. This creates a hotspot of no preset shape—you specify the shape of the hotspot in the **COORDS** attribute by listing the coordinates of every vertex, or corner of the hotspot. The browser will automatically connect these points with lines to form the area of the hotspot.

SHAPE = "circle" is the last shape attribute that is commonly used in image maps. It creates a *circular hotspot*, and requires both the coordinates of the center of the circle and the radius of the circle, in pixels.

To use the image map with an **IMG** element, you must insert the **USEMAP = "#***name***"** attribute into the **IMG** element, where *name* is the value of the **NAME** attribute in the **MAP** element. Lines 42 and 43

```
<IMG SRC = "deitel.gif" WIDTH = "200" HEIGHT="144" BORDER="1"
    ALT = "Harvey and Paul Deitel" USEMAP = "#picture">
```

show how the image map **NAME = "picture"** is applied to the **IMG** element being inserted in the page.

Good Programming Practice 10.5

Keep the **<MAP>...</MAP>** *tags on the same page as the image that will use them. This will save time if you have to edit the image map.*

10.10 <META> Tags

People use search engines to find interesting Web sites. Search engines usually catalog sites by following links from page to page and saving identification and classification information for each page visited. The main HTML element that interacts with the search engines is the *META* tag (Fig. 10.11).

```
1   <!DOCTYPE HTML PUBLIC "-//W3C//DTD HTML 4.0 Transitional//EN">
2   <HTML>
3
4   <!-- Fig. 10.11: main.html       -->
5   <!-- <META> and <!DOCTYPE> tags -->
6
7   <HEAD>
8   <!-- <META> tags give search engines information they need -->
9   <!-- to catalog your site                                  -->
10  <META NAME = "keywords" CONTENT = "Webpage, design, HTML,
11     tutorial, personal, help, index, form, contact, feedback,
12     list, links, frame, deitel">
13
14  <META NAME = "description" CONTENT = "This Web site will help
15     you learn the basics of HTML and Webpage design through the
16     use of interactive examples and instruction.">
17
18  <TITLE>Internet and WWW How to Program - Welcome</TITLE>
19  </HEAD>
20
21  <BODY>
22
23  <H1 ALIGN = "center"><U>Welcome to Our Web Site!</U></H1>
24
```

Fig. 10.11 Using **<META>** and **<DOCTYPE>** (part 1 of 2).

```
25   <P><FONT COLOR = "red" SIZE = "+1" FACE = "Arial">We have
26   designed this site to teach about the wonders of
27   <EM>HTML</EM>.</FONT>
28
29   <FONT COLOR = "purple" SIZE = "+2" FACE = "Verdana">We have been
30   using <EM>HTML</EM> since <U>version<STRONG> 2.0</STRONG></U>,
31   and we enjoy the features that have been added recently.</FONT>
32
33   <FONT COLOR = "blue" SIZE = "+1" FACE = "Helvetica">It
34   seems only a short time ago that we read our first <EM>HTML</EM>
35   book.</FONT>
36
37   <FONT COLOR = "green" SIZE = "+2" FACE = "Times">Soon you will
38   know about many of the great new feature of HTML 4.0.</FONT></P>
39
40   <H2 ALIGN = "center">Have Fun With the Site!</H2></P>
41
42   </BODY>
43   </HTML>
```

Fig. 10.11   Using **<META>** and **<DOCTYPE>** (part 2 of 2).

Line 1

```
<!DOCTYPE HTML PUBLIC "-//W3C//DTD HTML 4.0 Transitional//EN">
```

tells the browser that the following HTML conforms to a **Transitional** subset of HTML version 4.0. Although browsers do not require this element in order to read your HTML file, it useful to include it at the beginning of every HTML document.

 Portability Tip 10.1

HTML has evolved through many versions. Although the latest major version is 4, there are still many browsers and Web pages that are using version 3.2 or lower. Because each version of HTML introduces new features, it is important to tell the browser what version you are using, in order to get the best possible performance, compatibility and portability.

META tags contain two attributes that should always be used. The first of these, *NAME*, is an identification of the type of **META** tag you are including. The *CONTENT* attribute provides information the search engine will be cataloging about your site.

Lines 10 through 12 demonstrate the **META** tag.

```
<META NAME = "keywords" CONTENT = "Webpage, design, HTML,
    tutorial, personal, help, index, form, contact, feedback,
    list, links, frame, deitel">
```

The **CONTENT** of a **META** tag with *NAME = "keywords"* provides search engines with a list of words that describe key aspects of your site. These words are used to match with searches—if someone searches for some of the terms in your **keywords META** tag, they have a better chance of being informed about your site in the search engine output. Thus, including **META** tags and their **CONTENT** information will draw more viewers—and better qualified viewers—to your site.

The ***description*** attribute value appears on lines 14 through 16:

```
<META NAME = "description" CONTENT = "This Web site will help
you learn the basics of HTML and Webpage design through the
use of interactive examples and instruction.">
```

It is quite similar to the **keywords** value. Instead of giving a list of words describing your page, the **CONTENTS** of the keywords **META** element should be a readable 3-to-4 line description of your site, written in sentence form. This description is also used by search engines to catalog and display your site.

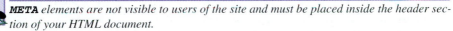

Software Engineering Observation 10.1

META elements are not visible to users of the site and must be placed inside the header section of your HTML document.

10.11 <FRAMESET> Tag

All of the Web pages we have designed so far have the ability to link to other pages but can display only one page at a time. Figure 10.12 introduces *frames*, which can help you display more than one HTML file at a time. Frames, when used properly, can make your site more readable and usable for your users.

```
1   <!DOCTYPE HTML PUBLIC "-//W3C//DTD HTML 4.0 Frameset//EN">
2   <HTML>
3
4   <!-- Fig. 10.12: index.html -->
5   <!-- HTML Frames I         -->
6
7   <HEAD>
8   <META NAME = "keywords" CONTENT = "Webpage, design, HTML,
9       tutorial, personal, help, index, form, contact, feedback,
10      list, links, frame, deitel">
11
12  <META NAME = "description" CONTENT = "This Web site will help
13      you learn the basics of HTML and Webpage design through the
14      use of interactive examples and instruction.">
15
16  <TITLE>Internet and WWW How to Program - Main</TITLE>
17  </HEAD>
18
19  <!-- The <FRAMESET> tag gives the dimensions of your frame -->
20  <FRAMESET COLS = "110,*">
21
22      <!-- The individual FRAME elements specify which pages -->
23      <!-- appear in the given frames                        -->
24      <FRAME NAME = "nav" SRC = "nav.html">
25      <FRAME NAME = "main" SRC = "main.html">
26
27      <NOFRAMES>
28      <P>This page uses frames, but your browser does not support
29      them.</P>
```

Fig. 10.12 Web site using two frames—navigational and content (part 1 of 2).

```
30          <P>Get Internet Explorer 5 at the
31              <A HREF = "http://www.microsoft.com/">
32              Microsoft Web Site</A></P>
33          </NOFRAMES>
34
35      </FRAMESET>
36      </HTML>
```

Fig. 10.12 Web site using two frames—navigational and content (part 2 of 2).

On line 1

```
<!DOCTYPE HTML PUBLIC "-//W3C//DTD HTML 4.0 Frameset//EN">
```

we encounter a slightly different **<!DOCTYPE>** tag. It now says **Frameset** instead of **Transitional**. This tag tells the browser that we will be using frames in the following code. You should include this modified version of the **<!DOCTYPE>** tag whenever you use frames in your HTML document.

The framed page begins with the opening *FRAMESET* tag, on line 20:

```
<FRAMESET COLS = "110,*">
```

This tag tells the browser that the page contains frames, the details of which will be set between the **<FRAMESET>**...**</FRAMESET>** tags. The **COLS** attribute of the opening **FRAMESET** tag gives the layout of the frameset. The value of *COLS* (or *ROWS*, if you will be writing a frameset with a horizontal layout) gives the width of each frame, either in pixels or as a percentage of the screen. In this case, the attribute **COLS = "110,*"** tells the browser that there are two frames. The first one extends 110 pixels from the left edge of the screen, and the second frame fills the remainder of the screen (as indicated by the asterisk).

Now that we have defined the page layout, we have to specify what files will make up the frameset. We do this with the **FRAME** element in lines 24 and 25:

```
<FRAME NAME = "nav" SRC = "nav.html">
<FRAME NAME = "main" SRC = "main.html">
```

In each **FRAME** element, the **SRC** attribute gives the URL of the page that will be displayed in the specified frame. In the preceding example, the first frame (which covers 110 pixels on the left side of the **FRAMESET**) will display the page **nav.html** and has the attribute **NAME = "nav"**. The second frame will display the page **main.html** and has the attribute **NAME = "main"**.

The purpose of a **NAME** attribute in the **FRAME** element is to identify that specific frame, enabling hyperlinks in a **FRAMESET** to load in their intended **FRAME**. For example,

```
<A HREF = "links.html" TARGET = "main">
```

would load **links.html** in the frame whose **NAME** attribute is **"main"**.

A target in an anchor element can also be set to a number of preset values: **TARGET="_blank"** loads the page in a new blank browser window, **TARGET="_self"** loads the page into the same window as the anchor element, **TARGET="_parent"** loads it in the parent **FRAMESET** (i.e., the **FRAMESET** which encapsulates the current frame) and **TARGET="_top"** loads the page into the full browser window (the page loads over the **FRAMESET**).

In lines 26 through 32 of the code example in Fig. 10.12, the **NOFRAMES** element displays HTML in those browsers that do not support frames.

Portability Tip 10.2

*Not everyone uses a browser that supports frames. Use the **NOFRAMES** element inside the **FRAMESET**, either to direct users to a non-framed version of your site or to provide links for downloading a frames-enabled browser.*

Look-and-Feel Observation 10.5

Frames are capable of enhancing your page, but are often misused. Never use frames to accomplish what you could with tables or other, simpler HTML formatting.

10.12 Nested <FRAMESET> Tags

You can use the **FRAMESET** element to create more complex layouts in a framed Web site by nesting **FRAMESET** areas as in Fig. 10.13.

The first level of **FRAMESET** tags is on lines 17 through 18:

```
<FRAMESET COLS="110,*">
<FRAME NAME="nav" SCROLLING="no" NORESIZE SRC="nav.html">
```

The **FRAMESET** and **FRAME** elements here are constructed in the same manner as in Fig. 10.12. To this point, we have one frame that extends over the first 110 pixels of the screen starting at the left edge. The **SCROLLING** attribute, when set to **"no"**, prevents the browser from placing a scrolling bar on that frame. The **NORESIZE** attribute prevents the user from resizing the frame by using the mouse.

The second (nested) level of the **FRAMESET** element covers only the remaining **FRAME** area that was not included in the primary **FRAMESET**. Thus, any frames included in the second **FRAMESET** will not include the left-most 110 pixels of the screen. Lines 22 through 24 show the second level of **FRAMESET** tags.

```
<FRAMESET ROWS = "175,*">
   <FRAME NAME = "picture" SRC = "picture.html" NORESIZE>
   <FRAME NAME = "main" SRC = "main.html">
```

In this **FRAMESET** area, the first frame extends 175 pixels from the top of the screen, as indicated by the **ROWS = "175,*"**. Be sure to include the correct number of **FRAME** elements inside the second **FRAMESET** area. Also, be sure to include a **NOFRAME** element and to close both of the **FRAMESET** areas at the end of the Web page.

```
1   <!DOCTYPE html PUBLIC "-//W3C//DTD HTML 4.0 Frameset//EN">
2   <HTML>
3
4   <!-- Fig. 10.13: index.html -->
5   <!-- HTML Frames II         -->
6
7   <HEAD>
8
9   <META NAME = "keywords" CONTENT = "Webpage, design, HTML,
10     tutorial, personal, help, index, form, contact, feedback,
11     list, links, frame, deitel">
12
13  <META NAME = "description" CONTENT = "This Web site will help
14     you learn the basics of HTML and Webpage design through the
15     use of interactive examples and instruction.">
16
17  <TITLE>Internet and WWW How to Program - Main</TITLE>
18  </HEAD>
19
20  <FRAMESET COLS = "110,*">
21     <FRAME NAME = "nav" SCROLLING = "no" SRC = "nav.html">
22
23     <!-- Nested Framesets are used to change the formatting -->
24     <!-- and spacing of the frameset as a whole            -->
25     <FRAMESET ROWS = "175,*">
26        <FRAME NAME = "picture" SRC = "picture.html" NORESIZE>
27        <FRAME NAME = "main" SRC = "main.html">
28     </FRAMESET>
29
30     <NOFRAMES>
31        <P>This page uses frames, but your browser doesn't
32           support them.</P>
33        <P>Get Internet Explorer 5 at the
34           <A HREF = "http://www.microsoft.com/">Microsoft
35           Web Site</A></P>
36
37     </NOFRAMES>
38
```

Fig. 10.13 Framed Web site with a nested frameset (part 1 of 2).

```
39  </FRAMESET>
40  </HTML>
```

Fig. 10.13 Framed Web site with a nested frameset (part 2 of 2).

Testing and Debugging Tip 10.1

*When using nested **FRAMESET** elements, indent every level of **FRAME** tag. This makes the page clearer and easier to debug.*

Look-and-Feel Observation 10.6

*Nested **FRAMESET**s can help you create visually pleasing, easy-to-navigate Web sites.*

10.13 Internet and WWW Resources

There are many Web sites that cover the more advanced and difficult features of HTML. Several of these sites are featured here.

markradcliffe.co.uk/html/advancedhtml.htm
This site gives pointers on techniques that can be used in addition to knowledge of basic HTML tags. The site mainly focuses on frames and tables.

www.geocities.com/SiliconValley/Orchard/5212/
Adam's Advanced HTML Page is geared to those looking to master the more advanced techniques of HTML. It includes instructions for creating tables, frames and marquees and other advanced topics.

`www.webdeveloper.com`

An excellent resource for creating and maintaining Web pages. This site contains extensive coverage of almost all topics related to creating Web pages and keeping them running. Its clean examples make learning even advanced topics very easy.

SUMMARY

- The unordered list element begins every line with a bullet mark. All entries in an unordered list must be enclosed within **`<UL>`**…**`</UL>`** tags, which open and close the unordered list element.

- Each entry in an unordered list is inserted with the **`<LI>`** tag, which creates a line break and inserts a bullet mark at the beginning of the line. You then insert and format any text. The closing list element tag (**`</LI>`**) is optional.

- Nested lists display information in outline form. A nested list is a list that appears in the bounds of another list element. Nesting the new list inside the original indents the list one level and changes the bullet type to reflect the nesting.

- Browsers insert a line of whitespace after every closed list.

- An ordered list (**`<OL>`**…**`</OL>`**) begins every new line with a sequence number instead of a bullet. By default, ordered lists use decimal sequence numbers (1,2,3, …).

- To change the sequence type of a list, use the **`TYPE`** attribute in the **`<OL>`** opening tag or in an individual **`<LI>`** tag. The default type is **`TYPE="1"`**, which uses the 1, 2, 3, … sequence. The second type, **`TYPE="I"`**, makes a capital Roman numeral sequence: I, II, III, and so on. **`TYPE="i"`** creates the lowercase Roman numeral sequence: i, ii, iii, etc. The last two types are **`TYPE="A"`** and **`TYPE="a"`**, which produce uppercase and lowercase alphabetic sequences, respectively.

- HTML tables organize data into rows and columns. All tags and text that apply to a table go inside the **`<TABLE>`**…**`</TABLE>`** tags. The **`BORDER`** attribute lets you set the width of the table's border in pixels. The **`WIDTH`** attribute sets the width of the table—you specify either a number of pixels or a percentage of the screen width.

- The text inside the **`<CAPTION>`**…**`</CAPTION>`** tags is inserted directly above the table in the browser window. The caption text is also used to help text-based browsers interpret the table data.

- Tables can be split into distinct horizontal and vertical sections. Put all header information (such as table titles and column headers) inside the **`<THEAD>`**…**`</THEAD>`** tags. The **`TR`** (table row) element is used for formatting the cells of individual rows. All of the cells in a row belong within the **`<TR>`**…**`</TR>`** tags of that row.

- The smallest area of the table that we are able to format is the data cell. There are two types of data cells: ones located in the header (**`<TH>`**…**`</TH>`**) and ones located in the table body (**`<TD>`**…**`</TD>`**). Header cells, usually placed in the **`<THEAD>`** area, are suitable for titles and column headings.

- Like **`THEAD`**, the **`TBODY`** is used for formatting and grouping purposes. Most tables use **`TBODY`** to house the majority of their content.

- **`TD`** table data cells are left aligned by default. **`TH`** cells are centered by default.

- Just as you can use the **`THEAD`** and **`TBODY`** elements to format groups of table rows, you can use the **`COLGROUP`** element to group and format columns. **`COLGROUP`** is used by setting in its opening tag the number of columns it affects and the formatting it imposes on that group of columns.

- Each **`COL`** element contained inside the **`<COLGROUP>`**…**`</COLGROUP>`** tags can in turn format a specified number of columns.

- You can add a background color or image to any table row or cell with either the **`BGCOLOR`** or **`BACKGROUND`** attributes, which are used in the same way as in the **`BODY`** element.

- It is possible to make some table data cells larger than others by using the **`ROWSPAN`** and **`COL-SPAN`** attributes. The attribute value extends the data cell to span the specified number of cells.

- The **VALIGN** (vertical alignment) attribute of a table data cell accepts the following values: **"top"**, **"middle"**, **"bottom"** and **"baseline"**.

- All cells in a table row whose **VALIGN** attribute is set to **"baseline"** will have the first text line on a common baseline.

- The default vertical alignment in all data and header cells is **VALIGN="middle"**.

- HTML provides several mechanisms—including the **FORM**—to collect information from people viewing your site.

- Use **METHOD = "post"** in a form that causes changes to server data, for example when updating a database. The form data will be sent to the server as an *environment variable,* which scripts are able to access (you will learn how to do this in Chapter 29 when we cover Perl). The other possible value, **METHOD = "get"**, should be used when your form does not cause any changes in server-side data, for example when making a database request. The form data from **METHOD = "get"** is appended to the end of the URL. Because of this, the amount of data submitted using this **METHOD** is limited to 4K. Also be aware that **METHOD = "get"** is limited to standard characters, and cannot submit any special characters.

- A Web server is a machine that runs a software package such as Apache or IIS; servers are designed to handle browser requests. When a user uses a browser to request a page or file somewhere on the server, the server processes this request and returns an answer to the browser.

- The **ACTION** attribute in the **FORM** tag is the path to a script that processes the form data.

- The input element is common in forms, and always requires the **TYPE** attribute. Two other attributes are **NAME**, which provides a unique identification for the **INPUT**, and **VALUE**, which indicates the value that the **INPUT** element sends to the server upon submission.

- The input **TYPE="text"** inserts a one-line text bar into the form. The value of this **INPUT** element and the information that the server sends to you from this **INPUT** is the text that the user types into the bar. The **SIZE** attribute determines the width of the text input, measured in characters. You can also set a maximum number of characters that the text input will accept by inserting the **MAXLENGTH="***length***"** attribute.

- You must make sure to include a textual identifier (in this case, "**Name:**") adjacent to the **INPUT** element to indicate the function of the element.

- The **TYPE="submit" INPUT** element places a button in the form that submits data to the server when clicked. The **VALUE** attribute of the **submit** input changes the text displayed on the button.

- The **TYPE="reset"** input element places a button on the form that, when clicked, will clear all entries the user has entered into the form.

- The **TEXTAREA** element inserts a box into the form. You specify the size of the box (which is scrollable) inside the opening **<TEXTAREA>** tag with the **ROWS** attribute and the **COLS** attribute.

- Data entered in a **TYPE="password"** input appears on the screen as asterisks. The password is used for submitting sensitive information that the user would not want others to be able to read. It is just the browser that displays asterisks—the real form data is still submitted to the server.

- Every **INPUT** element with **TYPE="checkbox"** creates a new checkbox in the form. Checkboxes can be used individually or in groups. Each checkbox in a group should have the same **NAME** (in this case, **NAME="things"**).

- Inserted into forms by means of the **INPUT** attribute **TYPE="radio"**, radio buttons are different from checkboxes in that only one in the group may be selected at any time. All of the **NAME** attributes of a group of radio inputs must be the same and all of the **VALUE** attributes different.

- Insert the attribute **CHECKED** to indicate which radio button you would like selected initially.

- The **SELECT** element places a selectable list of items inside your form. To add an item to the list, insert an **OPTION** element in the **<SELECT>**...**</SELECT>** area and type what you want the list item to display on the same line. You can change the number of list options visible at one time by including the **SIZE=**"*size*" attribute inside the **<SELECT>** tag. Use this attribute if you prefer an expanded version of the list to the one-line expandable list.

- A location on a page is marked by including a **NAME** attribute in an **A** element. Clicking on this hyperlink in a browser would scroll the browser window to that point on the page.

- An image map allows you to designate certain sections of the image as hotspots and then use these hotspots as anchors for linking.

- All elements of an image map are contained inside the **<MAP>…</MAP>** tags. The required attribute for the **MAP** element is **NAME**.

- A hotspot on the image is designated with the **AREA** element. Every **<AREA>** tag has the following attributes: **HREF** sets the target for the link on that spot, **SHAPE** and **COORDS** set the characteristics of the area and **ALT** function just as it does in **<IMG>** tags.

- **SHAPE="rect"** creates a rectangular hotspot around the *coordinates* of a **COORDS** element.

- A coordinate pair consists of two numbers, which are the locations of the point on the *x* and *y* axes. The *x* axis extends horizontally from the upper-left corner and the *y* axis vertically. Every point on an image has a unique *x–y* coordinate, annotated as *(x, y)*.

- In the case of a rectangular hotspot, the required coordinates are those of the upper-left and lower-right corners of the rectangle.

- The **SHAPE="poly"** creates a hotspot of no preset shape—you specify the shape of the hotspot in the **COORDS** attribute by listing the coordinates of every vertex, or corner of the hotspot.

- **SHAPE="circle"** creates a circular hotspot; it requires both the coordinates of the center of the circle and the length of the radius, in pixels.

- To use an image map with a graphic on your page, you must insert the **USEMAP="#*name*"** attribute into the **IMG** element, where "name" is the value of the **NAME** attribute in the **MAP** element.

- The main HTML element that interacts with search engines is the **META** element.

- **<!DOCTYPE HTML PUBLIC "-//W3C//DTD HTML 4.0 Transitional//EN">** tells the browser that the following HTML conforms to a transitional subset of HTML version 4.0.

- **META** tags contain two attributes that should always be used. The first of these, **NAME**, is an identification of the type of **META** tag you are including. The **CONTENT** attribute gives the information the search engine will be cataloging.

- The **CONTENT** of a **META** tag with **NAME="keywords"** provides the search engines with a list of words that describe the key aspects of your site. By including **META** tags and their content information, you can give precise information about your site to search engines. This will help you draw a more focused audience to your site.

- The **description** value of the **NAME** attribute in the **META** tag should be a 3-to-4 line description of your site, written in sentence form. This description is used by the search engine to catalog and display your site.

- **META** elements are not visible to users of the site and should be placed inside the header section of your HTML document.

- **<!DOCTYPE html PUBLIC "-//W3C//DTD HTML 4.0 Frameset//EN">** tells the browser that we are using frames in the following code. You should include this modified version of **<!DOCTYPE>** whenever you use frames in your HTML document.

- The **FRAMESET** tag tells the browser that the page contains frames.

- **COLS** or **ROWS** gives the width of each frame in pixels or as a percentage of the screen.

- In each **FRAME** element, the **SRC** attribute gives the URL of the page that will be displayed in the specified frame.

- The purpose of a **NAME** attribute in the **FRAME** element is to give an identity to that specific frame, in order to enable hyperlinks in a **FRAMESET** to load their intended **FRAME**. The **TARGET** attribute in an anchor element is set to the **NAME** of the **FRAME** in which the new page should load.

- A target in an anchor element can be set to a number of preset values: **TARGET="_blank"** loads the page in a new blank browser window, **TARGET="self"** loads the page into the same window as the anchor element, **TARGET="_parent"** loads the page into the parent **FRAMESET** and **TARGET="_top"** loads the page into the full browser window.

- Not everyone viewing a page has a browser that can handle frames. You therefore need to include a **NOFRAMES** element inside of the **FRAMESET**. You should include regular HTML tags and elements within the **<NOFRAMES>...</NOFRAMES>** tags. Use this area to direct the user to a non-framed version of the site or to provide links for downloading a frame-enabled browser.

- By nesting **FRAMESET** elements, you can create more complex layouts.

TERMINOLOGY

ACTION attribute in **FORM** element
AREA
BORDER property of **TABLE** element
CAPTION element
cell of a table
CELLSPACING property of **TABLE** element
CGI script
CHECKED
circular hotspot
COL element
COLGROUP element
COLS attribute of **TABLE** element
COLSPAN attribute of **TD** element
column of a table
COORDS attribute inside **AREA** element
data cell
DATAFIELD property of **TD** element
<!DOCTYPE...>
environment variable
form
FRAME element (**<FRAME>...</FRAME>**)
FRAMESET element
header cell
hotspot
image map
indenting lists
INPUT element (**<INPUT>...</INPUT>**)
INPUT Type="button"
INPUT Type="checkbox"
INPUT Type="password"
INPUT Type="radio"
INPUT Type="reset"
INPUT Type="submit"
INPUT Type="text"
INPUT Type="textarea"

internal linking
list
MAP element
MAXLENGTH="#"
<META> Tag
METHOD="get"
METHOD="post"
NAME attribute in **INPUT** element
NAME="recipient" in **INPUT** element
NAME="redirect" in **INPUT** element
NAME="subject" in **INPUT** element
nested lists
NOFRAMES
NORESIZE attribute in **FRAME**
OL (ordered list) element (**<OL>...</OL>**)
<OPTION>
rectangular hotspot
row of a table
ROWSPAN attribute of **TD** element
SCROLLING attribute in **FRAME**
SELECT element (**<SELECT>...</SELECT>**)
SHAPE attribute inside **AREA** element
SIZE attribute in **SELECT**
SRC attribute of **FRAME** element
table
TABLE element (**<TABLE>...</TABLE>**)
TARGET="_blank"
TARGET="_blank"
TARGET="_parent"
TARGET="_top"
TBODY
TD (table data) element (**<TD>...</TD>**)
text-based browser
TH (header cell) element (**<TH>...</TH>**)
THEAD element (**<THEAD>...</THEAD>**)

TR (table row) element (**<TR>...</TR>**)   **UL** (unordered list) element (**<UL>...</UL>**)
TYPE=1 attribute of **<OL>**   **USEMAP="name"** attribute in **IMG**
TYPE=a attribute of **<OL>**   **VALUE** attribute of **INPUT** element
TYPE=A attribute of **<OL>**   Web server
TYPE=i attribute of **<OL>**   *x–y* scale
TYPE=I attribute of **<OL>**

SELF-REVIEW EXERCISES

10.1 State whether the following are *true* or *false*. If the answer is *false*, explain why.
  a) There is no limit to the number of levels to which you can nest an ordered or unordered list.
  b) The width of all data cells in a table must be the same.
  c) An ordered list can have only one type of numbering system. To initiate a new type of numbering, you must make a new ordered list.
  d) The **THEAD** element is mandatory in a **TABLE**.
  e) You are limited to a maximum of 100 internal links per page.
  f) All browsers can render **FRAMESET**s.

10.2 Fill in the blanks in each of the following statements.
  a) The _____ attribute in an **INPUT** element inserts a button that, when clicked, will clear the contents of the form.
  b) The spacing of a **FRAMESET** is set by including the _____ attribute or the _____ attribute inside of the **<FRAMESET>** tag.
  c) The _____ element inserts a new item in a list.
  d) The _____ element tells the browser what version of HTML is included on the page. Two types of this element are _____ and _____.
  e) The common shapes used in image maps are _____, _____ and _____.

10.3 Write HTML tags to accomplish the following.
  a) Insert a framed Web page with the first frame extending 300 pixels across the page from the left side.
  b) Insert an ordered list that will have numbering by lowercase Roman numerals.
  c) Insert a scrollable list (in a form) that will always display four entries of the list.
  d) Insert an image map onto a page using **deitel.gif** as an image and **MAP** with **NAME="hello"** as the image map, and have "hello" be the **ALT** text.

ANSWERS TO SELF-REVIEW EXERCISES

10.1 a) True.
  b) False. You can specify the width of any column either in pixels or as a percentage of the total width of the table.
  c) False. You can specify a numbering type for an individual list element by including the attribute **TYPE = "*name*"**.
  d) False. The **THEAD** element is used only for formatting purposes and is optional (but it is recommended that you include it).
  e) False. You can have an unlimited number of hyperlink locations on any page.
  f) False. Text-based browsers are unable to render a **FRAMESET** and must therefore rely on the information that you include inside the **<NOFRAMES>...</NOFRAMES>** tag.

10.2 a) **TYPE = "reset"**. b) **COLS**, **ROWS**. c) **LI**. d) **<!DOCTYPE...>**, **TRANSITIONAL**, **FRAMESET**. e) **poly**, **circle**, **rect**.

10.3 a) **<FRAMESET COLS = "300,*">...</FRAMESET>**
  b) **<OL TYPE = "i">...</OL>**

   c) `<SELECT SIZE = "4">...</SELECT>`
   d) `<IMG SRC = "deitel.gif" ALT = "hello" USEMAP = "#hello">`

EXERCISES

10.4   Categorize each of the following as an element or an attribute:
   a) `SIZE`
   b) `OL`
   c) `LI`
   d) `FRAME`
   e) `CAPTION`
   f) `SELECT`
   g) `TYPE`

10.5   What will the **FRAMESET** produced by the following code look like? Assume that the pages being imported are blank with white backgrounds and that the dimensions of the screen are 800 by 600. Sketch the layout, approximating the dimensions.

```
<FRAMESET ROWS = "20%,*">
<FRAME SRC = "hello.html" NAME = "hello">
   <FRAMESET COLS = "150,*">
   <FRAME SRC = "nav.html" NAME = "nav">
   <FRAME SRC = "deitel.html" NAME = "deitel">
   </FRAMESET>
</FRAMESET>
```

10.6   Write the HTML code that produces the following Web page. The width of the table is 400 pixels and the border is one pixel wide. The header is enclosed in an **H2** element.

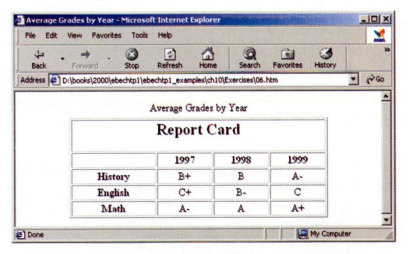

10.7   Assume that you have a document with many subsections. Write the HTML code to create a frame with a table of contents on the left side of the window, and have each entry in the table of contents use internal linking to scroll down the document frame to the appropriate subsection.

11

Ultimate Paint

Objectives

- To learn the basics of Ultimate Paint.
- To understand the difference between the GIF and JPEG formats.
- To become familiar with the Portable Network Graphics format.
- To be able to design professional quality images for your Web pages.
- To be able to use a variety of brushes.
- To be able to apply a wide variety of effects to an image.

Now follow in this direction, now turn a different hue.
Theognis

There are occasions when it is undoubtedly better to incur loss than to make gain.
Titus Maccius Plautus

Beware lest you lose the substance by grasping at the shadow.
Aesop

Outline

11.1 Introduction

Web pages are more than HTML. They contain text, images, animations, etc. The most popular Web sites are often the ones with fancy graphics and dazzling animations. In Chapters 30 through 34 you will learn how to create these animations using Dynamic HTML, multimedia and Flash. In this chapter we discuss how to create graphical images using Megalux's *Ultimate Paint* (included on the CD with this book). This easy-to-use graphics package offers much of the functionality of more expensive graphics packages. The freeware version can be used with Windows 95/98 systems. If you are running Windows NT or Windows 2000, you can download the shareware version of Ultimate Paint (which has more features) from **www.ultimatepaint.com**. We use Ultimate Paint to demonstrate how to create a few images that can add pizzazz to your Web pages. In particular, we create a title image and a button. We also demonstrate a few advanced photographic effects.

11.2 Image Basics

In this section, we introduce Ultimate Paint's tool bar and their basic properties. We begin by creating a basic title image for a Web page. The title image is important because it is normally the first part of your Web site that users see when they visit your site. Once you know the look and feel you would like for your Web page, open Ultimate Paint and click **New...** in the **File** menu. The ***New Image*** *dialog* (Fig. 11.1) that appears allows you to choose the size for your image measured in pixels. Create a new image where the ***Size X*** (*width*) value is 300 and the ***Size Y*** (*height*) value is 150. Next, take a few moments to familiarize yourself with Ultimate Paint. Figure 11.2 points out several of the key features.

Fig. 11.1   **New Image** dialog. (Courtesy of Megalux Light Techniques, Ltd.)

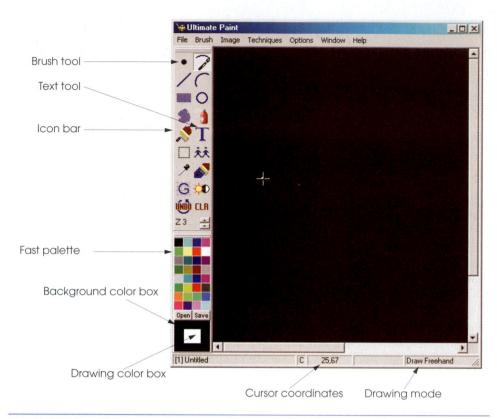

Brush tool
Text tool
Icon bar
Fast palette
Background color box
Drawing color box
Cursor coordinates   Drawing mode

Fig. 11.2   Creating a new image in Ultimate Paint. (Courtesy of Megalux Light Techniques, Ltd.)

Notice the *icon bar* in the upper-left corner of the window. Each icon represents a basic drawing function. Moving the mouse cursor over an icon displays a "tool tip" describing that particular tool. Clicking and holding the left-mouse button on most icons displays a pop-up submenu. This submenu enables you to choose different drawing methods for tools of a similar type. For example, if you click and hold the left mouse button on the *brush tool* (located in the upper-left corner of the icon bar), a pop-up submenu appears allowing you to change the shape and size of your brush. As you move the mouse over the submenu icons, "tool tips" appear to describe each submenu tool. We discuss each tool in more depth in Section 11.4.

Click the **Text** tool and place your mouse cursor over the image. Notice that the status bar on the bottom shows information about the tool you are using as well as the cursor's location in the image's coordinate system. Image coordinates are measure from the upper-left corner coordinate of 0, 0.

The toolbar on the lower-left side of the window is the *fast palette*, from which you can select new colors and in which you can store custom colors you define. There are always two active colors—the *drawing color* (or *foreground color*) and the *background color*. The drawing color can be changed by clicking the left mouse button on a fast palette color. Similarly, the background color can be changed by clicking the right mouse button. Choose a background color which is the same as the background color of your Web page. If the background of your Web page is not a solid color, you may have to use other software to make the background of the images you create with Ultimate Paint *transparent*. A transparent image allows the Web page background to show through the image. This allows you to change the Web page background without having to redesign all your images. The freeware version of Ultimate Paint does not support transparency but the shareware version does.

Click the drawing color box to display the **Select Drawing Color** *dialog* shown in Fig. 11.3. To select a color, either move the three vertical slider controls or enter the RGB (red/green/blue) values as numbers in the range 0 through 255 until you find the precise color you want. A simpler but less accurate way to select a color is by clicking the color field above the horizontal slider. Move the horizontal slider to change the starting base color. You can store your new custom color in the fast palette by clicking an appropriate fast palette entry while holding one of the *Shift*, *Ctrl* or *Alt* keys down.

You can also use the **Preferences...** *dialog* to add colors to your fast palette toolbox. Open the dialog by clicking **Preferences...** in the **Options** menu. Set the **Palette Entries** value to 32 to have a full range of colors available in your palette. While in this dialog, set the **Level** to **Expert** to access each tool's full range of capabilities. Most tools have a customized *property bar* containing their capabilities that appears at the bottom of the Ultimate Paint window (above the status bar) when you select the tool from the icon bar.

Now we construct our title image. Click the drawing color box to enter the **Select Drawing Color** dialog again (see Fig. 11.3). In this example, we use RGB values 190, 180 and 140 for the red, green and blue parts of the drawing color. Select the color by adjusting the vertical RGB slider controls until the numbers below reflect these values. Click **OK** to accept the color change or click **Cancel** to keep using the current color. You should now see the color displayed in the foreground color box on the left side of the screen.

Look-and-Feel Observation 11.1

Too many colors will make your site look confusing and erratic. Pick three or four main colors, and use these as the prominent colors in your images and text. This will be easier for you to do with Cascading Style Sheets, discussed later in the book.

Now try to place your text. Select the **Text** tool on the tool palette and notice the *text tool properties bar* that appears above the status bar at the bottom of the window. The tool properties bar allows you to fine-tune the properties of the currently selected tool (see Fig. 11.4). Select a font, a style and a large type size (25 "points" is a good place to start; a point is 1/72 of an inch).

Fig. 11.3   Selecting a new color. (Courtesy of Megalux Light Techniques, Ltd.)

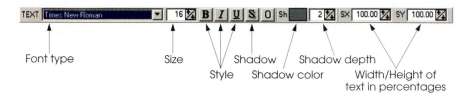

Fig. 11.4   Text Property Bar. (Courtesy of Megalux Light Techniques, Ltd.)

Open the **Preferences** dialog again and be sure that the ***Anti-alias*** *checkbox* in the **General** tab is selected. *Anti-aliasing* is a process that smooths edges of scalable fonts by blending the color of the edge pixels with the color of the background on which the text is being placed (see Fig. 11.5). Without it, fonts appear jagged on the screen—an unattractive and distracting effect.

After typing the text, you can use the mouse to move the text around the image. The text properties can still be changed until you press *Enter*. When the text looks good and is in its proper position, press *Enter*, then press *Esc* or choose another tool from the palette to close the operation. The text's color is the drawing color you selected previously.

Fig. 11.5   Anti-aliased text. (Courtesy of Megalux Light Techniques, Ltd.)

Next, let us create a *drop-shadow effect* to help bring your image out from the background, creating a 3-D illusion. This effect is one of the most widely used image effects on the Web. Click the **Text** tool to begin. Type the text to which you will apply the drop-shadow effect, but do not press *Enter* yet. Now, click the *shadow* button (containing the letter **S**) on the text tool properties bar at the bottom of the window. Here, you can adjust the *shadow color* and *depth*. Once again, we used RGB values 190, 180 and 140 as our text color with a shadow color value of RGB 128, 128 and 128. The shadow depth is set at 2. The results are shown in Fig. 11.6.

Look-and-Feel Observation 11.2

The drop shadow is one of the most widely used image effects on the Web. If you are striving for originality in your pages, you might want to vary the settings or explore other effects Ultimate Paint has to offer.

The title image for your Web page is now finished. In the **Save** menu (beneath **File**), choose **CompuServe's GIF (*.gif)** format for the picture. You can now insert the picture into your page using an **<IMG>** tag, as described in Chapter 9.

11.3 File Formats: GIF or JPEG?

The two major file formats used for images on the Web are *GIF (Graphics Interchange Format)* and *JPEG (Joint Photographic Experts Group)*. You should know the differences between these formats so you can choose the format that best suits your needs.

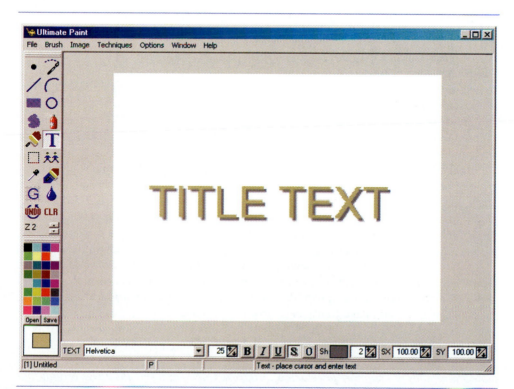

Fig. 11.6   Drop shadow text. (Courtesy of Megalux Light Techniques, Ltd.)

The Graphics Interchange Format (GIF), developed by CompuServe, uses a palette of 256 colors. It is best used for screenshots, line drawings and other images with sharp edges. It is commonly used on the Web because it supports background transparency.

JPEG is actually not a file format but a compression algorithm named after its developers the Joint Photographic Experts Group. It supports a palette of 16.7 million colors and is best used for photographs and other images which have *continuous tones*. JPEG does not support transparency. The file format which is primarily associated with JPEG compression is called the *JPEG File Interchange Format (JFIF)*. Although JFIF is the proper name for files that use JPEG compression, many people use the name JPEG in place of JFIF. As a result, files that use JPEG compression have either the JFIF extension (`.jif`, `.jfif`) or the JPEG extension (`.jpg`, `.jpeg`). For consistency, we use the name JPEG where JFIF is also applicable.

Each format (JPEG and GIF) uses a different compression algorithm. Sometimes, it is preferable to use one format over another. JPEG is best used with photographs because it is designed to compress high-color images with continuous tones. Saving a photograph as a JPEG file retains the image quality and minimizes the file size. If the same photograph were to be saved as a GIF file, the image would appear grainy and the file size would be larger. In the same manner, the GIF format maximizes image quality while reducing file size on images with sharp color changes such as line art and abstract images. Using JPEG with these types of images would reduce image quality and increase file size.

Performance Tip 11.1

A GIF file is typically larger than a JPEG file. If server space is a problem and your image has more than 256 colors, it is better to use a JPEG format.

Another issue that must be considered when choosing between these formats is that the GIF compression method is *lossless* while JPEG is *lossy*. When a JPEG image is saved to disk, it loses data to minimize the file size. This data loss does not have a noticeable effect on the image quality unless the image has sharp edges. GIF files do not lose any data when they are saved to disk but as a consequence they are often larger than JPEG files. In general, choose the GIF format for drawings and abstract images and choose the JPEG format for photographs and photo-realistic images that do not require transparency.

Both GIF and JPEG share a feature known as *interlacing* (in GIF terminology) or *progressive encoding* (in JPEG terminology). As an interlaced image downloads, the entire image appears and gradually increases in clarity. Normally, images are downloaded and displayed from the top of the image down (resulting in partial images until the download completes). Interlacing can often keep a user's attention focused while a page loads. However, placing too many interlaced images on any one Web page can slow the rendering of the page.

A newer image standard is making its mark on the Web. The *Portable Network Graphics (PNG*, pronounced *ping*) format incorporates the qualities of both GIF and JPEG formats. PNG encodes in *RGBA format*—the A stands for *alpha transparency*, which helps make an image transparent. PNG is also a lossless format and it provides more colors than JPEG. The PNG format is supported by the latest versions of both Netscape Communicator and Internet Explorer. More information about the PNG format can be found at **www.w3.org/Graphics/PNG**. *(Note: The freeware version of Ultimate Paint does not support interlacing, progressive encoding or the PNG format, but the shareware version does.)*

11.4 Tool Palette

The power of Ultimate Paint lies in its filters and its easy-to-use tools. The icon bar groups the tools on a single toolbar, that by default appears on the left side of the image editing area. The icon bar can be dragged to other locations. Figure 11.7 shows the default Ultimate Paint tool bar.

Figure 11.8 shows the default tool bar items and specifies the name of each tool. The default drawing mode is *draw freehand*. The icon for the tool in use remains pressed until another tool is selected. To deactivate a tool, click another icon in the icon bar. All options in the tool bar are repeatable (i.e., you can perform the task again without re-selecting the tool) except for *cut brush, get color, undo last action* and *clear image*.

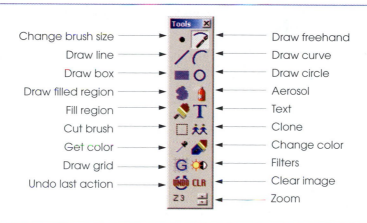

Change brush size		Draw freehand
Draw line		Draw curve
Draw box		Draw circle
Draw filled region		Aerosol
Fill region		Text
Cut brush		Clone
Get color		Change color
Draw grid		Filters
Undo last action		Clear image
		Zoom

Fig. 11.7   Ultimate Paint's tool bar. (Courtesy of Megalux Light Techniques, Ltd.)

Icon	Submenu Options	Description
•		Changes brush size and shape. Choose from four different sizes and two shapes. Resize these brush shapes interactively by selecting a standard shape (circle or square) and right clicking this icon. Additional sizes and shapes can be created using the brush cutting method (see the second-to-last row of this table).
⟋		Changes the brush drawing method. Choose from *Continuous Freehand, Dotted Freehand*, and *Single Freehand*.
／		Changes the line drawing method. Choose from *Single Line* and *Continuous Line*.

Fig. 11.8   Toolbox submenus (part 1 of 2).
(Courtesy of Megalux Light Techniques, Ltd.)

Icon	Submenu Options	Description
		Changes the curve drawing method. Choose from *Single Curve* and *Continuous Curve.*
		Changes the box drawing method. Choose from *Rectangle, Filled Rectangle, Square* and *Filled Square.*
		Changes the ellipse drawing method. Choose from *Circle, Filled Circle, Ellipse* and *Filled Ellipse.*
		Changes the filled region drawing method. Choose from *Filled Shape* and *Filled Polygon.*
		Changes the aerosol drawing method. Choose from *Spray* and *Airbrush.*
		Changes the fill region method. *Solid Fill* will fill the enclosed space with the currently selected color. *Pattern Fill* fills the enclosed space with the current brush.
		Changes the brush cutting method. Choose from *Cut Rectangle, Cut Predefined Rectangle, Cut Freehand, Cut Polygon* and *Cut with Magic Wand.*
		Changes the filter method. These filters are applied to the image with the current brush. Choose from Brightness/Contrast, Blur, Median, Sharpen, Remove Noise and Mosaic.

Fig. 11.8   Toolbox submenus (part 2 of 2).
(Courtesy of Megalux Light Techniques, Ltd.)

The undo last action tool is useful for correcting mistakes. It is limited in its use to the last action performed, so save frequently. The shareware version of Ultimate Paint (downloadable from **www.ultimatepaint.com**) has unlimited undo and redo functions so you can experiment freely.

To change the background color, right click the color of your choice in the fast palette. You can use the *fill region* tool to fill the background with the selected color. Left clicking a fast palette color selects the foreground (drawing) color.

The *get color* tool selects a color from your image as the background or foreground color. Again, right clicking the mouse sets the background color and left clicking sets the foreground color.

The *zoom* tool enlarges the view of an image in the Ultimate Paint window. Clicking the upper arrow zooms in to a maximum ratio of 32:1 (32 times the original image size). Conversely, the lower arrow zooms out to a minimum ratio of 1:4 (one fourth of the original image size).

The *filters* tool is useful when working with photos. These filters are similar to the filters under the **Image** menu with one important difference—they must be applied using a brush. This unique feature allows you to "paint" a filter over your image. Clicking the filters tool button brings up its pop-up properties window. Choosing another tool will close the properties window. Remember that a brush must be selected to apply the filter tool.

The *grid option* allows you to constrain the shapes you draw to an invisible grid. Unlike other buttons in the icon bar, the grid button stays pressed until you click it again to turn off the grid. When the grid is enabled (i.e., the grid button is pressed), shapes you draw align to the grid. To use the grid, click the grid button, then use the tool properties bar below the image to specify the distance between grid lines in the *x* (horizontal) and *y* (vertical) directions. When you draw a shape, notice that the shape "jumps" between grid lines as you drag the mouse. To align the grid with your image, set one of the corners as the *origin point* on the grid menu. Your other shapes will align with that edge when you move them around. Using the grid is recommended when you are working with text to keep it aligned properly and create balance in your image.

Testing and Debugging Tip 11.1

Keep in mind that most of your viewers will be using an 800 x 600 screen resolution. Two other common resolutions are 640 x 480 and 1024 x 768. Check your Web pages in each of these resolutions to ensure that it displays as you intended.

11.5 Brushes

Ultimate Paint has the ability to create custom brushes from portions of an image. This feature allows you to quickly and easily create a brush of any shape, size and color you desire. A custom brush can be used for drawing, copying and editing your work. Part of the fun of Ultimate Paint lies in experimentation. Brushes are a great way to be creative and use your imagination.

As we discussed in Fig. 11.8, Ultimate Paint has four brush sizes for each shape (circle or square). To create your own brush, use a tool from the *cut brush* group to select the area of your image to use as a custom brush. The *cut rectangle* tool creates a rectangular brush. The *cut predefined rectangle* tool in its property bar allows you to specify precisely the dimensions of your rectangular brush. The *cut freehand* tool and *cut polygon* tool allow you to draw the shape of your custom brush. The *magic wand* works like the fill region tool. Instead of filling a region with a color, it creates a brush using a region of the image. After creating the new brush, all the line drawing tools (i.e., freehand, line, ellipse, rectangle and curve) will use the new brush to draw (until you select a different brush). You can also use the *pattern fill* (see Fig. 11.8) tool to fill shapes with the new brush. The drawing mode is automatically reset to freehand after the brush is cut. Save your brush by clicking **Save** in the **Brush** menu.

The **Brush** menu also provides options for modifying the brush shape and size. Remember that a brush is created from whatever you select using the cut brush tool. In Ultimate Paint, you can use the cut brush tool to select the entire image and use the entire image as a brush! If you select text with the cut brush tool, you can actually draw with text.

Figure 11.9 illustrates some of the possibilities for modifying a brush using the **Brush** menu. This image was originally identical to the title picture we created in Fig. 11.6 only with a black background. The cut rectangle tool was used to create a brush from the text portion of the image. Next, the custom brush was modified using the **Brush** menu items **Bend**, **Stretch** and **Rotate**. Drawing the image was accomplished with a simple drag of the mouse from bottom-left to top-right in the drawing area.

Look-and-Feel Observation 11.3

*If you want to return to the previous brush, simply right-click the cut brush tool. Remember that your custom brush can be saved by clicking **Save** in the **Brush** menu.*

There are three options in the **Techniques** *menu* for drawing with a custom brush. The options are **Paint**, **Color** and **Replace**. **Paint** mode allows you to draw with the custom brush you selected using the cut brush tool. When drawing in this mode, note that the brush's background color brush is now invisible in the brush. **Color** mode allows you to use the custom brush shape with the selected drawing color. **Replace** mode is like the **Paint** mode except the background color is visible in the brush. The current technique is displayed in the status bar next to the cursor coordinates (see Fig. 11.9).

11.6 Effects

In addition to text and graphics, photographs are important components in the design of a Web site. Ultimate Paint enables you to alter photographs with the **Image** *menu*. The first four options in the menu allow you to stretch, mirror, rotate and get statistics on your image. The next nine options have submenus that allow you to mutate the image color and shape using predefined effects. You may feel your photograph does not require the use of an effect. In this case, Ultimate Paint can be your aid in touching up minor imperfections. Effects are an easy way to create interesting backgrounds for your Web page. To demonstrate how effects work, we will use them to create a navigation button and to modify a scanned photograph.

Current brush drawing technique

Fig. 11.9 Drawing with a custom brush. (Courtesy of Megalux Light Techniques, Ltd.)

Begin by creating a new image that is 100 pixels wide and 40 pixels high—this will be the size of your button. Click the background color box and enter the RGB value 136, 136 and 0. We would like our button to have a three-dimensional appearance. One way to achieve this effect is with *beveling* which uses lighting to provide the 3D appearance. To bevel the edge of the image select **Fun...** in the **Image** menu, then select **Bevel**. In the **Bevel** properties dialog (Fig. 11.10), set the *depth* (the amount of beveling) at 285 and the *angle* (the direction of the light source) at 110. Click **Preview** to display a full preview. Click **OK** to accept the current settings and your image is altered.

Select the text tool and configure the attributes of the text. We chose the 18 point Arial font and we chose white as our drawing color. Type the text you want to appear on your button (**LINKS** in our example). Use the grid tool to help center the text. Press *Enter* to set the text and your button is complete (Fig. 11.11).

Next let us apply a filter to a photo. Filters help tailor your photographs to match the personality of your Web page. First, open a photograph using the **Open...** command in the **File** menu. After importing the image, you are ready to apply filters to create images for the Web. Figure 11.12 shows the original image in Ultimate Paint.

You can view the variety of effect options in the **Image** menu. To avoid the time consuming task of independently previewing each effect, go to the **Effect browser** (Fig. 11.13) by clicking the **Browse** option in the **Artistic** submenu. The window that appears displays thumbnail views of your photo modified by the filters. To view another group of options, select a different effect category in the window's bottom-right corner.

Fig. 11.10   Bevel Properties. (Courtesy of Megalux Light Techniques, Ltd.)

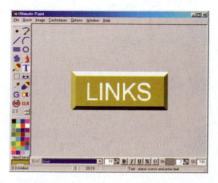

Fig. 11.11   Creating a Button. (Courtesy of Megalux Light Techniques, Ltd.)

Fig. 11.12   Original Image. (Courtesy of Megalux Light Techniques, Ltd.)

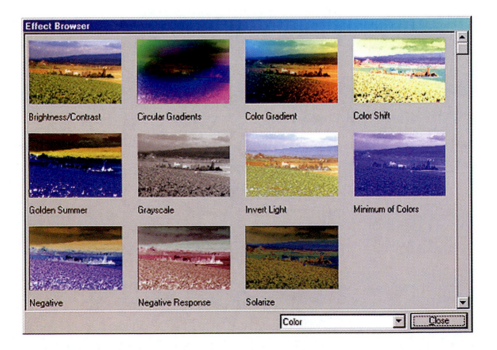

Fig. 11.13   **Effect Browser**. (Courtesy of Megalux Light Techniques, Ltd.)

To choose an effect, double click the thumbnail to display the properties window for that effect. If you do not change the settings, Ultimate Paint will use the default settings for that effect. Click **Preview** to display a full preview. Click **OK** to accept the current settings and your image is altered.

The variety of effects offered by Ultimate Paint impose different moods on your image. The image on the left in Fig. 11.14 was changed to *grayscale* and combined with a simple font to create a classic, professional look. The **neon** effect was applied to the image on the right, giving it more pizazz and life. The effects used on your images should not counter the overall design of your site. It is important to maintain integrity between your images and icons to create designs with a professional look and feel.

11.7 Internet and World Wide Web Resources

Many resources are available for Ultimate Paint. Visit **www.ultimatepaint.com** to software updates and general information about Ultimate Paint. There is also a beginner's tutorial on the site and the technical support staff is helpful. Other information about Ultimate Paint is available at user-run sites. If you are looking for more diverse effects than those included in Ultimate Paint, you can download new filters. The PlugIn Com HQ site (**pico.i-us.com**) is a storehouse of filters and effects, free for download and use. If you plan to develop images, make sure to look at the W3C site about the PNG image format, located at **www.w3.org/Graphics/PNG**.

SUMMARY

- Images liven up your pages.
- Many images are available on the Internet for free download and use.
- The **New Image** dialog allows you to choose the size for your image measured in pixels.
- The icon bar contains the basic drawing functions.
- Placing the mouse cursor over an icon and lingering for a moment displays a "tool tip" describing that tool. A pop-up submenu containing different drawing methods appears over most icons if you hold the left mouse button down for a few seconds.

Fig. 11.14 Grayscale and Neon Effects.

- The fast palette allows new colors to be selected and custom colors to be stored. There are always two active colors—the drawing color (or foreground color) and the background color. The drawing color can be changed by clicking the left mouse button on a fast palette color. The background color can be changed by clicking the right mouse button on any fast palette color.

- A transparent image allows the background of the Web page to show through the image as the background of the image. The freeware version of Ultimate Paint does not support transparency but the shareware version does.

- The **Select Drawing Color** dialog allows the user to choose a color by moving the three vertical slider controls or by entering the RGB (red/green/blue) values as numbers in the range 0 through 255. The horizontal slider in the dialog changes the base color. You can store new custom colors in the fast palette by clicking an appropriate fast palette entry while holding the *Shift*, *Ctrl* or *Alt* key.

- Most tools have a customized tool property bar that allows you to fine-tune the properties of the currently selected tool. The tool property bar appears above the status bar at the bottom of the Ultimate Paint window when you select the tool from the icon bar.

- Anti-aliasing is a process that smooths edges of scalable fonts by blending the color of the edge pixels with the color of the background on which the text is being placed. Without it, fonts appear jagged on the screen.

- The drop-shadow effect is one of the most widely used image effects on the Web. The drop shadow helps to bring your image out from the background, creating a 3-D illusion.

- The two major file formats used for images on the Web are GIF (Graphics Interchange Format) and JPEG (Joint Photographic Experts Group).

- The Graphics Interchange Format (GIF), developed by CompuServe, is based on a palette of 256 colors. It is best used for screenshots, line drawings and other images with sharp edges. It is well suited to the Web because it enables transparency.

- JPEG is actually not a file format but a compression algorithm developed by the Joint Photographic Experts Group. It supports a palette of 16.7 million colors and is best used for photographs and other images which have continuous tones. JPEG does not support transparency.

- An issue to consider when choosing between GIF and JPEG is that the GIF compression method is lossless while JPEG is lossy. When a JPEG image is saved, it loses data to minimize file size. This data loss does effect the image quality unless the image has sharp edges. GIF files do not lose data when they are saved to disk, but they are often larger than JPEG files. In general, choose the GIF format for drawings and abstract images and choose the JPEG format for photographs and photo-realistic images that do not require transparency.

- Both GIF and JPEG share a feature known as interlacing (in GIF terminology) or progressive encoding (in JPEG terminology). This technique downloads a rough whole image and gradually increases the image's clarity.

- The Portable Network Graphics (PNG, pronounced ping) format incorporates the qualities of both GIF and JPEG formats. PNG encodes in RGBA format—the A stands for alpha transparency, which can make any image transparent against any background. PNG is also a lossless format and it provides more colors than JPEG. The PNG format is supported by the latest versions of both Netscape Communicator and Internet Explorer.

- The icon for the drawing tool in use remains pressed until another tool is selected. To deactivate a tool, click another icon in the icon bar. All options in the tool bar are repeatable except for cut brush, get color, undo last action and clear image.

- The undo last action tool is useful for correcting mistakes. It is limited to the last action performed.

- To change the background color, right click the color of your choice in the fast palette. Left clicking a fast palette color selects the foreground (drawing) color.

- The get color tool selects a color from your image as the background or foreground color. Right clicking the mouse sets the background color and left clicking sets the foreground color.

- Clicking the upper arrow of the zoom tool zooms in to a maximum ratio of 32:1. Clicking the lower arrow zooms out to a minimum ratio of 1:4.

- The filters tool allows you to use a brush to "paint" a filter over an image.

- The grid option allows you to constrain the shapes you draw to an invisible grid.

- Ultimate Paint has the ability to create custom brushes from portions of an image. This feature allows you to quickly and easily create a brush of any shape, size and color you desire.

- Ultimate Paint has four default brush sizes in both circle and square shapes.

- To create your own brush, use a tool from the cut brush group to select the area of your image to use as a custom brush. After creating the new brush, all the line drawing tools (i.e. freehand, line, ellipse, rectangle and curve) will use the new brush to draw (until you select a different brush). You can also use the pattern fill tool to fill shapes with the new brush.

- The **Brush** menu provides options for modifying the brush shape and size.

- There are three options in the **Techniques** menu for drawing with a custom brush. **Paint** mode draws with a custom brush. In this mode, the brush's background color brush is invisible in the brush. **Color** mode uses the custom brush shape with the currently selected drawing color. **Replace** mode is like the **Paint** mode except the background color is visible in the brush.

- Ultimate Paint enables you to alter images with the **Image** menu. The first four options in the menu allow you to stretch, mirror, rotate and get statistics on your image. The next nine options have submenus that allow you to mutate the image color and shape using predefined effects.

- The **Effect browser** allows you to preview each effect.

TERMINOLOGY

airbrush tool	fast palette
alpha transparency	filters
Anti-alias checkbox	flood fill tool
antialiasing	foreground color
background color	get color tool
bevel effect	GIF (Graphics Interchange Format)
Blur filter	gradient
Brush filter	greyscale image
brushes	**Icon Bar**
brush cutting	**Image** menu
brush size tool	interlacing
clear picture tool	JPEG (Joint Photographic Experts Group)
Color mode	line tool
Color of shadow	lossless format
custom cut brush	magic wand tool
cut brush tool	neon effect
dithering	**New Image** dialog
draw freehand	**Paint** mode
drawing color	palette
drop shadow effect	PNG (Portable Network Graphics) format
dropper tool	**Preferences** dialog
effects browser	progressive encoding
Effects submenu of **Image** menu	**Replace** mode

RGB value
Select Drawing Color dialog
shadow color
shadow depth
shape of a brush
shapes tool
size of a brush

Techniques menu
text tool
text tool property bar
tool tip window
tool property bar
undo last action tool
zoom tool

SELF-REVIEW EXERCISES

11.1   Identify either GIF or JPEG as the optimal format for the following situations:
  a) Line drawings
  b) Photographs
  c) Computer art
  d) Transparent logos
  e) Scanned images

11.2   Fill in the blank for each of the following:
  a) JPEG originally was developed by the _____.
  b) PNG uses _____ to make images transparent against any background.
  c) The compression method in GIF is _____ while in JPEG it is _____.
  d) The bevel tool and other effects are found in the _____ menu.
  e) _____ is the JPEG version of interlacing.

11.3   State whether the following are *true* or *false*. If the answer is *false*, explain why.
  a) There are a maximum of 16.7 million colors in a GIF image.
  b) The Cut Rectangle feature is used to cut a rectangular region of an image so that region can be pasted into another location in the image.
  c) The right mouse button is used to select the foreground color.
  d) The effects browser displays thumbnail views of your image modified by the nine categories of effects.
  e) There are two active colors at any time in Ultimate Paint.
  f) There are five modes of drawing that can be used by custom brushes.
  g) Anti-aliasing prevents blurred edges on scalable text.
  h) Activating the grid tool aids in aligning objects in an image.
  i) The JIFF format is another name for the GIF format.

ANSWERS TO SELF-REVIEW EXERCISES

11.1   a) GIF. b) JPEG. c) JPEG. d) GIF. e) JPEG.

11.2   a) Joint Photographers Expert Group. b) alpha transparency. c) lossless, lossy. d) **Image**. e) progressive encoding.

11.3   a) False. There are 256 colors in a GIF image.
  b) False. The Cut Rectangle feature is used to create a rectangular brush.
  c) False. Foreground color is selected with the left mouse button.
  d) True.
  e) True.
  f) False. There are only three drawing modes for custom brushes.
  g) False. Anti-aliasing prevents jagged edges, not blurred edges. The blurred edges help smooth the appearance of fonts on the screen.
  h) True.
  i) False. The JIFF format is another name for the JPEG format.

EXERCISES

11.4   Create a new title image that reads "Welcome to my Web page." Outline the text and fill it in with the **Dolphin** pattern (located in the **Image** menu under **Pattern**).

11.5   Create a background pattern for your Web site. Use the **Mirror** tool (located in the **Brush** menu) to make the pattern symmetrical.

11.6   Use the **Blur** filter (on the **Icon Bar**) to add a drop shadow to text without using the built-in **Drop Shadow...** effect.

11.7   Create another button like the one in Section 11.6. This time apply one of the **Emboss** tools to the text to create the appearance that the text is carved into the button.

12

Microsoft FrontPage Express

Objectives

- To be able to use FrontPage Express effectively.
- To become familiar with developing Web pages in a visual environment.
- To understand how to insert images and links into Web pages.
- To use FrontPage to create advanced HTML elements such as tables and forms.
- To understand how to use the **MARQUEE** element to create dynamically scrolling text.
- To understand how to insert scripts into pages.

The test of greatness is the page of history.
William Hazlitt

The one in front has reached there, the one behind only hears about it.
West African saying

We must select the illusion which appeals to our temperament, and embrace it with passion, if we want to be happy.
Cyril Connolly

The symbolic view of things is a consequence of long absorption in images. Is sign language the real language of Paradise?
Hugo Ball

What you see is what you get (WYSIWYG).
Anonymous

All human knowledge takes the form of interpretation.
Walter Benjamin

Outline

12.1 Introduction

Now that you have a working knowledge of HTML, you are ready to start making your own Web pages. Successful Web pages are often huge undertakings. They need constant attention, maintenance and updating. They can also attract more attention if they are visually appealing. Many tools have appeared on the market to help the aspiring Web developer.

Many companies have written Web design software for nonprogrammers, making it easier for a wider range of people to establish a presence on the World Wide Web. This software is also useful for programmers. However, if you plan to build complex Web sites, then these graphics-based editing programs should only serve as aids. They often disrupt indentation and insert unnecessary tags, making it difficult to code manually when necessary. They are no substitute for in-depth knowledge of HTML, but are quite useful for speeding up tasks such as coding large tables.

In this chapter we discuss the features of Microsoft *FrontPage Express,* which is on the CD that accompanies this book. Perhaps the most popular of the graphics-based HTML editors, FrontPage Express is a versatile tool with a familiar interface similar to that of Microsoft Word. The short amount of time it takes to learn FrontPage Express is well worth the amount of effort it saves. FrontPage Express can more easily perform many of the tasks already discussed in previous chapters. It can insert text and font changes, and it can also create more complex HTML, such as for creating tables, forms, frames and much more.

12.2 Microsoft FrontPage Express

Upon starting FrontPage Express, you are welcomed with a blank page in the default viewing mode. This is a *WYSIWYG* (What You See Is What You Get) display. Unlike editors that simply display HTML code, FrontPage Express renders HTML elements exactly as a browser would. This is intended to give you more insight into how people will see your page on the Web, and saves you the often substantial amount of time that can be spent switching between browser and editor when writing HTML directly, tweaking code to make sure your page was displayed correctly.

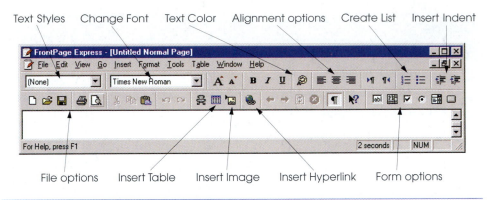

Text Styles   Change Font   Text Color   Alignment options   Create List   Insert Indent

File options   Insert Table   Insert Image   Insert Hyperlink   Form options

Fig. 12.1   A FrontPage Express window.

We can now easily recreate the example in Fig. 9.1 using FrontPage Express. Type in

```
Welcome to our Web Site!
```

in the text window. FrontPage express will automatically enclose this in a **P** element for proper formatting. Now to insert a title as we did in Fig. 9.1, right-click (click the second button on a two-button mouse) in the text area, and select ***Page Properties...*** from the pop-up menu. This causes the **Page Properties** dialog of Fig. 12.2 to appear.

Type in the title as shown and click **OK**. This inserts a **<TITLE>** tag inside the **<HEAD>**...**</HEAD>** element in your HTML code. Your page now appears exactly as it is in Fig. 9.1, shown here in FrontPage Express's WYSIWYG display instead of the browser window.

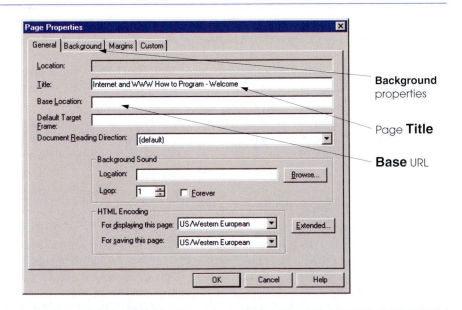

Background properties

Page **Title**

Base URL

Fig. 12.2   Setting overall **Page Properties**.

Fig. 12.3   Using FrontPage Express on example of Fig. 9.1.

Now that you have seen a basic example of WYSIWYG editing, remember that you are still programming in HTML. To view or edit your HTML directly select the ***HTML...*** option in the ***View*** menu. FrontPage automatically color codes your HTML to make viewing easier. The tag names, tag attributes, attribute values and page text are all displayed in different colors. This feature can be turned off by clicking off the checkbox titled ***Show Color Coding*** at the bottom of the dialog box.

There is also an option to switch between your **Current** code and your **Original** code. If you have modified your code since your last save, this is a useful option for reviewing any changes or updates you have made.

To save your file, click **Save** in the ***File*** menu. FrontPage Express will first give you a dialog box with the `TITLE` of your page and the address of a Web server on which to save the file. This will only work if your server has FrontPage Extensions installed. If it does not, simply click the **As File...** button in the dialog box and you can browse your hard drive for a location to save the file.

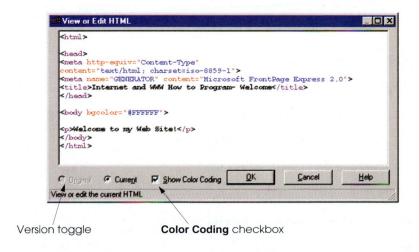

Version toggle   **Color Coding** checkbox

Fig. 12.4   Viewing the HTML source code.

Title ────────▶ (Page Title: Internet and WWW How to Program - Welcome)

Location ──────▶ (Page Location: http://dellxps300_14/internet.htm)
on server

Save locally ◀──── (As File...)

Fig. 12.5   Saving your HTML file.

12.3 Text Styles

FrontPage's screen appearance is like Microsoft Word's. There is a drop-down menu for changing text styles. Using this menu, you can quickly apply header tags (**<H1>**, **<H2>**, etc.), list tags (**<OL>**, **<UL>**), and several other tags used for stylizing text. Text can also be aligned left, right or centered using buttons on the top toolbar. Text can be increased or decreased in size indented and colored.

Type the screen text as shown in Fig. 12.6 into the window. Drag the mouse to highlight one line at a time and use the **Change Style** pull-down menu to apply the appropriate header tags. Now highlight all of the text, and click the align center button on the toolbar. Alignment options and text styles are also accessible through the **Paragraph...** option in the **Format** menu. The resulting HTML produced by FrontPage Express is shown in Fig. 12.6 (line 6 is split because it is too wide to fit on the page).

```
1   <html>
2   <head>
3
4   <meta http-equiv="Content-Type"
5   content="text/html; charset=iso-8859-1">
6   <meta name="GENERATOR" content="Microsoft FrontPage Express 2.0">
7   <title>Untitled Normal Page</title>
8   </head>
9
10  <body bgcolor="#FFFFFF">
11
12  <h1 align="center">Level 1 Header</h1>
13
14  <h2 align="center">Level 2 Header</h2>
15
16  <h3 align="center">Level 3 Header</h3>
17
18  <h4 align="center">Level 4 Header</h4>
19
20  <h5 align="center">Level 5 Header</h5>
21
22  <h6 align="center">Level 6 Header</h6>
23  </body>
24  </html>
```

Fig. 12.6   Applying header tags and centering using FrontPage Express (part 1 of 2).

Fig. 12.6   Applying header tags and centering using FrontPage Express (part 2 of 2).

As you can see, FrontPage Express is prone to producing inefficient code. In this case, enclosing all the headers in a **CENTER** element would save both time and file space.

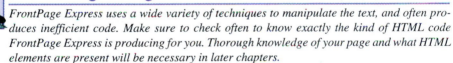

Software Engineering Observation 12.1

FrontPage Express uses a wide variety of techniques to manipulate the text, and often produces inefficient code. Make sure to check often to know exactly the kind of HTML code FrontPage Express is producing for you. Thorough knowledge of your page and what HTML elements are present will be necessary in later chapters.

FrontPage Express is capable of much more extensive text formatting. Perhaps you needed to place a mathematical formula on your Web page. For example, type

```
E=mc2
```

in the window, then highlight the text. You can now change the formatting of the equation by opening the **Font...** dialog box in the **Format** menu, and switching to the **Special Styles** tab. Click on the **Code** checkbox and return to the text by clicking **OK**. This applies a **CODE** element to the highlighted text, which designates formulas or computer code. Select the "2" in our formula and return to the **Special Styles** tab. Change the text to superscript as indicated in Fig. 12.7.

You can also access the **Font** dialog box by right-clicking highlighted text, and selecting **Font Properties...** from the pop-up menu that appears. The formula can be further emphasized by highlighting the text and using the **Text Color** button on the upper toolbar to make it stand out from surrounding text.

Good Programming Practice 12.1

When you press Enter *after typing text, FrontPage Express will enclose that text in a new set of* **<P>...</P>** *tags. If you want to insert only a* **
** *tag into your page hold down* Shift *while you press* Enter.

Code checkbox

Height selector

Vertical position
pull-down list

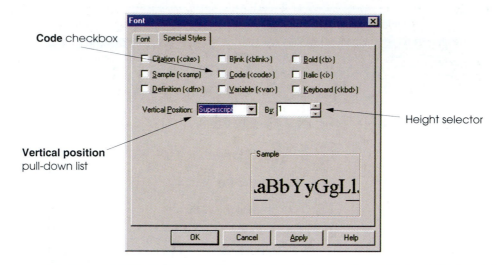

Fig. 12.7   Changing **Font** settings and adding special styles.

 Good Programming Practice 12.2

You can manipulate the properties of almost any element displayed in the FrontPage Express window by right-clicking that element and selecting that element's properties from the window that pops up.

The **Change Style** pull-down menu (which we used previously in Fig. 12.6) is also useful for creating lists. Try entering the contents of a shopping list as shown Fig. 12.8, and applying the **Bulleted List** style.

Fig. 12.8   Applying an unordered list and a header to text.

Apply an **H2** element to the title of the list. The **Change Style** pull-down menu has many more useful tags that were not covered in Chapters 9 and 10, such as the *definition list* (**<DL>**). There are two list elements in a definition list—the *defined term* (**<DT>**) and the *definition* (**<DD>**). Figure 12.9 shows the formatting produced by the definition list and the code FrontPage Express used to produce it.

To apply the definition list as shown, pull down the **Change Style** menu to **Defined Term**, and type in the term you want to define. When you press *Enter*, FrontPage Express then changes the style to **Definition**. The bold style was applied using the appropriate toolbar button (this applies to the **STRONG** element).

12.4 Images and Links

Inserting images using FrontPage Express is simply a matter of clicking a button and typing the image's path. The example of Fig. 12.10 is a repeat of the example in Fig. 9.8, using an image as a hyperlink.

Select ***Image...*** from the ***Insert*** menu, and browse your local hard drive directory for the image. You can also select ***From Location*** to use an image from the Web.

```
1   <dl>
2       <dt><strong>FTP</strong></dt>
3       <dd>File Transfer Protocol</dd>
4       <dt><strong>GIF</strong></dt>
5       <dd>Graphics Interchange Format</dd>
6       <dt><strong>HTML</strong></dt>
7       <dd>HyperText Markup Language</dd>
8       <dt><strong>PNG</strong></dt>
9       <dd>Portable Network Graphics</dd>
10  </dl>
```

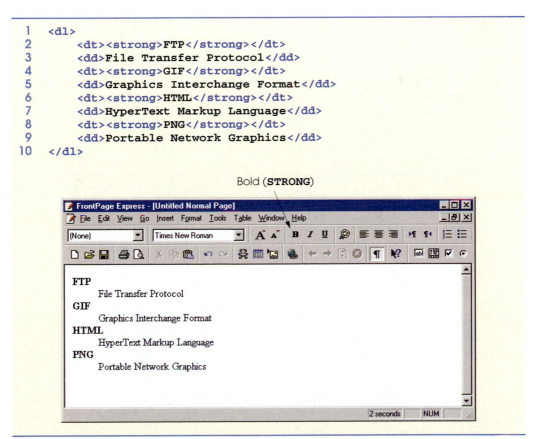

Fig. 12.9   Inserting a definition list using the **Change Style** menu.

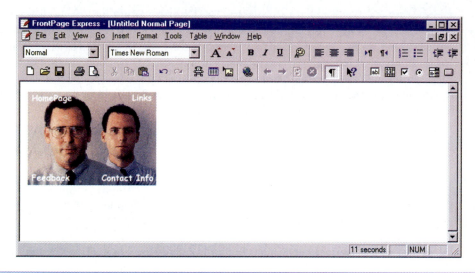

Fig. 12.10   Inserting an image into a Web page.

 Common Programming Error 12.1

When you insert a local image into your code by using the **Browse...** *button, FrontPage Express sets an absolute path such as* `C:/images/deitel.gif`*. This will not work on the Web, so be sure to change this to a relative path such as* `images/deitel.gif`*.*

After inserting your image, highlight it and create a hyperlink using the *Hyperlink...* option in the **Insert** menu. First select the *Hyperlink Type...* that you want to use. There are some we have seen in previous chapters, such as `http` and `mailto`, and there are many new ones, such as `https`. `https` (Secure HyperText Transfer Protocol) is used to transfer sensitive information such as credit card numbers and personal data.

Fig. 12.11   Inserting a Hyperlink in a Web page.

Type in the URL to which the hyperlink will point. FrontPage Express adds a **BORDER=0** attribute to the **<IMG>** tag, removing the blue rectangle that would usually appear around the image.

You can add other attributes to the tag by using the *Extended...* button at the bottom of the dialog box. This button appears in many places throughout FrontPage Express and is often useful for adding unlisted attributes to fine-tune the appearance of the element.

12.5 Symbols and Lines

FrontPage Express also allows you to insert characters that are not located on the standard keyboard. This feature, accessed by the *Symbol...* option in the **Insert** menu, functions much like the Windows program **Character Map**. Select any listed character and click **Insert** to copy it into the text window.

In the coming example, we demonstrate how these symbols can be used in a Web page, along with another feature in FrontPage express, the **Horizontal Line Properties** menu. Begin by typing

```
This sentence is <π of the way down the page.
```

Use the **Symbol** menu to insert the two special characters into the sentence. Now click the **Horizontal Line** option in the **Insert** menu. This will insert the line (an **HR** element) directly into the page, so right-click the line and select **Horizontal Line Properties...** from the popup menu. Make this line 1 pixel high, spanning 40% of the width of the page.

Fig. 12.12   Adding symbols and nonstandard letters.

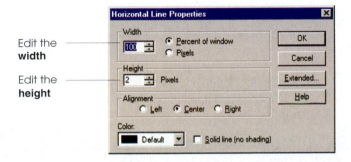

Fig. 12.13   Setting the properties of a **Horizontal Line** element.

Next type the following text

> `This sentence is <⌠ of the way down the page.`

Again, insert a horizontal rule. This time set it 3 pixels high and spanning 60% of the page width. Type in the last two sentences as they appear in Fig. 12.14. The third horizontal line is 80% of the page width and 10 pixels high.

12.6 Tables

As useful as tables are, they are hard and confusing to code accurately in HTML. FrontPage Express offers a simple method of dealing with this problem. To create a table click **Insert Table...** in the **Table** menu. You can select the number of rows and columns, the overall width of the table and several other related settings. Figure 12.15 is a simple table created this way with the default size of 2 rows by 2 columns.

Once the table is placed, you can manipulate the table size. You can click in a cell and press the *Delete* key to remove the cell. You can highlight two adjacent cells and use the **Merge Cells...** option in the **Table** menu to merge the cells into one. FrontPage Express uses the **COLSPAN** and **ROWSPAN** attributes of the **<TD>** tag to accomplish this. Using the **Split Cells...** option allows you to split a cell into any number of rows or columns. Figure 12.16 shows a table two cells high and two cells wide that has had its top two cells merged, and its lower left cell split into five columns. A caption has also been added using the **Insert Caption** command, also located in the **Table** menu.

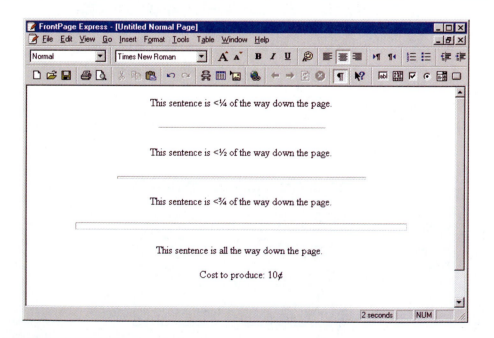

Fig. 12.14 Demonstrating symbols and horizontal lines on one page.

More complex tables are created with the ***Table Properties...*** command (Fig. 12.17). You can add colors or background images and change the width and alignment. Individual cells are customized by clicking a cell and clicking ***Cell Properties...*** in the **Table** menu.

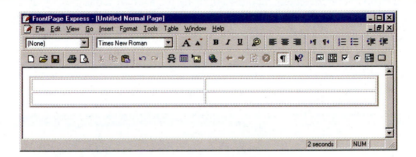

Fig. 12.15 A default table.

Fig. 12.16 A basic table.

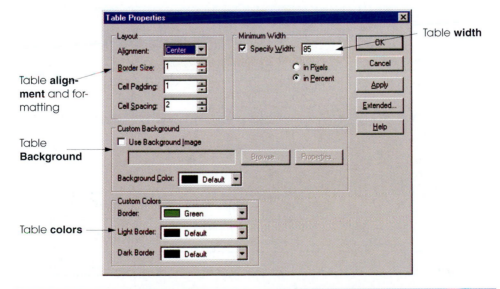

Fig. 12.17 Adjusting table colors and alignment in **Table Properties**.

In Fig. 12.18, we recreate the table of Fig. 10.5. Begin by making a table 4 rows tall and 5 columns wide. Click the top left cell, and click **Select Column** in the **Table** menu. This will highlight the left-most column in the table. Now control-click (hold control down as you click) the lower two selected cells; this will deselect them and turn them white again. Now that only the top two are selected, merge them using the **Merge Cells** command.

Now to make space for the title, click in the same cell as before, but this time use the **Select Row** command. Unselect the top left cell, and click on **Merge Cells.** Repeat this process for the rest of the oversized cells, and then start typing in the text and insert the image (Fig 12.19).

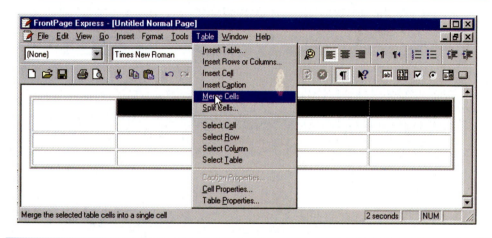

Fig. 12.18 A 4x5 table with the top left cell expanded.

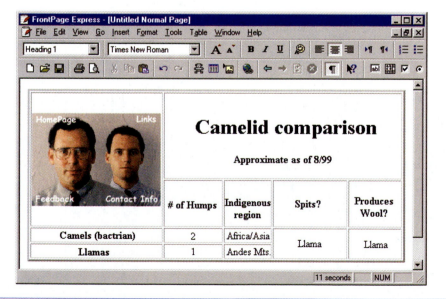

Fig. 12.19 An almost completed table.

Remember to shade the upper rows just as they were in Fig. 10.5. Do this by right-clicking the cells and selecting **Cell Properties...** from the pop-up menu that appears. Select the proper color from the **Background Color** pull-down menu.

12.7 Forms

All the necessary HTML coding needed for installing a feedback form or other form on your page can be done with FrontPage Express. After you insert any form field, a dotted line will be drawn around the field. Any other form fields placed inside this line will lie inside the same set of `<FORM>`...`</FORM>` tags as the original form.

A text box is easily inserted by clicking the ***One-Line Text Box*** button on the toolbar or by clicking **One-Line Text Box** in the ***Form-Field*** submenu of the **Insert** menu. Once placed, the placed text box can be stretched wider or narrower with the mouse, or its width can be changed in the ***Form Field Properties...*** menu, accessed by right-clicking on the field or by double-clicking the text box.

In the **Text Box Properties** dialog that appears, the `NAME` and `VALUE` attributes of the form field can be set along with the width (this corresponds to the `SIZE` attribute) and whether this box is a `TYPE = "password"`.

Multiline text boxes can also be placed from the ***Form-Field*** submenu, and their properties are almost identical to normal text boxes, except that they have an additional attribute of height (measured in lines).

The drop-down `SELECT` menu is also added through the **Form Field** submenu. In the **Form Field Properties...** menu, new entries can be added, removed, modified or moved up and down in the order you want them to appear on the page. A single entry can also be made the default selection by toggling **Selected** or **Not Selected** when you add or modify a menu item (Fig 12.20).

Now that we have completed the basics of forms in FrontPage Express, we are ready to make a real form that could be used on any Web page—a typical "rate-my-Web site" form. To start, place all the form fields as they appear in Fig. 12.21.

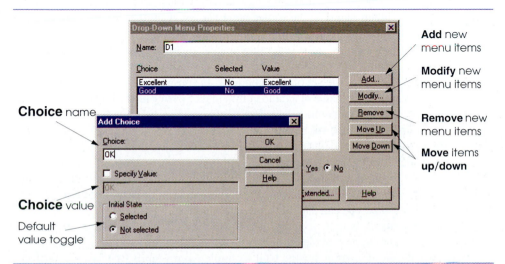

Fig. 12.20 Adding a new item to a drop-down form menu.

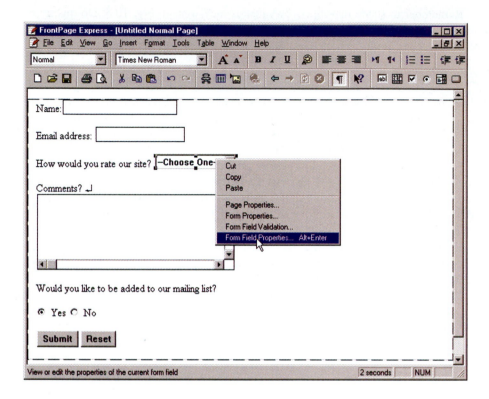

Fig. 12.21 A brief form for user input.

Stretch the text boxes to the proper width using your mouse. Now right-click on the drop-down menu and click on the **Form Field Properties...** menu. You can also access the properties dialog box by double-clicking that form field. Begin adding choices by clicking **Add...** and then typing in the choice name. If you want the **VALUE** of the choice to be different than the name, click on **Specify Value** and type in the value. You can also move any choices up or down in the order they appear on screen with the **Move Up** and **Move Down** buttons.

This example only has one set of radio buttons. If you want to put more than one set in, you can change the group name of a radio button in its **Form Field Properties...**. Only one radio button in each set may be selected and only one may be set as default.

To set the **Reset** and **Submit** buttons, click **Push Button** in the Form section on the toolbar. The placed button defaults to **Submit**, but by accessing their **Form Field Properties**, you can change them to **Normal** or **Reset** buttons.

Now that all the fields have been placed, modify the form itself by right-clicking anywhere inside the dotted line that delineates the form, and select **Form Properties...**. In the resulting dialog box, you can add any hidden fields that a CGI script might require. By clicking the **Settings...** button, you can also set the **ACTION** and **METHOD** attributes of your form, which should be provided to you by your ISP (Fig. 12.22).

Here we add the properties for the CGI example from Figure 10.6 using FrontPage Express' **Form Properties** dialog box.

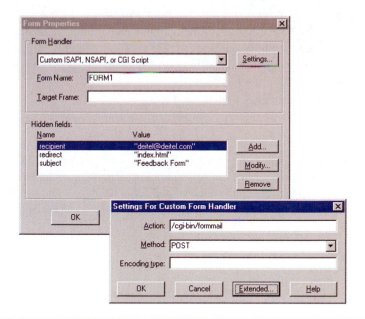

Fig. 12.22 Using the **Form Properties** dialog box.

12.8 Marquees and Scripts

The **<MARQUEE>** tag is a nonstandard tag, supported only by Microsoft Internet Explorer. It is meant as a mimic of the Marquee screen saver, included with Windows. Any text inside a **<MARQUEE>**...**</MARQUEE>** element will scroll slowly across the screen and repeat, depending on the settings you choose. Figure 12.23 illustrates the *Marquee...* properties box, located in the **Insert** menu.

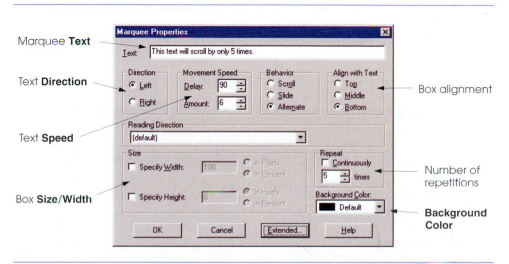

Fig. 12.23 Inserting a **MARQUEE** element for scrolling Web page text.

You can choose the **Text** that scrolls by, the **Direction** it scrolls, and the **Speed** at which it scrolls by. You can also specify the width and height of the box in which the text will scroll, and its background color. You can also choose whether it will scroll by continuously and, if not, how many times it will iterate. Figure 12.24 shows two screen captures of the **MARQUEE** element in action.

Good Programming Practice 12.3

Netscape will not display any **<MARQUEE>** *elements that you put on your page, so use them sparingly, and do not put any critical information inside them.*

While not providing much support for scripts, FrontPage Express does give you the ability to insert them into your Web page. By clicking **Script...** in the **Insert** menu, you are given a dialog box (Fig. 12.25) in which you can type your complete script in JavaScript or VBScript. We discuss how to program JavaScripts for use in your Web pages in Chapters 13 through 18.

SUMMARY

- Upon starting FrontPage Express, you are welcomed with a blank page in the default viewing mode. This is a WYSIWYG (What You See Is What You Get) display. FrontPage Express renders HTML elements as a browser would.

- FrontPage express automatically encloses text that you type in a **P** element for proper formatting.

- To insert a title right-click in the text area, and select **Page Properties...** from the pop-up menu. Type in the title as shown, and click **OK**. This inserts a **<TITLE>** tag inside the **<HEAD>**...**</HEAD>** element in your HTML code.

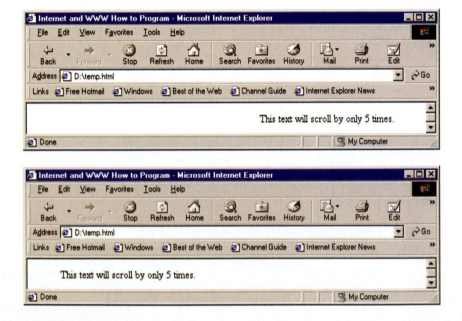

Fig. 12.24 The **MARQUEE** element in action.

Script **Language**

Script text

Fig. 12.25 Adding a script to the HTML file.

- To view or edit HTML directly, select the **HTML...** option in the **View** menu. FrontPage automatically color codes HTML to make viewing easier. The tag names, tag attributes, attribute values and page text are all displayed in different colors. This feature can be turned off by clicking off the checkbox titled **Show Color Coding** at the bottom of the dialog box.

- To save your file, click **Save** in the **File** menu. FrontPage Express will first give you a dialog box with the **TITLE** of your page, and the address of a Web server on which to save the file. This will only work if your server has FrontPage Extensions installed. If it does not, click the **As File...** button in the dialog box and you can browse your hard drive for a location to save the file.

- Using the **Change Style** menu, you can quickly apply header tags (**<H1>**, **<H2>**, etc.), list tags (**<OL>**, **<UL>**) and several other tags used for stylizing text.

- Text can be aligned left, center or right using buttons on the top toolbar. Text can be increased or decreased in size, indented and colored.

- The **Font...** dialog box in the **Format** menu allows you to apply special styles to selected text. You can also access the **Font** dialog box by right-clicking highlighted text and selecting **Font Properties...** from the pop-up menu that appears.

- The **Change Style** pull-down menu is useful for creating lists.

- The items in a definition list (**<DL>**) are the defined term (**<DT>**) and the definition (**<DD>**). To apply the definition list, pull down the **Change Style** menu to **Defined Term** and type the term you want to define. When you press Enter, FrontPage Express changes the style to **Definition**.

- To insert an image select **Image...** from the **Insert** menu and type the image's path. You can **Browse** the local hard drive for the image or select **From Location** to use an image on the Web.

- Create a hyperlink using the **Hyperlink...** option in the **Insert** menu. First select the **Hyperlink Type...** that you want to use, then type in the address of the link.

- **https** (Secure HyperText Transfer Protocol) is used in transfer of sensitive information such as credit card numbers and personal data.

- FrontPage Express allows you to insert characters that are not on a standard keyboard. This feature, accessed by the **Symbol...** option in the **Insert** menu, functions like the Windows **Character Map**. Select any listed character and click **Insert** to copy it into the text window.

- Click on the **Horizontal Line** option in the **Insert** menu to insert a line (an **HR** element) directly into the page. Right-click the line and select **Horizontal Line Properties...** from the popup menu to change the properties of this line.

- To create a table, click **Insert Table...** in the **Table** menu. You can select the number of rows and columns, the overall width of the table and other related settings. Once the table is placed, options exist for manipulating the table size. You can click in a cell and press the Delete key to remove the cell. The **Merge Cells...** option in the **Table** menu merges selected cells into one. The **Split Cells...** option splits a cell into any number of rows or columns. A caption may be added using the **Insert Caption** command located in the **Table** menu.

- More advanced tables can be created by using the **Table Properties...** command. You can add colors or background images to the whole table and change width and alignment. This can also be done to individual cells by clicking on a cell and clicking **Cell Properties...** in the **Table** menu.

- All the necessary HTML coding needed for installing a feedback or other form on your page can be done with FrontPage Express. After you insert any form field, a dotted line will be automatically drawn around the field. Any other form fields placed inside this line will lie inside the same set of **<FORM>**...**</FORM>** tags as the original form.

- A text box is inserted by clicking the **One-Line Text Box** button on the toolbar, or by clicking **One-Line Text Box** in the **Form-Field** submenu of the **Insert** menu. The placed text box can be stretched wider or narrower with the mouse, or its width can be changed in the **Form Field Properties...** menu, accessed by right-clicking on the field. In this menu both the **NAME** and **VALUE** attributes of the form field can also be set. Multiline text boxes can be placed from the same submenu, and their properties are almost identical to normal text boxes, except that they have an additional attribute of height.

- A drop-down menu is added through the **Form-Field** submenu. In the **Form Field Properties...** menu, new entries can be added, removed, modified or moved up and down in the order you want them to appear on the page. A single entry is made the default selection by toggling **Selected** or **Not Selected** when you add or modify a menu item. When adding entries, if you want the **VALUE** of the choice to be different than the name, click on **Specify Value** and type the value.

- If you want to insert more than one set of radio buttons in your form, you can change the group name of a radio button in its **Form Field Properties...**. Only one radio button in each set may be selected, and only one may be set as default.

- To insert the **Reset** and **Submit** buttons, click **Push Button** in the Form section on the toolbar. The placed buttons default to **Submit**, but by accessing their **Form Field Properties...**, you can change them to **Normal** or **Reset** buttons.

- You can modify a form by right-clicking anywhere inside the dotted line that delineates the form, and select **Form Properties...**. In the resulting dialog box, you can add any hidden fields that your CGI script might require. By clicking the **Settings...** button, you can also set the **ACTION** and **METHOD** attributes of your form, which should be provided to you by your ISP.

- The **<MARQUEE>** tag is a nonstandard tag supported only by Microsoft Internet Explorer. It is meant as a mimic of the Marquee screen saver, included with Windows. Any text inside a **<MARQUEE>**...**</MARQUEE>** element will scroll slowly across the screen and repeat, depending on the settings you choose.

- FrontPage Express gives you the ability to insert scripts into your Web page. By clicking **Script...** in the **Insert** menu, you are given a dialog box in which you can type your complete script.

TERMINOLOGY

absolute path
Add... in **Form Field Properties...**
Align Center button
As File... in the **Save** menu
Background Color in **Cell Properties**

Cell Properties... in **Table** menu
Change Style pull-down menu
Code checkbox
COLSPAN
Current toggle and **Original** toggle.

DD element (definition; **<DD>**...)

Direction of a **MARQUEE** tag

DL element (definition list; **<DL>**...**</DL>**)

DT element (defined term; **<DT>**...**</DT>**)

Font Properties... pop-up menu

Font... in the **Format** menu

Form Field Properties... menu

Form Properties...

From Location in **Image**

ftp

Horizontal Line in **Insert** menu

Horizontal Line Properties menu

HTML... in *View* menu

https

Hyperlink Type...

Hyperlink... in the **Insert** menu

Image... in **Insert** menu

Insert Caption in **Table** menu

Insert in **Symbol** menu

Insert Table... in **Table** menu

mailto

<MARQUEE>

Marquee... in **Insert** menu

Merge Cells... in **Table** menu

Move Down in *Add* menu

Move Up in *Add* menu

Normal option in **Push Button** menu

One-Line Text Box button

Page Properties... *pop-up* menu.

Paragraph... in the **Format** menu

Push Button button

relative path

Reset option in **Push Button** menu

ROWSPAN

Save in the **File** menu

Script... in **Insert** menu

Select Column in the **Table** menu

Select Row in **Table** menu

Selected and **Not Selected** toggles

Show Color Coding

Special Styles tab

Specify value in **Add** menu

Speed of a **MARQUEE** tag

Split Cells... in **Table** menu

Symbol... option in the **Insert** menu

Table Properties...

Text Color button

Text of a **MARQUEE** tag

VALUE

WYSIWYG

SELF-REVIEW EXERCISES

12.1 What color does FrontPage Express use for the following types of code in the *HTML...* option in the View menu?
   a) Plain text
   b) Tags
   c) Attributes
   d) Attribute Values

12.2 What button that appears in many dialog boxes allows you to insert unlisted attributes directly into your HTML code?

12.3 What action gives you access to the properties of an item?

12.4 State whether the following are true or false:
   a) FrontPage Express renders most HTML elements correctly in its WYSIWYG display.
   b) FrontPage Express sometimes inserts superfluous HTML tags.
   c) The **MARQUEE** element can be rendered properly by all browsers.
   d) **https** is the same as **http**.
   e) FrontPage Express delineates a **FORM** element with a dotted line.
   f) FrontPage Express inserts local images using a relative path.

ANSWERS TO SELF-REVIEW EXERCISES

12.1 a) Black. b) Purple. c) Red. d) Blue.

12.2 **Extended...**

12.3 Right-clicking.

12.4   a) True. b) True.   c) False. The **MARQUEE** element is supported only by Internet Explorer. d) False. **https** is a secure version of **http**, permitting the transmission of sensitive information such as credit card numbers. e) True. f) False. FrontPage Express inserts images with an absolute path. You must change this to a relative path so the images may be displayed properly on the Web.

EXERCISES

12.5   Create the following table using FrontPage Express:

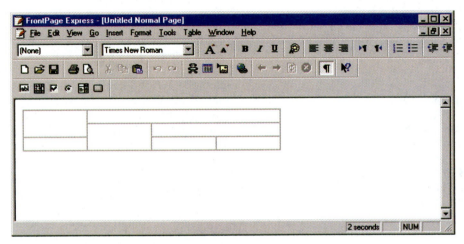

12.6   Create the following form using FrontPage Express.

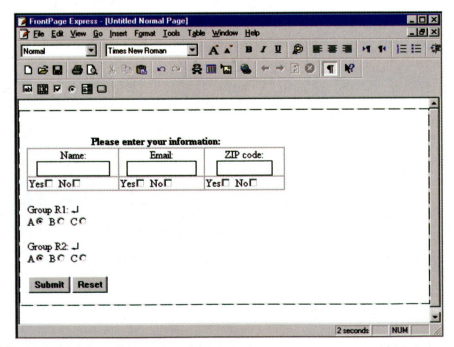

12.7   Create a personal Web page using FrontPage Express.

13

JavaScript/JScript: Introduction to Scripting

Objectives

- To be able to write simple JavaScript programs.
- To be able to use input and output statements.
- To understand basic memory concepts.
- To be able to use arithmetic operators.
- To understand the precedence of arithmetic operators.
- To be able to write decision-making statements.
- To be able to use relational and equality operators.

Comment is free, but facts are sacred.
C. P. Scott

The creditor hath a better memory than the debtor.
James Howell

When faced with a decision, I always ask, "What would be the most fun?"
Peggy Walker

Equality, in a social sense, may be divided into that of condition and that of rights.
James Fenimore Cooper

13.1 Introduction

In the first twelve chapters, we introduced the Internet and World Wide Web, e-Business and e-Commerce, creating HTML documents, and several tools that help Web page designers create HTML documents. In this chapter, we begin our introduction to the *JavaScript scripting language,* which facilitates a disciplined approach to designing computer programs that enhance the functionality and appearance of Web pages.

We now introduce JavaScript programming and present examples that illustrate several important features of JavaScript. Each example is analyzed one line at a time. In Chapters 14 and 15, we present a detailed treatment of *program development* and *program control* in JavaScript. *Note:* Microsoft's version of JavaScript is called *JScript.* JavaScript was originally created by Netscape. Both Netscape and Microsoft have been instrumental in the standardization of JavaScript/JScript by the *ECMA (European Computer Manufacturer's Association)* as *ECMAScript.* For information on the current ECMAScript standard, visit:

```
www.ecma.ch/stand/ecma-262.htm
```

Throughout this book we refer to JavaScript and JScript generically as JavaScript—the most commonly used name in industry.

13.2 A Simple Program: Printing a Line of Text in a Web Page

JavaScript uses notations that may appear strange to nonprogrammers. We begin by considering a simple *script* (or *program*) that displays the line of text "**Welcome to JavaScript Programming!**" in the body of an HTML document. The Internet Explorer Web browser contains the *JavaScript interpreter,* which processes the commands in a script written in JavaScript. The script and its output are shown in Fig. 13.1.

This program illustrates several important features of implementing a JavaScript in an HTML document. We consider each line of the HTML document and script in detail. We have given each HTML document line numbers for the reader's convenience; those line numbers are not part of the HTML document or of the JavaScript programs. Lines 9 and 10 do the "real work" of the script, namely displaying the phrase **Welcome to JavaScript Programming!** in the Web page. But let us consider each line in order.

```
1   <!DOCTYPE html PUBLIC "-//W3C//DTD HTML 4.0 Transitional//EN">
2   <!-- Fig. 13.1: welcome.html -->
3
4   <HTML>
5   <HEAD>
6   <TITLE>A First Program in JavaScript</TITLE>
7
8   <SCRIPT LANGUAGE = "JavaScript">
9      document.writeln(
10         "<H1>Welcome to JavaScript Programming!</H1>" );
11   </SCRIPT>
12
13   </HEAD><BODY></BODY>
14   </HTML>
```

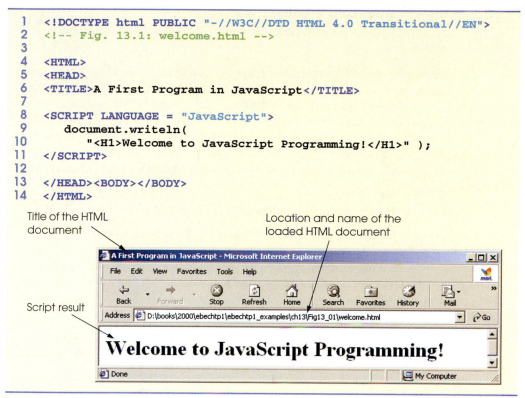

Title of the HTML document

Location and name of the loaded HTML document

Script result

Fig. 13.1   A first program in JavaScript.

The **DOCTYPE** element in line 1 indicates that the document type is an HTML 4.0 document. Line 2

```
<!-- Fig. 13.1: welcome.html -->
```

is an HTML comment indicating the figure number and file name for this HTML document. Programmers insert HTML comments to *document* or *describe* the purpose of parts of an HTML document and to improve readability. Comments also help other people read and understand your HTML documents. We begin every HTML document with a comment indicating figure number and file name.

 Good Programming Practice 13.1

HTML documents should begin with a comment describing the purpose of the document.

Line 3 is simply a blank line. Blank lines and space characters are often used throughout HTML documents and scripts to make them easier to read. Together, blank lines, space characters and tab characters are known as *whitespace* (space characters and tabs are known specifically as *whitespace characters*). Such characters are generally ignored by the browser. In many cases, such characters are used for readability and clarity. The spacing displayed by a browser in a Web page is determined by the HTML elements used to format the page. Several conventions for using whitespace characters are discussed in this chapter and the next several chapters, as these spacing conventions become needed.

Good Programming Practice 13.2

Use blank lines, space characters and tab characters in an HTML document to enhance readability.

The **\<HTML\>** tag at line 4 indicates the beginning of the HTML document. Line 5 indicates the beginning of the **\<HEAD\>** section of the HTML document. For the moment, the JavaScripts we write will appear in the **\<HEAD\>** section of the HTML document. The browser interprets the contents of the **\<HEAD\>** section first, so the JavaScript programs we write in the **\<HEAD\>** section will be executed before the **\<BODY\>** of the HTML document is displayed. In later JavaScript chapters and in the Dynamic HTML chapters, we illustrate *inline scripting,* in which JavaScript code is written in the **\<BODY\>** section of an HTML document. Line 6

```
<TITLE>A First Program in JavaScript</TITLE>
```

specifies the title of this HTML document. The title of the document appears in the title bar of the browser when the document is loaded.

Line 7 is simply a blank line to separate the **\<SCRIPT\>** tag at line 8 from the other HTML elements. This effect helps the script stand out in the HTML document and makes the document easier to read.

Good Programming Practice 13.3

*Place a blank line before the **\<SCRIPT\>** tag and after the **\</SCRIPT\>** tag to separate the script from the surrounding HTML elements and to make the script stand out in the document.*

Line 8

```
<SCRIPT LANGUAGE = "JavaScript">
```

uses the **\<SCRIPT\>** tag to indicate to the browser that the text that follows is part of a script. The **LANGUAGE** attribute specifies the *scripting language* used in the script—in this case, **JavaScript**. [*Note:* Even though Microsoft calls the language JScript, the **LANGUAGE** attribute specifies **JavaScript**, to adhere to the ECMAScript standard.] Both Microsoft Internet Explorer and Netscape Navigator use JavaScript as the default scripting language. Therefore, the preceding line can be written simply as

```
<SCRIPT>
```

with no **LANGUAGE** attribute specified.

Portability Tip 13.1

*Specify the scripting language with the **LANGUAGE** attribute of the **\<SCRIPT\>** tag, to ensure that all browsers in which the HTML document is loaded know the language of the script. Although it is unlikely at this time, future Web browsers may not use **JavaScript** as the default scripting language.*

Lines 9 and 10

```
document.writeln(
   "<H1>Welcome to JavaScript Programming!</H1>" );
```

instruct the browser's JavaScript interpreter to perform an *action,* namely to display in the Web page the *string* of characters contained between the *double quotation (") marks*. A string is sometimes called a *character string*, a *message* or a *string literal*. We refer to characters between double quotation marks generically as strings. Whitespace characters in strings are not ignored by the browser.

Software Engineering Observation 13.1

Strings in JavaScript can also be enclosed in single quotation (') marks.

Lines 9 and 10 use the browser's *document object*, which represents the HTML document currently being displayed in the browser. The **document** object allows a script programmer to specify HTML text to be displayed in the HTML document. The browser contains a complete set of objects that allow script programmers to access and manipulate every element of an HTML document. In the next several chapters, we overview some of these objects. Chapters 19 through 24 and Chapters 30 through 32 provide in-depth coverage of many more objects that a script programmer can manipulate.

An object resides in the computer's memory and contains information used by the script. The term *object* normally implies that *attributes* (*data*) and *behaviors* (*methods*) are associated with the object. The object's methods use the attributes to provide useful services to the *client of the object*—the script that calls the methods. In the preceding statement, we call the **document** object's *writeln* method to write a line of HTML text in the HTML document being displayed. The parentheses following the method name **writeln** contain the *arguments* that the method requires to perform its task (or its action). Method **writeln** instructs the browser to display the argument string. If the string contains HTML elements, the browser interprets these elements and renders them on the screen. In this example, the browser displays the phrase **Welcome to JavaScript Programming!** as an **H1**-level HTML head, because the phrase is enclosed in an **H1** element. [*Note:* Using **writeln** to write a line of HTML text into the **document** does not necessarily write a line of text in the HTML document. The text displayed in the browser is entirely dependent on the contents of the string written, which is subsequently rendered by the browser. The browser will interpret the HTML elements as it normally does to render the final text in the document.]

The code elements in lines 9 and 10, including **document.writeln**, its *argument* in the parentheses (the string) and the *semicolon* (**;**), together are called a *statement*. Every statement should end with a semicolon (also known as the *statement terminator*), although this practice is not required by JavaScript.

Good Programming Practice 13.4

Always include the semicolon at the end of a statement to explicitly terminate the statement. This clarifies where one statement ends and the next statement begins.

Line 11

```
</SCRIPT>
```

indicates the end of the script.

Common Programming Error 13.1

Forgetting the ending **</SCRIPT>** *tag for a script may prevent the browser from interpreting the script properly and may prevent the HTML document from loading properly.*

The **</HEAD>** tag at line 13 indicates the end of the **<HEAD>** section. Also on line 13, the tags **<BODY>** and **</BODY>** specify that this HTML document has an empty body—no HTML appears in the **BODY** element. Line 14 indicates the end of this HTML document.

We are now ready to view our HTML document in Internet Explorer. Open this HTML document in the browser. If the script contains no syntax errors, the preceding script should produce the output shown in Fig. 13.1.

Common Programming Error 13.2

JavaScript is case sensitive. Not using the proper uppercase and lowercase letters is a syntax error. A syntax error occurs when the script interpreter cannot recognize a statement. The interpreter normally issues an error message to help the programmer locate and fix the incorrect statement. Syntax errors are violations of the language rules. You will be notified of a syntax error when the interpreter attempts to execute the statement containing the error. The JavaScript interpreter in Internet Explorer reports all syntax errors by indicating in a separate popup window that a "runtime error" occurred (a problem occurred while the interpreter was running the script).

Testing and Debugging Tip 13.1

When the interpreter reports a syntax error, the error may not be on the line indicated by the error messages. First, check the line where the error was reported. If that line does not contain errors, check the preceding several lines in the script.

Some older Web browsers do not support scripting. In such browsers, the actual text of a script will often display in the Web page. To prevent this from happening, many script programmers enclose the script code in an HTML comment so the browser ignores the script if it does not support scripts. The syntax used is as follows:

```
<SCRIPT LANGUAGE = "JavaScript">
<!--
    script code here
// -->
</SCRIPT>
```

When a browser that does not support scripts encounters the preceding code, it ignores the **<SCRIPT>** and **</SCRIPT>** tags and the script code in the HTML comment. Browsers that do support scripting will interpret the JavaScript code as expected. [*Note:* The *JavaScript single-line comment* **//** (see section 13.3 for an explanation) before the ending HTML comment delimiter (**-->**) is required in some browsers for the script to interpret properly.]

Portability Tip 13.2

*Some browsers do not support the **<SCRIPT></SCRIPT>** tags. If your document is to be rendered with such browsers, the script code between these tags should be enclosed in an HTML comment so the script text does not display as part of the Web page.*

Welcome to JavaScript Programming! can be displayed in several ways. Figure 13.2 uses two JavaScript statements to produce one line of text in the HTML document. In this example, we also changed the color of the text displayed.

The majority of this HTML document is identical to Fig. 13.1, so we concentrate only on lines 9 and 10 of Fig. 13.2

```
document.write( "<FONT COLOR='magenta'><H1>Welcome to " );
document.writeln( "JavaScript Programming!</H1></FONT>" );
```

```
1   <!DOCTYPE html PUBLIC "-//W3C//DTD HTML 4.0 Transitional//EN">
2   <HTML>
3   <!-- Fig. 13.2: welcome.html -->
4
5   <HEAD>
6   <TITLE>Printing a Line with Multiple Statements</TITLE>
7
8   <SCRIPT LANGUAGE = "JavaScript">
9      document.write( "<FONT COLOR='magenta'><H1>Welcome to " );
10     document.writeln( "JavaScript Programming!</H1></FONT>" );
11  </SCRIPT>
12
13  </HEAD><BODY></BODY>
14  </HTML>
```

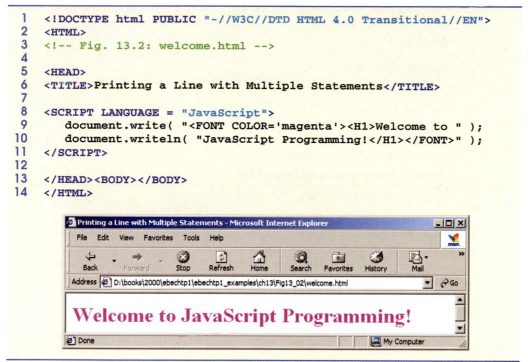

Fig. 13.2   Printing on one line with separate statements.

which display one line of text in the HTML document. The first statement uses **document** method *write* to display a string. Unlike **writeln**, **write** does not position the output cursor in the HTML document at the beginning of the next line after writing its argument. [*Note:* The output cursor keeps track of where the next character will be placed in the HTML document.] The next character written in the HTML document appears immediately after the last character written with **write**. Thus, when line 10 executes, the first character written, "**J**," appears immediately after the last character displayed with **write** (the space character inside the right double quote on line 9). Each **write** or **writeln** statement resumes writing characters where the last **write** or **writeln** stopped writing characters. So after a **writeln**, the next output appears on the next line. In effect, the preceding two statements result in one line of HTML text.

It is important to note that the preceding discussion has nothing to do with the actual rendering of the HTML text. Remember that the browser does not create a new line of text unless the browser window is too narrow for the text being rendered or an HTML element is encountered that causes the browser to start a new line—e.g., **
** to start a new line, **<P>** to start a new paragraph, etc.

Common Programming Error 13.3

Many people confuse the writing of HTML text with the rendering of HTML text. Writing HTML text creates the HTML that will be rendered by the browser for presentation to the user.

In the next example, we demonstrate that a single statement can cause the browser to display multiple lines by using line break HTML tags (**
**) throughout the string of

HTML text in a **write** or **writeln** method call. Figure 13.3 demonstrates using line break HTML tags.

Lines 8 and 9

```
document.writeln(
    "<H1>Welcome to<BR>JavaScript<BR>Programming!</H1>" );
```

produce three separate lines of text in the HTML document. Remember that statements in JavaScript are separated with semicolons (**;**). Therefore, lines 8 and 9 represent one statement. JavaScript allows large statements to be split over many lines. However, you cannot split a statement in the middle of a string.

Common Programming Error 13.4

Splitting a statement in the middle of a string is a syntax error.

The first several programs display text in the HTML document. Sometimes it is useful to display information in windows called *dialog boxes* that "pop up" on the screen to grab the user's attention. Dialog boxes are typically used to display important messages to the user who is browsing the Web page. JavaScript allows you to easily display a dialog box containing a message. The program of Fig. 13.4 displays **Welcome to JavaScript Programming**! as three lines in a predefined dialog box called an ***alert*** *dialog*.

```
1   <!DOCTYPE html PUBLIC "-//W3C//DTD HTML 4.0 Transitional//EN">
2   <HTML>
3   <!-- Fig. 13.3: welcome.html -->
4
5   <HEAD><TITLE>Printing Multiple Lines</TITLE>
6
7   <SCRIPT LANGUAGE = "JavaScript">
8      document.writeln(
9         "<H1>Welcome to<BR>JavaScript<BR>Programming!</H1>" );
10  </SCRIPT>
11
12  </HEAD><BODY></BODY>
13  </HTML>
```

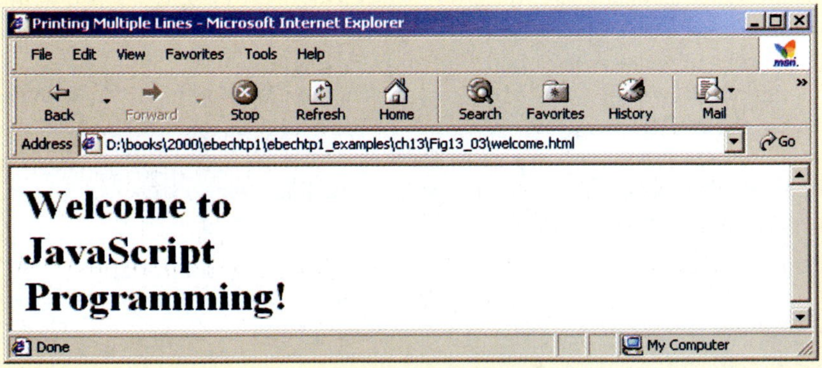

Fig. 13.3   Printing on multiple lines with a single statement.

```
 1  <!DOCTYPE HTML PUBLIC "-//W3C//DTD HTML 4.0 Transitional//EN">
 2  <HTML>
 3  <!-- Fig. 13.4: welcome.html -->
 4  <!-- Printing multiple lines in a dialog box -->
 5
 6  <HEAD>
 7
 8  <SCRIPT LANGUAGE = "JavaScript">
 9     window.alert( "Welcome to\nJavaScript\nProgramming!" );
10  </SCRIPT>
11
12  </HEAD>
13
14  <BODY>
15  <P>Click Refresh (or Reload) to run this script again.</P>
16  </BODY>
17  </HTML>
```

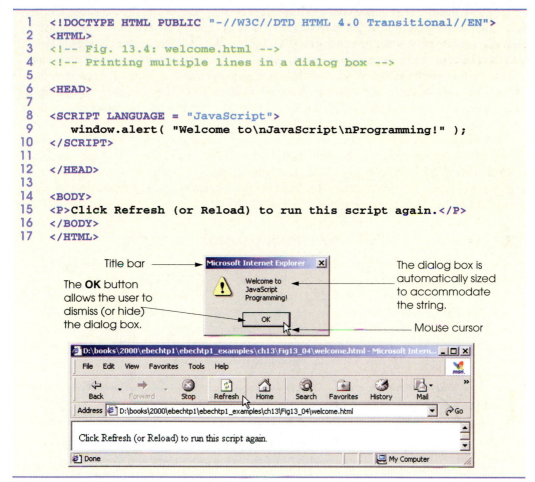

Fig. 13.4   Displaying multiple lines in a dialog box.

Line 9 in the script

```
window.alert( "Welcome to\nJavaScript\nProgramming!" );
```

uses the browser's **window** object to display an alert dialog box. Method **alert** of the **window** object requires as its argument the string to display. Executing the preceding statement displays the dialog box shown in the first window of Fig. 13.4. The *title bar* of the dialog contains the string **Microsoft Internet Explorer,** to indicate that the browser is presenting a message to the user. The dialog box automatically includes an **OK** button that allows the user to *dismiss (hide) the dialog* by pressing the button. This is accomplished by positioning the *mouse cursor* (also called the *mouse pointer*) over the **OK** button and clicking the mouse.

Common Programming Error 13.5

Dialog boxes display plain text—they do not render HTML. Therefore, specifying HTML elements as part of a string to display in a dialog box results in the actual characters of the tags being displayed.

Note that the alert dialog contains three lines of plain text. Normally the characters in a string are displayed in a dialog box exactly as they appear between the double quotes. Notice, however, that the two characters "****" and "**n**" are not displayed in the dialog box. The *backslash* (****) in a string is an *escape character.* It indicates that a "special" character is to be used in the string. When a backslash is encountered in a string of characters, the next character is combined with the backslash to form an *escape sequence.* The escape sequence **\n** is the *newline character.* In a dialog box, the newline character causes the *cursor* (the current screen position indicator) to move to the beginning of the next line in the dialog box. Some other common escape sequences are listed in Fig. 13.5. The **\n**, **\t** and **\r** escape sequences in the table do not affect HTML rendering unless they are in a **PRE** element (this element displays the text between its tags in a fixed-width font exactly as it is formatted between the tags). The other escape sequences result in characters that will be displayed in plain text dialog boxes and in HTML.

13.3 Another JavaScript Program: Adding Integers

Our next script inputs two *integers* (whole numbers such as 7, –11, 0, 31914) typed by a user at the keyboard, computes the sum of these values and displays the result.

This script uses another predefined dialog box from the **window** object, one called a ***prompt*** *dialog,* that allows the user to input a value for use in the script. The program displays the results of the addition in the HTML document. Figure 13.6 shows the script and some sample screen captures. [Note: In later JavaScript chapters, we will obtain input via GUI components in HTML forms, as introduced in Chapter 10].

Escape sequence	Description
\n	Newline. Position the screen cursor to the beginning of the next line.
\t	Horizontal tab. Move the screen cursor to the next tab stop.
\r	Carriage return. Position the screen cursor to the beginning of the current line; do not advance to the next line. Any characters output after the carriage return overwrite the previous characters output on that line.
****	Backslash. Used to represent a backslash character in a string.
\"	Double quote. Used to represent a double quote character in a string contained in double quotes. For example, `    window.alert( "\"in quotes\"" );` displays **"in quotes"** in an **alert** dialog.
\'	Single quote. Used to represent a single quote character in a string. For example, `    window.alert( '\'in quotes\'' );` displays **'in quotes'** in an **alert** dialog.

Fig. 13.5   Some common escape sequences.

```
1   <!DOCTYPE html PUBLIC "-//W3C//DTD HTML 4.0 Transitional//EN">
2   <HTML>
3   <!-- Fig. 13.6: Addition.html -->
4
5   <HEAD>
6   <TITLE>An Addition Program</TITLE>
7
8   <SCRIPT LANGUAGE = "JavaScript">
9      var firstNumber,     // first string entered by user
10         secondNumber,    // second string entered by user
11         number1,         // first number to add
12         number2,         // second number to add
13         sum;             // sum of number1 and number2
14
15      // read in first number from user as a string
16      firstNumber = window.prompt( "Enter first integer", "0" );
17
18      // read in second number from user as a string
19      secondNumber = window.prompt( "Enter second integer", "0" );
20
21      // convert numbers from strings to integers
22      number1 = parseInt( firstNumber );
23      number2 = parseInt( secondNumber );
24
25      // add the numbers
26      sum = number1 + number2;
27
28      // display the results
29      document.writeln( "<H1>The sum is " + sum + "</H1>" );
30   </SCRIPT>
31
32   </HEAD>
33   <BODY>
34   <P>Click Refresh (or Reload) to run the script again</P>
35   </BODY>
36   </HTML>
```

Explorer User Prompt ✕

JavaScript Prompt:
Enter first integer

OK
Cancel

45

Explorer User Prompt ✕

JavaScript Prompt:
Enter second integer

OK
Cancel

72

Fig. 13.6   An addition script "in action" (part 1 of 2).

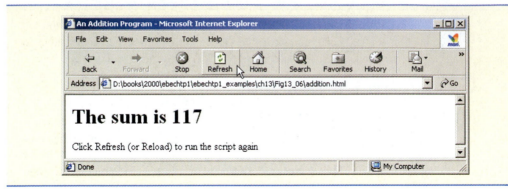

Fig. 13.6 An addition script "in action" (part 2 of 2).

Lines 9 through 13

```
var firstNumber,     // first string entered by user
    secondNumber,    // second string entered by user
    number1,         // first number to add
    number2,         // second number to add
    sum;             // sum of number1 and number2
```

are a *declaration*. The keyword **var** at the beginning of the statement indicates that the words **firstNumber**, **secondNumber**, **number1**, **number2** and **sum** are the names of *variables*. A variable is a location in the computer's memory where a value can be stored for use by a program. All variables should be declared with a name in a **var** statement before they are used in a program. Although using **var** to declare variables is not required, we will see in Chapter 16, "JavaScript/JScript: Functions," that **var** sometimes ensures proper behavior of a script.

A variable name can be any valid *identifier*. An identifier is a series of characters consisting of letters, digits, underscores (_) and dollar signs ($) that does not begin with a digit and does not contain any spaces. Some valid identifiers are **Welcome**, **$value**, **_value**, **m_inputField1** and **button7**. The name **7button** is not a valid identifier because it begins with a digit, and the name **input field** is not a valid identifier because it contains a space. Remember that JavaScript is *case sensitive*—uppercase and lowercase letters are different, so **firstNumber**, **FiRsTnUmBeR** and **FIRSTNUMBER** are different identifiers.

Good Programming Practice 13.5

Choosing meaningful variable names helps a script to be "self-documenting" (one that is easy to understand by simply reading it, rather than having to read manuals or excessive comments).

Good Programming Practice 13.6

*By convention, variable name identifiers begin with a lowercase first letter. Every word in the name after the first word should begin with a capital first letter. For example, identifier **firstNumber** has a capital **N** in its second word **Number**.*

Common Programming Error 13.6

Splitting a statement in the middle of an identifier is normally a syntax error.

Declarations (like statements) end with a semicolon (**;**) and can be split over several lines (as shown here) with each variable in the declaration separated by a comma—known as a *comma-separated list* of variable names. Several variables may be declared either in one declaration or in multiple declarations. We could have written five declarations, one for each variable, but the preceding single declaration is more concise.

Programmers often indicate the purpose of each variable in the program by placing a JavaScript comment at the end of each line in the declaration. In lines 9 through 13, *single-line comments* that begin with the characters **//** are used to state the purpose of each variable in the script. This form of comment is called a single-line comment because the comment terminates at the end of the line. A **//** comment can begin at any position in a line of JavaScript code and continues until the end of that line. Comments do not cause the browser to perform any action when the script is interpreted; rather, comments are ignored by the JavaScript interpreter.

Good Programming Practice 13.7

Some programmers prefer to declare each variable on a separate line. This format allows for easy insertion of a descriptive comment next to each declaration.

Another comment notation facilitates writing *multiple-line comments*. For example,

```
/* This is a multiple-line
   comment. It can be
   split over many lines. */
```

is a comment that can spread over several lines. Such comments begin with delimiter **/*** and end with delimiter ***/**. All text between the delimiters of the comment is ignored by the compiler.

Common Programming Error 13.7

Forgetting one of the delimiters of a multiple-line comment is a syntax error.

Common Programming Error 13.8

Nesting multiple-line comments (placing a multiple-line comment between the delimiters of another multiple-line comment) is a syntax error.

Note: JavaScript adopted comments delimited with **/*** and ***/** from the C programming language and single-line comments delimited with **//** from the C++ programming language. JavaScript programmers generally use C++-style single-line comments in preference to C-style comments. Throughout this book, we use C++-style single-line comments.

Line 15

```
// read in first number from user as a string
```

is a single-line comment indicating the purpose of the statement at line 16.

Line 16

```
firstNumber = window.prompt( "Enter first integer", "0" );
```

allows the user to enter a string representing the first of the two integers that will be added. The **window** object's *prompt* method displays the following **prompt** dialog:

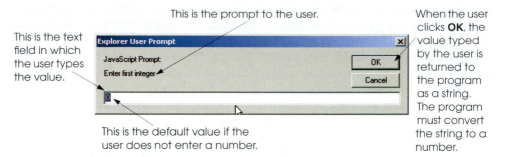

This is the prompt to the user.

This is the text field in which the user types the value.

When the user clicks **OK**, the value typed by the user is returned to the program as a string. The program must convert the string to a number.

This is the default value if the user does not enter a number.

The first argument to **prompt** indicates to the user what to do in the text field. This message is called a *prompt* because it directs the user to take a specific action. The optional second argument is the default string to display in the text field—if the second argument is not supplied, the text field does not contain a default value. The user types characters in the text field, then clicks the **OK** button to return the string to the program. [If you type and nothing appears in the text field, position the mouse pointer in the text field and click the mouse to activate the text field.] Unfortunately, JavaScript does not provide a simple form of input that is analogous to writing a line of text with **document.write** and **document.writeln**. For this reason, we normally receive input from a user through a GUI component such as the **prompt** dialog in this program or through an HTML form GUI component, as we will see in later chapters.

Technically, the user can type anything in the text field of the **prompt** dialog. For this program, if the user either types a non-integer value or clicks the **Cancel** button, a run-time logic error will occur and the sum of the two values will appear in the HTML document as *NaN* (*not a number*). In Chapter 18, "JavaScript: Objects," we discuss the **Number** object and its methods that can be used to determine whether a value is not a number.

The result of the call to **window.prompt** (a string containing the characters typed by the user) is given to variable **firstNumber** with the *assignment operator =*. The statement is read as, "**firstNumber**, *gets* the value of **window.prompt("Enter first integer", "0")**." The = operator is called a *binary operator* because it has two *operands*—**firstNumber** and the result of the expression **window.prompt("Enter first integer", "0")**. This whole statement is called an *assignment statement*, because it assigns a value to a variable. The expression to the right of the assignment operator = is always evaluated first.

Lines 18 and 19

```
// read in second number from user as a string
secondNumber = window.prompt( "Enter second integer", "0" );
```

consist of a single-line comment (line 18) that indicates the purpose of the statement at line 19. The statement displays a **prompt** dialog in which the user types a string representing the second of the two integers that will be added.

Lines 22 and 23

```
number1 = parseInt( firstNumber );
number2 = parseInt( secondNumber );
```

convert the two strings input by the user to **int** values that can be used in a calculation. Function **parseInt** converts its string argument to an integer. The integer returned by

parseInt in line 22 is assigned to variable **number1**. Any subsequent references to **number1** in the program use this same integer value. The integer returned by **parseInt** in line 23 is assigned to variable **number2**. Any subsequent references to **number2** in the program use this same integer value. [Note: We refer to **parseInt** as a *function* rather than a *method* because we do not precede the function call with an object name (such as **document** or **window**) and a dot operator (**.**). The term method implies that the function belongs to a particular object. For example, method **writeln** belongs to the **document** object and method **prompt** belongs to the **window** object.]

The assignment statement at line 26

```
sum = number1 + number2;
```

calculates the sum of the variables **number1** and **number2** and assigns the result to variable **sum** by using the assignment operator **=**. The statement is read as, "**sum** *gets* the value of **number1 + number2**." Most calculations are performed in assignment statements.

Good Programming Practice 13.8

Place spaces on either side of a binary operator. This makes the operator stand out and makes the program more readable.

After performing the calculation on line 26, on line 29 of the script,

```
document.writeln( "<H1>The sum is " + sum + "</H1>" );
```

displays the result of the addition using **document.writeln**. The expression

```
"<H1>The sum is " + sum + "</H1>"
```

from the preceding statement uses the operator **+** to "add" a string (the literal **"<H1>The sum is "**) and **sum** (the variable containing the integer result of the addition on line 26). JavaScript has a version of the **+** operator for *string concatenation* that enables a string and a value of another data type (including another string) to be concatenated—the result of this operation is a new (and normally longer) string. If we assume that **sum** contains the value **117**, the expression evaluates as follows: JavaScript determines that the two operands of the **+** operator (the string **"<H1>The sum is "** and the integer **sum**) are different types and one of them is a string. Next, the value of variable **sum** is automatically converted to a string and concatenated with **"<H1>The sum is "**, which results in the string **"<H1>The sum is 117"**. Next, the string **"</H1>"** is concatenated to produce the string **"<H1>The sum is 117</H1>"**. This string is rendered by the browser as part of the HTML document. Note that the automatic conversion of integer **sum** occurs because it is concatenated with the string literal **"<H1>The sum is "**. Also note that the space between **is** and **117** is part of the string **"<H1>The sum is "**.

Common Programming Error 13.9

Confusing the + operator used for string concatenation with the + operator used for addition can lead to strange results. For example, assuming integer variable y has the value 5, the expression "y + 2 = " + y + 2 results in the string "y + 2 = 52", not "y + 2 = 7", because first the value of y is concatenated with the string "y + 2 = ", then the value 2 is concatenated with the new larger string "y + 2 = 5". The expression "y + 2 = " + (y + 2) produces the desired result.

After the browser interprets the **<HEAD>** section of the HTML document (which contains the JavaScript), it then interprets the **<BODY>** of the HTML document (lines 33 through 35) and renders the HTML. If you click your browser's **Refresh** (or **Reload**) button, the browser will reload the HTML document so that you can execute the script again and add two new integers. [*Note:* In some cases, it may be necessary to hold the Shift key while clicking your browser's **Refresh** (or **Reload**) button to ensure that the HTML document reloads properly.]

13.4 Memory Concepts

Variable names such as **number1**, **number2** and **sum** actually correspond to *locations* in the computer's memory. Every variable has a *name,* a *type* and a *value*.

In the addition program of Fig. 13.6, when the statement

```
number1 = parseInt( firstNumber );
```

executes, the string **firstNumber** (previously entered by the user in a **prompt** dialog) is converted to an integer and placed into a memory location to which the name **number1** has been assigned by the compiler. Suppose the user entered the string **45** as the value for **firstNumber**. The program converts **firstNumber** to an integer, and the computer places that integer value **45** into location **number1** as shown in Fig. 13.7.

Whenever a value is placed in a memory location, this new value replaces the previous value in that location. The previous value is lost.

When the statement

```
number2 = parseInt( secondNumber );
```

executes, suppose the user entered the string **72** as the value for **secondNumber**. The program converts **secondNumber** to an integer and the computer places that integer value **72** into location **number2** and memory appears as shown in Fig. 13.8.

Once the program has obtained values for **number1** and **number2**, it adds these values and places the sum into variable **sum**. The statement

```
sum = number1 + number2;
```

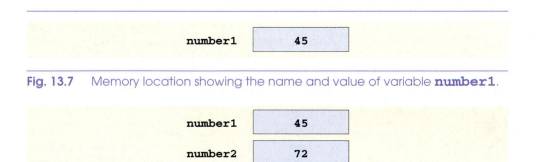

Fig. 13.7   Memory location showing the name and value of variable **number1**.

Fig. 13.8   Memory locations after values for variables **number1** and **number2** have been input.

performs the addition also replaces **sum**'s previous value. After **sum** is calculated, memory appears as shown in Fig. 13.9. Note that the values of **number1** and **number2** appear exactly as they did before they were used in the calculation of **sum**. These values were used, but not destroyed, as the computer performed the calculation. When a value is read from a memory location, the process is nondestructive.

13.5 Arithmetic

Many scripts perform arithmetic calculations. The *arithmetic operators* are summarized in Fig. 13.10. Note the use of various special symbols not used in algebra. The *asterisk (*)* indicates multiplication; the *percent sign (%)* is the *modulus operator*, which is discussed shortly. The arithmetic operators in Fig. 13.10 are called binary operators, because each operates on two operands. For example, the expression **sum + value** contains the binary operator + and the two operands **sum** and **value**.

JavaScript provides the modulus operator, **%**, which yields the remainder after division. The expression **x % y** yields the remainder after **x** is divided by **y**. Thus, **7.4 % 3.1** yields **1.2** and **17 % 5** yields **2**. In later chapters, we consider many interesting applications of the modulus operator such as determining whether one number is a multiple of another. There is no arithmetic operator for exponentiation in JavaScript. (Chapter 15 shows how to perform exponentiation in JavaScript.)

number1	45
number2	72
sum	117

Fig. 13.9 Memory locations after a calculation.

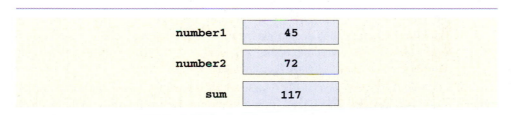

JavaScript operation	Arithmetic operator	Algebraic expression	JavaScript expression
Addition	+	$f + 7$	**f + 7**
Subtraction	–	$p - c$	**p - c**
Multiplication	*	bm	**b * m**
Division	/	$x / y \ or \ \dfrac{x}{y} \ or \ x \div y$	**x / y**
Modulus	%	$r \bmod s$	**r % s**

Fig. 13.10 Arithmetic operators.

Arithmetic expressions in JavaScript must be written in *straight-line form* to facilitate entering programs into the computer. Thus, expressions such as "**a** divided by **b**" must be written as **a / b** so that all constants, variables and operators appear in a straight line. The following algebraic notation is generally not acceptable to computers:

$$\frac{a}{b}$$

Parentheses are used in JavaScript expressions in the same manner as in algebraic expressions. For example, to multiply **a** times the quantity **b + c** we write:

```
a * ( b + c )
```

JavaScript applies the operators in arithmetic expressions in a precise sequence determined by the following *rules of operator precedence,* which are generally the same as those followed in algebra:

1. Operators in expressions contained between a left parenthesis and its corresponding right parenthesis are evaluated first. Thus, *parentheses may be used to force the order of evaluation to occur in any sequence desired by the programmer.* Parentheses are said to be at the "highest level of precedence." In cases of *nested* or *embedded* parentheses, the operators in the innermost pair of parentheses are applied first.

2. Multiplication, division and modulus operations are applied next. If an expression contains several multiplication, division and modulus operations, operators are applied from left to right. Multiplication, division and modulus are said to have the same level of precedence.

3. Addition and subtraction operations are applied last. If an expression contains several addition and subtraction operations, operators are applied from left to right. Addition and subtraction have the same level of precedence.

The rules of operator precedence enable JavaScript to apply operators in the correct order. When we say that operators are applied from left to right, we are referring to the *associativity* of the operators—the order in which operators of equal priority are evaluated. We will see that some operators associate from right to left. Figure 13.11 summarizes these rules of operator precedence. This table will be expanded as additional JavaScript operators are introduced. A complete precedence chart is included in Appendix D.

Now let us consider several expressions in light of the rules of operator precedence. Each example lists an algebraic expression and its JavaScript equivalent.

The following is an example of an arithmetic mean (average) of five terms:

Algebra: $m = \dfrac{a+b+c+d+e}{5}$

JavaScript: `m = (a + b + c + d + e) / 5;`

The parentheses are required because division has higher precedence than addition. The entire quantity **(a + b + c + d + e)** is to be divided by **5**. If the parentheses are erroneously omitted, we obtain **a + b + c + d + e / 5**, which evaluates as

$$a+b+c+d+\frac{e}{5}$$

Operator(s)	Operation(s)	Order of evaluation (precedence)
( )	Parentheses	Evaluated first. If the parentheses are nested, the expression in the innermost pair is evaluated first. If there are several pairs of parentheses "on the same level" (not nested), they are evaluated left to right.
*, / or %	Multiplication Division Modulus	Evaluated second. If there are several, they are evaluated left to right.
+ or −	Addition Subtraction	Evaluated last. If there are several, they are evaluated left to right.

Fig. 13.11 Precedence of arithmetic operators.

The following is an example of the equation of a straight line:

Algebra: $y = mx + b$

JavaScript: `y = m * x + b;`

No parentheses are required. The multiplication is applied first, because multiplication has a higher precedence than addition. The assignment occurs last because it has a lower precedence than multiplication and addition.

The following example contains modulus (**%**), multiplication, division, addition and subtraction operations:

Algebra: $z = pr\%q + w/x - y$

JavaScript: `z = p * r % q + w / x - y;`
                  ⑥   ①   ②   ④   ③   ⑤

The circled numbers under the statement indicate the order in which JavaScript applies the operators. The multiplication, modulus and division are evaluated first in left-to-right order (they associate from left to right), because they have higher precedence than addition and subtraction. The addition and subtraction are applied next. These are also applied left to right.

Not all expressions with several pairs of parentheses contain nested parentheses. For example, the expression

      `a * (b + c) + c * (d + e)`

does not contain nested parentheses. Rather, the parentheses are said to be "on the same level." To develop a better understanding of the rules of operator precedence, consider how a second-degree polynomial ($y = ax^2 + bx + c$) is evaluated.

```
y = a * x * x + b * x + c;
     ⑥   ①   ②   ④   ③   ⑤
```

The circled numbers under the statement indicate the order in which JavaScript applies the operators. There is no arithmetic operator for exponentiation in JavaScript, so x^2 is represented as **x * x**.

Suppose **a**, **b**, **c** and **x** are initialized as follows: **a = 2, b = 3, c = 7** and **x = 5**. Figure 13.12 illustrates the order in which the operators are applied in the preceding second-degree polynomial.

As in algebra, it is acceptable to place unnecessary parentheses in an expression to make the expression clearer. These unnecessary parentheses are also called *redundant parentheses*. For example, the preceding assignment statement might be parenthesized as

```
y = (a * x * x) + (b * x) + c;
```

Good Programming Practice 13.9

Using parentheses for more complex arithmetic expressions even when the parentheses are not necessary can make the arithmetic expressions easier to read.

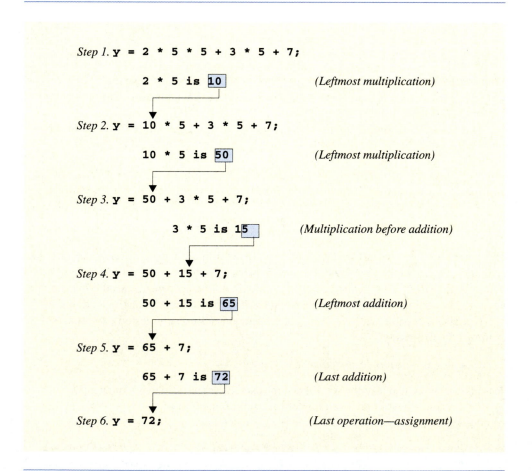

Fig. 13.12   Order in which a second-degree polynomial is evaluated.

13.6 Decision Making: Equality and Relational Operators

This section introduces a version of JavaScript's *if structure* that allows a program to make a decision based on the truth or falsity of a *condition*. If the condition is met (the condition is *true*), the statement in the body of the **if** structure is executed. If the condition is not met (the condition is *false*), the body statement is not executed. We will see an example shortly.

Conditions in **if** structures can be formed by using the *equality operators* and *relational operators* summarized in Fig. 13.13. The relational operators all have the same level of precedence and associate left to right. The equality operators both have the same level of precedence, which is lower than the precedence of the relational operators. The equality operators also associate left to right.

Common Programming Error 13.10
It is a syntax error if the operators ==, !=, >= and <= contain spaces between their symbols, as in = =, ! =, > = and < =, respectively.

Common Programming Error 13.11
Reversing the operators !=, >= and <=, as in =!, => and =<, are all syntax errors.

Common Programming Error 13.12
Confusing the equality operator == with the assignment operator = is a logic error. The equality operator should be read "is equal to" and the assignment operator should be read "gets" or "gets the value of." Some people prefer to read the equality operator as "double equals" or "equals equals."

The following script uses six **if** statements to compare two values input into **prompt** dialogs by the user. If the condition in any of these **if** statements is satisfied, the assignment statement associated with that **if** is executed. The user inputs two values through input dialogs. The values are stored in the variables **first** and **second**. Then, the comparisons are performed and the results of the comparison are displayed in an information dialog. The script and sample outputs are shown in Fig. 13.14.

Standard algebraic equality operator or relational operator	JavaScript equality or relational operator	Sample JavaScript condition	Meaning of JavaScript condition
Equality operators			
=	==	x == y	**x** is equal to **y**
≠	!=	x != y	**x** is not equal to **y**
Relational operators			
>	>	x > y	**x** is greater than **y**
<	<	x < y	**x** is less than **y**
≥	>=	x >= y	**x** is greater than or equal to **y**
≤	<=	x <= y	**x** is less than or equal to **y**

Fig. 13.13 Equality and relational operators.

```
1    <!DOCTYPE html PUBLIC "-//W3C//DTD HTML 4.0 Transitional//EN">
2    <HTML>
3    <!-- Fig. 13.14: comparison.html -->
4    <!-- Using if statements, relational operators, -->
5    <!-- and equality operators -->
6
7    <HEAD>
8    <TITLE>Performing Comparisons</TITLE>
9
10   <SCRIPT LANGUAGE = "JavaScript">
11      var first,    // first string entered by user
12          second;   // second string entered by user
13
14      // read first number from user as a string
15      first = window.prompt( "Enter first integer:", "0" );
16
17      // read second number from user as a string
18      second = window.prompt( "Enter second integer:", "0" );
19
20      document.writeln( "<H1>Comparison Results</H1>" );
21      document.writeln( "<TABLE BORDER = '1' WIDTH = '100%'>" );
22
23      if ( first == second )
24         document.writeln( "<TR><TD>" + first + " == " + second +
25                           "</TD></TR>" );
26
27      if ( first != second )
28         document.writeln( "<TR><TD>" + first + " != " + second +
29                           "</TD></TR>" );
30
31      if ( first < second )
32         document.writeln( "<TR><TD>" + first + " < " + second +
33                           "</TD></TR>" );
34
35      if ( first > second )
36         document.writeln( "<TR><TD>" + first + " > " + second +
37                           "</TD></TR>" );
38
39      if ( first <= second )
40         document.writeln( "<TR><TD>" + first + " <= " + second +
41                           "</TD></TR>" );
42
43      if ( first >= second )
44         document.writeln( "<TR><TD>" + first + " >= " + second +
45                           "</TD></TR>" );
46
47      // Display results
48      document.writeln( "</TABLE>" );
49   </SCRIPT>
50
51   </HEAD>
```

Fig. 13.14 Using equality and relational operators (part 1 of 4).

```
52   <BODY>
53   <P>Click Refresh (or Reload) to run the script again</P>
54   </BODY>
55   </HTML>
```

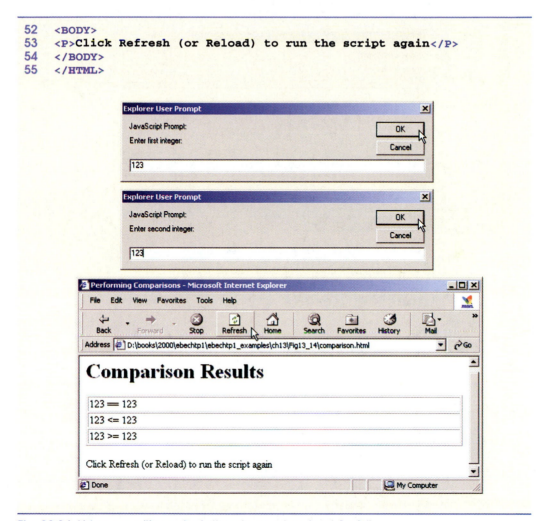

Fig. 13.14 Using equality and relational operators (part 2 of 4).

Lines 11 and 12

```
var first,    // first string entered by user
    second;   // second string entered by user
```

declare the variables used in the script. Remember that variables may be declared in one declaration or in multiple declarations. If more than one name is declared in a declaration (as in this example), the names are separated by commas (**,**). This is referred to as a comma-separated list. Once again, notice the comment at the end of each line indicating the purpose of each variable in the program.

Line 15

```
first = window.prompt( "Enter first integer:", "0" );
```

uses **window.prompt** to allow the user to input the first value and store it in **first**.

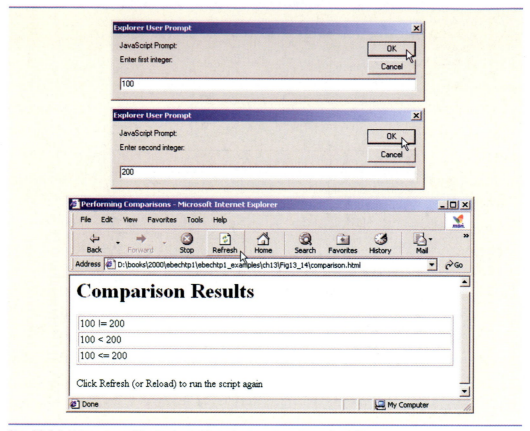

Fig. 13.14 Using equality and relational operators (part 3 of 4).

Line 18

```
second = window.prompt( "Enter second integer:", "0" );
```

uses **window.prompt** to allow the user to input the second value and store it in **second**.

Line 20 outputs a line of HTML text containing the **<H1>** head **Comparison Results**. Line 21 outputs a line of HTML text that indicates the start of a **<TABLE>** that has a 1-pixel border and is 100% of the browser window's width.

The **if** structure from lines 23 though 25

```
if ( first == second )
    document.writeln( "<TR><TD>" + first + " == " + second +
                      "</TD></TR>" );
```

compares the values of variables **number1** and **number2** to test for equality. If the values are equal, the statement at lines 24 and 25 outputs a line of HTML text representing one row of an HTML table (as indicated with the **<TR>** and **</TR>** tags). The text in the row contains the result of **first + " == " + second**. As in Fig. 13.6, the **+** operator is used in this expression to perform string concatenation. If the conditions are true in one or more of the **if** structures starting at lines 27, 31, 35, 39 and 43, the corresponding **document.writeln** statement(s) output a line of HTML text representing a row in the HTML table.

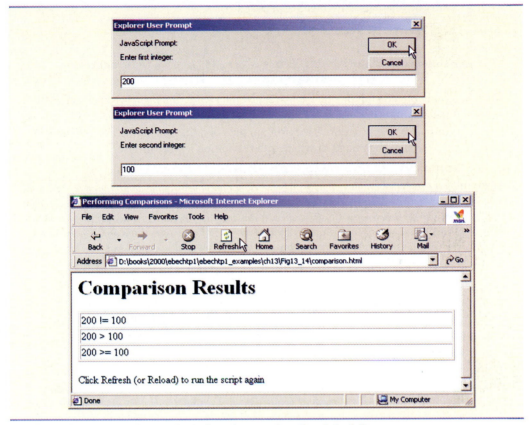

Fig. 13.14 Using equality and relational operators (part 4 of 4).

Notice the indentation in the **if** statements throughout the program. Such indentation enhances program readability.

Good Programming Practice 13.10

*Indent the statement in the body of an **if** structure to make the body of the structure stand out and to enhance program readability.*

Good Programming Practice 13.11

Place only one statement per line in a program. This enhances program readability.

Common Programming Error 13.13

*Forgetting the left and right parentheses for the condition in an **if** structure is a syntax error. The parentheses are required.*

Notice that there is no semicolon (**;**) at the end of the first line of each **if** structure. Such a semicolon would result in a logic error at execution time. For example,

```
if ( first == second ) ;
   document.writeln( "<TR><TD>" + first + " == " + second +
                     "</TD></TR>" );
```

would actually be interpreted by JavaScript as

```
if ( first == second )
    ;

document.writeln( "<TR><TD>" + first + " == " + second +
                  "</TD></TR>" );
```

where the semicolon on the line by itself—called the *empty statement*—is the statement to execute if the condition in the **if** structure is true. When the empty statement executes, no task is performed in the program. The program then continues with the assignment statement, which executes regardless of whether the condition is true or false.

Common Programming Error 13.14

*Placing a semicolon immediately after the right parenthesis of the condition in an **if** structure is normally a logic error. The semicolon would cause the body of the **if** structure to be empty, so the **if** structure itself would perform no action, regardless of whether its condition is true. Worse yet, the intended body statement of the **if** structure would now become a statement in sequence with the **if** structure and would always be executed.*

Notice the use of spacing in Fig. 13.14. Remember that whitespace characters such as tabs, newlines and spaces are normally ignored by the compiler. So, statements may be split over several lines and may be spaced according to the programmer's preferences without affecting the meaning of a program. It is incorrect to split identifiers and string literals. Ideally, statements should be kept small, but it is not always possible to do so.

Good Programming Practice 13.12

A lengthy statement may be spread over several lines. If a single statement must be split across lines, choose breaking points that make sense, such as after a comma in a comma-separated list, or after an operator in a lengthy expression. If a statement is split across two or more lines, indent all subsequent lines.

The chart in Fig. 13.15 shows the precedence of the operators introduced in this chapter. The operators are shown top to bottom in decreasing order of precedence. Notice that all these operators, with the exception of the assignment operator **=**, associate from left to right. Addition is left associative, so an expression like **x + y + z** is evaluated as if it had been written **(x + y) + z**. The assignment operator **=** associates from right to left, so an expression like **x = y = 0** is evaluated as if it had been written **x = (y = 0)**, which, as we will soon see, first assigns the value **0** to variable **y** and then assigns the result of that assignment, **0**, to **x**.

Good Programming Practice 13.13

Refer to the operator precedence chart when writing expressions containing many operators. Confirm that the operators in the expression are performed in the order you expect. If you are uncertain about the order of evaluation in a complex expression, use parentheses to force the order, exactly as you would do in algebraic expressions. Be sure to observe that some operators, such as assignment (=), associate right to left rather than left to right.

We have introduced many important features of JavaScript, including displaying data, inputting data from the keyboard, performing calculations and making decisions. In Chapter 14, we build on the techniques of Chapter 13 as we introduce *structured programming*. You will become more familiar with indentation techniques. We will study how to specify and vary the order in which statements are executed—this order is called *flow of control*.

Operators	Associativity	Type
( )	left to right	parentheses
* / %	left to right	multiplicative
+ -	left to right	additive
< <= > >=	left to right	relational
== !=	left to right	equality
=	right to left	assignment

Fig. 13.15   Precedence and associativity of the operators discussed so far.

13.7 JavaScript Internet and World Wide Web Resources

There are a tremendous number of resources for JavaScript programmers on the Internet and World Wide Web. This section lists a variety of JScript, JavaScript and ECMAScript resources available on the Internet and provides a brief description of each. Additional resources for these topics are presented in the subsequent JavaScript chapters and in other chapters as necessary.

www.ecma.ch/stand/ecma-262.htm
JScript is Microsoft's version of *JavaScript*—a scripting language that is standardized by the *ECMA (European Computer Manufacturer's Association)* as *ECMAScript*. This site is the home of the standard document for ECMAScript.

msdn.microsoft.com/scripting/default.htm
The *Microsoft Windows Script Technologies* page includes an overview of JScript complete with tutorials, FAQ, demos, tools for download and newsgroups.

www.webteacher.com/javatour/framehol.htm
Webteacher.com is an excellent source for tutorials that focus on teaching with detailed explanations and examples. This site is particularly useful for nonprogrammers.

wsabstract.com/
Website Abstraction is devoted to JavaScript with specialized tutorials and many free scripts. This is a good site for beginners, as well as those with experience who are looking for help in a specific area of JavaScript.

builder.cnet.com/Programming/JsTips/
This site provides 30 tips for using JavaScript to improve your HTML programming. Tips are divided into the following categories: controlling windows, tips to add fun and functionality, tips to simplify your scripts and tips to master syntax.

SUMMARY

• The JavaScript language facilitates a disciplined approach to designing computer programs that enhance Web pages.

• JScript is Microsoft's version of JavaScript—a scripting language that is standardized by the ECMA (European Computer Manufacturer's Association) as ECMAScript.

• Together, blank lines, space characters and tab characters are known as whitespace (space characters and tabs are known specifically as whitespace characters).

- The spacing displayed by a browser in a Web page is determined by the HTML elements used to format the page.
- The **<HTML>** tag indicates the beginning of the HTML document.
- Often JavaScripts appear in the **<HEAD>** section of the HTML document.
- The browser interprets the contents of the **<HEAD>** section first.
- The **<SCRIPT>** tag indicates to the browser that the text that follows is part of a script. Attribute **LANGUAGE** specifies the scripting language used in the script—such as **JavaScript**.
- A string of characters can be contained between the double (**"**) or single quotation (**'**) marks.
- A string is sometimes called a character string, a message or a string literal.
- The browser's **document** object represents the HTML document currently being displayed in the browser. The **document** object allows a script programmer to specify HTML text to be displayed in the HTML document.
- The browser contains a complete set of objects that allow script programmers to access and manipulate every element of an HTML document.
- An object resides in the computer's memory and contains information used by the script. The term object normally implies that attributes (data) and behaviors (methods) are associated with the object. The object's methods use the attributes to provide useful services to the client of the object—the script that calls the methods.
- The **document** object's **writeln** method writes a line of HTML text in the HTML document.
- The parentheses following a method name contain the arguments that the method requires to perform its task (or its action).
- Using **writeln** to write a line of HTML text into the **document** does not guarantee that a corresponding line of text will appear in the HTML document. The text displayed is dependent on the contents of the string written which is subsequently rendered by the browser. The browser will interpret the HTML elements as it normally does to render the final text in the document.
- Every statement should end with a semicolon (also known as the statement terminator), although none is required by JavaScript.
- JavaScript is case sensitive. Not using the proper uppercase and lowercase letters is a syntax error.
- Sometimes it is useful to display information in windows called dialog boxes that "pop up" on the screen to grab the user's attention. Dialog boxes are typically used to display important messages to the user who is browsing the Web page. The browser's **window** object displays an alert dialog box with method **alert**. Method **alert** requires as its argument the string to display.
- When a backslash is encountered in a string of characters, the next character is combined with the backslash to form an escape sequence. The escape sequence **\n** is the newline character. It causes the cursor in the HTML document to move to the beginning of the next line in the dialog box.
- The keyword **var** is used to declare the names of variables. A variable is a location in the computer's memory where a value can be stored for use by a program. Though not required, all variables should be declared with a name in a **var** statement before they are used in a program.
- A variable name can be any valid identifier consisting of letters, digits, underscores (**_**) and dollar signs (**$**) that does not begin with a digit and does not contain any spaces.
- Declarations end with a semicolon (**;**) and can be split over several lines with each variable in the declaration separated by a comma (a comma-separated list of variable names). Several variables may be declared in one declaration or in multiple declarations.
- Programmers often indicate the purpose of each variable in the program by placing a JavaScript comment at the end of each line in the declaration. A single-line comment begins with the charac-

ters **//** and terminate at the end of the line. Comments do not cause the browser to perform any action when the script is interpreted; rather, comments are ignored by the JavaScript interpreter.

- Multiple-line comments begin with delimiter **/*** and end with delimiter ***/**. All text between the delimiters of the comment is ignored by the compiler.

- The **window** object's **prompt** method displays a dialog into which the user can type a value. The first argument is a message (called a prompt) that directs the user to take a specific action. The optional second argument is the default string to display in the text field.

- A variable is assigned a value with an assignment statement using the assignment operator **=**. The **=** operator is called a binary operator because it has two operands.

- Function **parseInt** converts its string argument to an integer.

- JavaScript has a version of the **+** operator for string concatenation that enables a string and a value of another data type (including another string) to be concatenated.

- Variable names correspond to locations in the computer's memory. Every variable has a name, a type, a size and a value.

- When a value is placed in a memory location, this value replaces the previous value in that location. When a value is read out of a memory location, the process is nondestructive.

- The arithmetic operators are binary operators because they each operate on two operands.

- Operators in arithmetic expressions are applied in a precise sequence determined by the rules of operator precedence.

- Parentheses may be used to force the order of evaluation of operators to occur in any sequence desired by the programmer.

- When we say operators are applied from left to right, we are referring to the associativity of the operators. Some operators associate from right to left.

- Java's **if** structure allows a program to make a decision based on the truth or falsity of a condition. If the condition is met (the condition is true), the statement in the body of the **if** structure is executed. If the condition is not met (the condition is false), the body statement is not executed.

- Conditions in **if** structures can be formed by using the equality operators and relational operators.

TERMINOLOGY

\n newline escape sequence.
<HEAD> section of the HTML document
<SCRIPT></SCRIPT>
addition operator (**+**)
alert dialog
alert method of the **window** object
argument to a method
arithmetic expressions in straight-line form
arithmetic operator
assignment operator (**=**)
assignment statement
attribute
automatic conversion
backslash (****) escape character
behavior
binary operator
blank line

case sensitive
character string
client of an object
comma-separated list
comment
condition
data
decision making
declaration
dialog box
division operator (**/**)
document object
double quotation (**"**) marks
ECMA
ECMAScript
empty statement
equality operators

error message
escape sequence
European Computer Manufacturer's Association
false
identifier
if structure
inline scripting
integer
interpreter
JavaScript
JavaScript interpreter
JScript
LANGUAGE attribute of the **<SCRIPT>** tag
location in the computer's memory
logic error
meaningful variable names
method
modulus operator (**%**)
multiple-line comment (**/*** and ***/**)
multiplication operator (*****)
name of a variable
object
operand
operator associativity
operator precedence
parentheses
parseInt function
perform an action
program
prompt
prompt dialog

prompt method of the **window** object
redundant parentheses
relational operators
remainder after division
rules of operator precedence
runtime error
script
scripting language
self-documenting
semicolon (**;**) statement terminator
single quotation (**'**) marks
single-line comment (**//**)
statement
string concatenation
string concatenation operator (**+**)
string literal
string of characters
subtraction operator (**-**)
syntax error
text field
true
type of a variable
value of a variable
var keyword
variable
violation of the language rules
whitespace characters
whole number
window object
write method of the **document** object
writeln method of the **document** object

SELF-REVIEW EXERCISES

13.1   Fill in the blanks in each of the following.
  a) _____ begins a single-line comment.
  b) Every statement should end with a _____.
  c) The _____ structure is used to make decisions.
  d) _____, _____, _____ and _____ are known as whitespace.
  e) The _____ object displays alert dialogs and prompt dialogs.
  f) _____ are reserved for use by JavaScript.
  g) Methods _____ and _____ of the _____ object write HTML text into an HTML document.

13.2   State whether each of the following is *true* or *false*. If *false*, explain why.
  a) Comments cause the computer to print the text after the **//** on the screen when the program is executed.
  b) JavaScript considers the variables **number** and **NuMbEr** to be identical.
  c) The modulus operator (**%**) can be used only with any numeric operands.
  d) The arithmetic operators *****, **/**, **%**, **+** and **-** all have the same level of precedence.
  e) Method **parseInt** converts an integer to a string.

13.3 Write JavaScript statements to accomplish each of the following:
   a) Declare variables **c**, **thisIsAVariable**, **q76354** and **number**.
   b) Display a dialog asking the user to enter an integer. Show a default value of **0** in the text field.
   c) Convert a string to an integer and store the converted value in variable **age**. Assume that the string is stored in **stringValue**.
   d) If the variable **number** is not equal to **7**, display **"The variable number is not equal to 7"** in a message dialog.
   e) Output a line of HTML text that will display the message **"This is a JavaScript program"** on one line in the HTML document.
   f) Output a line of HTML text that will display the message **"This is a JavaScript program"** on two lines in the HTML document. Use only one statement.

13.4 Identify and correct the errors in each of the following statements:
   a) `if ( c < 7 );`
           `window.alert( "c is less than 7" );`
   b) `if ( c => 7 )`
           `window.alert( "c is equal to or greater than 7" );`

13.5 Write a statement (or comment) to accomplish each of the following:
   a) State that a program will calculate the product of three integers.
   b) Declare the variables **x**, **y**, **z** and **result**.
   c) Declare the variables **xVal**, **yVal** and **zVal**.
   d) Prompt the user to enter the first value, read the value from the user and store it in the variable **xVal**.
   e) Prompt the user to enter the second value, read the value from the user and store it in the variable **yVal**.
   f) Prompt the user to enter the third value, read the value from the user and store it in the variable **zVal**.
   g) Convert **xVal** to an integer and store the result in the variable **x**.
   h) Convert **yVal** to an integer and store the result in the variable **y**.
   i) Convert **zVal** to an integer and store the result in the variable **z**.
   j) Compute the product of the three integers contained in variables **x**, **y** and **z**, and assign the result to the variable **result**.
   k) Write a line of HTML text containing the string **"The product is "** followed by the value of the variable **result**.

13.6 Using the statements you wrote in Exercise 13.5, write a complete program that calculates and prints the product of three integers.

ANSWERS TO SELF-REVIEW EXERCISES

13.1 a) `//`. b) Semicolon (`;`). c) `if`. d) Blank lines, space characters, newline characters and tab characters. e) **window**. f) Keywords. g) **write, writeln, document**.

13.2 a) False. Comments do not cause any action to be performed when the program is executed. They are used to document programs and improve their readability. b) False. JavaScript is case sensitive, so these variables are distinct. c) True. d) False. The operators *****, **/** and **%** are on the same level of precedence and the operators **+** and **–** are on a lower level of precedence. e) False. Function **parseInt** converts a string to an integer value.

13.3 a) `var c, thisIsAVariable, q76354, number;`
       b) `value = window.prompt( "Enter an integer", "0" );`
       c) `var age = parseInt( stringValue );`

d) `if ( number != 7 )`
     `window.alert( "The variable number is not equal to 7" );`
e) `document.writeln( "This is a JavaScript program" );`
f) `document.writeln( "This is a<BR>JavaScript program" );`

13.4 a) Error: Semicolon after the right parenthesis of the condition in the **if** statement.
      Correction: Remove the semicolon after the right parenthesis. [*Note:* The result of this error is that the output statement is executed whether or not the condition in the **if** statement is true. The semicolon after the right parenthesis is considered an empty statement—a statement that does nothing. We discuss the empty statement in the next chapter.]
      b) Error: The relational operator **=>** is incorrect.
      Correction: Change **=>** to **>=**.

13.5 a) `// Calculate the product of three integers`
      b) `var x, y, z, result;`
      c) `var xVal, yVal, zVal;`
      d) `xVal = window.prompt( "Enter first integer:", "0" );`
      e) `yVal = window.prompt( "Enter second integer:", "0" );`
      f) `zVal = window.prompt( "Enter third integer:", "0" );`
      g) `x = parseInt( xVal );`
      h) `y = parseInt( yVal );`
      i) `z = parseInt( zVal );`
      j) `result = x * y * z;`
      k) `document.writeln(`
           `<H1>"The product is " + result + "</H1>" );`

13.6   The program is:

```
1   <!DOCTYPE html PUBLIC "-//W3C//DTD HTML 4.0 Transitional//EN">
2   <!-- Exercise 13.6: product.html -->
3
4   <HTML>
5   <HEAD>
6   <TITLE>Product of Three Integers</TITLE>
7
8   <SCRIPT LANGUAGE = "JavaScript">
9      // Calculate the product of three integers
10     var x, y, z, result;
11     var xVal, yVal, zVal;
12
13     xVal = window.prompt( "Enter first integer:", "0" );
14     yVal = window.prompt( "Enter second integer:", "0" );
15     zVal = window.prompt( "Enter third integer:", "0" );
16
17     x = parseInt( xVal );
18     y = parseInt( yVal );
19     z = parseInt( zVal );
20
21     result = x * y * z;
22     document.writeln( "<H1>The product is " + result + "<H1>" );
23  </SCRIPT>
24
25  </HEAD><BODY></BODY>
26  </HTML>
```

EXERCISES

13.7   Fill in the blanks in each of the following:
   a) _____ are used to document a program and improve its readability.
   b) A dialog capable of receiving input from the user is displayed with method _____ of object _____.
   c) A JavaScript statement that makes a decision is _____.
   d) Calculations are normally performed by _____ statements.
   e) A dialog capable of showing a message to the user is displayed with method _____ of object _____.

13.8   Write JavaScript statements that accomplish each of the following:
   a) Display the message **"Enter two numbers"** using the **window** object.
   b) Assign the product of variables **b** and **c** to variable **a**.
   c) State that a program performs a sample payroll calculation (*Hint:* use text that helps to document a program).

13.9   State whether each of the following is *true* or *false*. If *false*, explain why.
   a) JavaScript operators are evaluated from left to right.
   b) The following are all valid variable names: **_under_bar_, m928134, t5, j7, her_sales$, his_$account_total, a, b$, c, z, z2**.
   c) A valid JavaScript arithmetic expression with no parentheses is evaluated from left to right.
   d) The following are all invalid variable names: **3g, 87, 67h2, h22, 2h.**

13.10   Fill in the blanks in each of the following:
   a) What arithmetic operations have the same precedence as multiplication? _____.
   b) When parentheses are nested, which set of parentheses is evaluated first in an arithmetic expression? _____.
   c) A location in the computer's memory that may contain different values at various times throughout the execution of a program is called a _____.

13.11   What displays in the message dialog when each of the following JavaScript statements is performed? Assume **x = 2** and **y = 3**.
   a) **window.alert("x = " + x);**
   b) **window.alert("The value of x + x is " + (x + x));**
   c) **window.alert("x =");**
   d) **window.alert((x + y) + " = " + (y + x));**

13.12   Which of the following JavaScript statements contain variables whose values are destroyed (changed or replaced)?
   a) **p = i + j + k + 7;**
   b) **window.alert("variables whose values are destroyed");**
   c) **window.alert("a = 5");**
   d) **stringVal = window.prompt("Enter string:");**

13.13   Given $y = ax^3 + 7$, which of the following are correct statements for this equation?
   a) **y = a * x * x * x + 7;**
   b) **y = a * x * x * (x + 7);**
   c) **y = (a * x) * x * (x + 7);**
   d) **y = (a * x) * x * x + 7;**
   e) **y = a * (x * x * x) + 7;**
   f) **y = a * x * (x * x + 7);**

13.14   State the order of evaluation of the operators in each of the following JavaScript statements and show the value of **x** after each statement is performed.

```
a) x = 7 + 3 * 6 / 2 - 1;
b) x = 2 % 2 + 2 * 2 - 2 / 2;
c) x = ( 3 * 9 * ( 3 + ( 9 * 3 / ( 3 ) ) ) );
```

13.15 Write a script that displays the numbers 1 to 4 on the same line with each pair of adjacent numbers separated by one space. Write the program using the following methods.
  a) Using one **document.writeln** statement.
  b) Using four **document.write** statements.

13.16 Write a script that asks the user to enter two numbers, obtains the two numbers from the user and outputs HTML text that displays the sum, product, difference and quotient of the two numbers. Use the techniques shown in Fig. 13.6.

13.17 Write a script that asks the user to enter two integers, obtains the numbers from the user and outputs HTML text that displays the larger number followed by the words "**is larger**" in an information message dialog. If the numbers are equal, output HTML text that displays the message "**These numbers are equal**." Use the techniques shown in Fig. 13.14.

13.18 Write a script that inputs three integers from the user and displays the sum, average, product, smallest and largest of these numbers in an **alert** dialog.

13.19 Write a script that inputs from the user the radius of a circle and outputs HTML text that displays the circle's diameter, circumference and area. Use the constant value 3.14159 for π. Use the GUI techniques shown in Fig. 13.6. [*Note:* You may also use the predefined constant **Math.PI** for the value of π. This constant is more precise than the value 3.14159. The **Math** object is defined by JavaScript and provides many common mathematical capabilities.] Use the following formulas (*r* is the radius): *diameter* = 2r, *circumference* = 2πr, *area* = πr^2.

13.20 Write a script that outputs HTML text that displays in the HTML document an oval, an arrow and a diamond using asterisks (*****) as follows (Note: Use the **<PRE>** and **</PRE>** tags to specify that the asterisks should be displayed using a fixed-width font):

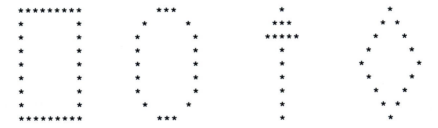

13.21 Modify the program you created in Exercise 13.20 to display the shapes without using the **<PRE>** and **</PRE>** tags. Does the program display the shapes exactly as in Exercise 13.20?

13.22 What does the following code print?

```
document.writeln( "*\n**\n***\n****\n*****" );
```

13.23 What does the following code print?

```
document.writeln( "*" );
document.writeln( "***" );
document.writeln( "*****" );
document.writeln( "****" );
document.writeln( "**" );
```

13.24　What does the following code print?

```
document.write( "*<BR>" );
document.write( "***<BR>" );
document.write( "*****<BR>" );
document.write( "****<BR>" );
document.writeln( "**" );
```

13.25　What does the following code print?

```
document.write( "*<BR>" );
document.writeln( "***" );
document.writeln( "*****" );
document.write( "****<BR>" );
document.writeln( "**" );
```

13.26　Write a script that reads five integers and determines and outputs HTML text that displays the largest and the smallest integers in the group. Use only the programming techniques you learned in this chapter.

13.27　Write a script that reads an integer and determines and outputs HTML text that displays whether it is odd or even. (*Hint:* Use the modulus operator. An even number is a multiple of 2. Any multiple of 2 leaves a remainder of zero when divided by 2.)

13.28　Write a script that reads in two integers and determines and outputs HTML text that displays whether the first is a multiple of the second. (*Hint:* Use the modulus operator.)

13.29　Write a script that outputs HTML text that displays in the HTML document a checkerboard pattern as follows:

```
* * * * * * * *
 * * * * * * * *
* * * * * * * *
 * * * * * * * *
* * * * * * * *
 * * * * * * * *
* * * * * * * *
 * * * * * * * *
```

13.30　Write a script that inputs five numbers and determines and outputs HTML text that displays the number of negative numbers input, the number of positive numbers input and the number of zeros input.

13.31　Using only the programming techniques you learned in this chapter, write a script that calculates the squares and cubes of the numbers from 0 to 10 and outputs HTML text that displays the resulting values in an HTML table format as follows:

```
number   square   cube
0        0        0
1        1        1
2        4        8
3        9        27
4        16       64
5        25       125
6        36       216
7        49       343
8        64       512
9        81       729
10       100      1000
```

[*Note:* This program does not require any input from the user.]

14

JavaScript/JScript: Control Structures I

Objectives

- To understand basic problem-solving techniques.
- To be able to develop algorithms through the process of top-down, stepwise refinement.
- To be able to use the **if** and **if/else** selection structures to choose among alternative actions.
- To be able to use the **while** repetition structure to execute statements in a script repeatedly.
- To understand counter-controlled repetition and sentinel-controlled repetition.
- To be able to use the increment, decrement and assignment operators.

Let's all move one place on.
Lewis Carroll

The wheel is come full circle.
William Shakespeare, *King Lear*

How many apples fell on Newton's head before he took the hint!
Robert Frost, Comment

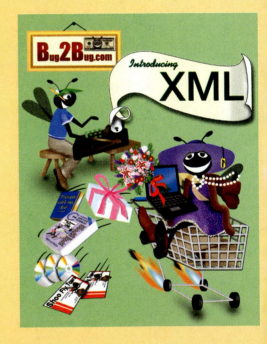

Outline

14.1 Introduction

Before writing a script to solve a problem, it is essential to have a thorough understanding of the problem and a carefully planned approach to solving the problem. When writing a script, it is equally essential to understand the types of building blocks that are available and to employ proven program construction principles. In this chapter and in Chapter 15, we discuss these issues in our presentation of the theory and principles of structured programming. The techniques you learn here are applicable to most high-level languages, including JavaScript.

14.2 Algorithms

Any computing problem can be solved by executing a series of actions in a specific order. A *procedure* for solving a problem in terms of

1. the *actions* to be executed, and

2. the *order* in which these actions are to be executed

is called an *algorithm*. The following example demonstrates that correctly specifying the order in which the actions are to be executed is important.

Consider the "rise-and-shine algorithm" followed by one junior executive for getting out of bed and going to work: (1) get out of bed, (2) take off pajamas, (3) take a shower, (4) get dressed, (5) eat breakfast, (6) carpool to work.

This routine gets the executive to work well-prepared to make critical decisions. Suppose, however, that the same steps are performed in a slightly different order: (1) get out of bed, (2) take off pajamas, (3) get dressed, (4) take a shower, (5) eat breakfast, (6) carpool to work.

In this case, our junior executive shows up for work soaking wet. Specifying the order in which statements are to be executed in a computer program is called *program control*. In this chapter and Chapter 15, we investigate the program control capabilities of JavaScript.

14.3 Pseudocode

Pseudocode is an artificial and informal language that helps programmers develop algorithms. The pseudocode we present here is particularly useful for developing algorithms that will be converted to structured portions of JavaScript programs. Pseudocode is similar to everyday English; it is convenient and user-friendly, although it is not an actual computer programming language.

Pseudocode is not actually executed on computers. Rather, it helps the programmer "think out" a program before attempting to write it in a programming language, such as JavaScript. In this chapter, we give several examples of pseudocode.

Software Engineering Observation 14.1

Pseudocode is often used to "think out" a program during the program design process. Then the pseudocode program is converted to a programming language such as JavaScript.

The style of pseudocode we present consists purely of characters, so programmers may conveniently type pseudocode using an editor program. The computer can produce a fresh printed copy of a pseudocode program on demand. Carefully prepared pseudocode may be converted easily to a corresponding JavaScript program. This is done in many cases simply by replacing pseudocode statements with their JavaScript equivalents.

Pseudocode normally describes only executable statements—the actions that are performed when the program is converted from pseudocode to JavaScript and is run. Declarations are not executable statements. For example, the declaration

```
var value1;
```

instructs the JavaScript interpreter to reserve space in memory for the variable **value1**. This declaration does not cause any action—such as input, output or a calculation—to occur when the script executes. Some programmers choose to list variables and mention the purpose of each at the beginning of a pseudocode program.

14.4 Control Structures

Normally, statements in a program are executed one after the other in the order in which they are written. This is called *sequential execution*. Various JavaScript statements we will soon discuss enable the programmer to specify that the next statement to be executed may be one other than the next one in sequence. This is called *transfer of control*.

During the 1960s, it became clear that the indiscriminate use of transfers of control was the root of much difficulty experienced by software development groups. The finger of blame was pointed at the **goto** *statement,* which allows the programmer to specify a transfer of control to one of a very wide range of possible destinations in a program. The notion of so-called *structured programming* became almost synonymous with "**goto elimination.**" JavaScript does not have a **goto** statement.

The research of Bohm and Jacopini[1] had demonstrated that programs could be written without any **goto** statements. The challenge of the era for programmers was to shift their styles to "**goto**-less programming." It was not until the 1970s that programmers started taking structured programming seriously. The results have been impressive, as software development groups have reported reduced development times, more frequent on-time delivery of systems and more frequent within-budget completion of software projects. The key to these successes is that structured programs are clearer, easier to debug and modify, and more likely to be bug-free in the first place.

Bohm and Jacopini's work demonstrated that all programs could be written in terms of only three *control structures*, namely the *sequence structure*, the *selection structure* and the *repetition structure*. The sequence structure is built into JavaScript. Unless directed otherwise, the computer executes JavaScript statements one after the other in the order in which they are written. The *flowchart* segment of Fig. 14.1 illustrates a typical sequence structure in which two calculations are performed in order.

A flowchart is a graphical representation of an algorithm or of a portion of an algorithm. Flowcharts are drawn using certain special-purpose symbols such as rectangles, diamonds, ovals and small circles; these symbols are connected by arrows called *flowlines,* which indicate the order in which the actions of the algorithm execute.

Like pseudocode, flowcharts are often useful for developing and representing algorithms, although pseudocode is strongly preferred by many programmers. Flowcharts show clearly how control structures operate; that is all we use them for in this text. The reader should carefully compare the pseudocode and flowchart representations of each control structure.

Consider the flowchart segment for the sequence structure on the left side of Fig. 14.1. We use the *rectangle symbol* (or *action symbol*) to indicate any type of action, including a calculation or an input/output operation. The flowlines in the figure indicate the order in which the actions are performed—first, **grade** is added to **total**, then **1** is added to **counter**. JavaScript allows us to have as many actions as we want in a sequence structure. As we will soon see, anywhere a single action may be placed, we may place several actions in sequence.

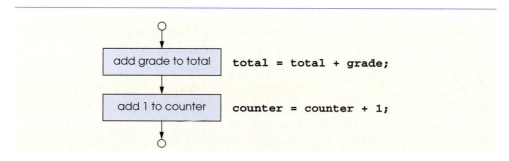

Fig. 14.1   Flowcharting JavaScript's sequence structure.

---

1. Bohm, C., and G. Jacopini, "Flow Diagrams, Turing Machines, and Languages with Only Two Formation Rules," *Communications of the ACM,* Vol. 9, No. 5, May 1966, pp. 336–371.

In a flowchart that represents a *complete* algorithm, an *oval symbol* containing the word "Begin" is the first symbol used in the flowchart; an oval symbol containing the word "End" indicates where the algorithm ends. In a flowchart that shows only a portion of an algorithm, as in Fig. 14.1, the oval symbols are omitted in favor of using *small circle symbols,* also called *connector symbols*.

Perhaps the most important flowcharting symbol is the *diamond symbol*, also called the *decision symbol,* which indicates that a decision is to be made. We will discuss the diamond symbol in the next section.

JavaScript provides three types of selection structures; we discuss each of these in this chapter and in Chapter 15. The **if** selection structure performs (selects) an action if a condition is true or skips the action if the condition is false. The **if/else** selection structure performs an action if a condition is true and performs a different action if the condition is false. The **switch** selection structure (Chapter 15) performs one of many different actions, depending on the value of an expression.

The **if** structure is called a *single-selection structure* because it selects or ignores a single action (or, as we will soon see, a single group of actions). The **if/else** structure is called a *double-selection structure* because it selects between two different actions (or groups of actions). The **switch** structure is called a *multiple-selection structure* because it selects among many different actions (or groups of actions).

JavaScript provides four types of repetition structures, namely **while**, **do/while**, **for** and **for/in** (**do/while** and **for** are covered in Chapter 15; **for/in** is covered in Chapter 17). Each of the words **if**, **else**, **switch**, **while**, **do**, **for** and **in** is a JavaScript *keyword*. These words are reserved by the language to implement various features, such as JavaScript's control structures. Keywords cannot be used as identifiers (such as for variable names). A complete list of JavaScript keywords is shown in Fig. 14.2.

Common Programming Error 14.1

Using a keyword as an identifier is a syntax error.

JavaScript Keywords				
break	case	continue	delete	do
else	false	for	function	if
in	new	null	return	switch
this	true	typeof	var	void
while	with			
Keywords that are reserved but not used by JavaScript				
catch	class	const	debugger	default
enum	export	extends	finally	import
super	try			

Fig. 14.2   JavaScript keywords.

As we have shown, JavaScript has only eight control structures: sequence, three types of selection and four types of repetition. Each program is formed by combining as many of each type of control structure as is appropriate for the algorithm the program implements. As with the sequence structure of Fig. 14.1, we will see that each control structure is flow-charted with two small circle symbols, one at the entry point to the control structure and one at the exit point.

Single-entry/single-exit control structures make it easy to build programs—the control structures are attached to one another by connecting the exit point of one control structure to the entry point of the next. This process is similar to the way a child stacks building blocks, so we call this *control-structure stacking*. We will learn that there is only one other way control structures may be connected—*control-structure nesting*. Thus, algorithms in JavaScript programs are constructed from only eight different types of control structures combined in only two ways.

14.5 The `if` Selection Structure

A selection structure is used to choose among alternative courses of action in a program. For example, suppose that the passing grade on an examination is 60 (out of 100). Then the pseudocode statement

> *If student's grade is greater than or equal to 60*
>   *Print "Passed"*

determines if the condition "student's grade is greater than or equal to 60" is true or false. If the condition is true, then "Passed" is printed, and the next pseudocode statement in order is "performed" (remember that pseudocode is not a real programming language). If the condition is false, the print statement is ignored, and the next pseudocode statement in order is performed. Note that the second line of this selection structure is indented. Such indentation is optional, but it is highly recommended because it emphasizes the inherent structure of structured programs. The JavaScript interpreter ignores whitespace characters: blanks, tabs and newlines used for indentation and vertical spacing. Programmers insert these whitespace characters to enhance program clarity.

Good Programming Practice 14.1

Consistently applying reasonable indentation conventions throughout your programs improves program readability. We suggest a fixed-size tab of about 1/4 inch or three spaces per indent.

The preceding pseudocode *If* statement may be written in JavaScript as

```
if ( studentGrade >= 60 )
   document.writeln( "Passed" );
```

Notice that the JavaScript code corresponds closely to the pseudocode. This similarity is why pseudocode is a useful program development tool. The statement in the body of the `if` structure outputs the character string **"Passed"** in the HTML document.

The flowchart of Fig. 14.3 illustrates the single-selection `if` structure. This flowchart contains what is perhaps the most important flowcharting symbol—the *diamond symbol* (or *decision symbol*) which indicates that a decision is to be made. The decision symbol contains an expression, such as a condition, that can be either **true** or **false**. The decision symbol has two flowlines emerging from it. One indicates the path to follow in the program when the expression in the symbol is true; the other indicates the path to follow in the program when the expression is false. A decision can be made on any expression that evaluates to a value of JavaScript's boolean type (any expression that evaluates to **true** or **false**).

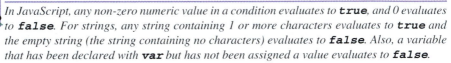

Software Engineering Observation 14.2

*In JavaScript, any non-zero numeric value in a condition evaluates to **true**, and 0 evaluates to **false**. For strings, any string containing 1 or more characters evaluates to **true** and the empty string (the string containing no characters) evaluates to **false**. Also, a variable that has been declared with **var** but has not been assigned a value evaluates to **false**.*

Note that the **if** structure is a single-entry/single-exit structure. We will soon learn that the flowcharts for the remaining control structures also contain (besides small circle symbols and flowlines) only rectangle symbols to indicate the actions to be performed and diamond symbols to indicate decisions to be made. This is the *action/decision model of programming*.

We can envision eight bins, each containing only control structures of one of the eight types. These control structures are empty. Nothing is written in the rectangles or in the diamonds. The programmer's task, then, is to assemble a program from as many of each type of control structure as the algorithm demands, combining those control structures in only two possible ways (stacking or nesting) and then filling in the actions and decisions in a manner appropriate for the algorithm. We will discuss the variety of ways in which actions and decisions may be written.

14.6 The `if/else` Selection Structure

The **if** selection structure performs an indicated action only when the condition evaluates to **true**; otherwise, the action is skipped. The **if/else** selection structure allows the programmer to specify that a different action is to be performed when the condition is true than when the condition is false. For example, the pseudocode statement

> *If student's grade is greater than or equal to 60*
> *   Print "Passed"*
> *else*
> *   Print "Failed"*

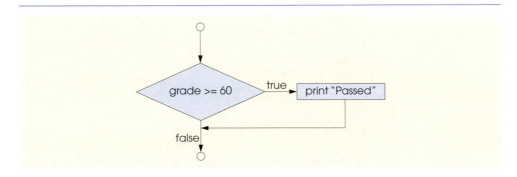

Fig. 14.3   Flowcharting the single-selection **if** structure.

prints *Passed* if the student's grade is greater than or equal to 60 and prints *Failed* if the student's grade is less than 60. In either case, after printing occurs, the next pseudocode statement in sequence (the next statement after the whole **if/else** structure) is "performed." Note that the body of the *else* is also indented.

Good Programming Practice 14.2

Indent both body statements of an **if/else** *structure.*

The indentation convention you choose should be carefully applied throughout your programs (both in pseudocode and in JavaScript). It is difficult to read programs that do not use uniform spacing conventions.

The preceding pseudocode *if/else* structure may be written in JavaScript as

```
if ( studentGrade >= 60 )
    document.writeln( "Passed" );
else
    document.writeln( "Failed" );
```

The flowchart of Fig. 14.4 nicely illustrates the flow of control in the **if/else** structure. Once again, note that the only symbols in the flowchart (besides small circles and arrows) are rectangles (for actions) and a diamond (for a decision). We continue to emphasize this action/decision model of computing. Imagine again a deep bin containing as many empty double-selection structures as might be needed to build a JavaScript algorithm. The programmer's job is to assemble the selection structures (by stacking and nesting) with other control structures required by the algorithm and to fill in the empty rectangles and empty diamonds with actions and decisions appropriate to the algorithm being implemented.

JavaScript provides an operator called the *conditional operator (?:)* that is closely related to the **if/else** structure. The operator **?:** is JavaScript's only *ternary operator*—it takes three operands. The operands together with the **?:** form a *conditional expression.* The first operand is a boolean expression, the second is the value for the conditional expression if the condition evaluates to true and the third is the value for the conditional expression if the condition evaluates to false. For example, the statement

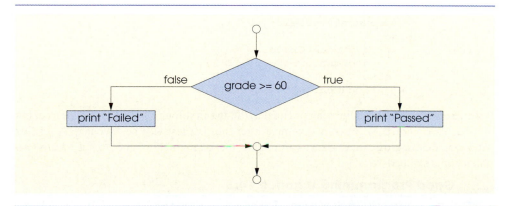

Fig. 14.4   Flowcharting the double-selection **if/else** structure.

```
document.writeln(
    studentGrade >= 60 ? "Passed" : "Failed" );
```

contains a conditional expression that evaluates to the string **"Passed"** if the condition
studentGrade >= 60 is true and evaluates to the string **"Failed"** if the condition is
false. Thus, this statement with the conditional operator performs essentially the same operation as the preceding **if/else** statement. The precedence of the conditional operator is
low, so the entire conditional expression is normally placed in parentheses.

*Nested **if/else** structures* test for multiple cases by placing **if/else** structures
inside **if/else** structures. For example, the following pseudocode statement will print **A**
for exam grades greater than or equal to 90, **B** for grades in the range 80 to 89, **C** for grades
in the range 70 to 79, **D** for grades in the range 60 to 69 and **F** for all other grades:

> *If student's grade is greater than or equal to 90*
> > *Print "A"*
>
> *else*
> > *If student's grade is greater than or equal to 80*
> > > *Print "B"*
> >
> > *else*
> > > *If student's grade is greater than or equal to 70*
> > > > *Print "C"*
> > >
> > > *else*
> > > > *If student's grade is greater than or equal to 60*
> > > > > *Print "D"*
> > > >
> > > > *else*
> > > > > *Print "F"*

This pseudocode may be written in JavaScript as

```
if ( studentGrade >= 90 )
    document.writeln( "A" );
else
    if ( studentGrade >= 80 )
        document.writeln( "B" );
    else
        if ( studentGrade >= 70 )
            document.writeln( "C" );
        else
            if ( studentGrade >= 60 )
                document.writeln( "D" );
            else
                document.writeln( "F" );
```

If **studentGrade** is greater than or equal to 90, the first four conditions will be true, but
only the **document.writeln** statement after the first test will be executed. After that
particular **document.writeln** is executed, the **else** part of the "outer" **if/else**
statement is skipped.

 Good Programming Practice 14.3

*If there are several levels of indentation, each level should be indented the same additional
amount of space.*

Most JavaScript programmers prefer to write the preceding **if** structure as

```
if ( grade >= 90 )
   document.writeln( "A" );
else if ( grade >= 80 )
   document.writeln( "B" );
else if ( grade >= 70 )
   document.writeln( "C" );
else if ( grade >= 60 )
   document.writeln( "D" );
else
   document.writeln( "F" );
```

The two forms are equivalent. The latter form is popular because it avoids the deep indentation of the code to the right. Such deep indentation often leaves little room on a line, forcing lines to be split and decreasing program readability.

It is important to note that the JavaScript interpreter always associates an **else** with the previous **if**, unless told to do otherwise by the placement of braces (**{}**). This is referred to as the *dangling-else problem*. For example,

```
if ( x > 5 )
   if ( y > 5 )
      document.writeln( "x and y are > 5" );
else
   document.writeln( "x is <= 5" );
```

appears to indicate with its indentation that if **x** is greater than **5**, the **if** structure in its body determines whether **y** is also greater than **5**. If so, the string **"x and y are > 5"** is output. Otherwise, it *appears* that if **x** is not greater than **5**, the **else** part of the **if/else** structure outputs the string **"x is <= 5"**.

Beware! The preceding nested **if** structure does not execute as it appears. The interpreter actually interprets the preceding structure as

```
if ( x > 5 )
   if ( y > 5 )
      document.writeln( "x and y are > 5" );
   else
      document.writeln( "x is <= 5" );
```

in which the body of the first **if** structure is an **if/else** structure. This structure tests whether **x** is greater than **5**. If so, execution continues by testing whether **y** is also greater than **5**. If the second condition is true, the proper string—**"x and y are > 5"**—is displayed. However, if the second condition is false, the string **"x is <= 5"** is displayed, even though we know **x** is greater than **5**.

To force the preceding nested **if** structure to execute as it was originally intended, the structure must be written as follows:

```
if ( x > 5 ) {
   if ( y > 5 )
      document.writeln( "x and y are > 5" );
}
else
   document.writeln( "x is <= 5" );
```

The braces (**{}**) indicate to the interpreter that the second **if** structure is in the body of the first **if** structure and that the **else** is matched with the first **if** structure. In Exercises 14.21 and 14.22 you will investigate the dangling-else problem further.

The **if** selection structure normally expects only one statement in its body. To include several statements in the body of an **if**, enclose the statements in braces (**{** and **}**). A set of statements contained within a pair of braces is called a *compound statement*.

Software Engineering Observation 14.3

A compound statement can be placed anywhere in a program that a single statement can be placed.

Software Engineering Observation 14.4

Unlike individual statements, a compound statement does not end with a semicolon. However, each statement within the braces of a compound statement should end with a semicolon.

The following example includes a compound statement in the **else** part of an **if/else** structure.

```
if ( grade >= 60 )
   document.writeln( "Passed" );
else {
   document.writeln( "Failed<BR>" );
   document.writeln( "You must take this course again." );
}
```

In this case, if **grade** is less than 60, the program executes both statements in the body of the **else** and prints

```
Failed.
You must take this course again.
```

Notice the braces surrounding the two statements in the **else** clause. These braces are important. Without the braces, the statement

```
document.writeln( "You must take this course again." );
```

would be outside the body of the **else** part of the **if** and would execute regardless of whether the grade is less than 60.

Common Programming Error 14.2

Forgetting one or both of the braces that delimit a compound statement can lead to syntax errors or logic errors.

Syntax errors (such as when one brace in a compound statement is left out of the program) are caught by the interpreter when it attempts to interpret the code containing the syntax error. A *logic error* (such as the one caused when both braces in a compound statement are left out of the program) also has its effect at execution time. A *fatal logic error* causes a program to fail and terminate prematurely. A *nonfatal logic error* allows a program to continue executing, but the program produces incorrect results.

Software Engineering Observation 14.5

Just as a compound statement can be placed anywhere a single statement can be placed, it is also possible to have no statement at all (the empty statement). The empty statement is represented by placing a semicolon (;) where a statement would normally be.

Common Programming Error 14.3

*Placing a semicolon after the condition in an **if** structure leads to a logic error in single-selection **if** structures and a syntax error in double-selection **if** structures (if the **if** part contains a nonempty body statement).*

Good Programming Practice 14.4

Some programmers prefer to type the beginning and ending braces of compound statements before typing the individual statements within the braces. This helps avoid omitting one or both of the braces.

14.7 The `while` Repetition Structure

A *repetition structure* allows the programmer to specify that an action is to be repeated while some condition remains true. The pseudocode statement

> *While there are more items on my shopping list*
> *Purchase next item and cross it off my list*

describes the repetition that occurs during a shopping trip. The condition "there are more items on my shopping list" may be true or false. If it is true, then the action "Purchase next item and cross it off my list" is performed. This action will be performed repeatedly while the condition remains true. The statement(s) contained in the *while* repetition structure constitute the body of the *while*. The *while* structure body may be a single statement or a compound statement. Eventually, the condition will become false (when the last item on the shopping list has been purchased and crossed off the list). At this point, the repetition terminates, and the first pseudocode statement after the repetition structure is executed.

Common Programming Error 14.4

*Not providing in the body of a **while** structure an action that eventually causes the condition in the **while** to become false is a logic error. Normally, such a repetition structure will never terminate—an error called an "infinite loop." Browsers handle infinite loops differently. For example, Internet Explorer allows the user to terminate the script containing the infinite loop.*

Common Programming Error 14.5

*Spelling the keyword **while** with an uppercase **W** as in **While** (remember that JavaScript is a case-sensitive language) is a syntax error. All of JavaScript's reserved keywords, such as **while**, **if** and **else**, contain only lowercase letters.*

As an example of a `while` structure, consider a program segment designed to find the first power of 2 larger than 1000. Suppose variable `product` has been initialized to 2. When the following `while` structure finishes executing, `product` contains the result:

```
var product = 2;

while ( product <= 1000 )
   product = 2 * product;
```

The flowchart of Fig. 14.5 illustrates the flow of control of the preceding `while` repetition structure. Once again, note that (besides small circles and arrows) the flowchart contains only a rectangle symbol and a diamond symbol.

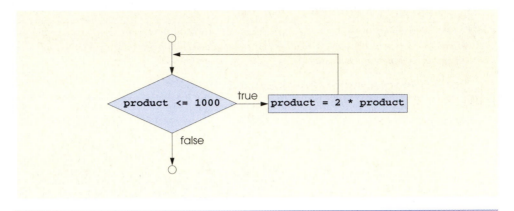

Fig. 14.5   Flowcharting the `while` repetition structure.

When the **while** structure is entered, **product** is 2. Variable **product** is repeatedly multiplied by 2, taking on the values 4, 8, 16, 32, 64, 128, 256, 512 and 1024 successively. When **product** becomes 1024, the condition **product <= 1000** in the **while** structure becomes **false**. This terminates the repetition with 1024 as **product**'s final value. Execution continues with the next statement after the **while**. [*Note:* If a **while** structure's condition is initially **false** the body statement(s) will never be performed.]

Imagine, again, a deep bin of empty **while** structures that may be stacked and nested with other control structures to form a structured implementation of an algorithm's flow of control. The empty rectangles and diamonds are then filled in with appropriate actions and decisions. The flowchart clearly shows the repetition. The flowline emerging from the rectangle wraps back to the decision, which is tested each time through the loop until the decision eventually becomes false. At this point, the **while** structure is exited, and control passes to the next statement in the program.

14.8 Formulating Algorithms: Case Study 1 (Counter-Controlled Repetition)

To illustrate how algorithms are developed, we solve several variations of a class-averaging problem. Consider the following problem statement:

> *A class of ten students took a quiz. The grades (integers in the range 0 to 100) for this quiz are available to you. Determine the class average on the quiz.*

The class average is equal to the sum of the grades divided by the number of students (10 in this case). The algorithm for solving this problem on a computer must input each of the grades, perform the averaging calculation and display the result.

Let us use pseudocode to list the actions to be executed and specify the order in which these actions should be executed. We use *counter-controlled repetition* to input the grades one at a time. This technique uses a variable called a *counter* to control the number of times a set of statements will execute. In this example, repetition terminates when the counter exceeds 10. In this section, we present a pseudocode algorithm (Fig. 14.6) and the corresponding program (Fig. 14.7). In the next section, we show how pseudocode algorithms are developed. Counter-controlled repetition is often called *definite repetition* because the number of repetitions is known before the loop begins executing.

Set total to zero
Set grade counter to one

While grade counter is less than or equal to ten
    Input the next grade
    Add the grade into the total
    Add one to the grade counter

Set the class average to the total divided by ten
Print the class average

Fig. 14.6   Pseudocode algorithm that uses counter-controlled repetition to solve the class-average problem.

Note the references in the algorithm to a total and a counter. A *total* is a variable used to accumulate the sum of a series of values. A counter is a variable used to count—in this case, to count the number of grades entered. Variables used to store totals should normally be initialized to zero before being used in a program.

Good Programming Practice 14.5

Variables to be used in calculations should be initialized before their use.

```
1   <!DOCTYPE html PUBLIC "-//W3C//DTD HTML 4.0 Transitional//EN">
2   <HTML>
3   <!-- Fig. 14.7: average.html -->
4
5   <HEAD>
6   <TITLE>Class Average Program</TITLE>
7
8   <SCRIPT LANGUAGE = "JavaScript">
9      var total,              // sum of grades
10         gradeCounter,       // number of grades entered
11         gradeValue,         // grade value
12         average,            // average of all grades
13         grade;              // grade typed by user
14
15     // Initialization Phase
16     total = 0;              // clear total
17     gradeCounter = 1;       // prepare to loop
18
19     // Processing Phase
20     while ( gradeCounter <= 10 ) {  // loop 10 times
21
22        // prompt for input and read grade from user
23        grade = window.prompt( "Enter integer grade:", "0" );
24
25        // convert grade from a String to an integer
26        gradeValue = parseInt( grade );
```

Fig. 14.7   Class-average program with counter-controlled repetition (part 1 of 3).

```
27
28        // add gradeValue to total
29        total = total + gradeValue;
30
31        // add 1 to gradeCounter
32        gradeCounter = gradeCounter + 1;
33     }
34
35     // Termination Phase
36     average = total / 10;   // calculate the average
37
38     // display average of exam grades
39     document.writeln(
40        "<H1>Class average is " + average + "</H1>" );
41  </SCRIPT>
42
43  </HEAD>
44  <BODY>
45  Click Refresh (or Reload) to run the script again
46  </BODY>
47  </HTML>
```

Fig. 14.7   Class-average program with counter-controlled repetition (part 2 of 3).

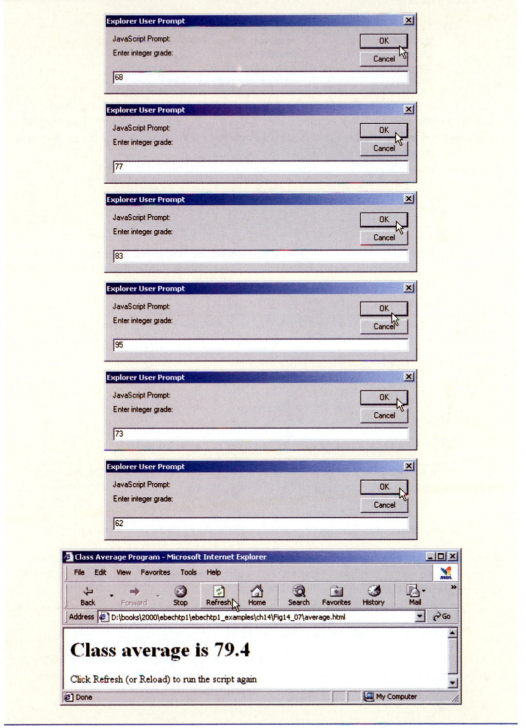

Fig. 14.7   Class-average program with counter-controlled repetition (part 3 of 3).

Lines 9 through 13,

```
var total,            // sum of grades
    gradeCounter,     // number of grades entered
    gradeValue,       // grade value
    average,          // average of all grades
    grade;            // grade typed by user
```

declare variables **total**, **gradeCounter**, **gradeValue**, **average** and **grade**. The variable **grade** will store the string the user types into the **prompt** dialog. The variable **gradeValue** will store the value of **grade** when its string representation that was returned from the **prompt** dialog is converted to an integer.

Lines 16 and 17

```
total = 0;            // clear total
gradeCounter = 1;     // prepare to loop
```

are assignment statements that initialize **total** to **0** and **gradeCounter** to **1**.

Note that variables **total** and **gradeCounter** are initialized before they are used in a calculation. Uninitialized variables used in calculations result in logic errors and produce the value *NaN* (not a number).

Common Programming Error 14.6

Not initializing a variable that will be used in a calculation results in a logic error. You must initialize the variable before it is used in a calculation.

Testing and Debugging Tip 14.1

Initialize variables that will be used in calculations.

Line 20

```
while ( gradeCounter <= 10 ) {  // loop 10 times
```

indicates that the **while** structure should continue as long as the value of the variable **gradeCounter** is less than or equal to 10.

Line 23

```
grade = window.prompt( "Enter integer grade:", "0" );
```

corresponds to the pseudocode statement *"Input the next grade."* The statement displays a **prompt** dialog with the prompt "**Enter integer grade:**" on the screen. The default value displayed in the dialog box's text field is **0**.

After the user enters the **grade**, it is converted from a string to an integer with line 26:

```
gradeValue = parseInt( grade );
```

Note that we must convert the string to an integer in this example. Otherwise, the addition statement at line 29 will be a string concatenation statement rather than a numeric sum.

Next, the program updates the **total** with the new **gradeValue** entered by the user. Line 29

```
total = total + gradeValue;
```

adds **gradeValue** to the previous value of **total** and assigns the result to **total**. This statement seems a bit strange, because it does not follow the rules of algebra. Keep in mind that operator precedence causes JavaScript to evaluate the addition (**+**) operation before the assignment (**=**) operation. The value of the expression on the right side of the assignment always replaces the value of the variable on the left side of the assignment.

The program is now ready to increment the variable **gradeCounter** to indicate that a grade has been processed and read the next grade from the user. Line 32

```
gradeCounter = gradeCounter + 1;
```

adds **1** to **gradeCounter**, so the condition in the **while** structure will eventually become **false** and terminate the loop. After this statement executes, the program continues by testing the condition in the **while** at line 20. If the condition is still true, the statements from lines 23 through 32 are repeated. Otherwise the program continues execution with the first statement in sequence after the body of the loop.

Line 36

```
average = total / 10;  // calculate the average
```

assigns the results of the average calculation to variable **average**. Lines 39 and 40

```
document.writeln(
    "<H1>Class average is " + average + "</H1>" );
```

write a line of HTML text in the document that displays the string **"Class average is "** followed by the value of variable **average** as an **<H1>** head in the browser.

After saving the HTML document, load it into Internet Explorer to execute the script. Note that this script reads only integer values from the user. In the sample program execution of Fig. 14.7, the sum of the values entered (100, 88, 93, 55, 68, 77, 83, 95, 73 and 62) is 794. Although the script reads only integers, the averaging calculation in the program does not produce an integer. Rather, the calculation produces a *floating-point number* (a number containing a decimal point). The average for the 10 integers input by the user in this example is 79.4.

Software Engineering Observation 14.6

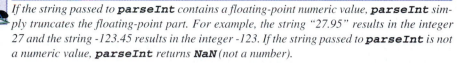

*If the string passed to **parseInt** contains a floating-point numeric value, **parseInt** simply truncates the floating-point part. For example, the string "27.95" results in the integer 27 and the string -123.45 results in the integer -123. If the string passed to **parseInt** is not a numeric value, **parseInt** returns **NaN** (not a number).*

JavaScript actually represents all numbers as floating-point numbers in memory. Floating-point numbers often develop through division, as shown in this example. When we divide 10 by 3, the result is 3.3333333…, with the sequence of 3s repeating infinitely. The computer allocates only a fixed amount of space to hold such a value, so the stored floating-point value can only be an approximation. Despite the fact that floating-point numbers are not always "100% precise," they have numerous applications. For example, when we speak of a "normal" body temperature of 98.6 we do not need to be precise to a large number of digits. When we view the temperature on a thermometer and read it as 98.6, it may actually be 98.5999473210643. The point here is that few applications require high-precision floating-point values, so calling this number simply 98.6 is fine for most applications.

Common Programming Error 14.7

Using floating-point numbers in a manner that assumes they are precisely represented real numbers can lead to incorrect results. Real numbers are represented only approximately by computers. For example, no fixed-size floating-point representation of PI can ever be precise because PI is a transcendental number whose value cannot be expressed in a finite amount of space.

14.9 Formulating Algorithms with Top-Down, Stepwise Refinement: Case Study 2 (Sentinel-Controlled Repetition)

Let us generalize the class-average problem. Consider the following problem:

> *Develop a class-averaging program that will process an arbitrary number of grades each time the program is run.*

In the first class-average example, the number of grades (10) was known in advance of our inputting the data. In this example, no indication is given of how many grades are to be entered. The program must process an arbitrary number of grades. How can the program determine when to stop the input of grades? How will it know when to calculate and display the class average?

One way to solve this problem is to use a special value called a *sentinel value* (also called a *signal value*, a *dummy value* or a *flag value*) to indicate "end of data entry." The user types grades in until all legitimate grades have been entered. The user then types the sentinel value to indicate that the last grade has been entered. Sentinel-controlled repetition is often called *indefinite repetition,* because the number of repetitions is not known before the loop begins executing.

Clearly, the sentinel value must be chosen so that it cannot be confused with an acceptable input value. Because grades on a quiz are normally nonnegative integers from 0 to 100, –1 is an acceptable sentinel value for this problem. Thus, a run of the class-average program might process a stream of inputs such as 95, 96, 75, 74, 89 and –1. The program would then compute and print the class average for the grades 95, 96, 75, 74 and 89 (–1 is the sentinel value, so it should not enter into the average calculation).

Common Programming Error 14.8

Choosing a sentinel value that is also a legitimate data value results in a logic error and may prevent a sentinel-controlled loop from terminating properly.

We approach the class-average program with a technique called *top-down, stepwise refinement*, a technique that is essential to the development of well-structured algorithms. We begin with a pseudocode representation of the *top:*

> *Determine the class average for the quiz*

The top is a single statement that conveys the overall purpose of the program. As such, the top is, in effect, a complete representation of a program. Unfortunately, the top rarely conveys a sufficient amount of detail from which to write the JavaScript algorithm. So, we now begin the refinement process. We divide the top into a series of smaller tasks and list these in the order in which they need to be performed, creating the following *first refinement*:

> *Initialize variables*
> *Input, sum up and count the quiz grades*
> *Calculate and print the class average*

Here, only the sequence structure has been used—the steps listed are to be executed in order, one after the other.

Software Engineering Observation 14.7

Each refinement, as well as the top itself, is a complete specification of the algorithm; only the level of detail varies.

To proceed to the next level of refinement (the *second refinement*), we commit to specific variables. We need a running total of the numbers, a count of how many numbers have been processed, a variable to receive the string representation of each grade as it is input, a variable to store the value of the grade after it is converted to an integer and a variable to hold the calculated average. The pseudocode statement

> *Initialize variables*

may be refined as follows:

> *Initialize total to zero*
> *Initialize gradeCounter to zero*

Notice that only the variables *total* and *gradeCounter* are initialized before they are used; the variables *average*, *grade* and *gradeValue* (for the calculated average, the user input and the integer representation of the *grade*, respectively) need not be initialized, because their values are determined as they are calculated or input.

The pseudocode statement

> *Input, sum up and count the quiz grades*

requires a repetition structure (a loop) that successively inputs each grade. Because we do not know how many grades are to be processed, we will use sentinel-controlled repetition. The user at the keyboard will type legitimate grades in one at a time. After the last legitimate grade is typed, the user will type the sentinel value. The program will test for the sentinel value after each grade is input and will terminate the loop when the sentinel value is entered by the user. The second refinement of the preceding pseudocode statement is then

> *Input the first grade (possibly the sentinel)*
> *While the user has not as yet entered the sentinel*
>> *Add this grade into the running total*
>> *Add one to the grade counter*
>> *Input the next grade (possibly the sentinel)*

Notice that in pseudocode, we do not use braces around the pseudocode that forms the body of the *while* structure. We simply indent the pseudocode under the *while* to show that it belongs to the body of the *while*. Remember, pseudocode is only an informal program development aid.

The pseudocode statement

> *Calculate and print the class average*

may be refined as follows:

> *If the counter is not equal to zero*
>> *Set the average to the total divided by the counter*
>> *Print the average*
> *else*
>> *Print "No grades were entered"*

Notice that we are testing for the possibility of division by zero—a *logic error* that, if undetected, would cause the program to produce invalid output. The complete second refinement of the pseudocode algorithm for the class-average problem is shown in Fig. 14.8.

Testing and Debugging Tip 14.2

When performing division by an expression whose value could be zero, explicitly test for this case and handle it appropriately in your program (such as printing an error message) rather than allowing the division by zero to occur.

Good Programming Practice 14.6

Include completely blank lines in pseudocode programs to make the pseudocode more readable. The blank lines separate pseudocode control structures and separate the phases of the programs.

Software Engineering Observation 14.8

Many algorithms can be divided logically into three phases: an initialization phase that initializes the program variables; a processing phase that inputs data values and adjusts program variables accordingly; and a termination phase that calculates and prints the results.

The pseudocode algorithm in Fig. 14.8 solves the more general class-averaging problem. This algorithm was developed after only two levels of refinement. Sometimes more levels are necessary.

Software Engineering Observation 14.9

The programmer terminates the top-down, stepwise refinement process when the pseudocode algorithm is specified in sufficient detail for the programmer to be able to convert the pseudocode to a JavaScript program. Implementing the JavaScript program is then normally straightforward.

Initialize total to zero
Initialize gradeCounter to zero

Input the first grade (possibly the sentinel)
While the user has not as yet entered the sentinel
    Add this grade into the running total
    Add one to the grade counter
    Input the next grade (possibly the sentinel)

If the counter is not equal to zero
    Set the average to the total divided by the counter
    Print the average
else
    Print "No grades were entered"

Fig. 14.8   Pseudocode algorithm that uses sentinel-controlled repetition to solve the class-average problem.

Good Programming Practice 14.7

When converting a pseudocode program to JavaScript, keep the pseudocode in the Java-Script program as comments.

Software Engineering Observation 14.10

Experience has shown that the most difficult part of solving a problem on a computer is developing the algorithm for the solution. After a correct algorithm has been specified, the process of producing a working JavaScript program from the algorithm is normally straightforward.

Software Engineering Observation 14.11

Many experienced programmers write programs without ever using program development tools like pseudocode. These programmers feel that their ultimate goal is to solve the problem on a computer, and that writing pseudocode merely delays the production of final outputs. Although this may work for simple and familiar problems, it can lead to serious errors on large, complex projects.

The JavaScript program and a sample execution are shown in Fig. 14.9. Although each grade is an integer, the averaging calculation is likely to produce a number with a decimal point (a real number).

```
1   <!DOCTYPE html PUBLIC "-//W3C//DTD HTML 4.0 Transitional//EN">
2   <HTML>
3   <!-- Fig. 14.9: Average2.html -->
4
5   <HEAD>
6   <TITLE>Class Average Program:
7          Sentinel-controlled Repetition</TITLE>
8
9   <SCRIPT LANGUAGE = "JavaScript">
10     var gradeCounter,   // number of grades entered
11         gradeValue,     // grade value
12         total,          // sum of grades
13         average,        // average of all grades
14         grade;          // grade typed by user
15
16     // Initialization phase
17     total = 0;          // clear total
18     gradeCounter = 0;   // prepare to loop
19
20     // Processing phase
21     // prompt for input and read grade from user
22     grade = window.prompt(
23             "Enter Integer Grade, -1 to Quit:", "0" );
24
25     // convert grade from a String to an integer
26     gradeValue = parseInt( grade );
27
```

Fig. 14.9   Class-average program with sentinel-controlled repetition (part 1 of 3).

```
28        while ( gradeValue != -1 ) {
29            // add gradeValue to total
30            total = total + gradeValue;
31
32            // add 1 to gradeCounter
33            gradeCounter = gradeCounter + 1;
34
35            // prompt for input and read grade from user
36            grade = window.prompt(
37                      "Enter Integer Grade, -1 to Quit:", "0" );
38
39            // convert grade from a String to an integer
40            gradeValue = parseInt( grade );
41        }
42
43        // Termination phase
44        if ( gradeCounter != 0 ) {
45            average = total / gradeCounter;
46
47            // display average of exam grades
48            document.writeln(
49                "<H1>Class average is " + average + "</H1>" );
50        }
51        else
52            document.writeln( "<P>No grades were entered</P>" );
53    </SCRIPT>
54    </HEAD>
55
56    <BODY>
57    <P>Click Refresh (or Reload) to run the script again</P>
58    </BODY>
59    </HTML>
```

Fig. 14.9   Class-average program with sentinel-controlled repetition (part 2 of 3).

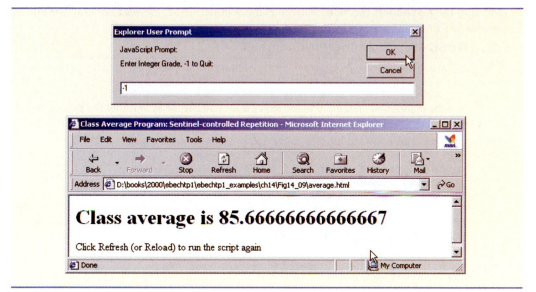

Fig. 14.9   Class-average program with sentinel-controlled repetition (part 3 of 3).

In this example, we see that control structures may be stacked on top of one another (in sequence) just as a child stacks building blocks. The **while** structure (lines 28 through 41) is immediately followed by an **if/else** structure (lines 44 through 52) in sequence. Much of the code in this program is identical to the code in Fig. 14.7, so we concentrate in this example on the new features and issues.

Line 18 initializes **gradeCounter** to **0**, because no grades have been entered yet. Remember that this program uses sentinel-controlled repetition. To keep an accurate record of the number of grades entered, variable **gradeCounter** is incremented only when a valid grade value is entered.

Notice the difference in program logic for sentinel-controlled repetition compared with the counter-controlled repetition in Fig. 14.7. In counter-controlled repetition, we read a value from the user during each iteration of the **while** structure's body for the specified number of iterations. In sentinel-controlled repetition, we read one value (lines 22 and 23) and convert it to an integer (line 26) before the program reaches the **while** structure. This value is used to determine whether the program's flow of control should enter the body of the **while** structure. If the **while** structure condition is **false** (the user typed the sentinel as the first grade), the body of the **while** structure does not execute (no grades were entered). If, on the other hand, the condition is **true**, the body begins execution and the value entered by the user is processed (added to the **total** at line 30). After the value is processed, **gradeCounter** is incremented by 1 (line 33), the next **grade** is input from the user (lines 36 and 37) and the **grade** is converted to an integer (line 40), before the end of the **while** structure's body. As the closing right brace (**}**) of the body is reached, at line 41, execution continues with the next test of the **while** structure condition (line 28) using the new value just entered by the user to determine whether the **while** structure's body should execute again. Notice that the next value is always input from the user immediately before the **while** structure condition is evaluated. This order allows us to determine whether the value just entered by the user is the sentinel value *before* that value is processed (added to the **total**). If the value entered is the sentinel value, the **while** structure terminates and the value is not added to the **total**.

Good Programming Practice 14.8

In a sentinel-controlled loop, the prompts requesting data entry should explicitly remind the user what the sentinel value is.

Notice the compound statement in the **while** loop in Fig 14.9. Without the braces, the last four statements in the body of the loop would fall outside the loop, causing the computer to interpret this code incorrectly as follows:

```
while ( gradeValue != -1 )
   // add gradeValue to total
   total = total + gradeValue;

// add 1 to gradeCounter
gradeCounter = gradeCounter + 1;

// prompt for input and read grade from user
grade = window.prompt(
          "Enter Integer Grade, -1 to Quit:", "0" );

// convert grade from a String to an integer
gradeValue = parseInt( grade );
```

This interpretation would cause an infinite loop in the program if the user does not input the sentinel **-1** as the input value at lines 22 and 23 (before the **while** structure) in the program.

Common Programming Error 14.9

Omitting the curly braces that are needed to delineate a compound statement can lead to logic errors such as infinite loops.

14.10 Formulating Algorithms with Top-Down, Stepwise Refinement: Case Study 3 (Nested Control Structures)

Let us work through another complete problem. We will once again formulate the algorithm using pseudocode and top-down, stepwise refinement, and we will write a corresponding JavaScript program.

Consider the following problem statement:

A college offers a course that prepares students for the state licensing exam for real estate brokers. Last year, several of the students who completed this course took the licensing examination. Naturally, the college wants to know how well its students did on the exam. You have been asked to write a program to summarize the results. You have been given a list of these 10 students. Next to each name is written a 1 if the student passed the exam and a 2 if the student failed.

Your program should analyze the results of the exam as follows:

1. *Input each test result (a 1 or a 2). Display the message "Enter result" on the screen each time the program requests another test result.*

2. *Count the number of test results of each type.*

3. *Display a summary of the test results indicating the number of students who passed and the number of students who failed.*

4. *If more than 8 students passed the exam, print the message "Raise tuition."*

After reading the problem statement carefully, we make the following observations about the problem:

1. The program must process test results for 10 students. A counter-controlled loop will be used.

2. Each test result is a number—either a 1 or a 2. Each time the program reads a test result, the program must determine whether the number is a 1 or a 2. We test for a 1 in our algorithm. If the number is not a 1, we assume that it is a 2. (An exercise at the end of the chapter considers the consequences of this assumption.)

3. Two counters are used to keep track of the exam results—one to count the number of students who passed the exam, and one to count the number of students who failed the exam.

4. After the program has processed all the results, it must decide whether more than eight students passed the exam.

Let us proceed with top-down, stepwise refinement. We begin with a pseudocode representation of the top:

Analyze exam results and decide if tuition should be raised

Once again, it is important to emphasize that the top is a complete representation of the program but that several refinements are likely to be needed before the pseudocode can be naturally evolved into a JavaScript program. Our first refinement is

Initialize variables
Input the ten exam grades and count passes and failures
Print a summary of the exam results and decide whether tuition should be raised

Here, too, even though we have a complete representation of the entire program, further refinement is necessary. We now commit to specific variables. Counters are needed to record the passes and failures, a counter will be used to control the looping process and a variable is needed to store the user input. The pseudocode statement

Initialize variables

may be refined as follows:

Initialize passes to zero
Initialize failures to zero
Initialize student to one

Notice that only the counters for the number of passes, number of failures and number of students are initialized. The pseudocode statement

Input the ten quiz grades and count passes and failures

requires a loop that successively inputs the result of each exam. Here it is known in advance that there are precisely 10 exam results, so counter-controlled looping is appropriate. Inside the loop (*nested* within the loop), a double-selection structure will determine whether each exam result is a pass or a failure and will increment the appropriate counter accordingly. The refinement of the preceding pseudocode statement is then

> *While student counter is less than or equal to ten*
> > *Input the next exam result*
>
> > *If the student passed*
> > > *Add one to passes*
> > *else*
> > > *Add one to failures*
>
> > *Add one to student counter*

Notice the use of blank lines to set off the *if/else* control structure to improve program readability. The pseudocode statement

> *Print a summary of the exam results and decide whether tuition should be raised*

may be refined as follows:

> *Print the number of passes*
> *Print the number of failures*
> *If more than eight students passed*
> > *Print "Raise tuition"*

The complete second refinement appears in Fig. 14.10. Notice that blank lines are also used to set off the *while* structure for program readability.

This pseudocode is now sufficiently refined for conversion to JavaScript. The JavaScript program and two sample executions are shown in Fig. 14.11.

> *Initialize passes to zero*
> *Initialize failures to zero*
> *Initialize student to one*
>
> *While student counter is less than or equal to ten*
> > *Input the next exam result*
>
> > *If the student passed*
> > > *Add one to passes*
> > *else*
> > > *Add one to failures*
>
> > *Add one to student counter*
>
> *Print the number of passes*
> *Print the number of failures*
> *If more than eight students passed*
> > *Print "Raise tuition"*

Fig. 14.10 Pseudocode for examination-results problem.

```
1   <!DOCTYPE html PUBLIC "-//W3C//DTD HTML 4.0 Transitional//EN">
2   <HTML>
3   <!-- Fig. 14.11: analysis.html -->
4
5   <HEAD>
6   <TITLE>Analysis of Examination Results</TITLE>
7
8   <SCRIPT LANGUAGE = "JavaScript">
9      // initializing variables in declarations
10     var passes = 0,        // number of passes
11         failures = 0,      // number of failures
12         student = 1,       // student counter
13         result;            // one exam result
14
15     // process 10 students; counter-controlled loop
16     while ( student <= 10 ) {
17        result = window.prompt(
18                    "Enter result (1=pass,2=fail)", "0" );
19
20        if ( result == "1" )
21           passes = passes + 1;
22        else
23           failures = failures + 1;
24
25        student = student + 1;
26     }
27
28     // termination phase
29     document.writeln( "<H1>Examination Results</H1>" );
30     document.writeln(
31        "Passed: " + passes + "<BR>Failed: " + failures );
32
33     if ( passes > 8 )
34        document.writeln( "<BR>Raise Tuition" );
35  </SCRIPT>
36
37  </HEAD>
38  <BODY>
39  <P>Click Refresh (or Reload) to run the script again</P>
40  </BODY>
41  </HTML>
```

Fig. 14.11 JavaScript program for examination-results problem (part 1 of 5).

Fig. 14.11   JavaScript program for examination-results problem (part 2 of 5).

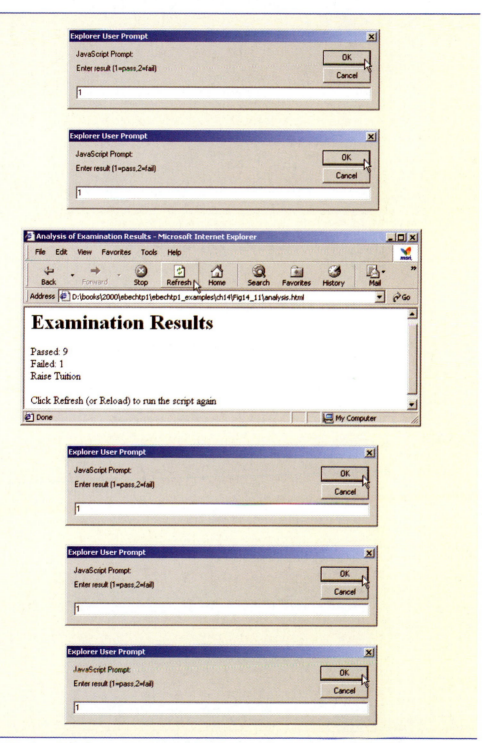

Fig. 14.11 JavaScript program for examination-results problem (part 3 of 5).

Fig. 14.11   JavaScript program for examination-results problem (part 4 of 5).

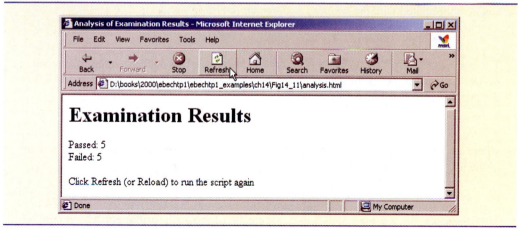

Fig. 14.11   JavaScript program for examination-results problem (part 5 of 5).

Lines 10 through 13,

```
var passes = 0,      // number of passes
    failures = 0,    // number of failures
    student = 1,     // student counter
    result;          // one exam result
```

declare the variables used to process the examination results. Note that we have taken advantage of a feature of JavaScript that allows variable initialization to be incorporated into
declarations (**passes** is assigned **0**, **failures** is assigned **0** and **student** is assigned
1). Looping programs may require initialization at the beginning of each repetition; such
initialization would normally occur in assignment statements.

Testing and Debugging Tip 14.3

*Initializing variables when they are declared in methods helps the programmer avoid incor-
rect results and interpreter messages warning of uninitialized data.*

The processing of the exam results occurs in the **while** structure at lines 16 through
26. Notice that the **if/else** structure at lines 20 through 23 in the loop tests only whether
the exam result was 1; it assumes that all other exam results are 2. Normally, you should
validate the values input by the user (determine whether the values are correct). In the exercises, we ask you to modify this example to validate the input values to ensure that they are
either 1 or 2.

Good Programming Practice 14.9

*When inputting values from the user, validate the input to ensure that it is correct. If an input
value is incorrect, prompt the user to input the value again.*

14.11 Assignment Operators

JavaScript provides several assignment operators for abbreviating assignment expressions.
For example, the statement

```
c = c + 3;
```

can be abbreviated with the *addition assignment operator* **+=** as

```
c += 3;
```

The **+=** operator adds the value of the expression on the right of the operator to the value of the variable on the left of the operator and stores the result in the variable on the left of the operator. Any statement of the form

   variable **=** *variable operator expression***;**

where *operator* is one of the binary operators **+**, **−**, *****, **/** or **%** (or others we will discuss later in the text), can be written in the form

   *variable operator***=** *expression***;**

Thus the assignment **c += 3** adds **3** to **c**. Figure 14.12 shows the arithmetic assignment operators, sample expressions using these operators and explanations.

Performance Tip 14.1

Programmers can write programs that execute a bit faster when the "abbreviated" assignment operators are used, because the variable on the left side of the assignment does not have to be evaluated twice.

Performance Tip 14.2

Many of the performance tips we mention in this text result in nominal improvements, so the reader may be tempted to ignore them. Significant performance improvement is often realized when a supposedly nominal improvement is placed in a loop that may repeat a large number of times.

14.12 Increment and Decrement Operators

JavaScript provides the unary *increment operator* (**++**) and *decrement operator* (**−−**) which are summarized in Fig. 14.13. If a variable **c** is incremented by 1, the increment operator **++** can be used rather than the expressions **c = c + 1** or **c += 1**. If an increment or decrement operator is placed before a variable, it is referred to as the *preincrement* or *predecrement operator*, respectively. If an increment or decrement operator is placed after a variable, it is referred to as the *postincrement* or *postdecrement operator*, respectively.

Assignment operator	Initial variable value	Sample expression	Explanation	Assigns
+=	c = 3	c += 7	c = c + 7	10 to c
-=	d = 5	d -= 4	d = d - 4	1 to d
*=	e = 4	e *= 5	e = e * 5	20 to e
/=	f = 6	f /= 3	f = f / 3	2 to f
%=	g = 12	g %= 9	g = g % 9	3 to g

Fig. 14.12 Arithmetic assignment operators.

Operator	Called	Sample expression	Explanation
++	preincrement	++a	Increment **a** by 1, then use the new value of **a** in the expression in which **a** resides.
++	postincrement	a++	Use the current value of **a** in the expression in which **a** resides, then increment **a** by 1.
--	predecrement	--b	Decrement **b** by 1, then use the new value of **b** in the expression in which **b** resides.
--	postdecrement	b--	Use the current value of **b** in the expression in which **b** resides, then decrement **b** by 1.

Fig. 14.13 The increment and decrement operators.

Preincrementing (predecrementing) a variable causes the variable to be incremented (decremented) by 1, then the new value of the variable is used in the expression in which it appears. Postincrementing (postdecrementing) the variable causes the current value of the variable to be used in the expression in which it appears, then the variable value is incremented (decremented) by 1.

The script of Fig. 14.14 demonstrates the difference between the preincrementing version and the postincrementing version of the **++** increment operator. Postincrementing the variable **c** causes it to be incremented after it is used in the **document.writeln** method call (line 14). Preincrementing the variable **c** causes it to be incremented before it is used in the **document.writeln** method call (line 20). The program displays the value of **c** before and after the **++** operator is used. The decrement operator (**--**) works similarly.

Good Programming Practice 14.10

For readability, unary operators should be placed next to their operands with no intervening spaces.

```
1   <!DOCTYPE html PUBLIC "-//W3C//DTD HTML 4.0 Transitional//EN">
2   <HTML>
3   <!-- Fig. 14.14: increment.html -->
4
5   <HEAD>
6   <TITLE>Preincrementing and Postincrementing</TITLE>
7
8   <SCRIPT LANGUAGE = "JavaScript">
9      var c;
10
11     c = 5;
12     document.writeln( "<H3>Postincrementing</H3>" );
13     document.writeln( c );                 // print 5
14     document.writeln( "<BR>" + c++ ); // print 5 then increment
15     document.writeln( "<BR>" + c );   // print 6
16
```

Fig. 14.14 Differences between preincrementing and postincrementing (part 1 of 2).

```
17      c = 5;
18      document.writeln( "<H3>Preincrementing</H3>" );
19      document.writeln( c );                   // print 5
20      document.writeln( "<BR>" + ++c ); // increment then print 6
21      document.writeln( "<BR>" + c );   // print 6
22   </SCRIPT>
23
24   </HEAD><BODY></BODY>
25   </HTML>
```

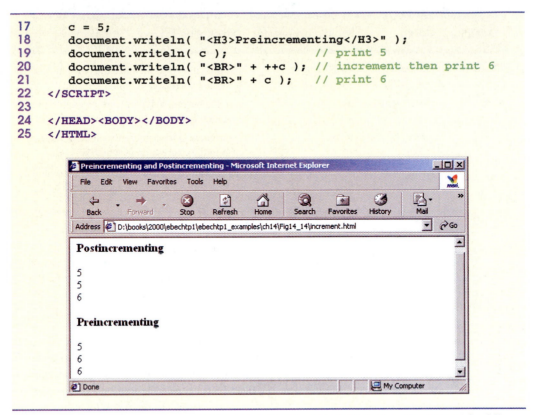

Fig. 14.14 Differences between preincrementing and postincrementing (part 2 of 2).

The three assignment statements in Fig 14.11 (lines 21, 23 and 25, respectively),

```
passes = passes + 1;
failures = failures + 1;
student = student + 1;
```

can be written more concisely with assignment operators as

```
passes += 1;
failures += 1;
student += 1;
```

with preincrement operators as

```
++passes;
++failures;
++student;
```

or with postincrement operators as

```
passes++;
failures++;
student++;
```

It is important to note here that when incrementing or decrementing a variable in a statement by itself, the preincrement and postincrement forms have the same effect and the predecrement and postdecrement forms have the same effect. It is only when a variable appears in the context of a larger expression that preincrementing the variable and post-incrementing the variable have different effects. Predecrementing and postdecrementing behave similarly.

Common Programming Error 14.10

Attempting to use the increment or decrement operator on an expression other than an lvalue *is a syntax error. An* lvalue *is a variable or expression that can appear on the left side of an assignment operation. For example, writing* **++(x + 1)** *is a syntax error because* **(x + 1)** *is not an* lvalue.

The chart in Fig. 14.15 shows the precedence and associativity of the operators introduced up to this point. The operators are shown from top to bottom in decreasing order of precedence. The second column describes the associativity of the operators at each level of precedence. Notice that the conditional operator (**?:**), the unary operators increment (**++**) and decrement (**--**) and the assignment operators **=, +=, -=, *=, /=** and **%=** associate from right to left. All other operators in the operator precedence chart of Fig. 14.15 associate from left to right. The third column names the groups of operators.

14.13 A Note on Data Types

Unlike its predecessor languages C, C++ and Java, JavaScript does not require variables to have a type before they can be used in a program. A variable in JavaScript can contain a value of any data type, and in many situations JavaScript automatically converts between values of different types for you. For this reason, JavaScript is referred to as a *loosely typed language*.

When a variable is declared in JavaScript but is not given a value, that variable has an *undefined* value. Attempting to use the value of such a variable is normally a logic error.

When variables are declared, they are not assigned default values unless specified otherwise by the programmer. To indicate that a variable does not contain a value, you can assign the value **null** to the variable.

Operators	Associativity	Type
( )	left to right	parentheses
++ --	right to left	unary
* / %	left to right	multiplicative
+ -	left to right	additive
< <= > >=	left to right	relational
== !=	left to right	equality
?:	right to left	conditional
= += -= *= /= %=	right to left	assignment

Fig. 14.15 Precedence and associativity of the operators discussed so far.

14.14 JavaScript Internet and World Wide Web Resources

There are a tremendous number of resources for JavaScript programmers on the Internet and World Wide Web. This section lists a variety of JavaScript, JavaScript and ECMA-Script resources available on the Internet and provides a brief description of each. Additional resources for these topics are presented at the ends of chapters 15 through 18 (on JavaScript) and in other chapters as necessary.

www.javascriptmall.com/
The *JavaScript Mall* provides free scripts, FAQs, tools for web pages and a class in JavaScript. The mall is a helpful resource for web page design.

builder.cnet.com/Programming/kahn
This site offers recent and backdated columns containing tips on JavaScript. It also includes nifty tools to aid in JavaScript programming.

developer.netscape.com/docs/manuals/communicator/
jsref/contents.htm
This *JavaScript Reference* explores JavaScript syntax piece by piece.

www.javascripts.com/toc.cfm
Javascripts.com contains an archive of over 2700 scripts to cut and paste and a tutorial section comprised of 30 demo scripts with explanations.

www.hidaho.com/colorcenter/
JavaScript for testing backgrounds by combining colors and textures.

javascript.internet.com
"Cut & Paste" JavaScript Library has more than 300 free scripts! Simply click on the source code to obtain JavaScript buttons, clocks, games, cookies and more.

www.infohiway.com/javascript/indexf.htm
Here you will find close to 200 free JavaScripts.

SUMMARY

- Any computing problem can be solved by executing a series of actions in a specific order.
- A procedure for solving a problem in terms of the actions to be executed and the order in which these actions are to be executed is called an algorithm.
- Specifying the order in which statements are to be executed in a computer program is called program control.
- Pseudocode is an artificial and informal language that helps programmers develop algorithms.
- Carefully prepared pseudocode may be converted easily to a corresponding JavaScript program.
- Pseudocode normally describes only executable statements—the actions that are performed when the program is converted from pseudocode to JavaScript and is run.
- Normally, statements in a program are executed one after the other, in the order in which they are written. This is called sequential execution.
- Various JavaScript statements enable the programmer to specify that the next statement to be executed may be other than the next one in sequence. This is called transfer of control.
- All programs can be written in terms of only three control structures, namely the sequence structure, the selection structure and the repetition structure.
- A flowchart is a graphical representation of an algorithm or of a portion of an algorithm. Flowcharts are drawn using certain special-purpose symbols, such as rectangles, diamonds, ovals and

small circles; these symbols are connected by arrows called flowlines, which indicate the order in which the actions of the algorithm execute.

- JavaScript provides three selection structures. The **if** structure either performs (selects) an action if a condition is true or skips the action if the condition is false. The **if/else** structure performs an action if a condition is true and performs a different action if the condition is false. The **switch** structure performs one of many different actions, depending on the value of an expression.

- JavaScript provides four repetition structures, namely **while, do/while, for** and **for/in**.

- Keywords cannot be used as identifiers (such as for variable names).

- *Single*-entry/single-exit control structures make it easy to build programs. Control structures are attached to one another by connecting the exit point of one control structure to the entry point of the next—this is called control-structure stacking. There is only one other way control structures may be connected—control-structure nesting.

- The JavaScript interpreter ignores whitespace characters: blanks, tabs and newlines used for indentation and vertical spacing. Programmers insert whitespace characters to enhance program clarity.

- A decision can be made on any expression that evaluates to a value of JavaScript's boolean type (any expression that evaluates to **true** or **false**).

- The indentation convention you choose should be carefully applied throughout your programs. It is difficult to read programs that do not use uniform spacing conventions.

- JavaScript provides an operator called the conditional operator (**?:**) that is closely related to the **if/else** structure. Operator **?:** is JavaScript's only ternary operator—it takes three operands. The operands together with the **?:** form a conditional expression. The first operand is a boolean expression, the second is the value for the conditional expression if the condition evaluates to true and the third is the value for the conditional expression if the condition evaluates to false.

- Nested **if/else** structures test for multiple cases by placing **if/else** structures inside **if/else** structures.

- The JavaScript interpreter always associates an **else** with the previous **if** unless told to do otherwise by the placement of braces (**{}**).

- The **if** selection structure normally expects only one statement in its body. To include several statements in the body of an **if**, enclose the statements in braces (**{** and **}**). A set of statements contained within a pair of braces is called a compound statement.

- A logic error has its effect at execution time. A fatal logic error causes a program to fail and terminate prematurely. A nonfatal logic error allows a program to continue executing, but the program produces incorrect results.

- A repetition structure allows the programmer to specify that an action is to be repeated while some condition remains true.

- Counter-controlled repetition is often called definite repetition, because the number of repetitions is known before the loop begins executing.

- Uninitialized variables used in mathematical calculations result in logic errors and produce the value **NaN** *(not a number)*.

- JavaScript represents all numbers as floating-point numbers in memory. Floating-point numbers often develop through division. The computer allocates only a fixed amount of space to hold such a value, so the stored floating-point value can only be an approximation.

- In sentinel-controlled repetition, a special value called a sentinel value (also called a signal value, a dummy value or a flag value) indicates "end of data entry." Sentinel-controlled repetition is often called indefinite repetition, because the number of repetitions is not known in advance.

- The sentinel value must be chosen so that it is not confused with an acceptable input value.

- Top-down, stepwise refinement is a technique that is essential to the development of well-structured algorithms. The top is a single statement that conveys the overall purpose of the program. As such, the top is, in effect, a complete representation of a program. The stepwise refinement process divides the top into a series of smaller tasks. The programmer terminates the top-down, stepwise refinement process when the pseudocode algorithm is specified in sufficient detail for the programmer to be able to convert the pseudocode to a JavaScript program.

- JavaScript provides the arithmetic assignment operators **+=**, **-=**, ***=**, **/=** and **%=** that help abbreviate certain common types of expressions.

- The increment operator, **++**, and the decrement operator, **--**, increment or decrement a variable by 1. If the operator is prefixed to the variable, the variable is incremented or decremented by 1 first, then used in its expression. If the operator is postfixed to the variable, the variable is used in its expression, then incremented or decremented by 1.

- JavaScript does not require variables to have a type before they can be used in a program. A variable in JavaScript can contain a value of any data type, and in many situations JavaScript automatically converts between values of different types for you. For this reason, JavaScript is referred to as a *loosely typed language*.

- When a variable is declared in JavaScript but is not given a value, that variable has an *undefined* value. Attempting to use the value of such a variable is normally a logic error.

- When variables are declared, they are not assigned default values unless specified otherwise by the programmer. To indicate that a variable does not contain a value, you can assign the value **null** to the variable.

TERMINOLOGY

-- operator
?: operator
++ operator
action
action/decision model
algorithm
arithmetic assignment operators:
    +=, -=, *=, /= and **%=**
block
body of a loop
compound statement
conditional operator (**?:**)
control structure
counter-controlled repetition
decision
decrement operator (**--**)
definite repetition
double-selection structure
empty statement (**;**)
if selection structure
if/else selection structure
increment operator (**++**)
indefinite repetition
infinite loop

initialization
logic error
loop counter
loop-continuation condition
nested control structures
postdecrement operator
postincrement operator
predecrement operator
preincrement operator
pseudocode
repetition
repetition structures
selection
sentinel value
sequential execution
single-entry/single-exit control structures
single-selection structure
stacked control structures
structured programming
syntax error
top-down, stepwise refinement
unary operator
while repetition structure
whitespace characters

SELF-REVIEW EXERCISES

14.1 Answer each of the following questions.
  a) All programs can be written in terms of three types of control structures: _____, _____ and _____.
  b) The _____ selection structure is used to execute one action when a condition is true and another action when that condition is false.
  c) Repetition of a set of instructions a specific number of times is called _____ repetition.
  d) When it is not known in advance how many times a set of statements will be repeated, a _____ value can be used to terminate the repetition.

14.2 Write four JavaScript statements that each add 1 to variable **x** which contains a number.

14.3 Write JavaScript statements to accomplish each of the following:
  a) Assign the sum of **x** and **y** to **z** and increment the value of **x** by 1 after the calculation. Use only one statement.
  b) Test whether the value of the variable **count** is greater than 10. If it is, print **"Count is greater than 10"**.
  c) Decrement the variable **x** by 1, then subtract it from the variable **total**. Use only one statement.
  d) Calculate the remainder after **q** is divided by **divisor** and assign the result to **q**. Write this statement two different ways.

14.4 Write a JavaScript statement to accomplish each of the following tasks.
  a) Declare variables **sum** and **x**.
  b) Assign **1** to variable **x**.
  c) Assign **0** to variable **sum**.
  d) Add variable **x** to variable **sum** and assign the result to variable **sum**.
  e) Print **"The sum is: "** followed by the value of variable **sum**.

14.5 Combine the statements that you wrote in Exercise 14.4 into a JavaScript program that calculates and prints the sum of the integers from 1 to 10. Use the **while** structure to loop through the calculation and increment statements. The loop should terminate when the value of **x** becomes 11.

14.6 Determine the values of each variable after the calculation is performed. Assume that, when each statement begins executing, all variables have the integer value 5.
  a) **product *= x++;**
  b) **quotient /= ++x;**

14.7 Identify and correct the errors in each of the following:

```
a) while ( c <= 5 ) {
      product *= c;
      ++c;
b) if ( gender == 1 )
      document.writeln( "Woman" );
   else;
      document.writeln( "Man" );
```

14.8 What is wrong with the following **while** repetition structure?
```
while ( z >= 0 )
   sum += z;
```

ANSWERS TO SELF-REVIEW EXERCISES

14.1 a) Sequence, selection and repetition. b) **if/else**. c) Counter-controlled (or definite). d) Sentinel, signal, flag or dummy.

14.2   `x = x + 1;`
        `x += 1;`
        `++x;`
        `x++;`

14.3   a) `z = x++ + y;`
        b) `if ( count > 10 )`
           `    document.writeln( "Count is greater than 10" );`
        c) `total -= --x;`
        d) `q %= divisor;`
           `q = q % divisor;`

14.4   a) `var sum, x;`
        b) `x = 1;`
        c) `sum = 0;`
        d) `sum += x;` or `sum = sum + x;`
        e) `document.writeln( "The sum is: " + sum );`

14.5   The solution is:

```
1   <!DOCTYPE html PUBLIC "-//W3C//DTD HTML 4.0 Transitional//EN">
2   <!-- Exercise 14.5: sum.html -->
3
4   <HTML>
5   <HEAD><TITLE>Sum the Integers from 1 to 10</TITLE>
6
7   <SCRIPT LANGUAGE = "JavaScript">
8      var sum, x;
9
10     x = 1;
11     sum = 0;
12
13     while ( x <= 10 ) {
14        sum += x;
15        ++x;
16     }
17
18     document.writeln( "The sum is: " + sum );
19  </SCRIPT>
20
21  </HEAD><BODY></BODY>
22  </HTML>
```

14.6   a) `product = 25, x = 6;`
        b) `quotient = 0.833333..., x = 6;`

14.7   a) Error: Missing the closing right brace of the **while** body.
           Correction: Add closing right brace after the statement **++c;**.
        b) Error: Semicolon after **else** results in a logic error. The second output statement will
           always be executed.
           Correction: Remove the semicolon after **else**.

14.8   The value of the variable **z** is never changed in the **while** structure body. Therefore, if the
loop-continuation condition **(z >= 0)** is true, an infinite loop is created. To prevent the infinite loop,
z must be decremented so that it eventually becomes less than 0.

EXERCISES

14.9   Identify and correct the errors in each of the following. [*Note:* There may be more than one error in each piece of code.]

```
a) if ( age >= 65 );
       document.writeln( "Age greater than or equal to 65" );
   else
       document.writeln( "Age is less than 65 )";
b) var x = 1, total;
   while ( x <= 10 ) {
      total += x;
      ++x;
   }
c) While ( x <= 100 )
      total += x;
      ++x;
d) while ( y > 0 ) {
      document.writeln( y );
      ++y;
```

14.10   What does the following program print?

```
1   <!DOCTYPE html PUBLIC "-//W3C//DTD HTML 4.0 Transitional//EN">
2   <HTML>
3   <HEAD><TITLE>Mystery Script</TITLE>
4
5   <SCRIPT LANGUAGE = "JavaScript">
6      var y, x = 1, total = 0;
7
8      while ( x <= 10 ) {
9         y = x * x;
10        document.writeln( y + "<BR>" );
11        total += y;
12        ++x;
13     }
14
15     document.writeln( "<BR>Total is " + total );
16  </SCRIPT>
17
18  </HEAD><BODY></BODY>
19  </HTML>
```

For Exercises 14.11 through 14.14, perform each of these steps:
   a) Read the problem statement.
   b) Formulate the algorithm using pseudocode and top-down, stepwise refinement.
   c) Write a JavaScript program.
   d) Test, debug and execute the JavaScript program.
   e) Process three complete sets of data.

14.11   Drivers are concerned with the mileage obtained by their automobiles. One driver has kept track of several tankfuls of gasoline by recording miles driven and gallons used for each tankful. Develop a JavaScript program that will input the miles driven and gallons used (both as integers) for each tankful. The program should calculate and output HTML text that displays the miles per gallon obtained for each tankful and print the combined miles per gallon obtained for all tankfuls up to this point. Use **prompt** dialogs to obtain the data from the user.

14.12 Develop a JavaScript program that will determine whether a department store customer has exceeded the credit limit on a charge account. For each customer, the following facts are available:

a) Account number
b) Balance at the beginning of the month
c) Total of all items charged by this customer this month
d) Total of all credits applied to this customer's account this month
e) Allowed credit limit

The program should input each of these facts from **prompt** dialogs as integers, calculate the new balance (= *beginning balance + charges – credits*), display the new balance and determine whether the new balance exceeds the customer's credit limit. For those customers whose credit limit is exceeded, the program should output HTML text that displays the message, "Credit limit exceeded."

14.13 A large company pays its salespeople on a commission basis. The salespeople receive $200 per week plus 9% of their gross sales for that week. For example, a salesperson who sells $5000 worth of merchandise in a week receives $200 plus 9% of $5000, or a total of $650. You have been supplied with a list of items sold by each salesperson. The values of these items are as follows:

Item	Value
1	239.99
2	129.75
3	99.95
4	350.89

Develop a program that inputs one salesperson's items sold for last week, calculates that salesperson's earnings and outputs HTML text that displays that salesperson's earnings.

14.14 Develop a JavaScript program that will determine the gross pay for each of three employees. The company pays "straight-time" for the first 40 hours worked by each employee and pays "time-and-a-half" for all hours worked in excess of 40 hours. You are given a list of the employees of the company, the number of hours each employee worked last week and the hourly rate of each employee. Your program should input this information for each employee, determine the employee's gross pay and output HTML text that displays the employee's gross pay. Use **prompt** dialogs to input the data.

14.15 The process of finding the largest value (the maximum of a group of values) is used frequently in computer applications. For example, a program that determines the winner of a sales contest would input the number of units sold by each salesperson. The salesperson who sells the most units wins the contest. Write a pseudocode program and then a JavaScript program that inputs a series of 10 single-digit numbers as characters, determines the largest of the numbers and outputs HTML text that displays the largest number. Your program should use three variables as follows:

counter: A counter to count to 10 (to keep track of how many numbers have been input, and to determine when all 10 numbers have been processed)

number: The current digit input to the program

largest: The largest number found so far.

14.16 Write a JavaScript program that utilizes looping to print the following table of values. Output the results in an HTML table.

N	10*N	100*N	1000*N
1	10	100	1000
2	20	200	2000
3	30	300	3000
4	40	400	4000
5	50	500	5000

14.17 Using an approach similar to Exercise 14.15, find the *two* largest values among the 10 digits entered. (*Note:* You may input each number only once.)

14.18 Modify the program in Fig. 14.11 to validate its inputs. On any input, if the value entered is other than 1 or 2, keep looping until the user enters a correct value.

14.19 What does the following program print?

```
1   <!DOCTYPE html PUBLIC "-//W3C//DTD HTML 4.0 Transitional//EN">
2   <HTML>
3   <HEAD><TITLE>Mystery Script</TITLE>
4
5   <SCRIPT LANGUAGE = "JavaScript">
6      var count = 1;
7
8      while ( count <= 10 ) {
9         document.writeln(
10           count % 2 == 1 ? "****<BR>" : "++++++++<BR>" );
11        ++count;
12     }
13  </SCRIPT>
14
15  </HEAD><BODY></BODY>
16  </HTML>
```

14.20 What does the following program print?

```
1   <!DOCTYPE html PUBLIC "-//W3C//DTD HTML 4.0 Transitional//EN">
2   <HTML>
3   <HEAD><TITLE>Mystery Script</TITLE>
4
5   <SCRIPT LANGUAGE = "JavaScript">
6      var row = 10, column;
7
8      while ( row >= 1 ) {
9         column = 1;
10
11        while ( column <= 10 ) {
12           document.write( row % 2 == 1 ? "<" : ">" );
13           ++column;
14        }
15
16        --row;
17        document.writeln( "<BR>" );
18     }
19  </SCRIPT>
20
21  </HEAD><BODY></BODY>
22  </HTML>
```

14.21 *(Dangling-Else Problem)* Determine the output for each of the following when **x** is **9** and **y** is **11** and when **x** is **11** and **y** is **9**. Note that the interpreter ignores the indentation in a JavaScript program. Also, the JavaScript interpreter always associates an **else** with the previous **if** unless told to do otherwise by the placement of braces (**{}**). Because, on first glance, the programmer may not be sure which **if** an **else** matches, this is referred to as the "dangling-else" problem. We have eliminated the indentation from the following code to make the problem more challenging. (*Hint:* Apply indentation conventions you have learned.)

a)
```
if ( x < 10 )
if ( y > 10 )
document.writeln( "*****<BR>" );
else
document.writeln( "#####<BR>" );
document.writeln( "$$$$$<BR>" );
```

b)
```
if ( x < 10 ) {
if ( y > 10 )
document.writeln( "*****<BR>" );
}
else {
document.writeln( "#####<BR>" );
document.writeln( "$$$$$<BR>" );
}
```

14.22 *(Another Dangling-Else Problem)* Modify the following code to produce the output shown. Use proper indentation techniques. You may not make any changes other than inserting braces and changing the indentation of the code. The interpreter ignores indentation in a JavaScript program. We have eliminated the indentation from the following code to make the problem more challenging. [*Note:* It is possible that no modification is necessary.]

```
if ( y == 8 )
if ( x == 5 )
document.writeln( "@@@@@<BR>" );
else
document.writeln( "#####<BR>" );
document.writeln( "$$$$$<BR>" );
document.writeln( "&&&&&<BR>" );
```

a) Assuming **x = 5** and **y = 8**, the following output is produced.

```
@@@@@
$$$$$
&&&&&
```

b) Assuming **x = 5** and **y = 8**, the following output is produced.

```
@@@@@
```

c) Assuming **x = 5** and **y = 8**, the following output is produced.

```
@@@@@
&&&&&
```

d) Assuming **x = 5** and **y = 7**, the following output is produced. [*Note:* The last three output statements after the **else** are all part of a compound statement.]

```
#####
$$$$$
&&&&&
```

14.23 Write a script that reads in the size of the side of a square and outputs HTML text that displays a hollow square of that size out of asterisks. Use a **prompt** dialog to read the size from the user. Your program should work for squares of all side sizes between 1 and 20.

14.24 A palindrome is a number or a text phrase that reads the same backward as forward. For example, each of the following five-digit integers is a palindrome: 12321, 55555, 45554 and 11611. Write a script that reads in a five-digit integer and determines whether it is a palindrome. If the number is not five digits, output HTML text that displays an **alert** dialog indicating the problem to the user. When the user dismisses the **alert** dialog, allow the user to enter a new value.

14.25 Write a script that outputs HTML text that displays the following checkerboard pattern:

Your program may use only three output statements, one of the form

```
document.write( "* " );
```

one of the form

```
document.write( " " );
```

and one of the form

```
document.writeln( "<BR>" );
```

[*Hint:* Repetition structures are required in this exercise.]

14.26 Write a script that outputs HTML text that keeps displaying in the browser window the multiples of the integer 2, namely 2, 4, 8, 16, 32, 64, etc. Your loop should not terminate (you should create an infinite loop). What happens when you run this program?

14.27 A company wants to transmit data over the telephone, but they are concerned that their phones may be tapped. All of their data is transmitted as four-digit integers. They have asked you to write a program that will encrypt their data so that it may be transmitted more securely. Your script should read a four-digit integer entered by the user in a **prompt** dialog and encrypt it as follows: Replace each digit by *(the sum of that digit plus 7) modulus 10*. Then swap the first digit with the third, and swap the second digit with the fourth. Then output HTML text that displays the encrypted integer. Write a separate program that inputs an encrypted four-digit integer and decrypts it to form the original number.

15

JavaScript/JScript: Control Structures II

Objectives

- To be able to use the **for** and **do/while** repetition structures to execute statements in a program repeatedly.
- To understand multiple selection using the **switch** selection structure.
- To be able to use the **break** and **continue** program control statements.
- To be able to use the logical operators.

Who can control his fate?
William Shakespeare, *Othello*

The used key is always bright.
Benjamin Franklin

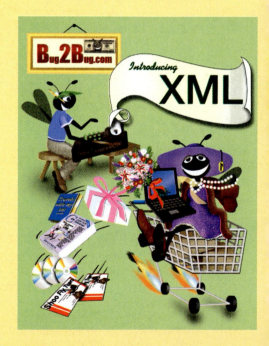

Outline

15.1 Introduction

Before you write a program to solve a particular problem, it is essential to have a thorough understanding of the problem and a carefully planned approach to solving the problem. When you are writing a program, it is equally essential to understand the types of building blocks that are available and to employ proven program construction principles. In this chapter, we discuss all of these issues in our presentation of the theory and principles of structured programming. The techniques that you will learn here are applicable to most high-level languages, including JavaScript.

15.2 Essentials of Counter-Controlled Repetition

Counter-controlled repetition requires:

1. The *name* of a control variable (or loop counter).

2. The *initial value* of the control variable.

3. The *increment* (or *decrement*) by which the control variable is modified each time through the loop (also known as *each iteration of the loop*).

4. The condition that tests for the *final value* of the control variable to determine whether looping should continue.

To see the four elements of counter-controlled repetition, consider the simple script shown in Fig. 15.1, which displays lines of HTML text that illustrate the seven different font sizes supported by HTML. The declaration at line 9

```
var counter = 1;                    // initialization
```

names the control variable (**counter**), reserves space for it in memory and sets it to an *initial value* of **1**. Declarations that include initialization are, in effect, executable statements.

```
1   <!DOCTYPE html PUBLIC "-//W3C//DTD HTML 4.0 Transitional//EN">
2   <HTML>
3   <!-- Fig. 15.1: WhileCounter.html -->
4
5   <HEAD>
6   <TITLE>Counter-Controlled Repetition</TITLE>
7
8   <SCRIPT LANGUAGE = "JavaScript">
9      var counter = 1;                  // initialization
10
11     while ( counter <= 7 ) {       // repetition condition
12        document.writeln( "<P><FONT SIZE = '" + counter +
13           "'>HTML font size " + counter + "</FONT></P>" );
14        ++counter;                     // increment
15     }
16  </SCRIPT>
17
18  </HEAD><BODY></BODY>
19  </HTML>
```

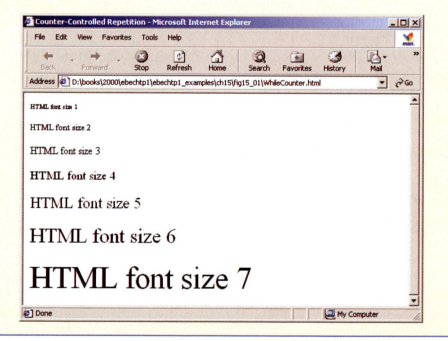

Fig. 15.1   Counter-controlled repetition.

The declaration and initialization of **counter** could also have been accomplished with the following declaration and statement:

```
var counter;               // declare counter
counter = 1;               // initialize counter to 1
```

The declaration is not executable, but the assignment statement is. We use both methods of initializing variables throughout the book.

Lines 12 and 13 in the **while** structure

```
document.writeln( "<P><FONT SIZE = '" + counter +
    "'>HTML font size " + counter + "</FONT></P>" );
```

write a paragraph consisting of the string "**HTML font size**" concatenated with the control variable **counter**'s value that represents the font size. This text is enclosed in a **<FONT>** tag that specifies the font size of the text. Notice the use of the single quotes that are placed around the value of **counter** in the concatenated string. For example, if **counter** is 5, the preceding statement produces the HTML

```
<P><FONT SIZE='5'>HTML font size 5</FONT></P>
```

Because the double quote character is used to specify the beginning and end of a string literal in JavaScript, it cannot be used in the contents of the string unless it is preceded by a \ to create the escape sequence **\"**. HTML allows either single quotes (**'**) or double quotes (**"**) to be placed around the value specified for an attribute (such as the **SIZE** attribute of the **<FONT>** tag). JavaScript allows single quotes to be placed in a string literal and HTML allows single quotes to delimit an attribute value, so we use single quotes to delimit the attribute value for **SIZE** in the script. [*Note:* Although it is considered a good programming practice, HTML does not require attribute values to be enclosed in quotes. Therefore, the preceding HTML can be written as

```
<P><FONT SIZE=5>HTML font size 5</FONT></P>
```

without quotes around **SIZE** value **5**, and the browser will produce the same output.]

Common Programming Error 15.1

Placing a double-quote (**"** *) character inside a string literal causes a runtime error when the script is interpreted. To display a double-quote (* **"** *) character as part of a string literal, the double quote (* **"** *) character must be preceded by a \ to form the escape sequence* **\"** *.*

Testing and Debugging Tip 15.1

When writing HTML text from a script, use single-quote (**'** *) characters to delimit attribute values in string literals.*

Line 14 in the **while** structure

```
++counter;                 // increment
```

increments the control variable by 1 for each iteration of the loop (i.e., each time the body of the loop is performed). The loop-continuation condition (line 11) in the **while** structure tests whether the value of the control variable is less than or equal to **7** (the *final value* for which the condition is **true**). Note that the body of this **while** is performed even when the control variable is **7**. The loop terminates when the control variable exceeds **7** (**counter** becomes **8**).

Good Programming Practice 15.1

Control counting loops with integer values.

Good Programming Practice 15.2

Indent the statements in the body of each control structure.

Good Programming Practice 15.3

Put a blank line before and after each major control structure, to make it stand out in the program.

Good Programming Practice 15.4

Too many levels of nesting can make a program difficult to understand. As a general rule, try to avoid using more than three levels of nesting.

Good Programming Practice 15.5

Vertical spacing above and below control structures, and indentation of the bodies of control structures within the control structure headers, gives programs a two-dimensional appearance that enhances readability.

15.3 The `for` Repetition Structure

The **for** *repetition structure* handles all the details of counter-controlled repetition. Figure 15.2 illustrates the power of the **for** structure by reimplementing the script of Fig. 15.1.

The script operates as follows. When the **for** structure (line 11) begins executing, the control variable **counter** is declared and is initialized to **1** (the first two elements of counter-controlled repetition—declaring the control variable's *name* and providing the control variable's *initial value*). Next, the loop-continuation condition **counter <= 7** is checked. The condition contains the *final value* (**7**) of the control variable. Because the initial value of **counter** is **1**, the condition is satisfied (i.e., **true**), so the body statement (lines 12 and 13) writes a line of HTML text in the document. Variable **counter** is then incremented in the expression **++counter** and the loop continues execution with the loop-continuation test. Because the control variable is now equal to 2, the final value is not exceeded, so the program performs the body statement again (i.e., performs the next iteration of the loop). This process continues until the control variable **counter** is incremented to 8—this causes the loop-continuation test to fail and repetition terminates.

```
1   <!DOCTYPE html PUBLIC "-//W3C//DTD HTML 4.0 Transitional//EN">
2   <HTML>
3   <!-- Fig. 15.2: ForCounter.html -->
4
5   <HEAD>
6   <TITLE>Counter-Controlled Repetition</TITLE>
7
8   <SCRIPT LANGUAGE = "JavaScript">
9      // Initialization, repetition condition and incrementing
10     // are all included in the for structure header.
11     for ( var counter = 1; counter <= 7; ++counter )
12        document.writeln( "<P><FONT SIZE = '" + counter +
13           "'>HTML font size " + counter + "</FONT></P>" );
14  </SCRIPT>
15
16  </HEAD><BODY></BODY>
17  </HTML>
```

Fig. 15.2   Counter-controlled repetition with the **for** structure (part 1 of 2).

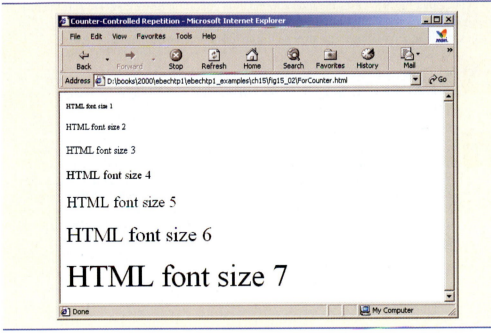

Fig. 15.2   Counter-controlled repetition with the **for** structure (part 2 of 2).

The program continues by performing the first statement after the **for** structure (in this case, the script terminates, because the interpreter reaches the end of the script).

Note that **counter** is declared inside the **for** in this example, but this practice is not required. Variable **counter** could have been declared before the **for** structure or not declared at all. Remember that JavaScript does not explicitly require variables to be declared before they are used. If a variable is used without being declared, the JavaScript interpreter creates the variable at the point of its first use in the script.

Figure 15.3 takes a closer look at the **for** structure of Fig. 15.2. The **for** structure's first line (including the keyword **for** and everything in parentheses after **for**) is often called the **for** *structure header*. Notice that the **for** structure "does it all"—it specifies each of the items needed for counter-controlled repetition with a control variable. If there is more than one statement in the body of the **for**, braces (**{** and **}**) are required to define the body of the loop.

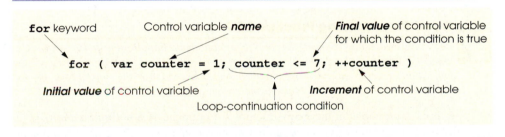

Fig. 15.3   Components of a typical **for** header.

Notice that Fig. 15.3 uses the loop-continuation condition **counter <= 7**. If the programmer incorrectly wrote **counter < 7**, the loop would be executed only 6 times. This is an example of a common logic error called an *off-by-one error*.

Common Programming Error 15.2

Using an incorrect relational operator or using an incorrect final value of a loop counter in the condition of a **while**, **for** *or* **do/while** *structure can cause an off-by-one error or an infinite loop.*

Good Programming Practice 15.6

Using the final value in the condition of a **while** *or* **for** *structure and using the* **<=** *relational operator will help avoid off-by-one errors. For a loop used to print the values 1 to 10, for example, the loop-continuation condition should be* **counter <= 10** *rather than* **counter < 10** *(which is an off-by-one error) or* **counter < 11** *(which is correct). Many programmers prefer so-called zero-based counting, in which, to count 10 times through the loop,* **counter** *would be initialized to zero and the loop-continuation test would be* **counter < 10**.

The general format of the **for** structure is

    for (initialization; loopContinuationTest; increment)
        statement

where the *initialization* expression names the loop's control variable and provides its initial value, *loopContinuationTest* is the expression that tests the loop-continuation condition (containing the final value of the control variable for which the condition is true) and *increment* is an expression that increments the control variable. The **for** structure can be represented by an equivalent **while** structure, with *initialization*, *loopContinuationTest* and *increment* placed as follows:

    initialization;

    while (loopContinuationTest) {
        statement
        increment;
    }

There is an exception to this rule that we will discuss in Section 15.7.

If the *initialization* expression in the **for** structure header is the first definition of the control variable, the control variable can still be used after the **for** structure in the script. The part of a script in which a variable name can be used is known as the variable's *scope*. Scope is discussed in detail in Chapter 16, "JavaScript: Functions."

Good Programming Practice 15.7

Place only expressions involving the control variables in the initialization and increment sections of a **for** *structure. Manipulations of other variables should appear either before the loop (if they execute only once, like initialization statements) or in the loop body (if they execute once per iteration of the loop, like incrementing or decrementing statements).*

The three expressions in the **for** structure are optional. If *loopContinuationTest* is omitted, JavaScript assumes that the loop-continuation condition is **true**, thus creating an infinite loop. One might omit the *initialization* expression if the control variable is initialized elsewhere in the program before the loop. One might omit the *increment* expression if the increment is calculated by statements in the body of the **for** or if no increment is needed. The increment expression in the **for** structure acts like a stand-alone statement at the end of the body of the **for**. Therefore, the expressions

```
counter = counter + 1
counter += 1
++counter
counter++
```

are all equivalent in the incrementing portion of the **for** structure. Many programmers prefer the form **counter++** because the incrementing of the control variable occurs after the loop body is executed. The postincrementing form therefore seems more natural. Because the variable being incremented here does not appear in an expression, preincrementing and postincrementing both have the same effect. The two semicolons in the **for** structure are required.

Common Programming Error 15.3

*Using commas instead of the two required semicolons in a **for** header is a syntax error.*

Common Programming Error 15.4

*Placing a semicolon immediately to the right of the right parenthesis of a **for** header makes the body of that **for** structure an empty statement. This is normally a logic error.*

Software Engineering Observation 15.1

*Placing a semicolon immediately after a **for** header is sometimes used to create a so-called delay loop. Such a **for** loop with an empty body still loops the indicated number of times, doing nothing other than the counting. You might use a delay loop, for example, to slow down a program that is producing outputs on the screen too quickly for you to read them. [Chapter 20 introduces better techniques to create delays in programs, so you should never use delay loops.]*

The initialization, loop-continuation condition and increment portions of a **for** structure can contain arithmetic expressions. For example, assume that **x = 2** and **y = 10**. If **x** and **y** are not modified in the loop body, the statement

```
for ( var j = x; j <= 4 * x * y; j += y / x )
```

is equivalent to the statement

```
for ( var j = 2; j <= 80; j += 5 )
```

The "increment" of a **for** structure may be negative, in which case it is really a decrement and the loop actually counts downward.

If the loop-continuation condition is initially **false**, the body of the **for** structure is not performed. Instead, execution proceeds with the statement following the **for** structure.

The control variable is frequently printed or used in calculations in the body of a **for** structure, but it does not have to be. It is common to use the control variable for controlling repetition while never mentioning it in the body of the **for** structure.

Testing and Debugging Tip 15.2

*Although the value of the control variable can be changed in the body of a **for** loop, avoid changing it, because doing so can lead to subtle errors.*

The **for** structure is flowcharted much like the **while** structure. For example, the flowchart of the **for** statement

```
for ( var counter = 1; counter <= 7; ++counter )
    document.writeln( "<P><FONT SIZE = '" + counter +
        "'>HTML font size " + counter + "</FONT></P>" );
```

is shown in Fig. 15.4. This flowchart makes it clear that the initialization occurs only once and that incrementing occurs each time *after* the body statement is performed. Note that (besides small circles and arrows) the flowchart contains only rectangle symbols and a diamond symbol. Imagine, again, that the programmer has access to a deep bin of empty **for** structures—as many as the programmer might need to stack and nest with other control structures to form a structured implementation of an algorithm's flow of control. The rectangles and diamonds are then filled with actions and decisions appropriate to the algorithm.

15.4 Examples Using the **for** Structure

The following examples show methods of varying the control variable in a **for** structure. In each case, we write the appropriate **for** header. Note the change in the relational operator for loops that decrement the control variable.

a) Vary the control variable from **1** to **100** in increments of **1**.

```
for ( var i = 1; i <= 100; ++i )
```

b) Vary the control variable from **100** to **1** in increments of **−1** (decrements of **1**).

```
for ( var i = 100; i >= 1; --i )
```

Common Programming Error 15.5

*Not using the proper relational operator in the loop-continuation condition of a loop that counts downward (such as using **i <= 1** in a loop counting down to 1) is usually a logic error that will yield incorrect results when the program runs.*

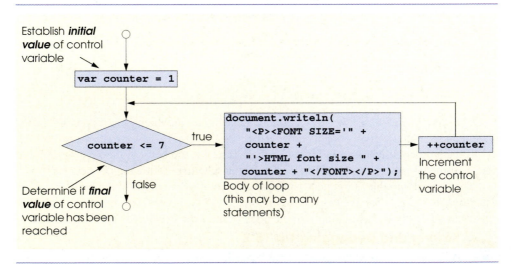

Fig. 15.4   Flowcharting a typical **for** repetition structure.

c) Vary the control variable from **7** to **77** in steps of **7**.

```
for ( var i = 7; i <= 77; i += 7 )
```

d) Vary the control variable from **20** to **2** in steps of **-2**.

```
for ( var i = 20; i >= 2; i -= 2 )
```

e) Vary the control variable over the following sequence of values: **2, 5, 8, 11, 14, 17, 20**.

```
for ( var j = 2; j <= 20; j += 3 )
```

f) Vary the control variable over the following sequence of values: **99, 88, 77, 66, 55, 44, 33, 22, 11, 0**.

```
for ( var j = 99; j >= 0; j -= 11 )
```

The next two scripts demonstrate the **for** repetition structure. Figure 15.5 uses the **for** structure to sum all the even integers from **2** to **100**. Notice the increment expression adds **2** to the control variable **number** after the body is executed during each iteration of the loop. The loop terminates when **number** has the value 102 (which is not added to the sum).

```
1   <!DOCTYPE html PUBLIC "-//W3C//DTD HTML 4.0 Transitional//EN">
2   <HTML>
3   <!-- Fig. 15.5: Sum.html -->
4
5   <HEAD>
6   <TITLE>Sum the Even Integers from 2 to 100</TITLE>
7
8   <SCRIPT LANGUAGE = "JavaScript">
9      var sum = 0;
10
11     for ( var number = 2; number <= 100; number += 2 )
12        sum += number;
13
14     document.writeln( "<BIG>The sum of the even integers " +
15        "from 2 to 100 is " + sum + "</BIG>" );
16  </SCRIPT>
17
18  </HEAD><BODY></BODY>
19  </HTML>
```

The sum of the even integers from 2 to 100 is 2550

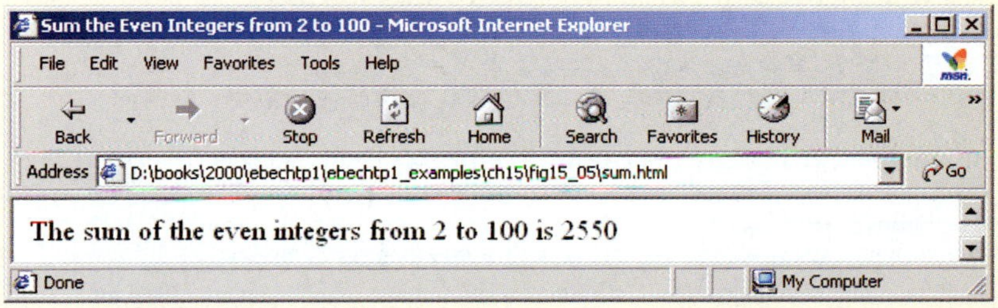

Fig. 15.5   Summation with **for**.

Note that the body of the **for** structure in Fig. 15.5 could actually be merged into the rightmost portion of the **for** header, by using a *comma* as follows:

```
for ( var number = 2; number <= 100;
        sum += number, number += 2)
    ;
```

Similarly, the initialization **sum = 0** could be merged into the initialization section of the **for** structure.

Good Programming Practice 15.8

*Although statements preceding a **for** and in the body of a **for** can often be merged into the **for** header, avoid doing so because it makes the program more difficult to read.*

Good Programming Practice 15.9

For clarity, limit the size of control structure headers to a single line if possible.

The next example computes compound interest (compounded yearly) using the **for** structure. Consider the following problem statement:

> *A person invests $1000.00 in a savings account yielding 5% interest. Assuming that all interest is left on deposit, calculate and print the amount of money in the account at the end of each year for 10 years. Use the following formula for determining these amounts:*
>
> $$a = p \, (1 + r)^{\,n}$$
>
> *where*
>
> p is the principal (original) amount invested,
> r is the annual interest rate,
> n is the number of years and
> a is the amount on deposit at the end of the nth year.

This problem involves a loop that performs the indicated calculation for each of the 10 years the money remains on deposit. The solution is the script shown in Fig. 15.6.

```
1   <!DOCTYPE html PUBLIC "-//W3C//DTD HTML 4.0 Transitional//EN">
2   <HTML>
3   <!-- Fig. 15.6: interest.html -->
4
5   <HEAD>
6   <TITLE>Calculating Compound Interest</TITLE>
7
8   <SCRIPT LANGUAGE = "JavaScript">
9      var amount, principal = 1000.0, rate = .05;
10
11     document.writeln( "<TABLE BORDER = '1' WIDTH = '100%'>" );
12     document.writeln( "<TR><TD WIDTH = '100'><B>Year</B></TD>" );
13     document.writeln(
14        "<TD><B>Amount on deposit</B></TD></TR>" );
15
```

Fig. 15.6   Calculating compound interest with **for** (part 1 of 2).

```
16      for ( var year = 1; year <= 10; ++year ) {
17         amount = principal * Math.pow( 1.0 + rate, year );
18         document.writeln( "<TR><TD>" + year + "</TD><TD>" +
19            Math.round( amount * 100 ) / 100 + "</TD></TR>" );
20      }
21
22      document.writeln( "</TABLE>" );
23   </SCRIPT>
24
25   </HEAD><BODY></BODY>
26   </HTML>
```

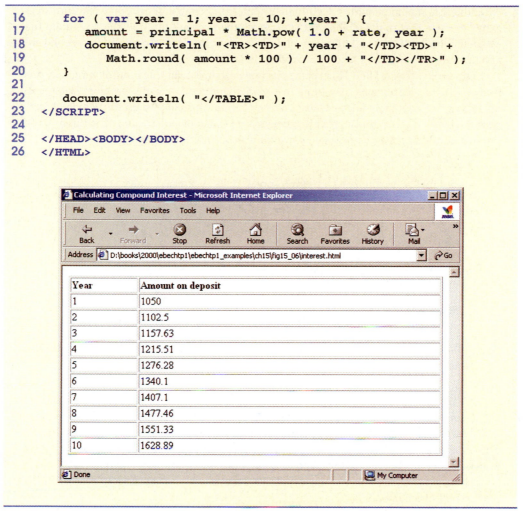

Fig. 15.6   Calculating compound interest with **for** (part 2 of 2).

Line 9

```
var amount, principal = 1000.0, rate = .05;
```

declares three variables and initializes **principal** to **1000.0** and **rate** to **.05**.
Lines 11 through 14

```
document.writeln( "<TABLE BORDER = '1' WIDTH = '100%'>" );
document.writeln( "<TR><TD WIDTH='100'><B>Year</B></TD>" );
document.writeln(
   "<TD><B>Amount on deposit</B></TD></TR>" );
```

write HTML text that begins the definition of an HTML **<TABLE>** element that has a
BORDER of **1** and a **WIDTH** of **100%** (the table is the entire width of the browser window).

After the first statement writes the initial attributes of the table, the second and third statements create a row in the table (**<TR>**) in which the first column (indicated with the first **<TD>** tag) has a **WIDTH** of **100** pixels and contains the bold text **Year** and the second column contains the bold text **Amount on deposit**.

The **for** structure (line 16) executes its body 10 times, varying control variable **year** from 1 to 10 in increments of 1 (note that **year** represents n in the problem statement). JavaScript does not include an exponentiation operator. Instead, we use the **Math** object's **pow** method for this purpose. **Math.pow(x, y)** calculates the value of **x** raised to the **y**th power. Method **Math.pow** takes two numbers as arguments and returns the result.

Line 17

```
amount = principal * Math.pow( 1.0 + rate, year );
```

performs this calculation from the problem statement

$$a = p\,(1 + r)^{\,n}$$

where a is **amount**, p is **principal**, r is **rate** and n is **year** in line 17.

Lines 18 and 19

```
document.writeln( "<TR><TD>" + year + "</TD><TD>" +
    Math.round( amount * 100 ) / 100 + "</TD></TR>" );
```

write a line of HTML text that creates another row in the table. The first column is the current **year** value, and the second column is the result of the expression

```
Math.round( amount * 100 ) / 100
```

which multiplies the current value of **amount** by 100 to convert the value from dollars to cents, then uses the **Math** object's *round* method to round the value to the closest integer. The result is then divided by 100, to produce a dollar value that has a maximum of 2 digits to the right of the decimal point. Unlike many other programming languages, JavaScript does not provide numeric formatting capabilities that allow you to precisely control the display format of a number.

When the loop terminates, line 22

```
document.writeln( "</TABLE>" );
```

writes the **</TABLE>** tag to terminate the HTML table definition.

Variables **amount**, **principal** and **rate** are used to represent numbers in this script. Remember that JavaScript represents all numbers as floating-point numbers. This is convenient in this example, because we are dealing with fractional parts of dollars and we need a type that allows decimal points in its values. Unfortunately, this can cause trouble. Here is a simple explanation of what can go wrong when using floating-point numbers to represent dollar amounts (assuming that dollar amounts are displayed with two digits to the right of the decimal point): Two dollar amounts stored in the machine could be 14.234 (which would normally be rounded to 14.23 for display purposes) and 18.673 (which would normally be rounded to 18.67 for display purposes). When these amounts are added, they produce the internal sum 32.907, which would normally be rounded to 32.91 for display purposes. Thus your printout could appear as

```
    14.23
  + 18.67
  _____
    32.91
```

but a person adding the individual numbers as printed would expect the sum 32.90! You have been warned!

15.5 The `switch` Multiple-Selection Structure

Previously, we discussed the `if` single-selection structure and the `if`/`else` double-selection structure. Occasionally, an algorithm will contain a series of decisions in which a variable or expression is tested separately for each of the values it may assume and different actions are taken for each. JavaScript provides the `switch` multiple-selection structure to handle such decision making. The script of Fig. 15.7 demonstrates one of three different HTML list formats determined by the value input by the user.

```
1   <!DOCTYPE html PUBLIC "-//W3C//DTD HTML 4.0 Transitional//EN">
2   <HTML>
3   <!-- Fig. 15.7: SwitchTest.html -->
4
5   <HEAD>
6   <TITLE>Switching between HTML List Formats</TITLE>
7
8   <SCRIPT LANGUAGE = "JavaScript">
9      var choice,               // user's choice
10         startTag,              // starting list item tag
11         endTag,                // ending list item tag
12         validInput = true,     // indicates if input is valid
13         listType;              // list type as a string
14
15      choice = window.prompt( "Select a list style:\n" +
16                  "1 (bullet), 2 (numbered), 3 (lettered)", "1" );
17
18      switch ( choice ) {
19         case "1":
20            startTag = "<UL>";
21            endTag = "</UL>";
22            listType = "<H1>Bullet List</H1>"
23            break;
24         case "2":
25            startTag = "<OL>";
26            endTag = "</OL>";
27            listType = "<H1>Ordered List: Numbered</H1>"
28            break;
29         case "3":
30            startTag = "<OL TYPE = 'A'>";
31            endTag = "</OL>";
32            listType = "<H1>Ordered List: Lettered</H1>"
33            break;
```

Fig. 15.7   An example using `switch` (part 1 of 3).

```
34          default:
35              validInput = false;
36      }
37
38      if ( validInput == true ) {
39          document.writeln( listType + startTag );
40
41          for ( var i = 1; i <= 3; ++i )
42              document.writeln( "<LI>List item " + i + "</LI>" );
43
44          document.writeln( endTag );
45      }
46      else
47          document.writeln( "Invalid choice: " + choice );
48  </SCRIPT>
49
50  </HEAD>
51  <BODY>
52  <P>Click Refresh (or Reload) to run the script again</P>
53  </BODY>
54  </HTML>
```

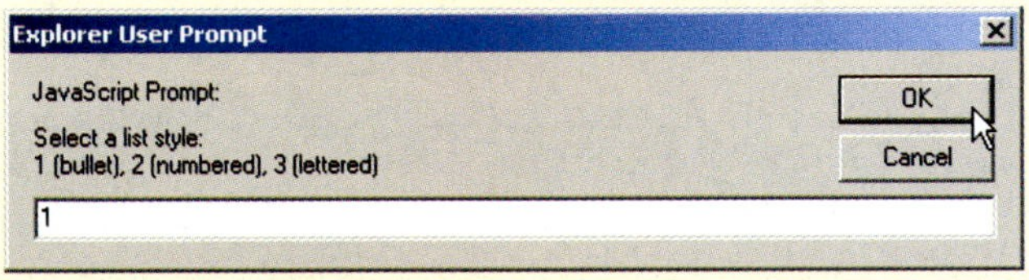

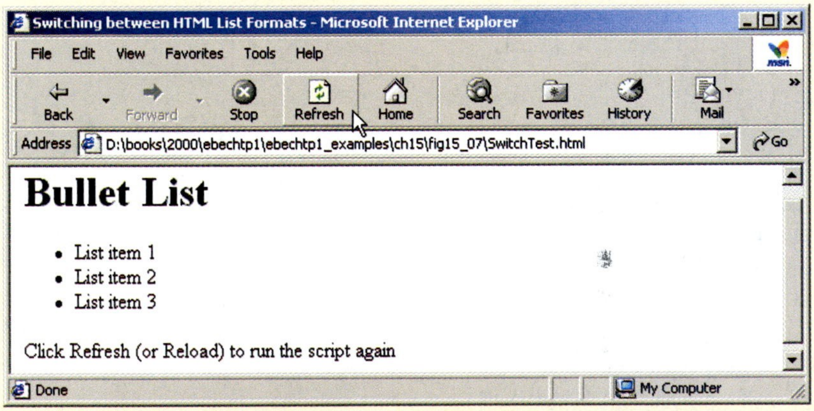

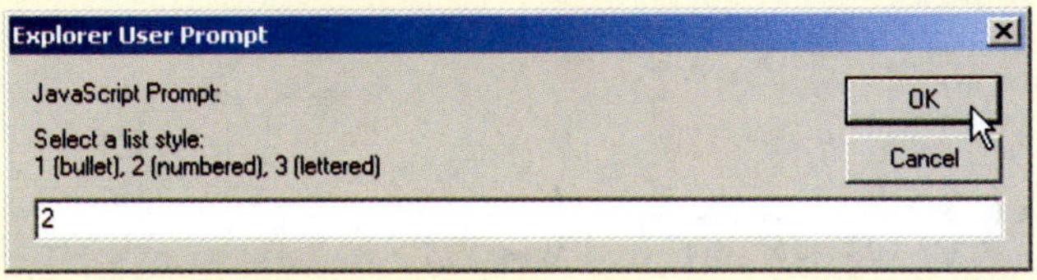

Fig. 15.7   An example using **switch** (part 2 of 3).

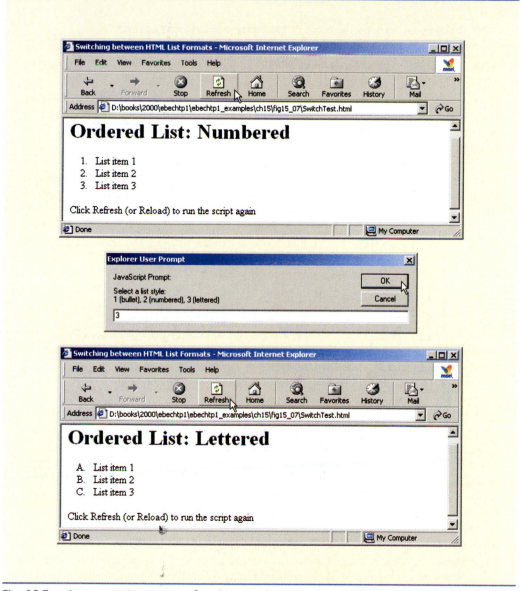

Fig. 15.7 An example using **switch** (part 3 of 3).

Line 9 in the script declares the instance variable **choice**. This variable will store the user's choice that determines which type of HTML list to display. Lines 10 and 11 declare variables **startTag** and **endTag** that store the HTML tags that indicate the HTML list type the user chooses. Line 12 declares variable **validInput** and initializes it to **true**. This boolean variable is used in the script to determine whether the user made a valid choice (**true**). If a choice is invalid, the script will set this variable's value to **false**. Line 13 declares variable **listType** that will store a string indicating the HTML list type. This string will appear before the list in the HTML document.

Lines 15 and 16

```
choice = window.prompt( "Select a list style:\n" +
              "1 (bullet), 2 (numbered), 3 (lettered)", "1" );
```

prompt the user to enter a 1 to display a bullet (unordered) list, a 2 to display a numbered (ordered) list and a 3 to display a lettered (ordered) list.

Lines 18 through 36 define a **switch** structure that assigns to the variables **startTag**, **endTag** and **listType** values based on the value input by the user in the **prompt** dialog. The **switch** structure consists of a series of *case labels* and an optional *default case*.

When the flow of control reaches the **switch** structure, the *controlling expression* (**choice** in this example) in the parentheses following keyword **switch** is evaluated. The value of this expression is compared with the value in each of the *case labels* starting with the first **case** label. Assume the user entered **2**. Remember that the value typed by the user in a **prompt** dialog is returned as a string. So, the string **2** is compared to the string in each **case** in the **switch**. If a match occurs (**case "2":**), the statements for that **case** are executed. For the string **2**, lines 25 through 27,

```
startTag = "<OL>";
endTag = "</OL>";
listType = "<H1>Ordered List: Numbered</H1>"
```

set **startTag** to **"<OL>"** to indicate an ordered list (such lists are numbered by default), set **endTag** to **"</OL>"** to indicate the end of an ordered list and set **listType** to **"<H1>Ordered List: Numbered</H1>"**. Line 28

```
break;
```

exits the **switch** structure immediately with the **break** statement. The **break** statement causes program control to proceed with the first statement after the **switch** structure. The **break** statement is used because the **case**s in a **switch** statement would otherwise run together. If **break** is not used anywhere in a **switch** structure, then each time a match occurs in the structure, the statements for all the remaining **case**s will be executed. If no match occurs between the controlling expression's value and a **case** label, the **default** case executes and sets boolean variable **validInput** to **false**.

Next, the flow of control continues with the **if** structure at line 38, which tests variable **validInput** to determine whether its value is **true**. If so, lines 39 through 44 write the **listType**, the **startTag**, three list items (**<LI>**) and the **endTag**. Otherwise, the script writes text in the HTML document indicating that an invalid choice was made.

Each **case** can have multiple actions (statements). The **switch** structure is different from other structures in that braces are not required around multiple actions in a **case** of a **switch**. The general **switch** structure (using a **break** in each **case**) is flowcharted in Fig. 15.8. [*Note:* As an exercise, flowchart the general **switch** structure without **break** statements.]

The flowchart makes it clear that each **break** statement at the end of a **case** causes control to exit from the **switch** structure immediately. The **break** statement is not required for the last **case** in the **switch** structure (or the **default** case, when it appears last), because program control automatically continues with the next statement after the **switch** structure.

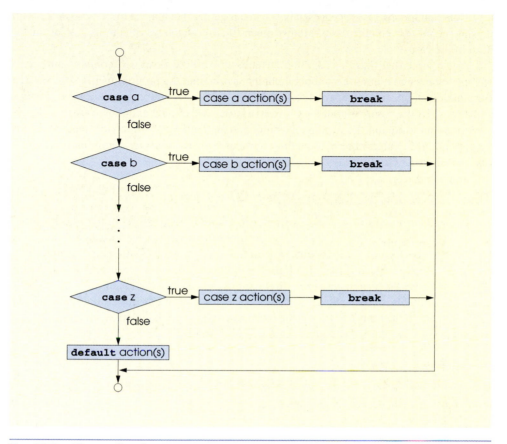

Fig. 15.8 The **switch** multiple-selection structure.

Common Programming Error 15.6

*Forgetting a **break** statement when one is needed in a **switch** structure is a logic error.*

Good Programming Practice 15.10

*Provide a **default** case in **switch** statements. Cases not explicitly tested in a **switch** statement without a **default** case are ignored. Including a **default** case focuses the programmer on processing exceptional conditions. However, there are situations in which no **default** processing is needed.*

Good Programming Practice 15.11

*Although the **case** clauses and the **default** case clause in a **switch** structure can occur in any order, it is considered a good programming practice to place the **default** clause last.*

Good Programming Practice 15.12

*In a **switch** structure, when the **default** clause is listed last, the **break** for that **case** statement is not required. Some programmers include this **break** for clarity and for symmetry with other cases.*

Note that having several **case** labels listed together (such as **case 1: case 2:** with no statements between the cases) simply means that the same set of actions is to occur for each of the cases.

Again, note that (besides small circles and arrows) the flowchart contains only rectangle symbols and diamond symbols. Imagine, again, that the programmer has access to a deep bin of empty **switch** structures—as many as the programmer might need to stack and nest with other control structures to form a structured implementation of an algorithm's flow of control. Again, the rectangles and diamonds are filled with actions and decisions appropriate to the algorithm. Although nested control structures are common, it is rare to find nested **switch** structures in a program.

15.6 The do/while Repetition Structure

The **do/while** repetition structure is similar to the **while** structure. In the **while** structure, the loop-continuation condition is tested at the beginning of the loop before the body of the loop is performed. The **do/while** structure tests the loop-continuation condition *after* the loop body is performed; therefore, *the loop body is always executed at least once.* When a **do/while** terminates, execution continues with the statement after the **while** clause. Note that it is not necessary to use braces in the **do/while** structure if there is only one statement in the body. However, the braces are usually included to avoid confusion between the **while** and **do/while** structures. For example,

```
while ( condition )
```

is normally regarded as the header to a **while** structure. A **do/while** with no braces around the single statement body appears as

```
do
    statement
while ( condition );
```

which can be confusing. The last line—**while(** *condition* **);**—may be misinterpreted by the reader as a **while** structure containing an empty statement (the semicolon by itself). Thus, the **do/while** with one statement is often written as follows, to avoid confusion:

```
do {
    statement
} while ( condition );
```

Good Programming Practice 15.13
*Some programmers always include braces in a **do/while** structure even if the braces are not necessary. This helps eliminate ambiguity between the **while** structure and the **do/while** structure containing one statement.*

Common Programming Error 15.7
*Infinite loops are caused when the loop-continuation condition never becomes **false** in a **while**, **for** or **do/while** structure. To prevent this, make sure there is not a semicolon immediately after the header of a **while** or **for** structure. In a counter-controlled loop, make sure the control variable is incremented (or decremented) in the body of the loop. In a sentinel-controlled loop, make sure the sentinel value is eventually input.*

The script in Fig. 15.9 uses a **do/while** structure to display each of the six different HTML header types (**H1** through **H6**). Control variable **counter** is declared is and initialized to **1** at line 9. Upon entering the **do/while** structure, lines 12 and 13 write a line of HTML text in the document. The value of control variable **counter** is used both to create the starting and ending header tags (e.g., **<H1>** and **</H1>**) and to create the line of text to display (e.g., **This is an H1 level head**). Line 15 increments the **counter** before the loop-continuation test is performed at the bottom of the loop.

```
1   <!DOCTYPE html PUBLIC "-//W3C//DTD HTML 4.0 Transitional//EN">
2   <HTML>
3   <!-- Fig. 15.9: DoWhileTest.html -->
4
5   <HEAD>
6   <TITLE>Using the do/while Repetition Structure</TITLE>
7
8   <SCRIPT LANGUAGE = "JavaScript">
9      var counter = 1;
10
11     do {
12        document.writeln( "<H" + counter + ">This is an H" +
13           counter + " level head" + "</H" + counter + ">" );
14
15        ++counter;
16     } while ( counter <= 6 );
17  </SCRIPT>
18
19  </HEAD><BODY></BODY>
20  </HTML>
```

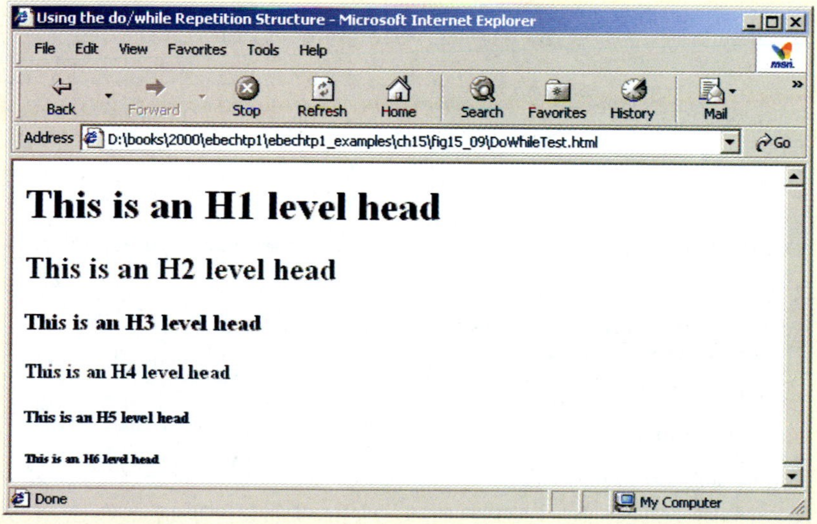

Fig. 15.9   Using the **do/while** repetition structure.

The **do/while** flowchart (Fig. 15.10) makes it clear that the loop-continuation condition is not executed until the action is performed at least once. The flowchart contains only a rectangle and a diamond. Imagine, also, that the programmer has access to a bin of empty **do/while** structures—as many as the programmer might need to stack and nest with other control structures to form a structured implementation of an algorithm. The rectangles and diamonds are filled with actions and decisions appropriate to the algorithm.

15.7 The **break** and **continue** Statements

The **break** and **continue** statements alter the flow of control. The **break** statement, when executed in a **while**, **for**, **do/while** or **switch** structure, causes immediate exit from that structure. Execution continues with the first statement after the structure. Common uses of the **break** statement are to escape early from a loop or to skip the remainder of a **switch** structure (as in Fig. 15.7). Figure 15.11 demonstrates the **break** statement in a **for** repetition structure.

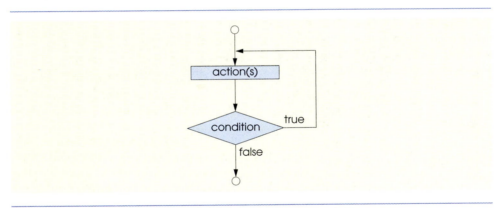

Fig. 15.10 Flowcharting the **do/while** repetition structure.

```
1   <!DOCTYPE html PUBLIC "-//W3C//DTD HTML 4.0 Transitional//EN">
2   <HTML>
3   <!-- Fig. 15.11: BreakTest.html -->
4
5   <HEAD>
6   <TITLE>Using the break Statement in a for Structure</TITLE>
7
8   <SCRIPT LANGUAGE = "JavaScript">
9      for ( var count = 1; count <= 10; ++count ) {
10        if ( count == 5 )
11           break;   // break loop only if count == 5
12
13        document.writeln( "Count is: " + count + "<BR>" );
14     }
15
16     document.writeln( "Broke out of loop at count = " + count );
17  </SCRIPT>
```

Fig. 15.11 Using the **break** statement in a **for** structure (part 1 of 2).

```
18
19   </HEAD><BODY></BODY>
20   </HTML>
```

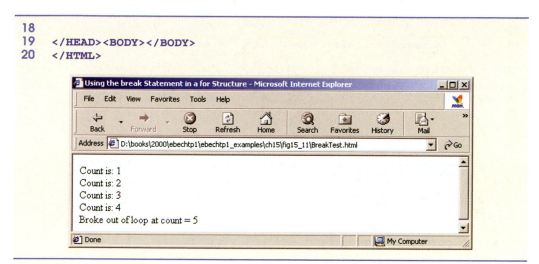

Fig. 15.11   Using the **break** statement in a **for** structure (part 2 of 2).

During each iteration of the **for** structure at line 9, the value of **count** is written in the HTML document. When the **if** structure at line 10 in the **for** structure detects that **count** is **5**, **break** (line 11) is executed. This statement terminates the **for** structure, and the program proceeds to line 16 (the next statement in sequence immediately after the **for**), where the script writes the value of **count** when the loop terminated (i.e., 5). The loop fully executes its body only four times.

The **continue** statement, when executed in a **while**, **for** or **do/while** structure, skips the remaining statements in the body of that structure and proceeds with the next iteration of the loop. In **while** and **do/while** structures, the loop-continuation test is evaluated immediately after the **continue** statement is executed. In the **for** structure, the increment expression is executed, then the loop-continuation test is evaluated.

Figure 15.12 uses **continue** in a **for** structure to the **document.writeln** statement at line 14 when the **if** structure at line 10 determines that the value of **count** is **5**. When the **continue** statement executes, the remainder of the **for** structure's body is skipped. Program control continues with the increment of the **for** structure control variable followed by the loop-continuation test to determine whether the loop should continue executing.

```
1    <!DOCTYPE html PUBLIC "-//W3C//DTD HTML 4.0 Transitional//EN">
2    <HTML>
3    <!-- Fig. 15.12: ContinueTest.html -->
4
5    <HEAD>
6    <TITLE>Using the break Statement in a for Structure</TITLE>
7
8    <SCRIPT LANGUAGE = "JavaScript">
9       for ( var count = 1; count <= 10; ++count ) {
10          if ( count == 5 )
11             continue;  // skip remaining code in loop
12                        // only if count == 5
```

Fig. 15.12   Using the **continue** statement in a **for** structure (part 1 of 2).

```
13
14           document.writeln( "Count is: " + count + "<BR>" );
15       }
16
17       document.writeln( "Used continue to skip printing 5" );
18   </SCRIPT>
19
20   </HEAD><BODY></BODY>
21   </HTML>
```

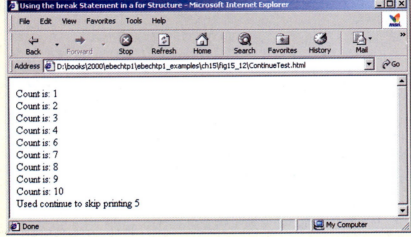

Fig. 15.12 Using the **continue** statement in a **for** structure (part 2 of 2).

Good Programming Practice 15.14

*Some programmers feel that **break** and **continue** violate structured programming. Because the effects of these statements can be achieved by structured programming techniques, these programmers do not use **break** and **continue**.*

Performance Tip 15.1

*The **break** and **continue** statements, when used properly, perform faster than the corresponding structured techniques.*

Software Engineering Observation 15.2

There is a tension between achieving quality software engineering and achieving the best-performing software. Often, one of these goals is achieved at the expense of the other. For all but the most performance-intensive situations, the following "rule of thumb" should be followed: First make your code simple and correct; then make it fast and small, but only if necessary.

15.8 The Labeled break and continue Statements

The **break** statement can break out of an immediately enclosing **while**, **for**, **do/while** or **switch** structure. To break out of a nested set of structures, you can use the *labeled break* statement. This statement, when executed in a **while**, **for**, **do/while** or

switch, causes immediate exit from that structure and any number of enclosing repetition structures; program execution resumes with the first statement after the enclosing *labeled statement* (a statement preceded by a label). The labeled statement can be a compound statement (a set of statements enclosed in curly braces, **{}**). Labeled **break** statements are commonly used to terminate nested looping structures containing **while**, **for**, **do/while** or **switch** structures. Figure 15.13 demonstrates the labeled **break** statement in a nested **for** structure.

```
1   <!DOCTYPE html PUBLIC "-//W3C//DTD HTML 4.0 Transitional//EN">
2   <HTML>
3   <!-- Fig. 15.13: BreakLabelTest.html -->
4
5   <HEAD>
6   <TITLE>Using the break Statement with a Label</TITLE>
7
8   <SCRIPT LANGUAGE = "JavaScript">
9      stop: {    // labeled compound statement
10         for ( var row = 1; row <= 10; ++row ) {
11            for ( var column = 1; column <= 5 ; ++column ) {
12
13               if ( row == 5 )
14                  break stop; // jump to end of stop block
15
16               document.write( "* " );
17            }
18
19            document.writeln( "<BR>" );
20         }
21
22         // the following line is skipped
23         document.writeln( "This line should not print" );
24      }
25
26      document.writeln( "End of script" );
27   </SCRIPT>
28
29   </HEAD><BODY></BODY>
30   </HTML>
```

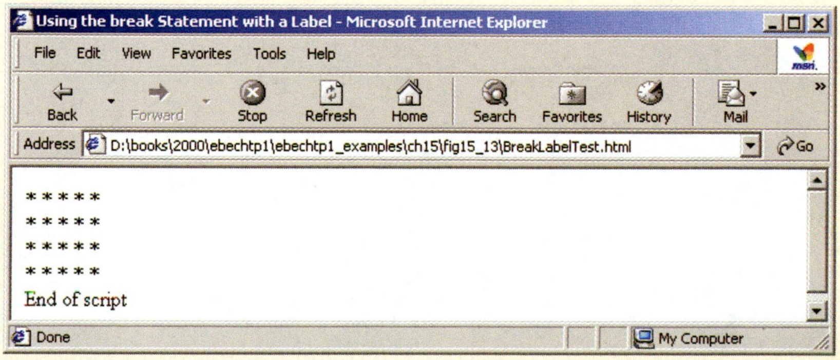

Fig. 15.13 Using a labeled **break** statement in a nested **for** structure.

The labeled compound statement (lines 9 through 24) begins with a *label* (an identifier followed by a colon). Here we use the label "**stop:**." The compound statement is enclosed between the braces at the end of line 9 and line 24, and includes both the nested **for** structure starting at line 10 and the **document.writeln** statement at line 23. When the **if** structure at line 13 detects that **row** is equal to **5**, the statement at line 14

```
break stop;
```

executes. This statement terminates both the **for** structure at line 11 and its enclosing **for** structure at line 10, and the program proceeds to the statement at line 26 (the first statement in sequence after the labeled compound statement). The inner **for** structure fully executes its body only four times. Notice that the **document.writeln** statement at line 23 never executes, because it is included in the labeled compound statement and the outer **for** structure never completes.

The **continue** statement proceeds with the next iteration (repetition) of the immediately enclosing **while**, **for** or **do/while** structure. The *labeled* **continue** *statement*, when executed in a repetition structure (**while**, **for** or **do/while**), skips the remaining statements in that structure's body and any number of enclosing repetition structures, then proceeds with the next iteration of the enclosing *labeled repetition structure* (a repetition structure preceded by a label). In labeled **while** and **do/while** structures, the loop-continuation test is evaluated immediately after the **continue** statement is executed. In a labeled **for** structure, the increment expression is executed, then the loop-continuation test is evaluated. Figure 15.14 uses the labeled **continue** statement in a nested **for** structure to cause execution to continue with the next iteration of the outer **for** structure.

```
1   <!DOCTYPE html PUBLIC "-//W3C//DTD HTML 4.0 Transitional//EN">
2   <HTML>
3   <!-- Fig. 15.14: ContinueLabelTest.html -->
4
5   <HEAD>
6   <TITLE>Using the continue Statement with a Label</TITLE>
7
8   <SCRIPT LANGUAGE = "JavaScript">
9      nextRow:    // target label of continue statement
10        for ( var row = 1; row <= 5; ++row ) {
11           document.writeln( "<BR>" );
12
13           for ( var column = 1; column <= 10; ++column ) {
14
15              if ( column > row )
16                 continue nextRow; // next iteration of
17                                   // labeled loop
18
19              document.write( "* " );
20           }
21        }
22   </SCRIPT>
23
```

Fig. 15.14 Using a labeled **continue** statement in a nested **for** structure (part 1 of 2).

```
24    </HEAD><BODY></BODY>
25    </HTML>
```

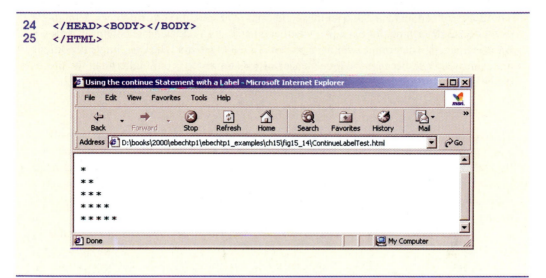

Fig. 15.14 Using a labeled **continue** statement in a nested **for** structure (part 2 of 2).

The labeled **for** structure (lines 9 through 21) starts with the **nextRow** label at line 9. When the **if** structure at line 15 in the inner **for** structure detects that **column** is greater than **row**, the statement

```
continue nextRow;
```

executes and program control continues with the increment of the control variable of the outer **for** loop. Even though the inner **for** structure counts from 1 to 10, the number of * characters output on a row never exceeds the value of **row**.

15.9 Logical Operators

So far we have studied only such *simple conditions* as **count <= 10**, **total > 1000** and **number != sentinelValue**. These conditions were expressed in terms of the relational operators **>**, **<**, **>=** and **<=** and in terms of the equality operators **==** and **!=**. Each decision tested one condition. To test multiple conditions in the process of making a decision, we performed these tests in separate statements or in nested **if** or **if/else** structures.

JavaScript provides *logical operators* that may be used to form more complex conditions by combining simple conditions. The logical operators are **&&** *(logical AND)*, **||** *(logical OR)* and **!** *(logical NOT,* also called *logical negation).* We will consider examples of each of these.

Suppose that at some point in a program we wish to ensure that two conditions are *both* **true** before we choose a certain path of execution. In this case, we can use the logical **&&** operator as follows:

```
if ( gender == 1 && age >= 65 )
    ++seniorFemales;
```

This **if** statement contains two simple conditions. The condition **gender == 1** might be evaluated to determine, for example, whether a person is a female. The condition **age >= 65** is evaluated to determine whether a person is a senior citizen. The two simple conditions are evaluated first, because the precedences of **==** and **>=** are both higher than the precedence of **&&**. The **if** statement then considers the combined condition

```
gender == 1 && age >= 65
```

This condition is **true** *if and only if* both of the simple conditions are **true**. Finally, if this combined condition is indeed **true**, the count of **seniorFemales** is incremented by **1**. If either or both of the simple conditions are **false**, the program skips the incrementing and proceeds to the statement following the **if** structure. The preceding combined condition can be made more readable by adding redundant parentheses:

```
( gender == 1 ) && ( age >= 65 )
```

The table of Fig. 15.15 summarizes the **&&** operator. The table shows all four possible combinations of **false** and **true** values for *expression1* and *expression2*. Such tables are often called *truth tables*. JavaScript evaluates to **false** or **true** all expressions that include relational operators, equality operators and/or logical operators.

Now let us consider the **||** (logical OR) operator. Suppose we wish to ensure that either *or* both of two conditions are **true** before we choose a certain path of execution. In this case, we use the **||** operator as in the following program segment:

```
if ( semesterAverage >= 90 || finalExam >= 90 )
    document.writeln( "Student grade is A" );
```

This statement also contains two simple conditions. The condition **semesterAverage >= 90** is evaluated to determine whether the student deserves an "A" in the course because of a solid performance throughout the semester. The condition **finalExam >= 90** is evaluated to determine whether the student deserves an "A" in the course because of an outstanding performance on the final exam. The **if** statement then considers the combined condition

```
semesterAverage >= 90 || finalExam >= 90
```

and awards the student an "A" if either or both of the simple conditions are **true**. Note that the message "**Student grade is A**" is *not* printed only when both of the simple conditions are **false**. Figure 15.16 is a truth table for the logical OR operator (**||**).

expression1	expression2	expression1 && expression2
false	false	false
false	true	false
true	false	false
true	true	true

Fig. 15.15 Truth table for the **&&** (logical AND) operator.

expression1	expression2	expression1 || expression2
false	false	false
false	true	true
true	false	true
true	true	true

Fig. 15.16 Truth table for the `||` (logical OR) operator.

The `&&` operator has a higher precedence than the `||` operator. Both operators associate from left to right. An expression containing `&&` or `||` operators is evaluated only until truth or falsity is known. Thus, evaluation of the expression

```
gender == 1 && age >= 65
```

will stop immediately if **gender** is not equal to **1** (the entire expression is **false**), and continue if **gender** is equal to **1** (the entire expression could still be **true** if the condition **age >= 65** is **true**). This performance feature for evaluation of logical AND and logical OR expressions is called *short-circuit evaluation.*

JavaScript provides the `!` (logical negation) operator to enable a programmer to "reverse" the meaning of a condition (a **true** value becomes **false** and a **false** value becomes **true**). Unlike the logical operators `&&` and `||` which combine two conditions (binary operators), the logical negation operator has only a single condition as an operand (unary operator). The logical negation operator is placed before a condition to choose a path of execution if the original condition (without the logical negation operator) is **false**, such as in the following program segment:

```
if ( ! ( grade == sentinelValue ) )
    document.writeln( "The next grade is " + grade );
```

The parentheses around the condition **grade == sentinelValue** are needed because the logical negation operator has a higher precedence than the equality operator. Figure 15.17 is a truth table for the logical negation operator.

In most cases, the programmer can avoid using logical negation by expressing the condition differently with an appropriate relational or equality operator. For example, the preceding statement may also be written as follows:

```
if ( grade != sentinelValue )
    document.writeln( "The next grade is " + grade );
```

expression	!expression
false	true
true	false

Fig. 15.17 Truth table for operator `!` (logical negation).

This flexibility can help a programmer express a condition in a more convenient manner.

The script of Fig. 15.18 demonstrates all the logical operators by producing their truth tables. The script produces an HTML table containing the results.

In the output of Fig. 15.18, the strings "false" and "true" indicate **false** and **true** for the operands in each condition. The result of the condition is shown as **true** or **false**. Note that when you add a boolean value to a string, JavaScript automatically adds the string "false" or "true" based on the boolean value. Lines 9 through 30 build an HTML table containing the results.

An interesting feature of JavaScript is that most non-boolean values can be converted by JavaScript into a boolean **true** or **false** value. Non-zero numeric values are considered to be **true**. The numeric value zero is considered to be **false**. Any string that contains characters is considered to be **true**. The empty string (i.e., the string containing no characters) is considered to be **false**. The value **null** and a variable that has been declared but not initialized are considered to be **false**. All objects (such as the browser's **document** and **window** objects and JavaScript's **Math** object) are considered **true**.

```html
1   <!DOCTYPE html PUBLIC "-//W3C//DTD HTML 4.0 Transitional//EN">
2   <HTML>
3   <!-- Fig. 15.18: LogicalOperators.html -->
4
5   <HEAD>
6   <TITLE>Demonstrating the Logical Operators</TITLE>
7
8   <SCRIPT LANGUAGE = "JavaScript">
9      document.writeln( "<TABLE BORDER = '1' WIDTH = '100%'>" );
10
11     document.writeln(
12        "<TR><TD WIDTH = '25%'>Logical AND (&&)</TD>" +
13        "<TD>false && false: " + ( false && false ) +
14        "<BR>false && true: " + ( false && true ) +
15        "<BR>true && false: " + ( true && false ) +
16        "<BR>true && true: " + ( true && true ) + "</TD>" );
17
18     document.writeln(
19        "<TR><TD WIDTH = '25%'>Logical OR (||)</TD>" +
20        "<TD>false || false: " + ( false || false ) +
21        "<BR>false || true: " + ( false || true ) +
22        "<BR>true || false: " + ( true || false ) +
23        "<BR>true || true: " + ( true || true ) + "</TD>" );
24
25     document.writeln(
26        "<TR><TD WIDTH = '25%'>Logical NOT (!)</TD>" +
27        "<TD>!false: " + ( !false ) +
28        "<BR>!true: " + ( !true ) + "</TD>" );
29
30     document.writeln( "</TABLE>" );
31  </SCRIPT>
32
33  </HEAD><BODY></BODY>
34  </HTML>
```

Fig. 15.18 Demonstrating the logical operators (part 1 of 2).

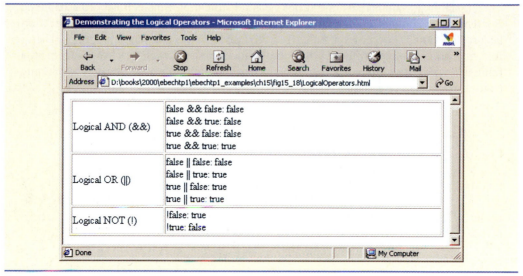

Fig. 15.18 Demonstrating the logical operators (part 2 of 2).

The chart in Fig. 15.19 shows the precedence and associativity of the JavaScript operators introduced up to this point. The operators are shown from top to bottom in decreasing order of precedence.

15.10 Structured Programming Summary

Just as architects design buildings by employing the collective wisdom of their profession, so should programmers design programs. Our field is younger than architecture is, and our collective wisdom is considerably sparser. We have learned that structured programming produces programs that are easier than unstructured programs to understand and hence are easier to test, debug, modify and even prove correct in a mathematical sense.

Operators	Associativity	Type
( )	left to right	parentheses
++ -- !	right to left	unary
* / %	left to right	multiplicative
+ -	left to right	additive
< <= > >=	left to right	relational
== !=	left to right	equality
&&	left to right	logical AND
||	left to right	logical OR
?:	right to left	conditional
= += -= *= /= %=	right to left	assignment

Fig. 15.19 Precedence and associativity of the operators discussed so far.

Figure 15.20 summarizes JavaScript's control structures. Small circles are used in the figure to indicate the single entry point and the single exit point of each structure. Connecting individual flowchart symbols arbitrarily can lead to unstructured programs. Therefore, the programming profession has chosen to combine flowchart symbols to form a limited set of control structures and to build structured programs by properly combining control structures in two simple ways.

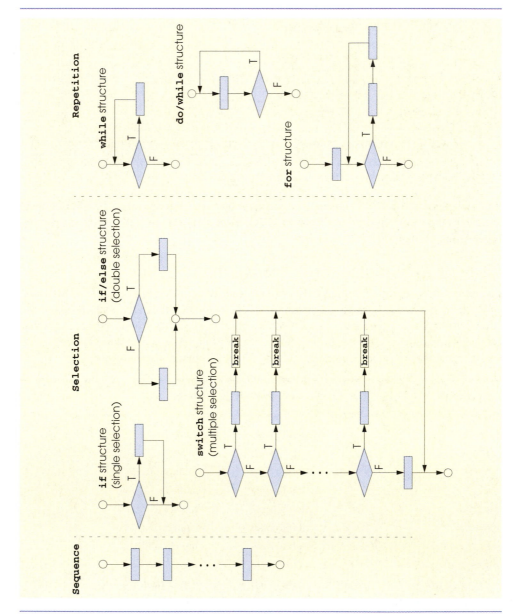

Fig. 15.20   JavaScript's single-entry/single-exit sequence, selection and repetition structures.

For simplicity, only single-entry/single-exit control structures are used—there is only one way to enter and only one way to exit each control structure. Connecting control structures in sequence to form structured programs is simple—the exit point of one control structure is connected to the entry point of the next control structure (the control structures are simply placed one after another in a program)—we have called this "control structure stacking." The rules for forming structured programs also allow for control structures to be nested.

Figure 15.21 shows the rules for forming properly structured programs. The rules assume that the rectangle flowchart symbol may be used to indicate any action, including input/output.

Applying the rules of Fig. 15.21 always results in a structured flowchart with a neat, building-block appearance. For example, repeatedly applying rule 2 to the simplest flowchart (Fig. 15.22) results in a structured flowchart containing many rectangles in sequence (Fig. 15.23). Notice that rule 2 generates a stack of control structures; so, let us call rule 2 the *stacking rule*.

Rule 3 is called the *nesting rule*. Repeatedly applying rule 3 to the simplest flowchart results in a flowchart with neatly nested control structures. For example, in Fig. 15.24, the rectangle in the simplest flowchart is first replaced with a double-selection (**if/else**) structure. Then rule 3 is applied again to both of the rectangles in the double-selection structure, by replacing each of these rectangles with double-selection structures. The dashed box around each of the double-selection structures represent the rectangle in the original simplest flowchart that was replaced.

Rules for Forming Structured Programs

1)   Begin with the "simplest flowchart" (Fig. 15.22).

2)   Any rectangle (action) can be replaced by two rectangles (actions) in sequence.

3)   Any rectangle (action) can be replaced by any control structure (sequence, **if**, **if/else**, **switch**, **while**, **do/while** or **for**).

4)   Rules 2 and 3 may be applied as often as you like and in any order.

Fig. 15.21 Rules for forming structured programs.

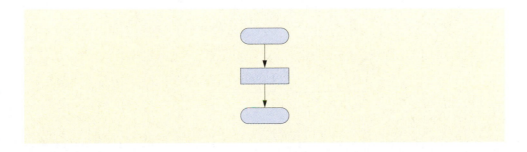

Fig. 15.22 The simplest flowchart.

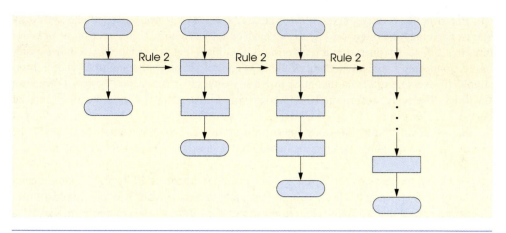

Fig. 15.23 Repeatedly applying rule 2 of Fig. 15.21 to the simplest flowchart.

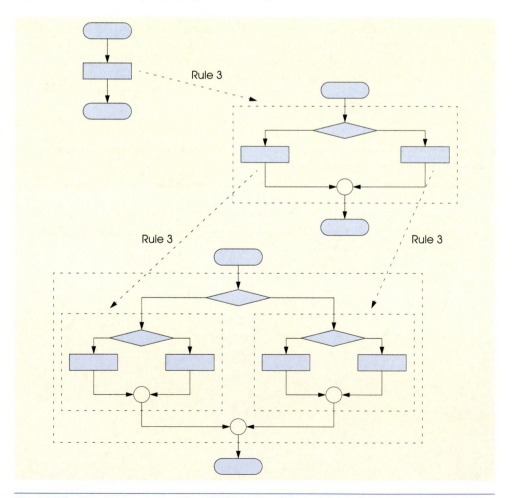

Fig. 15.24 Applying rule 3 of Fig. 15.21 to the simplest flowchart.

Rule 4 generates larger, more involved and more deeply nested structures. The flow-charts that emerge from applying the rules in Fig. 15.21 constitute the set of all possible structured flowcharts and hence the set of all possible structured programs.

The beauty of the structured approach is that we use only seven simple single-entry/single-exit pieces and that we assemble them in only two simple ways. Figure 15.25 shows the kinds of stacked building blocks that emerge from applying rule 2 and the kinds of nested building blocks that emerge from applying rule 3. The figure also shows the kind of overlapped building blocks that cannot appear in structured flowcharts (because of the elimination of the **goto** statement).

If the rules in Fig. 15.21 are followed, an unstructured flowchart (such as that in Fig. 15.26) cannot be created. If you are uncertain about whether a particular flowchart is structured, apply the rules of Fig. 15.21 in reverse to try to reduce the flowchart to the simplest flowchart. If the flowchart is reducible to the simplest flowchart, the original flowchart is structured; otherwise, it is not.

Structured programming promotes simplicity. Bohm and Jacopini have given us the result that only three forms of control are needed:

- sequence
- selection
- repetition

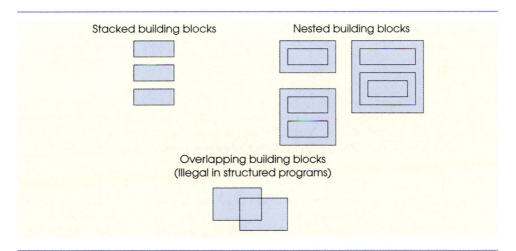

Fig. 15.25 Stacked, nested and overlapped building blocks.

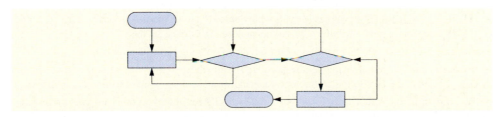

Fig. 15.26 An unstructured flowchart.

Sequence is trivial. Selection is implemented in one of three ways:

- **if** structure (single selection)
- **if/else** structure (double selection)
- **switch** structure (multiple selection)

In fact, it is straightforward to prove that the simple **if** structure is sufficient to provide any form of selection—everything that can be done with the **if/else** structure and the **switch** structure can be implemented by combining **if** structures (although perhaps not as smoothly).

Repetition is implemented in one of four ways:

- **while** structure
- **do/while** structure
- **for** structure
- **for/in** structure (discussed in Chapter 17)

It is straightforward to prove that the **while** structure is sufficient to provide any form of repetition. Everything that can be done with the **do/while** structure and the **for** structure can be done with the **while** structure (although perhaps not as elegantly).

Combining these results illustrates that any form of control ever needed in a JavaScript program can be expressed in terms of:

- sequence
- **if** structure (selection)
- **while** structure (repetition)

These control structures can be combined in only two ways—stacking and nesting. Indeed, structured programming promotes simplicity.

In this chapter, we discussed composing programs from control structures containing actions and decisions. In Chapter 16, we introduce another program structuring unit called the *function*. We will learn to compose large programs by combining functions that are composed of control structures. We will also discuss how functions promote software reusability.

SUMMARY

- Counter-controlled repetition requires the name of a control variable (or loop counter), the initial value of the control variable, the increment (or decrement) by which the control variable is modified each time through the loop (also known as *each iteration of the loop*) and the condition that tests for the final value of the control variable to determine whether looping should continue.
- The double quote character cannot be used in the contents of the string unless it is preceded by a \ to create the escape sequence **\"**.
- HTML allows either single quotes (**'**) or double quotes (**"**) to be placed around an attribute value. HTML does not require attribute values to be enclosed in quotes.
- The **for** repetition structure handles all the details of counter-controlled repetition.
- JavaScript does not require variables to be declared before they are used. If a variable is used without being declared, the JavaScript interpreter creates the variable at the point of its first use in the script.
- The **for** structure's first line (including the keyword **for** and everything in parentheses after **for**) is often called the **for** structure header.
- Braces (**{** and **}**) are required to define the body of a **for** loop with multiple statements in its body.

- The general format of the **for** structure is

    for (*initialization*; *loopContinuationTest*; *increment*)
        statement

    where the *initialization* expression names the loop's control variable and provides its initial value, the *loopContinuationTest* expression is the loop-continuation condition and *increment* is an expression that increments the control variable.

- In most cases the **for** structure can be represented by an equivalent **while** structure with initialization, loopContinuationTest and increment placed as follows:

    initialization;

    while (*loopContinuationTest*) {
        statement
        increment;
    }

- The three expressions in the **for** structure are optional. If *loopContinuationTest* is omitted, the loop-continuation condition is **true**, thus creating an infinite loop. Omit the *initialization* expression if the control variable is initialized in the program before the loop. Omit the *increment* expression if the increment is calculated in the body of the **for** or if no increment is needed.

- The increment expression in a **for** acts like a stand-alone statement at the end of the **for**'s body.

- The initialization, loop-continuation condition and increment portions of a **for** structure can contain arithmetic expressions.

- The "increment" of a **for** structure may be negative, in which case it is really a decrement and the loop actually counts downward.

- If the loop-continuation condition is initially **false**, the body of the **for** structure is not performed.

- JavaScript does not include an exponentiation operator. The **Math** object's **pow** method calculates the value of **x** raised to the **y**th power and returns the result.

- The **Math** object's *round* method rounds its argument to the closest integer.

- The **switch** multiple-selection structure handles a series of decisions in which a variable or expression is tested separately for each of the values it may assume and different actions are taken.

- The **switch** structure consists of a series of **case** labels and an optional **default** case. When the flow of control reaches the **switch** structure, the controlling expression in the parentheses following keyword **switch** is evaluated. The value of this expression is compared with the value in each of the **case** labels, starting with the first **case** label. If a match occurs, the statements for that **case** are executed. If no match occurs between the controlling expression's value and the value in a **case** label, the statements in the **default** case execute.

- Each **case** can have multiple actions (statements). The **switch** structure is different from other structures, in that braces are not required around multiple actions in a **case** of a **switch**.

- The **break** statement at the end of a **case** causes control to immediately exit the **switch**. The **break** statement is not required for the last **case** (or the **default** case when it appears last) because program control automatically continues with the next statement after the **switch**.

- Listing several **case** labels together means that the same actions is to occur for each of the cases.

- The **do/while** structure tests the loop-continuation condition after the loop body is performed; therefore, the loop body is always executed at least once.

- Braces are not necessary in the **do/while** structure if there is only one statement in the body. The braces are usually included to avoid confusion between the **while** and **do/while** structures.

- The **break** statement, when executed in a **while**, **for**, **do/while** or **switch** structure, causes immediate exit from that structure.

- The **continue** statement, when executed in a **while**, **for** or **do/while** structure, skips the remaining statements in the body of that structure and proceeds with the next iteration of the loop.

- The labeled **break** statement, when executed in a **while**, **for**, **do/while** or **switch**, causes immediate exit from that structure and any number of enclosing repetition structures; program execution resumes with the first statement after the enclosing labeled (compound) statement.

- The labeled **continue** statement, when executed in a repetition structure (**while**, **for** or **do/while**), skips the remaining statements in that structure's body and in any number of enclosing repetition structures, and proceeds with the next iteration of the enclosing labeled loop.

- JavaScript provides logical operators **&&** (logical AND), **||** (logical OR) and **!** (logical NO) that may be used to form more complex conditions by combining simple conditions.

- A logical AND (**&&**) condition is **true** if and only if both of its operands are **true**. A logical OR (**||**) condition is **true** if either or both of its operands are **true**.

- An expression containing **&&** or **||** operators is evaluated only until truth or falsity is known. This performance feature is called short-circuit evaluation.

- The unary logical negation (**!**) operator reverses the meaning of a condition.

- JavaScript uses only single-entry/single-exit control structures—there is only one way to enter and only one way to exit each control structure.

- Structured programming promotes simplicity. Any form of control ever needed in a program can be expressed in terms of: the sequence structure, the **if** structure (selection) and the **while** structure (repetition). These control structures can be combined in only two ways—stacking and nesting.

- Selection is implemented in one of three ways: the **if** structure (single selection), the **if/else** structure (double selection) and the **switch** structure (multiple selection).

- Repetition is implemented in one of four ways: the **while** structure, the **do/while** structure, the **for** structure and the **for/in** structure.

TERMINOLOGY

! operator	logical AND (**&&**)
&& operator	logical negation (**!**)
|| operator	logical operators
break	logical OR (**||**)
case label	loop-continuation condition
continue	multiple selection
counter-controlled repetition	nested control structures
default case in **switch**	off-by-one error
definite repetition	repetition structures
do/while repetition structure	scroll box
for repetition structure	scrollbar
infinite loop	short-circuit evaluation
labeled **break** statement	single-entry/single-exit control structures
labeled compound statement	stacked control structures
labeled **continue** statement	**switch** selection structure
labeled repetition structure	**while** repetition structure

SELF-REVIEW EXERCISES

15.1 State whether each of the following is *true* or *false*. If *false*, explain why.
   a) The **default** case is required in the **switch** selection structure.
   b) The **break** statement is required in the default case of a **switch** selection structure.
   c) The expression (**x > y && a < b**) is true if either **x > y** is true or **a < b** is true.

d) An expression containing the || operator is true if either or both of its operands is true.

15.2 Write a JavaScript statement or a set of statements to accomplish each of the following:
a) Sum the odd integers between 1 and 99. Use a **for** structure. Assume that the variables **sum** and **count** have been declared.
b) Calculate the value of **2.5** raised to the power of **3**. Use the **pow** method.
c) Print the integers from 1 to 20 by using a **while** loop and the counter variable **x**. Assume that the variable **x** has been declared but not initialized. Print only five integers per line. [*Hint:* Use the calculation **x % 5**. When the value of this is 0, print a newline character; otherwise, print a tab character. Use the **document.write("<BR>")** to output a line break in the HTML document.]
d) Repeat Exercise 15.2 c), but using a **for** structure.

15.3 Find the error in each of the following code segments and explain how to correct it.
```
a) x = 1;
   while ( x <= 10 );
      x++;
   }
b) for ( y = .1; y != 1.0; y += .1 )
      document.write( y + " " );
c) switch ( n ) {
      case 1:
         document.writeln( "The number is 1" );
      case 2:
         document.writeln( "The number is 2" );
         break;
      default:
         document.writeln( "The number is not 1 or 2" );
         break;
   }
```
d) The following code should print the values 1 to 10.
```
   n = 1;
   while ( n < 10 )
      document.writeln( n++ );
```

ANSWERS TO SELF-REVIEW EXERCISES

15.1 a) False. The **default** case is optional. If no default action is needed, then there is no need for a **default** case. b) False. The **break** statement is used to exit the **switch** structure. The **break** statement is not required for the last case in a **switch** structure. c) False. Both of the relational expressions must be true in order for the entire expression to be true when using the **&&** operator. d) True.

15.2
```
a) sum = 0;
   for ( count = 1; count <= 99; count += 2 )
      sum += count;
b) Math.pow( 2.5, 3 )
c) x = 1;
   while ( x <= 20 ) {
      document.write( x + " " );
      if ( x % 5 == 0 )
         document.write( "<BR>" );
      ++x;
   }
```

d)
```
for ( x = 1; x <= 20; x++ ) {
    document.write( x + " " );

    if ( x % 5 == 0 )
        document.write( "<BR>" );
}
```

or

```
for ( x = 1; x <= 20; x++ )

    if ( x % 5 == 0 )
        document.write( x + "<BR>" );
    else
        document.write( x + " " );
```

15.3   a) Error: The semicolon after the **while** header causes an infinite loop and there is a missing left brace. Correction: Replace the semicolon by a **{** or remove both the **;** and the **}**.

b) Error: Using a floating-point number to control a **for** repetition structure may not work, because floating-point numbers are represented approximately by most computers. Correction: Use an integer, and perform the proper calculation in order to get the values you desire.
```
for ( y = 1; y != 10; y++ )
    document.writeln( y / 10 );
```

c) Error: Missing **break** statement in the statements for the first **case**. Correction: Add a **break** statement at the end of the statements for the first **case**. Note that this is not necessarily an error if the programmer wants the statement of **case 2:** to execute every time the **case 1:** statement executes.

d) Error: Improper relational operator used in the **while** repetition-continuation condition. Correction: Use **<=** rather than **<** or change **10** to **11**.

EXERCISES

15.4   Find the error in each of the following. [*Note:* There may be more than one error.]

a)
```
For ( x = 100, x >= 1, x++ )
    document.writeln( x );
```

b) The following code should print whether integer **value** is odd or even:
```
switch ( value % 2 ) {
    case 0:
        document.writeln( "Even integer" );
    case 1:
        document.writeln( "Odd integer" );
}
```

c) The following code should output the odd integers from 19 to 1:
```
for ( x = 19; x >= 1; x += 2 )
    document.writeln( x );
```

d) The following code should output the even integers from 2 to 100:
```
counter = 2;
do {
    document.writeln( counter );
    counter += 2;
} While ( counter < 100 );
```

15.5   What does the following script do?

```
1   <!DOCTYPE html PUBLIC "-//W3C//DTD HTML 4.0 Transitional//EN">
2   <HTML>
3   <HEAD><TITLE>Mystery</TITLE>
4
5   <SCRIPT LANGUAGE = "JavaScript">
6      for ( var i = 1; i <= 10; i++ ) {
7
8         for ( var j = 1; j <= 5; j++ )
9            document.writeln( "@" );
10
11         document.writeln( "<BR>" );
12      }
13   </SCRIPT>
14
15   </HEAD><BODY></BODY>
16   </HTML>
```

15.6   Write a script that finds the smallest of several integers. Assume that the first value read specifies the number of values to be input from the user.

15.7   Write a script that calculates the product of the odd integers from 1 to 15 and then outputs HTML text that displays the results.

15.8   Modify the compound interest program of Fig. 15.6 to repeat its steps for interest rates of 5, 6, 7, 8, 9 and 10%. Use a **for** loop to vary the interest rate.

15.9   Write a script that outputs HTML to display the following patterns separately one below the other. Use **for** loops to generate the patterns. All asterisks (*) should be printed by a single statement of the form **document.write("*");** (this causes the asterisks to print side by side). A statement of the form **document.writeln("<BR>");** can be used to position to the next line. A statement of the form **document.write(" ");** can be used display a space for the last two patterns. There should be no other output statements in the program. (*Hint:* The last two patterns require that each line begin with an appropriate number of blanks. You may need to use the HTML **<PRE></PRE>** tags.)

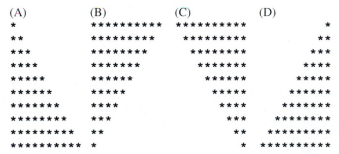

15.10   One interesting application of computers is the drawing of graphs and bar charts (sometimes called "histograms"). Write a script that reads five numbers between 1 and 30. For each number read, output HTML text that displays a line containing that number of adjacent asterisks. For example, if your program reads the number seven, it should output HTML text that displays *******.

15.11   (*"The Twelve Days of Christmas" Song*) Write a script that uses repetition and **switch** structures to print the song "The Twelve Days of Christmas." One **switch** structure should be used to print the day (i.e., "First," "Second," etc.). A separate **switch** structure should be used to print the remainder of each verse. You can find the words at the site

www.santas.net/twelvedaysofchristmas.htm

15.12 A mail order house sells five different products whose retail prices are: product 1— $2.98, product 2—$4.50, product 3—$9.98, product 4—$4.49, and product 5—$6.87. Write a script that reads a series of pairs of numbers as follows:

   a) Product number
   b) Quantity sold for one day

Your program should use a **switch** structure to help determine the retail price for each product. Your program should calculate and ouput HTML that displays the total retail value of all products sold last week. Use a **prompt** dialog to obtain the product number from the user. Use a sentinel-controlled loop to determine when the program should stop looping and display the final results.

15.13 Assume **i = 1**, **j = 2**, **k = 3** and **m = 2**. What does each of the following statements print? Are the parentheses necessary in each case?

   a) `document.writeln( i == 1 );`
   b) `document.writeln( j == 3 );`
   c) `document.writeln( i >= 1 && j < 4 );`
   d) `document.writeln( m <= 99 && k < m );`
   e) `document.writeln( j >= i || k == m );`
   f) `document.writeln( k + m < j | 3 - j >= k );`
   g) `document.writeln( !( k > m ) );`

15.14 Modify Exercise 15.9 to combine your code from the four separate triangles of asterisks into a single script that prints all four patterns side by side making clever use of nested **for** loops.

```
*                 **********    **********             *
**                *********     *********             **
***               ********      ********             ***
****              *******       *******             ****
*****             ******        ******             *****
******            *****         *****             ******
*******           ****          ****             *******
********          ***           ***             ********
*********         **            **             *********
**********        *             *             **********
```

15.15 *(De Morgan's Laws)* In this chapter, we discussed the logical operators **&&**, **||** and **!**. De Morgan's Laws can sometimes make it more convenient for us to express a logical expression. These laws state that the expression **!** (*condition1* **&&** *condition2*) is logically equivalent to the expression (**!***condition1* **||** **!***condition2*). Also, the expression **!** (*condition1* **||** *condition2*) is logically equivalent to the expression (**!***condition1* **&&** **!***condition2*). Use De Morgan's Laws to write equivalent expressions for each of the following, and then write a program to show that the original expression and the new expression are equivalent in each case.

   a) `!( x < 5 ) && !( y >= 7 )`
   b) `!( a == b ) || !( g != 5 )`
   c) `!( ( x <= 8 ) && ( y > 4 ) )`
   d) `!( ( i > 4 ) || ( j <= 6 ) )`

15.16 Write a script that prints the following diamond shape. You may use output statements that print a single asterisk (*****), a single space or a single newline character. Maximize your use of repetition (with nested **for** structures) and minimize the number of output statements.

15.17   Modify the program you wrote in Exercise 15.16 to read an odd number in the range 1 to 19 to specify the number of rows in the diamond. Your program should then display a diamond of the appropriate size.

15.18   A criticism of the **break** statement and the **continue** statement is that each is unstructured. Actually, **break** statements and **continue** statements can always be replaced by structured statements, although coding the replacement can be awkward. Describe in general how you would remove any **break** statement from a loop in a program and replace that statement with some structured equivalent. (*Hint:* The **break** statement "jumps out of" a loop from the body of that loop. The other way to leave is by failing the loop-continuation test. Consider using in the loop-continuation test a second test that indicates "early exit because of a 'break' condition.") Use the technique you developed here to remove the break statement from the program of Fig. 15.11.

15.19   What does the following script do?

```
1   <!DOCTYPE html PUBLIC "-//W3C//DTD HTML 4.0 Transitional//EN">
2   <HTML>
3   <HEAD><TITLE>Mystery</TITLE>
4
5   <SCRIPT LANGUAGE = "JavaScript">
6      for ( i = 1; i <= 5; i++ ) {
7         for ( j = 1; j <= 3; j++ ) {
8            for ( k = 1; k <= 4; k++ )
9               document.write( "*" );
10           document.writeln( "<BR>" );
11        }
12        document.writeln( "<BR>" );
13     }
14   </SCRIPT>
15
16   </HEAD><BODY></BODY>
17   </HTML>
```

15.20   Describe in general how you would remove any **continue** statement from a loop in a program and replace that statement with some structured equivalent. Use the technique you developed here to remove the **continue** statement from the program of Fig. 15.12.

16

JavaScript/JScript: Functions

Objectives

- To understand how to construct programs modularly from small pieces called functions.
- To be able to create new functions.
- To understand the mechanisms used to pass information between functions.
- To introduce simulation techniques using random number generation.
- To understand how the visibility of identifiers is limited to specific regions of programs.

Form ever follows function.
Louis Henri Sullivan

E pluribus unum.
(One composed of many.)
Virgil

O! call back yesterday, bid time return.
William Shakespeare, *Richard II*

Call me Ishmael.
Herman Melville, *Moby Dick*

When you call me that, smile.
Owen Wister

Outline

16.1 Introduction

Most computer programs that solve real-world problems are much larger than the programs presented in the first few chapters. Experience has shown that the best way to develop and maintain a large program is to construct it from small, simple pieces or *modules*. This technique is called *divide and conquer*. This chapter describes many key features of JavaScript that facilitate the design, implementation, operation and maintenance of large scripts.

16.2 Program Modules in JavaScript

Modules in JavaScript are called *functions*. JavaScript programs are written by combining new functions that the programmer writes with "prepackaged" functions and objects available in JavaScript. The "prepackaged" functions that belong to JavaScript objects (such as **Math.pow** and **Math.round**, introduced previously) are often called *methods*. The term method implies that the function belongs to a particular object; however, the terms function and method can be used interchangeably. We will refer to functions that belong to a particular JavaScript object as methods; all others are referred to as functions.

JavaScript provides several objects that have a rich collection of methods for performing common mathematical calculations, string manipulations, date and time manipulations, and manipulations of collections of data called **Array**s. These make the programmer's job easier, because they provide many of the capabilities programmers need. Some common predefined objects of JavaScript and their methods are discussed in Chapter 17, "JavaScript: Arrays" and Chapter 18, "JavaScript: Objects."

Good Programming Practice 16.1

Familiarize yourself with the rich collection of objects and methods provided by JavaScript.

Software Engineering Observation 16.1

Avoid reinventing the wheel. If possible, use JavaScript objects, methods and functions instead of writing new functions. This reduces program development time and avoids introducing new errors.

Portability Tip 16.1

Using the methods built into JavaScript objects helps make programs more portable.

Performance Tip 16.1

Do not try to rewrite existing methods of JavaScript objects to make them more efficient. You usually will not be able to increase the performance of these methods.

The programmer can write functions to define specific tasks that may be used at many points in a script. These are sometimes referred to as *programmer-defined functions.* The actual statements defining the function are written only once and these statements are hidden from other functions.

A function is *invoked* (i.e., made to perform its designated task) by a *function call.* The function call specifies the function name and provides information (as *arguments*) that the called function needs to do its task. A common analogy for this structure is the hierarchical form of management. A boss (the *calling function* or *caller*) asks a worker (the *called function*) to perform a task and *return* (i.e., report back) the results when the task is done. The boss function does not know *how* the worker function performs its designated tasks. The worker may call other worker functions, and the boss will be unaware of this. We will soon see how this "hiding" of implementation details promotes good software engineering. Figure 16.1 shows the **boss** function communicating with several worker functions in a hierarchical manner. Note that **worker1** acts as a "boss" function to **worker4** and **worker5**. Relationships among functions may be other than the hierarchical structure shown in this figure.

Functions (and methods) are called (invoked) by writing the name of the function (or method), followed by a left parenthesis, followed by the argument (or a comma-separated list of arguments) of the function, followed by a right parenthesis. For example, a programmer desiring to convert a string stored in variable **inputValue** to a floating-point number, to add it to variable **total**, might write

```
total += parseFloat( inputValue );
```

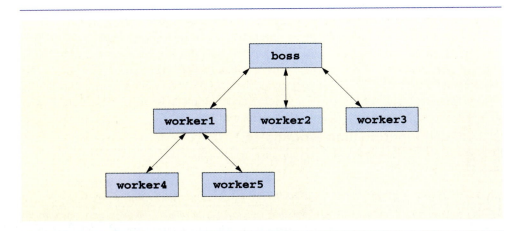

Fig. 16.1   Hierarchical boss function/worker function relationship.

When this statement executes, JavaScript function ***parseFloat*** converts the string contained in the parentheses (stored in variable **inputValue** in this case) to a floating-point value, then that value is added to **total**. The variable **inputValue** is the argument of the **parseFloat** function. Function **parseFloat** takes a string representation of a floating-point number as an argument and returns the corresponding floating-point numeric value.

Function (and method) arguments may be constants, variables or expressions. If **s1 = "22.3"** and **s2 = "45"**, then the statement

```
total += parseFloat( s1 + s2 );
```

evaluates the expression **s1 + s2**, concatenates the strings **s1** and **s2** (resulting in the string **"22.345"**), converts the result into a floating-point number and adds the floating-point number to variable **total**.

16.3 Programmer-Defined Functions

Functions allow the programmer to modularize a program. All variables declared in function definitions are *local variables*—they are known only in the function in which they are defined. Most functions have a list of *parameters* that provide the means for communicating information between functions via function calls. A function's parameters are also considered to be local variables. When a function is called, the arguments in the function call are assigned to the corresponding parameters in the function definition.

There are several motivations for modularizing a program with functions. The divide-and-conquer approach makes program development more manageable. Another motivation is *software reusability*—using existing functions as building blocks to create new programs. With good function naming and definition, programs can be created from standardized functions rather than being built by using customized code. For example, we did not have to define how to convert strings to integers and floating-point numbers—JavaScript already provides function **parseInt** to convert a string to an integer and function **parseFloat** to convert a string to a floating-point number. A third motivation is to avoid repeating code in a program. Packaging code as a function allows that code to be executed from several locations in a program by calling the function.

Software Engineering Observation 16.2

Each function should be limited to performing a single, well-defined task and the function name should effectively express that task. This promotes software reusability.

Software Engineering Observation 16.3

If you cannot choose a concise name that expresses what the function does, it is possible that your function is attempting to perform too many diverse tasks. It is usually best to break such a function into several smaller functions.

16.4 Function Definitions

Each script we have presented has consisted of a series of statements and control structures in sequence. These scripts have been executed as the browser loads the Web page and evaluates the **<HEAD>** section of the page. We now consider how programmers write their own customized functions and call them in a script.

Consider a script (Fig. 16.2) that uses a function **square** to calculate the squares of the integers from 1 to 10. [*Note:* We continue to show many examples in which the **BODY** element of the HTML document is empty and the document is created directly by a Java-Script. In later chapters we show many examples in which JavaScripts interact with the elements in the **BODY** of a document.]

```
1   <!DOCTYPE html PUBLIC "-//W3C//DTD HTML 4.0 Transitional//EN">
2   <HTML>
3   <!-- Fig. 16.2: SquareInt.html -->
4
5   <HEAD>
6   <TITLE>A Programmer-Defined square Function</TITLE>
7
8   <SCRIPT LANGUAGE = "JavaScript">
9      document.writeln(
10        "<H1>Square the numbers from 1 to 10</H1>" );
11
12     // square the numbers from 1 to 10
13     for ( var x = 1; x <= 10; ++x )
14        document.writeln( "The square of " + x + " is " +
15                          square( x ) + "<BR>" );
16
17     // The following square function's body is executed only
18     // when the function is explicitly called.
19
20     // square function definition
21     function square( y )
22     {
23        return y * y;
24     }
25  </SCRIPT>
26
27  </HEAD><BODY></BODY>
28  </HTML>
```

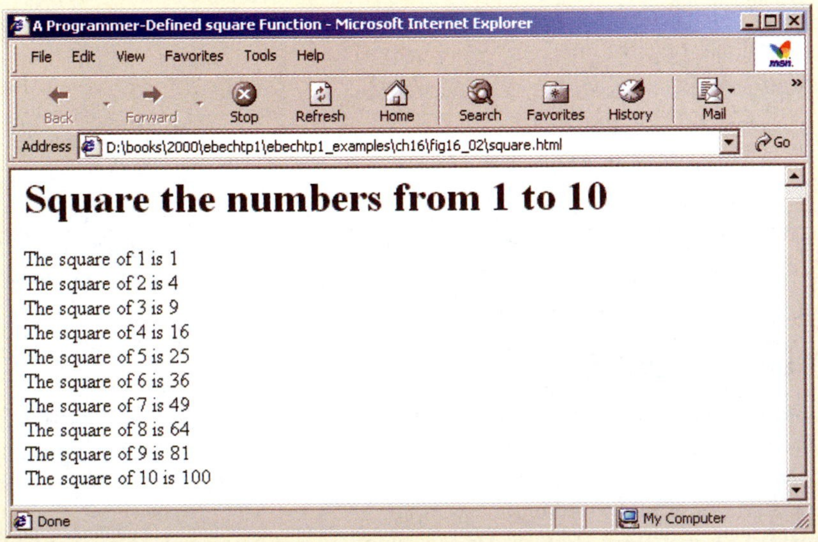

Fig. 16.2   Using programmer-defined function **square**.

The **for** structure at lines 13 through 15

```
for ( var x = 1; x <= 10; ++x )
   document.writeln( "The square of " + x + " is " +
                       square( x ) + "<BR>" );
```

outputs HTML that displays the results of squaring the integers from 1 to 10. Each iteration of the loop calculates the **square** of the current value of control variable **x** and outputs the result by writing a line in the HTML document. Function **square** is *invoked* or *called* on line 15 in the **for** structure with the expression

```
square( x )
```

When program control reaches this expression, function **square** (defined at line 21) is called. In fact, the **( )** represent the *function call operator*, which has high precedence. At this point, a copy of the value of **x** (the argument to the function call) is made automatically by the program and program control transfers to the first line of function **square**. Function **square** receives the copy of the value of **x** in the parameter **y**. Then **square** calculates **y * y**. The result is passed back to the point in line 15 where **square** was invoked. Lines 14 and 15 concatenate **"The square of "**, the value of **x**, **" is "**, the value returned by function **square** and a **
** tag, then write that line of text in the HTML document. This process is repeated ten times.

The definition of function **square** (line 21) shows that **square** expects a single parameter **y**—this will be the name used in the body of function **square** to manipulate the value passed to **square** from line 15. Note that the JavaScript keyword **var** is not used to declare variables in the parameter list of a function. The **return** *statement* in **square** passes the result of the calculation **y * y** back to the calling function.

Common Programming Error 16.1

*Using the JavaScript **var** keyword to declare a variable in a function parameter list results in a JavaScript runtime error.*

Note that function **square** follows the rest of the script. When the **for** structure terminates, JavaScript will not continue to flow sequentially into function **square**. A function must explicitly be called for the code in its body to execute. Thus, when the **for** structure terminates in this example, the script terminates.

Good Programming Practice 16.2

Place a blank line between function definitions to separate the functions and enhance program readability.

Software Engineering Observation 16.4

Statements that are enclosed in the body of a function definition will not be executed by the JavaScript interpreter unless the function is explicitly invoked (called).

The format of a function definition is

```
function function-name ( parameter-list )
{
     declarations and statements
}
```

The *function-name* is any valid identifier. The *parameter-list* is a comma-separated list containing the names of the parameters received by the function when it is called (remember that the arguments in the function call are assigned to the corresponding parameter in the function definition). There should be one argument in the function call for each parameter in the function definition. If a function does not receive any values, the *parameter-list* is empty (the function name is followed by an empty set of parentheses).

The *declarations* and *statements* within braces form the *function body*. The function body is also referred to as a *block*. A block is a compound statement that includes declarations.

Common Programming Error 16.2

Forgetting to return a value from a function that is supposed to return a value is a logic error.

Common Programming Error 16.3

Placing a semicolon after the right parenthesis enclosing the parameter list of a function definition results in a JavaScript runtime error.

Common Programming Error 16.4

Redefining a function parameter as a local variable in the function is a logic error.

Common Programming Error 16.5

Passing to a function an argument that is not compatible with the corresponding parameter's expected type is a logic error and may result in a JavaScript runtime error.

Good Programming Practice 16.3

Although it is not incorrect to do so, do not use the same name for an argument passed to a function and the corresponding parameter in the function definition. This avoids ambiguity.

Good Programming Practice 16.4

Choosing meaningful function names and meaningful parameter names makes programs more readable and helps avoid excessive use of comments.

Software Engineering Observation 16.5

A function should usually be no longer than one printed page. Better yet, a function should usually be no longer than half a printed page. Regardless of how long a function is, it should perform one task well. Small functions promote software reusability.

Software Engineering Observation 16.6

Scripts should be written as collections of small functions. This makes programs easier to write, debug, maintain and modify.

Software Engineering Observation 16.7

A function requiring a large number of parameters may be performing too many tasks. Consider dividing the function into smaller functions that perform the separate tasks. The function header should fit on one line if possible.

Software Engineering Observation 16.8

Modularizing programs in a neat, hierarchical manner promotes good software engineering, sometimes at the expense of performance.

Performance Tip 16.2

A heavily modularized program—as compared to a monolithic (i.e., one-piece) program without functions—makes potentially large numbers of function calls, and these consume execution time and space on a computer's processor(s). But monolithic programs are difficult to program, test, debug, maintain and evolve. So modularize your programs judiciously, always keeping in mind the delicate balance between performance and good software engineering.

Testing and Debugging Tip 16.1

Small functions are easier to test, debug and understand than large ones.

There are three ways to return control to the point at which a function was invoked. If the function does not return a result, control is returned when the function-ending right brace is reached or by executing the statement

```
return;
```

If the function does return a result, the statement

```
return expression;
```

returns the value of *expression* to the caller. When a **return** statement is executed, control returns immediately to the point at which a function was invoked.

The script in our next example (Fig. 16.3) uses a programmer-defined function called **maximum** to determine and return the largest of three floating-point values.

```
1   <!DOCTYPE html PUBLIC "-//W3C//DTD HTML 4.0 Transitional//EN">
2   <HTML>
3   <!-- Fig. 16.3: maximum.html -->
4
5   <HEAD>
6   <TITLE>Finding the Maximum of Three Values</TITLE>
7
8   <SCRIPT LANGUAGE = "JavaScript">
9      var input1 = window.prompt( "Enter first number", "0" );
10     var input2 = window.prompt( "Enter second number", "0" );
11     var input3 = window.prompt( "Enter third number", "0" );
12
13     var value1 = parseFloat( input1 );
14     var value2 = parseFloat( input2 );
15     var value3 = parseFloat( input3 );
16
17     var maxValue = maximum( value1, value2, value3 );
18
19     document.writeln( "First number: " + value1 +
20                       "<BR>Second number: " + value2 +
21                       "<BR>Third number: " + value3 +
22                       "<BR>Maximum is: " + maxValue );
23
```

Fig. 16.3 Programmer-defined **maximum** function (part 1 of 2).

```
24        // maximum method definition (called from line 17)
25        function maximum( x, y, z )
26        {
27            return Math.max( x, Math.max( y, z ) );
28        }
29    </SCRIPT>
30
31    </HEAD>
32    <BODY>
33    <P>Click Refresh (or Reload) to run the script again</P>
34    </BODY>
35    </HTML>
```

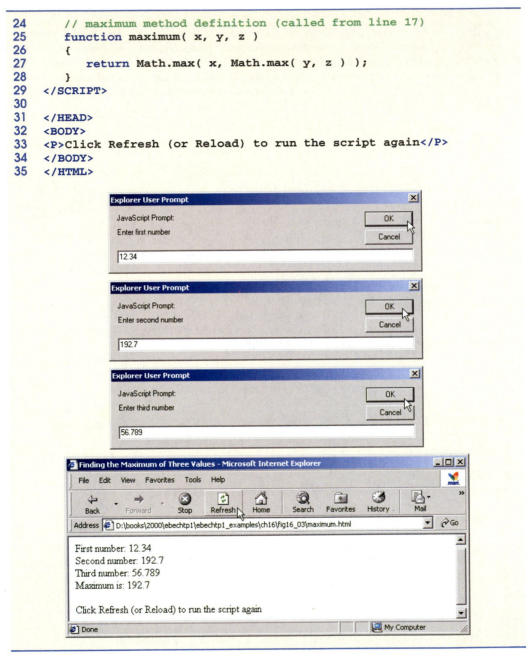

Fig. 16.3   Programmer-defined **maximum** function (part 2 of 2).

The three floating-point values are input by the user via **prompt** dialogs (lines 9 through 11). Lines 13 through 15 use function **parseFloat** to convert the strings input by the user to floating-point values. The statement at line 17

```
var maxValue = maximum( value1, value2, value3 );
```

passes the three floating-point values to function **maximum** (defined at line 25), which determines the largest floating-point value. This value is returned to line 17 by the **return** statement in function **maximum**. The value returned is assigned to variable **maxValue**. The three floating-point values input by the user and the **maxValue** value are concatenated and displayed by the **document.writeln** statement at lines 19 through 22.

Notice the implementation of the function **maximum** (line 25). The first line indicates that the function's name is **maximum** and that the function takes three parameters (**x**, **y** and **z**) to accomplish its task. Also, the body of the function contains the statement

```
return Math.max( x, Math.max( y, z ) );
```

which returns the largest of the three floating-point values using two calls to the **Math** object's **max** method. First, method **Math.max** is invoked with the values of variables **y** and **z** to determine the larger of these two values. Next, the value of variable **x** and the result of the first call to **Math.max** are passed to method **Math.max**. Finally, the result of the second call to **Math.max** is returned to the point at which **maximum** was invoked (i.e., line 17). Note once again that the script terminates before sequentially reaching the definition of function **maximum**. The statement in the body of function **maximum** is executed only when the function is invoked from line 17.

16.5 Random Number Generation

We now take a brief and, it is hoped, entertaining diversion into a popular programming application, namely simulation and game playing. In this section and the next section, we will develop a nicely structured game-playing program that includes multiple functions. The program uses most of the control structures we have studied.

There is something in the air of a gambling casino that invigorates people, from the high-rollers at the plush mahogany-and-felt craps tables to the quarter-poppers at the one-armed bandits. It is the *element of chance,* the possibility that luck will convert a pocketful of money into a mountain of wealth. The element of chance can be introduced through the **Math** object's *random* method. (Remember, we are calling **random** a method because it belongs to the **Math** object.)

Consider the following statement:

```
var randomValue = Math.random();
```

Method **random** generates a floating-point value from 0.0 up to (but not including) 1.0. If **random** truly produces values at random, every value from 0.0 up to (but not including) 1.0 has an equal *chance* (or *probability*) of being chosen each time **random** is called.

The range of values produced directly by **random** is often different from what is needed in a specific application. For example, a program that simulates coin tossing might require only 0 for "heads" and 1 for "tails." A program that simulates rolling a six-sided die would require random integers in the range 1 to 6. A program that randomly predicts the next type of spaceship (out of four possibilities) that will fly across the horizon in a video game might require random integers in the range 0 through 3 or 1 through 4.

To demonstrate method **random**, let us develop a program (Fig. 16.4) that simulates 20 rolls of a six-sided die and displays the value of each roll. We use the multiplication operator (*****) in conjunction with **random** as follows:

```
Math.floor( 1 + Math.random() * 6 )
```

```
1    <!DOCTYPE html PUBLIC "-//W3C//DTD HTML 4.0 Transitional//EN">
2    <HTML>
3    <!-- Fig. 16.4: RandomInt.java -->
4
5    <HEAD>
6    <TITLE>Shifted and Scaled Random Integers</TITLE>
7
8    <SCRIPT LANGUAGE = "JavaScript">
9       var value;
10
11      document.writeln( "<H1>Random Numbers</H1>" +
12                        "<TABLE BORDER = '1' WIDTH = '50%'><TR>" );
13
14      for ( var i = 1; i <= 20; i++ ) {
15         value = Math.floor( 1 + Math.random() * 6 );
16         document.writeln( "<TD>" + value + "</TD>" );
17
18         if ( i % 5 == 0 && i != 20 )
19            document.writeln( "</TR><TR>" );
20      }
21
22      document.writeln( "</TR></TABLE>" );
23   </SCRIPT>
24
25   </HEAD>
26   <BODY>
27   <P>Click Refresh (or Reload) to run the script again</P>
28   </BODY>
29   </HTML>
```

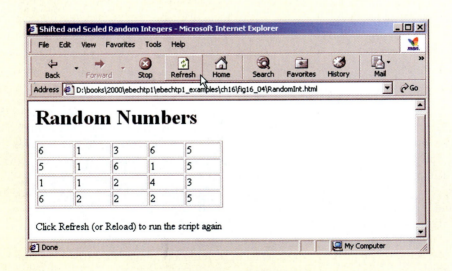

Fig. 16.4   Shifted and scaled random integers (part 1 of 2).

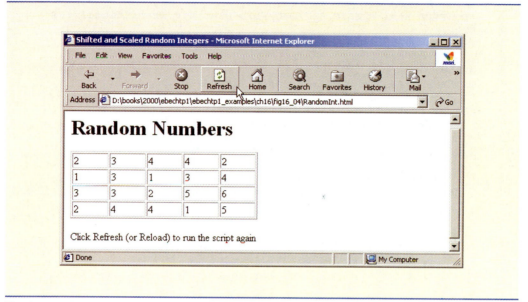

Fig. 16.4   Shifted and scaled random integers (part 2 of 2).

First, the preceding expression multiplies the result of a call to **Math.random()** by **6** to produce a number in the range 0.0 up to (but not including) 6.0. This is called *scaling* the range of the random numbers. The number 6 is called the *scaling factor.* Next, we add 1 to this result to *shift* the range of numbers to produce a number in the range 1.0 up to (but not including 7.0. Finally, we use method *Math.floor* to *round* the result down to the closest integer value in the range 1 to 6. **Math** method **floor** rounds its floating-point number argument to the closest integer not greater than its argument's value—e.g., 1.75 is rounded to 1 and -1.25 is rounded to -2. Figure 16.4 confirms that the results are in the range 1 to 6.

To show that these numbers occur with approximately equal likelihood, let us simulate 6000 rolls of a die with the program of Fig. 16.5. Each integer from 1 to 6 should appear approximately 1000 times. Use your browser's **Refresh** (or **Reload**) button to execute the script again.

As the program output shows, by scaling and shifting we used **Math** method **random** to realistically simulate the rolling of a six-sided die. Note that we used nested control structures to determine the number of times each side of the six-sided die occurred. The **for** loop at lines 14 through 37 iterates 6000 times. During each iteration of the loop, line 15 produces a value from 1 to 6. The nested **switch** structure at lines 17 through 36 uses the **face** value that was randomly chosen as its controlling expression. Based on the value of **face**, one of the six counter variables is incremented during each iteration of the loop. Note that *no* **default** case is provided in this **switch** structure because the statement at line 15 only produces the values 1, 2, 3, 4, 5 and 6. In this example, the **default** case would never be executed. After we study **Array**s in Chapter 17, we will show how to replace the entire **switch** structure in this program with a single-line statement. Run the program several times and observe the results. Notice that a *different* sequence of random numbers is obtained each time the script executes, so the results should vary.

```
1   <!DOCTYPE html PUBLIC "-//W3C//DTD HTML 4.0 Transitional//EN">
2   <HTML>
3   <!-- Fig. 16.5: RollDie.html -->
4
5   <HEAD>
6   <TITLE>Roll a Six-Sided Die 6000 Times</TITLE>
7
8   <SCRIPT LANGUAGE = "JavaScript">
9      var frequency1 = 0, frequency2 = 0,
10         frequency3 = 0, frequency4 = 0,
11         frequency5 = 0, frequency6 = 0, face;
12
13     // summarize results
14     for ( var roll = 1; roll <= 6000; ++roll ) {
15        face = Math.floor( 1 + Math.random() * 6 );
16
17        switch ( face ) {
18           case 1:
19              ++frequency1;
20              break;
21           case 2:
22              ++frequency2;
23              break;
24           case 3:
25              ++frequency3;
26              break;
27           case 4:
28              ++frequency4;
29              break;
30           case 5:
31              ++frequency5;
32              break;
33           case 6:
34              ++frequency6;
35              break;
36        }
37     }
38
39     document.writeln( "<TABLE BORDER = '1' WIDTH = '50%'>" );
40     document.writeln( "<TR><TD><B>Face</B></TD>" +
41                       "<TD><B>Frequency</B></TD></TR>" );
42     document.writeln( "<TR><TD>1</TD><TD>" + frequency1 +
43                       "</TD></TR>" );
44     document.writeln( "<TR><TD>2</TD><TD>" + frequency2 +
45                       "</TD></TR>" );
46     document.writeln( "<TR><TD>3</TD><TD>" + frequency3 +
47                       "</TD></TR>" );
48     document.writeln( "<TR><TD>4</TD><TD>" + frequency4 +
49                       "</TD></TR>" );
50     document.writeln( "<TR><TD>5</TD><TD>" + frequency5 +
51                       "</TD></TR>" );
52     document.writeln( "<TR><TD>6</TD><TD>" + frequency6 +
53                       "</TD></TR></TABLE>" );
```

Fig. 16.5   Rolling a six-sided die 6000 times (part 1 of 2).

```
54   </SCRIPT>
55
56   </HEAD>
57   <BODY>
58   <P>Click Refresh (or Reload) to run the script again</P>
59   </BODY>
60   </HTML>
```

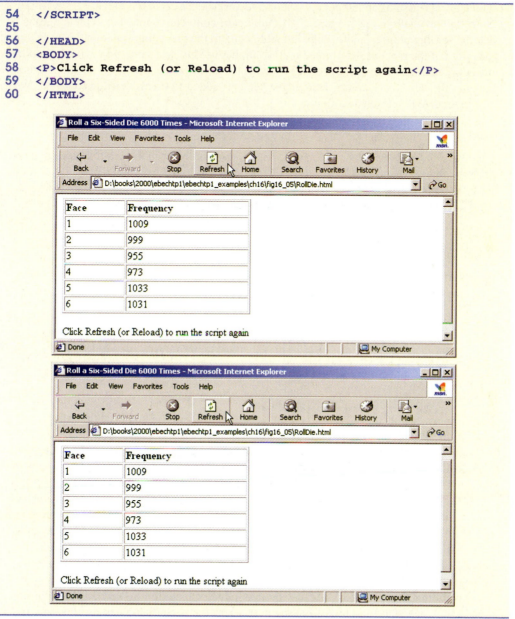

Fig. 16.5   Rolling a six-sided die 6000 times (part 2 of 2).

The values produced directly by **random** are always in the range

```
0.0 ≤ Math.random() < 1.0
```

Previously we demonstrated how to write a single statement to simulate the rolling of a six-sided die with the statement

```
face = Math.floor( 1 + Math.random() * 6 );
```

which always assigns an integer (at random) to variable **face** in the range $1 \leq$ **face** ≤ 6. Note that the width of this range (i.e., the number of consecutive integers in the range) is 6 and the starting number in the range is 1. Referring to the preceding statement, we see that the width of the range is determined by the number used to scale **random** with the multiplication operator (6 in the preceding statement) and the starting number of the range is equal to the number (1 in the preceding statement) added to **Math.random() * 6**. We can generalize this result as follows:

```
face = Math.floor( a + Math.random() * b );
```

where **a** is the *shifting value* (which is equal to the first number in the desired range of consecutive integers) and **b** is the *scaling factor* (which is equal to the width of the desired range of consecutive integers). In the exercises, we will see that it is possible to choose integers at random from sets of values other than ranges of consecutive integers.

16.6 Example: A Game of Chance

One of the most popular games of chance is a dice game known as "craps," which is played in casinos and back alleys throughout the world. The rules of the game are straightforward:

> *A player rolls two dice. Each die has six faces. These faces contain 1, 2, 3, 4, 5 and 6 spots, respectively. After the dice have come to rest, the sum of the spots on the two upward faces is calculated. If the sum is 7 or 11 on the first throw, the player wins. If the sum is 2, 3 or 12 on the first throw (called "craps"), the player loses (i.e., the "house" wins). If the sum is 4, 5, 6, 8, 9 or 10 on the first throw, that sum becomes the player's "point." To win, you must continue rolling the dice until you "make your point" (i.e., roll your point value). The player loses by rolling a 7 before making the point.*

The script in Fig. 16.6 simulates the game of craps.

Notice that the player must roll two dice on the first and all subsequent rolls. When you execute the script, click the **Roll Dice** button to play the game. The *status bar* in the lower-left corner of the browser window displays the results of each roll. The screen captures show four separate executions of the script (a win and a loss on the first roll, and a win and a loss after the first roll).

Until now, all user interactions with scripts have been through either a **prompt** dialog (into which the user could type an input value for the program) or an **alert** dialog (in which a message was displayed to the user and the user could click **OK** to dismiss the dialog). Although these are valid ways to receive input from a user and to display messages in a JavaScript program, they are fairly limited in their capabilities—a **prompt** dialog can obtain only one value at a time from the user, and a message dialog can display only one message. It is much more common to receive multiple inputs from the user at once via an HTML *form* (such as the user entering name and address information) or to display many pieces of data at once (such as the values of the dice, the sum of the dice and the point, in this example). To begin our introduction to more elaborate user interfaces, this program uses an HTML form (discussed in Chapter 10) and introduces a new graphical user interface concept—graphical user interface *event handling*. This is our first example in which the JavaScript executes in response to the user's interaction with a GUI component in an HTML form. This interaction causes an *event*. Scripts are often used to respond to events.

```
61   <!DOCTYPE html PUBLIC "-//W3C//DTD HTML 4.0 Transitional//EN">
62   <HTML>
63   <!-- Fig. 16.6: Craps.html -->
64
65   <HEAD>
66   <TITLE>Program that Simulates the Game of Craps</TITLE>
67
68   <SCRIPT LANGUAGE = "JavaScript">
69      // variables used to test the state of the game
70      var WON = 0, LOST = 1, CONTINUE_ROLLING = 2;
71
72      // other variables used in program
73      var firstRoll = true,               // true if first roll
74          sumOfDice = 0,                   // sum of the dice
75          myPoint = 0,     // point if no win/loss on first roll
76          gameStatus = CONTINUE_ROLLING;   // game not over yet
77
78      // process one roll of the dice
79      function play()
80      {
81         if ( firstRoll ) {               // first roll of the dice
82            sumOfDice = rollDice();
83
84            switch ( sumOfDice ) {
85               case 7: case 11:           // win on first roll
86                  gameStatus = WON;
87                document.craps.point.value = ""; // clear point field
88                  break;
89               case 2: case 3: case 12:   // lose on first roll
90                  gameStatus = LOST;
91                document.craps.point.value = ""; // clear point field
92                  break;
93               default:                    // remember point
94                  gameStatus = CONTINUE_ROLLING;
95                  myPoint = sumOfDice;
96                  document.craps.point.value = myPoint;
97                  firstRoll = false;
98            }
99         }
100        else {
101           sumOfDice = rollDice();
102
103           if ( sumOfDice == myPoint )    // win by making point
104              gameStatus = WON;
105           else
106              if ( sumOfDice == 7 )        // lose by rolling 7
107                 gameStatus = LOST;
108        }
109
```

Fig. 16.6   Program to simulate the game of craps (part 1 of 5).

```
110          if ( gameStatus == CONTINUE_ROLLING )
111             window.status = "Roll again";
112          else {
113             if ( gameStatus == WON )
114                window.status = "Player wins. " +
115                   "Click Roll Dice to play again.";
116             else
117                window.status = "Player loses. " +
118                   "Click Roll Dice to play again.";
119
120             firstRoll = true;
121          }
122       }
123
124       // roll the dice
125       function rollDice()
126       {
127          var die1, die2, workSum;
128
129          die1 = Math.floor( 1 + Math.random() * 6 );
130          die2 = Math.floor( 1 + Math.random() * 6 );
131          workSum = die1 + die2;
132
133          document.craps.firstDie.value = die1;
134          document.craps.secondDie.value = die2;
135          document.craps.sum.value = workSum;
136
137          return workSum;
138       }
139   </SCRIPT>
140
141   </HEAD>
142   <BODY>
143   <FORM NAME = "craps">
144      <TABLE BORDER = "1">
145      <TR><TD>Die 1</TD>
146         <TD><INPUT NAME = "firstDie" TYPE = "text"></TD></TR>
147      <TR><TD>Die 2</TD>
148         <TD><INPUT NAME = "secondDie" TYPE = "text"></TD></TR>
149      <TR><TD>Sum</TD>
150         <TD><INPUT NAME = "sum" TYPE = "text"></TD></TR>
151      <TR><TD>Point</TD>
152         <TD><INPUT NAME = "point" TYPE = "text"></TD></TR>
153      <TR><TD><INPUT TYPE = "button" VALUE = "Roll Dice"
154                     ONCLICK = "play()"></TD></TR>
155      </TABLE>
156   </FORM>
157   </BODY>
158   </HTML>
```

Fig. 16.6   Program to simulate the game of craps (part 2 of 5).

A **text**
HTML GUI
component

A **button**
HTML GUI
component

Browser's
status bar

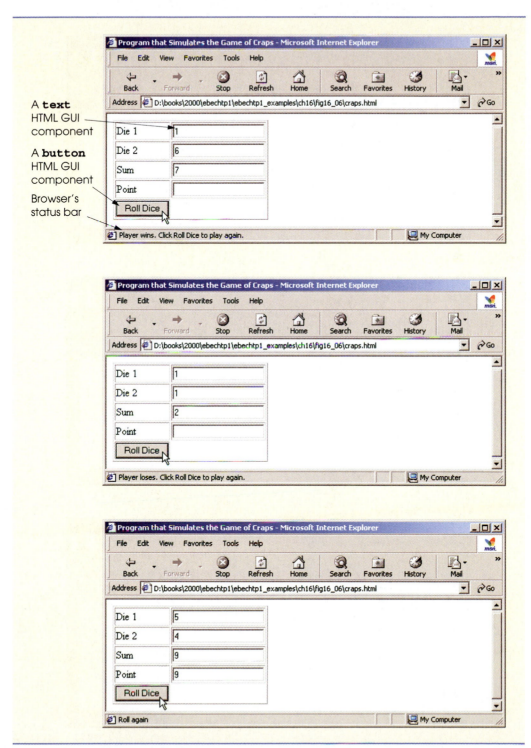

Fig. 16.6   Program to simulate the game of craps (part 3 of 5).

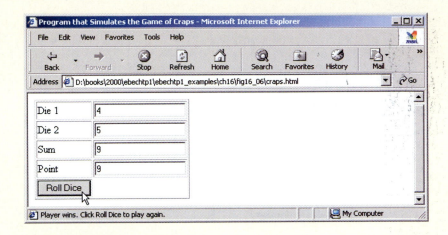

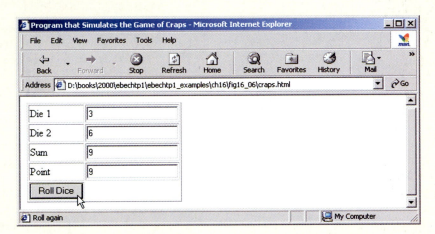

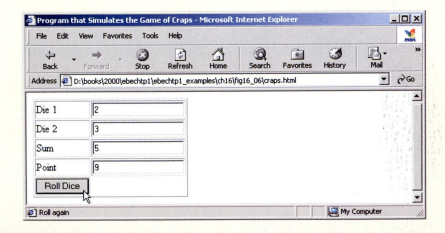

Fig. 16.6   Program to simulate the game of craps (part 4 of 5).

Fig. 16.6   Program to simulate the game of craps (part 5 of 5).

Before we discuss the script code, we first discuss the **<BODY>** section (lines 82 through 97) of the HTML document. The GUI components in this section are used extensively in the script.

Line 83,

```
<FORM NAME = "craps">
```

begins the definition of an HTML **<FORM>** with its **NAME** attribute set to **craps**. The **NAME** attribute **craps** enables script code to refer to the elements of the form. This attribute helps a script distinguish between multiple forms in the same HTML document. Similarly, the **NAME** attribute is specified for each GUI component in the form, so that the script code can individually refer to each GUI component.

In this example, we decided to place the form's GUI components in an HTML **<TABLE>**, so line 84

```
<TABLE BORDER = "1">
```

begins the definition of the HTML table and indicates that it has a 1-pixel border.

Lines 85 and 86

```
<TR><TD>Die 1</TD>
    <TD><INPUT NAME = "firstDie" TYPE = "text"></TD></TR>
```

define the first row of the table. The left column contains the text **Die 1** and the right column contains the text field named **firstDie**.

Lines 87 and 88

```
<TR><TD>Die 2</TD>
    <TD><INPUT NAME = "secondDie" TYPE = "text"></TD></TR>
```

define the second row of the table. The left column contains the text **Die 2** and the right column contains the text field named **secondDie**.

Lines 89 and 90

```
<TR><TD>Sum</TD>
    <TD><INPUT NAME = "sum" TYPE = "text"></TD></TR>
```

define the third row of the table. The left column contains the text **Sum** and the right column contains the text field named **sum**.

Lines 91 and 92

```
<TR><TD>Point</TD>
    <TD><INPUT NAME = "point" TYPE = "text"></TD></TR>
```

define the fourth row of the table. The left column contains the text **Point** and the right column contains the text field named **point**.

Lines 93 and 94

```
<TR><TD><INPUT TYPE = "button" VALUE = "Roll Dice"
                ONCLICK = "play()"></TD></TR>
```

define the last row of the table. The left column contains the button **Roll Dice**. The button's attribute **ONCLICK** is used to indicate the action to take when the user of this HTML document clicks the **Roll Dice** button. In this example, the script function **play** will be called in response to a button click.

This style of programming is known as *event-driven programming*—the user interacts with a GUI component, the script is notified of the event and the script processes the event. The user's interaction with the GUI "drives" the program. The clicking of the button is known as the *event*. The function that is called when an event occurs is known as an *event handling function* or *event handler*. When a GUI event occurs in a form, the browser *automatically calls* the specified event handling function. Before any event can be processed, each GUI component must know which event handling function will be called when a particular event occurs. Most HTML GUI components have several different event types. The event model is discussed in detail in Chapter 21, "Dynamic HTML: Event Model." By specifying **ONCLICK = "play()"** for the **Roll Dice** button, we enable the browser to *listen for events* (button click events in particular). This is called *registering the event handler* with the GUI component (we also like to call it the *start listening* line, because the browser is now listening for button click events from the button). If not event handler is specified for the **Roll Dice** button, the script will not respond when the user presses the button.

Lines 95 and 96 end the **<TABLE>** and **<FORM>** definitions, respectively.

The game is reasonably involved. The player may win or lose on the first roll, or may win or lose on any roll. Line 10 of the program

```
var WON = 0, LOST = 1, CONTINUE_ROLLING = 2;
```

creates variables that define the three states of a game of craps—game won, game lost or continue rolling the dice. Unlike many other programming languages, JavaScript does not provide a mechanism to define a *constant variable* (the value of such a variable cannot be modified). For this reason, we purposely used all capital letters for these variable names to indicate that we do not intend to modify their values and to make them stand out in the code.

Good Programming Practice 16.5

Use only uppercase letters (with underscores between words) in the names of variables that should be used as constants. This makes these constants stand out in a program.

Good Programming Practice 16.6

Use meaningfully named variables rather than constants (such as 2) to make programs more readable.

Lines 13 through 16

```
var firstRoll = true,              // true if first roll
    sumOfDice = 0,                 // sum of the dice
    myPoint = 0,   // point if no win/loss on first roll
    gameStatus = CONTINUE_ROLLING;  // game not over yet
```

declare several variables that are used throughout the script. Variable **firstRoll** indicates whether the next roll of the dice is the first roll in the current game. Variable **sumOfDice** maintains the sum of the dice for the last roll. Variable **myPoint** stores the "point" if the player does not win or lose on the first roll. Variable **gameStatus** keeps track of the current state of the game (**WON**, **LOST** or **CONTINUE_ROLLING**).

We define a function **rollDice** (line 65) to roll the dice and to compute and display their sum. Function **rollDice** is defined once, but it is called from two places in the program (lines 22 and 41). Function **rollDice** takes no arguments, so it has an empty parameter list. Function **rollDice** returns the sum of the two dice.

The user clicks the "**Roll Dice**" button to roll the dice. This invokes function **play** (line 19) of the script. Function **play** checks the boolean variable **firstRoll** (line 21) to determine whether it is **true** or **false**. If it is **true**, this is the first roll of the game. Line 22 calls **rollDice** (defined at line 65), which picks two random values from 1 to 6, displays the value of the first die, the second die and the sum of the dice in the first three text fields and returns the sum of the dice (we discuss function **rollDice** in detail shortly). After the first roll, the nested **switch** structure at line 24 determines whether the game is won or lost, or whether the game should continue with another roll. After the first roll, if the game is not over, **sumOfDice** is saved in **myPoint** and displayed in the text field **point** in the HTML form. Notice how the text field's value is changed at lines 27, 31 and 36. The expression

```
craps.point.value
```

specifies that the script would like to change the **value** property of the text field **point**. The **value** property specifies the text to display in the text field. To access this property, we specify the name of the form (**craps**) that contains the text field followed by a *dot operator* (**.**) followed by the name of the text field we would like to manipulate. The dot operator is also known as the *field access operator* or the *member access operator*. In the preceding expression, the dot operator is used to access the **point** member of the **craps** form. Similarly, the second member access operator is used to access the **value** member (or property) of the **point** text field. Actually, we will see in the Dynamic HTML chapters that every element of an HTML document can be accessed in a manner similar to that shown here.

The program proceeds to the nested **if**/**else** structure at line 50, which sets the **window** object's **status** property (**window.status** at lines 51, 54 and 57) to

```
Roll again.
```

if **gameStatus** is equal to **CONTINUE**, to

```
Player wins. Click Roll Dice to play again.
```

if **gameStatus** is equal to **WON** and to

```
Player loses. Click Roll Dice to play again.
```

if **gameStatus** is equal to **LOST**. The **window** object's **status** property displays the string assigned to it in the status bar of the browser. If the game was won or lost, line 60 sets **firstRoll** to **true** to indicate that the next roll of the dice begins the next game.

The program then waits for the user to click the button "**Roll Dice**" again. Each time the user presses **Roll Dice**, function **play** is called, which, in turn, calls the **rollDice** function to produce a new value for **sumOfDice**. If **sumOfDice** matches **myPoint**, **gameStatus** is set to **WON**, the **if/else** structure at line 50 executes and the game is complete. If **sum** is equal to **7**, **gameStatus** is set to **LOST**, the **if/else** structure at line 50 executes and the game is complete. Clicking the "**Roll Dice**" button starts a new game. Throughout the program, the four text fields in the HTML form are updated with the new values of the dice and the sum on each roll, and the text field **point** is also updated each time a new game begins.

Function **rollDice** (line 65) defines its own local variables **die1**, **die2** and **workSum** at line 67. Because these variables are defined inside the body of **rollDice**, they are known only in that function. If these three variable names are used elsewhere in the program, they will be entirely separate variables in memory. Lines 69 and 70 pick two random values in the range 1 to 6 and assign them to variables **die1** and **die2** respectively. Lines 73 through 75

```
craps.firstDie.value = die1;
craps.secondDie.value = die2;
craps.sum.value = workSum;
```

assign the values of **die1**, **die2** and **workSum** to the corresponding text fields in the HTML form **craps**. Note that the integer values are automatically converted to strings when they are assigned to each text field's **value** property. Line 77 returns the value of workSum for use in function **play**.

Software Engineering Observation 16.9

Variables that are defined inside the body of a function are known only in that function. If the same variable names are used elsewhere in the program, they will be entirely separate variables in memory.

Note the interesting use of the various program control mechanisms we have discussed. The craps program uses two functions—**play** and **rollDice**—and the **switch**, **if/else** and nested **if** structures. Note also the use of multiple **case** labels in the **switch** structure to execute the same statements (lines 25 and 29). In the exercises, we investigate various interesting characteristics of the game of craps.

16.7 Duration of Identifiers

Chapters 13 through 15 used identifiers for variable names. The attributes of variables include name, value and data type (such as string, number or boolean). We also use identifiers as names for user-defined functions. Actually, each identifier in a program has other attributes, including *duration* and *scope* (discussed in section 16.8).

An identifier's *duration* (also called its *lifetime*) is the period during which that identifier exists in memory. Some identifiers exist briefly, some are repeatedly created and destroyed and others exist for the entire execution of a script.

Identifiers that represent local variables in a function (i.e., parameters and variables declared in the function body) have *automatic duration*. Automatic duration variables are *automatic*ally created when program control enters the function in which they are declared, they exist while the function in which they are declared is active; and they are *automatic*ally destroyed when the function in which they are declared is exited. For the remainder of the text, we will refer to variables of automatic duration as local variables.

Software Engineering Observation 16.10

Automatic duration is a means of conserving memory, because automatic duration variables are created when program control enters the function in which they are declared and are destroyed when the function in which they are declared is exited.

Software Engineering Observation 16.11

Automatic duration is an example of the principle of least privilege. *This principle states that each component of a system should have sufficient rights and privileges to accomplish its designated task, but no additional rights or privileges. This helps prevent accidental and/or malicious errors from occurring in systems. Why have variables stored in memory and accessible when they are not needed?*

JavaScript also has identifiers of *static duration*. Such identifiers are typically defined in the **<HEAD>** of the HTML document and exist from the point at which the **<HEAD>** of the HTML document is interpreted until the browsing session terminates (the browser is closed by the user). Even though static duration variables exist after the **<HEAD>** section of the document is interpreted, this does not mean that these identifiers can be used throughout the script. Duration and *scope* (where a name can be used) are separate issues, as shown in Section 16.8. Static duration variables are globally accessible to the script—i.e., every function in the script can potentially use these variables. For the remainder of the text, we refer to variables of static duration as *global variables* or *script-level variables*.

16.8 Scope Rules

The *scope* of an identifier for a variable or function is the portion of the program in which the identifier can be referenced. A local variable declared in a function can be used only in that function. The scopes for an identifier are *global scope* and *function* (or *local*) *scope*.

Identifiers declared inside a function have *function* (or *local*) *scope*. Function scope begins with the opening left brace (**{**) of the function in which the identifier is declared and ends at the terminating right brace (**}**) of the function. Local variables of a function have function scope; so do function parameters, which are also local variables of the function. If a local variable in a function has the same name as a global variable, the global variable is "hidden" from the body of the function.

Good Programming Practice 16.7

Avoid local variable names that hide global variable names. This can be accomplished by avoiding the use of duplicate identifiers in a script.

The script of Fig. 16.7 demonstrates scoping issues in JavaScript with global variables and local variables. This example also demonstrates the event **ONLOAD**, which calls an event handler when the **<BODY>** of the HTML document is completely loaded into the browser window.

```
1   <!DOCTYPE html PUBLIC "-//W3C//DTD HTML 4.0 Transitional//EN">
2   <HTML>
3   <!-- Fig. 16.7: scoping.html -->
4
5   <HEAD>
6   <TITLE>A Scoping Example</TITLE>
7
8   <SCRIPT LANGUAGE = "JavaScript">
9      var x = 1;        // global variable
10
11     function start()
12     {
13        var x = 5;    // variable local to function start
14
15        document.writeln( "local x in start is " + x );
16
17        functionA();   // functionA has local x
18        functionB();   // functionB uses global variable x
19        functionA();   // functionA reinitializes local x
20        functionB();   // global variable x retains its value
21
22        document.writeln(
23           "<P>local x in start is " + x + "</P>" );
24     }
25
26     function functionA()
27     {
28        var x = 25;   // initialized each time functionA is called
29
30        document.writeln( "<P>local x in functionA is " + x +
31                          " after entering functionA" );
32        ++x;
33        document.writeln( "<BR>local x in functionA is " + x +
34                          " before exiting functionA</P>" );
35     }
36
37     function functionB()
38     {
39        document.writeln( "<P>global variable x is " + x +
40                          " on entering functionB" );
41        x *= 10;
42        document.writeln( "<BR>global variable x is " + x +
43                          " on exiting functionB</P>" );
44     }
45   </SCRIPT>
46
47   </HEAD>
48   <BODY ONLOAD = "start()"></BODY>
49   </HTML>
```

Fig. 16.7   A scoping example (part 1 of 2).

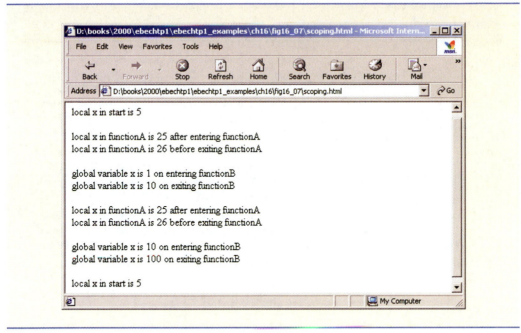

Fig. 16.7   A scoping example (part 2 of 2).

Global variable **x** (line 9) is declared and initialized to 1. This global variable is hidden in any block (or function) that declares a variable named **x**. Function **start** (line 11) declares a local variable **x** (line 13) and initializes it to **5**. This variable is output in a line of HTML text to show that the global variable **x** is hidden in **start**. The script defines two other functions—**functionA** and **functionB**—that each take no arguments and return nothing. Each function is called twice from function **start**.

Function **functionA** defines local variable **x** (line 28) and initializes it to **25**. When **functionA** is called, the variable is output in a line of HTML text to show that the global variable **x** is hidden in **functionA**, then the variable is incremented and output in a line of HTML text again before exiting the function. Each time this function is called, local variable **x** is recreated and initialized to **25**.

Function **functionB** does not declare any variables. Therefore, when it refers to variable **x**, the global variable **x** is used. When **functionB** is called, the global variable is output in a line of HTML text, multiplied by **10** and output in a line of HTML text again before exiting the function. The next time function **functionB** is called, the global variable has its modified value, **10**. Finally, the program outputs local variable **x** in **start** in a line of HTML text again to show that none of the function calls modified the value of **x** in **start** because the functions all referred to variables in other scopes.

16.9 JavaScript Global Functions

JavaScript provides seven functions that are available globally in a JavaScript. We have already used two of these functions—**parseInt** and **parseFloat**. The global functions are summarized in Fig. 16.8.

Global function	Description
escape	This function takes a string argument and returns a string in which all spaces, punctuation, accent characters and any other character that is not in the ASCII character set (see Appendix C, "ASCII Character Set") are encoded in a hexadecimal format (see the "Number Systems" document on the CD that accompanies this book) that can be represented on all platforms.
eval	This function takes a string argument representing JavaScript code to execute. The JavaScript interpreter evaluates the code and executes it when the **eval** function is called. This function allows JavaScript code to be stored as strings and executed dynamically.
isFinite	This function takes a numeric argument and returns **true** if the value of the argument is not **NaN**, **Number.POSITIVE_INFINITY** or **Number.NEGATIVE_INFINITY**; otherwise the function returns **false**.
isNaN	This function takes a numeric argument and returns **true** if the value of the argument is not a number; otherwise the function returns **false**. The function is commonly used with the return value of **parseInt** or **parseFloat** to determine whether the result is a proper numeric value.
parseFloat	This function takes a string argument and attempts to convert the beginning of the string into a floating-point value. If the conversion is not successful, the function returns **NaN**; otherwise, it returns the converted value (e.g., **parseFloat("abc123.45")** returns **NaN** and **parseFloat("123.45abc")** returns the value **123.45**.
parseInt	This function takes a string argument and attempts to convert the beginning of the string into an integer value. If the conversion is not successful, the function returns **NaN**; otherwise, it returns the converted value (e.g., **parseInt("abc123")** returns **NaN** and **parseInt("123abc")** returns the integer value **123**. This function takes an optional second argument from 2 to 36 specifying the *radix* (or *base*) of the number. Base 2 indicates that the first argument string is in *binary* format, 8 indicates that the first argument string is in *octal* format and 16 indicates that the first argument string is in *hexadecimal* format. See see the "Number Systems" document on the CD that accompanies this book for more information on binary, octal and hexadecimal numbers.
unescape	This function takes a string as its argument and returns a string in which all characters that we previously encoded with **escape** are decoded.

Fig. 16.8   **JavaScript** global functions.

Actually, the global functions in Fig. 16.8 are all part of JavaScript's **Global** *object*. The **Global** object contains all the global variables in the script, all the user-defined functions in the script and the functions of Fig. 16.8. Because global functions and user-defined functions are part of the **Global** object, some JavaScript programmers refer to these functions as methods. We will use the term "method" only when referring to a function that is called for a particular object (such as **Math.random()**). As a JavaScript programmer, you do not need to use the **Global** object directly; JavaScript does this for you.

SUMMARY

- Experience has shown that the best way to develop and maintain a large program is to construct it from small, simple pieces or modules. This technique is called divide and conquer.
- Modules in JavaScript are called functions. JavaScript programs are written by combining new functions that the programmer writes with "prepackaged" functions and objects available in JavaScript.
- The "prepackaged" functions that belong to JavaScript objects are often called *methods*. The term *method* implies that the function belongs to a particular object.
- The programmer can write programmer-defined functions to define specific tasks that may be used at many points in a script. The actual statements defining the function are written only once, and these statements are hidden from other functions.
- A function is invoked by a function call. The function call specifies the function name and provides information (as arguments) that the called function needs to do its task.
- Functions allow the programmer to modularize a program.
- All variables declared in function definitions are local variables—they are known only in the function in which they are defined.
- Most functions have parameters that provide the means for communicating information between functions via function calls. A function's parameters are also considered to be local variables.
- The divide-and-conquer approach to program development makes program development more manageable.
- Using existing functions as building blocks to create new programs promotes software reusability. With good function naming and definition, programs can be created from standardized functions rather than be built by using customized code.
- The **()** represent the *function call operator.*
- The **return** *statement* passes the result of a function call back to the calling function.
- The format of a function definition is

    function *function-name* **(** *parameter-list* **)**
    {
    　　 declarations and statements
    }

    The *function-name* is any valid identifier. The *parameter-list* is a comma-separated list containing the names of the parameters received by the function when it is called. There should be one argument in the function call for each parameter in the function definition. If a function does not receive any values, the *parameter-list* is empty (i.e., the function name is followed by an empty set of parentheses).
- The declarations and statements within braces form the function body. The function body is also referred to as a block. A block is a compound statement that includes declarations. Variables can be declared in any block and blocks can be nested.
- There are three ways to return control to the point at which a function was invoked. If the function does not return a result, control is returned when the function-ending right brace is reached or by executing the statement

    return;
- If the function does return a result, the statement

    return *expression***;**

    returns the value of *expression* to the caller. When a **return** statement is executed, control returns immediately to the point at which a function was invoked.

- The **Math** object **max** method determines the larger of its two argument values.
- The **Math** object **random** method generates numeric values from 0.0 up to but not including 1.0.
- **Math** method **floor** rounds its floating-point number argument to the closest integer not greater than its argument's value.
- The values produced directly by **random** are always in the range

  $$0.0 \leq \texttt{Math.random()} < 1.0$$

- We can generalize picking a random number from a range of values by writing:

  $$\texttt{value = Math.floor(a + Math.random() * b);}$$

  where a is the shifting value (the first number in the desired range of consecutive integers) and b is the scaling factor (the width of the desired range of consecutive integers).
- Graphical user interface event handling enables JavaScript code to execute in response to the user's interaction with a GUI component in an HTML form. This interaction causes an event. Scripts are often used to respond to events.
- Specifying the **NAME** attribute of an HTML **<FORM>** enables script code to refer to the elements of the form. This attribute helps a script distinguish between multiple forms in the same HTML document. Similarly, the **NAME** attribute is specified for each GUI component in the form, so the script code can individually refer to each GUI component.
- An HTML button's attribute **ONCLICK** indicates the action to take when the user clicks the button.
- When the user interacts with a GUI component, the script is notified of the event, and the script processes the event. The user's interaction with the GUI "drives" the program. This style of programming is known as event-driven programming.
- The clicking of the button (or any other GUI interaction) is known as the event. The function that is called when an event occurs is known as an event handling function or event handler. When a GUI event occurs in a form, the browser automatically calls the specified event handling function.
- The **value** property specifies the text to display in an HTML text field GUI component.
- The dot operator (**.**) is known as the field access operator or the member access operator.
- Each identifier in a program has many attributes, including duration and scope.
- An identifier's duration or lifetime is the period during which that identifier exists in memory.
- Identifiers that represent local variables in a function have automatic duration. Automatic duration variables are automatically created when program control enters the function in which they are declared, they exist while the function in which they are declared is active; and they are automatically destroyed when the function in which they are declared is exited.
- Identifiers of static duration are typically defined in the **<HEAD>** section of the HTML document and exist from the point at which the **<HEAD>** section of the HTML document is interpreted until the browsing session terminates.
- Variables of static duration are normally called global variables or script-level variables.
- The scope of an identifier for a variable or function is the portion of the program in which the identifier can be referenced. The scopes for an identifier are global scope and function (or local) scope.
- Event **ONLOAD** calls an event handler when the **<BODY>** of the HTML document is loaded into the browser.
- Identifiers declared inside a function have function (or local) scope. Function scope begins with the opening left brace (**{**) of the function in which the identifier is declared and ends at the terminating right brace (**}**) of the function. Local variables of a function have function scope, as do function parameters, which are also local variables of the function.

- If a local variable in a function has the same name as a global variable, the global variable is "hidden" from the body of the function.

- Function **escape** takes a string argument and returns a string in which all spaces, punctuation, accent characters and any other character that is not in the ASCII character set are encoded in a hexadecimal format that can be represented on all platforms.

- Function **eval** takes a string argument representing JavaScript code to execute. The JavaScript interpreter evaluates the code and executes it when the **eval** function is called.

- Function **isFinite** takes a numeric argument and returns **true** if the value of the argument is not **NaN**, **Number.POSITIVE_INFINITY** or **Number.NEGATIVE_INFINITY**; otherwise the function returns **false**.

- Function **isNaN** takes a numeric argument and returns **true** if the value of the argument is not a number; otherwise the function returns **false**.

- Function **parseFloat** takes a string argument and attempts to convert the beginning of the string into a floating-point value. If the conversion is not successful, the function returns **NaN**; otherwise, it returns the converted value.

- Function **parseInt** takes a string argument and attempts to convert the beginning of the string into an integer value. If the conversion is not successful, the function returns **NaN**; otherwise, it returns the converted value. This function takes an optional second argument between 2 and 36 specifying the *radix* (or *base*) of the number.

- Function **unescape** takes a string as its argument and returns a string in which all characters that we previously encoded with **escape** are decoded.

- JavaScript's global functions are all part of the **Global** object, which also contains all the global variables in the script and all the user-defined functions in the script.

TERMINOLOGY

argument in a function call
automatic duration
automatic variable
block
call a function
called function
caller
calling function
compound statement
converge on the base case
copy of a value
divide and conquer
dot operator (**.**)
duration
escape function
eval function
event
event handler
event-driven programming
field access operator (**.**)
floor method of the **Math** object
function
function argument

function body
function call
function call operator, **( )**
function definition
function keyword
function name
function parameter
function scope
Global object
global scope
global variable
invoke a function
isFinite function
isNaN function
lifetime
local scope
local variable
max method of the **Math** object
member access operator (**.**)
method
modularize a program
module
NAME attribute of an HTML **<FORM>**

ONCLICK	scope
ONLOAD	script-level variable
parameter in a function definition	shifting
parseFloat function	shifting value
parseInt function	side effect
programmer-defined function	signature
random method of the **Math** object	simulation
random number generation	software engineering
respond to an event	software reusability
return statement	static duration
scaling	**unescape** function
scaling factor	**value** property of an HTML text field

SELF-REVIEW EXERCISES

16.1   Answer each of the following:
  a) Program modules in JavaScript are called _____.
  b) A function is invoked with a _____.
  c) A variable known only within the function in which it is defined is called a _____.
  d) The _____ statement in a called function can be used to pass the value of an expression back to the calling function.
  e) The keyword _____ indicates the beginning of a function definition.

16.2   For the following program, state the scope (either global scope or function scope) of each of the following elements.
  a) The variable **x**.
  b) The variable **y**.
  c) The function **cube**.
  d) The function **output**.

```
1   <!DOCTYPE html PUBLIC "-//W3C//DTD HTML 4.0 Transitional//EN">
2   <!-- Exercise 16.2: scoping.html -->
3
4   <HEAD>
5   <TITLE>Scoping</TITLE>
6
7   <SCRIPT LANGUAGE = "JavaScript">
8      var x;
9
10     function output()
11     {
12        for ( var x = 1; x <= 10; x++ )
13           document.writeln( cube( x ) + "<BR>" );
14     }
15
16     function cube( y )
17     {
18        return y * y * y;
19     }
20  </SCRIPT>
21
22  </HEAD><BODY ONLOAD = "output()"></BODY>
23  </HTML>
```

16.3 Answer each of the following:

a) Programmer-defined functions, global variables and JavaScript's global functions are all part of the _____ object.

b) Function _____ determines if its argument is or is not a number.

c) Function _____ takes a string argument and returns a string in which all spaces, punctuation, accent characters and any other character that is not in the ASCII character set are encoded in a hexadecimal format.

d) Function _____ takes a string argument representing JavaScript code to execute.

e) Function _____ takes a string as its argument and returns a string in which all characters that we previously encoded with **escape** are decoded.

16.4 Answer each of the following:

a) The _____ of an identifier is the portion of the program in which the identifier can be used.

b) The three ways to return control from a called function to a caller are _____, _____ and _____.

c) The _____ function is used to produce random numbers.

d) Variables declared in a block or in a function's parameter list are of _____ duration.

16.5 Find the error in each of the following program segments and explain how to correct the error:

a)
```
method g() {
    document.writeln( "Inside method g" );
}
```

b)
```
// This function should return the sum of its arguments
function sum( x, y ) {
    var result;
    result = x + y;
}
```

c)
```
function f( a ); {
    document.writeln( a );
}
```

16.6 Write a complete JavaScript script to prompt the user for the radius of a sphere and call function **sphereVolume** to calculate and display the volume of that sphere. Use the statement

```
volume = ( 4.0 / 3.0 ) * Math.PI * Math.pow( radius, 3 )
```

to calculate the volume. The user should input the radius through an HTML text field in a **<FORM>** and press an HTML button to initiate the calculation.

ANSWERS TO SELF-REVIEW EXERCISES

16.1 a) functions. b) function call. c) Local variable. d) **return**. e) **function**.

16.2 a) Global scope. b) Function scope. c) Global scope. d) Global scope.

16.3 a) **Global**. b) **isNaN**. c) **escape**. d) **eval**. e) **unescape**.

16.4 a) Scope. b) **return;** or **return** *expression;* or encountering the closing right brace of a function. c) **Math.random**. e) Automatic.

16.5 a) Error: **method** is not a keyword used to begin a function definition.
Correction: Change **method** to **function**.

b) Error: The function is supposed to return a value, but does not. Correction: Delete variable **result** and place the following statement in the function:
```
return x + y;
```

or add the following statement at the end of the function body:

```
return result;
```

c) Error: The result of **n + sum(n - 1)** is not returned by this recursive function, resulting in a syntax error.

Correction: Rewrite the statement in the **else** clause as

```
return n + sum(n - 1);
```

d) Error: The semicolon after the right parenthesis that encloses the parameter list.

Correction: Delete the semicolon after the right parenthesis of the parameter list.

16.6   The following solution calculates the volume of a sphere using the radius entered by the user.

```
1   <!DOCTYPE html PUBLIC "-//W3C//DTD HTML 4.0 Transitional//EN">
2   <HTML>
3   <!-- Exercise 16.6: volume.html -->
4
5   <HEAD>
6   <TITLE>Calculating Sphere Volumes</TITLE>
7
8   <SCRIPT LANGUAGE = "JavaScript">
9       function displayVolume()
10      {
11          var radius = parseFloat( myForm.radiusField.value );
12          window.status = "Volume is " + sphereVolume( radius );
13      }
14
15      function sphereVolume( r )
16      {
17          return ( 4.0 / 3.0 ) * Math.PI * Math.pow( r, 3 );
18      }
19  </SCRIPT>
20
21  </HEAD>
22
23  <BODY>
24  <FORM NAME = "myForm">
25      Enter radius of sphere<BR>
26      <INPUT NAME = "radiusField" TYPE = "text">
27      <INPUT NAME = "calculate" TYPE = "button" VALUE = "Calculate"
28              ONCLICK = "displayVolume()">
29  </FORM>
30  </BODY>
31  </HTML>
```

EXERCISES

16.7   Write a script that uses a function **circleArea** to prompt the user for the radius of a circle and to calculate and print the area of that circle.

16.8   A parking garage charges a $2.00 minimum fee to park for up to three hours. The garage charges an additional $0.50 per hour for each hour *or part thereof* in excess of three hours. The maximum charge for any given 24-hour period is $10.00. Assume that no car parks for longer than 24 hours at a time. Write a script that calculates and displays the parking charges for each customer who parked a car in this garage yesterday. You should input from the user the hours parked for each customer. The program should display the charge for the current customer and should calculate and display the running total of yesterday's receipts. The program should use the function **calculateCharges** to determine the charge for each customer. Use the techniques described in Self-Review Exercise 16.6 to obtain the input from the user.

16.9   Write function **distance**, which calculates the distance between two points (x1, y1) and (x2, y2). All numbers and return values should be floating-point values. Incorporate this function into a script that enables the user to enter the coordinates of the points through an HTML form.

16.10   Answer each of the following questions.
   a)   What does it mean to choose numbers "at random?"
   b)   Why is the **Math.random** function useful for simulating games of chance?
   c)   Why is it often necessary to scale and/or shift the values produced by **Math.random**?
   d)   Why is computerized simulation of real-world situations a useful technique?

16.11   Write statements that assign random integers to the variable n in the following ranges:
   a) $1 \le n \le 2$
   b) $1 \le n \le 100$
   c) $0 \le n \le 9$
   d) $1000 \le n \le 1112$
   e) $-1 \le n \le 1$
   f) $-3 \le n \le 11$

16.12   For each of the following sets of integers, write a single statement that will print a number at random from the set.
   a)   2, 4, 6, 8, 10.
   b)   3, 5, 7, 9, 11.
   c)   6, 10, 14, 18, 22.

16.13   Write a function **integerPower(base, exponent)** that returns the value of

$$base^{\ exponent}$$

For example, **integerPower(3, 4) = 3 * 3 * 3 * 3**. Assume that **exponent** is a positive, nonzero integer and **base** is an integer. Function **integerPower** should use **for** or **while** to control the calculation. Do not use any math library functions. Incorporate this function into a script that reads integer values from an HTML form for **base** and **exponent** and performs the calculation with the **integerPower** function. The HTML form should consist of two text fields and a button to initiate the calculation. The user should interact with the program by typing numbers in both text fields then clicking the button.

16.14   Write a function **multiple** that determines for a pair of integers whether the second integer is a multiple of the first. The function should take two integer arguments and return **true** if the second is a multiple of the first and **false** otherwise. Incorporate this function into a script that inputs a series of pairs of integers (one pair at a time using **JTextField**s). The HTML form should consist of two text fields and a button to initiate the calculation. The user should interact with the program by typing numbers in both text fields, then clicking the button.

16.15   Write a script that inputs integers (one at a time) and passes them one at a time to function **isEven**, which uses the modulus operator to determine if an integer is even. The function should take an integer argument and return **true** if the integer is even and **false** otherwise. Use sentinel-controlled looping and a **prompt** dialog.

16.16   Write a function **squareOfAsterisks** that displays a solid square of asterisks whose side is specified in integer parameter **side**. For example, if **side** is **4**, the function displays

```
****
****
****
****
```

Incorporate this function into a script that reads an integer value for **side** from the user at the keyboard and performs the drawing with the **squareOfAsterisks** function.

16.17   Modify the function created in Exercise 16.16 to form the square out of whatever character is contained in parameter **fillCharacter**. Thus if **side** is **5** and **fillCharacter** is "**#**", this function should print

```
#####
#####
#####
#####
#####
```

16.18   Write program segments that accomplish each of the following:
   a) Calculate the integer part of the quotient when integer **a** is divided by integer **b**.
   b) Calculate the integer remainder when integer **a** is divided by integer **b**.
   c) Use the program pieces developed in a) and b) to write a function **displayDigits** that receives an integer between **1** and **99999** and prints it as a series of digits, each pair of which is separated by two spaces. For example, the integer **4562** should be printed as
      4   5   6   2.
   d) Incorporate the function developed in c) into a script that inputs an integer from a **prompt** dialog and invokes **displayDigits** by passing the function the integer entered.

16.19   Implement the following functions:
   a) Function **celsius** returns the Celsius equivalent of a Fahrenheit temperature using the calculation
      ```
      C = 5.0 / 9.0 * ( F - 32 );
      ```
   b) Function **fahrenheit** returns the Fahrenheit equivalent of a Celsius temperature using the calculation
      ```
      F = 9.0 / 5.0 * C + 32;
      ```
   c) Use these functions to write a script that enables the user to enter either a Fahrenheit temperature and display the Celsius equivalent or enter a Celsius temperature and display the Fahrenheit equivalent.

Your HTML document should contain two buttons—one to initiate the conversion from Fahrenheit to Celcius and one to initiate the conversion from Celcius to Fahrenheit.

16.20   Write a function **minimum3** that returns the smallest of three floating-point numbers. Use the **Math.min** function to implement **minimum3**. Incorporate the function into a script that reads three values from the user and determines the smallest value. Display the result in the status bar.

16.21   An integer number is said to be a *perfect number* if its factors, including 1 (but not the number itself), sum to the number. For example, 6 is a perfect number because 6 = 1 + 2 + 3. Write a function

perfect that determines whether parameter **number** is a perfect number. Use this function in a script that determines and displays all the perfect numbers between 1 and 1000. Print the factors of each perfect number to confirm that the number is indeed perfect. Challenge the computing power of your computer by testing numbers much larger than 1000. Display the results in a **<TEXTAREA>**.

16.22 An integer is said to be *prime* if it is divisible by only 1 and itself. For example, 2, 3, 5 and 7 are prime, but 4, 6, 8 and 9 are not.
 a) Write a function that determines whether a number is prime.
 b) Use this function in a script that determines and prints all the prime numbers between 1 and 10,000. How many of these 10,000 numbers do you really have to test before being sure that you have found all the primes? Display the results in a **<TEXTAREA>**.
 c) Initially you might think that $n/2$ is the upper limit for which you must test to see whether a number is prime, but you only need go as high as the square root of n. Why? Rewrite the program and run it both ways. Estimate the performance improvement.

16.23 Write a function that takes an integer value and returns the number with its digits reversed. For example, given the number 7631, the function should return 1367. Incorporate the function into a script that reads a value from the user. Display the result of the function in the status bar.

16.24 The *greatest common divisor (GCD)* of two integers is the largest integer that evenly divides each of the two numbers. Write a function **gcd** that returns the greatest common divisor of two integers. Incorporate the function into a script that reads two values from the user. Display the result of the function in the browser's status bar.

16.25 Write a function **qualityPoints** that inputs a student's average and returns 4 if a student's average is 90–100, 3 if the average is 80–89, 2 if the average is 70–79, 1 if the average is 60–69 and 0 if the average is lower than 60. Incorporate the function into a script that reads a value from the user. Display the result of the function in the browser's status bar.

16.26 Write a script that simulates coin tossing. Let the program toss the coin each time the user presses the "**Toss**" button. Count the number of times each side of the coin appears. Display the results. The program should call a separate function **flip** that takes no arguments and returns **false** for tails and **true** for heads. [*Note:* If the program realistically simulates the coin tossing, each side of the coin should appear approximately half the time.]

16.27 Computers are playing an increasing role in education. Write a program that will help an elementary school student learn multiplication. Use **Math.random** to produce two positive one-digit integers. It should then display a question such as

        How much is 6 times 7?

The student then types the answer into a text field. Your program checks the student's answer. If it is correct, display the string **"Very good!"** in the browser's status bar and generate a new question. If the answer is wrong, display the string **"No. Please try again."** in the browser's status bar, and let the student try the same question again repeatedly until the student finally gets it right. A separate function should be used to generate each new question. This function should be called once when the script begins execution and each time the user answers the question correctly.

16.28 The use of computers in education is referred to as *computer-assisted instruction* (CAI). One problem that develops in CAI environments is student fatigue. This can be eliminated by varying the computer's dialogue to hold the student's attention. Modify the program of Exercise 16.27 so the various comments are printed for each correct answer and each incorrect answer. Correct answer responses:

        Very good!
        Excellent!
        Nice work!
        Keep up the good work!

Incorrect answer responses:

```
No. Please try again.
Wrong. Try once more.
Don't give up!
No. Keep trying.
```

Use random number generation to choose a number from 1 to 4 that will be used to select an appropriate response to each answer. Use a **switch** structure to issue the responses.

16.29 More sophisticated computer-aided instruction systems monitor the student's performance over a period of time. The decision to begin a new topic is often based on the student's success with previous topics. Modify the program of Exercise 16.28 to count the number of correct and incorrect responses typed by the student. After the student types 10 answers, your program should calculate the percentage of correct responses. If the percentage is lower than 75%, print **Please ask your instructor for extra help** and reset the program so another student can try the program.

16.30 Write a script that plays the "guess the number" game as follows: Your program chooses the number to be guessed by selecting a random integer in the range 1 to 1000. The script displays the prompt **Guess a number between 1 and 1000** next to a text field. The player types a first guess into the text field and presses a button to submit the guess to the script. If the player's guess is incorrect, your program should display **Too high. Try again.** or **Too low. Try again.** in the browser's status bar to help the player "zero in" on the correct answer and should clear the text field so the user can enter the next guess. When the user enters the correct answer, display **Congratulations. You guessed the number!** in the status bar and clear the text field so the user can play again. [*Note:* The guessing technique employed in this problem is similar to a *binary search.*]

16.31 Modify the program of Exercise 16.30 to count the number of guesses the player makes. If the number is 10 or fewer, display **Either you know the secret or you got lucky!** If the player guesses the number in 10 tries, display **Ahah! You know the secret!** If the player makes more than 10 guesses, display **You should be able to do better!** Why should it take no more than 10 guesses? Well with each "good guess" the player should be able to eliminate half of the numbers. Now show why any number 1 to 1000 can be guessed in 10 or fewer tries.

16.32 Exercises 16.27 through 16.29 developed a computer-assisted instruction program to teach an elementary school student multiplication. This exercise suggests enhancements to that program.
  a) Modify the program to allow the user to enter a grade-level capability. A grade level of 1 means to use only single-digit numbers in the problems, a grade level of 2 means to use numbers as large as two digits, etc.
  b) Modify the program to allow the user to pick the type of arithmetic problems he or she wishes to study. An option of 1 means addition problems only, 2 means subtraction problems only, 3 means multiplication problems only, 4 means division problems only and 5 means to randomly intermix problems of all these types.

16.33 Modify the craps program of Fig. 16.6 to allow wagering. Initialize variable **bankBalance** to 1000 dollars. Prompt the player to enter a **wager**. Check that **wager** is less than or equal to **bankBalance**, and if not, have the user reenter **wager** until a valid **wager** is entered. After a correct **wager** is entered, run one game of craps. If the player wins, increase **bankBalance** by **wager** and print the new **bankBalance**. If the player loses, decrease **bankBalance** by **wager**, print the new **bankBalance**, check if **bankBalance** has become zero, and if so, print the message **"Sorry. You busted!"** As the game progresses, print various messages to create some "chatter," such as **"Oh, you're going for broke, huh?"** or **"Aw c'mon, take a chance!"** or **"You're up big. Now's the time to cash in your chips!"**. Implement the "chatter" as a separate function that randomly chooses the string to display.

17

JavaScript/JScript: Arrays

Objectives

- To introduce the array data structure.
- To understand the use of arrays to store, sort and search lists and tables of values.
- To understand how to declare an array, initialize an array and refer to individual elements of an array.
- To be able to pass arrays to functions.
- To be able to search and sort an array.
- To be able to declare and manipulate multiple-subscript arrays.

With sobs and tears he sorted out
Those of the largest size …
Lewis Carroll

Attempt the end, and never stand to doubt;
Nothing's so hard, but search will find it out.
Robert Herrick

Now go, write it before them in a table,
and note it in a book.
Isaiah 30:8

'Tis in my memory lock'd,
And you yourself shall keep the key of it.
William Shakespeare

17.1 Introduction

This chapter serves as an introduction to the important topic of data structures. *Arrays* are data structures consisting of related data items (sometimes called *collections* of data items). JavaScript arrays are "dynamic" entities, in that they can change size after they are created. Many of the techniques demonstrated in this chapter are used frequently in the Dynamic HTML chapters, as we introduce the collections that allow a script programmer to manipulate every element of an HTML document dynamically.

17.2 Arrays

An array is a group of memory locations that all have the same name and are normally of the same type (although this is not required). To refer to a particular location or element in the array, we specify the name of the array and the *position number* of the particular element in the array.

Figure 17.1 shows an array of integer values called **c**. This array contains 12 *elements*. Any one of these elements may be referred to by giving the name of the array followed by the position number of the particular element in square brackets (**[]**). The first element in every array is the *zeroth element*. Thus, the first element of array **c** is referred to as **c[0]**, the second element of array **c** is referred to as **c[1]**, the seventh element of array **c** is referred to as **c[6]** and, in general, the *i*th element of array **c** is referred to as **c[i-1]**. Array names follow the same conventions as other identifiers.

The position number in square brackets is formally called a *subscript* (or an index). A subscript must be an integer or an integer expression. If a program uses an expression as a subscript, the expression is evaluated first, to determine the subscript. For example, if we assume that variable **a** is equal to **5** and that variable **b** is equal to **6**, then the statement

```
c[ a + b ] += 2;
```

adds 2 to array element **c[11]**. Note that a subscripted array name is an *lvalue*—it can be used on the left side of an assignment to place a new value into an array element.

Let us examine array **c** in Fig. 17.1 more closely. The *name* of the array is **c**. The *length* of the array is determined by the following expression:

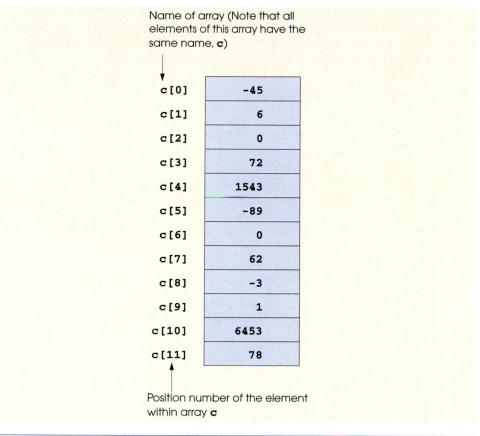

Name of array (Note that all elements of this array have the same name, **c**)

c[0]	-45
c[1]	6
c[2]	0
c[3]	72
c[4]	1543
c[5]	-89
c[6]	0
c[7]	62
c[8]	-3
c[9]	1
c[10]	6453
c[11]	78

Position number of the element within array **c**

Fig. 17.1   A 12-element array.

```
c.length
```

Every array in JavaScript *knows* its own length. The array's 12 elements are referred to as **c[0], c[1], c[2], …, c[11]**. The *value* of **c[0]** is **-45**, the value of **c[1]** is **6**, the value of **c[2]** is **0**, the value of **c[7]** is **62** and the value of **c[11]** is **78**. To calculate the sum of the values contained in the first three elements of array **c** and store the result in variable **sum**, we would write

```
sum = c[ 0 ] + c[ 1 ] + c[ 2 ];
```

To divide the value of the seventh element of array **c** by **2** and assign the result to the variable **x**, we would write

```
x = c[ 6 ] / 2;
```

Common Programming Error 17.1

It is important to note the difference between the "seventh element of the array" and "array element seven." Because array subscripts begin at 0, the "seventh element of the array" has a subscript of 6, while "array element seven" has a subscript of 7 and is actually the eighth element of the array. This confusion is a source of "off-by-one" errors.

The brackets used to enclose the subscript of an array are an operator in JavaScript. Brackets have the same level of precedence as parentheses. The chart in Fig. 17.2 shows the precedence and associativity of the operators introduced to this point in the text. They are shown top to bottom in decreasing order of precedence with their associativity and type.

17.3 Declaring and Allocating Arrays

Arrays occupy space in memory. Actually, an array in JavaScript is an **Array** object. The programmer uses *operator* **new** to dynamically allocate the number of elements required by each array. Operator **new** creates an object as the program executes by obtaining enough memory to store an object of the type specified to the right of **new**. The process of creating new objects is also known as *creating an instance* or *instantiating an object,* and operator **new** is known as the *dynamic memory allocation operator*. **Array** objects are allocated with **new** because arrays are considered to be objects and all objects must be created with **new**. To allocate 12 elements for integer array **c**, use the statement

```
var c = new Array( 12 );
```

The preceding statement can also be performed in two steps as follows:

```
var c;                // declares the array
c = new Array( 12 );  // allocates the array
```

When arrays are allocated, the elements are not initialized.

Common Programming Error 17.2

Assuming that the elements of an array are initialized when the array is allocated may result in logic errors.

Memory may be reserved for several arrays with a single declaration. The following declaration reserves 100 elements for array **b** and 27 elements for array **x**:

```
var b = new Array( 100 ), x = new Array( 27 );
```

Operators	Associativity	Type
( ) [ ] .	left to right	highest
++ -- !	right to left	unary
* / %	left to right	multiplicative
+ -	left to right	additive
< <= > >=	left to right	relational
== !=	left to right	equality
&&	left to right	logical AND
||	left to right	logical OR
?:	right to left	conditional
= += -= *= /= %=	right to left	assignment

Fig. 17.2   Precedence and associativity of the operators discussed so far.

17.4 Examples Using Arrays

The script of Fig. 17.3 uses the **new** operator to dynamically allocate an **Array** of five elements and an empty array. The script demonstrates initializing an **Array** of existing elements and also shows that an **Array** can grow dynamically to accommodate new elements. The two **Array** objects are displayed as HTML tables. [*Note:* Many of the scripts in this chapter are executed in response to the **<BODY>**'s **ONLOAD** event.]

```
1   <!DOCTYPE HTML PUBLIC "-//W3C//DTD HTML 4.0 Transitional//EN">
2   <HTML>
3   <!-- Fig. 17.3: InitArray.html -->
4
5   <HEAD>
6   <TITLE>Initializing an Array</TITLE>
7
8   <SCRIPT LANGUAGE = "JavaScript">
9      // this function is called when the <BODY> element's
10     // ONLOAD event occurs
11     function initializeArrays()
12     {
13        var n1 = new Array( 5 );    // allocate 5-element Array
14        var n2 = new Array();       // allocate empty Array
15
16        // assign values to each element of Array n1
17        for ( var i = 0; i < n1.length; ++i )
18           n1[ i ] = i;
19
20        // create and initialize five-elements in Array n2
21        for ( i = 0; i < 5; ++i )
22           n2[ i ] = i;
23
24        outputArray( "Array n1 contains", n1 );
25        outputArray( "Array n2 contains", n2 );
26     }
27
28     // output "header" followed by a two-column table
29     // containing subscripts and elements of "theArray"
30     function outputArray( header, theArray )
31     {
32        document.writeln( "<H2>" + header + "</H2>" );
33        document.writeln( "<TABLE BORDER = '1' WIDTH = '100%'>" );
34        document.writeln( "<TR><TD WIDTH = '100'><B>Subscript</B>"
35                          + "<TD><B>Value</B></TR>" );
36
37        for ( var i = 0; i < theArray.length; i++ )
38           document.writeln( "<TR><TD>" + i + "<TD>" +
39                             theArray[ i ] + "</TR>" );
40
41        document.writeln( "</TABLE>" );
42     }
43  </SCRIPT>
44
```

Fig. 17.3   Initializing the elements of an array (part 1 of 2).

```
45   </HEAD><BODY ONLOAD = "initializeArrays()"></BODY>
46   </HTML>
```

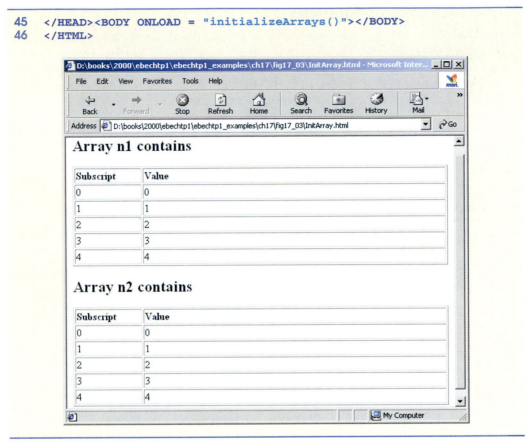

Fig. 17.3   Initializing the elements of an array (part 2 of 2).

Function **initializeArrays** (defined at line 11) is called by the browser as the event handler for the **<BODY>**'s **ONLOAD** event. Line 13 creates **Array n1** as an array of 5 elements. Line 14 creates **Array n2** as an empty array.

Lines 17 and 18

```
for ( var i = 0; i < n1.length; ++i )
   n1[ i ] = i;
```

use a **for** structure to initialize the elements of **n1** to their subscript numbers (0 to 4). Note the use of zero-based counting (remember, subscripts start at 0), so the loop can access every element of the array. Also, note the expression **n1.length** in the **for** structure condition to determine the length of the array. In this example, the length of the array is 5, so the loop continues executing as long as the value of control variable **i** is less than 5. For a five-element array, the subscript values are 0 through 4, so using the less than operator, **<**, guarantees that the loop does not attempt to access an element beyond the end of the array.

Lines 21 and 22

```
for ( i = 0; i < 5; ++i )
   n2[ i ] = i;
```

use a **for** structure to add five elements to the **Array n2** and initialize each element to its subscript numbers (0 to 4). Note that **Array n2** grows dynamically to accommodate the values assigned to each element of the array.

Software Engineering Observation 17.1

*JavaScript automatically reallocates an **Array** when a value is assigned to an element that is outside the bounds of the original **Array**. Elements between the last element of the original **Array** and the new element have undefined values.*

Lines 24 and 25 invoke function **outputArray** (defined at line 30) to display the contents of each array as HTML tables. Function **outputArray** receives two arguments—a string to be output before the HTML table that displays the contents of the array and the array to output. Lines 32 through 35 output the header string and begin the definition of the HTML table with two columns—**Subscript** and **Value**. Lines 37 through 39

```
for ( var i = 0; i < theArray.length; i++ )
    document.writeln( "<TR><TD>" + i + "<TD>" +
                      theArray[ i ] + "</TR>" );
```

use a **for** structure to output HTML text that defines each row of the table. Once again, note the use of zero-based counting so that the loop can access every element of the array. Line 41 terminates the definition of the HTML table.

Common Programming Error 17.3

*Referring to an element outside the **Array** bounds is normally a logic error.*

Testing and Debugging Tip 17.1

*When looping through an **Array** using subscripts, the subscript should never go below 0 and should always be less than the number of elements in the **Array** (one less than the **Array** size). Make sure the loop-terminating condition prevents accessing elements outside this range.*

If an **Array**'s element values are known in advance, the elements of the **Array** can be allocated and initialized in the array declaration. There are two ways in which the initial values can be specified. The statement

```
var n = [ 10, 20, 30, 40, 50 ];
```

uses a comma-separated *initializer list* enclosed in square brackets (**[** and **]**) to create a five-element **Array** with subscripts of **0**, **1**, **2**, **3** and **4**. The array size is determined by the number of values in the initializer list. Note that the preceding declaration does not require the **new** operator to create the **Array** object—this is provided by the interpreter when it encounters an array declaration that includes an initializer list. The statement

```
var n = new Array( 10, 20, 30, 40, 50 );
```

also creates a five-element array with subscripts of **0**, **1**, **2**, **3** and **4**. In this case, the initial values of the array elements are specified as arguments in the parentheses following **new Array**. The array size is determined by the number of values in parentheses. It is also possible to reserve a space in an **Array** for a value to be specified later by using a comma as a *place holder* in the initializer list. For example, the statement

```
var n = [ 10, 20, , 40, 50 ];
```

creates a five-element array with no value specified for the third element (**n[2]**).

The script of Fig. 17.4 creates three **Array** objects to demonstrate initializing arrays with initializer lists and displays each array in an HTML table using the same function **outputArray** discussed in Fig. 17.3. Notice that when **Array integers2** is displayed in the Web page, the elements with subscripts 1 and 2 (the second and third elements of the array) appear in the Web page as "**undefined**." These are the two elements of the array for which we did not supply values in the declaration at line 16 in the script.

The script of Fig. 17.5 sums the values contained in the 10-element integer array called **theArray**—declared, allocated and initialized at line 11 in function **start** (which is called in response to the **<BODY>**'s **ONLOAD** event). The statement at line 15 in the body of the first **for** loop does the totaling. It is important to remember that the values being supplied as initializers for array **theArray** normally would be read into the program. For example, in a script the user could enter the values through an HTML form.

```
1   <!DOCTYPE HTML PUBLIC "-//W3C//DTD HTML 4.0 Transitional//EN">
2   <HTML>
3   <!-- Fig. 17.4: InitArray.html -->
4
5   <HEAD>
6   <TITLE>Initializing an Array with a Declaration</TITLE>
7
8   <SCRIPT LANGUAGE = "JavaScript">
9      function start()
10     {
11        // Initializer list specifies number of elements and
12        // value for each element.
13        var colors = new Array( "cyan", "magenta",
14                                "yellow", "black" );
15        var integers1 = [ 2, 4, 6, 8 ];
16        var integers2 = [ 2, , , 8 ];
17
18        outputArray( "Array colors contains", colors );
19        outputArray( "Array integers1 contains", integers1 );
20        outputArray( "Array integers2 contains", integers2 );
21     }
22
23     // output "header" followed by a two-column table
24     // containing subscripts and elements of "theArray"
25     function outputArray( header, theArray )
26     {
27        document.writeln( "<H2>" + header + "</H2>" );
28        document.writeln( "<TABLE BORDER = '1' WIDTH = '100%'>" );
29        document.writeln( "<TR><TD WIDTH = '100'><B>Subscript</B>"
30                    + "<TD><B>Value</B></TR>" );
31
32        for ( var i = 0; i < theArray.length; i++ )
33           document.writeln( "<TR><TD>" + i + "<TD>" +
34                             theArray[ i ] + "</TR>" );
35
36        document.writeln( "</TABLE>" );
37     }
38  </SCRIPT>
```

Fig. 17.4   Initializing the elements of an array (part 1 of 2).

```
39
40   </HEAD><BODY ONLOAD = "start()"></BODY>
41   </HTML>
```

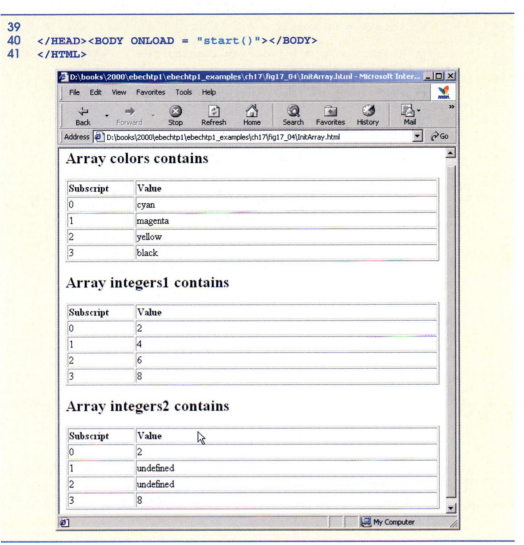

Array colors contains

Subscript	Value
0	cyan
1	magenta
2	yellow
3	black

Array integers1 contains

Subscript	Value
0	2
1	4
2	6
3	8

Array integers2 contains

Subscript	Value
0	2
1	undefined
2	undefined
3	8

Fig. 17.4 Initializing the elements of an array (part 2 of 2).

```
1    <!DOCTYPE HTML PUBLIC "-//W3C//DTD HTML 4.0 Transitional//EN">
2    <HTML>
3    <!-- Fig. 17.5: SumArray.html -->
4
5    <HEAD>
6    <TITLE>Sum the Elements of an Array</TITLE>
7
8    <SCRIPT LANGUAGE = "JavaScript">
9       function start()
10      {
11         var theArray = [ 1, 2, 3, 4, 5, 6, 7, 8, 9, 10 ];
```

Fig. 17.5 Computing the sum of the elements of an array (part 1 of 2).

```
12          var total1 = 0, total2 = 0;
13
14          for ( var i = 0; i < theArray.length; i++ )
15             total1 += theArray[ i ];
16
17          document.writeln( "Total using subscripts: " + total1 );
18
19          for ( var element in theArray )
20             total2 += theArray[ element ];
21
22          document.writeln( "<BR>Total using for/in: " + total2 );
23       }
24    </SCRIPT>
25
26    </HEAD><BODY ONLOAD = "start()"></BODY>
27    </HTML>
```

D:\books\2000\ebechtp1\ebechtp1_examples\ch17\fig17_05\SumArray.html - Microsoft Inte...

File   Edit   View   Favorites   Tools   Help

Back   Forward   Stop   Refresh   Home   Search   Favorites   History   Mail

Address D:\books\2000\ebechtp1\ebechtp1_examples\ch17\fig17_05\SumArray.html   Go

Total using subscripts: 55
Total using for/in: 55

My Computer

Fig. 17.5   Computing the sum of the elements of an array (part 2 of 2).

In this example, we introduce for the first time JavaScript's ***for/in*** control structure, which enables a script to perform a task ***for*** *each element **in** an array* (or, as we will see in the Dynamic HTML chapters, for each element in a collection). This is also known as *iterating over the array elements.* Lines 19 and 20

```
for ( var element in theArray )
   total2 += theArray[ element ];
```

show the syntax of a **for/in** structure. Inside the parentheses, we declare the **element** variable that will be used to select each element in the object to the right of keyword **in** (**theArray**, in this case). In the preceding **for/in** structure, JavaScript automatically determines the number of elements in the array. As the JavaScript interpreter iterates over **theArray**'s elements, variable **element** is assigned a value that can be used as a subscript for **theArray**. In the case of an **Array**, the value assigned is a subscript in the range from 0 up to (but not including) **theArray.length**. Each value is added to **total2** to produce the sum of the elements in the array.

Testing and Debugging Tip 17.2

*When iterating over all the elements of an **Array**, use a **for/in** control structure to ensure that you manipulate only the existing elements of the **Array**.*

Chapter 16 indicated that there is a more elegant way to implement the dice-rolling program of Fig. 16.5. The program rolled a single six-sided die 6000 times and used a **switch** structure to total the number of times each value was rolled. An array version of this script is shown in Fig. 17.6. The **switch** structure in lines 17 through 36 of the script in Fig. 16.5 are replaced by line 16 of this program, which uses the random **face** value as the subscript for the array **frequency** to determine which element should be incremented during each iteration of the loop. Because the random number calculation on line 15 produces numbers from 1 to 6 (the values for a six-sided die), the **frequency** array must be large enough to allow subscript values of 1 to 6. The smallest number of elements required for an array to have these subscript values is seven elements (subscript values from 0 to 6). In this program, we ignore element 0 of array **frequency**. Also, lines 23 through 25 of this program replace lines 42 through 53 from Fig. 16.5. Because we can loop through array **frequency** to help product the output, we do not have to enumerate each HTML table row as we did in Fig. 16.5.

```
1   <!DOCTYPE HTML PUBLIC "-//W3C//DTD HTML 4.0 Transitional//EN">
2   <HTML>
3   <!-- Fig. 17.6: RollDie.html -->
4
5   <HEAD>
6   <TITLE>Roll a Six-Sided Die 6000 Times</TITLE>
7
8   <SCRIPT LANGUAGE = "JavaScript">
9      var face, frequency = [ , 0, 0, 0, 0, 0, 0 ];
10
11     // summarize results
12     for ( var roll = 1; roll <= 6000; ++roll ) {
13        face = Math.floor( 1 + Math.random() * 6 );
14        ++frequency[ face ];
15     }
16
17     document.writeln( "<TABLE BORDER = '1' WIDTH = '100%'>" );
18     document.writeln( "<TR><TD WIDTH = '100'><B>Face</B>" +
19        "<TD><B>Frequency</B></TR>" );
20
21     for ( face = 1; face < frequency.length; ++face )
22        document.writeln( "<TR><TD>" + face + "<TD>" +
23                           frequency[ face ] + "</TR>" );
24
25     document.writeln( "</TABLE>" );
26   </SCRIPT>
27
28   </HEAD>
29   <BODY>
30   <P>Click Refresh (or Reload) to run the script again</P>
31   </BODY>
32   </HTML>
```

Fig. 17.6   Dice-rolling program using arrays instead of **switch** (part 1 of 2).

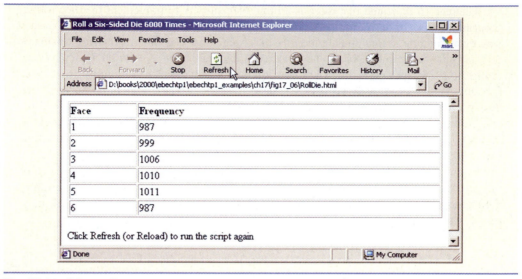

Fig. 17.6   Dice-rolling program using arrays instead of **switch** (part 2 of 2).

17.5 References and Reference Parameters

Two ways to pass arguments to functions (or methods) in many programming languages are *call-by-value* and *call-by-reference* (also called *pass-by-value* and *pass-by-reference*). When an argument is passed to a function using call-by-value, a *copy* of the argument's value is made and is passed to the called function. In JavaScript, numbers and boolean values are passed to functions by value.

Testing and Debugging Tip 17.3

With call-by-value, changes to the called function's copy do not affect the original variable's value in the calling function. This prevents the accidental side effects that so greatly hinder the development of correct and reliable software systems.

With call-by-reference, the caller gives the called function the ability to directly access the caller's data and to modify that data if the called function so chooses. This is accomplished by passing to the called function the actual *location in memory* (also called the *address*) where the data resides. Call-by-reference can improve performance because it can eliminate the overhead of copying large amounts of data, but call-by-reference can weaken security because the called function can access the caller's data. In JavaScript, all objects and **Array**s are passed to functions by reference.

Software Engineering Observation 17.2

Unlike other languages, JavaScript does not allow the programmer to choose whether to pass each argument by value or by reference. Numbers and boolean values are passed by value. Objects are not passed to functions; rather, references to objects are passed to functions. When a function receives a reference to an object, the function can manipulate the object directly.

Software Engineering Observation 17.3

*When returning information from a function via a **return** statement, numbers and boolean values are always returned by value (i.e., a copy is returned) and objects are always returned by reference (i.e., a reference to the object is returned).*

To pass a reference to an object into a function, simply specify in the function call the reference name. Normally, the reference name is the identifier that is used to manipulate the object in the program. Mentioning the reference by its parameter name in the body of the called function actually refers to the original object in memory, and the original object can be accessed directly by the called function.

Because **Array**s are objects in JavaScript, **Array**s are passed to functions call-by-reference—a called function can access the elements of the caller's original **Array**s. The name of an array is actually a reference to an object that contains the array elements and the **length** variable, which indicates the number of elements in the array. In the next section, we demonstrate call-by-value and call-by-reference, using arrays.

Performance Tip 17.1

Passing arrays by reference makes sense for performance reasons. If arrays were passed by value, a copy of each element would be passed. For large, frequently passed arrays, this would waste time and would consume considerable storage for the copies of the arrays.

17.6 Passing Arrays to Functions

To pass an array argument to a function, specify the name of the array (a reference to the array) without brackets. For example, if array **hourlyTemperatures** has been declared as

```
var hourlyTemperatures = new Array( 24 );
```

the function call

```
modifyArray( hourlyTemperatures );
```

passes array **hourlyTemperatures** to function **modifyArray**. In JavaScript, every array object "knows" its own size (via the **length** instance variable). Thus, when we pass an array object into a function, we do not separately pass the size of the array as an argument. In fact, Fig. 17.3 illustrated this concept when we passed **Array**s **n1** and **n2** to function **outputArray** to display each **Array**'s contents.

Although entire arrays are passed by using call-by-reference, *individual numeric and boolean array elements are passed by call-by-value exactly as simple numeric and boolean variables are passed* (the objects referred to by individual elements of an Array of objects are still passed by call-by-reference). Such simple single pieces of data are called *scalars* or *scalar quantities.* To pass an array element to a function, use the subscripted name of the array element as an argument in the function call.

For a function to receive an **Array** through a function call, the function's parameter list must specify a parameter that will be used to refer to the **Array** in the body of the function. Unlike other programming languages, JavaScript does not provide a special syntax for this purpose. JavaScript simply requires specifying the identifier for the **Array** in the parameter list. For example, the function header for function **modifyArray** might be written as

```
function modifyArray( b )
```

indicating that **modifyArray** expects to receive a parameter named **b** (the argument supplied in the calling function must be an **Array**). Because arrays are passed by reference, when the called function uses the array name **b**, it refers to the actual array in the caller (array **hourlyTemperatures** in the preceding call).

Software Engineering Observation 17.4

JavaScript does not check the number of arguments or types of arguments that are passed to a function. It is possible to pass any number of values to a function. JavaScript will attempt to perform conversions when the values are used

The script of Fig. 17.7 demonstrates the difference between passing an entire array and passing an array element. [*Note:* Function **start** (defined at line 10) is called in response to the **<BODY>**'s **ONLOAD** event.]

```
1   <!DOCTYPE HTML PUBLIC "-//W3C//DTD HTML 4.0 Transitional//EN">
2   <HTML>
3   <!-- Fig. 17.7: PassArray.html -->
4
5   <HEAD>
6   <TITLE>Passing Arrays and Individual Array
7          Elements to Functions</TITLE>
8
9   <SCRIPT LANGUAGE = "JavaScript">
10     function start()
11     {
12        var a = [ 1, 2, 3, 4, 5 ];
13
14        document.writeln( "<H2>Effects of passing entire " +
15                          "array call-by-reference</H2>" );
16        outputArray(
17           "The values of the original array are: ", a );
18
19        modifyArray( a );   // array a passed call-by-reference
20
21        outputArray(
22           "The values of the modified array are: ", a );
23
24        document.writeln( "<H2>Effects of passing array " +
25           "element call-by-value</H2>" +
26           "a[3] before modifyElement: " + a[ 3 ] );
27
28        modifyElement( a[ 3 ] );
29
30        document.writeln(
31           "<BR>a[3] after modifyElement: " + a[ 3 ] );
32     }
33
34     // outputs "header" followed by the contents of "theArray"
35     function outputArray( header, theArray )
36     {
37        document.writeln(
38           header + theArray.join( " " ) + "<BR>" );
39     }
40
41     // function that modifies the elements of an array
42     function modifyArray( theArray )
43     {
```

Fig. 17.7   Passing arrays and individual array elements to functions (part 1 of 2).

```
44              for ( var j in theArray )
45                  theArray[ j ] *= 2;
46          }
47
48          // function that attempts to modify the value passed
49          function modifyElement( e )
50          {
51              e *= 2;
52              document.writeln( "<BR>value in modifyElement: " + e );
53          }
54      </SCRIPT>
55
56      </HEAD><BODY ONLOAD = "start()"></BODY>
57      </HTML>
```

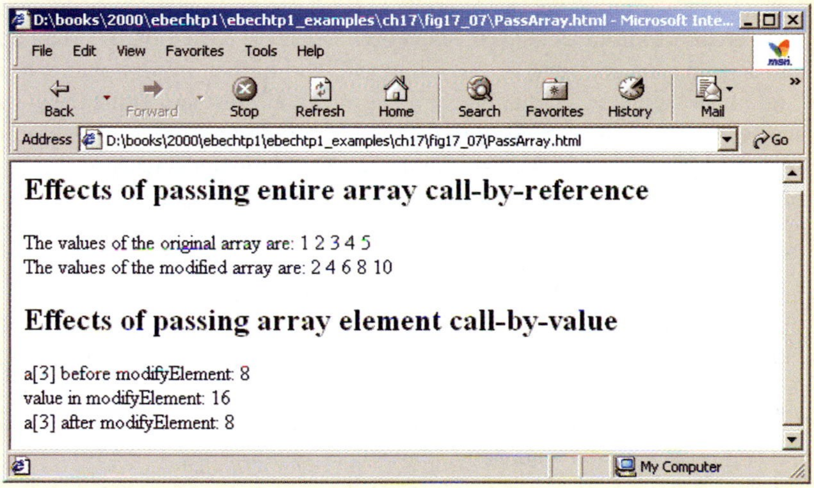

Fig. 17.7   Passing arrays and individual array elements to functions (part 2 of 2).

The statement at lines 16 and 17 invokes function **outputArray** to display the contents of array **a** before it is modified. Function outputArray (defined at line 35) receives a string to output and the array to output. The statement at lines 37 and 38

```
document.writeln(
    header + theArray.join( " " ) + "<BR>" );
```

uses **Array** method **join** to create a string containing all the elements in **theArray**. Method **join** takes as its argument a string containing the *separator* that should be used to separate the elements of the array in the string that is returned. If the argument is not specified, the empty string is used as the separator.

Line 19 invokes function **modifyArray** and passes it array **a**. The **modifyArray** function multiplies each element by 2. To illustrate that array **a**'s elements were modified, the statement at lines 21 and 22 invokes function **outputArray** again to display the contents of array **a** after it is modified. As the screen capture shows, the elements of **a** are indeed modified by **modifyArray**.

To show the value of **a[3]** before the call to **modifyElement**, lines 24 through 26 output the value of **a[3]** (and other information). Line 28 invokes **modifyElement** and passes **a[3]**. Remember that **a[3]** is actually one integer value in the array **a**. Also, remember that numeric values and boolean values are always passed to functions call-by-value. Therefore, a copy of **a[3]** is passed. Function **modifyElement** multiplies its argument by 2 and stores the result in its parameter **e**. The parameter of function **modify-Element** is a local variable in that function, so when the function terminates, the local variable is destroyed. Thus, when control is returned to **start**, the unmodified value of **a[3]** is displayed by the statement at lines 30 and 31.

17.7 Sorting Arrays

Sorting data (placing the data into some particular order, such as ascending or descending) is one of the most important computing scripts. A bank sorts all checks by account number, so that it can prepare individual bank statements at the end of each month. Telephone companies sort their lists of accounts by last name and, within that, by first name, to make it easy to find phone numbers. Virtually every organization must sort some data—in many cases, massive amounts of data. Sorting data is an intriguing problem that has attracted some of the most intense research efforts in the field of computer science.

The **Array** object in JavaScript has a built-in method *sort* for sorting arrays. Figure 17.8 demonstrates the **Array** object's **sort** method.

By default, **Array** method **sort** (with no arguments) uses string comparisons to determine the sorting order of the **Array** elements. The strings are compared by the ASCII values of their characters. [*Note:* String comparison is discussed in more detail in Chapter 18, "JavaScript: Objects."] In this example, we would like once again to sort an array of integers.

Method **sort** takes as its optional argument the name of a function (called the *comparator function*) that compares its two arguments and returns one of the following:

- a negative value if the first argument is less than the second,
- zero if the arguments are equal, or
- a positive value if the first argument is greater than the second.

Function **compareIntegers** (defined at line 27) is used in this example as the comparator function for method **sort**. It calculates the difference between the integer values of its two arguments (function **parseInt** is used to ensure that the arguments are properly handled as integers). If the first argument is less than the second, the difference will be a negative value. If the arguments are equal, the difference will be zero. If the first argument is greater than the second, the difference will be a positive value.

Line 15

```
a.sort( compareIntegers );  // sort the array
```

invokes **Array** object **a**'s **sort** method and passes function **compareIntegers** as an argument. In JavaScript, functions are actually considered to be data and can be assigned to variables and passed to functions like any other data. Here, method **sort** receives function **compareIntegers** as an argument, then uses the function to compare elements of the **Array a** to determine their sorting order.

Software Engineering Observation 17.5

*Functions in JavaScript are considered to be data. Therefore, functions can be assigned to variables, stored in **Array**s and passed to functions like other data types.*

```
1  <!DOCTYPE html PUBLIC "-//W3C//DTD HTML 4.0 Transitional//EN">
2  <HTML>
3  <!-- Fig. 17.8: sort.html -->
4
5  <HEAD>
6  <TITLE>Sorting an Array with Array Method sort</TITLE>
7
8  <SCRIPT LANGUAGE = "JavaScript">
9     function start()
10    {
11       var a = [ 10, 1, 9, 2, 8, 3, 7, 4, 6, 5 ];
12
13       document.writeln( "<H1>Sorting an Array</H1>" );
14       outputArray( "Data items in original order: ", a );
15       a.sort( compareIntegers );  // sort the array
16       outputArray( "Data items in ascending order: ", a );
17    }
18
19    // outputs "header" followed by the contents of "theArray"
20    function outputArray( header, theArray )
21    {
22       document.writeln( "<P>" + header +
23          theArray.join( " " ) + "</P>" );
24    }
25
26    // comparison function for use with sort
27    function compareIntegers( value1, value2 )
28    {
29       return parseInt( value1 ) - parseInt( value2 );
30    }
31 </SCRIPT>
32
33 </HEAD><BODY ONLOAD = "start()"></BODY>
34 </HTML>
```

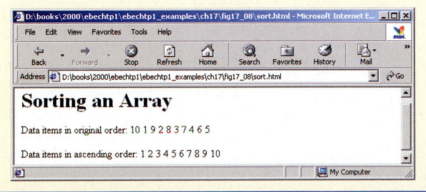

Fig. 17.8   Sorting an array with **sort**.

17.8 Searching Arrays: Linear Search

Often, a programmer will be working with large amounts of data stored in arrays. It may be necessary to determine whether an array contains a value that matches a certain *key value*. The process of locating a particular element value in an array is called *searching*. In this section we discuss the *linear search* technique (Fig. 17.9).

```
1  <!DOCTYPE HTML PUBLIC "-//W3C//DTD HTML 4.0 Transitional//EN">
2  <HTML>
3  <!-- Fig. 17.9: LinearSearch.html -->
4
5  <HEAD>
6  <TITLE>Linear Search of an Array</TITLE>
7
8  <SCRIPT LANGUAGE = "JavaScript">
9     var a = new Array( 100 );  // create an Array
10
11    // fill Array with even integer values from 0 to 198
12    for ( var i = 0; i < a.length; ++i )
13       a[ i ] = 2 * i;
14
15    // function called when "Search" button is pressed
16    function buttonPressed()
17    {
18       var searchKey = searchForm.inputVal.value;
19
20       // Array a is passed to linearSearch even though it
21       // is a global variable. Normally an array will
22       // be passed to a method for searching.
23       var element = linearSearch( a, parseInt( searchKey ) );
24
25       if ( element != -1 )
26          searchForm.result.value =
27             "Found value in element " + element;
28       else
29          searchForm.result.value = "Value not found";
30    }
31
32    // Search "theArray" for the specified "key" value
33    function linearSearch( theArray, key )
34    {
35       for ( var n = 0; n < theArray.length; ++n )
36          if ( theArray[ n ] == key )
37             return n;
38
39       return -1;
40    }
41 </SCRIPT>
42
43 </HEAD>
44
45 <BODY>
```

Fig. 17.9 Linear search of an array (part 1 of 2).

```
46   <FORM NAME = "searchForm">
47      <P>Enter integer search key<BR>
48      <INPUT NAME = "inputVal" TYPE = "text">
49      <INPUT NAME = "search" TYPE = "button" VALUE = "Search"
50           ONCLICK = "buttonPressed()"><BR></P>
51
52      <P>Result<BR>
53      <INPUT NAME = "result" TYPE = "text" SIZE = "30"></P>
54   </FORM>
55   </BODY>
56   </HTML>
```

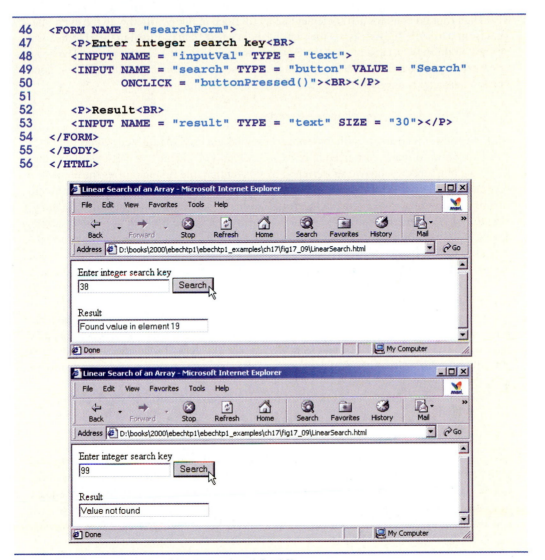

Fig. 17.9   Linear search of an array (part 2 of 2).

In the script of Fig. 17.9, function **linearSearch** (defined at line 33) uses a **for** structure containing an **if** structure to compare each element of an array with a *search key* (lines 35 through 37). If the search key is found, the function returns the subscript value (line 37) for the element to indicate the exact position of the search key in the array. [*Note:* The loop in the **linearSearch** function terminates and the function returns control to the caller as soon as the **return** statement in its body executes.] If the search key is not found, the function returns **−1** to indicate that the search key was not found. (We the value return **−1** because it is not a valid subscript number.)

If the array being searched is not in any particular order, it is just as likely that the value will be found in the first element as the last. On average, therefore, the program will have to compare the search key with half the elements of the array.

The program contains a 100-element array (defined at line 9) filled with the even integers from 0 to 198. The user types the search key in a text field (defined in the HTML form at lines 46 through 54) and presses the **Search** button to start the search. [*Note:* The array is passed to **linearSearch** even though the array is a global variable. This is done because an array is normally passed to a function for searching.]

17.9 Multiple-Subscripted Arrays

Multiple-subscripted arrays with two subscripts are often used to represent *tables* of values consisting of information arranged in *rows* and *columns*. To identify a particular table element, we must specify the two subscripts—by convention, the first identifies the element's row and the second identifies the element's column. Arrays that require two subscripts to identify a particular element are called *double-subscripted arrays* (also called *two-dimensional arrays*). Note that multiple-subscripted arrays can have more than two subscripts. JavaScript does not support multiple-subscripted arrays directly, but does allow the programmer to specify single-subscripted arrays whose elements are also single-subscripted arrays, thus achieving the same effect. Figure 17.10 illustrates a double-subscripted array, **a**, containing three rows and four columns (i.e., a 3-by-4 array). In general, an array with *m* rows and *n* columns is called an *m-by-n array*.

Every element in array **a** is identified in Fig. 17.10 by an element name of the form **a[i][j]**; **a** is the name of the array and **i** and **j** are the subscripts that uniquely identify the row and column of each element in **a**. Notice that the names of the elements in the first row all have a first subscript of **0**; the names of the elements in the fourth column all have a second subscript of **3**.

Multiple-subscripted arrays can be initialized in declarations like a single-subscripted array. Array **b** with two rows and two columns could be declared and initialized with

```
var b = [ [ 1, 2 ], [ 3, 4 ] ];
```

The values are grouped by row in square brackets. So, **1** and **2** initialize **b[0][0]** and **b[0][1]**, and **3** and **4** initialize **b[1][0]** and **b[1][1]**. The compiler determines the number of rows by counting the number of sub-initializer lists (represented by sets of square brackets) in the main initializer list. The compiler determines the number of columns in each row by counting the number of initializer values in the sub-initializer list for that row.

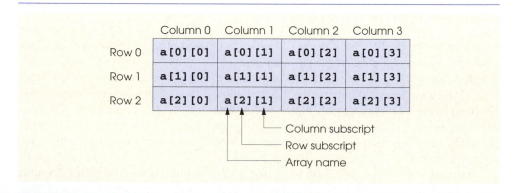

Fig. 17.10   A double-subscripted array with three rows and four columns.

Multiple-subscripted arrays are maintained as arrays of arrays. The declaration

```
var b = [ [ 1, 2 ], [ 3, 4, 5 ] ];
```

creates array **b** with row **0** containing two elements (**1** and **2**) and row **1** containing three elements (**3, 4** and **5**).

A multiple-subscripted array in which each row has a different number of columns can be allocated dynamically as follows:

```
var b;
b = new Array( 2 );    // allocate rows
b[ 0 ] = new Array( 5 ); // allocate columns for row 0
b[ 1 ] = new Array( 3 ); // allocate columns for row 1
```

The preceding code creates a two-dimensional array with two rows. Row **0** has five columns and row **1** has three columns.

Figure 17.11 initializes double-subscripted arrays in declarations and uses nested **for/in** loops to *traverse the arrays* (i.e., manipulate every element of the array).

The program declares two arrays in function **start** (which is called in response to the **<BODY>**'s **ONLOAD** event). The declaration of **array1** (line 11) provides six initializers in two sublists. The first sublist initializes the first row of the array to the values 1, 2 and 3; and the second sublist initializes the second row of the array to the values 4, 5 and 6. The declaration of **array2** (line 13) provides six initializers in three sublists. The sublist for the first row explicitly initializes the first row to have two elements, with values 1 and 2, respectively. The sublist for the second row initializes the second row to have one element with value 3. The sublist for the third row initializes the third row to the values 4, 5 and 6.

```
1   <!DOCTYPE html PUBLIC "-//W3C//DTD HTML 4.0 Transitional//EN">
2   <HTML>
3   <!-- Fig. 17.11: InitArray.html -->
4
5   <HEAD>
6   <TITLE>Initializing Multidimensional Arrays</TITLE>
7
8   <SCRIPT LANGUAGE = "JavaScript">
9      function start()
10     {
11        var array1 = [ [ 1, 2, 3 ],      // first row
12                       [ 4, 5, 6 ] ];    // second row
13        var array2 = [ [ 1, 2 ],         // first row
14                       [ 3 ],            // second row
15                       [ 4, 5, 6 ] ];    // third row
16
17        outputArray( "Values in array1 by row", array1 );
18        outputArray( "Values in array2 by row", array2 );
19     }
20
21     function outputArray( header, theArray )
22     {
23        document.writeln( "<H2>" + header + "</H2><TT>" );
24
```

Fig. 17.11 Initializing multidimensional arrays (part 1 of 2).

```
25          for ( var i in theArray ) {
26
27              for ( var j in theArray[ i ] )
28                  document.write( theArray[ i ][ j ] + " " );
29
30              document.writeln( "<BR>" );
31          }
32
33          document.writeln( "</TT>" );
34      }
35  </SCRIPT>
36
37  </HEAD><BODY ONLOAD = "start()"></BODY>
38  </HTML>
```

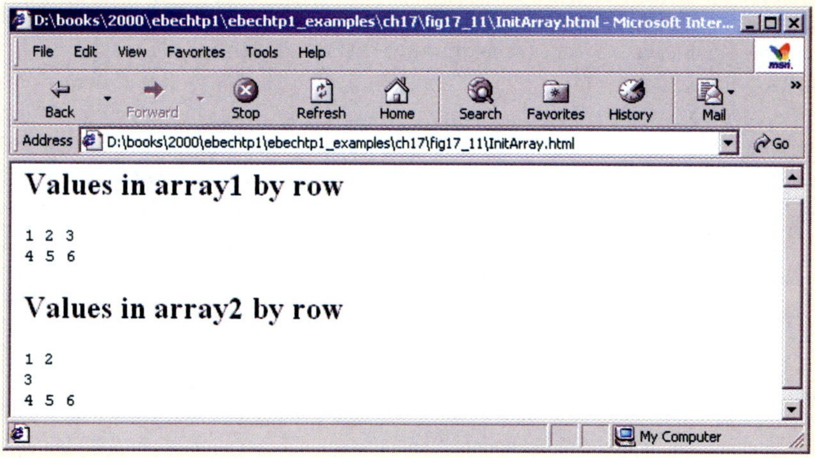

Fig. 17.11 Initializing multidimensional arrays (part 2 of 2).

Function **start** calls function **outputArray** from lines 17 and 18 to display each array's elements in the Web page. Function **outputArray** receives two arguments—a string **header** to output before the array and the array to output (called **theArray**). Note the use of a nested **for/in** structure to output the rows of each double-subscripted array. The outer **for/in** structure iterates over the rows of the array. The inner **for/in** structure iterates over the columns of the current row being processed. The nested **for/in** structure in this example could have been written with **for** structures as follows:

```
for ( var i = 0; i < theArray.length; ++i ) {
   for ( var j = 0; j < theArray[ i ].length; ++j )
      document.write( theArray[ i ][ j ] + " " );
   document.writeln( "<BR>" );
}
```

In the outer **for** structure, the expression **theArray.length** determines the number of rows in the array. In the inner **for** structure, the expression **theArray[i].length** determines the number of columns in each row of the array. This condition enables the loop to determine, for each row, the exact number of columns.

Many common array manipulations use **for** or **for/in** repetition structures. For example, the following **for** structure sets all the elements in the third row of array **a** in Fig. 17.10 to zero:

```
for ( var col = 0; col < a[ 2 ].length; ++col )
    a[ 2 ][ col ] = 0;
```

We specified the *third* row, therefore we know that the first subscript is always **2** (**0** is the first row and **1** is the second row). The **for** loop varies only the second subscript (i.e., the column subscript). The preceding **for** structure is equivalent to the assignment statements

```
a[ 2 ][ 0 ] = 0;
a[ 2 ][ 1 ] = 0;
a[ 2 ][ 2 ] = 0;
a[ 2 ][ 3 ] = 0;
```

The following **for/in** structure is also equivalent to the preceding **for** structure

```
for ( var col in a[ 2 ] )
    a[ 2 ][ col ] = 0;
```

The following nested **for** structure determines the total of all the elements in array **a**.

```
var total = 0;

for ( var row = 0; row < a.length; ++row )
    for ( var col = 0; col < a[ row ].length; ++col )
        total += a[ row ][ col ];
```

The **for** structure totals the elements of the array, one row at a time. The outer **for** structure begins by setting the **row** subscript to **0**, so the elements of the first row may be totaled by the inner **for** structure. The outer **for** structure then increments **row** to **1**, so the second row can be totaled. Then, the outer **for** structure increments **row** to **2**, so the third row can be totaled. The result can be displayed when the nested **for** structure terminates. The preceding **for** structure is equivalent to the following **for/in** structure

```
var total = 0;

for ( var row in a )
    for ( var col in a[ row ] )
        total += a[ row ][ col ];
```

SUMMARY

- Arrays are data structures consisting of related data items (sometimes called collections).
- Arrays are "dynamic" entities, in that they can change size after they are created.
- An array is a group of memory locations that all have the same name and are normally of the same type (although this is not required).
- To refer to a particular location or element in the array, specify the name of the array and the position number of the particular element in the array.
- The first element in every array is the zeroth element.
- The length of an array is determined by *arrayName*.**length**.
- An array in JavaScript is an **Array** object. Operator **new** is used to dynamically allocate the number of elements required by an array. Operator **new** creates an object as the program executes, by obtaining enough memory to store an object of the type specified to the right of **new**.

- The process of creating new objects is also known as creating an instance or instantiating an object, and operator **new** is known as the dynamic memory allocation operator.

- An array can be initialized with a comma-separated initializer list enclosed in square brackets (**[** and **]**). The array size is determined by the number of values in the initializer list. When using an initializer list in an array declaration, the **new** operator is not required to create the **Array** object—this operator is provided automatically by the interpreter.

- It is possible to reserve a space in an **Array** for a value to be specified later, by using a comma as a place holder in the initializer list.

- JavaScript's **for/in** control structure enables a script to perform a task for each element in an array. This is also known as iterating over the array elements.

- The basic syntax of a **for/in** structure is

  > **for (var** *element* **in** *arrayName* **)**
  >   *statement*

  where **element** is the name of the variable to which the **for/in** structure assigns a subscript number and **arrayName** is the array over which to iterate.

- When a value is assigned to an element of an **Array** that is outside the current bounds, JavaScript automatically allocates more memory so the **Array** contains the appropriate number of elements. The new elements of the array are not initialized.

- Two ways to pass arguments to functions (or methods) in many programming languages are call-by-value and call-by-reference (also called pass-by-value and pass-by-reference).

- When an argument is passed to a function by using call-by-value, a copy of the argument's value is made and passed to the called function. Numbers and boolean values are passed by value.

- With call-by-reference, the caller gives the called function the ability to directly access the caller's data and to modify that data. This is accomplished by passing to the called function the location or address in memory where the data resides. All objects and **Array**s are passed by reference.

- To pass a reference to an object into a function, specify in the function call the reference name. The reference name is the identifier that is used to manipulate the object in the program.

- The name of an array is actually a reference to an object that contains the array elements and the **length** variable, which indicates the number of elements in the array.

- Placing data into some particular order, such as ascending or descending, is called sorting the data.

- The **Array** object in JavaScript has a built-in method, **sort**, for sorting arrays. By default, **Array** method **sort** uses string comparisons to determine the sorting order of the **Array** elements.

- Method **sort** takes as its optional argument the comparator function that compares its two arguments and returns a negative value if the first argument is less than the second, zero if the arguments are equal or a positive value if the first argument is greater than the second.

- The process of locating a particular element value (the key value) in an array is called searching.

- Linear search compares each element of an array with a search key. If the search key is found, the linear search normally returns the subscript for the element to indicate the exact position of the search key in the array. If the search key is not found, the linear search normally returns **−1** to indicate that the search key was not found.

- If the array being searched with a linear search is not in any particular order, it is just as likely that the value will be found in the first element as the last. On average, the program will have to compare the search key with half the elements of the array.

- Multiple-subscripted arrays with two subscripts are often used to represent tables of values consisting of information arranged in rows and columns. Two subscripts identify a particular table element—the first identifies the element's row and the second identifies the element's column.

- Arrays requiring two subscripts to identify a particular element are called double-subscripted arrays (or two-dimensional arrays). Multiple-subscripted arrays can have more than two subscripts.
- JavaScript does not support multiple-subscripted arrays directly, but does allow single-subscripted arrays whose elements are also single-subscripted arrays, thus achieving the same effect.
- In general, an array with *m* rows and *n* columns is called an *m*-by-*n* array.
- Multiple-subscripted arrays can be initialized with initializer lists. The compiler determines the number of rows by counting the number of sub-initializer lists (represented by sets of square brackets) in the main initializer list. The compiler determines the number of columns in each row by counting the number of initializer values in the sub-initializer list for that row.

TERMINOLOGY

a[i]	linear search of an array
a[i][j]	location in an array
array	lvalue
array initializer list	*m*-by-*n* array
Array object	multiple-subscripted array
bounds of an array	name of an array
call by reference	off-by-one error
call by value	pass by reference
column subscript	pass by value
comma-separated initializer list	passing arrays to functions
comparator function	place holder in an initializer list (**,**)
creating an instance	position number of an element
data structure	reserve a space in an **Array**
declare an array	row subscript
double-subscripted array	search key
dynamic memory allocation operator (**new**)	searching an array
element of an array	single-subscripted array
for/in repetition structure	**sort** method of the **Array** object
index of an element	sorting an array
initialize an array	square brackets **[]**
initializer	subscript
initializer list	table of values
instantiating an object	tabular format
iterating over an array's elements	value of an element
length of an **Array**	zeroth element

SELF-REVIEW EXERCISES

17.1 Answer each of the following:
   a) Lists and tables of values can be stored in _____.
   b) The elements of an array are related by the fact that they have the same _____ and normally the same _____.
   c) The number used to refer to a particular element of an array is called its _____.
   d) The process of placing the elements of an array in order is called _____ the array.
   e) Determining whether an array contains a certain key value is called _____ the array.
   f) An array that uses two subscripts is referred to as a _____ array.

17.2 State whether each of the following is *true* or *false*. If *false*, explain why.
   a) An array can store many different types of values.

      b) An array subscript should normally be a floating-point value.

      c) An individual array element that is passed to a function and modified in that function will contain the modified value when the called function completes execution.

17.3 Answer the following questions regarding an array called **fractions**.

      a) Declare an array with 10 elements and initialize the elements of the array to **0**.

      b) Name the fourth element of the array.

      c) Refer to array element 4.

      d) Assign the value **1.667** to array element 9.

      e) Assign the value **3.333** to the seventh element of the array.

      f) Sum all the elements of the array using a **for/in** repetition structure. Define variable **x** as a control variable for the loop.

17.4 Answer the following questions regarding an array called **table**.

      a) Declare and create the array with 3 rows and 3 columns.

      b) How many elements does the array contain?

      c) Use a **for/in** repetition structure to initialize each element of the array to the sum of its subscripts. Assume the variables **x** and **y** are declared as control variables.

17.5 Find the error in each of the following program segments and correct the error.

      a) Assume **var b = new Array(10);**

```
for ( var i = 0; i <= b.length; ++i )
    b[ i ] = 1;
```

      b) Assume **var a = [[1, 2], [3, 4]];**

```
a[ 1, 1 ] = 5;
```

ANSWERS TO SELF-REVIEW EXERCISES

17.1 a) Arrays. b) Name, type. c) Subscript. d) Sorting. e) Searching. f) Double-subscripted.

17.2 a) True. b). False. An array subscript must be an integer or an integer expression. c) False for individual primitive-data-type elements of an array because they are passed with call-by-value. If a reference to an array is passed, then modifications to the array elements are reflected in the original. Also, an individual element of an object type passed to a function is passed with call-by-reference, and changes to the object will be reflected in the original array element.

17.3 a) **var fractions = [0, 0, 0, 0, 0, 0, 0, 0, 0, 0];**

      b) **fractions[3]**

      c) **fractions[4]**

      d) **fractions[9] = 1.667;**

      e) **fractions[6] = 3.333;**

      f) **var total = 0;**

```
for ( var x in fractions )
    total += fractions[ x ];
```

17.4 a) **var table = new Array(new Array(3), new Array(3),**
new Array(3));

      b) Nine.

      c)
```
for ( var x in table )
    for ( var y in table[ x ] )
        table[ x ][ y ] = x + y;
```

17.5 a) Error: Referencing an array element outside the bounds of the array (**b[10]**). [*Note:* This is actually a logic error, not a syntax error.]

      Correction: Change the **<=** operator to **<**.

b) Error: Array subscripting done incorrectly.

Correction: Change the statement to a[1][1] = 5;.

EXERCISES

17.6   Fill in the blanks in each of the following:

a) JavaScript stores lists of values in _____.

b) The names of the four elements of array **p** are _____, _____, _____ and

_____.

c) The process of placing the elements of an array into either ascending or descending order

is called _____.

d) In a double-subscripted array, the first subscript identifies the _____ of an element

and the second subscript identifies the _____ of an element.

e) An *m*-by-*n* array contains _____ rows, _____ columns and _____ elements.

f) The name of the element in row 3 and column 5 of array **d** is _____.

g) The name of the element in the third row and fifth column of array **d** is _____.

17.7   State whether each of the following is *true* or *false*. If *false*, explain why.

a) To refer to a particular location or element within an array, we specify the name of the

array and the value of the particular element.

b) An array declaration reserves space for the array.

c) To indicate that 100 locations should be reserved for integer array **p**, the programmer

writes the declaration

```
p[ 100 ];
```

d) A JavaScript program that initializes the elements of a 15-element array to zero must con-

tain at least one **for** statement.

e) A JavaScript program that totals the elements of a double-subscripted array must contain

nested **for** statements.

17.8   Write JavaScript statements to accomplish each of the following:

a) Display the value of the seventh element of array **f**.

b) Initialize each of the five elements of single-subscripted array **g** to **8**.

c) Total the elements of array **c** of 100 numeric elements.

d) Copy 11- element array **a** into the first portion of array **b**, containing 34 elements.

e) Determine and print the smallest and largest values contained in 99-element floating-

point array **w**.

17.9   Consider a 2-by-3 array **t** that will store integers.

a) Write a statement that declares and creates array **t**.

b) How many rows does **t** have?

c) How many columns does **t** have?

d) How many elements does **t** have?

e) Write the names of all the elements in the second row of **t**.

f) Write the names of all the elements in the third column of **t**.

g) Write a single statement that sets the element of **t** in row 1 and column 2 to zero.

h) Write a series of statements that initializes each element of **t** to zero. Do not use a repe-

tition structure.

i) Write a nested **for** structure that initializes each element of **t** to zero.

j) Write a series of statements that determines and prints the smallest value in array **t**.

k) Write a statement that displays the elements of the first row of **t**.

l) Write a statement that totals the elements of the fourth column of **t**.

m) Write a series of statements that prints the array **t** in neat, tabular format. List the column

subscripts as headings across the top and list the row subscripts at the left of each row.

17.10 Use a single-subscripted array to solve the following problem: A company pays its salespeople on a commission basis. The salespeople receive $200 per week plus 9% of their gross sales for that week. For example, a salesperson who grosses $5000 in sales in a week receives $200 plus 9% of $5000, or a total of $650. Write a script (using an array of counters) that obtains the gross sales for each employee through an HTML form and determines how many of the salespeople earned salaries in each of the following ranges (assume each salesperson's salary is truncated to an integer amount):

    a) $200-$299
    b) $300-$399
    c) $400-$499
    d) $500-$599
    e) $600-$699
    f) $700-$799
    g) $800-$899
    h) $900-$999
    i) $1000 and over

17.11 Write statements that perform the following single-subscripted array operations:

    a) Set the 10 elements of array **counts** to zeros.
    b) Add 1 to each of the 15 elements of array **bonus**.
    c) Display the five values of array **bestScores** separated by spaces.

17.12 Use a single-subscripted array to solve the following problem. Read in 20 numbers, each of which is between 10 and 100, inclusive. As each number is read, print it only if it is not a duplicate of a number already read. Provide for the "worst case" in which all 20 numbers are different. Use the smallest possible array to solve this problem.

17.13 Label the elements of 3-by-5 double-subscripted array **sales** to indicate the order in which they are set to zero by the following program segment:

```
for ( var row in sales )
   for ( var col in sales[ row ] )
      sales[ row ][ col ] = 0;
```

17.14 Write a script to simulate the rolling of two dice. The script should use **Math.random** to roll the first die and should use **Math.random** again to roll the second die. The sum of the two values should then be calculated. [*Note:* Since each die can show an integer value from 1 to 6, the sum of the values will vary from 2 to 12, with 7 being the most frequent sum and 2 and 12 being the least frequent sums. Figure 17.12 shows the 36 possible combinations of the two dice. Your program should roll the dice 36,000 times. Use a single-subscripted array to tally the numbers of times each possible sum appears. Display the results in an HTML table. Also, determine whether the totals are reasonable (e.g., there are six ways to roll a 7, so approximately one sixth of all the rolls should be 7).]

17.15 Write a script that runs 1000 games of craps and answers the following questions:

    a) How many games are won on the first roll, second roll, ..., twentieth roll and after the twentieth roll?
    b) How many games are lost on the first roll, second roll, ..., twentieth roll and after the twentieth roll?
    c) What are the chances of winning at craps? [*Note:* You should discover that craps is one of the fairest casino games. What do you suppose this means?]
    d) What is the average length of a game of craps?
    e) Do the chances of winning improve with the length of the game?

17.16 (*Airline Reservations System*) A small airline has just purchased a computer for its new automated reservations system. You have been asked to program the new system. You are to write a program to assign seats on each flight of the airline's only plane (capacity: 10 seats).

	1	2	3	4	5	6
1	2	3	4	5	6	7
2	3	4	5	6	7	8
3	4	5	6	7	8	9
4	5	6	7	8	9	10
5	6	7	8	9	10	11
6	7	8	9	10	11	12

Fig. 17.12 The 36 possible outcomes of rolling two dice.

Your program should display the following menu of alternatives—**Please type 1 for "First Class"** and **Please type 2 for "Economy"**. If the person types **1**, your program should assign a seat in the first class section (seats 1-5). If the person types **2**, your program should assign a seat in the economy section (seats 6-10). Your program should print a boarding pass indicating the person's seat number and whether it is in the first class or economy section of the plane.

Use a single-subscripted array to represent the seating chart of the plane. Initialize all the elements of the array to 0 to indicate that all seats are empty. As each seat is assigned, set the corresponding elements of the array to 1 to indicate that the seat is no longer available.

Your program should, of course, never assign a seat that has already been assigned. When the first class section is full, your program should ask the person if it is acceptable to be placed in the nonsmoking section (and vice versa). If yes, then make the appropriate seat assignment. If no, then print the message **"Next flight leaves in 3 hours."**

17.17 Use a double-subscripted array to solve the following problem. A company has four salespeople (1 to 4) who sell five different products (1 to 5). Once a day, each salesperson passes in a slip for each different type of product actually sold. Each slip contains

1. the salesperson number,
2. the product number, and
3. the total dollar value of that product sold that day.

Thus, each salesperson passes in between 0 and 5 sales slips per day. Assume that the information from all of the slips for last month is available. Write a script that will read all this information for last month's sales and summarize the total sales by salesperson by product. All totals should be stored in the double-subscripted array **sales**. After processing all the information for last month, display the results in an HTML table format with each of the columns representing a particular salesperson and each of the rows representing a particular product. Cross total each row to get the total sales of each product for last month; cross total each column to get the total sales by salesperson for last month. Your tabular printout should include these cross totals to the right of the totaled rows and to the bottom of the totaled columns.

17.18 (*Turtle Graphics*) The Logo language, which is popular among young computer users, made the concept of *turtle graphics* famous. Imagine a mechanical turtle that walks around the room under the control of a JavaScript program. The turtle holds a pen in one of two positions, up or down. While the pen is down, the turtle traces out shapes as it moves; while the pen is up, the turtle moves about freely without writing anything. In this problem you will simulate the operation of the turtle and create a computerized sketchpad as well.

Use a 20-by-20 array **floor** that is initialized to zeros. Read commands from an array that contains them. Keep track of the current position of the turtle at all times and of whether the pen is currently up or down. Assume that the turtle always starts at position (0,0) of the floor, with its pen up. The set of turtle commands your script must process are as follows:

Command	Meaning
1	Pen up
2	Pen down
3	Turn right
4	Turn left
5,10	Move forward 10 spaces (or a number other than 10)
6	Print the 20-by-20 array
9	End of data (sentinel)

Suppose that the turtle is somewhere near the center of the floor. The following "program" would draw and print a 12-by-12 square, then leave the pen in the up position:

```
2
5,12
3
5,12
3
5,12
3
5,12
1
6
9
```

As the turtle moves with the pen down, set the appropriate elements of array **floor** to **1**s. When the **6** command (print) is given, wherever there is a **1** in the array, display an asterisk or some other character you choose. Wherever there is a zero, display a blank. Write a script to implement the turtle graphics capabilities discussed here. Write several turtle graphics programs to draw interesting shapes. Add other commands to increase the power of your turtle graphics language.

17.19 (*The Sieve of Eratosthenes*) A prime integer is an integer that is evenly divisible by only itself and 1. The Sieve of Eratosthenes is an algorithm for finding prime numbers. It operates as follows:

    a) Create an array with all elements initialized to 1 (true). Array elements with prime subscripts will remain 1. All other array elements will eventually be set to zero.

    b) Starting with array subscript 2 (subscript 1 must be prime), every time an array element is found whose value is 1, loop through the remainder of the array and set to zero every element whose subscript is a multiple of the subscript for the element with value 1. For array subscript 2, all elements beyond 2 in the array that are multiples of 2 will be set to zero (subscripts 4, 6, 8, 10, etc.); for array subscript 3, all elements beyond 3 in the array that are multiples of 3 will be set to zero (subscripts 6, 9, 12, 15, etc.); and so on.

When this process is complete, the array elements that are still set to one indicate that the subscript is a prime number. These subscripts can then be printed. Write a script that uses an array of 1000 elements to determine and print the prime numbers between 1 and 999. Ignore element 0 of the array.

17.20 (*Simulation: The Tortoise and the Hare*) In this problem you will recreate one of the truly great moments in history, namely, the classic race of the tortoise and the hare. You will use random number generation to develop a simulation of this memorable event.

Our contenders begin the race at "square 1" of 70 squares. Each square represents a possible position along the race course. The finish line is at square 70. The first contender to reach or pass square 70 is rewarded with a pail of fresh carrots and lettuce. The course weaves its way up the side of a slippery mountain, so occasionally the contenders lose ground.

There is a clock that ticks once per second. With each tick of the clock, your script should adjust the position of the animals according to the following rules:

Animal	Move type	Percentage of the time	Actual move
Tortoise	Fast plod	50%	3 squares to the right
	Slip	20%	6 squares to the left
	Slow plod	30%	1 square to the right
Hare	Sleep	20%	No move at all
	Big hop	20%	9 squares to the right
	Big slip	10%	12 squares to the left
	Small hop	30%	1 square to the right
	Small slip	20%	2 squares to the left

Use variables to keep track of the positions of the animals (i.e., position numbers are 1–70). Start each animal at position 1 (i.e., the "starting gate"). If an animal slips left before square 1, move the animal back to square 1.

Generate the percentages in the preceding table by producing a random integer, i, in the range $1 \leq i \leq 10$. For the tortoise, perform a "fast plod" when $1 \leq i \leq 5$, a "slip" when $6 \leq i \leq 7$ or a "slow plod" when $8 \leq i \leq 10$. Use a similar technique to move the hare.

Begin the race by printing

```
BANG !!!!!
AND THEY'RE OFF !!!!!
```

Then, for each tick of the clock (i.e., each repetition of a loop), print a 70-position line showing the letter **T** in the position of the tortoise and the letter **H** in the position of the hare. Occasionally, the contenders will land on the same square. In this case, the tortoise bites the hare and your script should print **OUCH!!!** beginning at that position. All print positions other than the **T**, the **H** or the **OUCH!!!** (in case of a tie) should be blank.

After each line is printed, test whether either animal has reached or passed square 70. If so, print the winner and terminate the simulation. If the tortoise wins, print **TORTOISE WINS!!! YAY!!!** If the hare wins, print **Hare wins. Yuch.** If both animals win on the same tick of the clock, you may want to favor the turtle (the "underdog") or you may want to print **It's a tie**. If neither animal wins, perform the loop again to simulate the next tick of the clock. When you are ready to run your script, assemble a group of fans to watch the race. You'll be amazed at how involved your audience gets!

Later in the book we introduce a number of Dynamic HTML capabilities, such as graphics, images, animation and sound. As you study those features, you might enjoy enhancing your tortoise-and-hare contest simulation.

18

JavaScript/JScript: Objects

Objectives

- To understand object-based programming terminology and concepts.
- To understand encapsulation and data hiding.
- To appreciate the value of object orientation.
- To be able to use the **Math** object.
- To be able to use the **String** object.
- To be able to use the **Date** object.
- To be able to use the **Boolean** and **Number** objects.

My object all sublime
I shall achieve in time.
W. S. Gilbert

Is it a world to hide virtues in?
William Shakespeare, *Twelfth Night*

Good as it is to inherit a library, it is better to collect one.
Augustine Birrell

A philosopher of imposing stature doesn't think in a vacuum.
Even his most abstract ideas are, to some extent, conditioned
by what is or is not known in the time when he lives.
Alfred North Whitehead

18.1 Introduction

Most JavaScript programs demonstrated to this point illustrate basic computer programming concepts. These programs provide you with the foundation you need to build powerful and complex scripts as part of your Web pages. As you proceed beyond this chapter, you will use JavaScript to manipulate every element of an HTML document from a script.

This chapter presents a more formal treatment of *objects*. The chapter overviews—and serves as a reference for—several of JavaScript's built-in objects and demonstrates many of their capabilities. In the chapters on Dynamic HTML that follow this chapter, you will be introduced to a wide variety of objects provided by the browser that enable scripts to interact with the different elements of an HTML document.

18.2 Thinking About Objects

Now we begin our introduction to objects. We will see that objects are a natural way of thinking about the world and of writing scripts that manipulate HTML documents.

In Chapters 13 through 17, we used built-in JavaScript objects—**Math** and **Array**—and we used objects provided by the Web browser—**document** and **window**—to perform tasks in our scripts. Because JavaScript uses objects to perform many tasks, JavaScript is commonly referred to as an *object-based programming language*. As we have seen, JavaScript also contains many constructs from the "conventional" methodology of structured programming supported by many other programming languages. In the first six JavaScript chapters, we concentrated on these "conventional" parts of JavaScript, as they are important components of all JavaScript programs.

Our strategy in this section is to introduce the basic concepts (i.e., "object think") and terminology (i.e., "object speak") of object-based programming, so we can properly refer to the object-based concepts as we encounter them in the remainder of the text.

Let us start by introducing some of the key terminology of object orientation. Look around you in the real world. Everywhere you look you see them—objects! People, animals, plants, cars, planes, buildings, computers and the like. Humans think in terms of objects. We have the marvelous ability of *abstraction,* which enables us to view screen images as objects such as people, planes, trees and mountains rather than as individual dots of color (called *pixels,* for "picture elements"). We can, if we wish, think in terms of beaches rather than grains of sand, forests rather than trees and houses rather than bricks.

We might be inclined to divide objects into two categories—animate objects and inanimate objects. Animate objects are "alive" in some sense. They move around and do things. Inanimate objects, like towels, seem not to do much at all. They just kind of "sit around." All these objects, however, do have some things in common. They all have *attributes,* such as size, shape, color, weight and the like; and they all exhibit *behaviors*—for example, a ball rolls, bounces, inflates and deflates; a baby cries, sleeps, crawls, walks and blinks; a car accelerates, decelerates, brakes and turns; a towel absorbs water.

Humans learn about objects by studying their attributes and observing their behaviors. Different objects can have similar attributes and can exhibit similar behaviors. Comparisons can be made, for example, between babies and adults and between humans and chimpanzees. Cars, trucks, little red wagons and skateboards have much in common.

Objects *encapsulate* data (attributes) and methods (behavior); the data and methods of an object are intimately tied together. Objects have the property of *information hiding*. Programs communicate with objects through well-defined *interfaces*. Normally, implementation details of objects are hidden within the objects themselves.

Most people reading this book probably drive (or have driven) an automobile—a perfect example of an object. Surely it is possible to drive an automobile effectively without knowing the details of how engines, transmissions and exhaust systems work internally. Millions of human years of research and development have been performed for automobiles and have resulted in extremely complex objects containing thousands of parts (attributes). All of this complexity is hidden (encapsulated) from the driver. The driver only sees the friendly user interface of behaviors that enable the driver to make the car go faster by pressing the gas pedal, go slower by pressing the brake pedal, turn left or right by turning the steering wheel, go forward or backward by selecting the gear and turn on and off by turning the key in the ignition.

Like the designers of an automobile, the designers of World Wide Web browsers have defined a set of objects that encapsulate the elements of an HTML document and expose to a JavaScript programmer attributes and behaviors that enable a JavaScript program to interact with (or script) the elements (objects) in an HTML document. The browser's **window** object provides attributes and behaviors that enable a script to manipulate a browser window. When a string is assigned to the **window** object's **status** property (attribute), that string is displayed in the status bar of the browser window. The **window** object's **alert** method (behavior) allows the programmer to display a message in a separate window. We will soon see that the browser's **document** object contains attributes and behaviors that provide access to every element of an HTML document. Similarly, JavaScript provides objects that encapsulate various capabilities in a script. For example, the

JavaScript **Array** object provides attributes and behaviors that enable a script to manipulate a collection of data. The **Array** object's **length** property (attribute) contains the number of elements in the **Array**. The **Array** object's **sort** method (behavior) orders the elements of the **Array**.

Indeed, with object technology, we will build most future software by combining "standardized, interchangeable parts" called objects. These parts allow programmers to create new programs without having to "reinvent the wheel." Objects will allow programmers to speed and enhance the quality of future software development efforts.

18.3 Math Object

The **Math** object's methods allow the programmer to perform many common mathematical calculations. As shown previously, an object's methods are called by writing the name of the object followed by a dot operator (**.**) and the name of the method. In parentheses following the method name is the argument (or a comma-separated list of arguments) to the method. For example, a programmer desiring to calculate and display the square root of **900.0** might write

```
document.writeln( Math.sqrt( 900.0 ) );
```

When this statement is executed, the method **Math.sqrt** is called to calculate the square root of the number contained in the parentheses (**900.0**). The number **900.0** is the argument of the **Math.sqrt** method. The preceding statement would display **30.0**. Invoking the **sqrt** method of the **Math** object is also referred to as *sending the sqrt message to Math object*. Similarly, invoking the **writeln** method of the **document** object is also referred to as *sending the writeln message to the document object*.

Common Programming Error 18.1

*Forgetting to invoke a **Math** method by preceding the method name with the object name **Math** and a dot operator (.) is an error.*

Software Engineering Observation 18.1

The primary difference between invoking a function and invoking a method is that a function does not require an object name and a dot operator to call the function.

Some **Math** object methods are summarized in Fig. 18.1.

Method	Description	Example
abs(x)	absolute value of *x*	if **x > 0** then **abs(x)** is **x** if **x = 0** then **abs(x)** is **0** if **x < 0** then **abs(x)** is **-x**
ceil(x)	rounds *x* to the smallest integer not less than *x*	**ceil(9.2)** is **10.0** **ceil(-9.8)** is **-9.0**

Fig. 18.1   Commonly used **Math** object methods (part 1 of 2).

Method	Description	Example
`cos( x )`	trigonometric cosine of x (x in radians)	`cos( 0.0 )` is `1.0`
`exp( x )`	exponential method e^x	`exp( 1.0 )` is `2.71828` `exp( 2.0 )` is `7.38906`
`floor( x )`	rounds x to the largest integer not greater than x	`floor( 9.2 )` is `9.0` `floor( -9.8 )` is `-10.0`
`log( x )`	natural logarithm of x (base e)	`log( 2.718282 )` is `1.0` `log( 7.389056 )` is `2.0`
`max( x, y )`	larger value of x and y	`max( 2.3, 12.7 )` is `12.7` `max( -2.3, -12.7 )` is `-2.3`
`min( x, y )`	smaller value of x and y	`min( 2.3, 12.7 )` is `2.3` `min( -2.3, -12.7 )` is `-12.7`
`pow( x, y )`	x raised to power y (x^y)	`pow( 2.0, 7.0 )` is `128.0` `pow( 9.0, .5 )` is `3.0`
`round( x )`	rounds x to the closest integer	`round( 9.75 )` is `10` `round( 9.25 )` is `9`
`sin( x )`	trigonometric sine of x (x in radians)	`sin( 0.0 )` is `0.0`
`sqrt( x )`	square root of x	`sqrt( 900.0 )` is `30.0` `sqrt( 9.0 )` is `3.0`
`tan( x )`	trigonometric tangent of x (x in radians)	`tan( 0.0 )` is `0.0`

Fig. 18.1   Commonly used **Math** object methods (part 2 of 2).

The **Math** object also defines several commonly used mathematical constants, summarized in Fig. 18.2. [Note: By convention, the names of these constants are written in all uppercase letters.]

Good Programming Practice 18.1

*Use the mathematical constants of the **Math** object rather than explicitly typing the numeric value of the constant.*

Constant	Description	Value
`Math.E`	Euler's constant.	Approximately 2.718.
`Math.LN2`	Natural logarithm of 2.	Approximately 0.693.
`Math.LN10`	Natural logarithm of 10.	Approximately 2.302.
`Math.LOG2E`	Base 2 logarithm of Euler's constant.	Approximately 1.442.

Fig. 18.2   Properties of the **Math** object (part 1 of 2).

Constant	Description	Value
`Math.LOG10E`	Base 10 logarithm of Euler's constant.	Approximately 0.434.
`Math.PI`	PI—the ratio of a circle's circumference to its diameter.	Approximately 3.141592653589793.
`Math.SQRT1_2`	Square root of 0.5.	Approximately 0.707.
`Math.SQRT2`	Square root of 2.0.	Approximately 1.414.

Fig. 18.2   Properties of the **Math** object (part 2 of 2).

18.4 `String` Object

In this section, we introduce Java's string and character processing capabilities. The techniques discussed here are appropriate for developing text editors, word processors, page layout software, computerized typesetting systems and other kinds of text-processing software.

18.4.1 Fundamentals of Characters and Strings

Characters are the fundamental building blocks of JavaScript programs. Every program is composed of a sequence of characters that—when grouped together meaningfully—is interpreted by the computer as a series of instructions used to accomplish a task.

A string is a series of characters treated as a single unit. A string may include letters, digits and various *special characters,* such as **+, -, *, /, $** and others. A string is an object of type **String**. *String literals* or *string constants* (often called *anonymous **String** objects*) are written as a sequence of characters in double quotation marks or single quotation marks as follows:

```
"John Q. Doe"(a name)
'9999 Main Street'(a street address)
"Waltham, Massachusetts"(a city and state)
'(201) 555-1212'(a telephone number)
```

A **String** may be assigned to a variable in a declaration. The declaration

```
var color = "blue";
```

initializes variable **color** as a **String** object containing the string **"blue"**.

Strings can be compared with the relational operators (**<, <=, >** and **>=**) and the equality operators (**==** and **!=**).

18.4.2 Methods of the `String` Object

The **String** object encapsulates the attributes and behaviors of a string of characters. The **String** object provides many methods (behaviors) for selecting characters from a string, combining strings (called *concatenation*), obtaining substrings of a string, searching for substrings within a string, tokenizing a string and converting strings to all uppercase or lowercase letters. The **String** object also provides several methods that generate HTML tags. Figure 18.3 summarizes many **String** methods. Figures 18.4 through 18.7 demonstrate some of these methods.

Method	Description
charAt (*index* **)**	Returns the character at the specified *index*. If there is no character at that *index*, **charAt** returns an empty string. The first character is located at *index* 0.
charCodeAt (*index* **)**	Returns the Unicode value of the character at the specified *index*. If there is no character at that *index*, **charCodeAt** returns **NaN**.
concat (*string* **)**	Concatenates its argument to the end of the string that invokes the method. This method is the same as adding two strings with the string concatenation operator **+** (e.g., **s1.concat (s2)** is the same as **s1 + s2**). The original strings are not modified.
fromCharCode (*value1*, *value2*, …**)**	Converts a list of Unicode values into a string containing the corresponding characters.
indexOf (*substring*, *index* **)**	Searches for the first occurrence of *substring* starting from position *index* in the string that invokes the method. The method returns the starting index of *substring* in the source string (-1 if *substring* is not found). If the *index* argument is not provided, the method begins searching from index 0 in the source string.
lastIndexOf (*substring*, *index* **)**	Searches for the last occurrence of *substring* starting from position *index* and searching toward the beginning of the string that invokes the method. The method returns the starting index of *substring* in the source string (-1 if *substring* is not found). If the *index* argument is not provided, the method begins searching from end of the source string.
slice (*start*, *end* **)**	Returns a string containing the portion of the string from index *start* through index *end*. If the *end* index is not specified, the method returns a string from the *start* index to the end of the source string. A negative *end* index specifies an offset from the end of the string starting from a position one past the end of the last character (so, -1 indicates the last character position in the string).
split (*string* **)**	Splits the source string into an array of strings (tokens) where its *string* argument specifies the delimiter (i.e., the characters that indicate the end of each token in the source string).
substr (*start*, *length* **)**	Returns a string containing *length* characters starting from index *start* in the source string. If *length* is not specified, a string containing characters from *start* to the end of the source string is returned.
substring (*start*, *end* **)**	Returns a string containing the characters from index *start* up to but not including index *end* in the source string.
toLowerCase ()	Returns a string in which all uppercase letters are converted to lowercase letters. Non-letter characters are not changed.
toUpperCase ()	Returns a string in which all lowercase letters are converted to uppercase letters. Non-letter characters are not changed.
toString ()	Returns the same string as the source string.

Fig. 18.3   Methods of the **String** object (part 1 of 2).

Method	Description
`valueOf()`	Returns the same string as the source string.

Methods that generate HTML tags

Method	Description
`anchor( name )`	Wraps the source string in an anchor element (`<A></A>`) with *name* as the anchor name.
`big()`	Wraps the source string in a `<BIG></BIG>` element.
`blink()`	Wraps the source string in a `<BLINK></BLINK>` element.
`bold()`	Wraps the source string in a `<B></B>` element.
`fixed()`	Wraps the source string in a `<TT></TT>` element.
`fontcolor( color )`	Wraps the source string in a `<FONT></FONT>` element with *color* as the font color.
`fontsize( size )`	Wraps the source string in a `<FONT></FONT>` element with *size* as the HTML font size.
`italics()`	Wraps the source string in an `<I></I>` element.
`link( url )`	Wraps the source string in an anchor element (`<A></A>`) with *url* as the hyperlink location.
`small()`	Wraps the source string in a `<SMALL></SMALL>` element.
`strike()`	Wraps the source string in a `<STRIKE></STRIKE>` element.
`sub()`	Wraps the source string in a `<SUB></SUB>` element.
`sup()`	Wraps the source string in a `<SUP></SUP>` element.

Fig. 18.3 Methods of the **String** object (part 2 of 2).

18.4.3 Character Processing Methods

The script of Fig. 18.4 demonstrates some of the **String** object's character processing methods: ***charAt*** (returns the character at a specific position); ***charCodeAt*** (returns the Unicode value of the character at a specific position); ***fromCharCode*** (creates a string from a list of Unicode values); ***toLowerCase*** (returns the lowercase version of a string); and ***toUpperCase*** (returns the uppercase version of a string).

```
1   <!DOCTYPE HTML PUBLIC "-//W3C//DTD HTML 4.0 Transitional//EN">
2   <HTML>
3   <!-- Fig. 18.4: CharacterProcessing.html -->
4
5   <HEAD>
6   <TITLE>Character Processing Methods</TITLE>
7
8   <SCRIPT LANGUAGE = "JavaScript">
9      var s = "ZEBRA";
10     var s2 = "AbCdEfG";
```

Fig. 18.4 String methods **charAt**, **charCodeAt**, **fromCharCode**, **toLowercase** and **toUpperCase** (part 1 of 2).

```
11
12      document.writeln( "<P>Character at index 0 in '" +
13          s + "' is " + s.charAt( 0 ) );
14      document.writeln( "<BR>Character code at index 0 in '" +
15          s + "' is " + s.charCodeAt( 0 ) + "</P>" );
16
17      document.writeln( "<P>'" +
18          String.fromCharCode( 87, 79, 82, 68 ) +
19          "' contains character codes 87, 79, 82 and 68</P>" )
20
21      document.writeln( "<P>'" + s2 + "' in lowercase is '" +
22          s2.toLowerCase() + "'" );
23      document.writeln( "<BR>'" + s2 + "' in uppercase is '" +
24          s2.toUpperCase() + "'</P>" );
25  </SCRIPT>
26
27  </HEAD><BODY></BODY>
28  </HTML>
```

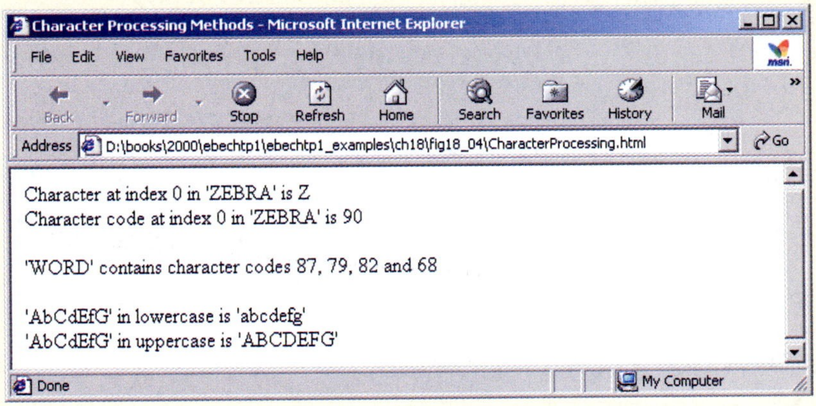

Fig. 18.4   String methods **charAt**, **charCodeAt**, **fromCharCode**, **toLowercase** and **toUpperCase** (part 2 of 2).

Lines 12 and 13

```
document.writeln( "<P>Character at index 0 in '" +
    s + "' is " + s.charAt( 0 ) );
```

display the first character in **String s** (**"ZEBRA"**) using **String** method **charAt**. Method *charAt* returns a string containing the character at the specified index (**0** in this example). Indices for the characters in a string start at 0 (the first character) and go up to (but not including) the string's **length** (i.e., if the string contains five characters, the indices are 0 through 4). If the index is outside the bounds of the string, the method returns an empty string.

Lines 14 and 15

```
document.writeln( "<BR>Character code at index 0 in '" +
    s + "' is " + s.charCodeAt( 0 ) + "</P>" );
```

display the character code for the first character in **String s** (**"ZEBRA"**) by using **String** method *charCodeAt*. Method **charCodeAt** returns the Unicode value of the character at the specified index (**0** in this example). If the index is outside the bounds of the string, the method returns **NaN**.

String method *fromCharCode* receives as its argument a comma-separated list of Unicode values and builds a string containing the character representation of those Unicode values. Lines 17 through 19

```
document.writeln( "<P>'" +
    String.fromCharCode( 87, 79, 82, 68 ) +
    "' contains character codes 87, 79, 82 and 68</P>" )
```

display the string "**WORD**", which consists of the character codes 87, 79, 82 and 68. Notice that the **String** object is used to call method **fromCharCode**. Appendix C, "ASCII Character Set," contains the character codes ASCII character set—a subset of the Unicode character set that contains only English characters.

The statements at lines 21 and 23 use **String** methods *toLowerCase* and *toUpperCase* to display versions of **String s2** (**"AbCdEfG"**) in all lowercase letters and all uppercase letters, respectively.

18.4.4 Searching Methods

Often it is useful to search for a character or a sequence of characters in a string. For example, if you are creating your own word processor, you may want to provide a capability for searching through the document. The script of Fig. 18.5 demonstrates the **String** object methods *indexOf* and *lastIndexOf* that search for a specified substring in a string. All the searches in this example are performed on the global string **letters** (initialized at line 9 with **"abcdefghijklmnopqrstuvwxyzabcdefghijklm"** in the script).

The user types a substring in the HTML form **searchForm**'s **inputVal** text field and presses button **search** (with the label **Search** on the screen) to search for the substring in **letters**. Function **buttonPressed** (defined at line 11) is called to respond to the **ONCLICK** event of button **search** and perform the searches. The results of each search are displayed in the appropriate text field of **searchForm**.

```
1  <!DOCTYPE HTML PUBLIC "-//W3C//DTD HTML 4.0 Transitional//EN">
2  <HTML>
3  <!-- Fig. 18.5: SearchingStrings.html -->
4
5  <HEAD>
6  <TITLE>Searching Strings with indexOf and lastIndexOf</TITLE>
7
8  <SCRIPT LANGUAGE = "JavaScript">
9     var letters = "abcdefghijklmnopqrstuvwxyzabcdefghijklm";
10
11    function buttonPressed()
12    {
13       searchForm.first.value =
14          letters.indexOf( searchForm.inputVal.value );
```

Fig. 18.5 Searching **String**s with **indexOf** and **lastIndexOf** (part 1 of 3).

```
15            searchForm.last.value =
16                letters.lastIndexOf( searchForm.inputVal.value );
17            searchForm.first12.value =
18                letters.indexOf( searchForm.inputVal.value, 12 );
19            searchForm.last12.value =
20                letters.lastIndexOf( searchForm.inputVal.value, 12 );
21        }
22    </SCRIPT>
23
24    </HEAD>
25    <BODY>
26    <FORM NAME = "searchForm">
27        <H1>The string to search is:<BR>
28            abcdefghijklmnopqrstuvwxyzabcdefghijklm</H1>
29        <P>Enter substring to search for
30        <INPUT NAME = "inputVal" TYPE = "text">
31        <INPUT NAME = "search" TYPE = "button" VALUE = "Search"
32            ONCLICK = "buttonPressed()"><BR></P>
33
34        <P>First occurrence located at index
35        <INPUT NAME = "first" TYPE = "text" SIZE = "5">
36        <BR>Last occurrence located at index
37        <INPUT NAME = "last" TYPE = "text" SIZE = "5">
38        <BR>First occurrence from index 12 located at index
39        <INPUT NAME = "first12" TYPE = "text" SIZE = "5">
40        <BR>Last occurrence from index 12 located at index
41        <INPUT NAME = "last12" TYPE = "text" SIZE = "5"></P>
42    </FORM>
43    </BODY>
44    </HTML>
```

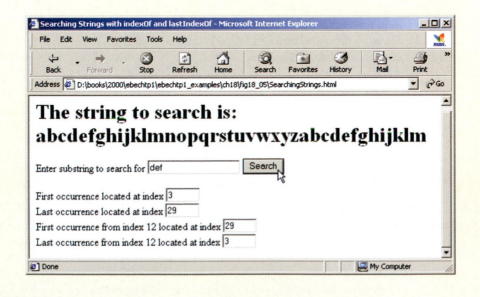

Fig. 18.5   Searching **String**s with **indexOf** and **lastIndexOf** (part 2 of 3).

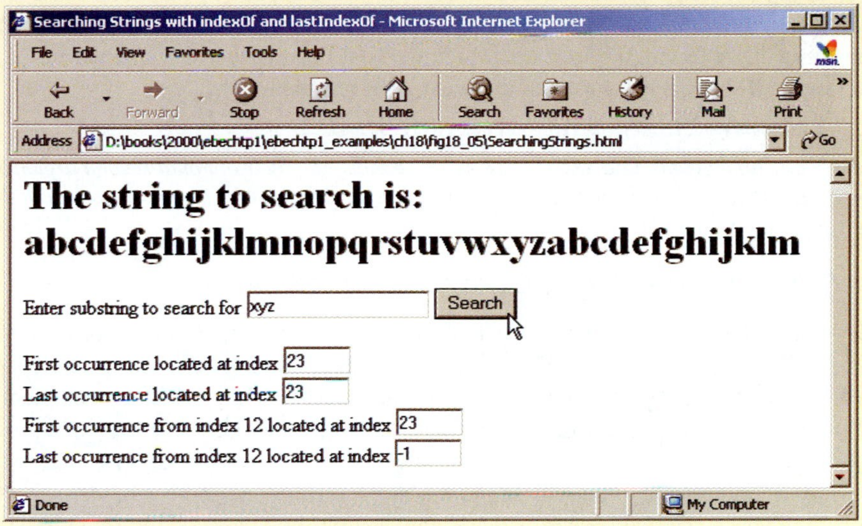

Fig. 18.5 Searching **String**s with **indexOf** and **lastIndexOf** (part 3 of 3).

Lines 13 and 14

```
searchForm.first.value =
    letters.indexOf( searchForm.inputVal.value );
```

use **String** method **indexOf** to determine the location of the first occurrence in string **letters** of the string **searchForm.inputVal.value** (i.e., the string the user typed in the **inputVal** text field). If the substring is found, the index at which the first occurrence of the substring begins is returned; otherwise, -1 is returned.

Lines 15 and 16

```
searchForm.last.value =
    letters.lastIndexOf( searchForm.inputVal.value );
```

use **String** method **lastIndexOf** to determine the location of the last occurrence in **letters** of the string in the **inputVal** text field. If the substring is found, the index at which the last occurrence of the substring begins is returned; otherwise, -1 is returned.

Lines 17 and 18

```
searchForm.first12.value =
    letters.indexOf( searchForm.inputVal.value, 12 );
```

use **String** method **indexOf** to determine the location of the first occurrence in string **letters** of the string in the **inputVal** text field, starting from index **12** in **letters**. If the substring is found, the index at which the first occurrence of the substring (starting from index **12**) begins is returned; otherwise, -1 is returned.

Lines 19 and 20

```
searchForm.last12.value =
    letters.lastIndexOf( searchForm.inputVal.value, 12 );
```

use **String** method **lastIndexOf** to determine the location of the last occurrence in **letters** of the string in the **inputVal** text field starting from index **12** in **letters**. If the substring is found, the index at which the first occurrence of the substring (starting from index **12**) begins is returned; otherwise, -1 is returned.

Software Engineering Observation 18.2

String methods indexOf or lastIndexOf, with their optional second argument (the starting index from which to search), are particularly useful for continuing a search through a large amount of text.

18.4.5 Splitting Strings and Obtaining Substrings

When you read a sentence, your mind breaks the sentence into individual words, or *tokens,* each of which conveys meaning to you. The process of breaking a string into tokens is called *tokenization*. Interpreters also perform tokenization. They break up statements into such individual pieces as keywords, identifiers, operators and other elements of a programming language. In this section, we demonstrate **String** method *split* that breaks a string into its component tokens. Tokens are separated from one another by *delimiters*, typically white-space characters such as blank, tab, newline and carriage return. Other characters may also be used as delimiters to separate tokens. The program of Fig. 18.6 demonstrates **String** method **split**. The HTML document displays a form containing a text field where the user types a sentence to tokenize. The results of the tokenization process are displayed in an HTML **TEXTAREA** GUI component. The script of Fig. 18.6 also demonstrates **String** method *substring* which returns a portion of a string.

```
1   <!DOCTYPE HTML PUBLIC "-//W3C//DTD HTML 4.0 Transitional//EN">
2   <HTML>
3   <!-- Fig. 18.6: SplitAndSubString.html -->
4
5   <HEAD>
6   <TITLE>String Method split and substring</TITLE>
7
8   <SCRIPT LANGUAGE = "JavaScript">
9      function splitButtonPressed()
10     {
11        var strings = myForm.inputVal.value.split( " " );
12        myForm.output.value = strings.join( "\n" );
13
14        myForm.outputSubstring.value =
15           myForm.inputVal.value.substring( 0, 10 );
16     }
17  </SCRIPT>
18  </HEAD>
19
20  <BODY>
21  <FORM NAME = "myForm">
22     <P>Enter a sentence to split into words<BR>
23     <INPUT NAME = "inputVal" TYPE = "text" SIZE = "40">
24     <INPUT NAME = "splitButton" TYPE = "button" VALUE = "Split"
25            ONCLICK = "splitButtonPressed()"></P>
```

Fig. 18.6   Using **String** method **split** and **Array** method **join** (part 1 of 2).

```
26
27        <P>The sentence split into words is<BR>
28        <TEXTAREA NAME = "output" ROWS = "8" COLS = "34">
29        </TEXTAREA></P>
30
31        <P>The first 10 characters of the input string are
32        <INPUT NAME = "outputSubstring" TYPE = "text" SIZE = "15">
33        </P>
34     </FORM>
35     </BODY>
36     </HTML>
```

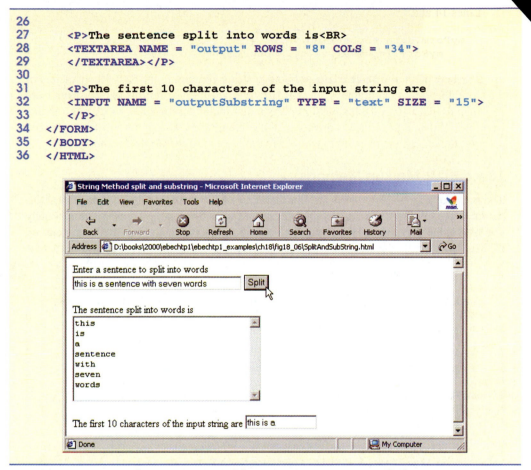

Fig. 18.6   Using **String** method **split** and **Array** method **join** (part 2 of 2).

The user types a sentence into form **myForm**'s **inputVal** text field and presses button **splitButton** (labeled **Split** on the screen) to tokenize the string. Function **splitButtonPressed** (line 9) handles **splitButton**'s **ONCLICK** event.

Line 11

```
var strings = myForm.inputVal.value.split( " " );
```

uses **String** method **split** to tokenize the string **myForm.inputVal.value**. The argument to method **split** is the *delimiter string*—the string that determines the end of each token in the original string. In this example, the space character is used as the delimiter for tokens. The delimiter string can contain multiple characters that should be used as delimiters. Method **split** returns an array of strings containing the tokens. Line 12

```
myForm.output.value = strings.join( "\n" );
```

uses **Array** method **join** to combine the strings in array **strings** and separate each string with a newline character (**\n**). The resulting string is assigned to the **value** property of the HTML form's **output** GUI component (an HTML **TEXTAREA**).

nd 15

```
.outputSubstring.value =
rm.inputVal.value.substring( 0, 10 );
```

...ing method **substring** to obtain a string containing the first 10 characters of the string the user entered in text field **inputVal**. The method returns the substring from the *starting index* (**0** in this example) up to but not including the *ending index* (**10** in this example). If the ending index is greater than the length of the string, the substring returned includes the characters from the starting index to the end of the original string.

18.4.6 HTML Markup Methods

The script of Fig. 18.7 demonstrates the **String** object's methods that generate HTML markup tags. When a markup method is applied to a string, the string is automatically wrapped in the appropriate HTML tag. These methods are particularly useful for generating HTML dynamically during script processing. [*Note:* Internet Explorer ignores the **BLINK** element.]

```
1  <!DOCTYPE HTML PUBLIC "-//W3C//DTD HTML 4.0 Transitional//EN">
2  <HTML>
3  <!-- Fig. 18.7: MarkupMethods.html -->
4
5  <HEAD>
6  <TITLE>HTML Markup Methods of the String Object</TITLE>
7
8  <SCRIPT LANGUAGE = "JavaScript">
9     var anchorText = "This is an anchor",
10        bigText = "This is big text",
11        blinkText = "This is blinking text",
12        boldText = "This is bold text",
13        fixedText = "This is monospaced text",
14        fontColorText = "This is red text",
15        fontSizeText = "This is size 7 text",
16        italicText = "This is italic text",
17        linkText = "Click here to go to anchorText",
18        smallText = "This is small text",
19        strikeText = "This is strike out text",
20        subText = "subscript",
21        supText = "superscript";
22
23     document.writeln( anchorText.anchor( "top" ) );
24     document.writeln( "<BR>" + bigText.big() );
25     document.writeln( "<BR>" + blinkText.blink() );
26     document.writeln( "<BR>" + boldText.bold() );
27     document.writeln( "<BR>" + fixedText.fixed() );
28     document.writeln(
29        "<BR>" + fontColorText.fontcolor( "red" ) );
30     document.writeln( "<BR>" + fontSizeText.fontsize( 7 ) );
31     document.writeln( "<BR>" + italicText.italics() );
32     document.writeln( "<BR>" + smallText.small() );
```

Fig. 18.7   HTML markup methods of the **String** object (part 1 of 2).

```
33      document.writeln( "<BR>" + strikeText.strike() );
34      document.writeln(
35         "<BR>This is text with a " + subText.sub() );
36      document.writeln(
37         "<BR>This is text with a " + supText.sup() );
38      document.writeln( "<BR>" + linkText.link( "#top" ) );
39   </SCRIPT>
40
41   </HEAD><BODY></BODY>
42   </HTML>
```

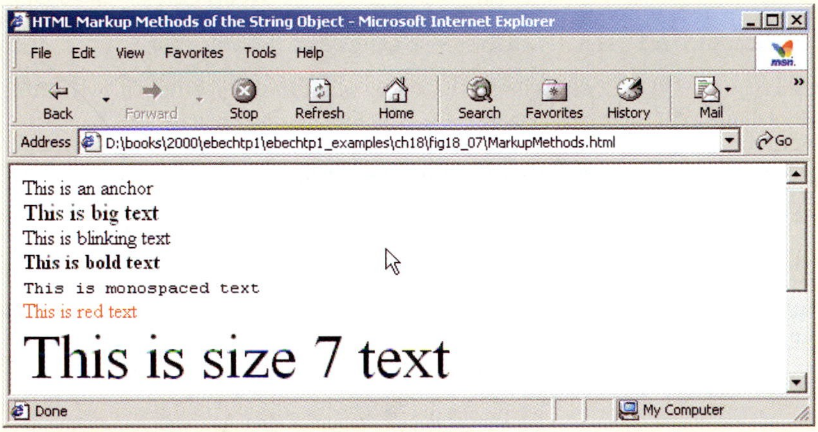

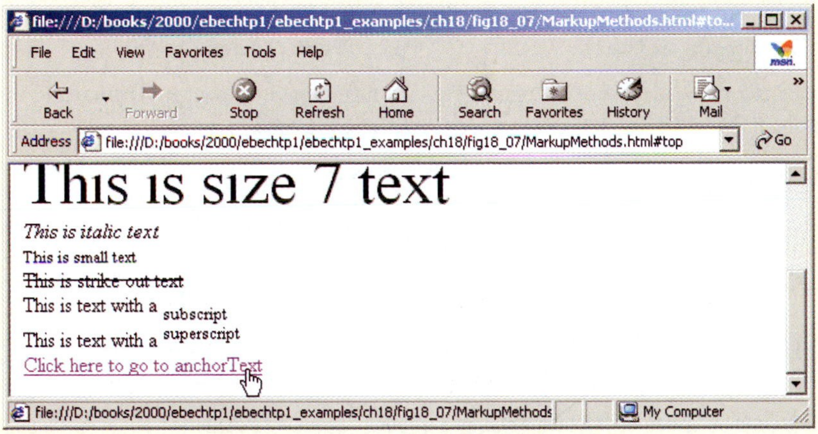

Fig. 18.7 HTML markup methods of the **String** object (part 2 of 2).

Lines 9 through 21 define the strings that are used to call each of the HTML markup methods of the **String** object. Line 23

```
document.writeln( anchorText.anchor( "top" ) );
```

uses **String** method *anchor* to format the string in variable **anchorText** (**"This is an anchor"**) as

```
<A NAME = "top">This is an anchor</A>
```

The **NAME** of the anchor is supplied as the argument to the method. This anchor will be used later in the example as the target of a hyperlink.

Line 24

```
document.writeln( "<BR>" + bigText.big() );
```

uses **String** method *big* to make the size of the displayed text bigger than normal text by formatting the string in variable **bigText** (**"This is big text"**) as

```
<BIG>This is big text</BIG>
```

Line 25

```
document.writeln( "<BR>" + blinkText.blink() );
```

uses **String** method *blink* to make the string blink in the Web page by formatting the string in variable **blinkText** (**"This is blinking text"**) as

```
<BLINK>This is blinking text</BLINK>
```

Line 26

```
document.writeln( "<BR>" + boldText.bold() );
```

uses **String** method *bold* to display bold text by formatting the string in the variable **boldText** (**"This is bold text"**) as

```
<B>This is bold text</B>
```

Line 27

```
document.writeln( "<BR>" + fixedText.fixed() );
```

uses **String** method *fixed* to display text in a fixed-width font by formatting the string in variable **fixedText** (**"This is monospaced text"**) as

```
<TT>This is monospaced text</TT>
```

Lines 28 and 29

```
document.writeln(
    "<BR>" + fontColorText.fontcolor( "red" ) );
```

uses **String** method *fontcolor* to change the color of the displayed text by formatting the string in variable **fontColorText** (**"This is red text"**) as

```
<FONT COLOR = "red">This is red text</FONT>
```

The argument to the method is the HTML color for the text. This color can be specified either as the HTML color name or as a hexadecimal value. For example, red in hexadecimal format would be **"FF0000"**.

Line 30

```
document.writeln( "<BR>" + fontSizeText.fontsize( 7 ) );
```

uses **String** method *fontsize* to change the HTML size of the displayed text by formatting the string in variable **fontSizeText** (**"This is size 7 text"**) as

```
<FONT SIZE = "7">This is size 7 text</FONT>
```

The argument to the method is the HTML font size (1 to 7) for the text.
   Line 31

```
document.writeln( "<BR>" + italicText.italics() );
```

uses **String** method *italics* to display italic text by formatting the string in variable **italicText** (**"This is italic text"**) as

```
<I>This is italic text</I>
```

   Line 32

```
document.writeln( "<BR>" + smallText.small() );
```

uses **String** method *small* to make the size of the displayed text smaller than normal text by formatting the string in variable **smallText** (**"This is small text"**) as

```
<SMALL>This is small text</SMALL>
```

   Line 33

```
document.writeln( "<BR>" + strikeText.strike() );
```

uses **String** method *strike* to display struck-out text (i.e., text with a line through it) by formatting the string in variable **strikeText** (**"This is strike out text"**) as

```
<STRIKE>This is strike out text</STRIKE>
```

   Lines 34 and 35

```
documentv.writeln(
   "<BR>This is text with a " + subText.sub() );
```

use **String** method *sub* to display subscript text by formatting the string in variable **subText** (**"subscript"**) as

```
<SUB>subscript</SUB>
```

Notice that the resulting line in the HTML document displays the word **subscript** smaller than the rest of the line and slightly below the line. Lines 36 and 37

```
document.writeln(
   "<BR>This is text with a " + supText.sup() );
```

use **String** method *sup* to display superscript text by formatting the string in variable **supText** (**"superscript"**) as

```
<SUP>superscript</SUP>
```

Notice that the resulting line in the HTML document displays the word **superscript** smaller than the rest of the line and slightly above the line.
   Line 38

```
document.writeln( "<BR>" + linkText.link( "#top" ) );
```

uses **String** method *link* to create a hyperlink by formatting the string in variable **linkText** (**"Click here to go to anchorText"**) as

```
<A HREF = "#top">Click here to go to anchorText</A>
```

The target of the hyperlink (**#top** in this example) is the argument to the method and can be any URL. In this example, the hyperlink target is the anchor created at line 23. If you make your browser window short and scroll to the bottom of the Web page, then click this link, the browser will reposition to the top of the Web page.

18.5 Date Object

JavaScript's *Date* object provides methods for date and time manipulations. Date and time processing can be performed based on the computer's *local time zone* or based on World Time Standard's *Universal Coordinated Time (UTC)*—formerly called *Greenwich Mean Time (GMT)*. Most methods of the **Date** object have a local time zone and a UTC version. The methods of the **Date** object are summarized in Fig. 18.8.

Method	Description
getDate() getUTCDate()	Returns a number from 1 to 31 representing the day of the month in local time or UTC, respectively.
getDay() getUTCDay()	Returns a number from 0 (Sunday) to 6 (Saturday) representing the day of the week in local time or UTC, respectively.
getFullYear() getUTCFullYear()	Returns the year as four-digit number in local time or UTC, respectively.
getHours() getUTCHours()	Returns a number from 0 to 23 representing hours since midnight in local time or UTC, respectively.
getMilliseconds() getUTCMilliSeconds()	Returns a number from 0 to 999 representing the number of milliseconds in local time or UTC, respectively. The time is stored in hours, minutes, seconds and milliseconds.
getMinutes() getUTCMinutes()	Returns a number from 0 to 59 representing the minutes for the time in local time or UTC, respectively.
getMonth() getUTCMonth()	Returns a number from 0 (January) to 11 (December) representing the month in local time or UTC, respectively.
getSeconds() getUTCSeconds()	Returns a number from 0 to 59 representing the seconds for the time in local time or UTC, respectively.
getTime()	Returns the number of milliseconds between January 1, 1970 and the time in the **Date** object.
getTimezoneOffset()	Returns the difference in minutes between the current time on the local computer and UTC—previously known as Greenwich Mean Time (GMT).
setDate(*val*) setUTCDate(*val*)	Sets the day of the month (1 to 31) in local time or UTC, respectively.
setFullYear(*y, m, d*) setUTCFullYear(*y, m, d*)	Sets the year in local time or UTC, respectively. The second and third arguments representing the month and the date are optional. If an optional argument is not specified, the current value in the **Date** object is used.

Fig. 18.8   Methods of the **Date** object (part 1 of 2).

Method	Description
`setHours( h, m, s, ms )` `setUTCHours( h, m, s, ms )`	Sets the hour in local time or UTC, respectively. The second, third and fourth arguments representing the minutes, seconds and milliseconds are optional. If an optional argument is not specified, the current value in the **Date** object is used.
`setMilliSeconds( ms )` `setUTCMilliseconds( ms )`	Sets the number of milliseconds in local time or UTC, respectively.
`setMinutes( m, s, ms )` `setUTCMinutes( m, s, ms )`	Sets the minute in local time or UTC, respectively. The second and third arguments representing the seconds and milliseconds are optional. If an optional argument is not specified, the current value in the **Date** object is used.
`setMonth( m, d )` `setUTCMonth( m, d )`	Sets the month in local time or UTC, respectively. The second argument representing the date is optional. If the optional argument is not specified, the current date value in the **Date** object is used.
`setSeconds( s, ms )` `setUTCSeconds( s, ms )`	Sets the second in local time or UTC, respectively. The second argument representing the milliseconds is optional. If this argument is not specified, the current millisecond value in the **Date** object is used.
`setTime( ms )`	Sets the time based on its argument—the number of elapsed milliseconds since January 1, 1970.
`toLocaleString()`	Returns a string representation of the date and time in a form specific to the locale of the computer. For example, September 13, 1999 at 3:42:22 PM is represented as *09/13/99 15:47:22* in the United States and *13/09/99 15:47:22* in Europe.
`toUTCString()`	Returns a string representation of the date and time in the form: *13 Sep 1999 15:47:22 UTC*
`toString()`	Returns a string representation of the date and time in a form specific to the locale of the computer (*Mon Sep 13 15:47:22 EDT 1999* in the United States).
`valueOf()`	The time in number of milliseconds since midnight, January 1, 1970.

Fig. 18.8   Methods of the **Date** object (part 2 of 2).

The script of Fig. 18.9 demonstrates many of the local time zone methods in Fig. 18.8. Line 9 creates a new **Date** object with the statement

```
var current = new Date();
```

The **new** operator allocates the memory for the **Date** object, then the **Date** object's *constructor* is called with no arguments. A constructor is an initializer method for an object. Constructors are called automatically when an object is allocated with **new**. The **Date** constructor with no arguments initializes the **Date** object with the current date and time.

```
1   <!DOCTYPE HTML PUBLIC "-//W3C//DTD HTML 4.0 Transitional//EN">
2   <HTML>
3   <!-- Fig. 18.9: DateTime.html -->
4
5   <HEAD>
6   <TITLE>Date and Time Methods</TITLE>
7
8   <SCRIPT LANGUAGE = "JavaScript">
9      var current = new Date();
10
11     document.writeln(
12        "<H1>String representations and valueOf</H1>" );
13     document.writeln( "toString: " + current.toString() +
14        "<BR>toLocaleString: " + current.toLocaleString() +
15        "<BR>toUTCString: " + current.toUTCString() +
16        "<BR>valueOf: " + current.valueOf() );
17
18     document.writeln(
19        "<H1>Get methods for local time zone</H1>" );
20     document.writeln( "getDate: " + current.getDate() +
21        "<BR>getDay: " + current.getDay() +
22        "<BR>getMonth: " + current.getMonth() +
23        "<BR>getFullYear: " + current.getFullYear() +
24        "<BR>getTime: " + current.getTime() +
25        "<BR>getHours: " + current.getHours() +
26        "<BR>getMinutes: " + current.getMinutes() +
27        "<BR>getSeconds: " + current.getSeconds() +
28        "<BR>getMilliseconds: " + current.getMilliseconds() +
29        "<BR>getTimezoneOffset: " +
30        current.getTimezoneOffset() );
31
32     document.writeln(
33        "<H1>Specifying arguments for a new Date</H1>" );
34     var anotherDate = new Date( 1999, 2, 18, 1, 5, 0, 0 );
35     document.writeln( "Date: " + anotherDate );
36
37     document.writeln(
38        "<H1>Set methods for local time zone</H1>" );
39     anotherDate.setDate( 31 );
40     anotherDate.setMonth( 11 );
41     anotherDate.setFullYear( 1999 );
42     anotherDate.setHours( 23 );
43     anotherDate.setMinutes( 59 );
44     anotherDate.setSeconds( 59 );
45     document.writeln( "Modified date: " + anotherDate );
46  </SCRIPT>
47
48  </HEAD><BODY></BODY>
49  </HTML>
```

Fig. 18.9   Demonstrating date and time methods of the **Date** object (part 1 of 2).

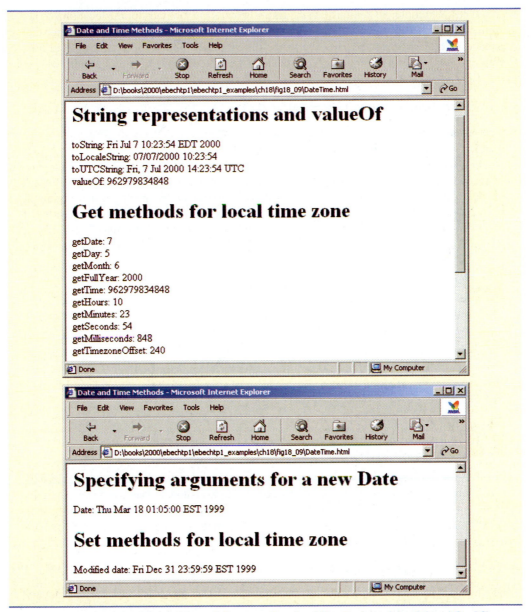

Fig. 18.9   Demonstrating date and time methods of the **Date** object (part 2 of 2).

Software Engineering Observation 18.3

When an object is allocated with **new**, *the object's constructor is called automatically to initialize the object before it is used in the program.*

Lines 13 through 16 demonstrate the methods **toString**, **toLocaleString**, **toUTCString** and **valueOf**. Notice that method **valueOf** returns a large integer value representing the total number of milliseconds between midnight, January 1, 1970 and the date and time stored in **Date** object **current**.

Lines 20 through 30 demonstrate the **Date** object's *get* methods for the local time zone. Notice that method **getFullYear** returns the year as a four-digit number. Also, notice that method **getTimeZoneOffset** returns the difference in minutes between the local time zone and UTC time (a difference of four hours at the time of the sample execution).

Line 34

```
var anotherDate = new Date( 1999, 2, 18, 1, 5, 0, 0 );
```

demonstrates creating a new **Date** object and supplying arguments to the **Date** constructor for *year*, *month*, *date*, *hours*, *minutes*, *seconds* and *milliseconds*. Note that the *hours*, *minutes*, *seconds* and *milliseconds* arguments are all optional. If any one of these arguments is not specified, a zero is supplied in its place. For the *hours*, *minutes* and *seconds* arguments, if the argument to the right of any of these arguments is specified, that argument must also be specified (e.g., if the *minutes* argument is specified, the *hours* argument must be specified; if the *milliseconds* argument is specified, all the arguments must be specified).

Lines 39 through 44 demonstrate the **Date** object *set* methods for the local time zone.

Software Engineering Observation 18.4

*Methods **getFullYear** and **setFullYear** use four-digit years to avoid problems with dates at the beginning of the 21st century. In particular, two-digit year format would cause a problem for year 2000–00 could be treated by many computers as 1900 rather than 2000. This is commonly known as the Y2K (year 2000) bug.*

Date objects represent the month internally as a integer from 0 to 11. These values are off-by-one from what you might expect (i.e., 1 for January, 2 for February, …, and 12 for December). When creating a **Date** object, you must specify 0 to indicate January, 1 to indicate February, …, and 11 to indicate December.

Common Programming Error 18.2

*Assuming months are represented as numbers from 1 to 12 leads to off-by-one errors when you are processing **Date**s.*

The **Date** object provides two other methods that can be called without creating a new **Date** object—*Date.parse* and *Date.UTC*. Method **Date.parse** receives as its argument a string representing a date and time, and returns the number of milliseconds between midnight, January 1, 1970 and the specified date and time. This value can be converted to a **Date** object with the statement

```
var theDate = new Date( numberOfMilliseconds );
```

which passes to the **Date** constructor the number of milliseconds since midnight, January 1, 1970 for the **Date** object.

Method **parse** converts the string using the following rules:

- Short dates can be specified in the form **MM-DD-YY**, **MM-DD-YYYY**, **MM/DD/YY** or **MM/DD/YYYY**. The month and day are not required to be two-digits. The year should be specified as a four-digit number to avoid the Y2K problem mentioned previously.

- Long dates that specify the complete month name (e.g., "January"), date and year can specify the month, date and year in any order. The year should be specified as a four-digit number to avoid the Y2K problem mentioned previously.

- Text in parentheses within the string is treated as a comment and ignored. Commas and whitespace characters are treated as delimiters.

- All month and day names must have at least two characters. The names are not required to be unique. If the names are identical, the name is resolved as the last match (e.g., "Ju" represents "July" rather than "June").

- If the name of the day of the week is supplied, it is ignored.

- All standard time zones (e.g., EST for Eastern Standard Time), Universal Coordinated Time (UTC) and Greenwich Mean Time (GMT) are recognized.

- When specifying hours, minutes, and seconds, separate each by colons.

- When using 24-hour clock format, "PM" should not be used for times after 12 noon.

Date method **UTC** returns the number of milliseconds between midnight, January 1, 1970 and the date and time specified as its arguments. The arguments to the **UTC** method include the required *year*, *month* and *date*, and the optional *hours*, *minutes*, *seconds* and *milliseconds*. If any of the *hours*, *minutes*, *seconds* or *milliseconds* arguments is not specified, a zero is supplied in its place. For the *hours*, *minutes* and *seconds* arguments, if the argument to the right of any of these arguments is specified, that argument must also be specified (e.g., if the *minutes* argument is specified, the *hours* argument must be specified; if the *milliseconds* argument is specified, all the arguments must be specified). As with the result of **Date.parse**, the result of **Date.UTC** can be converted to a **Date** object by creating a new **Date** object with the result of **Date.UTC** as its argument.

18.6 Boolean and Number Objects

JavaScript provides the **Boolean** and **Number** objects as object *wrappers* for boolean **true**/**false** values and numbers, respectively. These wrappers define methods and properties useful in manipulating boolean values and numbers.

When a boolean value is required in a JavaScript program, JavaScript automatically creates a **Boolean** object to store the value. JavaScript programmers can create **Boolean** objects explicitly with the statement

```
var b = new Boolean( booleanValue );
```

The constructor argument *booleanValue* specifies whether the value of the **Boolean** object should be **true** or **false**. If *booleanValue* is **false**, **0**, **null**, **Number.NaN** or the empty string (**""**), or if no argument is supplied, the new **Boolean** object contains **false**. Otherwise, the new **Boolean** object contains **true**. Figure 18.10 summarizes the methods of the **Boolean** object.

Method	Description
toString()	Returns the string "**true**" if the value of the **Boolean** object is true; otherwise, returns the string "**false**."
valueOf()	Returns the value **true** if the **Boolean** object is **true**; otherwise, returns **false**.

Fig. 18.10 Methods of the **Boolean** object.

JavaScript automatically creates **Number** objects to store numeric values in a JavaScript program. JavaScript programmers can create a **Number** object with the statement

```
var n = new Number( numericValue );
```

The constructor argument *numericValue* is the number to store in the object. Although you can explicitly create **Number** objects, normally they are created when needed by the JavaScript interpreter. Figure 18.11 summarizes the methods and properties of the **Number** object.

SUMMARY

- Objects are a natural way of thinking about the world.

- Because JavaScript uses objects to perform many tasks, JavaScript is commonly referred to as an object-based programming language.

- Humans think in terms of objects. We have the marvelous ability of abstraction, which enables us to view screen images as objects such as people, planes, trees and mountains rather than as individual dots of color (called pixels for "picture elements").

Method or property	Description
toString(*radix* **)**	Returns the string representation of the number. The optional *radix* argument (a number from 2 to 36) specifies the base of the number. For example, radix 2 results in the binary representation of the number, 8 results in the octal representation of the number, 10 results in the decimal representation of the number and 16 results in the hexadecimal representation of the number. See the document "Number Systems" on the CD that accompanies this book for a review of the binary, octal, decimal and hexadecimal number systems.
valueOf()	Returns the numeric value.
Number.MAX_VALUE	This property represents the largest value that can be stored in a JavaScript program—approximately 1.79E+308
Number.MIN_VALUE	This property represents the smallest value that can be stored in a JavaScript program—approximately 2.22E–308
Number.NaN	This property represents *not a number*—a value returned from arithmetic expressions that do not result in a number (e.g., the expression **parseInt("hello")** cannot convert the string **"hello"** into a number, so **parseInt** would return **Number.NaN**). To determine whether a value is **NaN**, test the result with function **isNaN** which returns **true** if the value is **NaN**; otherwise, it returns **false**.
Number.NEGATIVE_INFINITY	This property represents a value less than **-Number.MAX_VALUE**.
Number.POSITIVE_INFINITY	This property represents a value greater than **Number.MAX_VALUE**.

Fig. 18.11   Methods and properties of the **Number** object.

- All objects have attributes and exhibit behaviors. Humans learn about objects by studying their attributes and observing their behaviors.
- Objects encapsulate data (attributes) and methods (behavior).
- Objects have the property of information hiding.
- Programs communicate with objects by using well-defined interfaces.
- World Wide Web browsers have a set of objects that encapsulate the elements of an HTML document and expose to a JavaScript programmer attributes and behaviors that enable a JavaScript program to interact with (or script) the elements (i.e., objects) in an HTML document.
- **Math** object methods allow programmers to perform many common mathematical calculations.
- An object's methods are called by writing the name of the object followed by a dot operator (**.**) and the name of the method. In parentheses following the method name is the argument (or a comma-separated list of arguments) to the method.
- Invoking (or calling) a method of an object is called "sending a message to the object."
- Characters are the fundamental building blocks of JavaScript programs. Every program is composed of a sequence of characters that—when grouped together meaningfully—is interpreted by the computer as a series of instructions used to accomplish a task.
- A string is a series of characters treated as a single unit.
- A string may include letters, digits and various special characters, such as **+, -, *, /, $** and others.
- String literals or string constants (often called anonymous **String** objects) are written as a sequence of characters in double quotation marks or single quotation marks.
- String method **charAt** returns the character at a specific index in a string. Indices for the characters in a string start at 0 (the first character) and go up to (but not including) the string's **length** (i.e., if the string contains five characters, the indices are 0 through 4). If the index is outside the bounds of the string, the method returns an empty string.
- **String** method **charCodeAt** returns the Unicode value of the character at a specific index in a string. If the index is outside the bounds of the string, the method returns **NaN**.
- **String** method **fromCharCode** creates a string from a list of Unicode values.
- **String** method **toLowerCase** returns the lowercase version of a string.
- **String** method **toUpperCase** returns the uppercase version of a string.
- **String** method **indexOf** determines the location of the first occurrence of its argument in the string used to call the method. If the substring is found, the index at which the first occurrence of the substring begins is returned; otherwise, -1 is returned. This method receives an optional second argument specifying the index from which to begin the search.
- **String** method **lastIndexOf** determines the location of the last occurrence of its argument in the string used to call the method. If the substring is found, the index at which the first occurrence of the substring begins is returned; otherwise, -1 is returned. This method receives an optional second argument specifying the index from which to begin the search.
- The process of breaking a string into tokens is called tokenization. Tokens are separated from one another by delimiters, typically white-space characters such as blank, tab, newline and carriage return. Other characters may also be used as delimiters to separate tokens.
- **String** method **split** breaks a string into its component tokens. The argument to method **split** is the delimiter string—the string that determines the end of each token in the original string. Method **split** returns an array of strings containing the tokens.
- **String** method **substring** returns the substring from the starting index (its first argument) up to but not including the ending index (its second argument). If the ending index is greater than the

length of the string, the substring returned includes the characters from the starting index to the end of the original string.

- **String** method **anchor** wraps the string that calls the method in HTML element **<A></A>** with the **NAME** of the anchor supplied as the argument to the method.

- **String** method **big** makes the size of the displayed text bigger than normal text by wrapping the string that calls the method in a **<BIG></BIG>** HTML element.

- **String** method **blink** make a string blink in a Web page by wrapping the string that calls the method in a **<BLINK></BLINK>** HTML element.

- **String** method **bold** displays bold text by wrapping the string that calls the method in HTML element **<B></B>**.

- **String** method **fixed** displays text in a fixed-width font by wrapping the string that calls the method in a **<TT></TT>** HTML element.

- **String** method **fontcolor** changes the color of the displayed text by wrapping the string that calls the method in a **<FONT></FONT>** element. The argument to the method is the HTML color for the text, which can be specified as either the HTML color name or as a hexadecimal value.

- **String** method **fontsize** changes the HTML size of the displayed text by wrapping the string that calls the method in a **<FONT></FONT>** element. The argument to the method is the HTML font size (1 to 7) for the text.

- **String** method **italics** displays italic text by wrapping the string that calls the method in an **<I></I>** HTML element.

- **String** method **small** makes the size of the displayed text smaller than normal text by wrapping the string that calls the method in a **<SMALL></SMALL>** HTML element.

- **String** method **strike** displays struck-out text (i.e., text with a line through it) by wrapping the string that calls the method in a **<STRIKE></STRIKE>** HTML element.

- **String** method **sub** displays subscript text by wrapping the string that calls the method in a **** HTML element.

- **String** method **sup** displays superscript text by wrapping the string that calls the method in a **** HTML element.

- **String** method **link** creates a hyperlink by wrapping the string that calls the method in HTML element **<A></A>**. The target of the hyperlink (i.e, value of the **HREF** property) is the argument to the method and can be any URL.

- JavaScript's **Date** object provides methods for date and time manipulations.

- Date and time processing can be performed based on the computer's local time zone or based on World Time Standard's Universal Coordinated Time (UTC)—formerly called Greenwich Mean Time (GMT).

- Most methods of the **Date** object have a local time zone and a UTC version.

- **Date** method **parse** receives as its argument a string representing a date and time and returns the number of milliseconds between midnight, January 1, 1970 and the specified date and time.

- **Date** method **UTC** returns the number of milliseconds between midnight, January 1, 1970 and the date and time specified as its arguments. The arguments to the **UTC** method include the required year, month and date, and the optional hours, minutes, seconds and milliseconds. If any of the hours, minutes, seconds or milliseconds arguments is not specified, a zero is supplied in its place. For the hours, minutes and seconds arguments, if the argument to the right of any of these arguments is specified, that argument must also be specified (e.g., if the minutes argument is specified, the hours argument must be specified; if the milliseconds argument is specified, all the arguments must be specified).

- JavaScript provides the **Boolean** and **Number** objects as object wrappers for boolean **true**/**false** values and numbers, respectively.

- When a boolean value is required in a JavaScript program, JavaScript automatically creates a **Boolean** object to store the value.

- JavaScript programmers can create **Boolean** objects explicitly with the statement

```
var b = new Boolean( booleanValue );
```

The argument *booleanValue* specifies whether the value of the **Boolean** object should be **true** or **false**. If *booleanValue* is **false**, **0**, **null**, **Number.NaN** or the empty string (**""**), or if no argument is supplied, the new **Boolean** object contains **false**. Otherwise, the new **Boolean** object contains **true**.

- JavaScript automatically creates **Number** objects to store numeric values in a JavaScript program.

- JavaScript programmers can create a **Number** object with the statement

```
var n = new Number( numericValue );
```

The argument *numericValue* is the number to store in the object. Although you can explicitly create **Number** objects, normally they are created when needed by the JavaScript interpreter.

TERMINOLOGY

abs method of **Math**
abstraction
anchor method of **String**
anonymous **String** object
attribute
behavior
big method of **String**
blink method of **String**
bold method of **String**
Boolean object
bounds of the string
ceil method of **Math**
character
charAt method of **String**
charCodeAt method of **String**
concat method of **String**
cos method of **Math**
date
Date object
delimiters
double quotation marks
E property of Math
empty string
encapsulation
ending index
exp method of **Math**
fixed method of **String**
floor method of **Math**
fontcolor method of **String**
fontsize method of **String**

fromCharCode method of **String**
getDate method of **Date**
getDay method of **Date**
getFullYear method of **Date**
getHours method of **Date**
getMilliseconds method of **Date**
getMinutes method of **Date**
getMonth method of **Date**
getSeconds method of **Date**
getTime method of **Date**
getTimezoneOffset method of **Date**
getUTCDate method of **Date**
getUTCDay method of **Date**
getUTCFullYear method of **Date**
getUTCHours method of **Date**
getUTCMilliSeconds method of **Date**
getUTCMinutes method of **Date**
getUTCMonth method of **Date**
getUTCSeconds method of **Date**
Greenwich Mean Time (GMT)
hiding
index in a string
indexOf method of **String**
information hiding
italics method of **String**
lastIndexOf method of **String**
link method of **String**
local time zone
LN10 property of Math
LN2 property of Math

log method of **Math**
LOG10E property of Math
LOG2E property of Math
Math object
max method of **Math**
MAX_SIZE property of **Number**
min method of **Math**
MIN_SIZE property of **Number**
NaN property of **Number**
NEGATIVE_INFINITY property of **Number**
Number object
object
object-based programming language
object wrapper
parse method of **Date**
PI property of Math
POSITIVE_INFINITY property of **Number**
pow method of **Math**
round method of **Math**
search a string
sending a message to an object
setDate method of **Date**
setFullYear method of **Date**
setHours method of **Date**
setMilliSeconds method of **Date**
setMinutes method of **Date**
setMonth method of **Date**
setSeconds method of **Date**
setTime method of **Date**
setUTCDate method of **Date**
setUTCFullYear method of **Date**
setUTCHours method of **Date**
setUTCMilliseconds method of **Date**
setUTCMinutes method of **Date**
setUTCMonth method of **Date**
setUTCSeconds method of **Date**
single quotation marks
sin method of **Math**

slice method of **String**
small method of **String**
special characters
split method of **String**
sqrt method of **Math**
SQRT1_2 property of Math
SQRT2 property of Math
starting index
strike method of **String**
string
string constant
string literal
sub method of **String**
substring
substring method of **String**
substr method of **String**
sup method of **String**
sup method of **String**
tan method of **Math**
time
token
tokenization
toLocaleString method of **Date**
toLowerCase method of **String**
toString method of **Date**
toString method of **String**
toUpperCase method of **String**
toUTCString method of **Date**
Unicode
Universal Coordinated Time (UTC)
UTC method of **Date**
valueOf method of **Boolean**
valueOf method of **Date**
valueOf method of **Number**
valueOf method of **String**
well-defined interfaces
wrap in HTML tags

SELF-REVIEW EXERCISES

18.1 Fill in the blank(s) in each of the following:
   a) Because JavaScript uses objects to perform many tasks, JavaScript is commonly referred to as an _____.
   b) All objects have _____ and exhibit _____.
   c) The methods of the _____ object allow programmers to perform many common mathematical calculations.
   d) Invoking (or calling) a method of an object is referred to as _____.
   e) String literals or string constants are written as a sequence of characters in _____ or _____.
   f) Indices for the characters in a string start at _____.

g) **String** methods _____ and _____ search for the first and last occurrence of a substring in a **String**, respectively.

h) The process of breaking a string into tokens is called _____.

i) **String** method _____ formats a **String** as a hyperlink.

j) Date and time processing can be performed based on the _____ or based on World Time Standard's _____.

k) **Date** method _____ receives as its argument a string representing a date and time, and returns the number of milliseconds between midnight, January 1, 1970 and the specified date and time.

ANSWERS TO SELF-REVIEW EXERCISES

18.1 a) object-based programming language. b) attributes, behaviors. c) **Math**. d) sending a message to the object. e) double quotation marks, single quotation marks. f) 0. g) **indexOf, lastIndexOf**. h) tokenization. i) **link**. j) computer's local time zone, Universal Coordinated Time (UTC). k) **parse**.

EXERCISES

18.2 Write a script that tests whether the examples of the **Math** method calls shown in Fig. 18.1 actually produce the indicated results.

18.3 Write a script that tests as many of the math library functions in Fig. 18.1 as you can. Exercise each of these functions by having your program display tables of return values for a diversity of argument values in an HTML **TEXTAREA**.

18.4 **Math** method **floor** may be used to round a number to a specific decimal place. For example, the statement

        y = Math.floor(x * 10 + .5) / 10;

rounds **x** to the tenths position (the first position to the right of the decimal point). The statement

        y = Math.floor(x * 100 + .5) / 100;

rounds **x** to the hundredths position (i.e., the second position to the right of the decimal point). Write a script that defines four functions to round a number **x** in various ways:

a) **roundToInteger(number)**
b) **roundToTenths(number)**
c) **roundToHundredths(number)**
d) **roundToThousandths(number)**

For each value read, your program should display the original value, the number rounded to the nearest integer, the number rounded to the nearest tenth, the number rounded to the nearest hundredth and the number rounded to the nearest thousandth.

18.5 Modify the solution to Exercise 18.4 to use **Math** method **round** instead of method **floor**.

18.6 Write a script that uses relational and equality operators to compare two **String**s input by the user through an HTML form. Output in an HTML **TEXTAREA** whether the first string is less than, equal to or greater than the second.

18.7 Write a script that uses random number generation to create sentences. Use four arrays of strings called **article, noun, verb** and **preposition**. Create a sentence by selecting a word at random from each array in the following order: **article, noun, verb, preposition, article** and **noun**. As each word is picked, concatenate it to the previous words in the sentence. The words should be separated by spaces. When the final sentence is output, it should start with a capital letter and end with a period. The program should generate 20 sentences and output them to an HTML **TEXTAREA**.

The arrays should be filled as follows: the **article** array should contain the articles **"the"**, **"a"**, **"one"**, **"some"** and **"any"**; the **noun** array should contain the nouns **"boy"**, **"girl"**, **"dog"**, **"town"** and **"car"**; the **verb** array should contain the verbs **"drove"**, **"jumped"**, **"ran"**, **"walked"** and **"skipped"**; the **preposition** array should contain the prepositions **"to"**, **"from"**, **"over"**, **"under"** and **"on"**.

After the preceding script is written, modify the script to produce a short story consisting of several of these sentences. (How about the possibility of a random term paper writer!)

18.8   *(Limericks)* A limerick is a humorous five-line verse in which the first and second lines rhyme with the fifth, and the third line rhymes with the fourth. Using techniques similar to those developed in Exercise 18.7, write a script that produces random limericks. Polishing this program to produce good limericks is a challenging problem, but the result will be worth the effort!

18.9   *(Pig Latin)* Write a script that encodes English language phrases into pig Latin. Pig Latin is a form of coded language often used for amusement. Many variations exist in the methods used to form pig Latin phrases. For simplicity, use the following algorithm:

To form a pig Latin phrase from an English language phrase, tokenize the phrase into an array of words using **String** method **split**. To translate each English word into a pig Latin word, place the first letter of the English word at the end of the word and add the letters "**ay**." Thus the word "**jump**" becomes "**umpjay**," the word "**the**" becomes "**hetay**," and the word "**computer**" becomes "**omputercay**." Blanks between words remain as blanks. Assume the following: The English phrase consists of words separated by blanks, there are no punctuation marks and all words have two or more letters. Function **printLatinWord** should display each word. Each token (i.e., word in the sentence) is passed to method **printLatinWord** to print the pig Latin word. Enable the user to input the sentence through an HTML form. Keep a running display of all the converted sentences in an HTML **TEXTAREA**.

18.10   Write a script that inputs a telephone number as a string in the form **(555) 555-5555**. The script should use **String** method **split** to extract the area code as a token, the first three digits of the phone number as a token and the last four digits of the phone number as a token. Display the area code in one text field and the seven-digit phone number in another text field.

18.11   Write a script that inputs a line of text, tokenizes the line with **String** method **split** and outputs the tokens in reverse order.

18.12   Write a script that inputs text from an HTML form and outputs the text in uppercase and lowercase letters.

18.13   Write a script that inputs several lines of text and a search character and uses **String** method **indexOf** to determine the number of occurrences of the character in the text.

18.14   Write a script based on the program of Exercise 18.13 that inputs several lines of text and uses **String** method **indexOf** to determine the total number of occurrences of each letter of the alphabet in the text. Uppercase and lowercase letters should be counted together. Store the totals for each letter in an array, and print the values in tabular format in an HTML **TEXTAREA** after the totals have been determined.

18.15   Write a script that reads a series of strings and outputs in an HTML **TEXTAREA** only those strings beginning with the letter "**b**."

18.16   Write a script that reads a series of strings and outputs in an HTML **TEXTAREA** only those strings ending with the letters "**ED**."

18.17   Write a script that inputs an integer code for a character and displays the corresponding character.

18.18   Modify your solution to Exercise 18.17 so that it generates all possible three-digit codes in the range 000 to 255 and attempts to display the corresponding characters. Display the results in an HTML **TEXTAREA**.

18.19 Write your own version of the **String** method **indexOf** and use it in a script.

18.20 Write your own version of the **String** method **lastIndexOf** and use it in a script.

18.21 Write a program that reads a five-letter word from the user and produces all possible three-letter words that can be derived from the letters of the five-letter word. For example, the three-letter words produced from the word "bathe" include the commonly used words "ate", "bat", "bet", "tab", "hat", "the" and "tea." Output the results in an HTML **TEXTAREA**.

18.22 *(Printing Dates in Various Formats)* Dates are printed in several common formats. Write a script that reads a date from an HTML form and creates a **Date** object in which to store that date. Then, use the various methods of the **Date** object that convert **Date**s into strings to display the date in several formats.

SPECIAL SECTION: ADVANCED STRING MANIPULATION EXERCISES

The preceding exercises are keyed to the text and designed to test the reader's understanding of fundamental string manipulation concepts. This section includes a collection of intermediate and advanced string manipulation exercises. The reader should find these problems challenging, yet entertaining. The problems vary considerably in difficulty. Some require an hour or two of program writing and implementation. Others are useful for lab assignments that might require two or three weeks of study and implementation. Some are challenging term projects.

18.23 *(Text Analysis)* The availability of computers with string manipulation capabilities has resulted in some rather interesting approaches to analyzing the writings of great authors. Much attention has been focused on whether William Shakespeare ever lived. Some scholars believe there is substantial evidence indicating that Christopher Marlowe or other authors actually penned the masterpieces attributed to Shakespeare. Researchers have used computers to find similarities in the writings of these two authors. This exercise examines three methods for analyzing texts with a computer.

    a) Write a script that reads several lines of text from the keyboard and prints a table indicating the number of occurrences of each letter of the alphabet in the text. For example, the phrase

To be, or not to be: that is the question:

    contains one "a," two "b's," no "c's," etc.

    b) Write a script that reads several lines of text and prints a table indicating the number of one-letter words, two-letter words, three-letter words, etc. appearing in the text. For example, the phrase

Whether 'tis nobler in the mind to suffer

    contains

Word length	Occurrences
1	0
2	2
3	1
4	2 (including 'tis)
5	0
6	2
7	1

c) Write a script that reads several lines of text and prints a table indicating the number of occurrences of each different word in the text. The first version of your program should include the words in the table in the same order in which they appear in the text. For example, the lines

```
To be, or not to be: that is the question:
Whether 'tis nobler in the mind to suffer
```

contain the words "to" three times, the word "be" two times, the word "or" once, etc. A more interesting (and useful) printout should then be attempted in which the words are sorted alphabetically.

18.24 *(Check Protection)* Computers are frequently employed in check-writing systems such as payroll and accounts payable applications. Many strange stories circulate regarding weekly paychecks being printed (by mistake) for amounts in excess of $1 million. Incorrect amounts are printed by computerized check-writing systems because of human error and/or machine failure. Systems designers build controls into their systems to prevent such erroneous checks from being issued.

Another serious problem is the intentional alteration of a check amount by someone who intends to cash a check fraudulently. To prevent a dollar amount from being altered, most computerized check-writing systems employ a technique called *check protection.*

Checks designed for imprinting by computer contain a fixed number of spaces in which the computer may print an amount. Suppose a paycheck contains eight blank spaces in which the computer is supposed to print the amount of a weekly paycheck. If the amount is large, then all eight of those spaces will be filled, for example:

```
1,230.60 (check amount)
--------
12345678 (position numbers)
```

On the other hand, if the amount is less than $1000, then several of the spaces would ordinarily be left blank. For example,

```
   99.87
--------
12345678
```

contains three blank spaces. If a check is printed with blank spaces, it is easier for someone to alter the amount of the check. To prevent a check from being altered, many check-writing systems insert *leading asterisks* to protect the amount as follows:

```
***99.87
--------
12345678
```

Write a script that inputs a dollar amount to be printed on a check, and then prints the amount in check-protected format with leading asterisks if necessary. Assume that nine spaces are available for printing the amount.

18.25 *(Writing the Word Equivalent of a Check Amount)* Continuing the discussion of the previous exercise, we reiterate the importance of designing check-writing systems to prevent alteration of check amounts. One common security method requires that the check amount be written both in numbers and "spelled out" in words as well. Even if someone is able to alter the numerical amount of the check, it is extremely difficult to change the amount in words.

Many computerized check-writing systems do not print the amount of the check in words. Perhaps the main reason for this omission is the fact that most high-level languages used in commercial applications do not contain adequate string manipulation features. Another reason is that the logic for writing word equivalents of check amounts is somewhat involved.

Write a script that inputs a numeric check amount and writes the word equivalent of the amount. For example, the amount 112.43 should be written as

```
ONE HUNDRED TWELVE and 43/100
```

18.26 *(Morse Code)* Perhaps the most famous of all coding schemes is the Morse code, developed by Samuel Morse in 1832 for use with the telegraph system. The Morse code assigns a series of dots and dashes to each letter of the alphabet, each digit and a few special characters (such as period, comma, colon, and semicolon). In sound-oriented systems, the dot represents a short sound and the dash represents a long sound. Other representations of dots and dashes are used with light-oriented systems and signal-flag systems.

Separation between words is indicated by a space, or, quite simply, by the absence of a dot or dash. In a sound-oriented system, a space is indicated by a short period of time during which no sound is transmitted. The international version of the Morse code appears in Fig. 18.12.

Write a script that reads an English language phrase and encodes the phrase into Morse code. Also write a program that reads a phrase in Morse code and converts the phrase into the English language equivalent. Use one blank between each Morse-coded letter and three blanks between each Morse-coded word.

Character	Code	Character	Code
A	.−	T	−
B	−...	U	..−
C	−.−.	V	...−
D	−..	W	.−−
E	.	X	−..−
F	..−.	Y	−.−−
G	−−.	Z	−−..
H	....		
I	..	Digits	
J	.−−−	1	.−−−−
K	−.−	2	..−−−
L	.−..	3	...−−
M	−−	4	....−
N	−.	5	.....
O	−−−	6	−....
P	.−−.	7	−−...
Q	−−.−	8	−−−..
R	.−.	9	−−−−.
S	...	0	−−−−−

Fig. 18.12 The letters of the alphabet as expressed in international Morse code.

18.27 *(A Metric Conversion Program)* Write a script that will assist the user with metric conversions. Your program should allow the user to specify the names of the units as strings (i.e., centimeters, liters, grams etc. for the metric system and inches, quarts, pounds etc. for the English system) and should respond to simple questions such as

> ```
> "How many inches are in 2 meters?"
> "How many liters are in 10 quarts?"
> ```

Your program should recognize invalid conversions. For example, the question

> ```
> "How many feet in 5 kilograms?"
> ```

is not a meaningful question because **"feet"** is a unit of length while **"kilograms"** is a unit of mass.

SPECIAL SECTION: CHALLENGING STRING MANIPULATION PROJECTS

18.28 *(Project: A Spelling Checker)* Many popular word processing software packages have built-in spell checkers.

In this project, you are asked to develop your own spell-checker utility. We make suggestions to help get you started. You should then consider adding more capabilities. Use a computerized dictionary (if you have access to one) as a source of words.

Why do we type so many words with incorrect spellings? In some cases, it is because we simply do not know the correct spelling, so we make a "best guess." In some cases, it is because we transpose two letters (e.g., "defualt" instead of "default"). Sometimes we double-type a letter accidentally (e.g., "hanndy" instead of "handy"). Sometimes we type a nearby key instead of the one we intended (e.g., "biryhday" instead of "birthday"). And so on.

Design and implement a spell-checker application in Java. Your program should maintain an array **wordList** of strings. Enable the user to enter these strings.

Your program should ask a user to enter a word. The program should then look up that word in the **wordList** array. If the word is present in the array, your program should print "**Word is spelled correctly**."

If the word is not present in the array, your program should print "**word is not spelled correctly**." Then your program should try to locate other words in **wordList** that might be the word the user intended to type. For example, you can try all possible single transpositions of adjacent letters to discover that the word "default" is a direct match to a word in **wordList**. Of course, this implies that your program will check all other single transpositions, such as "edfault," "dfeault," "deafult," "defalut," and "defautl." When you find a new word that matches one in **wordList**, print that word in a message, such as "**Did you mean "default?"**."

Implement other tests, such as replacing each double letter with a single letter and any other tests you can develop to improve the value of your spell checker.

18.29 *(Project: A Crossword Puzzle Generator)* Most people have worked a crossword puzzle, but few have ever attempted to generate one. Generating a crossword puzzle is suggested here as a string manipulation project requiring substantial sophistication and effort.

There are many issues the programmer must resolve to get even the simplest crossword puzzle generator program working. For example, how does one represent the grid of a crossword puzzle inside the computer? Should one use a series of strings, or should double-subscripted arrays be used?

The programmer needs a source of words (i.e., a computerized dictionary) that can be directly referenced by the program. In what form should these words be stored to facilitate the complex manipulations required by the program?

The really ambitious reader will want to generate the "clues" portion of the puzzle, in which the brief hints for each "across" word and each "down" word are printed for the puzzle worker. Merely printing a version of the blank puzzle itself is not a simple problem.

19

Dynamic HTML: Cascading Style Sheets™ (CSS)

- Objectives
- To take control of the appearance of a Web site by creating your own style sheets.
- To use a style sheet to give all the pages of a Web site the same look and feel.
- To use the **CLASS** attribute to apply styles.
- To specify the precise font, size, color and other properties of displayed text.
- To specify element backgrounds and colors.
- To understand the box model and be able to control the margins, borders, padding.
- To truly separate content and presentation.

Fashions fade, style is eternal.
Yves Saint Laurent

A style does not go out of style as long as it adapts itself to its period. When there is an incompatibility between the style and a certain state of mind, it is never the style that triumphs.
Coco Chanel

How liberating to work in the margins, outside a central perception.
Don DeLillo

Our words have wings, but fly not where we would.
George Eliot

There are aphorisms that, like airplanes, stay up only while they are in motion.
Vladimir Nabokov

19.1 Introduction

Cascading Style Sheets (*CSS*) allow you to specify the style of your page elements (spacing, margins, etc.) separately from the structure of your document (section headers, body text, links, etc.). This *separation of structure from content* allows greater manageability and makes changing the style of your document easier.

19.2 Inline Styles

There are many ways to declare styles for a document. Figure 19.1 presents *inline styles* in which an individual element's style is declared using the ***STYLE*** attribute.

```
1   <!DOCTYPE html PUBLIC "-//W3C//DTD HTML 4.0 Transitional//EN">
2   <HTML>
3
4   <!-- Fig. 19.1: inline.html -->
5   <!-- Using inline styles      -->
6
7   <HEAD><TITLE>Inline Styles</TITLE></HEAD>
8
9   <BODY>
10
11  <P>Here is some text</P>
12
13  <!-- The STYLE attribute allows you to declare inline   -->
14  <!-- styles. Separate multiple styles with a semicolon. -->
15  <P STYLE = "font-size: 20pt">Here is some more text</P>
16  <P STYLE = "font-size: 20pt; color: #0000FF">Even more text</P>
```

Fig. 19.1   Inline styles (part 1 of 2).

```
17
18     </BODY>
19     </HTML>
```

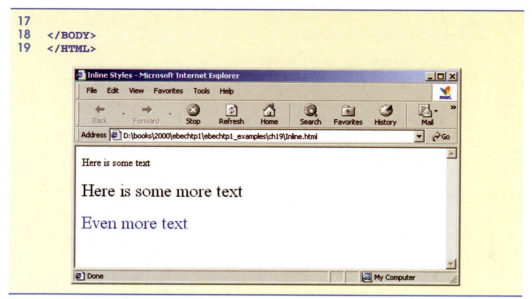

Fig. 19.1   Inline styles (part 2 of 2).

Our first inline style declaration appears on line 15:

```
<P STYLE = "font-size: 20pt">Here is some more text</P>
```

The **STYLE attribute** allows you to specify a style for an element. Each *CSS property* (in this case, **font-size**) is followed by a colon then the value of that attribute. In the preceding HTML line we declare the **P** element (of only that line) to have 20-point text size.
    Line 16

```
<P STYLE = "font-size: 20pt; color: #0000FF">Even more text</P>
```

specifies two properties separated by a semicolon. In this line we also set the **color** of the text to blue using the hex code **#0000FF**. Color names (see Appendix B) may be used in place of hex codes as we will see in the next example. Note that inline styles override any other styles applied by the methods we cover later in this chapter.

19.3 Creating Style Sheets with the STYLE Element

In Fig. 19.2 we declare, in the header section of the document, styles that may be applied to the entire document.

```
1     <!DOCTYPE html PUBLIC "-//W3C//DTD HTML 4.0 Transitional//EN">
2     <HTML>
3
4     <!-- Fig. 19.2: declared.html                              -->
5     <!-- Declaring a style sheet in the header section. -->
6
```

Fig. 19.2   Declaring styles in the header section of a document (part 1 of 2).

```
 7    <HEAD>
 8    <TITLE>Style Sheets</TITLE>
 9
10    <!-- This begins the style sheet section. -->
11    <STYLE TYPE = "text/css">
12
13        EM      { background-color: #8000FF;
14                  color: white }
15
16        H1      { font-family: Arial, sans-serif }
17
18        P       { font-size: 18pt }
19
20        .blue { color: blue }
21
22    </STYLE>
23    </HEAD>
24
25    <BODY>
26
27    <!-- This CLASS attribute applies the .blue style -->
28    <H1 CLASS = "blue">A Heading</H1>
29    <P>Here is some text. Here is some text. Here is some text.
30    Here is some text. Here is some text.</P>
31
32    <H1>Another Heading</H1>
33    <P CLASS = "blue">Here is some more text. Here is some more text.
34    Here is some <EM>more</EM> text. Here is some more text.</P>
35
36    </BODY>
37    </HTML>
```

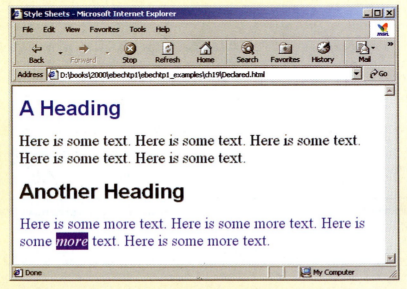

Fig. 19.2   Declaring styles in the header section of a document (part 2 of 2).

The element in the header section on line 11

```
<STYLE TYPE = "text/css">
```

begins the *style sheet*. Styles that are placed here apply to the whole document, not just a single element. The **TYPE attribute** specifies the *MIME type* of the following style sheet. MIME is a standard for specifying the format of content—some other MIME types are **text/html**, **image/gif**, and **text/javascript**. Regular text style sheets always use the MIME type **text/css**.

Look-and-Feel Observation 19.1

Without style sheets, the browser completely controls the look and feel of Web pages. With style sheets, the designer can specify the look and feel of all elements on a Web page.

The body of the **STYLE** sheet on lines 13 through 20

```
EM     { background-color: #8000FF;
         color: white }

H1     { font-family: Arial, sans-serif }

P      { font-size: 18pt }

.blue { color: blue }
```

declares the *CSS rules* for this style sheet. We declare rules for the **EM**, **H1** and **P** elements. All **EM**, **H1** and **P** elements in this document will be modified in the specified manner. CSS is a powerful tool for applying universal formatting. Notice that each rule body begins and ends with a curly brace (**{** and **}**). We also declare a *style class* named **blue** on line 20. All class declarations are preceded with a period and are applied to elements only of that specific class (as we will see below).

The CSS rules in a style sheet use the same format as inline styles—the property is followed by a colon (**:**) and the value of that property. Multiple properties are separated with a semicolon (**;**) as in the preceding **EM** style rule.

The **color** property specifies the color of text in an element. The **background-color** property specifies the background color of the element (like the **BGCOLOR** attribute in HTML does).

The **font-family** property (line 16) specifies the name of the font that should be displayed. In this case, we use the **Arial** font. The second value, **sans-serif**, is a *generic font family*. Generic font families allow you to specify a type of font instead of a specific font. This allows much greater flexibility in your site display. In this example, if the **Arial** font is not found on the system, the browser will instead display another **sans-serif** font (such as **Helvetica** or **Verdana**). Other generic font families are *serif* (e.g., **Times New Roman** or **Georgia**), *cursive* (e.g., *Script*), *fantasy* (e.g., **Critter**) and *monospace* (e.g., **Courier** or **Fixedsys**).

The **font-size** property specifies the size to use to render the font—in this case we use 18 points. Other possible measurements besides **pt** are covered later in the chapter. You can also use the relative values *xx-small*, *x-small*, *small*, *smaller*, *medium*, *large*, *larger*, *x-large* and *xx-large*.

On line 28

```
<H1 CLASS = "blue">A Heading</H1>
```

the **CLASS attribute** applies a style class, in this case **blue** (this was declared as **.blue** in the **STYLE** sheet). Note that the text appears on screen with *both* the properties of an **H1** element and the properties of the **.blue** style class applied.

On lines 33 and 34

```
<P CLASS = "blue">Here is some more text. Here is some more text.
Here is some <EM>more</EM> text. Here is some more text.</P>
```

The **P** element and the **.blue** class style are both applied to the whole text. All styles applied to an element (the *parent element*) also apply to elements inside that element (*child elements*). The word inside the **EM** element *inherits* the **P** style (namely, the 18-point font size of line 18), but it conflicts with the **color** attribute of the **blue** class. Because styles declared in child element are more specific (have greater *specificity*) than parent element styles, the **EM** style overrides the styles set in the **blue** class.

19.4 Conflicting Styles

Figure 19.3 has more examples of *inheritance* and *specificity*.

```
1   <!DOCTYPE html PUBLIC "-//W3C//DTD HTML 4.0 Transitional//EN">
2   <HTML>
3
4   <!-- Fig 19.3: advanced.html    -->
5   <!-- More advanced style sheets -->
6
7   <HEAD>
8   <TITLE>More Styles</TITLE>
9   <STYLE TYPE = "text/css">
10
11      A.nodec   { text-decoration: none }
12
13      A:hover   { text-decoration: underline;
14                  color: red;
15                  background-color: #CCFFCC }
16
17      LI EM     { color: red;
18                  font-weight: bold }
19
20      UL        { margin-left: 75px }
21
22      UL UL     { text-decoration: underline;
23                  margin-left: 15px }
24
```

Fig. 19.3   Inheritance in style sheets (part 1 of 2).

```
25    </STYLE>
26    </HEAD>
27
28    <BODY>
29
30    <H1>Shopping list for <EM>Monday</EM>:</H1>
31    <UL>
32    <LI>Milk</LI>
33    <LI>Bread
34       <UL>
35       <LI>White bread</LI>
36       <LI>Rye bread</LI>
37       <LI>Whole wheat bread</LI>
38       </UL></LI>
39    <LI>Rice</LI>
40    <LI>Potatoes</LI>
41    <LI>Pizza <EM>with mushrooms</EM></LI>
42    </UL>
43
44    <P><A CLASS = "nodec" HREF = "http://food.com">Go to the Grocery
45       store</A></P>
46
47    </BODY>
48    </HTML>
```

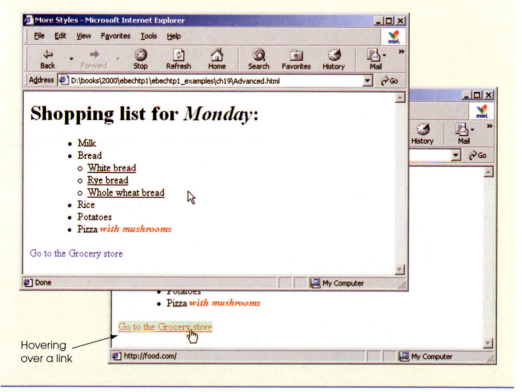

Fig. 19.3 Inheritance in style sheets (part 2 of 2).

Line 11

```
A.nodec   { text-decoration: none }
```

applies the ***text-decoration property*** to all **A** elements whose **CLASS** attribute is set to **nodec**. The default browser rendering of an **A** element is to underline, but here we set it to **none**. The **text-decoration** property applies *decorations* to text within an element. Other possible values are ***overline***, ***line-through*** and ***blink***.

The **.nodec** appended to **A** is an extension of class styles—this style will apply only to **A** elements that specify **nodec** as their class.

Lines 13 through 15

```
A:hover   { text-decoration: underline;
            color: red;
            background-color: #CCFFCC }
```

specify a style for **hover**, which is a *pseudo-class*. Pseudo-classes give the author access to content not specifically declared in the document. The **hover** pseudo-class is dynamically activated when the user moves the mouse cursor over an **A** element.

Portability Tip 19.1

*Browsers are not required to support the **blink** value of the **text-decoration** property, so do not use it as a mechanism for important highlighting.*

Portability Tip 19.2

Always test DHTML programs on all intended client platforms to ensure that the display is reasonable, especially for those client platforms with older browsers.

Lines 17 and 18

```
LI EM    { color: red;
           font-weight: bold }
```

declare a style for all **EM** elements that are children of **LI** elements. In the screen output of Fig. 19.3 notice that **Monday** is not made red and bold, because it is not encapsulated by an **LI** element as **with mushrooms** is.

The declaration syntax for applying rules to multiple elements is similar. If you instead wanted to apply the rule on lines 17 and 18 to both **LI** and **EM** elements, you would separate the elements with commas, as follows:

```
LI, EM   { color: red;
           font-weight: bold }
```

Lines 22 and 23

```
UL UL    { text-decoration: underline;
           margin-left: 15px }
```

specify that all nested lists (**UL** elements that are children of **UL** elements) will be underlined and have a left-hand margin of 15 pixels (margins and the box model will be covered in Section 19.9).

A pixel is a *relative-length* measurement—it varies in size based on screen resolution. Other relative lengths are **em** (the size of the font), **ex** (the so-called "x-height" of the font, which is usually set to the height of a lowercase x) and percentages (e.g., **margin-left: 10%**). To set an element to display text at 150% of its normal size, you could use the syntax

    font-size: 1.5em

The other units of measurement available in CSS are *absolute-length* measurements, i.e., units that do not vary in size based on the system. These are **in** (inches), **cm** (centimeters), **mm** (millimeters), **pt** (points—1 **pt**=1/72 **in**) and **pc** (picas—1 **pc** = 12 **pt**).

Good Programming Practice 19.1

Whenever possible, use relative length measurements. If you use absolute length measurements, you might override styles preset by the user.

Software Engineering Observation 19.1

*There are three possible sources for styles sheets—browser defaults, preset user styles, and author styles (e.g., in the **STYLE** section of a document). Author styles have a greater precedence than preset user styles, so any conflicts will be resolved in favor of the author styles.*

In Fig. 19.3, the whole list is indented because of the 75-pixel left-hand margin for top-level **UL** elements, but the nested list is indented only 15 pixels (not another 75 pixels) because the child **UL** element's **margin-left** property overrides the parent **UL** element's **margin-left** property.

19.5 Linking External Style Sheets

As we have seen, style sheets are an efficient way to give a document a uniform theme. With *external linking*, you can give your whole Web site the same uniform look—separate pages on your site could all use the same style sheet, and you would have to modify only a single file to make changes to styles across your whole Web site. Figure 19.4 shows the external style sheet, and Fig. 19.5 shows the syntax for including the external style sheet.

```
1   A        { text-decoration: none }
2
3   A:hover  { text-decoration: underline;
4                color: red;
5                background-color: #CCFFCC }
6
7   LI EM    { color: red;
8                font-weight: bold}
9
10  UL       { margin-left: 2cm }
11
12  UL UL    { text-decoration: underline;
13               margin-left: .5cm }
```

Fig. 19.4   An external style sheet (**styles.css**).

```
1   <!DOCTYPE html PUBLIC "-//W3C//DTD HTML 4.0 Transitional//EN">
2   <HTML>
3
4   <!-- Fig. 19.5: imported.html        -->
5   <!-- Linking external style sheets   -->
6
7   <HEAD>
8   <TITLE>Importing style sheets</TITLE>
9   <LINK REL = "stylesheet" TYPE = "text/css" HREF = "styles.css">
10  </HEAD>
11
12  <BODY>
13
14  <H1>Shopping list for <EM>Monday</EM>:</H1>
15  <UL>
16  <LI>Milk</LI>
17  <LI>Bread
18      <UL>
19      <LI>White bread</LI>
20      <LI>Rye bread</LI>
21      <LI>Whole wheat bread</LI>
22      </UL></LI>
23  <LI>Rice</LI>
24  <LI>Potatoes</LI>
25  <LI>Pizza <EM>with mushrooms</EM></LI>
26  </UL>
27
28  <A HREF = "http://food.com">Go to the Grocery store</A>
29
30  </BODY>
31  </HTML>
```

Fig. 19.5   Linking an external style sheet.

Line 9

```
<LINK REL = "stylesheet" TYPE = "text/css" HREF =
"styles.css">
```

shows a **LINK element**, which specifies a *relationship* between the current document and another document using the **REL attribute**. In this case, we declare the linked document to be a **stylesheet** for this document. We use the **TYPE** attribute to specify the MIME type as **text/css** and provide the URL for the stylesheet with the **HREF** attribute.

Software Engineering Observation 19.2

Style sheets are reusable. Creating style sheets once and reusing them reduces programming effort.

Software Engineering Observation 19.3

*The **LINK** element can be placed only in the header section. Other relationships you can specify between documents are **next** and **previous**, which would allow you to link a whole series of documents. This could let browsers print a large collection of related documents at once (in Internet Explorer, select **Print all linked documents** in the **Print...** submenu of the **File** menu).*

19.6 Positioning Elements

In the past, controlling the positioning of elements in an HTML document was difficult; positioning was basically up to the browser. CSS introduces the **position** property and a capability called *absolute positioning*, which gives us greater control over how our documents are displayed (Fig. 19.6).

```
1   <!DOCTYPE html PUBLIC "-//W3C//DTD HTML 4.0 Transitional//EN">
2   <HTML>
3
4   <!-- Fig 19.6: positioning.html        -->
5   <!-- Absolute positioning of elements -->
6
7   <HEAD>
8   <TITLE>Absolute Positioning</TITLE>
9   </HEAD>
10
11  <BODY>
12
13  <IMG SRC = "i.gif" STYLE = "position: absolute; top: 0px;
14      left: 0px; z-index: 1">
15  <H1 STYLE = "position: absolute; top: 50px; left: 50px;
16      z-index: 3">Positioned Text</H1>
17  <IMG SRC = "circle.gif" STYLE = "position: absolute; top: 25px;
18      left: 100px; z-index: 2">
19
20  </BODY>
21  </HTML>
```

Fig. 19.6   Positioning elements with CSS (part 1 of 2).

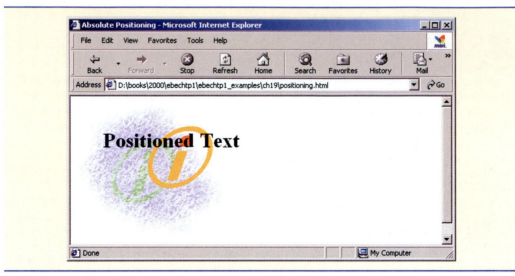

Fig. 19.6   Positioning elements with CSS (part 2 of 2).

Lines 13 and 14

```
<IMG SRC = "i.gif" STYLE = "position: absolute; top: 0px;
    left: 0px; z-index: 1">
```

position the first **IMG** element (**i.gif**) on the page. Specifying an element's **position** as *absolute* removes it from the normal flow of elements on the page and instead, positions the element according to distance from the *top*, *left*, *right* or *bottom* margins of its parent element. Here we position the element to be **0** pixels away from both the **top** and **left** margins of the **BODY** element (the parent element).

The *z-index   attribute* allows you to properly layer overlapping elements. Elements that have higher **z-index** values are displayed in front of elements with lower **z-index** values. In this example, **i.gif**, with a **z-index** of 1, is displayed at the back; **circle.gif**, with a **z-index** of 2, is displayed in front of that; the **H1** element ("Positioned Text"), with a **z-index** of 3, is displayed in front of both of the others. If you do not specify **z-index**, the elements that occur later in the document are displayed in front of those that occur earlier.

Absolute positioning is not the only way to specify page layout—*relative positioning* is shown in Fig. 19.7.

```
1   <!DOCTYPE html PUBLIC "-//W3C//DTD HTML 4.0 Transitional//EN">
2   <HTML>
3
4   <!-- Fig 19.7: positioning2.html      -->
5   <!-- Relative positioning of elements -->
6
7   <HEAD>
8   <TITLE>Relative Positioning</TITLE>
```

Fig. 19.7   Relative positioning of elements (part 1 of 2).

```
9
10   <STYLE TYPE = "text/css">
11
12      P        { font-size: 2em;
13                 font-family: Verdana, Arial, sans-serif }
14
15      SPAN     { color: red;
16                 font-size: .6em;
17                 height: 1em }
18
19      .super  { position: relative;
20                 top: -1ex }
21
22      .sub     { position: relative;
23                 bottom: -1ex }
24
25      .shiftl { position: relative;
26                 left: -1ex }
27
28      .shiftr { position: relative;
29                 right: -1ex }
30   </STYLE>
31   </HEAD>
32
33   <BODY>
34
35   <P>
36   Text text text text <SPAN CLASS = "super">superscript</SPAN>
37   text text text text <SPAN CLASS = "sub">subscript</SPAN>
38   text Text text <SPAN CLASS = "shiftl">left-shifted</SPAN>
39   text text text <SPAN CLASS = "shiftr">right-shifted</SPAN>
40   Text text text text text
41   </P>
42
43   </BODY>
44   </HTML>
```

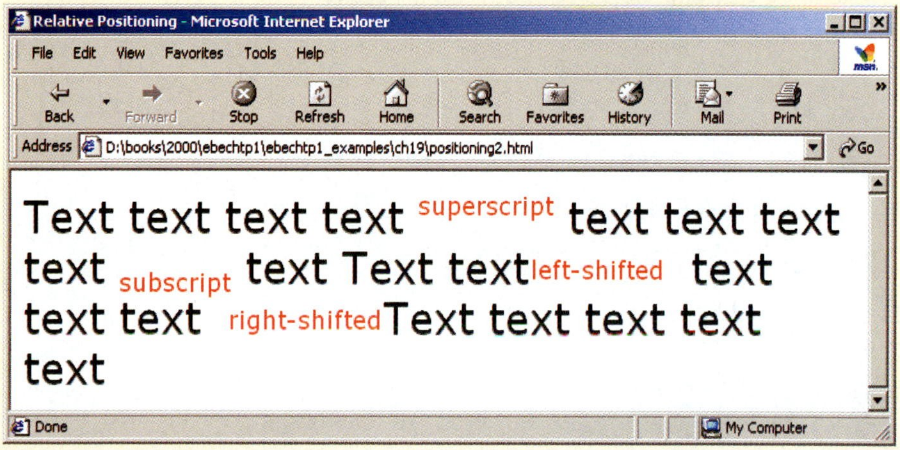

Fig. 19.7   Relative positioning of elements (part 2 of 2).

Setting the **position** property to *relative*, as in lines 19 and 20,

```
.super  { position: relative;
          top: -1ex }
```

will first lay out the element on the page, then offset the element by the specified **top**, **bottom**, **left** or **right** values. Unlike absolute positioning, relative positioning keeps elements in the general flow of elements on the page.

Common Programming Error 19.1

Because relative positioning keeps elements in the flow of text in your documents, be careful to avoid overlapping text unintentionally.

19.7 Backgrounds

CSS also gives you more control over backgrounds than simple HTML attributes. We have used the **background-color** property in previous examples. You can also add background images to your documents using CSS. In Fig. 19.8, we add a corporate watermark to the bottom-right corner of the document—this watermark stays fixed in the corner, even when the user scrolls up or down the screen.

```
1   <!DOCTYPE html PUBLIC "-//W3C//DTD HTML 4.0 Transitional//EN">
2   <HTML>
3
4   <!-- Fig. 19.8: background.html              -->
5   <!-- Adding background images and indentation -->
6
7   <HEAD>
8   <TITLE>Background Images</TITLE>
9
10  <STYLE TYPE = "text/css">
11
12     BODY  { background-image: url(watermark.gif);
13             background-position: bottom right;
14             background-repeat: no-repeat;
15             background-attachment: fixed }
16
17     P     { font-size: 2em;
18             color: #AA5588;
19             text-indent: 1em;
20             font-family: Arial, sans-serif }
21
22     .dark { font-weight: bold }
23
24  </STYLE>
25  </HEAD>
26
27  <BODY>
28
29  <P>
30  This is some sample text to fill in the page.
```

Fig. 19.8   Adding a background image with CSS (part 1 of 2).

```
31    <SPAN CLASS = "dark">This is some sample
32    text to fill in the page.</SPAN>
33    This is some sample text to fill in the page.
34    This is some sample text to fill in the page.
35    This is some sample text to fill in the page.
36    This is some sample text to fill in the page.
37    </P>
38
39    </BODY>
40    </HTML>
```

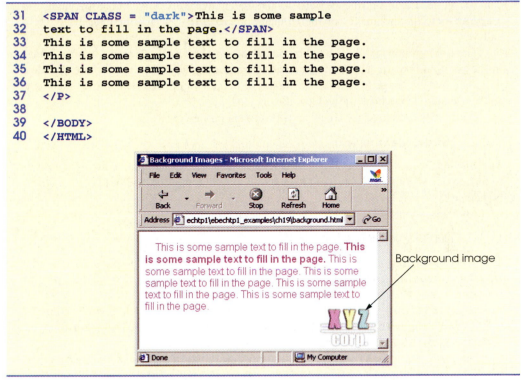

Fig. 19.8   Adding a background image with CSS (part 2 of 2).

The code that adds the background image in the bottom-right corner of the window is on lines 12 through 15:

```
BODY   { background-image: url(watermark.gif);
         background-position: bottom right;
         background-repeat: no-repeat;
         background-attachment: fixed }
```

The ***background-image property*** specifies the URL of the image to use, in the format **url(fileLocation)**. You can also specify ***background-color*** to use in case the image is not found.

The ***background-position property*** positions the image on the page. You can use the keywords **top**, **bottom**, **center**, **left** and **right** individually or in combination for vertical and horizontal positioning. You can also position using lengths, specifying the horizontal length followed by the vertical length. For example, to position the image centered vertically (positioned at 50% of the distance across the screen) and 30 pixels from the top, you would use

```
background-position: 50% 30px;
```

The **background-repeat** property controls the *tiling* of the background image (tiling was discussed in Section 9.8). Here we set the tiling to **no-repeat** so that only one copy of the background image is placed on screen. The **background-repeat** property can be set to **repeat** (the default) to tile the image vertically and horizontally, to **repeat-x** to tile the image only horizontally or **repeat-y** to tile the image only vertically.

The final property setting, **background-attachment: fixed**, fixes the image in the position specified by **background-position**. Scrolling the browser window will not move the image from its set position. The default value, **scroll**, moves the image as the user scrolls the browser window down.

On line 19, we introduce a new text-formatting property:

```
text-indent: 1em;
```

This indents the first line of text in the element by the specified amount. You might use this to make your Web page read more like a novel, in which the first line of every paragraph is indented.

Another new property is introduced on line 22

```
.dark { font-weight: bold }
```

The **font-weight property** specifies the "boldness" of affected text. Values besides **bold** and **normal** (the default) are **bolder** (bolder than **bold** text) and **lighter** (lighter than **normal** text). You can also specify the value using multiples of 100 from 100 to 900 (i.e., **100, 200, ..., 900**). Text specified as **normal** is equivalent to **400** and **bold** text is equivalent to **700**. Most systems do not have fonts that can be scaled this finely so using the **100...900** values might not display the desired effect.

Another CSS property you can use to format text is the **font-style property**, which allows you to set text to **none**, **italic** or **oblique** (**oblique** will default to **italic** if the system does not have a separate font file for oblique text, which is normally the case).

We introduce the **SPAN element** in lines 31 and 32:

```
<SPAN CLASS = "dark">This is some sample
text to fill in the page.</SPAN>
```

SPAN is a generic grouping element—it does not apply any inherent formatting to its contents. Its main use is to apply styles or **ID attributes** to a block of text. It is displayed inline (a so-called *inline-level element*) with other text, with no line breaks. A similar element is the **DIV element**, which also applies no inherent styles, but is displayed on its own line, with margins above and below (a so-called *block-level element*).

19.8 Element Dimensions

The dimensions of each element on the page can be set using CSS (Fig. 19.9).

```
1   <!DOCTYPE html PUBLIC "-//W3C//DTD HTML 4.0 Transitional//EN">
2   <HTML>
3
4   <!-- Fig. 19.9: width.html                    -->
5   <!-- Setting box dimensions and aligning text -->
6
```

Fig. 19.9   Setting box dimensions and aligning text (part 1 of 2).

```
 7   <HEAD>
 8   <TITLE>Box Dimensions</TITLE>
 9   <STYLE TYPE = "text/css">
10
11      DIV { background-color: #FFCCFF;
12            margin-bottom: .5em }
13
14   </STYLE>
15   </HEAD>
16
17   <BODY>
18
19   <DIV STYLE = "width: 20%">Here is some
20   text that goes in a box which is
21   set to stretch across twenty precent
22   of the width of the screen.</DIV>
23
24   <DIV STYLE = "width: 80%; text-align: center">
25   Here is some CENTERED text that goes in a box
26   which is set to stretch across eighty precent of
27   the width of the screen.</DIV>
28
29   <DIV STYLE = "width: 20%; height: 30%; overflow: scroll">
30   This box is only twenty percent of
31   the width and thirty percent of the height.
32   What do we do if it overflows? Set the
33   overflow property to scroll!</DIV>
34
35   </BODY>
36   </HTML>
```

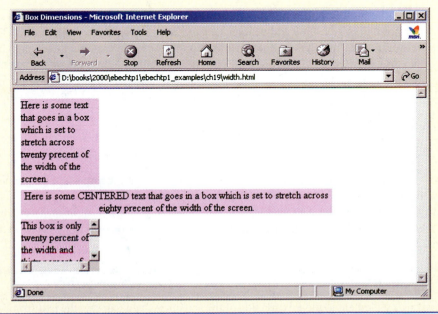

Fig. 19.9   Setting box dimensions and aligning text (part 2 of 2).

The inline style of line 19

```
<DIV STYLE = "width: 20%">Here is some
```

shows how to set the **width** of an element on screen; here we indicate that this **DIV** element should occupy 20% of the screen width (which 20% of the screen depends on how the element is aligned, most elements are left-aligned by default). The height of an element can be set similarly, using the **height** property. Relative lengths and absolute lengths may also be used to specify **height** and **width**. For example, you could set the width of an element using

```
width: 10em
```

to have the element's width be equal to 10 times the size of the font.
    Line 24

```
<DIV STYLE = "width: 80%; text-align: center">
```

shows that text within an element can be **center**ed—other values for the **text-align** property are **left** and **right**.
    One problem with setting both element dimensions is that content inside might sometimes exceed the set boundaries, in which case the element is simply made large enough for all the content to fit. However, as we see on line 29

```
<DIV STYLE = "width: 20%; height: 30%; overflow: scroll">
```

we can set the **overflow property** to **scroll**; this adds scrollbars if the text overflows the boundaries.

19.9 Text Flow and the Box Model

A browser normally places text and elements on screen in the order they are in the HTML file. However, as we saw with absolute positioning, it is possible to remove elements from the normal flow of text. *Floating* allows you to move an element to one side of the screen—other content in the document will then flow around the floated element. In addition, each block-level element has a box drawn around it, known as the *box model*—the properties of this box are easily adjusted (Fig. 19.10).
    Line 21

```
<DIV STYLE = "text-align: center">Centered Text</DIV>
```

shows that text inside an element can be aligned by setting the **text-align** property, whose possible values are **left**, **center**, **right** and **justify**.
    In addition to text, whole elements can be *floated* to the left or right of a document. This means that any nearby text will wrap around the floated element. For example, in lines 24 and 25

```
<DIV STYLE = "float: right; margin: .5em">This is some floated
    text, floated text, floated text, floated text.</DIV>
```

we float a **DIV** element to the **right** side of the screen. As you can see, the text from lines 27 through 34 flows cleanly to the left and underneath this **DIV** element.

The second property we set in line 24, **margin**, determines the distance between the edge of the element and any text outside the element. When elements are rendered on the screen using the box model, the content of each element is surrounded by *padding*, a *border* and *margins* (Fig. 19.11).

```
1   <!DOCTYPE html PUBLIC "-//W3C//DTD HTML 4.0 Transitional//EN">
2   <HTML>
3
4   <!-- Fig. 19.10: floating.html              -->
5   <!-- Floating elements and element boxes -->
6
7   <HEAD>
8   <TITLE>Flowing Text Around Floating Elements</TITLE>
9   <STYLE TYPE = "text/css">
10
11      DIV { background-color: #FFCCFF;
12            margin-bottom: .5em;
13            font-size: 1.5em;
14            width: 50% }
15
16  </STYLE>
17  </HEAD>
18
19  <BODY>
20
21  <DIV STYLE = "text-align: center">Centered text</DIV>
22  <DIV STYLE = "text-align: right">Right-aligned text</DIV>
23
24  <DIV STYLE = "float: right; margin: .5em">This is some floated
25  text, floated text, floated text, floated text.</DIV>
26  <P>
27  Here is some flowing text, flowing text, flowing text.
28  Here is some flowing text, flowing text, flowing text.
29  Here is some flowing text, flowing text, flowing text.
30  Here is some flowing text, flowing text, flowing text.
31  Here is some flowing text, flowing text, flowing text.
32  Here is some flowing text, flowing text, flowing text.
33  Here is some flowing text, flowing text, flowing text.
34  Here is some flowing text, flowing text, flowing text.
35  </P>
36
37  <P><DIV STYLE ="float: right; padding: .5em">This is some floated
38  text, floated text, floated text, floated text.</DIV>
39  Here is some flowing text, flowing text, flowing text.
40  Here is some flowing text, flowing text, flowing text.
41  Here is some flowing text, flowing text, flowing text.
42  <SPAN STYLE = "clear: right">Here is some unflowing text.
43  Here is some unflowing text.</SPAN>
44  </P>
45
46  </BODY>
47  </HTML>
```

Fig. 19.10   Floating elements, aligning text and setting box dimensions (part 1 of 2).

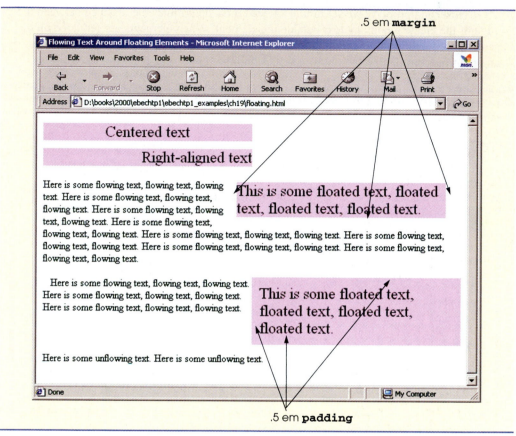

Fig. 19.10 Floating elements, aligning text and setting box dimensions (part 2 of 2).

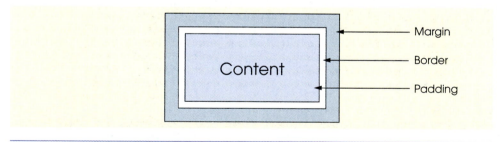

Fig. 19.11 Box model for block-level elements.

Margins for individual sides of an element can be specified by using **margin-top**, **margin-right**, **margin-left**, and **margin-bottom**.

A related property, **padding**, is set for the **DIV** element in line 37:

```
<DIV STYLE = "float: right; padding: .5em">This is some floated
```

The *padding* is the distance between the content inside an element and the edge of the element. Like the margin, the padding can be set for each side of the box with **padding-top**, **padding-right**, **padding-left**, and **padding-bottom**.

Line 42

```
<SPAN STYLE = "clear: right">Here is some unflowing text.
```

shows that you can interrupt the flow of text around a **float**ed element by setting the *clear property* to the same direction the element is **float**ed—**right** or **left**. Setting the **clear** property to **all** interrupts the flow on both sides of the document. Note that the box model only applies to block-level elements such as **DIV**, **P** and **H1**—the box model does not apply to inline-level elements such as **EM**, **STRONG** and **SPAN**.

Another property included around every block-level element on screen is the border. The border lies between the padding space and the margin space, and has numerous properties to adjust its appearance (Fig. 19.12).

```
1   <!DOCTYPE html PUBLIC "-//W3C//DTD HTML 4.0 Transitional//EN">
2   <HTML>
3
4   <!-- Fig. 19.12: borders.html       -->
5   <!-- Setting borders of an element -->
6
7   <HEAD>
8   <TITLE>Borders</TITLE>
9   <STYLE TYPE = "text/css">
10
11      BODY    { background-color: #CCFFCC }
12
13      DIV     { text-align: center;
14                margin-bottom: 1em;
15                padding: .5em }
16
17      .thick  { border-width: thick }
18
19      .medium { border-width: medium }
20
21      .thin   { border-width: thin }
22
23      .groove { border-style: groove }
24
25      .inset  { border-style: inset }
26
27      .outset { border-style: outset }
28
29      .red    { border-color: red }
30
31      .blue   { border-color: blue }
32
33   </STYLE>
34   </HEAD>
35
36   <BODY>
37
38   <DIV CLASS = "thick groove">This text has a border</DIV>
```

Fig. 19.12 Applying borders to elements (part 1 of 2).

```
39    <DIV CLASS = "medium groove">This text has a border</DIV>
40    <DIV CLASS = "thin groove">This text has a border</DIV>
41
42    <P CLASS = "thin red inset">A thin red line...</P>
43    <P CLASS = "medium blue outset">And a thicker blue line</P>
44
45    </BODY>
46    </HTML>
```

Fig. 19.12   Applying borders to elements (part 2 of 2).

In this example, we set three properties: the **border-width**, **border-style** and **border-color**. The **border-width** property may be set to any of the CSS lengths, or the predefined values of **thin**, **medium** or **thick**. The **border-color** sets the color used for the border (this has different meanings for different borders).

As with padding and margins, each of the border properties may be set for individual sides of the box (e.g., **border-top-style** or **border-left-color**).

Also, as shown on line 38,

```
<DIV CLASS = "thick groove">This text has a border</DIV>
```

it is possible to assign more than one class to an HTML element using the **CLASS** attribute.

The **border-style**s are **none**, **hidden**, **dotted**, **dashed**, **solid**, **double**, **groove**, **ridge**, **inset** and **outset**. Figure 19.13 illustates these border styles.

Portability Tip 19.3

*Keep in mind that the **dotted** and **dashed** styles are available only for Macintosh systems.*

As you can see, the **groove** and **ridge border-style**s have opposite effects, as do **inset** and **outset**.

```
1   <!DOCTYPE html PUBLIC "-//W3C//DTD HTML 4.0 Transitional//EN">
2   <HTML>
3
4   <!-- Fig. 19.13: borders2.html   -->
5   <!-- Various border-styles       -->
6
7   <HEAD>
8   <TITLE>Borders</TITLE>
9
10  <STYLE TYPE = "text/css">
11
12      BODY    { background-color: #CCFFCC }
13
14      DIV     { text-align: center;
15                margin-bottom: .3em;
16                width: 50%;
17                position: relative;
18                left: 25%;
19                padding: .3em }
20  </STYLE>
21  </HEAD>
22
23  <BODY>
24
25  <DIV STYLE = "border-style: solid">Solid border</DIV>
26  <DIV STYLE = "border-style: double">Double border</DIV>
27  <DIV STYLE = "border-style: groove">Groove border</DIV>
28  <DIV STYLE = "border-style: ridge">Ridge border</DIV>
29  <DIV STYLE = "border-style: inset">Inset border</DIV>
30  <DIV STYLE = "border-style: outset">Outset border</DIV>
31  </BODY>
32  </HTML>
```

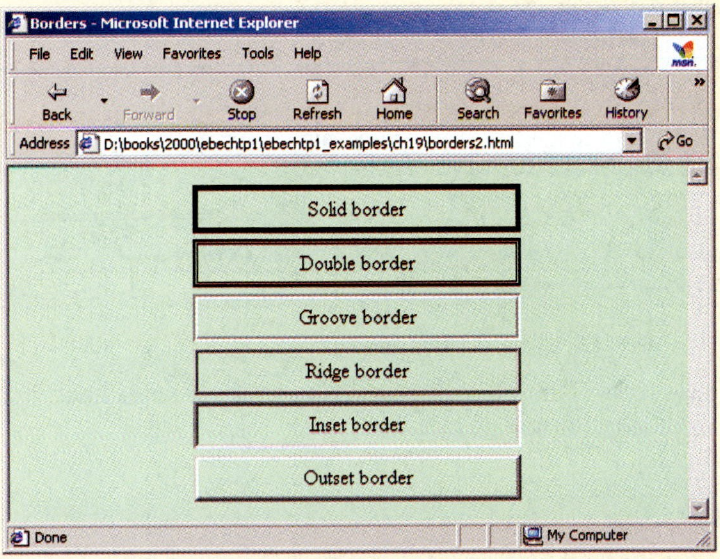

Fig. 19.13   Various **border-style**s.

19.10 User Style Sheets

An important issue to keep in mind when adding style sheets to your site is what kind of users will be viewing your site. Users have the option to define their own *user style sheets* to format pages based on their own preferences—for example, visually impaired people might want to increase the text size on all pages they view. As a Web-page author, if you are not careful, you might inadvertently override user preferences with the styles defined on your Web pages. This section explores possible conflicts between *user styles* and *author styles*. Figure 19.14 is a simple example of a Web page using the **em** measurement for the **font-size** property to increase text size on the page.

```
1   <!DOCTYPE html PUBLIC "-//W3C//DTD HTML 4.0 Transitional//EN">
2   <HTML>
3
4   <!-- Fig. 19.14: user.html   -->
5   <!-- User styles            -->
6
7   <HEAD>
8   <TITLE>User Styles</TITLE>
9
10  <STYLE TYPE = "text/css">
11
12      .note { font-size: 1.5em }
13
14  </STYLE>
15  </HEAD>
16
17  <BODY>
18
19  <P>Thanks for visiting my Web site. I hope you enjoy it.</P>
20  <P CLASS = "note">Please Note: This site will be moving soon.
21  Please check periodically for updates.</P>
22
23  </BODY>
24  </HTML>
```

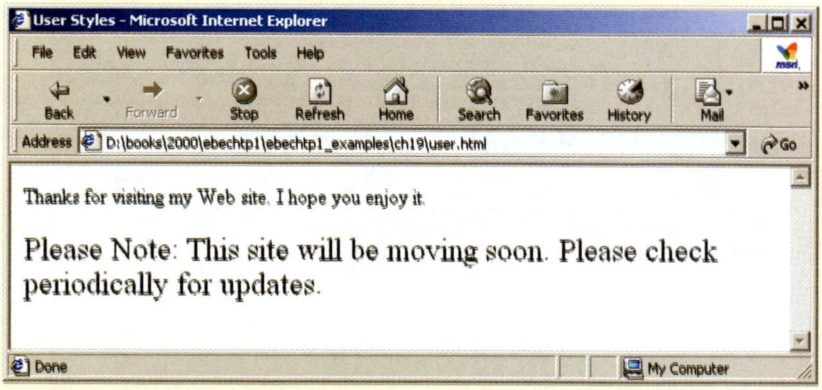

Fig. 19.14 Modifying text size with the **em** measurement.

In line 12

```
.note { font-size: 1.5em }
```

we multiply by 1.5 the font size of all elements with **CLASS = "note"** (see lines 20 and 21). Assuming the default browser font size of 12 points, this same text size increase could also have been accomplished by specifying

```
.note { font-size:  18pt }
```

However, what if the user had defined their own **font-size** in a user style sheet? Because the CSS specification gives precedence to author styles over user styles, this conflict would be resolved with the author style overriding the user style. This can be avoided by using relative measurements (such as **em** or **ex**) instead of absolute measurements (such as **pt**).

Adding a user style sheet (Fig. 19.15) in Internet Explorer 5 is done by selecting **Internet Options...** located in the **Tools** menu. In the dialog box that appears, click on **Accessibility...**, check the **Format documents using my style sheet** check box and type in the location of your user style sheet. Note that you also have the option of overriding colors, font styles, and font sizes specified on Web pages with your own user styles.

User style sheets are created in the same format as the linked external style sheet shown in Fig. 19.4. A sample user style sheet is shown in Fig. 19.16.

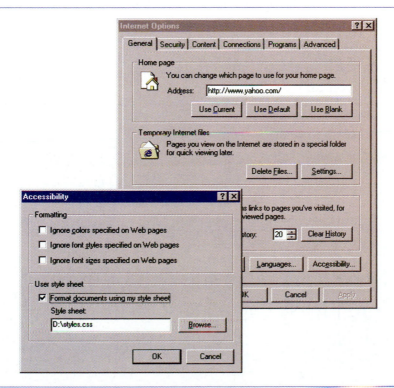

Fig. 19.15 Adding a user style sheet in Internet Explorer 5.

The Web page shown in Fig. 19.14 is re-rendered in Figure 19.17, this time with the user style sheet from 19.16 applied.

Because the code for this page uses a relative **font-size** measurement of **1.5em**, it multiplies the original size of the affected text (**20pt**) by **1.5** times, giving it an effective size of **30pt**.

19.11 Internet and World Wide Web Resources

www.w3.org/TR/REC-CSS2/
The W3C *Cascading Style Sheets, Level 2* specification contains a list of all the CSS properties. The specification is also filled with helpful examples detailing the use of many of the properties.

style.webreview.com
This site has several charts of CSS properties, including a listing of which browsers support which attributtes, and to what extent.

www.w3.org/TR/REC-CSS1-961217.html
This site contains the W3C *Cascading Style Sheets, Level 1* specification.

SUMMARY

- The inline style allows you to declare a style for an individual element using the **STYLE** attribute in that element's opening HTML tag.
- Each CSS property is followed by a colon, then the value of that attribute.
- The **color** property sets the color of text. Color names and hex codes may be used as the value.
- Styles that are placed in the **<STYLE>** section apply to the whole document.

```
1   BODY      { font-size: 20pt;
2               background-color: #CCFFCC }
3   A         { color: red }
```

Fig. 19.16   A sample user style sheet.

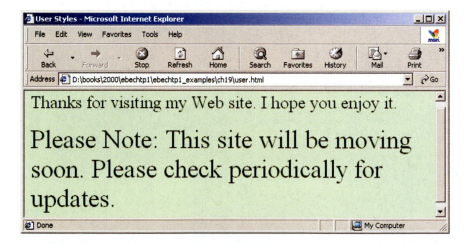

Fig. 19.17   A Web page with user styles enabled.

- The **TYPE** attribute of the **STYLE** element specifies the MIME type (the specific format of binary encoding) of the following style sheet. Regular text style sheets always use **text/css**.
- Each rule body begins and ends with a curly brace (**{** and **}**).
- Style class declarations are preceded with a period and are applied to elements of that specific class.
- The CSS rules in a style sheet use the same format as inline styles—the property is followed by a colon (**:**) and the value of that property. Multiple properties are separated with a semicolon (**;**).
- The **background-color** attribute specifies the background color of the element.
- The **font-family** attribute specifies the name of the font that should be displayed. Generic font families allow you to specify a type of font instead of a specific font for greater display flexibility. The **font-size** property specifies the size to use to render the font.
- The **CLASS** attribute applies a style class to an element.
- All styles applied to a parent element also apply to child elements inside that element.
- Pseudo-classes give the author access to content not specifically declared in the document. The **hover** pseudo-class is activated when the user moves the mouse cursor over an **A** element.
- The **text-decoration** property applies decorations to text within an element, such as **underline**, **overline**, **line-through** and **blink**
- To apply rules to multiple elements separate the elements with commas in the stylesheet.
- A pixel is a relative-length measurement—it varies in size based on screen resolution. Other relative lengths are **em** (font size), **ex** ("x-height" of the font—the height of a lowercase x) and percentages.
- The other units of measurement available in CSS are absolute-length measurements, i.e., units that do not vary in size based on the system. These are **in** (inches), **cm** (centimeters), **mm** (millimeters), **pt** (points—1 **pt**=1/72 **in**) and **pc** (picas—1 **pc** = 12 **pt**).
- External linking can help give a Web site a uniform look—separate pages on a site can all use the same styles. Modifying a single file can then make changes to styles across an entire Web site.
- The **LINK** element's **REL** attribute specifies a relationship between the current document and another document.
- The CSS **position** property allows absolute positioning, which gives us greater control over how documents are displayed. Specifying an element's **position** as **absolute** removes it from the normal flow of elements on the page, and positions it according to distance from the **top**, **left**, **right** or **bottom** margins of its parent element.
- The **z-index** property allows you to properly layer overlapping elements. Elements that have higher **z-index** values are displayed in front of elements with lower **z-index** values.
- Unlike absolute positioning, relative positioning keeps elements in the general flow of elements on the page, and offsets them by the specified **top**, **left**, **right** or **bottom** values.
- Property **background-image** specifies the URL of the image to use, in the format **url** (*fileLocation*). Specify the **background-color** to use if the image is not found. The property **background-position** positions the image on the page using the values **top**, **bottom**, **center**, **left** and **right** individually or in combination for vertical and horizontal positioning. You can also position using lengths.
- The **background-repeat** property controls the tiling of the background image. Setting the tiling to **no-repeat** displays one copy of the background image on screen. The **background-repeat** property can be set to **repeat** (the default) to tile the image vertically and horizontally, to **repeat-x** to tile the image only horizontally or **repeat-y** to tile the image only vertically.
- The property setting **background-attachment: fixed** fixes the image in the position specified by **background-position**. Scrolling the browser window will not move the image from its set position. The default value, **scroll**, moves the image as the user scrolls the window.

- The **text-indent** property indents the first line of text in the element by the specified amount.

- The **font-weight** property specifies the "boldness" of text. Values besides **bold** and **normal** (the default) are **bolder** (bolder than **bold** text) and **lighter** (lighter than **normal** text). You can also specify the value using multiples of 100 from 100 to 900 (i.e., **100**, **200**, ..., **900**). Text specified as **normal** is equivalent to **400** and **bold** text is equivalent to **700**.

- The **font-style** property allows you to set text to **none**, **italic** or **oblique** (**oblique** will default to **italic** if the system does not have a separate font file for oblique text, which is normally the case).

- **SPAN** is a generic grouping element—it does not apply any inherent formatting to its contents. Its main use is to apply styles or **ID** attributes to a block of text. It is displayed inline (a so-called in-line element) with other text, with no line breaks. A similar element is the **DIV** element, which also applies no inherent styles, but is displayed on a separate line, with margins above and below (a so-called block-level element).

- The dimensions of page elements can be set using CSS using the **height** and **width** properties.

- Text within an element can be **center**ed using **text-align**—other values for the **text-align** property are **left** and **right**.

- One problem with setting both element dimensions is that content inside might sometimes exceed the set boundaries, in which case the element is simply made large enough for all the content to fit. However, you can set the **overflow** property to **scroll**; this adds scroll bars if the text overflows the boundaries we have set for it.

- Browsers normally place text and elements on screen in the order they appear in the HTML file. Elements can be removed from the normal flow of text. Floating allows you to move an element to one side of the screen—other content in the document will then flow around the floated element.

- Each block-level element has a box drawn around it, known as the box model—the properties of this box are easily adjusted.

- The **margin** property determines the distance between the element's edge and any outside text.

- CSS uses a box model to render elements on screen—the content of each element is surrounded by padding, a border and margins

- Margins for individual sides of an element can be specified by using **margin-top**, **margin-right**, **margin-left** and **margin-bottom**.

- The padding, as opposed to the margin, is the distance between the content inside an element and the edge of the element. Padding can be set for each side of the box with **padding-top**, **padding-right**, **padding-left** and **padding-bottom**.

- You can interrupt the flow of text around a **float**ed element by setting the **clear** property to the same direction the element is **float**ed—**right** or **left**. Setting the **clear** property to **all** interrupts the flow on both sides of the document.

- A property of every block-level element on screen is its border. The border lies between the padding space and the margin space and has numerous properties to adjust its appearance.

- The **border-width** property may be set to any of the CSS lengths, or the predefined values of **thin**, **medium** or **thick**.

- The **border-style**s available are **none**, **hidden**, **dotted**, **dashed**, **solid**, **double**, **groove**, **ridge**, **inset** and **outset**. Keep in mind that the **dotted** and **dashed** styles are available only for Macintosh systems.

- The **border-color** property sets the color used for the border.

- It is possible to assign more than one class to an HTML element using the **CLASS** attribute.

TERMINOLOGY

<LINK> element
absolute positioning
absolute-length measurement
Arial font
background
background-attachment
background-color
background-image
background-position
background-repeat
blink
block-level element
border
border-color
border-style
border-width
box model
Cascading Style Sheet (CSS) specification
child element
CLASS attribute of an element
clear: all
clear: left
clear: right
cm (centimeters)
colon (**:**) in a CSS rule
color
CSS rule
cursive generic font family
dashed border style
dotted border style
double border style
em (size of font)
embedded style sheet
ex (x-height of font)
float property
font-style property
generic font family
groove border style
hidden border style
hover pseudo-class
HREF attribute of **<LINK>** element
importing a style sheet
in (inches)
inline styles
inline-level element
inset border style
large font size
larger font size
left

line-through text decoration
linking to an external style sheet
margin
margin-bottom property
margin-left property
margin-right property
margin-top property
medium border width
medium font size
mm (millimeters)
monospace generic font family
none border style
outset border style
overflow property
overline text decoration
padding
parent element
pc (picas)
position: absolute
position: relative
pseudo-class
pt (points)
REL attribute of **<LINK>** element
relative positioning
relative-length measurement
repeat-x
repeat-y
ridge border style
right
rule in CSS
sans-serif generic font family
scroll
separation of structure from content
serif generic font family
small font size
smaller font size
solid border style
style
STYLE attribute
style class
style in header of document
style sheet (CSS rules separate text file)
text flow
text/css MIME type
text-align
text-decoration
text-indent
thick border width
thin border width

user style sheet   **xx-large** font size
x-large font size   **xx-small** font size
x-small font size   **z-index**

SELF-REVIEW EXERCISES

19.1   Assume that the size of the base font on a system is 12 points.
   a) How big is 36 point font in ems?
   b) How big is 8 point font in ems?
   c) How big is 24 point font in picas?
   d) How big is 12 point font in inches?
   e) How big is 1 inch font in picas?

19.2   Fill in the blanks in the following questions:
   a) Using the _____ element allows you to use external style sheets in your pages.
   b) To apply a CSS rule to more than one element at a time, separate the element names with a _____.
   c) Pixels are a _____ length measurement unit.
   d) The **hover** _____-_____ is activated when the user moves the mouse cursor over the specified element.
   e) Setting the **overflow** property to _____ provides a mechanism for containing inner content without compromising specified box dimensions.
   f) While _____ is a generic inline element that applies no inherent formatting, the _____ is a generic block-level element that applies no inherent formatting.
   g) Setting the **background-repeat** property to _____ will tile the specified **background-image** only vertically.
   h) If you **float** an element, you can stop the flowing text by using the _____ property.
   i) The _____ property allows you to indent the first line of text in an element.
   j) Three components of the box model are the _____, _____ and _____.

ANSWERS TO SELF-REVIEW EXERCISES

19.1   a) 3 ems. b) .75 ems. c) 2 picas. d) 1/6 inch. e) 6 picas.

19.2   a) **LINK**. b) comma. c) relative. d) pseudo-element. e) **scroll**. f) **SPAN**, **DIV**. g) **y-repeat**. h) **clear**. i) **text-indent**. j) content, padding, border or margin.

EXERCISES

19.3   Write a CSS rule that makes all text 1.5 times larger than the base font of the system and colors it red.

19.4   Write a CSS rule that removes the underline from all links inside list items (**LI**) and shifts them left by 3 **em**s.

19.5   Write a CSS rule that places a background image halfway down the page, tiling horizontally. The image should remain in place when the user scrolls up or down.

19.6   Create a CSS rule that changes the effect of an **EM** element from italic text to underlined text.

19.7   Write a CSS rule that gives all **H1** and **H2** elements a padding of .5 **em**s, a **groove**d border style and a margin of .5 **em**s.

19.8   Write a CSS rule that changes the color of all elements with attribute **CLASS="greenMove"** to green and shifts them down 25 pixels and right 15 pixels.

19.9   Write a CSS rule that centers an element horizontally in 60% of the browser window's width.

20

Dynamic HTML: Object Model and Collections

Objectives

- To use the Dynamic HTML Object Model and scripting to create dynamic Web pages.
- To understand the Dynamic HTML object hierarchy.
- To use the **all** and **children** collections to enumerate all of the HTML elements of a Web page.
- To use dynamic styles and dynamic positioning.
- To use the **frames** collection to access objects in a separate frame on your Web page.
- To use the **navigator** object to determine which browser is being used to access your page.

Absolute freedom of navigation upon the seas...
Woodrow Wilson

Our children may learn about heroes of the past. Our task is to make ourselves architects of the future.
Jomo Mzee Kenyatta

The complex is made over into the simple, the hypothetical into the dogmatic, and the relative into an absolute.
Walter Lippmann

The thing that impresses me most about America is the way parents obey their children.
Duke of Windsor

The test of greatness is the page of history.
William Hazlitt

Outline

20.1 Introduction

In this chapter we introduce the Dynamic HTML object model. The object model gives Web authors great control over the presentation of their pages by giving them access to all elements on their Web page. The whole Web page—elements, forms, frames, tables, etc. is represented in an object hierarchy. Using scripting, an author is able to retrieve and modify any properties or attributes of the Web page dynamically.

This chapter begins by examining several of the objects available in the object hierarchy. Toward the end of the chapter there is a diagram of the extensive object hierarchy, with explanations of the various objects and properties and links to Web sites with further information on the topic.

Software Engineering Observation 20.1

*With Dynamic HTML, HTML elements can be treated as objects and attributes of these elements can be treated as properties of those objects. Then, objects identified with an **ID** attribute can be scripted with languages like JavaScript and VBScript to achieve dynamic effects.*

20.2 Object Referencing

The simplest way to reference an element is by its **ID** attribute. The element is represented as an object, and its various HTML attributes become properties that can be manipulated by scripting. Figure 20.1 uses this method to read the ***innerText*** *property* of a **P** element.

```
1   <!DOCTYPE html PUBLIC "-//W3C//DTD HTML 4.0 Transitional//EN">
2   <HTML>
3
4   <!-- Fig. 20.1: reference.html   -->
5   <!-- Object Model Introduction -->
6
7   <HEAD>
8   <TITLE>Object Model</TITLE>
9
```

Fig. 20.1   Object referencing with the Dynamic HTML Object Model (part 1 of 2).

```
10   <SCRIPT LANGUAGE = "JavaScript">
11      function start()
12      {
13         alert( pText.innerText );
14         pText.innerText = "Thanks for coming.";
15      }
16   </SCRIPT>
17
18   </HEAD>
19
20   <BODY ONLOAD = "start()">
21
22   <P ID = "pText">Welcome to our Web page!</P>
23
24   </BODY>
25   </HTML>
```

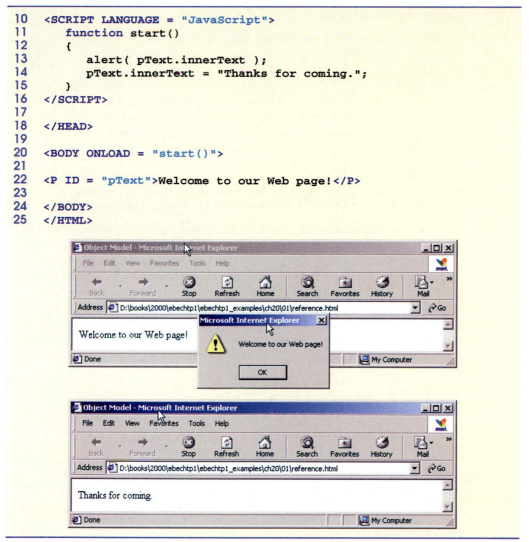

Fig. 20.1   Object referencing with the Dynamic HTML Object Model (part 2 of 2).

Line 20

```
<BODY ONLOAD = "start()">
```

uses the **ONLOAD** *event* to call the JavaScript **start** function when the document is finished loading. Events are covered in depth in the next chapter. Once function **start** has been called, it pops up an **alert** box with the value **pText.innerText**. The object **pText** refers to the **P** element whose **ID** is set to **pText** (line 22). The **innerText** property of the object refers to the text contained in that element (**Welcome to our Web page!**). The next line of the **start** function, line 14, sets the **innerText** property of **pText** to a different value—changing the text displayed on screen, as we do here, is an example of a Dynamic HTML ability called *dynamic content*.

20.3 Collections `all` and `children`

Included in the Dynamic HTML Object Model is the notion of *collections*. Collections are basically arrays of related objects on a page. There are several special collections in the object model (some collections are listed at the end of this chapter, in Figs. 20.10 and 20.11). The Dynamic HTML Object Model includes a special collection, **all**. The ***all*** *collection* is a collection of all the HTML elements in a document, in the order in which they appear. This provides an easy way of referring to any specific element, especially if it does not have an **ID**. The script in Fig. 20.2 loops through the **all** collection, and displays the list of HTML elements on the page by writing to the ***innerHTML*** *property* of a **P** element.

Lines 15 and 16 in function **start**

```
for ( var loop = 0; loop < document.all.length; ++loop )
    elements += "<BR>" + document.all[ loop ].tagName;
```

loop through the elements of the **all** collection and displays each element's name. The **all** collection is a property of the **document** object (discussed in more detail later in this chapter). The ***length*** *property* of the **all** collection (and other collections) specifies the number of elements in the collection. For each element in the collection, we append to **elements** the name of the HTML element (determined with the ***tagName*** *property*). When the loop terminates, we write the names of the elements to **pText.innerHTML**—the ***innerHTML*** *property* is similar to the **innerText** property, but it can include HTML formatting. Note that both the **!DOCTYPE** element and the **<!--** (comment) elements are represented with a **tagName** property of **!** in the document.

```
1   <!DOCTYPE html PUBLIC "-//W3C//DTD HTML 4.0 Transitional//EN">
2   <HTML>
3
4   <!-- Fig 20.2: all.html        -->
5   <!-- Using the all collection -->
6
7   <HEAD>
8   <TITLE>Object Model</TITLE>
9
10  <SCRIPT LANGUAGE = "JavaScript">
11     var elements = "";
12
13     function start()
14     {
15         for ( var loop = 0; loop < document.all.length; ++loop )
16             elements += "<BR>" + document.all[ loop ].tagName;
17
18         pText.innerHTML += elements;
19     }
20  </SCRIPT>
21  </HEAD>
22
23  <BODY ONLOAD = "start()">
24
25  <P ID = "pText">Elements on this Web page:</P>
```

Fig. 20.2   Looping through the **all** collection (part 1 of 2).

```
26
27    </BODY>
28    </HTML>
```

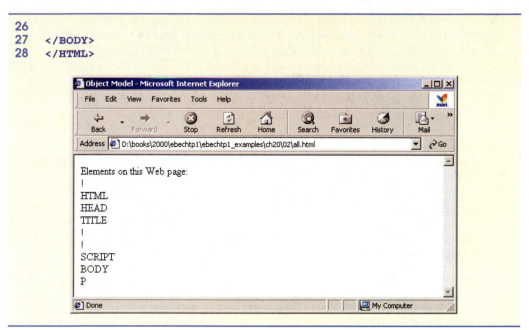

Fig. 20.2   Looping through the **all** collection (part 2 of 2).

When we use the **document.all** collection, we refer to all the HTML elements in the document. However, every element has its own **all** collection, consisting of all the elements contained within that element. For example, the **all** collection of the **BODY** element contains the **P** element in line 25.

A collection similar to the **all** collection is the **children** collection. The **children** collection of any element contains only those elements that are direct child elements of that element. For example, an **HTML** element has only two children: the **HEAD** element and the **BODY** element. In Fig. 20.3, we use the **children** collection to walk through all the elements in the document. When you look at the script in this HTML document, do you notice anything different about this script's use of functions compared to the uses of functions in our prior scripts? The difference is that function **child** (defined at line 13) calls itself at line 22 in the program. This is a programming technique called *recursion*. Recursion is an alternative problem solving approach to looping and iteration.

The scripts we have discussed are generally structured as functions that call one another in a disciplined, hierarchical manner. For some problems, it is useful to have functions call themselves. A *recursive function* is a function that calls itself, either directly, or indirectly (through another function). Recursion is an important topic discussed at length in upper-level computer science courses. The script of Fig. 20.3 pesents a simple example of recursion.

We first consider recursion conceptually and then examine the script containing recursive function **child**. Recursive problem-solving approaches have a number of elements in common. A recursive function is called to solve a problem. The function actually knows how to solve only the simplest case(s), or so-called *base case(s)*. If the function is called with a base case, the function simply returns a result. If the function is called with a more complex problem, the function divides the problem into two conceptual pieces: a piece that the function knows how to do and a piece that the function does not know how to do. To make recursion feasible, the latter piece must resemble the original problem, but be a slightly simpler or slightly smaller version of the original problem. Because this new problem looks like the original problem, the function launches (calls) a fresh copy of itself to go to work on the smaller problem—this is referred to as a *recursive call* and is also called the *recursion step*. The recursion step often includes the keyword **return**, because its result often will be combined with the portion of the problem the function knew how to solve to form a result that will be passed back to the original caller.

```
1   <!DOCTYPE html PUBLIC "-//W3C//DTD HTML 4.0 Transitional//EN">
2   <HTML>
3
4   <!-- Fig 20.3: children.html -->
5   <!-- The children collection -->
6
7   <HEAD>
8   <TITLE>Object Model</TITLE>
9
10  <SCRIPT LANGUAGE = "JavaScript">
11     var elements = "<UL>";
12
13     function child( object )
14     {
15        var loop = 0;
16
17        elements += "<LI>" + object.tagName + "<UL>";
18
19        for ( loop = 0; loop < object.children.length; loop++ ) {
20
21           if ( object.children[loop].children.length )
22              child( object.children[ loop ] );
23           else
24              elements += "<LI>" + object.children[ loop ].tagName
25                             + "</LI>";
26        }
27
28        elements += " </UL> ";
29     }
30  </SCRIPT>
31  </HEAD>
32
33  <BODY ONLOAD = "child( document.all[ 1 ] );
34                  myDisplay.outerHTML += elements;">
35
36  <P>Welcome to our <STRONG>Web</STRONG> page!</P>
37
38  <P ID = "myDisplay">
39  Elements on this Web page:
40  </P>
41
42  </BODY>
43  </HTML>
```

Fig. 20.3   Navigating the object hierarchy using collection **children** (part 1 of 2).

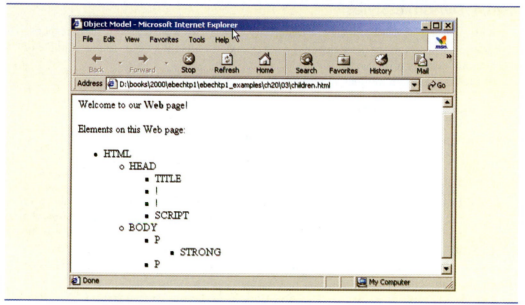

Fig. 20.3   Navigating the object hierarchy using collection **children** (part 2 of 2).

The recursion step executes while the original call to the function is still open, i.e., it has not yet finished executing. The recursion step can result in many more such recursive calls as the function keeps dividing each new subproblem with which the function is called into two conceptual pieces. For the recursion to eventually terminate, each time the function calls itself with a slightly simpler version of the original problem this sequence of smaller and smaller problems must eventually converge on the base case. At that point, the function recognizes the base case, returns a result to the previous copy of the function, and a sequence of returns ensues all the way up the line until the original call of the function eventually returns the final result to the original caller. All of this sounds quite exotic compared to the kind of conventional problem solving we have been using to this point. As an example of these concepts at work, let us discuss the function **child** in Fig. 20.3.

Function **child** uses recursion to view all the elements on the page—it starts at the level of the **HTML** element (**document.all[1]** on line 33) and begins walking through all the children of that element. If it encounters an element that has its own children (line 21), it recursively calls the **child** function, passing the object of the new element through which the function should loop. As that loop finishes, the loop which called it proceeds to the next element in its own array of **children**. We use the **tagName** property to gather the names of the tags we encounter while looping through the document, and place them in the string **elements**. The script adds **UL** and **LI** tags to display the element in a hierarchical manner on the page. When the original call to function child completes, line 34

```
myDisplay.outerHTML += elements;">
```

changes the *outerHTML* property of the **P** element **myDisplay** to string **elements**. Property **outerHTML** is similar to property **innerHTML** we introduced in the previous example, but it includes the enclosing HTML tags (tags **<P ID = "myDisplay">** and **</P>** in this case) as well as the content inside them.

20.4 Dynamic Styles

An element's style can be changed dynamically. Often such a change is made in response to user events, which are discussed in the next chapter. Figure 20.4 is a simple example of changing styles in response to user input.

Function **start**, in lines 11 through 16

```
function start()
{
    var inputColor = prompt( "Enter a color name for the " +
                            "background of this page", "" );
    document.body.style.backgroundColor = inputColor;
}
```

prompts the user to enter a color name, then sets the background color to that value. We refer to the background color as **document.body.style.backgroundColor**—the **body** property of the **document** object refers to the **BODY** element. We then use the **style** object (a property of most HTML elements) to set the **background-color** CSS property. (This is referred to as **backgroundColor** in JavaScript, to avoid confusion with the subtraction (**-**) operator. This naming convention is consistent for most of the CSS properties. For example, **borderWidth** correlates to the **border-width** CSS property, and **fontFamily** correlates to the **font-family** CSS property).

```
1   <!DOCTYPE html PUBLIC "-//W3C//DTD HTML 4.0 Transitional//EN">
2   <HTML>
3
4   <!-- Fig. 20.4: dynamicstyle.html -->
5   <!-- Dynamic Styles              -->
6
7   <HEAD>
8   <TITLE>Object Model</TITLE>
9
10  <SCRIPT LANGUAGE = "JavaScript">
11     function start()
12     {
13        var inputColor = prompt( "Enter a color name for the " +
14                                "background of this page", "" );
15        document.body.style.backgroundColor = inputColor;
16     }
17  </SCRIPT>
18  </HEAD>
19
20  <BODY ONLOAD = "start()">
21
22  <P>Welcome to our Web site!</P>
23
24  </BODY>
25  </HTML>
```

Fig. 20.4   Dynamic styles (part 1 of 2).

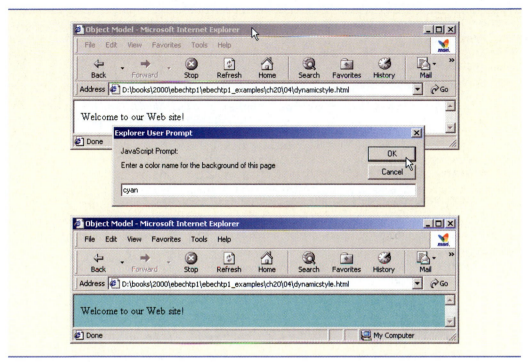

Fig. 20.4   Dynamic styles (part 2 of 2).

The Dynamic HTML object model also allows you to change the **CLASS** attribute of an element—instead of changing many individual styles at a time, you can have preset style classes for easily altering element styles. Fig 20.5 prompts the user to enter the name of a style class, and then changes the screen text to that style.

As in the previous example, we prompt the user for information—in this case, we ask for the name of a style class to apply, either **bigText** or **smallText**. Once we have this information, we then use the **className** property to change the style class of **pText**.

```
1   <!DOCTYPE html PUBLIC "-//W3C//DTD HTML 4.0 Transitional//EN">
2   <HTML>
3
4   <!-- Fig. 20.5: dynamicstyle2.html -->
5   <!-- More Dynamic Styles           -->
6
7   <HEAD>
8   <TITLE>Object Model</TITLE>
9
10  <STYLE>
11
12      .bigText    { font-size: 3em;
13                    font-weight: bold }
14
15      .smallText { font-size: .75em }
```

Fig. 20.5   Dynamic styles in action (part 1 of 2).

```
16
17   </STYLE>
18
19   <SCRIPT LANGUAGE = "JavaScript">
20      function start()
21      {
22         var inputClass = prompt( "Enter a className for the text "
23                                  + "(bigText or smallText)", "" );
24         pText.className = inputClass;
25      }
26   </SCRIPT>
27   </HEAD>
28
29   <BODY ONLOAD = "start()">
30
31   <P ID = "pText">Welcome to our Web site!</P>
32
33   </BODY>
34   </HTML>
```

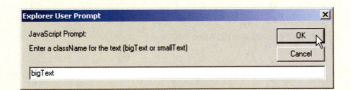

Fig. 20.5   Dynamic styles in action (part 2 of 2).

20.5 Dynamic Positioning

Another important feature of Dynamic HTML is *dynamic positioning*, by means of which HTML elements can be positioned with scripting. This is done by declaring an element's CSS **position** property to be either **absolute** or **relative**, and then moving the element by manipulating any of the **top**, **left**, **right** or **bottom** CSS properties.

The example of Fig. 20.6 is a combination of dynamic positioning, dynamic styles, and dynamic content—we vary the position of the element on the page by accessing its CSS **left** attribute, we use scripting to vary the **color**, **fontFamily** and **fontSize** attributes, and we use the element's **innerHTML** property to alter the content of the element.

To constantly update the content of the **P** element, in line 20

```
window.setInterval( "run()", 100 );
```

```
 1  <!DOCTYPE html PUBLIC "-//W3C//DTD HTML 4.0 Transitional//EN">
 2  <HTML>
 3
 4  <!-- Fig. 20.6: dynamicposition.html -->
 5  <!-- Dynamic Positioning              -->
 6
 7  <HEAD>
 8  <TITLE>Dynamic Positioning</TITLE>
 9
10  <SCRIPT LANGUAGE = "JavaScript">
11     var speed = 5;
12     var count = 10;
13     var direction = 1;
14     var firstLine = "Text growing";
15     var fontStyle = [ "serif", "sans-serif", "monospace" ];
16     var fontStylecount = 0;
17
18     function start()
19     {
20        window.setInterval( "run()", 100 );
21     }
22
23     function run()
24     {
25        count += speed;
26
27        if ( ( count % 200 ) == 0 ) {
28           speed *= -1;
29           direction = !direction;
30
31           pText.style.color =
32              ( speed < 0 ) ? "red" : "blue" ;
33           firstLine =
34              ( speed < 0 ) ? "Text shrinking" : "Text growing";
35           pText.style.fontFamily =
36              fontStyle[ ++fontStylecount % 3 ];
37        }
```

Fig. 20.6 Dynamic positioning (part 1 of 2).

```
38
39          pText.style.fontSize = count / 3;
40          pText.style.left = count;
41          pText.innerHTML = firstLine + "<BR> Font size: " +
42                             count + "px";
43      }
44   </SCRIPT>
45   </HEAD>
46
47   <BODY ONLOAD = "start()">
48
49   <P ID = "pText" STYLE = "position: absolute; left: 0;
50                            font-family: serif; color: blue">
51   Welcome!</P>
52
53   </BODY>
54   </HTML>
```

Fig. 20.6   Dynamic positioning (part 2 of 2).

we use a new function, *setInterval*. This function takes two parameters—a function name, and how often to *run* that function (in this case, every **100** milliseconds). A similar JavaScript function is **setTimeout**, which takes the same parameters but instead waits the specified amount of time before calling the named function only once. There are also JavaScript functions for stopping either of these two timers—the **clearTimeout** and **clearInterval** functions. To stop a specific timer, the parameter you pass to either of these functions should be the value that the corresponding set time function returned. For example, if you started a **setTimeout** timer with

```
timer1 = window.setTimeout( "timedFunction()", 2000 );
```

you could then stop the timer by calling

```
window.clearTimeout( timer1 );
```

which would stop the timer before it fired.

20.6 Using the `frames` Collection

One problem that you might run into while developing applications is communication between frames in the browsers. The referencing we have used certainly allows for access to objects and HTML elements on the same page, but what if those elements and objects are on separate pages? Figures 20.7 and 20.8 solve this problem by using the **frames** collection. [*Note:* Because Fig. 20.7 and Fig. 20.8 compose one example, we use consecutive lines numbers across the two figures.]

```
1   <!DOCTYPE html PUBLIC "-//W3C//DTD HTML 4.0 Frameset//EN">
2   <HTML>
3
4   <!-- Fig 20.7: index.html         -->
5   <!-- Using the frames collection -->
6
7   <HEAD>
8       <TITLE>Frames collection</TITLE>
9   </HEAD>
10
11  <FRAMESET ROWS = "100, *">
12      <FRAME SRC = "top.html" NAME = "upper">
13      <FRAME SRC = "" NAME = "lower">
14  </FRAMESET>
15
16  </HTML>
```

Fig. 20.7   **FRAMESET** file for cross-frame scripting.

```
17  <!DOCTYPE html PUBLIC "-//W3C//DTD HTML 4.0 Transitional//EN">
18  <HTML>
19
```

Fig. 20.8   Accessing other frames.

```
20   <!-- Fig 20.8: top.html     -->
21   <!-- Cross-frame scripting -->
22
23   <HEAD>
24   <TITLE>The frames collection</TITLE>
25
26   <SCRIPT LANGUAGE = "JavaScript">
27      function start()
28      {
29         var text = prompt( "What is your name?", "" );
30         parent.frames( "lower" ).document.write( "<H1>Hello, " +
31                                                  text + "</H1>" );
32      }
33   </SCRIPT>
34   </HEAD>
35
36   <BODY ONLOAD = "start()">
37
38   <H1>Cross-frame scripting!</H1>
39
40
41   </BODY>
42   </HTML>
```

Fig. 20.8   Accessing other frames.

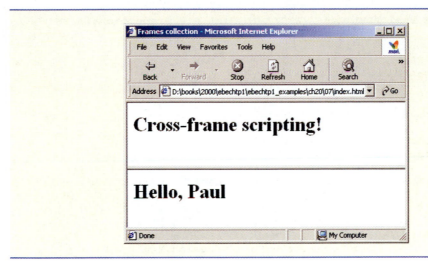

Fig. 20.8   Accessing other frames.

Lines 30 and 31 of Fig. 20.8

```
parent.frames( "lower" ).document.write( "<H1>Hello, " +
                                       text + "</H1>" );
```

apply changes to the lower frame. To reference the lower frame, we first reference the
parent frame of the current frame, then use the **frames** collection. We use a new notation here—**frames("lower")**—to refer to the element in the frames collection with
an **ID** or **NAME** of lower. The **<FRAME>** tag for the lower frame appears second in the
HTML file, so the frame is second in the **frames** collection. We then use the familiar
document.write method in that frame to update it with the user input from our
prompt on line 29.

20.7 navigator Object

One of the most appealing aspects of the Internet is its diversity. Unfortunately, because of
this diversity, standards are often compromised. Of the most popular browsers currently on
the market, Netscape's Navigator and Microsoft's Internet Explorer, each has many features that give the Web author great control over the browser, but most of their features are
incompatible. Each, however, supports the **navigator** object, which contains information about the Web browser that is viewing the page. This allows Web authors to determine
which browser the user has—this is especially important when the page uses browser-specific features, because it allows the author to redirect users to a page that can be viewed
properly in their own browsers. (This is done in Fig. 20.9.)

When the page loads, function **start** is called. It checks the value of the property
navigator.appName—this property of the **navigator** object contains the name of
the application (for IE, this property is "**Microsoft Internet Explorer**"; for
Netscape, it is "**Netscape**"). If the browser viewing this page is not Internet Explorer, in
line 21 we redirect the browser to the file "**NSversion.html**" by using the property
document.location. (This is the URL of the document being viewed.) .

```
1   <!DOCTYPE html PUBLIC "-//W3C//DTD HTML 4.0 Transitional//EN">
2   <HTML>
3
4   <!-- Fig 20.9: navigator.html    -->
5   <!-- Using the navigator object -->
6
7   <HEAD>
8   <TITLE>The navigator Object</TITLE>
9
10  <SCRIPT LANGUAGE = "JavaScript">
11     function start()
12     {
13        if ( navigator.appName == "Microsoft Internet Explorer" ) {
14
15           if ( navigator.appVersion.substring( 1, 0 ) >= "4" )
16              document.location = "newIEversion.html";
17           else
18              document.location = "oldIEversion.html";
19        }
20        else
21           document.location = "NSversion.html";
22     }
23  </SCRIPT>
24  </HEAD>
25
26  <BODY ONLOAD = "start()">
27
28  <P>Redirecting your browser to the appropriate page,
29  please wait...</P>
30
31  </BODY>
32  </HTML>
```

Fig. 20.9   Using the **navigator** object to redirect users.

In line 15, we also check the version of the browser by using the property **navigator.appVersion**. The value of **appVersion** is not a simple integer, however—it is a string containing other information, such as the current Operating System. We therefore use the **substring** method to retrieve the first character of the string, which is the actual version number. If the version number is **4** or greater, we redirect to **newIEversion.html**. Otherwise, we redirect the browser to **oldIEversion.html**

As we see here, the **navigator** object is crucial in providing browser-specific pages so that as many users as possible can view your site properly.

Portability Tip 20.1

Always make provisions for other browsers if you are using a browser-specific technology or feature on your Web page

20.8 Summary of the DHTML Object Model

As you have seen in the preceding sections, the objects and collections supported by Internet Explorer allow the script programmer tremendous flexibility in manipulating the elements of a Web page. We have shown how to access the objects in a page, how to navigate the objects in a collection, how to change element styles dynamically and how to change the position of elements dynamically.

The Dynamic HTML object model provided by Internet Explorer allows a script programmer to access every element in an HTML document. Literally every element in a document is represented by a separate object. The diagram in Fig. 20.10 shows many of the important objects and collections supported in Internet Explorer. The table of Fig. 20.11 provides a brief description of each object and collection in the diagram of Fig. 20.10. For a comprehensive listing of all objects and collections supported by Internet Explorer, browse the Microsoft *DHTML, HTML and CSS* Web site,

```
msdn.microsoft.com/workshop/c-frame.htm#/workshop/author/
default.asp
```

This site provides detailed information on HTML, Dynamic HTML and Cascading Style Sheets technologies. The *DHTML References* section of this site provides detailed descriptions of every object, event and collection used in DHTML. For each object, all the properties, methods and collections supported by that object are discussed. For each collection, all the properties and methods supported by that collection are discussed.

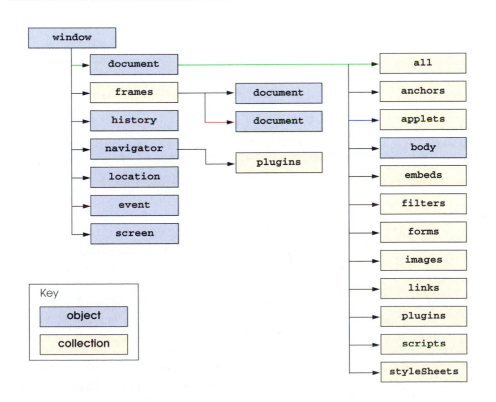

Fig. 20.10   The DHTML Object Model.

Object or collection	Description
Objects	
window	This object represents the browser window and provides access to the **document** object contained in the **window**. If the **window** contains frames, a separate **window** object is created automatically for each frame, to provide access to the **document** rendered in that frame. Frames are considered to be subwindows in the browser.
document	This object represents the HTML document rendered in a **window**. The document object provides access to every element in the HTML document and allows dynamic modification of the HTML document.
body	This object provides access to the **BODY** element of an HTML document.
history	This object keeps track of the sites visited by the browser user. The object provides a script programmer with the ability to move forward and backward through the visited sites, but for security reasons does not allow the actual site URLs to be manipulated.
navigator	This object contains information about the Web browser, such as the name of the browser, the version of the browser, the operating system on which the browser is running and other information that can help a script writer customize the user's browsing experience.
location	This object contains the URL of the rendered document. When this object is set to a new URL, the browser immediately switches (navigates) to the new location.
event	This object can be used in an event handler to obtain information about the event that occurred (e.g., the mouse coordinates during a mouse event).
screen	The object contains information about the computer screen for the computer on which the browser is running. Information such as the width and height of the screen in pixels can be used to determine the size at which elements should be rendered in a Web page.
Collections	
all	Many objects have an **all** collection that provides access to every element contained in the object. For example, the **body** object's **all** collection provides access to every element in the **BODY** element of an HTML document.
anchors	This collection contains all anchor elements (**A**) that have a **NAME** or **ID** attribute. The elements appear in the collection in the order they were defined in the HTML document.
applets	This collection contains all the **APPLET** elements in the HTML document. Currently, the most common **APPLET** elements are Java™ applets.
embeds	This collection contains all the **EMBED** elements in the HTML document.

Fig. 20.11   Objects in the Internet Explorer 5 object model (part 1 of 2).

Object or collection	Description
forms	This collection contains all the **FORM** elements in the HTML document. The elements appear in the collection in the order they were defined in the HTML document.
frames	This collection contains **window** objects that represent each frame in the browser window. Each frame is treated as its own subwindow.
images	This collection contains all the **IMG** elements in the HTML document. The elements appear in the collection in the order they were defined in the HTML document.
links	This collection contains all the anchor elements (**A**) with an **HREF** property. This collection also contains all the **AREA** elements that represent links in an image map.
plugins	Like the **embeds** collection, this collection contains all the **EMBED** elements in the HTML document.
scripts	This collection contains all the **SCRIPT** elements in the HTML document.
styleSheets	This collection contains **styleSheet** objects that represent each **STYLE** element in the HTML document and each style sheet included in the HTML document via **LINK**.

Fig. 20.11 Objects in the Internet Explorer 5 object model (part 2 of 2).

SUMMARY

- The Dynamic HTML object model gives Web authors great control over the presentation of their pages by giving them access to all elements on their Web page. The whole Web page—elements, forms, frames, tables, etc. is represented in an object hierarchy. Using scripting, an author is able to retrieve and modify any properties or attributes of the Web page dynamically.

- The simplest way to reference an element by its **ID** attribute. The element is represented as an object and its various HTML attributes become properties that can be manipulated by scripting.

- The **innerText** property of the object refers to the text contained in that element

- Changing the text displayed on screen is a Dynamic HTML ability called dynamic content.

- Collections are basically arrays of related objects on a page. There are several special collections in the object model.

- The **all** collection is a collection of all the HTML elements in a document in the order in which they appear.

- The **length** property of the a collection specifies the size of the collection.

- Property **innerHTML** is similar to property **innerText**, but it can include HTML formatting.

- Every element has its own **all** collection consisting of all the elements contained in that element.

- The **children** collection of any element contains only elements which are direct children elements of that element. For example, an **HTML** element has only two children: the **HEAD** element and the **BODY** element.

- A recursive function is a function that calls itself either directly or indirectly.

- If a recursive function is called with a base case, the function simply returns a result. If the function is called with a more complex problem, the function divides the problem into two conceptual piec-

es: a piece that the function knows how to do, and a slightly smaller version of the original problem. Because this new problem looks like the original problem, the function launches a recursive
call to work on the smaller problem.

- For recursion to terminate, each time the recursive function calls itself with a slightly simpler version of the original problem, the sequence of smaller and smaller problems must converge on the
  base case. When the function recognizes the base case, the result is returned to the previous function call, and a sequence of returns ensues all the way up the line until the original call of the function eventually returns the final result.

- The **tagName** property contains the name of the tags we encounter while looping through the
  document, and place them in the string **elements**.

- The **outerHTML** property is similar to the **innerHTML** property, but it includes the enclosing
  HTML tags as well as the content inside them.

- The **className** property of an element is used to change that element's style class.

- An important feature of Dynamic HTML is dynamic positioning, in which HTML elements can
  be positioned with scripting. This is done by declaring an element's CSS **position** property to
  be either **absolute** or **relative**, and then moving the element by manipulating any of the
  top, **left**, **right**, or **bottom** CSS properties.

- Function **setInterval** takes two parameters—a function name and how often to call it.

- Function **setTimeout** takes the same parameters as **setInterval**, but instead waits the specified amount of time before calling the named function only once.

- There are also JavaScript functions for stopping the **setTimeout** and **setInterval** timers—
  the **clearTimeout** and **clearInterval** functions. To stop a specific timer, the parameter you
  pass to either of these functions should be the value that the corresponding set time function returned.

- The **frames** collections contains all the frames in a document.

- The **navigator** object contains information about the Web browser that is viewing the page.
  This allows Web authors to determine which browser the user has.

- The **navigator.appName** property contains the name of the application—for IE, this property
  is "**Microsoft Internet Explorer**", and for Netscape it is "**Netscape**".

- The version of the browser is accessible through the **navigator.appVersion** property. The
  value of **appVersion** is not a simple integer, however—it is a string containing other information such as the current Operating System. The **navigator** object is crucial in providing browser-specific pages so that as many users as possible can view your site properly.

TERMINOLOGY

all
all collection of an element
background-color CSS property
base case
body property of **document** object
bottom CSS property
children collection
className property
clearInterval JavaScript function
clearTimeout JavaScript function
collection
collection
document object

document.all.length
dynamic content
Dynamic HTML Object Model
dynamic positioning
dynamic style
fontSize property
ID attribute
innerHTML property
innerText property
iteration
JavaScript
left CSS property
length property of a collection

loop through a collection
object referencing
onload event
outerHTML property
position: absolute
position: relative
prompt dialog box
recursion
recursion
recursion step

recursive call
reference an object
right CSS property
setInterval JavaScript function
setTimeout JavaScript function
style object
tagName property
top CSS property
window.setInterval
window.setTimeout

SELF-REVIEW EXERCISES

20.1 Answer the following questions true or false; If false, state why.
  a) An HTML element may be referred to in JavaScript by its **ID** attribute.
  b) Only the **document** object has an **all** collection.
  c) An element's tag is accessed with the **tagName** property.
  d) You can change an element's style class dynamically with the **style** property.
  e) The **frames** collection contains all the frames on a page.
  f) The **setTimeout** method calls a function repeatedly at a set time interval.
  g) The **browser** object is often used to determine which Web browser is viewing the page.
  h) The browser may be sent to a new URL by setting the **document.url** property.
  i) Collection **links** contains all links in a document with specified **NAME** or **ID** attributes.

20.2 Fill in the blanks for each of the following.
  a) The _____ property refers to the text inside an element
  b) The _____ property refers to the text inside an element, including HTML tags.
  c) The _____ property refers to the text and HTML inside an element *and* the enclosing HTML tags.
  d) The _____ property contains the length of a collection.
  e) An element's CSS **position** property must be set to _____ or _____ in order to reposition it dynamically.
  f) The _____ property contains the name of the browser viewing the Web page.
  g) The _____ property contains the version of the browser viewing the Web page.
  h) The _____ collection contains all **IMG** elements on a page.
  i) The _____ object contains information about the sites that a user previously visited.
  j) CSS properties may be accessed using the _____ object.

ANSWERS TO SELF-REVIEW EXERCISES

20.1   a) True. b) False. All elements have an **all** collection. c) True. d) False; this is done with the **className** property. e) True. f) False; the **setInterval** method does this. g) False; the navigator object does this. h) False; use the **document.location** object to send the browser to a different URL. i) False; the **anchors** collection contains all links in a document.

20.2   a) **innerText**. b) **innerHTML**. c) **outerHTML**. d) **length**. e) **absolute, relative**. f) **navigator.appName**. g) **navigator.appVersion**. h) **images**. i) **history**. j) **style**.

EXERCISES

20.3   Modify Fig.20.9 to display a greeting to the user which contains the name and version of their browser.

20.4   Use the **screen** object to get the size of the user's screen, then use this information to place an image (using dynamic positioning) in the middle of the page.

20.5   Write a script that loops through the elements in a page and places enclosing **<STRONG>**...**</STRONG>** tags around all text inside all **P** elements.

20.6   Write a script that prints out the length of all collections on a page.

20.7   Create a Web page in which users are allowed to select their favorite layout and formatting through the use of the **className** property.

20.8   *(15 Puzzle)* Write a Web page that enables the user to play the game of 15. There is a 4-by-4 board (implemented as an HTML table) for a total of 16 slots. One of the slots is empty. The other slots are occupied by 15 tiles, randomly numbered from 1 through 15. Any tile next to the currently empty slot can be moved into the currently empty slot by clicking on the tile. Your program should create the board with the tiles out of order. The user's goal is to arrange the tiles into sequential order row by row. Using the DHTML object model and the **ONCLICK** event presented in Chapter 16, write a script that allows the user swap the positions of a tile and the open position. [*Hint:* The **ONCLICK** event should be specified for each table cell.]

20.9   Modify your solution to Exercise 20.8 to determine when the game is over, then prompt the user to determine if they would like to play again. If so, scramble the numbers.

20.10   Modify your solution to Exercise 20.9 to use an image that is split into 16 equally sized pieces. Discard one of the pieces ad randomly place the other 15 pieces in the HTML table.

21

Dynamic HTML:
Event Model

Objectives

- To understand the notion of events, event handlers and event bubbling.
- To be able to create event handlers that respond to mouse and keyboard events.
- To be able to use the event object to be made aware of, and ultimately, respond to user actions.
- To understand how to recognize and respond to the most popular events.

The wisest prophets make sure of the event first.
Horace Walpole

Do you think I can listen all day to such stuff?
Lewis Carroll

The user should feel in control of the computer; not the other way around. This is achieved in applications that embody three qualities: responsiveness, permissiveness, and consistency.
Inside Macintosh, Volume 1
Apple Computer, Inc., 1985

We are responsible for actions performed in response to circumstances for which we are not responsible.
Allan Massie

Outline

21.1 Introduction

We have seen that HTML pages can be controlled via scripting. Dynamic HTML with the *event model* exists so that scripts can respond to user actions and change the page accordingly. This makes Web applications more responsive and user-friendly, and can reduce server load—a concern we will learn more about in Chapters 25 through 29.

With the event model, scripts can respond to a user moving the mouse, scrolling up or down the screen or entering keystrokes. Content becomes more dynamic while interfaces become more intuitive.

In this chapter we discuss how to use the event model to respond to user actions. We give examples of event handling for 10 of the most common and useful events, which range from mouse capture to error handling to form processing. For example, we use the **ONRESET** event to prompt a user to confirm that they want to reset a form. Included at the end of the chapter is a table of all DHTML events.

21.2 Event ONCLICK

One of the most common events is **ONCLICK**. When the user clicks the mouse, the **ONCLICK** event *fires*. With JavaScript we are able to respond to **ONCLICK** and other events. Figure 21.1 is an example of simple event handling for the **ONCLICK** event.

The script beginning on line 12

```
<SCRIPT LANGUAGE = "JavaScript" FOR = "para" EVENT = "onclick">
```

introduces a new notation. The **FOR** attribute of the **SCRIPT** element specifies another element (in this case, the **<P>** element in line 22) that is identified by its **ID** attribute (in this case, **para**). When the event specified in the **EVENT** attribute occurs for the element with **ID** specified in the **FOR** attribute, the enclosed script (line 14) runs. Notice that the **EVENT** attribute value is in lowercase letters. This is often required to ensure that JavaScript recognizes the event name.

Good Programming Practice 21.1

When defining a script for a particular object in a document, use lowercase letters for the ***EVENT*** *attribute's value.*

```
1   <!DOCTYPE html PUBLIC "-//W3C//DTD HTML 4.0 Transitional//EN">
2   <HTML>
3
4   <!-- Fig 21.1: onclick.html              -->
5   <!-- Demonstrating the ONCLICK event -->
6
7   <HEAD>
8   <TITLE>DHTML Event Model - ONCLICK</TITLE>
9
10  <!-- The FOR attribute declares the script for a certain -->
11  <!-- element, and the EVENT for a certain event.         -->
12  <SCRIPT LANGUAGE = "JavaScript" FOR = "para" EVENT = "onclick">
13
14      alert( "Hi there" );
15
16  </SCRIPT>
17  </HEAD>
18
19  <BODY>
20
21  <!-- The ID attribute gives a unique identifier -->
22  <P ID = "para">Click on this text!</P>
23
24  <!-- You can specify event handlers inline -->
25  <INPUT TYPE = "button" VALUE = "Click Me!"
26      ONCLICK = "alert( 'Hi again' )">
27
28  </BODY>
29  </HTML>
```

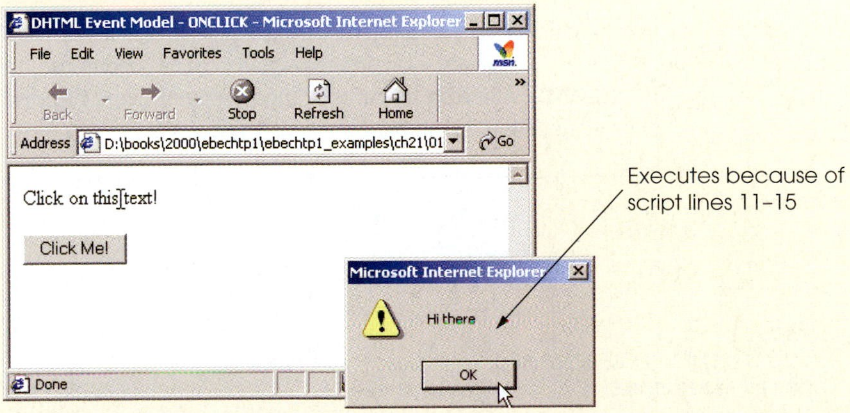

Executes because of
script lines 11–15

Fig. 21.1   Triggering an **ONCLICK** event (part 1 of 2).

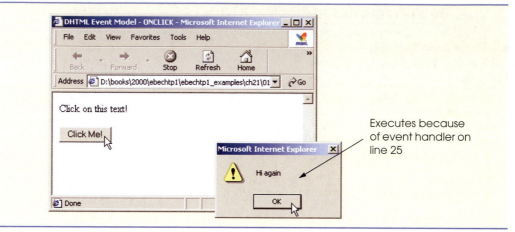

Fig. 21.1   Triggering an **ONCLICK** event (part 2 of 2).

Line 22

```
<P ID = "para">Click on this text!</P>
```

sets the **ID** for this **P** element to match that mentioned **SCRIPT** tag. The **ID** *attribute* specifies a unique identifier for an HTML element. When the **ONCLICK** event for this element is *fired* the script in line 14 executes.

Another way to handle events is with inline scripting. As we see in lines 25 and 26,

```
<INPUT TYPE = "button" VALUE = "Click Me!"
    ONCLICK = "alert( 'Hi again' )";>
```

specifying the event as an HTML attribute allows you to insert script directly. Inline scripting like this is often used to pass a value to an event handler, based on the clicked element.

21.3 Event ONLOAD

The **ONLOAD** event fires whenever an element finishes loading successfully, and is often used in the **BODY** tag to initiate scripts as soon as the page has been loaded into the client. In Fig. 21.2 we use the **ONLOAD** event for this purpose, updating a timer that indicates how many seconds have elapsed since the document has been loaded.

```
1   <HTML>
2
3   <!-- Fig. 21.2: onload.html          -->
4   <!-- Demonstrating the ONLOAD event -->
5
6   <HEAD>
7   <TITLE>DHTML Event Model - ONLOAD</TITLE>
8   <SCRIPT LANGUAGE = "JavaScript">
9
```

Fig. 21.2   Demonstrating the **ONLOAD** event (part 1 of 2).

```
10   var seconds = 0;
11
12   function startTimer(){
13      // 1000 milliseconds = 1 second
14      window.setInterval( "updateTime()", 1000 );
15   }
16
17   function updateTime(){
18      seconds++;
19      soFar.innerText = seconds;
20   }
21
22   </SCRIPT>
23   </HEAD>
24
25   <BODY ONLOAD = "startTimer()">
26
27   <P>Seconds you have spent viewing this page so far:
28   <A ID = "soFar" STYLE = "font-weight: bold">0</A></P>
29
30   </BODY>
31   </HTML>
```

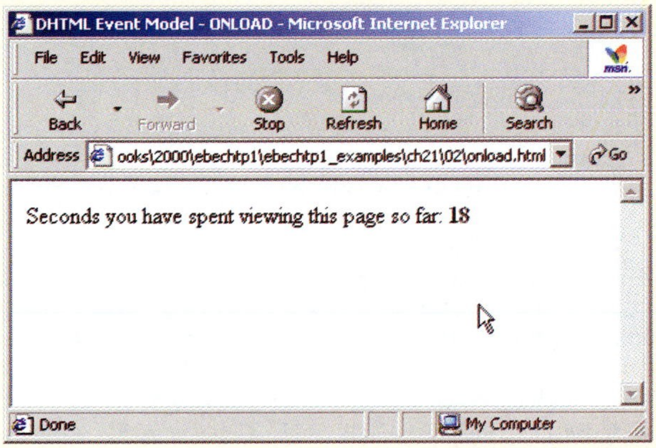

Fig. 21.2   Demonstrating the **ONLOAD** event (part 2 of 2).

Our reference to the **ONLOAD** event occurs in line 26:

```
<BODY ONLOAD = "startTimer()">
```

After the **BODY** section is loaded, the **ONLOAD** event is triggered. This calls function **startTimer**, which in turn uses the **window.setInterval** method to call function **updateTime** every **1000** milliseconds. Other uses of the **ONLOAD** event are to open a popup window once your page has loaded, or to trigger a script when an image or applet loads.

21.4 Error Handling with ONERROR

With the Web being as dynamic a medium as it is, there are occasions when, for example, the object your script refers to might change location, rendering your scripts invalid. The error dialog box presented by browsers is usually confusing to the user. To prevent this dialog box from appearing in order and to handle errors more elegantly, you can use the **ONERROR** event to launch error-handling code. In Fig. 21.3, we use the **ONERROR** event to launch a script that writes error messages to the status bar of the browser. Note: p. 542: *Note:* This program will works correctly only if "Script debugging" is turned off in Internet Explorer. In the **Tools** menu's **Internet Options** dialog click the **Advanced** tab and selecting **Disable script debugging** under the **Browsing** section.

```
1   <!DOCTYPE html PUBLIC "-//W3C//DTD HTML 4.0 Transitional//EN">
2   <HTML>
3
4   <!-- Fig 21.3: onerror.html              -->
5   <!-- Demonstrating the ONERROR event     -->
6
7   <HEAD>
8   <TITLE>DHTML Event Model - ONERROR</TITLE>
9   <SCRIPT LANGUAGE = "JavaScript">
10
11  // Specify that if an ONERROR event is triggered in the window
12  // function handleError should execute
13  window.onerror = handleError;
14
15  function doThis() {
16      alrrt( "hi" ); // alert misspelled, creates an error
17  }
18
19  // The ONERROR event passes three values to the function: the
20  // name of the error, the url of the file, and the line number.
21  function handleError( errType, errURL, errLineNum )
22  {
23      // Writes to the status bar at the bottom of the window.
24      window.status = "Error: " + errType + " on line " +
25          errLineNum;
26
27      // Returning a value of true cancels the browser's reaction.
28      return true;
29  }
30
31  </SCRIPT>
32  </HEAD>
33
34  <BODY>
35
36  <INPUT ID = "mybutton" TYPE = "button" VALUE = "Click Me!"
37      ONCLICK = "doThis()">
38
```

Fig. 21.3   Handling script errors by handling an **ONERROR** event (part 1 of 2).

```
39    </BODY>
40    </HTML>
```

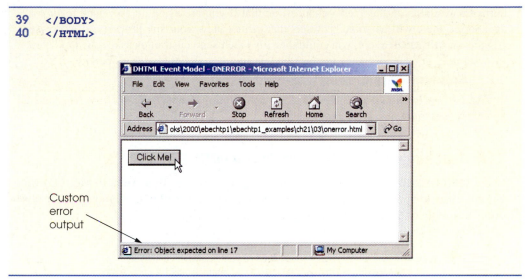

Custom error output

Fig. 21.3   Handling script errors by handling an **ONERROR** event (part 2 of 2).

Line 13

```
window.onerror = handleError;
```

indicates that function **handleError** is to execute when an **ONERROR** event is triggered in the **window** object.

The misspelled function name (**alrrt**) in line 16

```
alrrt( "hi" );
```

intentionally creates an error; the code in line 13 then calls the **handleError** function.

The function definition beginning in line 21

```
function handleError( errType, errURL, errLineNum )
```

accepts three parameters from the **ONERROR** event, which is one of the few events that passes parameters to an event handler. The parameters are the type of error that occurred, the URL of the file that had the error, and the line number on which the error occurred.

In lines 24 and 25

```
window.status = "Error: " + errType + " on line " +
    errLineNum;
```

we use the parameters passed to the function by **ONERROR** to write information about the scripting error to the status bar at the bottom of the browser window (Fig. 21.3). This mechanism provides a neat way of handling errors without confusing users browsing your site.

Line 28

```
return true;
```

returns **true** to the event handler, stopping the browser's default response (the intrusive dialog box we choose to avoid). Error handling is useful because of the diversity of browser software available on the Web—chances are that if you are using an advanced feature of JavaScript, there will be some browsers that cannot view your site properly. If a browser triggers an **ONERROR** event, you could then give the user a custom message such as "Your browser does not support some features on this site. It may not render properly."

Software Engineering Observation 21.1

Use error handling on your Web site to prevent incompatible browsers from complaining about scripts they cannot process.

21.5 Tracking the Mouse with Event ONMOUSEMOVE

Event **ONMOUSEMOVE** fires constantly whenever the mouse is in motion. In Fig. 21.4 we use this event to update a coordinate display that gives the position of the mouse in the coordinate system of the object containing the mouse cursor.

Our event handling in this example occurs in lines 12 and 13

```
coordinates.innerText = event.srcElement.tagName +
    " (" + event.offsetX + ", " + event.offsetY + ")";
```

The **event** object (line 12) contains much information about the triggered event. Property **srcElement** is a pointer to the element object that triggered the event. We use this pointer to access the name (**tagName**) of the element and display it in the **innerText** (line 12) of **coordinates** (line 21).

```
1   <!DOCTYPE html PUBLIC "-//W3C//DTD HTML 4.0 Transitional//EN">
2   <HTML>
3
4   <!-- Fig 21.4: onmousemove.html          -->
5   <!-- Demonstrating the ONMOUSEMOVE event -->
6
7   <HEAD>
8   <TITLE>DHTML Event Model - ONMOUSEMOVE event</TITLE>
9   <SCRIPT LANGUAGE = "JavaScript">
10     function updateMouseCoordinates()
11     {
12        coordinates.innerText = event.srcElement.tagName +
13           " (" + event.offsetX + ", " + event.offsetY + ")";
14     }
15
16  </SCRIPT>
17  </HEAD>
18
19  <BODY ONMOUSEMOVE = "updateMouseCoordinates()">
20
21  <SPAN ID = "coordinates">(0, 0)</SPAN><BR>
22  <IMG SRC = "deitel.gif" STYLE = "position: absolute; top: 100;
23     left: 100">
24
25  </BODY>
26  </HTML>
```

Fig. 21.4   Demonstrating the **ONMOUSEMOVE** event (part 1 of 2).

Updated text (keeps changing as you move the mouse)

Fig. 21.4   Demonstrating the **ONMOUSEMOVE** event (part 2 of 2).

The **offsetX** and **offsetY** properties of the **event** object give the location of the mouse cursor relative to the top-left corner of the object on which the event was triggered. Notice that when you move the cursor over the image, the coordinate display changes to the image's coordinate system. This is because it is now the image over which the **ONMOUSEMOVE** event is being triggered. Figure 21.5 is a table of 14 of the 28 properties of the **event** object.

Property of **event**	Description
altkey	This value is **true** if *ALT* key was pressed when event fired.
button	Returns which mouse button was pressed by user (1: left- mouse button, 2: right-mouse button, 3: left and right buttons, 4: middle button, 5: left and middle buttons, 6: right and middle, 7: all three buttons).
cancelBubble	Set to **false** to prevent this event from bubbling.
clientX / **clientY**	The coordinates of the mouse cursor inside the client area (i.e., the active area where the Web page is displayed, excluding scrollbars, navigation buttons, etc.).
ctrlKey	This value is **true** if *CTRL* key was pressed when event fired.
offsetX / **offsetY**	The coordinates of the mouse cursor relative to the object that fired the event.
propertyName	The name of the property that changed in this event.
recordset	A reference to a datafield's recordset (see Chapter 23, "Data Binding").

Fig. 21.5   Properties of the **event** object (part 1 of 2).

Property of **event**	Description
returnValue	Set to **false** to cancel the default browser action.
screenX / screenY	The coordinates of the mouse cursor on the screen coordinate system.
shiftKey	This value is **true** if *Shift* key was pressed when event fired.
srcElement	A reference to the object that fired the event.
type	The name of the event that fired.
x / y	The coordinates of the mouse cursor relative to this element's parent element.

Fig. 21.5   Properties of the **event** object (part 2 of 2).

The properties of the **event** object contain much information any events that occur on your page, and are easily used to create Web pages that are truly dynamic and responsive to the user.

21.6 Rollovers with ONMOUSEOVER and ONMOUSEOUT

Two more events fired by mouse movement are **ONMOUSEOVER** and **ONMOUSEOUT**. When the mouse cursor moves over an element, **ONMOUSEOVER** is fired for that element. When the mouse cursor leaves the element, the **ONMOUSEOUT** event is fired. Figure 21.6 uses these events to achieve a *rollover effect* that updates text when the mouse cursor moves over that text. We also introduce a technique for creating rollover images.

```
1   <!DOCTYPE html PUBLIC "-//W3C//DTD HTML 4.0 Transitional//EN">
2   <HTML>
3
4   <!-- Fig 21.6: onmouseoverout.html     -->
5   <!-- Events ONMOUSEOVER and ONMOUSEOUT -->
6
7   <HEAD>
8   <TITLE>DHTML Event Model - ONMOUSEOVER and ONMOUSEOUT</TITLE>
9   <SCRIPT LANGUAGE = "JavaScript">
10
11     captionImage1 = new Image();
12     captionImage1.src = "caption1.gif";
13     captionImage2 = new Image();
14     captionImage2.src = "caption2.gif";
15
16     function mOver()
17     {
18        if ( event.srcElement.id == "tableCaption" ) {
19           event.srcElement.src = captionImage2.src;
20           return;
21        }
22
```

Fig. 21.6   Events **ONMOUSEOVER** and **ONMOUSEOUT**.

```
23              // If the element which triggered ONMOUSEOVER has an ID,
24              // Change its color to its ID.
25              if ( event.srcElement.id )
26                  event.srcElement.style.color = event.srcElement.id;
27          }
28
29          function mOut()
30          {
31            if ( event.srcElement.id == "tableCaption" ) {
32                event.srcElement.src = captionImage1.src;
33                return;
34            }
35
36            // If it has an ID, change the text inside to the text of
37            // the ID.
38            if ( event.srcElement.id )
39                event.srcElement.innerText = event.srcElement.id;
40          }
41
42          document.onmouseover = mOver;
43          document.onmouseout = mOut;
44
45      </SCRIPT>
46      </HEAD>
47
48      <BODY STYLE = "background-color: wheat">
49
50      <H1>Guess the Hex Code's Actual Color</H1>
51
52      <P>Can you tell a color from its hexadecimal RGB code value?
53      Look at the hex code, guess the color. To see what color it
54      corresponds to, move the mouse over the hex code. Moving the
55      mouse out will display the color name.</P>
56
57      <TABLE STYLE = "width: 50%; border-style: groove;
58          text-align: center; font-family: monospace;
59          font-weight: bold">
60
61          <CAPTION>
62              <IMG SRC = "caption1.gif" ID = "tableCaption">
63          </CAPTION>
64
65          <TR>
66              <TD><A ID = "Black">#000000</A>
67              <TD><A ID = "Blue">#0000FF</A>
68              <TD><A ID = "Magenta">#FF00FF</A>
69              <TD><A ID = "Gray">#808080</A>
70          </TR>
71          <TR>
72              <TD><A ID = "Green">#008000</A>
73              <TD><A ID = "Lime">#00FF00</A>
74              <TD><A ID = "Maroon">#800000</A>
```

Fig. 21.6   Events **ONMOUSEOVER** and **ONMOUSEOUT**.

```
75            <TD><A ID = "Navy">#000080</A>
76        </TR>
77        <TR>
78            <TD><A ID = "Olive">#808000</A>
79            <TD><A ID = "Purple">#800080</A>
80            <TD><A ID = "Red">#FF0000</A>
81            <TD><A ID = "Silver">#C0C0C0</A>
82        </TR>
83        <TR>
84            <TD><A ID = "Cyan">#00FFFF</A>
85            <TD><A ID = "Teal">#008080</A>
86            <TD><A ID = "Yellow">#FFFF00</A>
87            <TD><A ID = "White">#FFFFFF</A>
88        <TR>
89    </TABLE>
90
91    </BODY>
92    </HTML>
```

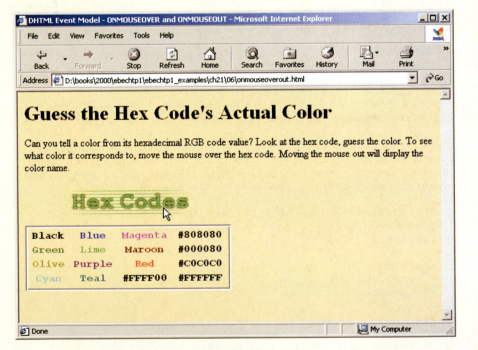

Fig. 21.6   Events **ONMOUSEOVER** and **ONMOUSEOUT**.

To create a rollover effect for the image in the table caption, lines 11 through 14

```
captionImage1 = new Image();
captionImage1.src = "caption1.gif";
captionImage2 = new Image();
captionImage2.src = "caption2.gif";
```

create two new JavaScript **Image** objects—**captionImage1** and **captionImage2**. The image **captionImage2** will be displayed when the mouse is hovering over the image. The image **captionImage1** is displayed when the mouse is not over the image. We set the **src** properties of the **Image** objects to the two images we are using (lines 12 and 14). Creating **Image** objects allows us to pre-load the desired images—if we had not done this, then the browser would only begin to download the rollover image once we moved the mouse over the image. If the image is large or the connection is slow, this causes a noticeable delay in the image update.

Lines 18 through 21 in the **mOver** function

```
if ( event.srcElement.id == "tableCaption" ) {
    event.srcElement.src = captionImage2.src;
    return;
}
```

handle the **ONMOUSEOVER** event for the image by setting its **SRC** attribute (**event.srcElement.src**) to the **src** property of the appropriate **Image** object (**captionImage2.src**). The same task is performed with the **captionImage1** object in the **mOut** function (lines 31 through 34).

We handle the **ONMOUSEOVER** event for the table cells in lines 25 and 26

```
if ( event.srcElement.id )
    event.srcElement.style.color = event.srcElement.id;
```

As mentioned earlier, the **event** object contains much information about the triggered event. In particular, the **id** property of the **srcElement** object is the **ID** attribute of that element. This code checks whether an **ID** is specified, and if it is, the code changes the color of the element to match the color name in the **ID**. As you can see in the code for the table (lines 57 through 89), each **ID** is one of the 16 basic HTML colors.

Lines 38 and 39

```
if ( event.srcElement.id )
    event.srcElement.innerText = event.srcElement.id;
```

handle the **ONMOUSEOUT** event by changing the text in the table cell the cursor just left to match the color that it represents.

21.7 Form Processing with ONFOCUS and ONBLUR

The **ONFOCUS** and **ONBLUR** events are particularly useful when dealing with forms (Fig. 21.7).

```
1   <!DOCTYPE html PUBLIC "-//W3C//DTD HTML 4.0 Transitional//EN">
2   <HTML>
3
4   <!-- Fig 21.7: onfocusblur.html                    -->
5   <!-- Demonstrating the ONFOCUS and ONBLUR events   -->
6
```

Fig. 21.7   Events **ONFOCUS** and **ONBLUR** (part 1 of 3).

```
 7    <HEAD>
 8    <TITLE>DHTML Event Model - ONFOCUS and ONBLUR</TITLE>
 9    <SCRIPT LANGUAGE = "JavaScript">
10
11       var helpArray =
12          [ "Enter your name in this input box.",
13            "Enter your email address in this input box, " +
14            "in the format user@domain.",
15            "Check this box if you liked our site.",
16            "In this box, enter any comments you would " +
17            "like us to read.",
18            "This button submits the form to the " +
19            "server-side script",
20            "This button clears the form",
21            "This TEXTAREA provides context-sensitive " +
22            "help. Click on any input field or use the TAB " +
23            "key to get more information about the input field." ];
24
25       function helpText( messageNum )
26       {
27          myForm.helpBox.value = helpArray[ messageNum ];
28       }
29    </SCRIPT>
30    </HEAD>
31
32    <BODY>
33
34    <FORM ID = "myForm">
35    Name: <INPUT TYPE = "text" NAME = "name"
36       ONFOCUS = "helpText(0)" ONBLUR = "helpText(6)"><BR>
37    Email: <INPUT TYPE = "text" NAME = "email"
38       ONFOCUS = "helpText(1)" ONBLUR = "helpText(6)"><BR>
39    Click here if you like this site
40    <INPUT TYPE = "checkbox" NAME = "like" ONFOCUS = "helpText(2)"
41       ONBLUR = "helpText(6)"><BR><HR>
42
43    Any comments?<BR>
44    <TEXTAREA NAME = "comments" ROWS = 5 COLS = 45 ONFOCUS =
45       "helpText(3)" ONBLUR = "helpText(6)"></TEXTAREA><BR>
46    <INPUT TYPE = "submit" VALUE = "Submit" ONFOCUS = "helpText(4)"
47       ONBLUR = "helpText(6)">
48    <INPUT TYPE = "reset" VALUE = "Reset" ONFOCUS = "helpText(5)"
49       ONBLUR = "helpText(6)">
50
51    <TEXTAREA NAME = "helpBox" STYLE = "position: absolute;
52       right: 0; top: 0" ROWS = 4 COLS = 45>
53    This TEXTAREA provides context-sensitive help. Click on any
54    input field or use the TAB key to get more information about the
55    input field.</TEXTAREA>
56    </FORM>
57
58    </BODY>
59    </HTML>
```

Fig. 21.7   Events **ONFOCUS** and **ONBLUR** (part 2 of 3).

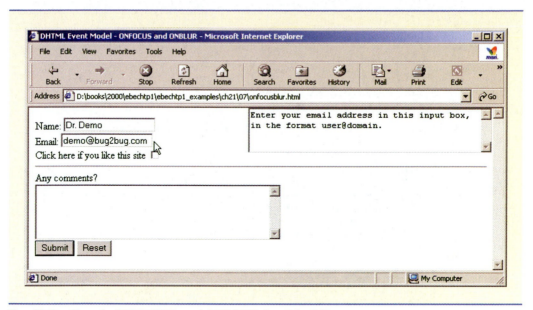

Fig. 21.7   Events **ONFOCUS** and **ONBLUR** (part 3 of 3)

The **ONFOCUS** event fires when an element gains focus (i.e., when the user clicks on a form field or when the user uses the *Tab* key to highlight the element) and **ONBLUR** fires when an element loses focus. In line 27 of function **helpText**

```
myForm.helpBox.value = helpArray[ messageNum ];
```

we see that the function simply changes the text inside the text box in the upper-right corner based on the **messageNum** passed to it. The elements of the form, for example on lines 35 and 36

```
Name: <INPUT TYPE = "text" NAME = "name"
        ONFOCUS = "helpText(0)" ONBLUR = "helpText(6)"><BR>
```

each pass a different value to the **helpText** function when they gain focus and the **ONFOCUS** event is fired. When elements lose focus, they all pass the value 6 to **helpText** so that the default message ("**This TEXTAREA provides context-sensitive help. Click on any**...") is displayed in **helpBox**. In this way, there is constantly a message in the help box—if the user clicks elsewhere on the page without specifically focusing on another form field, the default message is displayed again.

21.8 More Form Processing with ONSUBMIT and ONRESET

Two more functions that are useful for dealing with forms are **ONSUBMIT** and **ONRESET**. These events fire when a form is submitted or reset, respectively (Fig. 21.8).
Line 31

```
window.event.returnValue = false;
```

sets the **returnValue** property to **false** and cancels the default action of the event on the element, which in this case is for the browser to submit the form.

```
1    <!DOCTYPE html PUBLIC "-//W3C//DTD HTML 4.0 Transitional//EN">
2    <HTML>
3
4    <!-- Fig 21.8: onsubmitreset.html                    -->
5    <!-- Demonstrating the ONSUBMIT and ONRESET events -->
6
7    <HEAD>
8    <TITLE>DHTML Event Model - ONSUBMIT and ONRESET events</TITLE>
9    <SCRIPT LANGUAGE = "JavaScript">
10
11      var helpArray =
12         [ "Enter your name in this input box.",
13           "Enter your email address in this input box, " +
14           "in the format user@domain.",
15           "Check this box if you liked our site.",
16           "In this box, enter any comments you would " +
17           "like us to read.",
18           "This button submits the form to the " +
19           "server-side script",
20           "This button clears the form",
21           "This TEXTAREA provides context-sensitive " +
22           "help. Click on any input field or use the TAB " +
23           "key to get more information about the input field." ];
24
25      function helpText( messageNum )
26      {
27         myForm.helpBox.value = helpArray[ messageNum ];
28      }
29
30      function formSubmit() {
31         window.event.returnValue = false;
32
33         if ( confirm ( "Are you sure you want to submit?" ) )
34            window.event.returnValue = true;
35      }
36
37      function formReset() {
38         window.event.returnValue = false;
39
40         if ( confirm ( "Are you sure you want to reset?" ) )
41            window.event.returnValue = true;
42      }
43
44    </SCRIPT>
45    </HEAD>
46
47    <BODY>
48
49    <FORM ID = "myForm" ONSUBMIT = "formSubmit()"
50       ONRESET = "formReset()">
51    Name: <INPUT TYPE = "text" NAME = "name" ONFOCUS =  "helpText(0)"
52       ONBLUR = "helpText(6)"><BR>
```

Fig. 21.8   Events **ONSUBMIT** and **ONRESET** (part 1 of 2)

```
53   Email: <INPUT TYPE = "text" NAME = "email"
54      ONFOCUS = "helpText(1)" ONBLUR = "helpText(6)"><BR>
55   Click here if you like this site
56   <INPUT TYPE = "checkbox" NAME = "like" ONFOCUS = "helpText(2)"
57      ONBLUR = "helpText(6)"><HR>
58
59   Any comments?<BR>
60   <TEXTAREA NAME = "comments" ROWS = 5 COLS = 45
61      ONFOCUS = "helpText(3)" ONBLUR = "helpText(6)"></TEXTAREA><BR>
62   <INPUT TYPE = "submit" VALUE = "Submit" ONFOCUS = "helpText(4)"
63      ONBLUR = "helpText(6)">
64   <INPUT TYPE = "reset" VALUE = "Reset" ONFOCUS = "helpText(5)"
65      ONBLUR = "helpText(6)">
66
67   <TEXTAREA NAME = "helpBox" STYLE = "position: absolute; right:0;
68      top: 0" ROWS = 4 COLS = 45>
69   This TEXTAREA provides context-sensitive help. Click on any
70   input field or use the TAB key to get more information about the
71   input field.</TEXTAREA>
72   </FORM>
73
74   </BODY>
75   </HTML>
```

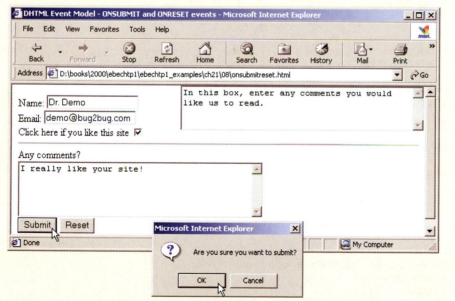

Fig. 21.8   Events **ONSUBMIT** and **ONRESET** (part 2 of 2)

Line 33

```
if ( confirm ( "Are you sure you want to submit?" ) )
```

pops up a dialog box asking the user a question. If the user clicks **OK**, function **confirm** returns **true**. If the user clicks **Cancel**, **confirm** returns **false**.

Based on this information, line 34

```
window.event.returnValue = true;
```

sets the **returnValue** back to **true**, since the user has confirmed that the form should indeed be submitted (based on the **if** statement on line 33, which executes line 34 if the user clicks **OK**).

21.9 Event Bubbling

Event bubbling, a crucial part of the event model, is the process whereby events fired in child elements also "bubble" up to their parent elements for handling. If you intend to handle an event in a child element, you might need to cancel the bubbling of that event in that child element's event-handling code using the **cancelBubble** property of the **event** object, as shown in Fig. 21.9.

```
1   <!DOCTYPE html PUBLIC "-//W3C//DTD HTML 4.0 Transitional//EN">
2   <HTML>
3
4   <!-- Fig 21.9: bubbling.html   -->
5   <!-- Disabling event bubbling -->
6
7   <HEAD>
8   <TITLE>DHTML Event Model - Event Bubbling</TITLE>
9
10  <SCRIPT LANGUAGE = "JavaScript">
11     function documentClick()
12     {
13        alert( "You clicked in the document" );
14     }
15
16     function paragraphClick( value )
17     {
18        alert( "You clicked the text" );
19        if ( value )
20           event.cancelBubble = true;
21     }
22
23     document.onclick = documentClick;
24  </SCRIPT>
25  </HEAD>
26
27  <BODY>
28
29  <P ONCLICK = "paragraphClick( false )">Click here!</P>
30  <P ONCLICK = "paragraphClick( true )">Click here, too!</P>
31  </BODY>
32  </HTML>
```

Fig. 21.9   Event bubbling (part 1 of 2).

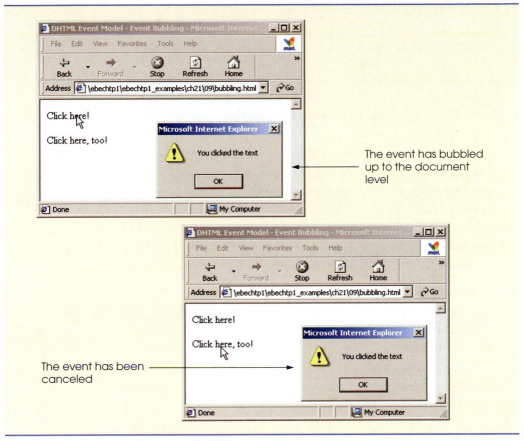

Fig. 21.9   Event bubbling (part 2 of 2).

Common Programming Error 21.1

Forgetting to cancel event bubbling when necessary may cause unexpected results in your scripts.

As we see, clicking on the first **P** element (line 29) first triggers the statement

```
ONCLICK = paragraphClick( false )
```

then also triggers the

```
document.onclick = documentClick
```

statement in line 23, since the **ONCLICK** event has bubbled up to the document level. This is probably not the desired result. However, clicking on the second **P** element (line 30) passes a value of **true** to function **paragraphClick**, so that the **if** statement on line 19 executes line 20

```
event.cancelBubble = true;
```

which disables the event bubbling for this event by setting the **cancelBubble** property of the **event** object to **true**.

21.10 More DHTML Events

The events we covered in this chapter are among the most common in use. The remaining DHTML events and their descriptions are listed in Fig. 21.10.

Event	Description
Clipboard events	
ONBEFORECUT	Fires before a selection is cut to the clipboard.
ONBEFORECOPY	Fires before a selection is copied to the clipboard.
ONBEFOREPASTE	Fires before a selection is pasted from the clipboard.
ONCOPY	Fires when a selection is copied to the clipboard.
ONCUT	Fires when a selection is cut to the clipboard.
ONABORT	Fires if image transfer has been interrupted by user.
ONPASTE	Fires when a selection is pasted from the clipboard.
Data binding events	
ONAFTERUPDATE	Fires immediately after a databound object has been updated.
ONBEFOREUPDATE	Fires before a data source is updated.
ONCELLCHANGE	Fires when a data source has changed.
ONDATAAVAILABLE	Fires when new data from a data source become available.
ONDATASETCHANGED	Fires when content at a data source has changed.
ONDATASETCOMPLETE	Fires when transfer of data from the data source has completed.
ONERRORUPDATE	Fires if an error occurs while updating a data field.
ONROWENTER	Fires when a new row of data from the data source is available.
ONROWEXIT	Fires when a row of data from the data source has just finished.
ONROWSDELETE	Fires when a row of data from the data source is deleted.
ONROWSINSERTED	Fires when a row of data from the data source is inserted.
Keyboard Events	
ONHELP	Fires when the user initiates help (i.e., by pressing the *F1* key).
ONKEYDOWN	Fires when the user pushes down a key.
ONKEYPRESS	Fires when the user presses a key.
ONKEYUP	Fires when the user ends a keypress.
MARQUEE *Events*	
ONBOUNCE	Fires when a scrolling **MARQUEE** bounces back in the other direction.
ONFINISH	Fires when a **MARQUEE** finishes its scrolling.

Fig. 21.10 Dynamic HTML events (part 1 of 2).

Event	Description
ONSTART	Fires when a **MARQUEE** begins a new loop.
Mouse events	
ONCONTEXTMENU	Fires when the context menu is shown (right-click).
ONDBLCLICK	Fires when the mouse is double-clicked.
ONDRAG	Fires during a mouse drag.
ONDRAGEND	Fires when a mouse drag ends.
ONDRAGENTER	Fires when something is dragged onto an area.
ONDRAGLEAVE	Fires when something is dragged out of an area.
ONDRAGOVER	Fires when a drag is held over an area.
ONDRAGSTART	Fires when a mouse drag begins.
ONDROP	Fires when a mouse button is released over a valid target during a drag.
ONMOUSEDOWN	Fires when a mouse button is pressed down.
ONMOUSEUP	Fires when a mouse button is released.
Miscellaneous Events	
ONAFTERPRINT	Fires immediately after the document prints.
ONBEFOREEDITFOCUS	Fires before an element gains focus for editing.
ONBEFOREPRINT	Fires before a document is printed.
ONBEFOREUNLOAD	Fires before a document is unloaded (i.e., the window was closed or a link was clicked).
ONCHANGE	Fires when a new choice is made in a **SELECT** element, or when a text input is changed and the element loses focus.
ONFILTERCHANGE	Fires when a filter changes properties or finishes a transition (see Chapter 17, Filters and Transitions).
ONLOSECAPTURE	Fires when the **releaseCapture** method is invoked.
ONPROPERTYCHANGE	Fires when the property of an object is changed.
ONREADYSTATECHANGE	Fires when the **readyState** property of an element changes.
ONRESET	Fires when a form resets (i.e., the user clicks an `<INPUT TYPE = "reset">`).
ONRESIZE	Fires when the size of an object changes (i.e., the user resizes a window or frame).
ONSCROLL	Fires when a window or frame is scrolled.
ONSELECT	Fires when a text selection begins (applies to **INPUT** or **TEXTAREA**).
ONSELECTSTART	Fires when the object is selected.
ONSTOP	Fires when the user stops loading the object.
ONUNLOAD	Fires when a page is about to unload.

Fig. 21.10 Dynamic HTML events (part 2 of 2).

SUMMARY

- The event model allows scripts to respond to user actions and change a page accordingly. This makes Web applications responsive and user-friendly, and can lessen server load greatly.
- With the event model, scripts can respond to a user moving the mouse, scrolling up or down the screen or entering keystrokes. Content becomes more dynamic and interfaces become more intuitive.
- One of the most common events is **ONCLICK**. When the user clicks the mouse, **ONCLICK** fires.
- The **FOR** attribute of the **SCRIPT** element specifies an element by its **ID** attribute. When the event specified in the **EVENT** attribute occurs for the element with **ID** specified in the **FOR** attribute, the designated script runs.
- Specifying an event as an HTML attribute allows you to insert script directly into your HTML. Inline scripting is usually used to pass a value to a event handler based on the element that was clicked.
- The **ONLOAD** event fires whenever an element finishes loading successfully, and is often used in the **BODY** tag to initiate scripts as soon as the page has been loaded into the client.
- You can use the **ONERROR** event to write error-handling code.
- The syntax **window.onerror** = *functionName* says that *functionName* will run if the **ONERROR** event is triggered in the **window** object.
- Event handlers can accept three parameters from the **ONERROR** event (one of the few events that passes parameters to an event handler). The **ONERROR** event passes the type of error that occurred, the URL of the file that had the error and the line number on which the error occurred.
- Returning **true** in an error handler prevents the browser's from displaying an error dialog box.
- Writing a function to ignore other script errors is not a good idea—try writing scripts that will adjust or stop their actions if an error in loading the page has been detected.
- Event **ONMOUSEMOVE** fires constantly whenever the mouse is in motion.
- The **event** object contains much information about the triggered event.
- Property **srcElement** of the **event** object is a pointer to the element that triggered the event. The **offsetX** and **offsetY** properties of the **event** object give the location of the cursor relative to the top-left corner of the object on which the event was triggered.
- Notice that when you move the mouse cursor over an element like an image, the **offsetX** and **offsetY** properties change to that element's coordinate system. This is because it is now the element over which the **ONMOUSEMOVE** is being triggered.
- Whenever the mouse cursor moves over an element, it fires event **ONMOUSEOVER** for that element. Once the mouse cursor leaves the element, an **ONMOUSEOUT** event is fired.
- The **id** property of the **srcElement** object is the **ID** attribute of that element.
- Events **ONFOCUS** and **ONBLUR** fire when an element gains or loses focus, respectively.
- The events **ONSUBMIT** and **ONRESET** fire when a form is submitted or reset, respectively.
- The code **window.event.returnValue = false** cancels the default browser action.
- Event bubbling, a crucial part of the event model, is the process whereby events fired in child elements also "bubble" up to their parent elements for handling. If you intend to handle an event in a child element, you might need to cancel the bubbling of that event in that child element's event-handling code using the **cancelBubble** property of the **event** object.

TERMINOLOGY

altKey property of **event** object
button property of **event** object
cancelBubble property of **event** object

clientX property of **event** object
clientY property of **event** object
confirm method of **window** object

ctrlKey property of **event** object
Dynamic HTML event model
EVENT attribute of **SCRIPT** element
event bubbling
event handler
event model
event object (property of the **window** object)
events in DHTML
fire an event
FOR attribute of **SCRIPT** element
innerText property of an HTML element
keyboard events
mouse events
offsetX property of **event** object
offsetY property of **event** object
ONAFTERPRINT event
ONAFTERUPDATE event
ONBEFORECOPY event
ONBEFORECUT event
ONBEFOREEDITFOCUS event
ONBEFOREPASTE event
ONBEFOREPRINT event
ONBEFOREUNLOAD event
ONBEFOREUPDATE event
ONBLUR event
ONBOUNCE event
ONCELLCHANGE event
ONCHANGE event
ONCLICK event
ONCONTEXTMENU event
ONCOPY event
ONCUT event
ONDATAAVAILABLE event
ONDATASETCHANGED event
ONDATASETCOMPLETE event
ONDBLCLICK event
ONDRAG event
ONDRAGEND event
ONDRAGENTER event
ONDRAGLEAVE event
ONDRAGOVER event
ONDRAGSTART event
ONDROP event
ONERRORUPDATE event

ONFINISH event
ONFOCUS event
ONHELP event
ONKEYDOWN event
ONKEYPRESS event
ONKEYUP event
ONLOAD event
ONLOSECAPTURE event
ONMOUSEDOWN event
ONMOUSEMOVE event
ONMOUSEOUT event
ONMOUSEOVER event
ONMOUSEUP event
ONPASTE event
ONPROPERTYCHANGE event
ONREADYSTATECHANGE event
ONRESET event
ONRESIZE event
ONROWEXIT event
ONROWSDELETE event
ONROWSINSERTED event
ONSCROLL event
ONSELECT event
ONSELECTSTART event
ONSTART event
ONSTOP event
ONSUBMIT event
ONUNLOAD event
position of the mouse cursor
propertyName property of **event** object
returnValue property of **event**
screenX property of event
screenY property of event
setInterval method of **window** object
shiftkey property of **event**
srcElement property of **event**
status bar at bottom of a window
status property of **window** object
Tab key to switch between fields on a form
tagName property of **event** object
trigger an event
type property of event
x property of **event** object
y property of **event** object

SELF-REVIEW EXERCISES

21.1   Fill in the blanks in each of the following:
   a) The state of three special keys can be retrieved using the **event** object. These keys are
        _____, _____ and _____.

b) If a child element does not handle an event, _____ lets the event rise through the object hierarchy handling.

c) Using the _____ property of the **SCRIPT** element allows you to specify to which element the script applies.

d) The _____ property of the **event** object specifies whether to continue bubbling the current event.

e) Setting **window.returnValue** to _____ cancels the default browser action for the event.

f) In an event handler, the reference for the **ID** of an element that fired an event is _____.

g) Three events that fire when the user clicks the mouse are _____, _____ and _____.

ANSWERS TO SELF-REVIEW EXERCISES

21.1 a) *Ctrl*, *Alt* and *Shift*. b) event bubbling. c) **FOR**. d) **returnValue**. e) false. f) **event.srcElement.id**. g) ONCLICK, ONMOUSEDOWN, ONMOUSEUP.

EXERCISES

21.2 Write an error handler that changes the **ALT** text of an image to "Error Loading" if the image loading is not completed.

21.3 You have a server-side script that cannot handle any ampersands (**&**) in the form data. Write a function that converts all ampersands in a form field to "and" when the field loses focus (**ONBLUR**).

21.4 Write a function that responds to a click anywhere on the page by displaying with **alert()** the event name if the user held *Shift* during the mouse click, or the name of the element that triggered the event if the user held *Ctrl* during the mouse click.

21.5 Use CSS absolute positioning, **ONMOUSEMOVE** and **event.x/event.y** to have a sentence of text follow the mouse as the user moves the mouse over the Web page. Disable this feature if the user double-clicks (**ONDBLCLICK**).

21.6 Modify Exercise 21.5 to have an image follow the mouse as the user moves the mouse over the Web page.

22

Dynamic HTML:
Filters and Transitions

Objectives

- To use filters to achieve special effects.
- To combine filters to achieve an even greater variety of special effects.
- To be able to create animated visual transitions between Web pages.
- To be able to modify filters dynamically using DHTML.

Between the motion and the act falls the shadow.
Thomas Stearns Eliot, *The Hollow Men*

...as through a filter, before the clear product emerges.
F. Scott Fitzgerald

There is strong shadow where there is much light.
Johann Wolfgang von Goethe

When all things are equal, translucence in writing is more effective than transparency, just as glow is more revealing than glare.
James Thurber

...one should disdain the superficial and let the true beauty of one's soul shine through.
Fran Lebowitz

Modernity exists in the form of a desire to wipe out whatever came earlier, in the hope of reaching at least a point that could be called a true present, a point of origin that marks a new departure.
Paul de Man

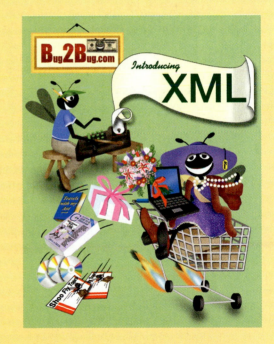

Outline

22.1 Introduction

Just a few years back it was not realistic to offer the kinds of dramatic visual effects you will see in this chapter because desktop processing power was insufficient. Today with powerful processors, these visual effects are realizable without delays. Just as you expect to see dramatic visual effects on TV weather reports, Web users appreciate visual effects when browsing Web pages.

In the past, achieving these kinds of effects, if you could get them at all, demanded frequent trips back and forth to the server. With the consequent delays, the beauty of the effects was lost.

Performance Tip 22.1

With Dynamic HTML, many visual effects are implemented directly in the client-side browser (Internet Explorer 5 for this book), so no server-side processing delays are incurred. The DHTML code that initiates these effects is generally quite small and is coded directly into the HTML Web page.

You will be able to achieve a great variety of effects. You may transition between pages with *random dissolves* and *horizontal and vertical blinds* effects, among others. You can convert colored images to gray in response to user actions; this could be used, for example, to indicate that some option is not currently selectable. You can make letters *glow* for emphasis. You can create *drop shadows* to give text a three-dimensional appearance.

In this chapter we discuss both *filters* and *transitions*. Applying filters to text and images causes changes that are persistent. Transitions are temporary phenomena: applying a transition allows you to transfer from one page to another with a pleasant visual effect such as a random dissolve. Filters and transitions do not add content to your pages—rather, they present existing content in an engaging manner to help hold the user's attention.

Each of the visual effects achievable with filters and transitions is programmable, so these effects may be adjusted dynamically by programs that respond to user-initiated events like mouse clicks and keystrokes. Filters and transitions are so easy to use that virtually any Web page designer or programmer can incorporate these effects with minimal effort.

Look-and-Feel Observation 22.1

Experiment by applying combinations of filters to the same element. You may discover some eye-pleasing effects that are particularly appropriate for your applications.

Part of the beauty of DHTML filters and transitions is that they are built right into Internet Explorer. You do not need to spend time working with sophisticated graphics packages preparing images that will be downloaded (slowly) from servers. When Internet Explorer renders your page, it applies all the special effects and does this while running on the client computer without lengthy waits for files to download from the server.

Look-and-Feel Observation 22.2

DHTML's effects are programmable. They can be applied dynamically to elements of your pages in response to user events such as mouse clicks and keystrokes.

Filters and transitions are included with the *CSS* **filter** *property.* They give you the same kind of graphics capabilities you get through presentation software like Microsoft's PowerPoint. You can have new pages or portions of pages fade in and fade out. You can have a page randomly dissolve into the next page. You can make portions of the page transparent or semitransparent so that you can see what is behind them. You can make elements glow for emphasis. You can blur text or an image to give it the illusion of motion. You can create drop shadows on elements to give them a three-dimensional effect. And you can combine effects to generate an even greater variety of effects.

Software Engineering Observation 22.1

*Filters and transitions can be applied to block-level elements such as **DIV** or **P**, and can only be applied to inline-level elements such as **STRONG** or **EM** if the element has its **height** or **width** CSS properties set.*

Portability Tip 22.1

Filters and transitions are a Microsoft technology available only in Windows-based versions of Internet Explorer 5. Do not use these capabilities if you are writing for other browsers. If you are writing for an audience with a diversity of browsers and you use DHTML filters and transitions, you should also make alternate provisions.

22.2 Flip filters: `flipv` and `fliph`

The **flipv** and **fliph** *filters* mirror text or images vertically and horizontally, respectively. In Fig. 22.1 we demonstrate these effects using both filters to flip text.

In line 30

```
<TD STYLE = "filter: fliph">Text</TD>
```

filters are applied in the **STYLE** attribute. The value of the **filter** property is the name of the filter. In this case, the filter is **fliph**, which flips the affected object horizontally.

In line 36

```
<TD STYLE = "filter: flipv fliph">Text</TD>
```

we see that more than one filter can be applied at once. Enter multiple filters as values of the **filter** attribute, separated by spaces. In this case the **flipv** filter is also applied, which flips the affected object vertically.

```
1   <!DOCTYPE html PUBLIC "-//W3C//DTD HTML 4.0 Transitional//EN">
2   <HTML>
3
4   <!-- Fig. 22.1: flip.html    -->
5   <!-- Using the flip filters -->
6
7   <HEAD>
8   <TITLE>The flip filter</TITLE>
9
10  <STYLE TYPE = "text/css">
11     BODY  { background-color: #CCFFCC }
12
13     TABLE { font-size: 3em;
14             font-family: Arial, sans-serif;
15             background-color: #FFCCCC;
16             border-style: ridge ;
17             border-collapse: collapse }
18
19     TD    { border-style: groove;
20             padding: 1ex }
21  </STYLE>
22  </HEAD>
23
24  <BODY>
25
26  <TABLE>
27
28     <TR>
29        <!-- Filters are applied in style declarations -->
30        <TD STYLE = "filter: fliph">Text</TD>
31        <TD>Text</TD>
32     </TR>
33
34     <TR>
35        <!-- More than one filter can be applied at once -->
36        <TD STYLE = "filter: flipv fliph">Text</TD>
37        <TD STYLE = "filter: flipv">Text</TD>
38     </TR>
39
40  </TABLE>
41
42  </BODY>
43  </HTML>
```

Fig. 22.1   Using the **flip** filter (part 1 of 2).

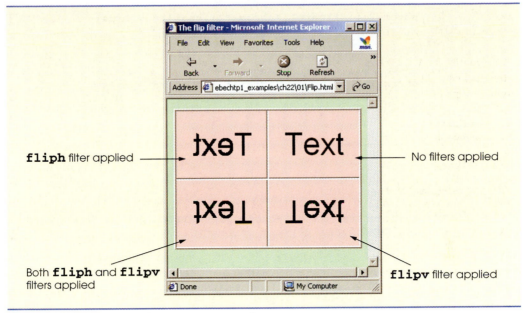

fliph filter applied

No filters applied

Both fliph and flipv filters applied

flipv filter applied

Fig. 22.1 Using the **flip** filter (part 2 of 2).

22.3 Transparency with the chroma Filter

The *chroma filter* allows you to apply *transparency effects* dynamically, without using a graphics editor to hard-code transparency into the image. However, as we noted in Chapter 5, using transparency on images that have antialiasing often produces unsightly effects. In Fig. 22.2 we alter the transparency of an image using object model scripting, based on a user selection from a **SELECT** element.

```
1  <!DOCTYPE html PUBLIC "-//W3C//DTD HTML 4.0 Transitional//EN">
2  <HTML>
3
4  <!-- Fig 22.2: chroma.html                              -->
5  <!-- Applying transparency using the chroma filter  -->
6
7  <HEAD>
8  <TITLE>Chroma Filter</TITLE>
9
10 <SCRIPT LANGUAGE = "JavaScript">
11
12    function changecolor()
13    {
14       if ( colorSelect.value ) { // if the user selected a color,
15
16          // parse the value to hex and set the filter color.
17          chromaImg.filters( "chroma" ).color =
18             parseInt( colorSelect.value, 16 );
```

Fig. 22.2 Changing values of the **chroma** filter (part 1 of 2).

```
19              chromaImg.filters( "chroma" ).enabled = true;
20          }
21          else // if the user selected "None",
22
23              // disable the filter.
24              chromaImg.filters( "chroma" ).enabled = false;
25      }
26
27  </SCRIPT>
28  </HEAD>
29
30  <BODY>
31
32  <H1>Chroma Filter:</H1>
33
34  <IMG ID = "chromaImg" SRC = "trans.gif" STYLE =
35      "position: absolute; filter: chroma">
36
37  <!-- The ONCHANGE event fires when a selection is changed -->
38  <SELECT ID = "colorSelect" ONCHANGE = "changecolor()">
39      <OPTION VALUE = "">None
40      <OPTION VALUE = "00FFFF">Cyan
41      <OPTION VALUE = "FFFF00">Yellow
42      <OPTION VALUE = "FF00FF">Magenta
43      <OPTION VALUE = "000000" SELECTED>Black
44  </SELECT>
45
46  </BODY>
47  </HTML>
```

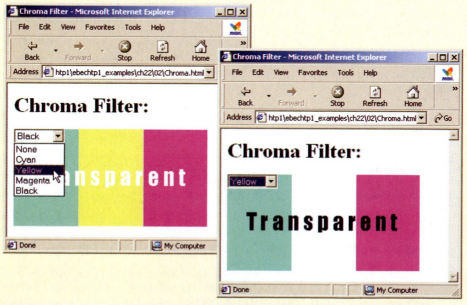

Fig. 22.2   Changing values of the **chroma** filter (part 2 of 2).

In lines 17 and 18

```
chromaImg.filters( "chroma" ).color =
    parseInt( colorSelect.value, 16 );
```

we set the filter properties dynamically using JavaScript. In this case **colorSelect.value**, the value of the **colorSelect** drop-down list (line 38), is a string. We use the **parseInt** function to convert the value to a hexadecimal integer for setting the **color** property of the **chroma** filter. The second parameter of **parseInt**, **16** in this case, specifies the base of the integer (base 16 is hexadecimal).

In line 19

```
chromaImg.filters( "chroma" ).enabled = true;
```

we turn on the filter. Each filter has a property named **enabled**. If this property is set to **true**, the filter is applied. If it is set to **false**, the filter is not applied. So, in line 24

```
chromaImg.filters( "chroma" ).enabled = false;
```

we say that if the user selected **None** (line 39) from the drop-down list, the filter is disabled.

In line 38

```
<SELECT ID = "trSelect" ONCHANGE = "changecolor()">
```

we use a new event, *ONCHANGE*. This event fires whenever the **VALUE** of a form field changes, which in this case happens whenever the user makes a different selection in the **colorSelect** drop-down list.

22.4 Creating Image masks

Applying the **mask** *filter* to an image allows you to create an *image mask*, in which the background of an element is a solid color and the foreground of an element is transparent to the image or color behind it. In Fig. 22.3 we add the **mask** filter to an **H1** element which overlaps an image. The foreground of that **H1** element (the text inside it) is transparent to the image behind it.

```
1   <!DOCTYPE html PUBLIC "-//W3C//DTD HTML 4.0 Transitional//EN">
2   <HTML>
3
4   <!-- Fig 22.3: mask.html          -->
5   <!-- Placing a mask over an image -->
6
7   <HEAD>
8   <TITLE>Mask Filter</TITLE>
9   </HEAD>
10
11  <BODY>
12
13  <H1>Mask Filter</H1>
14
```

Fig. 22.3   Using the **mask** filter (part 1 of 2).

```
15   <!-- Filter parameters are specified in parentheses, in  -->
16   <!-- the form param1 = value1, param2 = value2, etc.      -->
17   <DIV STYLE = "position: absolute; top: 125; left: 20;
18      filter: mask( color = #CCFFFF )">
19   <H1 STYLE = "font-family: Courier, monospace">
20   AaBbCcDdEeFfGgHhIiJj<BR>
21   KkLlMmNnOoPpQqRrSsTt
22   </H1>
23   </DIV>
24
25   <IMG SRC = "gradient.gif" WIDTH = "400" HEIGHT = "200">
26   </BODY>
27   </HTML>
```

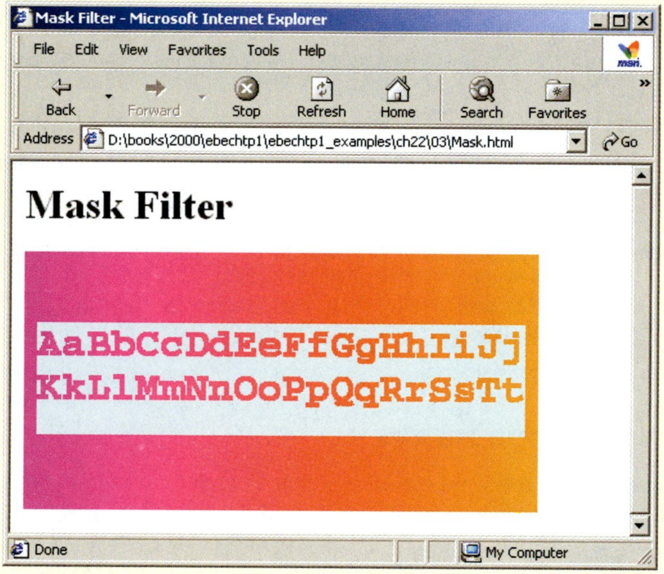

Fig. 22.3   Using the **mask** filter (part 2 of 2).

In line 18

```
filter: mask( color = #CCFFFF )
```

is a color parameter for the **mask** filter that specifies what color the mask will be. Parameters are always specified in the format *param = value*.

22.5 Miscellaneous Image filters: `invert`, `gray` and `xray`

The following three image filters apply simple image effects to images or text. The *invert filter* applies a *negative image effect*—dark areas become light, and light areas become dark. The *gray filter* applies a *grayscale image effect*, in which all color is stripped from the image and all that remains is brightness data. The *xray filter* applies an x-ray effect, which is basically just an inversion of the grayscale effect. Figure 22.4 demonstrates applying these filters, alone and in combination, to a simple image.

```
1   <!DOCTYPE html PUBLIC "-//W3C//DTD HTML 4.0 Transitional//EN">
2   <HTML>
3
4   <!-- Fig 22.4: misc.html                              -->
5   <!-- Image filters to invert, grayscale, or xray an image -->
6
7   <HEAD>
8   <TITLE>Misc. Image filters</TITLE>
9
10  <STYLE TYPE = "text/css">
11     .cap { font-weight: bold;
12            background-color: #DDDDAA;
13            text-align: center }
14  </STYLE>
15  </HEAD>
16
17  <BODY>
18  <TABLE>
19     <TR CLASS = "cap">
20        <TD>Normal</TD>
21        <TD>Grayscale</TD>
22        <TD>Xray</TD>
23        <TD>Invert</TD>
24     </TR>
25
26     <TR>
27        <TD><IMG SRC = "harvey.jpg"></TD>
28        <TD><IMG SRC = "harvey.jpg" STYLE = "filter: gray"></TD>
29        <TD><IMG SRC = "harvey.jpg" STYLE = "filter: xray"></TD>
30        <TD><IMG SRC = "harvey.jpg" STYLE = "filter: invert"></TD>
31     </TR>
32  </TABLE>
33
34  </BODY>
35  </HTML>
```

Fig. 22.4　Filters **invert**, **gray** and **xray**.

Each of our filters in lines 28 through 30 applies a separate image effect to `harvey.jpg`.

Look-and-Feel Observation 22.3

A good use of the **invert** *filter is to signify that something has just been clicked or selected.*

22.6 Adding **shadows** to Text

A simple filter that adds depth to your text is the ***shadow*** *filter*. This filter creates a shadowing effect that gives your text a three-dimensional look (Fig. 22.5).

In lines 31 through 33

```
<H1 ID = "shadowText" STYLE = "position: absolute; top: 50;
          left: 50; padding: 10; filter: shadow(direction = 0,
          color = red )">Shadow Direction: 0</H1>
```

```
1  <!DOCTYPE html PUBLIC "-//W3C//DTD HTML 4.0 Transitional//EN">
2  <HTML>
3
4  <!-- Fig 22.5: shadow.html      -->
5  <!-- Applying the shadow filter -->
6
7  <HEAD>
8  <TITLE>Shadow Filter</TITLE>
9
10 <SCRIPT LANGUAGE = "JavaScript">
11    var shadowDirection = 0;
12
13    function start()
14    {
15       window.setInterval( "runDemo()", 500 );
16    }
17
18    function runDemo()
19    {
20       shadowText.innerText =
21          "Shadow Direction: " + shadowDirection % 360;
22       shadowText.filters( "shadow" ).direction =
23          ( shadowDirection % 360 );
24       shadowDirection += 45;
25    }
26 </SCRIPT>
27 </HEAD>
28
29 <BODY ONLOAD = "start()">
30
31 <H1 ID = "shadowText" STYLE = "position: absolute; top: 50;
32          left: 50; padding: 10; filter: shadow( direction = 0,
33          color = red )">Shadow Direction: 0</H1>
34 </BODY>
35 </HTML>
```

Fig. 22.5   Applying a **shadow** filter to text (part 1 of 2).

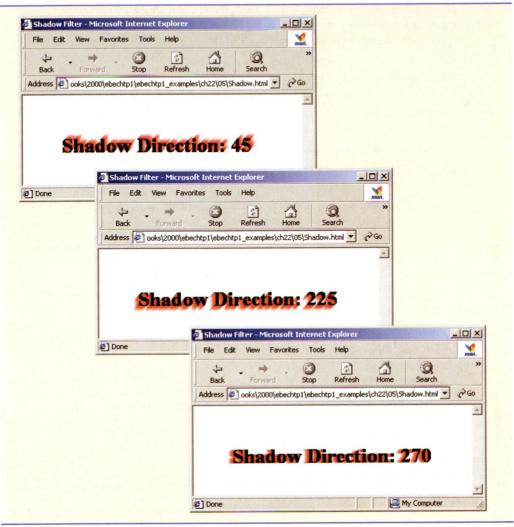

Fig. 22.5   Applying a **shadow** filter to text (part 2 of 2).

we apply the **shadow** filter to text. Property **direction** of the **shadow** filter determines in which direction the shadow effect is applied—this can be set to any of eight directions expressed in angular notation: **0** (up), **45** (above-right), **90** (right), **135** (below-right), **180** (below), **225** (below-left), **270** (left) and **315** (above-left). Property **color** specifies the color of the shadow that is applied to the text. Lines 20 through 24 in function **runDemo**

```
shadowText.innerText =
    "Shadow Direction: " + shadowDirection % 360;
shadowText.filters( "shadow" ).direction =
    ( shadowDirection % 360 );
shadowDirection += 45;
```

cycle through all values of the **direction** property, from **0** to **315**, and update property **innerText** of the **H1** element (**shadowText**) to match the current shadow direction.

Note that we apply a **padding** CSS style to the **H1** element. Otherwise, the shadow effect is partially cut off by the border of the element. Increasing the **padding** gives greater distance between the text and the border of the element, allowing the full effect to be displayed.

Software Engineering Observation 22.2

Some filters may be cut off by element borders—make sure to increase the padding in that element if this happens.

22.7 Creating Gradients with `alpha`

In Chapter 11 we saw a brief example of the gradient effect, which is a gradual progression from a starting color to a target color. Internet Explorer 5 allows you to create the same type of effect dynamically using the ***alpha*** *filter* (Fig 22.6). It is also often used for transparency effects not achievable with the ***chroma*** *filter*.

```
1   <!DOCTYPE html PUBLIC "-//W3C//DTD HTML 4.0 Transitional//EN">
2   <HTML>
3
4   <!-- Fig 22.6: alpha.html                        -->
5   <!-- Applying the alpha filter to an image -->
6
7   <HEAD>
8   <TITLE>Alpha Filter</TITLE>
9   <SCRIPT LANGUAGE = "JavaScript">
10     function run()
11     {
12        pic.filters( "alpha" ).opacity = opacityButton.value;
13        pic.filters( "alpha" ).finishopacity = opacityButton2.value;
14        pic.filters( "alpha" ).style = styleSelect.value;
15     }
16  </SCRIPT>
17  </HEAD>
18
19  <BODY>
20
21  <DIV ID = "pic"
22      STYLE = "position: absolute; left:0; top: 0;
23                filter: alpha( style = 2, opacity = 100,
24                finishopacity = 0 )">
25    <IMG SRC = "flag.gif">
26  </DIV>
27
28  <TABLE STYLE = "position: absolute; top: 250; left: 0;
29     background-color: #CCFFCC" BORDER = "1">
30
31     <TR>
32        <TD>Opacity (0-100):</TD>
33        <TD><INPUT TYPE = "text" ID = "opacityButton" SIZE = "3"
34           MAXLENGTH = "3" VALUE = "100"></TD>
35     </TR>
```

Fig. 22.6   Applying the **alpha** filter (part 1 of 2).

```
36
37      <TR>
38          <TD>FinishOpacity (0-100):</TD>
39          <TD><INPUT TYPE = "text" ID = "opacityButton2" SIZE = "3"
40              MAXLENGTH = "3" VALUE = "0"></TD>
41      </TR>
42
43      <TR>
44          <TD>Style:</TD>
45          <TD><SELECT ID = "styleSelect">
46              <OPTION VALUE = "1">Linear
47              <OPTION VALUE = "2" SELECTED>Circular
48              <OPTION VALUE = "3">Rectangular
49              </SELECT></TD>
50      </TR>
51
52      <TR>
53          <TD ALIGN = "center" COLSPAN = "2"><INPUT TYPE = "button"
54              VALUE = "Apply" ONCLICK = "run()"></TD>
55      </TR>
56   </TABLE>
57
58   </BODY>
59   </HTML>
```

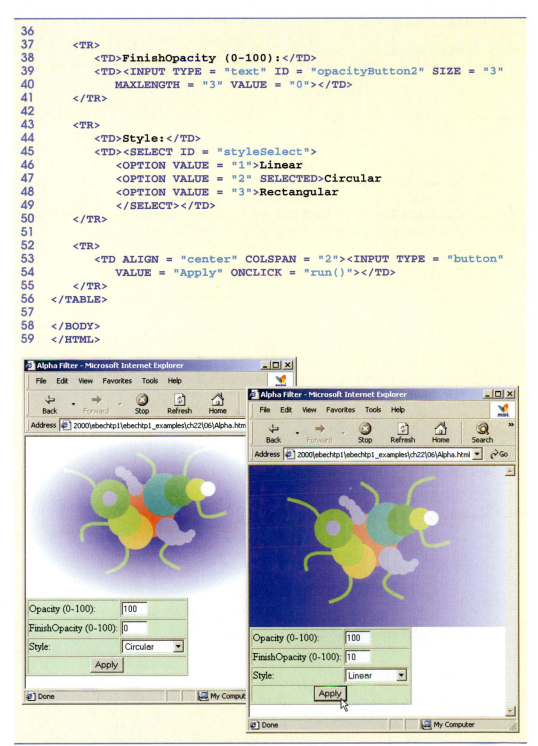

Fig. 22.6 Applying the **alpha** filter (part 2 of 2).

In lines 21 through 24

```
<DIV ID = "pic"
     STYLE = "position: absolute; left:0; top: 0; filter:
              alpha( style = 2, opacity = 100,
              finishopacity = 0 )">
```

we apply the **alpha** filter to a **DIV** element containing an image. The **style** property of the filter determines in what style the opacity is applied; a value of 0 applies *uniform opacity*, a value of 1 applies a *linear gradient*, a value of 2 applies a *circular gradient*, and a value of 3 applies a *rectangular gradient*.

The **opacity** and **finishopacity** properties are both percentages determining at what percent opacity the specified gradient will start and finish, respectively. Additional attributes are **startX**, **startY**, **finishX**, and **finishY**. These allow you to specify at what *x-y* coordinates the gradient starts and finishes in that element.

22.8 Making Text glow

The *glow filter* allows you to add an aura of color around your text. The color and strength can both be specified (Fig. 22.7).

```
1   <!DOCTYPE html PUBLIC "-//W3C//DTD HTML 4.0 Transitional//EN">
2   <HTML>
3
4   <!-- Fig 22.7: glow.html      -->
5   <!-- Applying the glow filter -->
6
7   <HEAD>
8   <TITLE>Glow Filter</TITLE>
9   <SCRIPT LANGUAGE = "JavaScript">
10     var strengthIndex = 1;
11     var counter = 1;
12     var upDown = true;
13     var colorArray = [ "FF0000", "FFFF00", "00FF00",
14                        "00FFFF", "0000FF", "FF00FF" ];
15     function apply()
16     {
17        glowSpan.filters( "glow" ).color =
18           parseInt( glowColor.value, 16 );
19        glowSpan.filters( "glow" ).strength =
20           glowStrength.value;
21     }
22
23     function startdemo()
24     {
25        window.setInterval( "rundemo()", 150 );
26     }
27
```

Fig. 22.7   Applying changes to the **glow** filter (part 1 of 3).

```
28      function rundemo()
29      {
30         if ( upDown )
31            glowSpan.filters( "glow" ).strength = strengthIndex++;
32         else
33            glowSpan.filters( "glow" ).strength = strengthIndex--;
34
35         if ( strengthIndex == 1 ) {
36            upDown = !upDown;
37            counter++;
38            glowSpan.filters( "glow" ).color =
39               parseInt( colorArray[ counter % 6 ], 16 );
40         }
41
42         if ( strengthIndex == 10 ) {
43            upDown = !upDown;
44         }
45      }
46   </SCRIPT>
47   </HEAD>
48
49   <BODY STYLE = "background-color: #00AAAA">
50   <H1>Glow Filter:</H1>
51
52   <SPAN ID = "glowSpan" STYLE = "position: absolute; left: 200;
53      top: 100; padding: 5; filter: glow( color = red,
54      strength = 5 )">
55      <H2>Glowing Text</H2>
56   </SPAN>
57
58   <TABLE BORDER = 1 STYLE = "background-color: #CCFFCC">
59      <TR>
60         <TD>Color (Hex)</TD>
61         <TD><INPUT ID = "glowColor" TYPE = "text" SIZE = 6
62            MAXLENGTH = 6 VALUE = FF0000></TD>
63      </TR>
64      <TR>
65         <TD>Strength (1-255)</TD>
66         <TD><INPUT ID = "glowStrength" TYPE = "text" SIZE = 3
67            MAXLENGTH = 3 VALUE = 5></TD>
68      </TR>
69      <TR>
70         <TD COLSPAN = 2>
71            <INPUT TYPE = "button" VALUE = "Apply"
72               ONCLICK = "apply()">
73            <INPUT TYPE = "button" VALUE = "Run Demo"
74               ONCLICK = "startdemo()"></TD>
75      </TR>
76   </TABLE>
77
78   </BODY>
79   </HTML>
```

Fig. 22.7   Applying changes to the **glow** filter (part 2 of 3).

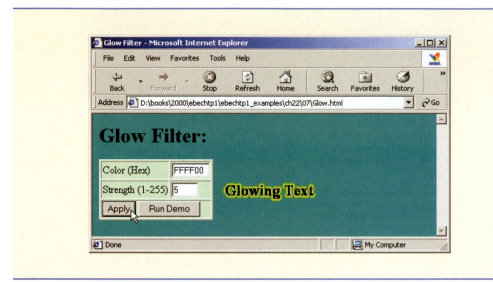

Fig. 22.7   Applying changes to the **glow** filter (part 3 of 3).

Lines 13 and 14

```
var colorArray = [ "FF0000", "FFFF00", "00FF00",
                   "00FFFF", "0000FF", "FF00FF" ];
```

establish an array of color values to cycle through in the demo.
    Lines 38 and 39

```
glowSpan.filters( "glow" ).color =
   parseInt( colorArray[ counter % 6 ], 16 );
```

change the **color** attribute of the **glow** filter based on **counter**, which is incremented
(line 37) every time the value of **strengthIndex** becomes 1. As in the example with the
chroma filter, we use the **parseInt** function to assign a proper hex value (taken from
the **colorArray** we declared in lines 13 and 14) to the **color** property.
    Lines 30 through 33

```
if ( upDown )
   glowSpan.filters( "glow" ).strength = strengthIndex++;
else
   glowSpan.filters( "glow" ).strength = strengthIndex--;
```

are an **if/else** structure that increments or decrements the **strength** property of the
glow filter based on the value of **upDown**, which is toggled in the **if** structures at lines
35 and 42 when **strengthIndex** reaches either 1 or 10.
    Clicking the **Run Demo** button starts a cycle that oscillates the filter **strength**,
cycling through the colors in **colorArray** after every loop.

Common Programming Error 22.1

*When the **glow** filter is set to a large **strength**, the effect is often cut off by the borders of
the element. Add CSS **padding** to prevent this.*

22.9 Creating Motion with `blur`

The *blur filter* creates an illusion of motion by blurring text or images in a certain direction. As we see in Fig 22.8, the `blur` filter can be applied in any of eight directions and its strength may vary.

```
1   <!DOCTYPE html PUBLIC "-//W3C//DTD HTML 4.0 Transitional//EN">
2   <HTML>
3
4   <!-- Fig 22.8: blur.html -->
5   <!-- The blur filter      -->
6
7   <HEAD>
8   <TITLE>Blur Filter</TITLE>
9   <SCRIPT LANGUAGE = "JavaScript">
10     var strengthIndex = 1;
11     var blurDirection = 0;
12     var upDown = 0;
13     var timer;
14
15     function reBlur()
16     {
17        blurImage.filters( "blur" ).direction =
18           document.forms( "myForm" ).Direction.value;
19        blurImage.filters( "blur" ).strength =
20           document.forms( "myForm" ).Strength.value;
21        blurImage.filters( "blur" ).add =
22           document.forms( "myForm" ).Add.checked;
23     }
24
25     function startDemo()
26     {
27        timer = window.setInterval( "runDemo()", 5 );
28     }
29
30     function runDemo( )
31     {
32        document.forms( "myForm" ).Strength.value = strengthIndex;
33        document.forms( "myForm" ).Direction.value =
34           ( blurDirection % 360 );
35
36        if( strengthIndex == 35 || strengthIndex == 0 )
37           upDown = !upDown;
38
39        blurImage.filters( "blur" ).strength =
40           ( upDown ? strengthIndex++ : strengthIndex-- );
41
42        if ( strengthIndex == 0 )
43           blurImage.filters( "blur" ).direction =
44              ( ( blurDirection += 45 ) % 360 );
45     }
46
47   </SCRIPT>
```

Fig. 22.8   Using the `blur` filter with the `add` property `false` then `true` (part 1 of 3).

```
48    </HEAD>
49
50    <BODY>
51    <FORM NAME = "myForm">
52
53    <TABLE BORDER = "1" STYLE = "background-color: #CCFFCC">
54    <CAPTION>Blur filter controls</CAPTION>
55
56       <TR>
57          <TD>Direction:</TD>
58          <TD><SELECT NAME = "Direction">
59             <OPTION VALUE = "0">above
60             <OPTION VALUE = "45">above-right
61             <OPTION VALUE = "90">right
62             <OPTION VALUE = "135">below-right
63             <OPTION VALUE = "180">below
64             <OPTION VALUE = "225">below-left
65             <OPTION VALUE = "270">left
66             <OPTION VALUE = "315">above-left
67          </SELECT></TD>
68       </TR>
69
70       <TR>
71          <TD>Strength:</TD>
72          <TD><INPUT NAME = "Strength" SIZE = "3" MAXLENGTH = "3"
73             VALUE = "0"></TD>
74       </TR>
75
76       <TR>
77          <TD>Add original?</TD>
78          <TD><INPUT TYPE = "checkbox" NAME = "Add"></TD>
79       </TR>
80
81       <TR>
82          <TD ALIGN = "center" COLSPAN = "2"><INPUT TYPE = "button"
83             VALUE = "Apply" ONCLICK = "reBlur();"></TD>
84       </TR>
85
86       <TR>
87          <TD COLSPAN = "2">
88          <INPUT TYPE = "button" VALUE = "Start demo"
89             ONCLICK = "startDemo();">
90          <INPUT TYPE = "button" VALUE = "Stop demo"
91             ONCLICK = "window.clearInterval( timer );"></TD>
92       </TR>
93
94    </TABLE>
95    </FORM>
96
97    <DIV ID = "blurImage" STYLE = "position: absolute; top: 0;
98       left: 300; padding: 0; filter:
99       blur( add = 0, direction = 0, strength = 0 );
100      background-color: white;">
```

Fig. 22.8   Using the **blur** filter with the **add** property **false** then **true** (part 2 of 3).

```
101        <IMG ALIGN = "center" SRC = "shapes.gif">
102    </DIV>
103
104    </BODY>
105    </HTML>
```

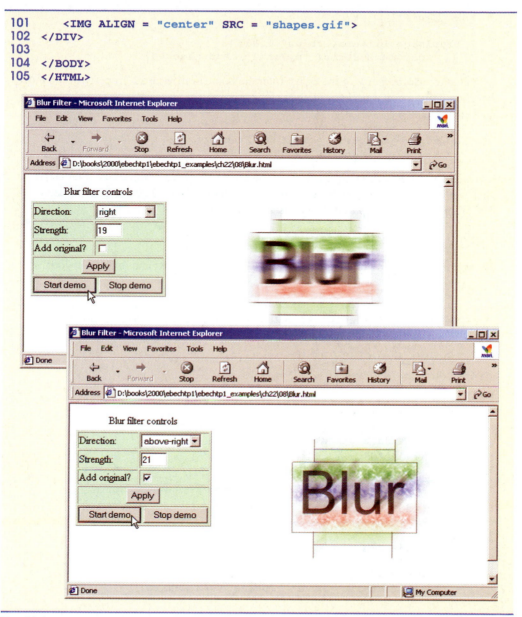

Fig. 22.8   Using the **blur** filter with the **add** property **false** then **true** (part 3 of 3).

The three properties of the **blur** filter are **add**, **direction** and **strength**. The **add** property, when set to **true**, adds a copy of the original image over the blurred image, creating a more subtle blurring effect; Fig. 22.8 demonstrates the contrast between setting this to **true** or **false**.

The **direction** property determines in which direction the **blur** filter will be applied. This is expressed in angular form (as we saw in Fig. 22.5 with the **shadow** filter). The **strength** property determines how strong the blurring effect will be.

Lines 21 and 22

```
blurImage.filters( "blur" ).add =
     document.forms( "myForm" ).Add.checked;
```

assign to the **add** property of the **blur** filter the boolean **checked** property of the **Add** checkbox—if the box was checked, the value is **true**.

Lines 43 and 44

```
blurImage.filters( "blur" ).direction =
     ( ( blurDirection += 45 ) % 360 )
```

increment the **direction** property whenever the **strength** of the **blur** filter is 0 (i.e., whenever an iteration has completed). The value assigned to the **direction** property cycles through all the multiples of 45 between 0 and 360.

22.10 Using the wave Filter

The **wave** *filter* allows you to apply *sine-wave distortions* to text and images on your Web pages (Fig. 22.9).

```
1   <!DOCTYPE html PUBLIC "-//W3C//DTD HTML 4.0 Transitional//EN">
2   <HTML>
3
4   <!-- Fig 22.9: wave.html        -->
5   <!-- Applying the wave filter -->
6
7   <HEAD>
8   <TITLE>Wave Filter</TITLE>
9
10  <SCRIPT LANGUAGE = "JavaScript">
11     var wavePhase = 0;
12
13     function start()
14     {
15        window.setInterval( "wave()", 5 );
16     }
17
18     function wave()
19     {
20        wavePhase++;
21        flag.filters( "wave" ).phase = wavePhase;
22     }
23  </SCRIPT>
24  </HEAD>
25
26  <BODY ONLOAD = "start();">
27
28  <SPAN ID = "flag"
29     STYLE = "align: center; position: absolute;
30     left: 30; padding: 15;
31     filter: wave(add = 0, freq = 1, phase = 0, strength = 10)">
```

Fig. 22.9   Adding a **wave** filter to text (part 1 of 2).

```
32    <H1>Here's some waaaavy text</H1>
33    </SPAN>
34
35    </BODY>
36    </HTML>
```

Fig. 22.9   Adding a **wave** filter to text (part 2 of 2).

The **wave** filter, as seen in line 31,

```
filter: wave(add = 0, freq = 1, phase = 0, strength = 10)">
```

has many properties. The **add** property, as in the case of the **blur** filter, adds a copy of the text or image underneath the filtered effect. The **add** property is usually useful only when applying the **wave** filter to images.

> **Performance Tip 22.2**
>
> *Applying the **wave** filter to images is processor intensive—if your viewers have inadequate processor power, your pages may act sluggishly on their systems.*

The **freq** property determines the *frequency of the wave* applied—i.e., how many complete sine waves will be applied in the affected area. Increasing this property creates a more pronounced wave effect, but makes the text harder to read.

The **phase** property indicates the *phase shift of the wave*. Increasing this property does not modify any physical attributes of the wave, but merely shifts it in space. This property is useful for creating a gentle waving effect, as we do in this example. The last property, **strength**, is the amplitude of the sine wave that is applied.

In the script, lines 20 and 21

```
wavePhase++;
flag.filters( "wave" ).phase = wavePhase;
```

increment the phase shift of the wave in every call to the **wave** function.

22.11 Advanced Filters: dropShadow and light

Two filters that apply advanced image processing effects are the ***dropShadow*** and ***light*** *filters*. The **dropShadow** filter, as you can probably tell, applies an effect similar to the drop shadow we applied to our images with Paint Shop Pro in Chapter 5—it creates a blacked-out version of the image, and places it behind the image, offset by a specified number of pixels.

The **light** filter is the most powerful and advanced filter available in Internet Explorer 5. It allows you to simulate the effect of a light source shining on your page. With scripting, this filter can be used with dazzling results. Figure 22.10 combines these two filters to create an interesting effect.

```
1   <!DOCTYPE html PUBLIC "-//W3C//DTD HTML 4.0 Transitional//EN">
2   <HTML>
3
4   <!-- Fig 22.10: dropshadow.html                      -->
5   <!-- Using the light filter with the dropshadow filter -->
6
7   <HEAD>
8   <TITLE>DHTML dropShadow and light Filters</TITLE>
9
10  <SCRIPT LANGUAGE = "JavaScript">
11     function setlight( )
12     {
13        dsImg.filters( "light" ).addPoint( 150, 150,
14           125, 255, 255, 255, 100);
15     }
16
17     function run()
18     {
19        eX = event.offsetX;
20        eY = event.offsetY;
21
22        xCoordinate = Math.round( eX-event.srcElement.width/2, 0 );
23        yCoordinate = Math.round( eY-event.srcElement.height/2, 0 );
24
```

Fig. 22.10 Applying **light** filter with a **dropshadow** (part 1 of 2).

```
25          dsImg.filters( "dropShadow" ).offx = xCoordinate / -3;
26          dsImg.filters( "dropShadow" ).offy = yCoordinate / -3;
27
28          dsImg.filters( "light" ).moveLight(0, eX, eY, 125, 1);
29      }
30  </SCRIPT>
31  </HEAD>
32
33  <BODY ONLOAD = "setlight()" STYLE = "background-color: green">
34
35  <IMG ID = "dsImg" SRC = "circle.gif"
36     STYLE = "top: 100; left: 100; filter: dropShadow( offx = 0,
37     offy = 0, color = black ) light()" ONMOUSEMOVE = "run()">
38
39  </BODY>
40  </HTML>
```

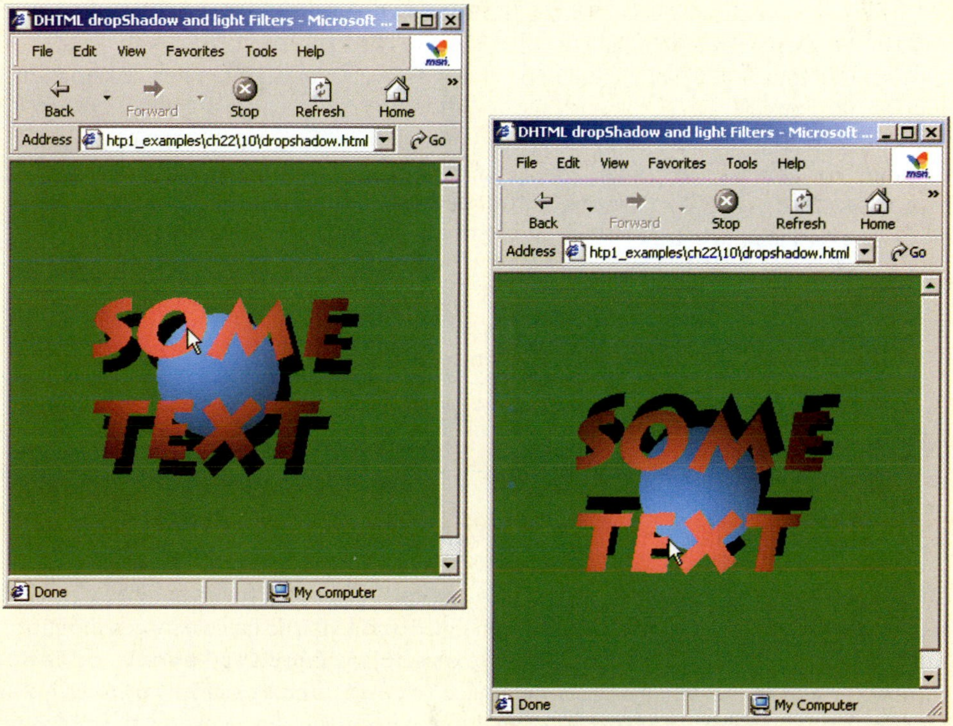

Fig. 22.10 Applying **light** filter with a **dropshadow** (part 2 of 2).

Let us begin by examining the **dropshadow** filter. In lines 35 through 37

```
<IMG ID = "dsImg" SRC = "circle.gif"
   STYLE = "top: 100; left: 100; filter: dropShadow( offx = 0,
   offy = 0, color = black ) light()" ONMOUSEMOVE = "run()">
```

we apply the **dropShadow** filter to our image. The **offx** and **offy** properties determine by how many pixels the drop shadow will be offset (see Chapter 5). The **color** property specifies the color of the drop shadow. Note that we also declare the **light** filter in line 37, although we do not give it any initial parameters—all the parameters and methods of the **light** filter are set by scripting. Lines 13 and 14

```
dsImg.filters( "light" ).addPoint(150, 150,
    125, 255, 255, 255, 100);
```

call the **addPoint** method of the **light** filter. This adds a *point light source*—a source of light which emanates from a single point and radiates in all directions. The first two parameters (**150, 150**) set the *x-y* coordinates at which to add the point source. In this case we place the source at the center of the image, which is 300-by-300 pixels.

The next parameter (**125**) sets the *height* of the point source. This simulates how far above the surface the light is situated. Small values create a small but high-intensity circle of light on the image, while large values cast a circle of light which is darker, but spreads over a greater distance.

The next three parameters (**255, 255, 255**) specify the RGB value of the light, in decimal. In this case we set the light to a color of white (**#FFFFFF**).

The last value (**100**), is a strength percentage—we set our light in this case to radiate with 100% strength.

This point light source will create a pleasant lighting effect, but it is static. We can use scripting to animate the light source in response to user actions. We use the **ONMOUSEMOVE** event (line 37) to have the light source follow the mouse cursor as the user moves it over the image. Lines 19 through 28

```
eX = event.offsetX;
eY = event.offsetY;

xCoordinate = Math.round( eX-event.srcElement.width/2, 0 );
yCoordinate = Math.round( eY-event.srcElement.height/2, 0 );

dsImg.filters( "dropShadow" ).offx = xCoordinate / -3;
dsImg.filters( "dropShadow" ).offy = yCoordinate / -3;

dsImg.filters( "light" ).moveLight(0, eX, eY, 125, 1);
```

of the **run** function animate both the **dropshadow** and **light** filters in response to user actions. First we set the variables **xCoord** and **yCoord** to the distance between the current cursor position (**eX** and **eY**, which were set to **event.offsetX** and **event.offsetY** on lines 19 and 20) to the middle of the image (**event.srcElement.width / 2** or **event.srcElement.height / 2**). In the next two lines of code we set the **offx** and **offy** properties of the **dropShadow** filter relative to the current *x-y* coordinates of the image. We divide by a certain amount to create an effect of height (shadows cast by objects far from light sources only move a small amount when the light source moves by a larger amount).

We then call the **moveLight** method to update the position of the light source as well. The first parameter (**0**) is the index of the light source on the page. Multiple light sources have index numbers assigned to them in the order in which they are added. The next two parameters (**event.offsetX, event.offsetY**) specify the *x-y* coordinates to which we should move the light source. We use the **offsetX** and **offsetY** properties of the

event object to move the light source to the current mouse cursor position over the image. The next parameter (**125**) specifies the height to which we move the light source. In this case, we keep the light source as the same level it was when we declared it. The last parameter (**1**) indicates that the values we are using are absolute. To move your light source by relative amounts instead, use a value of **0** for the last parameter of the **moveLight** function.

As you can see, combining the **dropShadow** and **light** filters creates a stunning effect that responds to user actions. The point source is not the only type of light source available for the light filter. Figure 22.11 demonstrates the use of a *cone light source* for illuminating an image.

```
1   <!DOCTYPE html PUBLIC "-//W3C//DTD HTML 4.0 Transitional//EN">
2   <HTML>
3
4   <!-- Fig 22.11: conelight.html          -->
5   <!-- Automating the cone light source -->
6
7   <HEAD><TITLE>Cone lighting</TITLE>
8
9   <SCRIPT LANGUAGE = "JavaScript">
10     var upDown = true;
11     var counter = 0;
12     var moveRate = -2;
13
14     function setLight()
15     {
16        marquee.filters( "light" ).addCone( 0, marquee.height, 8,
17           marquee.width/2, 30, 255, 150, 255, 50, 15 );
18        marquee.filters( "light" ).addCone( marquee.width,
19           marquee.height, 8, 200, 30, 150, 255, 255, 50, 15 );
20        marquee.filters( "light" ).addCone( marquee.width/2,
21           marquee.height, 4, 200, 100, 255, 255, 150, 50, 50 );
22
23        window.setInterval( "moveLight()", 100 );
24     }
25
26     function moveLight()
27     {
28        counter++;
29
30        if ( ( counter % 30 ) == 0 )
31           upDown = !upDown;
32
33        if ( ( counter % 10 ) == 0 )
34           moveRate *= -1;
35
36        if ( upDown ) {
37           marquee.filters( "light" ).moveLight( 0,-1,-1,3,0 );
38           marquee.filters( "light" ).moveLight( 1,1,-1,3,0 );
39           marquee.filters( "light" ).moveLight(2,moveRate,0,3,0);
40        }
```

Fig. 22.11 Dynamic cone source lighting (part 1 of 2).

```
41          else {
42             marquee.filters( "light" ).moveLight( 0,1,1,3,0 );
43             marquee.filters( "light" ).moveLight( 1,-1,1,3,0 );
44             marquee.filters( "light" ).moveLight(2,moveRate,0,3,0);
45          }
46       }
47   </SCRIPT>
48
49   <BODY STYLE = "background-color: #000000" ONLOAD = "setLight()">
50
51   <IMG ID = "marquee" SRC = "marquee.gif"
52      STYLE = "filter: light; position: absolute; left: 25;
53      top: 25">
54
55   </BODY>
56   </HTML>
```

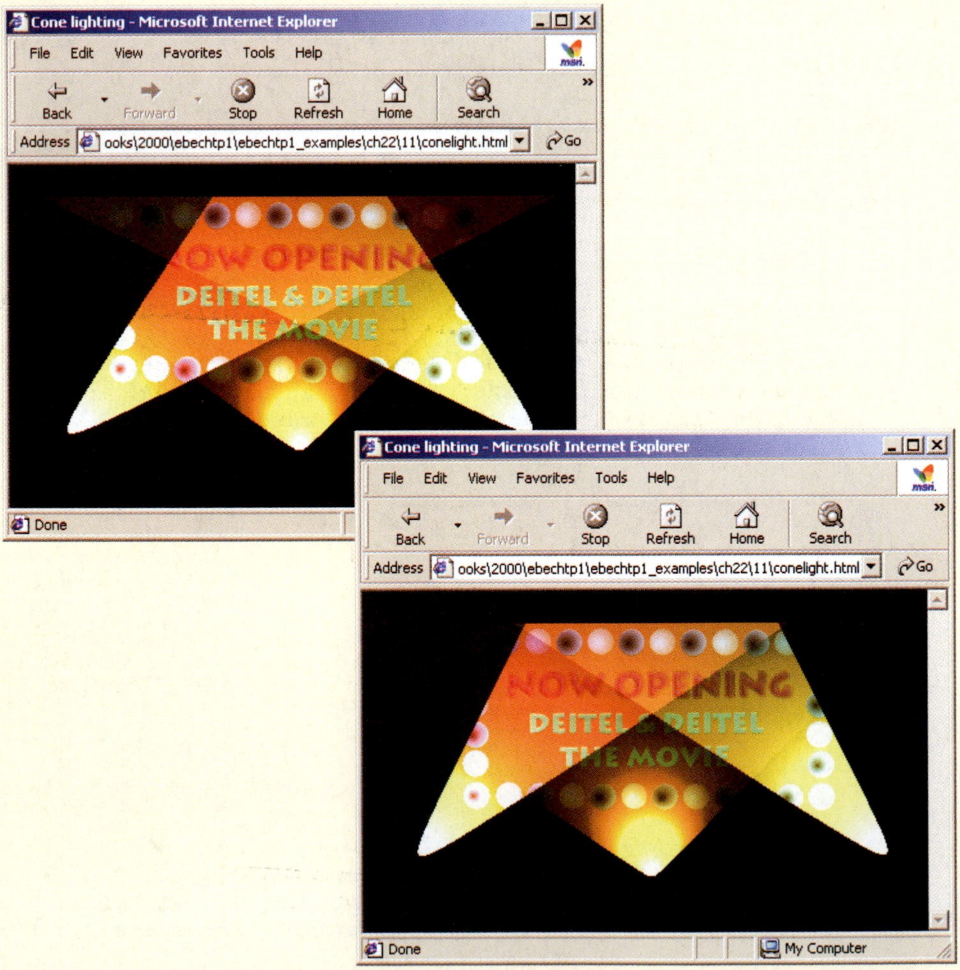

Fig. 22.11   Dynamic cone source lighting (part 2 of 2).

In lines 16 and 17

```
marquee.filters( "light" ).addCone( 0, marquee.height, 8,
    marquee.width/2, 30, 255, 150, 255, 50, 15 );
```

we add our first cone light source using the **addCone** method. The parameters of this method are similar to the **addPoint** method. The first two parameters specify the *x-y* coordinates of the light source, and the third parameter specifies the simulated height above the page at which the light should be placed. The next two parameters (**marquee.width/2**, **30**) are new—they specify the *x-y* coordinates at which the cone source is targeted. The next three parameters (**255**, **150**, **255**) specify the RGB value of the light which is cast, just as we did in the **addPoint** method. The next parameter (**50**) specifies the strength of the cone source, in a percentage (also equivalent to the strength parameter in the **addPoint** method). The last value (**15**) specifies the *spread* of the light source, in degrees (this can be set in the range **0–90**). In this case we set the spread of the cone to **15** degrees, illuminating a relatively narrow area.

In line 37

```
marquee.filters( "light" ).moveLight( 0,-1,-1,3,0 );
```

we use the **moveLight** method once again. When used on cone sources, the **moveLight** method moves the target of the light. In this case we set the last parameter to **0** to move the light by a relative amount, not an absolute amount, as we did in Fig 22.10.

22.12 Transitions I: Filter blendTrans

The transitions included with Internet Explorer 5 give the author control of many scriptable PowerPoint type effects. Transitions are set as values of the **filter** CSS property, just as regular filters are. We then use scripting to begin the transition. Figure 22.12 is a simple example of the ***blendTrans*** *transition*, which creates a smooth fade-in/fade-out effect.

```
1   <!DOCTYPE html PUBLIC "-//W3C//DTD HTML 4.0 Transitional//EN">
2   <HTML>
3
4   <!-- Fig 22.12: blendtrans.html -->
5   <!-- Blend transition          -->
6
7   <HEAD>
8   <TITLE>Using blendTrans</TITLE>
9
10  <SCRIPT LANGUAGE = "JavaScript">
11     function blendOut()
12     {
13        textInput.filters( "blendTrans" ).apply();
14        textInput.style.visibility = "hidden";
15        textInput.filters( "blendTrans" ).play();
16     }
17  </SCRIPT>
18  </HEAD>
```

Fig. 22.12 Using the **blendTrans** transition (part 1 of 2).

```
19
20    <BODY>
21
22    <DIV ID = "textInput" ONCLICK = "blendOut()"
23       STYLE = "width: 300; filter: blendTrans( duration = 3 )">
24       <H1>Some fading text</H1>
25    </DIV>
26
27    </BODY>
28    </HTML>
```

Fig. 22.12   Using the **blendTrans** transition (part 2 of 2).

First, line 23

```
STYLE = "width: 300; filter:blendTrans( duration = 3 )">
```

sets the filter to **blendTrans** and the **duration** parameter to 3. This determines how long the transition will take. All the rest of our work is done by scripting. In lines 13 through 15

```
textInput.filters( "blendTrans" ).apply();
textInput.style.visibility = "hidden";
textInput.filters( "blendTrans" ).play();
```

we invoke two methods of **blendTrans**. The **apply** method (line 13) initializes the transition for the affected element. Once this is done, we set the **visibility** of the element to **hidden**—this takes effect when we invoke the **play** method on line 15.

Figure 22.13 is a more complex example of the **blendTrans** transition. We use this to transition between two separate images.

```
1    <!DOCTYPE html PUBLIC "-//W3C//DTD HTML 4.0 Transitional//EN">
2    <HTML>
3
4    <!-- Fig 22.13: blendtrans2.html -->
5    <!-- Blend Transition            -->
6
7    <HEAD>
8    <TITLE>Blend Transition II</TITLE>
```

Fig. 22.13   Blending between images with **blendTrans** (part 1 of 3).

```
9
10   <SCRIPT LANGUAGE = "JavaScript">
11      var whichImage = true;
12
13      function blend()
14      {
15         if ( whichImage ) {
16            image1.filters( "blendTrans" ).apply();
17            image1.style.visibility = "hidden";
18            image1.filters( "blendTrans" ).play();
19         }
20         else {
21            image2.filters( "blendTrans" ).apply();
22            image2.style.visibility = "hidden";
23            image2.filters( "blendTrans" ).play();
24         }
25      }
26
27      function reBlend ( fromImage )
28      {
29         if ( fromImage ) {
30            image1.style.zIndex -= 2;
31            image1.style.visibility = "visible";
32         }
33         else {
34            image1.style.zIndex += 2;
35            image2.style.visibility = "visible";
36         }
37
38         whichImage = !whichImage;
39         blend();
40      }
41   </SCRIPT>
42   </HEAD>
43
44   <BODY STYLE = "color: darkblue; background-color: lightblue"
45         ONLOAD = "blend()">
46
47   <H1>Blend Transition Demo</H1>
48
49   <IMG ID = "image2" SRC = "cool12.jpg"
50      ONFILTERCHANGE = "reBlend( false )"
51      STYLE = "position: absolute; left: 50; top: 50; width: 300;
52      filter: blendTrans( duration = 4 ); z-index: 1">
53
54   <IMG ID = "image1" SRC = "cool8.jpg"
55      ONFILTERCHANGE = "reBlend( true )"
56      STYLE = "position: absolute; left: 50; top: 50; width: 300;
57      filter: blendTrans( duration = 4 ); z-index: 2">
58
59   </BODY>
60   </HTML>
```

Fig. 22.13 Blending between images with **blendTrans** (part 2 of 3).

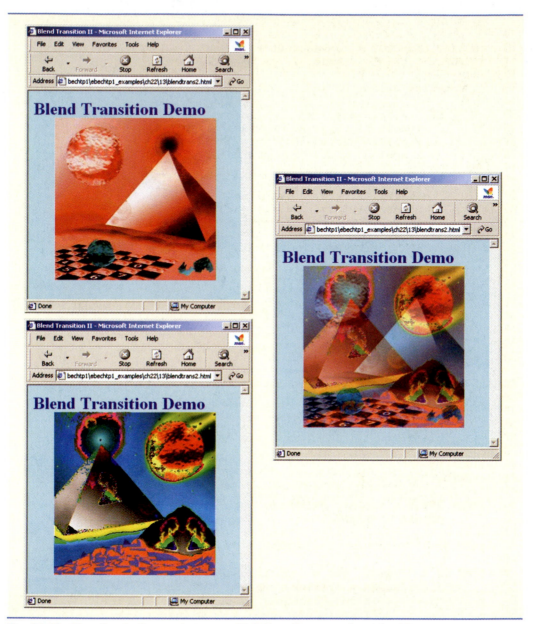

Fig. 22.13 Blending between images with **blendTrans** (part 3 of 3).

We begin by placing two overlapping images on the page, with IDs **image1** and **image2** (lines 49 though 57). The **BODY** tag's **ONLOAD** event (line 45) calls function **blend** as the body loads. The **blend** function checks the value of the **whichImage** variable, and because it is set to **true**, begins a fade transition on **image1**. Because there are two images in the same place, when **image1** fades out it appears that **image2** fades in to replace it. When the transition is complete, **image1**'s **ONFILTERCHANGE** event (line 55) fires. This calls function **reBlend**, which in lines 30 and 31

```
image1.style.zIndex -= 2;
image1.style.visibility = "visible";
```

changes the **zIndex** (the JavaScript version of the **z-index** CSS property) of **image1** so that it is now below **image2**. Once this is done, the image is made visible again. The function then toggles the **whichImage** property, and calls function **blend** so that the whole process starts again, now transitioning from **image2** back to **image1**.

22.13 Transitions II: Filter `revealTrans`

The *revealTrans* *filter* allows you to transition using professional-style transitions, from *box out* to *random dissolve*. Figure 22.14 cycles through all 24 of these, transitioning from one image to another.

The script in this example is almost the same as the script in the **blendTrans** example. In line 48

```
image2.filters("revealTrans").transition = counter % 24;
```

we set the **transition** property of the image, which determines what visual transition will be used here. There are 24 different visual transitions (their names are listed in the **transitionName** array for updating the **DIV** element **transitionDisplay**.

```
1    <!DOCTYPE html PUBLIC "-//W3C//DTD HTML 4.0 Transitional//EN">
2    <HTML>
3
4    <!-- Fig 22.14: revealtrans.html -->
5    <!-- Cycling through 24 transitions -->
6    <HEAD>
7    <TITLE>24 DHTML Transitions</TITLE>
8
9    <SCRIPT>
10      var transitionName =
11        ["Box In", "Box Out",
12         "Circle In", "Circle Out",
13         "Wipe Up", "Wipe Down", "Wipe Right", "Wipe Left",
14         "Vertical Blinds", "Horizontal Blinds",
15         "Checkerboard Across", "Checkerboard Down",
16         "Random Dissolve",
17         "Split Vertical In", "Split Vertical Out",
18         "Split Horizontal In", "Split Horizontal Out",
19         "Strips Left Down", "Strips Left Up",
20         "Strips Right Down", "Strips Right Up",
21         "Random Bars Horizontal", "Random Bars Vertical",
22         "Random"];
23
24      var counter = 0;
25      var whichImage = true;
26
27      function blend()
28      {
29         if ( whichImage ) {
30            image1.filters( "revealTrans" ).apply();
```

Fig. 22.14 Transitions using **revealTrans** (part 1 of 4).

```
31              image1.style.visibility = "hidden";
32              image1.filters( "revealTrans" ).play();
33          }
34      else {
35              image2.filters( "revealTrans" ).apply();
36              image2.style.visibility = "hidden";
37              image2.filters( "revealTrans" ).play();
38          }
39      }
40
41      function reBlend( fromImage )
42      {
43          counter++;
44
45          if ( fromImage ) {
46              image1.style.zIndex -= 2;
47              image1.style.visibility = "visible";
48              image2.filters("revealTrans").transition = counter % 24;
49          }
50          else {
51              image1.style.zIndex += 2;
52              image2.style.visibility = "visible";
53              image1.filters("revealTrans").transition = counter % 24;
54          }
55
56          whichImage = !whichImage;
57          blend();
58          transitionDisplay.innerHTML = "Transition " + counter % 24 +
59              ":<BR> " + transitionName[ counter % 24 ];
60      }
61  </SCRIPT>
62  </HEAD>
63
64  <BODY STYLE = "color: white; background-color: lightcoral"
65      ONLOAD = "blend()">
66
67     <IMG ID = "image2" SRC = "icontext.gif"
68          STYLE = "position: absolute; left: 10; top: 10;
69          width: 300; z-index:1; visibility: visible;
70          filter: revealTrans( duration = 2, transition = 0 )"
71          ONFILTERCHANGE = "reBlend( false )">
72
73     <IMG ID = "image1" SRC = "icons2.gif"
74          STYLE = "position: absolute; left: 10; top: 10;
75          width: 300; z-index:1; visibility: visible;
76          filter: revealTrans( duration = 2, transition = 0 )"
77          ONFILTERCHANGE = "reBlend( true )">
78
79  <DIV ID = "transitionDisplay" STYLE = "position: absolute;
80      top: 10; left: 325">Transition 0:<BR> Box In</DIV>
81
82  </BODY>
83  </HTML>
```

Fig. 22.14 Transitions using **revealTrans** (part 2 of 4).

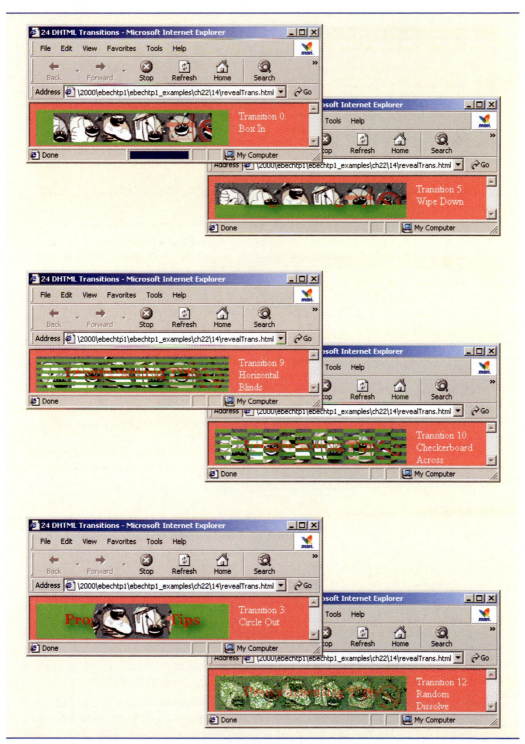

Fig. 22.14   Transitions using **revealTrans** (part 3 of 4).

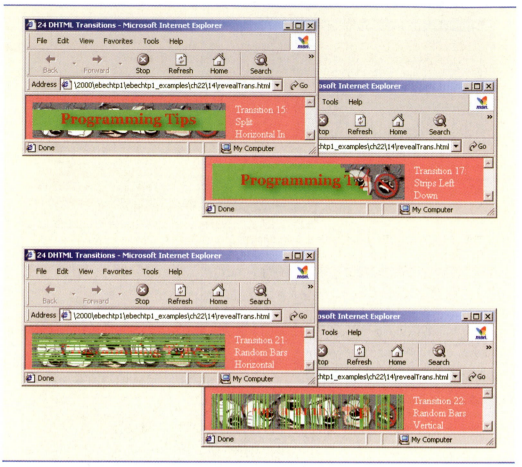

Fig. 22.14 Transitions using **revealTrans** (part 4 of 4).

SUMMARY

- Applying filters to text and images causes changes that are persistent.

- Transitions are temporary phenomena: applying a transition allows you to transfer from one page to another with a pleasant visual effect such as a random dissolve.

- Filters and transitions do not add content to your pages—rather, they present existing content in an engaging manner to help hold the user's attention.

- Each of the visual effects achievable with filters and transitions is programmable, so these effects may be adjusted dynamically by programs that respond to user-initiated events like mouse clicks and keystrokes.

- When Internet Explorer renders your page, it applies all the special effects and does this while running on the client computer without lengthy waits for files to download from the server.

- The **flipv** and **fliph** filters mirror text or images vertically and horizontally, respectively.

- Filters are applied in the **STYLE** attribute. The **filter** property's value is the name of the filter.

- One filter can be applied at once. Enter multiple filters as values of the **filter** attribute, separated by spaces.

- The **chroma** filter allows you to apply transparency effects dynamically, without using a graphics editor to hard-code transparency into the image.

- Use the **parseInt** function to convert a string to a hexadecimal integer for setting the **color** property of the **chroma** filter. The second parameter of **parseInt** specifies the base of the integer.

- Each filter has a property named **enabled**. If this property is set to **true**, the filter is applied. If it is set to **false**, the filter is not applied.

- The **ONCHANGE** event fires whenever the **VALUE** of a form field changes.

- Applying the **mask** filter to an image allows you to create an image mask, in which the background of an element is a solid color and the foreground of an element is transparent to the image or color behind it.

- Parameters for filters are always specified in the format *param = value*.

- The **invert** filter applies a negative image effect—dark areas become light, and light areas become dark.

- The **gray** filter applies a grayscale image effect, in which all color is stripped from the image and all that remains is brightness data.

- The **xray** filter applies an xray effect which is basically just an inversion of the grayscale effect.

- A simple filter that adds depth to your text is the **shadow** filter. This filter creates a shadowing effect that gives your text a three-dimensional look. The **direction** property of the **shadow** filter determines in which direction the shadow effect will be applied—this can be set to any of eight directions, expressed in angular notation: **0** (up), **45** (above-right), **90** (right), **135** (below-right), **180** (below), **225** (below-left), **270** (left), and **315** (above-left). The **color** property of the **shadow** filter specifies the color of the shadow which will be applied to the text.

- Internet Explorer 5 allows you to create gradient effects dynamically using the **alpha** filter. The **style** property of the filter determines in what style the opacity is applied; a value of **0** applies uniform opacity, a value of **1** applies a linear gradient, a value of **2** applies a circular gradient, and a value of **3** applies a rectangular gradient. The **opacity** and **finishopacity** properties are both percentages determining at what percent opacity the specified gradient will start and finish, respectively. Additional attributes are **startX**, **startY**, **finishX**, and **finishY**. These allow you to specify at what *x-y* coordinates the gradient starts and finishes in that element.

- The **glow** filter allows you to add an aura of color around your text. The **color** and **strength** can both be specified.

- The **blur** filter creates an illusion of motion by blurring text or images in a certain direction. The **blur** filter can be applied in any of eight directions, and its strength may vary. The **add** property, when set to **true**, adds a copy of the original image over the blurred image, creating a more subtle blurring effect. The **direction** property determines in which direction the **blur** filter will be applied. This is expressed in angular form (as with the **shadow** filter). The **strength** property determines how strong the blurring effect will be.

- The **wave** filter allows you to apply sine-wave distortions to text and images on your Web pages.

- The **add** property, as in the case of the **blur** filter, adds a copy of the text or image underneath the filtered effect. The **add** property is usually only useful when applying the **wave** filter to images. The **freq** property determines the frequency of the wave applied—i.e., how many complete sine waves will be applied in the affected area. Increasing this property would create a more pronounced wave effect, but makes the text harder to read. The **phase** property indicates the phase shift of the wave. Increasing this property does not modify any physical attributes of the wave, but merely shifts it in space. This property is useful for creating a gentle waving effect, as we do in this example. The last property, **strength**, is the amplitude of the sine wave that is applied.

- Two filters that apply advanced image processing effects are the **dropShadow** and **light** filters. The **dropShadow** filter applies an effect similar to the drop shadow we applied to our images in Chapter 11—it creates a blacked-out version of the image, and places it behind the image, offset by a specified number of pixels.

- The **light** filter is the most powerful and advanced filter available in Internet Explorer 5. It allows you to simulate the effect of a light source shining on your page.

- The **offx** and **offy** properties of the **dropShadow** filter determine by how many pixels the drop shadow will be offset. The **color** property specifies the color of the drop shadow.

- All the parameters and methods of the light **filter** are done by scripting. The **addPoint** method adds a point light source—a source of light which emanates from a single point and radiates in all directions. The first two parameters set the *x-y* coordinates at which to add the point source. The next parameter sets the height of the point source.This simulates how far above the surface the light is situated. Small values create a small but high-intensity circle of light on the image, while large values cast a circle of light which is darker, but spreads over a greater distance. The next three parameters specify the RGB value of the light, in decimal. In this case we set the light to a color of white. The last parameter is a strength percentage.

- The **moveLight** method updates the position of the light source. The first parameter is the index of the light source on the page. Multiple light sources have index numbers assigned to them in the order they are added. The next two parameters specify the *x-y* coordinates to which we should move the light source. The next parameter specifies the height to which we move the light source. Setting the last parameter to **1** indicates that the values we are using are absolute. To move your light source by relative amounts instead, use a value of **0** for the last parameter of the **moveLight** function.

- The parameters of the **addCone** method are similar to the **addPoint** method. The first two parameters specify the *x-y* coordinates of the light source, and the third parameter specifies the simulated height above the page at which the light should be placed. The next two parameters specify the *x-y* coordinates at which the cone source is targeted. The next three parameters specify the RGB value of the light which is cast, just as we did in the **addPoint** method. The next parameter specifies the strength of the cone source, in a percentage. The last value specifies the spread of the light source, in degrees (this can be set in the range **0-90**).

- The transitions included with Internet Explorer 5 give the author control of scriptable PowerPoint type effects. Transitions are set as values of the **filter** CSS property, just as regular filters are. We then use scripting to begin the transition.

- The **duration** parameter of **blendTrans** determines how long the transition will take.

- The **apply** method initializes the transition for the affected element. The **play** method then begins the transition.

- The **revealTrans** filter allows you to transition using professional-style transitions, from Box Out to Random Dissolve. The **transition** property determines what visual transition will be used. There are 24 different visual transitions.

TERMINOLOGY

add property of **blur** filter
add property of **wave** filter
addCone method of **light** filter
addPoint method of **light** filter
alpha filter
blendTrans filter

blur filter
chroma filter
circular gradient
color property of **chroma** filter
color property of **dropshadow** filter
color property of **glow** filter

color property of **shadow** filter
combining filters
cone light source
CSS **filter** property
direction property of **blur** filter
direction property of **shadow** filter
dropShadow filter
duration of **blendTrans** filter
enabled property of each filter
fade-in/fade-out effect
filter
filter property with **STYLE** attribute
filter **strength**
filter:alpha
filter:blur
filter:chroma
filter:dropshadow
filter:flipH
filter:flipV
filter:glow
filter:gray
filter:invert
filter:light
filter:mask
filter:shadow
filter:wave
filter:xray
finishopacity property of **alpha** filter
finishx property of **alpha** filter
finishy property of **alpha** filter
flipH filter
flipV filter
freq property of **wave** filter
glow filter
gradient
gray filter
grayscale image effect
height of light source

horizontal blinds transition
illusion of motion by blurring
image mask
invert filter
light filter
linear opacity
mask filter
moveLight property of **light** filter
negative image effect with **invert** filter
offx property of **dropshadow** filter
offy property of **dropshadow** filter
opacity property of **alpha** filter
padding (CSS)
phase property of **wave** filter
phase shift of a wave
point light source
radial opacity
random dissolve transition
rectangular opacity
revealTrans filter
shadow filter
sine-wave distortions
spread of cone light source
startx property of **alpha** filter
starty property of **alpha** filter
strength property of **blur** filter
strength property of **glow** filter
strength property of **wave** filter
style property of **alpha** filter
three-dimensional effect with **shadow** filter
transition effects
transparency effects
uniform opacity
vertical blinds transition
visibility
visual filters
wave filter
xray filter

SELF-REVIEW EXERCISES

22.1   State whether each of the following is *true* or *false*; if *false* state why:
a) You can determine the strength of the **shadow** filter.
b) The **flip** filter flips text horizontally.
c) The **mask** filter makes the foreground of an element transparent.
d) The **freq** property of the wave filter determines how many sine waves are applied to that element.
e) Increasing the margin of an element prevents the **glow** filter from being clipped by the element's border.
f) The **apply** method begins a transition.
g) The **invert** filter creates a negative image effect.

h) The **add** property adds a duplicate image below the affected image.

22.2 Fill in the blanks in the following questions:

a) You must use the _____ function to pass a value to the **color** property.

b) The last parameter of the **moveLight** method determines whether the move is _____ or _____.

c) The amplitude of the **wave** filter is controlled by the _____ property.

d) There are _____ **direction**s in which the **blur** filter can be applied.

e) There are two coordinate pairs in the parameters of the **addCone** method: the _____ and the _____.

f) There are _____ different transition styles for the **revealTrans** transition.

g) The two properties of the **dropShadow** filter that specify the offset of the shadow are _____ and _____.

h) The four styles of opacity are _____, _____, _____ and _____.

i) The _____ filter creates a grayscale version of the effected image.

ANSWERS TO SELF-REVIEW EXERCISES

22.1   a) False; there is no **strength** property for the **shadow** filter. b) False; the **flipH** filter flips text horizontally. c) True. d) True. e) False; increasing the padding of an element prevents clipping. f) False; the **play** method begins a transition. g) True. h) True.

22.2   a) **parseInt**. b) relative, absolute. c) **strength**. d) eight. e) source, target. f) 24 g) **offx**, **offy**. h) uniform, linear, circular, rectangular. i) **gray**.

EXERCISES

22.3   Create a Web page which applies the **invert** filter to an image if the user moves the mouse over the image.

22.4   Create a Web page which applies the **glow** filter to a hyperlink if the user moves the mouse over the over the link.

22.5   Write a script that **blur**s images and slowly unblurs them when they are finished loading into the browser (use event **ONLOAD** for the image).

22.6   Write a script that creates a cone **light** filter which tracks mouse movements across the page.

22.7   Write a script which uses the **blendTrans** filter to transition into an image after the image fully loads (use event **ONLOAD** for the image).

22.8   Write a script that changes the attributes of an **alpha** filter every 20 seconds (see **setInterval** in Chapter 20). Change both the color and the style of the **alpha** filter every time.

22.9   *(Slide Show)* Use the **revealTrans** filter to present your own slide show in a Web page. On each transition display a new image.

22.10   *(Image Selector)* Design a Web page that allows the user to choose from a series of images and allows the user to view the image in color and in grayscale.

23

Dynamic HTML: Data Binding with Tabular Data Control

Objectives

- To understand Dynamic HTML's notion of data binding and how to bind data to HTML elements.
- To be able to sort and filter data directly on the client without involving the server.
- To be able to bind a **TABLE** and other HTML elements to data source objects (DSOs).
- To be able to filter data to select only records appropriate for a particular application.
- To be able to navigate backwards and forwards through a database with the **Move** methods.

Let's look at the record.
Alfred Emanuel Smith

It is a capital mistake to theorize before one has data.
Sir Arthur Conan Doyle

The more the data banks record about each one of us, the less we exist.
Marshall McLuhan

Poor fellow, he suffers from files.
Aneurin Bevan

23.1 Introduction

This is one of the most important chapters for people who will build substantial, real-world, Web-based applications. Businesses and organizations thrive on data. Dynamic HTML helps Web application developers produce more responsive data-intensive applications.

Performance Tip 23.1

Prior to Dynamic HTML, the kinds of data manipulations we discuss in this chapter had to be done on the server, increasing the server load and the network load and resulting in choppy application responsiveness. With Dynamic HTML, these manipulations, such as sorting and filtering data, can now be done directly on the client without involving the server and the network.

With *data binding*, data need no longer reside exclusively on the server. The data can be maintained on the client and in a manner that distinguishes that data from the HTML code on the page. Typically, the data is sent to the client and then all subsequent manipulations take place on that data directly on the client thus eliminating server activity and network delays.

Performance Tip 23.2

With Dynamic HTML (rather than server-based database processing) it is more likely that a larger amount of data will be sent to the client on the first request. This initial downloading of the data by Internet Explorer is performed in a manner that enables processing to begin immediately on the portion of the data that has arrived.

Also, with the kind of data binding technology we discuss in this chapter, changes to data made on the client do not propagate back to the server. This is not a problem for a great many popular applications. If you do need to access the database directly and have the changes that you make on the client actually update the original database, you can use techniques we demonstrate in Chapters 25 through 29.

Once the data is available on the client, the data can then be sorted and filtered in various ways. We present examples of each of these operations.

To bind external data to HTML elements, Internet Explorer employs software capable of connecting the browser to live data sources. These are known as *Data Source Objects*

(DSOs). There are several DSOs available in IE5—in this chapter we discuss the most popular DSO, namely the *Tabular Data Control (TDC)*.

> ### Software Engineering Observation 23.1
> *Data-bound properties can be modified with Dynamic HTML even after the browser renders the page.*

23.2 Simple Data Binding

The Tabular Data Control (TDC) is an *ActiveX control* (a proprietary Microsoft software technology), and is added to the page with an **OBJECT** element. Figure 23.2 demonstrates a simple use of data binding with the TDC to update the contents of a **SPAN** element (the data file used in this example is listed in Fig. 23.1).

```
1   @ColorName@|@ColorHexRGBValue@
2   @aqua@|@#00FFFF@
3   @black@|@#000000@
4   @blue@|@#0000FF@
5   @fuchsia@|@#FF00FF@
6   @gray@|@#808080@
7   @green@|@#008000@
8   @lime@|@#00FF00@
9   @maroon@|@#800000@
10  @navy@|@#000080@
11  @olive@|@#808000@
12  @purple@|@#800080@
13  @red@|@#FF0000@
14  @silver@|@#C0C0C0@
15  @teal@|@#008080@
16  @yellow@|@#FFFF00@
17  @white@|@#FFFFFF@
```

Fig. 23.1   HTML color table data (**HTMLStandardColors.txt**).

```
1   <!DOCTYPE html PUBLIC "-//W3C//DTD HTML 4.0 Transitional//EN">
2   <HTML>
3
4   <!-- Fig 23.2: introdatabind.html                    -->
5   <!-- Simple data binding and recordset manipulation  -->
6
7   <HEAD>
8   <TITLE>Intro to Data Binding</TITLE>
9
10  <!-- This OBJECT element inserts an ActiveX control for -->
11  <!-- handling and parsing our data. The PARAM tags      -->
12  <!-- give the control starting parameters such as URL.  -->
13  <OBJECT ID = "Colors"
14      CLASSID = "CLSID:333C7BC4-460F-11D0-BC04-0080C7055A83">
15      <PARAM NAME = "DataURL" VALUE = "HTMLStandardColors.txt">
16      <PARAM NAME = "UseHeader" VALUE = "TRUE">
```

Fig. 23.2   Simple data binding. (part 1 of 3)

```
17          <PARAM NAME = "TextQualifier" VALUE = "@">
18          <PARAM NAME = "FieldDelim" VALUE = "|">
19   </OBJECT>
20
21   <SCRIPT LANGUAGE = "JavaScript">
22       var recordSet = Colors.recordset;
23
24       function reNumber()
25       {
26           if ( !recordSet.EOF )
27               recordNumber.innerText = recordSet.absolutePosition;
28           else
29               recordNumber.innerText = " ";
30       }
31
32       function forward()
33       {
34           if ( !recordSet.EOF )
35               recordSet.MoveNext();
36           else
37               recordSet.MoveFirst();
38
39           colorSample.style.backgroundColor = colorRGB.innerText;
40           reNumber();
41       }
42
43   </SCRIPT>
44   </HEAD>
45
46   <BODY ONLOAD = "reNumber()" ONCLICK = "forward()">
47
48   <H1>HTML Color Table</H1>
49   <H3>Click to move forward in the recordset.</H3>
50
51   <P><STRONG>Color Name: </STRONG>
52   <SPAN ID = "colorName" STYLE = "font-family: monospace"
53       DATASRC = "#Colors" DATAFLD = "ColorName"></SPAN><BR>
54
55   <STRONG>Color RGB Value: </STRONG>
56   <SPAN ID = "colorRGB" STYLE = "font-family: monospace"
57       DATASRC = "#Colors" DATAFLD = "ColorHexRGBValue"></SPAN>
58   <BR>
59
60   Currently viewing record number
61   <SPAN ID = "recordNumber" STYLE = "font-weight: 900"></SPAN>
62   <BR>
63
64   <SPAN ID = "colorSample" STYLE = "background-color: aqua;
65       color: 888888; font-size: 30pt">Color Sample</SPAN>
66   </P>
67
68   </BODY>
69   </HTML>
```

Fig. 23.2   Simple data binding. (part 2 of 3)

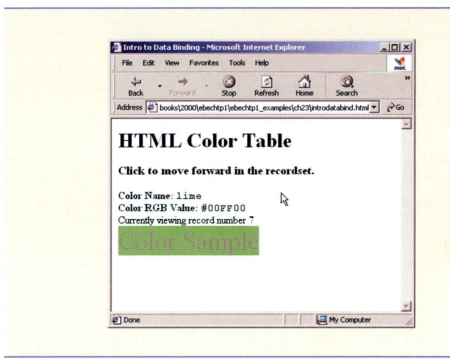

Fig. 23.2   Simple data binding. (part 3 of 3)

Line 1 of Fig. 23.1

```
@ColorName@|@ColorHexRGBValue@
```

begins our data file with a *header row*. This row specifies the names of the columns below (**ColorName** and **ColorHexRGBValue**). In this case, the data in each field is encapsulated in *text qualifiers* (**@**), and the fields are separated with a *field delimiter* (**|**).

Moving on to Fig. 23.2, the first thing you probably notice is the new **OBJECT** element, on lines 13 through 19

```
<OBJECT ID = "Colors"
    CLASSID = "CLSID:333C7BC4-460F-11D0-BC04-0080C7055A83">
    <PARAM NAME = "DataURL" VALUE = "HTMLStandardColors.txt">
    <PARAM NAME = "UseHeader" VALUE = "TRUE">
    <PARAM NAME = "TextQualifier" VALUE = "@">
    <PARAM NAME = "FieldDelim" VALUE = "|">
</OBJECT>
```

The **OBJECT** element here inserts the Tabular Data Control—one of the Microsoft ActiveX controls built into Internet Explorer 5. Attribute **CLASSID** specifies the ActiveX control to add to the Web page—here we use the **CLASSID** of the Tabular Data Control.

The **PARAM** tag specifies parameters for the object in the **OBJECT** element. Attribute **NAME** is the parameter name and attribute **VALUE** is the value. Parameter **DataURL** is the URL of the data source (**HTMLStandrardColors.txt**). Parameter **UseHeader**, when set to **true**, specifies that the first line of our data file has a header row.

Common Programming Error 23.1

*Forgetting to set the **UseHeader** parameter to **true** when you have a header row in your data source is an error that can cause problems in referencing columns.*

The third parameter, **TextQualifier**, sets the *text qualifier* of our data (in this case to **@**). A text qualifier is the character placed on both ends of the field data. The fourth parameter, **FieldDelim**, sets the *field delimiter* of our data (in this case to **|**). The field is the character delimiting separate data fields.

Lines 52 and 53

```
<SPAN ID = "colorName" STYLE = "font-family: monospace"
    DATASRC = "#Colors" DATAFLD = "ColorName"></SPAN><BR>
```

bind the data to a **SPAN** element. The **DATASRC** attribute refers to the **ID** of the TDC object (**Colors**, in this case) preceded with a hash mark (**#**), and the **DATAFLD** attribute specifies the name of the field to bind it to (**ColorName**, in this case). This will place the data contained in the first *record* (i.e., row) of the **ColorName** column into the **SPAN** element.

So far, we only have a static display of data. We can update it dynamically with some simple scripting. Line 22

```
recordSet = Colors.recordset;
```

assigns the **recordset** *property* of the **Colors** object (our TDC **OBJECT** element) to the variable **recordSet**. A *recordset* is simply a set of data—in our case, it is the data from our **HTMLStandardColors.txt** data source. To move the recordset to a different row in the data source, line 35

```
recordSet.MoveNext();
```

calls the **MoveNext** *method* of the **recordSet** object. This will move the current recordset forward by one row, automatically updating the **SPAN** to which we bound our data. Note that line 34

```
if( !recordSet.EOF )
```

checks to make sure that the boolean **EOF** property of the **recordSet** is not **true**. If it were, that would indicate that we had reached the end of the data source.

Common Programming Error 23.2

*Trying to use the **MoveNext** or **MovePrevious** methods past the boundaries of the data source creates a JavaScript error.*

If **EOF** is **true**, line 37

```
recordSet.MoveFirst();
```

uses the **MoveFirst** *method* to move back to the first recordset in the file.

23.3 Moving a Recordset

Most applications will probably need more functionality than simply moving forward. Figure 23.3 demonstrates creating a user interface for moving throughout a data source.

```
1   <!DOCTYPE html PUBLIC "-//W3C//DTD HTML 4.0 Transitional//EN">
2   <HTML>
3
4   <!-- Fig 23.3: moving.html       -->
5   <!-- Moving through a recordset -->
6
7   <HEAD>
8   <TITLE>Dynamic Recordset Viewing</TITLE>
9   <OBJECT ID = "Colors"
10     CLASSID = "CLSID:333C7BC4-460F-11D0-BC04-0080C7055A83">
11     <PARAM NAME = "DataURL" VALUE = "HTMLStandardColors.txt">
12     <PARAM NAME = "UseHeader" VALUE = "TRUE">
13     <PARAM NAME = "TextQualifier" VALUE = "@">
14     <PARAM NAME = "FieldDelim" VALUE = "|">
15   </OBJECT>
16
17   <SCRIPT LANGUAGE = "JavaScript">
18     var recordSet = Colors.recordset;
19
20     function update()
21     {
22         h1Title.style.color = colorRGB.innerText;
23     }
24
25     function move( whereTo )
26     {
27         switch ( whereTo ) {
28
29            case "first":
30               recordSet.MoveFirst();
31               update();
32               break;
33
34            // If recordset is at beginning, move to end.
35            case "previous":
36
37               if ( recordSet.BOF )
38                  recordSet.MoveLast();
39               else
40                  recordSet.MovePrevious();
41
42               update();
43               break;
44
45            // If recordset is at end, move to beginning.
46            case "next":
47
48               if ( recordSet.EOF )
49                  recordSet.MoveFirst();
50               else
51                  recordSet.MoveNext();
52
```

Fig. 23.3   Moving through a recordset using JavaScript (part 1 of 3).

```
53                  update();
54                  break;
55
56              case "last":
57                  recordSet.MoveLast();
58                  update();
59                  break;
60          }
61      }
62
63  </SCRIPT>
64
65  <STYLE TYPE = "text/css">
66    INPUT { background-color: khaki;
67            color: green;
68            font-weight: bold }
69  </STYLE>
70  </HEAD>
71
72  <BODY STYLE = "background-color: darkkhaki">
73
74  <H1 STYLE = "color: black" ID = "h1Title">HTML Color Table</H1>
75
76  <SPAN STYLE = "position: absolute; left: 200; width: 270;
77      border-style: groove; text-align: center;
78      background-color: cornsilk; padding: 10">
79  <STRONG>Color Name: </STRONG>
80  <SPAN ID = "colorName" STYLE = "font-family: monospace"
81      DATASRC = "#Colors" DATAFLD = "ColorName">ABC</SPAN><BR>
82
83  <STRONG>Color RGB Value: </STRONG>
84  <SPAN ID = "colorRGB" STYLE = "font-family: monospace"
85      DATASRC = "#Colors" DATAFLD = "ColorHexRGBValue">ABC
86  </SPAN><BR>
87
88  <INPUT TYPE = "button" VALUE = "First"
89      ONCLICK = "move( 'first' );">
90
91  <INPUT TYPE = "button" VALUE = "Previous"
92      ONCLICK = "move( 'previous' );">
93
94  <INPUT TYPE = "button" VALUE = "Next"
95      ONCLICK = "move( 'next' );">
96
97  <INPUT TYPE = "button" VALUE = "Last"
98      ONCLICK = "move( 'last' );">
99  </SPAN>
100
101  </BODY>
102  </HTML>
```

Fig. 23.3   Moving through a recordset using JavaScript (part 2 of 3).

Fig. 23.3   Moving through a recordset using JavaScript (part 3 of 3).

The **switch** on lines 27 through 60 handles the commands issued by clicking the buttons. The two new functions we use are **MoveLast** and **MovePrevious**, which are self-explanatory.

Line 37

```
if( recordSet.BOF )
```

determines if the recordset is pointing to the beginning of the file (**BOF**), so that we can redirect it. This is for the same reason that we checked for **EOF** in Fig. 23.2—using the **MovePrevious** when the recordset points to the first record in a data file that causes an error.

23.4 Binding to an **IMG**

Many different types of HTML elements can be bound to data sources. In Fig. 23.5 we bind an **IMG** element to the data source shown in Fig. 23.4.

```
1   image
2   numbers/0.gif
3   numbers/1.gif
4   numbers/2.gif
5   numbers/3.gif
6   numbers/4.gif
7   numbers/5.gif
8   numbers/6.gif
9   numbers/7.gif
10  numbers/8.gif
11  numbers/9.gif
```

Fig. 23.4   The **images.txt** data source file for Fig. 23.5 .

```
1   <!DOCTYPE html PUBLIC "-//W3C//DTD HTML 4.0 Transitional//EN">
2   <HTML>
3
4   <!-- Fig. 23.5: bindimg.html   -->
5   <!-- Binding data to an image -->
6
7   <HEAD>
8   <TITLE>Binding to a IMG</TITLE>
9
10  <OBJECT ID = "Images"
11     CLASSID = "CLSID:333C7BC4-460F-11D0-BC04-0080C7055A83">
12     <PARAM NAME = "DataURL" VALUE = "images.txt">
13     <PARAM NAME = "UseHeader" VALUE = "True">
14  </OBJECT>
15
16  <SCRIPT LANGUAGE = "JavaScript">
17
18     recordSet = Images.recordset;
19
20     function move( whereTo )
21     {
22        switch( whereTo ) {
23
24           case "first":
25              recordSet.MoveFirst();
26              break;
27
28           case "previous":
29
30              if ( recordSet.BOF )
31                 recordSet.MoveLast();
32              else
33                 recordSet.MovePrevious();
34
35              break;
36
37           case "next":
38
39              if ( recordSet.EOF )
40                 recordSet.MoveFirst();
41              else
42                 recordSet.MoveNext();
43
44              break;
45
46           case "last":
47              recordSet.MoveLast();
48              break;
49        }
50     }
51
52  </SCRIPT>
53  </HEAD>
```

Fig. 23.5   Binding data to an **IMG** element (part 1 of 2).

```
54
55   <BODY>
56
57   <IMG DATASRC = "#Images" DATAFLD = "image"
58      STYLE = "position: relative; left: 45px"><BR>
59
60   <INPUT TYPE = "button" VALUE = "First"
61      ONCLICK = "move( 'first' );">
62
63   <INPUT TYPE = "button" VALUE = "Previous"
64      ONCLICK = "move( 'previous' );">
65
66   <INPUT TYPE = "button" VALUE = "Next"
67      ONCLICK = "move( 'next' );">
68
69   <INPUT TYPE = "button" VALUE = "Last"
70      ONCLICK = "move( 'last' );">
71
72   </BODY>
73   </HTML>
```

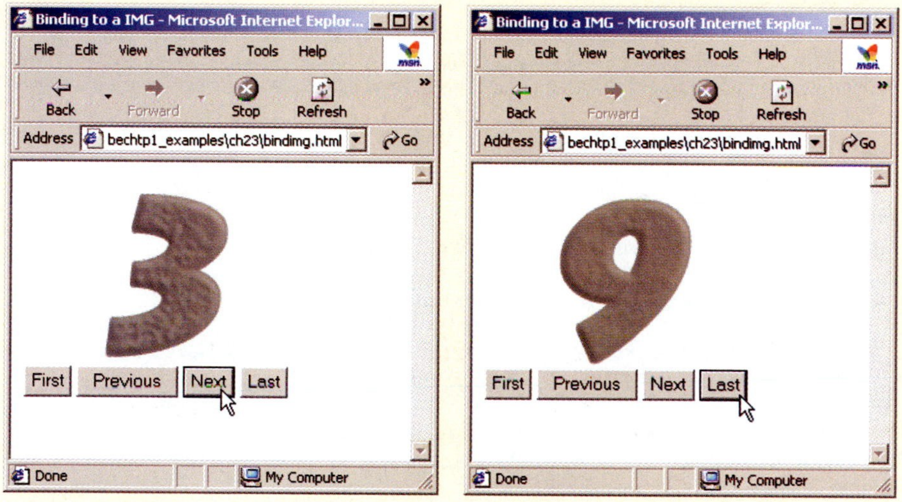

Fig. 23.5   Binding data to an **IMG** element (part 2 of 2).

Lines 57 and 58

```
<IMG DATASRC = "#Images" DATAFLD = "image"
   STYLE = "position: relative; left: 45px"><BR>
```

bind our data source to an **IMG** element. When binding to an **IMG** element, changing the recordset updates the **SRC** attribute of the image. Thus, clicking any of the navigation buttons under the image changes the image displayed on screen.

23.5 Binding to a TABLE

Binding data to a **TABLE** element (Fig. 23.6) is perhaps the most useful feature of data binding. This is done somewhat differently from the data binding we have seen thus far.

Lines 22 and 23

```
<TABLE DATASRC = "#Colors" STYLE = "border-style: ridge;
    border-color: darkseagreen; background-color: lightcyan">
```

begin binding the table by adding the **DATASRC** attribute to the opening **TABLE** tag. We complete the data binding in lines 34 through 36

```
<TD><SPAN DATAFLD = "ColorName"></SPAN></TD>
<TD><SPAN DATAFLD = "ColorHexRGBValue"
    STYLE = "font-family: monospace"></SPAN></TD>
```

```
1    <!DOCTYPE html PUBLIC "-//W3C//DTD HTML 4.0 Transitional//EN">
2    <HTML>
3
4    <!-- Fig 23.6: tablebind.html        -->
5    <!-- Using Data Binding with tables -->
6
7    <HEAD>
8    <TITLE>Data Binding and Tables</TITLE>
9    <OBJECT ID = "Colors"
10       CLASSID = "CLSID:333C7BC4-460F-11D0-BC04-0080C7055A83">
11       <PARAM NAME = "DataURL" VALUE = "HTMLStandardColors.txt">
12       <PARAM NAME = "UseHeader" VALUE = "TRUE">
13       <PARAM NAME = "TextQualifier" VALUE = "@">
14       <PARAM NAME = "FieldDelim" VALUE = "|">
15   </OBJECT>
16   </HEAD>
17
18   <BODY STYLE = "background-color: darkseagreen">
19
20   <H1>Binding Data to a <CODE>TABLE</CODE></H1>
21
22   <TABLE DATASRC = "#Colors" STYLE = "border-style: ridge;
23       border-color: darkseagreen; background-color: lightcyan">
24
25       <THEAD>
26       <TR STYLE = "background-color: mediumslateblue">
27          <TH>Color Name</TH>
28          <TH>Color RGB Value</TH>
29       </TR>
30       </THEAD>
31
32       <TBODY>
33          <TR STYLE = "background-color: lightsteelblue">
34             <TD><SPAN DATAFLD = "ColorName"></SPAN></TD>
35             <TD><SPAN DATAFLD = "ColorHexRGBValue"
36                 STYLE = "font-family: monospace"></SPAN></TD>
37          </TR>
38       </TBODY>
39
40   </TABLE>
41
```

Fig. 23.6   Binding data to a **TABLE** element (part 1 of 2).

```
42    </BODY>
43    </HTML>
```

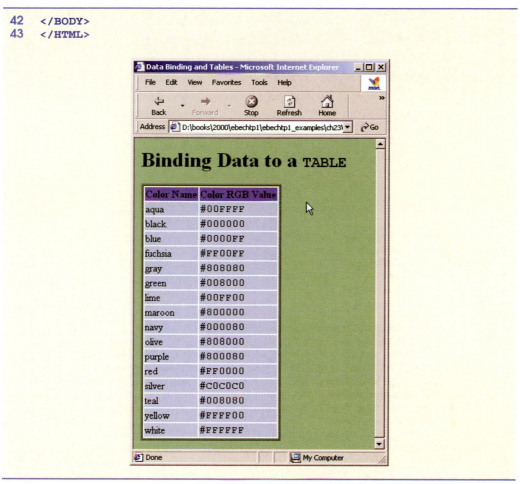

Fig. 23.6   Binding data to a **TABLE** element (part 2 of 2).

by adding the **DATAFLD** attribute to **SPAN** tags that reside in the table cells. Note that in the file we only have one row of table cells—Internet Explorer iterates through the data file, and creates a table row for each record it finds.

23.6 Sorting TABLE Data

If you are working with a large data source, your client will probably need some way to sort the data. This is accomplished with the **Sort** *property* of the TDC (Fig 23.7).

```
1    <!DOCTYPE html PUBLIC "-//W3C//DTD HTML 4.0 Transitional//EN">
2    <HTML>
3
```

Fig. 23.7   Sorting data in a **TABLE** (part 1 of 3).

```
 4   <!-- Fig 23.7: sorting.html -->
 5   <!-- Sorting TABLE data      -->
 6
 7   <HEAD>
 8   <TITLE>Data Binding and Tables</TITLE>
 9   <OBJECT ID = "Colors"
10      CLASSID = "CLSID:333C7BC4-460F-11D0-BC04-0080C7055A83">
11      <PARAM NAME = "DataURL" VALUE = "HTMLStandardColors.txt">
12      <PARAM NAME = "UseHeader" VALUE = "TRUE">
13      <PARAM NAME = "TextQualifier" VALUE = "@">
14      <PARAM NAME = "FieldDelim" VALUE = "|">
15   </OBJECT>
16   </HEAD>
17
18   <BODY STYLE = "background-color: darkseagreen">
19
20   <H1>Sorting Data</H1>
21
22   <TABLE DATASRC = "#Colors" STYLE = "border-style: ridge;
23      border-color: darkseagreen; background-color: lightcyan">
24      <CAPTION>
25      Sort by:
26
27      <SELECT ONCHANGE = "Colors.Sort = this.value;
28         Colors.Reset();">
29         <OPTION VALUE = "ColorName">Color Name (Ascending)
30         <OPTION VALUE = "-ColorName">Color Name (Descending)
31         <OPTION VALUE = "ColorHexRGBValue">Color RGB Value
32            (Ascending)
33         <OPTION VALUE = "-ColorHexRGBValue">Color RGB Value
34            (Descending)
35      </SELECT>
36      </CAPTION>
37
38      <THEAD>
39      <TR STYLE = "background-color: mediumslateblue">
40         <TH>Color Name</TH>
41         <TH>Color RGB Value</TH>
42      </TR>
43      </THEAD>
44
45      <TBODY>
46      <TR STYLE = "background-color: lightsteelblue">
47         <TD><SPAN DATAFLD = "ColorName"></SPAN></TD>
48         <TD><SPAN DATAFLD = "ColorHexRGBValue"
49            STYLE = "font-family: monospace"></SPAN></TD>
50      </TR>
51      </TBODY>
52
53   </TABLE>
54
55   </BODY>
56   </HTML>
```

Fig. 23.7   Sorting data in a **TABLE** (part 2 of 3).

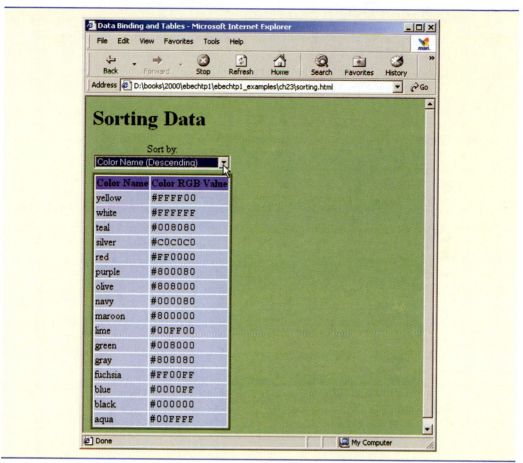

Fig. 23.7 Sorting data in a **TABLE** (part 3 of 3).

Lines 27 and 28

```
<SELECT ONCHANGE = "Colors.Sort = this.value;
    Colors.Reset();">
```

sort our data by specifying the column by which to sort in the **Sort** property of the TDC.
This example sets property **Sort** to the value of the selected **OPTION** tag (**this.value**)
when the **ONCHANGE** event is fired. JavaScript keyword **this** refers to the element in
which the statement resides (i.e., the **SELECT** element). Therefore, the **value** property refers to the currently selected **OPTION** tag. After setting the **Sort** property, we invoke the
Reset *method* of the TDC to display our data in its new sort order.

Lines 29 and 30

```
<OPTION VALUE = "ColorName">Color Name (Ascending)
<OPTION VALUE = "-ColorName">Color Name (Descending)
```

set the **VALUE** attributes of the **OPTION** tags to the column names in our data file. By default, a column will be sorted in ascending order. To sort in descending order, the column
name is preceded with a minus sign (**-**).

23.7 Advanced Sorting and Filtering

The TDC allows for sorting by multiple columns. Combined with *filtering*, this provides a powerful means of data rendering (Fig. 23.9).

Note that line 16

```
<PARAM NAME = "Sort" VALUE = "+Title">
```

sets the **Sort** property of the TDC using a **PARAM** tag instead of scripting. This is useful for providing an initial sorting order (in this case alphabetically by **Title**).

Line 28

```
SPAN     { cursor: hand; }
```

introduces the **cursor** CSS attribute, which specifies what the mouse cursor will look like when hovering over an object. In this case we set the property to **hand** (the same hand that appears when you move your cursor over a link). This lets the user know that a **SPAN** is clickable when the cursor is moved over it.

When a user clicks the **Ascending** or **Descending** links in any of the column heads, the table resorts by that column. To do this, each column head has an associated **ONCLICK** event that calls the **reSort** function, passing the name of the column to sort and a boolean value that specifies the sort order (**true** for ascending, **false** for descending).

```
 1   @Title:String@|@Authors:String@|@Copyright:String@|
@Edition:String@|@Type:String@
 2   @C How to Program@|@Deitel,Deitel@|@1992@|@1@|@BK@
 3   @C How to Program@|@Deitel,Deitel@|@1994@|@2@|@BK@
 4   @C++ How to Program@|@Deitel,Deitel@|@1994@|@1@|@BK@
 5   @C++ How to Program@|@Deitel,Deitel@|@1998@|@2@|@BK@
 6   @Java How to Program@|@Deitel,Deitel@|@1997@|@1@|@BK@
 7   @Java How to Program@|@Deitel,Deitel@|@1998@|@2@|@BK@
 8   @Java How to Program@|@Deitel,Deitel@|@2000@|@3@|@BK@
 9   @Visual Basic 6 How to Program@|@Deitel,Deitel,Nieto@|@1999@|
@1@|@BK@
10   @Internet and World Wide Web How to Program@|@Deitel,Deitel@|
@2000@|@1@|@BK@
11   @The Complete C++ Training Course@|@Deitel,Deitel@|@1996@|
@1@|@BKMMCD@
12   @The Complete C++ Training Course@|@Deitel,Deitel@|@1998@|
@2@|@BKMMCD@
13   @The Complete Java Training Course@|@Deitel,Deitel@|@1997@|
@1@|@BKMMCD@
14   @The Complete Java Training Course@|@Deitel,Deitel@|@1998@|
@2@|@BKMMCD@
15   @The Complete Java Training Course@|@Deitel,Deitel@|@2000@|
@3@|@BKMMCD@
16   @The Complete Visual Basic 6 Training Course@|
@Deitel,Deitel,Nieto@|@1999@|@1@|@BKMMCD@
17   @The Complete Internet and World Wide Web Programming Training
Course@|@Deitel,Deitel@|@2000@|@1@|@BKMMCD@
```

Fig. 23.8   DBPublications.txt data file for Fig. 23.9.

```
1    <!DOCTYPE html PUBLIC "-//W3C//DTD HTML 4.0 Transitional//EN">
2    <HTML>
3
4    <!-- Fig 23.9: advancedsort.html -->
5    <!-- Sorting and filtering data   -->
6
7    <HEAD>
8    <TITLE>Data Binding - Sorting and Filtering</TITLE>
9
10   <OBJECT ID = "Publications"
11      CLASSID = "CLSID:333C7BC4-460F-11D0-BC04-0080C7055A83">
12      <PARAM NAME = "DataURL" VALUE = "DBPublications.txt">
13      <PARAM NAME = "UseHeader" VALUE = "TRUE">
14      <PARAM NAME = "TextQualifier" VALUE = "@">
15      <PARAM NAME = "FieldDelim" VALUE = "|">
16      <PARAM NAME = "Sort" VALUE = "+Title">
17   </OBJECT>
18
19   <STYLE>
20
21   A        { font-size: 9pt;
22                text-decoration: underline;
23                cursor: hand;
24                color: blue }
25
26   CAPTION { cursor: hand; }
27
28   SPAN     { cursor: hand; }
29
30   </STYLE>
31
32   <SCRIPT LANGUAGE = "JavaScript">
33      var sortOrder;
34
35      function reSort( column, order )
36      {
37         if ( order )
38            sortOrder = "";
39         else
40            sortOrder = "-";
41
42         if ( event.ctrlKey ) {
43            Publications.Sort += "; " + sortOrder + column;
44            Publications.Reset();
45         }
46         else {
47            Publications.Sort = sortOrder + column;
48            Publications.Reset();
49         }
50
51         spanSort.innerText = "Current sort: " + Publications.Sort;
52      }
53
```

Fig. 23.9   Advanced sorting and filtering (part 1 of 4).

```
54      function filter( filterText, filterColumn )
55      {
56          Publications.Filter = filterColumn + "=" + filterText;
57          Publications.Reset();
58          spanFilter.innerText =
59             "Current filter: " + Publications.Filter;
60      }
61
62      function clearAll()
63      {
64          Publications.Sort = " ";
65          spanSort.innerText = "Current sort: None";
66          Publications.Filter = " ";
67          spanFilter.innerText = "Current filter: None";
68          Publications.Reset();
69      }
70   </SCRIPT>
71   </HEAD>
72
73   <BODY>
74   <H1>Advanced Sorting</H1>
75   Click on the link next to a column head to sort by that column.
76   To sort by more than one column at a time, hold down CTRL while
77   you click another sorting link. Click on any cell to filter by
78   the data of that cell. To clear filters and sorts, click on the
79   green caption bar.
80
81   <TABLE DATASRC = "#Publications" BORDER = 1 CELLSPACING = 0
82      CELLPADDING = 2 STYLE = "background-color: papayawhip;">
83
84      <CAPTION STYLE = "background-color: lightgreen; padding: 5"
85         ONCLICK = "clearAll()">
86         <SPAN ID = "spanFilter" STYLE = "font-weight: bold;
87            background-color: lavender">Current filter: None
88            </SPAN>
89         <SPAN ID = "spanSort" STYLE = "font-weight: bold;
90            background-color: khaki">Current sort: None</SPAN>
91      </CAPTION>
92
93      <THEAD>
94      <TR>
95         <TH>Title <BR>
96            (<A ONCLICK = "reSort( 'Title', true )">
97               Ascending</A>
98            <A ONCLICK = "reSort( 'Title', false )">
99               Descending</A>)
100        </TH>
101
102        <TH>Authors <BR>
103           (<A ONCLICK = "reSort( 'Authors', true )">
104              Ascending</A>
105           <A ONCLICK = "reSort( 'Authors', false )">
106              Descending</A>)
```

Fig. 23.9   Advanced sorting and filtering (part 2 of 4).

```
107          </TH>
108
109          <TH>Copyright <BR>
110             (<A ONCLICK = "reSort( 'Copyright', true )">
111                Ascending</A>
112             <A ONCLICK = "reSort( 'Copyright', false )">
113                Descending</A>)
114          </TH>
115
116          <TH>Edition <BR>
117             (<A ONCLICK = "reSort( 'Edition', true )">
118                Ascending</A>
119             <A ONCLICK = "reSort( 'Edition', false )">
120                Descending</A>)
121          </TH>
122
123          <TH>Type <BR>
124             (<A ONCLICK = "reSort( 'Type', true )">
125                Ascending</A>
126             <A ONCLICK = "reSort( 'Type', false )">
127                Descending</A>)
128          </TH>
129       </TR>
130       </THEAD>
131
132       <TR>
133          <TD><SPAN DATAFLD = "Title" ONCLICK =
134             "filter( this.innerText, 'Title' )"></SPAN></A>
135          </TD>
136
137          <TD><SPAN DATAFLD = "Authors" ONCLICK =
138             "filter( this.innerText, 'Authors')"></SPAN>
139          </TD>
140
141          <TD><SPAN DATAFLD = "Copyright" ONCLICK =
142             "filter( this.innerText, 'Copyright' )"></SPAN>
143          </TD>
144
145          <TD><SPAN DATAFLD = "Edition" ONCLICK =
146             "filter( this.innerText, 'Edition' )"></SPAN>
147          </TD>
148
149          <TD><SPAN DATAFLD = "Type" ONCLICK =
150             "filter( this.innerText, 'Type' )"></SPAN>
151          </TD>
152
153       </TR>
154
155    </TABLE>
156
157    </BODY>
158    </HTML>
```

Fig. 23.9   Advanced sorting and filtering (part 3 of 4).

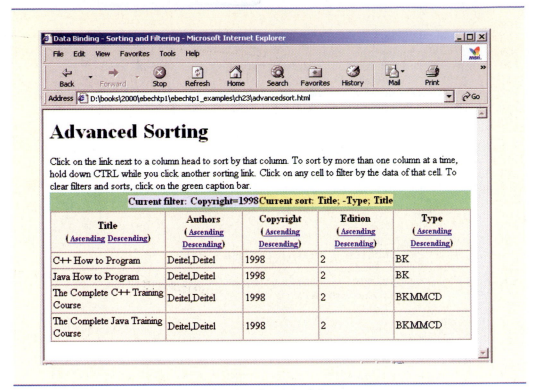

Fig. 23.9 Advanced sorting and filtering (part 4 of 4).

The user can sort by multiple columns by holding *CTRL* while clicking a link. Line 42

```
if ( event.ctrlKey )
```

checks the boolean value **event.ctrlKey**, which returns **true** if *CTRL* was pressed when the event was triggered. If the user did press *CTRL*, line 43

```
Publications.Sort += "; " + sortOrder + column;
```

adds another sort criterion to property **Sort**, separated from the first with a semicolon (**"; "**).

The **Filter** property allows you to filter out all records that do not have a cell matching the text you specify. It should be in the format *ColumnName = FilterText*. In this example, the user can click on any cell to filter by the text inside that cell. Any cell, when clicked, calls the **filter** function, passing as parameters the text of the cell (**this.innerText**) and the column by which to filter. In the **filter** function, line 56

```
Publications.Filter = filterColumn + "=" + filterText;
```

sets the **Filter** property of the TDC to the column and text by which that column should be filtered. In this case the filter tests for equality using the equality operator **=** (which is different from the JavaScript equality operator **==**). Any of the normal equality operators (**=, <>**) and relational operators (**>, <, >=, <=**) may be used for filtering.

23.8 Data Binding Elements

Exactly how a data source is displayed by the browser depends on the HTML element the data is bound to—different elements may use the data for different purposes. Figure 23.10 lists some elements that can be bound to data with the TDC, and the attributes of those elements that reflect data changes.

23.9 Internet and the World Wide Web Resources

www.microsoft.com/data
The Microsoft *Universal Data Access Technologies* Web site provides information about Microsoft database access strategies and data source objects.

www.msdn.microsoft.com/resources/schurmandhtml.asp
This Web site for the Microsoft Press book for *Dynamic HTML in Action, Second Edition* (by Eric M. Schurman and William J. Pardi) provides information about Dynamic HTML and Microsoft database access.

SUMMARY

- With data binding, data need no longer reside exclusively on the server. The data can be maintained on the client and in a manner that distinguishes that data from the HTML code on the page.
- If you need to access the database directly and have changes you make on the client to update the original database, you can use Microsoft's Remote Data Services.

Element	Bindable property/attribute
A	HREF
DIV	Contained text
FRAME	HREF
IFRAME	HREF
IMG	SRC
INPUT TYPE = "button"	VALUE (button text)
INPUT TYPE = "checkbox"	CHECKED (use a boolean value in the data)
INPUT TYPE = "hidden"	VALUE
INPUT TYPE = "password"	VALUE
INPUT TYPE = "radio"	CHECKED (use a boolean value in the data)
INPUT TYPE = "text"	VALUE
MARQUEE	Contained text
PARAM	VALUE
SELECT	Selected OPTION
SPAN	Contained text
TABLE	Cell elements (see Section 23.6)
TEXTAREA	Contained text (VALUE)

Fig. 23.10 HTML elements that allow data binding.

- Once the data is available on the client, the Web application designer can provide various functionality, especially the ability to sort and filter the data in various ways.

- When a Web page is loaded with data-bound elements, the client retrieves the data from the data source specified by the TDC. The data is then formatted for display on the Web page and remains accessible on the client.

- The Tabular Data Control (TDC) is an ActiveX control that can be added to the page with an **OBJECT** tag.

- A header row in a data source specifies the names of the columns. The data in each field can be encapsulated in text qualifiers and the fields are separated with a field delimiter.

- An **OBJECT** tag is used to insert the ActiveX Tabular Data Control. The **CLASSID** attribute specifies the ActiveX control identifier.

- The **PARAM** tag specifies parameters for the object in the **OBJECT** tag. The **NAME** attribute is the parameter name, and the **VALUE** attribute is the value. The **DataURL** parameter is the URL of the data source. The **UseHeader** parameter specifies that the first line of the data file have a header row when set to **TRUE**. The **TextQualifier** parameter sets the text qualifier of our data. The **FieldDelim** parameter sets the field delimiter of our data.

- The **DATASRC** attribute refers to the **ID** of the TDC object, and the **DATAFLD** attribute specifies the name of the field to bind it to (**ColorName**, in this case).

- A recordset is simply a set of data—in our case, it is the current row of data from the data source.

- The **MoveNext** method moves the current recordset forward by one row, automatically updating the **bound** element.

- The **EOF** property indicates whether the recordset has reached the end of the data source.

- The **MoveFirst** method moves the recordset to the first row in the file.

- The **BOF** property indicates whether the recordset points to the first row of the data source.

- When binding to an **IMG** element, changing the recordset updates the **SRC** attribute of the image.

- To bind to a table, add the **DATASRC** attribute to the opening **TABLE** tag. Then add the **DATAFLD** attribute to **SPAN** tags that reside in the table cells. Internet Explorer iterates through the data file, and creates a table row for each row it finds.

- The **Sort** property of the ActiveX control determines by what column the data is sorted. Once the **Sort** property is set, call the **Reset** method to display the data in its new sort order. By default, a column will be sorted in ascending order—to sort in descending order, the column name is preceded with a minus sign (-).

- Setting the **Sort** property of the TDC using a **PARAM** tag instead of scripting is useful for providing an initial sorting order.

- The **cursor** CSS attribute specifies what the mouse cursor will look like when hovering over an object. The value **hand** makes the mouse appear as the same hand that appears when you move your cursor over a link.

- The boolean value **event.ctrlKey** returns **true** if *CTRL* was held down when the event was triggered.

- An additional sort criterion can be added to the **Sort** property, separated from the first with a semicolon.

- The **Filter** property allows you to filter out all records that do not have a cell that matches the text you specify. It should be in the format *ColumnName = FilterText*.

- Any of the normal equality operators (**=**, **<>**) and relational operators (**>**, **<**, **>=**, **<=**) can be used for filtering.

TERMINOLOGY

ActiveX control
ascending sort order
ASP (Active Server Pages)
binding
BOF (beginning-of-file) property of **recordset**
bound elements
CLASSID property
column in a database
current record of a **recordset**
data binding
data source
data source object (DSO)
data-bound elements
database
DATAFLD attribute
DATASRC attribute
DataURL property of Tabular Data Control
descending sort order
DSO (data source object)
EOF (end-of-file) property of **recordset**
field delimiter
field of a record
FieldDelim property of Tabular Data Control

filter data
Filter property of Tabular Data Control
header row
minus sign (-) for descending sort order
Move methods
MoveFirst method of **recordset**
MoveLast method of **recordset**
MoveNext method of **recordset**
MovePrevious method of **recordset**
multicolumn sort
record
recordset
Remote Data Services (RDS)
sort in ascending order
sort in descending order
Sort property of Tabular Data Control
Tabular Data Control (**CLSID:333C7BC4-**
460F-11D0-BC04-0080C7055A83)
Tabular Data Control (TDC) DSO of IE5
text qualifier
TextQualifer property of TDC
UseHeader property of Tabular Data Control

SELF-REVIEW EXERCISES

23.1 Answer the following questions true or false; if false, state why:
  a) A TDC recordset is one row of data.
  b) You can bind any HTML element to data sources.
  c) The **CLASSID** attribute for the TDC never changes.
  d) **SPAN** elements display bound data as inner text.
  e) **IMG** elements display bound data as **ALT** text.
  f) You separate multiple sort criteria of the **Sort** property with a comma (**,**).
  g) The equality operator (**=**) is the only operator that can be used in filtering data.
  h) Calling **MoveNext** when **EOF** is true will move the recordset to the first row of data.
  i) Calling **MoveLast** when **EOF** is true causes an error.

23.2 Fill in the blank for each of the following:
  a) When binding data to a table, the _____ attribute is placed in the opening **TABLE**
      tag and the _____ attribute is placed inside the table cells.
  b) The TDC is an _____ control.
  c) To sort in descending order, precede the sort criterion with a _____.
  d) To display data with recently applied sorting, call the _____ method.
  e) The _____ parameter specifies that the data source has a header row.
  f) A _____ encapsulates text in a data source and a _____ separates fields in a
      data source.
  g) The _____ CSS property changes the appearance of the mouse cursor.

ANSWERS TO SELF-REVIEW EXERCISES

23.1   a) True. b) False; only some HTML elements may be bound to data (Fig. 23.1). c) True. d) True. e) False; data bound to **IMG** elements affects the **SRC** attribute of that **IMG**. f) False; you separate them with a semicolon (**;**). g) False; any of the equality operators or relational operators can be used. h) False; this causes an error. i) False; the recordset will move to the last row of data.

23.2   a) **DATASRC, DATAFLD**. b) ActiveX. c) minus sign. (**-**). d) **Reset**. e) **UseHeader**. f) text qualifier, field delimiter. g) **cursor**.

EXERCISES

23.3   Create a data source file with two columns: one for URLs, and one for URL descriptions. Bind the first column to an **A** element on a page and the second to a **SPAN** element contained within the **A** element.

23.4   Bind the data source file you created in Exercise 23.3 to a **TABLE** to create a table of clickable links.

23.5   Add a dropdown **SELECT** list to Fig. 23.9 that allows you to choose the binary operator used for filter matching, from any of **=, >, <, >=** or **<=**.

23.6   Create a data source with a set of name/password pairs. Bind these fields to an **INPUT TYPE = "text"** and **INPUT TYPE = "password"** and provide navigation buttons to allow the user to move throughout the data source.

23.7   Apply the transitions you learned in Chapter 22 to Fig. 23.5 to create a virtual slideshow.

24

Dynamic HTML: Client-Side Scripting with VBScript

Objectives

- To become familiar with the VBScript language.
- To use VBScript keywords, operators and functions to write client-side scripts.
- To be able to write **Sub** and **Function** procedures.
- To use VBScript arrays and regular expressions.
- To be able to write VBScript abstract data types called **Class**es.
- To be able to create objects from **Class**es.
- To be able to write **Property Let**, **Property Get** and **Property Set** procedures.

When they call the roll in the Senate, the senators do not know whether to answer "present" or "not guilty."
Theodore Roosevelt

While I nodded, nearly napping,
suddenly there came a tapping,
As of someone gently rapping, rapping at my chamber door.
Edgar Allan Poe

Basic research is what I am doing when I don't know what I am doing.
Wernher von Braun

A problem is a chance for you to do your best.
Duke Ellington

Everything comes to him who hustles while he waits.
Thomas Alva Edison

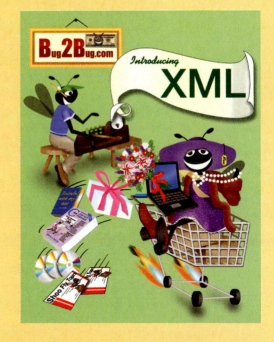

Outline

24.1 Introduction

Visual Basic Script (VBScript) is a subset of Microsoft Visual Basic® used in World Wide Web HTML documents to enhance the functionality of a Web page displayed in a Web browser. Microsoft's Internet Explorer Web browser contains a *VBScript scripting engine* (i.e., an interpreter) that executes VBScript code. In this chapter, we introduce client-side VBScript for use in HTML documents. Because JavaScript has become the de facto client-side scripting language in industry, you are not likely to use client-side VBScript.

Earlier in the text we used JavaScript to introduce fundamental computer programming concepts in the context of HTML documents and the World Wide Web. In this chapter, we overview VBScript, which provides capabilities similar to those of JavaScript. The material presented in this chapter is valuable for two reasons. First, company Intranets tend to standardize on a particular Web browser, and, if that browser is Internet Explorer, the VBScript techniques introduced in this chapter can readily be used on the client side to enhance HTML documents. Second, VBScript is particularly valuable when used with Microsoft Web servers to create *Active Server Pages* (*ASP*)—a technology that allows a server-side script to create dynamic content that is sent to the client's browser. Although other scripting languages can be used, VBScript is the de facto language for ASP. You will learn about ASP in Chapters 25 and 26.

24.2 Operators

VBScript is a case-insensitive language that provides arithmetic operators, logical operators, concatenation operators, comparison operators and relational operators. VBScript's arithmetic operators (Fig. 24.1) are similar to the JavaScript arithmetic operators. Two major differences are the *division operator*, \, which returns an integer result and the *exponentiation operator*, ^, which raises a value to a power. [*Note*: the precedence of operators is different in JavaScript. See Appendix D, "Operator Precedence Charts," for a list of VB-Script operators and their precedences.]

Figure 24.2 lists VBScript's comparison operators. Only the symbols for the equality operator and the inequality operator are different in JavaScript. In VBScript, these comparison operators may also be used to compare strings.

VBScript operation	Arithmetic operator	Algebraic expression	VBScript expression
Addition	+	$x + y$	`x + y`
Subtraction	–	$z - 8$	`z - 8`
Multiplication	*	yb	`y * b`
Division (floating-point)	/	$v \div u$ or $\dfrac{v}{u}$	`v / u`
Division (integer)	\	none	`v \ u`
Exponentiation	^	q^p	`q ^ p`
Negation	–	$-e$	`-e`
Modulus	**Mod**	$q \bmod r$	`q Mod r`

Fig. 24.1   Arithmetic operators.

Standard algebraic equality operator or relational operator	VBScript comparison operator	Example of VBScript condition	Meaning of VBScript condition
=	=	`d = g`	**d** is equal to **g**
≠	<>	`s <> r`	**s** is not equal to **r**
>	>	`y > x`	**y** is greater than **x**
<	<	`p < m`	**p** is less than **m**
≥	>=	`c >= z`	**c** is greater than or equal to **z**
≤	<=	`m <= s`	**m** is less than or equal to **s**

Fig. 24.2   Comparison operators.

The VBScript logical operators are **And** (logical AND), **Or** (logical OR), **Not** (logical negation), **Imp** (logical implication), **Xor** (exclusive OR) and **Eqv** (logical equivalence). Figure 24.3 shows truth tables for these logical operators. *Note*: Despite the mixture of case in keywords, functions, etc., VBScript is not case-sensitive—uppercase and lowercase letters are treated the same, except, as we will see, in *character string constants* (also called *character string literals*).

Performance Tip 24.1

VBScript logical operators do not use "short-circuit" evaluation. Both conditions are always evaluated.

VBScript provides the *plus sign*, +, and *ampersand*, **&**, operators for string concatenation as follows:

```
s1 = "Pro"
s2 = "gram"
s3 = s1 & s2
```

Truth tables for VBScript Logical Operators

Logical And:
```
True And True = True
True And False = False
False And True = False
False And False = False
```

Logical Or:
```
True Or True = True
True Or False = True
False Or True = True
False Or False = False
```

Logical Imp:
```
True Imp True = True
True Imp False = False
False Imp True = True
False Imp False = True
```

Logical Eqv:
```
True Eqv True = True
True Eqv False = False
False Eqv True = False
False Eqv False = True
```

Logical Xor:
```
True Xor True = False
True Xor False = True
False Xor True = True
False Xor False = False
```

Logical Not:
```
Not True = False
Not False = True
```

Fig. 24.3   Truth tables for VBScript logical operators.

or

```
s3 = s1 + s2
```

The ampersand is more formally called the *string concatenation operator*. The above statements would concatenate (or append) **s2** to the right of **s1** to create an entirely new string, **s3**, containing **"Program"**.

If both operands of the concatenation operator are strings, these two operators can be used interchangeably; however, if the **+** operator is used in an expression consisting of varying data types, there can be a problem. For example, consider the statement

```
s1 = "hello" + 22
```

VBScript first tries to convert the string **"hello"** to a number, then add **22** to it. The string **"hello"** cannot be converted to a number, so a type mismatch error occurs at run time. For this reason, the **&** operator should be used for string concatenation.

Testing and Debugging Tip 24.1

*Always use the ampersand (**&**) operator for string concatenation.*

24.3 Data Types and Control Structures

VBScript has only one data type—*variant*—that is capable of storing different types of data (e.g., strings, integers, floating-point numbers etc.). The data types (or *variant subtypes*) a variant stores are listed in Fig. 24.4. VBScript interprets a variant in a manner that is suitable to the type of data it contains. For example, if a variant contains numeric information, it will be treated as a number; if it contains string information, it will be treated as a string.

Subtype	Range/Description
Boolean	**True** or **False**
Byte	Integer in the range 0 to 255
Currency	–922337203685477.5808 to 922337203685477.5807
Date/Time	1 January 100 to 31 December 9999 0:00:00 to 23:59:59.
Double	–1.79769313486232E308 to –4.94065645841247E–324 (negative) 1.79769313486232E308 to 4.94065645841247E–324 (positive)
Empty	Uninitialized. This value is 0 for numeric types (e.g., double), **False** for booleans and the *empty string* (i.e., **""**) for strings.
Integer	–32768 to 32767
Long	–2147483648 to 2147483647
Object	Any object type.
Single	–3.402823E38 to –1.401298E–45 (negative) 3.402823E38 to 1.401298E–45 (positive)
String	0 to ~2000000000 characters.

Fig. 24.4   Some VBScript variant subtypes.

Software Engineering Observation 24.1

Because all variables are of type variant, the programmer does not specify a data type when declaring a variable in VBScript.

Variable names cannot be keywords and must begin with a letter. The maximum length of a variable name is 255 characters containing only letters, digits (0-9) and underscores. Variables can be declared simply by using their name in the VBScript code. The statement **Option Explicit** can be used to force all variables to be declared before they are used.

Common Programming Error 24.1

Attempting to declare a variable name that does not begin with a letter is an error.

Testing and Debugging Tip 24.2

*Forcing all variables to be declared, by using **Option Explicit**, can help eliminate various kinds of subtle errors.*

Common Programming Error 24.2

*If a variable name is misspelled (when not using **Option Explicit**), a new variable is declared, usually resulting in an error.*

VBScript provides control structures (Fig. 24.5) for controlling program execution. Many of the control structures provide the same capabilities as their JavaScript counterparts. Syntactically, every VBScript control structure ends with one or more keywords (e.g., **End If**, **Loop**, etc.). Keywords delimit a control structure's body—not curly braces (i.e., **{}**, as in JavaScript).

JavaScript Control Structure	VBScript Control Structure Equivalent
sequence	sequence
if	If/Then/End If
if/else	If/Then/Else/End If
while	While/Wend or Do While/Loop
for	For/Next
do/while	Do/Loop While
switch	Select Case/End Select
none	Do Until/Loop
none	Do/Loop Until

Fig. 24.5   Comparing VBScript control structures to JavaScript control structures.

The **If/Then/End If** and **If/Then/Else/End If** control structures behave identically to their JavaScript counterparts. VBScript's multiple selection version of **If/Then/Else/End If** uses a different syntax from JavaScript's version because it includes keyword **ElseIf** (Fig. 24.6).

Common Programming Error 24.3

*Writing an **If** control structure that does not contain keyword **Then** is an error.*

Notice that VBScript does not use a statement terminator like the semicolon (**;**) in JavaScript. Unlike in JavaScript, placing parentheses around conditions in VBScript is optional. A condition evaluates to **True** if the variant subtype is boolean **True** or if the variant subtype is considered non-zero. A condition evaluates to **False** if the variant subtype is boolean **False** or if the variant subtype is considered to be 0.

VBScript's **Select Case/End Select** structure provides all the functionality of JavaScript's **switch** structure, and more (Fig. 24.7).

JavaScript	VBScript
1 `if ( s == t )`	1 `If s = t Then`
2 `    u = s + t;`	2 `    u = s + t`
3 `else if ( s > t )`	3 `ElseIf s > t Then`
4 `    u = r;`	4 `    u = r`
5 `else`	5 `Else`
6 `    u = n;`	6 `    u = n`
	7 `End If`

Fig. 24.6   Comparing JavaScript's **if** structure to VBScript's **If** structure.

JavaScript	VBScript
| ```
1   switch ( x ) {
2      case 1:
3         alert("1");
4         break;
5      case 2:
6         alert("2");
7         break;
8      default:
9         alert("?");
10   }
``` | ```
1   Select Case x
2      Case 1
3         Call MsgBox("1")
4      Case 2
5         Call MsgBox("2")
6      Case Else
7         Call MsgBox("?")
8   End Select
``` |

Fig. 24.7   Comparing JavaScript's **switch** with VBScript's **Select Case**.

Notice that the **Select Case/End Select** structure does not require the use of a statement like **break**. One **Case** cannot accidentally run into another. The VBScript **Select Case/End Select** structure is equivalent to VBScript's **If/Then/Else/End If** multiple selection structure. The only difference is syntax. Any variant subtype can be used with the **Select Case/End Select** structure.

VBScript's *While/Wend* repetition structure and *Do While/Loop* behave identically to JavaScript's **while** repetition structure. VBScript's *Do/Loop While* structure behaves identically to JavaScript's **do/while** repetition structure.

VBScript contains two additional repetition structures, *Do Until/Loop* and *Do/ Loop Until*, that do not have direct JavaScript equivalents. Figure 24.8 shows the closest comparison between VBScript's **Do Until/Loop** structure and JavaScript's **while** structure. The **Do Until/Loop** structure loops until its condition becomes **True**. In this example, the loop terminates when **x** becomes 10. We used the condition **! (x == 10)** in JavaScript here, so both control structures have a test to determine whether **x** is **10**. The JavaScript **while** structure loops while **x** is not equal to 10 (i.e., until **x** becomes 10).

Figure 24.9 shows the closest comparison between VBScript's **Do/Loop Until** structure and JavaScript's **do/while** structure. The **Do/Loop Until** structure loops until its condition becomes **True**. In this example, the loop terminates when **x** becomes 10. Once again, we used the condition **! (x == 10)** in JavaScript here so both control structures have a test to determine if **x** is **10**. The JavaScript **do/while** structure loops while **x** is not equal to 10 (i.e., until **x** becomes 10).

JavaScript	VBScript
| ```
1   while ( !( x == 10 ) )
2      ++x;
``` | ```
1   Do Until x = 10
2      x = x + 1
3   Loop
``` |

Fig. 24.8   Comparing JavaScript's **while** to VBScript's **Do Until**.

JavaScript	VBScript
| ```
1   do {
2      ++x;
3   } while ( !( x == 10 ) );
``` | ```
1   Do
2      x = x + 1
3   Loop Until x = 10
``` |

Fig. 24.9 Comparing JavaScript's **do/while** to VBScript's **Do Loop/Until**.

Notice that these **Do Until** repetition structures iterate until the condition becomes **True**. VBScript *For* repetition structure behaves differently from JavaScript's **for** repetition structure. Consider the side-by-side comparison in Fig. 24.10.

Unlike JavaScript's **for** repetition structures condition, VBScript's **For** repetition structure's condition cannot be changed during the loop's iteration. In the JavaScript **for**/VBScript **For** loop side-by-side code comparison, the JavaScript **for** loop would iterate exactly two times, because the condition is evaluated on each iteration. The VBScript **For** loop would iterate exactly eight times because the condition is fixed as **1 To 8**—even though the value of **x** is changing in the body. VBScript **For** loops may also use the optional **Step** keyword to indicate an increment or decrement. By default, **For** loops increment in units of 1. Figure 24.11 shows a **For** loop that begins at **2** and counts to **20** in **Step**s of **2**.

Common Programming Error 24.4

*Attempting to use a relational operator in a **For/Next** loop (e.g., **For x = 1 < 10**) is an error.*

The *Exit Do* statement, when executed in a **Do While/Loop**, **Do/Loop While**, **Do Until/Loop** or **Do/Loop Until**, causes immediate exit from that structure. The fact that a **Do While/Loop** may contain **Exit Do** is the only difference, other than syntax, between **Do While/Loop** and **While/Wend**. Statement *Exit For* causes immediate exit from the **For/Next** structure. With **Exit Do** and **Exit For**, program execution continues with the first statement after the exited repetition structure.

JavaScript	VBScript
| ```
1   x = 8;
2   for ( y = 1; y < x; y++ )
3      x /= 2;
``` | ```
1   x = 8
2   For y = 1 To x
3      x = x \ 2
4   Next
``` |

Fig. 24.10 Comparing JavaScript's **for** to VBScript's **For**.

```
1   ' VBScript
2   For y = 2 To 20 Step 2
3      Call MsgBox( "y = " & y )
4   Next
```

Fig. 24.11 Using keyword **Step** in VBScript's **For** repetition structure.

Common Programming Error 24.5

*Attempting to use **Exit Do** or **Exit For** to exit a **While/Wend** repetition structure is an error.*

Common Programming Error 24.6

*Attempting to place the name of a **For** repetition structures's control variable after **Next** is an error.*

24.4 VBScript Functions

VBScript provides several predefined functions, many of which are summarized in this section. We overview variant functions, math functions, functions for interacting with the user, formatting functions and functions for obtaining information about the interpreter.

Figure 24.12 summarizes several functions that allow the programmer to determine which subtype is currently stored in a variant. VBScript provides function **IsEmpty** to determine if the variant has ever been initialized by the programmer. If **IsEmpty** returns **True** the variant has not been initialized by the programmer.

VBScript math functions allow the programmer to perform common mathematical calculations. Figure 24.13 summarizes some VBScript math functions. Note that trigonometric functions such as **Cos**, **Sin**, etc. take arguments expressed in radians. To convert from degrees to radians use the formula: *radians = degrees $\times \pi$ / 180.*

Function	Variant subtype returned	Description
IsArray	Boolean	Returns **True** if the variant subtype is an array and **False** otherwise.
IsDate	Boolean	Returns **True** if the variant subtype is a date or time and **False** otherwise.
IsEmpty	Boolean	Returns **True** if the variant subtype is **Empty** (i.e., has not been explicitly initialized by the programmer) and **False** otherwise.
IsNumeric	Boolean	Returns **True** if the variant subtype is numeric and **False** otherwise.
IsObject	Boolean	Returns **True** if the variant subtype is an object and **False** otherwise.
TypeName	String	Returns a string that provides subtype information. Some strings returned are **"Byte"**, **"Integer"**, **"Long"**, **"Single"**, **"Double"**, **"Date"**, **"Currency"**, **"String"**, **"Boolean"** and **"Empty"**.
VarType	Integer	Returns a value indicating the subtype (e.g., **0** for **Empty**, **2** for integer, **3** for long, **4** for single, **5** for double, **6** for currency, **7** for date/time, **8** for string, **9** for object, etc.).

Fig. 24.12 Some variant functions.

Function	Description	Example

`Abs(x)`	Absolute value of `x`	`Abs(-7)` is `7`
		`Abs(0)` is `0`
		`Abs(76)` is `76`

`Atn(x)`	Trigonometric arctangent of `x` (in radians)	`Atn(1)*4` is `3.14159265358979`
`Cos(x)`	Trigonometric cosine of `x` (in radians)	`Cos(0)` is `1`
`Exp(x)`	Exponential function e^x	`Exp(1.0)` is `2.71828` `Exp(2.0)` is `7.38906`

`Int(x)`	Returns the whole-number part of `x`. `Int` rounds to the next smallest number.	`Int(-5.3)` is `-6`
		`Int(0.893)` is `0`
		`Int(76.45)` is `76`

`Fix(x)`	Returns the whole-number part of `x` (*Note*: `Fix` and `Int` are different. When `x` is negative, `Int` rounds to the next smallest number, while `Fix` rounds to the next-largest number.)	`Fix(-5.3)` is `-5`
		`Fix(0.893)` is `0`
		`Fix(76.45)` is `76`

`Log(x)`	Natural logarithm of `x` (base *e*)	`Log(2.718282)` is `1.0` `Log(7.389056)` is `2.0`

`Rnd()`	Returns a pseudo-random floating-point number in the range $0 \leq$ `Rnd` < 1. Call function *Randomize* once before calling `Rnd` to get a different sequence of random numbers each time the program is run.	`Call Randomize`
		`...`
		`z = Rnd()`

`Round(x, y)`	Rounds `x` to `y` decimal places. If `y` is omitted, `x` is returned as an `Integer`.	`Round(4.844)` is `5` `Round(5.7839, 2)` is `5.78`

`Sgn(x)`	Sign of `x`	`Sgn(-1988)` is `-1`
		`Sgn(0)` is `0`
		`Sgn(3.3)` is `1`

`Sin(x)`	Trigonometric sine of `x` (in radians)	`Sin(0)` is `0`
`Sqr(x)`	Square root of `x`	`Sqr(900.0)` is `30.0` `Sqr(9.0)` is `3.0`
`Tan(x)`	Trigonometric tangent of `x` (in radians)	`Tan(0)` is `0`

Fig. 24.13 VBScript math functions.

VBScript provides two functions, **InputBox** and **MsgBox**, for interacting with the user. Function **InputBox** displays a dialog in which the user can input data. For example, the statement

```
intValue = InputBox( "Enter an integer", "Input Box", , _
                     1000, 1000 )
```

displays an *input dialog* (as shown in Fig. 24.15) containing the prompt (**"Enter an integer"**) and the caption (**"Input Box"**) at position *(1000, 1000)* on the screen. VBScript coordinates are measured in units of *twips* (1440 twips equal 1 inch). Position *(1000, 1000)* is relative to the upper-left corner of the screen, which is position *(0, 0)*. On the screen, *x* coordinates increase from left to right and *y* coordinates increase from top to bottom.

VBScript functions often take *optional arguments* (i.e., arguments that programmers can pass if they wish or that can be omitted). Notice, in the preceding call to **InputBox**, the consecutive commas (between **"Input Box"** and **1000**)—these indicate that an optional argument is being omitted. In this particular case, the optional argument corresponds to a file name for a help file—a feature we do not wish to use in this particular call to **InputBox**. Before using a VBScript function, check the VBScript documentation

msdn.microsoft.com/scripting/default.htm?/scripting/vbscript

to determine whether the function allows for optional arguments.

The *underscore character*, _, is VBScript's *line-continuation character*. A statement cannot extend beyond the current line without using this character. A statement may use as many line-continuation characters as necessary.

Common Programming Error 24.7

Splitting a statement over several lines without the line-continuation character is an error.

Common Programming Error 24.8

Placing anything, including comments, after a line-continuation character is an error.

When called, function **MsgBox** displays a *message dialog* (a sample is shown in Fig. 24.15). For example, the statement

```
Call MsgBox( "VBScript is fun!", , "Results" )
```

displays a message dialog containing the string **"VBScript is fun!"** with **"Results"** in the title bar. Although not used here, the optional argument allows the programmer to customize the **MsgBox**'s buttons (e.g., **OK**, **Yes**, etc.) and icon (e.g., question mark, exclamation point, etc.)—see the VBScript documentation for more information on these features. The preceding statement could also have been written as

```
MsgBox "VBScript is fun!", , "Results"
```

which behaves identically to the version of the statement that explicitly uses **Call**. In VBScript, function calls that wrap arguments in parentheses must be preceded with keyword *Call*—unless the function call is assigning a value to a variable, as in

```
a = Abs( z )
```

We prefer the more formal syntax that uses **Call** and parentheses to clearly indicate a function call.

VBScript provides formatting functions for currency values, dates, times, numbers and percentages. Figure 24.14 summarizes these formatting functions.

Although they are not discussed in this chapter, VBScript provides many functions for manipulating dates and times. Manipulations include adding dates, subtracting dates, parsing dates, etc. Consult the VBScript documentation for a list of these functions.

Function	Description
FormatCurrency	Returns a string formatted according to the local machine's currency **Regional Settings** (in the **Control Panel**). For example, the call **FormatCurrency("-1234.789")** returns **"($1,234.79)"** and the call **FormatCurrency(123456.789)** returns **"$123,456.79"**. Note the rounding to the right of the decimal place.
FormatDateTime	Returns a string formatted according to the local machine's date/time **Regional Settings** (in the **Control Panel**). For example, the call **FormatDateTime(Now, vbLongDate)** returns the current date in the format **"Wednesday, September 01, 1999"** and the call **FormatDateTime(Now, vbShortTime)** returns the current time in the format **"17:26"**. Function *Now* returns the local machine's time and date. Constant *vbLongDate* indicates that the day of the week, month, day and year is displayed. Constant *vbShortTime* indicates that the time is displayed in 24-hour format. Consult the VBScript documentation for additional constants that specify other date and time formats.
FormatNumber	Returns a string formatted according to the number **Regional Settings** (in the **Control Panel**) on the local machine. For example, the call **FormatNumber("3472435")** returns **"3,472,435.00"** and the call **FormatNumber(-123456.789)** returns **"-123,456.79"**. Note the rounding to the right of the decimal place.
FormatPercent	Returns a string formatted as a percentage. For example the call **FormatPercent(".789")** returns **"78.90%"** and the call **FormatPercent(0.45)** returns **"45.00%"**.

Fig. 24.14   Some VBScript formatting functions.

VBScript also provides functions for getting information about the scripting engine (i.e., the VBScript interpreter). These functions are *ScriptEngine* (which returns "JScript", "VBScript" or "VBA"), *ScriptEngineBuildVersion* (which returns the current *build version*—i.e., the identification number for the current release), *ScriptEngineMajorVersion* (which returns the major version number for the script engine) and *ScriptEngineMinorVersion* (which returns the minor release number). For example, the expression

```
ScriptEngine() & ", " & ScriptEngineBuildVersion() & ", " _
& ScriptEngineMajorVersion() & ", " & _
ScriptEngineMajorVersion()
```

evaluates to **"VBScript, 4615, 5, 5"** (where the numbers are the build version, major version and minor version of the script engine at the time of this writing).

Testing and Debugging Tip 24.3

VBScript functions ScriptEngine, ScriptEngineBuildVersion, ScriptEngineMajorVersion and ScriptEngineMinorVersion are useful if you are experiencing difficulty with the scripting engine and need to report information about the scripting engine to Microsoft.

Portability Tip 24.1

VBScript   functions   ScriptEngine,   ScriptEngineBuildVersion, ScriptEngineMajorVersion and ScriptEngineMinorVersion can be used to determine whether the browser's script engine version is different from the script engine version you used to develop the page. Older script engines do not support the latest VBScript features.

24.5 VBScript Example Programs

In this section, we present several complete VBScript "live-code" programs and show the screen inputs and outputs produced as the programs execute. The HTML document of Fig. 24.15 includes VBScript code that enables users to click a button to display an input dialog in which they can type an integer to be added into a running total. When the input dialog's **OK** button is clicked, a message dialog is displayed with a message indicating the number that was entered and the total of all the numbers entered so far.

```
1   <!DOCTYPE HTML PUBLIC "-//W3C//DTD HTML 4.0 Transitional//EN">
2   <HTML>
3   <!--Fig. 24.15: addition.html -->
4
5   <HEAD>
6   <TITLE>Our first VBScript</TITLE>
7
8   <SCRIPT LANGUAGE = "VBScript">
9   <!--
10      Option Explicit
11      Dim intTotal
12
13      Sub cmdAdd_OnClick()
14         Dim intValue
15
16         intValue = InputBox("Enter an integer", "Input Box", , _
17                            1000, 1000)
18         intTotal = CInt( intTotal ) + CInt( intValue )
19         Call MsgBox("You entered " & intValue & _
20                    "; total so far is " & intTotal, , "Results")
21      End Sub
22   -->
23   </SCRIPT>
24   </HEAD>
25
26   <BODY>
27   Click the button to add an integer to the total.
28   <HR>
29   <FORM>
30   <INPUT NAME = "cmdAdd" TYPE = "BUTTON"
31         VALUE = "Click Here to Add to the Total">
32   </FORM>
33   </BODY>
34   </HTML>
```

Fig. 24.15 Adding integers on a Web page using VBScript (part 1 of 2).

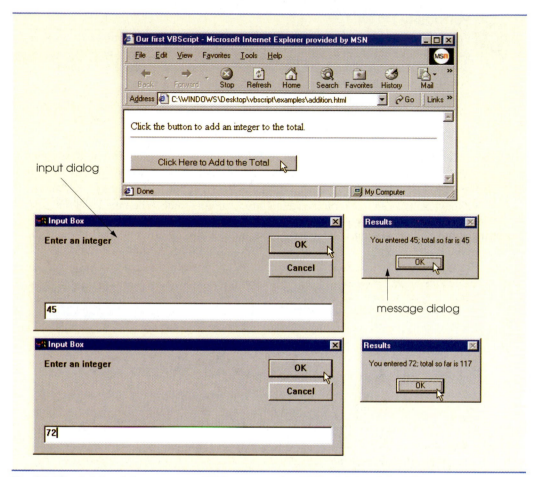

input dialog

message dialog

Fig. 24.15   Adding integers on a Web page using VBScript (part 2 of 2).

On Line 8, the HTML tag **SCRIPT** sets the **LANGUAGE** attribute to **VBScript**. This tag tells the browser to use its built-in VBScript interpreter to interpret the script code. Notice the HTML comment tags on lines 9 and 22 which appear to "comment out" the VBScript code.

If the browser understands VBScript, these HTML comments are ignored, and the VBScript is interpreted. If the browser does not understand VBScript, the HTML comment prevents the VBScript code from being displayed as text.

 Portability Tip 24.2

Always place client-side VBScript code inside HTML comments to prevent the code from being displayed as text in browsers that do not understand VBScript.

Line 10 uses the **Option Explicit** statement to force all variables in the VBScript code to be declared. Statement **Option Explicit**, if present, must be the first statement in the VBScript code. Line 11 declares variant variable **intTotal**, which is visible to all procedures within the script. Variables declared outside of procedures are called *script variables*.

Common Programming Error 24.9

Placing VBScript code before the **Option Explicit** *statement is an error.*

Lines 13 through 21 define a *procedure* (i.e., VBScript's equivalent of a function in JavaScript) called **OnClick** for the **cmdAdd** button. VBScript procedures that do not return a value begin with the keyword **Sub** (line 13) and end with the keywords **End Sub** (line 21). We will discuss VBScript procedures that return values later in this chapter. Line 14 declares the *local variable* **intValue**. Variables declared within a VBScript procedure are visible only within that procedure's body. Procedures that perform event handling (such as the **cmdAdd_OnClick** procedure in lines 13 through 21) are more properly called *event procedures.*

Line 16 calls the function **InputBox** to display an input dialog. The value entered into the input dialog is assigned to the **intValue** variable and is treated by VBScript as a string subtype. When using variants, conversion functions are often necessary to ensure that you are using the proper type. Line 18 calls VBScript function **CInt** twice to convert from the string subtype to the integer subtype. VBScript also provides conversion functions **CBool** for converting to the boolean subtype, **CByte** for converting to the byte subtype, **CCur** for converting to the currency subtype, **CDate** for converting to the date/time subtype, **CDbl** for converting to the double subtype, **CLng** for converting to the long subtype, **CSng** for converting to the single subtype and **CStr** for converting to the string subtype. Lines 19 and 20 display a message dialog indicating the last value input and the running total.

VBScript provides many predefined constants for use in your VBScript code. The constant categories include color constants, comparison constants (to specify how values are compared), date/time constants, date format constants, drive type constants, file attribute constants, file I/O constants, **MsgBox** constants, special folder constants, string constants, **VarType** constants (to help determine the type stored in a variable) and miscellaneous other constants. VBScript constants usually begin with the prefix **vb**. For a list of VBScript constants, see the VBScript documentation. You can also create your own constants by using keyword **Const**, as in

```
Const PI = 3.14159
```

Figure 24.16 provides another VBScript example. The HTML form provides a **SELECT** component, to allow the user to select a Web site from a list of sites. When the selection is made, the new Web site is displayed in the browser. Lines 30 through 35

```
<SCRIPT FOR = "SiteSelector" EVENT = "ONCHANGE"
        LANGUAGE = "VBScript">
<!--
    Document.Location = Document.Forms( 0 ).SiteSelector.Value
-->
</SCRIPT>
```

specify a VBScript. In such code, the **<SCRIPT>** tag's **FOR** attribute indicates the HTML component on which the script operates (**SiteSelector**), the **EVENT** attribute indicates the event to which the script responds (**OnChange**, which occurs when the user makes a selection) and the **LANGUAGE** attribute specifies the scripting language (**VBScript**).

```
1   <!DOCTYPE HTML PUBLIC "-//W3C//DTD HTML 4.0 Transitional//EN">
2   <HTML>
3   <!-- Fig. 24.16: site.html -->
4
5   <HEAD>
6      <TITLE>Select a site to browse</TITLE>
7   </HEAD>
8
9   <BODY>
10  Select a site to browse<P>
11  <HR>
12  <FORM>
13  <SELECT NAME = "SiteSelector" SIZE = "1">
14
15     <OPTION VALUE = "http://www.deitel.com">
16        Deitel & Associates, Inc.
17     </OPTION>
18
19     <OPTION VALUE = "http://www.prenhall.com">
20        Prentice Hall
21     </OPTION>
22
23     <OPTION VALUE = "http://www.phptr.com/phptrinteractive">
24        Prentice Hall Interactive
25     </OPTION>
26
27  </SELECT>
28
29  <!-- VBScript code -->
30  <SCRIPT FOR = "SiteSelector" EVENT = "ONCHANGE"
31          LANGUAGE = "VBScript">
32  <!--
33     Document.Location = Document.Forms( 0 ).SiteSelector.Value
34  -->
35  </SCRIPT>
36  </FORM>
37  </BODY>
38  </HTML>
```

Fig. 24.16 Using VBScript code to respond to an event (part 1 of 2).

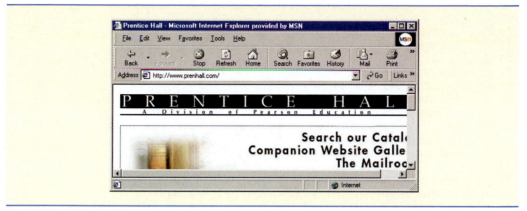

Fig. 24.16 Using VBScript code to respond to an event (part 2 of 2).

Line 33

```
Document.Location = Document.Forms( 0 ).SiteSelector.Value
```

causes the browser to change to the selected location. This line uses Internet Explorer's **Document** object to change the location. The **Document** object's *Location* property specifies the URL of the page to display. The expression **SiteSelector.Value** gets the **VALUE** of the selected **OPTION** in the **SELECT**. When the assignment is performed, Internet Explorer automatically loads and displays the Web page for the selected location.

Fig. 24.17 uses programmer-defined procedures: **Minimum**, to determine the smallest of three numbers; and **OddEven**, to determine whether the smallest number is odd or even.

```
1   <!DOCTYPE HTML PUBLIC "-//W3C//DTD HTML 4.0 Transitional//EN">
2   <HTML>
3   <!--Fig. 24.17: minimum.html -->
4
5   <HEAD>
6   <TITLE>Using VBScript Procedures</TITLE>
7
8   <SCRIPT LANGUAGE = "VBScript">
9   <!--
10      Option Explicit
11
12      ' Find the minimum value. Assume that first value is
13      ' the smallest.
14      Function Minimum( min, a, b )
15
16         If a < min Then
17            min = a
18         End If
19
20         If b < min Then
21            min = b
22         End If
```

Fig. 24.17 Program that determines the smallest of three numbers (part 1 of 2).

```
23
24          Minimum = min          ' Return value
25       End Function
26
27       Sub OddEven( n )
28          If n Mod 2 = 0 Then
29             Call MsgBox( n & " is the smallest and is even" )
30          Else
31             Call MsgBox( n & " is the smallest and is odd" )
32          End If
33       End Sub
34
35       Sub cmdButton_OnClick()
36          Dim number1, number2, number3, smallest
37
38          ' Convert each input to Long subtype
39          number1 = CLng( Document.Forms( 0 ).txtBox1.Value )
40          number2 = CLng( Document.Forms( 0 ).txtBox2.Value )
41          number3 = CLng( Document.Forms( 0 ).txtBox3.Value )
42
43          smallest = Minimum( number1, number2, number3 )
44          Call OddEven( smallest )
45       End Sub
46    -->
47    </SCRIPT>
48    </HEAD>
49
50    <BODY>
51    <FORM> Enter a number
52    <INPUT TYPE = "text" NAME = "txtBox1" SIZE = "5" VALUE = "0">
53    <P>Enter a number
54    <INPUT TYPE = "text" NAME = "txtBox2" SIZE = "5" VALUE = "0">
55    <P>Enter a number
56    <INPUT TYPE = "text" NAME = "txtBox3" SIZE = "5" VALUE = "0">
57    <P><INPUT TYPE = "BUTTON" NAME = "cmdButton" VALUE = "Enter">
58
59    </FORM>
60    </BODY>
61    </HTML>
```

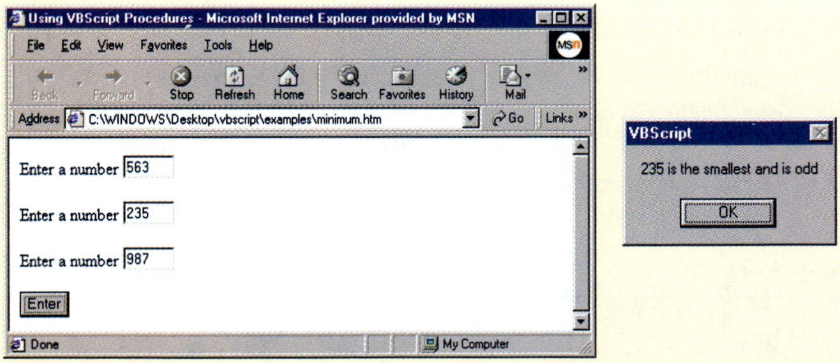

Fig. 24.17   Program that determines the smallest of three numbers (part 2 of 2).

Lines 12 and 13 are VBScript single-line comments. VBScript code is commented by either using a single quote (**'**) or the keyword **Rem** (for *remark*) before the comment. [*Note*: Keyword **Rem** can be used only at the beginning of a line of VBScript code.]

Good Programming Practice 24.1

*VBScript programmers use the single-quote character for comments. The use of **Rem** is considered archaic.*

Lines 14 through 25 define the programmer-defined procedure **Minimum**. VBScript procedures that return a value are delimited with the keywords ***Function*** (line 14) and ***End Function*** (line 25). This procedure determines the smallest of its three arguments by using **If/Then/Else** structures. A value is returned from a **Function** procedure by assigning a value to the **Function** procedure name (line 24). A **Function** procedure can return only one value.

Procedure **OddEven** (lines 27 through 33) takes one argument and displays a message dialog indicating the smallest value and whether or not it is odd or even. The modulus operator **Mod** is used to determine whether the number is odd or even. Because the data stored in the variant variable can be viewed as a number, VBScript performs any conversions between subtypes implicitly before performing the modulus operation. The advantage of placing these procedures in the **HEAD** is that other VBScripts can call them.

Lines 35 through 45 define an event procedure for handling **cmdButton**'s **OnClick** event. The statement

```
smallest = Minimum( number1, number2, number3 )
```

calls **Minimum**, passing **number1**, **number2** and **number3** as arguments. Parameters **min**, **a** and **b** are declared in **Minimum** to receive the values of **number1**, **number2** and **number3**, respectively. Procedure **OddEven** is passed the smallest number, on line 44.

Common Programming Error 24.10

Declaring a variable in a procedure body with the same name as a parameter variable is an error.

One last word about procedures—VBScript provides statements **Exit Sub** and **Exit Function** for exiting **Sub** procedures and **Function** procedures, respectively. Control is returned to the caller and the next statement in sequence after the call is executed.

24.6 Arrays

Arrays are data structures consisting of related data items of the same type. A *fixed-size array*'s size does not change during program execution; a *dynamic array*'s size can change during execution. A dynamic array is also called a *redimmable array* (short for a "re-dimensionable" array). Individual array elements are referred to by giving the array name followed by the element position number in parentheses, **( )**. The first array element is at position zero.

The position number contained within parentheses is more formally called an *index*. An index must be in the range 0 to 2,147,483,648 (any floating-point number is rounded to the nearest whole number).

The declaration

```
Dim numbers(2)
```

instructs the interpreter to reserve three elements for array **numbers**. The value **2** defines the *upper bound* (i.e., the highest valid index) of **numbers**. The *lower bound* (the lowest valid index) of **numbers** is **0**. When an upper bound is specified in the declaration, a fixed-size array is created.

Common Programming Error 24.11

Attempting to access an index that is less than the lower bound or greater than the upper bound is an error.

The programmer can explicitly initialize the array with assignment statements. For example, the lines

```
numbers(0) = 77
numbers(1) = 68
numbers(2) = 55
```

initialize **numbers**. Repetition statements can also be used to initialize arrays. For example, the statements

```
Dim h( 11 ), x, i
For x = 0 to 30 Step 3
   h(i) = CInt( x )
   i = CInt( i ) + 1
Next
```

initializes the elements of **h** to the values 0, 3, 6, 9, …, 30.

The program in Fig. 24.18 declares, initializes and prints three arrays. Two of the arrays are fixed-size arrays and one of the arrays is a dynamic array. The program introduces function **UBound**, which returns the upper bound (i.e., the highest-numbered index). [*Note*: VBScript does provide function **LBound** for determining the lowest-numbered index. However, the current version of VBScript does not permit the lowest-numbered index to be non-zero.]

```
1   <!DOCTYPE HTML PUBLIC "-//W3C//DTD HTML 4.0 Transitional//EN">
2   <HTML>
3   <!--Fig. 24.18: arrays.html -->
4
5   <HEAD>
6   <TITLE>Using VBScript Arrays</TITLE>
7
8   <SCRIPT LANGUAGE = "VBScript">
9   <!--
10     Option Explicit
11
12     Public Sub DisplayArray( x, s )
13        Dim j
14
15        Document.Write( s & ": " )
16        For j = 0 to UBound( x )
17           Document.Write( x( j ) & " " )
18        Next
19
```

Fig. 24.18 Using VBScript arrays (part 1 of 2).

```
20          Document.Write( "<BR>" )
21      End Sub
22
23      Dim fixedSize( 3 ), fixedArray, dynamic(), k
24
25      ReDim dynamic( 3 )   ' Dynamically size array
26      fixedArray = Array( "A", "B", "C" )
27
28      ' Populate arrays with values
29      For k = 0 to UBound( fixedSize )
30          fixedSize( k ) = 50 - k
31          dynamic( k ) = Chr( 75 + k )
32      Next
33
34      ' Display contents of arrays
35      Call DisplayArray( fixedSize, "fixedSize" )
36      Call DisplayArray( fixedArray, "fixedArray" )
37      Call DisplayArray( dynamic, "dynamic" )
38
39      ' Resize dynamic, preserve current values
40      ReDim Preserve dynamic( 5 )
41      dynamic( 3 ) = 3.343
42      dynamic( 4 ) = 77.37443
43
44      Call DisplayArray( dynamic, _
45                          "dynamic after ReDim Preserve" )
46  -->
47  </SCRIPT>
48  </HEAD>
49  </HTML>
```

```
Using VBScript Error Handling - Microsoft Internet Explorer provided by MSN

File   Edit   View   Favorites   Tools   Help

Back   Forward   Stop   Refresh   Home   Search   Favorites   History   Mail

Address  C:\WINDOWS\Desktop\vbscript\examples\arrays.htm                    Go   Links

fixedSize: 50 49 48 47
fixedArray: A B C
dynamic: K L M N
dynamic after ReDim Preserve: K L M 3.343 77.37443

Done                                              My Computer
```

Fig. 24.18 Using VBScript arrays (part 2 of 2).

Testing and Debugging Tip 24.4

*Array upper bounds can vary. Use function **UBound** to ensure that each index is in range (i.e., within the bounds of the array).*

Lines 12 through 21 define **Sub** procedure **DisplayArray**. VBScript procedures are **Public** by default; therefore, they are accessible to scripts on other Web pages. Keyword **Public** can be used explicitly to indicate that a procedure is public. A procedure can be marked as **Private** to indicate that the procedure can be called only from the HTML document in which it is defined.

Procedure **DisplayArray** receives arguments **x** and **s** and declares local variable **j**. Parameter **x** receives an array and parameter **s** receives a string. The **For** header (line 16) calls function **UBound** to get the upper bound of **x**. The **Document** object's **Write** method is used to print each element of **x**.

The declaration at line 23

```
Dim fixedSize( 3 ), fixedArray, dynamic(), k
```

declares a four element fixed-sized array named **fixedSize** (the value in parentheses indicates the highest index in the array, and the array has a starting index of 0), variants **fixedArray** and **k**, and dynamic array **dynamic**.

Statement **ReDim** (line 25) allocates memory for array **dynamic** (four elements, in this example). All dynamic array memory must be allocated via **ReDim**. Dynamic arrays are more flexible than fixed-sized arrays, because they can be resized anytime by using **ReDim**, to accommodate new data.

Performance Tip 24.2

Dynamic arrays allow the programmer to manage memory more efficiently than do fixed-size arrays.

Performance Tip 24.3

Resizing dynamic arrays consumes processor time and can slow a program's execution speed.

Common Programming Error 24.12

*Attempting to use **ReDim** on a fixed-size array is an error.*

Line 26

```
fixedArray = Array( "A", "B", "C" )
```

creates an array containing three elements and assigns it to **fixedArray**. VBScript function **Array** takes any number of arguments and returns an array containing those arguments. Lines 35 through 37 pass the three arrays and three strings to **DisplayArray**. Line 40

```
ReDim Preserve dynamic( 5 )
```

reallocates **dynamic**'s memory to 5 elements. When keyword **Preserve** is used with **ReDim**, VBScript maintains the current values in the array; otherwise, all values in the array are lost when the **ReDim** operation occurs.

Common Programming Error 24.13

*Using **ReDim** without **Preserve** and assuming that the array still contains previous values is a logic error.*

Testing and Debugging Tip 24.5

Failure to **Preserve** *array data can result in unexpected loss of data at run time. Always double check every array* **ReDim** *to determine whether* **Preserve** *is needed.*

If **ReDim Preserve** creates a larger array, every element in the original array is preserved. If **ReDim Preserve** creates a smaller array, every element up to (and including) the new upper bound is preserved (e.g., if there were 10 elements in the original array and the new array contains five elements, the first five elements of the original array are preserved). Lines 41 and 42 assign values to the new elements. Procedure **DisplayArray** is called to display array **dynamic**.

Arrays can have multiple dimensions. VBScript supports at least 60 array dimensions, but most programmers will need to use only two- or three-dimensional arrays.

Common Programming Error 24.14

Referencing a two-dimensional array element **u(x, y)** *incorrectly as* **u(x)(y)** *is an error.*

A multidimensional array is declared much like a one-dimensional array. For example, consider the following declarations

```
Dim b(2, 2), tripleArray(100, 8, 15)
```

which declares **b** as a two-dimensional array and **tripleArray** as a three-dimensional array. Functions **UBound** and **LBound** can also be used with multidimensional arrays. When calling **UBound** or **LBound**, the dimension is passed as the second argument. Array dimensions always begin at one. If a dimension is not provided, the default dimension 1 is used. For example, the **For** header

```
For x = 0 To UBound(tripleArray, 3)
```

would increment **x** from the third dimension's lower bound, **0**, to the third dimension's upper bound, **15**.

Multidimensional arrays can also be created dynamically. Consider the declaration

```
Dim threeD()
```

which declares a dynamic array **threeD**. The number of dimensions is not set until the first time **ReDim** is used. Once the number of dimensions is set, the number of dimensions cannot be changed by **ReDim** (e.g., if the array is a two-dimensional array, it cannot become a three-dimensional array). The statement

```
ReDim threeD(11, 8, 1)
```

allocates memory for **threeD** and sets the number of dimensions at 3.

Common Programming Error 24.15

Attempting to change the total number of array dimensions using **ReDim** *is an error.*

Common Programming Error 24.16

Attempting to change the upper bound for any dimension except the last dimension in a dynamic-multidimensional array (when using **ReDim Preserve**) *is an error.*

Memory allocated for dynamic arrays can be *deallocated* (*released*) at run-time using the keyword **Erase**. A dynamic array that has been deallocated must be redimensioned with **ReDim** before it can be used again. **Erase** can also be used with fixed-sized arrays to initialize all the array elements to the empty string. For example, the statement

```
Erase mDynamic
```

releases **mDynamic**'s memory.

Common Programming Error 24.17

Accessing a dynamic array that has been deallocated is an error.

24.7 String Manipulation

One of VBScript's most powerful features is its string-manipulation functions, some of which are summarized in Fig. 24.19. For a complete list consult the VBScript documentation. VBScript strings are case sensitive. The first character in a string has index 1 (as opposed to arrays which begin at index 0). [*Note:* Almost all VBScript string-manipulation functions do not modify their string argument(s); rather, they return new strings containing the results. Most VBScript string-manipulation functions take optional arguments.]

Function	Description
Asc	Returns the ASCII numeric value of a character. For example, **Asc("x")** returns **120**.
Chr	Returns the character representation for an ASCII value. For example the call **Chr(120)** returns "**x**." The argument passed must be in the range 0 to 255 inclusive, otherwise an error occurs.
InStr	Searches a string (i.e., the first argument) for a substring (i.e., the second argument). Searching is performed from left to right. If the substring is found, the index of the found substring in the search string is returned. For example, the call **Instr("sparrow","arrow")** returns **3** and the call **Instr("japan","wax")** returns **0**.
Len	Returns the number of characters in a string. For example, the call **Len("hello")** returns **5**.
LCase	Returns a lowercase string. For example, the call **LCase("HELLO@97[")** returns "**hello@97[**."
UCase	Returns an uppercase string. For example, the call **UCase("hello@97[")** returns "**HELLO@97[**."
Left	Returns a string containing characters from the left side of a string argument. For example, the call **Left("Web",2)** returns "**We**."
Mid	Function **Mid** returns a string containing a range of characters from a string. For example, the call **Mid("abcd",2,3)** returns "**bcd**."
Right	Returns a string containing characters from the right side of a string argument. For example, the call **Right("Web",2)** returns "**eb**."

Fig. 24.19   Some string-manipulation functions (part 1 of 3).

Function	Description
Space	Returns a string of spaces. For example, the call **Space(4)** returns a string containing four spaces.
StrComp	Compares two strings for equality. Returns **1** if the first string is greater than the second string, returns **-1** if the first string is less than the second string and returns **0** if the strings are equivalent. The default is a binary comparison (i.e., case-sensitive). An optional third argument of *vbTextCompare* indicates a case-insensitive comparison. For example the call **StrComp("bcd", "BCD")** returns **1**, the call **StrComp("BCD", "bcd")** returns **-1**, the call **StrComp("bcd", "bcd")** returns **0** and the call **StrComp("bcd", "BCD", vbTextCompare)** returns **0**.
String	Returns a string containing a repeated character. For example, the call **String(4,"u")** returns "**uuuu**."
Trim	Returns a string that does not contain leading or trailing space characters. For example the call **Trim(" hi ")** returns "**hi**."
LTrim	Returns a string that does not contain any leading space characters. For example, the call **LTrim(" yes")** returns "**yes**."
RTrim	Returns a string that does not contain any trailing space characters. For example, the call **RTrim("no ")** returns "**no**".
Filter	Returns an array of strings containing the result of the **Filter** operation. For example, the call **Filter(Array("A","S","D","F","G","D"),"D")** returns a two-element array containing **"D"** and **"D"**, and the call **Filter(Array("A","S","D","F","G","D"),"D",False)** returns an array containing **"A"** , **"S"**, **"F"** and **"G"**.
Join	Returns a string containing the concatenation of array elements separated by a delimiter. For example, the call **Join(Array("one","two","three"))** returns "**one two three**." The default delimiter is a space which can be changed by passing a delimiter string for the second argument. For example, the call **Join(Array("one","two","three"),"$^")** returns "**one$^two$^three**."
Replace	Returns a string containing the results of a **Replace** operation. Function **Replace** requires three string arguments: the string where characters will be replaced, the substring to search for and the replacement string. For example, **Replace("It's Sunday and the sun is out","sun","moon")** returns "**It's Sunday and the moon is out**." Note the case-sensitive replacement.
Split	Returns an array containing substrings. The default delimiter for **Split** is a space character. For example, the call **Split("I met a traveller")** returns an array containing elements **"I"**, **"met"**, **"a"** and **"traveller"** and **Split("red,white,and blue", ",")** returns an array containing elements **"red"**, **"white"** and **"and blue"**. The optional second argument changes the delimiter.

Fig. 24.19 Some string-manipulation functions (part 1 of 3).

Function	Description
StrReverse	Returns a string in reverse order. For example, the call **StrReverse("deer")** returns "**reed**."
InStrRev	Searches a string (i.e., the first argument) for a substring (i.e., the second argument). Searching is performed from right to left. If the substring is found, the index of the found substring in the search string is returned. For example, the call **InstrRev("sparrow","arrow")** returns **3**, the call **InstrRev("japan","wax")** returns **0** and the call **InstrRev("to be or not to be","to be")** returns **14**.

Fig. 24.19 Some string-manipulation functions (part 1 of 3).

We now present a VBScript program that converts a line of text into its pig Latin equivalent. Pig Latin is a form of coded language often used for amusement. Many variations exist in the methods used to form pig Latin phrases. For simplicity, we use the following algorithm:

> *To form a pig Latin phrase from an English language phrase, the translation proceeds one word at a time. To translate an English word into a pig Latin word, place the first letter of the English word (if it is not a vowel) at the end of the English word and add the letters "**ay**." If the first letter of the English word is a vowel place it at the end of the word and add "**y**." Thus, the word "**jump**" becomes "**umpjay**," the word "**the**" becomes "**hetay**," and the word "**ace**" becomes "**ceay**." Blanks between words remain as blanks. Make the following assumptions: the English phrase consists of words separated by blanks, there are no punctuation marks and all words have two or more letters.*

Lines 12 through 38 define the **Function** procedure **TranslateToPigLatin** which translates the string input by the user from English to pig Latin. Line 18 calls function **Split** to extract each word in the sentence. By default, **Split** uses spaces as delimiters. The condition (line 22)

```
InStr( 1, "aeiou", _
         LCase( Left( words( k ), 1 ) ) )
```

calls functions **InStr**, **LCase** and **Left** to determine whether the first letter of a word is a vowel. Function **Left** is called to retrieve the first letter in **words(k)**—which is then converted to lowercase using **LCase**. Function **InStr** is called to search the string **"aeiou"** for the string returned by **LCase**. The starting index in every string is **1**, and this is where **Instr** begins searching.

```
1    <!DOCTYPE HTML PUBLIC "-//W3C//DTD HTML 4.0 Transitional//EN">
2    <HTML>
3    <!--Fig. 24.20: piglatin.html -->
4
5    <HEAD>
6    <TITLE>Using VBScript String Functions</TITLE>
7
```

Fig. 24.20 Using VBScript string processing functions (part 1 of 3).

```
8   <SCRIPT LANGUAGE="VBScript">
9   <!--
10     Option Explicit
11
12     Public Function TranslateToPigLatin( englishPhrase )
13        Dim words          ' Stores each individual word
14        Dim k, suffix
15
16        ' Get each word and store in words the
17        ' default delimiter for Split is a space
18        words = Split( englishPhrase )
19
20        For k = 0 to UBound( words )
21           ' Check if first letter is a vowel
22           If InStr( 1, "aeiou", _
23                     LCase( Left( words( k ), 1 ) ) ) Then
24              suffix = "y"
25           Else
26              suffix = "ay"
27           End If
28
29           ' Convert the word to pig Latin
30           words( k ) = Right( words( k ), _
31                        Len( words( k ) ) - 1 ) & _
32                        Left( words( k ), 1 ) & suffix
33        Next
34
35        ' Return translated phrase, each word
36        ' is separated by spaces
37        TranslateToPigLatin = Join( words )
38     End Function
39
40     Sub cmdButton_OnClick()
41        Dim phrase
42
43        phrase = Document.Forms( 0 ).txtInput.Value
44
45        Document.forms( 0 ).txtPigLatin.Value = _
46           TranslateToPigLatin( phrase )
47     End Sub
48   -->
49   </SCRIPT>
50   </HEAD>
51
52   <BODY>
53   <FORM> Enter a sentence
54   <INPUT TYPE="text" NAME="txtInput" SIZE="50"><P>
55   Pig Latin
56   <INPUT TYPE="text" NAME="txtPigLatin" SIZE="70"><P>
57   <INPUT TYPE="button" NAME="cmdButton" VALUE="Translate">
58   </SCRIPT>
59   </FORM>
60   </BODY>
```

Fig. 24.20   Using VBScript string processing functions (part 2 of 3).

```
61    </HTML>
```

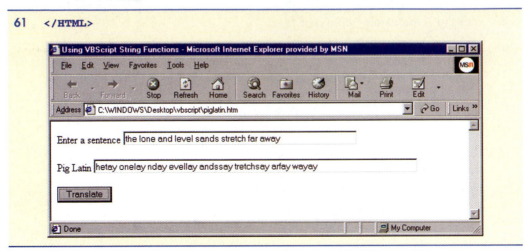

Fig. 24.20   Using VBScript string processing functions (part 3 of 3).

Lines 30 through 33

```
words( k ) = Right( words( k ), _
                    Len( words( k ) ) - 1 ) & _
                    Left( words( k ), 1 ) & suffix
```

translate an individual word to pig Latin. Function **Len** is called to get the number of characters in **words(k)**. One is subtracted from the value returned by **Len**, to ensure that the first letter in **words(k)** is not included in the string returned by **Right**. Function **Left** is called to get the first letter of **words(k)**, which is then concatenated to the string returned by **Right**. Finally the contents of **suffix** (either **"ay"** or **"y"**) and a space are concatenated.

Lines 40 through 47 define an event procedure for **cmdButton**'s **OnClick** event. Line 46 calls function **TranslateToPigLatin**, passing the string input by the user. The pig Latin sentence returned by **TranslateToPigLatin** is displayed in a text box (line 45).

24.8 Classes and Objects

In this section, we introduce the concepts (i.e., "object think") and the terminology (i.e., "object speak") of object-oriented programming in VBScript. Objects *encapsulate* (i.e., wrap together) data (*attributes*) and methods (*behaviors*); the data and methods of an object are intimately related. Objects have the property of *information hiding*. This phrase means that, although objects may communicate with one another, objects do not know how other objects are implemented—implementation details are hidden within the objects themselves. Surely it is possible to drive a car effectively without knowing the details of how engines and transmissions work. Information hiding is crucial to good software engineering.

In VBScript, the unit of object-oriented programming is the *Class* from which objects are *instantiated* (i.e., created). *Methods* are VBScript procedures that are encapsulated with the data they process within the "walls" of classes.

VBScript programmers can create their own *user-defined types* called *classes*. Classes are also referred to as *programmer-defined types*. Each class contains data as well as the set of methods which manipulate that data. The data components of a class are called *instance variables*. Just as an instance of a variant is called a *variable,* an instance of a class is called an *object.* The focus of attention in object-oriented programming with VBScript is on classes rather than methods.

The *nouns* in a system-requirements document help the VBScript programmer determine an initial set of classes with which to begin the design process. These classes are then used to instantiate objects that will work together to implement the system. The *verbs* in a system-requirements document help the VBScript programmer determine what methods to associate with each class.

This section explains how to create and use objects, a subject we call *object-based programming (OBP).* VBScript programmers craft new classes and reuse existing classes. Software is then constructed by combining new classes with existing, well-defined, carefully tested, well-documented, widely available components. This kind of *software reusability* speeds the development of powerful, high-quality software. *Rapid applications development (RAD)* is of great interest today.

Early versions of VBScript did not allow programmers to create their own classes, but VBScript programmers can now indeed develop their own classes, a powerful capability also offered by such object-oriented languages as C++ and Java.

Packaging software as classes out of which we make objects makes more significant portions of major software systems reusable. On the Windows platform, these classes have been packaged into class libraries, such as Microsoft's *MFC (Microsoft Foundation Classes)* that provide C++ programmers with reusable components for handling common programming tasks, such as the creating and manipulating of graphical user interfaces.

Objects are endowed with the capabilities to do everything they need to do. For example, employee objects are endowed with a behavior to pay themselves. Video game objects are endowed with the ability to draw themselves on the screen. This is like a car being endowed with the ability to "go faster" (if someone presses the accelerator pedal), "go slower" (if someone presses the brake pedal) and "turn left" or "turn right" (if someone turns the steering wheel in the appropriate direction). The blueprint for a car is like a class. Each car is like an instance of a class. Each car comes equipped with all the behaviors it needs, such as "go faster," "go slower" and so on, just as every instance of a class comes equipped with each of the behaviors instances of that class exhibit. We will discuss how to create classes and how to add properties and methods to those classes.

Software Engineering Observation 24.2

It is important to write programs that are understandable and easy to maintain. Change is the rule rather than the exception. Programmers should anticipate that their code will be modified. As we will see, using classes improves program modifiability.

Classes normally hide their implementation details from the *clients* (i.e., users) of the classes. This is called *information hiding.* As an example of information hiding, let us consider a data structure called a *stack.*

Think of a stack in terms of a pile of dishes. When a dish is placed on the pile, it is always placed at the top (referred to as *pushing* the dish onto the stack). When a dish is removed from the pile, it is always removed from the top (referred to as *popping* the dish off the stack). Stacks are known as *last-in, first-out (LIFO) data structures*—the last item *push*ed (inserted) on the stack is the first item *pop*ped (removed) from the stack. So if we push 1, then 2, then 3 onto a stack, the next three pop operations will return 3, then 2, then 1.

The programmer may create a stack class and hide from its clients the implementation of the stack. Stacks can be implemented with arrays and other techniques such as linked lists. A client of a stack class need not know how the stack is implemented. The client simply requires that when data items are placed in the stack with *push* operations, they will be recalled with *pop* operations in last-in, first-out order. Describing an object in terms of behaviors without concern for how those behaviors are actually implemented is called *data abstraction,* and VBScript classes define *abstract data types (ADTs).* Although users may happen to know how a class is implemented, users should not write code that depends on these details. This allows a class to be replaced with another version without affecting the rest of the system, as long as the **Public** interface of that class does not change (i.e. every method still has the same name, return type and parameter list in the new class definition).

Most programming languages emphasize actions. In these languages, data exists in support of the actions programs need to take. Data is "less interesting" than actions, anyway. Data is "crude." There are only a few built-in data types, and it is difficult for programmers to create their own new data types. VBScript elevates the importance of data. A primary activity in VBScript is creating new data types (i.e., *classes*) and expressing the interactions among *objects* of those classes.

An ADT actually captures two notions, a *data representation of the ADT* and the *operations allowed on the data of the ADT.* For example, subtype integer defines addition, subtraction, multiplication, division and other operations in VBScript, but division by zero is undefined. The allowed operations and the data representation of negative integers are clear, but the operation of taking the square root of a negative integer is undefined.

Software Engineering Observation 24.3

The programmer creates new types through the class mechanism. These new types may be designed to be used as conveniently as built-in types. Thus, VBScript is an extensible language. Although it is easy to extend the language with these new types, the base language itself cannot be modified.

Access to **Private** data should be carefully controlled by the class's methods. For example, to allow clients to read the value of **Private** data, the class can provide a *get method* (also called an *accessor* method or a *query* method).

To enable clients to modify **Private** data, the class can provide a *set* method (also called a *mutator* method). Such modification would seem to violate the notion of **Private** data. But a *set* method can provide data validation capabilities (such as range checking) to ensure that the data is set properly and to reject attempts to set data to invalid values. A *set* method can also translate between the form of the data used in the interface and the form used in the implementation. A *get* method need not expose the data in "raw" format; rather, the *get* method can edit the data and limit the view of the data the client will see.

Software Engineering Observation 24.4

The class designer need not provide set *and/or* get *methods for each* **Private** *data member; these capabilities should be provided only when it makes sense and after careful thought.*

Testing and Debugging Tip 24.6

Making the instance variables of a class **Private** *and the methods* **Public** *facilitates debugging because problems with data manipulations are localized to the class's methods.*

Classes often provide **Public** methods to allow clients of the class to *set* (i.e., assign values to) or *get* (i.e., obtain the values of) **Private** instance variables. These methods are special methods in VBScript called ***Property Let***, ***Property Set*** and ***Property Get*** (collectively these methods and the internal class data they manipulate are called *properties*). More specifically, a method that sets variable **mInterestRate** would be named **Property Let InterestRate** and a method that gets the **InterestRate** would be called **Property Get InterestRate**.

Procedures **Property Let** and **Property Set** differ in that **Property Let** is used for non-object subtypes (e.g., integer, string, byte, etc.) and **Property Set** is used for object subtypes.

Testing and Debugging Tip 24.7

Property procedures should scrutinize every attempt to set the object's data and should reject invalid data to ensure that the object's data remains in a consistent state. This eliminates large numbers of bugs that have plagued systems development efforts.

Software Engineering Observation 24.5

Property Get procedures can control the appearance of data, possibly hiding implementation details.

A **Property Let Hour** that stores the hour in universal time as 0 to 23 is shown in Fig. 24.21. Notice the change in the declaration of variable **theHour**—we are using keyword **Private** rather than **Dim**. In this case, **Private** restricts the scope of **theHour** to its class. If **Dim** or **Public** is used, the variable is accessible outside the class. Method definitions that are not preceded by **Public** or **Private** default to **Public**. Variables declared with **Dim** default to **Public**.

Good Programming Practice 24.2

*Qualify all class members with either **Public** or **Private** to clearly show their access.*

Suppose **Property Let Hour** is a member of class **CTime1** (we discuss how to create classes momentarily). An object of class **CTime1** is created with the following code

```
Dim wakeUp
Set wakeUp = New CTime1
```

When creating an object, VBScript keyword ***New*** is used and followed by the class name. When assigning the object to a variable, keyword ***Set*** must be used. When a variable (e.g., **wakeUp**) refers to an object, the variable is called a *reference*.

```
1   Private theHour
2
3   Public Property Let Hour( hr )
4       If hr >= 0 And hr < 24 Then
5           theHour = hr
6       Else
7           theHour = 0
8       End If
9   End Property
```

Fig. 24.21 A simple **Property Let** procedure.

Common Programming Error 24.18

Attempting to call a method or access a property for a reference that does not refer to an object is an error.

Common Programming Error 24.19

*Attempting to assign a reference a value without using **Set** is an error.*

If we perform the assignments **wakeup.Hour = -6** or **wakeup.Hour = 27**, the **Property Let** procedure would reject these as invalid values and set **theHour** to 0. The **Property Get Hour** procedure is shown in Fig. 24.22.

Using **CTime1** class object **wakeUp**, we can store the value of **Hour** into variable **alarmClockHourValue**, as follows:

```
alarmClockHourValue = wakeup.Hour
```

which call **Property Get Hour** to get the value of **theHour**. The **Class** definition for **CTime1** is shown in Fig. 24.23. Keywords **Class** and **End Class** are used to encapsulate the class members.

Software Engineering Observation 24.6

To implement a read-only *property, simply provide a **Property Get** procedure but no **Property Let** (or **Property Set**) procedure.*

Suppose we have a **CEmployee** class that contains an object **mBirthDate** of class **CDate**. We cannot use a **Property Let** to assign a value to an object. Instead, we must use a **Property Set**, as in each of the following **Property** procedures:

```
1   Public Property Get Hour()
2       Hour = theHour
3   End Property
```

Fig. 24.22 A simple **Property Get** procedure.

```
1   Class CTime1
2       Private mHour
3
4       Public Property Let Hour( hr )
5           If hr >= 0 And hr < 24 Then
6               theHour = hr
7           Else
8               theHour = 0
9           End If
10      End Property
11
12      Public Property Get Hour()
13          Hour = theHour
14      End Property
15  End Class
```

Fig. 24.23 A simple **Class** definition.

```
Public Property Set BirthDay(bDay)
   Set mBirthDate = bDay
End Property

Public Property Get BirthDay()
   Set BirthDay = mBirthDate
End Property
```

Any **Property Get**, **Property Let** or **Property Set** method may contain the ***Exit Property*** statement that causes an immediate exit from a **Property** procedure.

Access methods can read or display data. Another common use for access methods is to test the truth or falsity of conditions—such methods are often called *predicate methods*. An example of a predicate method would be an **IsEmpty** method for any container class—a class capable of holding multiple objects—such as a linked list or a stack. A program might test **IsEmpty** before attempting to remove another item from a container object. A program might test **IsFull** before attempting to insert another item into a container object.

It would seem that providing *set* and *get* capabilities is essentially the same as making the instance variables **Public**. This is another subtlety of VBScript that makes the language desirable for software engineering. If an instance variable is **Public**, it may be read or written at will by any method in the program. If an instance variable is **Private**, a **Public** *get* method certainly seems to allow other methods to read the data at will but the *get* method controls the formatting and display of the data. A **Public** *set* method can—and most likely will—carefully scrutinize attempts to modify the instance variable's value. This ensures that the new value is appropriate for that data item. For example, an attempt to *set* the day of the month to 37 would be rejected, an attempt to *set* a person's weight to a negative value would be rejected, and so on.

Software Engineering Observation 24.7

*The benefits of data integrity are not automatic simply because instance variables are made **Private**. Methods that set the values of **Private** data should verify that the intended new values are proper; if they are not, the* set *methods should place the **Private** instance variables into an appropriate consistent state.*

Software Engineering Observation 24.8

*Every method that modifies the **Private** instance variables of an object should ensure that the data remains in a consistent state.*

Figure 24.24 demonstrates using a VBScript **Class**. The Web page allows the user to enter a first name, age and social security number which are displayed in a message dialog. This example briefly introduces a VBScript feature for complex pattern matching called *regular expressions*. We use regular expressions to validate the format of the social security number. Client-side scripts often validate information before sending it to the server. In this example, we briefly introduce regular expressions in the context of client-side validation. In Chapter 29, "Perl 5 and CGI," you will learn more about regular expressions.

Lines 12 through 65 define **Class Person**, which encapsulates **Private** data members, **Public Property** procedures and a **Private** method. Data members store the person's first name in **name**, the person's age in **yearsOld** and the person's social security number in **ssn**. Both **Property Let** and **Property Get** procedures are provided for the data members.

Procedure **Property Let SocialSecurityNumber** (lines 31 through 40) is the most interesting **Property** procedure because it calls **Private** method **Validate** to verify the correct format for the social security number that was input. If **Validate** returns **True**, the social security number input is assigned to **ssn**; if **Validate** returns **False**, **ssn** is assigned the string **"000-00-0000"** and a message dialog is displayed.

Method **Validate** (line 46) checks the format of the social security number by using a so-called regular expression—a concept we explain in the next paragraph. Methods designated as **Private** are often called *utility* or *helper* methods. These methods are considered to be part of a class's implementation detail and therefore clients do not have access to them.f

```
1    <!DOCTYPE HTML PUBLIC "-//W3C//DTD HTML 4.0 Transitional//EN">
2    <HTML>
3    <!--Fig. 24.24: classes.html -->
4
5    <HEAD>
6    <TITLE>Using a VBScript Class</TITLE>
7
8    <SCRIPT LANGUAGE = "VBScript">
9    <!--
10      Option Explicit
11
12      Class Person
13         Private name, yearsOld, ssn
14
15         Public Property Let FirstName( fn )
16            name = fn
17         End Property
18
19         Public Property Get FirstName()
20            FirstName = name
21         End Property
22
23         Public Property Let Age( a )
24            yearsOld = a
25         End Property
26
27         Public Property Get Age()
28            Age = yearsOld
29         End Property
30
31         Public Property Let SocialSecurityNumber( n )
32
33            If Validate( n ) Then
34               ssn = n
35            Else
36               ssn = "000-00-0000"
37               Call MsgBox( "Invalid Social Security Format" )
38            End If
39
40         End Property
41
```

Fig. 24.24 Using VBScript classes and regular expressions (part 1 of 3).

```
42          Public Property Get SocialSecurityNumber()
43             SocialSecurityNumber = ssn
44          End Property
45
46          Private Function Validate( expression )
47             Dim regularExpression
48             Set regularExpression = New RegExp
49
50             regularExpression.Pattern = "^\d{3}-\d{2}-\d{4}$"
51
52             If regularExpression.Test( expression ) Then
53                Validate = True
54             Else
55                Validate = False
56             End If
57
58          End Function
59
60          Public Function ToString()
61             ToString = name & Space( 3 ) & age & Space( 3 ) _
62                        & ssn
63          End Function
64
65       End Class     ' Person
66
67       Sub cmdButton_OnClick()
68          Dim p                   ' Declare object reference
69          Set p = New Person      ' Instantiate Person object
70
71          With p
72             .FirstName = Document.Forms(0).txtBox1.Value
73             .Age = CInt( Document.Forms(0).txtBox2.Value )
74             .SocialSecurityNumber = Document.Forms(0).txtBox3.Value
75             Call MsgBox( .ToString() )
76          End With
77
78       End Sub
79    -->
80    </SCRIPT>
81    </HEAD>
82
83    <BODY>
84    <FORM>Enter first name
85    <INPUT TYPE = "text" NAME = "txtBox1" SIZE = "10">
86    <P>Enter age
87    <INPUT TYPE = "text" NAME = "txtBox2" SIZE = "5">
88    <P>Enter social security number
89    <INPUT TYPE = "text" NAME = "txtBox3" SIZE = "10"> <P>
90    <INPUT TYPE = "button" NAME = "cmdButton" VALUE = "Enter">
91
92    </FORM>
93    </BODY>
94    </HTML>
```

Fig. 24.24 Using VBScript classes and regular expressions (part 2 of 3).

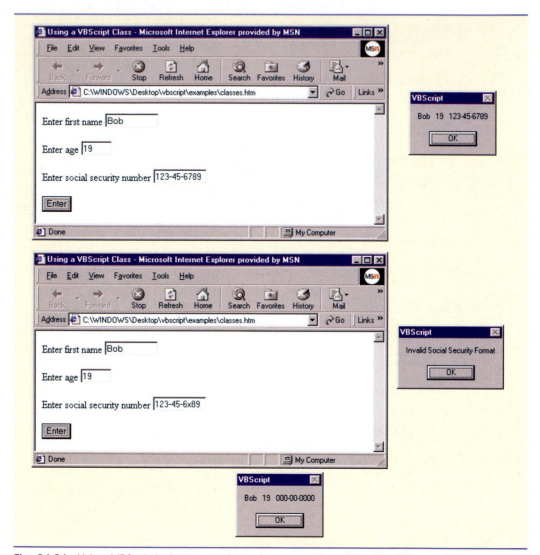

Fig. 24.24 Using VBScript classes and regular expressions (part 3 of 3).

The statement

```
Set regularExpression = New RegExp
```

instantiates a regular expression object (i.e., an object of VBScript class **RegExp**) and assigns it to reference **regularExpression**. Line 50

```
regularExpression.Pattern = "^\d{3}-\d{2}-\d{4}$"
```

sets the **Pattern** property to the pattern we wish to match—in this case a social security number which consists of three digits, a hyphen (i.e., **-**), two digits, a hyphen and four digits. This expression reads as follows: the beginning of the string should begin with exactly three digits followed by a hyphen, then two digits followed by a hyphen and end with exactly four digits. The *caret*, **^** indicates the beginning of the string and the **\d** indicates that any digit (i.e., 0 through 9) is a match. The **{3}**, **{2}** and **{4}** expressions indicate that exactly three occurrences of any digit, exactly two occurrences of any digit and exactly four occurrences of any digit, respectively, are a match. The *dollar sign*, **$** indicates the end of the string. The hyphens are treated as *literal characters* (i.e., a hyphen is not a special character used in a regular expression for pattern matching—so a hyphen literally is treated as a hyphen).

The **If**'s condition (line 52)

```
regularExpression.Test( expression )
```

calls function ***Test*** to determine whether the regular expression's pattern is a match for the string passed into **Test**. A successful match returns **True** and an unsuccessful match returns **False**. For more details on VBScript regular expressions, visit

```
msdn.microsoft.com/workshop/languages/clinic/
scripting051099.asp
```

Function **ToString** (line 60) returns a string containing the **name**, **age** and **ssn**. Function **Space** (line 61) is called to provide three spaces between words. Keywords ***End Class*** (line 65) designate the end of the class definition.

Lines 67 through 78 provide an event procedure for **cmdButton**'s **OnClick** event. Line 68 declares **p** as a variant—which can store object subtypes. The statement (line 69)

```
Set p = New Person
```

instantiates a **Person** object and assigns it to **p**. As mentioned earlier, VBScript requires the use of the **Set** keyword when assigning an object to a variable. To be more precise, we call **p** a reference, because it is used with an object. At any moment in time, a reference can refer to an object or **Nothing** (i.e., a special value that indicates the absence of an object).

Lines 71 through 76 use the ***With/End With*** statement to set several property values for **p** and to call **p**'s **ToString** method. The **With/End With** statement is provided for the convenience of the programmer, to minimize the number of times an object's name is written (when setting multiple properties or calling multiple methods). Note that lines 72 through 74 actually call the appropriate **Property Let** procedures—these lines are not directly accessing **p**'s data. Line 75

```
Call MsgBox( .ToString() )
```

calls **p**'s **ToString** method to get the string that the message dialog will display. Although the syntax may appear a bit strange, it is indeed correct.

24.9 Internet and World Wide Web Resources

Although the VBScript language contains far more features than can be presented in one chapter, there are many Web resources available that are related to VBScript. Visit the following sites for additional information.

msdn.microsoft.com/scripting/VBScript/doc/vbstutor.htm
The *VBScript tutorial* contains a short tutorial on VBScript.

msdn.microsoft.com/scripting/VBScript/doc/vbstoc.htm
The *VBScript language reference* contains links for constants, keywords, functions, etc.

www.msdn.microsoft.com/vbasic/technical/Documentation.asp
Visual Basic 6 documentation. Use the Visual Basic 6 documentation to get additional information on functions, constants etc. VBScript is a subset of Visual Basic.

msdn.microsoft.com/workshop/languages/clinic/scripting051099.asp
This is an article that discusses regular expressions in VBScript. One substantial example is provided at the end of the article.

SUMMARY

- Visual Basic Script (VBScript) is case-insensitive subset of Microsoft Visual Basic® used in World Wide Web HTML documents to enhance the functionality of a Web page displayed in a Web browser (such as Microsoft's Internet Explorer) that contains a VBScript scripting engine (i.e., interpreter) and used on servers to enhance the functionality of server-side applications.

- VBScript's arithmetic operators are similar to JavaScript arithmetic operators. Two major differences are the division operator, ****, which returns an integer result, and the exponentiation operator, **^**, which raises a value to a power. VBScript operator precedence differs from that of JavaScript.

- VBScript's symbols for the equality operator and inequality operators are different from JavaScript's symbols. VBScript comparison operators may also be used to compare strings.

- VBScript provides the following logical operators: **And** (logical AND), **Or** (logical Or), **Not** (logical negation), **Imp** (logical implication), **Xor** (exclusive Or) and **Eqv** (logical equivalence).

- Despite the mixture of case in keywords, functions, etc., VBScript is not case-sensitive—uppercase and lowercase letters are treated the same.

- VBScript provides the plus sign, **+**, the and ampersand, **&**, operators for string concatenation. The ampersand is more formally called the string concatenation operator. If both operands of the concatenation operator are strings, these two operators can be used interchangeably. However, if the **+** operator is used in an expression consisting of varying data types, there can be a problem.

- VBScript code is commented either by using a single quote (**'**) or by keyword **Rem**. As with JavaScript's two forward slashes, **//**, VBScript comments are single-line comments.

- Like JavaScript, VBScript has only one data type—variant—and it is capable of storing different types of data (e.g., strings, integers, floating-point numbers, etc.). A variant is interpreted by VBScript in a manner that is suitable to the type of data it contains.

- Variable names cannot be keywords and must begin with a letter. The maximum length of a variable name is 255 characters containing only letters, numbers and underscores. Variables can be declared simply by using their name in the VBScript code. Statement **Option Explicit** can be used to force all variables to be declared before they are used.

- VBScript provides nine control structures for controlling program execution. Many of the control structures provide the same capabilities as their JavaScript counterparts. Syntactically, every VBScript control structure ends with one or more keywords (e.g., **End If**, **Loop**, etc.). Keywords delimit a control structure's body—not curly braces (i.e., **{}**).

- The **If/Then/End If** and **If/Then/Else/End If** control structures behave identically to their JavaScript counterparts. VBScript's multiple selection version of **If/Then/Else/End If** uses a different syntax from JavaScript's version because it includes keyword **ElseIf**.

- VBScript does not use a statement terminator (e.g., a semicolon, **;**). Unlike JavaScript, placing parentheses around conditions in VBScript is optional. A condition evaluates to **True** if the variant subtype is boolean **True** or if the variant subtype is considered non-zero. A condition evaluates to **False** if the variant subtype is boolean **False** or if the variant subtype is considered to be 0.

- VBScript's **Select Case/End Select** structure provides the same functionality as JavaScript's **switch** structure and more. The **Select Case/End Select** structure does not require the use of a statement such as **break**. One **Case** cannot accidently run into another. The VBScript **Select Case/End Select** structure is equivalent to VBScript's **If/Then/Else/ End If** multiple selection structure. The only difference is syntax. Any variant subtype can be used with the **Select Case/End Select** structure.

- VBScript's **While/Wend** repetition structure and **Do While/Loop** behave identically to Java-Script's **while** repetition structure. VBScript's **Do/Loop While** structure behaves identically to JavaScript's **do/while** repetition structure. VBScript contains two additional repetition structures, **Do Until/Loop** and **Do/Loop Until**, that do not have direct JavaScript equivalents. These **Do Until** repetition structures iterate until the condition becomes **True**.

- The **Exit Do** statement, when executed in a **Do While/Loop, Do/Loop While, Do Until/ Loop** or **Do/Loop Until**, causes immediate exit from that structure and execution continues with the next statement in sequence. The fact that a **Do While/Loop** may contain **Exit Do** is the only difference, other than syntax, between **Do While/Loop** and **While/Wend**. Statement **Exit For** causes immediate exit from the **For/Next** structure.

- Function **IsEmpty** determines whether the variant has ever been initialized by the programmer. If **IsEmpty** returns **True**, the variant has not been initialized by the programmer.

- VBScript math functions allow the programmer to perform common mathematical calculations. Trigonometric functions such as **Cos**, **Sin**, etc. take arguments that are expressed in radians. To convert from degrees to radians use the formula: *radians = degrees* $\times \pi$ / *180*.

- Function **InputBox** displays a dialog in which the user can input data.

- VBScript coordinates are measured in units of twips (1440 twips equal 1 Inch). Coordinates are relative to the upper-left corner of the screen, which is position *(0, 0)*. *X* coordinates increase from left to right and *y* coordinates increase from top to bottom.

- Many VBScript functions often take optional arguments.

- The underscore character, _ is VBScript's line continuation character. A statement cannot extend beyond the current line without using this character. A statement may use as many line continuation characters as necessary.

- Function **MsgBox** displays a message dialog.

- In VBScript, function calls that wrap arguments in parentheses must be preceded with keyword **Call**—unless the function call is assigning a value to a variable.

- VBScript provides functions for getting information about the scripting engine (i.e., the interpreter). These functions are **ScriptEngine**—which returns either **"JScript"**, **"VBScript"** or **"VBA"**, **ScriptEngineBuildVersion**—which returns the current build version, **ScriptEngineMajorVersion**—which returns the major version number for the script engine and **ScriptEngineMinorVersion**—which returns the minor release number.

- HTML comment tags comment out the VBScript code. If the browser understands VBScript, these tags are ignored and the VBScript is interpreted. If the browser does not understand VBScript, the HTML comment prevents the VBScript code from being displayed as text.

- Procedures that do not return a value begin with keyword **Sub** and end with keywords **End Sub**.

- Variables declared within a VBScript procedure are visible only within the procedure body. Procedures that perform event handling are more properly called event procedures.

- VBScript provides functions **CBool, CByte, CCur, CDate, CDbl, CInt, CLng, CSng** and **CStr** for converting between variant subtypes.

- Programmer-defined constants are created by using keyword **Const**.

- Because the **HEAD** section of an HTML document is decoded first by the browser, VBScript code is normally placed there, so it can be decoded before it is invoked in the document.

- VBScript procedures that return a value are delimited with keywords **Function** and **End Function**. A value is returned from a **Function** procedure by assigning a value to the procedure name. As in JavaScript, a **Function** procedure can return only one value at a time.

- VBScript provides statements **Exit Sub** and **Exit Function** for exiting **Sub** procedures and **Function** procedures, respectively. Control is returned to the caller, and the next statement in sequence after the call is executed.

- A fixed-size array's size does not change during program execution; a dynamic array's size can change during execution. A dynamic array is also called a redimmable array. Array elements may be referred to by giving the array name followed by the element position number in parentheses, **()**. The first array element is at index zero.

- Function **UBound** returns the upper bound (i.e., the highest-numbered index) and function **LBound** returns the lowest-numbered index (i.e., 0).

- Keyword **Public** explicitly indicates that a procedure is public. A procedure may also be marked as **Private**, to indicate that only scripts on the same Web page may call the procedure.

- Statement **ReDim** allocates memory for a dynamic array. All dynamic arrays must receive memory via **ReDim**. Dynamic arrays are more flexible than fixed-sized arrays, because they can be resized anytime using **ReDim** to accommodate new data.

- Function **Array** takes any number of arguments and returns an array containing those arguments.

- Keyword **Preserve** may be used with **ReDim** to maintain the current values in the array. When **ReDim** is executed without **Preserve**, all values contained in the array are lost.

- Arrays can have multiple dimensions. VBScript supports at least 60 array dimensions, but most programmers will need to use no more than two- or three-dimensional arrays. Multidimensional arrays can also be created dynamically.

- Memory allocated for dynamic arrays can be deallocated (released) at run-time using keyword **Erase**. A dynamic array that has been deallocated must be redimensioned with **ReDim** before it can be used again. **Erase** can also be used with fixed-sized arrays to initialize all the array elements to the empty string.

- VBScript strings are case sensitive and begin with an index of 1.

- Objects encapsulate data (attributes) and methods (behaviors); the data and methods of an object are intimately tied together. Objects have the property of information hiding. This means that although objects may communicate with one another, objects do not know how other objects are implemented—implementation details are hidden within the objects themselves.

- In VBScript, the unit of object-oriented programming is the **Class** from which objects are instantiated (i.e., created). Methods are VBScript procedures that are encapsulated with the data they process within the "walls" of classes.

- VBScript programmers can create their own user-defined types called classes. Classes are also referred to as programmer-defined types. Each class contains data as well as the set of methods which manipulate that data. The data components of a class are called instance variables. Just as an instance of a variant is called a variable, an instance of a class is called an object.

- Classes normally hide their implementation details from the clients (i.e., users) of the classes. This is called information hiding.

- Describing an object in terms of behaviors without concern for how those behaviors are actually implemented is called data abstraction, and VBScript classes define abstract data types (ADTs). Although users may happen to know how a class is implemented, users must not write code that depends on these details. This means that a class can be replaced with another version without affecting the rest of the system, as long as the **Public** interface of that class does not change (i.e. every method still has the same name, return type and parameter list in the new class definition).

- Access to **Private** data should be carefully controlled by the class's methods. For example, to allow clients to read the value of **Private** data, the class can provide a get method (also called an accessor method or a query method).

- To enable clients to modify **Private** data, the class can provide a set method (also called a mutator method). A set method can also translate between the form of the data used in the interface and the form used in the implementation. A get method need not expose the data in "raw" format; rather, the get method can edit the data and limit the view of the data the client will see.

- Classes often provide **Public** methods to allow clients of the class to set (i.e., assign values to) or get (i.e., obtain the values of) **Private** instance variables. These methods are special methods in VBScript called **Property Let**, **Property Set** and **Property Get** (collectively these methods and the internal class data they manipulate are called properties). Procedures **Property Let** and **Property Set** differ in that **Property Let** is used for non-object subtypes (e.g., integer, string, byte, etc.) and **Property Set** is used for object subtypes.

- Method definitions that are not preceded by **Public** or **Private** default to **Public**. Variables declared with **Dim** default to **Public**. Methods designated as **Private** are often called utility or helper methods. These methods are considered to be part of a class's implementation detail, and therefore clients do not have access to them.

- When creating an object, VBScript keyword **New** is used followed by the class name. When assigning the object to a variable, keyword **Set** must be used. When a variable (e.g., **wakeUp**) refers to an object, the variable is called a reference.

- Any **Property Get**, **Property Let** or **Property Set** method may contain the **Exit Property** statement that causes an immediate exit from a **Property** procedure.

- Class **RegExp** may be used to create a regular expression object. A **RegExp** object's **Pattern** property stores a regular expression. Function **Test** determines whether a regular expression's **Pattern** is a match for the string argument passed into it.

TERMINOLOGY

$	**CDbl** function
\d	**Chr** function
^	**CInt** function
Abs function	**Class** keyword
abstract data type (ADT)	client
accessor method	**CLng** function
Active Server Pages (ASP)	comment character, **'**
addition operator, **+**	comparison operator
And logical operator	**Const** keyword
Array function	**Cos** function
Asc function	**CStr** function
Atn function	currency subtype
attribute	date/time subtype
behavior	**Dim** keyword
boolean subtype	**Do Loop/Until** control structure
build version	**Do Loop/While** control structure
byte subtype	**Do Until/Loop** control structure
CBool function	**Do While/Loop** control structure
CByte function	double subtype
CCur function	dynamic array
CDate function	**ElseIf** keyword

Rem keyword
Replace function
Right function
Rnd function
Round function
RTrim function
ScriptEngine function
ScriptEngineBuildVersion function
ScriptEngineMajorVersion function
ScriptEngineMinorVersion function
Set keyword
set method
Sgn function
Sin function
single subtype
software reusability
Space function
Split function
Sqr function
Step keyword
StrComp function
string concatenation operator, **&**
String function
string subtype
StrReverse function
subtraction operator, **–**

subtype of a variant
Tan function
Test function
To keyword
Trim function
True keyword
twip
TypeName function
UBound function
UCase function
upper bound
user-defined type
variant data type
variant subtype
VarType function
vbLongDate constant
VBScript (Visual Basic Scripting Edition)
VBScript language attribute
VBScript scripting engine
vbShortTime constant
vbTextCompare constant
verb
Wend keyword
While/Wend control structure
With keyword
XOr logical operator

SELF-REVIEW EXERCISES

24.1 State whether the following are *true* or *false*. If the answer is *false*, explain why.
  a) VBScript is case-sensitive.
  b) **Option Explicit** forces all VBScript variables to be declared.
  c) The single quote character indicates a VBScript comment.
  d) The exponentiation operator's symbol is the caret, **^**.
  e) The starting index for an array may be set to either 0 or 1.
  f) Array dimensions begin at 0.

24.2 Fill in the blanks in each of the following:
  a) Keyword _____ is required when assigning an object to a reference.
  b) Keyword _____ is required when instantiating an object.
  c) VBScript variables are of type _____.
  d) Function _____ returns a string containing characters from the left side of a string.
  e) Class _____ defines a regular expression.
  f) Function _____ returns an uppercase string.

24.3 Briefly explain the difference between a **Function** procedure and a **Sub** procedure.

24.4 Fill in the blanks in each of the following:
  a) Keyword _____ is used to create a constant.
  b) By default, script variables declared with **Dim** are _____.
  c) Statement **ReDim** is used to allocate memory for a _____ array.

d) **Property** _____ returns a property's value.

e) _____ is the logical AND operator.

f) Function _____ returns the highest numbered array index.

ANSWERS TO SELF-REVIEW EXERCISES

24.1   a) False. VBScript is case-insensitive. b) True. c) True. d) True. e) False. An array's starting index is always 0. f) False. Array dimensions begin at 1.

24.2   a) **Set**. b) **New**. c) variant. d) **Left**. e) **RegExp**. f) **UCase**.

24.3   A **Function** procedure returns a value and a **Sub** procedure does not return a value.

24.4   a) **Const**. b) **Public**. c) dynamic. d) **Get**. e) **And**. f) **UBound**.

EXERCISES

24.5   *(Compound Interest Calculator)* Create an HTML document that enables the user to calculate compound interest. Provide several **TEXT** components in which the user can enter the *principal amount*, the yearly interest *rate* and the number of *years* (see the compound interest program of Fig. 10.6 for the calculation of interest). Provide a **BUTTON** to cause the VBScript to execute and calculate the interest. Display the result in another **TEXT** component. If any **TEXT** component is left empty, display a **MsgBox** indicating the error. Use a **Function** procedure to perform the calculation.

24.6   *(Monthly Compound Interest Calculator)* Modify Exercise 24.5 to calculate the compound interest on a monthly basis. Remember that you must divide the interest rate by 12 to get the monthly rate.

24.7   Write a VBScript that allows the user to enter a name, email address and phone number. Use regular expressions to perform the validation (e.g., names can only contain letters, email must be of the format *username@name.extension* and the phone number must have the format *(555) 555-5555)*. *Note*: you should read the article on regular expression (listed in the Web Resources section) before attempting this exercise.

24.8   Modify the script of Fig. 24.24 to use some of the string-related functions introduced in Section 24.7 to perform the validation instead of a regular expression. How does your new solution compare?

24.9   Write a VBScript that generates from the string **"abcdefghijklmnopqrstuvwxyz{"** the following:

```
            a
           bcb
          cdedc
         defgfed
        efghihgfe
       fghijkjihgf
      ghijklmlkjihg
     hijklmnonmlkjih
    ijklmnopqponmlkji
   jklmnopqrsrqponmlkj
  klmnopqrstutsrqponmlk
 lmnopqrstuvwvutsrqponml
mnopqrstuvwxyxwvutsrqponm
nopqrstuvwxyz{zyxwvutsrqpon
```

24.10 Law enforcement agencies often get partial descriptions of suspect license plate numbers and have to search for license plate numbers that match the description. Create a program that will allow a local law enforcement agency to determine how many license plate numbers match a partial description. Randomly create 500 6-character long license plate numbers and store them in an array. Allow the user to search for partial plate numbers of 3 or 4 digits. *Note*: License plate numbers can contain both digits and letters. The array should not contain any duplicates.

24.11 Write a program that reads a five-letter word from the user and produces all possible three-letter words that can be derived from the letters of the five-letter word. For example, the three-letter words produced from the word "bathe" include the commonly used words

ate   bat   bet   tab   hat   the   tea

24.12 Create a class called **CComplex** for performing arithmetic with complex numbers. Write a program to test your class.
    Complex numbers have the form

$$realPart + imaginaryPart \infty i$$

where *i* is

$$\sqrt{-1}$$

    Use floating-point subtypes to represent the **Private** data of the class. Provide **Public** methods for each of the following:

   a) Addition of two **CComplex** numbers: The real parts are added together and the imaginary parts are added together.

   b) Subtraction of two **CComplex** numbers: The real part of the right operand is subtracted from the real part of the left operand and the imaginary part of the right operand is subtracted from the imaginary part of the left operand.

   c) Printing **CComplex** numbers in the form **(A, B)**, where **A** is the real part and **B** is the imaginary part.

24.13 Create a class called **CRational** for performing arithmetic with fractions. Write a program to test your class.
    Use integer variables to represent the **Private** instance variables of the class—**mNumerator** and **mDenominator**. The class should store the fraction in reduced form (i.e., the fraction

2/4

would be stored in the object as 1 in the **mNumerator** and 2 in the **mDenominator**). Provide **Public** methods for each of the following:

   a) Addition of two **CRational** numbers. The result is stored in reduced form.

   b) Subtraction of two **CRational** numbers. The result is stored in reduced form.

   c) Multiplication of two **CRational** numbers. The result is stored in reduced form.

   d) Division of two **CRational** numbers. The result is stored in reduced form.

   e) Returning **CRational** numbers in the form **mNumerator/mDenominator** (i.e., a string with this format).

   f) Returning **CRational** numbers in floating-point format. (Consider providing formatting capabilities that enable the user of the class to specify the number of digits of precision to the right of the decimal point.)

24.14   Use a two-dimensional array to solve the following problem. A company has four salespeople (with salesperson numbers 1 to 4) who sell five different products (with product numbers 1 to 5). Once a day, each salesperson passes in a slip for each different type of product sold. Each slip contains the salesperson number, product number and the total dollar value of that product sold that day.

Write a program that reads this information and summarizes the total sales by salesperson by product. All totals should be stored in the two-dimensional array **sales**. After each input, print the results in tabular format, with each of the columns representing a particular salesperson and each of the rows representing a particular product. Cross-total each row to get the total sales of each product for last month; cross total each column to get the total sales by salesperson for last month. Your neat tabular printout should include these cross-totals to the right of the totaled rows and at the bottoms of the totaled columns. Use VBScript function **FormatCurrency** as part of your solution.

24.15   Use a one-dimensional array to solve the following problem. A company pays its salespeople on a commission basis. The salespeople receive $200 per week plus 9% of their gross sales for that week. For example, a salesperson who grosses $5000 in sales in a week receives $200 plus 9% of $5000, or a total of $650. Write a program (using an array of counters) that determines how many of the salespeople earned salaries in each of the following ranges (assume that each salesperson's salary is truncated to an integer amount):

Salary Ranges

1) $200-$299   6) $700-$799

2) $300-$399   7) $800-$899

3) $400-$499   8) $900-$999

4) $500-$599   9) $1000 and over

5) $600-$699

24.16   Use a one-dimensional dynamic array to solve the following problem. Read in 20 numbers, each of which is between 10 and 100, inclusive. As each number is input, print it only if it is not a duplicate of a number already input. Provide for the "worst case," in which all 20 numbers are different.

24.17   Write a Web page that allows the user to select one or more books by using check boxes. Display the name of each book and its price. Display the current total in a text box at the bottom of the page. When a book is selected (or unselected), update the total. Use VBScript to perform any arithmetic operations and to format the total.

24.18   (*VBScript Calculator*) Write a VBScript calculator that provides addition, subtraction, multiplication and division operations.

24.19   Modify your solution to Exercise 24.21 to include scientific features such as exponentiation, cosine, sine, etc. Use the Windows calculator as a guide.

24.20   In the chapter, we mentioned that VBScript contains various date/time manipulations. Study these date/time capabilities by visiting the resources listed in Section 24.9. Write a program that demonstrates as many of these capabilities as possible.

24.21   Write a **Function** procedure **ToMorseCode** that takes one string argument and returns a string containing the Morse code equivalent. Figure 18.12 lists the Morse code for letters and digits.

24.22 Write a program that plays the "guess the number" game as follows: Your program chooses the number to be guessed by selecting an **Integer** at random in the range 1 to 1000, then displays

```
I have a number between 1 and 1000.
Can you guess my number?
Please enter your first guess.
```

The player then types a first guess. The program responds with one of the following:

```
Excellent! You guessed the number!
Would you like to play again (y or n)?

Too low. Try again.
Too high. Try again.
```

If the player's guess is incorrect, your program should keep telling the player "**Too high**" or "**Too low**" to help the player "zero in" on the correct answer.

25

Active Server Pages (ASP)

Objectives

- To be able to program Active Server Pages using VBScript.
- To understand how Active Server Pages work.
- To understand the differences between client-side scripting and server-side scripting.
- To be able to pass data between Web pages.
- To be able to use server-side include statements.
- To be able to use server-side ActiveX components.
- To be able to create sessions.
- To be able to use cookies.
- To be able to use ActiveX Data Objects (ADO) to access a database.

A client is to me a mere unit, a factor in a problem.
Sir Arthur Conan Doyle

Rule One: Our client is always right.
Rule Two: If you think our client is wrong, see Rule One.
Anonymous

Protocol is everything.
Francoise Giuliani

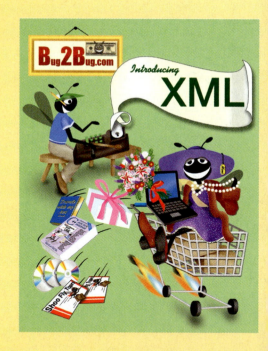

25.1　Introduction

In the previous chapters, we discussed client-side scripting and its function in creating interactive Web pages, form data validation, etc. In this chapter, we discuss server-side scripting, which is essential to e-commerce applications. In the next several chapters, we introduce many server-side technologies, such as database interaction, that are crucial to e-commerce applications. In this and the next chapter, we use server-side text files called *Active Server Pages* (*ASP*) that are processed in response to a client (e.g., browser) request. These pages are processed by an *ActiveX component* (i.e., a server-side ActiveX control) called a *scripting engine*. An ASP file has the file extension **.asp** and contains HTML tags and scripting code. Although other languages like JavaScript can be used for ASP scripting, VBScript is the most widely used language for ASP scripting. If you are not familiar with VBScript, please read Chapter 24, "VBScript," before reading this chapter.

Software Engineering Observation 25.1

Some independent software vendors (ISVs) provide scripting engines for use with ASP that support languages other than VBScript and JavaScript.

Server-side scripting uses information sent by clients, information stored on the server, information stored in the server's memory and information from the Internet to dynamically create Web pages. The examples in this chapter illustrate how Active Server Pages use server and client information to send dynamic Web pages to clients. We present a clock, advertisement rotator, guest book, Web-page creator and user verification system. In Chapter 26, we concentrate on e-commerce applications (i.e., a shopping cart, an online auction site and a comparison-pricing program) that feature Active Server Pages.

25.2 How Active Server Pages Work

The Active Server Pages in this chapter demonstrate communication between clients and servers via the HTTP protocol of the World Wide Web. When a server receives a client's HTTP request, the server loads the document (or page) requested by the client. HTML documents are *static documents*—all clients see the same content when requesting an HTML document. ASP is a Microsoft technology for sending to the client dynamic Web content—which includes HTML, Dynamic HTML, ActiveX controls, client-side scripts and *Java applets* (i.e., client-side Java programs that are embedded in a Web page). The Active Server Page processes the request (which often includes interacting with a database), and returns the results to the client—normally in the form of an HTML document, but other data formats (e.g., images, binary data, etc.) can be returned.

The two most common *HTTP request types* (also known as *request methods*) are **GET** and **POST**. These requests are frequently used to send client form data to a Web server. Although **GET** and **POST** both send information to the server, the method of sending the information is different. A **GET** request sends form content as part of the URL (e.g., **www.searchsomething.com/search?query=userquery**). A **POST** request *posts* form contents to the end of an HTTP request. An HTTP request contains information about the server, client, connection, authorization, etc.

Software Engineering Observation 25.2

*The data sent in a **POST** request is not part of the URL and cannot be seen by the user. Forms that contain many fields are most often submitted by a **POST** request. Sensitive form fields such as passwords are usually sent using this request type.*

An HTTP request is often used to post data to a server-side form handler that processes the data. For example, when the user responds to a Web-based survey, a request sends the Web server the information specified in the HTML form.

Browsers often *cache* (save on disk) Web pages for quick reloading. This speeds up the user's browsing experience by reducing the amount of data downloaded to view a Web page. Browsers typically do not cache the server's response to a **POST** request because the next **POST** request may not contain the same information. For example, several users might request the same Web page to participate in a survey. Each user's response changes the overall results of the survey.

When a Web-based search engine is used, a **GET** request normally supplies the search engine with the information specified in the HTML form. The search engine then performs the search and returns the results as a Web page. These pages are often cached in the event that the user performs the same search again.

When a client requests an ASP document, it is loaded into memory and parsed (top to bottom) by a scripting engine named ***asp.dll***. Script code is interpreted as it is encountered.

Portability Tip 25.1

*Because browsers are capable of rendering HTML, an ASP page that generates pure HTML can be rendered on any client browser—regardless of the fact that the page requested ends in **.asp**.*

Software Engineering Observation 25.3

*To take advantage of Active Server Page technology, a Web server must provide a component such as **asp.dll** to support ASP.*

25.3 Client-side Scripting versus Server-side Scripting

In earlier chapters, we focused on client-side scripting with JavaScript and VBScript. Client-side scripting is often used for validation, interactivity, accessing the browser and enhancing a Web page with ActiveX controls, Dynamic HTML and Java applets. Client-side validation reduces the number of requests the server receives and therefore reduces the amount of work the server must perform. Interactivity allows the user to make decisions, click buttons, play games, etc.—which is often more interesting than just reading text. ActiveX controls, Dynamic HTML and Java applets enhance a Web page's appearance by providing richer functionality than HTML. Client-side scripts can access the browser, use features specific to that browser and manipulate browser documents.

Client-side scripting does have limitations such as browser dependency, where the browser or *scripting host* must support the scripting language. Another limitation is that client-side scripts are viewable (e.g., using the **View** menu's **Source** command in Internet Explorer) to the client. Some Web developers do not like this, because people can easily steal their scripting code.

Software Engineering Observation 25.4

JavaScript is the most popular client-side scripting language and is supported by both Microsoft Internet Explorer and Netscape Communicator.

Performance Tip 25.1

To conserve server resources, perform as much processing as possible on the client side.

Because server-side scripts reside on the server, programmers have greater flexibility—especially when accessing databases. Scripts executed on the server usually generate custom responses for clients. For example, a client might connect to an airline's Web server and request a list of all flights from Boston to Dallas between September 18th and November 5th. The script queries the database, dynamically generates HTML content containing the flight list and sends HTML to the client. A client who connects to the airline's Web server always gets the most current database information.

Server-side scripts also have access to server-side ActiveX components that extend scripting language functionality. We discuss some of these components later in this chapter.

An HTML document can contain both client-side script (e.g., JavaScript) and server-side script (e.g., VBScript).

Portability Tip 25.2

Server-side scripts run exclusively on the server; therefore cross-platform issues are not a concern.

Software Engineering Observation 25.5

Server-side scripts are not visible to the client—only HTML (plus any client-side scripts) are sent to the client.

25.4 Using Personal Web Server or Internet Information Server

This chapter contains several examples that require Personal Web Server (PWS) 4.0 or *Internet Information Server (IIS)* 4.0 or higher to execute. Before attempting to execute any example, you should make sure PWS or IIS is running. For help installing and running PWS, see the "Web Server Installation" document on the CD that accompanies this book for instructions on how to install and set up a Web server.

[*Note*: Do not confuse Internet Information Server 4.0 (IIS 4.0) with *Internet Information Services 5.0 (IIS 5.0)*. IIS 5.0 is integrated into Windows 2000 and is similar to PWS. For more information on Internet Information Services 5.0, visit the following Web site: **www.microsoft.com/windows2000/guide/server/features/web.asp**.]

If you are going to execute the chapter examples, we recommend that you create a subdirectory beneath **C:\Webshare\Wwwroot** or **C:\Inetpub\Wwwroot** named **Deitel**. Copy all the **.asp** files from the Chapter 25 examples directory (included on the book's CD) to this directory. Create two other directories beneath **C:\Webshare\Wwwroot** named **includes** and **images**. Copy all **.shtml** files from the CD to **includes** and all **.gif** (or any other graphic file extension) files to **images**. [*Note*: you will need to modify some of the paths in the **.asp** files to reflect these directories.]

To execute a particular example, type **http://***machineName***/Deitel/***name***.asp** into the Web browser's **Address** field and press *Enter*. For example, to execute **clock.asp** on a machine named **thunder** type

```
http://thunder/Deitel/clock.asp
```

into the Web browser's **Address** field and press *Enter*. To determine the machine name, in Windows 98, right-click **Network Neighborhood** and select **Properties** from the context menu to display the **Network** dialog. In the **Network** dialog, click the **Identification** tab. Displayed in the **Computer name:** field is the computer name. Click **Cancel** to close the **Network** dialog.

In Windows 2000, right click **My Network Places** and select **Properties** from the context menu to display the **Network and Dialup Connections** explorer. In the explorer, click **Network Identification**. The computer name is displayed in the **Full Computer Name:** field in the **System Properties** window. Click **Cancel** to close the **System Properties** window.

Several Active Server Pages access a database. The database files (e.g., **.mdb** files) can be copied into any directory on your system. Before executing these examples, you must set up a System Data Source Name (DSN). See the "Setting up a System Data Source Name" document on the CD that accompanies this book for instructions on how to create a DSN.

25.5 Active Server Page Objects

Active Server Pages provide several built-in objects to offer programmers straightforward methods for communicating with a Web browser, gathering data sent by an HTTP request and distinguishing between users. Figure 25.1 provides a short description of the most commonly used ASP objects.

The ***Request*** *object* is commonly used to access the information passed by a **GET** or **POST** request. This information usually consists of data provided by the user in an HTML form. The **Request** object provides access to information, such as "cookies", that are stored on a client's machine. This object can also access binary information (e.g., a file upload) as well. The ***Response*** *object* sends information such as HTML, text, etc. to the client.

Object Name	Description
Request	Used to access information passed by an HTTP request.
Response	Used to control the information sent to the user.
Server	Used to access methods and properties on the server.

Fig. 25.1 Some built-in ASP objects.

The *Server object* provides access to methods and properties on the server. The **Server** object provides a method (**CreateObject**) to instantiate other objects. We can create instances of built-in objects, ActiveX components, etc.

25.6 A Simple ASP Example

In this section, we present a simple ASP example (Fig. 25.2) that represents a clock. Every 60 seconds, the page is updated with the server's time.

Notice the *scripting delimiters* **<%** and **%>** wrapped around the VBScript code—these indicate that the scripting code is executed on the server, not the client. Nothing enclosed in scripting delimiters is sent to the client; it is processed by the scripting engine. However, the scripting code inside the delimiters can generate information that is sent to the client. Everything outside of **<%** and **%>** is simply written to the client. The client's browser then interprets and renders the Web page (e.g., HTML sent to the client).

```
1   <% @LANGUAGE = VBScript %>
2   <% Option Explicit %>
3   <% ' Fig. 25.2 : clock.asp %>
4
5   <!DOCTYPE HTML PUBLIC "-//W3C//DTD HTML 4.0 Transitional//EN">
6   <HTML>
7   <HEAD>
8   <TITLE>A Simple ASP Example</TITLE>
9   <META HTTP-EQUIV = "REFRESH" CONTENT = "60; URL=CLOCK.ASP">
10  </HEAD>
11  <BODY>
12
13  <FONT FACE = "Arial" SIZE = "4"><STRONG>Simple ASP Example</STRONG>
14  </FONT><P>
15     <TABLE BORDER = "6">
16     <TR>
17     <TD BGCOLOR = "#000000">
18        <FONT FACE = "Arial" COLOR = "#00FF00" SIZE = "4">
19           <% =Time() %>
20        </FONT>
21     </TD>
22     </TR>
23     </TABLE>
```

Fig. 25.2 A simple Active Server Page (part 1 of 2).

```
24    </BODY>
25    </HTML>
```

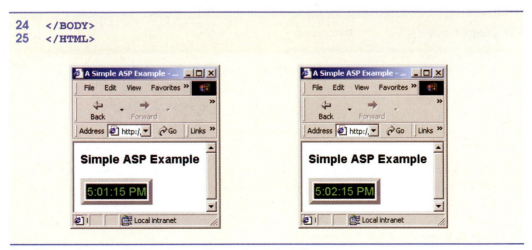

Fig. 25.2   A simple Active Server Page (part 2 of 2).

Common Programming Error 25.1

*Missing the opening delimiter, **<%**, or closing delimiter, **%>**, or both for a server-side script-ing statement is an error.*

Line 1

```
<% @LANGUAGE = "VBScript" %>
```

uses the optional ***@LANGUAGE*** *processing directive* to specify VBScript as the scripting language. This indicates the scripting engine needed to interpret the scripting code. In this chapter, we use VBScript exclusively to develop our Active Server Pages although other scripting languages such as JavaScript may be used. If the **@LANGUAGE** processing directive is not used, VBScript is the default.

Good Programming Practice 25.1

*When using VBScript code in an Active Server Page, use the **@LANGUAGE** statement for clarity.*

Common Programming Error 25.2

*When using the **@LANGUAGE** tag, not placing it inside the first statement in an ASP file is an error.*

Line 2 uses **Option Explicit** to indicate that the programmer must explicitly declare all VBScript variables. Remember that by simply mentioning a new name, VBScript variables are implicitly declared. This can lead to subtle errors. When used, the **Option Explicit** statement must be the first VBScript scripting statement after the **@LANGUAGE** statement. In this particular example, we do not declare any variables, but we include the **Option Explicit** statement as a good programming practice.

Testing and Debugging Tip 25.1

*Always include **Option Explicit** even if you are not declaring any VBScript variables. As a script evolves over time, you may need to declare variables and the presence of the **Option Explicit** statement can help eliminate subtle errors.*

We use the **META** tag on line 9 to set the refresh interval for the page. The **CONTENT** attribute specifies the number of seconds (**60**) until the **URL** attribute's value (**clock.asp**) is requested. Refreshing occurs every minute.

Line 19

```
<% =Time() %>
```

calls VBScript function *Time* to get the current time on the server. Function **Time** returns the time in the format, *hh:mm:ss*. This statement is short for

```
<% Call Response.Write( Time() ) %>
```

which calls the **Response** method *Write* to send the time as text to the client. One of the key points of this example is that the ASP indirectly requests itself. The **URL** attribute requests that the page reload itself every 60 seconds. This is perfectly valid and often done in ASP programming.

25.7 Server-side ActiveX Components

Server-side script functionality is extended with server-side ActiveX components—ActiveX controls that typically reside on the Web server and do not have a graphical user interface. These components make powerful features accessible to the ASP author. Figure 25.3 summarizes some of the ActiveX components included with Internet Information Server (IIS), Internet Information Services and Personal Web Server (PWS).

Component Name	Description
MSWC.BrowserType	ActiveX component for gathering information about the client's browser (e.g., type, version, etc.).
MSWC.AdRotator	ActiveX component for rotating advertisements on a Web page.
MSWC.NextLink	ActiveX component for linking Web pages together.
MSWC.ContentRotator	ActiveX component for rotating HTML content on a Web page.
MSWC.PageCounter	ActiveX component for storing the number of times a Web page has been requested.
MSWC.Counters	ActiveX components that provide general-purpose persistent counters.
MSWC.MyInfo	ActiveX component that provides information about a Web site (e.g., owner name, owner address, etc.).
Scripting.FileSystemObject	ActiveX component that provides an object library for accessing files on the server or on the server's network.
ActiveX Data Objects (ADO) Data Access Components	ActiveX components that provide an object library for accessing databases.

Fig. 25.3   Some server-side ActiveX components included with IIS and PWS.

Software Engineering Observation 25.6

If the scripting language you are using in an Active Server Page does not support a certain feature, an ActiveX server component can be created using Visual C++, Visual Basic, Delphi, etc., to provide that feature.

Performance Tip 25.2

Server-side ActiveX components usually execute faster than their scripting language equivalents.

Many Web sites sell advertising space—especially Web sites with large numbers of hits. In Fig. 25.4, we demonstrate the *AdRotator ActiveX component* for rotating advertisements on a Web page. Each time a client requests this Active Server Page, the AdRotator component randomly displays one of several advertisements—in this example, one of five flag images. When the user clicks a country's flag image, the country's corresponding Central Intelligence Agency (CIA) Fact book Web page is displayed. [*Note:* This is the first of several examples that consist of multiple files. When a file is part of the same example, we continue the line numbering from the last line number in the previous listing. We do this for discussion purposes and to connect all the example parts.]

Line 20

```
Set flagChanger = Server.CreateObject( "MSWC.AdRotator" )
```

```
1   <% @LANGUAGE = VBScript %>
2   <% Option Explicit %>
3   <% ' Fig. 25.4 : rotate.asp %>
4
5   <!DOCTYPE HTML PUBLIC "-//W3C//DTD HTML 4.0 Transitional//EN">
6   <HTML>
7   <HEAD>
8   <TITLE>AdRotator Example</TITLE>
9   </HEAD>
10
11  <BODY>
12  <FONT FACE = "Arial" SIZE = "4">
13  <STRONG>AdRotator Example</STRONG>
14  </FONT><P>
15  <%
16      ' Declare flagChanger
17      Dim flagChanger
18
19      ' Create an AdRotator object
20      Set flagChanger = Server.CreateObject( "MSWC.AdRotator" )
21
22      ' Use config.txt to send an advertisement to the client
23      Call Response.Write( _
24         flagChanger.GetAdvertisement( "config.txt" ) )
25  %>
26  </BODY>
27  </HTML>
```

Fig. 25.4   Demonstrating AdRotator ActiveX component (part 1 of 2).

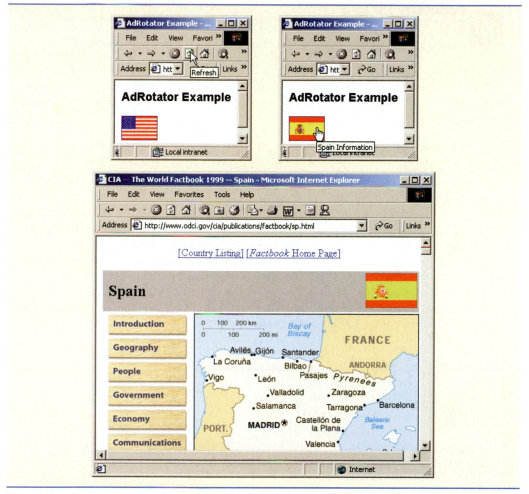

Fig. 25.4   Demonstrating AdRotator ActiveX component (part 2 of 2).

creates an instance of an AdRotator component and assigns it to reference **flagChanger**. Server-side ActiveX components are instantiated by passing the name of the component as a string to the **Server** object's method *CreateObject*.

Lines 23 and 24

```
Call Response.Write( _
    flagChanger.GetAdvertisement( "config.txt" ) )
```

call the **Response** object's **Write** method to send the advertisement as HTML to the client. Method *GetAdvertisement* is called using reference **flagChanger** to get the advertisements from the file **config.txt** (Fig. 25.5).

Software Engineering Observation 25.7

The AdRotator ActiveX component allows the page author to minimize the amount of space on a Web page committed to advertisements while at the same time maximizing the number of advertisements to display.

Portability Tip 25.3

Because the AdRotator ActiveX component is executed on the server, clients do not directly interact with the component and therefore do not have to support ActiveX technologies

The file's header (lines 28 through 31) includes the URL of the **REDIRECT** file, **redirect.asp** (discussed momentarily), the image **HEIGHT**, image **WIDTH** and image **BORDER** width. The asterisk (line 32) separates the header from the advertisements. Lines 33 through 36

```
/images/us.gif
http://www.odci.gov/cia/publications/factbook/us.html
United States Information
20
```

describe the first advertisement by providing the image's URL (the image's location), the destination URL for redirection upon clicking the ad, a value for the **ALT** tag (browsers that cannot display graphics display the specified text) and a number (between 0 and 1000) representing the ratio of time this particular image appears. The ratios must be numbers between 0 and 10000. For example, if four ads have the ratios 6, 9, 12 and 3, then the time ratios are calculated as 20% (6/30), 30% (9/30), 40% (12/30) and 10% (3/30), respectively. Lines 37 through 52 list the other four advertisements. [*Note*: If you are executing this example, copy **config.txt** to the **Deitel** directory you created in Section 25.4.]

```
28    REDIRECT redirect.asp
29    WIDTH 54
30    HEIGHT 36
31    BORDER 1
32    *
33    /images/us.gif
34    http://www.odci.gov/cia/publications/factbook/us.html
35    United States Information
36    20
37    /images/france.gif
38    http://www.odci.gov/cia/publications/factbook/fr.html
39    France Information
40    20
41    /images/germany.gif
42    http://www.odci.gov/cia/publications/factbook/gm.html
43    Germany Information
44    20
45    /images/italy.gif
46    http://www.odci.gov/cia/publications/factbook/it.html
47    Italy Information
48    20
49    /images/spain.gif
50    http://www.odci.gov/cia/publications/factbook/sp.html
51    Spain Information
52    20
```

Fig. 25.5   File **config.txt** that describes the advertisements.

File **redirect.asp** contains exactly one line:

```
<% Call Response.Redirect( Request( "url" ) ) %>
```

This redirects the user to the country page when the ad is clicked. Each time the ad is clicked, the document **redirect.asp** is requested and a *query string* is sent with the request. The query string contains an attribute **url** that is equal to the destination URL found in **config.txt** for this ad. For example, if you click the U.S. flag, the resulting behavior is equivalent to typing

> **http://localhost/Deitel/redirect.asp?url=http://www.odci.gov/
> cia/publications/factbook/us.html**

in the browser's **Address** field.

We arbitrarily chose the names **config.txt** and **redirect.asp**. You may choose any name you prefer. The redirect file loads (into the browser) the page referenced by the ad's URL. These files can be placed anywhere in the publishing directory (i.e., they do not have to be under the same directory as **rotate.asp**). For example, if you put **config.txt** under directory **X** in the publishing directory, then lines 23 and 24 would read

```
Call Response.Write( _
    flagChanger.GetAdvertisement( "/X/config.txt" ) )
```

Note that **GetAdvertisement** is passed a URL, not a physical disk path. Hence the use of the forward slash. Also note that **/X/config.txt** is short for **http://local-host/X/config.txt** (the server is **localhost** and the publishing directory is **C:\Webshare\Wwwroot**). You can replace **localhost** by the IP address **127.0.0.1**, which also refers to the local machine.

Figure 25.6 shows the HTML sent by **rotate.asp**. [*Note*: This file has been edited for presentation (e.g., the HTML **HEAD** and **BODY** tags have been omitted).]

25.8 File System Objects

File System Objects (*FSOs*) provide the programmer with the ability to manipulate files, directories and drives. FSOs also allow the programmer to read and write text and are an essential element for Active Server Pages that persist data. We first overview FSO features and then provide a "live-code" example that uses FSOs.

FSOs are objects in the *Microsoft Scripting Runtime Library*. Five FSO types exist: **FileSystemObject**, **File**, **Folder**, **Drive** and **TextStream**. Each type is summarized in Fig. 25.7.

```
53   <A HREF = "redirect.asp?url=http://www.odci.gov/cia/publications/
54      factbook/us.html&image=/images/us.gif">
55   <IMG SRC = "/images/us.gif" ALT = "United States Information"
56      WIDTH = "54" HEIGHT = "36" BORDER = "1"></A>
```

Fig. 25.6   HTML sent to the client by **rotate.asp** for the USA advertisement.

Object type	Description
FileSystemObject	Allows the programmer to interact with **File**s, **Folder**s and **Drive**s.
File	Allows the programmer to manipulate **File**s of any type.
Folder	Allows the programmer to manipulate **Folder**s (i.e., directories).
Drive	Allows the programmer to gather information about **Drive**s (hard disks, RAM disks—computer memory used as a substitute for hard disks to allow high-speed file operations, CD-ROMs, etc.). **Drive**s can be local or remote.
TextStream	Allows the programmer to read and write text files.

Fig. 25.7   File System Objects (FSOs).

The programmer can use **FileSystemObject**s to create directories, move files, determine whether a **Drive** exists, etc. Figure 25.8 summarizes some common methods of **FileSystemObject**.

The **File** object allows the programmer to gather information about files, manipulate files and open files. Figure 25.9 lists some common **File** properties and methods.

Methods	Description
CopyFile	Copies an existing **File**.
CopyFolder	Copies an existing **Folder**.
CreateFolder	Creates and returns a **Folder**.
CreateTextFile	Creates and returns a text **File**.
DeleteFile	Deletes a **File**.
DeleteFolder	Deletes a **Folder**.
DriveExists	Tests whether or not a **Drive** exists. Returns a boolean.
FileExists	Tests whether or not a **File** exists. Returns a boolean.
FolderExists	Tests whether or not a **Folder** exists. Returns a boolean.
GetAbsolutePathName	Returns the absolute path as a string.
GetDrive	Returns the specified **Drive**.
GetDriveName	Returns the **Drive** drive name.
GetFile	Returns the specified **File**.
GetFileName	Returns the **File** file name.
GetFolder	Returns the specified **Folder**.
GetParentFolderName	Returns a string representing the parent folder name.
GetTempName	Creates and returns a string representing a file name.
MoveFile	Moves a **File**.

Fig. 25.8   **FileSystemObject** methods (part 1 of 2).

Methods	Description
MoveFolder	Moves a **Folder**.
OpenTextFile	Opens an existing text **File**. Returns a **TextStream**.

Fig. 25.8 **FileSystemObject** methods (part 2 of 2).

Property/method	Description
Properties	
DateCreated	Date. The date the **File** was created.
DateLastAccessed	Date. The date the **File** was last accessed.
DateLastModified	Date. The date the **File** was last modified.
Drive	Drive object. The **Drive** where the file is located.
Name	String. The **File** name.
ParentFolder	String. The **File**'s parent folder name.
Path	String. The **File**'s path.
ShortName	String. The **File**'s name expressed as a short name.
Size	Variant. The size of the **File** in bytes.
Methods	
Copy	Copy the **File**. Same as **CopyFile** of **FileSystemObject**.
Delete	Delete the **File**. Same as **DeleteFile** of **FileSystemObject**.
Move	Move the **File**. Same as **MoveFile** of **FileSystemObject**.
OpenAsTextStream	Opens an existing **File** as a text **File**. Returns **TextStream**.

Fig. 25.9 Some common **File** properties and methods .

Property **Path** contains the **File**'s path in *long name format* (the operating system does not abbreviate the name when it exceeds the 8.3 format). Property **ShortName** contains, if applicable, the file name in *short name format* (a file name exceeding the 8.3 format is abbreviated). For example, a file name in long name format might be "**ABCD EFG HIJ.doc**." That same file name in short name format might be abbreviated as "**ABCDEF~1.doc**."

The **Folder** object allows the programmer to manipulate and gather information about directories. Figure 25.10 lists some common **Folder** properties and methods.

Property **IsRootFolder** indicates whether the folder is the *root folder* for the **Drive** (i.e., the folder that contains everything on the drive). If the folder is not the root folder, method **ParentFolder** may be called to get the folder's *parent folder* (i.e., the folder in which the selected folder is contained). Method **Size** returns the total number of bytes the folder contains. The size includes *subfolders* (i.e., folders inside the selected folder) and files.

Property/method	Description
Properties	
Attributes	Integer. Value indicating **Folder**'s attributes (read only, hidden, etc.).
DateCreated	Date. The date the folder was created.
DateLastAccessed	Date. The date the folder was last accessed.
DateLastModified	Date. The date the folder was last modified.
Drive	Drive object. The **Drive** where the folder is located.
IsRootFolder	Boolean. Indicates whether or not a **Folder** is the root folder.
Name	String. The **Folder**'s name.
ParentFolder	Folder object. The **Folder**'s parent folder.
Path	String. The **Folder**'s path.
ShortName	String. The **Folder**'s name expressed as a short name.
ShortPath	String. The **Folder**'s path expressed as a short path.
Size	Variant. The total size in bytes of all subfolders and files.
Type	String. The **Folder** type.
Methods	
Delete	Delete the **Folder**. Same as **DeleteFolder** of **FileSystemObject**.
Move	Move the **Folder**. Same as **MoveFolder** of **FileSystemObject**.
Copy	Copy the **Folder**. Same as **CopyFolder** of **FileSystemObject**.

Fig. 25.10   Some **Folder** properties and methods.

The **Drive** object allows the programmer to gather information about drives. Figure 25.11 lists some common **Drive** properties. Property **DriveLetter** contains the **Drive**'s letter. Property **SerialNumber** contains the **Drive**'s serial number. Property **FreeSpace** contains the number of bytes available.

Property	Description
AvailableSpace	Variant. The amount of available **Drive** space in bytes.
DriveLetter	String. The letter assigned to the **Drive** (e.g., "C").
DriveType	Integer. The **Drive** type. Constants **Unknown**, **Removable**, **Fixed**, **Remote**, **CDRom** and **RamDisk** represent **Drive** types and have the values 0–5, respectively.
FileSystem	String. The file system **Drive** description (FAT, FAT32, NTFS, etc.).

Fig. 25.11   **Drive** properties (part 1 of 2).

Property	Description
FreeSpace	Variant. Same as **AvailableSpace**.
IsReady	Boolean. Indicates whether or not a **Drive** is ready for use.
Path	String. The **Drive**'s path.
RootFolder	Folder object. The **Drive**'s root **Folder**.
SerialNumber	Long. The **Drive** serial number.
TotalSize	Variant. The total **Drive** size in bytes.
VolumeName	String. The **Drive** volume name.

Fig. 25.11 **Drive** properties (part 2 of 2).

Figure 25.12 is an Active Server Page for a *guest book* that allows the visitors to enter their name, email and comments. We use file system objects to write the visitor information to a file on the server.

```
1   <% @LANGUAGE = VBScript %>
2   <% Option Explicit %>
3
4   <% ' Fig. 25.12 : guestbook.asp %>
5
6   <!DOCTYPE HTML PUBLIC "-//W3C//DTD HTML 4.0 Transitional//EN">
7   <HTML>
8   <HEAD>
9   <TITLE>GuestBook Example</TITLE>
10  <BODY>
11  <FONT SIZE = "4" FACE = "Arial" COLOR = "blue">
12
13  <%
14     Dim fileObject, textFile, guestBook, mailtoUrl
15
16     ' If user has made an entry and thus the page is
17     ' reloading, then process this entry
18     If Request( "entry" ) = "true" Then
19
20        ' Print a thank you
21        Call Response.Write( "Thanks for your entry, " )
22        Call Response.Write( Request( "name" ) & "!" )
23  %>
24  <HR COLOR = "blue" SIZE = "1">
25  <%     ' Instantiate a FileSystemObject
26        Set fileObject = Server.CreateObject( _
27           "Scripting.FileSystemObject" )
28
29        ' Guestbook path must be modified to reflect the file
30        ' structure of the server.
31        guestBook = "c:\Inetpub\Wwwroot\Deitel\" & "guestbook.txt"
```

Fig. 25.12 Guest book Active Server Page (part 1 of 4).

```
32
33            ' Check if the file exists. If not, create it.
34            If fileObject.FileExists( guestbook ) <> True Then
35               Call fileObject.CreateTextFile( guestBook )
36            End If
37
38            ' Guestbook must be open for writing.
39            ' Open the guestbook, 8 is for appending
40            Set textFile = fileObject.OpenTextFile( guestbook, 8, True )
41
42            ' Build the mailtoUrl
43            mailtoUrl = Date() & " <A HREF = " & Chr( 34 ) _
44               & "mailto:" & Request( "email" ) & Chr( 34 ) _
45               & ">" & Request( "name" ) & "</A>:  "
46
47            ' Write data to guestbook.txt
48            Call textFile.WriteLine( "<HR COLOR = " & Chr( 34 ) _
49               & "blue" & Chr( 34 ) & " SIZE = " & Chr( 34 ) _
50               & "1" & Chr( 34 ) & ">" )
51            Call textFile.WriteLine( mailtoUrl )
52            Call textFile.WriteLine( Request( "comment" ) )
53            Call textFile.Close()
54         End If
55      %>
56
57      Please leave a message in our guestbook.
58
59      </FONT>
60      <FORM ACTION = "guestbook.asp?entry=true" METHOD = "POST">
61      <CENTER>
62      <TABLE>
63      <TR>
64      <TD><FONT FACE = "Arial" SIZE = "2">Your Name:  </FONT></TD>
65      <TD><INPUT TYPE = "text" FACE = "Arial"
66            SIZE = "60" NAME = "name"></TD>
67      </TR>
68      <TR>
69      <TD><FONT FACE = "Arial" SIZE = "2">Your email address:
70      </FONT></TD>
71      <TD><INPUT TYPE = "text" FACE = "Arial" SIZE = "60"
72            NAME = "email" VALUE = "user@isp.com"></TD>
73      </TR>
74      <TR>
75      <TD><FONT FACE = "Arial" SIZE = "2">Tell the world:  </FONT>
76      </TD>
77      <TD><TEXTAREA NAME = "comment" ROWS = "3" COLS = "50">
78      Replace this text with the information
79      you would like to post.
80      </TEXTAREA></TD>
81      </TR>
82      </TABLE>
83      <INPUT TYPE = "submit" VALUE = "SUBMIT">
84      <INPUT TYPE = "reset" VALUE = "CLEAR">
```

Fig. 25.12 Guest book Active Server Page (part 2 of 4).

```
85    </CENTER>
86    </FORM>
87
88    <%
89        Dim fileObject2, textFile2
90
91            ' Instantiate a FileSystemObject
92            Set fileObject2 = Server.CreateObject( _
93               "Scripting.FileSystemObject" )
94
95            ' Guestbook path must be modified to reflect
96            ' the file structure of the server.
97            guestBook = "c:\Inetpub\wwwroot\Deitel\" & "guestbook.txt"
98
99            ' Check if the file exists. If not, create it.
100           If fileObject2.FileExists( guestBook ) = True Then
101
102               ' Guestbook must be open for writing.
103               ' Open the guestbook, "1" is for reading.
104               Set textFile2 = fileObject2.OpenTextFile( guestbook, 1 )
105
106               ' Read the entries from the file and write them to
107               ' the client.
108               Call Response.Write( "Guestbook Entries:<BR>" )
109               Call Response.Write( textFile2.ReadAll() )
110               Call textFile2.Close()
111           End If
112    %>
113
114    </BODY>
115    </HTML>
```

Fig. 25.12   Guest book Active Server Page (part 3 of 4).

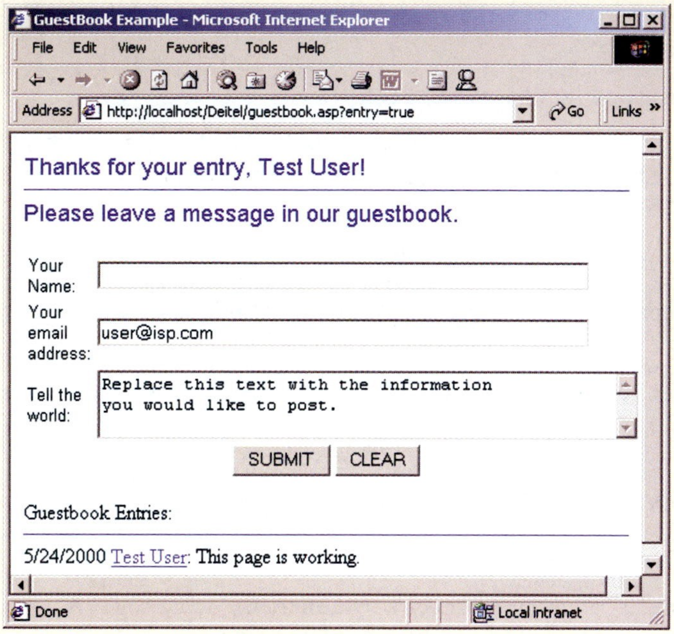

Fig. 25.12 Guest book Active Server Page (part 4 of 4).

The guest book page displayed in the browser consists of a form (to be filled in by the user) and a list of guest book entries (initially there are no entries in this list). We begin by discussing the form (lines 60 through 86). The form contains three text fields used to input the name, email and user comment.

Line 60

```
<FORM ACTION = "guestbook.asp?entry=true" METHOD = "POST">
```

indicates that a **POST** request occurs upon form submission. The action for the form requests the same ASP page in which the form is contained—**guestbook.asp**. As we demonstrated earlier, this is perfectly valid; a form's action is not required to request a different document. When the form is submitted, **guestbook.asp** is requested from the server. Notice that the form passes **guestbook.asp** a parameter in the URL. Passing parameters in a page's name simulates an HTTP **GET** request. We send the parameters in the page's name by appending a question mark to the page's URL followed by a list of parameters and values, separated by ampersands:

```
SomeURL?param1=value1&param2=value2& ... paramN=valueN
```

Our form passes one parameter named **entry**:

```
guestbook.asp?entry=true
```

This URL is a "virtual path" for:

```
http://localhost/Deitel/guestbook.asp?entry=true
```

Upon submission, **guestbook.asp** is requested and passed parameter **entry**—which is assigned **"true."** [*Note*: **"true"** is a string and not a boolean value.] The name **entry** is programmer-defined—you of course may choose any name you prefer. We use this technique to determine whether this ASP page is being requested by a form submit from **guestbook.asp**.

We want only lines 21 through 53 to execute when the page is loaded with a **POST** request. Line 18

```
If Request( "entry" ) = "true" Then
```

uses the **Request** object to get **entry**'s value and test it against the string **"true."** When this page is requested by a client for the first time, **entry** has the value **""** (an *empty string*) and lines 21 through 53 are not executed. Variable **entry** is only passed **"true"** during the **POST** operation (line 60). When **entry** is **"true"** lines 21 through 53 are executed.

Lines 21 and 22

```
Call Response.Write( "Thanks for your entry, " )
Call Response.Write( Request( "name" ) & "!" )
```

print **Thanks for your entry,** followed by the user's name. Notice that the **Request** object is used to get the value posted in the **name** text field of the submitted form.

Lines 26 and 27

```
Set fileObject = Server.CreateObject( _
    "Scripting.FileSystemObject" )
```

create an FSO instance (i.e., an object) and assign it to reference **fileObject**. When assigning an object to a reference in VBScript, keyword **Set** is required. We specify the location of the file that stores guest book information in line 31. *You may need to modify this path to conform to the directory structure on your machine.*

Before writing data to the guest book, we call **FileExists** in line 34 to determine if **guestbook.txt** exists. If it does not, method **CreateTextFile** is called to create the file.

Line 40

```
Set textFile = fileObject.OpenTextFile( guestbook, 8, True )
```

calls method **OpenTextFile** to get a **TextStream** object for accessing the text file **guestbook.txt**. The constant value **8** indicates *append mode* (writing to the end of the file) and **True** indicates that the file will be created if it does not already exist. Opening for read or write is specified with constant values **1** and **2**, respectively. The user's submitted name and email are combined with HTML tags and assigned to string **mailtoUrl** (lines 43 through 45). This string, when displayed in the browser, shows the submitted name as a *mailto link* (clicking this link opens an email message editor with the person's name in the **To:** field). Line 43 calls VBScript function **Date** to assign the current server date to the beginning of **mailtoUrl**. The **Request** object is used to retrieve the values from the **email** field (line 44) and the **name** field (line 45). We pass the value **34** to the VBScript function **Chr** to get a double quote (**"**) character. We store HTML tags in **mailtoUrl**. We choose to be formal and include quotations around HTML values. For example, we use **<FONT FACE="Arial">** instead of **<FONT FACE=Arial>**. Because the interpreter would treat a double quote as the end of the **mailtoUrl** string, we use function **Chr** to return a double quote.

Lines 48 through 52 write text to **guestbook.txt** using the **TextStream** method **WriteLine**. After writing the text to the file, **TextStream** method **Close** is called in line 53 to close the file.

Every time a client requests this Active Server Page, lines 89 through 111 execute. This VBScript code displays a list of all the users who have made guest book entries. If the **guestbook.txt** file exists, it is opened for reading in line 104. Lines 108 and 109 write HTML/text to the client. The entire contents of **guestbook.txt** is read by calling **Text-Stream** method **ReadAll**. This text is written to the client using **Response.Write**. Because the text contains HTML markup, it is rendered in the client browser.

25.9 Session Tracking and Cookies

HTTP does not support persistent information that could help a Web server distinguish between clients. In this section, we will introduce two related technologies that enable a Web server to distinguish between clients: session tracking and cookies.

Many Web sites provide custom Web pages and/or functionality on a client-by-client basis. For example, some Web sites allow you to customize their home page to suit your needs. An excellent example of this is the *Yahoo!* Web site (**my.yahoo.com**), which allows you to customize how the Yahoo! site appears. [*Note:* You need to get a free Yahoo! ID first.]

Another example of a service that is customized on a client-by-client basis is a *shopping cart* for shopping on the Web (see Chapter 26). Obviously, the server must distinguish between clients so the business can assign the proper items and charge each client the proper amount.

A third example of customizing on a client-by-client basis is marketing. Companies often track the pages you visit so they can display advertisements based upon your browsing trends. Many people consider tracking to be an invasion of their privacy, an increasingly sensitive issue in our information-based society. See Chapter 6 for more information on this and other legal, ethical and moral issues.

There are a number of popular techniques for uniquely identifying clients. For the purpose of this chapter, we introduce two techniques to track clients individually: *session tracking* and *cookies*.

The server handles session tracking. The first time a client connects to the server, the server assigns the user a unique *session ID*. When the client makes additional requests, the client's session ID is compared against the session IDs stored in the server's memory. Active Server Pages use the *Session* object to manage sessions. The **Session** object's *Timeout* property specifies the number of minutes that a session exists before it expires. The default value for property **Timeout** is 20 minutes. Calling **Session** method *Abandon* can also terminate an individual session.

We are now ready to present an example that uses session tracking. Figure 25.13 is an ASP page generator. Users who are not familiar with ASP can input their information in a form, submit the form, and the ASP page generator does all the work of creating the user's ASP page. This example consists of two Active Server Pages linked to each other through HTTP **POST** requests. We use session variables in this example to maintain a state between the two ASP pages. Multiple Active Server Pages connected in this manner are sometimes called an *ASP application*.

The first page, **instantpage.asp** (Fig. 25.13), consists of a form that requests information from the user. When submitted, the form is **POST**ed to **process.asp** (Fig. 25.17). If there are no errors, **process.asp** creates the user's ASP page. Otherwise, **process.asp** redirects the user back to **instantpage.asp**, passing it parameter **error=yes**. Also, **process.asp** stores a "welcome back" message in a session variable. Each time a user submits the form, **process.asp** stores a new "welcome back" message in the session variable. If a filename is not provided, **process.asp** returns an error to **instantpage.asp** (Fig. 25.14).

Line 15

```
<!-- #include virtual = "/includes/mgtheader.shtml" -->
```

is a *server side include* (*SSI*) statement that incorporates the contents of **mgtheader.shtml** (Fig. 25.15) into the ASP file. Server-side includes are commands embedded in HTML documents that add dynamic content. The SSI statement in line 15 is replaced with the contents of the file **mgtheader.shtml**. Not all Web servers support the available SSI commands. Therefore, SSI commands are written as HTML comments. SSI statements always execute before any scripting code executes.

We also use an SSI in line 69 to include **mgtfooter.shtml** (Fig. 25.16). The word **virtual** in the SSI refers to the include file's path as it appears below the server's root directory. This is often referred to as a *virtual path*. SSIs can also use **file** instead of **virtual** to indicate a *physical path* on the server. For example, line 15 could be rewritten as

```
1   <% @LANGUAGE = VBScript %>
2   <% Option Explicit %>
3
4   <% ' Fig. 25.13 : instantpage.asp %>
5
6   <!DOCTYPE HTML PUBLIC "-//W3C//DTD HTML 4.0 Transitional//EN">
7   <HTML>
8   <HEAD>
9   <TITLE>Instant Page Content Builder</TITLE>
10  </HEAD>
11
12  <BODY>
13
14  <% ' Include the header %>
15  <!-- #include virtual = "/includes/mgtheader.shtml" -->
16  <FONT FACE = "Arial" SIZE = "2">
17  <H2>Instant Page Content Builder</H2>
18
19  <% ' If process.asp signaled an error, print the error
20     ' message.
21     If Request( "error" ) = "yes" Then
22        Call Response.Write( Session( "errorMessage" ) )
23     ' Otherwise, print the welcome back message, if any.
```

Fig. 25.13 Listing for **instantpage.asp** (part 1 of 3).

```
24       Else
25          Call Response.Write( Session( "welcomeBack" ) )
26       End If
27
28       ' A form to get the information from the user.
29    %>
30    <FORM ACTION = "process.asp" METHOD = "POST">
31
32    <CENTER>
33
34    <TABLE>
35    <TR>
36    <TD><FONT FACE = "Arial" SIZE = "2">Your Name:
37    </FONT><BR></TD>
38    <TD><INPUT TYPE = "text" FACE = "Arial" SIZE = "60"
39             NAME = "name"><BR></TD>
40    </TR>
41    <TR>
42    <TD><FONT FACE = "Arial" SIZE = "2">Enter the Filename:
43    </FONT><BR></TD>
44    <TD><INPUT TYPE = "text" FACE = "Arial" SIZE = "60"
45             NAME = "filename" VALUE = "YourFileName.asp"><BR>
46    </TD>
47    </TR>
48    <TR>
49    <TD><FONT FACE = "Arial" SIZE = "2">Enter the Title:
50    </FONT><BR></TD>
51    <TD><INPUT TYPE = "text" FACE = "Arial" SIZE = "60"
52             NAME = "doctitle" VALUE = "Document Title"><BR>
53    </TD>
54    </TR>
55    <TR>
56    <TD><FONT FACE = "Arial" SIZE = "2">Enter the Content:
57    </FONT><BR></TD>
58    <TD><TEXTAREA NAME = "content" ROWS = "3" COLS = "50">
59    Replace this text with the
60    information you would like to post.
61    </TEXTAREA><BR></TD>
62    </TR>
63    </TABLE>
64    <INPUT TYPE = "submit" VALUE = "SUBMIT">
65    <INPUT TYPE = "reset" VALUE = "CLEAR">
66    </CENTER>
67    </FORM>
68
69    <!-- #include virtual = "/includes/mgtfooter.shtml" -->
70    </FONT>
71    </BODY>
72    </HTML>
```

Fig. 25.13 Listing for **instantpage.asp** (part 2 of 3).

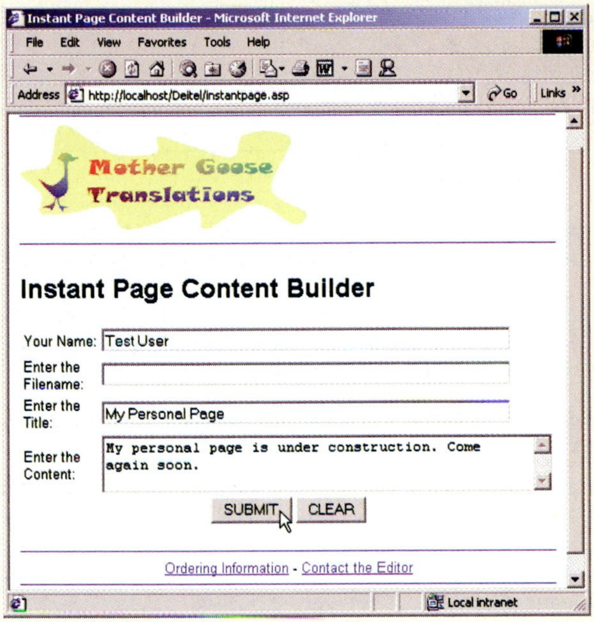

Fig. 25.13 Listing for **instantpage.asp** (part 3 of 3).

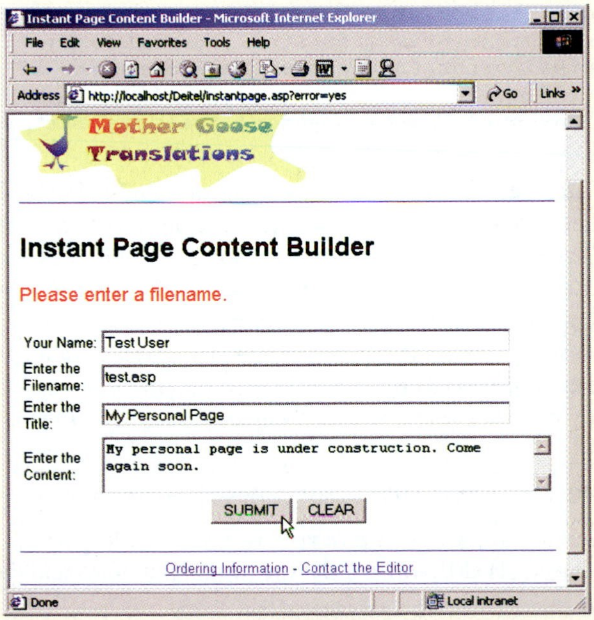

Fig. 25.14 Error message returned by **instantpage.asp**.

```
73    <HR SIZE = "1" COLOR = "blue">
74    <IMG HEIGHT = "100" SRC = "/images/mgheader.gif">
75    <HR SIZE = "1" COLOR = "blue">
```

Fig. 25.15   File listing for **mgtheader.shtml**.

```
76    <HR COLOR = "blue" SIZE = "1">
77    <CENTER>
78    <A HREF = "mailto:orders">Ordering Information</A> -
79    <A HREF = "mailto:editor">Contact the Editor</A><BR>
80    <HR COLOR = "blue" SIZE = "1">
81    </CENTER>
```

Fig. 25.16   File listing for **mgtfooter.shtml**.

```
<!-- #include file = "C:\Webshare\Wwwroot\includes\
mgtheader.shtml"-->
```

which assumes that **mgtheader.shtml** is in the directory **C:\Webshare\Wwwroot\includes** on the server.

Software Engineering Observation 25.8

Virtual paths hide the server's internal file structure.

The session variables used in this example are **errorMessage** for the error message and **welcomeBack** for the user's "welcome back" message. The **If** statement on lines 21 through 26

```
If Request( "error" ) = "yes" Then
   Call Response.Write( Session( "errorMessage" ) )
' Otherwise, print the welcome back message, if any.
Else
   Call Response.Write( Session( "welcomeBack" ) )
End If
```

test if the value of **error** is **"yes."** If true, the value of session variable **errorMessage** is written to the client. Otherwise, **welcomeBack**'s value is written to the client. A session variable's value is set and retrieved using the **Session** object. Note that **Request("error")** never equals **"yes"** unless **process.asp** passes **error=yes** as a parameter to **instantpage.asp**. Otherwise, **Request("error")** contains an empty string. A session variable that has not been explicitly given a value contains an empty string. When **instantpage.asp** is requested for the first time, and **Request("error")** is equal to an empty string, and the "welcome back" message is not written.
    Line 30

```
<FORM ACTION = "process.asp" METHOD = "POST">
```

requests Active Server Page **process.asp** when the form is posted. The remainder of **instantpage.asp** is HTML that defines the form input items and the page footer.

Software Engineering Observation 25.9
Server-side includes may include any type of information. Text files and HTML files are two of the most common server-side include files.

Software Engineering Observation 25.10

Server-side includes are performed before any scripting code is interpreted. Therefore, an Active Server Page cannot dynamically decide which server-side includes are used and which are not. Through scripting, an ASP can determine which SSI block is sent to the client.

Testing and Debugging Tip 25.2

*Server-side includes that contain scripting code should enclose the scripting code in **<SCRIPT>** tags or in **<% %>** delimiters to prevent one block of scripting code from running into another block of scripting code.*

Software Engineering Observation 25.11

*By convention, server-side include (SSI) files end with the **.shtml** extension.*

Software Engineering Observation 25.12

Server-side includes are an excellent technique for reusing HTML, Dynamic HTML, scripts and other programming elements.

The document **process.asp** (Fig. 25.17) creates the user's ASP document and presents a link to the user's page. This page is requested by **instantpage.asp** (line 30).

The **If** statement in line 91 validates the contents of field **Enter the Filename**. If the text box is empty or contains the default string **YourFileName.asp**, HTML text containing an error message is assigned to the session variable **errorMessage**:

```
Session( "errorMessage" ) = "<FONT COLOR = " & q _
   & "red" & q & " SIZE = " & q & "4" & q & ">" _
   & "Please enter a filename." & "</FONT>" & "<BR>"
```

```
82   <% @LANGUAGE = VBScript %>
83   <% Option Explicit %>
84
85   <% ' Fig. 25.17 : process.asp %>
86
87   <%  Dim q
88      q = Chr( 34 )
89
90      ' Check to make sure that they have entered a filename
91      If Request( "filename" ) = "YourFileName.asp" Or _
92         Request( "filename" ) = "" Then
93         Session( "errorMessage" ) = "<FONT COLOR = " & q _
94            & "red" & q & " SIZE = " & q & "4" & q & ">" _
95            & "Please enter a filename." & "</FONT>" & "<BR>"
96         Call Response.Redirect( "instantpage.asp?error=yes" )
97      End If
98
99      Dim directoryPath, filePath, fileObject
100
```

Fig. 25.17 Listing for **process.asp** (part 1 of 4).

```
101     ' Create a FileSystem Object
102     Set fileObject = Server.CreateObject( _
103        "Scripting.FileSystemObject" )
104
105     ' directoryPath must be modified to reflect the file
106     ' structure of your server
107     directoryPath = "c:\Inetpub\Wwwroot\userpages\"
108
109     ' See if the directory exists. If not, create it.
110     If Not fileObject.FolderExists( directoryPath ) Then
111        Call fileObject.CreateFolder( directoryPath )
112     End If
113
114     ' Build path for text file.
115     filePath = directoryPath & Request( "filename" )
116
117     ' Check if the file already exists
118     If fileObject.FileExists( filePath ) Then
119        Session( "errorMessage" ) = "<FONT COLOR = " & q _
120           & "red" & q & " SIZE = " & q & "4" & q & ">" _
121           & "This filename is in use. " _
122           & "Please enter another filename." & "</FONT>" _
123           & "<BR>"
124        Call Response.Redirect( "instantpage.asp?error=yes" )
125     End If
126
127     ' Save HTML for the welcome back message
128     ' in a session variable
129     Session( "welcomeBack" )= "<FONT COLOR = " _
130        & q & "blue"  & q & " SIZE = " _
131        & q & "4" & q & ">" _
132        & "Welcome Back, " & Request( "name" ) & "!</FONT>" _
133        & "<BR>"
134
135     Dim header, footer, textFile, openMark, closeMark
136     openMark = "<" & "%"
137     closeMark = "%" & ">"
138
139     ' Build the header.
140     ' vbCrLf inserts a carriage return/linefeed into the text
141     ' string which makes the HTML code more readable
142     header = openMark & " @LANGUAGE = VBScript " & closeMark _
143        & vbCrLf & openMark & " ' " & Request( "filename" ) _
144        & " " & closeMark & vbCrLf & vbCrLf _
145        & "<!DOCTYPE HTML PUBLIC " & q _
146        & "-//W3C//DTD HTML 4.0 Transitional//EN" & q & ">" _
147        & vbCrLf & "<HTML>" & vbCrLf & "<HEAD>" & vbCrLf _
148        & "<META NAME = " & q & "author" & q & " CONTENT = " _
149        & q & Request( "name" ) & q & ">" & vbCrLf _
150        & "<META NAME = " & q & "pubdate" & q _
151        & " CONTENT = " & q & Date() & q & ">" & vbCrLf _
152        & "<TITLE>" & Request( "doctitle" ) & "</TITLE>" _
153        & vbCrLf & "</HEAD>" & vbCrLf & "<BODY>" & vbCrLf _
```

Fig. 25.17 Listing for **process.asp** (part 2 of 4).

```
154          & "<FONT FACE = " & q & "arial" & q & " SIZE = " & q _
155          & "3" & q & " >" & vbCrLf _
156          & "<!-- #include virtual = " & q _
157          & "/includes/mgtheader.shtml" & q & " -->" & vbCrLf _
158          & "<CENTER><U><H2>" & Request( "doctitle" ) _
159          & "</H2></U>" & vbCrLf & "<BR>" & vbCrLf
160
161       ' Build the footer using a different style for
162       ' building the string
163       footer = vbCrLf & "</CENTER><BR><BR><BR>" & vbCrLf
164       footer = footer & "You have requested this page on "
165       footer = footer & openMark & " =Date() " & closeMark & ","
166       footer = footer & vbCrLf & "at " & openMark & " =Time() "
167       footer = footer & closeMark & "." & vbCrLf
168       footer = footer & "<!-- #include virtual = " & q
169       footer = footer & "/includes/mgtfooter.shtml" & q
170       footer = footer & " -->" & vbCrLf & "</FONT>"
171       footer = footer & vbCrLf & "</BODY>" & vbCrLf & "</HTML>"
172
173       ' Create the html file
174       Set textFile = fileObject.CreateTextFile( filePath, False )
175       Call textFile.WriteLine( header )
176       Call textFile.WriteLine( Request( "content" ) )
177       Call textFile.Write( footer )
178       Call textFile.Close
179    %>
180    <!DOCTYPE HTML PUBLIC "-//W3C//DTD HTML 4.0 Transitional//EN">
181    <HTML>
182    <HEAD>
183
184    <% ' Use the title given by the user %>
185    <TITLE>File Generated: <% =Request( "filename" ) %></TITLE>
186    </HEAD>
187
188    <BODY>
189
190    <!-- #include virtual = "/includes/mgtheader.shtml" -->
191
192    <FONT FACE = "Arial" SIZE = "3">
193    <CENTER><U><H2>
194       File Generated: <% =Request( "filename" ) %>
195    </H2></U></CENTER><BR>
196    <% ' Provide a link to the generated page %>
197    Your file is ready:
198    <A HREF = "/userpages/<% =Request( "filename" ) %>">
199    <% =Request( "doctitle" ) %></A>
200
201    <!-- #include virtual = "/includes/mgtfooter.shtml" -->
202
203    </FONT>
204    </BODY>
205    </HTML>
```

Fig. 25.17 Listing for **process.asp** (part 3 of 4).

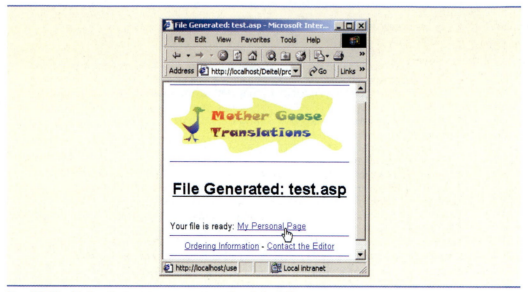

Fig. 25.17 Listing for `process.asp` (part 4 of 4).

Then, line 96

```
Call Response.Redirect( "instantpage.asp?error=yes" )
```

calls **Response** method *Redirect* to request **instantpage.asp** and pass it **error=yes**.

If the user has entered a valid filename, an FSO object is created in lines 102 and 103 and assigned to reference **fileObject**. Line 107 specifies the path on the server where the ASP file will eventually be written. We have chosen to store all the user pages in a directory that we created called **userpages** (beneath the publishing directory, **C:\Inetpub\Wwwroot**). *You will need to either create this directory or modify this path on your machine.*

The **If** statement in line 110 tests for the existence of the **C:\Inetpub\Wwwroot\userpages** folder by calling FSO method **FolderExists** to determine if the directory specified in line 107 exists. If the folder does not exist, FSO method **CreateFolder** is called to create it in line 111.

Line 115 builds the file path by concatenating the file name to the directory path. This **filePath** is passed to FSO method **FileExists**—which is called in line 118 to determine if the file exists. If it does exist, another user has already created an ASP document with the same filename. In this case, HTML containing an error message is saved to the session variable **errorMessage**. On line 124, **error=yes** is passed to **instantpage.asp** indicating that an error has occurred.

Lines 129 through 133 assign HTML for the "welcome back" message to session variable **welcomeBack**. The format of the message is:

```
Welcome back, X!
```

where **X** is the current user's name obtained from the form's **name** field.

Lines 136 and 137 assign the ASP scripting delimiters to string variables **openMark** and **closeMark**. We use two strings instead of one to represent the opening and closing delimiters (i.e., **"<"** & **"%"**) because the interpreter treats the single string **"<%"** as a scripting delimiter.

Next, we build the user's ASP file. For clarity, we divide the file into three parts: a header, a footer and the content (provided by the user in the form's **content** field).

Lines 142 through 159 construct HTML for the header and assign it to string **header**. VBScript constant **vbCrLf** is used to insert a carriage-return line-feed combination. The form's values are retrieved using the **Request** object. Note that character variable **q** is assigned the value **Chr(34)** in line 88, where **34** is the decimal ASCII code for the double-quote character. For more on ASCII characters, see Appendix C. Lines 163 through 171 create the page's footer and assign it to variable **footer**.

Lines 174 through 178 write **header**, text area **content**'s text and **footer** to the text file before closing it. Lines 180 through 205 send HTML to the client that contains a link to the created page. Figure 25.18 lists a sample ASP file—named **test.asp**—created by Active Server Page **process.asp**. [*Note*: We added line 2 for presentation purposes.] The first screen capture in Fig. 25.19 contains shows the message that is displayed when the user returns back to **instantpage.asp**. The second screen capture shows the error message generated when the user does not change the default file name in the **Enter the Filename** textfield.

```
 1  <% @LANGUAGE = VBScript %>
 2  <% ' Fig. 25.18 : test.asp %>
 3
 4  <!DOCTYPE HTML PUBLIC "-//W3C//DTD HTML 4.0 Transitional//EN">
 5  <HTML>
 6  <HEAD>
 7  <META NAME = "author" CONTENT = "Test User">
 8  <META NAME = "pubdate" CONTENT = "5/29/2000">
 9  <TITLE>My Personal Page</TITLE>
10  </HEAD>
11  <BODY>
12  <FONT FACE = "Arial" SIZE = "3">
13  <!-- #include virtual = "/includes/mgtheader.shtml" -->
14  <CENTER><U><H2>My Personal Page</H2></U>
15  <BR>
16
17  My personal page is under construction. Come again soon.
18
19  </CENTER><BR><BR><BR>
20  You have requested this page on <% =Date() %>,
21  at <% =Time() %>.
22  <!-- #include virtual = "/includes/mgtfooter.shtml" -->
23  </FONT>
24  </BODY>
25  </HTML>
```

Fig. 25.18 Listing for **test.asp**.

Fig. 25.18 Listing for `test.asp`.

Fig. 25.19 Output from `instantpage.asp` (part 1 of 2).

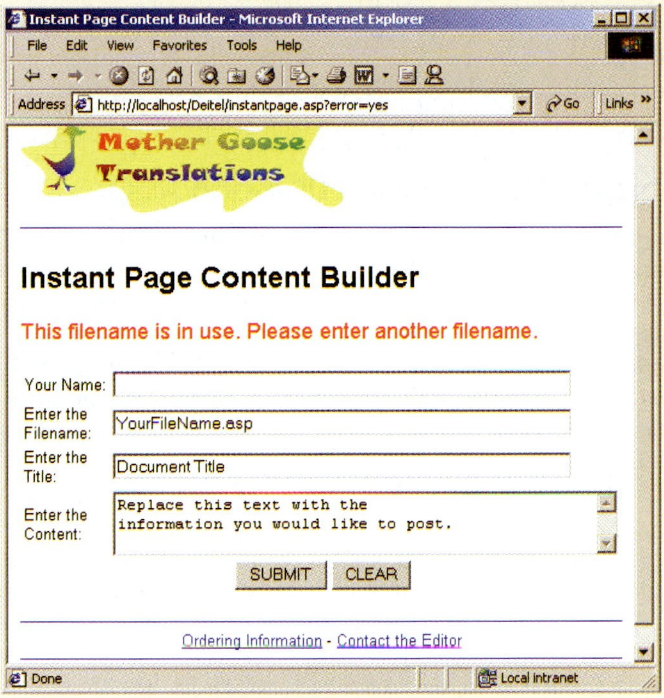

Fig. 25.19 Output from **instantpage.asp** (part 2 of 2).

Another popular way to customize Web pages is via *cookies*. Cookies can store information on the client's computer for retrieval later in the same browsing session or in future browsing sessions. For example, cookies could be used in a shopping application to keep track of the client's shopping-cart items.

Cookies are small files sent by an Active Server Page (or another similar technology such as Perl—discussed in Chapter 29) as part of a response to a client. Every HTTP-based interaction between a client and a server includes a *header* that contains information about either the request (when the communication is from the client to the server) or the response (when the communication is from the server to the client). When an Active Server Page receives a request, the header includes information such as the request type (e.g., **GET** or **POST**) and cookies stored on the client machine by the server. When the server formulates its response, the header information includes any cookies the server wants to store on the client computer.

Software Engineering Observation 25.13

Some clients do not allow cookies to be written on their machine. A refusal to accept cookies may prevent the client from being able to properly use the Web site that attempted to write the cookie.

Depending on the *maximum age* of a cookie, the Web browser either maintains the cookie for the duration of the browsing session (i.e., until the user closes the Web browser) or stores the cookie on the client computer for future use. When the browser makes a request to a server, cookies previously sent to the client by that server are returned to the server (if the cookies have not expired) as part of the request formulated by the browser. Cookies are automatically deleted when they *expire* (i.e., reach their maximum age). We use cookies in Section 25.11 to store user IDs.

25.10 Databases, SQL, Microsoft UDA and ADO

A *database* is an integrated collection of data. A *database management system (DBMS)* involves the data itself and the software that controls the storage and retrieval of data. Database management systems provide mechanisms for storing and organizing data in a manner that facilitates satisfying sophisticated queries and manipulations of the data.

The most popular database systems in use today are *relational databases*. A language called *Structured Query Language* (*SQL*—pronounced "sequel") is almost universally used with relational database systems to make *queries* (i.e., to request information that satisfies given criteria) and manipulate data. Some popular enterprise-level relational database systems include Microsoft SQL Server, Oracle, Sybase, DB2 and Informix. Enterprise-level database systems are used for large-scale database access. A popular personal relational database is Microsoft Access (which we use for simplicity in our examples). *Universal Data Access (UDA)* is a Microsoft architecture that provides data access to many data sources. We first discuss database structure and how to query a database using SQL, before briefly discussing the UDA architecture.

A relational database is composed of *tables*, which in turn are composed of *columns* (or *fields*). Figure 25.20 shows the table relationships in **catalog.mdb** (we use **catalog.mdb** in Chapter 26). The database contains four tables: **products**, **authorlist**, **authors** and **technologies**. Within each of these tables there are multiple fields. For example, the **technologies** table has **technologyID** and **technology** fields. The *records* (or *rows*) of the **technologies** table are also shown in Fig. 25.20. The **technologyID** field is the *primary key*. A primary key is a unique field that is used to identify a record. The records of the **technologies** table are ordered by a primary key. The first record has **technologyID** "1" and **technology** "C".

A line between two tables in Fig. 25.20 represents a relationship between those tables. Consider the line between the **products** and **technologies** tables. On the **technologies** end of the line, there is a **1**; on the **products** end, there is an infinity symbol. This indicates that every technology in the **technologies** table corresponds to an arbitrary number of products in the **products** table—a *one-to-many relationship*. The **products** and **technologies** tables are linked by their **technologyID** fields.

Different database users are often interested in different data and different relationships between those data. SQL statements are commonly used to specify which data to *select* from the table. SQL provides a complete set of keywords (including **SELECT**) that enable programmers to define complex queries for retrieving data from a table. Query results are commonly called *result sets* (or *record sets*).

Figure 25.21 lists some SQL keywords for querying a database, inserting records into a database and updating existing records in a database. For more information on SQL keywords, visit **www.aspin.com/home/references/database/sql**.

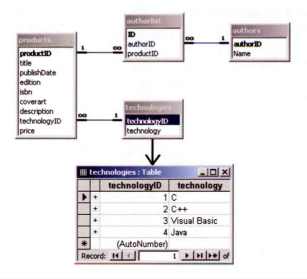

Fig. 25.20 Table relationships in `catalog.mbd`.

SQL keyword	Description
`SELECT`	Select (retrieve) fields from one or more tables.
`FROM`	Tables from which to get fields. Required in every `SELECT`.
`WHERE`	Criteria for selection that determine the rows to be retrieved.
`ORDER BY`	Criteria for ordering (sorting) of records.
`INSERT INTO`	Insert values into one or more tables. [*Note:* Some databases do not require the SQL keyword `INTO`.]
`UPDATE`	Update existing data in one or more tables.

Fig. 25.21 Some SQL query keywords.

A typical SQL query selects information from one or more tables in a database. Such selections are performed by ***SELECT*** *queries*. The simplest form of a `SELECT` query is

    SELECT * FROM *TableName*

In the preceding query, the asterisk (`*`) indicates that all rows and columns (fields) from table *TableName* should be selected. To select specific fields from a table, replace the asterisk (`*`) with a comma-separated list of the field names to select. For example,

    SELECT *FieldName1*, *FieldName2*, FROM *TableName*

selects all the *FieldName1* and *FieldName2* fields from the records in the *TableName* table.

Software Engineering Observation 25.14

For most SQL statements, the asterisk (`*`) should not be used to specify field names to select from a table (or several tables). In general, programmers process result sets by knowing in advance the order of the fields in the result set.

Software Engineering Observation 25.15

Specifying the actual field names to select from a table (or several tables) guarantees that the fields are always returned in the same order even if the actual order of the fields in the database table(s) changes.

Common Programming Error 25.3

When performing an SQL statement using the asterisk (*) to select fields, assuming that the fields in the result set of the query are always returned in the same order may result in incorrect processing of the data in the application receiving the result set. If the order of the fields in the database table(s) changes, the order of the fields in the result set changes accordingly

Common Programming Error 25.4

In a query, forgetting to enclose a field name containing spaces in square brackets (`[]`) is an error.

In most cases, it is necessary to locate only records in a database that satisfy certain *selection criteria*. SQL provides the optional **WHERE** clause in a **SELECT** query to specify the selection criteria for a query. The simplest form of a **SELECT** query with selection criteria is

    SELECT *fieldName1*, *fieldName2*, ... **FROM** *TableName* **WHERE** *criteria*

The **WHERE** clause condition can contain operators such as **<, >, <=, >=, =, <>** and **LIKE**. Operator **LIKE** is used for *pattern matching* with wildcard characters *asterisk (*)* and *question mark (?)*. Pattern matching allows SQL to search for similar strings that "match a pattern." An asterisk (*) in the pattern indicates any number of (i.e., zero or more) characters in a row at the asterisk's location in the pattern. [*Note:* Many databases use the **%** character in place of the ***** in a **LIKE** expression.]

It may be necessary to merge data from multiple tables into a single report for analysis purposes. This is accomplished using a *join condition*—a condition that joins, merges or extracts data from more than one table is considered a join condition. For example, to extract all of the Visual Basic products from the database in Fig. 25.20, we would use

    SELECT * FROM products, technologies WHERE technologyID = 3

This returns the **technologyID**, **technology** name, and all of the **products** associated with the **technologyID** for Visual Basic ("**3**") in a record set.

The query results can be sorted into ascending or descending order using the optional **ORDER BY** *clause*. The simplest forms of an **ORDER BY** clause are

    SELECT *field1*, *field2*, ... **FROM** *TableName* **ORDER BY** *fieldName* **ASC**
    SELECT *field1*, *field2*, ... **FROM** *TableName* **ORDER BY** *fieldName* **DESC**

where **ASC** specifies ascending (lowest to highest) order, **DESC** specifies descending (highest to lowest) order and *fieldName* represents the field (the column of the table) that is used for sorting purposes.

Often it is necessary to insert data into a table (i.e., add a new record). This is accomplished using an **INSERT INTO** keywords. The simplest form for an **INSERT INTO** statement is

    INSERT INTO *TableName* (*fieldName1*, *fieldName2*, ..., *fieldNameN*)
      VALUES (*value1*, *value2*, ..., *valueN*)

where *TableName* is the table into which the record will be inserted. The *TableName* is followed by a comma-separated list of field names in parentheses (this list is not required if the **INSERT INTO** operation fills a complete row in the table). The list of field names is followed by the SQL keyword **VALUES** and a comma-separated list of values in parentheses.

It is also often necessary to modify data in a table (i.e., update a record). This is accomplished using an **UPDATE** operation. The simplest form for an **UPDATE** statement is

```
UPDATE  TableName
   SET  fieldName1 = value1, fieldName2 = value2, ..., fieldNameN = valueN
   WHERE  criteria
```

where *TableName* is the table in which the record will be updated. The *TableName* is followed by the **SET** keyword and a comma-separated list of field name/value pairs in the format *fieldName = value*. The **WHERE** clause specifies the criteria used to determine which record(s) to update.

To execute an SQL query, a program must be able to access a database. Many different database vendors exist—each one potentially providing different database manipulation methods. Microsoft developed the *Open Database Connectivity (ODBC) Application Programming Interface (API)* to allow Windows applications to communicate in a uniform manner with disparate relational databases. Database vendors write a piece of software, called an *ODBC driver*, using the ODBC API to provide uniform access to the database (i.e., database programmers do not have to learn vendor-specific database implementations).

Microsoft *Universal Data Access* (*UDA*) is an architecture that is designed for high-performance data access to relational data sources, non-relational data sources and mainframe/legacy data sources. The UDA architecture (Fig. 25.22) consists of three primary components: *OLE DB*—the core of the UDA architecture that provides low-level access to any data source, *Open Database Connectivity* (*ODBC*)—a C programming language library that uses SQL to access data, and *ActiveX Data Objects* (*ADO*)—a simple object model that provides uniform access to any data source by interacting with OLE DB. [*Note:* OLE DB is required to implement a minimum set of data access services that can be used by ADO.]

More specifically, the *ADO object model* provides objects and *collections* (i.e., containers that hold one or more objects of a specific type). Figure 25.23 briefly describes some ADO objects and collections. Visit

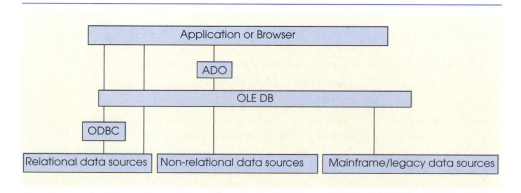

Fig. 25.22 Microsoft's UDA architecture.

`www.microsoft.com/data/ado/adords15/`

to access the ADO documentation and view a complete list of methods, properties and events for these ADO objects.

25.11 Accessing a Database from an Active Server Page

As discussed in the previous section, Active Server Pages can communicate with databases through ADO (ActiveX Data Objects). ADO provides a uniform way for a program to connect with a variety of databases in a general manner without having to deal with the specifics of those database systems.

Web applications are typically *three-tier distributed applications*, consisting of a *user interface*, *business logic* and *database access*. The user interface in such an application is often created using HTML, Dynamic HTML or XML (discussed in Chapter 27). The user interface can of course contain ActiveX controls and client-side scripts. In some cases, Java applets are also used for this tier. HTML is the preferred mechanism for representing the user interface in systems where portability is a concern. Because all browsers support HTML, designing the user interface to be accessed through a Web browser guarantees portability across all browser platforms. The user interface can communicate directly with the middle-tier business logic by using the networking provided automatically by the browser. The middle tier can then access the database to manipulate the data. All three tiers may reside on separate computers that are connected to a network or on a single machine.

In multi-tier architectures, Web servers are increasingly used to build the middle tier. They provide the business logic that manipulates data from databases and that communicates with client Web browsers. Active Server Pages, through ADO, can interact with popular database systems. Developers do not need to be familiar with the specifics of each database system. Rather, developers use SQL-based queries and ADO handles the specifics of interacting with each database system through OLE DB.

Object/Collection	Description
Connection object	The connection to the data source.
Command object	Contains the query that interacts with the database (the *data source*) to manipulate data.
Parameter object	Contains information needed by a **Command** object to query the data source.
Parameters collection	Contains one or more **Parameter** objects.
Error object	Created when an error occurs while accessing data.
Errors collection	Contains one or more **Error** objects.
Recordset object	Contains zero or more records that match the database query. Collectively this group of records is called a *record set*.
Field object	Contains the value (and other attributes) of one data source field.
Fields collection	Contains one or more **Field** objects.

Fig. 25.23 Some ADO object and collection types.

Databases can enhance applications by providing a data source that can be used to dynamically generate Web pages. Figure 25.13 (**instantpage.asp**) puts the power of Web page creation into the hands of individuals who are not familiar with HTML and ASP. However, we may want only a certain subset of pre-approved users to be able to access **instantpage.asp**. We can use password protection to restrict access. In Fig. 25.24, we provide an Active Server Page named **login.asp** that prompts the user for a login name and password. The login names and passwords are stored in an Access database.

This example uses cookies to identify users, which must be enabled by the browser before executing this example. If cookies are disable, the browser will not permit the example to write a cookie to the client machine and the example will not be able to properly identify the user. To enable cookies in Internet Explorer 5, select **Internet Options** from the **Tools** menu to display the **Internet Options** dialog. Click the **Security** tab at the top of this dialog to view the current security settings. Click the **Custom Level...** button, scroll down and find **Cookies**. Click **Enable** for both cookie options.

The Active Server Page **login.asp** prompts the user for a login ID and a password while **submitlogin.asp** is responsible for validating the user's login. Both **submitlogin.asp** and **login.asp** use session variable **loginFailure**. If login is successful, **loginFailure** is set to **False** and the client is redirected to **instantpage.asp**. If login is unsuccessful, the variable is set to **True** and the client is redirected back to **login.asp**. Because **login.asp** has access to session variable **loginFailure**, the page recognizes that there was an error in **submitlogin.asp** and displays the error message.

```
1    <% @LANGUAGE = VBScript %>
2    <% Option Explicit %>
3
4    <% ' Fig. 25.24 : login.asp %>
5
6    <% Dim connection, query, loginData
7
8       Set connection = Server.CreateObject( "ADODB.Connection" )
9       Call connection.Open( "login" )
10
11      ' Create the SQL query
12      query = "SELECT loginID FROM Users"
13
14      ' Create the record set
15      Set loginData = Server.CreateObject( "ADODB.Recordset" )
16      Call loginData.Open( query, connection )
17
18      ' If an error occurs, ignore it
19      On Error Resume Next
20   %>
21
22   <!DOCTYPE HTML PUBLIC "-//W3C//DTD HTML 4.0 Transitional//EN">
23   <HTML>
24   <HEAD><TITLE>Login Page</TITLE></HEAD>
25
26   <BODY>
```

Fig. 25.24 Listing for **login.asp** (part 1 of 4).

```
27
28   <!-- #include virtual="/includes/mgtheader.shtml" -->
29
30   <%
31      ' If this is a return after a failed attempt,
32      ' print an error
33      If Session( "loginFailure" ) = True Then %>
34   <FONT SIZE = "4" COLOR = "red"> Login attempt failed,
35   please try again <P></FONT>
36   <% End If
37
38      ' Begin the form %>
39   <FONT FACE = "Arial" SIZE = "2">
40   Please select your name and enter
41   your password to login:<BR>
42   </FONT>
43   <FORM ACTION = "submitlogin.asp" METHOD = "POST">
44
45   <% ' Format the form using a table %>
46   <TABLE BORDER = "0">
47   <TR>
48   <TD><FONT FACE = "Arial" SIZE = "2">Name:</FONT></TD>
49   <TD><SELECT NAME = "loginID">
50   <OPTION VALUE = "noSelection">Select your name
51
52   <% ' If the loginID cookie is an empty string then there is
53      ' no need to consider the returning case
54      If Request.Cookies( "loginID" ) <> "" Then
55         Call BuildReturning()
56      Else
57         Call BuildNewUser()
58      End If
59   %>
60
61   </SELECT>
62   </TD>
63   </TR>
64
65   <TR>
66   <TD><FONT FACE = "Arial" SIZE = "2">Password:</FONT></TD>
67   <TD><INPUT TYPE = "password" NAME = "password"></TD>
68   </TR>
69   <TR>
70   <TD>  </TD>
71   <TD ALIGN = "left">
72      <INPUT TYPE = "submit" VALUE = "Log Me In">
73   </TD>
74   </TR>
75   </TABLE>
76   </FORM>
77   </FONT>
78
79   <!-- #include virtual="/includes/mgtfooter.shtml" -->
```

Fig. 25.24 Listing for **login.asp** (part 2 of 4).

```
80
81   </BODY>
82   </HTML>
83
84   <% ' Builds the OPTION items for loginIDs and writes
85       ' selected for the loginID of the returning user
86      Sub BuildReturning()
87         Dim found
88
89         ' Pull user names from the record set to populate the
90         ' dropdown list
91         found = False
92         While Not loginData.EOF
93            ' Create this record's dropdown entry
94   %>        <OPTION
95   <%        ' If we did not write SELECTED for any OPTION
96            ' before
97            If ( Not found ) Then
98
99               ' If the current record's loginID is equal to
100              ' the loginID cookie, then it is the loginID of
101              ' the returning user, and thus we need to write
102              ' SELECTED for this option; in this case we also
103              ' need to signal that we have written SELECTED
104              ' for an OPTION by setting found to True.
105              If Request.Cookies( "loginID" ) _
106                 = loginData( "loginID" ) _
107              Then
108                 Call Response.Write( "SELECTED" )
109                 found = True
110              End If
111           End If
112  %>        VALUE = "<% =loginData( "loginID" ) %>">
113           <% =loginData( "loginID" ) %>
114  <%        Call loginData.MoveNext()
115        Wend
116     End Sub
117
118     ' Builds the OPTION items for loginIDs without writing
119     ' SELECTED for any loginID
120     Sub BuildNewUser()
121
122        ' Pull user names from the record set to populate the
123        ' dropdown list
124        While Not loginData.EOF
125           ' Create this record's dropdown entry
126  %>        <OPTION VALUE = "<% =loginData( "loginID" ) %>">
127           <% =loginData( "loginID" ) %>
128  <%        Call loginData.MoveNext()
129        Wend
130     End Sub
131  %>
```

Fig. 25.24 Listing for **login.asp** (part 3 of 4).

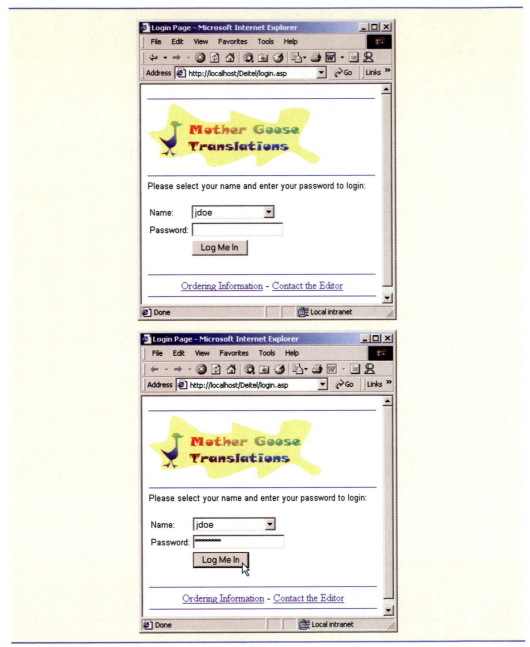

Fig. 25.24 Listing for `login.asp` (part 4 of 4).

The `loginID` and `password` fields are stored in table `Users` inside an Access database named `login.mdb`. For this particular example, all users have the same password (i.e., `password`). Before executing this example, an ODBC System DSN for this database must be created. See the "Setting up a System Data Source Name" document on the CD that accompanies this book for instructions on how to create a DSN.

Users select their **loginID** from a drop-down list populated from the **Users** table. Note that **submitlogin.asp** also accesses the database to verify login information.

To recognize returning users and have their **loginID** displayed in the drop-down list, **submitlogin.asp** writes a cookie (named **loginID**) to the client containing the user's **loginID** string. When the user returns, **login.asp** reads the cookie and selects the user's login name from the drop-down list.

Line 8

```
Set connection = Server.CreateObject( "ADODB.Connection" )
```

calls **Server** method **CreateObject** to create an **ADODB.Connection** object and **Set**s it to reference **connection**. An **ADODB.Connection** object encapsulates the functionality necessary to connect to a data source.

Line 9

```
Call connection.Open( "login" )
```

calls method *Open* to open the database referred to by the specified ODBC System DSN (i.e., **login**).

Line 12

```
query = "SELECT loginID FROM Users"
```

assigns the SQL query that **SELECT**s all the **loginID**s **FROM** the **Users** table.

Lines 15 and 16

```
Set loginData = Server.CreateObject( "ADODB.Recordset" )
Call loginData.Open( query, connection )
```

Set reference **loginData** to an **ADODB.Recordset** object and call method **Open** to execute the query (from line 12) against the database referenced by **connection**. Method **Open** is passed a string containing the SQL query and the **ADODB.Connection** object that **connection** references. When **Open** finishes executing, the **ADODB.Recordset** object referenced by **loginData** contains all records that match the SQL query and points to either the first record or *end of file* (*EOF*) if no records were found.

For simplicity, if an error occurs while the records are being retrieved, we choose to ignore them. Line 19

```
On Error Resume Next
```

specifies that any error caused by a statement from this point onward is ignored and control is transferred to the statement immediately following the statement that caused the error.

Lines 33 through 36 determine whether or not the session variable **loginFailure** is **True**, indicating that **submitlogin.asp** has detected an invalid login. If true, a message is displayed informing the client that the login attempt failed and prompting for another login.

Next, we use the HTML **SELECT** structure to build the drop-down list of **loginID**s. Line 50 writes the first **OPTION** that displays, **Select your name**. If no other **OPTION** is marked as **SELECTED**, this **OPTION** is displayed when the page is loaded. The next **OPTION**s are the **loginID**s retrieved from the database. If this is a returning user, we want to display their **loginID** as **SELECTED**.

Line 54 requests the **loginID** cookie. If this is the user's first visit, or if the cookie has expired, **Cookie** returns an empty string. [*Note*: It is possible for a cookie to store an empty string. If this is the case, **Cookie** returns the contents of the cookie, which is an empty string.] Otherwise, the user's **loginID** is returned otherwise. Lines 54 through 58

```
If Request.Cookies( "loginID" ) <> "" Then
   Call BuildReturning()
Else
   Call BuildNewUser()
End If
```

call procedure **BuildReturning** if **loginID** contains a login ID and call procedure **BuildNewUser** otherwise. Both **BuildReturning** and **BuildNewUser** build the login ID **OPTION**s. However, **BuildReturning** selects the returning user's login ID **OPTION** while **BuildNewUser** does not.

BuildReturning's **While** loop (lines 92 through 115) iterates through **login-Data**'s records. Recall that **loginData** contains the **loginID** column (field) of the **Users** table and points either to the first record or to **EOF**. Line 92

```
While Not loginData.EOF
```

tests for the end of the record set, indicating that there are no further records. Line 114

```
Call loginData.MoveNext()
```

increments the record set pointer to the next record.

Each iteration of the **While** loop builds an **OPTION** item for the current record. Line 94 simply writes the opening of the **OPTION** item. Next, we test whether or not this **OPTION** needs to be **SELECTED** with the **If** statement in lines 105 through 110. Note that once we have written **SELECTED** for an **OPTION**, there is no need to perform this check in further iterations—**SELECTED** is written for one and only one **OPTION**. The code that writes **SELECTED** for an option is thus wrapped in another **If** statement (lines 97 through 111). Variable **found** is set to **False** before the loop, in line 91. Once **SELECTED** is written for an **OPTION**, **found** is assigned **True**. Line 97 prevents the code that writes **SELECTED** for an option from being executed unnecessarily after an **OPTION** is already selected. Lines 105 and 106

```
If Request.Cookies( "loginID" ) _
   = loginData( "loginID" ) _
```

determine whether or not the current record's **loginID** field is equal to the value of the **loginID** cookie. If so, lines 108 and 109 write **SELECTED** and set **found** to **True**.

Line 112 sets the **VALUE** for the **OPTION** to current **loginID**. Finally, line 113 writes the display of this **OPTION** as the current **loginID**.

Active Server Page **submitlogin.asp** (Fig. 25.25) takes the values passed to it by **login.asp** and checks the values against the **Users** table in the database. If a match is found, the user is redirected to **instantpage.asp**. If no match is found, the user is redirected back to **login.asp**. The user never sees or knows about **submitlogin.asp** because the page is pure scripting code (i.e., its entire contents are enclosed in scripting delimiters).

```
132   <% @LANGUAGE = VBScript %>
133   <% Option Explicit %>
134
135   <% ' Fig. 25.25 : submitlogin.asp %>
136
137   <% ' First, make sure that a user name and a password were
138      ' entered. If not, redirect back to the login page.
139
140      If Request( "password" ) = "" Or _
141         Request( "loginID" ) = "noSelection" _
142      Then
143         Session( "loginFailure" ) = True
144         Call Response.Redirect( "login.asp" )
145      End If
146
147      Dim connection, query, loginData
148
149      Set connection = Server.CreateObject( "ADODB.Connection" )
150      Call connection.Open( "login" )
151
152      ' Create the SQL query
153      query = "SELECT * FROM Users WHERE loginID = '" _
154                & Request( "loginID" ) & "'"
155
156      ' Create the record set
157      Set loginData = Server.CreateObject( "ADODB.Recordset" )
158      Call loginData.Open( query, connection )
159
160      ' If an error occurs, ignore it
161      On Error Resume Next
162
163      If Request( "password" ) = loginData( "password" ) Then
164
165         ' Password is OK, adjust loginFailure
166         Session( "loginFailure" ) = False
167
168         ' Write a cookie to recognize them the next time they
169         ' go to login.asp
170         Response.Cookies( "loginID" ) = Request( "loginID" )
171
172         ' Give it three days to expire
173         Response.Cookies( "loginID" ).Expires = Date() + 3
174
175         ' Send them on to the next page
176         Call Response.Redirect( "instantpage.asp" )
177      Else
178         Session( "loginFailure" ) = True
179         Call Response.Redirect( "login.asp" )
180      End If
181   %>
```

Fig. 25.25 Listing for **submitlogin.asp**.

Lines 140 through 145 check whether the form's **password** field is empty or if the **loginID** field was submitted with the default value. If so, session variable **login-Failure** is set to **True** and the client is redirected to **login.asp**.

Lines 153 and 154

```
query = "SELECT * FROM Users WHERE loginID = '" _
        & Request( "loginID" ) & "'"
```

selects all the fields from the table. The **WHERE** clause in this SQL statement specifies a condition on which records are selected: Only the record(s) whose **loginID** field has the same value as the form's **loginID** field are selected. Also note that this SQL statement always finds a record because the form's **loginID** values are retrieved from the **Users**' **loginID** field. For example, if **loginID jdoe** is selected, then **query** contains

```
SELECT * FROM Users WHERE loginID = 'jdoe'
```

Line 163 checks the password against the password from the record set. Note that the submitted **loginID** is a valid login ID that was selected from the drop down list. Thus, we only need to check the password here to validate a login. If correct, line 170

```
Response.Cookies( "loginID" ) = Request( "loginID" )
```

writes the form's **loginID** value as a cookie named **loginID**.

Line 173

```
Response.Cookies( "loginID" ).Expires = Date() + 3
```

sets the expiration date of this cookie to the current date plus three days. If we do not set an expiration date for the cookie when we create it, it is treated as a session cookie (i.e., it is destroyed when the browser is closed). [*Note*: If an existing cookie's content is updated (we update cookies in Chapter 26), then the expiration date needs to be set again. Otherwise, the cookie is destroyed at the end of the session regardless of the expiration date it had before the update.] The cookie remains on the client's machine until it expires. At which time, the browser deletes it.

Next, line 176 calls method **Redirect** to redirect the client to **instantpage.asp**. Otherwise, the session variable **loginFailure** is set to **True**, and the client is redirected back to **login.asp** (lines 178 and 179).

25.12 Internet and World Wide Web Resources

http://www.microsoft.com/
Microsoft's home page. Provides a link to search Microsoft's entire Web-based information structure. Check this site first for answers. Some information is provided on a subscriber-only basis.

http://www.tcp-ip.com/
The *ASP Toolbox* home page is an excellent source for ASP information and resources. The site contains numerous links to free components and other resources helpful in Web development using Active Server Pages. The site tutorials includes an overview of Active Server technology as well as helpful hints and demos with source code provided. Other features of this page include ASP discussion forums and resources.

www.4guysfromrolla.com/webtech/index_asp.shtml
Contains FAQs, ASP-related articles, coding tips, message boards, etc.

www.aspin.com/index/
Contains ASP resources including applications, books, forums, references, examples and tutorials, links, etc.

www.kamath.com/default.asp
Contains downloads, FAQs, tutorials, book excerpts, columns, etc.

www.aspwatch.com/
Contains ASP-related articles and code examples.

www.developer.com/
Great source of information for developers. The ASP section contains working code, troubleshooting techniques and advice.

www.paessler.com/tools/ASPBeautify/
Home of a tool that formats ASP pages for readability.

SUMMARY

- Active Server Pages (ASP) are processed in response to a client (e.g., browser) request. An ASP file—which has file extension **.asp**—contains HTML and scripting code. Although other languages such as JavaScript can be used for ASP scripting, VBScript is the de facto language for ASP scripting.

- ASP is a Microsoft-developed technology for generating dynamic Web content—which includes HTML, Dynamic HTML, ActiveX controls, client-side scripts and Java applets (i.e., client-side Java programs that are embedded in a Web page).

- The two most common HTTP request types (also known as request methods) are **GET** and **POST**. These requests are frequently used to send client form data to a Web server.

- A **GET** request sends form content as part of the URL. A **POST** request posts form contents inside the HTTP request. The post data is appended to the end of an HTTP request.

- Browsers often cache (save on disk) Web pages so they can quickly reload the pages. There are no changes between the last version stored in the cache and the current version on the Web. Browsers typically do not cache the server's response to a **POST** request because the next **POST** may not return the same result.

- When a client requests an ASP file, the ASP file is parsed (top to bottom) by an ActiveX component named **asp.dll**. Scripting code is executed as it is encountered.

- The **@LANGUAGE** statement is used by the programmer to specify which scripting engine is needed to interpret the scripting code. If **@LANGUAGE** is not used, VBScript is assumed to be the default. As the script is interpreted, HTML (plus any client-side scripts) is sent to the client.

- Client-side scripting is often used for validation, interactivity, enhancing a Web page with ActiveX controls, Dynamic HTML and Java applets and for accessing the browser.

- Client-side scripting is browser dependent—the scripting language must be supported by the browser or scripting host. Because Microsoft Internet Explorer and Netscape Communicator both support JavaScript, JavaScript has become the de facto scripting language on the client.

- Because server-side scripts reside on the server, programmers have greater flexibility—especially with database access. Scripts executed on the server usually generate custom responses for clients.

- Server-side scripts have access to ActiveX server components—which extend scripting language functionality. Server-side ActiveX components typically do not have a graphical user interface. Many ActiveX components are included with Internet Information Server (IIS) and Personal Web Server (PWS).

- Scripting delimiters **<%** and **%>** indicate that the scripting code is to be executed on the server— not the client. Scripting code enclosed in a scripting delimiter is never sent to the client.
- Function **Time** returns the server's current time in the format, *hh:mm:ss*.
- The **Response** object provides functionality for sending information to the client.
- The AdRotator ActiveX component rotates advertisements on a Web page.
- Server-side ActiveX components are instantiated by passing the name of the component as a string to **Server** object method **CreateObject**. The **Server** object represents the Web server.
- **Response** object method **Write** writes text to the client.
- File System Objects (FSOs) provide the programmer with the ability to manipulate files, directories and drives. FSOs also allow the programmer to read and write text to sequential files. FSOs are an essential element for Active Server Pages with persistent data.
- FSOs are objects in the Microsoft Scripting Runtime Library. Five FSO types exist: **FileSystemObject**, **File**, **Folder**, **Drive** and **TextStream**.
- Type **FileSystemObject** allows the programmer to interact with **File**s, **Folder**s and **Drive**s. The programmer can use **FileSystemObject**s to create directories, move files, determine whether or not a **Drive** exists, etc. **File**s allow the programmer to gather information about files, manipulate files and open files. **Folder** objects allow the programmer to gather information about directories and to manipulate directories. **Drive** objects allow the programmer to gather information about drives.
- Many Web sites today provide custom Web pages and/or functionality on a client-by-client basis. The HTTP protocol does not support persistent information that could help a Web server determine that a request is from a particular client. As far as a Web server is concerned, every request could be from the same client or every request could be from a different client.
- Session tracking is handled by the server. The first time a client connects to the server, it is assigned a unique session ID by the server. When the client makes additional requests, the client's session ID is compared against the session IDs stored in the server's memory. Active Server Pages use the **Session** object to manage sessions. The **Session** object's **Timeout** property specifies the number of minutes a session exists for before it expires. The default value for property **Timeout** is 20 minutes. An individual session can also be terminated by calling **Session** method **Abandon**.
- Cookies can store information on the client's computer for retrieval later in the same browsing session or in future browsing sessions. Cookies are files that are sent by an Active Server Page as part of a response to a client. Every HTTP-based interaction between a client and a server includes a header that contains information about the request or information about the response. When an Active Server Page receives a request, the header includes information such as the request type and cookies stored on the client machine by the server. When the server formulates its response, the header information includes any cookies the server wants to store on the client computer.
- Server-side include (SSI) statements are always executed before any scripting code is executed. The word **virtual** in the SSI refers to the include file's path as it appears below the server root directory. This is often referred to as a virtual path. SSIs can also use **file** instead of **virtual** to indicate a physical path on the server.
- VBScript constant **vbCrLf** is used to insert a carriage-return line-feed combination.
- Method **Redirect** redirects the client to another Web page.
- A database is an integrated collection of data. A database management system (DBMS) involves the data itself and the software that controls the storage and retrieval of data.
- Database management systems provide mechanisms for storing and organizing data in a manner that facilitates satisfying sophisticated queries and manipulations of the data.

- A language called Structured Query Language (SQL) is almost universally used with relational database systems to make queries (i.e., to request information that satisfies given criteria) and manipulate data.
- Universal Data Access (UDA) is a Microsoft architecture that provides data access to many data sources.
- A relational database is composed of tables, which in turn are composed of columns (or fields).
- A primary key is a unique field that is used to identify a record.
- SQL provides a complete set of keywords that enable programmers to define complex queries for retrieving data from a table.
- Query results are commonly called result sets (or record sets).
- **SELECT** queries select information from one or more tables in a database.
- An asterisk (*****) indicates that all rows and columns (fields) from a table should be selected.
- SQL provides the optional **WHERE** clause in a **SELECT** query to specify the selection criteria for a query. The **WHERE** clause condition can contain operators such as **<, >, <=, >=, =, <>** and **LIKE**.
- Operator **LIKE** is used for pattern matching with wildcard characters asterisk (*****) and question mark (**?**).
- An asterisk (*****) in a pattern indicates any number of (i.e., zero or more) characters in a row at the asterisk's location in the pattern.
- Query results can be sorted into ascending (**ASC**) or descending (**DESC**) order using the optional **ORDER BY** clause.
- The **INSERT INTO** keywords inserts data into a table.
- The **UPDATE/SET** keywords modify data in a table.
- Microsoft developed the Open Database Connectivity (ODBC) Application Programming Interface (API) to allow Windows applications to communicate in a uniform manner with disparate relational databases.
- Web applications are three-tier distributed applications, consisting of a user interface (UI), business logic and database access. The UI in such an application is often created using HTML, Dynamic HTML or XML. All three tiers may reside on separate computers that are connected to a network or all three tiers may reside on a single machine.
- In multitier architectures, Web servers are increasingly used to build the middle tier. They provide the business logic that manipulates data from databases and that communicates with client Web browsers.
- Method **Open** opens a connection to the data source.
- Method **Execute** executes a query against the data source.
- **ADODB.Recordset** method **MoveFirst** moves to the first record in a recordset.
- **ADODB.RecordSet** constant **EOF** represents a recordset's end-of-file.

TERMINOLOGY

%> closing scripting delimiter	**#include**
<% opening script delimiter	**Abandon** method of **Session**
.asp file	**ActiveConnection** property
.shtml file	ActiveX Data Objects (ADO)
.mdb file	**ADODB.Command** object
@LANGUAGE directive	**ADODB.Connection** object

ADODB.RecordSet object
AdRotator ActiveX Control
appending to a file
asp.dll
business logic
cache Web pages
Chr method
client-side scripting
Close method
columns
CommandText property
CommandType property
configuration file
cookie
cookie expiration
CreateObject method
CreateTextFile method
database
database management system (DBMS)
database access
Drive
EOF constant
Execute method
expiration of a cookie
fields
File
file system object
FileExists method
FileSystemObject
Folder
GET HTTP request
GetAdvertisement method
guest book application
header
join condition
mailto link
maximum age of a cookie
MoveFirst method
MoveNext method
On Error Resume Next statement
one-to-many relationship
Open method

OpenTextFile method
Open Database Connectivity (ODBC) Application Programming Interface (API)
Option Explicit statement
physical path
POST HTTP request
primary key
ReadAll method
record
record set
Redirect method of **Response**
relational database
Request object
Response object
result set
script engine
script host
SELECT query
selection criteria
Server object
server-side ActiveX component
server-side include (SSI)
server-side scripting
session
session ID
Session object
session tracking
Set keyword
shopping cart application
short name format
Structured Query Language (SQL)
table
TextStream
three-tier distributed application
Timeout property of **Session**
Universal Data Access (UDA)
user interface
vbCrLf constant
VBScript
virtual path
Write method
WriteLine method

SELF-REVIEW EXERCISES

25.1 State whether each of the following is *true* or *false*. If *false*, explain why.
  a) VBScript is the only language that can be used in an Active Server Page.
  b) Active Server Page file names typically end in **.asp**.
  c) Only Microsoft Internet Explorer can render an Active Server Page.
  d) The **<% Option Explicit %>** statement is optional.

e) Variables can be passed from one Active Server Page to another without using a form.

f) VBScript statements cannot be present in a server-side include file.

g) Server-side ActiveX components typically do not have graphical user interfaces.

h) AdRotator is a client-side Activex control.

i) Server-side include files end in **.ssi** by convention.

j) Before an ASP can use ADO to access a database, the database must have a System DSN.

25.2   Fill in the blanks for each of the following:

a) Processing directive _____ informs **asp.dll** that scripting language is used.

b) Passing an integer value of _____ to function **Chr** returns the double quote (**"**) character.

c) Session variables retain their value during the duration of the _____.

d) Cookies are files placed on the _____ machine.

e) Constant _____ represents a carriage-return line-feed combination.

f) ASP is an acronym for _____.

g) Method _____ moves to the first record in a record set.

h) **Server** method _____ is called to create an object.

i) A recordset's **Fields** collection contains a series of _____ objects.

j) A _____ contains a database's name, location and driver.

ANSWERS TO SELF-REVIEW EXERCISES

25.1   a) False. Any scripting language recognized by the server can be used. b) True. c) False. Most browsers can render HTML returned by an Active Server Page. d) True. e) True. Variables can be embedded in a URL (e.g., **localhost/page.asp?var=true**). f) False. A server-side include can contain scripting code, HTML, text, etc. g) True. h) False. AdRotator is a server-side ActiveX component. i) False. Server-side include files end in **.shtml** by convention. j) True.

25.2   a) **@LANGUAGE**. b) **Chr(34)**. c) session. d) client. e) **vbCrLf**. f) data source name. g **MoveFirst**. h) **CreateObject**. i) **Field**. j) System Data Name Source (DNS).

EXERCISES

25.3   Create a server-side include file containing the AdRotator code listed in Fig. 25.3. Write an ASP that performs the same action as the AdRotator and uses this server-side include file.

25.4   Modify Fig. 25.2's **clock.asp** to also display different time zones.

25.5   Modify Fig. 25.12's **guestbook.asp** to read and write to a database rather than a text file. This exercise requires the use of a database development tool such as Microsoft Access.

25.6   Using the same techniques as Fig. 25.12 (**guestbook.asp**) develop an ASP application for a discussion group. Allow new links to be created for new topics.

25.7   Modify Fig. 25.24's **login.asp** to read and write to a text file rather than a database.

25.8   Create an ASP application that allows the user to customize a Web page. Store the user's name and preferences in a text file. The application should consist of three ASP files: one that asks the user to login and reads from the text file to determine if the user is known. If the user is not known, a second ASP file is loaded asking the user to choose their preference for foreground color, background color and image. Write the new user's name and preferences to the text file. Next, display the page customized to this user using the user's preferences that are stored in the text file. If the user is known at login, the normal page should be displayed.

26

ASP Case Studies

Objectives

- To understand the implementation of three-tier Web applications.
- To understand how HTML, VBScript and ASP can be combined to form e-Business solutions.
- To understand how a shopping cart is implemented.
- To understand how an online auction is implemented.
- To understand how a comparison pricing search engine is implemented.

If any man will draw up his case, and put his name at the foot of the first page, I will give him an immediate reply. Where he compels me to turn over the sheet, he must wait my leisure.
Lord Sandwich

You will come here and get books that will open your eyes, and your ears, and your curiosity, and turn you inside out or outside in.
Ralph Waldo Emerson

They also serve who only stand and wait.
John Milton

26.1 Introduction

In Chapters 9 and 10, we studied HTML, which allows content to be rendered in a Web browser. HTML is crucial to e-commerce applications, because it is the universal interface customers use. In Chapter 24, we studied VBScript, which is used to implement Active Server Pages (ASP). In Chapter 25, we studied ASP that introduced the concept of server-side scripting—an essential e-commerce technology. One of the most crucial aspects of server-side scripting studied in Chapter 25 is database access. An e-business typically uses a database to store customer information and track inventory. In this chapter, we present three e-commerce case studies that utilize HTML, VBScript and ASP. Each of these examples are three-tiered Web applications that use HTML on the client, ASP in the middle tier and a database for the third tier.

The first case study we present is a shopping cart. In Chapter 3, we discussed the theory of the shopping cart model; in this chapter, we implement it as a major case study. The example is an online bookstore that allows the user to add books to and remove books from their shopping cart. Cookies are used to implement the shopping cart.

Next, we present an online auction case study. We had also discussed the theory of online auctions in Chapter 3. The auction allows registered users to bid and sell items. This is the largest of the three case studies presented in the chapter. This case study contains 16 documents

Our final case study implements the comparison-pricing model discussed in Chapter 3. In this case study, we search the Web for the lowest price of a book. We search many different Web sites and sort the prices from lowest to highest.

26.2 Setup

In this section we present the setup and installation steps that are required to run each of the chapter's three case studies. Section 26.2.1 discusses the setup and installation steps for the shopping cart, Section 26.2.2 the auction site and Section 26.2.3 the comparison pricing search engine.

26.2.1 Shopping Cart

1. Copy the database file **Catalog.mdb** from the CD to your hard drive. You may place this file in any directory. **Catalog.mdb** is a Microsoft Access 2000 data-

base. In case you do not have the Access 2000 ODBC driver, we provide an Access 97 version of the same database called **Catalog_97.mdb** on the CD.

2. Create a System DSN named **Catalog** for the database. For instructions on creating a System DSN for a database, see the document titled "Setting up a System Data Source Name" on the CD that accompanies this book.

3. Copy the Chapter 26 **Includes** and **Images** folders from the CD to your publishing directory (e.g., **Inetpub/Wwwroot**).

4. Copy the Chapter 26 **ShoppingCart** folder from the CD to your publishing directory.

5.   Make sure your Web server (e.g., PWS) is running.

6. Document **catalog.asp** should be requested first. In IE5's **Address** bar, type:

```
http://localhost/ShoppingCart/catalog.asp
```

and press *Enter*.

26.2.2 Auction Site

1. Copy the database file **DeitelAuctions.mdb** from the CD to your hard drive. You may place this file in any directory. **DeitelAuctions.mdb** is a Microsoft Access 2000 database. In case you do not have the Access 2000 ODBC driver, we provide an Access 97 version of the same database called **DeitelAuctions_97.mdb** on the CD.

2. Create a System DSN named **DeitelAuctions** for the database. For instructions on creating a System DSN for a database, see the document titled "Setting up a System Data Source Name" on the CD that accompanies this book.

3. Copy the Chapter 26 **Images** folder from the CD to your publishing directory (e.g., **Inetpub/Wwwroot**).

4. Copy the Chapter 26 **DeitelAuctions** folder from the CD to your publishing directory.

5. Make sure your Web server (e.g., PWS) is running.

6. You will need to update several fields in the database before testing the auction site. A script named **update.asp** that updates the database is provided on the CD. It is located in the Chapter 26 **DeitelAuctions** folder. In IE5's **Address** bar, type:

```
http://localhost/DeitelAuctions/update.asp
```

and press *Enter*. A message indicating a successful update of the database should be displayed. The script updates records in the **DeitelAuctions.mdb** database so that two items are up for auction today and two items were won yesterday. Note that "today" is the date when the **update.asp** script is run. Because the auction site uses dates, you will need to run this script each day before testing the auction site.

7. The **index.asp** file is the home page of the auction site and should be requested first. In IE5's **Address** bar, type:

    `http://localhost/DeitelAuctions/index.asp`

and press *Enter*.

26.2.3 Comparison Pricing Search Engine

1. Copy the Chapter 26 **Asptear** folder from the CD to the root directory (**C:**) of the hard drive.

2. From the Windows **Start** menu, select **Run** and type:

    `regsvr32 C:\Asptear\AspTear.dll`

and press *Enter*. This installs the ASPTear component that is needed to run the comparison pricing search engine.

3. To prevent ASPTear from grabbing cached copies of Web pages, perform the following: Open the **Control Panel** and double click the **Internet Options** icon. Select the **General** tab. Click the **Settings** button in the **Temporary Internet Files** box. Make sure the **Every visit to the page** option is selected.

4. Copy the database file **Lowest.mdb** from the CD to your hard drive. You may place this file in any directory. **Lowest.mdb** is a Microsoft Access 2000 database. In case you do not have the Access 2000 ODBC driver, we provide an Access 97 version of the same database called **Lowest_97.mdb** on the CD.

5. Create a System DSN named **Lowest** for the database. For instructions on creating a System DSN for a database, see the document titled "Setting up a System Data Source Name" on the CD that accompanies this book.

6. Copy the Chapter 26 **Lowest** folder from the CD to your publishing directory (e.g., **Inetpub/Wwwroot**).

7. Make sure your Web server (e.g., PWS) is running.

8. The comparison-shopping search engine consists of a single file, **lowest.asp**. In IE5's **Address** bar, type:

    `http://localhost/Lowest/lowest.asp`

and press *Enter*.

26.3 Case Study: a Shopping Cart

Perhaps the most common e-business model is the shopping cart. This technology allows customers to store a list of items that they are considering purchasing. With the click of a button, the customer can add and remove items.

In this section, we create an online bookstore that sells Deitel books. The shopping cart functionality is implemented with cookies. Recall that cookies are text files written to the client machine. Each time the user visits the bookstore, any cookies previously written by the book store are retrieved. The shopping cart consists of six Active Server Pages that we summarize in Fig 26.1. We discuss each of these Active Server Pages in detail in this section. [*Note:* For simplicity, we do not implement the checkout and payment process.]

Before we begin discussing the Active Server Pages used in this example, let us first discuss the database used to store book information. An Access database (named **Catalog.mdb**) stores the book information. It has four tables: **Technologies**, **Products**, **Authors** and **Authorlist**. In Fig. 25.20, we showed the table relationships for **Catalog.mdb**. You may want to refer to this figure before proceeding. The **Technologies** table contains two fields: **technologyID** and **technology**. The **technology** field is a string containing the name of the technology, such as "C" or "Java." The **technologyID** field is a unique number assigned to each technology and is the **Technologies** table's primary key.

Table **Products** stores each book added to the cart. It consists of nine fields, including **title**, **publishDate**, **edition**, **isbn**, **coverart**, **description** and **price**. These fields contain the title, date published, edition number, ISBN number, image name, description and price of each book, respectively. The primary key field, **productID**, is a unique number assigned to each book. The **technologyID** field contains the number of the technology (from the **Technologies** table) the book covers.

The **Authorlist** table stores each book's author(s) in the **Products** table and contains three fields: **ID**, **authorID** and **productID**. The **authorID** field contains the unique number assigned to each author. The **productID** field contains the book's product number (from the **Products** table) that the author wrote. The **ID** field contains the unique number assigned to each author in the **Authorlist** table.

ASP document	Description
catalog.asp	Lists the different programming technologies for which books are available. When a technology is selected, the user is redirected to **titles.asp**.
titles.asp	Lists the book titles for the selected technology. When a title is selected, the user is redirected to **description.asp**.
description.asp	Displays the publication year, ISBN number, edition number, picture and a **Buy it now** shopping cart image. When the shopping cart image is clicked, the user is redirected to **buyit.asp**.
buyit.asp	Displays the title, author, ISBN number, price and book picture. The user enters in a form the quantity of the book to be purchased. When the form is submitted, the user is redirected to **addtocart.asp**.
addtocart.asp	Adds the quantity of the selected book to the user's cart. This document does not output any HTML. It simply adds the book to the cart and then redirects the user to **viewcart.asp**.
viewcart.asp	Lists the contents of the user's cart with prices.

Fig. 26.1   The Active Server Pages used to implement the shopping cart application.

The primary keys are used to retrieve relational records from different tables in the database. For example, if we know an **authorID** number, we can use it to extract the author's name (from the **Authors** table) and the books the author has written (from the **Authorlist** table). Similarly, if we know a **technologyID** number we can use it to extract the technology name (from the **Technology** table) and the books that cover that technology (from the **Products** table). The **Catalog.mdb** database must have a System DSN on the server before it can be accessed. For this example, we use **Catalog** for the System DSN.

Figure 26.2 (**catalog.asp**) creates a list of programming language links. When a link is clicked, the user is redirected to **titles.asp** (Fig. 26.3). Each programming language link passes its **technologyID** in the URL of **titles.asp**. For example, a link might be written as

```
<A HREF = "titles.asp?technologyid=1">
```

where **1** is the **technologyID**. The **titles.asp** document, which we will discuss in detail momentarily, uses this number to display titles of the selected programming language books.

```
1    <% @LANGUAGE = VBScript %>
2    <% Option Explicit %>
3
4    <% ' Fig 26.2 : catalog.asp %>
5
6    <!DOCTYPE HTML PUBLIC "-//W3C//DTD HTML 4.0 Transitional//EN">
7    <HTML>
8    <HEAD>
9    <TITLE>Textbook Information Center: Technology</TITLE>
10   </HEAD>
11   <BODY BGCOLOR = "#FFFFFF">
12
13   <!-- #include virtual = "/includes/header.shtml" -->
14
15   <CENTER>
16   <H2><FONT COLOR = "brown">
17   Welcome to the Textbook Information Center</FONT></H2>
18   </CENTER>
19
20   <TABLE BORDER = "0" WIDTH = "100%"
21     CELLPADDING = "0" CELLSPACING = "0">
22   <TR>
23   <TD WIDTH = "25%"> </TD>
24   <TD BGCOLOR = "#008080" WIDTH = "10%"> </TD>
25   <TD BGCOLOR = "#008080" WIDTH = "40%">
26   <FONT COLOR = "yellow" SIZE = "2">To view available titles
27   for a technology<BR>select a link from this list:</FONT>
28
29   <%
30       Dim connection, query, data
31
```

Fig. 26.2   Listing for **catalog.asp** (part 1 of 3).

```
32        Set connection = Server.CreateObject( "ADODB.Connection" )
33        Call connection.Open( "catalog" )
34
35        ' Create the SQL query and the record set
36        query = "SELECT * FROM technologies"
37        Set data = Server.CreateObject( "ADODB.Recordset" )
38        Call data.Open( query, connection )
39    %>
40    <UL>
41    <% ' Begin a while loop that iterates through each record
42        ' in the record set
43        While Not data.EOF
44
45           ' Create a link that passes the technologyID
46           ' number to titles.asp and uses the text
47           ' value of technology to label the link.
48    %>    <LI>
49        <A HREF = "titles.asp?technologyid=<%
50            =data( "technologyID" ) %>">
51            <FONT COLOR = "yellow" SIZE = "2">
52            <% =data( "technology" ) %>
53            </FONT>
54        </A>
55
56    <%    ' Move to the next record
57        Call data.MoveNext()
58    Wend
59    Call data.Close()
60    Call connection.Close()
61    %>
62
63    </UL></TD>
64
65    <TD WIDTH = "25%"></TD>
66    </TR></TABLE><BR>
67
68    <TABLE ALIGN = "center">
69    <TR>
70    <TD><IMG SRC = "/images/cartonly.gif"
71        ALT = "cartonly.gif"></TD>
72
73    <% ' The following form has 2 input items:
74        ' - A submit button that, when clicked, redirects
75        '   the user to viewcart.asp
76        ' - A hidden input item that holds the URL of this
77        '   this page. The viewcart.asp page uses this hidden
78        '   item to provide a link back to this page.
79    %>
80
81    <FORM ACTION = "viewcart.asp" METHOD = "POST">
82    <TD><INPUT TYPE = "submit" VALUE = "View Cart"></TD>
83    <INPUT TYPE = "hidden" NAME = "url" VALUE = "catalog.asp">
84    </FORM>
```

Fig. 26.2   Listing for **catalog.asp** (part 2 of 3).

```
85
86    <TD><IMG SRC = "/images/cartonly.gif"
87        ALT = "cartonly.gif"></TD>
88    </TR>
89    </TABLE>
90
91    <!-- #include virtual = "/includes/footer.shtml" -->
92
93    </BODY>
94    </HTML>
```

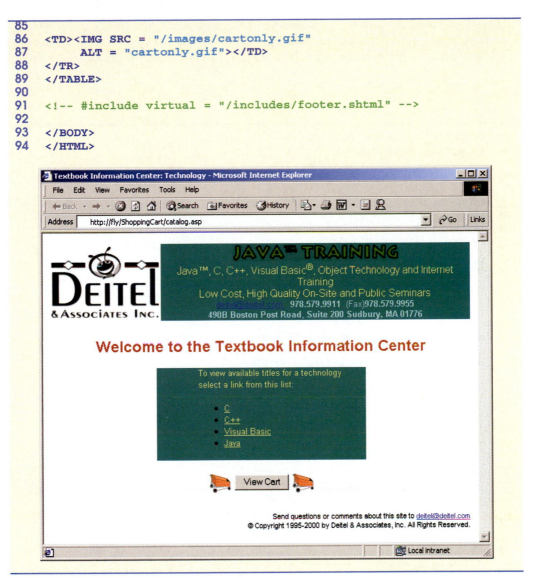

Fig. 26.2   Listing for `catalog.asp` (part 3 of 3).

A connection to the database is established in lines 32 and 33. When executed, the SQL query in line 36 retrieves all records from the **Technologies** table. The **While** loop in lines 43 through 58 iterates through the retrieved records and creates a link for each record's **technology** field (i.e., the name of the programming language).

The form in lines 81 through 84 creates a submit button labeled **View Cart** and a hidden input named **url**, that is given the value **catalog.asp**. When the button is clicked, the user is redirected to **viewcart.asp** (Fig. 26.7, which displays the shopping cart's content—we will discuss this ASP later in the chapter).

Figure 26.3 (**titles.asp**) uses the technology product number selected in **catalog.asp**, to build a list of book-title links from the **Products** table. When a link is clicked, the user is redirected to **description.asp**. Each link passes the product number in the URL of **description.asp** (lines 140 and 141). A link back to **catalog.asp** and a link to **viewcart.asp** are provided at the bottom of **titles.asp**.

```
95   <% @LANGUAGE = VBScript %>
96   <% Option Explicit %>
97
98   <% ' Fig 26.3 : titles.asp %>
99
100  <!DOCTYPE HTML PUBLIC "-//W3C//DTD HTML 4.0 Transitional//EN">
101  <HTML>
102  <HEAD>
103  <TITLE>Textbook Information Center: Titles</TITLE>
104  </HEAD>
105  <BODY BGCOLOR = "#FFFFFF">
106
107  <!-- #include virtual = "/includes/header.shtml" -->
108
109  <CENTER>
110  <H2><FONT COLOR = "brown">Welcome to the Textbook
111  Information Center</FONT></H2></CENTER>
112  <TABLE BORDER = "0" WIDTH = "100%"
113    CELLPADDING = "0" CELLSPACING = "0">
114  <TR>
115  <TD WIDTH = "15%"> </TD>
116  <TD BGCOLOR = "#008080" WIDTH = "5%"> </TD>
117  <TD BGCOLOR = "#008080" WIDTH = "60%">
118  <FONT COLOR = "yellow" SIZE = "2">Select a title from the
119  list below:</FONT>
120  <%
121      Dim connection, query, data
122
123      Set connection = Server.CreateObject( "ADODB.Connection" )
124      Call connection.Open( "catalog" )
125
126      ' Create the SQL query and the record set
127      query = "SELECT * FROM products WHERE technologyID = " _
128              & Request( "technologyid" )
129      Set data = Server.CreateObject( "ADODB.Recordset" )
130      Call data.Open( query, connection )
131  %>
132  <UL>
133  <% ' Begin a while loop that iterates through the records
134      ' in the record set
135      While Not data.EOF
136
137          ' Create a link that passes the productID number to
138          ' description.asp and uses the title and the edition
139          ' to label the link.
```

Fig. 26.3   Listing for **titles.asp** (part 1 of 3).

```
140  %>      <LI><A HREF="description.asp?productid=<%
141             =data( "productID" ) %>">
142         <FONT COLOR = "yellow" SIZE = "2">
143            <% =data( "title" ) %></A>  Edition
144            <% =data( "edition" ) %>
145         </FONT>
146         </LI>
147  <%     Call data.MoveNext() ' Move to the next record
148     Wend
149     Call data.Close()
150     Call connection.Close()
151  %>
152  </UL>
153  </TD>
154
155  <TD BGCOLOR = "#008080" WIDTH = "5%"> </TD>
156
157  <TD WIDTH = "15%"></TD>
158  </TR>
159  </TABLE>
160
161  <% ' Provide a link back to the previous page %>
162  <P ALIGN = "center"><FONT SIZE = "3">Back to<STRONG>
163  <A HREF = "catalog.asp">Technology List</FONT></A></STRONG>
164  </P>
165
166  <% Dim url
167
168     ' Store the URL of this page
169     url = "titles.asp?technologyid=" & Request( "technologyid" ) %>
170
171  <TABLE ALIGN = "center">
172  <TR>
173  <TD><IMG SRC = "/images/cartonly.gif" ALT = "cartonly.gif">
174  </TD>
175
176  <% ' A form similar to the form in catalog.asp %>
177  <FORM ACTION = "viewcart.asp" METHOD = "POST">
178     <TD><INPUT TYPE = "submit" VALUE = "View Cart"></TD>
179     <INPUT TYPE = "hidden" NAME = "url" VALUE = "<% =url %>">
180  </FORM>
181
182  <TD><IMG SRC = "/images/cartonly.gif" ALT = "cartonly.gif">
183  </TD>
184  </TR>
185  </TABLE>
186
187  <!-- #include virtual = "/includes/footer.shtml" -->
188
189  </BODY>
190  </HTML>
```

Fig. 26.3   Listing for **titles.asp** (part 2 of 3).

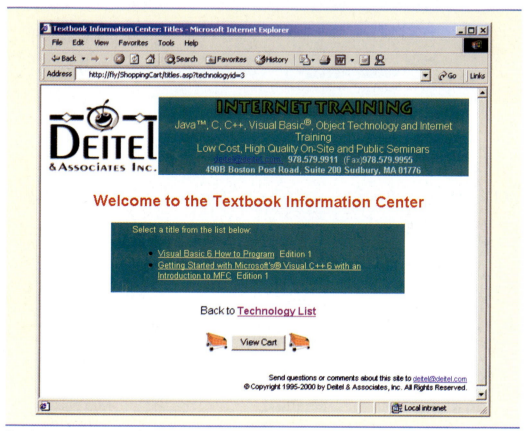

Fig. 26.3   Listing for `titles.asp` (part 3 of 3).

Figure 26.4 (`description.asp`) uses the product number (i.e., the `productID` value passed in the URL by `titles.asp` in lines 140 and 141) to display the book's information (i.e., the title, ISBN number and edition). When executed against the database, the SQL statement in lines 214 and 215 retrieves the book's record. The book title is displayed in line 222 and the book image is displayed in line 231. Lines 238 through 240 display the publication year, ISBN number and edition number.

```
191  <% @LANGUAGE = VBScript %>
192  <% Option Explicit %>
193
194  <% ' Fig. 26.4 : description.asp %>
195
196  <!DOCTYPE HTML PUBLIC "-//W3C//DTD HTML 4.0 Transitional//EN">
197  <HTML>
198  <HEAD>
199  <TITLE>Textbook Information Center: Description
200  </TITLE>
201  </HEAD>
```

Fig. 26.4   Listing for `description.asp` (part 1 of 3).

```
202
203   <BODY BGCOLOR = "#FFFFFF">
204
205   <!-- #include virtual = "/includes/header.shtml" -->
206
207   <%
208       Dim connection, query, data
209
210       Set connection = Server.CreateObject( "ADODB.Connection" )
211       Call connection.Open( "catalog" )
212
213       ' Create the SQL query and the record set
214       query = "SELECT * FROM products WHERE productID=" _
215               & Request( "productid" )
216       Set data = Server.CreateObject( "ADODB.Recordset" )
217       Call data.Open( query, connection )
218   %>
219
220   <CENTER><H2>
221   <FONT COLOR = "brown">
222   <% =data( "title" ) %>
223   </FONT>
224   </H2></CENTER>
225   <TABLE BORDER = "0" WIDTH = "100%"
226    CELLPADDING = "0" CELLSPACING = "0">
227   <TR>
228   <TD WIDTH = "25%"> </TD>
229   <TD BGCOLOR = "#008080" WIDTH = "10%">
230   <% ' Display the book image %>
231   <IMG SRC = "/images/<% =data( "coverart" ) %>">
232   </TD>
233
234   <TD BGCOLOR = "#008080" WIDTH = "40%">
235   <FONT COLOR = "yellow" SIZE = "2">
236
237   <% ' Display the record fields %>
238   <CENTER>Published in: <% =data( "publishDate" ) %><BR>
239   ISBN: <% =data( "isbn" ) %><BR>
240   EDITION: <% =data( "edition" ) %><BR>
241   </CENTER></FONT>
242
243   <P ALIGN = "center">
244   <FONT SIZE = "5" COLOR = "red">
245   <STRONG>Buy it now</STRONG></FONT><BR>
246
247   <A HREF = "buyit.asp?productid=<%
248    =data( "productID" ) %>">
249   <IMG SRC = "/images/cart.gif" ALT = "cart.gif"></A>
250   </P>
251   </TD>
252   <TD WIDTH = "25%"> </TD>
253
254   </TR>
```

Fig. 26.4   Listing for **description.asp** (part 2 of 3).

```
255   </TABLE>
256
257   <P ALIGN = "center"><FONT SIZE = "3">Back to<STRONG>
258   <A HREF = "titles.asp?technologyid=<% =data( "technologyID" ) %>">
259    Titles</FONT></A></STRONG></P>
260
261   <% Call data.Close()
262      Call connection.Close()
263      Dim url
264
265      ' Store the URL of this page
266      url = "description.asp?productid=" _
267            & Request( "productid" ) %>
268
269   <TABLE ALIGN = "center">
270   <TR>
271   <TD><IMG SRC = "/images/cartonly.gif" ALT = "cartonly.gif">
272   </TD>
273
274   <% ' A form similar to the form in catalog.asp %>
275   <FORM ACTION = "viewcart.asp" METHOD = "POST">
276      <TD><INPUT TYPE = "submit" VALUE = "View Cart"></TD>
277      <INPUT TYPE = "hidden" NAME = "url" VALUE = "<% =url %>">
278   </FORM>
279
280   <TD><IMG SRC = "/images/cartonly.gif" ALT = "cartonly.gif">
281   </TD>
282   </TR>
283   </TABLE>
284
285   <!-- #include virtual = "/includes/footer.shtml" -->
286
287   </BODY>
288   </HTML>
```

Fig. 26.4   Listing for **description.asp** (part 3 of 3).

The **description.asp** document provides three navigational links. One link is displayed as a shopping cart image that, when clicked, redirects the user to **buyit.asp** (Fig. 26.5, which allows the user to buy the book—we discuss this ASP momentarily). This link passes the product number in the URL of **buyit.asp** (lines 247 through 248). The two other links, **Titles** and **View Cart**, redirect the user to **titles.asp** and **viewcart.asp**, respectively.

Figure 26.5 (**buyit.asp**) allows a user to specify the number of books to add to the shopping cart. When the **Add to Cart** button is clicked, the form is posted and the user is redirected to **addtocart.asp** (Fig. 26.6).

The **buyit.asp** document displays the book's image, ISBN number, author(s) and price. These fields are retrieved from multiple tables in the database. The **Authors** and **Authorlist** tables are queried to retrieve the author(s), and the **Products** table is queried to retrieve the book information. When executed, the SQL query in lines 311 through 315 uses join clauses to retrieve book information from the **Authorlist**, **Authors** and **Products** tables.

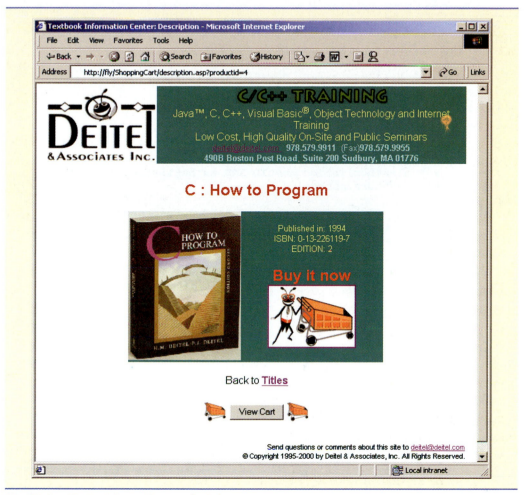

Fig. 26.4 Output from `description.asp`.

```
289  <% @LANGUAGE = VBScript %>
290  <% Option Explicit %>
291
292  <% ' Fig. 26.5 : buyit.asp %>
293
294  <!DOCTYPE HTML PUBLIC "-//W3C//DTD HTML 4.0 Transitional//EN">
295  <HTML>
296  <HEAD>
297  <TITLE>Textbook Information Center: BUY IT</TITLE>
298  </HEAD>
299
300  <BODY BGCOLOR = "#FFFFFF">
301
302  <!-- #include virtual = "/includes/header.shtml" -->
```

Fig. 26.5 Listing for `buyit.asp` (part 1 of 4).

```
303
304  <%
305      Dim connection, query, data, bookString
306
307      Set connection = Server.CreateObject( "ADODB.Connection" )
308      Call connection.Open( "catalog" )
309
310      ' Create the SQL query and the record set
311      query = "SELECT * FROM products, authors, " _
312         & "authorlist WHERE products.productID = " _
313         & Request( "productid" ) & " AND products.productID" _
314         & " = authorlist.productID AND authorlist.authorID " _
315         & "= authors.authorID"
316
317      Set data = Server.CreateObject( "ADODB.Recordset" )
318      Call data.Open( query, connection )
319  %>
320
321  <CENTER>
322  <H2>
323      <FONT COLOR = "brown">Buy it:</FONT>
324  </H2>
325
326  <IMG BORDER = "1" SRC = "/images/<% =data( "coverart" ) %>"
327  ALIGN = "center" VALIGN = "center">
328
329  </CENTER>
330
331  <TABLE BORDER = "0" align = "center" WIDTH = "100%"
332      CELLPADDING = "4" CELLSPACING = "1">
333  <TR>
334      <TD><STRONG><U>TITLE<STRONG></U></TD>
335      <TD><STRONG><U>AUTHOR(S)</STRONG></U></TD>
336      <TD><STRONG><U>ISBN</STRONG></U></TD>
337      <TD><STRONG><U>PRICE</STRONG></U></TD>
338  </TR>
339  <TR>
340
341  <% ' Fill the table and build the book string %>
342      <TD><STRONG><EM><% =data( "title" ) %></EM></STRONG>
343      </TD>
344
345      <TD><EM><% =data( "Name" ) %>
346
347  <% bookString = data( "title" ) & "|" & data( "Name" )
348      Call data.MoveNext()
349      While Not data.EOF
350         Call Response.Write( ", " & data( "Name" ) )
351         bookString = bookString & ", " & data( "Name" )
352         Call data.MoveNext()
353      Wend
354      Call data.MoveFirst()
```

Fig. 26.5 Listing for **buyit.asp** (part 2 of 4).

```
355     bookString = bookString & "|" & data( "isbn" ) & "|" _
356        & FormatCurrency( data( "price" ) )
357
358        ' Save the book string in a session variable so
359        ' that add.asp can use it
360        Session( "book" ) = bookString
361  %>
362     </EM></TD>
363
364     <TD><EM><% =data( "isbn" ) %></EM></TD>
365     <TD><EM><% =FormatCurrency( data( "price" ) ) %>
366     </EM></TD>
367   </TR>
368
369  </TABLE><BR><BR>
370
371  <% Dim url1, url2
372
373     ' Store the URL of titles.asp (the document the
374     ' user was just viewing)
375     url1 = "titles.asp?technologyid=" & _
376        data( "technologyID" )
377
378     ' Store the URL of this page
379     url2 = "buyit.asp?productid=" & Request( "productid" )
380
381     Call data.Close()
382     Call connection.Close()
383
384     ' Next we display two forms in a table. The first form
385     ' retrieves, from the user, the quantity to be added to
386     ' the cart. The first form also has a hidden item that
387     ' holds the URL of titles.asp (the document the user
388     ' was just viewing). This hidden item is passed to
389     ' addtocart.asp which will pass it along to viewcart.asp
390     ' for the back link. The second form is similar to the
391     ' form in catalog.asp.
392  %>
393
394  <TABLE>
395
396  <FORM ACTION = "addtocart.asp" METHOD = "POST">
397  <TR>
398
399  <TD>
400  <STRONG><FONT SIZE = "3">Quantity: </FONT></STRONG>
401  <INPUT TYPE = "text"  SIZE = "3"
402     NAME = "Quantity" VALUE = "1">
403  </TD>
404
405  <TD WIDTH = "50"></TD>
406
407  <TD COLSPAN = "3">
```

Fig. 26.5   Listing for **buyit.asp** (part 3 of 4).

```
408  <P ALIGN = "center">Back to<STRONG>
409  <A HREF="description.asp?productid=<%
410     =Request( "productid" ) %>">Description Page</A></STRONG>
411  </P>
412  </TD>
413  </TR>
414
415  <TR>
416  <TD>
417  <INPUT TYPE = "submit" value = "Add to Cart">
418  <INPUT TYPE = "reset" value = "Clear">
419  </TD>
420  <INPUT TYPE = "hidden" NAME = "url" VALUE = "<% =url1 %>">
421  </FORM>
422
423  <TD WIDTH = "50"></TD>
424
425  <TD><IMG  SRC = "/images/cartonly.gif" ALT = "cartonly.gif">
426  </TD>
427
428  <FORM ACTION = "viewcart.asp" METHOD = "POST">
429     <TD><INPUT TYPE = "submit" VALUE = "View Cart"></TD>
430     <INPUT TYPE = "hidden" NAME = "url" VALUE = "<% =url2 %>">
431  </FORM>
432
433  <TD><IMG SRC = "/images/cartonly.gif" ALT = "cartonly.gif">
434  </TD>
435
436  </TR>
437  </TABLE>
438
439  <!-- #include virtual = "/includes/footer.shtml" -->
440
441  </BODY>
442  </HTML>
```

Fig. 26.5   Listing for **buyit.asp** (part 4 of 4).

The title, author(s), ISBN number and price are stored in a temporary variable **bookString** in lines 347 through 356. We separate each field (e.g., title, ISBN number, etc.) by a pipe character (|). We chose this character because it is rarely used and unlikely to be part of a field's data.

The value of **bookString** is stored in the session variable **book** (line 360). We will see how this session variable is used by **addtocart.asp**, shortly. The format of the value stored by session variable **book** is:

```
title|author1, author2, ..., authorN|isbn|price
```

The table in lines 394 through 437 contains two forms and a link back to **description.asp**, that (when clicked) passes the book's **productID** number in the URL of **description.asp** (lines 409 and 410).

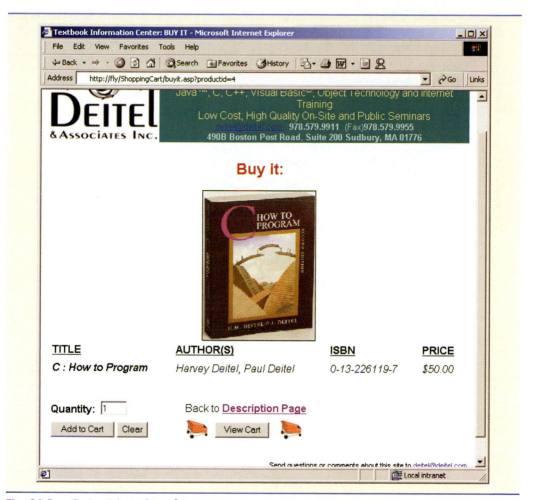

Fig. 26.5   Output from `buyit.asp`.

The first form (line 396) provides a text field for specifying the book quantity and submit button **Add to Cart**. The form also has a hidden input item that contains the URL of `titles.asp` and the `technologyID` number. When the form is submitted, the user is redirected to `addtocart.asp`—which adds the book quantity to the user's cart and then redirects the user to `viewcart.asp`. This document then uses the form's second hidden input item, `url`, to provide a link back to `titles.asp` (instead of to `buyit.asp`). We do this because the user has already added the book to the cart (by submitting this form) and does not need a link back to `buyit.asp`.

The second form's submit button (**View Cart**), when clicked, redirects the user to `viewcart.asp`. The form contains a hidden input item that contains the URL of `buyit.asp` and the `productID` (line 430). The `viewcart.asp` document provides a link back to `buyit.asp` that allows the user to buy the book after viewing the cart contents.

Figure 26.6 (`addtocart.asp`) adds the book quantity to the user's cart and redirects the user to `viewcart.asp` for confirmation. The `addtocart.asp` document does not send output to the client (i.e., the client sees nothing of this document other than the file-name in the browser's **Address** bar, before it is replaced by `viewcart.asp`).

```
443  <% @LANGUAGE = VBScript %>
444  <% Option Explicit %>
445
446  <% ' Fig 26.6 : addtocart.asp %>
447
448  <% ' If the submitted quantity is valid
449     If Request( "Quantity" ) <> "" Then
450        If CInt( Request( "Quantity" ) ) <> 0 Then
451
452           Dim count, i, found, s, quantity
453
454           ' How many books are in the cookie
455           count = Request.Cookies( "Books" ).Count / 2
456
457           ' Is the book already in the cookie?
458           found = False
459           For i = 1 To count
460              If Request.Cookies( "Books" )( _
461                 "book" & CStr( i ) ) = Session( "book" ) _
462              Then
463                 found = True
464                 Exit For
465              End If
466           Next
467
468           ' If the book is in the cookie, update the quantity
469           If found Then
470              quantity = CInt( Request.Cookies( "Books" ) _
471                 ( "quantity" & CStr( i ) ) )
472              Response.Cookies( "Books" )( "quantity" _
473                 & CStr( i ) ) = quantity + CInt( _
474                 Request( "Quantity" ) )
475
476              ' Set the expiration date
477              Response.Cookies( "Books" ).Expires = Date() + 2
478
479           ' Otherwise, create a new book item
480           Else
481              s = CStr( count + 1 )
482              Response.Cookies( "Books" )( "book" & _
483                 s ) = Session( "book" )
484              Response.Cookies( "Books" )( "quantity" & _
485                 s ) = Request( "Quantity" )
486
487              ' Set the expiration date
488              Response.Cookies( "Books" ).Expires = Date() + 2
489           End If
490        End If
491     End If
492  %>
```

Fig. 26.6   Listing for `addtocart.asp` (part 1 of 2).

```
493
494   <!DOCTYPE HTML PUBLIC "-//W3C//DTD HTML 4.0 Transitional//EN">
495   <HTML>
496
497   <% ' Force the form to submit when the page is loaded %>
498   <BODY ONLOAD = document.forms(0).submit()>
499
500   <% ' This form's purpose is to redirect the user to
501      ' viewcart.asp and pass the hidden input item that is
502      ' received from buyit.asp. The form is automatically
503      ' submitted when the page is loaded (see the <BODY> tag
504      ' above).
505   %>
506
507   <FORM ACTION = "viewcart.asp" METHOD = "POST">
508      <INPUT TYPE = "hidden" NAME = "url"
509       VALUE = "<% = Request( "url" ) %>">
510   </FORM>
511
512   </BODY>
513   </HTML>
```

Fig. 26.6   Listing for **addtocart.asp** (part 2 of 2).

As mentioned earlier, the shopping cart is implemented with cookies. In Chapter 25, we discussed writing cookies that store a single value. For e-commerce applications, this is not practical because many different values typically need to be written as part of the same cookie. For example, a cookie **Cars** might contain four-string *variables* **car1**, **car2**, **car3** and **car4**. The *Cookies collection* is used to set the value for each variable:

```
Response.Cookies( "Cars" )( "car1" ) = string1
Response.Cookies( "Cars" )( "car2" ) = string2
Response.Cookies( "Cars" )( "car3" ) = string3
Response.Cookies( "Cars" )( "car4" ) = string4
```

The **Cookies** collection is also used to read the values from a cookie:

```
string1 = Request.Cookies( "Cars" )( "car1" )
string2 = Request.Cookies( "Cars" )( "car2" )
string3 = Request.Cookies( "Cars" )( "car3" )
string4 = Request.Cookies( "Cars" )( "car4" )
```

We use two values in these statements: the cookie name (i.e., **Cars**) and the variable name (e.g., **car4**). Because one cookie may contain multiple values, it is often desirable to get the exact number of values a cookie contains. The **Cookie** collection's **Count** property contains the number of cookie items (line 455) in that cookie.

The cart must contain the quantities for each book. If the user has *n* books in their cart, the cookie contains data in the format:

book1, quantity1, book2, quantity2, ..., bookN, quantityN

Session variable **book** contains data (title, author, ISBN and price) in a similar format—each separated by a pipe character.

When **addtocart.asp** is requested, **book** stores the specified book the user has chosen to add to their cart. If the book is already in the cart, only the quantity is updated. If not, the book is added to the cart.

Line 455

```
count = Request.Cookies( "Books" ).Count / 2
```

sets **count** to the number of items in the **Books** cookie divided by two. This division is performed because each book has two values (i.e., the book string and the quantity). The **For** loop in line 459 through 466 iterates through the values stored in the cookie. If the book is found in the cookie, the quantity is updated in lines 469 through 477. If it is not found, the book is added to the cookie by writing the **book** session variable and the quantity in lines 480 through 488.

We use the **Cookies** collection's *Expires* property (in lines 477 and 488) to set the expiration date of the cookie to avoid the cookie being treated as a session cookie—which is deleted when the browser is closed. Function **Date** is called to get the current date, to which we add two days. After two days, the client's browser will delete the cookie. Notice that we set the cookie's expiration date both when the cookie is created and when the cookie is updated.

The statement **document.forms(0).submit()** in line 498 submits the form (of lines 507 through 510). When the form is submitted, the user is redirected to **viewcart.asp** to view their cart's contents. Recall that **buyit.asp** passes to **addtocart.asp** a hidden input item that contains the URL of **titles.asp** and the **technologyID** number of the programming language the selected book covers (lines 375 and 376). The form in lines 507 through 510 (in **addtocart.asp**) also has a hidden input item **url** that passes (to **viewcart.asp**) the URL and **technologyID** passed to it by **buyit.asp**. Document **viewcart.asp** uses this hidden input item to provide a link to the page (i.e., **titles.asp**) that lists the book titles of the selected technology.

Figure 26.7 (**viewcart.asp**) displays the contents of the user's cart with prices. If the **Books** cookie is empty, a message indicating that the cart is empty is displayed by line 539. If the cookie contains data, a table containing each book in the cookie is displayed. Each row contains the book title, ISBN number, author(s), price and quantity.

The **For** loop in lines 574 through 604 iterates through the books in the cart. Each book is read as a string from the cookie **Books** and is split on the pipe character (|) in lines 578 and 579 by function **Split**.

Each substring returned by **Split** is stored in array **splitArray**, whose element data is written in the table by the **For** loop in lines 583 through 585.

Each page in this case study provides a link to **viewcart.asp**. Each of these links passes a hidden input item **url** to **viewcart.asp**. Each page, except **addtocart.asp**, passes its URL and any other essential data in this hidden input item. For example, **titles.asp** passes **"titles.asp?technologyid=1"** as the value of **url**. The value **1** is the **technologyID** number that **titles.asp** uses to display a list of book titles. Document **viewcart.asp** uses the URL passed to it to provide a link, **Back to Shopping**. When **Back to Shopping** is clicked, the user is sent to the page that redirected the user to **viewcart.asp**.

```
514  <% @LANGUAGE = VBScript %>
515  <% Option Explicit %>
516
517  <% ' Fig. 26.7 : viewcart.asp %>
518
519  <!DOCTYPE HTML PUBLIC "-//W3C//DTD HTML 4.0 Transitional//EN">
520  <HTML>
521
522  <HEAD>
523  <TITLE>Textbook Information Center: View Cart
524  </TITLE>
525  </HEAD>
526
527  <BODY BGCOLOR = "#FFFFFF">
528
529  <!-- #include virtual = "/includes/header.shtml" -->
530
531  <% Dim i, j, splitArray, quantity, total, subtotal
532
533       ' If the Books cookie is equal to an empty string,
534       ' no items are in the cart.
535       If Request.Cookies( "Books" ) = "" Then %>
536          <CENTER>
537          <H3>
538             <FONT COLOR = "red">
539                Your cart is empty.
540             </FONT>
541          </H3>
542          </CENTER>
543
544  <% ' Otherwise, display the items in the cookie
545     Else %>
546          <TABLE BORDER = "1" ALIGN = "center" WIDTH = "100%"
547            CELLPADDING = "0" CELLSPACING = "3">
548          <CAPTION>
549             <H2>
550                <FONT COLOR = "brown">
551                   This is your current cart.
552                </FONT>
553             </H2>
554          </CAPTION>
555          <COLGROUP>
556             <COL SPAN = "6" ALIGN = "center">
557          </COLGROUP>
558          <TR>
559             <TH><U>TITLE</U></TH>
560             <TH><U>AUTHOR(S)</U></TH>
561             <TH><U>ISBN</U></TH>
562             <TH><U>PRICE</U></TH>
563             <TH><U>QUANTITY</U></TH>
564             <TH><U>SUBTOTAL</U></TH>
565          </TR>
566
```

Fig. 26.7 Listing for **viewcart.asp** (part 1 of 3).

```asp
567  <%      ' Initialize the total price to zero
568          total = 0
569
570          ' Loop through the books in the Books cookie and
571          ' and display each book's contents in the table.
572          ' Each iteration of this loop builds one row in the
573          ' table.
574          For i = 1 To Request.Cookies( "Books" ).Count / 2
575
576              ' Split the book string on | to get the book
577              ' information (e.g., title, author(s), etc.)
578              splitArray = Split( Request.Cookies( "Books" ) _
579                  ( "book" & CStr( i ) ), "|" )
580  %>          <TR>
581
582  <%          ' Display the book information
583              For j = 0 To UBound( splitArray ) %>
584                  <TD> <% =splitArray( j ) %> </TD>
585  <%          Next
586
587              ' Display the quantity of the book
588              quantity = Request.Cookies( "Books" )( "quantity" & _
589                  CStr( i ) ) %>
590              <TD>
591                  <% =quantity %>
592              </TD>
593
594  <%          ' Update the running total and display the subtotal
595              ' in a table cell
596                  subtotal = CCur( splitArray( 3 ) ) * _
597                      CInt( quantity )
598                  total = total + subtotal
599  %>          <TD>
600                  <% =FormatCurrency( subtotal ) %>
601              </TD>
602
603              </TR>
604  <%      Next
605
606          ' Finally, display the total
607  %>      <TR>
608          <TH COLSPAN = "5" ALIGN = "right"><U>Total:</U></TH>
609          <TD> <% =FormatCurrency( total ) %> </TD>
610          </TR>
611
612          </TABLE>
613  <% End If %>
614
615  <BR>
616
617  <P ALIGN = "center">
618  <FONT SIZE = "3">Back to<STRONG>
619  <A HREF = "<% =Request("url") %>">Shopping</FONT></A>
```

Fig. 26.7   Listing for **viewcart.asp** (part 2 of 3).

```
620  </STRONG></P>
621
622  <!-- #include virtual = "/includes/footer.shtml" -->
623
624  </BODY>
625  </HTML>
```

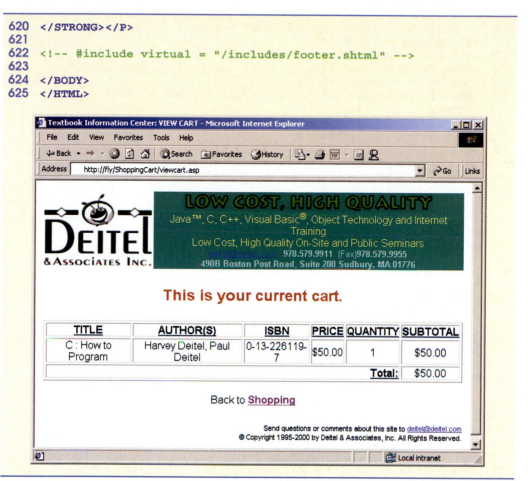

Fig. 26.7   Listing for **viewcart.asp** (part 3 of 3).

Document **addtocart.asp** adds a book to the user's cart and redirects the user to **viewcart.asp**. If **viewcart.asp** provided a link back to **addtocart.asp**, the book would be added to the user's cart a second time. Therefore, **addtocart.asp** passes the URL of **titles.asp** to **viewcart.asp**. Thus, after a user has added a book to their cart, **viewcart.asp** provides a link to **titles.asp** instead of to **addtocart.asp**.

In this case study, each Active Server Page that sends HTML to the client uses a server-side include for a header (**header.shtml**, Fig. 26.8) and a footer (**footer.shtml**, Fig. 26.9), to display the Deitel logo, banner and copyright information.

```
626  <BODY BGCOLOR = "#FFFFFF">
627  <TABLE BORDER = "0" WIDTH = "600">
628  <TR>
629  <TD><A HREF = "http://www.deitel.com"><IMG
```

Fig. 26.8   Listing for **header.shtml** (part 1 of 2).

```
630          SRC = "/images/logotiny.gif" BORDER = "0"></A></TD>
631    <TD BGCOLOR = "#008080">
632    <P ALIGN = "center">
633    <SPAN STYLE = "font-family: Arial, Helvetica, sans-serif">
634    <IMG SRC = "/images/banneranim.gif"
635     ALT = "banneranim.gif (185545 bytes)" WIDTH = "481"
636     HEIGHT = "28"><BR>
637    <FONT COLOR = "#FFFF00">Java&#153;, C, C++, Visual
638    Basic<SUP>&#174;</SUP>,
639    Object Technology and Internet Training<BR>
640    Low Cost, High Quality On-Site and Public Seminars<BR>
641    <SMALL><A HREF = "mailto:deitel@deitel.com">deitel@deitel.com
642    </A>
643    </FONT> 
644    <FONT COLOR = "#80FFFF"><STRONG>978.579.9911</STRONG> 
645    (Fax)<STRONG>978.579.9955</STRONG><BR>
646    <STRONG>490B Boston Post Road</STRONG>,
647    <STRONG>Suite 200 Sudbury, MA 01776</STRONG></FONT>
648    </SMALL></SPAN></P>
649    </TD>
650    </TR>
651    <TR><TD COLSPAN = "2"> </TD></TR>
652    <TR>
653    <TD COLSPAN = "2">
654    <FONT FACE = "Arial" SIZE = "2">
```

Fig. 26.8   Listing for **header.shtml** (part 2 of 2).

```
655    </FONT>
656    <TR><TD COLSPAN = "2"> </TD></TR>
657    <TR><TD COLSPAN = "2" ALIGN = "right">
658
659    <SPAN STYLE = "font-family: sans-serif, Helvetica, Arial;
660     font-size: 8pt">
661    Send questions or comments about this site to
662    <A HREF = "mailto:deitel@deitel.com">deitel@deitel.com</A><BR>
663    &copy; Copyright 1995-2000 by Deitel &amp; Associates, Inc.
664    All Rights Reserved.<BR>
665    </SPAN>
666
667    </TD></TR>
```

Fig. 26.9   Listing for **footer.shtml**.

26.4 Case Study: an Online Auction Site

In Chapter 3, we discussed the auction business model and the theory behind it. In this section, we build an online auction site where users can auction on and bid for Deitel products. These items are grouped into four categories: books, cyber classroom software packages, training seats and miscellaneous items. For simplicity, we implement only the books category. Figure 26.10 describes each ASP used in the implementation. Figure 26.11 shows some of the interactions between the Active Server Pages. You will find this diagram useful as you study this example. We discuss the significance of the dashed arrow later in this section.

ASP document	Description
`index.asp`	Lists the categories of items up for auction.
`newmember.asp`	Allows a new user to register. The new user inputs a user name and password in a form that, when submitted, redirects the user to `add.asp`.
`add.asp`	Adds the new member's user name and password to the database. If the selected user name is already in use, the user is redirected to `taken.asp`. Otherwise, the user is redirected to `confirmaccount.asp`.
`confirmaccount.asp`	Displays a message confirming the creation of a new member account.
`taken.asp`	Displays a message indicating that the user name is already in use.
`winning.asp`	Lists the auction items (if any) sold yesterday.
`bookitems.asp`	Lists the books that are up for auction.
`itemdata.asp`	Displays auction data for a selected item (i.e., seller, current bidder, high bid, etc.).
`bookdata.asp`	Displays book data for the selected book (i.e., title, author, ISBN number, etc.).
`login.asp`	Prompts the user to login with a user name and password. The user inputs these in a form that, when submitted, redirects the user to `checklogin.asp`.
`checklogin.asp`	Checks the validity of a login. If valid, the user is redirected to `bid.asp`. Otherwise, the user is redirected to `badlogin.asp`.
`badlogin.asp`	Displays a message indicating that the login attempt failed. Provides a link to `newmember.asp`.
`bid.asp`	Allows the user to bid on an item. When a bid is submitted, the user is redirected to `dobid.asp`.
`dobid.asp`	Checks the validity of a bid. If the bid is high enough, the auction database is updated. Otherwise, an error message is displayed.

Fig. 26.10 Active Server Pages used by the auction site.

We first begin by discussing the database used by the auction site. Auction data is stored in a Microsoft Access database named **DeitelAuctions.mdb**. This database contains three tables: **Products**, **AuctionItems** and **Members**. For this case study, the database contains only information about Deitel books. The **Products** table contains book information, such as the ISBN number, author, edition, year published, etc. The **AuctionItems** table contains information on the items which have been posted for auction. Before a user can bid on an item or place an item up for auction, the user must register by filling out an HTML form. Registered user information is stored in the **Members** table, which we discuss momentarily.

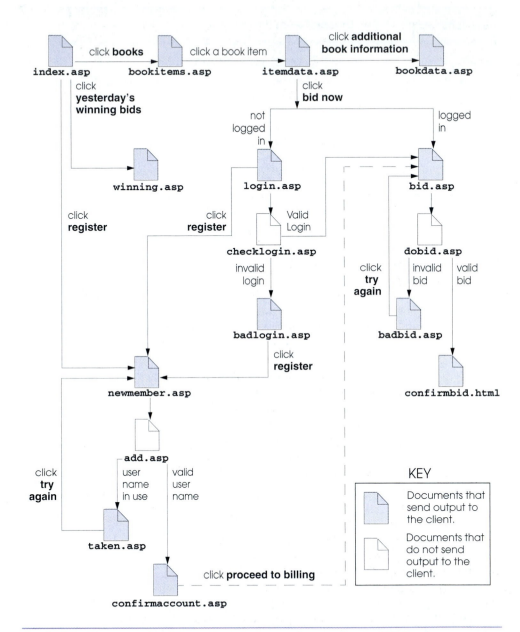

Fig. 26.11 Diagramming interactions between the auction's ASP files.

The **AuctionItems** table has several fields including primary key **ItemNumber**. The book description and the seller's user name are stored in the **Display** and **Seller** fields, respectively. Field **Ends** stores the item's expiration date and fields **Current-Bidder** and **CurrentPrice** contain the high bidder's user name and high bid. These fields are updated when one user outbids another. When the item is initially posted (on the **Sell an Item** page), **CurrentPrice** is set to the seller's minimum bid price. The **Pay-**

mentType field contains the methods of payment (i.e., check, credit card, cash, etc.) the seller accepts. The last field, **ProductNumber**, stores the item's product number.

The **Sell an Item** link allows registered users to auction a book. The implementation of selling an item is left as an exercise for the reader.

Users must login with a valid user name and password before selling or bidding on items. We leave the logout process as an exercise for the reader. The user names and passwords are stored in the **UserName** and **Password** fields in the **Members** table. New users are directed to a page that allows them to create a new account.

Now we are ready to begin discussing the ASP documents. Figure 26.12 lists **index.asp**, which is the auction site home page that contains links to the different categories (lines 24 through 29).

```
1   <% @LANGUAGE = VBSCRIPT %>
2   <% Option Explicit %>
3
4   <% ' Fig. 26.12 : index.asp %>
5
6   <!DOCTYPE HTML PUBLIC "-//W3C//DTD HTML 4.0 Transitional //EN">
7   <HTML>
8
9   <HEAD>
10  <TITLE>Deitel Auctions</TITLE>
11  </HEAD>
12
13  <BODY BGCOLOR = "#FFFF99">
14  <FONT COLOR = "magenta">
15  <% =Date() %>
16  </FONT>
17  <H1 ALIGN = "center"><U>Welcome to Deitel Auctions</U>
18  </H1><BR><BR><BR>
19  <P><STRONG><FONT SIZE = "+1">Categories:</FONT></STRONG>
20  </P>
21
22  <% ' A list of auction Categories %>
23  <UL>
24      <LI><A HREF = "bookitems.asp">Books</A></LI>
25      <LI><A HREF = "notimplemented.html">Cyber Classrooms</A>
26      </LI>
27      <LI><A HREF = "notimplemented.html">Training Seats</A>
28      </LI>
29      <LI><A HREF = "notimplemented.html">Miscellaneous</A>
30      </LI>
31  </UL>
32  <P><STRONG><FONT COLOR = "red"><CENTER>
33      All our auction items end at midnight on the same day
34      they are posted. Bid Now!
35  </CENTER></FONT></STRONG></P>
36
37  <% ' Save where the user came from in the "from" session
38     ' variable. Because we have several register links
39     ' in the site, we can use this variable to provide links
```

Fig. 26.12 Listing for **index.asp** (part 1 of 2).

```
40        ' in the registration pages, depending on where the
41        ' user came from.
42        Session( "from" ) = "home" %>
43
44    <% ' Provide a link to register a new user %>
45    <CENTER>
46        <A HREF = "newmember.asp">Register</A>
47    </CENTER>
48    <% ' Link to yesterday's winning bids %>
49    <A HREF = "winning.asp"><FONT COLOR = "magenta">
50        Yesterday's Winning Bids!</FONT>
51    </A><BR>
52    <% ' Link to Sell an item %>
53    <A HREF = "notimplemented.html">
54        <FONT COLOR = "green">Sell an item</FONT>
55    </A><BR><BR>
56    </BODY>
57    </HTML>
```

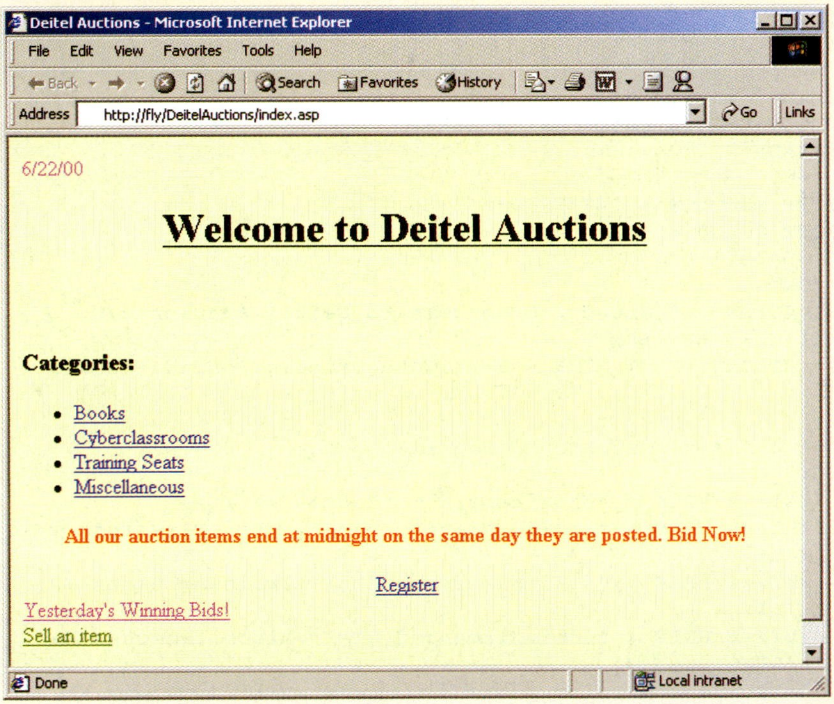

Fig. 26.12 Listing for **index.asp** (part 2 of 2).

The **Books** category is the only active link in this example. The other links are not fully implemented. If any other category link is clicked, the user is redirected to a page that displays a **Not Implemented** message. When **Books** is clicked, the user is redirected to **bookitems.asp** (Fig 26.18, which lists the books up for auction). When the **Register** link in line 46 is clicked, the user is redirected to the registration document **new-member.asp** (Fig. 26.13, which allows new users to register). When the **Yesterday's**

Winning Bids link (in lines 49 and 50) is clicked the user is redirected to **winning.asp** (Fig. 26.17, which lists the auction items won yesterday).

In line 42 the value **"home"** is stored in the session variable **from**, which is used throughout the auction site to keep track of the user's movement through the site. In this particular case, **"home"** represents **index.asp**, which is the home page. We will see exactly how this variable is used momentarily.

Figure 26.13 (**newmember.asp**) allows the user to enter a user name and password in a form (lines 74 through 99). When the form is submitted, the user is redirected to **add.asp** (Fig. 26.14, which creates a new account containing a user name and password).

```
58   <% @LANGUAGE = VBSCRIPT %>
59   <% Option Explicit %>
60
61   <% ' Fig. 26.13 : newmember.asp %>
62
63   <!DOCTYPE HTML PUBLIC "-//W3C//DTD HTML 4.0 Transitional //EN">
64   <HTML>
65
66   <HEAD>
67   <TITLE>New Member</TITLE>
68   </HEAD>
69
70   <BODY BGCOLOR = "#FFFF99">
71   <CENTER><H1><U>Welcome New Member!</U></H1></CENTER><BR>
72
73   <% ' Form to get user name and password %>
74   <FORM METHOD = "post" ACTION = "add.asp">
75      <TABLE>
76      <TR>
77         <TH>Choose your user name:</TH>
78         <TD>
79         <INPUT TYPE = "text" NAME = "UserName" SIZE = "25">
80         </TD>
81      </TR>
82
83      <TR>
84         <TH>Choose your password:</TH>
85         <TD>
86         <INPUT TYPE = "password" NAME = "Password"
87            SIZE = "25">
88         </TD>
89      </TR>
90
91      <TR>
92         <TD></TD>
93         <TD>
94         <INPUT TYPE = "submit" VALUE = "Submit">
95         <INPUT TYPE = "reset" VALUE = "Clear">
96         </TD>
97      </TR>
98      </TABLE>
```

Fig. 26.13 Listing for **newmember.asp** (part 1 of 2).

```
99   </FORM>
100
101  <CENTER><A HREF = "index.asp">Home</A>
102
103  <% ' If the user came to this page from login.asp,
104     ' provide an additional link to the item description
105     ' page.
106     If Session( "from" ) = "login" Then %>
107        <A HREF =
108        "itemdata.asp?ItemNumber=<% =Session( "ItemNumber" ) %>">
109        Back to Item Description</A>
110  <% End If %>
111  </CENTER>
112  </BODY>
113  </HTML>
```

Fig. 26.13 Listing for **newmember.asp** (part 2 of 2).

The session variable **from** is used by **newmember.asp** to determine if a link back to **itemdata.asp** is needed. Remember, we set session variable **from** to **"home"** in **index.asp**. The **If** statement in line 106 determines whether or not the value of **from** equals **"login."** If the value equals **"login,"** the user attempted to bid on an item before logging in and was redirected to **login.asp** where session variable **from** was set to **"login."** The user then clicked the **Register** link and was redirected to **newmember.asp**. If **from** equals **"login,"** a link is provided back to the page (**itemdata.asp**) where the user attempted to bid on an item. The link contains the item number for the book on which the user attempted to bid, and is similar to

```
<A HREF = "itemdata.asp?ItemNumber=1">
```

where **1** is the item number of the book.

Figure 26.14 (**add.asp**) is requested when the form in **newmember.asp** is submitted. The **add.asp** document checks if another user has already taken the user name. If so, the user is redirected to **taken.asp** (Fig. 26.16, which displays an error message).

Otherwise, the new member's user name and password are inserted into the database and the user is redirected to **confirmaccount.asp** (Fig. 26.15, which confirms the creation of a new account).

```
114  <% @LANGUAGE = VBSCRIPT %>
115  <% Option Explicit %>
116
117  <% ' Fig 26.14 : add.asp %>
118
119  <%
120     Dim connection, insert, data, query
121
122     ' Open the database connection.
123     Set connection = Server.CreateObject( "ADODB.Connection" )
124     Call connection.Open( "DeitelAuctions" )
125
126     ' Create the SQL query to check if the chosen user name
127     ' exists in the Members table
128     query = "SELECT * FROM Members WHERE UserName = '" & _
129             CStr( Request( "UserName" ) ) & "'"
130     Set data = Server.CreateObject( "ADODB.RecordSet" )
131     Call data.Open( query, connection )
132     On Error Resume Next
133
134     ' Check for records with the same user name
135     If data.EOF Then
136
137        ' Give the new member the selected user name.
138        ' Insert a new name/password record into the Members
139        ' table. Build the SQL INSERT statement:
140        insert = "INSERT INTO Members VALUES ( '" & _
141                CStr( Request( "UserName" ) ) & "','" & _
142                CStr( Request( "Password" ) ) & "' )"
143
144        ' Insert the record
145        Call connection.Execute( insert )
146
147        ' Signal a successful login
148        Session( "LoggedIn" ) = True
149
150        ' Save the user name in a session variable
151        Session( "UserName" ) = Request( "UserName" )
152
153        ' Confirm account creation
154        Call data.Close()
155        Call connection.Close()
156        Call Response.Redirect( "confirmaccount.asp" )
157     Else
158
159        ' The selected user name is not available.
160        Call data.Close()
161        Call connection.Close()
```

Fig. 26.14 Listing for **add.asp** (part 1 of 2).

```
162          Call Response.Redirect( "taken.asp" )
163      End If
164  %>
```

Fig. 26.14 Listing for **add.asp** (part 2 of 2).

The **add.asp** document checks if the user name is already in use by attempting to retrieve the record from the **Members** table whose **UserName** field equals the user name. When executed, the SQL statement in lines 128 and 129 attempts to retrieve this record. If a record is retrieved, the user name is already in use and the user is redirected to **taken.asp**. If no record is retrieved, a new account is created for the user. When executed, the SQL statement in lines 140 through 142 inserts the user name and password into the **Members** table. The user is then redirected to **confirmaccount.asp**.

Figure 26.15 (**confirmaccount.asp**) displays a message confirming the creation of a new account. If the user was asked to create a new account when attempting to bid on an item, **confirmaccount.asp** provides a link to **bid.asp** to complete that bid. This conditional link is displayed as a dashed line in Fig. 26.11.

```
165  <% @LANGUAGE = VBSCRIPT %>
166  <% Option Explicit %>
167
168  <% ' Fig. 26.15 : confirmaccount.asp %>
169
170  <!DOCTYPE HTML PUBLIC "-//W3C//DTD HTML 4.0 Transitional //EN">
171  <HTML>
172
173  <HEAD>
174     <TITLE>Confirm</TITLE>
175  </HEAD>
176
177  <% ' Print message and provide navigation links. %>
178  <BODY BGCOLOR = "#FFFF99">
179  <H2>Account Created.</H2>
180
181  <CENTER>
```

Fig. 26.15 Listing for **confimaccount.asp** (part 1 of 2).

```
182      <A HREF = "index.asp">Home</A>
183  <% ' If the user came to this page from the login process,
184     ' provide a link to the bidding page
185     If Session( "from" ) = "login" Then %>
186         <A HREF = "bid.asp">Proceed to Bidding</A>
187  <% End If %>
188  </CENTER>
189  </BODY>
190  </HTML>
```

Fig. 26.15   Listing for **confimaccount.asp** (part 2 of 2).

A link to **index.asp** is provided in line 182. If the session variable **from** equals **"login,"** a link to **bid.asp** is provided to allow the new member to complete the attempted bid. Figure 26.16 (**taken.asp**) displays an alert message indicating that the user name is already in use.

```
191  <% @LANGUAGE = VBSCRIPT %>
192  <% Option Explicit %>
193
194  <% ' Fig. 26.16 : taken.asp %>
195
196  <!DOCTYPE HTML PUBLIC "-//W3C//DTD HTML 4.0 Transitional //EN">
197  <HTML>
198
199  <HEAD>
200    <TITLE>In use</TITLE>
201  </HEAD>
202
203  <BODY BGCOLOR = "FFFF99">
204  <% ' Print a message and provide navigation links. %>
205  <H2>User name already in use.</H2>
206
207  <CENTER>
208    <A HREF = "newmember.asp">Try Again</A>  
209    <A HREF = "index.asp">Home</A>
210
211  <%    ' If the user came to this page from the login process,
212        ' provide a link to the item description page
213        ' (itemdata.asp).
214        If Session( "from" ) = "login" Then %>
215            <A HREF =
216           "itemdata.asp?ItemNumber=<% =Session( "ItemNumber" ) %>">
217           Back to Item Description</A>
218  <%    End If %>
219
220  </CENTER>
221  </BODY>
222  </HTML>
```

Fig. 26.16   Listing for **taken.asp**.

Links to **newmember.asp** and **index.asp** are displayed in lines 208 and 209. Again, we use the session variable **from** to determine whether a link to **itemdata.asp** should be provided (lines 214 through 218).

Figure 26.17 (**winning.asp**) lists the winning bids from the previous day. The **winning.asp** document queries the **AuctionItems** table to retrieve the items won the previous day. All auction items end at midnight on the same day they are posted. The query in lines 236 through 239 selects all the records from the previous day that had at least one bid (i.e., that do not have a null **CurrentBidder** field). If no records were retrieved, line 265 displays a message indicating that there were no winners yesterday. Otherwise, lines 266 through 306 display the item number, item description, winner, seller and price of each item.

```
223  <% @LANGUAGE = VBSCRIPT %>
224  <% Option Explicit %>
225
226  <% ' Fig. 26.17 : winning.asp %>
227
228  <% Dim connection, query, data
229
230     ' Open a database connection
231     Set connection = Server.CreateObject( "ADODB.Connection" )
232     Call connection.Open( "DeitelAuctions" )
233
234     ' Create the SQL query to select yesterday's auction items
235     ' that were bid on. Remember, an item might not be bid on.
236     query = "SELECT * FROM AuctionItems " _
237             & "WHERE Ends = #" & Date() - 1 & "# " _
238             &    "AND CurrentBidder IS NOT NULL " _
239             & "ORDER BY Display"
240
241     ' Open a record set
242     Set data = Server.CreateObject( "ADODB.RecordSet" )
243     Call data.Open( query, connection )
244
245     On Error Resume Next
246  %>
247
248  <!DOCTYPE HTML PUBLIC "-//W3C//DTD HTML 4.0 Transitional //EN">
249  <HTML>
250  <HEAD>
251  <TITLE>Book Items</TITLE>
252  </HEAD>
253
254  <BODY BGCOLOR = "#FFFF99">
255  <FONT COLOR = "magenta">
256  <% =Date() %>
257  </FONT>
258
```

Fig. 26.17 Listing for **winning.asp** (part 1 of 3).

```
259    <H1 ALIGN = "center"><U>Yesterday's Winning Bids</U></H1>
260    <BR>
261
262    <% ' If no items were found, display a message. Otherwise,
263        ' display the items.
264        If data.EOF Then %>
265            <P><H2>There were no winners yesterday</H2></P>
266    <% Else %>
267
268    <%      ' A table to display the results %>
269            <TABLE BORDER = "1" ALIGN = "center">
270
271            <COLGROUP>
272                <COL SPAN = "5" ALIGN = "center">
273            </COLGROUP>
274
275            <CAPTION>Winners</CAPTION>
276            <THEAD>
277                <TR>
278                    <TH>Item Number</TH>
279                    <TH>Displayed</TH>
280                    <TH>Seller</TH>
281                    <TH>Winner</TH>
282                    <TH>Price</TH>
283                </TR>
284            </THEAD>
285            <TBODY>
286
287    <%      ' Iterate through the record set and create a new row
288            ' in the table for each record
289            While Not data.EOF %>
290                <TR>
291                    <TD><% =data( "ItemNumber" ) %></TD>
292                    <TD><% =data( "Display" ) %></TD>
293                    <TD><% =data( "Seller" ) %></TD>
294                    <TD><% =data( "CurrentBidder" ) %></TD>
295                    <TD><% =FormatCurrency( data( "CurrentPrice" ) )
296                        %> </TD>
297                </TR>
298    <%      Call data.MoveNext()
299            Wend
300
301            ' Close the record set and the connection
302            Call data.Close()
303            Call connection.close()
304    %>      </TBODY>
305            </TABLE><BR>
306    <% End If %><BR>
307
308    <% ' Provide a link back to home %>
309    <CENTER><A HREF = "index.asp">Home</A></CENTER>
310    </BODY>
311    </HTML>
```

Fig. 26.17 Listing for **winning.asp** (part 2 of 3).

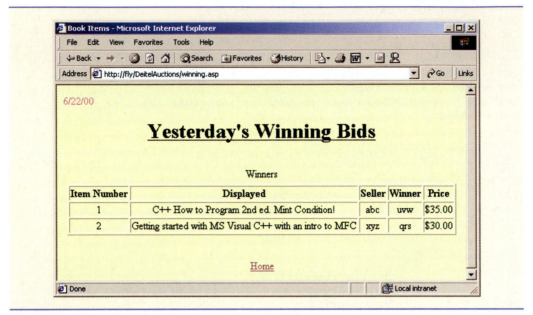

Fig. 26.17   Listing for **winning.asp** (part 3 of 3).

Figure 26.18 (**bookitems.asp**) lists all the books currently being auctioned, as hyperlinks. When a link is clicked, the user is redirected to a page (**itemdata.asp**—Fig. 26.19) that displays information for that particular book. Each link passes the item number in the URL of **itemdata.asp**.

```
312   <% @LANGUAGE = VBSCRIPT %>
313   <% Option Explicit %>
314
315   <% ' Fig. 26.18 : bookitems.asp %>
316
317   <% Dim connection, query, data
318
319       ' Open a database connection
320       Set connection = Server.CreateObject( "ADODB.Connection" )
321       Call connection.Open( "DeitelAuctions" )
322
323       ' Create the SQL query
324       query = "SELECT Display, ItemNumber FROM " _
325              & "AuctionItems " _
326              & "WHERE Ends = #" & Date() & "# " _
327              & "ORDER BY Display"
328
329       ' Open a record set
330       Set data = Server.CreateObject( "ADODB.RecordSet" )
331       Call data.Open( query, connection )
332       On Error Resume Next
333   %>
```

Fig. 26.18   Listing for **bookitems.asp** (part 1 of 3).

```
334
335   <!DOCTYPE HTML PUBLIC "-//W3C//DTD HTML 4.0 Transitional //EN">
336   <HTML>
337
338   <HEAD>
339   <TITLE>Book Items</TITLE>
340   </HEAD>
341
342   <BODY BGCOLOR = "#FFFF99">
343   <FONT COLOR = "magenta">
344   <% =Date() %>
345   </FONT>
346
347   <H1 ALIGN = "center"><U>Book Items In Auction</U></H1>
348   <BR>
349
350   <% ' If no items have been posted today, say so.
351      ' Otherwise, display the items.
352
353      If data.EOF Then
354   %>    <P><H2>No items have been put up for auction today.
355         </H2></P>
356   <% Else %>
357   <UL>
358   <%    ' Iterate through the record set and write the
359         ' Display fields to the client as links to the
360         ' corresponding item description page. Pass the item
361         ' number so that item description page can recognize the
362         ' item and display its description.
363         While Not data.EOF %>
364           <LI>
365           <A HREF =
366             "itemdata.asp?ItemNumber=<% =data( "ItemNumber" ) %>">
367              <% =data( "Display" ) %>
368           </A>
369           </LI>
370   <%      Call data.MoveNext()
371         Wend
372
373         ' Close the record set and the connection.
374         Call data.Close()
375         Call connection.close()
376   %>    </UL><BR>
377   <% End If
378
379      ' Provide a link back to home %>
380   <BR>
381   <CENTER><A HREF = "index.asp">Home</A></CENTER>
382   </BODY>
383   </HTML>
```

Fig. 26.18 Listing for **bookitems.asp** (part 2 of 3).

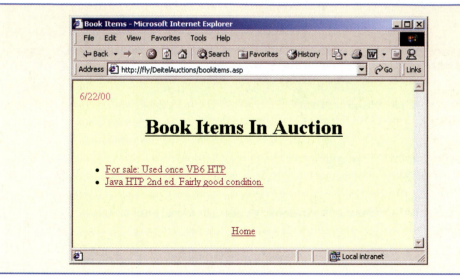

Fig. 26.18   Listing for **bookitems.asp** (part 3 of 3).

The query in lines 324 through 327 selects the records from the **AuctionItems** table that have ending dates equal to today's date. If the query returns no records, a message is displayed indicating that there are currently no items up for auction. Otherwise, the items found are displayed as links. When a link is clicked, the user is redirected to **itemdata.asp**. Each link passes the item number as a parameter.

Figure 26.19 (**itemdata.asp**) displays the selected book's information. The SQL query string (lines 396 and 397) retrieves the selected item's record from the **Auction-Items** table. Line 406 stores the item number in the session variable **ItemNumber**. [*Note*: To ensure users login before bidding, we use session variable **ItemNumber** to store the book's item number instead of passing it in the URL. A user could type the URL of the bidding page and the item number in their browser's **Address** bar. This would allow user to bid on items without logging in. A client cannot access a session variable because it is stored in the server's memory and not in a page's URL.]

```
384   <% @LANGUAGE = VBSCRIPT %>
385   <% Option Explicit %>
386
387   <% ' Fig. 26.19 : itemdata.asp %>
388
389   <% Dim connection, query, data
390
391      ' Open a database connection
392      Set connection = Server.CreateObject( "ADODB.Connection" )
393      Call connection.Open( "DeitelAuctions" )
394
395      ' Create the SQL query. Retrieve the selected item.
396      query = "SELECT * FROM AuctionItems WHERE ItemNumber = " _
397             & CStr( Request( "ItemNumber" ) )
```

Fig. 26.19   Listing for **itemdata.asp** (part 1 of 3).

```
398
399     ' Open the record set
400     Set data = Server.CreateObject( "ADODB.RecordSet" )
401     Call data.Open( query, connection )
402     On Error Resume Next
403
404     ' Save the item number in a session variable for the
405     ' bidding page.
406     Session( "ItemNumber" ) = data( "ItemNumber" )
407 %>
408
409 <!DOCTYPE HTML PUBLIC "-//W3C//DTD HTML 4.0 Transitional //EN">
410 <HTML>
411 <HEAD>
412 <TITLE>Item Description</TITLE>
413 </HEAD>
414 <BODY BGCOLOR = "#FFFF99">
415 <H1 ALIGN = "center"><U>Item Description</U></H1><BR>
416 <P>
417 <% ' Display the item's information %>
418 <FONT COLOR = "red"><% =data( "Display" ) %></FONT><BR>
419 <STRONG>Item#: </STRONG>
420 <% =data( "ItemNumber" ) %><BR>
421 <STRONG>Seller: </STRONG>
422 <% =data( "Seller" ) %><BR>
423 <STRONG>Ends: </STRONG>
424 <% =data( "Ends" ) %><BR>
425
426 <STRONG>Current Bidder: </STRONG>
427 <% ' If there are no bids yet, say so.
428     If IsNull( data( "CurrentBidder" ) ) Then %>
429         No bids on this item yet.<BR>
430 <% Else %>
431         <% =data( "CurrentBidder" ) %><BR>
432 <% End If %>
433
434 <STRONG>Current Price: </STRONG>
435 <% =FormatCurrency( data( "CurrentPrice" ) ) %><BR>
436 <STRONG>State: </STRONG>
437 <% =data( "State" ) %><BR>
438 <STRONG>Payment Type: </STRONG>
439 <% =data( "PaymentType" ) %><BR>
440 </P>
441
442 <% ' Create a link to bookdata.asp. Pass the product
443     ' number as a parameter.
444     Dim s
445     s = "bookdata.asp?ProductNumber=" & data( "ProductNumber" )
446     Call data.Close()
447     Call connection.Close()
448 %>
449
```

Fig. 26.19 Listing for `itemdata.asp` (part 2 of 3).

```
450  <A HREF = "<% =s %>">
451     Additional Book Information
452  </A>
453
454  <% If Session( "LoggedIn" ) Then
455        s = "bid.asp"
456     Else
457        s = "login.asp"
458     End If
459  %>
460
461  <CENTER>
462     <FORM METHOD = "POST" ACTION = "<% =s %>">
463        <INPUT TYPE = "submit" VALUE = "Bid Now">
464     </FORM>
465  </CENTER>
466
467  <% ' Provide links back to home and book items. %>
468  <BR><BR>
469  <CENTER>
470     <A HREF = "index.asp">Home</A> 
471     <A HREF = "bookitems.asp">Back to Book Items</A>
472  </CENTER>
473  </BODY>
474  </HTML>
```

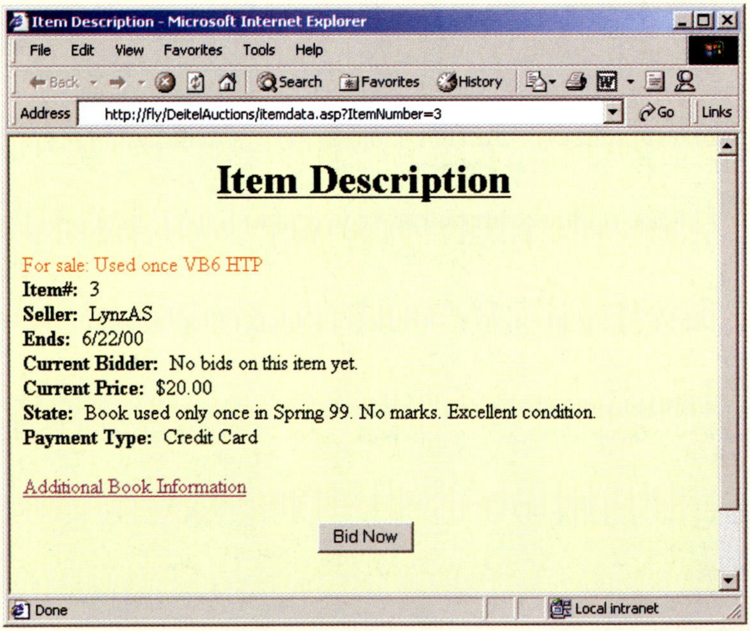

Fig. 26.19 Listing for **itemdata.asp** (part 3 of 3).

Lines 418 through 439 display the retrieved record's information. Line 428 tests the **CurrentBidder** field for null. If true, the item does not have any bids, and a message indicating this is displayed. If false, we display the **CurrentBidder** field. Line 445 creates a link to **bookdata.asp**—which lists the book information—e.g., title, author(s), ISBN number, etc. The link passes the item number as a parameter.

The form in lines 462 through 464 displays a submit button labeled **Bid Now**. When clicked, the user is redirected to either **bid.asp** or **login.asp**, based upon the value of **s**. Lines 454 through 458 assign **s** a value dependent upon whether or not the user has logged in (i.e., the session variable **LoggedIn** is **true**). If the user has logged in, **"bid.asp"** is assigned to **s**. Otherwise, **"login.asp"** is assigned to **s**. This prevents users from bidding on items before logging in.

When the session expires, session resources are released and all session variables are destroyed. Therefore, **LoggedIn** is set to **false** when the session expires. Users are required to login each session.

Figure 26.20 (**bookdata.asp**) displays the selected book's information. Remember this page is requested by **itemdata.asp**, which passes the book's product number as a parameter in the URL of **bookdata.asp** (see the **Address** bar in Fig. 26.20's screen capture). When executed, the SQL statement in lines 489 and 490 queries the **Products** table using this number. All the record fields, except the picture field, are displayed on this page. When a picture is available, a link to the picture is provided. When clicked, the link requests **bookdata.asp** and passes the **Picture** parameter in the URL (line 549). The **If** statement in line 528 tests this parameter's value and displays the picture if **Picture**'s value is **"yes"**. Otherwise, a link to a page that displays the picture is provided. If the book does not have a picture, a message is displayed indicating this.

```
475   <% @LANGUAGE = VBSCRIPT %>
476   <% Option Explicit %>
477
478   <% ' Fig. 26.20 : bookdata.asp %>
479
480   <%
481       Dim connection, query, data
482
483       ' Open a database connection
484       Set connection = Server.CreateObject( "ADODB.Connection" )
485       Call connection.Open( "DeitelAuctions" )
486
487       ' Create the SQL query. Retrieve the product with the same
488       ' product number as the number passed to this page.
489       query = "SELECT * FROM Products WHERE ProductNumber = " _
490             & CStr( Request( "ProductNumber" ) )
491
492       ' Open the record set
493       Set data = Server.CreateObject( "ADODB.RecordSet" )
494       Call data.Open( query, connection )
495       On Error Resume Next
496   %>
497
498
499   <!DOCTYPE HTML PUBLIC "-//W3C//DTD HTML 4.0 Transitional //EN">
```

Fig. 26.20 Listing for **bookdata.asp** (part 1 of 3).

```
500  <HTML>
501
502  <HEAD>
503  <TITLE>Book Information</TITLE>
504  </HEAD>
505
506  <BODY BGCOLOR = "#FFFF99">
507  <H1 ALIGN = "center"><U>Book Information</U></H1>
508
509  <BR>
510
511  <P>
512  <% ' Display the book information %>
513  <STRONG>Title: </STRONG>
514  <% =data( "Title" ) %><BR>
515  <STRONG>Language: </STRONG>
516  <% =data( "Language" ) %><BR>
517  <STRONG>Publication Year: </STRONG>
518  <% =data( "PublishYear" ) %><BR>
519  <STRONG>Edition: </STRONG>
520  <% =data( "Edition" ) %><BR>
521  <STRONG>ISBN: </STRONG>
522  <% =data( "ISBN" ) %><BR>
523  <STRONG>Description: </STRONG>
524  <% =data( "Description" ) %><BR>
525
526  <% ' If the Picture link was clicked, display the
527     ' picture.
528     If Request( "Picture" ) = "yes" Then %>
529        <STRONG>Picture:</STRONG><BR>
530        <CENTER>
531        <IMG SRC = "/images/<% =data( "PictureFile" ) %>"
532           BORDER = "1" ALT = "Book Picture">
533        </CENTER>
534
535  <% ' Otherwise, display the Picture link or Not
536     ' Available if there is no picture.
537     Else
538
539        ' If the book does not have a picture, say so
540        If IsNull( data( "PictureFile" ) ) Then
541  %>       <STRONG>Picture: </STRONG>Not Available<BR>
542  <%    Else
543
544           ' Provide a link that reloads the page
545           ' to display the picture.
546           Dim s
547           s = "bookdata.asp?Picture=yes&ProductNumber=" _
548              & Request( "ProductNumber" ) %>
549           <A HREF = "<% =s %>">Picture</A>
550  <%       End If
551     End If
552  %> </P>
```

Fig. 26.20 Listing for **bookdata.asp** (part 2 of 3).

```
553  <% Call data.Close()
554     Call connection.Close()
555  %> <BR><BR>
556
557  <CENTER>
558  <A HREF = "index.asp">Home</A>  
559  <A HREF =
560     "itemdata.asp?ItemNumber=<% =Session( "ItemNumber" ) %>">
561     Back to Item Description
562  </A>
563  </CENTER>
564  </BODY>
565  </HTML>
```

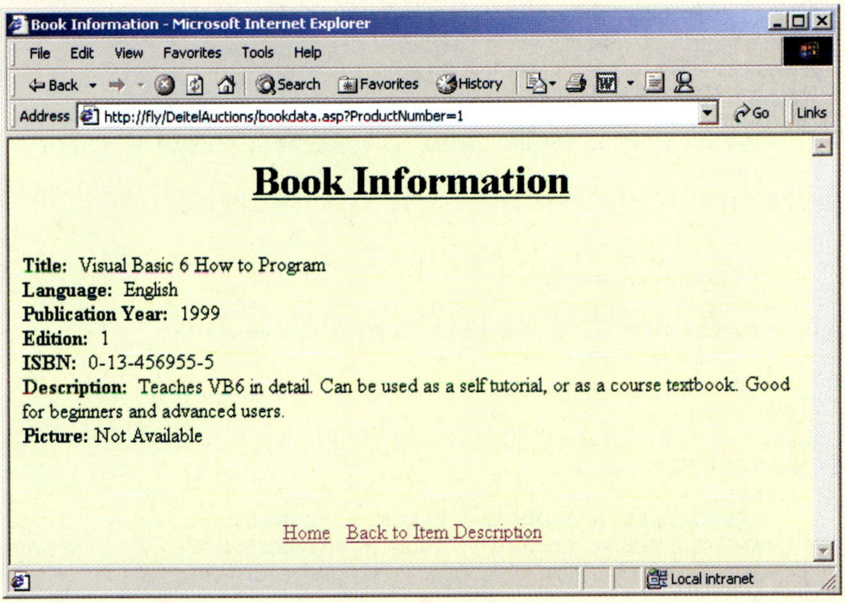

Book Information - Microsoft Internet Explorer

File Edit View Favorites Tools Help

←Back ▾ → ▾ ⊗ ⊗ ⌂ | ⊗Search ⊛Favorites ⊛History | ⬚▾ ⬚ ⬚ ▾ ⬚ ⬚

Address http://fly/DeitelAuctions/bookdata.asp?ProductNumber=1

Book Information

Title: Visual Basic 6 How to Program
Language: English
Publication Year: 1999
Edition: 1
ISBN: 0-13-456955-5
Description: Teaches VB6 in detail. Can be used as a self tutorial, or as a course textbook. Good for beginners and advanced users.
Picture: Not Available

Home   Back to Item Description

Fig. 26.20 Listing for **bookdata.asp** (part 3 of 3).

Finally, a link back to the item's description page (**itemdata.asp**) is provided (lines 559 and 560). Remember, the item number is stored in a session variable by **itemdata.asp**. The link (when clicked) passes this item number in the URL of **itemdata.asp**.

Figure 26.21 (**login.asp**) prompts the user to login before proceeding to the bidding page. The user inputs their user name and password in a form (lines 582 through 606). When this form is submitted, the user is redirected to **checklogin.asp** (Fig. 26.22). A link to create a new account is provided in line 618.

```
566  <% @LANGUAGE = VBSCRIPT %>
567  <% Option Explicit %>
```

Fig. 26.21 Listing for **login.asp** (part 1 of 3).

```
568
569   <% ' Fig. 26.21 : login.asp %>
570
571   <!DOCTYPE HTML PUBLIC "-//W3C//DTD HTML 4.0 Transitional //EN">
572   <HTML>
573
574   <HEAD>
575   <TITLE>Login</TITLE>
576   </HEAD>
577
578   <BODY BGCOLOR = "#FFFF99">
579
580   <CENTER><H2><U>Please Log In</U></H2></CENTER><BR><BR>
581   <% ' Form to post the login data %>
582   <FORM METHOD = "POST" ACTION = "checklogin.asp">
583      <TABLE>
584      <TR>
585         <TH>User Name:</TH>
586         <TD>
587         <INPUT TYPE = "text" NAME = "UserName" SIZE = "25">
588         </TD>
589      </TR>
590
591      <TR>
592         <TH>Password:</TH>
593         <TD>
594         <INPUT TYPE = "password" NAME = "Password"
595            SIZE = "25">
596         </TD>
597      </TR>
598      <TR>
599         <TD></TD>
600         <TD>
601         <INPUT TYPE = "submit" VALUE = "Submit">
602         <INPUT TYPE = "reset" VALUE = "Clear">
603         </TD>
604      </TR>
605      </TABLE>
606   </FORM><BR>
607
608   <% ' Save where the user came from in the "from" session
609      ' variable. Because we have several register links
610      ' in the site, we can use this variable to provide
611      ' links in the registration pages, depending on where
612      ' the user came from. %>
613
614   <% Session( "from" ) = "login" %>
615
616   <% ' Provide a link to register a new user %>
617   <P><STRONG>Do you not have an account?</STRONG>
618      <A HREF = "newmember.asp">Register</A></P>
619   </BODY>
620   </HTML>
```

Fig. 26.21 Listing for **login.asp** (part 2 of 3).

Fig. 26.21 Listing for **login.asp** (part 3 of 3).

Figure 26.22 (**checklogin.asp**) validates the user name and password submitted in **login.asp**. When executed, the SQL query in lines 634 through 637 retrieves the record from the **Members** table that matches the user name and password. If no record is retrieved, the user is redirected to **badlogin.asp** (Fig. 26.23). If the record is retrieved, the login is valid and we set the session variables **LoggedIn** and **UserName** to the value **true** and the user name, respectively, before redirecting to **bid.asp**.

```
621  <% @LANGUAGE = VBSCRIPT %>
622  <% Option Explicit %>
623
624  <% ' Fig 26.22 : checklogin.asp %>
625
626  <%
627     Dim connection, check, data
628
629     ' Open a database connection
630     Set connection = Server.CreateObject( "ADODB.Connection" )
631     Call connection.Open( "DeitelAuctions" )
632
633     ' Build the SQL query
634     check = "SELECT * FROM Members WHERE UserName = '" _
635             & CStr( Request( "UserName" ) ) & "'" _
636             & " AND Password = '" _
637             & CStr( Request( "Password" ) ) & "'"
638
639     ' Open the record set
640     Set data = Server.CreateObject( "ADODB.RecordSet" )
641     Call data.Open( check, connection )
642     On Error Resume Next
```

Fig. 26.22 Listing for **checklogin.asp** (part 1 of 2).

```
643
644     If data.EOF Then
645
646         ' The user's login is incorrect
647         Call data.Close()
648         Call connection.Close()
649         Call Response.Redirect( "badlogin.asp" )
650     Else
651
652         ' The user's login is correct
653         Session( "UserName" ) = Request( "UserName" )
654         Session( "LoggedIn" ) = True
655         Call data.Close()
656         Call connection.Close()
657         Call Response.Redirect( "bid.asp" )
658     End If
659  %>
```

Fig. 26.22   Listing for **checklogin.asp** (part 2 of 2).

Figure 26.23 (**badlogin.asp**) displays a message indicating an incorrect login. A link to **newmember.asp** is provided to allow new users to create an account.

```
660  <% @LANGUAGE = VBSCRIPT %>
661  <% Option Explicit %>
662
663  <% ' Fig 26.23 : badlogin.asp %>
664
665  <!DOCTYPE HTML PUBLIC "-//W3C//DTD HTML 4.0 Transitional //EN">
666  <HTML>
667
668  <HEAD>
669    <TITLE>Login Failure</TITLE>
670  </HEAD>
671
672  <BODY BGCOLOR = "#FFFF99">
673    <H2>Invalid username or password.</H2>
674
675  <CENTER>
676     <A HREF = "login.asp">Try Again</A> 
677     <A HREF = "index.asp">Home</A> 
678     <A HREF =
679        "itemdata.asp?ItemNumber=<% =Session( "ItemNumber" ) %>">
680        Back to Item Description
681     </A>
682  </CENTER>
683
684  <% ' Provide a link to register a new user %>
685  <BR><BR>
686  <P><STRONG>Do you not have an account?</STRONG>
687     <A HREF = "newmember.asp">Register</A>
688  </P>
```

Fig. 26.23   Listing for **badlogin.asp** (part 1 of 2).

```
689   </BODY>
690   </HTML>
```

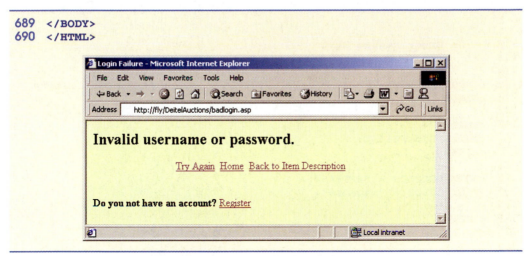

Fig. 26.23 Listing for **badlogin.asp** (part 2 of 2).

Figure 26.24 (**bid.asp**) allows users to bid on items. The book's description and current price are retrieved from the **AuctionItems** table and displayed (lines 731 through 734). The current date is also displayed in line 724. Lines 738 through 747 display the bidding form, which prompts the user to bid on the item. It has one input item: **Bid**. When the form is submitted, the user is redirected to **dobid.asp** (Fig. 26.25) which uses the form contents to update the database. Links back to **itemdata.asp** and to the home page (Fig. 26.12—**index.asp**) are provided.

```
691   <% @LANGUAGE = VBSCRIPT %>
692   <% Option Explicit %>
693
694   <% ' Fig 26.24 : bid.asp %>
695
696   <%
697      Dim connection, query, data
698
699      ' Open a database connection
700      Set connection = Server.CreateObject( "ADODB.Connection" )
701      Call connection.Open( "DeitelAuctions" )
702
703      ' Create the SQL query. Retrieve the record of the
704      ' item the user wants to bid on.
705      query = "SELECT CurrentPrice, ItemNumber, Display " & _
706              "FROM AuctionItems " & _
707              "WHERE ItemNumber = " & CStr( Session( "ItemNumber" ) ) )
708
709      ' Open the record set.
710      Set data = Server.CreateObject( "ADODB.RecordSet" )
711      Call data.Open( query, connection )
```

Fig. 26.24 Listing for **bid.asp** (part 1 of 3).

```
712     On Error Resume Next
713  %>
714
715  <!DOCTYPE HTML PUBLIC "-//W3C//DTD HTML 4.0 Transitional //EN">
716  <HTML>
717
718  <HEAD>
719  <TITLE>Bid</TITLE>
720  </HEAD>
721
722  <BODY BGCOLOR = "#FFFF99">
723  <FONT COLOR = "magenta">
724  <% =Date() %>
725  </FONT>
726  <H1 ALIGN = "center"><U>New Bid</U></H1>
727  <BR>
728  <P>
729  <% ' Display the item number and the current price.
730     ' Also, provide the display caption for the item.
731  %> <FONT COLOR = "red"><% =data( "Display" ) %></FONT><BR>
732  <STRONG>Item#: </STRONG><% =data( "ItemNumber" ) %><BR>
733  <STRONG>Current Price: </STRONG>
734  <% =FormatCurrency( data( "CurrentPrice" ) ) %><BR>
735  </P>
736
737  <% ' A form to post bidding data %>
738  <FORM METHOD = "POST" ACTION = "dobid.asp">
739     <P>
740        <STRONG>Your Bid:</STRONG>$
741        <INPUT TYPE = "text" NAME = "Bid" SIZE = "25">
742     </P>
743     <CENTER>
744        <INPUT TYPE = "submit" VALUE = "Submit">
745        <INPUT TYPE = "reset" VALUE = "Clear">
746     </CENTER><BR><BR>
747  </FORM><BR><BR>
748  <CENTER>
749     <A HREF = "index.asp">Home</A> 
750     <A HREF =
751        "itemdata.asp?ItemNumber=<% =data( "ItemNumber" )%>">
752        Back to Item Description
753     </A>
754  </CENTER>
755
756  <% ' Close the database connection and the record set
757     Call data.Close()
758     Call connection.Close()
759  %>
760  </BODY>
761  </HTML>
```

Fig. 26.24 Listing for `bid.asp` (part 2 of 3).

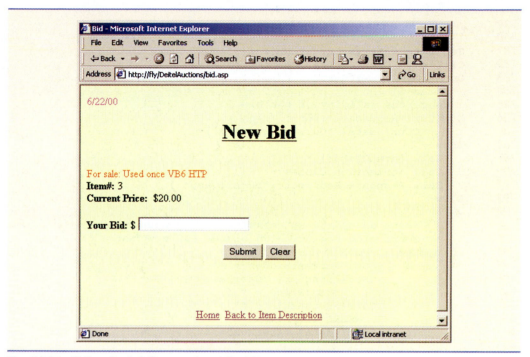

Fig. 26.24 Listing for **bid.asp** (part 3 of 3).

Figure 26.25 (**dobid.asp**) completes a valid bid (i.e., the bid is higher than the item's current price). If the bid is invalid, the user is redirected to **badbid.asp**. If the bid is valid, the SQL statement in lines 796 through 802 updates the item's **CurrentBidder** and **CurrentPrice** fields. Method **Execute** executes this SQL query against the database. Finally, the user is redirected to **confirmbid.html** (Fig. 26.26) where the bid is confirmed and navigational links are provided.

```
762  <% @LANGUAGE = VBSCRIPT %>
763  <% Option Explicit %>
764
765  <% ' Fig. 26.25 : dobid.asp %>
766
767  <%
768     Dim connection, data, query, update
769
770     ' Open a database connection.
771     Set connection = Server.CreateObject( "ADODB.Connection" )
772     Call connection.Open( "DeitelAuctions" )
773
774     ' Create the SQL query. Retrieve the record for this
775     ' item.
776     query = "SELECT ItemNumber, CurrentPrice " & _
777             "FROM AuctionItems WHERE ItemNumber = " & _
778             CStr( Session( "ItemNumber" ) )
```

Fig. 26.25 Listing for **dobid.asp** (part 1 of 2).

```
779
780        ' Open the record set
781        Set data = Server.CreateObject( "ADODB.RecordSet" )
782        Call data.Open( query, connection )
783        On Error Resume Next
784
785        ' Check the validity of the bid
786        If CCur( Request( "Bid" ) ) _
787           <= CCur( data( "CurrentPrice" ) ) _
788        Then
789           Call data.Close()
790           Call connection.Close()
791           Call Response.Redirect( "badbid.asp" )
792        Else
793
794           ' Create an update SQL statement that updates the item's
795           ' record with the new high bidder and new bid.
796           update = "UPDATE AuctionItems " & _
797                    "SET CurrentBidder = '" & _
798                    CStr( Session( "UserName" ) ) & "'" & _
799                    ", CurrentPrice = " & _
800                    CStr( Request( "Bid" ) ) & _
801                    " WHERE ItemNumber = " & _
802                    CStr( data( "ItemNumber" ) )
803
804           ' Execute the update statement.
805           Call connection.Execute( update )
806
807           ' Confirm the bid.
808           Call data.Close()
809           Call connection.Close()
810           Call Response.Redirect( "confirmbid.html" )
811        End If
812 %>
```

Fig. 26.25 Listing for **dobid.asp** (part 2 of 2).

```
813 <!DOCTYPE HTML PUBLIC "-//W3C//DTD HTML 4.0 Transitional //EN">
814 <!-- Fig. 26.26 : confirmbid.html -->
815 <HTML>
816 <HEAD>
817   <TITLE>Confirm Bid</TITLE>
818 </HEAD>
819 <!-- Display the message and provide navigational links -->
820 <BODY BGCOLOR = "#FFFF99">
821 <H2>Thanks. You are the high bidder now!</H2>
822
823 <CENTER>
824    <A HREF = "index.asp">Home</A> 
825    <A HREF = "bookitems.asp">Back to Book Items</A>
826 </CENTER>
```

Fig. 26.26 Listing for **confirmbid.html** (part 1 of 2).

```
827  </BODY>
828  </HTML>
```

Fig. 26.26 Listing for `confirmbid.html` (part 2 of 2).

Figure 26.27 (**badbid.asp**) displays an invalid bid message and provides navigational links. Again, notice the use of the session variable **ItemNumber** in line 851.

```
829  <% @LANGUAGE = VBSCRIPT %>
830  <% Option Explicit %>
831
832  <% ' Fig. 24.27 : badbid.asp %>
833
834  <!DOCTYPE HTML PUBLIC "-//W3C//DTD HTML 4.0 Transitional //EN">
835  <HTML>
836
837  <HEAD>
838     <TITLE>Invalid Bid</TITLE>
839  </HEAD>
840
841  <BODY BGCOLOR = "#FFFF99">
842
843  <% ' Print error message and provide navigational links %>
844  <H2>Invalid Bid.</H2>
845  <H2>You must bid higher than the current price.</H2>
846
847  <CENTER>
848  <A HREF = "bid.asp">Try Again</A> 
849  <A HREF = "index.asp">Home</A> 
850  <A HREF =
851     "itemdata.asp?ItemNumber=<% =Session( "ItemNumber" ) %>">
852     Back to Item Description
853  </A>
854  </CENTER>
855  </BODY>
856  </HTML>
```

Fig. 26.27 Listing for `badbid.asp` (part 1 of 2).

Fig. 26.27   Listing for **badbid.asp** (part 2 of 2).

26.5 Case Study: a Comparison Pricing Search Engine

In Chapter 3, we presented the comparison pricing model that allowed a variety of merchants to be polled in order to find the lowest price for a product or service. In this section, we present an implementation of the comparison pricing model using ASP. In this case study, we search several popular Web sites for Deitel book prices. This case study consists of a single Active Server Page—**lowest.asp**.

[*Note: This case study is highly sensitive to the format of the Web sites visited. Because of the Web's dynamic nature, a site's format may change at any time—which may result in this example not executing properly. You may need to modify this example if any of the Web sites searched change.*

*This example uses **Class**es and regular expressions. You may want to review Section 24.8 before proceeding.*]

First, we discuss the database used in this example. The Microsoft Access database **Lowest.mdb** contains information about the Deitel books, the list of Web sites to search and the methods (i.e., **GET** or **POST**) to use when searching the Web sites. When a search begins, each document listed in the database is requested and parsed for the book's price. After all the Web sites have been visited, the prices are listed from lowest to highest.

The **Lowest.mdb** database contains three tables: **Products**, **Sites** and **SpecialLinks**. The **Products** table contains information about each book. It has a primary key field, **ProductID**, and two other fields, **Title** and **ISBN**, which represent the book's unique identification number (used in this example), title and ISBN number, respectively.

The **Sites** table contains information about the Web sites that will be searched. Field **SiteID** is the primary key that stores the site's unique identification number, **Name** stores the site's name (e.g., **Amazon.com**) and **SearchURL** stores the site's URL.

Field **Label** is the text a Web site uses for a book's price (e.g., "**Our Price**", "**Online Price**", etc.). The prices found are written as hyperlinks to their corresponding Web sites. These hyperlinks (when clicked) send the ISBN number as part of the request by attaching it to the URL—which is the same behavior as an HTTP **GET** request. However, a site may require an HTTP **POST** request—which requires a direct link to the page. The last field, **DirectBookLink**, stores a **True-False** value that indicates whether or not a direct link is needed. Note that direct links are likely to change because they rely on the server's directory structure. For this reason, we have minimized the number of direct links used.

The **DirectLinks** table has three fields: **SiteID**, **LeftSubURL** and **RightSubURL**. A direct link contains the book's ISBN number. Because the ISBN number is not known until the user selects a book, we split the direct link into three strings: A left string (**LeftSubURL**), the ISBN number (which is provided by the user) and a right string (**RightSubURL**). Field **LeftSubURL** stores the page's URL and any data to the left of the ISBN parameter and **RightSubURL** stores any data specific to that Web site that is to the right of the ISBN parameter. For example, the direct link to **Amazon.com**'s **LeftSubURL** contains **http://www.amazon.com/exec/obidos/ASIN/** and **RightSubURL** contains **/102-8457819-5560832**. These might be combined to form the URL

```
http://www.amazon.com/exec/obidos/ASIN/0130161438/
102-8457819-5560832
```

where **0130161438** is the ISBN number. This links to the book's page on **Amazon.com**.

The **lowest.asp** document (Fig. 26.28) builds a drop-down list of Deitel books. When a user selects a book and clicks the **Search Prices** button, **lowest.asp** searches several predefined Web sites for the book's price. When the search is completed, a sorted price list is displayed in a table. For each price in the table, the Web site from which the price was obtained is displayed. Each price is a link to the specific page that contains the book.

```
1   <% @LANGUAGE = VBScript %>
2   <% Option Explicit %>
3
4   <% ' Fig. 26.28: lowest.asp %>
5
6   <% Dim connection, query, data
7
8       ' Open a database connection
9       Set connection = Server.CreateObject( "ADODB.Connection" )
10
11      ' System DSN named Lowest
12      Call connection.Open( "Lowest" )
13
14      query = "SELECT * FROM Products"
15
16      ' Open a record set
17      Set data = Server.CreateObject( "ADODB.RecordSet" )
18      Call data.Open( query, connection )
19
20      On Error Resume Next
21   %>
22
23   <!DOCTYPE HTML PUBLIC "-//W3C//DTD HTML 4.0 Transitional //EN">
24   <HTML>
25
26   <HEAD>
27   <TITLE>Lowest Price</TITLE>
28   </HEAD>
```

Fig. 26.28 Comparison-pricing search engine (part 1 of 9).

```
29
30    <BODY BGCOLOR = "FFFF99">
31
32    <CENTER><H1>Welcome to Deitel Lowest Price</H1></CENTER><BR>
33
34    <CENTER>
35    <STRONG>Please Select a book.</STRONG>
36    <FORM ACTION = "lowest.asp?entry=true" METHOD = "POST">
37
38    <SELECT NAME = "isbn">
39
40    <% ' Iterate through the records to form a book list
41       While Not data.EOF
42
43          ' Set the value of the OPTION to the book's
44          ' ISBN number %>
45          <OPTION VALUE = "<% =data( "ISBN" ) %>"
46
47             <% ' If the user has made a selection, keep their
48                ' selection by writing SELECTED for this OPTION
49                ' if it has the same ISBN number as the
50                ' selected ISBN number.
51                If Request( "entry" ) = "true" And _
52                   Request( "isbn" ) = data( "ISBN" ) _
53                Then
54                   Call Response.Write( "SELECTED" )
55                End If
56             %> >
57
58          <% ' Display the titles as OPTIONs for the user
59             Call Response.Write( data( "Title" ) )
60             Call data.MoveNext()
61
62       Wend
63       Call data.Close() %>
64
65    </SELECT>
66
67    <INPUT TYPE = "submit" VALUE = "Search Prices">
68
69    </FORM>
70    </CENTER>
71
72    <% ' If the user has made a selection, process the request
73       If Request( "entry" ) = "true" Then
74
75          Dim url, method, postData, label, _
76             isbn, s, ok, p, count, a()
77
78          p = 0
79
```

Fig. 26.28   Comparison-pricing search engine (part 2 of 9).

```
80           ' Count how many sites are in the database. This is
81           ' the number of entries needed in the price array.
82           ' Thus, dynamically allocate the array.
83           query = "SELECT Count(*) As C FROM Sites"
84           Call data.Open( query, connection )
85           count = data( "C" )
86           Call data.Close()
87           ReDim a( count - 1 )
88
89           ' This is the ISBN number to search for.
90           ' Store it in the variable isbn.
91           isbn = Request( "isbn" )
92
93           Call Response.Write( "<STRONG> Searching " )
94
95           ' Search all the Web sites in the database.
96           ' The query retrieves information about the Web sites
97           ' from the Sites table.
98           query = "SELECT * FROM Sites"
99           Call data.Open( query, connection )
100
101        ' Iterate through the sites and search them
102           While Not data.EOF
103              Set a( p ) = New CRecord
104
105              ' Set the variables to the corresponding fields of
106              ' the current record.
107              Call SetVariables()
108
109              ' Get the price
110              s = GetPrice( url, method, postData, label )
111
112              ' Insert the price into the array a
113              Call Insert( s )
114
115              ' Print search progress dots.
116              ' One dot is printed per site.
117              Call Response.Write(". ")
118
119              ' Move to the next record
120              Call data.MoveNext()
121
122              ' Increment the array index
123              p = p + 1
124           Wend
125           Call data.Close()
126           Call Response.Write( "</STRONG><BR>" )
127
128           ' Sort the array by price
129           Dim i, j, o
130
131           j = UBound( a )
```

Fig. 26.28 Comparison-pricing search engine (part 3 of 9).

```
132          While j >= 1
133
134             For i = 0 To j - 1
135
136                If a( i ).Price > a( i + 1 ).Price Then
137                   Set o = a( i )
138                   Set a( i ) = a( i + 1 )
139                   Set a( i + 1 ) = o
140                   Set o = Nothing
141                End If
142
143             Next
144             j = j - 1
145
146          Wend
147
148          ' Display the array elements in a table %>
149          <TABLE BORDER = "1" ALIGN = "CENTER">
150          <CAPTION><STRONG>Search Results</STRONG></CAPTION>
151
152   <%     For i = 0 To UBound( a ) %>
153             <TR>
154                <TD><STRONG><% =a( i ).Name %></STRONG></TD>
155                <TD><% =a( i ).Display %></TD>
156             </TR>
157   <%     Next %>
158
159          </TABLE>
160   <% End If
161
162       Call connection.Close()
163
164       ' A class to store the search results of a site
165       Class CRecord
166
167          ' Site name, book price and the display which is
168          ' either the book price as a link, "Failed" or "N/A".
169          Private n, p, d
170
171          Public Property Get Name()
172             Name = n
173          End Property
174
175          Public Property Let Name( parameter )
176             n = parameter
177          End Property
178
179          Public Property Get Price()
180             Price = p
181          End Property
182
```

Fig. 26.28 Comparison-pricing search engine (part 4 of 9).

```
183        Public Property Let Price( parameter )
184           p = parameter
185        End Property
186
187        Public Property Get Display()
188           Display = d
189        End Property
190
191        Public Property Let Display( parameter )
192           d = parameter
193        End Property
194     End Class
195
196     ' Sets the variables corresponding to the fields of the
197     ' current record.
198     Sub SetVariables()
199        a( p ).Name = data( "Name" )
200        url = data( "SearchURL" )
201        method = data( "Method" )
202
203        ' Append the current ISBN number to postData
204        postData = data( "PostData" ) & isbn
205        label = data( "Label" )
206     End Sub
207
208     ' This function returns the price of the book from the
209     ' current Web site. The parameters are: url is the URL of
210     ' the search script on a Web site; method is the request
211     ' type, 1 or 2; postData is the data to pass to the
212     ' site; label is the string used by the site to indicate
213     ' the price (e.g., "Our Price", "Online Price").
214     Function GetPrice( url, method, postData, label )
215        Dim s, aspTear, i, e, expression, b
216
217        Set aspTear = Server.CreateObject( "SOFTWING.AspTear" )
218
219        i = 1
220        e = 1
221
222        ' Make, at most, 3 attempts to grab a page
223        On Error Resume Next
224        While i <= 3 And e <> 0
225           s = aspTear.Retrieve( url, method, _
226                                  postData, "", "" )
227           e = Err.Number
228           i = i + 1
229        Wend
230
231        If Err.Number <> 0 Then
232           GetPrice = "Failed"
233           ok = False
234           Exit Function
235        End If
```

Fig. 26.28 Comparison-pricing search engine (part 5 of 9).

```
236
237        ' Split the string on the "$" character
238        b = Split( s, "$" )
239
240        ' If the "$" character was not found
241        If UBound( b ) = 0 Then
242           GetPrice = "N/A"
243           ok = False
244           Exit Function
245        End If
246
247        ' Look for the label
248        For i = UBound( b ) - 1 To 0 Step -1
249           If InStr( LCase( b( i ) ), LCase( label ) ) <> 0 Then
250              Exit For
251           End If
252        Next
253
254        ' If the label was not found
255        If i = -1 Then
256           GetPrice = "Failed"
257           ok = False
258           Exit Function
259        End If
260
261        ' Set s
262        s = b( i + 1 )
263
264        ' Find the "<" character and remove it and the
265        ' remaining characters to the right
266        s = Left( s, InStr( s, "<" ) - 1 )
267
268        ' Find the "~" character and remove it and the
269        ' remaining characters to the right
270        s = Left( s, InStr( s, "~" ) - 1 )
271
272        ' Find the characters, Chr(9) to Chr(13), and
273        ' remove them and the remaining characters to
274        ' the right
275        For i = 9 To 13
276           s = Left( s, InStr( s, Chr( i ) ) - 1 )
277        Next
278
279        ' Remove any remaining spaces from the string
280        s = Replace( s, " ", "" )
281
282        ' Check the pattern
283        Set expression = New RegExp
284        expression.Pattern = "^\d*\.{0,1}\d*$"
285
286        If expression.Test( s ) Then
287           GetPrice = "$" & s
288           ok = True
```

Fig. 26.28 Comparison-pricing search engine (part 6 of 9).

```
289          Else
290              GetPrice = "Failed"
291              ok = False
292          End If
293          Set expression = Nothing
294       End Function
295
296    ' Inserts the results of a Web site search in the
297    ' array a.
298    Sub Insert( s )
299       Dim display, href
300
301       ' If a price was found, set the price field at the
302       ' current array position, get the book's URL and
303       ' build the book's hyperlink.
304       If ok Then
305          a( p ).Price = CCur( s )
306          href = GetURL()
307          display = "<A HREF = """ & href & """>"
308       Else
309
310          ' If a price was not found, set the price field
311          ' at the current array position to a large number.
312          ' When the array is sorted, the "Failed" and "N/A"
313          ' items are moved to the end.
314          a( p ).Price = CCur( 60000 )
315
316       End If
317
318       ' Append what GetPrice returned to the display field.
319       display = display & s
320
321       ' If a price was found, the link needs to be closed.
322       If ok Then
323          display = display & "</A>"
324       End If
325
326       a( p ).Display = display
327    End Sub
328
329    ' Returns a link to the book we are searching for. The
330    ' link returned is on the Web site of the current
331    ' record.
332    Function GetURL()
333       Dim query2, data2
334
335       ' If a direct link to a page on the site is not
336       ' available, a link to the script that returns
337       ' the page containing the book is used.
338       If data( "DirectBookLink" ) = False Then
339          GetURL = url & "?" & postData
```

Fig. 26.28 Comparison-pricing search engine (part 7 of 9).

```
340        Else
341
342            ' If a hyperlink to a processing script on the site
343            ' does not work, a direct link to a page on the
344            ' site is needed. This link is stored in the
345            ' DirectLinks table.
346            query2 = "SELECT * FROM DirectLinks " &_
347                     "WHERE SiteID = " & data( "SiteID" )
348
349            ' Open a record set
350            Set data2 = _
351                Server.CreateObject( "ADODB.RecordSet" )
352            Call data2.Open( query2, Connection )
353            On Error Resume Next
354
355            ' Build the link by concatenating the left part
356            ' of the URL, the ISBN number and the right part
357            ' of the URL.
358            GetURL = data2( "LeftSubURL" ) & isbn _
359                    & data2( "RightSubURL" )
360            Call data2.Close()
361        End If
362    End Function
363 %>
364
365 </BODY>
366 </HTML>
```

Fig. 26.28 Comparison-pricing search engine (part 8 of 9).

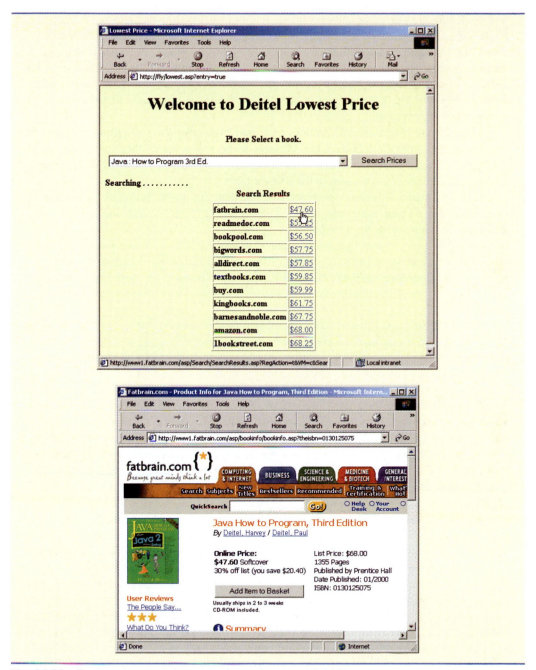

Fig. 26.28 Comparison-pricing search engine (part 9 of 9).

The form in lines 36 through 69 contains the drop-down list of book titles. To build this list, the query in line 14 indicates that all records in the **Products** table are to be retrieved. The **While** loop in lines 41 through 62 builds the book list. The ISBN number and book title are the value and text for each option. If the user has selected a book and clicked the submit button (i.e., **entry** is **true**), the selected book is retained in the drop-down list by writing **SELECTED** for the book's option. When the form is submitted, **lowest.asp** requests itself. We use parameter **entry** to prevent the search code from being executed unless the user has selected a book from the drop-down list and clicked **Search Prices**. The **If** statement in line 73 tests the value of **entry**. If **true**, lines 74 through 159 are executed.

Lines 75 and 76 declare the variables **url**, **method**, **postData**, **label**, etc., which get their values from the **Sites** table. Variable **isbn** stores the ISBN number, **ok** stores the success or failure of the search, **p** contains the current position in the array **a** and **count** contains the number of Web sites in the **Sites** table.

Line 78 initializes the array position to **0**. The query in line 83 retrieves the number of records in the **Sites** table and stores it in record **C**. Line 87 dynamically allocates **count - 1** elements for the array **a**.

The SQL query in line 98 is used in line 99 to retrieve all the records from the **Sites** table. The **While** loop in lines 102 through 124 iterates through the records in the database, calling procedures **SetVariables**, **GetPrice** and **Insert** for each. We will discuss each of these procedures momentarily. A search progress dot is printed after each site is searched.

Lines 131 through 146 sort the array using a *bubble sort*. The **For** loop in lines 152 through 157 iterates through the array and builds one row of the results table for each element in the array. Each table row has two cells that contain the **Name** and **Display** variable values. **Display**, contains either the price, "**N/A**" or "**Failed**."

Line 165 begins the class definition for **CRecord**. Objects of this class store the search results. This class contains three **Private** variables: **n**, **p** and **d**. We refer to these as **Name**, **Price** and **Display** because these are their respective **Get** and **Let** property names. **Name** stores the Web site's name, **Price** stores the book price and **Display** stores either the price (if found) as a link to the page containing the book or "**N/A**" or "**Failed**" (if a price was not found—for reasons we will discuss momentarily). The search results are stored in an array (**a**) of **CRecord**s. Each element in **a** stores the search results from an individual Web site.

Procedure **SetVariables** (line 198) sets the values for **url**, **method**, **postData** and **label**. Each variable is assigned its corresponding field value from the record set. Although we could have used the record fields directly in the program i.e., **data("fieldName")** instead of using variables, we use these variables for clarity.

We use ASP component *ASPTear* from SoftWing, to grab Web pages (see Section 26.2 for installation instructions for this component provided on the CD). The component (created in line 217) has one method—**Retrieve**, which takes the following parameters: **URL**, **Method**, **QueryString** or **PostData**, **UserName** and **Password**. All parameters are strings except for **Method**, which is a number. **URL** is the location of the page to retrieve. **Method** specifies the request method used to grab a Web page. This parameter is either a **1** or **2**—representing the **POST** and **GET** requests, respectively. The third parameter is either **PostData** (for a **POST** request) or **QueryString** (for a **GET** request). **PostData** is sent to the server inside the HTTP request, and **QueryString** is sent to the server as part of the URL. **UserName** and **Password** are used when the site requires user verification.

Function **Retrieve** returns a string containing the grabbed HTML document. If the requested page redirects the user to another page, function **Retrieve** returns the redirected page. For example, a call to **Retrieve** might be

```
s = ref.Retrieve( "http://www.amazon.com", 2, "", "", "" )
```

which uses the **GET** request (**2**) to retrieve **Amazon.com**'s home page and store it in **s**. This function does not contain any optional arguments—unused arguments (such as **PostData**, **UserName** and **Password**) are passed as empty strings (**""**).

To get the book price from a Web site, the user fills out and submits a form containing book information (e.g., ISBN number, etc.). The **lowest.asp** document simulates this form submission (i.e., as if the user had visited the site and requested the book). In order to place the URLs in the database, we viewed the HTML source of the documents (on each Web site) before writing the search engine. In particular, we examined the forms in detail. We extracted the form's **ACTION**, request method, input item names, hidden input items and their values. We stored this extracted information in the **Sites** table of the database and stored the form's **ACTION** in the **SearchURL** field. The **ACTION** of the form's URL must be stored as a complete URL (e.g., **http://www.Deitel.com/index.htm**); it cannot be stored as a virtual path (e.g., **index.htm**). The form's request method is stored as a **1** or **2** (**POST** or **GET**) in the **Method** field. We also store the form's input items and hidden-input items in the **PostData** field. This field stores the form's contents as a URL. For example, consider a form that asks for the user's first name and last name. **PostData** contains

```
field1=hidden1=hide&yourFirstName&field2=yourLastName
```

where **field1** and **field2** are the names of the input items, **hidden1** is the name of a hidden input item, **yourFirstName** and **yourLastName** are the user's name and **hide** is the value of **hidden1**. These fields, **SearchURL**, **Method** and **PostData**, are used as the first 3 parameters in calls to function **Retrieve**.

Form submission through the browser's address bar is permitted for most Web sites. That is, if you append a form's **ACTION** and contents to the URL (e.g., **http://www.Deitel.com/searchit.asp?param=value**) and type it in the browser's **Address** bar and press *Enter*, the results are the same as if you actually filled out and submitted the form. However, some Web sites do not allow this type of form submission. These sites require form contents be sent inside the request using HTTP **POST**.

Function **GetPrice** (line 214) retrieves the price of the selected book from the corresponding Web site. Line 217 instantiates an ASPTear object and assigns it to reference **aspTear**. Note that a call to function **Retrieve** may not be successful (i.e., the Web site may be down). If a call fails, a non-zero error code is returned and stored in the *error object*'s (**Err**) *Number* property. The **Err** object is provided by VBScript to store information about errors. The **While** loop in lines 224 through 229 makes at most three attempts to call function **Retrieve** and assigns the returned page to string **s**. Property **Number** contains a zero value if no errors occurred and a non-zero value otherwise. The **If** statement in line 231 checks the error status after the call(s) to function **Retrieve**. If an error was raised, the return value of **GetPrice** is set to "**Failed**" and variable **ok** is set to **False**. If **Err.Number** is zero, the Web page was successfully grabbed and stored in **s**. Line 238 splits **s** on the **$** character and stores the result in **b**. If the **$** character was not found, we assume that the page does not contain a book price and set the return value of **GetPrice** to "**N/A**." Variable **ok** is set to **False**. However, if the **$** character was found, the price is stored in **b**. Some Web sites may display more than one price. For example, a Web site might display

Retail: $68.00 New: $59.85 Wholesale $50.00 Used: $53.05

We search the page's HTML for the price label to avoid extracting the wrong price. The **For** loop in lines 248 through 252 searches for the label in **b**. The **If** statement in line 255 checks if the label was found. If the label was not found, the return value of **GetPrice** is set to "**Failed**" and variable **ok** is set to **False**. If the label was found, line 262 assigns **s** to the price string. Lines 266 through 280 remove any extraneous characters from the string.

The **If** statement in line 286 tests **s** against a string pattern. This pattern is a price pattern (e.g., **50.00**). If **s** matches the pattern, the price is returned. Otherwise, lines 290 and 291 indicate failure.

Procedure **Insert** (line 298) is passed either the price found, "**N/A**" or "**Failed**." Procedure **Insert** assigns values to **Price** and **Display** at the current position in the array **a**. Remember, **a** stores the search results. Line 305 converts **s** to a currency string and assigns the result to **Price**. Line 306 gets the book URL by calling the function **GetURL**. The hyperlink to the book's page is constructed in lines 305 through 307 and line 323.

Function **GetURL** (line 332) returns either the URL of the search script or the direct link. As explained earlier, if the **DirectBookLink** field is **False**, the site allows form submission through hyperlinks and we can thus use a search script. The **If** statement in line 338 tests if **DirectBookLink** is **False**. If it is, the return value of **GetURL** is set to the **SearchURL** plus the **PostData** fields. The **Else** block in line 340 is executed if a direct link to the page on the site is needed. Lines 358 and 359 build the direct link by concatenating the **LeftSubURL**, the book's **ISBN** and the **RightSubURL**.

26.6 Internet and World Wide Web Resources

www.alphasierrapapa.com/ComponentCenter/AspTear/
ASPTear component home page.

msdn.microsoft.com/library/psdk/iisref/iiapsess.htm
Contains information about the **Session** object and cookies.

msdn.microsoft.com/scripting/default.htm?/scripting/vbscript/doc/
vsmthExecute.htm
Contains information on the **Execute** method and regular expressions.

SUMMARY

- Three-tiered Web applications commonly use HTML on the client, ASP in the middle tier and a database for the third tier.
- Perhaps the most common e-Business model is the shopping cart. This technology allows customers to store a list of items that they are considering purchasing. With the click of a button, the customer can add and remove items.
- The **Cookies** collection is used to read and write cookies. Each collection member is a cookie.
- The **Cookies** collection **Count** property contains the number of cookie items in a cookie.
- The **Cookies** collection's **Expires** property sets a cookie's expiration date.
- In an online auction site, users auction items as well as bid on items.

- Comparison-pricing search engines poll Web merchants to find the lowest price for a product or service.
- Attaching a parameter to a URL is the same as an HTTP **GET** request.
- ASPTear from SoftWing grabs Web pages. This component has one method—**Retrieve**—which returns a string containing the grabbed HTML document. If the requested page redirects the user to another page, function **Retrieve** returns the redirected page.
- The **Err** object is provided by VBScript to store information about errors. Property **Number** stores a numeric value that identifies the error.
- Form submission through the browser's address bar is permitted for most Web sites. However, some Web sites do not allow this type of form submission. These sites require form contents be sent inside the request using HTTP **POST**.

TERMINOLOGY

ASPTear component
bubble sort
comparison pricing search engine
Cookies collection
Cookies.Count property
Cookies.Expires property
Cookies that store many values
Count property
Date method
document object
Execute method
Err object
Err object **Number** property
hidden input item

ISBN number
Nothing
online auction site
parameter passing in URLs
Pattern property
pipe character (|)
primary key field
RegExp class
relational record
session variable
shopping cart
Split method
SQL query
Test method

SELF-REVIEW EXERCISES

26.1   (True/False) A cookie stores exactly one values.

26.2   (True/False) A cookie's expiration date must be set each time the cookie is written.

26.3   (True/False) The **Execute** method can be used to retrieve information from a database.

26.4   Which of the following could have been used instead of the hidden input items to provide the **Back to Shopping** link in **viewcart.asp**?
   a) Session variables
   b) Cookies
   c) Parameter passing through URLs
   d) All of the above

26.5   (True/False) ASPTear function **Retrieve**'s **UserName** and **Password** parameters are optional.

ANSWERS TO SELF-REVIEW EXERCISES

26.1   False. A cookie can store multiple values.
26.2   True.
26.3   False. The **Execute** method is used to update or insert data into the database.
26.4   d) All of the above.
26.5   False. Function **Retrieve** requires all parameters be passed.

EXERCISES

26.6   Modify the shopping cart (Section 26.3) to include a feature that allows a user to update their cart. Modify **viewcart.asp** (Fig. 26.7) to allow users to edit an item's quantity. Use the value zero to indicate the removal of an item (i.e., set the quantity to zero). Write a document named **updatecart.asp** that updates the quantities stored in the cookie. After the quantities have been updated, the user is redirected to **viewcart.asp**. Also modify **viewcart.asp** to provide an **Update Cart** button that, when clicked, redirects the user to **updatecart.asp**.

26.7   Modify the online auction site (Section 26.4) to include a feature that allows users to sell items. Write a document named **sell.asp** that allows users to auction items. The user enters an item's information (e.g., price, description, etc.) in a form and submits it. Post the contents to **dosell.asp**, which inserts the information into the **AuctionItems** table of the **DeitelAuctions.mdb** database and redirects the user to **bookitems.asp**. Write **dosell.asp**.

   Next, modify the auction site to ensure that users are logged in before allowing them to sell an item. Modify **index.asp** (Fig. 26.12), **login.asp** (Fig. 26.21) and **checklogin.asp** (Fig. 26.22) as follows: If a user is not logged in when the **Sell an Item** link is clicked, redirect the user to **login.asp**. Once the user has successfully logged in, redirect the user to **sell.asp**.

   Next, modify the auction site to provide a logout feature. Modify **index.asp** (Fig. 26.12) and **confirmbid.html** (Fig. 26.26) to provide **Logout** links that request document **logout.asp**, which abandons the current session and redirects the user to **index.asp**. Write **logout.asp**.

   Now, modify **badlogin.asp** (Fig. 26.23), **newmember.asp** (Fig. 26.13) and **taken.asp** (Fig. 26.16) to only provide the **Back to Item Description** link if the user attempted to bid on an item before logging in.

26.8   Modify **itemdata.asp** (Fig. 26.19) to prevent seller from bidding on their items. If a seller attempts to do this, redirect them to **cannotbid.html**, which displays an alert message. Write **cannotbid.html**.

26.9   Write an Active Server Page (**partscookie.asp**) that displays two forms. The first contains one text box input, two drop-down lists and a submit button **Add to Cookie**. The user enters a number in the text box and selects a color (**Red**, **Green** or **Blue**) and size (**Small**, **Medium** or **Large**) from the drop-down lists. When the form is submitted, the ASP requests itself and **POST**s the form contents. The ASP then stores the number, color and size in a cookie named **Parts**. This cookie can contain multiple values. That is, the user can fill out the first form and submit it multiple times. Each time the form is submitted, a value is added to the **Parts** cookie. The second form contains a submit button **Display Cookie**. When the form is submitted, the ASP requests itself and passes a parameter (**Display**). The ASP displays, if parameter **Display** is **true**, all the cookie contents in a table.

26.10   Write an Active Server Page (**temperature.asp**) that displays the temperature for a specified ZIP code (i.e., a 5-digit number that uniquely identifies a region in the United States). The user enters a ZIP code in a form. When the form is submitted, the ASP requests itself and passes a parameter (**entry**). Use the ASPTear component to grab a Web page containing the current temperature at that ZIP code from **www.weather.com**. If the user enters an invalid ZIP code, display an error message (i.e., **The ZIP code you entered was not found**). If the temperature is not available, display **No Report**. Test the ASP with the following ZIP codes: Beverly Hills (90210), Boston (01776), Chicago (60606), Dallas (75205), Los Angeles (91108), Nashville (37235) and New York (10160).

27

XML (Extensible Markup Language)

Objectives

- To understand what XML is.
- To understand the relationship between HTML and XML.
- To understand how to create new markup tags.
- To be able to parse XML tags on a Web client.
- To understand the relationship between a DTD and an XML document.
- To understand the concept of schema.
- To be able to create style sheets using XSL.
- To understand the role of XHTML in Web publishing.

It is the huge buildings of commerce and trade which now align the people to attention.
Sean O'Casey

If you describe things as better than they are, you are considered to be romantic; if you describe things as worse than they are, you will be called a realist; and if you describe things exactly as they are, you will be thought of as a satirist.
Quentin Crisp

Like everything metaphysical, the harmony between thought and reality is to be found in the grammar of the language.
Ludwig Wittgenstein

Oh! what a snug little Island, A right little, tight little Island!
Thomas Dibdin

27.1 Introduction[1]

XML (*Extensible Markup Language*) was developed in 1996 by the *World Wide Web Consortium's (W3C's) XML Working Group* and—like HTML—is related to *Standard Generalized Markup Language (SGML)*. XML is a widely-supported, *open technology* (i.e., nonproprietary technology) for data exchange.

Although XML and HTML are both subsets of SGML (Fig. 27.1), XML provides distinct advantages over HTML. HTML is a markup language for describing how content is rendered. XML is a markup language for describing structured data—content is separated from presentation. Because an XML document contains only data, applications decide how to display the data. For example, a PDA (personal digital assistant) may render data differently than a cellular phone or desktop computer.

Unlike HTML, XML permits document authors to create their own markup for virtually any type of information. This extensibility enables document authors to create entirely new markup languages to describe specific types of data, including mathematical formulas, chemical molecular structures, music, recipes, etc. Some of the markup languages created with XML include MathML (for mathematics), VoiceXML™ (for speech), SMIL™ (the Synchronous Multimedia Interface Language—for multimedia presentations), CML (for chemistry) and XBRL (Extensible Business Reporting Language—for financial data exchange).

Because XML tags describe the data they contain, it is possible to search, sort, manipulate and render an XML document using related technologies, such as the *Extensible Stylesheet Language (XSL)*—which we discuss in detail later in the chapter.

XML documents are highly portable. Special software is not required to open an XML document—any text editor that supports ASCII/Unicode characters can be used. One important characteristic of XML is that it is both human readable and machine readable.

---

1. Deitel & Associates, Inc. is currently writing *XML How to Program*. We will be publishing historical and technical information about XML on our Web site (**www.deitel.com**).

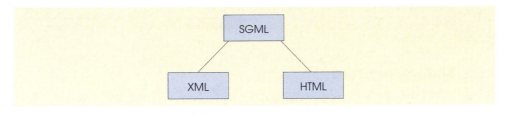

Fig. 27.1   Relationship between SGML, HTML and XML.

 Portability Tip 27.1

XML is defined by the World Wide Web Consortium (W3C) to be application and vendor neutral—which ensures maximum portability. [Deitel & Associates, Inc. is a W3C member.]

In order to process an XML document—which ends in the **.xml** extension—a software program called an *XML parser* (or an *XML processor*) is required. Most XML parsers are available at no charge and are available for a variety of programming languages (such as Java™, Python, C, etc.). Parsers check an XML document's syntax and can support the *Document Object Model (DOM)* and/or the *Simple API for XML (SAX)*. DOM-based parsers build a tree structure containing the XML document's data in memory. This allows the data to be programmatically manipulated. SAX-based parsers process the document and generate events when tags, text, comments, etc. are encountered. These events return data from the XML document. Several Independent Software Vendors (ISVs) have developed XML parsers, which can be found at **www.xml.com/xml/pub/Guide/ XML_Parsers**.

In this chapter, we use Internet Explorer 5's built-in DOM-based XML parser, **msxml**, to process XML documents.

An XML document can reference an optional *Document Type Definition (DTD)* file, which defines how the XML document is structured. When a DTD is provided, some parsers (called *validating* parsers) are able to read the DTD and check the XML document structure against it. If the XML document conforms to the DTD, then the XML document is *valid*. Parsers that cannot check for document conformity ignore the DTD and are called *non-validating* parsers. We discuss DTDs in more detail in Section 27.3.

If an XML parser is able to successfully process an XML document (that does not have a DTD), the XML document is considered *well formed* (i.e., it is syntactically correct). By definition, a valid XML document is also a well-formed XML document. Figure 27.2 shows a simple relationship between XML documents, DTDs, parsers and applications (i.e., programs such as IE5 that use XML).

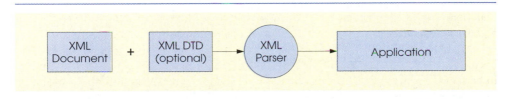

Fig. 27.2   XML documents and their corresponding DTDs are parsed and sent to an application.

Software Engineering Observation 27.1

To be usable by an application, an XML document must, as a minimum, be well formed.

27.2 Structuring Data

In this section and throughout this chapter, we will create our own XML markup. With XML, element types can be declared to describe data. This allows programmers an incredible amount of flexibility in using their own tags when describing different types of data. Tags delimit the beginning and end of each element.

Common Programming Error 27.1

XML is case sensitive. Using the wrong case for an XML tag is a syntax error.

Common Programming Error 27.2

In an XML document, the marked-up data must consist of a starting tag and a matching end tag.

Common Programming Error 27.3

*Unlike in HTML, attributes must have their value enclosed in double quotes (**""**) or single quotes (**' '**).*

In Fig. 27.3, we mark up a simple news article using XML tags the same way we would use HTML tags. We begin with the optional *XML declaration* on line 1. Attribute **version** indicates the XML version to which the document conforms. The current XML standard is version **1.0**. New versions of XML will be released by the World Wide Web Consortium as XML evolves to meet the requirements of many fields, especially e-commerce.

Good Programming Practice 27.1

An XML document should include a XML declaration.

```
1   <?xml version = "1.0"?>
2
3   <!-- Fig. 27.3: article.xml      -->
4   <!-- Article structured with XML -->
5
6   <article>
7
8      <title>Simple XML</title>
9
10     <date>September 6, 2000</date>
11
12     <author>
13        <FirstName>Tem</FirstName>
14        <LastName>Nieto</LastName>
15     </author>
16
```

Fig. 27.3   An article formatted with XML (part 1 of 2).

```
17        <summary>XML is pretty easy.</summary>
18
19        <content>Once you have mastered HTML, XML is easily
20           learned. You must remember that XML is not for
21           displaying information but for managing information.
22        </content>
23
24    </article>
```

Fig. 27.3   An article formatted with XML (part 2 of 2).

Comments (lines 3 and 4) in XML use the same syntax as HTML. Every XML document must contain exactly one element (called a *root element*) that contains every other element. In Fig. 27.3, **article** (line 6) is the root element. Lines preceding the root element are collectively called the *prolog*. XML element and attribute names can be of any length and may contain letters, digits, underscores, hyphens and periods. However, they must begin with either a letter or an underscore.

Common Programming Error 27.4

Using either a space or a tab in an XML element or attribute name is an error.

Good Programming Practice 27.2

XML elements and attributes should be meaningful and human readable. For example, use **<address>** *instead of* **<adr>**.

Common Programming Error 27.5

Attempting to create more than one root element is an error.

Element **title** (line 8) contains text that describes the article's title. Similarly, **date** (line 10), **summary** (line 17) and **content** (line 19) each contain text that describes the date, summary and content, respectively.

Any element (such as **article** and **author**) that contains other elements is called a *container element*. Elements inside a container element are collectively called *children*.

Common Programming Error 27.6

Overlapping XML tags is a syntax error. For example, **<x><y>hello</x><y>** *is illegal.*

XML is a technology for structuring data. Unlike HTML, an XML document does not contain any formatting information. When an XML document is loaded into IE5, it is parsed by IE5's parser **msxml** and displayed. Figure 27.4 shows **article.xml** (Fig. 27.3) displayed in IE5. Notice that what is displayed by IE5 is virtually identical to Fig. 27.3—because, again, an XML document does not contain formatting information. We will discuss how the data in an XML document can be formatted later in the chapter when we study the Extensible Stylesheet Language (XSL).

Notice the minus sign (**-**) and plus sign (**+**) in Fig. 27.4. These are not part of the XML document, but are placed there by IE5 next to all container elements. A minus sign indicates that all child elements arc being displayed. When clicked, a minus sign becomes a plus sign (which collapses the container element and hides all children) and vice versa. This behavior is similar to viewing the directory structure of your machine using Windows Explorer. In fact, a directory structure is often modelled as a series of tree structures with each drive letter (e.g., **C:**, etc.) representing the *root* of a tree. Each folder (that contains at least one folder inside it) is a *node* in the tree. XML documents (when they are parsed by a DOM-based parser) have their data placed into a tree structure. We will discuss in detail in Section 27.6 how to retrieve data items from a parsed XML document using the Document Object Model (DOM).

Now that we have seen a simple XML document, let us examine a slightly more complex XML document that marks up a business letter (Fig. 27.5).

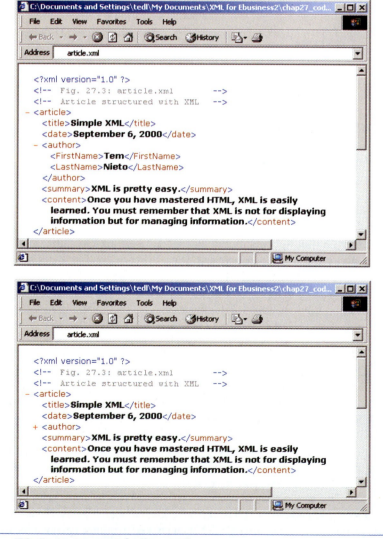

Fig. 27.4   IE5 displaying **article.xml**.

As with the previous example, we begin the document's definition with the **xml** declaration on line 1. This explicitly states the XML version to which the document conforms. Line 6

```
<!DOCTYPE letter SYSTEM "letter.dtd">
```

specifies that this XML document has a *document type definition (DTD)* file associated with it. DTD files define the grammatical rules for an XML document and are optional. E-commerce applications frequently use DTDs to ensure that XML documents are structured properly. This markup contains three items: the name of the root element (**letter**) to which the DTD is applied, the keyword **SYSTEM** (which in this case denotes an *external DTD*—a DTD declared in a separate file), and the DTD's name and location (i.e., **letter.dtd** in the current directory). DTD documents end with the **.dtd** extension. We discuss DTD files and **letter.dtd** in detail in the next section..

```
1   <?xml version = "1.0"?>
2
3   <!-- Fig. 27.5: letter.xml              -->
4   <!-- Business letter formatted with XML  -->
5
6   <!DOCTYPE letter SYSTEM "letter.dtd">
7
8   <letter>
9
10     <contact type = "from">
11        <name>      John Doe</name>
12        <address1>123 Main St.</address1>
13        <address2></address2>
14        <city>Anytown</city>
15        <state>Anystate</state>
16        <zip>12345</zip>
17        <phone>555-1234</phone>
18        <flag gender = "M"/>
19     </contact>
20
21     <contact type = "to">
22        <name>Joe Schmoe</name>
23        <address1>Box 12345</address1>
24        <address2>15 Any Ave.</address2>
25        <city>Othertown</city>
26        <state>Otherstate</state>
27        <zip>67890</zip>
28        <phone>555-4321</phone>
29        <flag gender = "M"/>
30     </contact>
31
32     <salutation>Dear Sir:</salutation>
33
34     <paragraph>It is our privilege to inform you about our new
35        database managed with XML. This new system allows
36        you to reduce the load of your inventory list server by
```

Fig. 27.5　A business letter marked up as XML (part 1 of 2).

```
37          having the client machine perform the work of sorting
38          and filtering the data.</paragraph>
39      <closing>Sincerely</closing>
40      <signature>Mr. Doe</signature>
41
42   </letter>
```

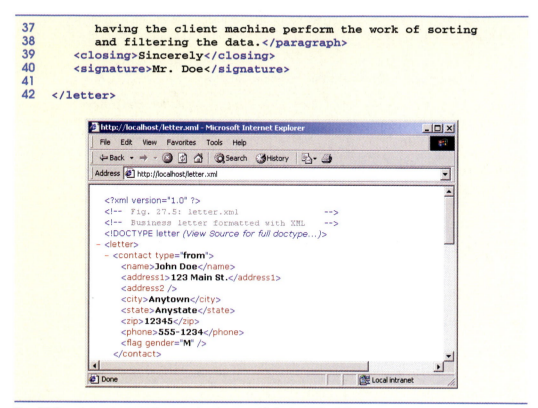

Fig. 27.5   A business letter marked up as XML (part 2 of 2).

Root element **letter** contains the child elements **contact**, **paragraph**, **salutation**, **closing** and **signature**. The first **contact** element (line 10) has attribute **type** which is assigned the value **from** (which identifies the letter's sender). The second **contact** element (line 21) has attribute **type** which is assigned value **to** (which identifies the letter's recipient). In a **contact** element, the contact's name, address and phone number are stored. Element **salutation** (line 32) marks up the letter's salutation. The letter's body is marked up with a **paragraph** element. Elements **closing** (line 39) and **signature** (line 40) mark up the closing sentence and the signature of the letter's author, respectively.

Notice that on line 18, we introduce *empty element* **flag**—which does not mark up any text. In previous chapters, we introduced to the HTML element **IMG**. Empty element **flag** indicates the gender of the contact. This allows us to correctly address the recipient as Mr. (if **gender** is **"M"**) or Ms. (if **gender** is **"F"**). Empty elements must be closed, either by placing a slash at the end of the element (as shown on line 18) or by explicitly writing a closing tag as in

```
<flag gender = "F"></flag>
```

Common Programming Error 27.7

Not terminating an empty element with a closing tag or a forward slash (/) is an error.

Common Programming Error 27.8

Omitting quotes (either single or double) around an XML attribute's value is an error.

XML treats consecutive white space, tabs and blank lines as a single space. Notice that, in the screen capture, **John Doe** is preceded by exactly one space. In order to preserve white space characters, use XML attribute ***xml:space*** and assign it the value ***preserve***. For example,

```
<myCProgram xml:space = "preserve">
            if ( x <= 0 )
                    x = 5;
</myCprogram>
```

uses attribute **xml:space** in element **myCProgram** to preserve the spaces used for indenting the C++ code. You may have noticed that five space characters precede the **name** element's data on line 11.

27.3 Document Type Definitions (DTD)

In Fig. 27.5, we presented a simple business letter marked up with XML. The business letter's list of element types, attributes and their relationships to each other are specified using a document type definition (DTD). Although a DTD is optional, it is recommended for document conformity. DTDs provide a method for type checking an XML document, thus verifying its *validity* (e.g., tags contain the proper attributes, elements are in proper sequence, etc.). The set of rules that structure a document is done with *EBNF* (*Extended Backus-Naur Form*) *grammar*—not XML syntax. XML processors need additional functionality to read a DTD because of the EBNF grammar. We define, in Fig. 27.6, the set of rules (i.e., the grammar) for structuring the business letter document of Fig. 27.5. This DTD file is the one referenced on line 6 of Fig. 27.5.

Software Engineering Observation 27.2

DTDs are inherited from SGML and are gradually being replaced by schema (see Section 27.8).

```
1    <!-- Fig 27.6: letter.dtd         -->
2    <!-- DTD document for letter.xml -->
3
4    <!ELEMENT letter (contact+, salutation, paragraph+,
5                         closing, signature )>
6
7    <!ELEMENT contact (name, address1, address2, city, state,
8                         zip, phone, flag)>
9    <!ATTLIST contact type CDATA #IMPLIED>
10
11   <!ELEMENT name (#PCDATA)>
12   <!ELEMENT address1 (#PCDATA)>
13   <!ELEMENT address2 (#PCDATA)>
14   <!ELEMENT city (#PCDATA)>
```

Fig. 27.6 Business letter DTD (part 1 of 2).

```
15   <!ELEMENT state (#PCDATA)>
16   <!ELEMENT zip (#PCDATA)>
17   <!ELEMENT phone (#PCDATA)>
18   <!ELEMENT flag EMPTY>
19   <!ATTLIST flag gender (M | F) "M">
20
21   <!ELEMENT salutation (#PCDATA)>
22   <!ELEMENT closing (#PCDATA)>
23   <!ELEMENT paragraph (#PCDATA)>
24   <!ELEMENT signature (#PCDATA)>
```

Fig. 27.6   Business letter DTD (part 2 of 2).

Line 4's *!ELEMENT* *element type declaration* defines the rules for element **letter**. In this case, **letter** contains one or more **contact** elements, one **salutation** element, one or more **paragraph** elements, one **closing** element and one **signature** element, in that sequence. The *plus sign (+) operator* indicates one or more occurrences for an element. Other operators include the *asterisk (*)*, which indicates any number of occurrences and the *question mark (?)*, which indicates either zero occurrences or exactly one occurrence. If an operator is omitted, exactly one occurrence is assumed.

The **contact** element definition in line 7 specifies that it contains the **name**, **address1**, **address2**, **city**, **state**, **zip**, **phone** and **flag** elements—in that order. Exactly one occurrence of each is expected.

Line 6

```
<!ATTLIST contact type CDATA #IMPLIED>
```

uses the *!ATTLIST* element type declaration to define an attribute (i.e., **type**) for the **contact** element. Keyword *#IMPLIED* specifies that if the parser finds a **contact** element without a **type** attribute, it is allowed to choose its own value or ignore it. So the XML document is still valid if a **contact** element does not have a **type** attribute. Other types of default values include *#REQUIRED* and *#FIXED*. Keyword *#REQUIRED* specifies that the attribute must be declared in the document, and the keyword *#FIXED* specifies that the attribute must be declared with the given fixed value. If it is not declared, then the parser, by default, uses the fixed value that is specified with the declaration. For example,

```
<!ATTLIST address zip #FIXED "02115">
```

indicates that the value **02115** is always used for attribute **zip**. Flag *CDATA* specifies that **type** attribute contains a string that will not be processed by the parser and is passed to the application as is.

Software Engineering Observation 27.3

DTD syntax does not provide any mechanism for describing an element's (or attribute's) data type.

Flag *#PCDATA* (line 11) specifies that the element can store *parsed character data* (i.e., text). Parsable character data should not contain markup. The characters less than (**<**), greater than (**>**) and ampersand (**&**) should be replaced by their entities (i.e., **<**, **>** and **&**). However, the ampersand (**&**) character can be inserted when used with entities.

Line 18

```
<!ELEMENT flag EMPTY>
```

creates an empty element named **flag**. Keyword **EMPTY** specifies that the element does not contain any text. Empty elements are commonly used for their attributes.

Portability Tip 27.2

DTDs ensure that XML documents created by different programs are consistent.

Common Programming Error 27.9

Any element, attribute, tag or relationship not explicitly defined by a DTD is an error.

27.4 Customized Markup Languages

XML allows authors to create their own tags to precisely describe data. Consequently, many different kinds of XML have been created for structuring data in various fields. Some of these markup languages are: *MathML (Mathematical Markup Language), Scalable Vector Graphics (SVG), Wireless Markup Language (WML), Extensible Business Reporting Language (XBRL), Extensible User Interface Language (XUL)* and *Product Data Markup Language (PDML)*. The following subsections describe MathML, XBRL and other custom markup languages.

27.4.1 MathML

Until recently, mathematical expressions have typically been displayed using images or specialized software packages such as TeX and LaTeX. This section introduces MathML, which was developed by the W3C for describing mathematical notations and expressions. One application that can parse and render MathML is the W3C's *Amaya*™ browser, which can be downloaded at no charge from

```
www.w3.org/Amaya/User/BinDist.html
```

This Web page contains several download links for Windows 95/98/NT, Linux® and Solaris™. Amaya documentation and installation notes are also available at the W3C Web site. Amaya is also an HTML/XML editor.

We now take a calculus expression and mark it up as MathML. Figure 27.7 marks up the expression which contains an integral symbol and a square-root symbol. We embed the MathML content directly into an HTML file by using the HTML **MATH** *element* (line 9).

```
1   <!DOCTYPE HTML PUBLIC "-//W3C//DTD HTML 4.0 Transitional//EN">
2   <HTML>
3
4   <!-- Fig. 27.7 mathml.html          -->
5   <!-- Calculus example using MathML -->
6
7   <BODY>
```

Fig. 27.7   A calculus expression marked up with MathML. (part 1 of 2)

```
8
9    <MATH>
10      <mrow>
11         <msubsup>
12            <mo>&Integral;</mo>
13            <mn>0</mn>
14            <mrow>
15               <mn>1</mn>
16               <mo>-</mo>
17               <mi>y</mi>
18            </mrow>
19         </msubsup>
20
21         <msqrt>
22            <mrow>
23               <mn>4</mn>
24               <mo>&InvisibleTimes;</mo>
25               <msup>
26                  <mi>x</mi>
27                  <mn>2</mn>
28               </msup>
29               <mo>+</mo>
30               <mi>y</mi>
31            </mrow>
32         </msqrt>
33
34         <mo>&delta;</mo>
35         <mi>x</mi>
36      </mrow>
37   </MATH>
38   </BODY>
39   </HTML>
```

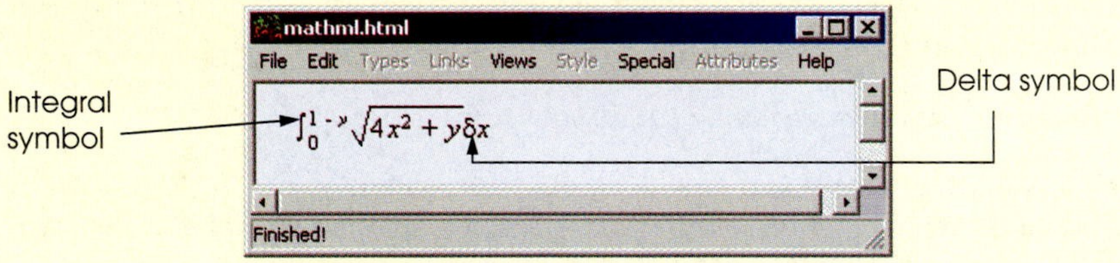

Integral symbol →

Delta symbol

mathml.html

File Edit Types Links Views Style Special Attributes Help

$\int_0^{1-y} \sqrt{4x^2 + y}\,\delta x$

Finished!

Fig. 27.7   A calculus expression marked up with MathML. (part 2 of 2)

Element **mrow** (line 10) is a container element. It allows the document's author to properly group together related elements. In this case we use **mrow** to group our calculus expression.

The integral symbol is represented by the entity **∫** (line 12), while the superscript and subscript markup is specified using **msubsup** (line 11). We use tag **<mo>** to mark up the integral operator. Element **msubsup** requires three child elements: The expression (e.g., the integral entity) to which the subscript and superscript are applied (line 12), the subscript expression (line 13) and the superscript expression (lines 14 through 18), respectively. Element **msqrt** represents a square root expression. We use element **mrow** (line 22) to group the expression contained in the square root.

Element **mn** (line 13) marks up the number (i.e., 0) that represents the subscript. Element **mrow** marks up the expression (i.e., **1-y**) that specifies the superscript expression used by **msubsup**. To mark up variables in MathML, element **mi** (line 17) is used. Collectively, the three child elements within **mrow** define the expression **1-y**.

Line 24 uses entity **⁢** to specify a multiplication operation without a *symbolic representation* (i.e., a multiplication symbol is not displayed between the **4** and the **x²**). Element **msup** (line 15) marks up an expression containing a base and an exponent. This element contains two child elements: The base and the exponent (i.e., the superscript). Because each argument contains exactly one element, additional **mrow** elements are not needed. Although not used in this example, MathML does provide element **msub** for marking up an expression that contains a subscript.

Line 34 introduces the entity **δ** for representing a delta symbol. Because it is an operator, it is marked up using element **mo**. To see other operations and symbols provided by MathML, visit **www.w3.org/Math**.

27.4.2 WML

The *Wireless Markup Language* (*WML*) is an XML-based language that allows text portions of Web pages to be displayed on wireless devices, such as cellular phones and personal digital assistants (PDA). WML works with the *Wireless Application Protocol* (*WAP*) to deliver this content. WML is similar to HTML but does not require input devices such as a keyboard or mouse for navigation.

Consider a PDA that requests a Web page on the Internet. A WAP gateway receives the request, translates it, and sends it to the appropriate Internet server. The server responds by sending the requested WML document. The WAP gateway parses this document's WML and sends the proper text to the PDA. For additional information on WML and WAP, visit **www.wapforum.org** or **www.xml.com/pub/Guide/WML**.

27.4.3 XBRL

XBRL (Extensible Business Reporting Language)—previously called *XFRML*—is a markup language derived from XML for facilitating the creation, exchange and validation of financial information (e.g., annual budgets, dividends, etc.) between vendors and corporations. XBRL was developed by the *American Institute of Certified Public Accountants (AICPA)* and other organizations. It conforms to the general principles of US *GAAP* (*General American Accounting Principles*) and complies to standards set by various committees such as *IASC (International Association for Statistical Computing)*. It sets no new standards in financial reporting; instead, it improves their usage and the efficiency of accessing information. XBRL is designed to be compatible with future changes in financial reporting standards.

Figure 27.8 is a financial statement marked up as XBRL for a fictitious company named ExComp. An XBRL document contains three elements: ***group***, ***item*** and ***label***. A **group** element groups **item**, **label** and other **group** elements. XBRL documents usually have **group** as the root element. An **item** element represents a single statement. Element **label** provides a caption for **group** and **item** elements.

```
1   <?xml version = "1.0" encoding = "utf-8"?>
2   <!DOCTYPE group SYSTEM "xbrl-core-00-04-04.dtd">
3
4   <!-- Fig. 27.8:financialHighlights.xml -->
5   <!-- XBRL example                        -->
6
7   <group
8       xmlns = "http://www.xbrl.org/us/aicpa-us-gaap-ci-00-04-04"
9       xmlns:ExComp = "http://www.example-ExComp.org/fHighlights.xml"
10      id = "XXXXXX-X-X-X"
11      entity = "NASDAQ:EXCOMP"
12      period = "2000-12-31"
13      scaleFactor = "3"
14      precision = "3"
15      type = "ExComp:statement.financialHighlights"
16      unit = "ISO4217:USD"
17      decimalPattern = "#,###.###">
18
19      <group id = "1" type = "ExComp:financialHighlights.introduction">
20          <item type = "ExComp:statement.declaration"
21                period = "2000-12-31">
22          ExComp has adopted all standard procedures for accounting.
23          This statement gives a financial highlight summary for the
24          last 4 years.
25          It also gives an account of percentage change in profit for
26          each year, which is useful in measuring the company's
27          performance.
28          </item>
29      </group>
30
31      <group id = "2" type = "ExComp:financialHighlights.statistics">
32          <group id = "21" type = "ExComp:sales.revenue">
33              <item period = "P1Y/2000-12-30">2961.5</item>
34              <item period = "P1Y/1999-12-30">3294.97</item>
35              <item period = "P1Y/1998-12-30">3593.78</item>
36              <item period = "P1Y/1997-12-30">4301.55</item>
37          </group>
38
39          <group id = "22" type = "ExComp:cost.production">
40              <item period = "P1Y/2000-12-30">1834.126</item>
41              <item period = "P1Y/1999-12-30">1923.226</item>
42              <item period = "P1Y/1998-12-30">2872.10</item>
43              <item period = "P1Y/1997-12-30">3101.11</item>
44          </group>
45
46          <group id = "23"
47                  type = "ExComp:cost.transportAndMaintenance">
48              <item period = "P1Y/2000-12-30">134.07</item>
49              <item period = "P1Y/1999-12-30">334.47</item>
50              <item period = "P1Y/1998-12-30">821.59</item>
51              <item period = "P1Y/1997-12-30">1007.12</item>
52          </group>
53
```

Fig. 27.8   XBRL example that marks up a company's financial highlights (part 1 of 2).

```
54            <group id = "24" type = "ExComp:net.profit">
55               <item period = "P1Y/2000-12-30">1335.5</item>
56               <item period = "P1Y/1999-12-30">1135.52</item>
57               <item period = "P1Y/1998-12-30">1142.03</item>
58               <item period = "P1Y/1997-12-30">1312.62</item>
59            </group>
60
61            <group id = "25" type = "ExComp:percentageChange.profit">
62               <item period = "P1Y/2000-12-30">18.35</item>
63               <item period = "P1Y/1999-12-30">11.11</item>
64               <item period = "P1Y/1998-12-30">10.25</item>
65               <item period = "P1Y/1997-12-30">24.98</item>
66            </group>
67
68            <!-- Labels -->
69            <label href = "#21">Revenue</label>
70            <label href = "#22">Production cost</label>
71            <label href = "#23">Transport and Maintenance</label>
72            <label href = "#24">Profit</label>
73            <label href = "#25">Percentage Change in profit</label>
74
75         </group>
76
77      </group>
```

Fig. 27.8   XBRL example that marks up a company's financial highlights (part 2 of 2).

Line 2 in Fig. 27.8 is the **DOCTYPE** declaration that specifies the DTD used by XBRL documents (i.e., **xbrl-core-00-04-04.dtd**). Line 7's root element (**group**) contains six other **group** elements and five **label** elements that describe the financial statement. Root element **group** specifies a set of attributes (or properties) that apply to all its child elements. If a child **group** element specifies an attribute that is the same as the parent's attribute, the child's attribute overrides the parent's attribute for the child element. Line 8

```
xmlns = "http://www.xbrl.org/us/aicpa-us-gaap-ci-00-04-04"
```

declares a *namespace* for XBRL elements using the attribute **xmlns**.

Common Programming Error 27.10

xmlns is a reserved attribute name. Redefining it is an error.

Because document authors are likely to create XML elements with the same name, XML provides namespaces to help minimize conflicts. Like elements, the document author defines namespaces. For example,

```
<subject>English</subject>
```

and

```
<subject>Thrombosis</subject>
```

can be differentiated by using namespaces, as in

```
<school:subject>English</school:subject>
<medical:subject>Thrombosis</medical:subject>
```

where **school** and **medical** are the *namespace prefixes*. A namespace declared for an element applies to all its child elements unless declared separately. Two predefined XML namespaces are **xml** and **xsl**, which are used in XML and XSL documents (Section 27.7), respectively. Namespaces are identified by *URIs (Uniform Resource Identifiers)* to ensure that namespaces are unique. An URI is an identifier that points to a resource. A resource can be anything that has an identity, such as a document, an image, a library, a service, etc. Because domain names are guaranteed to be unique, many document authors use their domain name for the namespace. In our example, the object is a string of characters (line 8). URIs can be further classified as URLs *(Uniform Resource Locators)* and URNs *(Uniform Resource Names)*. An example URL is **www.deitel.com**. URLs do not identify the resource directly. Instead they represent where the resource can be accessed. URLs are more commonly used by software applications. A URN labels each resource with a unique identifier. Even if the resource is unavailable or no longer exists, its URN still exists for it.

Line 9 declares a namespace prefix (**ExComp**) for elements specific to the company ExComp. Attribute **id** (line 10) specifies a unique identity for company. Attribute *entity* identifies *business entities*. For example, **entity** value **URI:www.deitel.com** would indicate that the company owns the URI **www.deitel.com**. Line 11 indicates that ExComp company bears the **NASDAQ** symbol **EXCOMP**. Attribute *period* (line 12) is used to specify the document creation date. Attribute *scalefactor* (line 13) specifies the power of 10 by which a numeric value appearing in the **group** should be multiplied by to arrive at the actual value; a value of **3** indicates thousands. Attribute *precision* (line 14) indicates the numeric precision of measurement that should be used for calculations; a value of **3** indicates an accuracy of three decimal places.

Attribute *type* (line 15) specifies the category of the group. It also differentiates one **group** element from another. Values of **type** attribute use "*parent.child*" naming convention where *parent* represents a category and *child* is its property.

Attribute *unit* (line 16) specifies the unit of currency adopted by the document and attribute *decimalPattern* (line 17) specifies the format for displaying numeric values using pound (**#**) symbols as placeholders.

The root element, **group** (line 7), contains two **group** child elements. The first **group** element (line 19) gives a brief introduction to the financial highlights statement. Its child element, **item** (line 20), contains the actual description. The **period** attribute (line 21) marks up the statement declaration date.

The second **group** element (line 31) contains ExComp's financial statistics (i.e., revenue, cost, profit, etc.), grouped by their respective categories. This **group** element also contains captions for each of the categories using *label elements* (lines 69 through 73). The **id** attribute uniquely identifies a **group** or an **item** element. Lines 31 through 66 declare **group** elements for revenue, cost of production, cost of transportation and maintenance, net profit and percentage change in profit. Each **group** element contains **item** elements that contain values for a period specified by its attribute **period**. The period **P1Y/2000-12-30** indicates a year that ends on December 30, 2000.

The **label** elements (lines 69 through 73) give each **group** element a caption. Their attribute **href** contains a reference to the **group** element which they label. More information about XBRL can be found at **www.xbrl.org**.

27.4.4 ebXML

Electronic Business XML (ebXML) is a markup language initiated by the *United Nations body for Trade Facilitation and Electronic Business (UN/CEFACT)* and *OASIS (Organization for the Advancement of Structured Information Standards)* to develop and standardize an XML document structure for exchanging business data. The goal of ebXML is to reduce the cost of electronic trading for small to medium sized businesses. Visit `www.ebxml.org` for more information.

27.4.5 FpML

Financial Products Markup Language (FpML) is an emerging standard for exchanging financial information over the Internet. Information exchanged includes interest rate swaps (a contractual agreement between two parties), forward rate agreements, etc. It is an easy-to-use and license-free protocol developed by a group of corporate bodies which includes banks, software companies and other financial institutions. The main advantage of adopting FpML is for platform independent data exchange. Visit `www.fpml.org` for more details.

27.4.6 Other Markup Languages

Literally hundreds of markup languages are derived from XML. Everyday developers are finding new uses for XML. In Fig. 27.9, we summarize some of these markup languages.

Markup Language	Description
Chemical Markup Language (CML)	CML was developed by Peter-Murray Rust. It is used by chemists to interchange descriptions of molecules, formulas and other chemical data. CML documents can be parsed and rendered by the Jumbo browser. Visit the CML home page at `www.xml-cml.org`.
VoiceXML™	VoiceXML was developed by the VoiceXML forum founded by AT&T, IBM, Lucent and Motorola. It provides interactive voice communication between humans and computers through a telephone, PDA (Personal Digital Assistant) or desktop computer. VoiceXML documents can be parsed using the VoiceXML SDK developed by IBM. Visit `www.voicexml.org` for more information on VoiceXML.
Synchronous Multimedia Integration Language (SMIL™)	SMIL is used for multimedia presentations. It was primarily developed by the W3C with contributions from other companies. Visit `www.w3.org/AudioVideo` for more on SMIL.
Vector Markup Language (VML)	VML marks up graphics information. It was developed by Microsoft, Hewlett-Packard and other companies and submitted to the W3C as a potential standard. For more information on VML, visit `www.w3.org/TR/NOTE-VML`.
Product Data Markup Language (PDML)	PDML is a markup language developed for product data interchange among businesses and government agencies. For more information on PDML, visit `www.pdml.org`.

Fig. 27.9   Various markup languages derived from XML (part 1 of 2).

Markup Language	Description
Commerce XML (cXML)	cXML is a markup language that provides a protocol for business transactions on the Internet. For more information on cXML, visit **www.cxml.org/home**.
XMI (XML Metadata Interchange)	XMI is used for metadata interchange between modelling applications/tools that are based on UML™ (Unified Modelling Language) and metadata repositories like MOF (Meta Object Facility). XMI is a specification submitted to the OMG™ (Object Management Group) by IBM, Oracle, Unisys and others. Visit **www.omg.org** for more information.
Trading Partner Agreement Markup Language (tpaML)	tpaML is an XML-based markup language developed by IBM that defines an electronic trading partner agreement (TPA) document. A TPA contains information about the organizations involved in the contract, the business protocols (e.g., cXML), etc. For more information on tpaML, visit **www-4.ibm.com/software/developer/library/tpaml.html**.
Small to Medium Business XML (SMBXML)	SMBXML was developed for small to medium sized business transactions. For more information on SMBXML, visit **www.smbxml.org**.
Financial XML (FinXML)	FinXML is an XML based framework developed by the Financial consortium that provides a standard format for exchanging financial data between financial institutions. For more information on FinXML, visit **www.finxml.org**.
Financial Information Exchange Markup Language (FixML)	FixML was developed by a consortium of over 20 financial firms and is a standard for data exchange between financial institutions. For more information on FixML visit **www.fixprotocol.org**.

Fig. 27.9   Various markup languages derived from XML (part 2 of 2).

27.5 Using XML with HTML

Because XML documents contain data, they are data sources. Internet Explorer 5 allows XML documents to be embedded into an HTML document using the *XML element*. An XML document that exists within an HTML page is called a *data island*. With data islands, binding data to a table requires minimal effort. Internet Explorer 5 handles many different data sources (e.g., XML, comma-delimited lists, ADO, etc.). Figure 27.10 uses a data island as a data source for an HTML table.

```
1   <!DOCTYPE HTML PUBLIC "-//W3C//DTD HTML 4.0 Transitional//EN">
2   <HTML>
3
4   <!-- Fig. 27.10: simple_contact.html   -->
5   <!-- A Simple Contact List Database    -->
6
```

Fig. 27.10   A simple contact list (part 1 of 2).

```
7   <BODY>
8
9   <XML ID = "xmlDoc">
10      <contacts>
11
12         <contact>
13            <lastName>Deitel</lastName>
14            <firstName>Harvey</firstName>
15         </contact>
16
17         <contact>
18            <lastName>Deitel</lastName>
19            <firstName>Paul</firstName>
20         </contact>
21
22         <contact>
23            <lastName>Nieto</lastName>
24            <firstName>Tem</firstName>
25         </contact>
26
27      </contacts>
28   </XML>
29
30   <TABLE BORDER = "1" DATASRC = "#xmlDoc">
31      <THEAD>
32      <TR>
33         <TH>Last Name</TH>
34         <TH>First Name</TH>
35      </TR>
36      </THEAD>
37
38      <TR>
39         <TD><SPAN DATAFLD = "lastName"></SPAN></TD>
40         <TD><SPAN DATAFLD = "firstName"></SPAN></TD>
41      </TR>
42   </TABLE>
43
44   </BODY>
45   </HTML>
```

Fig. 27.10 A simple contact list (part 2 of 2).

Line 9

```
<XML ID = "xmlDoc">
```

uses the **<XML>** tag to mark the beginning of the data island and line 28 uses the closing
</XML> *tag* to mark the end of the data island. *Attribute **ID*** is set to **xmlDoc**—the name
used by the document's author to reference the data island. This attribute's value is a au-
thor-defined name.

The data island contains the root element **contacts** (line 10), which contains three
contact elements. Each **contact** element contains a **lastName** and **firstName**
element representing the contact's last name and first name, respectively (lines 13 and 14).

In the HTML document, we add a **DATASRC** attribute (line 30) to the **TABLE** element's opening tag. This binds the data island (**xmlDoc**) to the table. To access the bound
data, we use **SPAN** elements with **DATAFLD** attributes (lines 39 and 40).

Portability Tip 27.3

*The **XML** tag is Microsoft specific.*

27.6 Document Object Model (DOM)

Although an XML document is a text file, retrieving data from the document using traditional sequential file access techniques is neither practical nor efficient, especially for documents where data needs to be dynamically added or deleted.

As mentioned earlier, when an XML document is successfully parsed, a tree structure
containing the document's data is stored in memory. Figure 27.11 shows the tree structure
for the document **article.xml** discussed in Fig. 27.3. This hierarchal tree structure is
called a *Document Object Model (DOM)*. Each name (e.g., **article**, **date**, **first-
Name**, etc.) is called a *node*. A node such as **author** that contains other nodes (called *child
nodes*) is called a *parent node*. Nodes that are peers (e.g., **firstName** and **lastName**)
are called *sibling nodes*.

The DOM has a single *root node* that contains all other nodes in the document. Each
node is an object that has properties, methods and events. Properties associated with a node
can be used to fetch its name, value, child nodes, etc. Methods allow us to create, delete and
append nodes, load XML documents, etc. Events are fired when an XML document finishes loading, a node property changes, etc. These properties, methods and events are
exposed by the XML parser as a programmatic library—called an *Application Programming Interface (API)*.

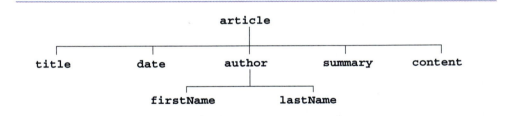

Fig. 27.11 Tree structure for **article.xml**.

We now present several tables that overview DOM API properties and methods. The purpose of these tables is to familiarize you with the DOM API capabilities used in this chapter and the next. In Chapter 28, we create an online bookstore that uses the majority of these properties and methods.

In the DOM, the entire XML document is represented by a **DOMDocument** object which includes the root node and all its child nodes. If we wish to programmatically access a document's content we must create a **DOMDocument** object. Figure 27.12 lists some **DOMDocument** properties and Fig. 27.13 lists some **DOMDocument** methods.\

Properties	Description
async	Sets the method of code execution. A setting of true allows code execution to continue even if the XML document has not finished loading. Microsoft specific.
childNodes	Contains a list of child nodes.
documentElement	Retrieves the document's root element.
text	Contains the value of the node and its child nodes. Microsoft specific.
xml	Contains the XML subtree of a node marked up as text. Microsoft specific.

Fig. 27.12 Some **DOMDocument** properties.

Methods	Description
cloneNode	Creates a new node that is a copy of the specified node.
createAttribute	Creates a new attribute node with the specified name.
createElement	Creates a new element node with the specified name.
load	Loads an XML document from a specified URL, file path or object. Microsoft specific.
loadXML	Loads an XML document from the specified string. Microsoft specific.
save	Saves an XML document to the specified location. Microsoft specific.
selectNodes	Returns a list of nodes that match the specified pattern. Microsoft specific.
selectSingleNode	Returns the first node that matches the specified pattern. Microsoft specific.
transformNode	Applies the supplied style sheet to a node and returns the result as a string. Microsoft specific. [*Note*: you will learn about style sheets in the next section.]
transformnodeToObject	Applies the supplied style sheet to a node and its children and returns the result in the supplied object. Microsoft specific. [*Note*: you will learn about style sheets in the next section.]

Fig. 27.13 Some **DOMDocument** methods .

Any node in the DOM can be represented with object **XMLDOMNode**. Figure 27.14 lists some **XMLDOMNode** properties and Fig. 27.15 lists some **XMLDOMNode** methods for adding new nodes, filtering nodes, etc.

Properties	Description
childNodes	Contains a list of child nodes.
dataType	Indicates the node content's data type defined by its schema. Microsoft specific. [*Note*: you will learn about schema in Section 27.8.]
nodeName	Contains the node's name (i.e., tag name, attribute name, etc.).
nodeType	Contains the node's type represented as an integer (an element is represented as one and an attribute as two).
nodeTypedValue	Contains the node's value expressed in the data type defined by its schema. Microsoft specific. [*Note*: you will learn about schema in Section 27.8.]
nodeTypeString	Returns the node's type represented as a string (e.g., "attribute", "element", "comment", etc.). Microsoft specific.
nodeValue	Contains the text contained by the node (i.e., an element's content, an attribute's value, etc.).
parentNode	Contains a node's parent node.
text	Contains the value of the node and its child nodes. Microsoft specific.
xml	Contains the XML subtree of a node marked up as text. Microsoft specific.

Fig. 27.14 Some **XMLDOMNode** properties .

Methods	Description
appendChild	Appends a new child to a node.
cloneNode	Creates a new node which is an exact copy of the node.
selectNodes	Returns a list of nodes that match the specified pattern. Microsoft specific.
selectSingleNode	Returns the first node that matches the specified pattern. Microsoft specific.
transformNode	Applies the supplied style sheet to a node and returns the result as a string. Microsoft specific. [*Note*: you will learn about style sheets in the next section.]
transformNodeToObject	Applies the supplied style sheet to a node and its children and returns the result in the supplied object. Microsoft specific. [*Note*: you will learn about style sheets in the next section.]

Fig. 27.15 Some **XMLDOMNode** methods.

Some properties and methods are the same for multiple objects, such as property **childNodes** or method **selectNodes**.

The DOM API provides object **XMLDOMElement** for manipulating nodes that are elements. Figure 27.16 lists some **XMLDOMElement** properties and Fig. 27.17 lists some **XMLDOMElement** methods. Although not discussed here, the DOM API provides object **XMLDOMAttribute** for manipulating nodes that are attributes.

Figure 27.18 demonstrates how we can programmatically access **article.xml**'s nodes using JavaScript. Line 14 instantiates an **DOMDocument** *object* and assigns it to reference **xmlDocument**. Method *load* loads the XML document **article.xml** into memory. Method **load** is a Microsoft extension to the DOM API. **DOMDocument** property *documentElement* (line 18) retrieves the document's root element and assigns it to reference **element**. To retrieve the name of the root node, we use property *nodeName* (line 21). In line 25, we determine the number of child nodes or the root element using the **length** property of *childNodes*. Property **childNodes** allows each child node to be accessed using method **item**. Each child node is identified using an integer value. The first child has the value zero, the second, one, and so on. Property *firstChild* (line 31) retrieves the first child of a node. To get the node's name, we use property **nodeName**. A sibling node object is retrieved using either the *nextSibling* (line 37) or *previousSibling* property. A parent node is retrieved using property *parentNode* (line 50).

Properties	Description
childNodes	Contains a list of child nodes.
text	Contains the value of the node and its child nodes. Microsoft specific.
xml	Contains the XML subtree of a node marked up as text. Microsoft specific.

Fig. 27.16 Some **XMLDOMElement** properties .

Method	Description
getAttribute	Returns the value of the specified attribute.
removeAttribute	The specified attribute is removed. If the attribute has a default value, the attribute is not removed and has its value replaced with the default value.
setAttribute	Assigns the supplied value to an attribute with the specified name.
transformNodeToObject	Applies the specified style sheet to this node and its child nodes and returns the result. Microsoft specific. [Note: you will learn about style sheets in the next section.]

Fig. 27.17 Some **XMLDOMElement** methods.

```
1    <!DOCTYPE HTML PUBLIC "-//W3C//DTD HTML 4.0 Transitional//EN">
2    <HTML>
3
4    <!-- Fig. 27.18: DOMExample.html -->
5    <!-- Using the DOM                 -->
6    <HEAD>
7       <TITLE>A DOM Example</TITLE>
8    </HEAD>
9
10   <BODY>
11
12   <SCRIPT LANGUAGE = "JavaScript">
13
14      var xmlDocument = new ActiveXObject( "Microsoft.XMLDOM" );
15
16      xmlDocument.load( "article.xml" );
17
18      var element = xmlDocument.documentElement;
19
20      document.writeln( "The root node of the document is:" );
21      document.writeln( "<STRONG>" + element.nodeName
22                          + "</STRONG>" );
23      document.writeln( "<BR>Its child elements are:" );
24
25      for ( i = 0; i < element.childNodes.length; i++ ) {
26         var curNode = element.childNodes.item( i );
27         document.writeln( "<LI><STRONG>" + curNode.nodeName
28                             + "</STRONG></LI>" );
29      }
30
31      var currentNode = element.firstChild;
32
33      document.writeln( "<BR>The first child of the root node is:" );
34      document.writeln( "<STRONG>" + currentNode.nodeName);
35      document.writeln( "</STRONG><BR>The next sibling is:" );
36
37      var nextSib = currentNode.nextSibling;
38
39      document.writeln( "<STRONG>" + nextSib.nodeName
40                          + "</STRONG>." );
41      document.writeln( "<BR/>Value of <STRONG>" + nextSib.nodeName
42                          + "</STRONG> element is:" );
43
44      var value = nextSib.firstChild;
45
46      document.writeln( "<EM>" + value.nodeValue + "</EM>" );
47      document.writeln( "<BR>The parent node of " );
48      document.writeln( "<STRONG>" + nextSib.nodeName
49                          + "</STRONG> is:" );
50      document.writeln( "<STRONG>" + nextSib.parentNode.nodeName
51                          + "</STRONG>." );
52
53   </SCRIPT>
```

Fig. 27.18 Accessing elements of `article.xml` (part 1 of 2).

```
54
55    </BODY>
56    </HTML>
```

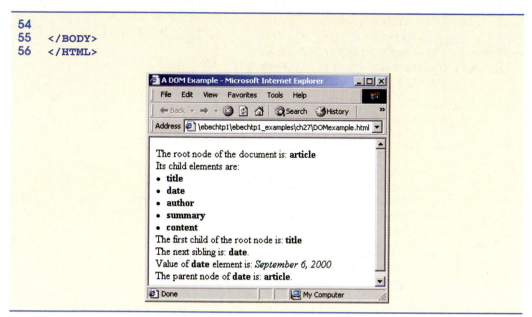

The root node of the document is: **article**
Its child elements are:
- **title**
- **date**
- **author**
- **summary**
- **content**
The first child of the root node is: **title**
The next sibling is: **date**.
Value of **date** element is: *September 6, 2000*
The parent node of **date** is: **article**.

Fig. 27.18 Accessing elements of `article.xml` (part 2 of 2).

27.7 Extensible Style Language (XSL)

Extensible Stylesheet Language (*XSL*) defines how an XML document's data is rendered. The relationship between XML and XSL is similar to the relationship between HTML and CSS (discussed in Chapter 19)—although XSL is much more powerful than CSS. An XML document's data does not have to be rendered using an XSL document, CSS can also be used. An *XSL document* provides the rules for displaying (or organizing) an XML document's data. XSL also provides elements that define rules for how one XML document is transformed into another text-based document (e.g., XML, HTML, etc.). The subset of XSL concerned with transformations is called *XSL Transformations (XSLT)*.

Software Engineering Observation 27.4

XSL allows data presentation to be separated from data description.

Figure 27.19 demonstrates a typical use of XSLT—sorting and selecting elements from an XML document. Notice in the screen capture that the XML document **contact.xml** is displayed. Recall from our discussion of Fig. 27.4 that an XML document does not contain formatting information and is simply displayed as "raw" XML by IE5. However, in the output of this example, the effects of the XSL document are evident.

```
1    <?xml version = "1.0"?>
2    <?xml:stylesheet type = "text/xsl" href = "contact_list.xsl"?>
3    <!-- Fig. 27.19: contact.xml -->
4
5    <contacts>
```

Fig. 27.19 A contact list database in XML (part 1 of 2).

```
 6
 7      <contact>
 8          <lastName>Black</lastName>
 9          <firstName>John</firstName>
10      </contact>
11
12      <contact>
13          <lastName>Green</lastName>
14          <firstName>Sue</firstName>
15      </contact>
16
17      <contact>
18          <lastName>Red</lastName>
19          <firstName>Bob</firstName>
20      </contact>
21
22      <contact>
23          <lastName>Blue</lastName>
24          <firstName>Mary</firstName>
25      </contact>
26
27      <contact>
28          <LastName>White</LastName>
29          <FirstName>Mike</FirstName>
30      </contact>
31
32      <contact>
33          <lastName>Brown</lastName>
34          <firstName>Jane</firstName>
35      </contact>
36
37      <contact>
38          <lastName>Gray</lastName>
39          <firstName>Bill</firstName>
40      </contact>
41
42  </contacts>
```

Fig. 27.19   A contact list database in XML (part 2 of 2).

```
43  <?xml version = "1.0"?>
44  <xsl:stylesheet xmlns:xsl = "http://www.w3.org/TR/WD-xsl">
45
46  <!-- Fig. 27.19: contact_list.xsl -->
47
48  <xsl:template match = "/">
49
50  <HTML>
51  <BODY>
52
53  <DIV ID = "data">
54      <xsl:apply-templates/>
```

Fig. 27.19   Using XSL style sheets (part 1 of 4).

```
55   </DIV>
56
57   <SCRIPT TYPE = "text/javascript" LANGUAGE = "JavaScript">
58    <xsl:comment><![CDATA[
59       var styleSheet = document.XSLDocument;
60       var xmlDocument = document.XMLDocument;
61
62       function update( scope, sortKey )
63       {
64          var sortBy = styleSheet.selectSingleNode( "//@order-by" );
65          sortBy.value = sortKey;
66          var scopeBy =
67            styleSheet.selectSingleNode( "//xsl:for-each/@select" );
68          scopeBy.value = scope;
69          data.innerHTML =
70            xmlDocument.documentElement.transformNode( styleSheet );
71       }
72
73       ]]>
74    </xsl:comment>
75   </SCRIPT>
76
77   <TABLE BORDER = "1" DATASRC = "#xmlData"  DATAPAGESIZE = "3"
78      ID = "tbl">
79      <THEAD>
80         <TR>
81            <TH>Last Name</TH>
82            <TH>First Name</TH>
83         </TR>
84      </THEAD>
85         <TR>
86            <TD><SPAN DATAFLD = "lastName"></SPAN></TD>
87            <TD><SPAN DATAFLD = "firstName"></SPAN></TD>
88         </TR>
89   </TABLE>
90
91   <INPUT TYPE = "button" VALUE = "Revert"
92      ONCLICK = "update('contact','+firstName;+lastName');"/>
93   <BR/>
94   <INPUT TYPE = "button" VALUE = "Sort By Last Name"
95      ONCLICK = "update('contact','+lastName;+firstName');"/>
96   <INPUT TYPE = "button" VALUE = "Sort By First Name"
97      ONCLICK = "update('contact','-firstName;+lastName');"/>
98   <BR/>
99   <INPUT TYPE = "button"
100     VALUE = "Filter for last name starting with 'B' "
101     ONCLICK = "update(
102     'contact[lastName &gt; \'B\' and lastName &lt; \'C\']',
103     '+firstName;+lastName');"/>
104  <BR/>
105  <INPUT TYPE = "button" VALUE = "|&lt;"
106         ONCLICK = "tbl.firstPage();"/>
```

Fig. 27.19 Using XSL style sheets (part 2 of 4).

```
107  <INPUT TYPE = "button" VALUE = "&lt;"
108                        ONCLICK = "tbl.previousPage();"/>
109  <INPUT TYPE = "button" VALUE = "&gt;"
110                        ONCLICK = "tbl.nextPage();"/>
111  <INPUT TYPE = "button" VALUE = "&gt;|"
112                        ONCLICK = "tbl.lastPage();"/>
113
114  </BODY>
115  </HTML>
116  </xsl:template>
117
118  <xsl:template match = "contacts">
119    <XML ID = "xmlData">
120      <contacts>
121        <xsl:for-each select = "contact"
122             order-by = "+firstName;+lastName">
123          <contact>
124            <lastName><xsl:value-of select = "lastName"/>
125            </lastName>
126            <firstName><xsl:value-of select = "firstName"/>
127            </firstName>
128          </contact>
129        </xsl:for-each>
130      </contacts>
131    </XML>
132  </xsl:template>
133
134  </xsl:stylesheet>
```

Fig. 27.19 Using XSL style sheets (part 3 of 4).

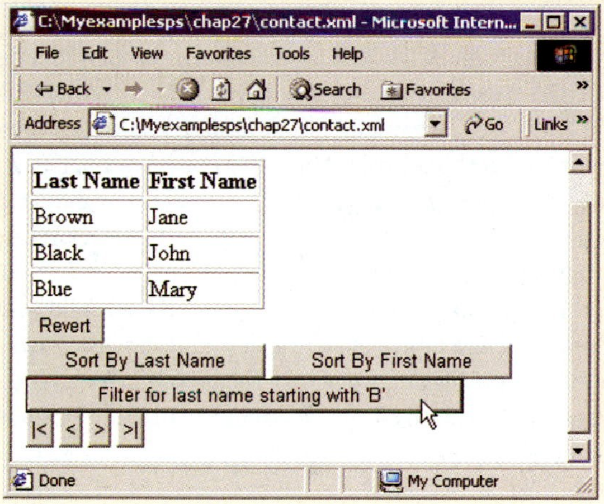

Fig. 27.19 Using XSL style sheets (part 4 of 4).

Instead of physically embedding the XML document in the HTML file, as we did in Fig. 27.10, we place the XML document in its own file, **contact.xml** (lines 1 through 42). Line 2 is a processing instruction that specifies the XSL file (**contact_list.xsl**) that transforms the XML document. XSL documents end in the **.xsl** extension.

Attribute **href** (line 2) specifies the XSL file's URI. Attribute **type** (line 2) specifies the type of style sheet (**text/xsl** for XSL files and **text/css** for CSS files).

Line 44

```
<xsl:stylesheet xmlns:xsl = "http://www.w3.org/TR/WD-xsl">
```

uses attribute **xmlns** to defines namespace **xsl**. Figure 27.19 uses Microsoft supported XSL namespace URI **http://www.w3.org/TR/WD-xsl**. The namespace URI for XSLT recommended by W3C is **http://www.w3.org/1999/XSL/Transform**.

An XSL document is also an XML document—this is the reason we included the processing instruction on line 43. The XSL document contains *template rules* that define how each node in the XML document should be processed. A template rule is specified by an **xsl:template** *element* (line 48). In a client/server environment, the XML document and the XSL document are parsed by the client XSL parser (built into IE5) to transform the XML document. XSL Transformations can also occur on the server, which sends the transformed document to its clients.

Element **xsl:template**'s **match** attribute specifies the element in an XML document for which the template rule should be applied. Line 48's match attribute value (**"/"**) specifies a *pattern* that indicates the **xsl:template** applies to the root node (**contacts**). HTML tags declared inside the template are directly inserted in the output.

HTML element **DIV** (line 53) contains the empty element **xsl:apply-template** (line 54). The **xsl:apply-templates** (line 54) element has a **select** attribute which select specific nodes. In the absence of a **select** attribute, all the child elements of the current node are selected.

For the moment, we will skip lines 57 through 75 and discuss other features in the document. Lines 77 through 89 create an HTML table that is populated with the XML document's data. Line 77 specifies the number of data records to display in the table with Microsoft-specific attribute **DATAPAGESIZE**. Attribute **DATASRC** refers to the data retrieved from the XML document by XSL elements (lines 118 through 132).

Contents of the **xsl:template** element (lines 118 through 132) are executed when a **contacts** node (root node) is parsed. The template builds up the data island from the XML file. The element **xsl:for-each** (line 121) iterates over each **contact** element in the XML document. Attribute **select** specifies the **contacts** elements over which the **xsl:for-each** iterates. Attribute **order-by** sorts the **contact** elements. A *plus sign* (**+**) indicates ascending order; a *minus sign* (**-**) indicates descending order. By default, an element without a sign is sorted in ascending order. By using a semicolon (**;**), we generate sort fields. On line 122, the item before the semicolon is the *primary sort field* and the item after the semicolon is the *secondary sort field*. When primary sort field values are identical (e.g., **Deitel** and **Deitel**), the secondary sort field values (e.g., **Harvey** and **Paul**) are used to determine the order.

Line 124

```
<lastName><xsl:value-of select = "lastName"/>
```

uses element *xsl:value-of* to retrieve the data specified by attribute **select**. The data returned replaces element **xsl:value-of**.

Lines 57 through 75 are the scripting code that changes the value of the attributes **order-by** and **select**. Lines 59 and 60 are executed when the document is loaded. Function **sort** is called each time a button is clicked.

Any material in the *CDATA* section (i.e., between **<![CDATA[** and **]]>**) is not processed by the XML parser. We place JavaScript (lines 57 through 75) in the **CDATA** section (line 58). Element *xsl:comment* is used to insert comments in the output.

Property **XSLDocument** (**document** object) retrieves a reference to the *XSL DOM* (line 59) as a **DOMDocument**. The XSL DOM is similar to the XML DOM but refers to the structure of an XSL document. This reference helps us traverse and modify the XSL DOM structure. In line 59, we declare variable **styleSheet**, which is initialized with the reference to the XSL DOM. Similarly, **xmlDocument** references the entire XML document.

Function **update** performs the action requested by the user. The variable **sortKey** (line 62) contains the item over which the table is to be sorted. Variable **scope** (line 62) contains the type of records that need to be selected (i.e., **contact**).

Method **selectSingleNode** (line 64) returns the first node that matches its *input pattern* (i.e., **//@order-by**). The input pattern **//@order-by** specifies a recursive search for first the **order-by** node (that is an attribute) in the XSL document. Similarly, the pattern **//xsl:for-each/@select** indicates a recursive search for the first **select** attribute node in an **xsl:for-each** element. This matches the **select** attribute at line 121. Lines 66 and 69 change the value of the nodes retrieved. To apply the style sheet, we call method **transformNode** (line 70). Method **transformNode** processes the XML document referenced by **xmlDocument** using the style sheet, which generates a new ordering of **contact** elements.

The **INPUT** elements (lines 91 through 103) provide buttons for the user to sort and filter the XML data. These buttons invoke function **update** and pass the sorting and querying parameters to it. When filtering for a **lastname** starting with **B**, the pattern (line 102)

```
contact[lastName &gt; \'B\' and lastName &lt; \'C\']
```

is passed as the first argument to method **update**. The *brackets ([ ])* contain the test criteria. This XSL pattern selects all names greater than **B** but less than **C**. All **contact** elements that satisfy this condition are selected. We use the entities **>(>)** and **<(<)** as conditional operators instead of **>** and **<** characters because they are not allowed in attribute values. The single quote character (**'**) is escaped using backslash (****) because it is passed as a parameter to JavaScript function **update**. Operator *and* is the logical AND operator that connects the two conditions.

ONCLICK event handlers (lines 105 through 112) call methods *firstPage*—to move to the first record, *previousPage*—to move to the previous record, *nextPage*—to move to the next record and *lastPage*—to move to the last record.

27.8 Microsoft Schema

Earlier in the chapter we introduced the concept of DTDs for validating XML documents. DTDs have two primary limitations—they do not use XML syntax and they do not provide a means of specifying element and attribute data types. *Schema* is an XML-based technology specifically aimed at addressing these limitations. Schema was initially pioneered by Microsoft and is currently a W3C working draft. Though schema and DTD serve the same purpose, there are considerable differences.

A schema is considered a valid XML document because the schema specification is defined using a DTD. The XML document that a schema defines is considered *schema valid*. An XML document is only valid when it conforms to a DTD—not a schema.

We use Microsoft's schema specification in this example. A W3C created schema called *XML Schema* is currently being created. Additional information on XML Schema can be found at **www.w3.org/TR/xmlschema-0**.

Figure 27.20 uses XML, XSL and Microsoft schema to display book information in Internet Explorer 5. When the user clicks a table header, the column sorts the table data. This example uses three XML documents: **books.xml**, **books-schema.xml** and **books.xsl**—which define the database, the document structure and the rendering style, respectively. This example requires Microsoft Internet Explorer 5..

The book database (i.e., **books.xml**) is straightforward. We have a **database** root-level element that contains an **author** element and many **book** elements. Each **book** element contains the title (**title**), ISBN number (**isbn**), page count (**pages**), **image** and **description**.

Line 2

```
<?xml:stylesheet type = "text/xsl" href = "books.xsl"?>
```

uses the processing instruction **xml:stylesheet** to indicate that the XML document uses style sheet **books.xsl**.

```
1   <?xml version = "1.0"?>
2   <?xml:stylesheet type = "text/xsl" href = "books.xsl"?>
3   <!-- Fig. 27.20: books.xml -->
4
5   <database xmlns = "x-schema:books-schema.xml">
```

Fig. 27.20 Book list database document (part 1 of 2).

```
6      <author>Deitel &amp; Associates, Inc.</author>
7
8      <book>
9         <title>C++ How to Program: Third Edition</title>
10        <isbn>0-13-089571-7</isbn>
11        <pages>1130</pages>
12        <description>C++ programming textbook.
13        </description>
14        <image>cplus.jpg</image>
15     </book>
16
17     <book>
18        <title>Getting Started with Microsoft's Visual C++ 6
19           with an Introduction to MFC</title>
20        <isbn>0-13-016147-0</isbn>
21        <pages>163</pages>
22        <description>Introductory MFC programming textbook.
23        </description>
24        <image>mfcvcplus.jpg</image>
25     </book>
26
27     <book>
28        <title>Java How to Program: Third Edition</title>
29        <isbn>0-13-012507-5</isbn>
30        <pages>1200</pages>
31        <description>Java Programming textbook.
32        </description>
33        <image>javahtp.jpg</image>
34     </book>
35
36  </database>
```

Fig. 27.20   Book list database document (part 2 of 2).

```
37  <?xml version = "1.0"?>
38
39  <!-- Fig. 27.20: books-schema.xml -->
40
41  <Schema xmlns = "urn:schemas-microsoft-com:xml-data">
42
43     <ElementType name = "author"/>
44     <ElementType name = "image"/>
45     <ElementType name = "title"/>
46     <ElementType name = "isbn"/>
47     <ElementType name = "pages"/>
48     <ElementType name = "description"/>
49
50     <ElementType name = "database" content = "eltOnly">
51        <group minOccurs = "0" maxOccurs = "1">
52           <element type = "author"/>
53        </group>
```

Fig. 27.20   Schema for the database document type (part 1 of 2).

```
54            <group minOccurs = "1" maxOccurs = "*">
55                <element type = "book"/>
56            </group>
57        </ElementType>
58
59        <ElementType name = "book" content = "eltOnly">
60            <element type = "title"/>
61            <element type = "isbn"/>
62            <element type = "pages"/>
63            <element type = "description"/>
64            <element type = "image"/>
65        </ElementType>
66
67    </Schema>
```

Fig. 27.20 Schema for the database document type (part 2 of 2).

```
68    <?xml version = "1.0"?>
69
70    <!-- Fig. 27.20: books.xsl -->
71
72    <xsl:stylesheet xmlns:xsl = "http://www.w3.org/TR/WD-xsl">
73        <xsl:template match = "/">
74            <HTML>
75            <HEAD>
76                <TITLE>
77                    <xsl:value-of select = "database/author"/>
78                </TITLE>
79                <STYLE>
80                    .head1 {font: bold}
81                    .head2 {font: bold; cursor: hand}
82                </STYLE>
83            </HEAD>
84
85        <SCRIPT FOR = "window" EVENT = "ONLOAD">
86            <xsl:comment><![CDATA[
87                stylesheet = document.XSLDocument;
88                source = document.XMLDocument;
89                sortBy = document.XSLDocument.selectSingleNode(
90                    "//@order-by" );
91            ]]></xsl:comment>
92        </SCRIPT>
93
94        <SCRIPT><xsl:comment><![CDATA[
95            var sortBy;    // To carry the sorting field
96            var source;    // Contains a reference to XML DOM
97            var stylesheet; // Contains a reference to XSL DOM
98
99            function sort( data )
100           {
101               sortBy.value  =  data;
```

Fig. 27.20 XSL specification for the book database (part 1 of 4).

```
102                  list.innerHTML =
103                     source.documentElement.transformNode(
104                     stylesheet );
105              }
106           ]]></xsl:comment></SCRIPT>
107
108       <BODY>
109          <H1>
110             <CENTER>
111                <xsl:value-of select = "database/author"/>
112             </CENTER>
113          </H1>
114
115          <DIV ID = "list">
116             <xsl:apply-templates select = "database"/>
117          </DIV>
118       </BODY>
119       </HTML>
120    </xsl:template>
121
122    <xsl:template match = "database">
123       <TABLE WIDTH = "100%" CELLSPACING = "0" BORDER = "1">
124          <THEAD>
125             <TD WIDTH = "200" ALIGN = "CENTER">
126                <DIV CLASS = "head1">Image</DIV>
127             </TD>
128             <TD WIDTH = "30%" ALIGN = "CENTER">
129                <DIV ONCLICK = "sort('title;isbn')"
130                   CLASS = "head2">Title</DIV>
131             </TD>
132             <TD WIDTH = "25%" ALIGN = "CENTER">
133                <DIV ONCLICK = "sort('isbn;title')"
134                   CLASS = "head2">ISBN</DIV>
135             </TD>
136             <TD WIDTH = "5%" ALIGN = "CENTER">
137                <DIV ONCLICK = "sort('pages;title')"
138                   CLASS = "head2">Pages</DIV>
139             </TD>
140             <TD WIDTH = "30%" ALIGN = "CENTER">
141                <DIV CLASS = "head1">Description</DIV>
142             </TD>
143          </THEAD>
144
145          <xsl:for-each select = "book" order-by = "title">
146             <TR>
147                <TD WIDTH = "200" ALIGN = "CENTER" VALIGN = "TOP">
148                   <xsl:choose>
149                      <xsl:when test = "image[.!='']">
150                         <xsl:element name = "IMG">
151                            <xsl:attribute name = "SRC">
152                               <xsl:value-of select = "image"/>
153                            </xsl:attribute>
154                         </xsl:element>
```

Fig. 27.20   XSL specification for the book database (part 2 of 4).

```
155                    </xsl:when>
156                    <xsl:otherwise>
157                       n/a
158                    </xsl:otherwise>
159                 </xsl:choose>
160              </TD>
161
162              <TD WIDTH = "25%" ALIGN = "LEFT" VALIGN = "TOP">
163                 <xsl:choose>
164                    <xsl:when test = "title[.!='']">
165                       <xsl:value-of select = "title"/>
166                    </xsl:when>
167                    <xsl:otherwise>
168                       n/a
169                    </xsl:otherwise>
170                 </xsl:choose>
171              </TD>
172
173              <TD WIDTH = "10%" ALIGN = "CENTER" VALIGN = "TOP">
174                 <xsl:choose>
175                    <xsl:when test = "isbn[.!='']">
176                       <xsl:value-of select = "isbn"/>
177                    </xsl:when>
178                    <xsl:otherwise>
179                       n/a
180                    </xsl:otherwise>
181                 </xsl:choose>
182              </TD>
183
184              <TD WIDTH = "5%" ALIGN = "CENTER" VALIGN = "TOP">
185                 <xsl:choose>
186                    <xsl:when test = "pages[.!=''] ">
187                       <xsl:value-of select = "pages"/>
188                    </xsl:when>
189                    <xsl:otherwise>
190                       n/a
191                    </xsl:otherwise>
192                 </xsl:choose>
193              </TD>
194
195              <TD WIDTH = "60%" ALIGN = "LEFT" VALIGN = "TOP">
196                 <xsl:choose>
197                    <xsl:when test = "description[.!='']">
198                       <xsl:value-of select = "description"/>
199                    </xsl:when>
200                    <xsl:otherwise>
201                       n/a
202                    </xsl:otherwise>
203                 </xsl:choose>
204              </TD>
205
206           </TR>
207        </xsl:for-each>
```

Fig. 27.20   XSL specification for the book database (part 3 of 4).

```
208            </TABLE>
209        </xsl:template>
210    </xsl:stylesheet>
```

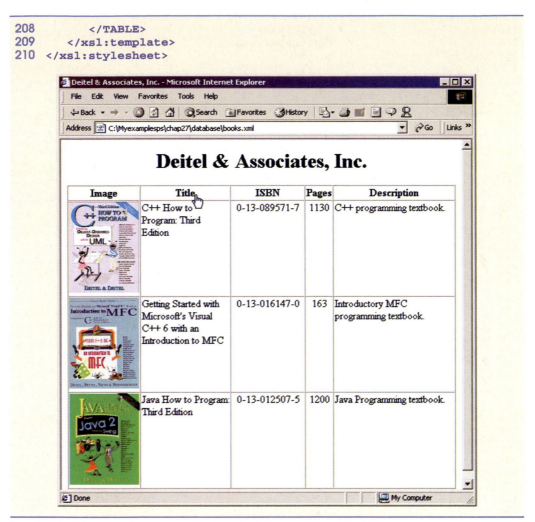

Fig. 27.20 XSL specification for the book database (part 4 of 4).

Line 5

```
<database xmlns = "x-schema:books-schema.xml">
```

defines the **database** element using the **books-schema.xml** file as a schema.

In the Microsoft schema file (**books-schema.xml**), we first declare our element types using element ***ElementType*** (line 43). *Attribute* **name** (line 43) defines the name of our element. *Attribute* ***content*** (line 50) defines the element's contents. In this example, the value ***eltOnly*** specifies that this element can only contain other elements. The other values that **content** may have are ***empty*** for empty elements, ***textOnly*** for text elements and ***mixed*** for both text and elements.

Element ***group*** (line 51) groups elements and specifies the order in which they occur. Attribute ***minOccurs*** defines an element's minimum number of occurrences. Assigning a value of **0** to **minOccurs** sets the element as optional, and assigning a value of **1** to

minOccurs sets the element as occurring at least once. *Attribute* **maxOccurs** defines an element's maximum number of occurrences. A value of **1** sets the element as occurring at most once and an asterisk (*****) specifies that the element occurs any number of times. Both the attributes are set to **1** by default.

Element **element** (line 52) references an element that can appear as part of the enclosing **ElementType** element's content model. In this case, the **author** element can occur at most once and the **book** element can occur one or more times within the **database** element. Similarly, attributes can be declared using the **AttributeType** element.

In lines 68 through 210, we define XSL style sheet **books.xsl**, which describes how to render the XML document. We start by using the **xsl:stylesheet** processing instruction (line 72). We use element **xsl:template** (line 73) to define a template rule. Attribute **match** selects the nodes (i.e., elements) to which the **xsl:template** is applied. In this case, the forward slash character (**/**) specifies that this template applies to the root element.

In line 89, method **selectSingleNode** returns the first **order-by** attribute node in the XSL style sheet. By doing this, we can dynamically set the value of attribute **order-by** in the **xsl:for-each** element on line 145. We use the **XSLDocument** property to access the **document**'s XSL style sheet.

In line 99, we define function **sort**, which sorts the XML document according to the passed arguments. We set variable **sortBy**'s value to the value of **data** and call method **transformNode** (line 103) to apply **stylesheet** to the XML document. The only data that are processed are the elements in the **database** element. The **xsl:apply-templates** element (line 116) selects the **database** node. Once selected, the **xsl:template** element for database is executed.

To perform conditional tests, we use the *xsl:choose* element (line 148). This element is composed of one or more *xsl:when* elements and an optional *xsl:otherwise* element. The **xsl:when** element (line 149) is a conditional statement with the condition placed in the *test* attribute. We test whether or not the **image** record item is equal to an empty string. Finally, the **xsl:otherwise** element (line 156) is used to define the default case.

The *xsl:element* element (line 150) generates the markup for an element of the specified name (i.e., **IMG**) in the output HTML. To add an attribute to a markup, we use the *xsl:attribute* element (line 151). These elements are useful when we need to change the value of an attribute, or the element itself.

27.9 Extensible Hypertext Markup Language (XHTML™)

This section introduces an XML-related technology called *Extensible Hypertext Markup Language (XHTML)*. XHTML is HTML's proposed successor, and the current version of XHTML includes HTML 4 (for backwards compatibility), to help Web authors make the transition from HTML to XHTML. Like XML, XHTML permits document authors to create their own markup.

XHTML's design is better equipped than HTML's to represent complex data on the internet. The majority of existing HTML code is not well formed, because browsers do not explicitly check the markup. Browsers can treat poorly written HTML documents differently, requiring browser vendors to write additional features to handle rendering problems. With the emergence of the wireless Web and Web-enabled appliances, smaller devices such as PDAs (personal digital assistants) have a limited amount of memory far below today's desktops and cannot provide the extra resources required to process poorly written HTML. Documents intended for these devices must be well formed to guarantee uniform processing.

XHTML documents follow the same rules for well-formedness as XML documents. Attribute values in XHTML must be enclosed in quotes and must have a value. HTML attributes that can be declared without a value are called *minimized attributes*. For example, an **HR** tag has attribute **NOSHADE**, which is a minimized attribute.

XHTML documents conform to one of three types of DTDs—*strict, transitional* and *frameset*. A strict DTD is used when the document does not contain HTML presentational elements (i.e., **H1**, **H2**, etc.). Strict is commonly used when an XHTML document is using a style sheets instead. A transitional DTD is used when the XHTML document contains HTML presentational elements. A frameset DTD is used when a browser window is partitioned with HTML frames.

Common Programming Error 27.11

All the elements in an XHTML file must be in lower case and must have proper open and close tags.

Figure 27.21 is an XHTML document that has been validated using the W3C's *HTML validation* service at **validator.w3.org**. Lines 1 and 2 define the frameset XHTML DTD to which the example conforms. All the elements in Fig. 27.21 are HTML 4 elements except for element **simple** (lines 39 through 49) which is programmer-defined. Elements in **simple** have their own programmer-defined namespace prefix **ct**..

```
1   <!DOCTYPE html PUBLIC "-//W3C//DTD XHTML 1.0 Frameset//EN"
2      "http://www.w3.org/TR/xhtml1/DTD/frameset.dtd">
3   <html>
4
5   <!-- Fig. 27.21: xhtmlExample.html -->
6   <!--An XHTML example-->
7   <head>
8
9   <meta name = "keywords" content = "Webpage, design, HTML,
10     tutorial, personal, help, index, form, contact, feedback,
11     list, links, frame, deitel"/>
12
13  <meta name = "description" content = "This Web site will help
14     you learn the basics of HTML and Webpage design through the
15     use of interactive examples and instruction."/>
16
17  </head>
18
19  <frameset cols = "110,*">
20     <frame name = "nav" scrolling = "no" src = "nav.html"/>
21
22     <!-- Nested Framesets are used to change the formatting -->
23     <!-- and spacing of the frameset as a whole            -->
24     <frameset rows = "175,*">
25        <frame name = "picture" src = "picture.html"
```

Fig. 27.21 XHTML Example (part 1 of 2). (Courtesy of World Wide Web Consortium)

```
26                    noresize = "noresize"/>
27          <frame name = "main" src = "main.html"/>
28      </frameset>
29
30      <noframes>
31         <p>This page uses frames, but your browser does not
32            support them.</p>
33         <p>Get Internet Explorer 5 at the
34            <a href = "http://www.microsoft.com/">Microsoft
35            Web-Site</a></p>
36      </noframes>
37   </frameset>
38
39      <simple xmlns:ct = "http://www.deitel.com">
40         <ct:contact>
41            <ct:LastName>Black</ct:LastName>
42            <ct:FirstName>John</ct:FirstName>
43         </ct:contact>
44
45         <ct:contact>
46            <ct:LastName>Green</ct:LastName>
47            <ct:FirstName>Sue</ct:FirstName>
48         </ct:contact>
49      </simple>
50
51   </html>
```

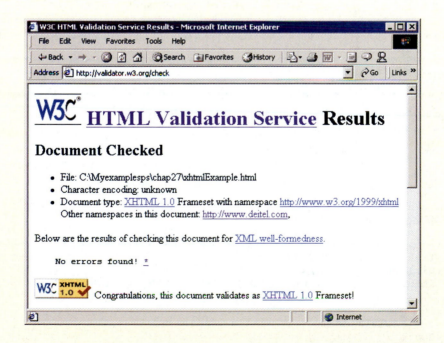

Fig. 27.21 XHTML Example (part 2 of 2). (Courtesy of World Wide Web Consortium)

Some authoring tools (e.g., XML Spy 3.0—**www.xmlspy.com**) include support for XHTML. This trend will continue to grow as XHTML increases in popularity. For more information on XHTML visit

www.w3.org/TR/xhtml1

and

wdvl.com/Authoring/Languages/XML/XHTML

27.10 Microsoft BizTalk™

Increasingly, more organizations are using the Internet to exchange data. Because organizations use different platforms, applications and data specifications, sending data between organizations is difficult. Sharing data with another business is simplified when XML is used. However, an easy method for transmitting and translating XML documents between businesses is also needed. Microsoft developed *BizTalk* for the purpose of managing and facilitating business transactions.

BizTalk consists of three parts: the BizTalk Server, the BizTalk Framework and the BizTalk Schema Library. The *BizTalk Server* (*BTS*) parses and translates all inbound and outbound messages (or documents) going to and from a business. The *BizTalk Framework* is a schema for structuring those messages. The *BizTalk Schema Library* is a collection of different Framework schemas. Businesses can design their own schema or choose one from the BizTalk Schema Library. Figure 27.22 summarizes the different BizTalk terminologies.

Figure 27.23 is an example of a BizTalk message for a product offer from a retail company. The message schema (lines 15 through 46) for this example was developed for Microsoft online shopping. We use this schema for a fictitious company named ExComp.

BizTalk	Description
Framework	A specification that defines the format for messages.
Schema library	A repository of Framework XML schemas.
Server	An application that helps vendors to convert their messages to BizTalk format. For more information visit **www.microsoft.com/biztalkserver**.
JumpStart Kit	A set of tools for developing BizTalk applications.

Fig. 27.22 BizTalk Terminologies.

```
1   <?xml version = "1.0"?>
2   <BizTalk
3    xmlns = "urn:schemas-biztalk-org:BizTalk/biztalk-0.81.xml">
4
5   <!-- Fig. 27.23: BizTalkexample.xml -->
6   <!-- BizTalk example                -->
7   <Route>
```

Fig. 27.23 BizTalk markup using an offer schema (part 1 of 2).

```
8        <From locationID = "8888888" locationType = "DUNS"
9              handle = "23" />
10
11       <To locationID = "454545445" locationType = "DUNS"
12             handle = "45" />
13    </Route>
14
15    <Body>
16     <Offers xmlns =
17     "x-schema:http://schemas.biztalk.org/eshop_msn_com/t7ntoqnq.xml">
18       <Offer>
19          <Model>12-a-3411d</Model>
20          <Manufacturer>ExComp, Inc.</Manufacturer>
21          <ManufacturerModel>DCS-48403</ManufacturerModel>
22          <MerchantCategory>Clothes | Sports wear</MerchantCategory>
23          <MSNClassId></MSNClassId>
24          <StartDate>2000-06-05 T13:12:00</StartDate>
25          <EndDate>2000-12-05T13:12:00</EndDate>
26          <RegularPrice>89.99</RegularPrice>
27          <CurrentPrice>25.99</CurrentPrice>
28          <DisplayPrice value = "3" />
29          <InStock value = "15" />
30          <ReferenceImageURL>
31             http://www.Example.com/clothes/index.jpg
32          </ReferenceImageURL>
33          <OfferName>Clearance sale</OfferName>
34         <OfferDescription>This is a clearence sale.</OfferDescription>
35          <PromotionalText>Free Shipping</PromotionalText>
36          <Comments>Clothes that you would love to wear.</Comments>
37          <IconType value = "BuyNow" />
38          <ActionURL>http://www.example.com/action.htm</ActionURL>
39          <AgeGroup1 value = "Infant" />
40          <AgeGroup2 value = "Adult" />
41          <Occasion1 value = "Birthday" />
42          <Occasion2 value = "Anniversary" />
43          <Occasion3 value = "Christmas" />
44       </Offer>
45     </Offers>
46    </Body>
47    </BizTalk>
```

Fig. 27.23 BizTalk markup using an offer schema (part 2 of 2).

All Biztalk documents have the root element, **BizTalk**. Lines 3 and 4 define a namespace for the BizTalk framework elements. Element **Route** contains the routing information, which is mandatory for all BizTalk documents. It also contains a **To** and **From** element. Element **To** specifies the document's destination and element **From** specifies the document's source. This makes it easier for the receiving application to communicate with the sender. Attributes **locationType** and **locationID** specify the type of business sending or receiving the information and a business identity (the unique identifier for a business) for source and destination organization. Attribute **handle** provides information to routing applications that handle the document.

Element **Body** contains the actual message, whose schema is defined by the businesses themselves. It contains the **Offers** element. Lines 16 and 17 specify the namespace for the **Offers**. Each offer is marked up using an **Offer** element which contains elements that describe the offer. For additional information on BizTalk, a list of Web sites is provided in Fig. 27.24.

Another organization with schema repositories is OASIS (Organization for the Advancement of Structured Information Standards—**www.oasis-open.org**). It is a non-profit organization consisting of vendors and software developers who are involved in development and standardization of schemas and DTDs.

27.11 Simple Object Access Protocol (SOAP)

Many applications use the Internet to transfer data. Some of these applications are run on clients with little processing power, so they invoke a method call on a different machine to process their data. Many of these applications use proprietary data specifications which makes communication between other applications difficult. The majority of these applications also reside behind firewalls (see Section 7.12.1) that restrict data communication to and from the application. The *Simple Object Access Protocol* (*SOAP*) is a protocol that addresses these problems. SOAP was developed and drafted by IBM, Lotus Development Corporation, Microsoft, DevelopMentor and Userland Software. SOAP is an HTTP/XML-based protocol that allows applications to communicate easily over the Internet using XML documents called *SOAP messages.*

A SOAP message contains an *envelope*—a structure for describing a method call. A SOAP message's body contains either a *request* or a *response.*

URL/Description

www.biztalk.com
Provides biztalk on finance, politics, law, etc. Also provides news on how to get your company noticed by the media.

www.biztalk.org/BizTalk/default.asp
Provides an introduction to BizTalk and contains many BizTalk resources.

www.extensibility.com/company/headlines/biztalk.htm
Provides information about the first commercial product utilizing the BizTalk Framework.

ipw.internet.com/development/software_development/937319431.html
Provides information about a free BizTalk jump start kit (see Fig. 27.22).

www.xmlglobal.com/biztalk
BizTalk toolkit for Perl (see Chapter 29).

**wdvl.internet.com/Authoring/Languages/XML/Conferences/
XMLWorld99/biztalk.html**
Provides various BizTalk resources.

Fig. 27.24 BizTalk reference Web sites .

A request message's body contains a *Remote Procedure Call* (*RPC*). An RPC is a request made to another machine to run a task. The RPC specifies the method to be invoked and any parameters the method takes. The message is sent via an HTTP POST. A SOAP-response message is an HTTP response document that contains the results from the method call (e.g., return values, error messages, etc.). For more information on SOAP, a list of Web sites is provided in Fig. 27.25.

27.12 Internet and World Wide Web Resources

www.xml.org
XML.org is a reference for XML, DTDs, schemas and namespaces.

www.w3.org/style/XSL
Provides information on XSL which includes the topics on what is new in XSL, learning XSL, XSL-enabled tools, XSL specification, FAQs, XSL history, etc.

www.w3.org/TR
W3C technical reports and publications page. Contains links to working drafts, proposed recommendations, recommendations, etc.

www.xmlbooks.com
Contains a list of recommended XML books by Charles GoldFarb—one of the original designers of GML (General Markup Language) from which SGML was derived.

www.xmlsoftware.com
Contains links for downloading XML-related software. Download links include XML browsers, conversion tools, database systems, DTD editors, XML editors, etc.

www.xml-zone.com/
The Development Exchange XML Zone is a complete resource for XML information. This site includes a FAQ, news, articles, links to other XML site and newsgroups.

wdvl.internet.com/Authoring/Languages/XML/
Web Developer's Virtual Library XML site includes tutorials, a FAQ, the latest news and extensive links to XML sites and software downloads.

URL/Description

msdn.microsoft.com/xml/general/soaptemplate.asp
Provides an introduction to SOAP. This site also contains links to examples and other information.

www.oasis-open.org/cover/soap.html
Provides information on SOAP and XML.

www.develop.com/soap
Provides downloads and FAQ.

www.whatis.com/soap.htm
Provides background information about SOAP and links for further information.

Fig. 27.25 SOAP reference Web sites .

www.xml.com/
Visit **XML.com** for the latest news and information about XML, conference listings, links to XML Web resources organized by topic, tools and more.

msdn.microsoft.com/xml/default.asp
The MSDN Online XML Development Center features articles on XML, Ask the Experts chat sessions, samples and demos, newsgroups and other helpful information.

www.w3.org/xml/
The W3C (World Wide Web Consortium) works to develop common protocols to ensure interoperability on the Web. Their XML page includes information about upcoming events, publications, software and discussion groups. Visit this site to read about the latest developments in XML.

www.oasis-open.org/cover/xml.html
The SGML/XML Web Page is an extensive resource that includes links to several FAQs, online resources, industry initiatives, demos, conferences and tutorials.

www.gca.org/whats_xml/default.htm
The GCA site has an XML glossary, list of books, brief descriptions of the draft standards for XML and links to online drafts.

www.xmlinfo.com/
XMLINFO is a resource site with tutorials, a list of recommended books, documentation, discussion forums and more.

xdev.datachannel.com/
The title of this site is xDev: The Definitive Site for Serious XML Developers. This Web site includes several short tutorials with code examples, toolkits downloads and a reference library.

www.ibm.com/developer/xml/
The IBM XML Zone site is a great resource for developers. You will find news, tools, a library, case studies, events and information about standards.

developer.netscape.com/tech/metadata/index.html
The XML and Metadata Developer Central site has demos, technical notes and news articles related to XML.

www.projectcool.com/developer/xmlz/
The Project Cool Developer Zone site includes several tutorials covering introductory through advanced XML.

www.poet.com/products/cms/xml_library/xml_lib.html
POET XML Resource Library includes links to white papers, tools, news, publications and Web links.

www.ucc.ie/xml/
This site is a detailed XML FAQ. Check out responses to some popular questions or submit your own questions through the site.

www.bell-labs.com/project/tts/sable.html
The Sable Markup Language is designed to markup text for input into speech synthesizers.

www.xml-cml.org/
This site is a resource for the Chemical Markup Language (CML). It includes a FAQ list, documentation, software and XML links.

www.tcf.nl/3.0/musicml/index.html
MusicML is a DTD for sheet music. Visit this site for examples and the specification.

www.hr-xml.org/
The HR-XML Consortium is a nonprofit organization working to set standardized XML tags for use in Human Resources.

www.textuality.com/xml/
Contains FAQ and the Lark non-validating XML parser.

SUMMARY

- XML (Extensible Markup Language) was developed in 1996 by the World Wide Web Consortium's (W3C's) XML Working Group and is related to Standard Generalized Markup Language (SGML).

- XML is a widely supported, open technology (i.e., non-proprietary technology) for data exchange.

- XML is a markup language for describing structured data—content is separated from presentation. Because an XML document contains only data, applications decide how to display the data.

- Unlike HTML, XML permits document authors to create their own markup for virtually any type of information. This extensibility enables document authors to create entirely new markup languages to describe specific types of data.

- Some of the markup languages created with XML include MathML (for mathematics), VoiceXML™ (for speech), SMIL™ (the Synchronous Multimedia Interface Language—for multimedia presentations), CML (for chemistry) and XBRL (Extensible Business Reporting Language—for financial data exchange).

- Because XML tags describe the data they contain, it is possible to search, sort, manipulate and render an XML document using related technologies such as the Extensible Stylesheet Language (XSL).

- Special software is not required to open an XML document—any text editor that supports ASCII/Unicode characters can be used.

- In order to process an XML document, a software program called an XML parser (or an XML processor) is required.

- Parsers check an XML document's syntax and can support the Document Object Model (DOM) and/or the Simple API for XML (SAX).

- DOM-based parsers build a tree structure containing the XML document's data in memory. This allows the data to be programmatically manipulated. SAX-based parsers process the document and generate events when tags, text, comments, etc. are encountered. These events return data from the XML document.

- Internet Explorer 5 has a built-in DOM-based XML parser called **msxml** that processes XML documents.

- An XML document can reference an optional Document Type Definition (DTD) file, which defines how the XML document is structured.

- Validating parsers check the XML document structure against the document's DTD.

- If the XML document conforms to the DTD, then the XML document is valid.

- Parsers that cannot check for document conformity ignore the DTD and are called nonvalidating parsers.

- If an XML parser is able to successfully process an XML document (that does not have a DTD), the XML document is considered well formed. By definition, a valid XML document is also a well-formed XML document.

- XML tags delimit the beginning and end of each element.

- XML declaration attribute **version** indicates the XML version to which the document conforms.

- Every XML document must contain exactly one element (called a root element) that contains every other element. Lines preceding the root element are collectively called the prolog.

- XML element and attribute names can be of any length and may contain letters, digits, underscores, hyphens and periods. However, they must begin with either a letter or an underscore.

- DTD files define the grammatical rules for an XML document and are optional.

- XML treats consecutive whitespace, tabs and blank lines as a single space. XML attribute **xml:space** preserves spaces.

- The set of rules that structure a document is done with EBNF (Extended Backus-Naur Form) grammar, not XML syntax. XML processors need additional functionality to read a DTD because of the EBNF grammar.

- The **!ELEMENT** element type declaration defines the rules for an element.

- The plus sign (**+**) operator indicates one or more occurrences for an element. Other operators include the asterisk (*****), which indicates any number of occurrences and the question mark (**?**), which indicates either zero occurrences or exactly one occurrence. If an operator is omitted, exactly one occurrence is assumed.

- The **!ATTLIST** element type declaration to define an attribute for an element.

- Keyword **#IMPLIED** specifies that if the parser finds an element without a **type** attribute, it is allowed to choose its own value or ignore it.

- Keyword **#REQUIRED** specifies that the attribute must be declared in the document, and keyword **#FIXED** specifies that the attribute must be declared with the given fixed value. If it is not declared, then the parser, by default, uses the fixed value that is specified with the declaration.

- Flag **#PCDATA** specifies that the element can store parsed character data (i.e., text). Parsable character data should not contain markup.

- The characters less than (**<**), greater than (**>**) and ampersand (**&**) should be replaced by their entities (i.e., **<**, **>** and **&**). However, the ampersand (**&**) character can be inserted when used with entities.

- Keyword **EMPTY** specifies that the element does not contain any text. Empty elements are commonly used for their attributes.

- MathML was developed by the W3C for describing mathematical notations and expressions.

- Because document authors are likely to create XML elements with the same name, XML provides namespaces to help minimize conflicts. Like elements, the document author defines namespaces. Because domain names are guaranteed to be unique, many document authors use their domain name for the namespace.

- Electronic Business XML (ebXML) is a markup language initiated by the United Nations body for Trade Facilitation and Electronic Business (UN/CEFACT) and OASIS (Organization for the Advancement of Structured Information Standards) to develop and standardize an XML document structure for exchanging business data.

- Financial Products Markup Language (FpML) is an emerging standard for exchanging financial information over the Internet. The main advantage of adopting XML standard for FpML is platform independent exchange of data.

- Because XML documents contain data, they are data sources.

- Internet Explorer 5 allows XML documents to be embedded into an HTML document using the **XML** element.

- A **DATASRC** attribute added to a **TABLE** element's opening tag binds a data island to the table. Bound data is accessed via **SPAN** elements with **DATAFLD** attributes.

- The Document Object Model (DOM) hierarchical tree structure is made up of nodes. A node that contains other nodes (called child nodes) is called a parent node. Nodes that are peers are called sibling nodes.

- The DOM has a single root node that contains all other nodes in the document.

- Each node is an object that has properties, methods and events. These properties, methods and events are exposed by the XML parser as a programmatic library—called an Application Programming Interface (API).

- Any node in the DOM can be represented with object **XMLDOMNode**.

- The DOM API provides object **XMLDOMElement** for manipulating nodes that are elements and object **XMLDOMAttribute** for manipulating nodes that are attributes

- In the DOM, the entire XML document is represented by a **DOMDocument** object—which includes the root node and all its child nodes. If we wish to programmatically access a document's content we must create a **DOMDocument** object.

- **DOMDocument** property **documentElement** retrieves the document's root element. Property **nodeName** retrieves the name of the node.

- **DOMDocument** property **childNodes** allows each child node to be accessed using method **item**. Each child node is identified using an integer value. The first child has the value zero, the second one, and so on.

- **DOMDocument** property **firstChild** retrieves the first child of a node. A sibling node object is retrieved using the **nextSibling** and **previousSibling** properties. A parent node is retrieved using property **parentNode**.

- The Extensible Stylesheet Language (XSL) defines how an XML document's data is rendered. An XML's data does not have to be rendered using an XSL document, CSS can also be used.

- XSL provides elements that define rules for how one XML document is transformed into another text-based document. The subset of XSL concerned with transformations is called XSL Transformations (XSLT). An XSL document is also an XML document.

- An XSL document contains template rules that define how each node in the XML document should be processed. A template rule is specified by an **xsl:template** element.

- Element **xsl:template**'s **match** attribute specifies the element in an XML document for which a template rule should be applied.

- Microsoft-specific attribute **DATAPAGESIZE** specifies the number of data records to display.

- The element **xsl:for-each** iterates over each **contact** element in the XML document. Attribute **select** specifies the **contacts** elements over which the **xsl:for-each** iterates.

- Attribute **order-by** sorts **contact** elements. A plus sign (**+**) indicates ascending order; a minus sign (**-**) indicates descending order.

- Element **xsl:value-of** to retrieve the data specified by attribute **select**.

- Any material in a **CDATA** section (i.e., between **<![CDATA[** and **]]>**) is not processed by the XML parser.

- Property **XSLDocument** (**document** object) retrieves a reference to the XSL DOM as a **DOMDocument**. XSL DOM is similar to XML DOM but refers to the structure of an XSL document.

- The input pattern **//@order-by** specifies a recursive search for the first **order-by** node (that is an attribute) in a XSL document. Similarly, the pattern **//xsl:for-each/@select** indicates a recursive search for the first **select** attribute node in an **xsl:for-each** element.

- Schema was initially pioneered by Microsoft and is currently a W3C working draft.

- Element **ElementType** declares schema element types. Attribute **name** defines the element's name. Attribute **content** defines the element's contents.

- Value **eltOnly** specifies that an element can only contain other elements. The other values that **content** may have are **empty** for empty elements, **textOnly** for text elements and **mixed** for both text and elements.

- Element **group** groups elements and specifies the order in which they occur.
- Attribute **minOccurs** defines an element's minimum number of occurrences. Assigning a value of **0** to **minOccurs** sets the element as optional, and assigning a value of **1** to **minOccurs** sets the element as occurring at least once.
- Attribute **maxOccurs** defines an element's maximum number of occurrences. A value of **1** sets the element as occurring at most once and an asterisk (*****) specifies any number of times.
- Element **element** references an element that can appear as part of the enclosing **ElementType** element's content model. Similarly, attributes can be declared using **AttributeType** element.
- The element **xsl:template** defines a template rule. Attribute **match** selects the nodes (i.e., elements) to which the **xsl:template** is applied.
- Property **XSLDocument** accesses a **document**'s XSL style sheet.
- Element **xsl:choose** element can be used to perform conditional tests. This element is composed of one or more **xsl:when** elements and an optional **xsl:otherwise** element.
- Element **xsl:when** is a conditional statement with the conditional placed in the **test** attribute.
- Element **xsl:element** generates the markup for an element of a specified name
- Element **xsl:attribute** adds an attribute to markup.
- Extensible Hypertext Markup Language (XHTML) is HTML's proposed successor, and the current version of XHTML includes HTML 4 (for backwards compatibility), to help Web authors make the transition from HTML to XHTML.
- XHTML documents follow the same rules for well-formedness as XML documents.
- XHTML documents conform to one of three types of DTDs—strict, transitional and frameset.
- Microsoft has developed BizTalk, an architecture that uses XML to facilitate application integration and data transactions.
- The Simple Object Access Protocol (SOAP) is an HTTP/XML-based protocol that developers can use to invoke remote methods.

TERMINOLOGY

!ATTLIST attribute type declaration
!ELEMENT element type declaration
#FIXED keyword
#IMPLIED flag
#IMPLIED keyword
#PCDATA (parsed character data)
#REQUIRED keyword
& entity (**&**)
&delta in MathML
∫ in MathML
⁢ in MathML
> entity (**>**)
< entity (**<**)
" entity (**"**)
.dtd extension
.xml extension
.xsl extension
Amaya editor from W3C
American Institute of Certified Public Accountants (AICPA)
Application Programming Interface (API)

asterisk,***** (any number of occurrences)
BizTalk
BizTalk element
Body element (BizTalk)
brackets, **[]** (XSL condition statement)
case sensitive
CDATA section
Chemical Markup Language (CML)
closing tag
CML (Chemical Markup Language)
Commerce XML (cXML)
container element
customized markup languages
data island
decimalPattern attribute in XBRL
describing data
displaying data
document type definition (DTD)
documentElement property
DOM parser
DOMDocument object

Uniform Resource Identifier (URI)
Uniform Resource Locator (URL)
Uniform Resource Name (URN)
United Nations body for Trade Facilitation and
    Electronic Business (UN/CEFACT)
URI (Uniform Resource Identifier)
URL (Uniform Resource Locator)
URN (Uniform Resource Name)
US GAAP (General American Accounting
    Principles)
valid document
validating parser
Vector Markup Language (VML)
version attribute
VoiceML (Voice Markup Language)
W3C XML working group
Web collection
well-formed document
whitespace
Wireless Markup Language (WML)
XHTML (Extensible Hypertext Markup
    Language)
XMI (XML Metadata Interchange)
XML (Extensible Markup Language)
XML Document Object Model (DOM)
XML editor
xml namespace (**xmlns**)

XML parser
XML specification
XML tag
xml:space attribute
XML-Data
XMLDocument property
XMLDOM object
XMLDOMAttribute object
XMLDOMElement object
XMLDOMNode object
xmlns (XML namespace)
XSL (Extensible Stylesheet Language)
XSL conditional statement
xsl namespace
xsl:apply-templates element
xsl:attribute element
xsl:choose element
xsl:comment element
xsl:element element
xsl:for-each element
xsl:otherwise element
xsl:stylesheet element
xsl:template element
xsl:value-of element
xsl:when element
XSLDocument property
XSLT (XSL Transformations)

SELF-REVIEW EXERCISES

27.1 Fill in the blanks for each of the following:
    a) Element _____ defines a mathematical operator.
    b) A data island uses attribute _____ to bind to a data source.
    c) To embed an XML document into an HTML file requires the _____ tag.
    d) Element _____ generates a markup tag in an HTML document.
    e) We use the _____ property to get the contents of an element in JavaScript.
    f) MathML symbol **∫** is an example of _____.
    g) To define a DTD element attribute, you use the _____ tag.
    h) Element _____ defines an XML stylesheet.
    i) Element _____ selects specific XML elements.
    j) Element _____ is used with the **preserve** value to preserve whitespace.

27.2 State which of the following statements are *true* and which are *false*. If *false*, explain why.
    a) XML is not case sensitive.
    b) An XML document can have exactly one root element.
    c) XML is used to display information.
    d) A DTD/Schema is used to define the style of a XML document.
    e) Schema **group** element with a **maxOccurs** attribute value of **2** specifies two occurrences of an element.
    f) MathML is a subset of XML.
    g) Data placed between **<![CDATA[** and **]]>** is not parsed by the XML parser.
    h) Element **xsl:otherwise** is used within an **xsl:when** element.

i) The `<!ELEMENT list (item*)>` tag defines a list element containing one or more `item` elements.

j) Element `MATH` is an XML element.

27.3 Find the error(s) in each of the following and explain how to correct it (them).

a)
```
<job>
    <title>Manager</title>
    <task number = "42">
</job>
```

b)
```
<statement>
    <costs>100<sales>
    </costs>200</sales>
    <net.profit>100</net.profit>
    <%profit>100</%profit>
</Statement>
```

27.4 In Fig. 27.2 we subdivided the `author` element into more detailed pieces. How would you subdivide the `date` element?

27.5 What is the `#PCDATA` flag used for?

27.6 In Fig. 27.18, how would you design an XSLT to filter for the first name, Sue?

27.7 What is the primary difference between HTML and XML?

ANSWERS TO SELF-REVIEW EXERCISES

27.1 a) `mo`. b) `DATASRC`. c) `XML`. d) `xsl:element`. e) `text`. f) an operator. **(mo)**. g) `!AT-TLIST`. h) `xsl:stylesheet`. i) `xsl:for-each`.

27.2 a) False. XML is case sensitive. b) True. c) False. XML is used to organize data in a structured manner. d) False. A DTD/schema is used to define the structure of an XML document. e) False. This is an invalid syntax. A `maxOccurs` attribute can only have a value of **1** or *****. f) True. g) True. h) False. Element `xsl:otherwise` is used within element `xsl:choose`. i) False. **(item*)** defines a `list` element containing any number of `item` elements. j) False. Element `MATH` is an HTML element.

27.3 a) A **/** in the empty element is missing:

```
<task number = "42"/>
```

b) Elements **costs** and **sales** are overlapping. The tag **%profit** cannot be used as percentage character is not allowed in XML names. The tag **statement** should have a matching tag.

27.4
```
<date>
    <month>September</month>
    <day>9</day>
    <year>1999</year>
</date>
```

27.5 The `#PCDATA` flag denotes that parsed character data can be contained by the element.

27.6 Use the `select` attribute value of `contact[FirstName='Sue']`.

27.7 Simply, the difference between HTML and XML is that HTML is a method for displaying data, while XML is a method for storing data.

EXERCISES

27.8 In Fig. 27.6 we defined a DTD for the business letter document. What would be a valid DTD for Fig. 27.3?

27.9   [*Note*: Before attempting to solve this exercise visit **www.w3.org/Math** to learn more about MathML's tags.] Using Amaya and MathML, generate the following:

a) $\int_{\frac{1}{2}}^{1} 5y\delta x$

b) $x = \sqrt{2y^{-3}} - 8y + \frac{\sqrt{y}}{3}$

27.10   Write an XML document that stores the following information:

Name	Job	Department	Cubicle
Joe	Programmer	Engineering	5E
Mary	Designer	Marketing	9M
Elaine	Designer	Human Resources	8H
Tim	Administrator	Engineering	4E
Peter	Project Coordinator	Marketing	3M
Bill	Programmer	Engineering	12E
Mark	Salesperson	Marketing	17M
Karin	Programmer	Technical Support	19T

27.11   Write a DTD for the XML document in Exercise 27.10.

27.12   Write an XSL that displays the XML document in Exercise 27.10.

27.13   Write an XSL style sheet for Fig. 27.19 that displays first names in blue and last names in red.

27.14   Write an HTML page that displays the XML data in Fig. 27.19, using data islands.

27.15   Create an Active Server Page that creates an XML document from the following database:

Product ID	Product
152341	Acme Anvil
015832	Big Bug
951324	Candy Crab
765421	Distorted Dinosaur
235231	Easy Exercise
882312	Foggy Freeway
441221	Green Grass
722345	Happy Heifer
523119	Icky Illness
612214	Jumpy Jellybeans

27.16   Write an Active Server Page that dynamically creates an XML data island as part of the HTML page sent to the client.

27.17   Write an XML schema document for Fig. 27.3.

27.18   Write an XML schema document for Fig. 27.19.

28

Case Study: An Online Bookstore

Objectives

- To be able to use persistence with Microsoft CSS behaviors.
- To be able to use Active Server Pages, Dynamic HTML and XML together to construct an e-Commerce application.
- To be able to send XML documents using HTTP POST requests.
- To understand how a Business-to-Consumer (B2C) model works.
- To understand the various Business-to-Business (B2B) models.

Knowing trees, I understand the meaning of patience.
Knowing grass, I can appreciate persistence.
Hal Borland

If it's a good script I'll do it. And if it's a bad script, and they pay me enough, I'll do it.
George Burns

The universe is like a safe to which there is a combination.
But the combination is locked up in the safe.
Peter De Vries

What's in a name? that which we call a rose
By any other name would smell as sweet.
William Shakespeare

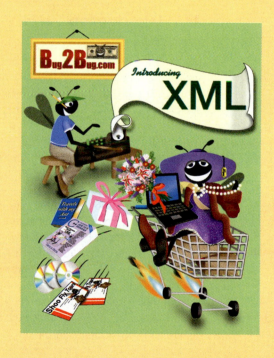

Outline

28.1 Introduction

In this chapter, we present a complete fully implemented case study of an e-commerce application using many of the programming technologies presented earlier in the book. We feel that a commitment to larger-scale case studies is something that has been lacking in introductory programming textbooks. This case study allows students to immerse themselves in a practical, substantial three-tier Web application.

The case study presented in this chapter is one of the most fundamental applications of e-commerce—an online store. In this particular case we sell books, but this example is easily adaptable to sell other products. Most online stores use a three-tier setup similar to what we describe in this chapter, though their implementation varies. We present one out of the many different possibilities.

This case study is divided into two parts: a business-to-client (B2C) scenario and a business-to-business (B2B) scenario. In the first five sections, we implement a B2C scenario and in the last two sections we consider a B2B scenario.

In order to create an online bookstore, a minimum of three fundamental pieces are required: client-side scripting, server-side scripting and a database. In Chapters 13 through 18, we introduced client-side scripting using JavaScript—the most widely used client-side scripting language. In this case study, we use JavaScript to validate client input and create a more dynamic Web site. In Chapters 19 through 23, we introduced Microsoft DHTML for dynamically enhancing the client-side browsing experience. We use DHTML to provide a cleaner user interface with Cascading Style Sheets (CSS) and to create content.

Active Server Pages (ASP) are used to implement server-side scripting. Active Server Pages (discussed in Chapters 25 and 26) allow the server to create and send custom, dynamic content to the client. We use ASP to generate an XML book list, handle customer information requests and input the submission of book orders.

We created a shopping cart using ASP in a previous chapter, but we can also use XML for shopping cart storage and transmission. To persist the shopping cart across browsing sessions, we introduce CSS persistence, implemented in Internet Explorer 5. By using XML (discussed in Chapter 27), we create a readable and structured document for storing book orders. We also create XML documents for transmission between businesses.

We present both the client-side and server-side files. Client-side validation and a client-side shopping cart are used to reduce the number of client-server interactions.

This case study involves many documents, which are summarized in Fig. 28.1 (client-side) and Fig. 28.2 (server-side). [*Note: Due to the size of the case study, we do not list the source code inline with the chapter. We include the source code with line numbers in a PDF (Adobe Portable Document Format) file named "Chapter 28 Code Listings" on the CD that accompanies this book. All source code documents are provided on the CD in the Chapter 28 examples directory and at www.deitel.com.*]

File Name	Description
index.html	Book browsing and shopping.
tableHighlight.js	Scripting used to highlight every other table row.
rowSelection.js	Scripting used to highlight and select table rows.
sortTable.js	Scripting used to sort the XML book list by ISBN, author, title or price.
productSearch.js	Scripting used to search the XML book list for ISBNs, authors or titles.
theCart.js	Scripting used to maintain the shopping cart table.
theItems.js	Scripting used to maintain the XML shopping cart data.
stringFunc.js	Scripting used to convert between currency amounts and strings.
style.css	CSS style sheet.

Fig. 28.1 Client-side documents.

File Name	Description
products.asp	Generates the XML book list.
productSchema.xml	Schema for products.asp.
sorting.xsl	XSL transformation for the book list.
server.asp	Processes the shopping cart submission.
verify.asp	Verifies the order.
account.asp	Navigation map for account information.
login.asp	Login page.
logoff.asp	Logout page.
profile.asp	Displays customer information. Also permits customer information to be modified.
orders.asp	Displays orders.
info.asp	Displays order details.
faq.asp	Displays Frequently Asked Questions.

Fig. 28.2 Server-side documents.

Figure 28.3 shows the bookstore in Internet Explorer 5 and Fig. 28.4 shows the key interactions between the store's documents. Section 28.2 explains the steps necessary to set up the case study for execution.

The storefront home page is **index.html** (Fig. 28.5). On the home page, the user can search for a specific book, view the list of available books, view a specific book's information and add/remove books to/from the shopping cart and checkout. This page contains JavaScript that provides user interface features and manages the shopping cart. If the user clicks **checkout**, **server.asp** (Fig 28.20) is requested to process the order. The order is placed into a database and set to be verified. If the order is valid, the user is sent to the order verification page (**verify.asp**, Fig. 28.21). The verification page completes the order by asking the user for their login and password. If an order is cancelled, the user is redirected to **index.html**.

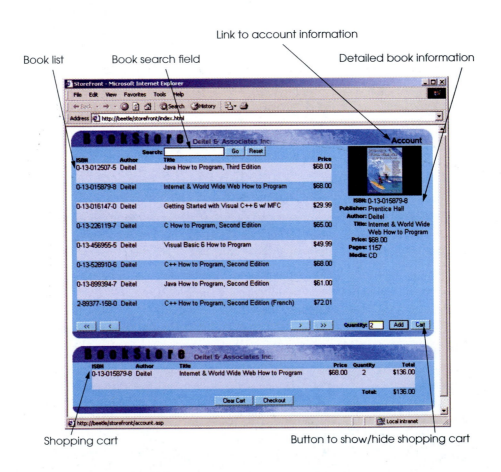

Fig. 28.3   The book store.

The account information page (**account.asp**, Fig. 28.22) provides links to the rest of the Web site. Each of the pages in the account information area can be navigated to from any other page. The link to frequently asked questions (**faq.asp**, Fig. 28.28) is available on all pages. If the user has not logged in, a link to the login page (**login.asp**, Fig. 28.23) is available. If the user has logged in, they can logout (**logoff.asp**, Fig. 28.24), view the customer profile (**profile.asp**, Fig. 28.25) or see previous orders (**orders.asp**, Fig. 28.26). The customer profile page shows the user's customer information. The user may modify this information if they so desire. The previous orders page shows a list of orders, which can be selected to show detailed order information (**info.asp**, Fig. 28.27). The detailed order information page shows all the books in order with their subtotals and also provides a link back to the previous orders page.

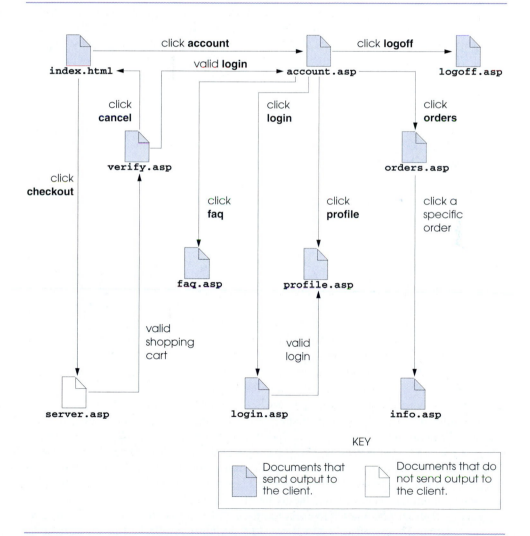

Fig. 28.4　Key interactions between the book store's documents.

28.2 Setup

This section describes the steps necessary to set up the bookstore.

1. Create the directory structure on your Web server. We recommend that you create a subdirectory beneath **C:\Inetpub\Wwwroot** named **storefront**. Into this directory, copy all the files and directories from the **storefront** subdirectory beneath the Chapter 28 examples directory on the CD found in the back of this book. The **images** directory contains the images used by the book store (i.e., background, header image and footer image) and the **books** directory contains the book images.

2. Register the Microsoft Access 2000 database **storefront2k.mdb** as a System DSN named **dbStorefront**. If you do not have the Access 2000 ODBC driver, we provide an Access 97 version of the same database called **storefront97.mdb**. See the document titled "Setting up a ODBC System Data Source Name" on the CD that accompanies this book for step-by-step instructions on registering a System DSN. The username and password for the bookstore is **new** and **new**. You can define new users by using Microsoft Access to add user records to the database.

3. Specify the location of the scripting code by changing line 27 of **index.html** (Fig. 28.5) to your Web site URL (e.g., **http://**_machineName_**/storefront/**). Line 47 of **request.asp** also needs to be changed to your Web server location to run the B2B example.

4. _You must use Internet Explorer 5 or higher to run this case study._ Remember that ASP files need to be served via a Web server (i.e., **http://localhost/**) and will not render correctly if you view the files directly by double-clicking them.

28.3 Client-Side Documents

In this section, we discuss the store's client-side documents and scripts. In Section 28.4, we will discuss the store's server-side documents and scripts. Client-side technologies used include HTML (discussed in Chapters 9 and 10), JavaScript (discussed in Chapters 13 through 17) and Dynamic HTML (discussed in Chapters 18 through 21).

For the client-side portion of the online bookstore, we decided to keep page refreshing at a minimum. A book store obviously needs a listing of books available for sale and a listing of what books have been selected. Because the space available for listing books is limited, we provide a place to view detailed information about a book. Another useful feature is the ability to search for specific books, so a search box is provided.

The first document (**index.html**) we discuss is shown in Fig. 28.5. Again, you will need to refer to the PDF file "Chapter 28 Code Listings" on the CD-ROM that accompanies this book to view the code listings. This page contains the book list (with clickable headers for sorting), buttons for navigating the book list, a text box and buttons for searching the book list, a book details section, a text box and buttons for adding items to the shopping cart, and a button for displaying and hiding the shopping cart.

Lines 9 through 22 contain references to external files that contain JavaScript. To reference an external file, use element **SCRIPT**'s **SRC** attribute. JavaScript files are commonly given the extension **.js**. We discuss each of these JavaScript files later in this section. We place the JavaScript into separate files for reuse purposes. Because the user interface elements are already grouped into specific categories (i.e., the search box, table highlighting, etc.), organizing the functions of a interface element makes finding functions easier.

Function **handleLoading** (lines 31 through 64) controls when user interface components are available for use. Initially, all clickable items (i.e., buttons and links) are disabled—using *attribute **DISABLED***—until the document's JavaScript files, images and XML data are loaded. When all the files have finished loading, the function enables the clickable items. This prevents errors from occurring during the loading process. JavaScript is used to enable the clickable items by changing the **DISABLED** attribute's value to **false**.

The bookstore table (lines 70 through 295) contains the search box (lines 82 through 92), the book details (lines 93 through 174), the book list (lines 183 through 225), the navigation bar (lines 230 through 259) and shopping cart functionality (lines 262 through 287).

The shopping cart table (lines 297 through 365) is initially hidden and contains no items. When the **Cart** button is clicked, the contents of the shopping cart are displayed.

The notice message table (lines 367 through 385) is also initially hidden, and is used to notify users that the shopping cart is being submitted. This block is displayed when the user enters the checkout process.

Finally, we have three XML storage elements. On line 387

```
<DIV ID = "xmlShoppingCart" CLASS = "userData"
```

the **DIV** element **xmlShoppingCart** is used to store the shopping cart contents over browser sessions by using Microsoft's *CSS persistence*.

Microsoft's CSS implementation contains a ***userData*** *behavior* which is used to persist element data on a page. There is a 64 KB data limitation per page, and a 640 KB data limit per Web domain (e.g., Web server). We need to be careful about the amount of information we store to be sure not to go over the data limit. We will cover the details of using **userData** later in this section.

On line 390

```
<XML ID = "xmlSortProducts" SRC = "sorting.xsl"
```

the **XML** element **xmlSortProducts** references the XSL document **sorting.xsl** which sorts and filters the book list.

Line 393 and 394

```
<XML ID = "xmlProducts" SRC = "products.asp"
    ONREADYSTATECHANGE = "handleLoading();"
```

reference the XML book list (**xmlProducts**) generated by **products.asp**. We use the **ONREADYSTATECHANGE** event to determine when the XML book list has finished loading and thus enable the page.

Figure 28.6 (**tableHighlight.js**) contains the scripting code that changes each individual row's color to make the book list easier to read. We place the scripting code in a separate file for reuse.

On line 405

```
var newColor = "#CCDDFF";
```

we assign the color **#CCDDFF** to variable **newColor**. This color is used to highlight every other row.

Function **hideTable** (lines 408 through 411) hides the book list. We hide the book list before showing a different page of books when navigating (for example, line 236) to prevent the browser from rendering the table each time a new row is displayed.

Function **highlightTable** (lines 414 through 426) iterates through the **productListing** table rows and changes the background color of every other row. It is called in function **refreshTable** on line 432 and also when **index.html** is first loaded (on line 62). Line 417

```
var objRow = window.productListing.rows;
```

uses the **TABLE** element's *rows* *collection* to return a collection of **row** (**TR**) elements. By using the **rows** collection, we access the table rows and assign **newColor** to every other row. For additional information on the **rows** collection, visit:

    msdn.microsoft.com/workshop/author/dhtml/reference/collec-
    tions/rows.asp

Function **refreshTable** (lines 429 through 435) is called on a **ONREADYSTATE-CHANGE** event (line 186). When a navigation button is pressed, the book list changes and the table is re-highlighted.

Function **refreshShoppingTable** (lines 438 through 450) is similar to function **refreshTable**, but refreshes the shopping cart's table instead.

Figure 28.7 (**rowSelection.js**) provides functionality for highlighting selected rows and retrieving detailed book information. We use the **ONMOUSEOVER**, **ONMOUSEOUT** and **ONMOUSECLICK** events of the book list and shopping cart table rows to call these functions.

Functions **rowSelect** (lines 457 through 466) and **rowUnselect** (lines 469 through 477) highlight and unhighlight table rows. When the mouse moves over each table row, these functions are called by the **ONMOUSEOVER** and **ONMOUSEOUT** events from the book list (lines 207 and 208) and shopping cart table.

Function **displayDetail** (lines 480 through 557) retrieves information from the XML book list and places the selected book's information into the detailed book information area. If information for a field does not exist, **N/A** is used.

On line 490 through 492

```
var theXMLnode =
   xmlProducts.documentElement.selectSingleNode(
   "book[ isbn = '" + object.cells[ 0 ].innerText + "' ]" );
```

we call method **selectSingleNode** to retrieve the **book** element from the book list. From this node, we use the **selectSingleNode** method to retrieve the node's children (**image**, **isbn**, **author**, **title**, **price**, **pages** and **media**) to populate the detail area. By using the *cells* *collection* of a **row** object, we retrieve the row's first cell which contains the book's ISBN. For more information on the **cells** collection, visit

    msdn.microsoft.com/workshop/author/dhtml/reference/collec-
    tions/cells.asp

In Fig. 28.8 (**sortTable.js**), we implement sorting and filtering of the book list using XSLT. On line 562, we define the variables that store the sort order—either a plus character (**+**) for ascending or a minus character (**-**) for descending—for the ISBN, author, title and price. Variable **lastNum** (line 563) stores the last field that was sorted to determine when to switch between ascending or descending sort methods. We initialize **lastNum** to **-1** to specify that there is no last sorted field.

Function **sortProducts** (lines 566 through 611) sets the sorting variables using the argument provided (e.g., the function call on line 190). Using these variables, we create a string, which is then used by XSLT to transform the book list.

On lines 608 through 610

```
xmlProducts.documentElement.transformNodeToObject(
    xmlSortProducts.documentElement,
    xmlProducts.XMLDocument );
```

method **transformNodeToObject** transforms the book list stored in the **xmlProducts** element according to the XSLT document in element **xmlSortProducts**. The resulting transformation is stored in **xmlProducts.XMLDocument**. The book list is automatically refreshed by Internet Explorer.

Figure 28.9 (**productSearch.js**) contains the JavaScript code that searches for items in the book list. Function **actSearchType** (lines 615 through 619) handles the event fired when keyboard buttons are pressed. If the *Enter* (or *Return*) key is pressed we perform a search by calling function **actSearchGo**. This function is bound to the search box via the **ONKEYPRESS** event (line 85).

Function **actSearchGo** (lines 622 through 642) performs an XSL transformation on the book list using the text entered into the text box when the **Go** button is pressed (line 87). The sorting expression is composed of three boolean expressions. Each of these expressions checks for a substring match on **ISBN**, **author** or **title**. This is performed using element **xsl:if**, which checks for instances of the query string in each of the three fields using the JavaScript method **indexOf**. Function **actSearchReset** (lines 645 through 650) sets the product listing to its original order when the **Reset** button is pressed (line 91).

We use XML as a structured data format for storing shopping cart items. We do not use cookies for storage because CSS data persistence already stores data as XML. The shopping cart data is stored with the structure

```
<cart>
    <item isbn = "0-13-015879-8" qty = "2"/>
    <item isbn = "0-14-039314-3" qty = "12"/>
</cart>
```

Because other data such as titles and prices are already stored on the server, we only need to store the ISBN and quantities of books in the shopping cart.

Figure 28.10 (**theCart.js**) contains the functions that add, modify and remove shopping cart table rows. Function **goCart** (lines 654 through 668) displays the shopping cart. When the **Cart** button is clicked (line 284), we either show the shopping cart by setting the CSS *display* property of the shopping cart table to **block**, or hide the shopping cart by setting the **display** property to **none**. Method **scrollIntoView** (line 660) brings the shopping cart into the browser's viewable area.

We create array **cartArray** (line 671) to store references to the shopping cart table rows. We use the ISBN string of a book to uniquely index **cartArray**.

Function **fillTable** (lines 674 through 769) adds items to the shopping cart table. If **null** is returned by the search for the ISBN, the item is considered invalid and rejected.

If an item already exists in the table, the existing entry is modified. If an item is new, it is appended to the table.

We use **table** element methods *insertRow* (line 690) and *insertCell* (line 696) to append a row to the table body and to append cells to the row. These methods return a **row** (**TR**) object and **cell** (**TD**) object, respectively.

Function **unfillTable** (lines 772 through 788) removes an item from the shopping cart table by using **table** element method *deleteRow*.

Function **loadShoppingCart** (lines 791 through 830) loads the XML shopping cart data into the shopping cart table. First, we remove the current table rows in the shopping cart table. We then create the shopping cart table by calling function **fillTable** on each book in the XML shopping cart.

The Microsoft CSS **userData** behavior is specified as an element's style using

```
behavior: url(#default#userData)
```

The behaviors that Microsoft has implemented for Internet Explorer 5 are called *default behaviors* (hence the *#default* namespace). Some **userData** behavior methods are listed in Fig. 28.11.

Function **clearShoppingCart** (lines 833 through 857) removes all the items from the shopping cart when the **Clear Cart** button is clicked—by removing all table rows and clearing the XML shopping cart.

Function **findItem** (lines 860 through 872) provides JavaScript code that retrieves a shopping cart item's quantity.

Figure 28.12 (**theItems.js**) contains the remaining shopping cart functionality. Here we modify the XML shopping cart and handle its submission to the Web server.

Function **changeAddButton** (lines 876 through 886) checks the text box for a valid item quantity. This function is called via an **ONKEYUP** event (line 273) of the quantity text box. If the input is valid, the **add** button is enabled.

Function **goBuy** (lines 889 through 940) adds a book to the shopping cart when the **add** button is clicked (line 279). We check for the existence of the book in our XML document and modify it accordingly or we create a new node. Functions **fillTable** (or **unfillTable**) and **refreshShoppingTable** are then called to update the shopping cart table.

Methods / Properties	Description
load(*string* **)**	Method. Loads the data referenced with *string*.
save(*string* **)**	Method. Saves the data with reference *string*.
setAttribute(*string, value* **)**	Method. Sets the *string* attribute to *value*.
getAttribute(*string* **)**	Method. Returns the value of attribute *string*.
XMLDocument	Property. Returns the XML document associated with the element.

Fig. 28.11 Some methods and properties of the Microsoft **userData** behavior.

Function **buyCheckOut** (lines 943 through 1012) submits the shopping cart to the server for verification when the **Checkout** button is clicked (line 358). In this function, we first verify that the user wants to continue the checkout process. We use the *XMLHttpRequest* object (**Microsoft.XMLHTTP**) to submit the data to the server. Some **XMLHttpRequest** object methods and properties are summarized in Fig. 28.13 and Fig. 28.14.

For more information on the **XMLHttpRequest** object, visit

```
msdn.microsoft.com/library/psdk/xmlsdk/xmld8bp0.htm
```

Figure 28.15 (**stringFunc.js**) contains JavaScript code that formats currency values into strings and coverts strings into currency values.

Function **createPriceNum** (lines 1016 through 1041) formats a floating-point number into a string with commas. For example, **12345.678** is formatted as **"12,345.68"**.

Function **parsePriceNum** (lines 1044 through 1053) converts a currency string with commas to a floating-point number. For example, **"12,345.67"** is converted to **12345.67**. This conversion is performed for mathematical calculations, because JavaScript does not automatically parse commas.

Figure 28.16 (**style.css**) contains the CSS stylesheet for the bookstore. On line 1158 we define the **userData** behavior, which is currently a Microsoft technology, but has been added to the W3C working draft for CSS3 (the behavioral extensions module). By using the **userData** behavior, we created a persistent data store for storing our shopping cart. For more information on other Microsoft CSS behaviors available for Internet Explorer 5 visit

```
msdn.microsoft.com/workshop/author/behaviors/reference/
reference.asp
```

Properties	Description
responseBody	The response from the server as raw undecoded bytes (i.e, a binary format).
responseXML	The response from the server in parsed XML form.
responseText	The response from the server as a Unicode string.
status	The numeric HTTP status code returned by the server.
statusText	The HTTP status text returned by the server.

Fig. 28.13 Some properties of the **XMLHttpRequest** object.

Methods	Description
open(*method, url, async*)	Sets up an HTTP request using *method* to *url*. If *async* is set to **true**, then method **send** returns immediately.
send(*object*)	Sends a request to the server with *object* as the content.

Fig. 28.14 Some methods of the **XMLHttpRequest** object.

28.4 XML Data (Book Listing)

Figure 28.17 (**products.asp**) is a server-side document that generates a book list (marked up as XML) from the **Products** table of Access database **storefront2k.mdb**. A screen capture of the generated XML is provided after the code.

If the book list stays constant, an XML document could be generated once and then used, instead of regenerating the XML document each time a client browser requests it. This would reduce the number of tasks the server performs.

On line 15

```
strQuery = "SELECT * FROM Products"
```

we select the records from the **Products** table of the database and return the records according to the structure defined in the schema.

Figure 28.18 (**productSchema.xml**) contains the book list schema. Figure 28.19 (**sorting.xsl**) contains the XSL transform code that sorts and searches for books.

On line 73

```
<xsl:if expr = "true">
```

the **xsl:if** element filters the data using the expression string that we created in **productSearch.js**. By setting the attribute **expr** to **true**, all records are initially displayed.

28.5 Other Server-Side Documents

With server-side documents, we provide the back-end of the bookstore. These documents depend on up-to-date information which is stored in the store database, such as the customer profile, a listing of what orders have been made and customer help. The first document that we discuss provides the connection between the client-side documents and the server.

Figure 28.20 (**server.asp**) shows the ASP code which accepts the shopping cart data from the client.

Line 98

```
Set xmlData = Server.CreateObject( "Microsoft.XMLDOM" )
```

creates a **DOMDocument** (**Microsoft.XMLDOM**) object to store the incoming XML data.

By setting the *Async* *property* to **False** (line 99), we make sure that we perform any XML operations synchronously so code will not continue executing until the data has completed loading. An asynchronous operation is performed parallel to executing code. If the operation is done asynchronously, the code continues executing even if the load operation has not completed. Because our code depends on the load operation, the operation must be synchronous to ensure proper behavior.

We then load the incoming data. On line 100

```
Call xmlData.Load( Request )
```

we use method **Load** to parse the data sent via the **XMLHttpRequest** object. The data is stored in the **Request** object. We now have our XML shopping cart data. Next, we verify that the data is valid (lines 102 through 113) and then insert the data into the database (lines 115 through 136). We store the order information using session variables (lines 132 through 134) and return the string **"OK"** to the client. On receiving **"OK"** the client redirects to the verification page (**verify.asp**).

On line 127

```
Call objRecord.AddNew()
```

we do not execute a SQL statement directly, but use the **RecordSet** *method* *AddNew*. This allows us to retrieve the **orderid** automatically generated (via the **AutoNumber** setting of the **orderid** field) by the database. To use method **AddNew**, we need to set the *CursorType* *property* (line 123) which defines how we use the **RecordSet**, the *Lock-Type* *property* (line 124) which defines the way to lock a **RecordSet** and the *Source* *property* (line 122) which defines the data source.

By using a **CursorType** of **1** (**vbOpenKeyset**), the **RecordSet** allows the movement of the cursor (a database object that handles navigation of records and how they are changed) anywhere in the **RecordSet**. The default **CursorType** has a value of **0** which only allows scrolling forward through records (i.e., the cursor can only move forward).

The **LockType** indicates the way to lock records when performing changes so other users cannot modify a record at the same time. By using a **LockType** of **2** (**vbLockPes-simistic**), we lock the record when editing. The default setting of **1** sets records as read-only, preventing them from being edited. The **Source** property is set to the database connection **objConn**.

Figure 28.21 (**verify.asp**) is the verification page for orders. The user is redirected here after the shopping cart information is written to the database.

We confirm that there is a valid order waiting to be verified, by checking the session variables (**storeFrontOrderID** and **storeFrontOrderDate**) set in the submission page (**server.asp**—Fig. 28.20). If the variables are **Empty** (i.e., not set), we redirect to **account.asp** (Fig. 28.22) with an error message (lines 157 and 158). We retrieve the order from the database and request a user name and password to complete the submission.

On lines 309 through 380, the book list is generated by matching the items in the XML shopping cart data to the items in the database. We also calculate the total price of the order.

On submission, we verify the user name and password (lines 186 through 198) and set the user and total price of the order into the record (lines 201 through 218). We flag the order as verified (line 209), clear the order session variables (lines 220 and 221) and redirect the user to the account status page (line 226).

If the user canceled the order (lines 160 through 178), we delete the record using method **Delete** (line 174) and redirect the user back to the book list (**index.html**).

Unverified orders may accumulate, so maintenance should be performed on the database to remove unverified orders that are older than a day. We do not perform this step in this case study, but this could be easily done with another server-side script.

Figure 28.22 (**account.asp**) shows the customer account navigation page. This page is the central hub for locating customer information, frequently asked questions and other information.

Figure 28.23 (**login.asp**) shows the login page for customer verification. After successfully logging in, the customer profile and orders pages are made available for viewing.

We perform client-side verification for the **username** and **password** fields. If these fields contain text, we query the database for the **username** and **password** pair and if successful we store the **userid** as a session variable named **StoreFrontLoggedIn**. Other pages that retrieve customer and order information use this session variable.

Figure 28.24 (**logout.asp**) shows the logout page used to log out of the account information pages. The only task that the logoff page performs is to clear the **Store-FrontLoggedIn** session variable by setting it to **Empty** (line 639).

Figure 28.25 (**profile.asp**) shows the customer profile page used to show information about the customer. This page also allows the modification of the customer profile.

The user profile page displays all the information about a customer. Client-side validation is performed in function **validate** (lines 766 through 815). Regular expressions are used to validate the dates and phone numbers. We also verify that both password fields match before submission.

On submission, we update the records. If a new credit card number was not entered, we do not change the credit card number field in the database. Similarly, if a new password was not entered, the password field is not modified.

Figure 28.26 (**orders.asp**) shows the orders made by the customer. All the user's records are retrieved to populate the order list. For each record item, the order number, order date and total are displayed. We provide a link on each table row to show detailed information about an order. Figure 28.27 (**info.asp**) shows the details on an order selected in **orders.asp**.

Detailed information on an order is generated in the same manner as the verification page. We locate the order selected and verify that the **userid** matches. Next, we retrieve the shopping cart, total amount and order date from the **Orders** table.

The shopping cart XML data is parsed and each **item** element's **isbn** attribute is used to query the **products** database to determine the book information. For each item, we also calculate the subtotal.

Figure 28.28 (**faq.asp**) contains the Frequently Asked Questions (FAQ) page used as a first step for customer help.

28.6 Business-to-Business (B2B) Models

In Chapter 3, we introduced various e-commerce business models. In this section, we discuss some of these business models in detail and in the next section we implement a B2B scenario.

In electronic commerce, B2B transactions involve transfer of data, such as purchase orders, invoices, payments, document specifications and other documents, such as articles and books.

Before the Internet, business documents were hand delivered by couriers. Depending on the courier and where these documents were being sent, a significant amount of time might have passed before business partners could complete a transaction. The Internet provides a means for data to be transmitted easily and almost instantaneously. Also, because data is always in an electronic format, transaction costs are low and information storage and retrieval is performed automatically.

There are three major B2B models: supplier-oriented, buyer-oriented and intermediary-oriented.

The *supplier-oriented B2B model* consists of suppliers providing a means for buyers to purchase products directly. Some companies which use this B2B model are Dell, Intel and Cisco, each of which sell large amounts of electronics. Dell, for example, devotes a large portion of computer sales to businesses, which need custom configurations in large quantities.

The *buyer-oriented B2B model* consists of buyers making available their product needs. Suppliers then place bids on products, which the buyer chooses. This model is used primarily by businesses that purchase many different items and do not have the money to search for suppliers which provide the products. For example, Boeing purchases thousands of parts and equipment to use in building airplanes. To search and compare suppliers for each necessary part is an incredibly complex task.

The *intermediary-oriented B2B model* consists of a business which manages the product information from multiple suppliers and provides buyers with an easy access point to the data. The intermediary then processes orders from the buyers or forwards the orders to the suppliers to fulfill.

For businesses to communicate, *electronic data interchange* (*EDI*) standards were created. These EDI standards provided a universal method for businesses to transmit documents electronically. Because of the complexity of setting up EDI in businesses, only large-scale corporations utilize it. Without EDI, companies such as Wal-Mart, Amazon.com, Dell and Intel would not be able to manage the amount of information transmitted. Currently, an XML-based EDI standard is being created to reduce the complexity involved in using EDI.

28.7 B2B Example

In the first part of this chapter, we discussed the interactions between the store and the user—a B2C scenario. In this section, we consider a business-to-business (B2B) scenario where the store places orders with another business (a warehouse) for books. In order for these two businesses to perform an electronic transaction, they must agree on the transmission method and document syntax for transactions.

Figure 28.29 (**request.asp**) creates a purchase request form for our book store. Because our book store carries a limited supply of books, we need to provide a means to order books from a warehouse. By using XML, we provide an easy method of transferring the purchase request. We defined our purchase request format as

```
<req>
   <book isbn = "9-21-912873-Y" qty = "200"/>
   <book isbn = "1-234-56789-0" qty = "1000"/>
</req>
```

To acquire new book inventory, we talk to a warehouse, which is a *B2B exchange*. In this case, we would be following an intermediary-oriented model. The buyer (the book store) browses the supplier's (the warehouse) book list and places orders for books. In our case, we have a local copy of the books that the warehouse stocks. The warehouse compiles book lists from many publishers and provides the compiled list to retailers. Retailers then search for books using this one access point, instead of searching over many lists. The warehouse would then fulfill the orders made by buyer.

We retrieve the book list from the **Products** table and create a form for submitting it. Function **submitRequest** (lines 17 through 57) creates the XML purchase request document and submits the data using the **XMLHttpRequest** object introduced in Section 28.3 when the **Submit** button is clicked (line 112).

Using the ISBNs and quantities stored in the form, we create an XML document by using the **DOMDocument** methods mentioned in Section 27.6. By using method **createElement** (lines 25 and 34) we create the root element, **req**. For each valid quantity, we create a **book** element and use method **setAttribute** to create and set the value of the **isbn** and **qty** attributes.

On line 38

```
xmlRoot.appendChild( xmlNode );
```

we append the **book** element to the **req** root element using method **appendChild**.

If the XML document contained books, we submit the document to **warehouse.asp** using the **XMLHttpRequest** object (line 45 through 49). After submission, we retrieve the response returned by the server and replace the document with the response (line 51). [*Note*: Line 47 will need to be changed to your Web server location, similarly to what was done in **index.html**.]

Figure 28.30 (**warehouse.asp**) acquires the data sent by **request.asp**, but only returns the XML document transmitted. In an actual transaction, we would use the XML document to create a shipping invoice for the books requested and fulfill the request.

28.8 Internet and World Wide Web Resources

msdn.microsoft.com/workshop/author/dhtml/reference/collections/ rows.asp
Reference information on the **table** element's **rows** collection.

msdn.microsoft.com/workshop/author/dhtml/reference/collections/ cells.asp
Reference information on the **table** element's **cells** collection.

msdn.microsoft.com/library/psdk/xmlsdk/xmld8bp0.htm
The XML reference section of the MSDN Web site.

msdn.microsoft.com/workshop/author/behaviors/reference/ reference.asp
Microsoft's CSS behaviors reference.

SUMMARY

- E-businesses are usually composed of three-tier setups comprised of an HTML client, ASP middle tier and a database. Some technologies used in these Web sites are DHTML, CSS and JavaScript. Heavy usage of client-side scripting is preferred to remove processing loads from the server.

- There are two types of business models: Business-to-Consumer (B2C) and Business-to-Business (B2B). The B2C model involves general consumer marketing, while the B2B model involves business marketing. There are three types of B2B models: supplier-oriented, buyer-oriented and intermediary-oriented. Another B2B model is electronic data interchange (EDI) which is used for information transmission between businesses.

- External scripting is referenced by using the **SCRIPT**'s **SRC** attribute. JavaScript files are commonly given the extension **.js**. With external scripting files, multiple Web pages can use the same script.

- An **INPUT** element can be disabled by using the **DISABLED** attribute. The element can be enabled by setting the element's **disabled** property to **false** via scripting.

- Persistence of data can be performed by using the **userData** behavior of Microsoft's CSS persistence. There is a 64 KB data limit per page and a 640 KB data limit per domain. To provide data persistence to an element, assign the **behavior** style the value **url(#default#userData)**.

- The **ONREADYSTATECHANGE** event can be attached to an **XML** element to determine the loading status of that element.

- To access the table rows of a **TABLE** element, use the **rows** collection of the element, which is composed of **row** objects. To access the table cells in a table row, use the **cells** collection of a **row** object, which is composed of **cell** objects.

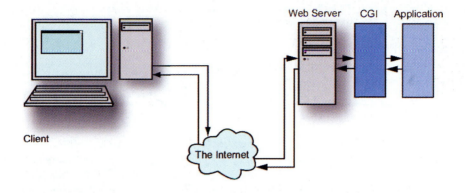

Fig. 29.1   Data path of a typical CGI-based application.

Applications typically interact with the user through *standard input* and s*tandard output.* Standard input is the stream of information received by a program from a user, typically through the keyboard, but also possibly from a file or another input device. Standard output is the information stream presented to the user by an application; it is typically displayed on the screen but may be printed by a printer, written to a file, etc.

For CGI scripts, the standard output is redirected (or *piped*) through the Common Gateway Interface to the server and then sent over the Internet to a Web browser for rendering. If the server-side script is correctly programmed, output will be readable to the client. Usually, that means that the output is a HTML document which can be viewed using a Web browser.

29.2 Perl

With the advent of the World Wide Web and Web browsers, the Internet gained tremendous popularity. This greatly increased the volume of requests users made for information from Web servers. It became evident that the degree of interactivity between the user and the server would be crucial. The power of the Web resides not only in serving content to users, but also in responding to requests from users and generating dynamic content. The framework for such communication already existed through CGI. Because most of the information users send to servers is text, Perl was a logical choice for programming the server side of interactive Web-based applications, due to its simple, yet powerful, text processing capabilities. It is arguably the most popular CGI scripting language. The Perl community, headed by Wall (who currently works for O'Reilly & Associates as a Perl developer and researcher) continuously works to evolve the language, keeping it competitive with newer server-side technologies such as Microsoft's Active Server Pages (see Chapter 25).

Figure 29.2 presents a simple Perl program that writes the text **"Welcome to Perl!"** to the screen. Because the program does not interact with the Common Gateway Interface, it is not a CGI script. Our first examples in Perl will be command-line programs to help explain the basics of the language. See Fig. 29.11 for our first example of a CGI script.

```
1  #!perl
2  # Fig. 29.2: first.pl
3  # A first program in Perl.
4
5  print "Welcome to Perl!\n";
```

```
Welcome to Perl!
```

Fig. 29.2   A simple program in Perl.

Lines 2 and 3 use the Perl *comment character* (**#**) to instruct the interpreter to ignore everything on the current line following the **#**. This syntax allows programmers to write descriptive comments inside their programs. The exception to this rule is the *"shebang" construct* (**#!**) in line 1. On Unix systems, this line indicates the path to the Perl interpreter (such as **#!/usr/bin/perl**). On other systems (such as Windows), the line may be ignored or it may indicate to the server (e.g., Apache) that a Perl program follows the statement.

The comment on line 2 indicates that the filename of the program is **first.pl**. Perl scripts file names typically end with the **.pl** extension. The program can be executed by running the Perl interpreter from the command-line prompt (e.g., DOS prompt in Windows).

In order to run the Perl script, Perl must first be installed on the system. Windows users, see the "ActiveState Perl Installation" document on the CD that accompanies this book for instructions on how to install ActivePerl, the standard Perl implementation for Windows. For installation on other platforms visit **www.perl.com**.

To run **first.pl** type

    perl first.pl

where **perl** is the interpreter and **first.pl** is the perl script. Alternatively, we could type

    perl -w first.pl

which instructs the Perl interpreter to output warnings to the screen if it finds possible bugs in your code.

Testing and Debugging Tip 29.1

*When running a Perl script from the command line, always use the **-w** option. The program may seem to execute correctly when there is actually something wrong with the source code. The **-w** option displays warnings encountered while executing a Perl program.*

On Windows systems, a Perl script may also be executed by double-clicking its programs icon. The program window closes automatically once the script terminates and any screen output is lost. For this reason, it is usually better to run a script from the DOS prompt.

Line 5 calls function ***print*** to write text to the screen. Note that since Perl is case-sensitive, writing **Print** or **PRINT** instead of **print** would yield an error. The text, **"Welcome to Perl!\n"**, is surrounded in quotes and called a *string*. The last portion of the string—the newline *escape sequence* **\n**—moves the cursor to the next line. The semicolon (**;**) at the end of line 5 is always used to terminate Perl statements.

Common Programming Error 29.1

*Forgetting to terminate a statement with a **;** is a syntax error.*

Good Programming Practice 29.1

*While not all servers require the "shebang" construct (**#!**) it is good practice to include it for program portability.*

Like other programming languages, Perl has built-in data types (Fig. 29.3) that represent the different kinds of data. Notice that each variable name has a specific character (i.e., **$**, **@** and **%**) preceding it. For example, the **$** character specifies that the variable contains a *scalar* value (i.e., strings, integer numbers and floating-point numbers). The script **variable.pl** (Fig. 29.4) demonstrates manipulation of scalar variables.

Common Programming Error 29.2

*Failure to place a preceding **$** character before a scalar variable name is a syntax error.*

Data type	Format for variable names of this type	Description
Scalar	*$scalarname*	Can be a string, an integer number or a floating-point number.
Array	*@arrayname*	An ordered list of scalar variables which can be accessed using integer indices.
Hash	*%hashname*	An unordered set of scalar variables whose values are accessed using unique scalar values (i.e., strings) called keys.

Fig. 29.3   Perl data types.

```
1   #!perl
2   # Fig. 29.4: variable.pl
3   # Program to illustrate the use of scalar variables.
4
5   $a = 5;
6   print "The value of variable a is: $a\n";
7
8   $a = $a + 5;
9   print "Variable a after adding 5 is: $a\n";
10
11  $a *= 2;
12  print "Variable a after multiplying by 2 is: $a\n";
13
14  # using an uninitialized variable in the context of a string
15  print "Using a variable before initializing: $var\n";
16
17  # using an uninitialized variable in a numeric context
18  $test = $num + 5;
19  print "Adding uninitialized variable \$num to 5 yields: $test.\n";
20
```

Fig. 29.4   Using scalar variables (part 1 of 2).

```
21   # using strings in numeric contexts
22   $str = "A string value";
23   $a = $a + $str;
24   print "Adding a string to an integer yields: $a\n";
25
26   $strnum = "15charactersand1";
27   $c = $a + $strnum;
28   print "Adding $a to string \"$strnum\" yields: $c\n";
```

```
The value of variable a is: 5
Variable a after adding 5 is: 10
Variable a after multiplying by 2 is: 20
Using a variable before initializing:
Adding uninitialized variable $num to 5 yields: 5.
Adding a string to an integer yields: 20
Adding 20 to string "15charactersand1" yields: 35
```

Fig. 29.4   Using scalar variables (part 2 of 2).

In Perl, a variable is created automatically the first time it is encountered by the inter-preter. Line 5 creates a variable with name **$a** and sets its value to **5**. Line 8 adds the integer **5** to **$a**. Line 9 calls function **print** to write text followed by the value of **$a**. Notice that the actual value of **$a** is printed, not "$a". When a variable is encountered inside a double quoted (**" "**) string, Perl uses a process called *interpolation* to replace the variable with its associated data. Line 11 uses an *assignment operator* ***=** to yield an expression equivalent to **$a = $a * 2** (thus assigning **$a** the value **20**). These assignment operators (i.e., **+=**, **-=**, ***=** and **/=**) are syntactical shortcuts.

Testing and Debugging Tip 29.2

Function **print** *can be used to display the value of a variable at a particular point during a program's execution. This is often helpful in debugging a program.*

In Perl, uninitialized variables have the value **undef**, which can evaluate to different things depending on context. When **undef** is found in a numeric context (e.g., **$num** in line 18), it evaluates to **0**. In contrast, when it is interpreted in a string context (such as **$var** in line 15), **undef** evaluates to the empty string (**" "**).

Lines 22 through 28 show the results of evaluating strings in numeric context. Unless a string begins with a digit it is evaluated as **undef** in a numeric context. If it does begin with a digit, every character up to (but not including) the first non-digit character is evalu-ated as a number and the remaining characters are ignored. For example, the string **"A string value"** (line 23) does not begin with a digit and therefore evaluates to **undef**. Because **undef** evaluates to **0**, variable **$a**'s value is unchanged. The string **"15charactersand1"** (line 27) begins with a digit and is therefore interpolated as **15**. The character **1** on the end is ignored because there are non-digit characters preceding it. Evaluating a string in numeric context does not actually change the value of the string. This is shown by line 28's output, which prints the **"15charactersand1"**.

Notice that the programmer does not need to differentiate between numeric and string data types because the interpreter evaluates scalar variables depending on the context in which they are used.

Common Programming Error 29.3

*Using an uninitialized variable might make a numerical calculation incorrect. For example, multiplying a number by an uninitialized variable results in **0**.*

Testing and Debugging Tip 29.3

While it is not always necessary to initialize variables before using them, errors can be avoided by doing so.

Perl provides the capability to store data in arrays. Arrays are divided into *elements* that each contain a scalar value. The script **arrays.pl** (Fig. 29.5) demonstrates some techniques for array initialization and manipulation.

Line 5 initializes array **@array** to contain the strings **"Bill"**, **"Bobby"**, **"Sue"** and **"Michelle"**. Note that in Perl, all array variable names must be preceded by the **@** symbol. Parentheses are necessary to group the strings in the array assignment; this group of elements surrounded by parentheses is called a *list* in Perl. In assigning the list to **@array**, each person's name is stored in an individual array element with a unique integer index value starting at 0.

When **print**ing an array inside double quotes (line 7), the array element values are printed with only one space separating them. If the array name is not enclosed in double quotes when it is **print**ed (line 8), the interpreter prints the element values without separating them with spaces.

```
1   #!perl
2   # Fig. 29.5: arrays.pl
3   # Program to demonstrate arrays in Perl
4
5   @array = ( "Bill", "Bobby", "Sue", "Michelle" );
6
7   print "The array contains: @array\n";
8   print "Printing array outside of quotes: ", @array, "\n\n";
9
10  print "Third element: $array[ 2 ]\n";
11
12  $number = 3;
13  print "Fourth element: $array[ $number ]\n\n";
14
15  @array2 = ( A..Z );
16  print "The range operator is used to create a list of\n";
17  print "all letters from capital A to Z:\n";
18  print "@array2 \n\n";
19
20  $array3[ 3 ] = "4th";
21  print "@array3 \n\n";
22
23  print 'Printing literal using single quotes: @array and \n', "\n";
24  print "Printing literal using backslashes: \@array and \\n\n";
```

Fig. 29.5   Using arrays (part 1 of 2).

```
The array contains: Bill Bobby Sue Michelle
Printing array outside of quotes: BillBobbySueMichelle

Third element: Sue
Fourth element: Michelle

The range operator is used to create a list of
all letters from capital A to Z:
A B C D E F G H I J K L M N O P Q R S T U V W X Y Z

   4th

Printing literal using single quotes: @array and \n
Printing literal using backslashes: @array and \n
```

Fig. 29.5   Using arrays (part 2 of 2).

Line 10 demonstrates how individual array elements are accessed using braces (**[ ]**). As mentioned above, if we use the **@** character followed by the array name we reference the array as a whole. But if the array name is prefaced by the **$** character and followed by an index number in square brackets (as in line 10), it refers instead to an individual array element, which is a scalar value. Line 13 demonstrates how a scalar variable can be used as an index. The value of **$number** (**3**) is used to get the value of the fourth array element.

Line 15 initializes array **@array2** to contain the capital letters from **A** to **Z** inclusive. The *range operator* (**..**), specifies that all values between uppercase **A** and uppercase **Z** be placed in the array. The range operator (**..**) can be used to create any consecutive series of values such as **1** through **15** or **a** through **z**.

The Perl interpreter handles memory management automatically. Therefore, it is not necessary to specify an array's size. If a value is assigned to a position outside the range of the array or to an uninitialized array, the interpreter automatically extends the array range to include the new element. Elements that are added by the interpreter during an adjustment of the range are initialized to the **undef** value. Lines 20 and 21 assign a value to the fourth element in the uninitialized array **@array3**. The interpreter recognizes that memory has not been allocated for this array and creates new memory for the array. The interpreter then sets the value of first three elements to **undef** and the value of the fourth element to the string **"4th"**. When the array is printed, the first three **undef** values are treated as empty strings and printed with a space between each one. This accounts for the three extra spaces in the output before the string **"4th"**.

In order to print special characters like **** and **@** and **"** and not have the interpreter treat them as an escape sequence or array, Perl provides two choices. The first is to ***print*** (line 23) the characters as a literal string (i.e., a string enclosed in single quotes). When strings are inside single quotes, the interpreter treats the string literally and does not attempt to interpret any escape sequence or variable substitution. The second choice is to use the backslash character (line 24) to *escape* special characters.

29.3 String Processing and Regular Expressions

One of Perl's most powerful capabilities is its ability to process textual data easily and efficiently, allowing for straightforward searching, substitution, extraction and concatenation of strings. Text manipulation in Perl is usually done with *regular expressions*—a series of characters that serve as pattern-matching templates (or search criteria) in strings, text files and databases. This feature allows complicated searching and string processing to be performed using relatively simple expressions.

Many string processing tasks can be accomplished by using Perl's *equality* and *comparison* operators (Fig. 29.6, **equals.pl**). Line 5 declares and initializes array **@fruits**. Operator **qw** ("quote word") takes the contents inside the parentheses and creates a comma-separated list with each element wrapped in double quotes. In this example, **qw(apple orange banana)** is equivalent to **("apple", "orange", "banana")**.

Lines 7 through 28 demonstrate our first examples of Perl *control structures*. The **foreach** loop beginning in line 7 iterates sequentially through the elements in the **@fruits** array. The value of each element is assigned in turn to variable **$item** and the body of the **foreach** is executed once for each array element. Notice that a semicolon does not terminate the **foreach**.

```perl
1   #!perl
2   # Fig. 29.6: equals.pl
3   # Program to demonstrate the eq, ne, lt, gt operators
4
5   @fruits = qw( apple orange banana );
6
7   foreach $item ( @fruits )
8   {
9      if ( $item eq "banana" )
10     {
11        print "String '$item' matches string 'banana'\n";
12     }
13
14     if ( $item ne "banana" )
15     {
16        print "String '$item' does not match string 'banana'\n";
17     }
18
19     if ( $item lt "banana" )
20     {
21        print "String '$item' is less than string 'banana'\n";
22     }
23
24     if ( $item gt "banana" )
25     {
26        print "String '$item' is greater than string 'banana'\n";
27     }
28  }
```

```
String 'apple' does not match string 'banana'
String 'apple' is less than string 'banana'
String 'orange' does not match string 'banana'
String 'orange' is greater than string 'banana'
String 'banana' matches string 'banana'
```

Fig. 29.6 Using the **eq, ne, lt, gt**, operators.

Line 9 introduces another control structure—the **if** statement. Parentheses surround the condition being tested and required curly braces surround the block of code that is executed when the condition is true. In Perl, anything except the number **0** and the empty string is defined as true. In our example, when the **$item**'s content is tested against **"banana"** (line 9) for equality, the condition evaluates to true, and the **print** command (line 11) is executed.

The remaining **if** statements (lines 14, 19 and 24) demonstrate the other string comparison operators. Operators **ne**, **lt**, and **gt** test strings for equality, less than, and greater than, respectively. These operators are only used with strings. When comparing numeric values, operators **==**, **!=**, **<**, **<=**, **>** and **>=** are used.

Common Programming Error 29.4

*Using **==** for string comparisons and **ne** for numerical comparisons can result in errors in the program.*

Common Programming Error 29.5

*While the number **0** and even the string **"0"** evaluate to false in Perl **if** statements, other string values that may look like zero (such as **"0.0"**) evaluate to true.*

For more powerful string comparisons, Perl provides the *match operator (**m//**)*, which uses regular expressions to search a string for a specified pattern. Figure 29.7 uses the match operator to perform a variety of regular expression tests.

```perl
1   #!perl
2   # Fig 29.7: expression.pl
3   # searches using the matching operator and regular expressions
4
5   $search = "Now is is the time";
6   print "Test string is: '$search'\n\n";
7
8   if ( $search =~ /Now/ )
9   {
10      print "String 'Now' was found.\n";
11  }
12
13  if ( $search =~ /^Now/ )
14  {
15      print "String 'Now' was found at the beginning of the line.\n";
16  }
17
18  if ( $search =~ /Now$/ )
19  {
20      print "String 'Now' was found at the end of the line.\n";
21  }
22
23  if ( $search =~ /\b ( \w+ ow ) \b/x )
24  {
25      print "Word found ending in 'ow': $1 \n";
26  }
```

Fig. 29.7   Using the match operator. (part 1 of 2)

```
27
28   if ( $search =~ /\b ( \w+ ) \s ( \1 ) \b/x )
29   {
30       print "Repeated words found: $1 $2\n";
31   }
32
33   @matches = ( $search =~ / \b ( t \w+ ) \b /gx );
34   print "Words beginning with 't' found: @matches\n";
```

```
String 'Now' was found.
String 'Now' was found at the beginning of the line.
Word found ending in 'ow': Now
Repeated words found: is is
Words beginning with 't' found: the time
```

Fig. 29.7   Using the match operator. (part 2 of 2)

We begin by assigning the string **"Now is is the time"** to variable **$search** (line 5). The expression

```
$search =~ /Now/
```

(line 8) uses the **m//** match operator to search for the *literal characters* **Now** inside variable **$search**. Note that the **m** character preceding the slashes of the **m//** operator is optional in most cases, and is thus omitted here.

The match operator takes two operands. The first of these is the regular expression pattern to search for (**Now**), which is placed between the slashes of the **m//** operator. The second operand is the string to search within, which is assigned to the match operator using the **=~** operator. This **=~** operator is sometimes called a binding operator, since it binds whatever is on its left side to a regular expression operator on the right.

In our example, the pattern **Now** is found in the string **"Now is is the time"**, the match operator returns true, and the body of the **if** statement is executed. In addition to literal characters like **Now** which match only themselves, regular expressions can include special characters called *metacharacters* which can specify patterns or contexts that cannot be defined using literal characters. For example, the caret metacharacter (**^**) matches the beginning of a string. The next regular expression (Line 13)

```
$search =~ /^Now/
```

uses this metacharacter to search the beginning of **$search** for the pattern **Now**.

The **$** metacharacter searches the end of a string for a pattern (line 18). Because the pattern **Now** is not found at the end of **$search**, the body of the **if** statement (line 20) is not executed. Note that **Now$** is not a variable, it is a search pattern that uses **$** to search specifically for **Now** at the end of a string.

The next condition (line 23),

```
$search =~ /\b ( \w+ ow ) \b/x
```

searches (from left to right) for the first word ending with the letters **ow**. As is in strings, backslashes are used in regular expressions to escape characters with special significance.

For example, the **\b** expression does not match the literal characters "**\b**". Instead, the expression matches any *word boundary (*generally, a boundary between an *alphanumeric character—***0–9**, **a–z**, **A–Z** and the underscore character—and something that is not an alphanumeric character). Between the **\b** characters is a set of parentheses; these will be explained momentarily.

The expression inside the parentheses, **\w+ ow**, indicates that we are looking for patterns ending in **ow**. The first part, **\w+**, is a combination of **\w** (an escape sequence which matches a single *alphanumeric character*) and the **+** *modifier*, which is a *quantifier* that instructs Perl to match the preceding character one or more times. Thus, **\w+** matches one or more alphanumeric characters. The characters **ow** are taken literally. Collectively, the whole expression **/\b (\w+ ow) \b/** matches one or more alphanumeric characters ending with **ow**, with word boundaries at the beginning and end. See Fig. 29.8 for a description of several other Perl regular expression quantifiers and Fig. 29.9 for a list of some regular expression metacharacters.

Parentheses indicate that the text matching the pattern is to be saved in a special Perl variable (e.g., **$1**, etc.). The parentheses in line 23 result in **Now** being stored in variable **$1**. Multiple sets of parentheses may be used in regular expressions, where each match results in a new Perl variable (**$1**, **$2**, **$3**, etc.) being created.

Quantifier	Matches
{n}	Exactly **n** times
{m,n}	Between **m** and **n** times inclusive
{n,}	**n** or more times
+	One or more times (same as {1,})
*	Zero or more times (same as {0,})
?	One or zero times (same as {0,1})

Fig. 29.8   Some of Perl's quantifiers.

Symbol	Matches	Symbol	Matches
^	Beginning of line	\d	Digit (i.e., **0** to **9**)
$	End of line	\D	Non-digit
\b	Word boundary	\s	Whitespace
\B	Non-word boundary	\S	Non-whitespace
\w	Word (alphanumeric) character	\n	Newline
\W	Non-word character	\t	Tab

Fig. 29.9   Some of Perl's metacharacters.

Adding *modifying characters* after a regular expression refines the pattern matching process. Modifying characters (Fig. 29.10) placed to the right of the forward slash that delimits the regular expression instruct the interpreter to treat the preceding expression in different ways. For example, the **i** after the regular expression

```
/computer/i
```

tells the interpreter to ignore case when searching, thus matching **computer**, **COMPUTER**, **Computer** and **CoMputER**.

When added to the end of a regular expression, the **x** modifying character indicates that whitespace characters are to be ignored. This allows programmers to add space characters to their regular expressions for readability without affecting the search. If the expression was written

```
$search =~ /\b ( \w+ ow ) \b/
```

without the **x** modifying character, then the script would be searching for a word boundary, two spaces, one or more alphanumeric characters, one space, the characters **ow**, two spaces and a word boundary. The expression would not match **$search**'s value.

The condition (line 28)

```
$search =~ /\b ( \w+ ) \s ( \1 ) \b/x
```

shows how the memory function of parentheses can be used in the regular expression itself. The first parenthetical expression matches any string containing one or more alphanumeric characters. The expression **\1** then evaluates to the word that was matched in the first parenthetical expression. The regular expression searches for two identical, consecutive words, separated by a whitespace character (**\s**)—in this case "**is is**".

Line 33's condition

```
$search =~ / \b ( t \w+ ) \b /gx
```

searches for words beginning with the letter **t** in the string **$search**. Modifying character **g** indicates a global search—one which does not stop after the first match is found. The array **@matches** is then assigned the value of a list of all matching words (line 33).

Modifying Character	Purpose
g	Perform a global search; find and return all matches, not just the first one found.
i	Ignores the case of the search string (case insensitive).
m	The string is evaluated as if it had multiple lines of text (i.e., newline characters are not ignored).
s	Ignore the newline character and treat it as whitespace. The text is seen as a single line.
x	All whitespace characters are ignored when searching the string.

Fig. 29.10 Some of Perl's modifying characters.

29.4 Viewing Client/Server Environment Variables

Knowing information about a client's execution environment can be useful to system administrators by allowing them to provide client-specific information. *Environment variables* contain information about the execution environment a script is being run in, such as the type of Web browser being used, the HTTP host and the HTTP connection. This information might be used by a server to send one Web page to a client using Microsoft Internet Explorer and a different Web page to a client using Netscape Communicator.

Until now, we have written simple Perl applications which output to the local user's screen. Through the use of CGI we can communicate with the Web server and its clients, allowing us to utilize the Internet as a method of input and output for our Perl applications. Note that in order to run Perl scripts as CGI applications, a Web server must first be installed and configured appropriately for your system. See the "Web Server Installation" document on the CD that accompanies this book for detailed information on how to install and set up a Web server.

Figure 29.11 generates an HTML table that displays the values of the clients' environment variables. The **use** *statement* (line 5) directs Perl programs to include the contents (e.g., functions, etc.) of predefined packages called *modules*. The **CGI** *module*, for example, contains many useful functions for CGI scripting in Perl, including functions that return strings representing HTML tags and HTTP headers. With the **use** statement we can specify which functions we would like to import from a particular module. In line 5, we use the *import tag* **:standard** to import a predefined set of standard functions.

```perl
1   #!perl
2   # Fig. 29.11: environment.pl
3   # Program to display CGI environment variables
4
5   use CGI qw( :standard );
6
7   print header;
8   print <<End_Begin;
9   <HTML>
10     <HEAD>
11        <TITLE>Environment Variables...</TITLE>
12     </HEAD>
13     <BODY TEXT = "BLACK" BGCOLOR = "WHITE">
14     <TABLE BORDER = "0" CELLPADDING = "2" CELLSPACING = "0"
15      WIDTH = 100%>
16   End_Begin
17
18   foreach $variable ( sort( keys( %ENV ) ) )
19   {
20      print <<End_Row;
21      <TR>
22      <TD BGCOLOR = "#11BBFF"><STRONG>$variable</STRONG></TD>
23      <TD><FONT COLOR = "BLACK" SIZE = "2">$ENV{$variable}
24      </FONT></TD>
25      </TR>
```

Fig. 29.11 Displaying CGI environment variables (part 1 of 2).

```
26  End_Row
27  }
28
29  print <<End_Finish;
30    </TABLE>
31    </BODY>
32  </HTML>
33  End_Finish
34  # Must include newline after End_Finish!
```

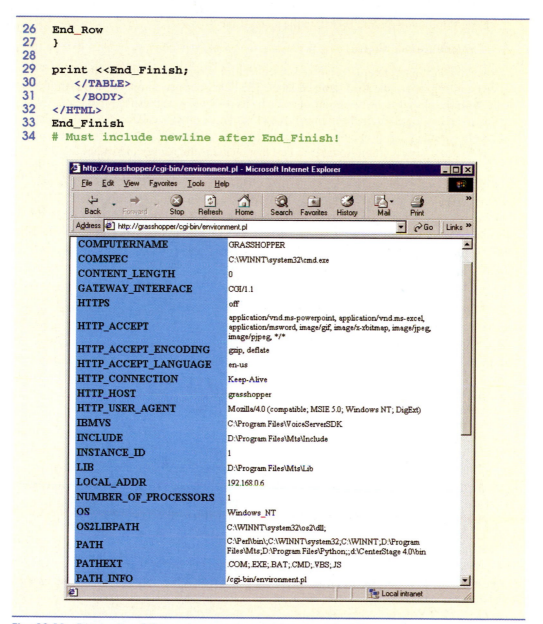

Fig. 29.11 Displaying CGI environment variables (part 2 of 2).

Line 7 directs the Perl program to **print** a valid *HTTP header* using function ***header*** from the **CGI** library. Browsers use HTTP headers to determine how to handle incoming data. The **header** function returns the string "**Content-type: text/html\n\n**", indicating to the client that what follows is HTML. The **text/html** portion of the header indicates that the browser must display the returned information as an HTML document. Since standard output is redirected when a CGI script is run, the function **print** outputs to the user's Web browser.

Lines 8 through 16 write HTML to the client. Line 8

```
print <<End_Begin;
```

instructs the Perl interpreter to print the subsequent lines verbatim (after variable interpolation) until it reaches the **End_Begin** label. This label consists simply of the identifier **End_Begin**, placed at the beginning of a line by itself, with no whitespace characters preceding it, and followed immediately with a newline. This syntax is called a *here document*, and is often used in CGI programs to eliminate the need to repeatedly call function *print*.

The **%ENV** *hash* is a built-in table in Perl that contains the names and values of all the environment variables. The *hash* data type is designated by the **%** character, and basically represents an unordered set of scalar-value pairs. Unlike an array, which accesses elements through integer subscripts (e.g., **$array[2]**), each element in a hash is accessed using a unique string *key* which is associated with that element's value. For this reason, hashes are also known as *associative arrays*, since the keys and values are associated in pairs. Hash values are accessed using the syntax **$hashName{keyName}**. In this example, each key in hash **%ENV** is the name of an environment variable (such as **HTTP_HOST**) which can be used to access the value of each environment variable (**$ENV{"HTTP_HOST"}**).

Function *keys* returns an array of all the keys in the **%ENV** hash (line 18) in no specific order, because hash elements have no defined order. We use function *sort* to order the array of keys alphabetically. Finally, the **foreach** loop iterates sequentially through the array returned by **sort**, repeatedly assigning the current key's value to scalar **$variable**. Lines 20 to 26 are executed for each element in the array of key values. Line 22 prints the key **$variable** (the name of the environment variable) in one column of the HTML table. Line 23 prints **$ENV{$variable}** in the other column, thus displaying the environment variable values associated with each key in hash **%ENV**.

29.5 Form Processing and Business Logic

HTML forms enable Web pages to collect data from users and send it to a Web server for processing by server-side programs and scripts, thus enabling users to purchase products, send and receive Web-based email, participate in a political poll, perform online paging or any number of other tasks. This type of Web communication allows users to interact with the server and is vital to electronic commerce.

Figure 29.12 uses an HTML **FORM** to collect information about users before adding them to a mailing list. This type of registration form could be used (for example) by a software company to get profile information for a company database before allowing the user to download software.

```
1  <!DOCTYPE html PUBLIC "-//W3C//DTD HTML 4.0 Transitional//EN">
2  <!-- Fig. 29.12: form.html -->
3
4  <HTML>
5  <HEAD>
6  <TITLE>Sample FORM to take user input in HTML</TITLE>
7  </HEAD>
8
```

Fig. 29.12 User entering a valid phone number (part 1 of 3).

```
9   <FONT FACE = "ARIAL,SANS-SERIF" SIZE = "2">
10
11      <FONT SIZE = "+2">
12         <STRONG>This is a sample registration form.</STRONG>
13      </FONT><BR>
14      Please fill in all fields and click Register.
15
16      <FORM METHOD = "POST" ACTION = "/cgi-bin/form.pl">
17         <IMG SRC = "images/user.gif"><BR>
18         <FONT COLOR = "BLUE">
19            Please fill out the fields below.<BR>
20         </FONT>
21
22         <IMG SRC = "images/fname.gif">
23         <INPUT TYPE = "TEXT" NAME = "FNAME"><BR>
24         <IMG SRC = "images/lname.gif">
25         <INPUT TYPE = "TEXT" NAME = "LNAME"><BR>
26         <IMG SRC = "images/email.gif">
27         <INPUT TYPE = "TEXT" NAME = "EMAIL"><BR>
28         <IMG SRC = "images/phone.gif">
29         <INPUT TYPE = "TEXT" NAME = "PHONE"><BR>
30
31         <FONT SIZE = "-2">
32            Must be in the form (555)555-5555<BR><BR>
33         </FONT>
34
35         <IMG SRC = "images/downloads.gif"><BR>
36         <FONT COLOR = "BLUE">
37            Which book would you like information about?<BR>
38         </FONT>
39
40         <SELECT NAME = "BOOK">
41            <OPTION>Internet and WWW How to Program 1e
42            <OPTION>C++ How to Program 2e
43            <OPTION>Java How to Program 3e
44            <OPTION>Visual Basic How to Program 1e
45         </SELECT>
46         <BR><BR>
47
48         <IMG SRC = "images/os.gif"><BR>
49         <FONT COLOR = "BLUE">
50            Which operating system are you
51            currently using?<BR>
52         </FONT>
53
54         <INPUT TYPE = "RADIO" NAME = "OS" VALUE = "Windows NT"
55         CHECKED>
56         Windows NT
57         <INPUT TYPE = "RADIO" NAME = "OS" VALUE = "Windows 2000">
58         Windows 2000
59         <INPUT TYPE = "RADIO" NAME = "OS" VALUE = "Windows 98">
60         Windows 98<BR>
61         <INPUT TYPE = "RADIO" NAME = "OS" VALUE = "Linux">
```

Fig. 29.12 User entering a valid phone number (part 2 of 3).

```
62          Linux
63          <INPUT TYPE = "RADIO" NAME = "OS" VALUE = "Other">
64          Other<BR>
65          <INPUT TYPE = "SUBMIT" VALUE = "Register">
66      </FORM>
67   </BODY>
68   </HTML>
```

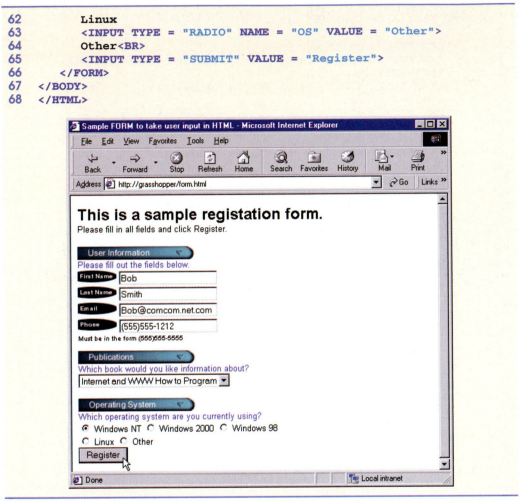

Fig. 29.12   User entering a valid phone number (part 3 of 3).

Except for line 16, the HTML code in Fig. 29.12 should look familiar. The **FORM** element (line 16) indicates that, when the user clicks **Register**, the form information is **POST**ed to the server. The statement **ACTION = "cgi-bin/form.pl"** directs the server to execute the **form.pl** Perl script (located in the **cgi-bin** directory) to process the posted form data. We assign a unique name (e.g., **EMAIL**) to each of the form's input fields. When **Register** is clicked, each field's **NAME** and **VALUE** is sent to the **form.pl** script, which can then access the submitted value for each specific field.

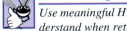

Good Programming Practice 29.2

*Use meaningful HTML object names for input fields. This makes Perl programs easier to understand when retrieving **FORM** data.*

Figure 29.13 (**form.pl**) processes the data posted by **form.html** and sends a Web page response back to the client. Function **param** (lines 8 through 13) is part of the Perl **CGI** module and is used to retrieve values for the form field elements and assign them to scalar variables. For example, in line 27 of Fig. 29.12, an HTML form text field is created with the name **EMAIL**; later, in line 11 of **form.pl**, we access the value that the user entered for that field by calling **param("EMAIL")**, and assign the value returned to scalar **$email**.

```perl
1   #!perl
2   # Fig. 29.13: form.pl
3   # Program to read information sent to the server
4   # from the FORM in the form.html document.
5
6   use CGI qw( :standard );
7
8   $os = param( "OS" );
9   $firstName = param( "FNAME" );
10  $lastName  = param( "LNAME" );
11  $email   = param( "EMAIL" );
12  $phone   = param( "PHONE" );
13  $book    = param( "BOOK" );
14
15  print header;
16  print "<BODY BACKGROUND = \"images/back.gif\">";
17  print "<BASEFONT FACE = \"ARIAL,SANS-SERIF\" SIZE = \"3\">";
18
19  if ( $phone =~ / ^ \( \d{3} \) \d{3} - \d{4} $ /x )
20  {
21     print <<End_Success;
22        Hi <FONT COLOR = "BLUE"><B>$firstName</B></FONT>.
23        Thank you for completing the survey.<BR>
24        You have been added to the
25        <FONT COLOR = "BLUE"><STRONG>$book</STRONG></FONT>
26        mailing list.<BR><BR>
27        <STRONG>The following information has been saved
28        in our database:</STRONG><BR>
29        <TABLE BORDER = "0" CELLPADDING = "0"
30           CELLSPACING = "10">
31        <TR><TD BGCOLOR = #FFFFAA>Name </TD>
32           <TD BGCOLOR = #FFFFBB>Email</TD>
33           <TD BGCOLOR = #FFFFCC>Phone</TD>
34           <TD BGCOLOR = #FFFFDD>OS</TD></TR>
35        <TR><TD>$firstName $lastName</TD><TD>$email</TD>
36           <TD>$phone</TD><TD>$os</TD></TR>
37        </TABLE>
38        <BR><BR><BR>
39        <CENTER><FONT SIZE = "-3">
40        This is only a sample form.
41        You have not been added to a mailing list.
42        </FONT></CENTER>
43  End_Success
44  }
45  else
46  {
47     print <<End_Failure;
```

Fig. 29.13 Script to process user data from **form.html** (part 1 of 2).

```
48         <FONT COLOR = "RED" SIZE = "+2">
49         INVALID PHONE NUMBER</FONT><BR>
50         A valid phone number must be in the form
51         <STRONG>(555)555-5555</STRONG>
52         <FONT COLOR = "BLUE"> Click the Back button,
53         enter a valid phone number and resubmit.<BR><BR>
54         Thank You.
55   End_Failure
56   }
```

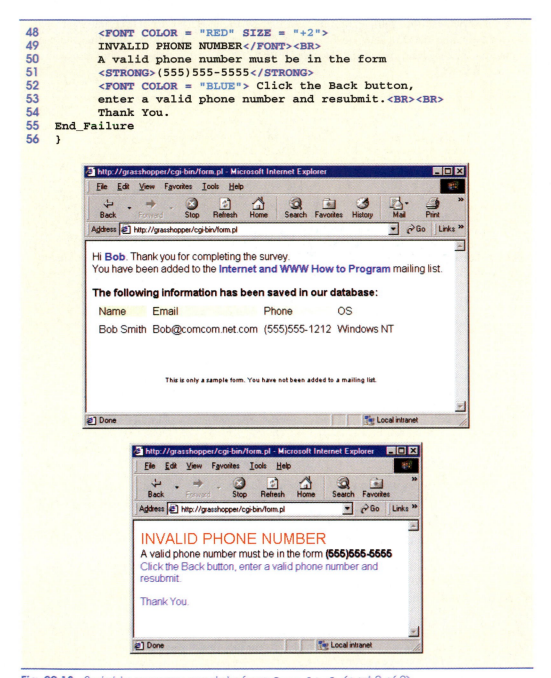

Fig. 29.13 Script to process user data from `form.html` (part 2 of 2).

In line 19, we determine whether the phone number entered by the user is valid. In this case, the format *(555)555-5555* is the only acceptable format. Validating information is crucial when you are maintaining a database or mailing list. For example, validation ensures that data is stored in the proper format in a database, that credit card numbers contain the proper number of digits before encrypting them for submission to a merchant, etc. The design of verifying information is called *business logic* (also called *business rules*).

Good Programming Practice 29.3

Use business logic to ensure that invalid information is not stored in databases.

Line 19's **if** condition

```
( $phone =~ / ^ \( \d{3} \) \d{3} - \d{4} $ /x )
```

uses a regular expression to validate the phone number. The expression **\(** matches the opening parenthesis of the phone number. Because we want to match the literal character **(**, we must escape its normal meaning by using the **** character. This must be followed by three digits (**\d{3}**), a closing parenthesis, three digits, a literal hyphen, and finally four more digits. Note that we use the **^** and **$** symbols to ensure that there are no extra characters at either end of the string.

If the regular expression is matched, then the phone number is valid and a Web page is sent to the client thanking the user for completing the form. If the user posts an invalid phone number, the **else** clause (lines 46 through 56) is executed, instructing the user to enter a valid phone number.

29.6 Server-Side Includes

Dynamic content greatly improves the look and feel of a Web page. Pages that include the current date or time, rotating banners or advertisements, a daily message or special offer, or the latest company news will always look new. Clients see new information upon every visit and thus will likely revisit the site in the future.

Server-side includes (SSIs) are commands embedded in HTML documents to allow simple dynamic content creation. SSI commands like **ECHO** and **INCLUDE** allow Web pages to include content that is constantly changing (like the current time) or information stored in a database. The command **EXEC** can be used to run CGI scripts and embed their output directly into a Web page.

Not all Web servers support the available SSI commands. Therefore, SSI commands are written as HTML comments (e.g., **<!--#ECHO VAR="DOCUMENT_NAME" -->**). Servers that do not recognize these commands will simply treat them as comments.

A document containing SSI commands is typically given the **.SHTML** file extension (the extra **S** at the front of the extension stands for server). The **.SHTML** files are parsed by the server. The server executes the SSI commands and writes any output to the client.

Figure 29.14 implements a *Web page hit counter*. Each time a client requests the document, the counter is incremented by one. Perl script **counter.pl** (Fig. 29.15) manipulates the counter.

Performance Tip 29.1

Parsing HTML documents on a server can dramatically increase the load on that server. To increase the performance of a heavily loaded server try to limit the use of Server Side Includes.

```
1   <!DOCTYPE html PUBLIC "-//W3C//DTD HTML 4.0 Transitional//EN">
2   <!-- Fig. 29.14: counter.shtml -->
3
4   <HTML>
5      <HEAD>
6         <TITLE>Using Server Side Includes</TITLE>
7      </HEAD>
8
9   <BODY>
10     <CENTER>
11        <H3>Using Server Side Includes</H3>
12     </CENTER>
13
14     <!--#EXEC CGI="/cgi-bin/counter.pl" --><BR>
15
16     The Greenwich Mean Time is
17     <FONT COLOR = "BLUE">
18     <!--#ECHO VAR="DATE_GMT" -->.
19     </FONT><BR>
20
21     The name of this document is
22     <FONT COLOR = "BLUE">
23     <!--#ECHO VAR="DOCUMENT_NAME" -->
24     </FONT><BR>
25
26     The local date is
27     <FONT COLOR = "BLUE">
28     <!--#ECHO VAR="DATE_LOCAL" -->
29     </FONT><BR>
30
31     This document was last modified on
32     <FONT COLOR = "BLUE">
33     <!--#ECHO VAR="LAST_MODIFIED" -->
34     </FONT><BR>
35
36     Your current IP Address is
37     <FONT COLOR = "BLUE">
38     <!--#ECHO VAR="REMOTE_ADDR" -->
39     </FONT><BR>
40
41     My server name is
42     <FONT COLOR = "BLUE">
43     <!--#ECHO VAR="SERVER_NAME" -->
44     </FONT><BR>
45
46     And I am using the
47     <FONT COLOR = "BLUE">
48     <!--#ECHO VAR="SERVER_SOFTWARE" -->
49     Web Server.</FONT><BR>
50
51     You are using
52     <FONT COLOR = "BLUE">
```

Fig. 29.14 Incorporating a Web-page hit counter and displaying environment variables (part 1 of 2).

```
53    <!--#ECHO VAR="HTTP_USER_AGENT" -->.
54    </FONT><BR>
55
56    This server is using
57    <FONT COLOR = "BLUE">
58    <!--#ECHO VAR="GATEWAY_INTERFACE" -->.
59    </FONT><BR>
60
61    <BR><BR>
62    <CENTER>
63    <HR>
64    <FONT SIZE = -5>This document was last modified on
65    <!--#ECHO VAR="LAST_MODIFIED" --></FONT>
66    </CENTER>
67 </BODY>
68 </HTML>
```

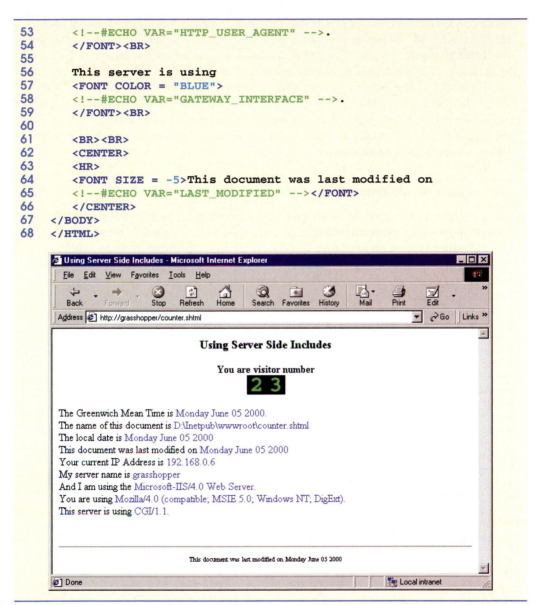

Fig. 29.14 Incorporating a Web-page hit counter and displaying environment variables (part 2 of 2).

Line 14 of the **counter.shtml** script executes the **counter.pl** script using the **EXEC** command. Before the HTML document is sent to the client, the SSI command is executed and any script output is sent to the client. This technique can increase the load on the server tremendously, depending on how many times the script has to be parsed and the size and work load of the scripts.

Line 18 uses the **ECHO** *command* to display variable information. The **ECHO** command is followed by the *keyword* **VAR** and the variable's name. For example, *variable*

DATE_GMT contains the current date and time in Greenwich Mean Time (GMT). In line 23, the name of the current document is included in the HTML page with the **DOCUMENT_NAME** *variable*. The **DATE_LOCAL** *variable* inserts the date in line 28 (in local format—different formats are used around the world).

Figure 29.15 (**counter.pl**) introduces file input and output in Perl. Line 7 opens (for input) the file **counter.dat**, which contains the number of hits to date for the **counter.shtml** Web page. Function *open* is called to create a *filehandle* to refer to the file during the execution of the script. In this example, the file opened is assigned a file-handle named **COUNTREAD** (line 7).

Line 8

```
$data = <COUNTREAD>;
```

uses the *diamond operator* **<>** to read one line of the file referred to by filehandle **COUNTREAD** and assign it to the variable **$data**. When the diamond operator is used in a scalar context, only one line is read. If assigned to an array, each line from the file is assigned to a successive array element. Because the file **counter.dat** contains only one line (in this case only one number), the variable **$data** is assigned the value of that number in line 8. Line 9 then increments **$data** by one.

Now that the counter has been incremented for this hit, we write the counter back to the **counter.dat** file. In line 12

```
open( COUNTWRITE, ">counter.dat" );
```

```
1   #!perl
2   # Fig. 29.15: counter.pl
3   # Program to track the number of times a web page has been accessed.
4
5   use CGI qw( :standard );
6
7   open( COUNTREAD, "counter.dat" );
8       $data = <COUNTREAD>;
9       $data++;
10  close( COUNTREAD );
11
12  open( COUNTWRITE, ">counter.dat" );
13      print COUNTWRITE $data;
14  close( COUNTWRITE );
15
16  print header;
17  print "<CENTER>";
18  print "<STRONG>You are visitor number</STRONG><BR>";
19
20  for ( $count = 0; $count < length( $data ); $count++ )
21  {
22      $number = substr( $data, $count, 1 );
23      print "<IMG SRC = \"images/counter/$number.jpg\">";
24  }
25
26  print "</CENTER>";
```

Fig. 29.15 Perl script for counting Web page hits

we open the **counter.dat** file for writing by preceding the file name with a **>** *character*. This immediately truncates (i.e., discards) any data in that file. If the file does not exist, Perl creates a new file with the specified name. Perl also provides an *append* mode (**>>**) for appending to the end of a file.

After line 12 is executed, data can be written to the file **counter.dat**. Line 13

```
print COUNTWRITE $data;
```

writes the counter number back to the file **counter.dat**. The first argument to **print** (**COUNTWRITE**) simply specifies the filehandle that refers to the file where data is written. If no filehandle is specified, **print** writes to standard out (**STDOUT**). In line 14, the connection to **counter.dat** is terminated by calling function *close*.

Good Programming Practice 29.4

When opening a text file to read its contents, open the file in read-only mode. Opening the file in other modes makes it possible to accidentally overwrite the data.

Good Programming Practice 29.5

Always close files as soon as you are finished with them.

Lines 20 through 24

```
for ( $count = 0; $count < length( $data ); $count++ )
{
    $number = substr( $data, $count, 1 ) ;
    print "<IMG SRC=\"images/counter/$number.jpg\">";
}
```

use a *for* loop to iterate through each digit of the number scalar **$data**. The **for** loop syntax consists of three semicolon-separated statements in parentheses followed by a body delimited by curly braces. In our example, we loop until **$count** is equal to **length($data)**. Because function *length* returns the length of a character string, the **for** iterates once for each digit in **$data**.

For each iteration, we obtain the current digit by calling function *substr*. The first parameter passed to function **substr** specifies the string from which to obtain a substring. The second parameter specifies the offset, in characters, from the beginning of the string, so an offset of 0 returns the first character, 1 returns the second, and so forth. The third argument specifies the length of the substring to be obtained (just one character in this case). The **for** loop, then, assigns each digit (possibly from a multiple-digit number) to the scalar variable **$number** in turn. Each digit's corresponding image is displayed using an HTML **IMG** tag (line 23).

29.7 Verifying a Username and Password

It is often desirable to have a *private Web site*—one that is visible only to certain people. Implementing privacy generally involves username and password verification. Figure 29.16 presents an example of an HTML form which queries the user for a username and a password to be verified. It posts the fields **USERNAME** and **PASSWORD** to the Perl script **password.pl** upon submission of the form. Note that for simplicity, this example does not encrypt the data before sending it to the server.

```
1   <!DOCTYPE html PUBLIC "-//W3C//DTD HTML 4.0 Transitional//EN">
2   <!-- Fig. 29.16: password.html -->
3
4   <HTML>
5   <HEAD>
6   <TITLE>Verifying a username and a password.</TITLE>
7   </HEAD>
8
9   <BODY>
10     <P>
11        <FONT FACE = "ARIAL">
12        Type in your username and password below.
13        </FONT><BR>
14        <FONT COLOR = "#0000FF" FACE = "ARIAL" SIZE = 1>
15        <STRONG>
16        Note that password will be sent as plain text
17        </STRONG>
18        </FONT>
19     </P>
20
21     <FORM ACTION = "/cgi-bin/password.pl" METHOD = "POST">
22     <BR>
23
24     <TABLE BORDER = "0" CELLSPACING = "0" STYLE = "HEIGHT: 90px;
25          WIDTH: 123px" CELLPADING = "0">
26        <TR>
27           <TD BGCOLOR = "#DDDDDD" COLSPAN = "3">
28           <FONT FACE = "ARIAL" SIZE = "2">
29           <STRONG>Username:</STRONG>
30           </FONT>
31           </TD>
32        </TR>
33        <TR>
34           <TD BGCOLOR = "#DDDDDD" COLSPAN = "3">
35           <INPUT SIZE = "40" NAME = "USERNAME"
36                  STYLE = "HEIGHT: 22px; WIDTH: 115px">
37           </TD>
38        </TR>
39        <TR>
40           <TD BGCOLOR = "#DDDDDD" COLSPAN = "3">
41           <FONT FACE = "ARIAL" SIZE = "2">
42           <STRONG>Password:</STRONG>
43           </FONT></TD>
44        </TR>
45        <TR>
46           <TD BGCOLOR = "#DDDDDD" COLSPAN = "3">
47           <INPUT SIZE = "40" NAME = "PASSWORD"
48                  STYLE = "HEIGHT: 22px; WIDTH: 115px"
49                  TYPE = "PASSWORD">
50           <BR></TD>
51        </TR>
52        <TR>
53           <TD COLSPAN = "3">
```

Fig. 29.16 Entering a username and password (part 1 of 3)

```
54                <INPUT TYPE = "SUBMIT" VALUE = "Enter"
55                   STYLE = "HEIGHT: 23px; WIDTH: 47px">
56             </TD>
57          </TR>
58       </TABLE>
59       </FORM>
60    </BODY>
61    </HTML>
```

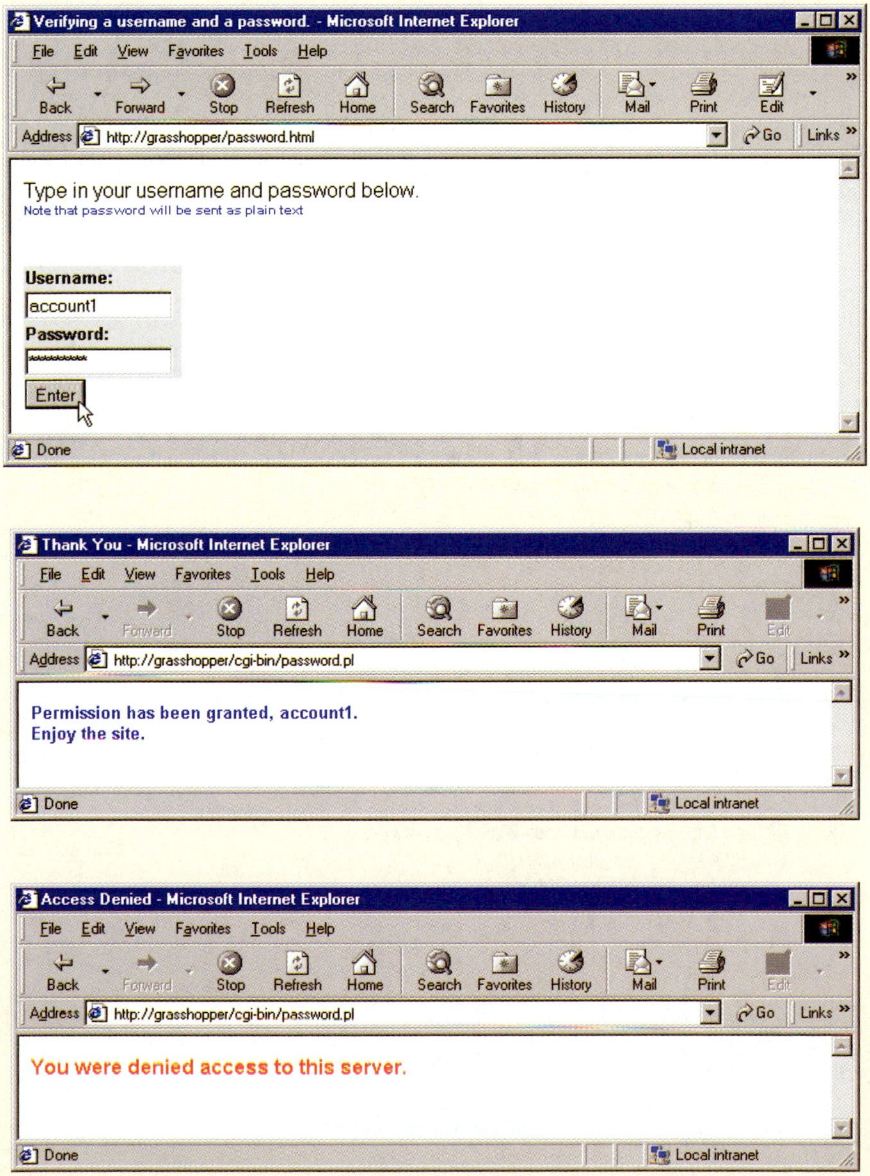

Fig. 29.16 Entering a username and password (part 2 of 3)

Fig. 29.16 Entering a username and password (part 3 of 3)

The script **password.pl** (Fig. 29.17) is responsible for verifying the username and password of the client by crosschecking against values from a database. The database list of valid users and their passwords is a simple text file: **password.txt** (Fig. 29.18).

```perl
1   #!perl
2   # Fig. 29.17: password.pl
3   # Program to search a database for usernames and passwords.
4
5   use CGI qw(:standard);
6
7   $testUsername = param( "USERNAME" );
8   $testPassword = param( "PASSWORD" );
9
10  open ( FILE, "password.txt" ) ||
11     die "The database could not be opened";
12
13  while ( $line = <FILE> )
14  {
15     chomp $line;
16     ( $username, $password ) = split( ",", $line );
17
18     if ( $testUsername eq $username )
19     {
20        $userVerified = 1;
21        if ( $testPassword eq $password )
22        {
23           $passwordVerified = 1;
24           last;
25        }
26     }
27  }
28
29  close( FILE );
30  print header;
31
32  if ( $userVerified && $passwordVerified )
33  {
```

Fig. 29.17 Contents of **password.pl** Perl script (part 1 of 2).

```
34          accessGranted();
35     }
36     elsif ( $userVerified && !$passwordVerified )
37     {
38          wrongPassword();
39     }
40     else
41     {
42          accessDenied();
43     }
44
45     sub accessGranted
46     {
47          print "<TITLE>Thank You</TITLE>";
48          print "<FONT FACE = \"ARIAL\" SIZE = 2 COLOR = \"BLUE\">";
49          print "<STRONG>Permission has been granted, $username.";
50          print "<BR>Enjoy the site.</STRONG></FONT>";
51     }
52
53     sub wrongPassword
54     {
55          print "<TITLE>Access Denied</TITLE>";
56          print "<FONT FACE = \"ARIAL\" SIZE =2 COLOR=\"RED\"><STRONG>";
57          print "You entered an invalid password.<BR>";
58          print "Access has been denied.</STRONG></FONT>";
59     }
60
61     sub accessDenied
62     {
63          print "<TITLE>Access Denied</TITLE>";
64          print "<FONT FACE = \"ARIAL\" SIZE = 3 COLOR =\"RED\"><STRONG>";
65          print "You were denied access to this server.";
66          print "</STRONG></FONT>";
67     }
```

Fig. 29.17   Contents of **password.pl** Perl script (part 2 of 2).

```
1     account1,password1
2     account2,password2
3     account3,password3
4     account4,password4
5     account5,password5
6     account6,password6
7     account7,password7
8     account8,password8
9     account9,password9
10    account10,password10
```

Fig. 29.18   Database **password.txt** containing user names and passwords.

Line 10 opens the file **password.txt** for reading, assigning it the filehandle **FILE**. To verify that the file was opened successfully, a test is performed using the *logical OR operator* (||). Operator OR returns true if either the left condition or the right condition.

If the condition on the left evaluates to true, then the condition on the right is not evaluated. In this case the *die* executes only if **open** returns false, indicating that the file did not open properly. If this happens, **die** displays an error message and the program terminates.

The *while* loop in line 13 is another control structure which repeatedly executes the code enclosed in curly braces (lines 14 through 27) until the test condition in parentheses returns false. In this case, the test condition assigns the next unread line of **password.txt** to **$line**, and evaluates to true as long as a line from the file was successfully read. When the end of the file is reached, **<FILE>** returns false and the loop terminates.

Each line in **password.txt** consists of an account name and password pair, separated by a comma, and followed with a newline character. For each line read, function *chomp* is called (line 15) to remove the newline character at the end of the line. Then, *split* is called to divide the string into substrings at the specified separator or *delimiter* (in this case, a comma). For example, the **split** of the first line in **password.txt** returns the list (**"account1", "password1"**). The syntax

```
( $username, $password ) = split( ",", $line );
```

sets **$username** and **$password** to the first and second elements returned by **split** (**account1** and **password1**), respectively.

If the username is equivalent to the one we have read from the text file, the conditional in line 18 returns true. The **$userVerified** variable is then set to **1**. Next, the value of **$testPassword** is tested against the value in the **$password** variable. If the password matches, the **$passwordVerified** variable is set to **1**. In this case, because a successful username-password match has been found, the *last* statement is used in line 24 to immediately exit the **while** loop. The **last** statement is often used to short-circuit a loop structure once a desired condition has been satisfied.

Because we are now finished reading from **password.txt** we **close** it on line 29. Line 32 checks if both the username and password were verified. Using, the Perl *logical AND operator*, **&&**. If both conditions are true (that is, if both variables evaluate to nonzero values), then the function **accessGranted** is called, which sends a Web page to the client indicating a successful login.

If the **if** statement returns false, the condition in the following **elsif** statement is then tested. Line 36, tests if the user was verified, but the password was not. In this case, the function **wrongPassword** is called. The unary *logical negation operator* **!** is used in line 36 to negate the value of **$passwordVerified** and thus test if it is false. If the user was not recognized at all, function **accessDenied** is called, and a message indicating that permission has been denied is sent to the client (line 42).

Perl allows programmers to define their own functions or *subroutines*. Keyword **sub** begins a function definition and curly braces delimit the function body (lines 45 and 53 and 61). To call a function, use the function name followed by a pair of parentheses (line 34 and 38 and 42).

29.8 Using ODBC to Connect to a Database

Database connectivity allows system administrators to maintain information on things such as user accounts, passwords, credit card information, mailing lists and product inventory. Databases allow companies to enter the world of electronic commerce and maintain crucial data. The Perl module *Win32::ODBC* installed with Perl 5.6 provides an interface for Perl programs to connect to **Windows ODBC (Open Database Connectivity)** data sources. To do interact with a database, a data source must first be defined with the Data Source Administrator in Microsoft Windows (see the "Setting up a System Data Source Name" document on the CD that accompanies this book). From a Web browser, the client enters an SQL query string that is sent to the Web server. The Perl script is then executed, querying the database and sending a record set in the form of an HTML document back to the client. This SQL query string is written following the rules and syntax discussed earlier in Chapter 25.

Figure 29.19 (**data.html**) is a Web page that **POST**s a form containing an SQL query to the server. Perl script **data.pl** (Fig. 29.20) processes the form data.

```
1   <!DOCTYPE html PUBLIC "-//W3C//DTD HTML 4.0 Transitional//EN">
2   <!-- Fig. 29.19: data.html -->
3
4   <HTML>
5   <HEAD>
6   <TITLE>Sample Database Query</TITLE>
7   </HEAD>
8
9   <BODY>
10  <FONT FACE = "ARIAL, SANS-SERIF" SIZE = "2">
11
12     <FONT SIZE = "+2">
13        <STRONG>Querying an ODBC database.</STRONG>
14     </FONT><BR>
15
16     <FORM METHOD = "POST" ACTION = "cgi-bin/data.pl">
17        <INPUT TYPE = "TEXT" NAME = "QUERY" SIZE = "40"
18               VALUE = "SELECT * FROM Authors"><BR><BR>
19        <INPUT TYPE = "SUBMIT" VALUE = "Send Query">
20     </FORM>
21  </BODY>
22  </HTML>
```

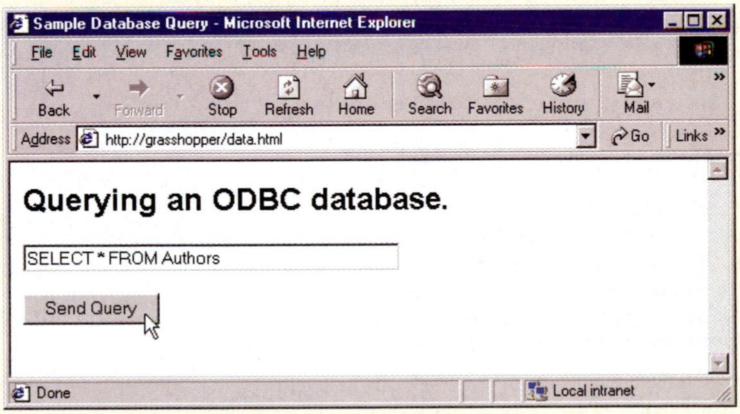

Fig. 29.19 Source code and output of the **data.html** document .

Line 16 creates an HTML **FORM**, indicating that the data submitted from the **FORM** will be sent to the Web server via the **POST METHOD** and the **ACTION** is to execute **data.pl** (Fig. 29.20). Line 17 adds a text field to the **FORM**, setting its name to **QUERY** and its **VALUE** to a default SQL query string. This query specifies that all records (**SELECT ***) are to be retrieved **FROM** the **Authors** table inside the **perl.mdb** database (for this example, we gave it the DSN **Products**. See the "Setting up a ODBC System Data Source Name" document on the CD that accompanies this book for instructions on how to create a DSN.

```perl
1   #!perl
2   # Fig. 29.20: data.pl
3   # Program to query a database and send results to the client.
4
5   use Win32::ODBC;
6   use CGI qw( :standard );
7
8   $queryString = param( "QUERY" );
9   $dataSourceName = "Products";
10
11  print header, start_html( "Search Results" );
12
13  if ( !( $data = new Win32::ODBC( $dataSourceName ) ) )
14  {
15     print "Error connecting to $dataSourceName: ";
16     print Win32::ODBC::Error();
17     exit;
18  }
19
20  if ( $data->Sql( $queryString ) )
21  {
22     print "SQL failed. Error: ", $data->Error();
23     $data->Close();
24     exit;
25  }
26
27  print "<FONT FACE = \"ARIAL,SANS-SERIF\" SIZE = 3>";
28  print "<FONT COLOR = \"BLUE\" SIZE = 4>Search Results</FONT>";
29  print "<TABLE BORDER = 0 CELLPADDING = 5 CELLSPACING = 0>";
30
31  for ( $counter = 0; $data->FetchRow(); $counter++ )
32  {
33     %rowHash = $data->DataHash();
34
35     print <<End_Row;
36     <TR BGCOLOR = "#9999CC">
37     <TD>$rowHash{'ID'}</TD>
38     <TD>$rowHash{'FirstName'}</TD>
39     <TD>$rowHash{'LastName'}</TD>
40     <TD>$rowHash{'Phone'}</TD>
41     </TR>
42  End_Row
43  }
```

Fig. 29.20 Contents of **data.pl** Perl script (part 1 of 2).

```
44
45  print <<End_Results;
46  </TABLE>
47  <BR>Your search yielded <B>$counter</B> results.<BR><BR>
48  <FONT SIZE = "2">
49  Please email comments to
50  <A href = "mailto:deitel\@deitel.com">
51  Deitel and Associates, Inc.</A>.
52  End_Results
53
54  print end_html;
55  $data->Close();
```

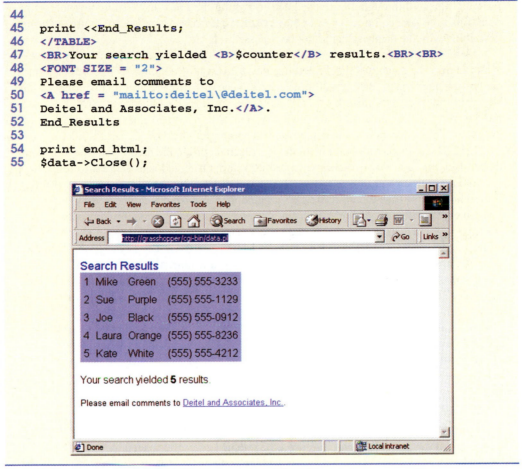

Fig. 29.20 Contents of **data.pl** Perl script (part 2 of 2).

Look-and-Feel Observation 29.1

Using tables to output fields in a database organizes information neatly into rows and columns

The **data.pl** script is responsible for taking the SQL query string and sending it on to the database management system. Line 5 imports the *Win32::ODBC* package to allow interaction with ODBC databases. In line 8, function **param** accesses the user input from the text field **QUERY**, and assigns the returned value to variable **$queryString**. Line 9 creates scalar variable **$dataSourceName** and assigns it the string **"Products"**.

Function *start_html* (line 11) from the CGI module prints the opening HTML tags, including the page's title, **Search Results**. Line 13 connects to the ODBC data source by passing the Data Source Name to the *new* constructor function for the **Win32::ODBC** object, which creates a new instance of the object. Specifically, the program uses Windows ODBC to look for and connect to the database named **Products**, and the variable **$data** becomes a reference to the object representing the Perl connection to that database. If the database cannot be accessed for any reason, the condition in line 13 is false and lines 14 through 18 are executed, reporting the error and terminating the script with function **exit**. Function **Win32::ODBC::Error** is called to return a string describing why the database could not be accessed.

Method **Sql** in line 20 executes the SQL query on the database, as specified by **$queryString**. The database object referenced by **$data** now contains the record set generated by the query on the database. If the query is successful, **Sql** returns an undefined value which is interpreted as false by the **if** statement in line 20. Otherwise, SQL returns a number representing an error code (which evaluates to true) and lines 21 through 25 are executed. The connection to the database is **Close**d on line 23.

Line 31 uses a **for** loop to iterate through each record in the record set. The loop condition uses function **FetchRow**, which either returns true and sets **$data** to return the next record in the set, or returns **undef** (false) indicating that the end of the record set has been reached. For each record retrieved, variable **$counter** is incremented by one.

Line 33 retrieves the fields from the current record using function **DataHash** and places this data into the hash **%rowHash**. The data can then be accessed using the field names (as specified in the **perl.mdb** database file) as keys. For example, **$rowHash{'Phone'}** yields the phone number of the current record.

In lines 37 through 40, the document accesses the values of certain fields for the current record using their keys and prints these values into table cells and rows. If a key is not contained in **%rowHash**, the corresponding table cell is simply left empty.

After all rows of the record set have been displayed, the **for** loop condition fails and the table's closing tag is written (line 46). The number of results contained in **$counter** is printed in line 47. Line 54 uses the CGI module's **end_html** in place of the closing HTML tag, and line 55 closes the connection to the database.

29.9 Cookies and Perl

Cookies maintain *state* information for a particular client that uses a Web browser. Preserving this information allows data and settings to be retained even after execution of a CGI script has ended. Cookies are often used to record user preferences (or other information) for the next time a client visits a Web site. For example, many Web sites use cookies to store a client's postal zip code. The zip code is used when the client requests a Web page to send current weather information or news updates for the client's region. On the server side, cookies may be used to help track information about client activity, to determine, for example, which sites are visited most frequently or how effective certain advertisements and products are.

Microsoft Internet Explorer stores cookies as small text files saved on the client's hard drive. The data stored in the cookie is sent back to the Web server that placed it there whenever the user requests a Web page from that particular server. The server can then serve up HTML content to the client that is specific to the information stored in the cookie.

Figure 29.21 uses a script to write a cookie to the client's machine. The **cookies.html** file is used to display an HTML **FORM** that allows a user to enter a name, height and favorite color. When the user clicks the **Write Cookie** button, the **cookies.pl** script (Fig. 29.22) is executed.

Good Programming Practice 29.6

Critical information such as credit card or password information should not be stored using cookies. Cookies cannot be used to retrieve information such as email addresses or data on the hard drive from a client's computer.

```
1   <!DOCTYPE html PUBLIC "-//W3C//DTD HTML 4.0 Transitional//EN">
2   <!-- Fig. 29.21: cookies.html -->
3
4   <HTML>
5      <HEAD>
6         <TITLE>Writing a cookie to the client computer</TITLE>
7      </HEAD>
8
9   <BODY>
10  <FONT FACE = "ARIAL,SANS-SERIF" SIZE = "2">
11
12     <FONT SIZE = "+2">
13        <B>Click Write Cookie to save your cookie data.</B>
14     </FONT><BR>
15
16     <FORM METHOD = "POST" ACTION = "cgi-bin/cookies.pl">
17        <STRONG>Name:</STRONG><BR>
18        <INPUT TYPE = "TEXT" NAME = "NAME"><BR>
19        <STRONG>Height:</STRONG><BR>
20        <INPUT TYPE = "TEXT" NAME = "HEIGHT"><BR>
21        <STRONG>Favorite Color</STRONG><BR>
22        <INPUT TYPE = "TEXT" NAME = "COLOR"><BR>
23        <INPUT TYPE = "SUBMIT" VALUE = "Write Cookie">
24     </FORM>
25  </BODY>
26  </HTML>
```

Fig. 29.21   Source for **cookies.html** Web page .

```
1   #!perl
2   # Fig. 29.22: cookies.pl
3   # Program to write a cookie to a client's machine
```

Fig. 29.22   Writing a cookie to the client (part 1 of 2).

```
4
5   use CGI qw( :standard );
6
7   $name = param( NAME );
8   $height = param( HEIGHT );
9   $color = param( COLOR );
10
11  $expires = "Tuesday, 05-JUL-05 16:00:00 GMT";
12
13  print "Set-Cookie: Name=$name; expires=$expires; path=\n";
14  print "Set-Cookie: Height=$height; expires=$expires; path=\n";
15  print "Set-Cookie: Color=$color; expires=$expires; path=\n";
16
17  print header, start_html( "Cookie Saved" );
18
19  print <<End_Data;
20  <FONT FACE = "ARIAL,SANS-SERIF" SIZE = "3">
21  The cookie has been set with the folowing data:<BR><BR>
22  <FONT COLOR = "BLUE">Name:</FONT> $name<BR>
23  <FONT COLOR = "BLUE">Height:</FONT> $height<BR>
24  <FONT COLOR = "BLUE">Favorite Color:</FONT>
25  <FONT COLOR = $color> $color<BR></FONT>
26  <BR>Click <A HREF = "readCookies.pl">here</A> to read saved cookie.
27  End_Data
28
29  print end_html;
```

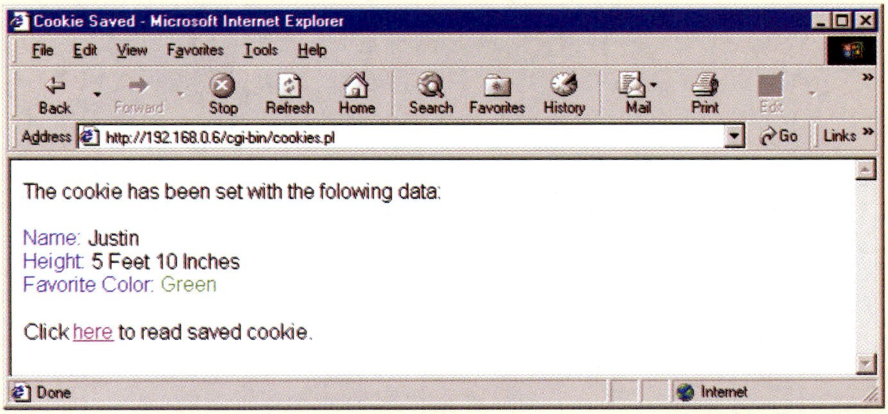

Fig. 29.22 Writing a cookie to the client (part 2 of 2).

The **cookies.pl** script reads the data sent from the client on lines 7 through 9. Line 11 declares and initializes variable **$expires** to contain the *expiration date of the cookie*. The browser deletes a cookie after it expires. Lines 13 through 15 call function **print** to output the cookie information. They use the ***Set-Cookie:*** *header* to indicate that the browser should store the incoming data in a cookie. They set three attributes for each cookie: a name-value pair containing the data to be stored, the expiration date and the URL path of the server domain over which the cookie is valid. For this example, no path is given, making the cookie readable from anywhere within the server's domain. Lines 17 through 29 send a Web page indicating that the cookie has been written to the client.

If the client is Internet Explorer, cookies are stored in the **Temporary Internet Files** directory on the client's machine. Figure 29.23 shows the contents of this directory prior to the execution of **cookies.pl**. After the cookie is written, a text file is added to this list. The file **Cookie:justin@196.168.0.6** can be seen in the **Temporary Internet Files** directory in Fig. 29.24. The IP address **196.168.0.6** is the domain for which the cookie is valid. The username **justin**, however, is just part of the filename Internet Explorer uses for cookies and is not actually a part of the cookie itself. A remote server, therefore, cannot access the username.

Fig. 29.23 Temporary Internet Files directory before a cookie is written.

Fig. 29.24 Temporary Internet Files directory after a cookie is written.

Figure 29.25 (**readCookies.pl**) reads the cookie written in Fig. 29.22 and displays the information in a table.

Environment variable **'HTTP_COOKIE'** contains the client's cookies. Line 12 calls subroutine **readCookies** and places the returned value into hash **%cookies**. The user-defined subroutine **readCookies** splits the environment variable containing the cookie information into separate cookies (using **split**) and stores these as distinct elements in **@cookieArray** (Line 29). For each cookie in **@cookieArray**, we call **split** again to obtain the original name-value pair, which in turn is stored in **%cookieHash** in line 33.

Note that the **split** function in line 32 makes reference to a variable named **$_**. The special Perl variable **$_** is used as a default for many Perl functions. In this case, because no variable was provided in the **foreach** loop (line 30), so **$_** is used by default. Thus, in this example, **$_** is assigned the value of the current element of **@cookieArray** as **foreach** loops though it.

Once **%cookieHash** has been created, it is *return*ed in line 36, and **%cookies** is assigned its value in line 12. The **foreach** loop (line 17) then iterates through the hash with the given key names, printing the key and value for the data from the cookie in an HTML table.

```perl
1   #!perl
2   # Fig. 29.25: readCookies.pl
3   # Program to read cookies from the client's computer
4
5   use CGI qw( :standard );
6
7   print header, start_html( "Read cookies" );
8   print "<FONT FACE = \"ARIAL,SANS-SERIF\" SIZE = 3>";
9   print "<STRONG>The folowing data is saved in a cookie on your ";
10  print "computer.<STRONG><BR><BR>";
11
12  %cookies = readCookies();
13
14  print "<TABLE BORDER = \"5\" CELLSPACING = \"0\" ";
15  print "CELLPADDING = \"10\">";
16
17  foreach $cookieName ( "Name", "Height", "Color" )
18  {
19     print "<TR>";
20     print "   <TD BGCOLOR=#AAAAFF>$cookieName</TD>";
21     print "   <TD BGCOLOR=#AAAAAA>$cookies{ $cookieName }</TD>";
22     print "</TR>";
23  }
24  print "</TABLE>";
25  print end_html;
26
27  sub readCookies
28  {
29     @cookieArray = split( "; ", $ENV{ 'HTTP_COOKIE' } );
30     foreach ( @cookieArray )
31     {
32        ( $cookieName, $cookieValue ) = split ( "=", $_ );
```

Fig. 29.25 Output displaying the cookie's content (part 1 of 2).

```
33              $cookieHash{ $cookieName } = $cookieValue;
34         }
35
36         return %cookieHash;
37    }
```

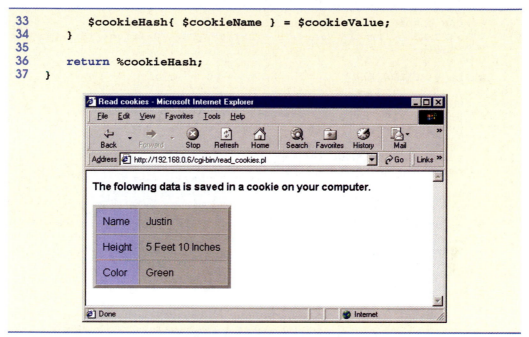

Fig. 29.25 Output displaying the cookie's content (part 2 of 2).

29.10 Example: An Internet Shopping Cart

Many e-businesses use shopping carts. The sites record what the consumer wants to purchase and provide an easy and understandable way to shop online. The user uses an electronic shopping cart just as one would use a physical shopping cart in a retail store. The user can add/remove items to/from their shopping cart and the site automatically updates the total. When the user "checks out," they pay for whatever items are in the shopping cart.

In this example, we will build a simple shopping cart that uses two CGI scripts written in Perl. The first, Fig. 29.26 (**books.pl**), displays the opening Web page, which displays a list of books available for purchase.

```
1    #!perl
2    # Fig. 29.26: books.pl
3    # Reads books from a database and prints them in a table
4
5    use CGI qw( :standard );
6    print header, start_html( "Shopping cart" );
7
8    open( FILE, "catalog.txt" ) ||
9       die "The database could not be opened.";
10
11   print <<End_Begin;
12   <CENTER><P>Books available for sale</P>
```

Fig. 29.26 Perl script **books.pl** displaying opening page of shopping cart example. (part 1 of 2).

```
13   <TABLE BORDER = "1" CELLPADDING = "7">
14   <TR><TH>Name</TH><TH>Year</TH><TH>ISBN</TH><TH>Price</TH></TR>
15   End_Begin
16
17   while ( <FILE> )
18   {
19      @data = split( "\t" );          # Variable $_ assumed
20      print "<FORM METHOD = \"POST\" ACTION = \"cart.pl\">";
21      param( "REMOVE" , 0 );
22      param( "NEWBOOK", @data );
23      print hidden( "REMOVE" );
24      print hidden( "NEWBOOK"), "\n<TR>";
25
26      foreach ( @data )
27      {
28         print "<TD>$_</TD>";          # print data item within a cell
29      }
30      print "<TD>", submit( "Buy" ), "</TD></TR></FORM>\n";
31   }
32
33   print "</TABLE>", end_html;
34   close( FILE );
```

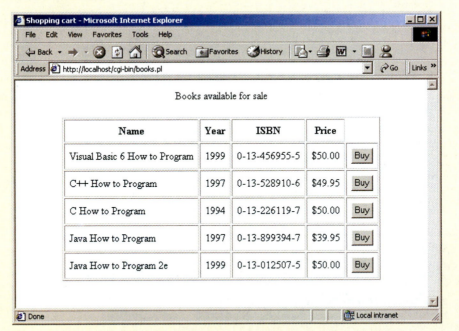

Fig. 29.26 Perl script **books.pl** displaying opening page of shopping cart example. (part 2 of 2)

The opening page contains a table displaying the title, year of publication, ISBN number, and price for each book. The actual book data is stored in a database file (**catalog.txt**) on the site's server. Each book and its data are stored on individual lines. Tabs separate the name, year, ISBN and price.

In line 8, we open **catalog.txt** for reading. Line 17 then iterates through the database books, line by line, storing the value of each line in the special default variable **$_**. Next, in line 19, we **split** each line on the tab delimiter (**\t**). Note that the second argument to **split** is implicitly assumed to be **$_**.

The **foreach** loop prints each line of book data into a row of the table (lines 26 through 29). Each book also gets a separate HTML form with opening and closing **FORM** tags. These multiple forms each include a submit button which calls **cart.pl** to add the given book to the shopping cart. In order to instruct the **cart.pl** script which book to add, we post that information in each form using *hidden fields*. These fields are "hidden" because they are not displayed on the Web page (as with other **FORM**s we have seen).

We first set the values for the fields in lines 21 and 22. This is done by calling **param** with a second argument to specify the new values for those fields. We then invoke function *hidden* (lines 23 and 24) to print the HTML tags which will post the hidden field data. This data will be posted just as if the user had entered it directly into any two visible form elements named **REMOVE** and **NEWBOOK**. Function **submit** (line 30) creates a submission button labeled **Buy** for each form. Upon clicking the button, the form's data is submitted to **cart.pl**, which is able to access the field data using function **param**.

Figure 29.27 (**cart.pl**) updates and displays the contents of the shopping cart in an HTML table similar to that displayed in **books.pl** (Fig. 29.26). First, line 7 reads the book data from a cookie and stores it in **@cart**. Note that the user-defined function **readCookie** beginning in line 81 is similar to that used in Fig. 29.25. The only difference is in lines 87 through 91. Rather than processing all readable cookies, we only want the data in the cookie named **CART**. Upon finding this cookie (line 87), we **split** its value into an array (line 89), terminate the **foreach** loop (line 90) and return the computed **@data** (line 93).

```perl
1   #!perl
2   # Fig. 29.27: cart.pl
3   # Add or remove a book from cart and print cart contents
4
5   use CGI qw( :standard );
6
7   @cart = readCookie();
8   $remove = param( "REMOVE" );
9
10  if ( $remove )
11  {
12     $number = param( "NUMBER" );
13     @book = splice( @cart, 4 * ($number - 1), 4 );
14
15     writeCookie( @cart );
16     print header;
17     print start_html( "Book removed" );
18
19     print <<End_Remove;
20     <CENTER><P>The book <I>$book[ 0 ]</I> has been removed.</P>
21     <A HREF = "cart.pl">Return to cart</A>
22  End_Remove
```

Fig. 29.27 Perl script **cart.pl** displaying shopping cart contents (part 1 of 3).

```perl
23
24   }
25   else
26   {
27      @book = param( "NEWBOOK" );
28      push ( @cart, @book );
29
30      if ( ! @cart )
31      {
32         print redirect( "books.pl" );
33         exit;
34      }
35
36      writeCookie( @cart );
37      print header;
38      print start_html( "Shopping Cart" );
39
40      print <<End_Add;
41   <CENTER><P>Here is your current order.</P>
42   <TABLE BORDER = "1" CELLPADDING = "7"><TR><TH>Item</TH>
43   <TH>Name</TH><TH>Year</TH><TH>ISBN</TH>
44   <TH>Price</TH><TH></TH></TR>
45   End_Add
46
47      $counter = 1;
48      $total = 0;
49      @cartCopy = @cart;
50      while ( @book = splice( @cartCopy, 0, 4 ) )
51      {
52         print "<TR><FORM METHOD=\"POST\" ACTION=\"cart.pl\">";
53         print "<TD>$counter</TD><TD>$book[ 0 ]</TD><TD>$book[ 1 ]";
54         print "</TD><TD>$book[ 2 ]</TD><TD>$book[ 3 ]</TD>";
55         print "<TD>", submit( "Remove" ), "</TD>";
56
57         param( "REMOVE", 1 );           # set REMOVE variable to true
58         param( "NUMBER", $counter );    # book number to remove
59         print hidden( "REMOVE" );
60         print hidden( "NUMBER" );
61         print "</FORM></TR>";
62
63         $book[ 3 ] =~ s/\$//;           # remove $ sign
64         $total += $book[ 3 ];           # calculate total price
65         $counter++;
66      }
67      print "<TR><TH COLSPAN= \"4\">Total Order</TH><TH>";
68      printf "\$%0.2f", $total;          # print the total
69      print "</TABLE><BR>";
70      print "<A HREF= \"books.pl\">Buy more books</A>";
71   }
72   print end_html;
73
74   sub writeCookie
75   {
```

Fig. 29.27   Perl script **cart.pl** displaying shopping cart contents (part 2 of 3).

```
76     $expires = "Tuesday, 05-JUL-05 16:00:00 GMT";
77     print "Set-Cookie: ";
78     print "CART=", join( "\t", @_ ), "; expires=$expires\n";
79  }
80
81  sub readCookie
82  {
83     @cookieValues = split( "; ", $ENV{ 'HTTP_COOKIE' } );
84     foreach ( @cookieValues )
85     {
86        ( $name, $value ) = split ( "=" );
87        if ($name eq "CART")
88        {
89           @data = split ( "\t", $value );
90           last;
91        }
92     }
93     return @data;
94  }
```

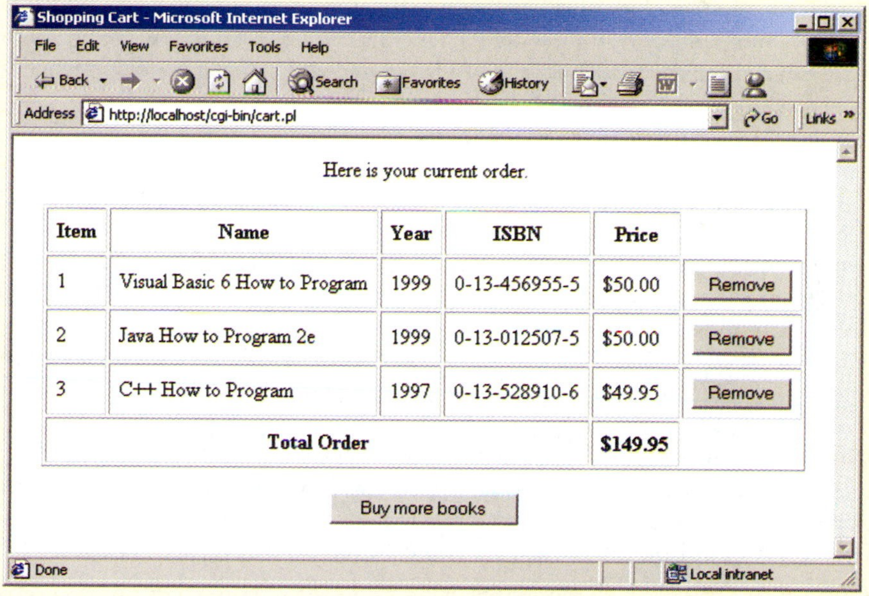
Shopping Cart - Microsoft Internet Explorer
File Edit View Favorites Tools Help
Back Search Favorites History
Address http://localhost/cgi-bin/cart.pl
Go Links
Here is your current order.
Item Name Year ISBN Price
1 Visual Basic 6 How to Program 1999 0-13-456955-5 $50.00 Remove
2 Java How to Program 2e 1999 0-13-012507-5 $50.00 Remove
3 C++ How to Program 1997 0-13-528910-6 $49.95 Remove
Total Order $149.95
Buy more books
Done
Local intranet

Fig. 29.27 Perl script **cart.pl** displaying shopping cart contents (part 3 of 3).

In line 8, the value of the form field **REMOVE** is assigned to variable **$remove**. Whether this script removes or adds a book depends on whether **$remove** is true (nonzero) or false, respectively (line 10). First, let us examine the code to add a book, beginning in line 27. We first put the **NEWBOOK** data into array **@book**. Then, in line 28, function ***push*** adds the four elements of **@book** to the end of array **@cart**—in essence, adding it to the cart. Next, line 30 checks if **@cart** is empty (i.e., all books have been removed). If true, function ***redirect*** sends the user to the original book selection page (**books.pl**). We will see how such a case might arise momentarily.

Otherwise, the new cart contents are stored in a cookie (line 36) with function **write-Cookie**. This function definition begins in line 74 and uses the HTTP **Cookie:** header to store the cart contents. The argument (**@cart**) passed to **writeCookie** is accessed in line 78 using special array variable **@_**. The elements of this array are by definition the arguments passed to the subroutine defined by the programmer. In this case, **@cart** is the argument to **writeCookie**, and so **@_** takes on the values in array **@cart**. In line 78, the elements of this array are then *join*ed together into a single string delimited by tab (**\t**) characters. This string is set as the value of the cookie named **CART**.

We begin printing the current cart contents in an HTML table in lines 37 through 45. In lines 47 and 48 we initialize variables **$counter** (to keep track of the total number of items in the cart) and **$total** (to record the total price of the cart's contents). The copy of **@cart** created in line 49 is used in the **while** loop beginning in line 50. The **while** loop uses function *splice* to repeatedly remove the first four elements (**4** elements beginning with index **0**) of **@cartCopy** and place those elements in **@book**. The index number and the data for each book is output to a table in lines 53 and 54. The book elements are accessed through array subscripts, so **$book[2]**, for example, corresponds to the book's ISBN number.

Again, a **FORM** is created for each line of the table (line 52). As in **books.pl**, these multiple forms each include a submit button (line 55) and hidden field data (lines 57 through 60). Submitting any of these forms posts the book number to remove (according to **$counter**) and sets the **REMOVE** field to 1 (true), indicating that a book removal must be performed. The data is sent to **cart.pl** (line 52).

To sum up the price of all books in the cart, one additional step is required. We cannot add up all of the prices in **$book[3]** because they are preceded with a dollar sign character. These strings would therefore be evaluated as **undef** in a numeric context. So we must remove the dollar sign character. Line 63 uses the *substitution pattern matching operator, s///*, to remove the dollar sign from the price in **$book[3]**. It searches for the pattern contained within the first two slashes (the dollar sign, escaped with a backslash) and replaces it with the contents between the second and third slashes (that is, nothing). This value is then added to **$total**. Finally, line 68 calls *printf* to format the output of the dollar amount with two digits following the decimal point. The link in line 70 returns the user to **books.pl**.

Now let us return to the code which removes a book from the cart, beginning in line 12. First we obtain the book number to be removed with **param**. Line 13 then uses method *splice* to remove the appropriate book from **@cart** by removing **4** elements, beginning with index **4 * ($number - 1)**, and assigning the removed elements to **@book**. Because each book in the cart contains four fields, the data for the first book in the **@cart** array begins at index 0, the second at index 4, and so on.

The new cart contents are written to a cookie in line 15 and a message is output informing the user that the book has been removed. The link to **cart.pl** in line 21 runs the script again, but without passing any form data. Thus, when the link is followed, the field **REMOVE** has no value, and the **if** statement in line 10 of **cart.pl** will return false on the following execution. The script then jumps to line 27, but because there is no field value for **NEWBOOK**, no book is added to the cart in line 28, and the remainder of the script simply outputs the current contents of the cart. This is why it is necessary to check (in lines 30 through 34) if the cart is empty—if all books have been removed from the cart, an empty table would be output.

29.11 Internet and World Wide Web Resources

There is a strong established Perl community online that has made available a wealth of information on the Perl language, Perl modules, CGI scripting, etc.

www.perl.com/
Perl.com is the first place to look for information about Perl. The homepage provides up-to-date news on Perl, answers to common questions about Perl, and an impressive collection of links to Perl resources of all kinds on the Internet. It includes sites for Perl software, tutorials, user groups and demos.

www.activestate.com/
From this site you can download ActivePerl—the Perl 5 implementation for Windows.

www.perl.com/CPAN/README.html
The "Comprehensive Perl Archive Network" is exactly what the name suggests. Here you will find an extensive listing of Perl related information.

www.perl.com/CPAN/scripts/index.html
This is the scripts index from the CPAN archive. Here you will find a wealth of scripts written in Perl.

www.pm.org/
This is the homepage of Perl Mongers, a group dedicated to supporting the Perl community. This site is helpful in finding others in the Perl community to converse with; Perl Mongers has established Perl user groups around the globe.

www.speakeasy.org/~cgires/
This is a collection of tutorials and scripts that can provide a thorough understanding of CGI and of how it is used.

www.cgi101.com/
CGI 101 is a site for those looking to improve their programming ability through familiarity with CGI. The site contains a six-chapter class outlining techniques for CGI programming in the Perl language. The class includes both basics and more sophisticated scripts, with working examples. Also included in the site are script libraries and links to other helpful sources.

www.jmarshall.com/easy/cgi/
A good, brief explanation of CGI for those with programming experience.

wdvl.internet.com/Authoring/Languages/Perl/Resources.html
This site contains many links to Perl resources.

wdvl.internet.com/Authoring/CGI/
The Web Developer's Virtual Library provides tutorials for learning both CGI and Perl, the language most commonly used in developing CGI applications.

www.perlmonth.com/
Perlmonth is a monthly online periodical devoted to Perl, with featured articles from professional programmers. This is a good source for those who use Perl frequently and wish to keep up on the latest developments involving Perl.

www.itknowledge.com/tpj/
The Perl Journal is a large magazine dedicated to Perl. Subscribers are provided with up-to-date Perl news and articles, on the Internet as well as in printed form.

home.t-online.de/home/wahls/perlnet.html
This page provides a brief tutorial on Perl network programming for those who already know the language. The tutorial uses code examples to explain the basics of network communication.

www.w3.org/CGI/
The World Wide Web Consortium page on CGI is concerned with security issues involving the Common Gateway Interface. This page provides links concerning CGI specifications, as indicated by the National Center for Super computing Applications (NCSA).

SUMMARY

- Practical Extraction and Report Language (Perl), developed by Larry Wall, is one of the most widely-used languages for Web programming today.

- Common Gateway Interface (CGI) is a standard protocol through which applications interact with Web servers.

- Permission is granted within the Web server to allow CGI scripts to be executed. They are typically either designated by filename extension (such as **.cgi** or **.pl**) or located within a special directory (such as **/cgi-bin**).

- For CGI scripts, standard output is redirected through the Common Gateway Interface to the server and then sent over the Internet to a Web browser for rendering.

- The Perl comment character (**#**) instructs the interpreter to ignore everything on the current line following the **#**.

- The "shebang" syntax (**#!**) indicates the path to the Perl interpreter or may indicate to the server (e.g., Apache) that a Perl program follows the statement.

- The **$** character specifies that the variable contains a scalar value (i.e., strings, integer numbers and floating-point numbers).

- In Perl, variables are created automatically the first time they are encountered by the interpreter.

- When a variable is encountered inside a double-quoted (**""**) string, Perl uses a process called interpolation to replace the variable with its associated data.

- In Perl, uninitialized variables have the value **undef**, which evaluates to **0** or the empty string (**""**), depending on context.

- Perl does not need to differentiate between numeric and string data types because the interpreter evaluates scalar variables depending on the context in which they are used.

- Perl arrays are named lists of elements, indexed by integer.

- Perl array variable names must be preceded by the **@** symbol.

- An array name prefixed by the **$** character and followed by an index number in square brackets accesses individual array elements.

- The range operator (**..**) creates a consecutive series of values in a list or array.

- The Perl interpreter automatically handles memory management.

- The backslash character (****) is used in Perl to escape special characters.

- One of Perl's most powerful capabilities is its ability to process textual data easily and efficiently, allowing for straightforward searching, substitution, extraction and concatenation of strings.

- Text manipulation in Perl is usually done with a regular expression—a series of characters that serves as a pattern-matching template (or search criteria) in strings, text files and databases.

- Perl has a collection of string operators used to compare and test strings for equality.

- A **foreach** loop iterates sequentially through the elements in a list or array.

- The match operator (**m//**) uses a regular expression to search a string for a specified pattern.

- The **=~** operator (or binding operator) assigns to the match operator a string to search.

- Regular expressions can include special characters called metacharacters which specify patterns or contexts that cannot be defined using literal characters.

- Parentheses in a regular expression indicate that the text matching the pattern is to be saved in special Perl variables `$1`, `$2`, `$3`, etc.
- Modifying characters following the match operator indicate additional search options.
- Environment variables contain information about the script's execution environment.
- In order to run Perl scripts as CGI applications, a Web server must first be installed and configured appropriately.
- The **use** statement directs Perl programs to include the contents (e.g., functions, etc.) of predefined packages called modules.
- The **CGI** module contains many functions for CGI scripting in Perl.
- Functions **header**, **start_html** and **end_html** in the CGI module return strings representing certain HTTP headers and HTML tags.
- The here document syntax is often used in CGI programs to eliminate the need to repeatedly call function **print**.
- The hash data type (or associative array), designated by the **%** character, represents an unordered set of scalar-value pairs.
- Elements in a hash are accessed using unique string keys which are associated with the elements' values: **$hashName{keyName}**.
- The **%ENV** hash is a built-in hash in Perl that contains the names and values of all environment variables.
- Function **keys** returns a list of all keys in a hash.
- Function **sort** orders an array of elements alphabetically.
- The design of verifying information entered into a database is called business logic or business rules.
- Server-side includes (SSIs) are commands embedded in HTML documents for simple dynamic content creation.
- Function **open** creates filehandles through which Perl scripts can read and write to files.
- The diamond operator **<>** reads information from a filehandle line by line.
- Function **print** writes to a filehandle.
- Function **die** displays an error message and terminates program execution.
- Function **chomp** removes the newline character at the end of a string.
- Function **split** divides a string into substrings at the specified separator or delimiter.
- The **last** statement short-circuits a loop structure once a desired condition is satisfied.
- Keyword **sub** begins a definition for a user-defined subroutine or function.
- Perl module **Win32::ODBC** provides an interface for Perl programs to connect to **Windows ODBC (Open Database Connectivity)** data sources.
- Cookies are used to maintain state information for a particular client that uses a Web browser.
- The **Set-Cookie:** HTTP header indicates that the browser should store the incoming data in a cookie.
- Function **hidden** in the CGI module prints HTML tags which post hidden field data (data which is not directly input by the client).
- Function **redirect** in the CGI module outputs an HTTP header which sends the client to another page.
- Function **join** concatenates the elements of a list into a single delimited string.
- Function **splice** removes and returns a subset of array elements.
- The substitution operator, **s///** uses regular expressions to search and replace within a string.

TERMINOLOGY

! logical negation operator
comment character
$_ variable in Perl
%ENV hash in Perl
&& logical AND operator
.pl extension for Perl programs
.SHTML file extension
@_ variable in Perl
\n newline character
{} braces denoting a block of code
|| logical OR operator
=~ operator
== numerical equality operator
ActivePerl
alphanumeric character
assignment operators
associative array
business logic
business rules
CGI environment variables
CGI module
cgi-bin directory
chomp function
client
command-line switches in Perl
Common Gateway Interface (CGI)
cookies
CPAN (Comprehensive Perl Archive Network)
Data Source Name (DSN)
DATE_GMT variable
DATE_LOCAL variable
delimiter
diamond operator (<>)
DOCUMENT_NAME variable
ECHO SSI command
elements (of an array)
end_html function from CGI module
environment variables
eq operator in Perl
escape character
EXEC SSI command
exit function
expiration date of a cookie
FLASTMOD SSI command
for statement in Perl
foreach statement in Perl
FSIZE command
GATEWAY_INTERFACE variable
GET command for HTTP

hash
here document
hidden fields
hit counter (for a Web page)
HTML
HTTP header
HTTP_USER_AGENT variable
HyperText Transfer Protocol (HTTP)
if statement in Perl
import tag
Internet
interpolation
interpreter
keys for a hash
LAST_MODIFIED
length function
literal characters
logical AND operator, &&
logical negation operator, !
logical OR operator, ||
m// match operator
metacharacters in regular expressions
modifying characters
modules
new constructor function
packages in Perl
param function
param function of Perl CGI module
Perl
Perl interpreter
Perl Package Manager (ppm)
perl.exe
POST command in HTTP
Practical Extraction and Report Language (Perl)
print function
push function
quantifier
range operator (..)
redirect function
regular expression
REMOTE_ADDR variable
scalar variable
script
server
SERVER_NAME variable
SERVER_SOFTWARE variable
server-side include (SSI) in Perl
sort function in Perl
splice function

`split` function	`undef`
SSI (Server-Side Include)	`use` statement in Perl
standard input	Wall, Larry
standard output	Web client
`start_html` function	Web server
string processing	`while` statement in Perl
subroutines	`Win32-ODBC` Perl module
`substr` function	word boundary

SELF-REVIEW EXERCISES

29.1   Answer each of the following:

a) The _____ Protocol is used by Web browsers and Web servers to communicate with each other.

b) Typically all CGI programs reside in directory _____.

c) To output warnings as a Perl program executes, the _____ command-line switch should be used.

d) The three data types in Perl are _____, _____ and _____.

e) _____ are divided into individual elements that can each contain an individual scalar variable.

f) To test the equality of two strings, operator _____ should be used.

g) Business _____ is used to ensure that invalid data is not entered into a database.

h) _____ includes allow Webmasters to include such things as the current time, date, or even the contents of a different HTML document.

i) The _____ control structure iterates once for each element in a list or array.

j) Many Perl functions take special variable _____ as a default argument.

29.2   State whether the following are *true* or *false*. If *false*, explain why.

a) Documents containing Server Side Includes must have a file extension of `.SSI` in order to be parsed by the server.

b) A valid HTTP header must be sent to the client to ensure that the browser displays the information correctly.

c) The numerical equality operator, `eq`, is used to determine if two numbers are equal.

d) The `^` metacharacter is used to match the beginning of a string.

e) Perl has a built-in matching operator, `=`, that tests if a matching string is found within a variable.

f) Cookies can read information from a client's hard drive such as email addresses and personal files.

g) An example of a valid HTTP header is: `Content-type text\html`.

h) CGI environment variables contain such information as the type of Web browser the client is running.

i) The characters `\w` in a regular expression only match a letter or number.

j) CGI is a programming language that can be used in conjunction with Perl to program for the Web.

ANSWERS TO SELF-REVIEW EXERCISES

29.1   a) Hypertext Transfer.   b) `/cgi-bin`.   c) `-w`. d) scalar variable, array and hash. e) Arrays.   f) `eq`.   g) logic.   h) Server-side.   i) `foreach`.   j) `$_`.

29.2   a) False. Documents containing Server Side Includes usually have a file extension of `.SH-TML`. b) True. c) False. The numerical equality operator is `==`. d) True. e) False. The built-in matching operator is, **=~**. f) False. Cookies do not have access to private information such as email addresses or private data stored on the hard drive. g) False. A valid HTTP header might be: **Content-type: text/html**. h) True. i) False. **\w** also matches the underscore character. j) False. CGI is an interface, not a programming language.

EXERCISES

29.3   How can a Perl program determine the type of browser a Web client is using?

29.4   Describe how input from an HTML **FORM** is retrieved in a Perl program.

29.5   How does a Web browser determine how to handle or display incoming data?

29.6   What is the terminology for a command that is embedded in an HTML document and parsed by a server prior to being sent?

29.7   Write a Perl program named **states.pl** that creates a scalar value **$states** with the value **"Mississippi Alabama Texas Massachusetts Kansas"**. Using only the techniques discussed in this chapter, write a program that does the following:

    a) Search for a word in scalar **$states** that ends in **xas**. Store this word in element 0 of an array named **@statesArray**.

    b) Search for a word in **$states** that begins with **k** and ends in **s**. Perform a case-insensitive comparison. Store this word in element 1 of **@statesArray**.

    c) Search for a word in **$states** that begins with **M** and ends in **s**. Store this element in element 2 of the array.

    d) Search for a word in **$states** that ends in **a**. Store this word in element 3 of the array.

    e) Search for a word in **$states** at the beginning of the string that begins with **M**. Store this word at element 4 of the array.

    f) Output the array **@statesArray** to the screen.

29.8   In the text we presented CGI environment variables. Develop a program that determines whether the client is using Internet Explorer. If so, determine the version number and send that information back to the client.

29.9   Modify the program of Fig. 29.17 to save information sent to the server into a text file.

29.10   Write a Perl program that tests whether an email addresses is input correctly. A valid email address contains a series of characters followed by the **@** character and a domain name.

29.11   Using CGI environment variables, write a program that logs the addresses (obtained with the **REMOTE_ADDR** CGI environment variable) that request information from the Web server.

29.12   Write a Perl program that stores URL information into a database using **Win32::ODBC**. The first field of the database should contain an actual URL and the second should contain a description of that URL.

29.13   Modify the program of Exercise 29.12 to query the database and return the results to the client.

30

Dynamic HTML: Structured Graphics ActiveX Control

Objectives

- To be able to use the Structured Graphics Control to create various shapes.
- To understand the Structured Graphics Control methods for modifying lines and borders
- To understand the Structured Graphics Control methods for modifying colors and fill styles
- To be able to enable event capturing for the Structured Graphics Control
- To be able to import external lists of methods into the Structured Graphics Control
- To be able to scale, rotate, and translate shapes in the Structured Graphics Control

One picture is worth ten thousand words.
Chinese proverb

Treat nature in terms of the cylinder, the sphere, the cone, all in perspective.
Paul Cezanne

Nothing ever becomes real till it is experienced—even a proverb is no proverb to you till your life has illustrated it.
John Keats

Capture its reality in paint!
Paul Cezanne

30.1 Introduction

Although high-quality content is what visitors to your site are usually looking for, it may not be enough to hold their attention and keep them coming back. Eye-catching graphics may help. This chapter explores the *Structured Graphics* ActiveX Control included with Internet Explorer 5.

The Structured Graphics Control, like the Tabular Data Control we discussed in the previous chapter, is an ActiveX control that you can add to your page with an **OBJECT** tag. Like the TDC, the Structured Graphics Control is easily accessible through scripting. Unlike the TDC, the Structured Graphics Control is meant primarily for visual presentations, and not for displaying data and content.

The Structured Graphics control is a Web interface for the widely used *DirectAnimation* subset of Microsoft's *DirectX* software, used in many high-end video games and graphical applications. To explore the Structured Graphics Control and DirectAnimation further, visit Microsoft's DirectAnimation reference site at

www.microsoft.com/directx/dxm/help/da/default.htm

30.2 Shape Primitives

The Structured Graphics Control allows you to create simple shapes by using methods that can be called via scripting or through **PARAM** tags inside **OBJECT** elements. Figure 30.1 demonstrates most of the shapes included in the Structured Graphics Control.

We begin in lines 13 through 15

```
<OBJECT ID = "shapes" STYLE = "background-color: #CCCCFF;
    width: 500; height: 400"
    CLASSID = "CLSID:369303C2-D7AC-11d0-89D5-00A0C90833E6">
```

by inserting the Structured Graphics ActiveX Control. We give it an **ID** of **shapes** for reference purposes. Note that this is a different **CLASSID** from that for the Tabular Data Control in Chapter 23.

The first **PARAM** tag in lines 17 and 18

```
<PARAM NAME = "Line0001"
    VALUE = "SetLineColor( 0, 0, 0 )">
```

calls the ***SetLineColor*** *method* of the Structured Graphics Control. The **NAME** attribute determines the order in which the function is called.

```
1    <!DOCTYPE html PUBLIC "-//W3C//DTD HTML 4.0 Transitional//EN">
2    <HTML>
3
4    <!-- Fig 30.1: shapes.html   -->
5    <!-- Creating simple shapes  -->
6
7    <HEAD>
8       <TITLE>Structured Graphics - Shapes</TITLE>
9    </HEAD>
10
11   <BODY>
12
13      <OBJECT ID = "shapes" STYLE = "background-color: #CCCCFF;
14         width: 500; height: 400"
15         CLASSID = "CLSID:369303C2-D7AC-11d0-89D5-00A0C90833E6">
16
17         <PARAM NAME = "Line0001"
18            VALUE = "SetLineColor( 0, 0, 0 )">
19         <PARAM NAME = "Line0002"
20            VALUE = "SetLineStyle( 1, 1 )">
21         <PARAM NAME = "Line0003"
22            VALUE = "SetFillColor( 0, 255, 255 )">
23         <PARAM NAME = "Line0004"
24            VALUE = "SetFillStyle( 1 )">
25
26         <PARAM NAME = "Line0005"
27            VALUE = "Oval( 0, -175, 25, 50, 45 )">
28         <PARAM NAME = "Line0006"
29            VALUE = "Arc( -200, -125, 100, 100, 45, 135, 0 )">
30         <PARAM NAME = "Line0007"
31            VALUE = "Pie( 100, -100, 150, 150, 90, 120, 0 )">
32         <PARAM NAME = "Line0008"
33            VALUE = "Polygon(5, 0, 0, 10, 20, 0, -30,
34                             -10, -10, -10, 25)">
35         <PARAM NAME = "Line0009"
36            VALUE = "Rect( -185, 0, 60, 30, 25 )">
37         <PARAM NAME = "Line0010"
38            VALUE = "RoundRect( 200, 100, 35, 60, 10, 10, 25 )">
39
40         <PARAM NAME = "Line0011"
41            VALUE = "SetFont( 'Arial', 65, 400, 0, 0, 0 )">
42         <PARAM NAME = "Line0012"
43            VALUE = "Text( 'Shapes', -200, 200 , -35 )">
44
45         <PARAM NAME = "Line0013"
46                VALUE = "SetLineStyle( 2,1 )">
47         <PARAM NAME = "Line0014"
48            VALUE = "PolyLine( 5, 100, 0, 120, 175, -150, -50,
49                              -75, -75, 75, -75)">
50      </OBJECT>
51
52   </BODY>
53   </HTML>
```

Fig. 30.1 Creating shapes with the Structured Graphics ActiveX Control (part 1 of 2).

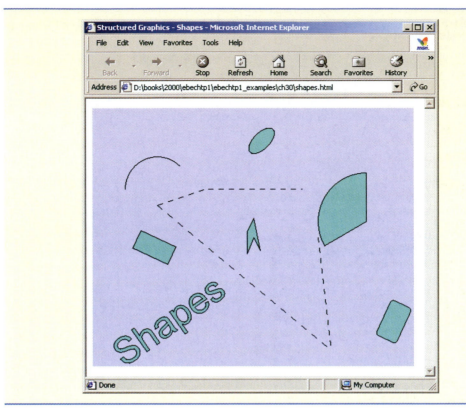

Fig. 30.1   Creating shapes with the Structured Graphics ActiveX Control (part 2 of 2).

Common Programming Error 30.1

*Forgetting to assign successive line numbers (i.e., **NAME = "Line0001"**, **NAME = "Line0002"**) to method calls prevents the intended methods from being called.*

The order of calls must be **Line0001**, **Line0002**, **Line0003**, and so on. Method **SetLineColor** sets the color of lines and borders of shapes. It takes an RGB triplet in decimal notation as its three parameters—in this case, we set the line color to black (**0, 0, 0**).
    Lines 19 and 20

```
<PARAM NAME = "Line0002"
   VALUE = "SetLineStyle( 1, 1 )">
```

call method **SetLineStyle**. Its two parameters set the *line style* and *line width*, respectively. Line style value **1** creates a solid line (the default), **0** does not draw any lines or borders, and **2** creates a dashed line. The line width is specified in pixels. In order to create a dashed line with the **SetLineStyle** method, you must set the line width to **1**.
    Method **SetFillColor** (lines 21 and 22) sets the foreground color with which to fill shapes. Like method **SetLineColor**, it takes a decimal RGB triplet as its parameters. We set the foreground color to cyan (**0, 255, 255**). The **SetFillStyle** method (lines 23 and 24) determines the style in which a shape is filled with color—a value of **1**, as we set here, fills shapes with the solid color we declared with the method **SetFillColor**.

There are 14 possible fill styles, some of which we demonstrate later in this chapter. Figure 30.2 lists all the possible fill styles available with the Structured Graphics Control.

Lines 26 and 27

```
<PARAM NAME = "Line0005"
    VALUE = "Oval( 0, -175, 25, 50, 45 )">
```

create our first shape with the *Oval* method. The first two parameters, (**0, -175**), specify *x*–*y* coordinates at which to place the oval. All shapes in the Structured Graphics Control effectively have a surrounding box—when you place the image at a certain *x*–*y* position, it is the upper-left corner of that box which is placed at that position. It is important to note that, inside the control, the point (0,0) (also known as the *origin*) is at the *center* of the control, not at the upper left.

The next two parameters (**25, 50**) specify the height and width of the oval, respectively. The last parameter (**45**) specifies the clockwise rotation of the oval relative to the *x*-axis, expressed in degrees.

Lines 28 and 29

```
<PARAM NAME = "Line0006"
    VALUE = "Arc( -200, -125, 100, 100, 45, 135, 0 )">
```

create another shape, an *arc*. The **Arc** method takes 7 parameters: the *x*-*y* coordinates of the arc, the height and width of the box that the arc encloses, the starting angle of the arc in degrees, the size of the arc relative to the starting angle, also in degrees, and the rotation of the arc. The **Pie** method (lines 30 and 31) takes the same parameters as the **Arc** method, but it fills the arc with the foreground color, thus creating a *pie* shape.

Number	Fill Style
0	None
1	Solid fill
2	None
3	Horizontal lines
4	Vertical lines
5	Diagonal lines
6	Diagonal lines
7	Cross-hatch
8	Diagonal cross-hatch
9	Horizontal Gradient
10	Vertical Gradient
11	Circular Gradient
12	Line Gradient
13	Rectangular Gradient
14	Shaped Gradient

Fig. 30.2   Fill styles available for the **SetFillStyle** method.

Lines 32 through 34, create a *polygon* using the **Polygon** method. The first parameter specifies the number of vertices in the polygon; each successive pair of parameters thereafter specifies the *x–y* coordinates of the next vertex of the polygon. The last point of the polygon is automatically connected to the first, to close the polygon.

Lines 35 and 36

```
<PARAM NAME = "Line0009"
    VALUE = "Rect( -185, 0, 60, 30, 25 )">
```

create a *rectangle* using the **Rect** method. Here the first two parameters specify the coordinates, the next two specify height and width respectively, and the last parameter specifies rotation in degrees.

Lines 37 and 38

```
<PARAM NAME = "Line0010"
    VALUE = "RoundRect( 200, 100, 35, 60, 10, 10, 25 )">
```

add a *rounded rectangle*. The **RoundRect** method is almost identical to the **Rect** method, but it adds two new parameters, which specify the width and height of the rounded arc at the corners of the rectangle—in this case, 10 pixels wide and 10 pixels high (**10, 10**).

Lines 40 through 43

```
<PARAM NAME = "Line0011"
    VALUE = "SetFont( 'Arial', 65, 400, 0, 0, 0 )">
<PARAM NAME = "Line0012"
    VALUE = "Text( 'Shapes', -200, 200 , -35 )">
```

add text to our Structured Graphics Control with two methods, **SetFont** and **Text**. The **SetFont** method sets the font style to use when we place text with the **Text** method. Here we tell **SetFont** to use a font face of **Arial** that is **65** points high, has a boldness of **400** (this is similar to the CSS **font-weight** property, with values ranging from 100 to 700) and is neither italic (**0**), underline (**0**) nor strikethrough (**0**). Then, we use the **Text** method to place the text (**Shapes**) on the screen, positioned at (**-200, 200**), with a rotation of **-35** degrees.

In lines 45 through 48 we use the **PolyLine** method to draw a line with multiple line segments. Before we draw the line, we call the **SetLineStyle** method again to override the settings we gave it before—in this case, we set the line style to dashed, with a width of **1** pixel (**2, 1**). The **PolyLine** method itself operates much like the **Polygon** method—the first parameter declares the number of points in the line, and each successive pair declares the *x–y* coordinates of the next vertex.

30.3 Moving Shapes with **Translate**

The Structured Graphics Control provides several scriptable methods that allow you to move and transform shapes on the screen. Figure 30.3 provides an example of using the **Translate** function to move an oval.

In this example, we create a ball that bounces around inside the Structured Graphics Control box. Instead of the **SetFillColor** method, we use the **SetTextureFill** method (line 49) to fill the oval we create with a *texture*. A texture is a picture that is placed on the surface of a polygon. The first two parameters, (**0, 0**), specify the *x–y* coordinates inside the shape at which the texture will begin. The next parameter (**'ball.gif'**) specifies the location of the texture to use, and the last parameter (**0**) specifies that the texture should be stretched to fit inside the shape. A last parameter of **1** would instead tile the texture as many times as necessary inside the shape.

```
1   <!DOCTYPE html PUBLIC "-//W3C//DTD HTML 4.0 Transitional//EN">
2   <HTML>
3
4   <!-- Fig 30.3: bounce.html                    -->
5   <!-- Textures and the Translate method -->
6
7   <HEAD>
8      <TITLE>Structured Graphics - Translate</TITLE>
9
10  <SCRIPT LANGUAGE = "JavaScript">
11     var x = 15;
12     var y = 15;
13     var upDown = -1;
14     var leftRight = 1;
15
16     function start()
17     {
18         window.setInterval( "run()", 50 );
19     }
20
21     function run()
22     {
23         // if the ball hits the top or bottom side...
24         if ( y == -100 || y == 50 )
25             upDown *= -1;
26
27         // if the ball hits the left or right side...
28         if ( x == -150 || x == 100 )
29             leftRight *= -1;
30
31         // Move the ball and increment our counters
32         ball.Translate( leftRight * 5, upDown * 5, 0 );
33         y += upDown * 5;
34         x += leftRight * 5;
35     }
36
37  </SCRIPT>
38  </HEAD>
39
40  <BODY ONLOAD = "start()">
41
42      <OBJECT ID = "ball" STYLE = "background-color: ffffff;
43         width: 300; height: 200; border-style: groove;
44         position: absolute;"
45         CLASSID = "CLSID:369303C2-D7AC-11d0-89D5-00A0C90833E6">
46
47         <PARAM NAME = "Line0001" VALUE = "SetLineStyle( 0 )">
```

Fig. 30.3   Methods **SetTextureFill** and **Translate** (part 1 of 2).

```
48              <PARAM NAME = "Line0002"
49                  VALUE = "SetTextureFill( 0, 0, 'ball.gif', 0 )">
50              <PARAM NAME = "Line0003"
51                  VALUE = "Oval( 15, 15, 50, 50 )">
52          </OBJECT>
53
54      </BODY>
55      </HTML>
```

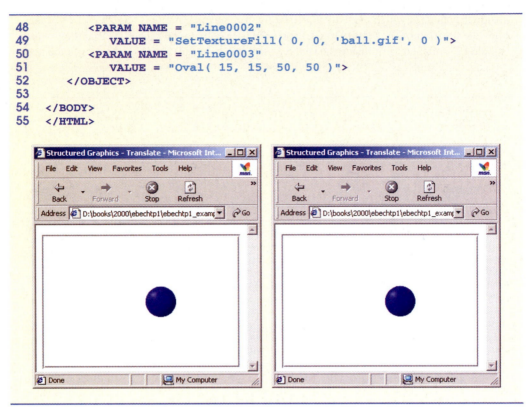

Fig. 30.3   Methods **SetTextureFill** and **Translate** (part 2 of 2).

Now that the shape is in place, we use the **Translate** method to *translate* the shape—that is, to move the shape in coordinate space without deforming it. In every call to function **run**, we determine whether the ball has reached the edge of the box (lines 24 and 28)—if this is the case, we reverse the ball's direction to simulate a bounce. Then, in line 32

```
        ball.Translate( leftRight * 5, upDown * 5, 0 );
```

we call the **Translate** function, passing it three parameters, which determine the relative distance to move the **ball** along the *x*, *y* and *z* axes, respectively.

30.4 Rotation

Another useful method for moving shapes is **Rotate**, which can rotate shapes in 3D space. Figure 30.4 demonstrates using the **Rotate** method, along with some new fill style effects.

In this example we create 3 pie shapes that we place together to form a circle. Line 30

```
        pies.Rotate( 0, 0, speed );
```

calls function **Rotate** to rotate the circle around the *z*-axis (like the **Translate** method, the three parameters of the **Rotate** function specify rotation in the *x*, *y* and *z* coordinate planes, respectively). Lines 23 through 29 in the JavaScript code provide a mechanism for varying the speed of rotation about the *z* axis.

```
1    <!DOCTYPE html PUBLIC "-//W3C//DTD HTML 4.0 Transitional//EN">
2    <HTML>
3
4    <!-- Fig 30.4: gradient.html -->
5    <!-- Gradients and rotation   -->
6
7    <HEAD>
8    <TITLE>Structured Graphics - Gradients</TITLE>
9
10   <SCRIPT LANGUAGE = "JavaScript">
11      var speed = 5;
12      var counter = 180;
13
14      function start()
15      {
16         window.setInterval( "run()", 100 );
17      }
18
19      function run()
20      {
21         counter += speed;
22
23         // accelerate half the time...
24         if ( ( counter % 360 ) > 180 )
25            speed *= ( 5 / 4 );
26
27         // deccelerate the other half.
28         if ( ( counter % 360 ) < 180 )
29            speed /= ( 5 / 4 );
30
31         pies.Rotate( 0, 0, speed );
32      }
33   </SCRIPT>
34
35   </HEAD>
36
37   <BODY ONLOAD = "start()">
38
39      <OBJECT ID = "pies" STYLE = "background-color:blue;
40         width: 300; height: 200;"
41         CLASSID = "CLSID:369303C2-D7AC-11d0-89D5-00A0C90833E6">
42
43         <PARAM NAME = "Line0001"
44            VALUE = "SetFillColor( 255, 0, 0, 0, 0, 0 )">
45         <PARAM NAME = "Line0002"
46            VALUE = "SetFillStyle( 13 )">
47         <PARAM NAME = "Line0003"
48            VALUE = "Pie( -75, -75, 150, 150, 90, 120, 300 )">
49
50         <PARAM NAME = "Line0004"
51            VALUE = "SetFillStyle( 9 )">
52         <PARAM NAME = "Line0005"
53            VALUE = "Pie( -75, -75, 150, 150, 90, 120, 180 )">
```

Fig. 30.4   Using gradients and **Rotate** (part 1 of 2).

```
54
55              <PARAM NAME = "Line0006"
56                 VALUE = "SetFillStyle( 11 )">
57              <PARAM NAME = "Line0007"
58                 VALUE = "Pie( -75, -75, 150, 150, 90, 120, 60 )">
59          </OBJECT>
60
61     </BODY>
62     </HTML>
```

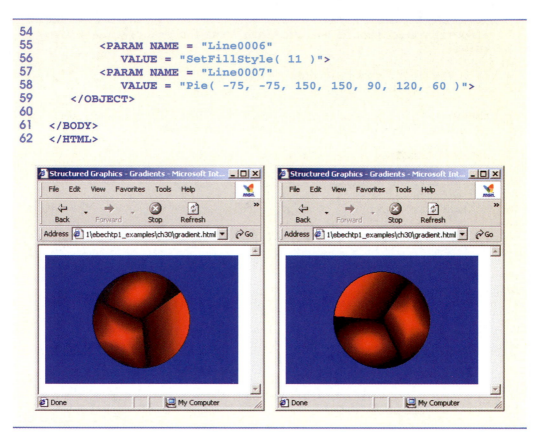

Fig. 30.4   Using gradients and **Rotate** (part 2 of 2).

The gradient fills are set with the **SetFillStyle** method (lines 46, 51, and 56). A parameter of **9** for **SetFillStyle** fills the shape with a linear gradient from the foreground color to the background color. The background color is specified with the method **SetFillColor** in lines 43 and 44

```
<PARAM NAME = "Line0001"
   VALUE = "SetFillColor( 255, 255, 255, 0, 0, 0 )">
```

by adding a second RGB triplet—here we set the foreground color to white (**255, 255, 255**) and the background color to black (**0,0,0**). The two other parameters we use for **SetFillStyle**, **11** and **13**, fill the pies with circular and rectangular gradients, respectively.

30.5 Mouse Events and External Source Files

To provide interaction with the user, the Structured Graphics Control can process the Dynamic HTML events **ONMOUSEUP**, **ONMOUSEDOWN**, **ONMOUSEMOVE**, **ONMOUSEOVER**, **ONMOUSEOUT**, **ONCLICK** and **ONDBLCLICK** (see Chapter 21). By default, the Structured Graphics Control does not capture these mouse events, because doing so takes a small amount of processing power. The **MouseEventsEnabled** property allows you to turn on capturing for these events. In Fig. 30.6, we use mouse events to trigger another feature of the Structured Graphics Control, one which allows you to keep a set of method calls in a separate source file (Fig. 30.5) and invoke them by calling the **SourceURL** method.

We toggle the mouse-event capturing in line 53

```
<PARAM NAME = "MouseEventsEnabled" VALUE = "1">
```

by setting the **MouseEventsEnabled** property to a value of **1** (true) to turn event capturing on.

```
1   SetLineStyle( 1, 3 )
2   SetFillStyle( 1 )
3   Oval( 20, 20, 50, 50, 0 )
4
5   SetLineStyle( 1, 1 )
6   PolyLine( 2, 45, 20, 45, 70, 0 )
7   PolyLine( 2, 45, 20, 45, 70, 90 )
8   PolyLine( 2, 45, 20, 45, 70, 45 )
9   PolyLine( 2, 45, 20, 45, 70, 135 )
10
11  SetFillColor( 0, 255, 0 )
12  Oval( 30, 30, 30, 30, 0 )
13  SetFillColor( 255,0,0 )
14  Oval( 35, 35, 20, 20, 0 )
```

Fig. 30.5   External source file **newoval.txt** for Fig. 30.6.

```
1   <!DOCTYPE html PUBLIC "-//W3C//DTD HTML 4.0 Transitional//EN">
2   <HTML>
3
4   <!-- Fig 30.6: bounce2.html          -->
5   <!-- SourceURL and MouseEventsEnabled -->
6
7   <HEAD>
8   <TITLE>Structured Graphics - Shapes</TITLE>
9
10  <SCRIPT FOR = "ball" EVENT = "onclick" LANGUAGE = "JavaScript">
11     ball.SourceURL = "newoval.txt";
12  </SCRIPT>
13
14  <SCRIPT LANGUAGE = "JavaScript">
15     var x = 20;
16     var y = 20;
17     var upDown = -1;
18     var leftRight = 1;
19
20     function start()
21     {
22         window.setInterval( "run()", 50 );
23     }
```

Fig. 30.6   Using **SourceURL** and **MouseEventsEnabled** (part 1 of 2).

```
24
25      function run()
26      {
27         if ( y == -100 || y == 50 )
28            upDown *= -1;
29
30         if ( x == -150 || x == 100 )
31            leftRight *= -1;
32
33         ball.Translate( leftRight * 5, upDown * 5, 0 );
34         y += upDown * 5;
35         x += leftRight *5;
36      }
37
38   </SCRIPT>
39   </HEAD>
40
41   <BODY ONLOAD = "start()">
42
43      <OBJECT ID = "ball"
44         STYLE = "width: 300; height: 200; border-style: groove;
45         position: absolute; top: 10; left: 10;"
46         CLASSID = "clsid:369303C2-D7AC-11d0-89D5-00A0C90833E6">
47
48         <PARAM NAME = "Line0001" VALUE = "SetLineStyle(0)">
49         <PARAM NAME = "Line0002"
50            VALUE = "SetTextureFill( 0, 0, 'ball.gif', 0 )">
51         <PARAM NAME = "Line0003"
52            VALUE = "Oval( 20, 20, 50, 50 )">
53         <PARAM NAME = "MouseEventsEnabled" VALUE = "1">
54      </OBJECT>
55
56   </BODY>
57   </HTML>
```

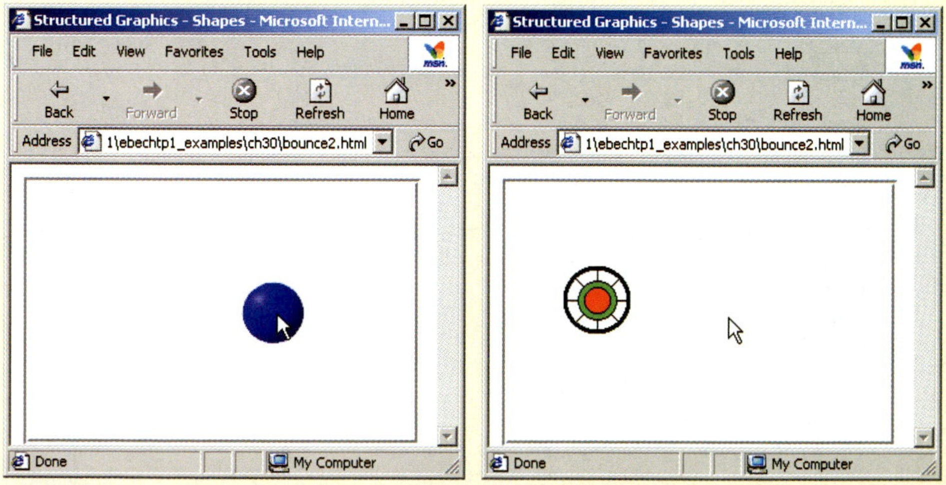

Fig. 30.6   Using **SourceURL** and **MouseEventsEnabled** (part 2 of 2).

Now lines 10 through 12

```
<SCRIPT FOR = "oval1" EVENT = "onclick" LANGUAGE = "JavaScript">
   ball.SourceURL = "newoval.txt";
</SCRIPT>
```

designate a script for the **onclick** event of our Structured Graphics object. This event sets property **SourceURL** to **newoval.txt** (Fig 30.5)—the new drawing instructions. Each command is on a separate line, consisting of only the method call and its parameters.

30.6 Scaling

The third type of shape transformation that the Structured Graphics Control provides is *scaling*, which modifies the size of an object while retaining its position and shape. Figure 30.7 provides an example of scaling, using the **Scale** method.

```
1   <!DOCTYPE html PUBLIC "-//W3C//DTD HTML 4.0 Transitional//EN">
2   <HTML>
3
4   <!-- Fig 30.7: scaling.html -->
5   <!-- Scaling a shape        -->
6
7   <HEAD>
8   <TITLE>Structured Graphics - Scaling</TITLE>
9
10  <SCRIPT LANGUAGE = "JavaScript">
11     var speedX = 0;
12     var speedY = 0;
13     var speedZ = 0;
14     var scale = 1;
15
16     function start()
17     {
18        window.setInterval( "run()", 100 );
19     }
20
21     function run()
22     {
23        drawing.Rotate( speedX, speedY, speedZ );
24        drawing.Scale( scale, scale, scale );
25     }
26
27     function rotate( axis )
28     {
29        axis = ( axis ? 0 : 5 );
30     }
31  </SCRIPT>
32
```

Fig. 30.7   Rotating a shape in three dimensions and scaling up and down (part 1 of 4).

```
33   </HEAD>
34
35   <BODY ONLOAD = "start()">
36
37   <DIV STYLE = "position: absolute; top: 25; left: 220">
38   <INPUT TYPE = "BUTTON" VALUE = "Rotate-X"
39      ONCLICK = "speedX = ( speedX ? 0 : 5 )"><BR>
40   <INPUT TYPE = "BUTTON" VALUE = "Rotate-Y"
41      ONCLICK = "speedY = ( speedY ? 0 : 5 )"><BR>
42   <INPUT TYPE = "BUTTON" VALUE = "Rotate-Z"
43      ONCLICK = "speedZ = ( speedZ ? 0 : 5 )"><BR>
44   <BR>
45   <INPUT TYPE = "BUTTON" VALUE = "Scale Up"
46      ONCLICK = "scale = ( scale * 10 / 9 )"><BR>
47   <INPUT TYPE = "BUTTON" VALUE = "Scale Down"
48      ONCLICK = "scale = ( scale * 9 / 10 )">
49   </DIV>
50
51   <OBJECT ID = "drawing" STYLE = " position: absolute;
52      z-index: 2; width: 200; height: 300;"
53      CLASSID = "CLSID:369303C2-D7AC-11d0-89D5-00A0C90833E6">
54
55      <PARAM NAME = "Line0001" VALUE = "SetFillColor( 0,0,0 )">
56      <PARAM NAME = "Line0002" VALUE = "SetFillStyle( 0 )">
57      <PARAM NAME = "Line0003" VALUE = "SetLineStyle( 1, 3 )">
58
59      <PARAM NAME = "Line0004"
60            VALUE = "Oval( -25, -100, 50, 50, 0 )">
61
62      <PARAM NAME = "Line0005"
63         VALUE = "PolyLine(2, 0, -50, 0, 50 )">
64
65      <PARAM NAME = "Line0006"
66         VALUE = "PolyLine( 3, -30, -25, 0, -15, 30, -25 )">
67
68      <PARAM NAME = "Line0007"
69         VALUE = "PolyLine( 3, -15, 90, 0, 50, 15, 90 )">
70
71      <PARAM NAME = "Line0008"
72         VALUE = "SetFillColor ( 255, 0, 0 )">
73      <PARAM NAME = "Line0009"
74         VALUE = "Oval( -15, -85, 7, 7, 0 )">
75      <PARAM NAME = "Line0010"
76         VALUE = "Oval( 5, -85, 7, 7, 0 )">
77
78      <PARAM NAME = "Line0011"
79         VALUE = "SetLineStyle( 1, 2 )">
80      <PARAM NAME = "Line0012"
81         VALUE = "SetLineColor( 255, 0, 0 )">
82      <PARAM NAME = "Line0013"
83         VALUE = "SetFont( 'Courier', 25, 200, 0, 0, 0 )">
84      <PARAM NAME = "Line0014"
85         VALUE = "Text( 'Hello', -35, -115 , 0 )">
```

Fig. 30.7   Rotating a shape in three dimensions and scaling up and down (part 2 of 4).

```
86   </OBJECT>
87
88   <OBJECT ID = "background" STYLE = " position:absolute;
89      z-index: 1; width: 200; height: 300; background-color: none"
90      CLASSID = "CLSID:369303C2-D7AC-11d0-89D5-00A0C90833E6">
91
92      <PARAM NAME = "Line0001"
93         VALUE = "SetFillColor( 38, 250, 38 )">
94      <PARAM NAME = "Line0002"
95         VALUE = "Oval( -75, -125, 150, 250, 0 )">
96   </OBJECT>
97   </BODY>
98   </HTML>
```

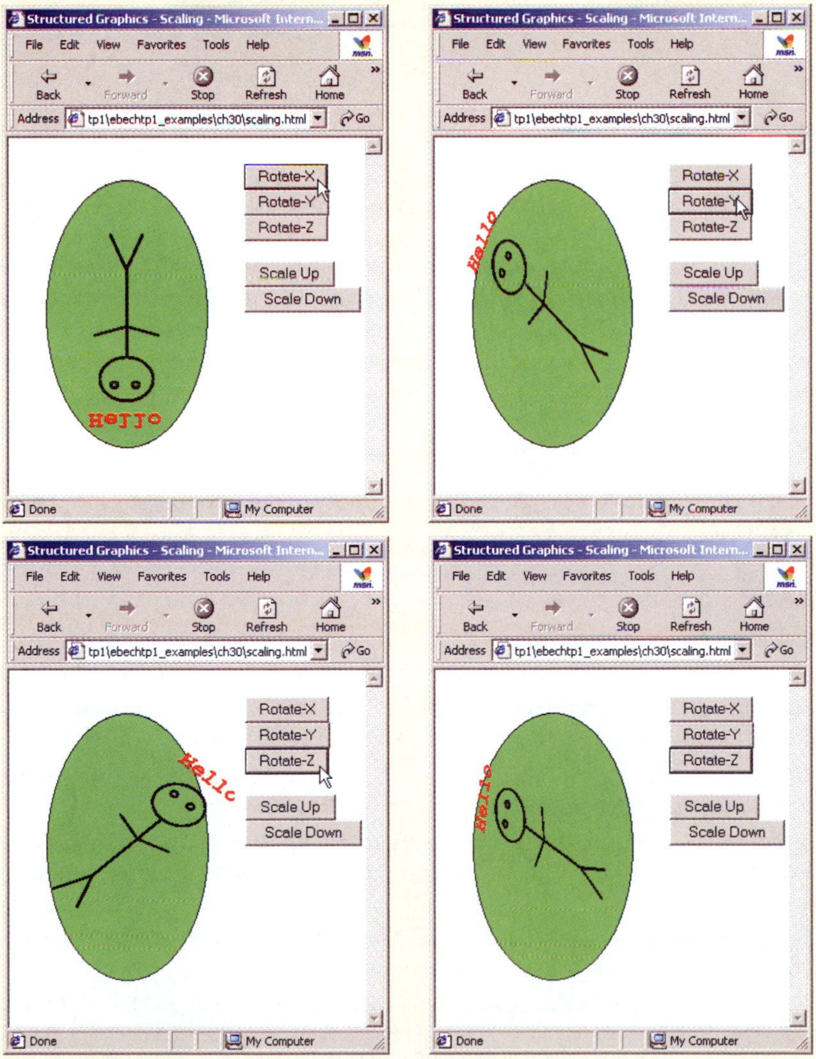

Fig. 30.7   Rotating a shape in three dimensions and scaling up and down (part 3 of 4).

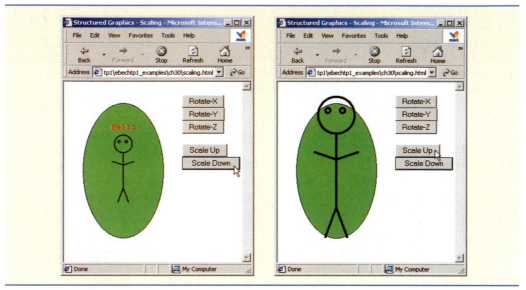

Fig. 30.7   Rotating a shape in three dimensions and scaling up and down (part 4 of 4).

In this example we use two separate controls—the first (lines 51 through 86) for our rotating foreground, and the second (lines 88 through 96) for the oval in the background. We position these over each other using the **position** and **z-index** CSS attributes. We then use the five buttons to the side of the Structured Graphics Controls to control rotation and scaling of the upper layer. In line 24

```
drawing.Scale( scale, scale, scale );
```

the **Scale** method scales object **drawing** uniformly in the three dimensions based on the variable **scale**.

SUMMARY

- The Structured Graphics Control is an ActiveX control that you can add with an **OBJECT** tag. The Structured Graphics Control is easily accessible through script for creating dynamic Web pages.
- The Structured Graphics Control is a Web interface for the widely used DirectAnimation subset of Microsoft's DirectX software, used in many high-end games and graphical applications.
- The Structured Graphics control allows you to create simple shapes by using functions that can be called via scripting or through **PARAM** tags inside **OBJECT** elements.
- The **NAME** attribute of the **PARAM** tag method determines the order in which the function specified in the **VALUE** attribute is called. The order of calls must be **Line0001**, **Line0002**, **Line0003**, and so on.
- The **SetLineColor** function sets the color of lines and borders of shapes that are drawn. It takes an RGB triplet in decimal notation as its three parameters.
- The two parameters of the **SetLineStyle** function set the line style and line width, respectively. A value of **1** for line style creates a solid line (the default). A value of **0** does not draw any lines or borders, and a value of **2** creates a dashed line. The line width is specified in pixels.
- The **SetFillColor** method sets the foreground color with which to fill shapes.

- The **SetFillStyle** method determines the style in which a shape is filled with color—a value of **1** fills shapes with the solid color declared with the **SetFillColor** method. There are 14 possible fill styles.

- The first two parameters of the **Oval** method specify *x–y* coordinates at which to place the oval. The next two parameters specify the height and width of the oval respectively. The last parameter specifies the clockwise rotation of the oval relative to the *x*-axis, expressed in degrees.

- All shapes in the Structured Graphics control effectively have a surrounding box—when you place the image at a certain *x–y* coordinate, it is the upper left corner of that box that is placed at that coordinate. Inside the control, the point *(0, 0)* (also known as the origin) is at the center of the control, not at the upper left.

- The **Arc** method takes 7 parameters: the *x–y* coordinates of the arc, the height and width of the box in which the arc is enclosed, the starting angle of the arc in degrees, the size of the arc relative to the starting angle (also in degrees) and the rotation of the arc.

- The **Pie** method takes the same parameters as the **Arc** method, but it fills in the arc with the foreground color, thus creating a pie shape.

- The first parameter of method **Polygon** specifies the number of vertices in the polygon, and then each successive pair of numbers specifies the *x–y* coordinates of the next vertex in the polygon.

- The **Rect** method creates a rectangle. The first two parameters specify the coordinates, the next two specify height and width respectively, and the last parameter specifies rotation in degrees.

- The **RoundRect** method is almost identical to the **Rect** method, but it adds two new parameters, which specify the height and width of the rounded arcs at the corners of the rectangle.

- The **SetFont** method sets the font style to use when placing text with the **Text** method.

- The **PolyLine** method draws a line with multiple segments. The **PolyLine** method functions much like the **Polygon** method—the first parameter declares the number of points in the line, and then each successive pair declares the *x–y* coordinates of another vertex.

- The **SetTextureFill** method fills a shape with a texture. A texture is a picture that is placed on the surface of a polygon. The first two parameters specify at what *x–y* coordinates inside the shape the texture will begin. The next parameter specifies the location of the texture to use. A last parameter of **0** specifies that the texture should be stretched to fit inside the shape. A last parameter of **1** would instead tile the texture as many times as necessary inside the shape.

- The **Translate** method moves a shape in coordinate space without deforming it. Its three parameters determine the relative distance to move along the *x*, *y* and *z* axes, respectively (the *z*-axis is the third-dimensional coordinate axis).

- The **Rotate** method rotates shapes in 3D space. The three parameters of the **Rotate** function specify rotation in the x, y and z coordinate planes, respectively.

- A parameter of **9** for **SetFillStyle** fills the shape with a linear gradient from the foreground color to the background color.

- A background color can be specified with the **SetFillColor** method by adding a second RGB triplet to the parameters.

- Two other parameters for **SetFillStyle**, **11** and **13**, fill shapes with circular and rectangular gradients, respectively.

- To provide interaction with the user, the Structured Graphics control can process the Dynamic HTML mouse events **ONMOUSEUP**, **ONMOUSEDOWN**, **ONMOUSEMOVE**, **ONMOUSEOVER**, **ONMOUSEOUT**, **ONCLICK** and **ONDBLCLICK**.

- By default, the Structured Graphics Control does not capture mouse events, because doing so takes a small amount of processing power.

- The Structure Graphics Control allows you to keep a set of method calls in a separate source file and to invoke those methods by calling the **SourceURL** function.

- Turn event capturing on by calling the **MouseEventsEnabled** method with a **VALUE** of **1** (true).

- Each command in a file targeted by **SourceURL** is on a separate line and consists of only the method call and its parameters.

TERMINOLOGY

arc	**Pie** method
Arc method	polygon
CLSID:369303C2-D7AC-11d0-89D5-	**Polygon** method
00A0C90833E6 (Structured Graphics Control)	**PolyLine** method
DirectAnimation	**Rect** method
DirectX	rectangle
line style	**Rotate** method
line width	rounded rectangle
Line0001 (Line0002, etc.)	**RoundRect** method
mouse events	**Scale** method
OBJECT tag	**SetFillColor** method
ONCLICK event	**SetFillStyle** method
ONDBLCLICK event	**SetFont** method
ONMOUSEDOWN event	**SetLineColor** method
ONMOUSEMOVE event	**SetLineStyle** method
ONMOUSEOUT event	**SetTextureFill** method
ONMOUSEOVER event	**SourceURL** method
ONMOUSEUP event	Structured Graphics
origin	**Text** method
oval	texture
Oval method	translate
PARAM tag	**Translate** method
pie	

SELF-REVIEW EXERCISES

30.1   Fill in the blanks for the following questions:
   a) The Structured Graphics control is a subset of Microsoft's _____ software package.
   b) The Structured Graphics control captures only _____-related events.
   c) The _____ method allows you to draw a multi-segmented line.
   d) There are _____ different styles for the **SetFillStyle** method.
   e) The _____ method allows you to import external lists of commands.
   f) A _____ is an image that is placed on the surface of a polygon.
   g) The _____ method moves shapes in the Structured Graphics Control without distorting or rotating them.
   h) To place text with the **Text** method, the _____ method must first be called to set the properties of the text to be placed.

30.2   Answer the following questions true or false; if false, state why.
   a) By default, event capturing is turned on for the Structured Graphics control.
   b) The **SetLineColor** and **SetLineStyle** methods also apply to shape borders.
   c) The **Pie** method has the same parameters as the **Arc** method.
   d) Calling **SetFillStyle** with an argument of **1** fills shapes with a solid color.

e) The dotted line style may be used at any line width.

f) The **SetFillTexture** method specifies whether the texture is tiled or stretched.

ANSWERS TO SELF-REVIEW EXERCISES

30.1   a) DirectX. b) mouse. c) **PolyLine**. d) 15. e) **SourceURL**. f) texture. g) **Translate**. h) **SetFont**.

30.2   a) False. It is off by default. b) True. c) True. d) True. e) False. It may be used only with lines that are 1 pixel wide. f) True.

EXERCISES

30.3   Modify example 30.2 to do the following:
  a) speed up when the ball is clicked;
  b) change the ball's shape when it hits a wall;
  c) have the ball stop if the user moves the mouse cursor over the ball and resume moving if the user moves the mouse cursor off the ball.

30.4   Use the Structured Graphics Control to create several ovals in different sizes, shapes, locations, colors and fill styles.

30.5   Use the primitive shapes to create simple pictures of a person, a car, a house, a bicycle, and a dog.

30.6   Look up the **Spline** method mentioned in the documentation at the URL provided in Section 30.1, and use it to create a figure-eight shape.

30.7   Draw a series of eight concentric circles, each separation being 10 pixels.

30.8   Draw four triangles of different sizes. Each triangle should be filled with a different color (or fill style).

30.9   Create a web page that uses JavaScript and the Structured Graphics Control to create an interactive hangman game.

30.10   Use the Structured Graphics Control to draw a cube.

30.11   Modify Exercise 30.10 to continuously rotate the cube.

30.12   Modify Exercise 30.10 to rotate the cube in response to the user moving the mouse. The cube should rotate in the direction the user drags the mouse. [Hint: Use the **ONMOUSEDOWN** event to determine when the user begins a drag and use the **ONMOUSEUP** event to determine when the drag operation terminates.]

30.13   Modify Exercise 30.12 to determine the speed at which the cube rotates by calculating the distance between two consecutive **ONMOUSEMOVE** events.

31

Dynamic HTML: Path, Sequencer and Sprite ActiveX Controls

Objectives

- To be able to use the DirectAnimation multimedia ActiveX controls, including the Path, Sequencer and Sprite controls.
- To add animation to Web pages with the DirectAnimation ActiveX controls.
- To use the Path Control to specify the path along which an animated Web page element moves.
- To use the Sequencer Control to control the timing and synchronization of actions on a Web page.
- To use the Sprite Control to create animated images for a Web page.

There is a natural hootchy-kootchy motion to a goldfish.
Walt Disney

Isn't life a series of images that change as they repeat themselves?
Andy Warhol

Between the motion and the act falls the shadow.
Thomas Stearns Eliot, *The Hollow Men*

The wheel is come full circle.
William Shakespeare

Grass grows, birds fly, waves pound the sand.
Muhammad Ali

31.1 Introduction

In this chapter we discuss the remaining three DirectAnimation ActiveX controls available for use with Internet Explorer 5: the *Path Control*, the *Sequencer Control*, and the *Sprite Control*. Each one of these controls allows a Web page designer to add certain multimedia effects to Web pages. When used with one another, with the Structured Graphics Control we discussed in the last chapter, and with other Dynamic HTML effects, they help create stunning visual presentations for your content.

Performance Tip 31.1

Multimedia is performance intensive. Internet bandwidth and processor speed are still precious resources. Multimedia-based Web applications must be carefully designed to use resources wisely, or they may perform poorly.

31.2 DirectAnimation Path Control

The *DirectAnimation Path Control* allows you to control the position of elements on your page. This is more advanced than dynamic CSS positioning, because it allows you to define paths that the targeted elements follow. This gives you the ability to create professional presentations, especially when integrated with other Dynamic HTML features such as filters and transitions. Figure 31.1 uses the Path Control to create a short linear path for an **H1** element.

```
1    <!DOCTYPE html PUBLIC "-//W3C//DTD HTML 4.0 Transitional//EN">
2    <HTML>
3
4    <!-- Fig. 31.1: path1.html        -->
5    <!-- Introducing the path control -->
6
7    <HEAD>
8       <TITLE>Path control</TITLE>
9    </HEAD>
10
11   <BODY STYLE = "background-color: #9C00FF">
```

Fig. 31.1   Demonstrating the DirectAnimation Path Control (part 1 of 2).

```
12
13   <H1 ID = "headerText" STYLE = "position: absolute">
14   Path animation:</H1>
15
16   <OBJECT ID = "oval"
17      CLASSID = "CLSID:D7A7D7C3-D47F-11D0-89D3-00A0C90833E6">
18      <PARAM NAME = "AutoStart" VALUE = "1">
19      <PARAM NAME = "Repeat" VALUE = "-1">
20      <PARAM NAME = "Duration" VALUE = "2">
21      <PARAM NAME = "Bounce" VALUE = "1">
22      <PARAM NAME = "Shape"
23         VALUE = "PolyLine( 2, 0, 0, 200, 50 )">
24      <PARAM NAME = "Target" VALUE = "headerText">
25   </OBJECT>
26
27   </BODY>
28   </HTML>
```

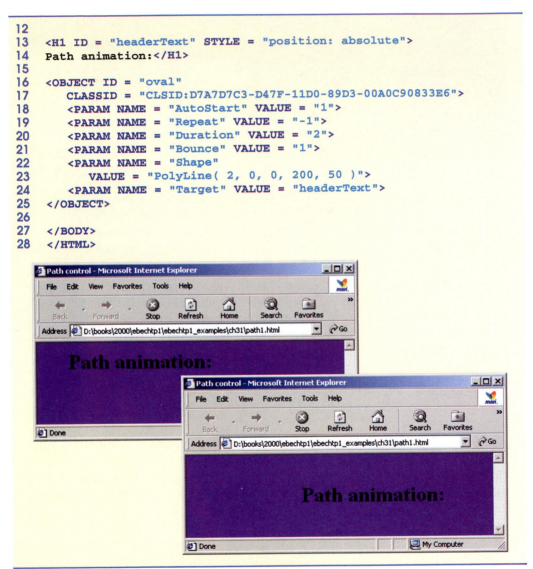

Fig. 31.1   Demonstrating the DirectAnimation Path Control (part 2 of 2).

Lines 16 through 25

```
<OBJECT ID = "oval"
   CLASSID = "CLSID:D7A7D7C3-D47F-11D0-89D3-00A0C90833E6">
   <PARAM NAME = "AutoStart" VALUE = "1">
   <PARAM NAME = "Repeat" VALUE = "-1">
   <PARAM NAME = "Duration" VALUE = "2">
   <PARAM NAME = "Bounce" VALUE = "1">
   <PARAM NAME = "Shape"
      VALUE = "PolyLine( 2, 0, 0, 200, 50 )">
   <PARAM NAME = "Target" VALUE = "headerText">
</OBJECT>
```

use the **OBJECT** element to place the Path Control on the page. The **CLASSID** attribute used here identifies the DirectAnimation Path Control. The **PARAM** tags in the **OBJECT** element specify certain properties of the control. Setting **AutoStart** to a nonzero value (**1** in this case) starts the element along the path as soon as the page loads (setting a zero value would prevent it from starting automatically, in which case a script would have to call the **Play** method to start the path). The **Repeat** method determines how many times the path will be traversed—setting the value to **-1**, as we do here, specifies that the path should loop continuously. The **Duration** method specifies the amount of time that it will take to traverse the path, in seconds.

Methof **Bounce**, when set to **1**, reverses the element's direction on the path when it reaches the end. Setting the value to **0** would instead return the element to the beginning of the path when the path has been traversed. The **Shape** method is what actually determines the path of the element—as we saw with the Structured Graphics Control, the **PolyLine** method creates a path with multiple line segments. In this case we declare a path with **2** points, located at (**0, 0**) and (**200, 50**). Finally, the **Target** method specifies the **ID** of the element that is targeted by the path control. Note that line 13

```
<H1 ID = "headertext" STYLE = "position: absolute">
```

sets the CSS attribute **position** to **absolute**—this allows the Path Control to actually move the element around the screen. Otherwise, the element would be static, locked in the position determined by the browser when the page loads.

31.3 Multiple Path Controls

The Path Control also allows you to set paths for multiple objects present on your page. To do this, you must add a separate **OBJECT** tag for each object you wish to control. Figure 31.2 creates **PolyLine** paths for seven separate objects for a pleasant splash screen effect.

Each **OBJECT** element in our program controls a separate **SPAN** element. As the page loads, these elements move separately into place, creating a visually pleasing effect. Note that because we did not specify the **z-index** properties, the **z-index** of elements that overlap each other is determined by their order of declaration in the HTML source. Elements declared later in the HTML file are displayed above elements declared earlier.

```
1   <!DOCTYPE html PUBLIC "-//W3C//DTD HTML 4.0 Transitional//EN">
2   <HTML>
3
4   <!-- Fig 31.2: path2.html       -->
5   <!-- Controlling multiple paths -->
6   <HEAD>
7      <TITLE>Path Control - Multiple paths</TITLE>
8
9   <STYLE TYPE = "text/css">
10
11    SPAN { position: absolute;
12            font-family: sans-serif;
13            font-size: 2em;
```

Fig. 31.2   Controlling multiple elements with the Path Control (part 1 of 4).

```
14              font-weight: bold;
15              filter: shadow( direction = 225 );
16              padding: 9px;
17          }
18
19   </STYLE>
20   </HEAD>
21
22   <BODY STYLE = "background-color: lavender">
23
24   <IMG SRC = "icons2.gif"
25       STYLE = "position: absolute; left: 30; top: 110">
26
27   <SPAN ID = "titleTxt"
28          STYLE = "left: 500; top: 500; color: white">
29   Multimedia Cyber Classroom<BR>
30   Programming Tip Icons</SPAN>
31
32   <SPAN ID = "CPEspan"
33          STYLE = "left: 75; top: 500; color: red">
34   Common Programming Errors</SPAN>
35
36   <SPAN ID = "GPPspan"
37          STYLE = "left: 275; top: 500; color: orange">
38   Good Programming Practices</SPAN>
39
40   <SPAN ID = "PERFspan"
41          STYLE = "left: 475; top: 500; color: yellow">
42   Performance Tips</SPAN>
43
44   <SPAN ID = "PORTspan"
45          STYLE = "left: 100; top: -50; color: green">
46   Portability Tips</SPAN>
47
48   <SPAN ID = "SEOspan"
49          STYLE = "left: 300; top: -50; color: blue">
50   Software Engineering Observations</SPAN>
51
52   <SPAN ID = "TDTspan"
53          STYLE = "left: 500; top: -50; color: violet">
54   Testing and Debugging Tips</SPAN>
55
56   <OBJECT ID = "CyberPath"
57      CLASSID = "CLSID:D7A7D7C3-D47F-11D0-89D3-00A0C90833E6">
58      <PARAM NAME = "Target" VALUE = "titleTxt">
59      <PARAM NAME = "Duration" VALUE = "10">
60      <PARAM NAME = "Shape"
61          VALUE = "PolyLine( 2, 500, 500, 100, 10 )">
62      <PARAM NAME = "AutoStart" VALUE = 1>
63   </OBJECT>
64
65   <OBJECT ID = "CPEPath"
66      CLASSID = "CLSID:D7A7D7C3-D47F-11D0-89D3-00A0C90833E6">
```

Fig. 31.2   Controlling multiple elements with the Path Control (part 2 of 4).

```
67          <PARAM NAME = "Target" VALUE = "CPEspan">
68          <PARAM NAME = "Duration" VALUE = "4">
69          <PARAM NAME = "Shape"
70             VALUE = "PolyLine( 3, 75, 500, 300, 170, 35, 175 )">
71          <PARAM NAME = "AutoStart" VALUE = 1>
72       </OBJECT>
73
74       <OBJECT ID = "GPPPath"
75          CLASSID = "CLSID:D7A7D7C3-D47F-11D0-89D3-00A0C90833E6">
76          <PARAM NAME = "Target" VALUE = "GPPspan">
77          <PARAM NAME = "Duration" VALUE = "5">
78          <PARAM NAME = "Shape"
79             VALUE = "PolyLine( 3, 275, 500, 300, 340, 85, 205 )">
80          <PARAM NAME = "AutoStart" VALUE = 1>
81       </OBJECT>
82
83       <OBJECT ID = "PERFPath"
84          CLASSID = "CLSID:D7A7D7C3-D47F-11D0-89D3-00A0C90833E6">
85          <PARAM NAME = "Target" VALUE = "PERFspan">
86          <PARAM NAME = "Duration" VALUE = "6">
87          <PARAM NAME = "Shape"
88             VALUE = "PolyLine( 3, 475, 500, 300, 340, 140, 235 )">
89          <PARAM NAME = "AutoStart" VALUE = 1>
90       </OBJECT>
91
92       <OBJECT ID = "PORTPath"
93          CLASSID = "CLSID:D7A7D7C3-D47F-11D0-89D3-00A0C90833E6">
94          <PARAM NAME = "Target" VALUE = "PORTspan">
95          <PARAM NAME = "Duration" VALUE = "7">
96          <PARAM NAME = "Shape"
97             VALUE = "PolyLine( 3, 600, -50, 300, 340, 200, 265 )">
98          <PARAM NAME = "AutoStart" VALUE = 1>
99       </OBJECT>
100
101      <OBJECT ID = "SEOPath"
102         CLASSID = "CLSID:D7A7D7C3-D47F-11D0-89D3-00A0C90833E6">
103         <PARAM NAME = "Target" VALUE = "SEOspan">
104         <PARAM NAME = "Duration" VALUE = "8">
105         <PARAM NAME = "Shape"
106            VALUE = "PolyLine( 3, 300, -50, 300, 340, 260, 295 )">
107         <PARAM NAME = "AutoStart" VALUE = 1>
108      </OBJECT>
109
110      <OBJECT ID = "TDTPath"
111         CLASSID = "CLSID:D7A7D7C3-D47F-11D0-89D3-00A0C90833E6">
112         <PARAM NAME = "Target" VALUE = "TDTspan">
113         <PARAM NAME = "Duration" VALUE = "9">
114         <PARAM NAME = "Shape"
115            VALUE = "PolyLine( 3, 500, -50, 300, 340, 310, 325 )">
116         <PARAM NAME = "AutoStart" VALUE = 1>
117      </OBJECT>
118   </BODY>
119   </HTML>
```

Fig. 31.2   Controlling multiple elements with the Path Control (part 3 of 4).

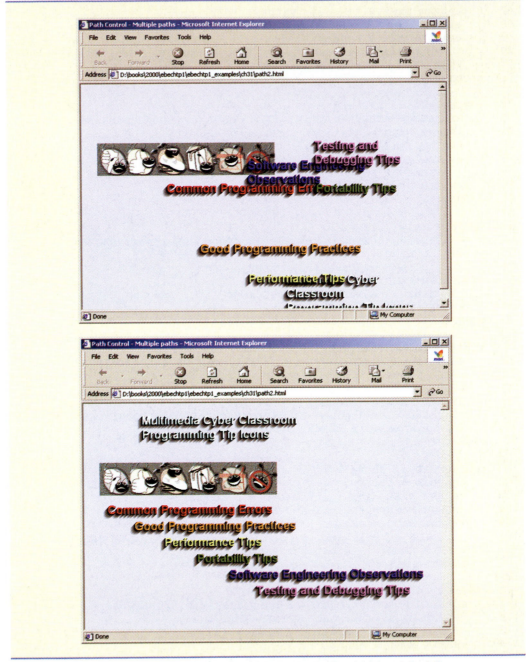

Fig. 31.2   Controlling multiple elements with the Path Control (part 4 of 4).

31.4 Time Markers for Path Control

A useful feature of the Path Control is the ability to execute certain actions at any point along an object's path. This is done with the **AddTimeMarker** method, which creates a *time marker* that can be handled with simple JavaScript event handling. Figure 31.3 has two separate time markers for an image that follows an *oval* path.

```
1   <!DOCTYPE html PUBLIC "-//W3C//DTD HTML 4.0 Transitional//EN">
2   <HTML>
3
4   <!-- Fig 31.3: path3.html       -->
5   <!-- Oval paths and time markers -->
6
7   <HEAD>
8   <TITLE>Path control - Advanced Paths</TITLE>
9
10  <SCRIPT LANGUAGE = "JavaScript" FOR = "oval"
11     EVENT = "ONMARKER ( marker )">
12
13     if ( marker == "mark1" )
14        pole.style.zIndex +=  2;
15
16     if ( marker == "mark2" )
17        pole.style.zIndex -=  2;
18  </SCRIPT>
19  </HEAD>
20
21  <BODY STYLE = "background-color: #9C00FF">
22
23  <IMG ID = "pole" SRC = "pole.gif" STYLE = "position: absolute;
24     left: 350; top: 80; z-index: 3; height: 300">
25
26  <IMG ID = "largebug" SRC = "animatedbug_large.gif"
27        STYLE = "position: absolute; z-index: 4">
28
29  <OBJECT ID = "oval"
30     CLASSID = "CLSID:D7A7D7C3-D47F-11D0-89D3-00A0C90833E6">
31     <PARAM NAME = "AutoStart" VALUE = "-1">
32     <PARAM NAME = "Repeat" VALUE = "-1">
33     <PARAM NAME = "Relative" VALUE = "1">
34     <PARAM NAME = "Duration" VALUE = "8">
35     <PARAM NAME = "Shape" VALUE = "Oval( 100, 80, 300, 60 )">
36     <PARAM NAME = "Target" VALUE = "largebug">
37     <PARAM NAME = "AddTimeMarker1" VALUE = "2, mark1, 0">
38     <PARAM NAME = "AddTimeMarker2" VALUE = "6, mark2, 0">
39  </OBJECT>
40
41  <OBJECT ID = "swarmPath"
42     CLASSID = "CLSID:D7A7D7C3-D47F-11D0-89D3-00A0C90833E6">
43     <PARAM NAME = "AutoStart" VALUE = "-1">
44     <PARAM NAME = "Repeat" VALUE = "-1">
45     <PARAM NAME = "Relative" VALUE = "1">
46     <PARAM NAME = "Duration" VALUE = "15">
47     <PARAM NAME = "Shape"
48        VALUE = "Polygon(6, 0, 0, 400, 300, 450, 50, 320, 300,
49                         150, 180, 50, 250 )">
50     <PARAM NAME = "Target" VALUE = "swarm">
```

Fig. 31.3   Adding time markers for script interaction (part 1 of 2).

```
51   </OBJECT>
52
53   <SPAN ID = "swarm"
54      STYLE = "position:absolute; top: 0; left: 0; z-index: 1">
55
56   <IMG SRC = "animatedbug_small.gif"
57      STYLE = "position:absolute; top: 25; left: -30">
58   <IMG SRC = "animatedbug_small.gif"
59      STYLE = "position:absolute; top: 0; left: 0">
60   <IMG SRC = "animatedbug_small.gif"
61      STYLE = "position:absolute; top: 15; left: 70">
62   <IMG SRC = "animatedbug_small.gif"
63      STYLE = "position:absolute; top: 30; left: 5">
64   <IMG SRC = "animatedbug_small.gif"
65      STYLE = "position: absolute; top: 10; left: 30">
66   <IMG SRC = "animatedbug_small.gif"
67      STYLE = "position: absolute; top: 40; left: 40">
68   <IMG SRC = "animatedbug_small.gif"
69      STYLE = "position: absolute; top: 65; left: 15">
70
71   </SPAN>
72   </BODY>
73   </HTML>
```

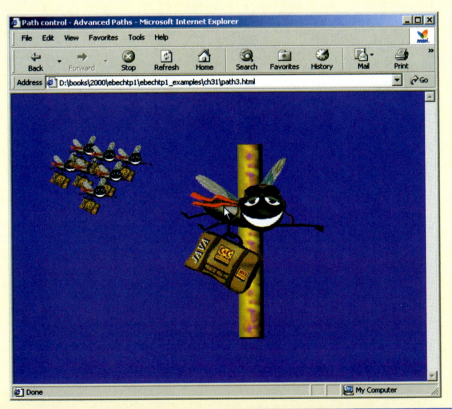

Fig. 31.3   Adding time markers for script interaction (part 2 of 2).

Line 35

```
<PARAM NAME = "Shape" VALUE = "Oval( 100, 80, 300, 60 )">
```

places the image with the **ID** of **largebug** on an oval path using the **Oval** method. This is very similar to the **Oval** method from the Structured Graphics Control in that the first two parameters specify the *x–y* coordinates of the oval and the next two parameters specify the width and height of the oval, respectively.

Line 37

```
<PARAM NAME = "AddTimeMarker1" VALUE = "2, mark1, 0">
```

introduces the **AddTimeMarker** method. The **1** appended to the **AddTimeMarker** function is a sequential identifier—much like **Line0001** is used in the Structured Graphics Control. The first parameter in the **VALUE** attribute determines at which point our time marker is placed along the path, specified in seconds—when this point is reached, event **ONMARKER** is fired. The second parameter gives an identifying name to the event, which is later passed on to the event handler for the **ONMARKER** function. The last parameter specifies whether to fire the **ONMARKER** event every time the object's path loops past the time marker (as we do here by setting the parameter to **0**) or to fire the event just the first time that the time marker is passed (by setting the parameter to **1**).

Lines 10 through 18

```
<SCRIPT LANGUAGE = "JavaScript" FOR = "oval"
   EVENT = "ONMARKER ( marker )">

   if ( marker == "mark1" )
      pole.style.zIndex += 2;

   if ( marker == "mark2" )
      pole.style.zIndex -= 2;
</SCRIPT>
```

create an event handler for the **ONMARKER** event. The parameter that the **ONMARKER** event receives (here defined as **marker** in line 11) identifies which marker fired the event. The **if** control structures following then change the **zIndex** attribute of element **pole** to correspond to the time marker in our Path Control that actually fired the event. These events fire when the large image is at the leftmost and rightmost extremes of its oval path, so this creates the appearance that the bee image is flying alternately behind and in front of the pole image.

31.5 DirectAnimation Sequencer Control

Thus far, we have been using the JavaScript function **window.setInterval** to control timed events on our Web pages. The Sequencer Control provides a simpler interface for calling functions or performing actions, at time intervals that you can set easily. Figure 31.4 uses the Sequencer Control to display 4 lines of text sequentially—when the fourth line of text has displayed, the Sequencer Control then starts that fourth line on a **PolyLine** path, using the **Play** method of the Path Control.

Lines 57 through 59

```
<OBJECT ID = "sequencer"
    CLASSID = "CLSID:B0A6BAE2-AAF0-11d0-A152-00A0C908DB96">
</OBJECT>
```

add the Sequencer Control to our Web page. Notice that we do not include any **PARAM** tags inside the **OBJECT** element—here, we set all the parameters for the Sequencer Control via scripting.

```
1   <!DOCTYPE html PUBLIC "-//W3C//DTD HTML 4.0 Transitional//EN">
2   <HTML>
3
4   <!-- Fig 31.4: sequencer.html -->
5   <!-- Sequencer Control        -->
6
7   <HEAD>
8
9   <STYLE TYPE = "text/css">
10
11     DIV { font-size: 2em;
12           color: white;
13           font-weight: bold }
14
15   </STYLE>
16
17   <SCRIPT FOR = "sequencer" EVENT = "oninit">
18     sequencer.Item( "showThem" ).at( 2.0, "show( line1 )" );
19     sequencer.Item( "showThem" ).at( 4.0, "show( line2 )" );
20     sequencer.Item( "showThem" ).at( 6.0, "show( line3 )" );
21     sequencer.Item( "showThem" ).at( 7.0, "show( line4 )" );
22     sequencer.Item( "showThem" ).at( 8.0, "runPath()" );
23   </SCRIPT>
24
25   <SCRIPT>
26     function show( object )
27     {
28        object.style.visibility = "visible";
29     }
30
31     function start()
32     {
33        sequencer.Item( "showThem" ).Play();
34     }
35
36     function runPath()
37     {
38        pathControl.Play();
39     }
40   </SCRIPT>
41   </HEAD>
```

Fig. 31.4   Using the DirectAnimation Sequencer Control (part 1 of 3).

```
42
43    <BODY STYLE = "background-color: limegreen" ONLOAD = "start()">
44
45    <DIV ID = "line1" STYLE = "position: absolute; left: 50;
46       top: 10; visibility: hidden">Sequencer DirectAnimation</DIV>
47
48    <DIV ID = "line2" STYLE = "position: absolute; left: 70;
49       top: 60; visibility: hidden">ActiveX Control</DIV>
50
51    <DIV ID = "line3" STYLE = "position: absolute; left: 90;
52       top: 110; visibility: hidden">Controls time intervals</DIV>
53
54    <DIV ID = "line4" STYLE = "position: absolute; left: 110;
55       top:160; visibility: hidden">For dynamic effects</DIV>
56
57    <OBJECT ID = "sequencer"
58       CLASSID = "CLSID:B0A6BAE2-AAF0-11d0-A152-00A0C908DB96">
59    </OBJECT>
60
61    <OBJECT ID = "pathControl"
62       CLASSID = "CLSID:D7A7D7C3-D47F-11D0-89D3-00A0C90833E6">
63       <PARAM NAME = "AutoStart" VALUE = "0">
64       <PARAM NAME = "Repeat" VALUE = "1">
65       <PARAM NAME = "Relative" VALUE = "1">
66       <PARAM NAME = "Duration" VALUE = "2">
67       <PARAM NAME = "Shape" VALUE = "PolyLine( 2, 0, 0, 250, 0 )">
68       <PARAM NAME = "Target" VALUE = "line4">
69    </OBJECT>
70
71    </BODY>
72    </HTML>
```

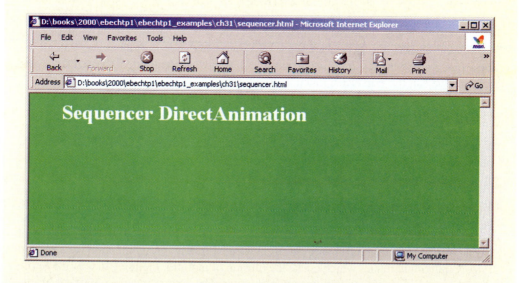

Fig. 31.4   Using the DirectAnimation Sequencer Control (part 2 of 3).

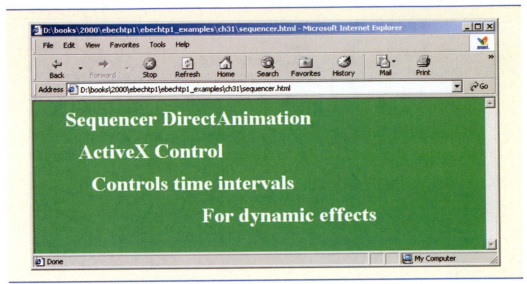

Fig. 31.4   Using the DirectAnimation Sequencer Control (part 3 of 3).

Lines 17 through 23

```
<SCRIPT FOR = "sequencer" EVENT = "ONINIT">
    sequencer.Item( "showThem" ).at( 2.0, "show( line1 )" );
    sequencer.Item( "showThem" ).at( 4.0, "show( line2 )" );
    sequencer.Item( "showThem" ).at( 6.0, "show( line3 )" );
    sequencer.Item( "showThem" ).at( 7.0, "show( line4 )" );
    sequencer.Item( "showThem" ).at( 8.0, "runPath()" );
</SCRIPT>
```

use a JavaScript event handler for the ***ONINIT*** *event* that fires when the sequencer loads. The **Item** object creates a grouping of events using a common name (in this case, **showThem**). The **at** method of the **Item** object takes two parameters: how many seconds to wait, and what action to perform when that time has expired. In this case, we call the **show** function for specific lines in the text at 2, 4, 6 and 7 seconds after the **ONINIT** event fires, and we call the **runPath** function after 8 seconds elapse.

We then use the **runPath** function to initiate a Path Control by scripting. Line 38

```
pathControl.Play();
```

calls the Path Control's **Play** method to start the targeted element (**line4**) along the path.

31.6 DirectAnimation Sprite Control

The images we have been using thus far have all been static. Some standards exist for standardized animation (the most common of which is an *animated GIF*), but none provides the dynamic control over animation that the Sprite Control provides. It allows you to control the rate of playback for images or even for individual *frames*. (An animation is composed of many individual frames which create the illusion of motion). Figure 31.6 uses the Sprite Control to add a simple animation to a Web page. The source image containing all the frames is displayed in Fig. 31.5.

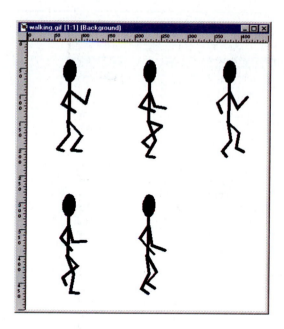

Fig. 31.5   Source image for Sprite Control (`walking.gif`).

```
1   <!DOCTYPE html PUBLIC "-//W3C//DTD HTML 4.0 Transitional//EN">
2   <HTML>
3
4   <!-- Fig 31.6: sprite.html -->
5   <!-- Sprite Control        -->
6
7   <HEAD>
8      <TITLE>Sprite Control</TITLE>
9   </HEAD>
10
11  <BODY>
12
13  <OBJECT ID = "walking" STYLE = "width: 150; height: 250"
14     CLASSID  = "CLSID:FD179533-D86E-11d0-89D6-00A0C90833E6">
15     <PARAM NAME = "Repeat" value = -1>
16     <PARAM NAME = "NumFrames" VALUE = 5>
17     <PARAM NAME = "NumFramesAcross" VALUE = 3>
18     <PARAM NAME = "NumFramesDown" VALUE = 2>
19     <PARAM NAME = "SourceURL" VALUE = "walking.gif">
20     <PARAM NAME = "AutoStart" VALUE = -1>
21  </OBJECT>
22
23  </BODY>
24  </HTML>
```

Fig. 31.6   Simple animation with the Sprite Control (part 1 of 2).

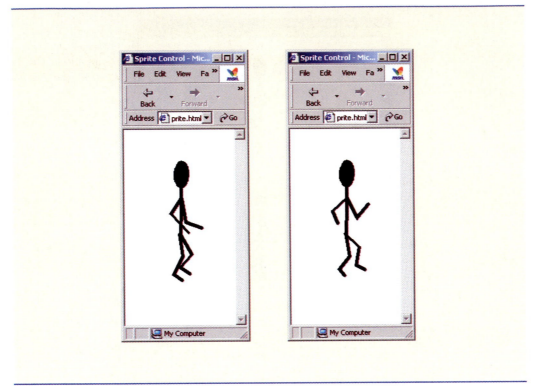

Fig. 31.6   Simple animation with the Sprite Control (part 2 of 2).

The **OBJECT** tag (lines 13 through 21) inserts the Sprite Control. The **height** and **width** CSS properties are needed to display the image correctly—they should be equal to the size of one frame in your file.

Setting the **REPEAT** attribute to a nonzero **VALUE** (**-1**) loops the animation indefinitely. The next attribute, **NumFrames**, specifies how many frames are present in the animation source image (Fig 31.5). The next two attributes—**NumFramesAcross** and **NumFramesDown**—specify how many rows and columns of frames there are in the animation file. The **SourceURL** property gives a path to the file containing all the frames of the animation, and setting the **AutoStart** property to a nonzero **VALUE** starts the animation automatically when the page loads.

What distinguishes Sprite Control from other animation formats is that it can do much more than simply loop through frames repeatedly—it can, through Dynamic HTML, respond to user actions, as we demonstrate in Fig. 31.7.

This example introduces several new aspects of the Sprite Control. The **PlayRate** method controls the rate at which frames are displayed—**1** is the default value. Method **MouseEventsEnabled**, as with the Structured Graphics Control, allows the object to capture certain mouse events.

In lines 10 through 16 and 18 through 24, we provide event handlers for the events **ONMOUSEOVER** and **ONMOUSEOUT**. When the user moves the mouse over the Sprite Control, the event handler calls the **Stop** method, which stops the animation in place, and sets the **PlayRate** method to **-3** . (The **PlayRate** method is writable only at runtime or when the animation is stopped.) This plays the animation in reverse at three times the normal speed. The script then calls the **Play** function to restart the animation. The **ONMOUSEOUT** event handler sets the **PlayRate** back to the default of **1** when the user moves the mouse cursor off the animation.

```
1   <!DOCTYPE html PUBLIC "-//W3C//DTD HTML 4.0 Transitional//EN">
2   <HTML>
3
4   <!-- Fig 31.7: sprite2.html      -->
5   <!-- Events with Sprite Control -->
6
7   <HEAD>
8   <TITLE>Sprite Control</TITLE>
9
10  <SCRIPT LANGUAGE = "JavaScript" FOR = "bounce"
11     EVENT = "ONMOUSEOVER">
12
13     bounce.Stop();
14     bounce.PlayRate = -3;
15     bounce.Play();
16  </SCRIPT>
17
18  <SCRIPT LANGUAGE = "JavaScript" FOR = "bounce"
19     EVENT = "ONMOUSEOUT">
20
21     bounce.Stop();
22     bounce.PlayRate = 1;
23     bounce.Play();
24  </SCRIPT>
25  </HEAD>
26
27  <BODY>
28
29  <H1>Sprite Control</H1>
30
31  <OBJECT ID = "bounce" STYLE = "width:75; height:75"
32     CLASSID  = "CLSID:FD179533-D86E-11d0-89D6-00A0C90833E6">
33     <PARAM NAME = "Repeat" value = -1>
34     <PARAM NAME = "PlayRate" VALUE = 1>
35     <PARAM NAME = "NumFrames" VALUE = 22>
36     <PARAM NAME = "NumFramesAcross" VALUE = 4>
37     <PARAM NAME = "NumFramesDown" VALUE = 6>
38     <PARAM NAME = "SourceURL" VALUE = "bounce.jpg">
39     <PARAM NAME = "MouseEventsEnabled" VALUE = "True">
40     <PARAM NAME = "AutoStart" VALUE = -1>
41  </OBJECT>
42
43  </BODY>
44  </HTML>
```

Fig. 31.7   Responding to mouse events with the Sprite Control (part 1 of 2).

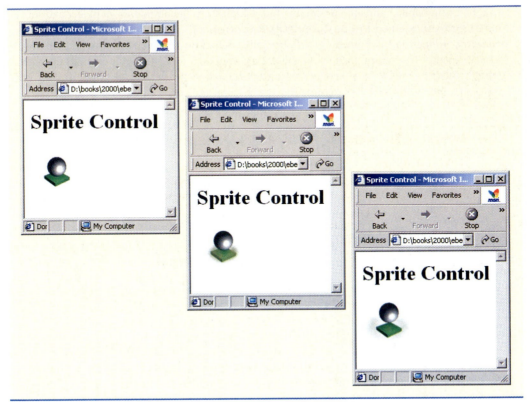

Fig. 31.7   Responding to mouse events with the Sprite Control (part 2 of 2).

31.7 Animated GIFs

Although the Sprite Control is useful for adding animation to Web pages, it is a new, proprietary format specific to Internet Explorer. The most popular method of creating animated graphics is a format known as *Animated GIF*. As with the Sprite Control, Animated GIFs are composed of a number of frames, which in this case are all in the GIF image format. However, unlike the images used with Sprite Control, GIF images must be assembled into animated GIF images by special graphics applications. One such program is Animation Shop, which is bundled with the Paint Shop Pro package on the CD included with this book. Figure 31.8 is a screen capture of the Animation Shop application. The screen capture the file **animatedbug_large.gif** loaded into Animation Shop. This image was used to demonstrate the Path Control in Figure 31.3.

As you can see here, the file is comprised of two separate frames. The Animated GIF format includes many features, such as specifying the amount of time each separate frame is displayed. Animation Shop itself has many useful features that you are able to apply, such as image transparency and transitions between frames (these are very similar to the transitions we covered in Chapter 22).

Performance Tip 31.2

Animated GIFs with a large number of frames can become extremely large. Make sure to use small images when possible and to minimize the amount of frames used.

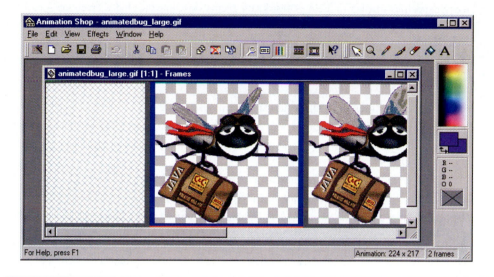

Fig. 31.8   Viewing an Animated Gif in Animation Shop

SUMMARY

- The DirectAnimation Path Control allows you to control the positions of elements on your page.

- Setting **AutoStart** to a nonzero value starts the element along a path as soon as the page loads. Setting a zero value would prevent it from starting automatically, in which case a script would have to call the **Play** method to start the path. The **Repeat** method determines how many times the path will be traversed—setting the value to **-1** specifies that the path should loop continuously. The **Duration** method specifies the amount of time that it will take to traverse the path, in seconds. The **Bounce** method, when set to **1**, reverses the element's direction on the path when it reaches the end. Setting the value to **0** would instead return the element to the beginning of the path when the path has been traversed.

- The **PolyLine** method creates a path with multiple line segments.

- The **Target** method specifies the **ID** of the element that is targeted by the Path Control.

- Setting the CSS attribute **position** to **absolute** allows the Path Control to move an element around the screen. Otherwise, the element would be static, locked in the position determined by the browser when the page loads.

- The Path Control also allows you to set paths for multiple objects present on your page. To do this, you must add a separate **OBJECT** tag for each object you wish to control.

- The **z-index** of elements that overlap is determined by their order of declaration in the HTML source (elements declared later in the HTML file are displayed above elements declared earlier).

- A useful feature of the Path Control is the ability to execute certain actions at any point along an object's path. This is done with the **AddTimeMarker** method, which creates a time marker that can be handled with simple JavaScript event handling.

- The number appended to the **AddTimeMarker** function is a sequential identifier, much like **Line0001** is used in Structured Graphics Control. The first parameter in the **VALUE** attribute determines at which point our time marker is placed along the path, specified in seconds—when this point is reached, the **ONMARKER** event is fired. The second parameter gives an identifying name to the event, which is later passed on to the event handler for the **ONMARKER** event. The last parameter specifies whether to fire the **ONMARKER** event every time the object's path loops past the time marker (as we do here by setting the parameter to **0**) or to fire the event just the first time that the time marker is passed (by setting the parameter to **1**).

- The parameter received by the **ONMARKER** event identifies which marker fired the event.
- The Sequencer Control provides a simpler interface for calling functions or performing actions at time intervals that you can set easily.
- The **ONINIT** event fires when the Sequencer Control has loaded.
- The **Item** object of the Sequencer Control creates a grouping of events using a common name.
- The **at** method of the **Item** object takes two parameters: how many seconds to wait, and what action to perform when that time has expired.
- The **Play** method of the Path Control starts the targeted element along the path.
- The Sprite Control allows you to display animated images composed of individual frames.
- The **OBJECT** tag inserts the Sprite Control. The **height** and **width** CSS properties are needed to display the image correctly—they should be equal to the size of one frame in your file. Setting attribute **REPEAT** to a nonzero **VALUE** loops the animation indefinitely. **NumFrames** specifies how many frames are present in the animation source image. Attributes **NumFramesAcross** and **NumFramesDown** specify how many rows and columns of frames there are in the animation file. Property **SourceURL** gives a path to the file containing the frames of the animation. Setting property **AutoStart** to a nonzero **VALUE** starts the animation automatically when the page loads.
- Sprite Control method **PlayRate** controls the rate at which frames are displayed (**1** is the default value). The **MouseEventsEnabled** method, as with the Structured Graphics Control, allows the object to capture certain mouse events. The **Stop** method stops the animation in place. Method **PlayRate** is writable only at runtime or when the animation is stopped.

TERMINOLOGY

AddTimeMarker method
animated GIF
at method of **Item** object
AutoStart
Bounce method
CLASSID
Duration method
Item object of Sequencer Control
MouseEventsEnabled
NumFrames
NumFramesAcross
NumFramesDown
ONINIT event
ONMARKER event
Oval method
Path Control
Play method

PlayRate method of the Sprite Control
PolyLine method
position: absolute
Relative method
REPEAT attribute
Repeat method
Sequencer Control
Shape method
SourceURL
splash screen effect
Sprite Control
Stop method
Target method
time marker
visibility: hidden
window.setInterval
z-index

SELF-REVIEW EXERCISES

31.1   Answer the following questions true or false; if false, explain why:
   a) The **z-index** of elements in which the **z-index** property is not declared specifically is determined by the order of their appearance in the HTML document.

b) The parameters for the Path Control **PolyLine** method are the same as those for the Structured Graphics Control **PolyLine**.
c) A time marker will fire the **ONMARKER** event only once.
d) You can control multiple paths with a single Path Control **OBJECT**.
e) The **ONINIT** event fires when the Sequencer Control has finished loading.
f) The **PlayRate** method of the Sprite Control is always writable.
g) All ActiveX controls use the same **CLASSID** attribute.

31.2 Fill in the blanks in the following questions:
a) The _____ Control allows you to perform scripted actions on your Web page at timed intervals.
b) The _____ Control allows you to place animated images on your web page.
c) The _____ Control can move elements around your page dynamically.
d) The _____ method is used to create a time marker for the Path Control.
e) An element's CSS **position** property must be set to _____ for the Path Control to successfully target that object.
f) The _____ method determines over how many iterations the Path Control will continue on a certain path.

ANSWERS TO SELF-REVIEW EXERCISES

31.1 a) True. b) True. c) False; this depends on the last parameter of the **AddTimeMarker** method and may be set to fire every time the time marker is reached. d) False; multiple controls are needed if you want to control multiple paths. e) True. f) False; it is writable only at run-time or when the animation is stopped. g) False; each uses a unique **CLASSID**.

31.2 a) Sequencer. b) Sprite. c) Path. d) **AddTimeMarker**. e) **absolute**. f) **Repeat**.

EXERCISES

31.3 Use the Path Control to have the logo on your Web page follow an **Oval** path around the page.

31.4 Use the Path Control to simulate the motion of text inside a **MARQUEE** tag.

31.5 Modify Exercise 31.4 by adding time markers that change the color of the text every loop.

31.6 Use the Sequencer Control to create a slideshow of images.

31.7 Use Paint Shop Pro to create a sprite that simulates a rotating planet. Modify Fig. 31.3 so that the sprite, animated with the Sprite control, rotates around a larger planet in the center of the page.

31.8 Create your own animated GIF with Animation Shop Pro.

32

Multimedia: Audio, Video, Speech Synthesis and Recognition

Objectives

- To enhance Web pages with sound and video.
- To use **<BGSOUND>** to add background sounds.
- To use the **<IMG>** element's **DYNSRC** property to incorporate video into Web pages.
- To use **<EMBED>** to add sound or video to Web pages.
- To use the Windows Media Player ActiveX control to play a variety of media formats in Web pages.
- To use the Microsoft Agent ActiveX control to create animated characters that speak to users and respond to spoken commands from users.
- To embed a RealPlayer™ ActiveX control to allow streaming audio and video to appear in a Web page.

The wheel that squeaks the loudest … gets the grease.
John Billings (Henry Wheeler Shaw)

We'll use a signal I have tried and found far-reaching and easy to yell. Waa-hoo!
Zane Grey

TV gives everyone an image, but radio gives birth to a million images in a million brains.
Peggy Noonan

Noise proves nothing. Often a hen who has merely laid an egg cackles as if she had laid an asteroid.
Mark Twain, *Following the Equator*

32.1 Introduction

Just a few years back, the typical desktop computer's power, although considered substantial at the time, made it impossible to think of integrating high-quality audio and video into applications. Today's computers typically include CD-ROMs, sound cards, and other hardware and special software to make computer multimedia a reality. Economical desktop machines are so powerful that they can store and play DVD-quality sound and video. Given this, we expect to see a huge advance in the kinds of programmable multimedia capabilities available through programming languages.

The multimedia revolution occurred first on the desktop, with the widespread availability of CD-ROMs. This platform is rapidly evolving towards DVD technology, but our focus in this chapter is on the explosion of sound and video technology appearing on the World Wide Web. In general, we expect the desktop to lead with the technology, because the Web is so dependent on bandwidth, and, for the foreseeable future, Internet bandwidths for the masses are likely to lag considerably behind those available on the desktop. One thing that we have learned—having been in this industry for nearly four decades now—is to plan for the impossible. In the computer and communications fields, the impossible has repeatedly become reality, and this has happened so many times as to be almost routine.

In this chapter, we discuss adding sound, video and animated characters to your Web-based applications. Your first reaction may be a sense of caution, because you realize that these are complex technologies and most readers have had little if any education in these areas. This is one of the beauties of today's programming languages. They give the programmer easy access to complex technologies and hide most of the complexity.

Performance Tip 32.1

Multimedia is performance intensive. Internet bandwidth and processor speed are still precious resources. Multimedia-based Web applications must be carefully designed to use resources wisely, or they may perform poorly.

Multimedia files can be quite large. Some multimedia technologies require that the complete multimedia file be downloaded to the client before the audio or video begins playing. With streaming audio and streaming video technologies, the audios and videos can begin playing while the files are downloading, thus reducing delays. Streaming technologies are becoming increasingly popular on the Web.

Creating audio and video to incorporate into Web pages often requires complex and powerful software. Rather than discuss how to create media clips, this chapter focuses on using existing audio and video clips to enhance Web pages. The chapter also includes an extensive set of Internet and World Wide Web resources. Some of these resources are Web sites that show you interesting ways in which Web site designers use multimedia to enhance Web pages. Many of the resource sites contain useful information for Web developers who plan to add multimedia to the sites they implement.

32.2 Adding Background Sounds with the BGSOUND Element

Some Web sites provide background audio to give the site some "atmosphere." There are several ways in which to add sound to a Web page. The simplest is the *BGSOUND* element.

Portability Tip 32.1

The BGSOUND element is specific to Internet Explorer.

The **BGSOUND** element has four key properties—*SRC*, *LOOP*, *BALANCE* and *VOLUME*. If you would like to change the property values via a script, you can assign a scripting name to the **BGSOUND** element's *ID* property.

Software Engineering Observation 32.1

The BGSOUND element should be placed in the HEAD section of the HTML document.

The **SRC** property specifies the URL of the audio clip to play. Internet Explorer supports a wide variety of audio formats.

Software Engineering Observation 32.2

The audio clip specified with BGSOUND's SRC property can be any type supported by Internet Explorer.

The **LOOP** property specifies the number of times the audio clip should play. The value **-1** (the default) specifies that the audio clip should loop until the user browses a different Web page or until the user clicks the browser's **Stop** button. A positive integer can be specified for this property, to indicate the exact number of times the audio clip should loop. Negative values (except **-1**) and zero values for this property result in the audio clip's playing once.

The **BALANCE** property specifies the balance between the left and right speakers. The value for this property is between **-10000** (sound only from the left speaker) and **10000** (sound only from the right speaker). The default value **0** indicates that the sound should be balanced between the two speakers.

Software Engineering Observation 32.3

BGSOUND property BALANCE cannot be set via scripting.

The **VOLUME** property determines the volume of the audio clip. The value for this property is between **-10000** (minimum volume) and **0** (maximum volume). The default value **0** indicates that the sound should play at its maximum volume.

Software Engineering Observation 32.4

The volume specified with **BGSOUND** *property* **VOLUME** *is relative to the current volume setting on the client computer. If the client computer has sound turned off, the* **VOLUME** *property has no effect.*

Portability Tip 32.2

On most computers, the minimum audible volume for **BGSOUND** *property* **VOLUME** *is a value much greater than* **-10000**. *This value will be machine dependent.*

The HTML document of Fig 32.1 demonstrates the **BGSOUND** element and scripting the element's properties. The audio clip used in this example came from the Microsoft Developer Network's downloads site,

msdn.microsoft.com/downloads/default.asp

This site contains many free images and sounds.

```
1   <!DOCTYPE HTML PUBLIC "-//W3C//DTD HTML 4.0 Transitional//EN">
2   <HTML>
3   <!-- Fig. 32.1: BackroundAudio.html -->
4
5   <HEAD><TITLE>The BGSOUND Element</TITLE>
6   <BGSOUND ID = "audio" SRC = "jazzgos.mid" LOOP = "1"></BGSOUND>
7
8   <SCRIPT LANGUAGE = "JavaScript">
9       function changeProperties()
10      {
11          var loop = parseInt( audioForm.loopit.value );
12          audio.loop = ( isNaN( loop ) ? 1 : loop );
13
14          var vol = parseInt( audioForm.vol.value );
15          audio.volume = ( isNaN( vol ) ? 0 : vol );
16      }
17  </SCRIPT>
18  </HEAD>
19
20  <BODY>
21      <H1>Background Music via the BGSOUND Element</H1>
22      <H2>Jazz Gospel</H2>
23
24      This sound is from the free sound downloads at the
25      <A HREF = "http://msdn.microsoft.com/downloads/default.asp">
26          Microsoft Developer Network</a> downloads site.
27      <HR>
28      Use the fields below to change the number of iterations
29      and the volume for the audio clip<BR>
30      Press <B>Stop</B> to stop playing the sound.<BR>
31      Press <B>Refresh</B> to begin playing the sound again.
```

Fig. 32.1   Demonstrating background audio with **BGSOUND** (part 1 of 2).

```
32
33      <FORM NAME = "audioForm"><P>
34         Loop [-1 = loop forever]
35         <INPUT NAME = "loopit" TYPE = "text" VALUE = "1"><BR>
36         Volume [-10000 (low) to 0 (high)]
37         <INPUT NAME = "vol" TYPE = "text" VALUE = "0"><BR>
38         <INPUT TYPE = "button" VALUE = "Set Properties"
39                ONCLICK = "changeProperties()">
40      </P></FORM>
41   </BODY>
42
43   </HTML>
```

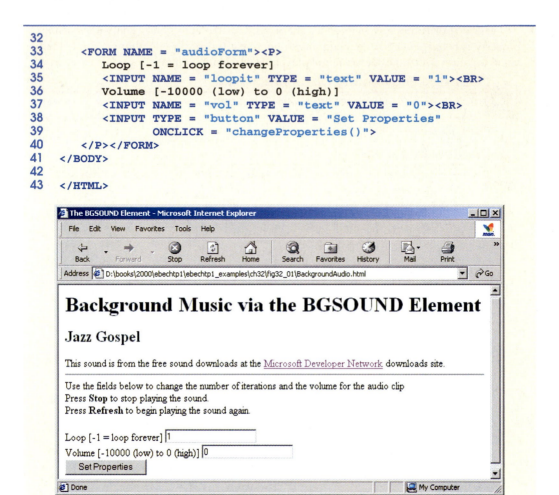

Fig. 32.1   Demonstrating background audio with **BGSOUND** (part 2 of 2).

Line 6

```
<BGSOUND ID = "audio" SRC = "jazzgos.mid" LOOP = "1">
</BGSOUND>
```

specifies that the audio clip **jazzgos.mid** should loop exactly once. Because the **BAL-ANCE** and **VOLUME** attributes are not specified, each will have the default **0** value.

Software Engineering Observation 32.5

The ending **</BGSOUND>** *tag is optional.*

Function **changeProperties** (line 9) is called when the user clicks the **Set Prop-erties** button in the HTML form. Lines 11 and 12

```
var loop = parseInt( audioForm.loopit.value );
audio.loop = ( isNaN( loop ) ? 1 : loop );
```

read the new value for property **LOOP** from the form's **loopit** text field, convert the value to an integer and set the new property value by assigning a value to **audio.loop** (where **audio** is the **ID** of the **BGSOUND** element and **loop** is the scripting name of the property).

Lines 14 and 15

```
var vol = parseInt( audioForm.vol.value );
audio.volume = ( isNaN( vol ) ? 0 : vol );
```

read the new value for the **VOLUME** property from the form's **vol** text field, convert the value to an integer and set the new property value by assigning a value to **audio.volume** (where **volume** is the scripting name of the property).

32.3 Adding Video with the **IMG** Element's **DYNSRC** Property

You can tremendously enhance the multimedia presentations on your Web site by incorporating a variety of video formats in your Web pages. The **IMG** element (introduced in Chapter 3) enables both images and videos to be included in a Web page. The **SRC** property, shown previously, indicates that the source is an image. The **DYNSRC** (i.e., dynamic source) property indicates that the source is a video clip. The HTML document of Fig. 32.2 demonstrates the **IMG** element and its **DYNSRC** property.

Portability Tip 32.3

*The **DYNSRC** property of the **IMG** element is specific to Internet Explorer.*

```
1   <!DOCTYPE HTML PUBLIC "-//W3C//DTD HTML 4.0 Transitional//EN">
2   <HTML>
3   <!-- Fig. 32.2: DynamicIMG.html -->
4
5   <HEAD>
6   <TITLE>An Embedded Image Using the DYNSRC Property</TITLE>
7   <BGSOUND SRC = "newage.mid" LOOP = "-1">
8   </HEAD>
9
10  <BODY>
11     <H1>An Embedded Video Using the IMG Element's
12        DYNSRC Property</H1>
13     <H2>Spinning Globe and New Age Music</H2>
14     This video is from the
15     <A HREF = "http://www.nasa.gov/gallery/">
16        NASA Multimedia Gallery</A><BR>
17     This sound is from the free sound downloads at the
18     <A HREF = "http://msdn.microsoft.com/downloads/default.asp">
19        Microsoft Developer Network</A> downloads site.
20     <HR>
21     <TABLE><TR>
22     <TD><IMG DYNSRC = "pathfinder.mpeg" START = "mouseover"
23             WIDTH = "180" HEIGHT = "135" LOOP = "-1"
24             ALT = "A spinning image of the Earth"></TD>
25     <TD>This page will play the audio clip and video in a
26     loop.<BR>The video will not begin playing until you move
```

Fig. 32.2   Playing a video with the **IMG** element's **DYNSRC** property (part 1 of 2).

```
27      the mouse over the video.<BR>Press <B>Stop</B> to stop
28      playing the sound and the video.</TD></TR></TABLE>
29  </BODY>
30  </HTML>
```

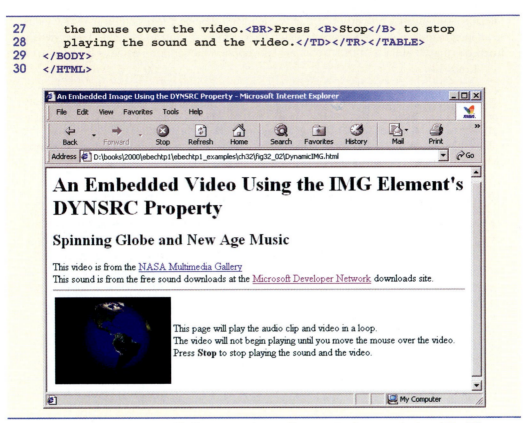

Fig. 32.2   Playing a video with the **IMG** element's **DYNSRC** property (part 2 of 2).

The **IMG** element in lines 22 through 24

```
<IMG DYNSRC = "pathfinder.mpeg" START = "mouseover"
     WIDTH = "180" HEIGHT = "135" LOOP = "-1"
     ALT = "A spinning image of the Earth"></TD>
```

uses the **DYNSRC** property to indicate that the video **pathfinder.mpeg** will be loaded and displayed. Property ***START*** indicates when the video should start playing. There are two possibilities—***fileopen*** indicates that the video should play as soon as it loads into the browser, and ***mouseover*** indicates that the video should play when the user first positions the mouse over the video.

The video used in this example is one of many videos that can be downloaded from the NASA Multimedia Gallery at

```
www.nasa.gov/gallery/
```

32.4 Adding Audio or Video with the **EMBED** Element

Previously, we used elements **BGSOUND** and **IMG** to embed audio and video in a Web page. In both cases, the user of the page is provided with little control over the media clip. In this section, we introduce the ***EMBED*** element, which embeds a media clip (audio or video) into a Web page. The **EMBED** element allows a graphical user interface to be displayed that gives the user direct control over the media clip. When the browser encounters a media clip in an **EMBED** element, the browser plays the clip with the player that is registered to handle that media type on the client computer. For example, if the media clip is a **wav** file (i.e., a Windows Wave file), Internet Explorer will typically use the Windows Media Player ActiveX control to play the clip. The Windows Media Player has a GUI that enables the user to play, pause and stop the media clip. It also allows the user to control the volume of audio and to move forward and backward quickly through the clip. [*Note:* Section 32.5 discusses embedding the Windows Media Player ActiveX control in a Web page.]

The HTML document of Fig. 32.3 modifies the **wave** filter example from Chapter 22 by using an **EMBED** element to add audio to the Web page.

```
1   <!DOCTYPE HTML PUBLIC "-//W3C//DTD HTML 4.0 Transitional//EN">
2   <HTML>
3   <!-- Fig. 32.3: EmbeddedAudio.html -->
4
5   <HEAD>
6   <TITLE>Background Audio via the EMBED Element</TITLE>
7   <STYLE TYPE = "text/css">
8      SPAN      { width: 600 }
9      .big      { color: blue;
10               font-family: sans-serif;
11               font-size: 50pt;
12               font-weight: bold }
13  </STYLE>
14
15  <SCRIPT LANGUAGE = "JavaScript">
16     var TimerID;
17     var updown  =  true;
18     var str = 1;
19
20     function start()
21     {
22        TimerID = window.setInterval( "wave()", 100 );
23     }
24
25     function wave()
26     {
27        if ( str > 20 || str < 1 )
28           updown = !updown;
29
30        if ( updown )
31           str++;
32        else
33           str--;
34
35        wft.filters( "wave" ).phase = str * 30;
36        wft.filters( "wave" ).strength = str;
37     }
38  </SCRIPT>
39  </HEAD>
```

Fig. 32.3   Embedding audio with the **EMBED** element (part 1 of 2).

```
40
41   <BODY ONLOAD = "start()">
42   <H1>Background Audio via the EMBED Element</H1>
43   <P>Click the text to stop the script.</P>
44
45   <SPAN ONCLICK = "window.clearInterval( TimerID )" ID = "wft"
46      STYLE =
47         "filter:wave(add=0, freq=3, light=0, phase=0, strength=5)">
48   <P CLASS = "big" ALIGN = "center">WAVE FILTER EFFECT</P></SPAN>
49
50   <P>These controls can be used to control the audio.</P>
51   <EMBED SRC = "humming.wav" LOOP = "true"></EMBED>
52   </BODY>
53   </HTML>
```

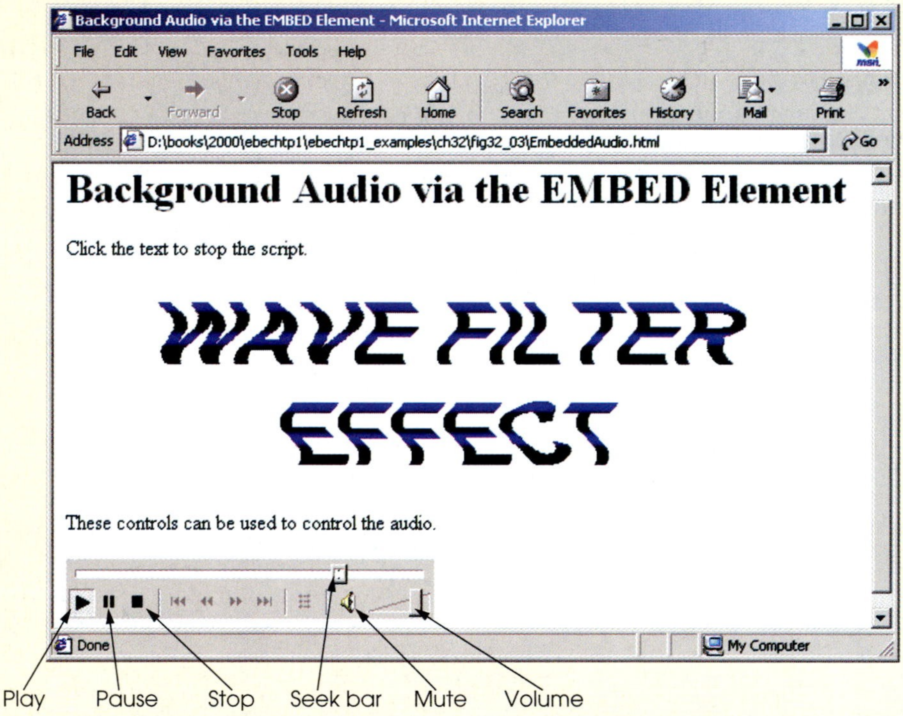

Fig. 32.3   Embedding audio with the **EMBED** element (part 2 of 2).

Line 51

```
<EMBED SRC = "humming.wav" LOOP = "true"></EMBED>
```

uses the **EMBED** element to specify that the audio file **humming.wav** should be embedded in the Web page. The *LOOP* property indicates that the media clip should loop forever. By default, the GUI for the media player is displayed. To prevent the GUI from appearing in the Web page, add the *HIDDEN* property to the **<EMBED>** element. If you want to script the element, specify a scripting name by adding the **ID** property to the **<EMBED>** element.

The **EMBED** element can specify video clips as well as audio clips. Figure 32.4 demonstrates an MPEG video from NASA's *Seaviewing Wide Field-of-view Sensor (SeaWiFS) Project*. The **EMBED** element that loads and plays the video is on line 14. This video and several others, which together make up a two-minute animation, can be found at

```
seawifs.gsfc.nasa.gov/OCEAN_PLANET/HTML/
oceanography_flyby.html
```

This video is part of the NASA Multimedia Gallery.

Software Engineering Observation 32.6

The **</EMBED>** *tag is required to terminate an* **<EMBED>** *tag.*

32.5 Using the Windows Media Player ActiveX Control

One benefit of Microsoft ActiveX controls is that they can be embedded in Web pages that are to be displayed in Internet Explorer and enhance the functionality of those Web pages. In this section, we embed the *Windows Media Player ActiveX control* in Web pages. Doing so gives us access to the wide range of media formats supported by the Windows Media Player. The Windows Media Player and other ActiveX controls are embedded into Web pages with the ***OBJECT*** element.

```
1   <!DOCTYPE HTML PUBLIC "-//W3C//DTD HTML 4.0 Transitional//EN">
2   <HTML>
3   <!-- Fig. 32.4: EmbeddedVideo.html -->
4
5   <HEAD>
6   <TITLE>Video via the EMBED Element</TITLE>
7   </HEAD>
8
9   <BODY>
10      <H1>Displaying a Video via the EMBED Element</H1>
11      <H2>Earth Fly-By</H2>
12
13      <TABLE><TR>
14      <TD><EMBED SRC = "approach_1_337.mpeg" LOOP = "false"></EMBED>
15      </TD>
16
17      <TD><P>This video is part of the NASA Multimedia Archives.
18      You can find this video and six additional videos that
19      continue the animation at the <A HREF = "http://
seawifs.gsfc.nasa.gov/OCEAN_PLANET/HTML/oceanography_flyby.html">
20      Sea-viewing Wide Field-of-view Sensor(SeaWiFS) Project
21      </A> site.</P></TD></TABLE>
22      <HR>
23      This page will play the video once.<BR>
24      Use the controls on the embedded video player to play the
25      video again.
26  </BODY>
27  </HTML>
```

Fig. 32.4   Embedding video with the **EMBED** element (part 1 of 2).

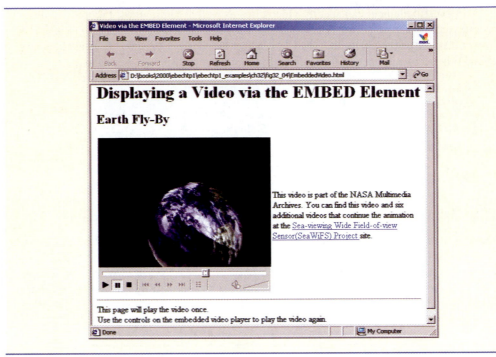

Fig. 32.4   Embedding video with the **EMBED** element (part 2 of 2).

The HTML document of Fig. 32.5 demonstrates using the **OBJECT** element to embed two Windows Media Player ActiveX controls in the Web page. One of the controls plays a video. The the other control plays an audio clip.

```
1   <!DOCTYPE HTML PUBLIC "-//W3C//DTD HTML 4.0 Transitional//EN">
2   <HTML>
3   <!-- Fig. 32.5: MediaPlayer.html -->
4
5   <HEAD><TITLE>Embedded Media Player Objects</TITLE>
6   <SCRIPT LANGUAGE = "JavaScript">
7      var videoPlaying = true;
8
9      function toggleVideo( b )
10     {
11        videoPlaying = !videoPlaying;
12        b.value = videoPlaying ? "Pause Video" : "Play Video";
13        videoPlaying ? VideoPlayer.Play() : VideoPlayer.Pause();
14     }
15  </SCRIPT>
16  </HEAD>
17
18  <BODY>
19  <H1>Audio and video through embedded Media Player objects</H1>
```

Fig. 32.5   Using the **OBJECT** element to Embed the Windows Media Player ActiveX control in a Web page (part 1 of 2).

```
20   <HR>
21   <TABLE>
22      <TR><TD VALIGN = "top" ALIGN = "center">
23      <OBJECT ID = "VideoPlayer" WIDTH = 200 HEIGHT = 225
24         CLASSID = "CLSID:22d6f312-b0f6-11d0-94ab-0080c74c7e95">
25         <PARAM NAME = "FileName" VALUE = "pathfinder.mpeg">
26         <PARAM NAME = "AutoStart" VALUE = "true">
27         <PARAM NAME = "ShowControls" VALUE = "false">
28         <PARAM NAME = "Loop" VALUE = "true">
29      </OBJECT></TD>
30      <TD VALIGN = "bottom" ALIGN = "center">
31      <P>Use the controls below to control the audio clip.</P>
32      <OBJECT ID = "AudioPlayer"
33         CLASSID = "CLSID:22d6f312-b0f6-11d0-94ab-0080c74c7e95">
34         <PARAM NAME = "FileName" VALUE = "newage.mid">
35         <PARAM NAME = "AutoStart" VALUE = "true">
36         <PARAM NAME = "Loop" VALUE = "true">
37      </OBJECT></TD></TR>
38
39      <TR><TD VALIGN = "top" ALIGN = "center">
40         <INPUT NAME = "video" TYPE = "button" VALUE = "Pause Video"
41                ONCLICK = "toggleVideo( this )"></TD>
42   </TABLE>
43   </BODY>
44   </HTML>
```

Fig. 32.5   Using the **OBJECT** element to Embed the Windows Media Player ActiveX
control in a Web page (part 2 of 2).

When the **BODY** of this document loads, two instances of the Windows Media Player ActiveX control are created. The **OBJECT** element at lines 23 through 29

```
<OBJECT ID = "VideoPlayer" WIDTH = 200 HEIGHT = 225
    CLASSID = "CLSID:22d6f312-b0f6-11d0-94ab-0080c74c7e95">
    <PARAM NAME = "FileName" VALUE = "pathfinder.mpeg">
    <PARAM NAME = "AutoStart" VALUE = "true">
    <PARAM NAME = "ShowControls" VALUE = "false">
    <PARAM NAME = "Loop" VALUE = "true">
</OBJECT>
```

creates a Media Player object for the file **pathfinder.mpeg** (specified on line 25). Line 23 indicates the start of the embedded **OBJECT** definition. The **ID** property specifies the scripting name of the element (i.e., **VideoPlayer**). The **WIDTH** and **HEIGHT** properties specify the width and height in pixels that the control will occupy in the Web page. On line 24, property **CLASSID** specifies the unique ActiveX control ID for the Windows Media Player.

Software Engineering Observation 32.7

Most HTML authoring tools that support embedding ActiveX controls enable you to insert the ActiveX controls in a Web page by selecting from a list of available control names.

Lines 25 through 28 specify *parameters* that should be passed to the control when it is created in the Web page. Each parameter is specified with a **PARAM** element that contains a **NAME** property and a **VALUE** property. The **FileName** parameter specifies the file containing the media clip. The **AutoStart** parameter is a boolean value indicating whether the media clip should play automatically when it is loaded (**true** indicates it should; **false** indicates it should not). The **ShowControls** parameter is a boolean value indicating whether the Media Player controls should be displayed (**true** indicates they should; **false** indicates they should not). The **Loop** parameter is a boolean value indicating whether the Media Player should play the media clip in an infinite loop (**true** indicates it should; **false** indicates it should not).

The **OBJECT** element at lines 32 through 37

```
<OBJECT ID = "AudioPlayer"
    CLASSID = "CLSID:22d6f312-b0f6-11d0-94ab-0080c74c7e95">
    <PARAM NAME = "FileName" VALUE = "newage.mid">
    <PARAM NAME = "AutoStart" VALUE = "true">
    <PARAM NAME = "Loop" VALUE = "true">
</OBJECT>
```

embeds another Media Player object in the Web page. This Media Player plays the MIDI file **newage.mid** (specified with the **FileName** parameter), automatically starts playing the clip when it is loaded (specified with the **AutoStart** parameter) and infinitely loops the audio clip (specified with the **Loop** parameter).

The script at lines 6 through 15 shows that the Media Player can be controlled from a script. Function **toggleVideo** (line 9) is called when the user clicks the button below the video clip. The button is defined in the HTML form in lines 40 and 41

```
<INPUT NAME = "video" TYPE = "button" VALUE = "Pause Video"
    ONCLICK = "toggleVideo( this )"></TD>
```

The **ONLCLICK** event specifies that function **toggleVideo** is the event handler and **this** button should be passed as an argument to the function. This allows us to change the text on the button at line 12. Line 13

```
videoPlaying ? VideoPlayer.Play() : VideoPlayer.Pause();
```

uses the boolean variable **videoPlaying** to determine whether to call **VideoPlayer**'s **Play** or **Pause** methods to play or pause the video clip, respectively.

32.6 Microsoft Agent Control

Microsoft Agent is an exciting technology for *interactive animated characters* in a Windows application or World Wide Web page. The *Microsoft Agent control* provides access to four predefined characters—*Peedy the Parrot*, *Genie*, *Merlin* and *Robby the Robot*. These characters allow users of your application to interact with the application using more natural human communication techniques. The control accepts both mouse and keyboard interactions, speaks (if a compatible text-to-speech engine is installed) and also supports speech recognition (if a compatible speech recognition engine is installed). With these capabilities, your Web pages can speak to users and can actually respond to their voice commands. You can also create your own characters with the help of the *Microsoft Agent Character Editor* and the *Microsoft Linguistic Sound Editing Tool* (both downloadable from the Microsoft Agent Web site).

In this section, we discuss some basic capabilities of the Microsoft Agent control. The software for Microsoft Agent is on the CD accompanying this book and can also be downloaded from the Microsoft Web site:

```
msdn.microsoft.com/workshop/imedia/agent
```

Here you will find tools for using Microsoft Agent in your own Web pages, including the Microsoft Agent ActiveX control, the *Lernout and Hauspie TruVoice text-to-speech (TTS) engine* and the *Microsoft Speech Recognition Engine*. In addition to the area of this Web site dedicated to Microsoft Agent, there are also discussions of several other multimedia technologies that are available for use in Windows applications and in Web pages. Simply visit

```
msdn.microsoft.com/workshop/imedia
```

for more information.

Figure 32.6 demonstrates the Microsoft Agent ActiveX control and the Lernout and Hauspie TruVoice text-to-speech engine (also an ActiveX control). The HTML document in Fig. 32.6 embeds each of these ActiveX controls into a Web page that acts as a tutorial for the various types of programming tips presented in this text. Peedy the Parrot will display and speak text that describes each of the programming tips. When the user clicks the icon for a programming tip, Peedy will fly to that tip and recite the appropriate text. *Note:* The examples in this section show a blue rounded rectangle in the position where Peedy the Parrot will appear when you run the examples with the included Microsoft Agent software.

Performance Tip 32.2

The Microsoft Agent control and the Lernout and Hauspie TruVoice TTS engine will be downloaded automatically from the Microsoft Agent Web site if they are not already installed on your computer. You may want to download these controls in advance, to allow the Web page to use Microsoft Agent and the TTS engine immediately when the Web page is loaded.

Testing and Debugging Tip 32.1

The Microsoft Agent characters and animations are downloaded from the Microsoft Agent Web site. If you are not connected to the Internet, these will not be able to download. You can download the character information onto your local computer and modify the Microsoft Agent examples to load character data from the local computer for demonstration purposes.

```
1   <!DOCTYPE HTML PUBLIC "-//W3C//DTD HTML 4.0 Transitional//EN">
2   <HTML>
3   <!-- Fig. 32.6: tutorial.html -->
4
5   <HEAD>
6   <TITLE>Microsoft Agent and the text to speech engine</TITLE>
7
8   <!-- Microsoft Agent ActiveX Control -->
9   <OBJECT ID = "agent" WIDTH = "0" HEIGHT = "0"
10      CLASSID = "CLSID:D45FD31B-5C6E-11D1-9EC1-00C04FD7081F"
11      CODEBASE = "#VERSION = 2,0,0,0">
12  </OBJECT>
13
14  <!-- Lernout & Hauspie TruVoice text to speech engine -->
15  <OBJECT WIDTH = "0" HEIGHT = "0"
16      CLASSID = "CLSID:B8F2846E-CE36-11D0-AC83-00C04FD97575"
17      CODEBASE = "#VERSION = 6,0,0,0">
18  </OBJECT>
19
20  <SCRIPT LANGUAGE = "JavaScript">
21     var parrot;
22     var currentImage = null;
23     var explanations = [
24        // Good Programming Practice Text
25        "Good Programming Practices highlight techniques for " +
26        "writing programs that are clearer, more " +
27        "understandable, more debuggable, and more " +
28        "maintainable.",
29
30        // Software Engineering Observation Text
31        "Software Engineering Observations highlight " +
32        "architectural and design issues that affect the " +
33        "construction of complex software systems.",
34
35        // Performance Tip Text
36        "Performance Tips highlight opportunities for " +
37        "improving program performance.",
38
39        // Portability Tip Text
40        "Portability Tips help students write portable code " +
41        "that can execute in different Web browsers.",
42
43        // Look-and-Feel Observation Text
44        "Look-and-Feel Observations highlight graphical user " +
45        "interface conventions. These observations help " +
```

Fig. 32.6   Demonstrating Microsoft Agent and the Lernout and Hauspie TruVoice text-to-speech (TTS) engine (part 1 of 5).

```
46          "students design their own graphical user interfaces " +
47          "in conformance with industry standards.",
48
49          // Testing and Debugging Tip Text
50          "Testing and Debugging Tips tell people how to test " +
51          "and debug their programs. Many of the tips also " +
52          "describe aspects of creating Web pages and scripts " +
53          "that reduce the likelihood of 'bugs' and thus " +
54          "simplify the testing and debugging process.",
55
56          // Common Programming Error Text
57          "Common Programming Errors focus the students' " +
58          "attention on errors commonly made by beginning " +
59          "programmers. This helps students avoid making the " +
60          "same errors. It also helps reduce the long lines " +
61          "outside instructors' offices during office hours!" ];
62
63      function loadAgent()
64      {
65          agent.Connected = true;
66          agent.Characters.Load( "peedy",
67              "http://agent.microsoft.com/agent2/" +
68              "chars/peedy/peedy.acf" );
69          parrot = agent.Characters.Character( "peedy" );
70          parrot.LanguageID = 0x0409;
71
72          // get states from server
73          parrot.Get( "state", "Showing" );
74          parrot.Get( "state", "Speaking" );
75          parrot.Get( "state", "Hiding" );
76
77          // get Greet animation and do Peedy introduction
78          parrot.Get( "animation", "Greet" );
79          parrot.MoveTo( screenLeft, screenTop - 100 );
80          parrot.Show();
81          parrot.Play( "Greet" );
82          parrot.Speak( "Hello. My name is Peedy the Parrot. " +
83              "Click a programming tip icon, and I will tell " +
84              "you about it." );
85          parrot.Play( "GreetReturn" );
86
87          // get other animations
88          parrot.Get( "animation", "Idling" );
89          parrot.Get( "animation", "MoveDown" );
90          parrot.Get( "animation", "MoveUp" );
91          parrot.Get( "animation", "MoveLeft" );
92          parrot.Get( "animation", "MoveRight" );
93          parrot.Get( "animation", "GetAttention" );
94      }
95
96      function imageSelectTip( tip )
97      {
```

Fig. 32.6   Demonstrating Microsoft Agent and the Lernout and Hauspie TruVoice text-to-speech (TTS) engine (part 2 of 5).

```
98          parrot.Stop();
99          for ( var i = 0; i < document.images.length; ++i )
100             if ( document.images( i ) == tip )
101                 tellMeAboutIt( i );
102     }
103
104     function tellMeAboutIt( element )
105     {
106         currentImage = document.images( element );
107         currentImage.style.background = "red";
108         parrot.MoveTo( currentImage.offsetParent.offsetLeft,
109             currentImage.offsetParent.offsetTop + 30 );
110         parrot.Speak( explanations[ element ] );
111     }
112 </SCRIPT>
113
114 <SCRIPT LANGUAGE="JavaScript" FOR = "agent" EVENT = "BalloonHide">
115     if ( currentImage != null ) {
116         currentImage.style.background = "lemonchiffon";
117         currentImage = null;
118     }
119 </SCRIPT>
120
121 <SCRIPT LANGUAGE = "JavaScript" FOR = "agent" EVENT = "Click">
122     parrot.Stop();
123     parrot.Play( "GetAttention" );
124     parrot.Speak( "Stop poking me with that pointer!" );
125 </SCRIPT>
126 </HEAD>
127
128 <BODY BGCOLOR = "lemonchiffon" ONLOAD = "loadAgent()">
129 <TABLE BORDER = "0">
130     <TH COLSPAN = "4"><H1 STYLE = "color: blue">
131         Deitel & Deitel Programming Tips</H1></TH>
132     <TR>
133     <TD ALIGN = "CENTER" VALIGN = "top" WIDTH = "120">
134         <IMG NAME = "gpp" SRC = "GPP_100h.gif"
135             ALT = "Good Programming Practice" BORDER = "0"
136             ONCLICK = "imageSelectTip( this )">
137         <BR>Good Programming Practices</TD>
138     <TD ALIGN = "CENTER" VALIGN = "top" WIDTH = "120">
139         <IMG NAME = "seo" SRC = "SEO_100h.gif"
140             ALT = "Software Engineering Observation" BORDER = "0"
141             ONCLICK = "imageSelectTip( this )">
142         <BR>Software Engineering Observations</TD>
143     <TD ALIGN = "CENTER" VALIGN = "top" WIDTH = "120">
144         <IMG NAME = "perf" SRC = "PERF_100h.gif"
145             ALT = "Performance Tip" BORDER = "0"
146             ONCLICK = "imageSelectTip( this )">
147         <BR>Performance Tips</TD>
148     <TD ALIGN = "CENTER" VALIGN = "top" WIDTH = "120">
149         <IMG NAME = "port" SRC = "PORT_100h.gif"
```

Fig. 32.6 Demonstrating Microsoft Agent and the Lernout and Hauspie TruVoice text-to-speech (TTS) engine (part 3 of 5).

```
150                 ALT = "Portability Tip" BORDER = "0"
151                 ONCLICK = "imageSelectTip( this )">
152          <BR>Portability Tips</TD>
153       </TR>
154       <TR>
155       <TD ALIGN = "CENTER" VALIGN = "top" WIDTH = "120">
156          <IMG NAME = "gui" SRC = "GUI_100h.gif"
157                 ALT = "Look-and-Feel Observation" BORDER = "0"
158                 ONCLICK = "imageSelectTip( this )">
159          <BR>Look-and-Feel Observations</TD>
160       <TD ALIGN = "CENTER" VALIGN = "top" WIDTH = "120">
161          <IMG NAME = "dbt" SRC = "DBT_100h.gif"
162                 ALT = "Testing and Debugging Tip" BORDER = "0"
163                 ONCLICK = "imageSelectTip( this )">
164          <BR>Testing and Debugging Tips</TD>
165       <TD ALIGN = "CENTER" VALIGN = "top" WIDTH = "120">
166          <IMG NAME = "cpe" SRC = "CPE_100h.gif"
167                 ALT = "Common Programming Error" BORDER = "0"
168                 ONCLICK = "imageSelectTip( this )">
169          <BR>Common Programming Errors</TD>
170       </TR>
171    </TABLE>
172    </BODY>
173    </HTML>
```

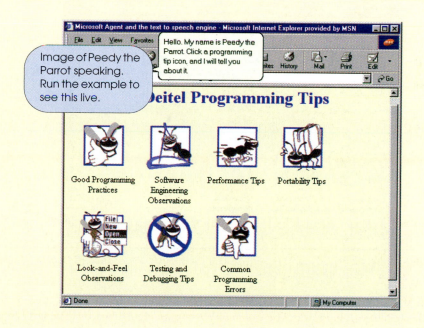

Fig. 32.6   Demonstrating Microsoft Agent and the Lernout and Hauspie TruVoice text-to-speech (TTS) engine (part 4 of 5).

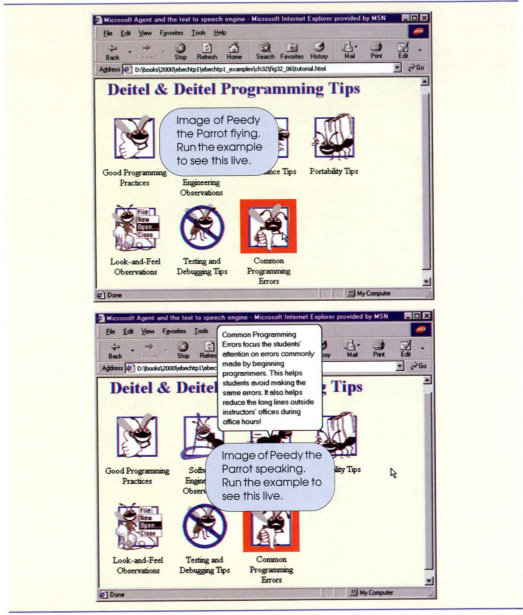

Fig. 32.6   Demonstrating Microsoft Agent and the Lernout and Hauspie TruVoice text-to-speech (TTS) engine (part 5 of 5).

The first screen capture illustrates Peedy finishing his introduction. The second screen capture shows Peedy flying toward the *Common Programming Error* icon. The last screen capture shows Peedy finishing his discussion of *Common Programming Errors.*

Before using Microsoft Agent or the Lernout and Hauspie TruVoice TTS engine in the Web page, they must both be loaded into the Web page via **OBJECT** elements. Lines 9 through 12 embed an instance of the Microsoft Agent ActiveX control into the Web page and give it the scripting name **agent** via the **ID** property. Similarly, lines 15 through 18 embed an instance of the Lernout and Hauspie TruVoice TTS engine into the Web page. This object is not scripted directly by the Web page. The TTS engine is used by the Microsoft Agent control to speak the text that Microsoft Agent displays. If either of these controls is not already installed on the computer browsing the Web page, the browser will attempt to download that control from the Microsoft Web site. The **CODEBASE** property (lines 11 and 17) specifies the URL from which to download the control and the version of the control to download (version 2 for the Microsoft Agent control and version 6 for the Lernout and Hauspie TruVoice TTS engine). The Microsoft Agent documentation discusses how to place these controls on your own server for download to your clients. [Note: Placing these controls on your own server requires a license from Microsoft.]

The **BODY** of the document (lines 128 through 172) defines a **TABLE** containing the seven programming tip icons. Each tip icon is given a scripting name via its **IMG** element's **NAME** property. This will be used to change the background color of the **IMG** element when the user clicks it to receive an explanation of that tip type. Each **IMG** element's **ONCLICK** event is registered as function **imageSelectTip**, defined at line 96. Each IMG element passes itself (i.e., **this**) to function **imageSelectTip** so the function can determine the particular image selected by the user.

The HTML document contains three separate **SCRIPT** elements. The **SCRIPT** element at lines 20 through 112 defines global variables used in all the **SCRIPT** elements and defines functions **loadAgent** (called in response to the **BODY** element's **ONLOAD** event), **imageSelectTip** (called when the user clicks an **IMG** element) and **tellMeAboutIt** (called by **imageSelectTip** to speak a few sentences about a tip).

Function **loadAgent** is particularly important, because it loads the Microsoft Agent character that is used in this example. Line 65

```
agent.Connected = true;
```

is provided mainly for backwards compatibility. This line may be needed to ensure that the Agent control executes properly in some older versions of Internet Explorer.

Lines 66 through 68

```
agent.Characters.Load( "peedy",
   "http://agent.microsoft.com/agent2/" +
   "chars/peedy/peedy.acf" );
```

use the Microsoft Agent control's **Characters** collection to load the character information for Peedy the Parrot from the Microsoft Web site. Method **Load** of the **Characters** collection takes two arguments—the first argument specifies a name for the character that can be used later to interact with that character, and the second argument specifies the URL of the character's data file (**peedy.acf** in this example).

Line 69

```
parrot = agent.Characters.Character( "peedy" );
```

assigns to global variable **parrot** a reference to the Peedy **Character** object. This object is used to interact with the character. Method **Character** of the **Characters** collection receives as its argument the name that was used to download the character data in lines 66 through 68. Line 70 sets the **Character**'s **LanguageID** property to 0x0409

(English). Microsoft Agent can actually be used with several different languages. See the documentation for more information.

Lines 73 through 75

```
parrot.Get( "state", "Showing" );
parrot.Get( "state", "Speaking" );
parrot.Get( "state", "Hiding" );
```

use the **Character** object's *Get* method to download the *Showing*, *Speaking* and *Hiding* states for the character. The method takes two arguments—the *type* of information to download (state in this case) and the *name* of the corresponding element (e.g., **Showing**). Each of these states has animation effects associated with it. When the character is displayed (i.e, the **Showing** state), its associated animation plays automatically (Peedy flies onto the screen). When the character is speaking (i.e, the **Speaking** state), the animations that make the character appear to be speaking are played. When the character hides (i.e, the **Hiding** state), the animations that make the character disappear are played (Peedy flies away).

Line 78

```
parrot.Get( "animation", "Greet" );
```

uses **Character** method **Get** to load an animation (**Greet**, in this example).

Lines 79 through 85

```
parrot.MoveTo( screenLeft, screenTop - 100 );
parrot.Show();
parrot.Play( "Greet" );
parrot.Speak( "Hello. My name is Peedy the Parrot. " +
    "Click a programming tip icon, and I will tell " +
    "you about it." );
parrot.Play( "GreetReturn" );
```

use a variety of **Character** methods to interact with Peedy. Line 79 uses the *MoveTo* method to specify Peedy's position on the screen. Line 80 uses method *Show* to display the character. When this occurs, the character goes into the **Showing** state, and its corresponding animation plays (i.e., Peedy flies onto the screen). Line 81 uses method *Play* to play the **Greet** animation (see the first screen capture). Lines 82 through 84 use method *Speak* to speak its string argument. If there is a compatible TTS engine installed, the character will display a bubble containing the text and will audibly speak the text as well. Finally, line 85 uses method **Play** to play the *GreetReturn* animation that returns the character to its normal standing state. Many animations have a "**Return**" animation that enables smooth transitions between different animations. The Microsoft Agent Web site contains complete lists of animations available for each character (some are standard to all characters, and others are specific to each character).

Lines 88 through 93 load several other animations. Line 88 loads the set of *Idling* animations that are used by Microsoft Agent when the user is not interacting with the character. When you run this example, be sure to leave Peedy alone for a while so you can see some of these animations. Lines 89 through 92 load the animations for moving the character up, down, left and right (*MoveUp*, *MoveDown*, *MoveLeft* and *MoveRight*, respectively).

Function **imageSelectTip** (lines 96 through 102) is called when the user clicks an image. The method first uses **Character** method *Stop* to terminate the current animation. Next, the **for** structure at lines 99 through 101 determines which image the user clicked. The condition at line 100

```
document.images( i ) == tip
```

uses the **document** object's *images* collection to determine the index of the clicked **IMG** element. If the current element of the collection is equal to **tip** (the clicked image), function **tellMeAboutIt** (defined at line 104) is called with the index of that **IMG** element.

Line 106 in function **tellMeAboutIt** assigns global variable **currentImage** a reference to the clicked **IMG** element. This will be used to change the background color of the **IMG** element the user clicked to highlight that image on the screen. Line 107 changes the background color of the image to red. Line 108 uses **Character** method **MoveTo** to position Peedy above the clicked image. When this statement executes, Peedy flies to the image. The **currentImage**'s *offsetParent* property determines the parent element that contains the image (in this example, the **TABLE** cell in which the image appears). The *offsetLeft* and *offsetTop* properties of the **TABLE** cell determine the location of the cell with respect to the upper-left corner of the browser window. Line 110 calls the **Character** object's **Speak** method to speak the text that is stored as strings in the array **explanations** for the selected tip.

The script for the **agent** control at lines 114 through 119 is invoked in response to the hiding of the text balloon. If the **currentImage** is not **null**, the background color of the image is changed to **lemonchiffon** (the document's background color) and variable **currentImage** is set to **null**.

The script for the **agent** control at lines 121 through 125 is invoked in response to the user's clicking the character. When this occurs, line 122 stops the current animation, line 123 plays the **GetAttention** animation and line 124 causes Peedy to speak the text "**Stop poking me with that pointer!**"

The HTML document of Fig. 32.7 enhances the example of Fig. 32.6 to include voice recognition. Most of the example is identical to Fig. 32.6, so here we discuss only the new features. The first screen capture illustrates Peedy finishing his introduction. The second screen capture shows Peedy after the user presses the *Scroll Lock* key to start issuing voice commands—this causes the voice recognition engine to initialize. The third screen capture shows Peedy ready to receive voice commands. The fourth screen capture shows Peedy after receiving a voice command (i.e., "Performance Tip"—this causes a *Command* event for the **agent** control). The last two screen captures show Peedy flying toward the Performance Tip icon and discussing Performance Tips, respectively.

To enable Microsoft Agent to recognize voice commands, a compatible voice recognition engine must be installed. Lines 21 through 24 use an **OBJECT** element to embed an instance of the Microsoft Speech Recognition Engine control in the Web page.

Next, the voice commands that the user can speak to interact with the Peedy must be registered in the **Character** object's *Commands* collection. The **for** structure at lines 118 through 120

```
for ( var i = 0; i < tips.length; ++i )
    parrot.Commands.Add( tips[ i ], tipNames[ i ],
        voiceTips[ i ], true, true );
```

uses the **Commands** collection's ***Add*** method to register each voice command. The method receives five arguments. The first argument is a string representing the command *name* (typically used in scripts that respond to voice commands). The second argument is a string that is displayed in a pop-up menu if you right-click the character or display the *Commands Window* (right-click the Microsoft Agent taskbar icon in the lower-right corner of your screen and select **Open Voice Commands Window**). The third argument is a string representing the words or phrases a user can speak for this command (stored in array **voiceTips** at lines 37 through 42). Optional words or phrases are enclosed in square brackets (**[]**). The last two arguments are boolean values indicating whether the command is currently enabled (i.e., the user can speak the command) and whether the command is currently visible in the pop-up menu and Commands Window for the character.

```
1   <!DOCTYPE HTML PUBLIC "-//W3C//DTD HTML 4.0 Transitional//EN">
2   <HTML>
3   <!-- Fig. 32.7: tutorial.html -->
4
5   <HEAD>
6   <TITLE>Speech Recognition</TITLE>
7
8   <!-- Microsoft Agent ActiveX Control -->
9   <OBJECT ID = "agent" WIDTH = "0" HEIGHT = "0"
10     CLASSID = "CLSID:D45FD31B-5C6E-11D1-9EC1-00C04FD7081F"
11     CODEBASE = "#VERSION = 2,0,0,0">
12  </OBJECT>
13
14  <!-- Lernout & Hauspie TruVoice text to speach engine -->
15  <OBJECT WIDTH = "0" HEIGHT = "0"
16     CLASSID = "CLSID:B8F2846E-CE36-11D0-AC83-00C04FD97575"
17     CODEBASE = "#VERSION = 6,0,0,0">
18  </OBJECT>
19
20  <!-- Microsoft Speech Recognition Engine -->
21  <OBJECT WIDTH = "0" HEIGHT = "0"
22     CLASSID = "CLSID:161FA781-A52C-11d0-8D7C-00A0C9034A7E"
23     CODEBASE = "#VERSION = 4,0,0,0">
24  </OBJECT>
25
26  <SCRIPT LANGUAGE = "JavaScript">
27     var parrot;
28     var currentImage = null;
29     var tips =
30         [ "gpp", "seo", "perf", "port", "gui", "dbt", "cpe" ];
31     var tipNames = [ "Good Programming Practice",
32                      "Software Engineering Observation",
33                      "Performance Tip", "Portability Tip",
34                      "Look-and-Feel Observation",
35                      "Testing and Debugging Tip",
36                      "Common Programming Error" ];
37     var voiceTips = [ "Good [Programming Practice]",
38                       "Software [Engineering Observation]",
```

Fig. 32.7 Microsoft Voice Recognition Engine and Microsoft Agent (part 1 of 8).

```
39                              "Performance [Tip]", "Portability [Tip]",
40                              "Look-and-Feel [Observation]",
41                              "Testing [and Debugging Tip]",
42                              "Common [Programming Error]" ];
43          var explanations = [
44              // Good Programming Practice Text
45              "Good Programming Practices highlight techniques for " +
46              "writing programs that are clearer, more " +
47              "understandable, more debuggable, and more " +
48              "maintainable.",
49
50              // Software Engineering Observation Text
51              "Software Engineering Observations highlight " +
52              "architectural and design issues that affect the " +
53              "construction of complex software systems.",
54
55              // Performance Tip Text
56              "Performance Tips highlight opportunities for " +
57              "improving program performance.",
58
59              // Portability Tip Text
60              "Portability Tips help students write portable code " +
61              "that can execute in different Web browsers.",
62
63              // Look-and-Feel Observation Text
64              "Look-and-Feel Observations highlight graphical user " +
65              "interface conventions. These observations help " +
66              "students design their own graphical user interfaces " +
67              "in conformance with industry standards.",
68
69              // Testing and Debugging Tip Text
70              "Testing and Debugging Tips tell people how to test " +
71              "and debug their programs. Many of the tips also " +
72              "describe aspects of creating Web pages and scripts " +
73              "that reduce the likelihood of 'bugs' and thus " +
74              "simplify the testing and debugging process.",
75
76              // Common Programming Error Text
77              "Common Programming Errors focus the students' " +
78              "attention on errors commonly made by beginning " +
79              "programmers. This helps students avoid making the " +
80              "same errors. It also helps reduce the long lines " +
81              "outside instructors' offices during office hours!" ];
82
83          function loadAgent()
84          {
85              agent.Connected = true;
86              agent.Characters.Load( "peedy",
87                  "http://agent.microsoft.com/agent2/" +
88                  "chars/peedy/peedy.acf" );
89              parrot = agent.Characters.Character( "peedy" );
90              parrot.LanguageID = 0x0409;  // needed in some conditions
91
```

Fig. 32.7   Microsoft Voice Recognition Engine and Microsoft Agent (part 2 of 8).

```
92          // get states from server
93          parrot.Get( "state", "Showing" );
94          parrot.Get( "state", "Speaking" );
95          parrot.Get( "state", "Hiding" );
96
97          // get Greet animation and do Peedy introduction
98          parrot.Get( "animation", "Greet" );
99          parrot.MoveTo( screenLeft, screenTop - 100 );
100         parrot.Show();
101         parrot.Play( "Greet" );
102         parrot.Speak( "Hello. My name is Peedy the Parrot. " +
103             "If you would like me to tell you about a " +
104             "programming tip, click its icon, or, press the " +
105             "'Scroll Lock' key, and speak the name of the " +
106             "tip, into your microphone." );
107         parrot.Play( "GreetReturn" );
108
109         // get other animations
110         parrot.Get( "animation", "Idling" );
111         parrot.Get( "animation", "MoveDown" );
112         parrot.Get( "animation", "MoveUp" );
113         parrot.Get( "animation", "MoveLeft" );
114         parrot.Get( "animation", "MoveRight" );
115         parrot.Get( "animation", "GetAttention" );
116
117         // set up voice commands
118         for ( var i = 0; i < tips.length; ++i )
119             parrot.Commands.Add( tips[ i ], tipNames[ i ],
120                 voiceTips[ i ], true, true );
121
122         parrot.Commands.Caption = "Programming Tips";
123         parrot.Commands.Voice = "Programming Tips";
124         parrot.Commands.Visible = true;
125     }
126
127     function imageSelectTip( tip )
128     {
129         for ( var i = 0; i < document.images.length; ++i )
130             if ( document.images( i ) == tip )
131                 tellMeAboutIt( i );
132     }
133
134     function voiceSelectTip( cmd )
135     {
136         var found = false;
137
138         for ( var i = 0; i < tips.length; ++i )
139             if ( cmd.Name == tips[ i ] ) {
140                 found = true;
141                 break;
142             }
143
```

Fig. 32.7   Microsoft Voice Recognition Engine and Microsoft Agent (part 3 of 8).

```
144        if ( found )
145            tellMeAboutIt( i );
146    }
147
148    function tellMeAboutIt( element )
149    {
150        currentImage = document.images( element );
151        currentImage.style.background = "red";
152        parrot.MoveTo( currentImage.offsetParent.offsetLeft,
153            currentImage.offsetParent.offsetTop + 30 );
154        parrot.Speak( explanations[ element ] );
155    }
156 </SCRIPT>
157
158 <SCRIPT LANGUAGE = "JavaScript" FOR = "agent"
159        EVENT = "Command( cmd )">
160    voiceSelectTip( cmd );
161 </SCRIPT>
162
163 <SCRIPT LANGUAGE="JavaScript" FOR = "agent" EVENT = "BalloonHide">
164    if ( currentImage != null ) {
165        currentImage.style.background = "lemonchiffon";
166        currentImage = null;
167    }
168 </SCRIPT>
169
170 <SCRIPT LANGUAGE = "JavaScript" FOR = "agent" EVENT = "Click">
171    parrot.Play( "GetAttention" );
172    parrot.Speak( "Stop poking me with that pointer!" );
173 </SCRIPT>
174
175 </HEAD>
176
177 <BODY BGCOLOR = "lemonchiffon" ONLOAD = "loadAgent()">
178 <TABLE BORDER = "0">
179    <TH COLSPAN = "4">
180      <H1 STYLE="color: blue">Deitel & Deitel Programming Tips</H1>
181    </TH>
182    <TR>
183    <TD ALIGN = "CENTER" VALIGN = "top" WIDTH = "120">
184      <IMG NAME = "gpp" SRC = "GPP_100h.gif"
185          ALT = "Good Programming Practice" BORDER = "0"
186          ONCLICK = "imageSelectTip( this )">
187      <BR>Good Programming Practices</TD>
188    <TD ALIGN = "CENTER" VALIGN = "top" WIDTH = "120">
189      <IMG NAME = "seo" SRC = "SEO_100h.gif"
190          ALT = "Software Engineering Observation" BORDER = "0"
191          ONCLICK = "imageSelectTip( this )">
192      <BR>Software Engineering Observations</TD>
193    <TD ALIGN = "CENTER" VALIGN = "top" WIDTH = "120">
194      <IMG NAME = "perf" SRC = "PERF_100h.gif"
195          ALT = "Performance Tip" BORDER = "0"
196          ONCLICK = "imageSelectTip( this )">
```

Fig. 32.7   Microsoft Voice Recognition Engine and Microsoft Agent (part 4 of 8).

```
197          <BR>Performance Tips</TD>
198      <TD ALIGN = "CENTER" VALIGN = "top" WIDTH = "120">
199          <IMG NAME = "port" SRC = "PORT_100h.gif"
200              ALT = "Portability Tip" BORDER = "0"
201              ONCLICK = "imageSelectTip( this )">
202          <BR>Portability Tips</TD>
203      </TR>
204      <TR>
205      <TD ALIGN = "CENTER" VALIGN = "top" WIDTH = "120">
206          <IMG NAME = "gui" SRC = "GUI_100h.gif"
207              ALT = "Look-and-Feel Observation" BORDER = "0"
208              ONCLICK = "imageSelectTip( this )">
209          <BR>Look-and-Feel Observations</TD>
210      <TD ALIGN = "CENTER" VALIGN = "top" WIDTH = "120">
211          <IMG NAME = "dbt" SRC = "DBT_100h.gif"
212              ALT = "Testing and Debugging Tip" BORDER = "0"
213              ONCLICK = "imageSelectTip( this )">
214          <BR>Testing and Debugging Tips</TD>
215      <TD ALIGN = "CENTER" VALIGN = "top" WIDTH = "120">
216          <IMG NAME = "cpe" SRC = "CPE_100h.gif"
217              ALT = "Common Programming Error" BORDER = "0"
218              ONCLICK = "imageSelectTip(this)">
219          <BR>Common Programming Errors</TD>
220      </TR>
221  </TABLE>
222  </BODY>
223  </HTML>
```

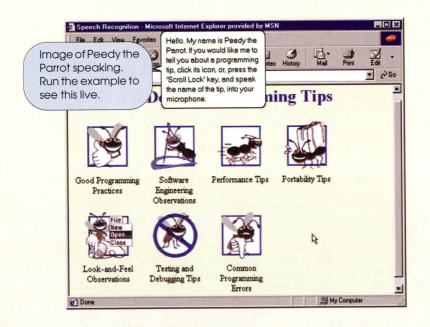

Fig. 32.7   Microsoft Voice Recognition Engine and Microsoft Agent (part 5 of 8).

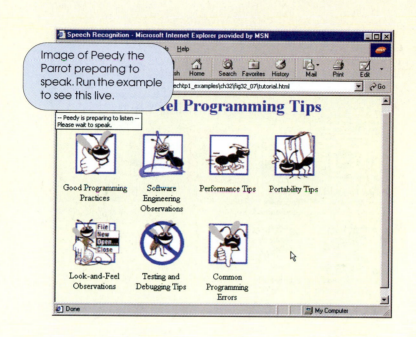

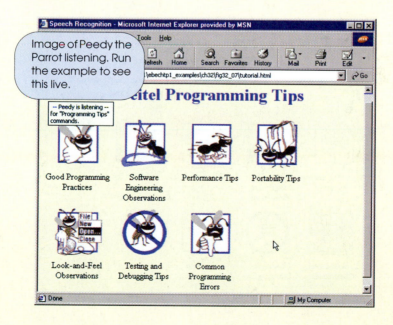

Fig. 32.7 Microsoft Voice Recognition Engine and Microsoft Agent (part 6 of 8).

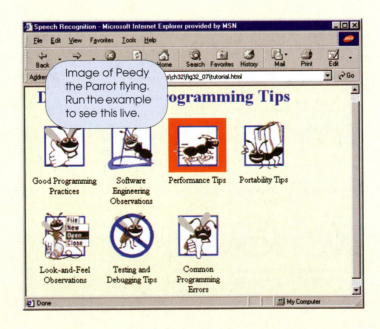

Fig. 32.7   Microsoft Voice Recognition Engine and Microsoft Agent (part 7 of 8).

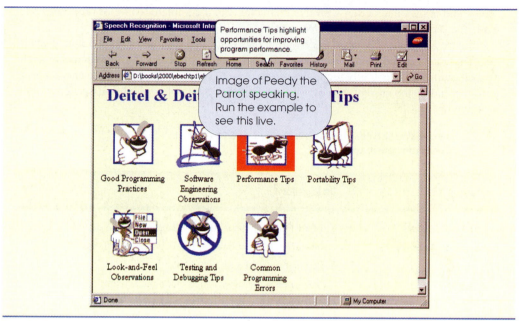

Fig. 32.7   Microsoft Voice Recognition Engine and Microsoft Agent (part 8 of 8).

Lines 122 through 124

```
parrot.Commands.Caption = "Programming Tips";
parrot.Commands.Voice = "Programming Tips";
parrot.Commands.Visible = true;
```

set the *Caption*, *Voice* and *Visible* properties of the **Commands** object. The **Caption** property specifies text that describes the voice command set. This text appears in the small rectangular area that appears below the character when the user presses the *Scroll Lock* key. The **Voice** property is similar to the **Caption** property except that the specified text appears in the Commands Window with the set of voice commands the user can speak below it. The **Visible** property is a boolean value that specifies whether the commands of this **Commands** object should appear in the popup menu.

When a voice command is received, the **agent** control's **Command** event handler (lines 158 through 161) executes. This script calls function **voiceSelectTip** and passes it the name of the command that was received. Function **voiceSelectTip** (lines 134 through 146) uses the name of the command in the **for** structure (line 138) to determine the index of the command in the **Commands** object. This value is then passed to function **tellMeAboutIt** (line 148) which causes Peedy to fly to the specified tip and discuss the tip.

These two examples have shown you the basic features and functionality of Microsoft Agent. However, there are many more features available. Figure 32.8 shows several other Microsoft Agent events. For a complete listing of Microsoft Agent events, see the site

```
msdn.microsoft.com/workshop/imedia/agent/
progagentcontrol.asp#TOPIC8
```

Figure 32.9 shows some other properties and methods of the **Character** object. Remember that the **Character** object represents a character that is displayed on the screen and allows interaction with that character. For a complete listing of properties and methods, see the Microsoft Agent Web site.

Figure 32.10 shows some speech output tags that can customize speech output properties. These tags are inserted in the text string that will be spoken by the animated character. Speech output tags generally remain in effect from the time at which they are encountered until the end of the current **Speak** method call. For a complete listing of speech output tags, see

```
msdn.microsoft.com/workshop/imedia/agent/
speechoutputtags.asp
```

Event	Description
BalloonHide	Called when the text balloon for a character is hidden.
BalloonShow	Called when the text balloon for a character is shown.
Hide	Called when a character is hidden.
Move	Called when a character is moved on the screen.
Show	Called when a character is displayed on the screen.
Size	Called when a character's size is changed.

Fig. 32.8 Other events for the Microsoft Agent control.

Property or method	Description
Properties	
Height	The height of the character in pixels.
Left	The left edge of the character in pixels from the left of the screen.
Name	The default name for the character.
Speed	The speed of the character's speech.
Top	The top edge of the character in pixels from the top of the screen.
Width	The width of the character in pixels.
Methods	
Activate	Sets the currently active character when multiple characters appear on the screen.
GestureAt	Specifies that the character should gesture toward a location on the screen that is specified in pixel coordinates from the upper-left corner of the screen.
Interrupt	Interrupts the current animation. The next animation in the queue of animations for this character is then displayed.
StopAll	Stops all animations of a specified type for the character.

Fig. 32.9 Other properties and methods for the **Character** object.

Tag	Description
\Chr=*string*\	Specifies the tone of the voice. Possible values for *string* are **Normal** (the default) for a normal tone of voice, **Monotone** for a monotone voice or **Whisper** for a whispered voice.
\Emp\	Emphasizes the next spoken word.
\Lst\	Repeats the last statement spoken by the character. This tag must be the only content of the string in the **Speak** method call.
\Pau=*number*\	Pauses speech for *number* milliseconds.
\Pit=*number*\	Changes the pitch of the character's voice. This value is specified in the range 50 to 400 hertz for the Microsoft Agent speech engine.
\Spd=*number*\	Changes the speech speed to a value in the range 50 to 250.
\Vol=*number*\	Changes the volume to a value in the range 0 (silent) to 65535 (maximum volume).

Fig. 32.10 Speech output tags.

32.7 RealPlayer™ Activex Control

In Chapter 2, we discussed using RealPlayer for listening to streaming audio and video. Via the **EMBED** element, you can embed RealPlayer objects in your Web pages to add streaming audio and video to your pages. Figure 32.11 demonstrates streaming audio in a Web page by embedding a RealPlayer object in the page. The user can select from several different audio sources. When a new source is selected, a JavaScript calls RealPlayer methods to start playing the selected audio stream.

```
1   <!DOCTYPE HTML PUBLIC "-//W3C//DTD HTML 4.0 Transitional//EN">
2   <HTML>
3
4   <!-- Fig 32.11: real.html                    -->
5   <!-- Embedding Realplayer into an HTML page -->
6
7   <HEAD>
8   <TITLE>Live Audio!</TITLE>
9
10  <SCRIPT LANGUAGE = "JavaScript">
11     var locations =
12        [ "http://kalx.berkeley.edu/kalx.ram",
13          "http://www.cjrt.org/live2.ra",
14          "http://www.1050chum.com/content/audiovideo/chumam_1.ram" ]
15
16     function change( loc )
17     {
18        raControl.SetSource( locations[ loc ] );
19        raControl.DoPlayPause();
20     }
```

Fig. 32.11 Embedding RealPlayer in a Web page (part 1 of 2).

```
21
22   </SCRIPT>
23   </HEAD>
24
25   <BODY>
26
27   <P>
28   Pick from my favorite audio streams:
29
30   <SELECT ID = "streamSelect" ONCHANGE = "change( this.value )">
31      <OPTION VALUE = "">Select a station</OPTION>
32      <OPTION VALUE = "0">KALX</OPTION>
33      <OPTION VALUE = "1">WMBR</OPTION>
34      <OPTION VALUE = "2">WFMU</OPTION>
35   </SELECT>
36
37   <BR>
38   <EMBED ID = "raControl" SRC = ""
39      TYPE = "audio/x-pn-realaudio-plugin" WIDTH = "275"
40      HEIGHT = "125" CONTROLS = "Default" AUTOSTART = "false">
41
42   </BODY>
43   </HTML>
```

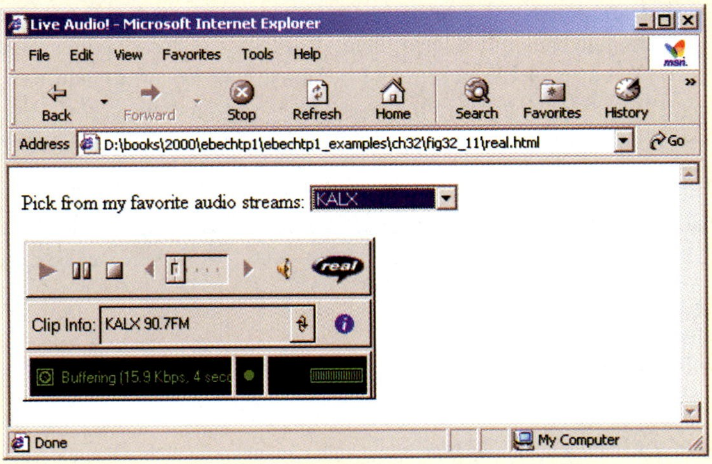

Fig. 32.11 Embedding RealPlayer in a Web page (part 2 of 2).

The **EMBED** element in lines 38 through 40

```
<EMBED ID = "raControl" SRC = ""
    TYPE = "audio/x-pn-realaudio-plugin" WIDTH = "275"
    HEIGHT = "125" CONTROLS = "Default" AUTOSTART = "false">
```

embeds the RealPlayer plug-in in your page. The **TYPE** *attribute* specifies the MIME type of the embedded file, which in this case is the MIME type for streaming audio. (Remember that MIME is a standard for specifying the format of content so the browser can determine how to handle the content). The **WIDTH** and **HEIGHT** *attributes* specify the dimensions the control will occupy on the page. The *AUTOSTART* *attribute* determines whether the audio should start playing when the page loads (here we set it to **false**). The *CONTROLS* *attribute* specifies which controls will be available to the user (i.e., *Play* button, *Pause* button, *volume control*, etc.). Setting **CONTROLS** to *Default* places the standard control buttons on screen. A list of the available controls can be found at the site

> `www.real.com/devzone/library/stream/plugtest/plugin.html`

We do not set the *SRC* *attribute* of the **EMBED** element. Normally this would be the location of the streaming audio, but in this example we use JavaScript to change the source dynamically based on the user's selection.

Now that the player is embedded in the Web page, we use scripting to activate the streaming audio. The **SELECT** menu (line 30) lists three radio stations, corresponding to the three entries in the array **locations** (defined at line 11), which contains the actual URLs for the live audio of those stations. When the selection changes, function **change** (line 16) is called by the **ONCHANGE** event. This function calls methods *SetSource* and *DoPlayPause* of the RealPlayer object. Method **SetSource** sets the source URL of the audio stream to be played. Then, method **DoPlayPause** toggles between pausing and playing the stream. (In this case the stream is paused because it has not started playing yet, so it begins playing in response to the call to **DoPlayPause**.)

In this example, we only explore streaming audio. The latest versions of RealPlayer have the ability to receive streaming video as well. If you would like to view streaming video with RealPlayer, check out the following sites:

> `www.cnn.com/`
> `www.msnbc.com/`
> `www.broadcast.com/television/`

If you'd like to learn more about programming with RealPlayer, visit the RealPlayer Dev-Zone at

> `www.real.com/devzone/index.html`

Broadcasting your own streaming audio and video requires a dedicated server and expensive software. As you see here however, embedding audio streams in your own pages is a simple way to enhance your page's look and feel.

32.8 Embedding VRML in a Web page

Another innovative technology for enhancing Web pages is *VRML*—the *Virtual Reality Modeling Language*. VRML is a markup language for specifying three-dimensional (3D) objects and scenes. Like HTML, VRML is purely text and can be created by hand in text editors such as Notepad. In addition, many leading 3D modeling programs can save three-dimensional designs in VRML format.

Both Netscape and Internet Explorer have free, downloadable plug-ins that allow them to view VRML *worlds* (VRML files are known as worlds and end with the *.wrl* *file extension*). The Web page shown in Fig. 32.12 uses the **EMBED** element to place a **.wrl** file in the page—the default VRML plug-in for IE is used to view the file (the VRML plug-in is included with the full install of IE5 on your CD).

```
1    <HTML>
2
3    <!-- Fig 32.11: vrml.html              -->
4    <!-- Embedding VRML into a Web page  -->
5
6    <HEAD>
7    <TITLE>Live VRML</TITLE>
8    </HEAD>
9
10   <BODY>
11
12   <EMBED SRC = "new.wrl" WIDTH = "400" HEIGHT = "400">
13
14   </BODY>
15   </HTML>
```

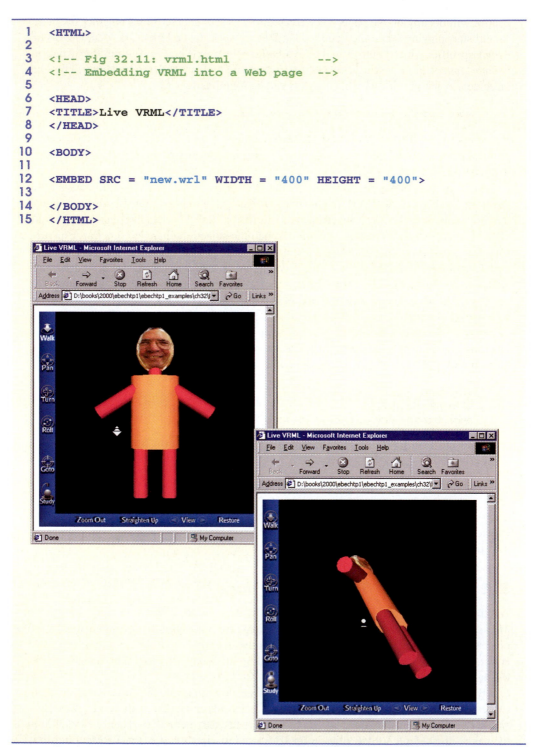

Fig. 32.12   Embedding VRML in a Web page (part 1 of 2).

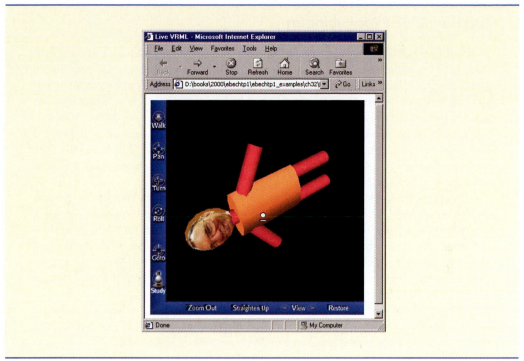

Fig. 32.12 Embedding VRML in a Web page (part 2 of 2).

Line 12

```
<EMBED SRC = "new.wrl" WIDTH = "400" HEIGHT = "400">
```

uses the **EMBED** element to embed the VRML world file **new.wrl** in the Web page, and specifies a width and height of 400 pixels for the viewing area. When the page loads and IE encounters the **EMBED** element, it sees that the file extension for the file specified in the SRC attribute is **.wrl**, and accordingly launches the VRML plug-in. The plug-in reads the **.wrl** file and renders the objects specified in the file on screen.

The controls on the left and bottom sides of the viewing area allow you to move around freely in the world—by clicking one of the controls and dragging the mouse in the viewing area, you can rotate the world, walk around or change which direction you are facing.

32.9 Using Streaming Media

In the past few years, Streaming Media companies (such as Real Networks discussed in the previous section) have been on the cutting edge of Internet technology. Streaming media companies have pushed Internet hardware and software to their limits to produce "acceptable" audio and video, all along hoping that the technology would improve and make high-quality, streaming media a viable option for content providers. The technology has improved to the point that streaming media companies are becoming major Internet players. This section introduces some of today's most important streaming media companies.

Feature: TellSoft Technologies

TellSoft Technologies (**www.tellsoft.com**) is a leading Application Service Provider of phone-to-Internet content and communications services. They add personality to the Web by offering services which use streaming audio to deliver informative content that anyone can create using a touch tone phone or Web interface. Their services (each is described below) include *iTalkWeb*, *iTalkLive*, *iTalkSlides* and *iTalkMail*.

iTalkWeb helps e-Businesses quickly update customers and partners with product highlights and other critical information. When a site contains an iTalkWeb URL, the site's content providers can add news to their Web pages without waiting for Web developers to modify those pages.

To add new iTalkWeb content to a site, the site's content provider dials a toll-free number and enters his/her message ID number. Next, the content provider records a message by speaking into the phone. The message ID associates the client's account and voice message with a hyperlink located on the client's Web site. When the content provider terminates the call, the recorded voice message is immediately available on the Web in streaming audio format. Messages can be delivered in both Windows Media Player or RealPlayer formats.

Gofish (**www.gofish.com**) uses iTalkWeb to deliver daily seafood industry news to their Web site visitors. They serve content for what they call "goRadio." The service offers Gofish a convenient way to deliver content that site visitors can listen to while they work. goRadio news is updated on a daily basis, providing visitors with new content that hopefully will attract them back to the site in the future (possibly daily).

TellSoft's iTalkLive service simplifies and personalizes internet communications by broadcasting live audio to groups of registered individuals. This makes conducting interviews, seminars and training sessions more convenient by eliminating the cost and hassle of in-person, organized meetings. Attendees access the information live from any Web browser. iTalkLive broadcasts can also be archived for retrieval at a later date.

TellSoft's iTalkSlides enables Web-based slide presentations that are accompanied by live audio delivered by telephone. iTalkSlides allows the presenter to upload slides, JPEG images, GIF images and other files directly to the Web. Unlike other online presentation services, iTalkSlides allows a presentation to be modified after it is uploaded. Presenters can apply critical last minute changes directly without uploading large presentations, repeatedly. The service offers a chat function for online discussions between the listeners and the presenter. The service also has the ability to let the presenter choose a moderator to manage the discussion. This option can be set for each listener—allowing the presenter to decide who takes an active role in the discussion.

iTalkMail allows people to send voice mail as part of an email message. The sender accesses his/her iTalkMail account via the Web and creates email distribution lists containing the email addresses of the people who will receive the message. Next, the sender dials a toll-free number, records a message and chooses a distribution list (or lists). An e-mail containing a hyperlink to the audio file is immediately sent to everyone on the list. The recipient simply clicks the hyperlink to listen to the message. Visit **www.italkservices.com/italkmail/index.asp** to open a free account (10 messages per month and upto 50 users per message).

Feature: TellSoft Technologies (Continued)

To demo iTalkServices, visit **www.tellsoft.com/demo.asp**, select a service and choose a user name and password. Click **Log In** to continue to the instructions Web page. Follow the instructions to record your sample message. When you are done, click the animated iTalk button in your Web browser to listen to your message. Your content should now be available on the Web. Figure 32.13 shows the iTalkWeb demo page. The X's in the image represent the personal Message ID number you receive with your individual account.

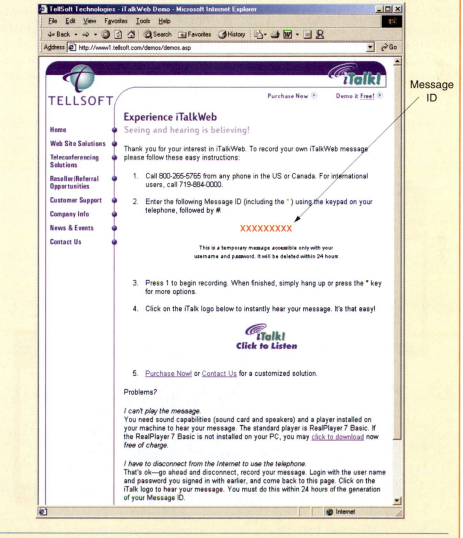

Fig. 32.13 iTalkWeb demo page. (Courtesy of TellSoft Technologies.)

Feature: Evoke Communications

Evoke Communications (**www.evoke.com**) is a leading Internet communications service provider. Among its free services is *Talking Email*, which allows users to record a 30-second message over the phone to be sent to the recipient(s) of their choice. Electronic greeting service **bluemountain.com** uses Talking Email to allow users to personalize electronic greeting cards.

To send a Talking Email, visit Evoke Communications's home page and click the **TALKING EMAIL** link located under the **ENGINES** interactive menu.

Evoke Communications' flagship service, *Evoke Webconferencing*, allows the Moderator of a Webconference to upload visuals, such as PowerPoint presentations, to a Web-enabled interface. Combining the Web with traditional telephone services allows an interactive conference with real-time audio and visual content. Figure 32.14 illustrates the user interface used to upload and preview a presentation.

To use Evoke Webconferencing, sign up at their Web site, **www.evoke.com**. Use the **SIGNUP** link located under the **WEBCONFERENCING** interactive menu. Evoke Communications also provides a demo of the Evoke Webconferencing features. The demo shows you how to load and view a PowerPoint presentation as well as how to use the **Conference Controls** (shown in Fig. 32.15). [*Note:* Evoke Webconferencing is a fee-based service.]

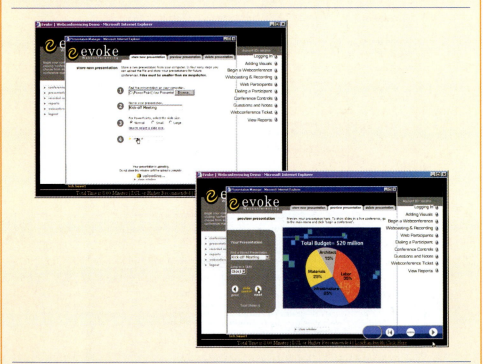

Fig. 32.14 Uploading and previewing a presentation using Evoke Webconferencing. (Courtesy of Evoke Communications.)

Feature: Evoke Communications (Continued)

Fig. 32.15 The Evoke Communications Webconferencing **Conference Controls** window. (Courtesy of Evoke Communications.)

Feature: iBEAM

iBEAM Broadcasting (**www.ibeam.com**) specializes in streaming media. Using a combination of satellites and land-based broadcasting facilities, iBEAM eliminates the usual problems of streaming media—*latency* and *jitter*. When information is transmitted across the Internet, it is broken up into packets. The delay in receiving these packets is called latency. When packets arrive out of order, it is called jitter. Latency and jitter are hard to detect for static Web documents such as a text-based Web page. However, when accessing streaming media, latency and jitter cause choppy audio and video. iBEAM's large, redundant network of satellite and terrestrial hubs delivers streaming media without latency and jitter, resulting in smooth streaming audio and video. This network also allows streaming media to be delivered to large audiences simultaneously, solving another problem of streaming media. Some of iBEAM's customers include Sony, Warner Bros. and MSNBC.

iBEAM has partnered with *Engage Inc.* to offer the streaming ad platform, *On-Target,* which allows advertisements to be inserted into streaming media. Allowing content providers to integrate advertisements with their streaming content. Engage Inc. offers online marketing solutions with a database of anonymous user profiles enabling advertisements to target users. This personalized advertising method is more effective than the traditional media. To find out about incorporating On-Target into your Web Site, visit **www.ibeam.com/ontarget/ontarget.htm**.

iBEAM also offers *Activecast*—an end-to-end solution for interactive Webcasting events. For example, if a company wants to create an employee-orientation event, iBEAM can incorporate streaming audio, streaming video, presentation slides and chats into a browser-based viewer customized to that company's needs. To learn more about Activecast, visit iBEAM's home page, **www.ibeam.com**.

Feature: Digital Island

Digital Island (`www.digitalisland.net`) offers hosting, network and application services as well as content delivery. Digital Island offers fast, reliable service for your e-Business. Some of Digital Island's customers include `aol.com`, `cnbc.com` and `latimes.com`.

Digital Island's *Footprint* streaming services provide a number of different streaming options. *Footprint Live* specializes in delivering live streaming media, such as news broadcasts. *Footprint On-Demand* provides users access to prerecorded videos that can be viewed at their request. Finally, *Footprint Media Services* include options such as streaming ad insertion for targeting the user based on geographic location, frequency of previously viewed ads or browsing patterns. For more information on Digital Island visit `www.digitalisland.net`.

32.10 Internet and World Wide Web Resources

There are many multimedia-related resources on the Internet and World Wide Web. This section lists a variety of resources that can help you learn about multimedia programming and provides a brief description of each.

`www.microsoft.com/windows/windowsmedia/`
The *Windows Media* Web site contains information to help get you started with Microsoft's streaming media technologies. The site also links you to various software.

`www.microsoft.com/ntserver/basics/netshowservices`
This is the *Windows NT Server site for Windows Media Technologies*. This site provides information for the serving of streaming media over the Internet.

`msdn.microsoft.com/workshop/imedia/agent/default.asp`
The *Microsoft Agent Home Page* provides you with everything you need to know about programming with Microsoft Agent.

`msdn.microsoft.com/workshop/imedia/agent/agentdl.asp`
The *Microsoft Agent downloads area* contains all the software downloads you need to build applications and Web pages that use Microsoft Agent.

`msdn.microsoft.com/downloads/default.asp`
The *Microsoft Developer Network Downloads* home page contains images, audio clips and other free downloads.

`www.macromedia.com`
This is the *Macromedia Home Page*. Macromedia specializes in tools for creating multimedia-rich Web sites. Check out this site for 30-day trial versions of their multimedia authoring tools.

`www.shockwave.com/`
The *Shockwave* Web site contains a wide variety of Web-based games, cartoons and music. The site was created with Macromedia authoring tools.

`xdude.com/`
This site is an example of the power of the Macromedia Flash technology.

`www.station.sony.com/`
The Station is one of the most popular sites on the Internet today. It is loaded with games that use a variety of multimedia techniques.

www.broadcast.com
Broadcast.com is one of the leading Web sites for streaming media on the World Wide Web. From this site, you can access a variety of live and pre-recorded audio and video.

www.real.com/
The *RealNetworks* site is the home of RealPlayer—one of the most popular software products for receiving streaming media over the Web. Also, with their RealJukebox, you can download MP3 files and other digital music.

service.real.com/help/library/guides/extend/embed.htm
This site provides the details of embedding RealPlayer in a Web page. The site also provides a detailed listing of the methods and events of the RealPlayer.

www.nasa.gov/gallery/index.html
This site is *NASA's Multimedia Gallery*. You can view audio, video, and images from NASA's exploration of space and of our planet.

disney.go.com/disneyvideos/bvhevideo/index.html
This *Disney* site contains streaming video clips from several Disney movies.

www.space-tv.com/
This site contains streaming video from past NASA space missions and the Russian Mir space station.

www.w3.org/WAI/
The World Wide Web Consortium's *Web Accessibility Initiative (WAI)* site promotes design of universally accessible Web sites. This site will help you keep up-to-date with current guidelines and forthcoming standards for Web accessibility.

web.ukonline.co.uk/ddmc/software.html
This site provides links to software for people with disabilities.

www.hj.com/
Henter-Joyce, Inc. provides software for the blind and visually impaired.

www.abledata.com/text2/icg_hear.htm
This page contains a consumer guide that discusses technologies for the hearing impaired.

www.washington.edu/doit/
The University of Washingtion's *DO-IT (Disabilities, Opportunities, Internetworking and Technology) Program* Web site provides information and Web development resources for creating Web sites that are universally accessible.

www.webable.com/
The WebABLE site contains links to many disability-related Internet resources. The site is geared to development of technologies for people with disabilities.

www.speech.cs.cmu.edu/comp.speech/SpeechLinks.html
The *Speech Technology Hyperlinks Page* has over 500 links to sites related to computer-based speech and speech recognition.

www.islandnet.com/~tslemko/
The *Micro Consulting Limited* site contains shareware speech-synthesis software.

www.chantinc.com/technology/
The *Chant* Web site discusses what speech technology can do for you and how it works. Chant also provides speech-synthesis and speech-recognition software.

www.dismusic.com/
The *Disney Music Page* offers free Disney music in MIDI (**.mid**) format. MIDI format is particularly useful for embedding sound into a Web page and having it play when someone enters onto the site.

www.Tx-Marketeers.com/musicroom/
The Music Room site has a great variety of MIDI format music.

www.spinner.com/
The *Spinner* site is an on-line radio station, with many genres from which to choose. Either download the player for your computer, or listen to the music through your browser with the RealPlayer plug-in.

www.netradio.com/
The *NetRadio* site is another on-line radio station that you can listen to with your browser and the RealPlayer plug-in.

www.discjockey.com/
The *DiscJockey.com* site is an on-line radio station with music from the 40s through the 90s. The music on this site can be played through RealPlayer or the Windows Media Player.

www.mp3.com/
The *mp3.com* site is an excellent resource for the MP3 audio format. The site offers files, info on the format, hardware info and software info.

home.cnet.com/category/0-4004.html
CNET is an Internet news group containing a variety of information about today's hottest computer and Internet topics. This page from the *CNET* Web site discusses the MP3 format, MP3 encoders and streaming MP3 format audio over the Internet.

www.mpeg.org/
The *MPEG.org* site is the primary reference site for information on the MPEG video format.

www.winamp.com/
Winamp is probably the most popular and well-known player for the MP3 format. Winamp has capabilities of allowing you to stream MP3 over the Internet.

www.shoutcast.com/
SHOUTcast is a streaming audio system. Anyone that has Winamp and a fast Internet connection can broadcast their own net radio!

www.microsoft.com/windows/mediaplayer/default.asp
Here is the official site of the *Windows Media Player*. Go here to learn all about its capabilities, especially of streaming audio and video over the net.

SUMMARY

- **BGSOUND** is an Internet Explorer-specific element that adds background audio to a Web site. The **SRC** property specifies the URL of the audio clip to play. The **LOOP** property specifies the number of times the audio clip should play. The **BALANCE** property specifies the balance between the left and right speakers. The **VOLUME** property determines the volume of the audio clip. To change the property values via a script, assign a scripting name to the **ID** property.

- The **IMG** element enables both images and videos to be included in a Web page. The **SRC** property indicates that the source is an image. The **DYNSRC** (i.e., dynamic source) property indicates that the source is a video clip. Property **START** indicates when the video should start playing (specify **fileopen** to play when the clip is loaded or **mouseover** to play when the user first positions the mouse over the video).

- The **EMBED** element embeds a media clip in a Web page. A graphical user interface can be displayed to give the user control over the media clip. The GUI typically enables the user to play, pause and stop the media clip, to specify the volume and to move forward and backward quickly through the clip. The **LOOP** property indicates that the media clip should loop forever. To prevent the GUI from appearing in the Web page, add the **HIDDEN** property to the **<EMBED>** element. To script the element, specify a scripting name by adding the **ID** property to the **<EMBED>** element.

- A benefit of Microsoft's ActiveX controls is that they can be incorporated into Web pages that are to be displayed in Internet Explorer and enhance the functionality of those Web pages.

- The **OBJECT** element is used to embed ActiveX controls in Web pages. The **WIDTH** and **HEIGHT** properties specify the width and height in pixels that the control will occupy in the Web page. Property **CLASSID** specifies the unique ActiveX control ID for the ActiveX control.

- The ActiveX control ID for the Windows Media Player ActiveX control is

  CLSID:22d6f312-b0f6-11d0-94ab-0080c74c7e95

- Parameters can be passed to an ActiveX control by placing **PARAM** elements between the **OBJECT** element's **<OBJECT>** and **</OBJECT>** tags. Each parameter is specified with a **PARAM** element that contains a **NAME** property and a **VALUE** property.

- The Windows Media Player ActiveX control's **FileName** parameter specifies the file containing the media clip. Parameter **AutoStart** is a boolean value indicating whether the media clip should play automatically when it is loaded (**true** if so; **false** if not). The **ShowControls** parameter is a boolean value indicating whether the Media Player controls should be displayed (**true** if so; **false** if not). The **Loop** parameter is a boolean value indicating whether the Media Player should play the media clip in an infinite loop (**true** if so; **false** if not).

- The Windows Media Player ActiveX control's **Play** and **Pause** methods can be called to play or pause a media clip, respectively.

- Microsoft Agent is a technology for interactive animated characters in a Windows application or World Wide Web page. These characters allow users of your application to interact with the application by using more natural human communication techniques. The control accepts both mouse and keyboard interactions, speaks (if a compatible text-to-speech engine is installed) and also supports speech recognition (if a compatible speech-recognition engine is installed). With these capabilities, your Web pages can speak to users and can respond to their voice commands.

- The *Microsoft Agent control* provides four predefined characters—*Peedy the Parrot, Genie, Merlin* and *Robby the Robot*.

- The Lernout and Hauspie TruVoice Text to Speech (TTS) engine is used by the Microsoft Agent ActiveX control to speak the text that Microsoft Agent displays.

- The Microsoft Agent control's **Characters** collection stores information about the characters that are currently available for use in a program. Method **Load** of the **Characters** collection loads character data. The method takes two arguments—a name for the character that can be used later to interact with that character, and the URL of the character's data file.

- A **Character** object is used to interact with the character. Method **Character** of the **Characters** collection receives as its argument the name that was used to download the character data and returns the corresponding **Character** object.

- The **Character** object's **Get** method downloads character animations and states.

- Each state has animation effects associated with it. When the character enters a state (such as the **Showing** state), the state's associated animation plays automatically.

- **Character** method **MoveTo** moves the character to a new position on the screen. Method **Show** displays the character. Method **Play** plays the specified animation. Method **Speak** speaks its string argument. If there is a compatible TTS engine installed, the character displays a bubble containing the text and audibly speaks the text as well.

- Many animations have a "**Return**" animation for smooth transitioning between animations.

- The **Idling** animations are displayed by Microsoft Agent when the user is not interacting with the character.

- **Character** method **Stop** terminates the current animation.

- To enable Microsoft Agent to recognize voice commands, a compatible voice-recognition engine, such as the Microsoft Speech Recognition Engine, must be installed.
- The voice commands that the user can speak to interact with a character must be registered in the **Character** object's **Commands** collection.
- The **Commands** collection's **Add** method registers each voice command. The method receives five arguments.
- The **Commands** object's **Caption** property specifies text that describes the voice command set. This text appears in the small rectangular area that appears below the character when the user presses the *Scroll Lock* key. The **Voice** property is similar to the **Caption** property, except that the specified text appears in the Commands Window with the set of voice commands the user can speak below it. The **Visible** property is a boolean value that specifies whether the commands of this **Commands** object should appear in the popup menu.
- When a voice command is received, the **agent** control's **Command** event handler executes.
- A RealPlayer object can be embedded (with the **EMBED** element) in a Web page to add streaming media to a Web page. The **TYPE** attribute specifies the MIME type of the embedded file. The **WIDTH** and **HEIGHT** attributes specify the dimensions the control will occupy on the page. The **AUTOSTART** attribute determines whether the audio should start playing when the page loads. The **CONTROLS** attribute specifies which controls will be available to the user. Setting **CONTROLS** to **Default** places the standard control buttons on screen. The SRC attribute specifies the location of the streaming audio.
- RealPlayer method **SetSource** sets the source URL of the audio stream to be played. Method **DoPlayPause** toggles between pausing and playing the stream.
- Both Netscape and Internet Explorer have free, downloadable plug-ins that allow them to view VRML worlds. The **EMBED** element can be used to place a .wrl file in a Web page.

TERMINOLOGY

ActiveX control
Add method of **Commands**
animated characters
audio
audio format
AutoStart parameter of Media Player
background sound
BALANCE property of the **BGSOUND** element
BGSOUND Element
Caption property of **Commands**
CD-ROM
character data file
Character method **Characters**
Character object (Microsoft Agent)
Characters collection (Microsoft Agent)
CLASSID property of **OBJECT**
CODEBASE property of **OBJECT**
Command event (Microsoft Agent)
Commands collection of **Character**
Commands Window
DoPlayPause method of RealPlayer
DVD

DYNSRC property of **IMG**
embed a media clip
EMBED element
FileName parameter of Media Player
Genie
Get method of **Character**
HEIGHT property of **OBJECT**
HIDDEN property of **EMBED**
Hiding state of a character
ID property of **BGSOUND**
ID property of **EMBED**
ID property of **OBJECT**
Idling animations
interactive animated character
Internet bandwidth
Lernout and Hauspie TruVoice TTS engine
load an animation
Load method of **Characters**
Loop parameter of Media Player
LOOP property of **BGSOUND**
LOOP property of **EMBED**
media clip

Merlin
Microsoft Agent
Microsoft Agent control
Microsoft Speech Recognition Engine
MoveTo method **Character**
multimedia
multimedia-based Web application
NAME property of **PARAM**
natural human communication techniques
OBJECT element
PARAM element
Pause method of Media Player
Peedy the Parrot
Play method of **Character**
Play method of Media Player
Robby the Robot
"**Return**" animation
SetSource method of RealPlayer
Show method **Character**
ShowControls parameter
Showing state of a character
sound cards
Speak method **Character**
Speaking state of a character

speech recognition
SRC property of **BGSOUND**
START property of **IMG**
START property value **fileopen**
START property value **mouseover**
streaming audio
streaming technology
streaming video
text-to-speech (TTS) engine
three-dimensional (3D) object
VALUE property of **PARAM**
video
video clip
video format
Virtual Reality Modeling Language (VRML)
Visible property of **Commands**
voice command
Voice property of **Commands**
VOLUME property of **BGSOUND**
WIDTH property of **OBJECT**
Windows Media Player
Windows Media Player ActiveX control
world file (**.wrl**)

SELF-REVIEW EXERCISES

32.1 Fill in the blanks in each of the following:
   a) _____ is a technology for interactive animated characters.
   b) The _____ element is used to play a background audio in Internet Explorer.
   c) The _____ property of the **IMG** element specifies a video clip should appear in the **IMG** element's location in the Web page.
   d) The _____ element can be used to embed an ActiveX control on a Web page.
   e) The _____ element can be used to place an audio or video clip on a Web page.
   f) The **IMG** element's _____ property has values **mouseover** and **fileopen**.
   g) The _____ property of the **EMBED** element prevents a GUI containing media clip controls from being displayed with the media clip.
   h) Microsoft Agent's _____ animations enable smooth transition between animations.
   i) When set to **true**, the _____ parameter to the Windows Media Player specifies that a GUI should be displayed so the user can control a media clip.
   j) When a compatible _____ engine is available to Microsoft Agent, characters have the ability to speak text.
   k) The Microsoft Agent control's _____ collection keeps track of the information about each loaded character.
   l) Macromedia Flash's _____ feature draws the in-between frames of an animation automatically.
   m) Graphics, Buttons, and Movie Clips are all types of _____.
   n) The two types of tweening in Macromedia Flash are _____ tweening and _____ tweening.
   o) Macromedia Flash's scripting language is called _____.

32.2   State whether each of the following is *true* or *false*. If *false*, explain why.

a) The **BGSOUND** element can be used with any browser.

b) The **IMG** element enables both images and videos to be included in a Web page.

c) **BGSOUND** property **BALANCE** cannot be set via scripting.

d) The **NAME** property of the **OBJECT** element specifies a scripting name for the element.

e) The Microsoft Agent **Character** object's **StopAnimation** method terminates the current animation for the character.

f) A Macromedia Flash button's **HIT** state is entered when the button is clicked.

g) To draw a circle in Flash, hold down the **SHIFT** key while using the Oval tool.

h) Motion tweening cannot be used on layers with more than one object or symbol.

i) The more frames you give to an animation, the slower it will be.

j) Setting the argument of Flash's Random function to 5 tells the function to generate a number between 1 and 5, inclusive.

ANSWERS TO SELF-REVIEW EXERCISES

32.1   a) Microsoft Agent. b) **BGSOUND**. c) **DYNSRC**. d) **OBJECT**. e) **EMBED**. f) **START**. g) **HIDDEN**. h) "**Return**." i) **ShowControls**. j) text-to-speech. k) **Characters**. l) tweening. m) symbols. n) shape, motion. o) ActionScript.

32.2   a) False. The **BGSOUND** element is specific to Internet Explorer. b) True. c) True. d) False. The **ID** property of the **OBJECT** element specifies a scripting name. e) False. The **STOP** method terminates the current animation for the character. f) False. The **DOWN** state is entered when the button is clicked. g) True. h) True. i) True. j) False. Setting the argument of Flash's Random function to 5 tells the function to generate a number between 0 and 4, inclusive.

EXERCISES

32.3   *(Story Teller)* Store a large number of nouns, verbs, articles, prepositions, etc. in arrays of strings. Then use random number generation to forms sentences and have your script speak the sentences with Microsoft Agent and the Lernout and Hauspie text-to-speech engine.

32.4   *(Limericks)* Modify the limerick-writing script you wrote in Exercise 18.8 to use a Microsoft Agent character and the Lernout and Hauspie text-to-speech engine to speak the limericks your program creates. Use the speech output tags in Fig. 32.10 to control the characteristics of the speech (i.e., emphasis on certain syllables, volume of the voice, pitch of the voice, etc.).

32.5   Modify the script of Exercise 32.4 to play character animations during pauses in the limerick.

32.6   *(Background Audio)* Write an HTML document and script that allows the user to choose from a list of the audio downloads available from the Microsoft Developer Network Downloads site

msdn.microsoft.com/downloads/default.asp

and listen to the chosen audio clip as background music with the **BGSOUND** element.

32.7   Modify Exercise 32.6 to use the **EMBED** element to play the audio clips.

32.8   Modify Exercise 32.6 to use the Windows Media Player ActiveX control to play the audio clips.

32.9   *(Video Browser)* Write an HTML document and script that allows the user to choose from a list of the videos available from the NASA Multimedia Gallery site

www.nasa.gov/gallery/

and view that video using the **EMBED** element.

32.10   Modify Exercise 32.9 to use the Windows Media Player ActiveX control to play the video clips.

32.11 Modify the program of Fig. 32.4 to download the other six videos from the SeaWiFs site and allow the user to select which video to play.

32.12 *(Image Flasher)* Create a script that repeatedly flashes an image on the screen. Do this by changing the visibility of the image. Allow the user to control the "blink speed."

32.13 *(Digital Clock)* Using features of the Dynamic HTML chapters, implement an application that displays a digital clock in a Web page. You might add options to scale the clock; to display day, month and year; to issue an alarm; to play certain audios at designated times; and the like.

32.14 *(Analog Clock)* Create a script that displays an analog clock with hour, minute and second hands that move as the time changes. Use the Structured Graphics Control to create the graphics and play a tick sound every second. Play other sounds to mark every half-hour and hour.

32.15 *(Karaoke)* Create a Karaoke system that plays the music for a song and displays the words for your user to sing at the appropriate time.

32.16 *(Calling Attention to an Image)* If you want to emphasize an image, you might place a row of simulated light bulbs around your image. You can let the light bulbs flash in unison, or you can let them fire on and off in sequence, one after the other.

32.17 *(On-Line Product Catalog)* Companies are rapidly realizing the potential for doing business on the Web. Develop an on-line multimedia catalog from which your customers may select products to be shipped. Use the data binding features of Chapter 23 to load data into tables. Use Microsoft Agent to speak descriptions of a selected product.

32.18 Modify Exercise 32.17 to support voice commands that allow the user to speak a product name to receive a description of the product.

32.19 *(Reaction Time/Reaction Precision Tester)* Create a Web page that moves an image around the screen. The user moves the mouse to catch and click on the shape. The shape's speed and size can be varied. Keep statistics on how much time the user typically takes to catch a shape of a given size. The user will probably have more difficulty catching faster-moving, smaller shapes.

32.20 *(Animation)* Create an animation by displaying a series of images that represent the frames in the animation. Allow the user to specify the speed at which the images are displayed.

32.21 *(Tortoise and the Hare)* Develop a multimedia version of the Tortoise and Hare simulation of Exercise 17.20. Record an announcer's voice calling the race, "The contenders are at the starting line." "And they're off!" "The Hare pulls out in front." "The Tortoise is coming on strong." and so forth. As the race proceeds, play the appropriate recorded audios. Play sounds to simulate the animals' running (and the crowd cheering!). Do an animation of the animals racing up the side of the slippery mountain.

32.22 *(Arithmetic Tutor)* Develop a multimedia version of the Computer-Assisted Instruction (CAI) systems you developed in Exercises 16.27, 16.28 and 16.29.

32.23 *(15 Puzzle)* Write a multimedia-based version of the game of 15. There is a 4-by-4 board for a total of 16 slots. One of the slots is empty. The other slots are occupied by 15 tiles, numbered 1 through 15. Any tile next to the currently empty slot can be moved into the currently empty slot by clicking the tile. Your program should create the board with the tiles out of order. The goal is to arrange the tiles into sequential order row by row. Play sounds with the movement of the tiles.

32.24 *(Morse Code)* Modify your solution to Exercise 18.26 to output the morse code using audio clips. Use two different audio clips for the dot and dash characters in Morse code.

32.25 *(Calendar/Tickler File)* Create a general purpose calendar and "tickler" file. The application should sing "Happy Birthday" to you when you use it on your birthday. Have the application display images and play audios associated with important events and remind you in advance of important events. For example, have the application give you a week's warning so you can pick up an appropriate greeting card for that special person. Store the calendar information in a file for use with the data-binding techniques of Chapter 23 to load the calendar information into a table in the Web page.

33

Macromedia® Flash™ 4: Building Interactive Animations

Objectives

- To learn Flash 4 multimedia development.
- To learn animation techniques using Flash.
- To learn to script with your Flash movies.
- To build a storefront and product demonstration.
- To add background and event sounds to Flash movies.
- To embed a Flash movie into a Web page.

A flash and where previously the brain held a dead fact, the soul grasps a living truth! At moments we are all artists.
Arnold Bennett

All the world's a stage and all the men and women merely players; they have their exits and their entrances; and one man in his time plays many parts…

William Shakespeare

Science and technology and the various forms of art, all unite humanity in a single and interconnected system.
Zhores Aleksandrovich Medvedev

Music hath charms to soothe a savage breast, To soften rocks, or bend a knotted oak.
William Congreve

The true art of memory is the art of attention.
Samuel Johnson

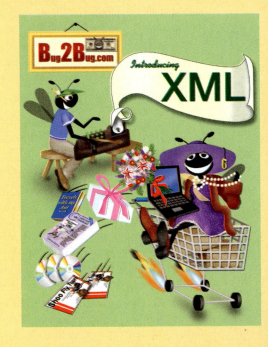

33.1 Introduction[1]

Macromedia Flash 4 is an application for creating interactive, animated *movies*. A Flash movie can be anything from a Web-based banner advertisement to a fully functional animated Web site. Flash movies can be embedded in Web pages, used on CD-ROMs or converted into standalone, executable programs. This chapter provides an introduction to Flash movie development.

Flash is arguably one of the most important advancements in Web multimedia since the addition of scripting capabilities. Flash allows you to build cross-platform audio, video,

---

1. We would like to thank Prof. Peter Kugel of the Boston College Computer Science Department for suggesting that we write this material and for his guidance throughout the writing process.

animations and still images. Flash movies also have small file sizes compared to other techniques of creating multimedia presentations. Advanced animation features such as *tweening*, which takes the first and last frames of an animation and automatically generates the middle animation frames from them, help to transform even the most artistically challenged developers into respectable animators.

Web users must have the *Flash Player plug-in* which enables a browser to display Flash content. According to a Macromedia press release dated July 12, 2000, 92% of Web users (approximately 248 million online users), have the ability to view Flash movies. Of those users, 51% never had to download the plug-in, because it was bundled with software they already owned. Both Netscape Communicator 4.06 and higher and Microsoft Internet Explorer 4 and higher are bundled with the Flash Player plug-in. The plug-in is also bundled with Microsoft Windows® 98, AOL 5.0, various Macintosh software and others.[1]

Web page implementors can use JavaScript to detect if the Flash Player plug-in is present on the user's computer. The few users who are unable to view Flash-enhanced Web sites can be given the option of viewing the same content formatted in HTML. They can also be offered an opportunity to download the plug-in. For an example of how to implement browser detection please see chapter 20. Macromedia offers technical support documents called TechNotes on thier Web site, one of which discusses the process of detecting the Flash player plug-in without the use of Javascipt. This TechNote can be found at:

```
http://www.macromedia.com/support/flash/ts/documents/
scriptfree_detection.htm
```

33.2 Learning Flash with Hands-on Examples

This chapter is intended to provide a foundation from which to begin building more advanced Flash movies. We focus on the Flash development environment for Windows, though most Flash features we discuss are similar to those used in the Apple Macintosh environment. Other Deitel & Associates, Inc. Flash publications are currently under development. Visit our Web site often for information and status updates.

If you do not already own a copy of Flash 4, there is a 30-day trial version available on the CD that accompanies this book. You may also download a 30-day trial copy from Macromedia, available at **www.macromedia.com/software/flash/trial**. After 30 days you have to buy the product to continue using it.

After setting up the Flash 4 trial version according to the detailed instructions provided by Macromedia, launch the program. Figure 33.1 provides a list of Flash and animation terms that are used throughout the chapter.

Though its layout should be fairly self-explanatory to Macromedia Director users and those who have used other timeline-based products such as Adobe® Premiere™, Flash 4 may be a bit overwhelming to the newcomer, Fig. 33.2 shows the Flash 4 development environment and points out several key features.

We begin by taking a look at the drawing toolbar. Compared to many multimedia products, Flash has a fairly simple one. Figure 33.3 shows the tools in the drawing toolbar. Figure 33.4 explains the function and modifiers of each tool. A tool's modifiers allow you to alter the way it works.

Term	Description
Movie	Macromedia Flash terminology is largely borrowed from the realm of animation and video. Thus, Flash animation files are known as movies.
Stage	The stage is the area where you create the movie. Objects are drawn directly on the stage.
Vector graphics	Vector graphics use geometric formulas to describe images that can be scaled to any size without distortion. Vector graphics require less memory than their bitmap counterparts, which are made up of tiny squares called pixels. Although vector graphics are small in size. Rendering a vector graphic is processor intensive. In other words, the speed of the your processor directly effects the speed at which your movie is played.
Timeline	The timeline is a graphical display of all frames in a movie. See Fig. 33.2 for a picture of the timeline.
Frame	A frame is a single moment in the timeline. Flash shows multiple frames in sequence to create animations.
Layers	Anyone who has ever seen an old fashioned cartoon being drawn may have seen the clear plastic *cells* on which animators draw. Later these cells are layered, combined and shown in sequence to provide the animation effect. Layers are Flash's computerized equivalent of traditional animation cells. In Flash, the timeline can be broken into multiple layers. Objects drawn in higher layers hide anything below them in other layers. Making a change in one layer does not affect any others, this allows each object to be changed individually.
Keyframes	The term keyframe also has its roots in traditional cartooning. Lead animators would often only draw the frames, or *cells*, that showed a significant change— the keyframes. Keyframes provide a frame of reference in animation. To draw an animation in Flash one only has to depict frames where important changes occur, i.e., the "keyframes."
Tweening	Drawing the frames between keyframes was left to junior animators who came to be called "tweeners." Thus, drawing the frames between keyframes was known as "tweening." Macromedia uses advanced algorithms to create the in-between frames. Drawing a complex animation now only requires animators to draw keyframes—Flash does the rest.
ActionScript	ActionScript is the scripting language that is used to add interactivity and events to Flash movies.
Shape	In Flash, a shape is a vector graphic which has not as yet been converted to a symbol. Shapes can be edited using the Paint Bucket and Ink Bottle tools and can be broken into smaller parts using the various selection tools. Shape tweening can only be applied to shapes. Breaking apart objects, such as imported bitmaps and text strings, converts them to editable shapes.

Fig. 33.1   Flash and animation terms.

Term	Description
Symbol	Flash's vector graphics can be converted to symbols to make them interactive and reusable. Symbol types include *Graphics*, *Buttons* and *Movie Clips*. Graphic symbols can have actions applied to them. This allows them to interact with the user, as well as other symbols. Buttons are specialized symbols which, like graphics, perform tasks in response to user interactions. Buttons also hold information, such as how they should appear when the mouse is over the button (known as a "roll over"). Movie clips are much like animated GIF images (see Chapter 32). A movie clip is a package of multiple frames. Any Flash animation can be converted into a movie clip. Doing so allows you to reuse that clip by dragging it onto the stage at any given time. Movie clips can even contain scripting.
Inspectors	Inspectors are windows that allow you to view and edit various shape and symbol information. There are five different inspectors in Flash. The **Object Inspector** provides access to properties such as the size and location of a given object. The **Frame Inspector** provides frame information such as whether tweening or audio is used in the frame. The **Transform Inspector** allows you to alter the scale, rotation and skew of an object. The **Scene Inspector** provides a list of all the movie's scenes and allows switching between them. The **Generator Inspector** provides access to attributes of Macromedia Flash Generator movies. This Inspector is inactive unless you have Macromedia Generator (a separate product). We do not cover this inspector.
Onionskinning	Onionskinning is the equivalent of laying traditional animation "cells" on top of each other. This allows the animator to see the motion of objects over time in a single frame. Onionskinning allows Flash developers to see multiple frames depicted on the stage at the same time. This is a valuable tool for verifying the quality of an animation and the interactions between objects in the animation.
Projector	Macromedia continues with its video analogy by calling movies that are published in standalone executable format *Projectors*. A projector can be one of two file formats. On a PC a Projector is simply a `.exe` file. On a Macintosh computer, a Projector is a `.hqx` file.

Fig. 33.1   *Flash and animation terms.*

The best way to learn how the Flash tools work is through hands-on examples. Let us begin by demonstrating how to build an interactive, animated button. With the help of some beginner-level scripting, the button produces a random string of advice to be displayed in a text field.

This exercise teaches you to use Flash to create a small executable program. Our program, which we call **CEO Assistant 1.0**, helps a corporate Chief Executive Officer make decisions. The program generates advice in a random manner.

The first step in building a Flash movie is to create the symbols to be used in the movie. In this example, we build a button and a title graphic. We use a text field to display the random text string. To begin, Open a new Flash movie and save it as `CeoAssistant.fla`.

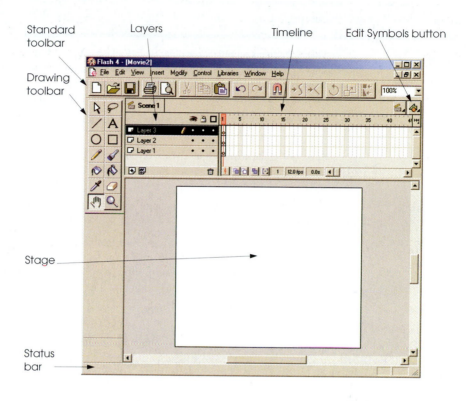

Fig. 33.2   Flash 4 development environment. (Courtesy of Macromedia, Inc.)

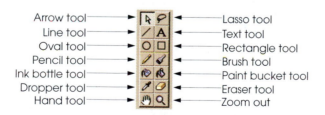

Fig. 33.3   Flash 4 toolbar. (Courtesy of Macromedia, Inc.)

Good Programming Practice 33.1

Save each project with a meaningful name in its own folder. Saving early and often is important for any work that you do. Using a new folder for each movie helps keep projects organized. When publishing, your movie files are placed in the same directory as the movie.

Tool		Description
Arrow		This tool selects an object (or objects) in a Flash movie. Modifiers, such as rotate and scale, allow it to be used to move, resize and rotate an object. Its modifiers can also be used to straighten lines and smooth curves. We demonstrate the use of modifiers later in the chapter.
Line		This tool creates straight lines in a movie. Its modifiers allow thickness, color and style to be altered.
Oval		This tool creates ovals and circles of any size. This tool's modifiers allow the user to change border color, fill colors, border thickness and style.
Rectangle		This tool creates rectangles and squares. Its modifiers are the same as the **Oval** tool.
Pencil		This tool enables free-hand drawing. Flash takes this familiar tool one step further by providing modifiers that allow smoothing and straightening of lines and shapes. This helps eliminate the rough edges often seen in computer drawings.
Dropper		This tool lifts a color from an existing object on the stage.
Hand		This tool allows the user to move the stage around the screen. This is useful for moving parts of a large stage into view.
Lasso		This tool is a selection tool. It allows you to select all or parts of objects on the stage.
Text		This tool adds text to a movie. It also adds fields for use in forms. Text written in fields can be updated using scripting, allowing the user to dynamically change the text in a movie.
Brush		This tool creates paint brush like strokes on the canvas. Brush sizes and shapes can be customized. The paint brush has an array of painting options such as **Paint Inside**, which causes the brush to paint only inside the boundaries of a given object. Examples of this are provided later in the chapter.
Paint Bucket		This tool changes the color inside an object's border, i.e., the *fill color* of an object. This tool does not change lines or borders; the **Ink Bottle** is used for that purpose.
Ink Bottle		This tool looks similar to the **Paint Bucket**, but its function is more specific. It is only used to change the ink color of lines and borders.
Eraser		Like the **Paint Brush**, the **Eraser** has various options. In its simplest form, the **Eraser** tool simply erases anything added to a layer or stage.
Magnifier		The **Magnifier** allows the developer to zoom in and out on the stage. Because Flash uses vector graphics, the movie does not distort even at a high zoom percentage.

Fig. 33.4   Flash development tools.

33.2.1 Changing the Appearance of the Stage

This section will teach you how to change a Flash movie's properties. In particular we will change the size and color of the stage. Click the **Modify** menu and select **Movie...** to display the **Movie Properties** dialog box (Fig. 33.5). Set the dimensions field labeled **Width** to **200 px** and set the field labeled **Height** to **180 px**. The letters **px** are an abbreviation for the word pixel, which is described in the vector graphics section of Fig. 33.1. This creates a small stage on which to work, but the stage can always be enlarged later without a decrease in quality. The size and the background color of a movie may also be changed by clicking on the square of color (commonly called a *swatch*) labeled **Background**. This displays a palette of colors. Select a pale blue in the palette and click **OK** when finished. Figure 33.8 shows a color being selected from the palette.

You should now have a small, colored stage. Use the **Magnifier** tool to enlarge the work area, this makes working on the small stage easier. The **Magnifier** tool has only two modifiers; they allow you to zoom in and zoom out. When a drawing tool is selected, it's modifiers appear below the drawing toolbar. Figure 33.6 depicts the **Magnifier** tool's modifiers. Click the stage once using the **Magnifier** tool. Save the movie.

33.2.2 Creating a Shape with the Oval Tool

Now that the stage is ready, we can build the symbols to be used in our movie. First, create a round button and click the **Oval** tool to activate it. Then, modify the **Oval** tool's attributes by specifying a black border and a red gradient fill (gradient fills are located at the bottom of the color palette). To change the gradient fill, click the **Fill Color** modifier, shown in Fig. 33.7.

Fig. 33.5   Flash 4 **Movie Properties** dialog box. (Courtesy of Macromedia, Inc.)

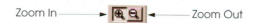

Fig. 33.6   Flash 4 **Magnifier** tool attributes. (Courtesy of Macromedia, Inc.)

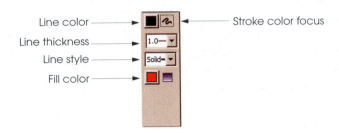

Line color ────────► █ 𝓷 ◄──── Stroke color focus
Line thickness ─────► 1.0─ ▼
Line style ─────────► Solid─ ▼
Fill color ─────────► █ █

Fig. 33.7   Flash 4 **Oval** tool attributes. (Courtesy of Macromedia, Inc.)

You should now see a color palette similar to the one seen when changing the background color; choose the red gradient at the bottom of the screen. See Fig. 33.8 for a diagram of Flash's fill color palette. Use the same technique to set the **Line Color** to black. Feel free to experiment with the **Line Thickness** and **Line Style** modifiers. We are now ready to build the button symbol

Move the cursor to the stage. Do not worry where you create the circle—you can move it later. Hold the *Shift* key and drag the mouse on the stage to draw a circle rather than an oval. Using the *shift* key in this manner allows you to *constrain* a shape. The same method can be used to create a square using the rectangle tool. Drag the mouse until you have a circle about the size of a dime and then release the mouse button. You should now have a small circle, with a black border and a gradient fill. Save the movie.

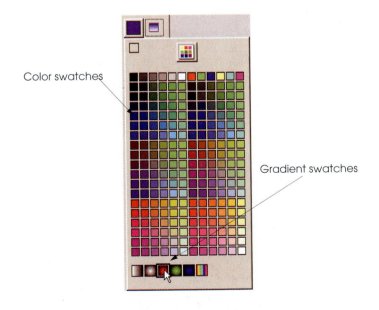

Color swatches

Gradient swatches

Fig. 33.8   Choosing a color from the Flash 4 **Fill Color** modifier's color palette. (Courtesy of Macromedia, Inc.)

33.2.3 Adding Text to a Button

Now let us add the button's text label. Click the **Text** tool. To ensure readability, we use the modifiers to change the font to **Arial** or **Helvetica**, which are less ornate than other fonts. Set the font size to 14 pt using the *Font Size* modifier and activate the *Bold* modifier pictured in Fig. 33.9 by clicking it. Finally, change the font color by clicking the *Font Color* modifier and selecting white from the palette.

After setting the modifiers, move the cursor directly above the red circle you just created and click the mouse. In the resulting text box, type GO in capital letters.

If the text did not appear in exactly the correct location, click the **Arrow** tool and then drag the text by keeping the mouse button pressed. You should now be able to drag the text to the middle of the red button. The button is almost complete and should now look similar to Fig. 33.10.

33.2.4 Converting a Shape into a Symbol

Now we create our first symbol. Because the button is made up of a graphic and some text, both have to be selected to make them one symbol. Once we create the symbol, the graphic and text will be treated as a single object.

Make sure that the **Arrow** tool is still active and select the circle and the text. To make the selection, click and hold the mouse button slightly above and to the left of the button as shown in Fig. 33.11. Next, drag the cursor until the circle and text are completely surrounded by the selection marquee and release the mouse button. Both the circle and the text should now be selected as shown in the rightmost image of Fig. 33.11. You can tell that an image has been selected if it is highlighted in grey. To make the symbol, select **Convert to Symbol...** from the **Insert** menu. You should now see the *Symbol Properties* dialog box on the screen. Give the button the name `gobutton` and click the radio button labeled **Button**. Click **OK** to create your first Flash **Button Symbol**. After the button has been created, use the **Arrow** tool to drag the **GO** button to the lower right-hand corner of the stage.

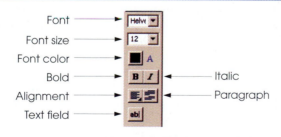

Font	Helve ▾
Font size	12 ▾
Font color	■ A
Bold	**B** *I* ◄—— Italic
Alignment	▤ ▤ ◄—— Paragraph
Text field	abl

Fig. 33.9   Flash 4 **Text** tool attributes. (Courtesy of Macromedia, Inc.)

Fig. 33.10   Nearly complete button. (Courtesy of Macromedia, Inc.)

Fig. 33.11 Selecting an object or objects using the **Arrow** tool. (Courtesy of Macromedia, Inc.)

33.2.5 Adding Keyframes

To complete later sections of this chapter, you must know how to add *keyframes*. Without keyframes, animation is impossible. Keyframes tell Flash how a shape or symbol should appear at the beginning and end of an animation. Tweening is then used to create the middle animation frames. Keyframes are also referred to quite frequently while using scripts.

To add a keyframe, first, click the frame in the timeline where you wish to add the keyframe. Once the desired frame is selected, either click **Keyframe**, which is located in the **Insert** menu, or press the *F6* key. Right-clicking the selected frame in the timeline and selecting **Insert Keyframe** from the pop up menu will also add a keyframe. The next section provides you with a hands on exercise for adding a keyframe.

33.2.6 Editing Button Symbols

The button is not yet complete—we will now make the button change color when the mouse rolls over it. Right-click the **GO** button to add these features. In the pop-up menu, select **Edit**. If you successfully switched to **Edit** mode, the stage should appear stretched across the entire development window and the button should be at the center of the screen.

In **Edit** mode, a symbol's pieces can be edited separately. As you can see, the frames in the timeline are labeled **UP**, **OVER**, **DOWN** and **HIT**. Each of the frames corresponds to a unique button state. The **UP** state is the default state, which we designed originally. **OVER** is activated when the mouse is positioned over the button; this is known as a *mouseover* in many programming languages. **DOWN** is the state of the button when it is clicked. The **HIT** state is used to define the clickable area of the button. Leaving the **Hit** state unchanged constrains the clickable area to the boundaries of the button.

First we will edit the **OVER** state. Add a keyframe in the **OVER** frame, as pictured in Fig. 33.12. Make sure that the **OVER** state is highlighted in the timeline before editing.

33.2.7 Using the Paint Bucket Tool

Next, change the fill of the circle from a red gradient to a green one. Activate the **Arrow** tool and click the area outside the stage to deselect everything. In **Edit** mode, the text and shape that you created earlier can once again be edited separately. Carefully click the filled portion of the circle. You know that the fill is selected if the entire center of the circle is highlighted. Be careful that you do not accidentally highlight the border or text. You may have to zoom in closer using the **Magnifier** tool to make the selection easier. After selecting the fill, activate the **Paint Bucket** tool. Use the **Fill Color** modifier to select the green gradient. The **Paint Bucket** tool's modifiers are pictured in Fig. 33.13. after adjusting the **Paint Bucket** modifiers, click the selected fill to change its color. The color of the button in the **OVER** state should now be green. To verify the color, click off the stage using the **Arrow** tool. Doing so causes the selection to disappear and will reveal the new fill. If you like, you can edit the **DOWN** state using the same techniques described for the **OVER** state. To exit the **Edit** mode click the tab labeled **Scene 1** above the timeline.

33.2.8 Using Test Movie to Verify Changes

Now we will test the movie to be sure that the new button works as it should. Click the **Control** menu and select **Test Movie**. Moving the cursor over the "GO" button should now cause the color to change as shown in Fig. 33.14. When you are done testing the movie, close the test window to return to the stage.

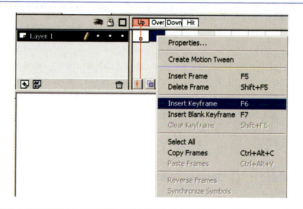

Fig. 33.12 Adding a keyframe in edit mode. (Courtesy of Macromedia, Inc.)

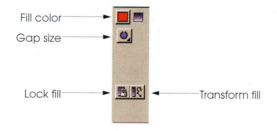

Fig. 33.13 Flash 4 **Paint Bucket** tool modifiers. (Courtesy of Macromedia, Inc.)

Fig. 33.14 **GO** button in its **UP** and **OVER** states. (Courtesy of Macromedia, Inc.)

33.2.9 Adding Layers to a Movie

Next, we demonstrate adding new layers to a movie. We also create a symbol representing the title for our movie. These symbols used later when we introduce form fields and scripting.

Let us make a new layer before we add the title. We could put the title in the same layer as the button. Adding a new layer gives us more flexibility, by allowing us to animate the title without affecting the button. The first step is to rename the first layer. Doing so makes keeping track of the project's elements easier. Do this by double clicking the label **Layer 1**, located on the left-hand side of the timeline. Notice that the label's text becomes editable. Change the text to **Button Layer** and press the *Enter* key.

Now we are ready to add a new layer. Click the **Insert** menu and select **Layer**. This places a layer called **Layer 2** above **Button Layer**. Rename **Layer 2** to `Title Layer` using the method we just described. This layer is used for the title. To activate the new layer, click its name.

Good Programming Practice 33.2

Always name all of a movie's layers with descriptive names. Naming layers is especially helpful when working with many layers.

Next, configure the **Text** tool to produce text in 20 pt., navy blue, Arial font, by using its modifiers. Using the tool, click the stage and begin typing as you did for the button label. Type the string `CEO Assistant 1.0`. Next, click the **View** menu and select **Antialias Text** (see Chapter 11 for a discussion of antialiasing). Notice that the text is smoother once this option is set. Center the text using the **Text** tool's alignment modifier. The Flash movie should now appear similar to Fig. 33.15.

33.2.10 Using Tweening to Animate Text

There are two types of tweening in Flash, *shape tweening* and *motion tweening*. Shape tweening is used to "morph" an object into a different shape. For instance, the word "star" could be morphed into the shape of a star. Shape tweening cannot be used with symbols or *grouped objects* (groups of shapes that have been combined using the **Group** option, which is found in the **Modify** menu). Motion tweening, which we are using to make the text appear to fly into view, also has specific guidelines. Motion tweening cannot be used with layers containing more than one object or symbol and cannot be used on shapes or grouped objects.

We need to convert the text to a symbol because we are going to use motion tweening. To do so, click the new text title and press the *F8* key. You should now see the symbol properties dialog box. Name the symbol `title` and be sure that the **Behavior** checkbox is set to **Graphic**. Click **OK,** when you are ready.

We have to designate frames in the timeline for our animation before we can create the motion tween and make the text fly. We want the title to fly into view at the start of the movie, so place the animation in the first few frames. The more frames you use, the slower an animation is. Currently, there is only one frame occupied in the timeline. To designate frames for the animation, we increase the number of frames used in the movie. First, let us move the button to a later frame where it will be used. Click the first frame in **Button Layer**. Once the frame is selected, if the cursor is still over the frame, a small white box will appear to the lower right of the cursor. This box indicates that you may now drag and drop the active frame. Click and hold the frame and move it to frame 15. For an illustration of this technique, see Fig. 33.16.

Fig. 33.15 CEO Assistant 1.0 early screen shot. (Courtesy of Macromedia, Inc.)

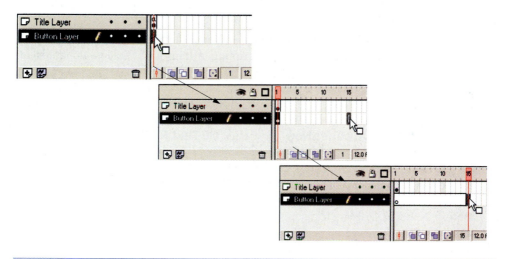

Fig. 33.16 Moving a frame. (Courtesy of Macromedia, Inc.)

We must still add another keyframe to the title layer to create our zooming effect. The animation should start at frame 1 and end at frame 15. Add a new keyframe to frame 15 of **Title Layer** using 1 of the methods discussed in section 33.2.5. Because each new keyframe always inherits the properties of the keyframe that directly precedes it, frame 15 will be identical to frame 1. Any future changes to a keyframe only effect the changed frame, unless tweening is used. The title symbol in frame 1 still has to be altered to make it appear as if it flies onto the stage. Click frame 1 to select it. The only object on the stage should be the title. Use the **Arrow** tool to select the title symbol by clicking it.

Click the **Window** menu, scroll down to the **Inspectors** submenu and select **Object** to open the **Object** inspector. We want the title to fly onto the screen from just outside of the top-left corner of the stage, so we must change the **x** and **y** coordinates of the title. We also change the width and height values to make the title appear to shrink as it enters the stage. To make these changes, all we have to do is change the form fields in the inspector. Set both the **x** and **y** fields to **-10** and press the **Apply** button. The title should now be partly off of the stage. Now set both the **width** and **height** values to **0** and press the **Apply** button. As a result, you should only see a small smudge outside the stage. We are now ready to apply the motion tween. [*Note:* As we mentioned in the terminology section at the beginning of this chapter, there are different types of inspectors. We use the **Object** inspector for this exercise. Be sure to experiment with the others at your leisure.]

To activate the motion tween, move the cursor to any frame between the keyframes in **Title Layer** and right click. Select **Properties…** from the pop-up menu to open the **Frame Properties** dialog box. Click the **Tweening** tab and select **Motion** from the drop down menu labeled **Tweening**. There should now be a number of options for motion tweening. For our purposes the default values are adequate, but feel free to experiment. Press **OK** to apply the tweening.

Congratulations, you have just created your first Flash animation! Press *Ctrl+Enter* to open the testing window and test the movie. Your movie should look similar to the one pictured in Fig. 33.15. Close the test window to return to the development environment.

33.2.11 Adding a Text Field

We have focused on artistic aspects of Flash. We now consider Flash scripting. We will create a text field that will be manipulated using scripting. Adding a text field is similar to adding text to the stage.

Let us add a new layer for the text field. Create a new layer called **Field Layer**. Next, click frame 15 of the timeline in the new layer and press the *F6* key to add a new keyframe. We are now ready to add the field. Select the **Text** tool and use its modifiers to set the font size to 12 and the font to **Courier New**. Now click the **Text Field** modifier (Fig. 33.9) at the bottom of the modifier tool bar to convert the text box into a **Text Field**. After completing the **Text Field** modifications, click the mouse near the left edge of the stage and somewhere between the **GO** button and the title. You should now see a familiar text box. Stretch the box so it appears as in Fig. 33.17.

Before we begin scripting let us give the text field a variable name that we can use in the script. Use the **Arrow** tool to select the new text field, then right click it and select **Properties…** from the pop-up menu to display the **Text Field Properties** window. First, change the value of the **Variable** field to **advice**. Be sure to remember the names of your variables—you need them when scripting. Now check the box labeled **Disable editing** and uncheck the box labeled **Draw border and background** to make the field uneditable and invisible. Click **OK** to complete the text field. You should now see only a selection box in its place.

33.2.12 Adding ActionScripting

We have now completed the object development phase, so the program is almost complete. We now use Flash's scripting language, *ActionScript*, to add interactivity to the project.

Fig. 33.17 Creating a text field. (Courtesy of Macromedia, Inc.)

When we push the **GO** button, we want the text field to display a random message that will help a CEO make decisions. Therefore, we need to add actions to the button that change the text field in response to button click events. Our program will use a built-in Flash function to generate a random number. We will use that random number to select from a list of possible messages to display. Spaces, line breaks, and indentation have been added to all Flash ActionScript in the Chapter to conform with the program-layout conventions we have used thourghout the book. The code you produce in Flash will be formatted slightly differently by the application.

Make sure that you are working in frame 15 of **Button Layer** and right-click the **GO** button on the stage. Select **Properties...** from the pop-up menu. In the **Instance Properties** window that appears, click the tab labeled **Actions**. This is the window in which we add script functions to our symbols. Figure 33.18 shows the **Actions** window.

Fig. 33.18   Actions tab of the **Instance Properties** window. (Courtesy of Macromedia, Inc.)

We want the action to occur when the user clicks on the button with the mouse. To add the action click the Add Action button, which is the button labeled **+**. From the pop-up menu, select **OnMouseEvent**. Notice that the white text area now has the following two lines of code:

```
On ( )
End on
```

Now check the box labeled **Press** next to the text area (Fig. 33.18). The code now reads:

```
On ( Press )
End on
```

This code tells Flash that something should be done when the mouse button is pressed. Next, add the functionality to the button. Press the **+** button again. This time select **Set Variable**; this changes the code to read:

```
On ( Press )
Set Variable: "" = ""
End on
```

Set the field labeled **Variable** to `randomnumber`. The variable `randomnumber` is assigned a specific expression as its value. Click the small button next to the **Value** text field to set the variable equal to an expression. Select *Expression Editor* from the list, see Fig. 33.19. Ensure that the radio button labeled **Expression** is selected then scroll down the list labeled **Functions** and double-click **Random** to select it. Set the argument for **Random** by replacing the word **number** inside the parentheses with the number **5**. This tells the function to generate a number from zero to four. When using the random function with an argument of some number, n, remember that the values returned are in the range of 0 to n-1. Click **OK** to continue.

The code should now read

```
On ( Press )
   Set Variable: "randomnumber" = Random ( 5 )
End On
```

The code now performs a function when the **GO** button is pressed. Each time the user pushes the button, the value of the variable `randomnumber` is set to a new random number. We will now use the random number to change the text in the text field. `If/Else` statements allow us to determine the value of `randomnumber` and to set the text field's value accordingly. To add `If/Else` statements, press the **+** button and select **If** from the list. Your code should now appear as follows:

```
On ( Press )
   Set Variable: "randomnumber" = Random ( 5 )
   If ( )
   End If
End On
```

We will use nested `If` statements to cause different text to appear in the advice text field by testing the variable `randomnumber` in the `If` condition. We now have a single `If` statement in the code. In the text box labeled **Condition**, type in the statement:

```
randomnumber = 0
```

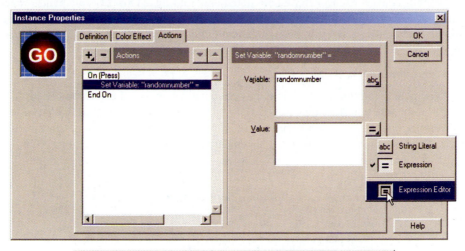

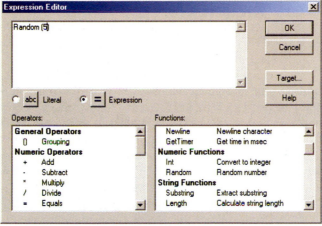

Fig. 33.19 Accessing the **Expression Editor**. (Courtesy of Macromedia, Inc.)

This causes the action in the **If** statement, which we will add later, to be performed only if **randomnumber** is equal to zero. Next, push the button labeled **Add Else\Else If clause** four times. We need five decisions in total because we need to perform one of five different actions depending on the value of the variable **randomnumber**. The code should appear as follows:

```
On ( Press )
    Set Variable: "randomnumber" = Random ( 5 )
    If ( randomnumber = 0 )
    Else
    Else
    Else
    Else
    End If
End On
```

We will convert each of the **Else** statements into an **Else If** statement to check **randomnumber**. Click the top **Else** in the code window. This will cause a few new attributes to be displayed. First, set the **Action** radio button to **Else If**, this allows us to give the statement a condition. Then set the condition to:

```
randomnumber = 1
```

This statement determines the action to be performed when **randomnumber** is given the value 1 by the function **Random**. Repeat this process for each one of the **Else** statements, incrementing the value of **randomnumber** each time. When you are done converting all of the **Else** statements to **Else If** statements and setting their conditions, your code should look like this:

```
On (Press)
    Set Variable: "randomnumber" = Random ( 5 )

    If ( randomnumber = 0 )
    Else If ( randomnumber = 1 )
    Else If ( randomnumber = 2 )
    Else If ( randomnumber = 3 )
    Else If ( randomnumber = 4 )
    End If
End On
```

We are now ready to add actions to the conditional statements. Click the code for the original **If** statement —**If (randomnumber = 0)**—and click the **+** button. Select **Set Variable** from the list. This is where the name of the text field becomes imporant. We called the text field **advice**, so set value of the **Variable** attribute to **advice**. Verify that the button next to the field labeled **Value** has **abc** written on it meaning that the value is a string; if not, change it. This tells Flash that the value we are assigning is a text string rather than an integer or expression. Now type the string **Hire Someone!** (do not use quotation marks) into the field labeled **Value,** Each time **randomnumber** is set to zero, the **advice** text field will read: **Hire Someone!**. Click each **Else** statement and add the **Set Variable** function. Your code should now resemble the following, though the advice you give may vary.

```
On ( Press )
    Set Variable: "randomnumber" = random( 5 )

    If ( randomnumber = 0 )
       Set Variable: "advice" = "Hire Someone!"
    Else If ( randomnumber = 1 )
       Set Variable: "advice" = "Buy a Yacht!"
    Else If ( randomnumber = 2 )
       Set Variable: "advice" = "Fire Someone!"
    Else If ( randomnumber = 3 )
       Set Variable: "advice" = "Go Golfing!"
    Else
       Set Variable: "advice" = "Hold A Meeting!"
    End If
End On
```

Of course, if you feel ambitious, you can increase the number of advice statements by making the argument for the **Random** function larger and adding more **Else If** statements. Click **OK** to continue. There is one important last step to complete before the movie will work—adding a `Stop` action into the movie's last frame to stop the movie and wait for user interaction. Double click Frame 15 of the timeline in any layer. In the **Frame Properties** window that opens, click the **Actions** tab and select **Stop** from the + menu.

Congratulations! You have now completed building the `CEO Assistant 1.0`. Press *Ctrl+Enter* to test your movie. When you are done close the test window. The previous sections should have given you an intermediate level understanding of many of Flash's features. The sections that follow should prepare you for more advanced Flash projects.

33.3 Creating a Projector (.exe) File Using Publish

We are now ready to create a Windows executable file (`.exe`) for the new movie. The **Publish** function in Flash is similar to the **Export** command in other programs, however it has more advanced features. For instance, choosing **Publish as HTML** outputs a Web page with your Flash movie embedded inside of it. For our purposes, we will only need to publish in three formats, Flash, HTML and *Windows Projector*. Select **Publish Settings...** from the **File** menu to create an executable. Click the check boxes corresponding to the three file types just mentioned and click **OK** to set the publishing settings. To publish the movie in all three formats click the **File** menu once again and select **Publish**. When the publish function is complete, you will have three new files in the directory in which you saved your movie. You can test the HTML file by opening it with a Web browser. The Windows Projector is an executable, so all you have to do is double click the `CeoAssistant.exe` file in Windows Explorer to run the program. Figure 33.20 shows the new Flash projector in action.

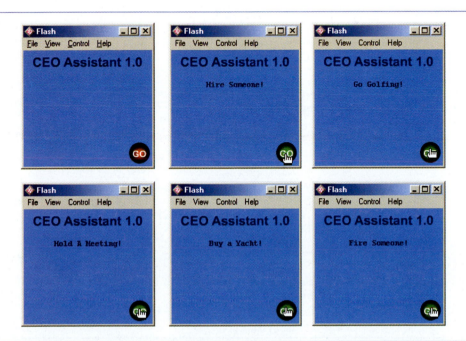

Fig. 33.20   The final **CEO Assistant 1.0** projector. (Courtesy of Macromedia, Inc.)

Flash is a feature-rich program. In our introductory treatment, we have discussed a few of these features. We have barely scratched the surface of scripting in Flash. ActionScript is a powerful scripting language that gives Flash the ability to create sophisticated programs and interactive movies. It even allows Flash to interact with Active Server Pages (Chapters 25 and 26), CGI (Chapter 29) and JavaScript (Chapters 13 through 18). For more information and for tutorials that helps you learn about ActionScripting and all other aspects of Flash, visit **www.flashaddict.com**.

33.4 Manually Embedding a Flash Movie in a Web page

Flash's interactive capabilities make it an attractive alternative to HTML. One of the most frustrating aspects of Web development is ensuring browser compatibility. Web sites written in HTML often render differently in different browsers. This is not the case with Flash movies. No matter which browser you use, as long as the Flash Player plug-in is supported, Flash movies appear as intended. There is one issue that can be a bit troublesome—to ensure that your Flash movie is visible in both Microsoft Internet Explorer and Netscape communicator, two different tags must be used in the same Web page. Like video and audio, Flash movies are added to a Web site with the **<OBJECT>** and **<EMBED>** tags. The **<OBJECT>** tag allows the movie to be seen using the Internet Explorer browser. The **<EMBED>** tag makes your movie viewable for Netscape users. Figure 33.21 provides source code for embedding Flash movies in a cross-platform manner.

```
1   <HTML>
2
3   <!-- Fig. 33.21: Embedding a Flash Movie into a Web site -->
4   <!-- ceoassist.html                                        -->
5
6   <!DOCTYPE HTML PUBLIC "-//W3C//DTD HTML 4.0 Transitional//EN">
7   <HTML>
8
9   <HEAD>
10  <TITLE>
11  Adding Flash to your Web site
12  </TITLE>
13  </HEAD>
14
15  <BODY>
16
17  <!-- The following OBJECT tag tells the Microsoft     -->
18  <!-- Internet Explorer browser to play the Flash Movie -->
19  <!-- and where to find the Flash Player plug-in if it  -->
20  <!-- is not installed.                                  -->
21
22  <OBJECT CLASSID = "clsid:D27CDB6E-AE6D-11cf-96B8-444553540000"
23  CODEBASE =
24  "http://download.macromedia.com/pub/shockwave/cabs
25  /flash/swflash.cab#version=4,0,2,0">
26  <PARAM NAME = "Movie" VALUE = "ceoassist.swf">
27
```

Fig. 33.21 Embedding a Flash Movie into a Web site (part 1 of 2).

```
28   <!-- The following EMBED tag tells the Netscape Navigator   -->
29   <!-- browser to play the Flash Movie and where to find the  -->
30   <!-- Flash Player plug-in if it is not installed.           -->
31
32   <EMBED SRC = "ceoassist.swf" PLUG-INSPAGE =
33   "http://www.macromedia.com/shockwave/download
34   /index.cgi?P1_Prod_Version=ShockwaveFlash">
35   </EMBED>
36
37   <NOEMBED>
38   This Web site contains the CEO Assistant 1.0 Flash movie.
39   You must have the Flash PLayer plug-in to see the Flash movie.
40   </NOEMBED>
41
42   </OBJECT>
43
44   </BODY>
45   </HTML>
```

Fig. 33.21 Embedding a Flash Movie into a Web site (part 2 of 2).

As you can see in Fig 33.21, the **<OBJECT>** tag has several attributes. The **CLASSID** and **CODEBASE** parameters must appear exactly as shown to embed the movie properly. **CODEBASE** allows users to be prompted to download the plug-in if they do not have it. It is also important to be sure that you place the **<EMBED>** tag inside the **<OBJECT>** tag. Microsoft Internet Explorer ignores tags placed inside the **<OBJECT>** tag. Netscape only reads the **<EMBED>** tag; it ignores the **<OBJECT>** information.

Earlier in this chapter, we mentioned using JavaScript to reroute visitors based on their browsers or even based on which plug-ins they use. There are alternatives to rerouting users. In Fig. 33.21, the **<NOEMBED>** tag (lines 37–40)provides alternative content. Any HTML elements can be placed within the **<NOEMBED>** section of the site.

33.5 Using Flash for Special Effects

The following sections introduce a variety of special effects you can get with Flash's more advanced capabilities. We assume that you completed the earlier examples and now have a solid understand of basic Flash development. We cover many topics from importing bitmaps to building a storefront.

33.5.1 Importing and Manipulating Bitmaps

Some of the later examples require you to import bitmap images and other media. We import images in this example, but the process is the same for all types of media, including sound and video. To begin, insert the CD-ROM that came with this book. Open Flash and start a new movie. Click **Import...** under the **File** menu and use the directory structure in the resulting **Import** window to navigate to your CD-ROM drive. Once there, open the **Examples** folder and click the **ch33** folder within it. Finally, open the folder labeled **ImportDemo** and select **bug.bmp**. Click **OK** to continue. You should now see the image of the bug on your stage. Images are imported as graphic symbols and can be accessed from the library as well. You can convert the imported bitmap into a shape by selecting it and pressing *Ctrl + B* or by choosing **Break Apart** from the **Modify** menu. After breaking the image apart, it is editable. You can apply shape tweening, select portions of it with the **Lasso** tool or even make use of the **Magic Wand** modifier of the **Lasso** tool to select portions of a shape based on color. For example, you could select just the bug's right wing simply by clicking it with the **Lasso** tool while the **Magic Wand** modifier is activated.

33.5.2 Using Masking to Create an Advertisement Banner

Masking can be used to add animation and color effects to your text, it is used to hide sections of a layer. The masking layer hides objects in the layer directly below it, while the layers underneath the layer being masked remain visible. In this example, we will build a banner that can be placed on a Web site for advertising purposes.

Open a new movie and set the size of the movie to 470 pixels wide by 60 pixels high using the **Movie Properties** window (**Movie...** in the **Modify** menu). Most users have computer monitors with screen resolutions of 640-by-480 or higher. Choosing a size of 470-by-60 pixels enables most users to see the entire banner.

Portability Tip 33.1

Build your Flash movies and other Web-based multimedia using the smallest possible size and web-safe colors, which are recognized by all browsers, while still preserving the intended look and feel. This ensures that the maximum number of people are able to view your work.

To create the masking effect you need to add two layers to the movie, making a total of three layers. Name the layers **top**, **middle** and **bottom**. This will help you to keep track of which layer is being masked and which layer is going to stay visible. For this example, import a graphic of our bug using the method discussed in section 33.5.1. This time choose the **Banner** folder in the **ch33** folder. Inside the folder you will find a file named **Logo.gif**. Import the graphic into frame 1 of the **top** layer. Resize it using the **Scale** modifier of the **Arrow** tool and move the image to the left side of the banner in the **top** layer. Next, use the **Text** tool to add text to your banner. Add your choice of text to the right side of the banner. Use any of the text modifiers you like, but be sure that the text fits inside the banner. Next, right click frame 1 of the **top** layer and select **Copy Frames**. Now, add a keyframe in frame 1 of the layer named **bottom**. Finally, right click frame 1 of the bottom layer again and select **Paste Frames** from the menu. This will duplicate the contents of frame1 of the **top** layer and put them in the first frame of the **bottom** layer.

In the middle layer, add a colorful animated graphic to change the look of the banner. In the first frame of the middle layer, use the **Oval** tool to draw a circle that is taller than the text (it does not have to fit inside the banner). Use the **Paint Bucket** tool to add color to the circle. We used the **Gradient Palette** to make a rainbow-colored circle (Fig. 33.22). Select the circle by double-clicking it with the **Arrow** tool and convert it to a graphic symbol by pressing *F8*. Name the symbol **circle**.

Now we will make the circle traverse the stage. Using the **Arrow** tool, move the circle and place it just outside the left edge of the stage. Next, place a keyframe in frame 20 and another in frame 40. Select frame 20 and move the circle just outside the right side of the banner. This frame will serve as the midpoint of the symbols animation. Now, double click frame 1 of the **middle** layer and chose **Motion** from the **Tweening** drop-down menu of the **Tweening** tab. Do this again for frame 20 of the **middle** layer. This makes the ball move from left to right and back.

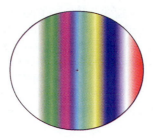

Fig. 33.22   The `circle` graphic. (Courtesy of Macromedia, Inc.)

Now that all of the supporting effects are in place, the **Masking** effect can by applied. Adding this effect is actually quite simple. Double click the paper sheet icon next to the label of the **top** layer (Fig. 33.23). This opens the **Layer Properties** window. Select the **Mask** radio button and click **OK**. The icon changes to one picturing a down-pointing purple arrow inside a white circle (Fig. 33.23). Next, click the paper icon in the **middle** layer. This time select the **Masked** radio button and click **OK**. This adds an icon picturing a white arrow enclosed in a purple circle (Fig. 33.23). These two icons indicate that the **middle** layer is now being masked by the **top** layer. Place a keyframe in frame 40 of both the **top** layer and the **bottom** layer to keep the bug graphic and the text present throughout the movie.The banner is now complete, click the main stage with the **Arrow** tool and press *Control + Enter* to play your movie and see the masking effect. Figure 33.24 displays the completed banner.

33.5.3 Adding Online Help to Your Forms

This example will cover adding online help to your forms. It uses motion tweening, shape tweening, basic scripting, graphic symbols and movie clip symbols. To save space we do not implement the forms in this section. Implementing forms is covered in depth in section 33.6, where you build an online storefront. Instead, this section provides you with an introduction to movie clips.

Fig. 33.23   Unmasked layers and masked layers. (Courtesy of Macromedia, Inc.)

Fig. 33.24   Completed banner. (Courtesy of Macromedia, Inc.)

Create a new Flash movie and use the **Movie Properties** dialog to adjust its height to 250 pixels. Do not change its width. Zoom in with the **Magnifier** tool, if necessary, to make working on the small stage easier. Rename **Layer 1** to `text`. Before building the shapes and symbols that are used in the project, add a `Stop` action to the current frame. Right click frame 1 of the **text** layer and select **Properties**. Click the **Actions** tab and add the `Stop` action (see section 33.2.12). Click **OK** to begin creating the movie.

Next, we will add some static text to the movie. First, give the form a title. In the example, we used multiple text boxes and called our form `Bug2Bug.com Registration Form`. Now add field labels to the form. Use the modifiers to alter the text style to your preferences and add three labels. They should read **Name:**, **Member#:** and **Password:**. Align the text as we did in Fig. 33.25.

Next, create a graphic symbol to take the place of what would normally be a form field. First, create a new layer and name it `Form`. In the new layer, draw a rectangle anywhere on the stage with roughly the same height as the label's text. We rounded the corners and used use a blue color, but you may wish to experiment withother shapes and colors. Use the arrow tool to select your completed rectangle (see Section 3.2.11) and select **Group** from the **Modify** menu. This groups the rectangle's fill and border into one object. Next, press *Ctrl + C (*or select **Copy** from the **Edit** menu*)* to copy the object, then press *Ctrl + V* (or select **Paste** from the **Edit** menu) twice. This places two more rectangles on the stage. Align the rectangles next to the three labels as shown in Fig. 33.26.

Next, you will create the help buttons. First, add a new layer and call it **helpButtons**. Use shapes and text to create a button. We made ours by creating a circle containing a question mark. Once your button looks the way you want it, select all of its pieces and press the *F8* key or select **Convert to Symbol...** from the **Insert** menu, to open the **Symbol Properties** dialog box. Check the radio button labeled **Button** and name the symbol `helpButton`. Right click the new help button symbol and select **Properties** from the pop-up menu. Then select the actions tab on the resulting window. Using the techniques discussed in Section 33.2.12, add the following ActionScripting to the button:

```
On ( Release )
Go to and Stop ( 2 )
End On
```

This scripting causes the movie to advance to frame 2. This is necessary because the `Stop` action that was added earlier prevents us from moving on automatically. Click **OK** to return to the stage. Now duplicate the button by selecting and copying it as we did with the rectangle. Paste two additional copies and place them to the right of each of the rectangles (Fig. 33.27).

Now, change the actions for the buttons associated with the **Member#** and **Password**. Set the action for the **Member#** field help button to:

```
On ( Release )
   Go to and Stop ( 3 )
End On
```

Set the action for the **Password** help button to:

```
On ( Release )
   Go to and Stop ( 4 )
End On
```

Bug2Bug.com

Registration Form

Name:

Member#:

Password:

Fig. 33.25 Form's **text** layer. (Courtesy of Macromedia, Inc.)

Bug2Bug.com

Registration Form

Name:

Member#:

Password:

Fig. 33.26 Transformation of help window. (Courtesy of Macromedia, Inc.)

Bug2Bug.com

Registration Form

Name:

Member#:

Password:

Fig. 33.27 The form with help buttons. (Courtesy of Macromedia, Inc.)

All three buttons now have actions that point to frames two, three and four, though these frames have yet to be created yet. Next, we will build the movie clips that fill those frames. Select **New Symbol...** from the **Insert** menu and name the symbol **nameWindow**. Be sure to select the **Movie Clip** radio button. Pressing **OK** opens the movie clip's stage and timeline. Use the rectangle tool to create a colored rectangle with no border. It does not matter how big the rectangle is, as it can be adjusted. Use the **Arrow** tool to select the new rectangle and open the **Object Inspector**. Now, resize the rectangle and position it on the stage using the **Object Inspector**. Set the **w** field in the inspector to 230; set the **h** field to 120. Click the **Use Center Point** checkbox to activate it and set both the **x** and **y** fields to 0.0. Press **Apply** to set the changes but do not close the inspector. Your rectangle should now be centered and has probably changed size. Now, add keyframes in frames 5 and 10. Click the **Apply** button in the **Object Inspector** once more to set the values for these frames. Click frame 5 to activate it and click the **Apply** button in the object inspector to activate the settings for the frame and set the height of the rectangle to 5.0. You may notice that the **y** value has changed. Set it back to 0.0. Now, right click frame 5 in the timeline and select **Copy Frames**. Right click frame 1 and select **Paste Frames**. While in frame 1, set the **y** value in the **Object Inspector** to **0.0** and the **w** to 5.0 and press the **Apply** button.

Now, we are ready to apply shape tweening to frames 1 and 5. Right click the frames and select **Properties...** from the pop-up menu. Click the **Tweening** tab and select **Shape** from the **Tweening** pull-down list. Then click **OK**. Figure 33.28 illustrates the way your rectangle should appear in frames 1, 5 and 10.

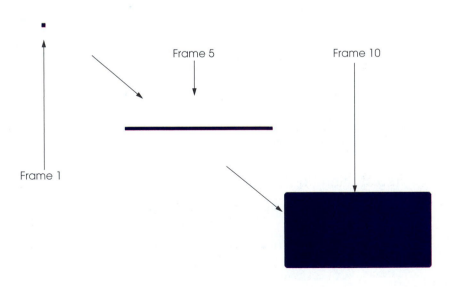

Frame 5   Frame 10

Frame 1

Fig. 33.28 Shape tweening for the help window. (Courtesy of Macromedia, Inc.)

Next, we will animate the rectangle. Rename the layer that contains the shapes we just tweened to **background** and add two new layers. Name the new layers **fieldLayer** and **text**. Add a keyframe to the **fieldLayer** and **background** layers in frame 10. While you are there, drag the `field` symbol we created into **fieldLayer**. Align the `field` symbol with the top left of the background rectangle as shown in Fig 33.29. Add a keyframe to both the **fieldLayer** and **background** layers in frame 40. Now, add more keyframes to **fieldLayer** in frames 20 and 25. Then, click frame 20 and open the **Transform Inspector**, by clicking **Transform** in the **Inspector** section of the **Window** menu. Click the `field` symbol and scale it to 150% of its size using the inspector. Now, click frame ten of the same layer and set the scale of the `field` symbol to 0%. Right click frames 10 and 20 and select **Create Motion Tween** from the pop-up menu for each. Lastly, add a keyframe to frame 40 in **fieldLayer**. See Fig. 33.29 for an illustration of the `nameWindow` movie clip after adding the `field` symbol.

Now add text to the movie clip. Add a keyframe in frame 25 of the **text** layer. Use the **Text** tool to add a label and description to the help window. Add another keyframe to the layer in frame 40. The three movie clips with the added text are shown in Fig. 33.30.

Next, open the project library by clicking on **Library** in the **Window** menu and right click the `nameWindow` movie clip. Select **Duplicate** from the pop-up menu and name the new clip `passwordWindow`. Duplicate it again, but this time call it `memberWindow`. Change the text in each movie clip's `text` layer to reflect the frames being described. In other words, `passwordMovie`'s text should label and describe the password field. After doing so you will be ready to add the last segment to each of the movie clips.

Double click the `nameMovie` movie clip in the project's library. Add a new layer to its timeline called **typedText**. Add a keyframe to the layer in frame 25 and add a text box on top of the field symbol, as demonstrated in Fig. 33.31.

Fig. 33.29 The `nameWindow` movie clip. (Courtesy of Macromedia, Inc.)

The Name field	The Member# field	The Password field
Type your first and last name into this field. We will use it to keep track of your orders.	Type your unique member number into this field. The default is 5551212. You will be able to change it later.	Type your desired password into this field. The default is newbie It can be changed later.

Fig. 33.30 The `nameWindow` movie clip with text descriptions. (Courtesy of Macromedia, Inc.)

Fig. 33.31   Adding a text box to the name field. (Courtesy of Macromedia, Inc.)

Type the name **Jon Doe** in the text box. Now add a keyframe to frame 40. To create the appearance of the name being typed into the field symbol, add keyframes in frames 26 through 31, then click the **Jon Doe** text in frame 25 and delete everything but the first **J**. In frame 26, delete all of the characters except the **J** and the **o**. Do this for each of the layers leaving one more letter each time. Frame 31 should show the entire name.

Repeat this process for the other two movie clips, using suitable words. In the example, we placed six asterisks in the **passwordWindow** movie clip and seven numbers in the movie clip we named **memberWindow**. You must also add a **Stop** action to frame 40 of all three of the movie clips.

The movie clips are now ready to be added to the main movie. Click the tab labeled **Scene 1** above the timeline to return to the main movie. Add the following layers to the timeline: **nameMovie, memberMovie** and **passwordMovie**, in that order. Add a keyframe in frame 2 of every layer. Click the **nameMovie** layer and drag the **nameWindow** movie clip onto the stage. Use the **Object Inspector** to set its **x** value to 340 and its **y** value to 175. Next, click the **memberMovie** layer and add a keyframe in frame 3. Also add keyframes to frame 3 of the **form**, **text** and **helpButtons** layers. Drag the **member-Window** movie clip to the stage in that layer and frame. Set its **x** and **y** location to 340 and 175, respectively. Finally, add a keyframe to frame 4 of the **passwordMovie** layer and the **form**, **text** and **helpButtons** layers. Drag the **passwordWindow** movie clip to the stage and set its **x** and **y** location to 340 and 175.

Your movie is now complete. Press *Ctrl + Enter* to preview it. In the example, we decorated the movie by adding a picture of a bug in a new layer and lowering its **Alpha** value which fades the colors. Be creative when decorating your movie. The final movie is pictured in Fig. 33.32.

Our movie can be found on the accompanying CD by going into the **Examples, ch33** and finally the **FormDemo** folder. After doing so choose **Open as Library...** from the **File** menu. This allows you to open the library of the movie and use the symbols we created.

33.5.4 Adding Sound

Several media libraries are included with Flash, one of which contains sound effects. The *Sound library* can be opened by clicking **Sound** in the **Libraries** menu. The library has several sound effects that can be played as a result of mouse events or that can be embedded in frames. If a sound is embedded in a frame it will be played when the frame is displayed. We will step you through adding sound to a button, so that when the button is pressed the sound effect is played.

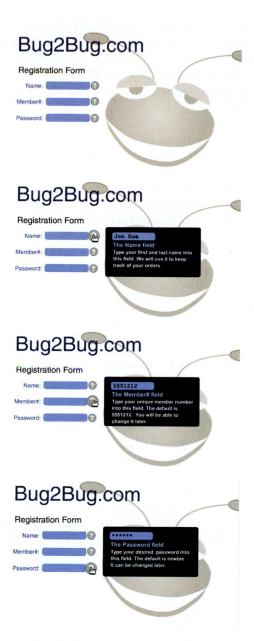

Fig. 33.32 Form help movie in all states. (Courtesy of Macromedia, Inc.)

Open a new movie and place a button on the main stage. In out example, we used a generic button from the Flash button library. Instead of using a Flash button, you can import your own button and follow the same steps. You can access the Flash buttons by opening the ***Button*** *library* found on the **Libraries** menu. Choose the button you want to use, then drag and drop it onto the main stage. The buttons in the library have predefined up, over and down states. To add a sound effect, open the **Edit Symbol** window. To open this window select the button and choose **Edit Symbols** from the **Edit window**.

In the **Edit Symbols** window, add a new layer to your button and name it **Sound Effect**. Click the **Down** frame in the **Sound Effect** layer and add a keyframe by pressing *F6*. Now, to make the sound effects available for later use transfer them from the **Flash** library to the **Project** library. The difference between the two is that the sounds that are in the **Flash** library are part of the software. The sounds in the **Project** library are ones we may have imported or borrowed from the **Flash** library. Open the **Flash** sounds library by clicking **Sounds** on the **Libraries** menu. Open the **Project** library by clicking **Library** on the **Window** menu. Drag and drop the sounds from the **Flash** library to the **Project** library to transfer the sounds from one library to the next (Fig. 33.33). To add the sound effect to your button, double-click the **Down** frame in the **Sound Effect** layer (or highlight the frame by clicking it once), then choose **Frame** from the **Modify** menu.

The **Frame Properties** window has four tabs. Choose the **Sound** tab and from the **Sound** drop-down menu choose the sound effect you want to add to your button; make sure that the **Sync** field is set to **Event** (Fig. 33.34). After clicking **OK**, pressing the button will play the sound effect. You can see that the effect has been added to your button by looking at the **Down** frame of the **Sound Effect** layer. It should have a blue wave form image in it (Fig. 33.35).

There are many other uses of sound effects. For example, instead of placing the sound effect in the **Down** frame, you can place it in the **Over** frame. Doing so will cause the sound effect to be played when the mouse moves over the button. Additionally, it is possible to have a music loop play as a result of a mouse event. Unfortunately, Flash does not provide music loops with its software. There are sites on the Internet that have sound loops available for download such as Flash Kit (**www.flashkit.com**). You can import sound loops into your Flash movie by choosing **Import** from the **File** menu. Imported sound loops become part of the **Project** library. To add a music loop to a button, follow the same steps outlines for adding a standard sound effect.

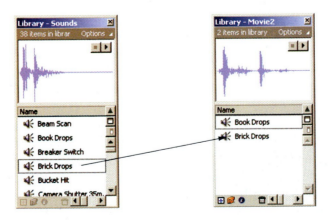

Fig. 33.33 Flash library and Project library. (Courtesy of Macromedia, Inc.)

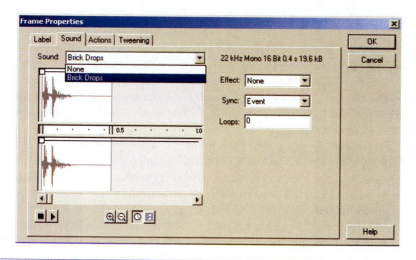

Fig. 33.34   **Frame Properties** window. (Courtesy of Macromedia, Inc.)

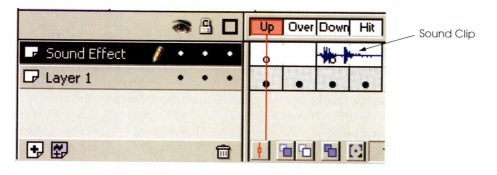

Fig. 33.35   Button layers with sound effect. (Courtesy of Macromedia, Inc.)

33.5.5 Creating a Web-Site Introduction

As you know, Flash is becoming an important part of e-Business. Many organizations use it for Web-site introductions, product demos or Web applications. Others use it to build games and other entertaining movies in an effort to attract new visitors. Waiting for Web pages to load often causes visitors—especially those with slow modems—to grow impatient and leave the site. One way to solve this problem is to entertain visitors with a site introduction built with Flash. Flash makes it possible to produce impressive animations that are surprisingly small in file size. A Flash animation can be downloaded quickly while the user is waiting for the rest of the page to load. Such pages are the Web-based equivalent of television commercials. If done well, these movies serve a dual purpose, they keep people at the site and help them forget that they are waiting. The following example demonstrates how to build one of these valuable movies.

Creating Three-Dimensional Numbers With Flash
One of the hottest trends in Flash is simulating three-dimensional graphics. One technique for doing this is to use a product specifically designed to create 3D objects and animations for Flash, such as Swift3d (**www.swift3d.com**) from Electronic Rain. This product allows the developer to create original 3D models or import them from other 3D modeling software such as Autodesk® Discreet™ 3D Studio Max™ (**www2.discreet.com/products/products.html?prod=3dsmax**) and Adobe®Illustrator™ (**www.adobe.com/products/illustrator/main.html**). Models imported into Swift3D are converted into vector graphics and can be exported in Flash format. Another option is to import Adobe Illustrator files or bitmap images directly into Flash. For example, animations created in many 3D modeling products can be exported as individual frames in bitmap format. These frames can then be imported into Flash and converted into vector-graphic animations. 3D animations can also be simulated directly in Flash. The following example illustrates how one can create three-dimensional symbols using Flash's built in drawing and text tools.

We use the **Text** tool, **Line** tool, **Arrow** tool, **Ink Bottle** tool and **Paint Bucket** tool, as well as graphic and movie-clip symbols and motion tweening in this example. You should be familiar with all of these having completed the **CEO Assistant** program and **Form Help** example. The three-dimensional numbers that we are going to create are used in a countdown animation.

First set the stage to 550 pixels by 400 pixels and set the background color to black using the **Movie Properties** dialog box. Next, using white, 72-point, Bold, Arial font, type the number 3 anywhere on the stage. Select the white number using the **Arrow** tool and press *Ctrl+B* to break it apart. By breaking apart the number, you have converted it into a shape. Now use the **Ink Bottle** tool to add a solid white border with thickness set at 1.0. Make sure that only the fill is selected and delete it—if you accidentally delete the border select **Undo** from the **Edit** menu. After deleting the fill, you should see only the outline of the number 3.

Double click the outline with the **Arrow** tool and press the *F8* key. Pressing *F8* opens the **Symbol Properties** dialog box. Name the symbol **three** and be sure that the radio button labeled **Graphic** is selected. Press **OK** to continue.

Now, we make a *wireframe* or image displaying only the outline of the three-dimensional number. Begin by right clicking in the symbol and selecting **Edit** from the popup menu. When the **Edit** window opens, make sure the border is selected. Open the **Transform Inspector** and scale the number by 500%. Do not forget to press **Apply** to apply the scaling transformation, as shown in Fig. 33.36.

Now we give the number depth to make it appear to be three-dimensional. Copy and paste the image so there are now two instances on the stage. You are not able to see the new number 3 that you pasted, because it is directly on top of the original one. Move the new number down and to the right of the original as shown in Fig. 33.37.

Now connect all of the corners of the two numbers as shown in Fig. 33.38. Using Flash's **Snap** feature makes this job much easier. Select **Snap** in the **View** menu to activate the **Snap** feature. The **Snap** feature attempts to place the line's endpoint at a logical location on the second shape. For instance, if you click the corner of the upper number while using the line tool and move the cursor near the corresponding position on the number to the lower right, the **Snap** feature automatically moves the line to the corner. This ensures that the lines are straight and that there are no gaps between connection points.

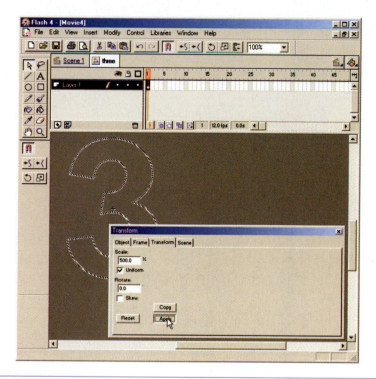

Fig. 33.36 Using the **Transform Inspector** to scale the symbol by 500%. (Courtesy of Macromedia, Inc.)

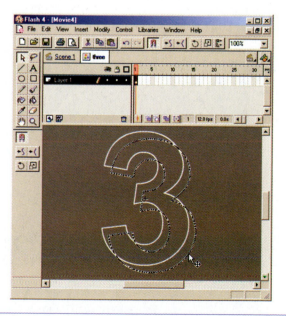

Fig. 33.37 Copying, pasting and moving the symbol to create the illusion of depth. (Courtesy of Macromedia, Inc.)

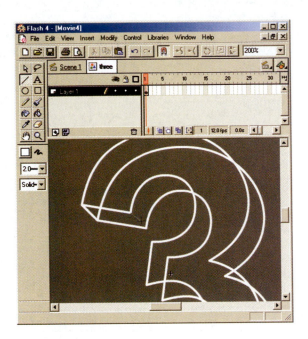

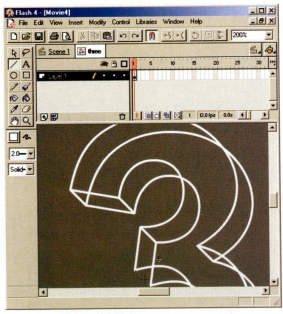

Fig. 33.38   Connecting shapes to create a wireframe. (Courtesy of Macromedia, Inc.)

After you have connected all seven corners you should now see what appears to be a wireframe of the number three. See Fig. 33.39 for an example of the wireframe. It may look a bit odd until the unneeded lines are deleted.

Adding a gradient fill to your image will create the illusion of three dimensions. the gradient fill should be added to a copy of the symbol which will require having one copy of the filled object and one of the unfilled object. This is to prepare for a future animation. To begin, choose **Select All** from the **Edit Menu** then copy the image.

Next, we create two more versions of the three-dimensional number. One retains some of the white border and is filled with a gradient. The other does not have a border. Open the **Library** by pressing *Ctrl+L* or by choosing **Library** from the **Window** menu. Right click the graphic symbol we called `three` and select **Duplicate**. Name the new symbol `threefilled`. Double click the symbol name in the library window, to ensure you are ready to edit. This brings the `threefilled` symbol into edit mode.

Common Programming Error 33.1

If you duplicate a symbol in the library while in edit mode, you must double click it before it shows up in the edit window. Forgetting to do so causes you to edit the original symbol.

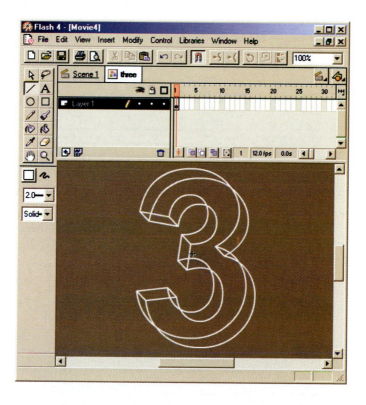

Fig. 33.39 Completed wireframe. (Courtesy of Macromedia, Inc.)

We are now ready to edit the new symbol. The first step is to delete the lines that should not be seen through the faces. See Fig. 33.40 for an example of how the symbol should look after deleting all of the unwanted lines. After deleting the lines, activate the **Paint Bucket** tool, set its fill color to the red gradient, and fill in all the faces of the number. Click the upper-right of each face to give the illusion of a common light source. When you are finished, our number should appear like the one pictured in Fig. 33.41. If it does not, apply the gradient again. The filled symbol is now complete. Duplicate this symbol just as you did the previous one. Name the new graphic symbol **threenolines**.

To complete the third symbol only one change needs to be made. Using the **Arrow** tool, double click the white border of the number and press the *Delete* key. If any of the border remains, repeat the last step. When there is no border left, your last symbol is finished and should appear like the one in Fig. 33.42.

Repeat the process for the numbers 1 and 2. When you are done you should have nine graphic symbols in your **Library**. Each number should have three symbols.

Creating a Movie Clip Symbol

Create a new symbol and name the movie clip **threemov**. The **Edit** window that results should have a complete timeline. First, double click the **Layer 1** label and rename the layer **wireframe**. Next, drag the symbol **three** onto the stage. While the symbol is still selected, center it by selecting **Align...** from the **Modify** menu. You should see various buttons dealing with the alignment and distribution of objects. Activate the buttons associated with horizontal and vertical center alignment (see Fig. 39.43) and make sure that the **Align to page** checkbox is checked. Click **OK** to continue. The symbol should now be centered.

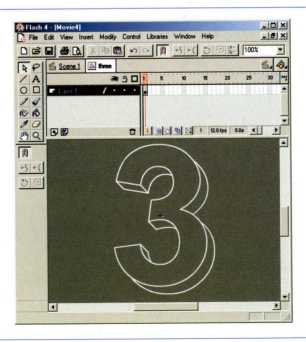

Fig. 33.40 3D shape after deleting all lines that should not be visible. (Courtesy of Macromedia, Inc.)

Fig. 33.41 3D shape with remaining wireframe border and gradient fill. (Courtesy of Macromedia, Inc.)

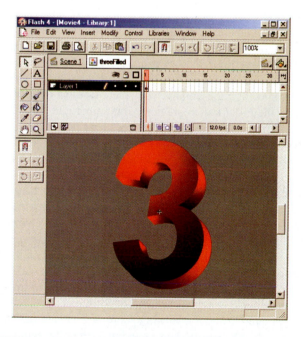

Fig. 33.42 The **threeNoLines** symbol after deleting the border. (Courtesy of Macromedia, Inc.)

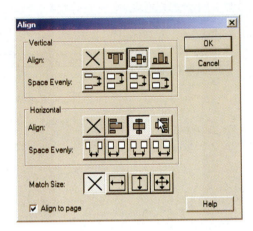

Fig. 33.43   **Align** dialog box set to center an object on the stage. (Courtesy of Macromedia, Inc.)

Click frame 20 and press *F6* to insert a new keyframe. This sets the end point for the first 20 frames of animation. Now, alter frame 1 and add a motion "tween" to the sequence. Click frame 1 in the timeline. Click the **three** symbol to be sure that it is selected and use the **Transform Inspector** to scale the symbol to 1500% of its original size. You should now be able to see only a small section of the middle of the number.

Next add the fade effect to your graphics; to do so, double click one of the symbols and when the **Instance Properties** window opens, go to the **Color Effects** tab and select **Alpha**. Set the **Alpha** slider to 0 and Click **OK**; this makes the graphic completely transparent. Right click frame 10 in the timeline and select **Create Motion Tween** from the resulting menu. Press the *Enter* key to preview your animation. Add another keyframe in frame 30 to prepare for the next animation sequence. This causes the wireframe version to remain on stage for ten frames. Add another keyframe at frame 40. In frame 40 set the **Alpha** of the **three** symbol to 0. Tween the frames between 30 and 40. Doing this causes your 3 to fade away over 10 frames.

Next, add the **threefilled** symbol in a new layer. Select **Layer** from the **Insert** menu. You should now see a layer labeled **Layer 2** above the **wireframe** layer. Rename this layer **fill**. Now, add a keyframe in **fill**'s 25th frame. Drag the **threefilled** symbol onto the stage while frame 25 of the **fill** layer is selected. Align the symbol just as we did with the **three** symbol. Add keyframes at frames 45, 55 and 65 in the **fill** layer. Set the **Alpha** of the **threefilled** symbol into frames 25 and 65 to 0. Add motion tweens to the frames between 25 and 45, and 55 and 65. Press the *Enter* key again to preview the animation. The wireframe should appear to be filled over time.

Add another layer and rename it **nolines** to complete the animation. Add a keyframe to frame 50 and drag in the **threenolines** symbol. Center the symbol as we did earlier. Add keyframes at frames 70, 80 and 90 and set the **Alpha** of the symbol to 0 in frames 50 and 90. Lastly, add tweening between frames 50 and 70. Do the same for the frames between 80 and 90. Repeat the entire process two more times to create two additional movie clips. Use the symbols of the number 2 for one of them and the symbols of the number 1 for the other. Name them **twomov** and **onemov**, respectively. Together the three movie clips are used to make a countdown.

When the movie clips are placed on the main stage, they are allotted one frame each. We must add a **Stop** action to each frame in the main movie that contains a movie clip. This will allow each movie clip to be able to play to completion. Actions must then be added to the last frame of each movie clip to advance the main movie. Double click frame 90 of the **nolines** layer; this brings up the **Frame Properties** window. Click the **Action** tab to add the actions. From the **+** drop-down menu, choose **Tell Target** and enter **/** to the **Target** field. The **/** is an indicator thta tells Flash to expect a name of a movie. Go back to the **+** drop down menu and select **Go To**. Click the **Next Frame** radio button on the right. Adding these actions to each of the three movie clips cause them to inform the main movie to continue to the next frame and play when they are finished playing. The following code should be added to the last frame of each of the movie clips.

```
Begin Tell Target ("/")
Go to Next Frame
End Tell Target
```

Getting back to the introduction movie, name the first layer of the movie **SkipIntro**. Because not all visitors will want to see the movie, we create a button that allows them to bypass the movie and access the Web site. From the **Insert** menu, choose **New symbol** to create a new button. Name the button **Skip**. Build a button consisting of a circle with the text **Skip Intro** (Fig. 33.44) and return to the main stage. Open the library by choosing **Library** from the **Window** drop-down menu. Do not close the window. Click the first frame of the timeline and place the button you just created on the main stage in the lower right corner. We would like clicking the button to bring the user to the Deitel & Associates, Inc. Web site. Double click the button to bring up the **Instance Properties** window. Click the **Action** tab and then the **+** button to open the **Actions** drop-down menu. From the list choose **Get URL** and in the **URL** field on the right, type the URL for the Deitel Web site— **www.deitel.com**. Click **OK** to return to the main stage. Once we finish building the introduction, place a keyframe in the **SkipIntro** layer at the end of the movie that keeps the button on the screen throughout the intro.

Fig. 33.44   The **Skip Intro** button. (Courtesy of Macromedia, Inc.)

We want to begin the intro with a countdown using the 3D number movie clips we built. Add three layers above the **SkipIntro** layer. Name the top layer **one**, the middle layer **two** and the bottom layer **three**. Click the second frame in the **three** layer and press *F5* to insert a blank frame. While in frame 2, drag the movie named **threemov** on to the main stage from the **Library** window. Although the movie clip takes 90 frames to complete, we do not need to allot 90 frames to the movie clip. We simply put the movie in the second frame and add a **Stop** action to the frame. This holds the movie in frame 2 until told to do otherwise by the code just added to the end of the movie clips. Double click the frame, click the **Action** tab in the resulting **Frame Properties** window and select **Stop** from the **+** menu to add the **Stop** action. To complete the countdown we need to do the same for the **Twomov** and the **Onemov**. Place the movies in their respective layers. **Twomov**, should be placed in frame three and **Onemov** should be placed in frame four (Fig. 33.45).

The next feature to be added will make three of the Deitel book covers spin and fade into the screen. Add a layer to your movie above the **one** layer named **internetCover**. Place a keyframe in frame 5 of the **internetCover** layer. Before adding any actions to the graphic, we need to import it into the movie. From the **File** menu choose **Import**. When the **Import** window opens, navigate through the directories to find the graphic called **iw3htp.jpg** located in the **Welcome** folder in the chapter 33 examples section of the CD that accompanies this book. When the graphic appears, resize it to fit the stage using the **Transform Inspector**. Use the **Align** tool to center the image on the stage as illustrated in Fig. 33.43. Place a keyframe in frame 25. Click frame 5 to highlight the graphic of the book cover. Shrink the book cover down to 2% of its original size using the **Transform** inspector. This makes the graphic a small dot on the stage. Use the **Arrow** tool to drag the tiny graphic off the upper-left corner of the stage and double click frame 5 to bring up the **Instance Properties** window. From the **Tweening** tab choose **Motion** from the drop-down menu. Choose **ClockWise** from the **Rotate** drop-down menu and set the number of rotations to 5 (Fig. 33.46). This gives the effect of the book cover spinning into the screen. Before the next book cover comes spinning onto the screen, we want to make the first book cover fade away. To do this for the *Internet and World Wide Web How To Program* cover, place keyframes in frames 35 and 45. Click frame 45 and then double click the image of the book cover which is on the main stage. This brings up the **Instance Properties** window. Set the symbols **Alpha** value to zero and click **OK** to make it transparent.

Add two more layers to the movie above the **internetCover** layer. Name the top layer **cCover** for the *C How To Program: Third Edition* book cover and name the other layer **javaCover** for the *JAVA How To Program: Third Edition* book cover. Repeat the steps you just used to make the *Internet and World Wide Web How To Program* book cover fly into the center of the screen to make the other two book covers do the same. Start each of the book animations in the exact frame where the proceeding book animation ends. For instance, the *Internet and World Wide Web How To Program* cover animation ends on frame 45, so start the *C How To Program: Third Edition* animation in that frame. To complete each process add four keyframes in each layer, import the images and resize and tween them between the first two keyframes (to spin them onto the stage) and the last two keyframes (to make them fade off the screen). Instead of having all three covers fly in from the left, make the *JAVA How To Program* cover fly in from the right and the *C How To Program: Third Edition* cover fly in from the center. No matter which direction they fly in, they should all finish centered on the stage.

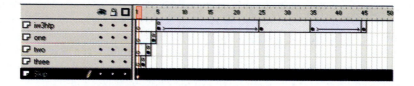

Fig. 33.45 Time line showing the **one, two** and **three** layers with stop actions. (Courtesy of Macromedia, Inc.)

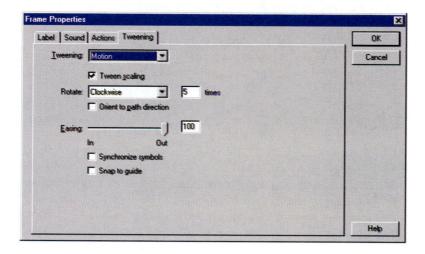

Fig. 33.46 **Tweening** window showing motion tweening with rotation. (Courtesy of Macromedia, Inc.)

Next add a graphic of the Deitel Bug. Once again, add another layer and call it **bug**. Add a keyframe at frame 125 (this should be the last keyframe of your **cCover** layer) and import the image of the bug, called **bug.bmp** which is also located in the **Welcome** folder in the Chapter 33 examples section of the accompanying CD. Size it to fit the stage using the **Transform Inspector** and center it on the stage. Add a keyframe further down the layer in frame 130. Go back to frame 125 and double click the image of the bug. Set the alpha to zero on the **Alpha** window and click **OK**. Double click the first frame of the bug layer and choose **Motion** from the drop-down menu on the **Tween** tab. This gives the bug image the effect of fading onto the screen. Place a keyframe in frame 150, resize the bug to make it smaller and move it to the top of the stage. Place a motion tween in frame 130. This will make the bug graphic move from the center of the stage to the top and also make it smaller. This gets it out of the way for the text graphic we are about to add.

Go to the **Insert** menu and choose **Insert symbol**. Enter the letter **D** in the **Name** field and make sure the **Graphic** radio button is selected and click **OK**. Use the **Text** tool to place a capital letter **D** on the stage. Use the font modifiers to alter the type, color and size of the letter. Make sure the font size is at least 48 pt. Repeat this process to make a lower case **e**, **i**, **t** and **l**. These letters are used to spell out **Deitel** on the screen—because you can reuse the **e** graphic, there is no need to make two of them. Once you are finished, return to the main stage by clicking the **Scene 1** tab. Add six more layers to the movie. Name the top layer **l**, the next **e** and so on until **Deitel** is spelled backwards ending with the capital **D**. Put a keyframe in each of these layers at frame 150. Drag the symbols one by one from the library onto the main stage in their respective layers. Use the **Align** tool to straighten the letters and to spell the name **Deitel** across the stage. Place a keyframe in each layer at frame 170. Next, double click each layer in frame 150 create a motion tween. While each letter is still highlighted, choose **Transform,** then **Flip Horizontal** from the **Modify** menu. Highlight each letter in frame 150 by holding the *Shift* key and clicking each individual letter. Use the **Arrow** tool to move each letter on the stage up about an inch, and use the **Align** tool to center the letters on top of each other in the middle of the stage. This gives the letters the effect of falling into place. Flipping them horizontally makes them twist while they fall. Take the beginning keyframe in each layer and move it two frames to the right of the keyframe where the animation begins in the layer above it. Move the ending keyframe one frame to the left of the ending keyframe in the layer below it (Fig. 33.47). This makes the letters fall at different times. Now create a new graphic consisting of an ampersand (**&**) and the words **Associates, Inc**. Place this symbol below the word **Deitel** in the last frame of the movie in its own layer named **assoc**.

Create a button with the text **Click here to go to our Web site** and call it **goto**, see Fig. 33.48. Place this button in a new layer named **goto** on the main stage. Place it below the words **& Associates, Inc.** by dragging it onto the stage from your Library. Double click the button to bring up the **Properties** window. On the **Action** tab, click the **(+)** button and choose **Get URL**. Enter the URL of the Deitel Web site, **www.deitel.com**, in the URL field and click **OK**. Additionally, place a **Stop** action in the last frame of the movie.

The final step is to place a keyframe in the second-to-last frame of the movie, frame 189, in the **skip** layer. This is the layer that includes the **SkipIntro** button. This makes the button visible throughout the movie until the last frame where the **goto** button appears.

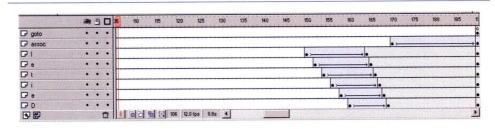

Fig. 33.47   Picture of the time line where the text effect is applied to the word Deitel. (Courtesy of Macromedia, Inc.)

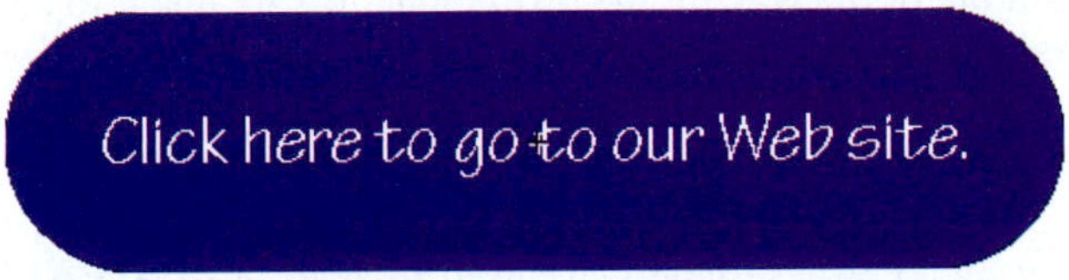

Fig. 33.48   Picture of the **goto** button. (Courtesy of Macromedia, Inc.)

33.6 Creating a Store Front

Another application for Flash is the development of interesting storefronts. With a bit of scripting, these storefronts can even communicate with databases through the use of Active Server Pages, JavaScript or CGI (each of which you have learned in this book.). Information on using these technologies with Flash can be found at the **flashaddict.com**'s intermediate tutorials section at **www.virtual-fx.net/tutorials/ tutresults.asp?level=intermediate**

The next exercise teaches you how to build a storefront that keeps a running total of current pizza orders. The storefront calculates a sub total, determines the delivery price for the order and totals the cost of all pizzas plus delivery.

When the storefront is complete it will include the functionality of the one pictured in Fig. 33.49. For this exercise you are free to design your own movie background. This exercise does not cover the creation of graphics.

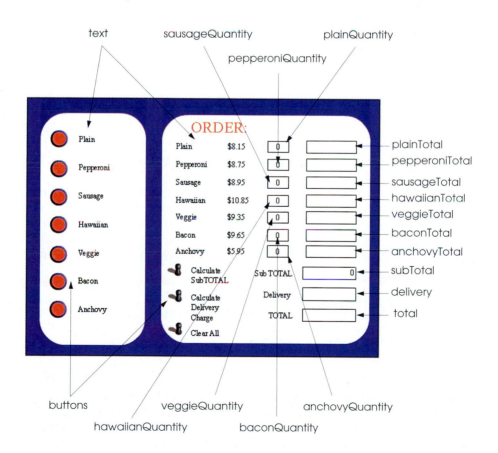

Fig. 33.49 Pizza store template. (Courtesy of Macromedia, Inc.)

The first step in building the storefront is to place a number of buttons on the stage which are used to update the order and to calculate the order price and delivery charge. Click the **Libraries** menu and choose **Buttons**; this brings up a list of buttons that are included with Flash. By using these buttons, you can save a considerable amount of development time. When the buttons are dragged onto the stage, they are fully functional. You do not have to set the their **Up**, **Over**, **Down** or **Hit** states. Choose a button from the list, we used the button labeled **Push Button Red.** Drag one instance of the button to the stage. The next step is to add functionality to the button and then duplicate it. Doing so prevents having to add the same scripts repeatedly. After all of the buttons are duplicated you can go back and alter each of their scripts as needed.

Software Engineering Observation 33.1

When using similar objects in a movie, build one of the symbols to completion and duplicate it as needed. After duplicating the object, alter the attributes of the copy where necessary. Using this technique minimizes repetition.

Next, create two **Text Fields** which serve as the templates for the rest. Like the buttons, we build these text fields to include the scripts needed and then duplicate them and alter the duplicates as needed. Use the **Text** tool to create one small text field about four characters wide. This field is used to display the total number of each type of pizza being ordered. Create another text field, one slightly larger than the last and eight characters wide which is used to display the total price for each type of pizza. Refer to the text boxes shown in Fig. 33.49. When creating these text fields, make sure the **Text Field** modifier is activated. Assign names to the text fields so they can be called in the ActionScripts. To name them, open the **Text Field Properties** window by right clicking the small field. Using meaningful text fields names makes remembering their functions easier when the text fields are used in scripts. Name the small field **plainQuantity**, because it displays the quantity of plain pizzas that the user orders. Name the larger one **plainTotal** because it displays the total due based on the price of the pizza and the quantity ordered. Add three more fields, **subTotal**, **Delivery** and **Total**. After you have assigned the names to all five of the fields currently on the stage, you are ready to begin scripting.

It is important to note that all of the code we ask you to copy is case sensitive. Using the techniques discussed in section 33.2.11, add the following ActionScripting to the button (again, Flash will align this a little differently).

```
On (Press)
   Set Variable: "plainQuantity" = plainQuantity + 1
   Set Variable: "plainSum" = plainQuantity * 8.15
   Set Variable: "plainTotal" = "$" & plainSum
End On
```

This code increments the number of plain pizzas ordered and calculates the total amount spent on plain pizza. Notice that the **&** character is used to concatenate the **$** symbol to the front of the price in the **plainTotal** variable. Using the concatenation operator always results in a string value, even if you started with an integer. To calculate the **subTotal** later we need a variable that holds an integer version of the amount spent on plain pizza. We created the variable **plainSum** to hold that value. Flash does not have the ability to convert decimal values into monetary format. Macromedia offers instructions for doing so on the **Calling the FormatCurrency script** Web site, which is part of a larger tutorial at

www.macromedia.com/support/flash/interactivity/orderform
Next, copy and paste the **plainQuantity** and **plainTotal** text fields six times. Arrange the new fields and rename all of them according to Fig. 33.49. This should give you a total of 14 text fields. Copy the red button six times. Use the text tool to label each of the red buttons with a type of pizzas. You should now have a total of seven red buttons from which to order pizza. Each button has a corresponding quantity field and total field. For each button, replace the variable names with the names of the **Text Fields** that correspond to them. Give each pizza its own unique price by changing the amount in its sum equation. In our example, we used $8.15 for the plain pizza so this is the value you should change. Notice that the variable names were created by taking the pizza names and concatenating the string **Quantity**, **Sum** or **Total**. For example, the names used for the anchovy pizza are **anchovyQuantity**, **anchovySum** and **anchovyTotal**.

We now add the buttons that will be used to calculate the subtotal, calculate the delivery charge, and clear the form. Use the **Switch 1 Silver** button from the Flash library to save time. Each switch button needs its own unique script, because they all have different actions to perform. Drag three instances of the switch symbol onto the satge, and align them and label them as we did in Fig. 33.51.

Next, give the **Calculate SubTOTAL** switch the following script using the **Actions** section of the **Instance Properties** window.

```
On ( Press )
   Set Variable: "subTotal" =
      plainSum + pepperoniSum + sausageSum +
      hawaiianSum + veggieSum + baconSum + anchovySum
End On
```

Fig. 33.50 Screen shot of the pizza buttons and price labels. (Courtesy of Macromedia, Inc.)

Calculate
SubTOTAL

Calculate
Delivery
Charge

Clear All

Fig. 33.51   Switch buttons for the pizza store and their labels. (Courtesy of Macromedia, Inc.)

This calculates the subtotal each time you click the switch. Now add the following code to the switch labeled **Calculate Delivery Charge**:

```
On ( Press )
    If ( subTotal > 50 )
        Set Variable: "delivery" = "FREE"
    Else
        Set Variable: "delivery" = subTotal * .1
    End If
        Set Variable: "total" = delivery + subTotal
End On
```

This small ActionScript determines the shipping charge. If the subtotal is less than $50, the delivery cost is set to 10% of the **subTotal** value; otherwise, shipping is free. Add the following code to the clear all button to clear all the variables and allow the user to start over.

```
On (Press)
    Set Variable: "plainSum" = 0
    Set Variable: "plainTotal" = 0
    Set Variable: "plainQuantity" = 0
    Set Variable: "pepperoniSum" = 0
    Set Variable: "pepeproniTotal" = 0
    Set Variable: "pepperoniQuantity" = 0
    Set Variable: "sausageSum" = 0
    Set Variable: "sausageTotal" = 0
    Set Variable: "sausageQuantity" = 0
    Set Variable: "hawaiianSum" = 0
    Set Variable: "hawaiianTotal" = 0
    Set Variable: "hawaiianQuantity" = 0
    Set Variable: "veggieSum" = 0
    Set Variable: "veggieTotal" = 0
    Set Variable: "veggieQuantity" = 0
    Set Variable: "baconSum" = 0
    Set Variable: "baconTotal" = 0
    Set Variable: "baconQuantity" = 0
    Set Variable: "anchovySum" = 0
    Set Variable: "anchovyTotal" = 0
    Set Variable: "anchovyQuantity" = 0
    Set Variable: "subTotal" = 0
End On
```

When you are done adding the code, test your movie to see that it functions like a storefront. With additional scripting this movie could be adapted to be a fully functioning store

Website. Doing so is beyond the scope of this chapter, however this topic is discussed in greater detail at **www.flashaddict.com**.

33.7 Using Loops

Flash offers only one repetition structure—the **Loop While**. In this example, we use a loop that dynamically creates multiple Movie Clip instances and places them in random locations on the stage. The user will specify the number of repetitions by typing a number into a text field. Each time through the loop, a duplicate of the original movie clip will be generated. In addition to the **Loop While** statement, this example will introduce the **Duplicate/Remove Movie Clip**, **Set Property**, and **Call** actions.

Open a new movie and save it as **LoopExample**. On the main stage place a text field named **createNumber**. Place a label next to the field with the text **Enter the number of flowers to create**. Place two buttons on the main stage, one to display the flowers and one to clear the flowers. Use buttons from Flash's **Button Library** to save time. Open the Flash **Movie Clip Library** and drag an instance of the **Animated Asterisk** just off-stage (Fig. 33.52). Assign the name **flower** to the **Animated Asterix** movie clip instance the name **flower**.

The **Duplicate/Remove Movie Clip** action is used to duplicate or remove any movie clip that exists on the stage. In our example, we use it to create and delete new movie clips. Each movie clip will be given its own unique name which will depend on the order in which the movie clips are created. We name the dynamically created movie clips by concatenating the value of a counter variable onto the word **flower** such that the clips are named **flower1**, **flower2**, **flower3** and so on.

Instead of applying scripts directly to the buttons which call them, it is possible to create the script elsewhere and use it with the **Call** action. These scripts are known as *subroutines (*reusable ActionScripts). Creating a subroutine involves applying a script to a labeled keyframe and calling the script using that frame's label. All subroutines should be placed beyond the end of your animation sequence in the timeline. The movie must have a **Stop** action applied to its final frame to be sure that the subroutines will not be accessed during play. In this example, our entire movie uses only the first frame allowing you to use any other frame for subroutines.

In this example we create two subroutines, **createFlowers** and **delete-Flowers**. We call the subroutines using scripts assigned to the buttons on the stage. To create a subroutine in a frame, place a keyframe in the frame, give the frame a label and add the script, then use the **Call** function to run it.

Common Programming Error 33.2
Be careful when deleting a layer, doing so also deletes anything off-stage that is part of the layer.

Insert a keyframe in frames 15 and 30. In frame 15 we will place the **create-Flowers** subroutine and in frame 30 we place the **deleteFlowers** subroutine. Click frame 15 and open the **Frame Properties** window. First, click on the **Label** tab and label the subroutine **createFlowers**. Figure 33.53 contains the code that you will use for the **createFlowers** subroutine. The paragraphs that follow explain some of the more complex aspects of ActionScripting.

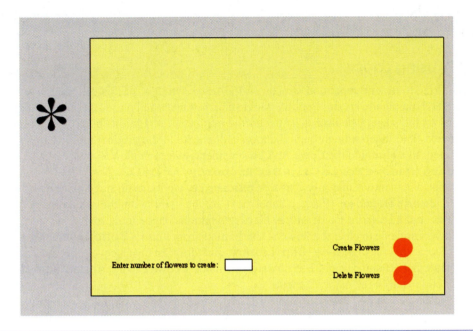

Fig. 33.52   Loop Example movie with all elements on stage. (Courtesy of Macromedia, Inc.)

The **Set Properties** action is used to set the new movie clip's attributes. In our example we use random numbers to decide the location, size and Alpha values of the clips. Be careful when you use the **Set Property** and **Duplicate/Remove Movie Clip** actions. By default, all text box values in the **Actions** window are set to **String Literal** which is denoted by the **abc** button. Pressing the **abc** button results in a drop-down menu with three options—**String Literal** (denoted by the **abc** button), **Expression** (denoted by the **=** button) and **Expression Editor** (denoted by a bordered **=** button). See Fig. 33.19 for an illustration of the options. [*Note:* The **Target** textbox menus also have a **Target Editor** option which allows you to choose your target from a list.]

Duplicate/Remove Movie Clip has specific requirements that must be met for it to work properly. Leave the **Target** text box as a **String Literal** and set its value to **/ flower**. The **/** symbol tells Flash that the target will be a movie clip. Set the **New Name** and **Depth** text boxes to **Expression** by clicking the small buttons next to them and selecting the **=** symbol from the drop-down lists. As shown in line 22 of Fig. 33.53, set the value of the **New Name** text box to **"flower" & count**. Putting the word **flower** in quotation marks indicates that it should be treated as a string. The word **count** is not in quotation marks because it is a variable. The entire value is set to expression, because it will concatenate a variable and a string. The **Depth** field is important. Whenever a Movie Clip is placed onto the stage it is given a unique depth index. The main movie always has a depth of **0**, the first movie dragged onto the stage is given a depth of **1**, etc. Type **count** into the **Depth** text box. This automatically gives each movie a depth equal to the value of the variable **count** which is increased each time through our loop. Thus, each of our movie clips will have its own unique name.

Common Programming Error 33.3

When duplicating a movie clip, it is important that you use a unique depth. Using a depth value that is already taken will replace the current movie clip at that depth.

When inserting the **Set Property** action, the **Target** and **Value** textboxes must be set to **Expression**. For instance, line 26 of Fig. 33.53 was created by typing **"flower" & count** into the **Target** textbox and setting it to an expression.

Next, select **X Position** from the **Set** drop down menu to make the **Set Property** action change the x position of each movie clip. Lastly, set the **Value** text box to **Expression** and type **randomX** into the box. This tells Flash to set the x location of each movie clip to a random number generated on line 17. Use the same values to set the **Target** and **Value** text boxes for each of the **Set Property** actions in lines 26 through 30. Change only the **Set** drop-down menu each time.

```
1   Comment: Initialize variables. Set all value types to
2   Comment: expression in the actions window.
3   Set Variable: "count" = 0
4   Set Variable: "randomX" = 0
5   Set Variable: "randomY" = 0
6
7   Comment: This variable keeps track of all movies created
8   Comment: while the movie plays.
9   Set Variable: "total" = total+createNumber
10
11  Comment: This number of repetitions this while loop
12  Comment: completes is decided by user input.
13  Loop While (count < createNumber)
14
15     Comment: Get random variables for location of each
16     Comment: movie clip.
17     Set Variable: "randomX" = Random(450) + 100
18     Set Variable: "randomY" = Random(300)
19
20     Comment: This action creates new movie clips based
21     Comment: on the value of count.
22     Duplicate Movie Clip ( "/flower", "flower" &count, count )
23
24     Comment: The following code sets the  attributes for each
25     Comment: movie clip that is created.
26     Set Property ( "/flower" & count, X Position ) = randomX
27     Set Property ( "/flower" & count, Y Position ) = randomY
28     Set Property ( "/flower" & count, Alpha ) = Random(50) + 50
29     Set Property ( "/flower" & count, X Scale ) = Random(200) + 5
30     Set Property ( "/flower" & count, Y Scale ) = Random(200) + 50
31
32     Comment: Increment count to prevent an infinite loop
33     Set Variable: "count" = count + 1
34  End Loop
```

Fig. 33.53 The **createFlowers** subroutine. (Courtesy of Macromedia, Inc.)

To create the **deleteFlowers** subroutine, select frame 30 and open the **Frame Properties** window. Label the frame **deleteFlowers** in the **Label** tab and add the following ActionScript. Remember to set the **Variable** text box for the **Set Variable** action to **String Literal** and all of the text boxes for **Remove Movie Clip** to **Expression** as we did for the **createFlowers** subroutine.

Now that the subroutines have been created, add them to the two buttons in frame 1 by using the call function, which uses the following syntax:

```
Call ( "/movie_name:subroutine_name" )
```

As noted earlier, the **/** is used to indicate a movie in Flash. When calling to a subroutine found within a movie clip, the **/** is followed by the name of the movie clip. If the subroutine is located in the timeline of the main movie, you simply need the **/** symbol. The **:** symbol separates the movie name from the subroutine name. Add the following ActionScript to the button you will use to call the **createFlowers** subroutine. Open the **Instance Properties** window for the button which creates the flowers. In the **Actions** window, insert the following ActionScript.

```
On ( Release )

    Comment: Call to the subroutine createFlowers.
    Call ( "/:createFlowers" )
End On
```

This script runs the subroutine **createFlowers** where the number of flowers had already been assigned by the input of the **createNumber** text field. When this button is pressed, the subroutine is run and the instances are displayed on the screen. Figure 33.54 shows ten movie clips that were created by the **createFlowers** subroutine.

Add the following ActionScript to the button that calls subroutine **deleteFlowers**.

```
On ( Release )

    Comment: Call to the subroutine deleteFlowers.

    Call ( "/:deleteFlowers" )
End On
```

When this button is pressed, the subroutine **deleteFlowers** is called clearing all instances of **flower** from the screen. To finish the movie add a **Stop** action in frame 1 this prevents it from playing any later frames.

```
1   Set Variable: "count" = 0
2
3   Comment: The total variable is used to be sure that all of the movie
4   Comment: clips are removed.
5   Loop While ( count < total )
6
7       Comment: This action removes the movie clips.
8       Remove Movie Clip ( "flower" & count )
9       Set Variable: "count" = count + 1
10  End Loop
```

Fig. 33.54 The **deleteFlowers** subroutine. (Courtesy of Macromedia, Inc.)

Fig. 33.55   Movie clips displayed after completing 20 loops. (Courtesy of Macromedia, Inc.)

33.8 ActionScripts

The following is a table of the ActionScript functions available in Flash. Figure 33.56 outlines all of the ActionScript commands.

Action	Description
`Go To`	Jump to a frame or scene in another part of the movie.
`Play`	Start a movie at certain points of the movie where the movie may have been stopped.
`Stop`	Stop a movie.
`Toggle High Quality`	Turn anti-aliasing on and off. By turning it off, the movie is able to play faster, but renders with rough edges.
`Stop All Sounds`	Stop the sound track without affecting the movie.
`Get URL`	Load a URL into a new or existing browser window.
`FS Command`	Insert JavaScript or other scripting languages into to your Flash movie.
`Load/Unload Movie`	Play consecutive Flash movies without closing the Flash Player window.
`Tell Target`	Navigate through a movie by assigning a specific frame to jump to, skipping all in-between frames.
`If Frame is Loaded`	Check whether certain frames have been loaded.

Fig. 33.56   Additional ActionScript functions (part 1 of 2).

Action	Description
OnMouseEvent	Assign actions such as **Press**, **Release** and **RollOver** to a button.
If	Set up condition statements that run only when that condition is true.
Loop	Run a collection of statements while a condition statement is true.
Call	Give multiple buttons or frames the same action.
Set Property	Change the attributes of a movie clip while the movie plays.
Set Variable	Assign a value to a variable within a Flash movie.
Duplicate/Remove Movie Clip	Dynamically add or remove a movie clip to or from you movie.
Drag Movie Clip	Move a movie clip while the movie is running.
Trace	Display programming notes or variable values while testing a movie.
Comment	Keep track of personal notes in a frame or action for future reference.

Fig. 33.56   Additional ActionScript functions (part 2 of 2).

33.9 Internet and World Wide Web Resources

www.macromedia.com
This is the *Macromedia Home Page*. Macromedia specializes in tools for creating multimedia-rich Web sites. Check out this site for the 30-day trial versions of their multimedia authoring tools.

www.macromedia.com/software/flash/trial
This is the Macromedia Flash download page. You can download the latest copies of the software here.

www.flashaddict.com
This site offer tutorials, news, discussion boards and other resources for Flash developers. The tutorials on this site are some of the most helpful on the Web.

www.swift3d.com
This is the Swift3d home page. Swift3d is a program that allows you to create 3D objects for use in Flash.

www2.discreet.com/products/products.html?prod=3dsma
This is Discreet's Web site for the 3D Studio Max product. 3D Studio Max is a high-end 3D modeling tool.

www.adobe.com/products/illustrator/main.html
This is the section of Adobe's Web site that is devoted to the Illustrator product line.

www.shockwave.com
The *Shockwave* Web site contains a wide variety of Web-based games, cartoons and music. The site was created with Macromedia authoring tools.

www.xdude.com
This site is an example of the power of the Macromedia Flash technology.

`www.real.com`

The *RealNetworks* site is the home of RealPlayer—one of the most popular software products for receiving streaming media over the Web. Also, with their RealJukebox, you can download MP3 files and other digital music.

`www.flashcentral.com/Xena3/Index.htm`

Flash Central is a great site which includes links to some great Flash galleries. Flash Central is also a great source for tutorials on upper-level scripting and other concepts.

SUMMARY

- Macromedia Flash 4 is an application for creating interactive, animated *movies*.

- Flash Movies can be embedded into Web pages, used on CD-ROMs and can be converted into standalone, executable programs.

- Flash movies also have small file sizes compared to other techniques for creating multimedia presentations.

- Advanced animation features such as *tweening*, which takes the first and last frames of an animation and automatically extrapolates the middle animation frames from them, help to transform even the most artistically challenged developers into respectable animators.

- Web users must have the *Flash Player plug-in* to see Flash content in a browser.

- Web page developers can use JavaScript to detect if the Flash Player plug-in is present on the users computer. The few users who are unable to view Flash-enhanced Web sites can also be offered the same content formatted in HTML.

- The first step in building a Flash movie is to create the symbols for use in the movie.

- To change a Flash movie's properties click the **Modify** menu and select **Movie...** to display the **Movie Properties** dialog box.

- The letters **px** are an abbreviation for the word pixel.

- The **Magnifier** tool enlarges the work area, this makes working on the smaller stage easier.

- The **Magnifier** tool has modifiers that allow you to zoom in and zoom out.

- When a drawing tool is selected, its modifiers appear below the drawing toolbar.

- Holding the *Shift* key while using the **Oval** tool allows the user to draw a perfect circle rather than an oval. You can use the same method to create a square using the rectangle tool.

- Because a button consists of a graphic and some text, both have to be selected to make them one symbol. Once the symbol is created, the graphic and text are treated as a single object.

- To select the items in a certain area, click and hold the mouse button slightly above and to the left of the area and drag the cursor until the entire area is inside the selection marquee and release the mouse button.

- To make a button symbol, select **Convert to Symbol...** from the **Insert** menu while it is highlighted. Be sure to click the radio button labeled **Button**.

- Keyframes tell Flash how a shape or symbol should appear at the beginning and end of an animation. Tweening is then used to create the middle animation frames.

- To add key frames click the frame in the timeline where you wish to add the keyframe. Once the desired frame is selected, you can either click **Keyframe** which is located in the **Insert** menu, or you can press the *F6* key. You can also right-click the selected frame in the timeline and selected **Insert Keyframe** from the pop up menu.

- To edit a symbol, right-click the symbol and in the pop-up menu, select **Edit**. If you successfully switched to **Edit** mode, the stage should appear stretched across the entire development window and the button should be at the center of the screen.

- In **Edit** mode, a symbol's pieces can be edited separately.
- The frames in the button symbol timeline are labeled **UP**, **OVER**, **DOWN** and **HIT**. Each of the frames corresponds to a unique button state. The **UP** state is the default state, which we designed originally. **OVER** is activated when the mouse is positioned over the button; this is known as a *mouseover* in many programming languages. **DOWN** is the state of the button when it is clicked. The **HIT** state is used to define the clickable area of the button. Leaving the **HIT** state unchanged constrains the area to the boundaries of the button.
- To change the fill of a symbol activate the **Arrow** tool and click the area outside the stage to de-select everything. In **Edit** mode text and shape can be edited separately. Click the Filled portion of the circle. You know that the fill is selected if the entire center of the circle is highlighted. After selecting the fill, activate the **Paint Bucket** tool. Use the **Fill Color** modifier to select the gradient. Click the selected fill to change its color. To verify the color, click outside the stage using the **Arrow** tool. This causes the selection to disappear revealing the new fill.
- Click the **Control** menu and select **Test Movie** to play a movie.
- Change the name of a layer by double clicking the label **Layer 1**, located on the left-hand side of the timeline. Notice that the label's text becomes editable.
- To add a new layer, click the **Insert** menu and select **Layer**.
- The **Antialias Text** option makes the text smoother once this option is set.
- There are two types of tweening in Flash, *shape tweening* and *motion tweening*.
- Shape tweening is used to "morph" an object into a different shape.
- Shape tweening cannot be used with symbols or *grouped objects* (groups of shapes that have been combined using the **Group** option which is found in the **Modify** menu).
- Motion tweening also has specific guidelines. Motion tweening cannot be used with layers with more than one object or symbol and cannot be used on shapes or grouped objects.
- The more frames you use, the slower an animation is.
- Each new keyframe always inherits the properties of the keyframe that directly precedes it.
- Any future changes to a keyframe only effect the changed frame, unless tweening is used.
- To activate a motion tween, move the cursor to any frame between the keyframes and right click. Select **Properties...** from the pop-up menu to open the **Frame Properties** dialog box. Click the **Tweening** tab and select **Motion** from the drop-down menu labeled **Tweening**. There should now be a number of options for motion tweening. Press **OK** to apply the tweening.
- To add a text field, select the **Text** tool and click the **Text Field** modifier at the bottom of the modifier tool bar to convert the text box into a **Text Field**. Next, use the mouse to draw the text field on the stage.
- To give a text field a variable name that we can use in the script, use the **Arrow** tool to select the text field, right click it and select **Properties...** from the pop-up menu to display the **Text Field Properties** window.
- Flash uses a built-in Flash function to generate a random number.
- To add ActionScript to an instance, select **Properties...** from the pop-up menu. In the **Instance Properties** window that appears, click the tab labeled **Actions**.
- To add the action click the **+** button.
- To create a new variable insert the name of the variable into the field labeled **Variable.**
- **If/Else** statements provide the ability to act only if certain conditions are met.
- The button next to the field labeled **Value** which has **abc** written on it tells Flash that the value we are assigning is a text string rather than an integer or expression.

- The **Publish** function in Flash is similar to the **Export** command in other programs, however it has more advanced features.
- Choosing to **Publish as HTML** outputs a Web page with your Flash movie embedded.
- The Windows Projector is an executable, so all you have to do is double click the file name in Windows explorer to run the program.
- ActionScripting is a powerful scripting language that gives Flash the ability to create sophisticated programs and interactive movies.
- ActionScript allows Flash to interact with Active Server Pages, CGI and JavaScript.
- Web sites written in HTML often render quite differently in each browser. This annoyance is not an issue with Flash movies. They are compatible across most browsers.
- No matter which browser you use, as long as the Flash player plug-in is supported, Flash movies appear as intended.
- Flash movies are added to a Web site with the **<OBJECT>** and **<EMBED>** tags. The **<OBJECT>** tag allows the movie to be seen using the Internet Explorer browser. The **<EMBED>** tag makes your movie viewable for Netscape users.
- The **<OBJECT>** tag has several attributes.
- **CODEBASE**, an attribute of the **<OBJECT>** tag, allows users to be prompted to download the plug-in if they do not have it.
- Microsoft Internet Explorer ignores tags placed inside **<OBJECT>** tag. Netscape only reads the **<EMBED>** tag; it ignores the **<OBJECT>** information.
- To import a bitmap, click **Import...** under the **File** menu and use the directory structure in the resulting **Import** window to navigate to find the desired file.
- You can convert the imported bitmap into a shape by selecting it and pressing *Ctrl + B* or by choosing **Break Apart** from the **Modify** menu.
- To create a masking effect you need a total of three layers.
- To mask a layer, double click the paper sheet icon next to the layer label to open the Layer Properties window. Select the Mask radio button and click OK. The icon changes to one picturing a down-pointing purple arrow inside a white circle.
- To assign the layer being masked, click the paper icon next to the layer label and select the Masked radio button and click OK. This adds an icon picturing a white arrow enclosed in a purple circle.
- An instance of an object can be duplicated in the library by clicking on **Library** in the **Window** menu and right click the instance name. Select **Duplicate** from the pop-up menu and assign a new name to the new instance. Several media libraries are included with Flash, one of which contains sound effects.
- The Sound library can be opened by clicking Sound in the Libraries menu. The library has several sound effects that can be played as a result of mouse events or they can be embedded into frames to be played when the frame is played.
- The buttons in Flash's button library have predefined up, over and down states.
- Flash does not provide music loops with its software. There are sites on the Internet that have sound loops available for download. You can import sound loops into your Flash movie by choosing Import from the File menu. Imported sound loops become part of the Project library.
- To create a movie clip, select **New Symbol...** from the **Insert** menu, click the radio button labeled **Movie Clip** in the **Symbol Properties** dialog box, and name the movie clip.
- Setting the **Alpha** slider to 0 makes the graphic completely transparent.

- Another application for Flash is the development of interesting storefronts. With a bit of scripting, these storefronts can even communicate with databases through the use of Active Server Pages, JavaScript or CGI.

- Assign names to the text fields to be able to call to them in the ActionScripts. To name them, open the **Text Field Properties** window by right clicking the small field.

- It is important to note that all of the code we ask you to copy is case sensitive.

- Using the concatenation operator always results in a string value, even if you started with an integer.

TERMINOLOGY

Actions menu	line style
ActionScript	line thickness
Align tool	**Loop**
Alpha	**Magic Wand**
Arrow tool	masking
background	**Magnifier** tool
Break Apart	**Modify** menu
Brush tool	movie
`CLASSID`	movie clip
constraining	**Movie Properties**
Copy Frames	New Symbol
Dropper	`NOEMBED` element
Duplicate	**Object Inspector**
`EMBED` element	onionskinning
Eraser tool	**OnMouseEvent**
Export	**Oval** tool
expression	**Paint Bucket** tool
Expression Editor	palette
event	**Paste Frames**
Fill tool	**Paste in Place**
Frame inspector	**Pencil** tool
Frame Properties window	projector
function	**Publish**
Generator Inspector	`random`
Go To	**Rectangle** tool
Gradient Palette	**Scale** tool
graphic	scene
Hand tool	**Scene 1**
`If/Else`	**Scene Inspector**
Import	shape
Ink Bottle tool	stage
inspector	**Stop**
Instance Properties window	subroutine
JavaScript	symbol
keyframe	**Symbol Properties**
Lasso tool	`sync`
Label	**Target**
layer	text field
library	**Text Field Properties** window
line color	timeline

Transform Inspector
tweening

Use Center Point
vector graphics

SELF-REVIEW EXERCISES

33.1 Fill in the blanks in each of the following.
a) Macromedia Flash's _____ feature draws the in-between frames of an animation automatically.
b) Graphics, buttons and movie clips are all types of _____.
c) The two types of tweening in Macromedia Flash are _____ tweening and _____ tweening.
d) Macromedia Flash's scripting language is called _____.
e) The area where the movie is created is called the _____.
f) Holding down the *Shift* key while using the **Oval** tool draws a perfect _____.
g) "Morphing" one shape into another over a period of time requires _____.
h) An object's transparency value is known as its _____ value in Flash.
i) The _____ feature provides help when drawing by automatically aligning items with each other and with the scene grid.
j) _____ tell Flash how a shape or symbol should look at the beginning and end of an animation.

33.2 State whether each of the following is *true* or *false*. If *false*, explain why.
a) A Macromedia Flash button's **HIT** state is entered when the button is clicked.
b) To draw a circle in Flash, hold down the *SHIFT* key while using the **Oval** tool.
c) Motion tweening cannot be used on layers with more than one object or symbol.
d) The more frames that you give to an animation, the slower it is.
e) Setting the argument of Flash's **random** function to 5 tells the function to generate a number between 1 and 5, inclusive.
f) The maximum number of layers allowed in a movie is ten.
g) Flash does not provide for text larger then 72 pt.
h) Flash can shape-tween only one shape per layer.
i) When a new layer is created, it is placed above the selected layer.
j) The **Lasso** tool can be used to select objects by drawing free-hand or straight-edge selection areas.

ANSWERS TO SELF-REVIEW EXERCISES

33.1   a) Tweening. b) symbols. c) shape, motion. d) ActionScript. e) stage. f) circle. g) shape tweening. h) Alpha. i) snapping j) Keyframes.

33.2   a) False. The **DOWN** state is entered when the button is clicked. b) True. c) True. d) True. e) False. Setting the argument of Flash's Random function to 5 tells the function to generate a number between 0 and 4, inclusive. f) False. Flash allows an unlimited number of layers for each movie. g) False. Although 72 pt is the highest you can select from the drop down menu, you can enter up to 999 by using the keyboard. h) False. Flash can tween as many shapes as there are on a layer. The effect is usually better when the shapes are placed on their own layers. i) True. j) True.

EXERCISES

33.3   Use the motion tweening techniques covered in this chapter to create an exploding text effect. Place a button in the movie, which when pressed, starts a spark traveling down a fuse to a string of text. When the spark reaches the text, make the text explode off the screen.

33.4   Use the masking effect, covered in Section 33.5.2 to simulate a rippling text effect. Create a movie which includes a string of text and a graphic of a drop of rain. Make the drop of rain fall from the top of the stage onto the middle of the text. When the drop hits the text, simulate a ripple effect which gives the text the appearance of being under water.[*Hint*: The movie should have four layers.: Layer one should hold a text string that does not change. Layer two should contain the same text string but should start slightly smaller and finish slightly larger when animated. The third should hold a thick ring-shaped graphic which starts small and gradually gets larger until it completely surrounds the text. The ring layer should mask layer two, see section 33.5.2. The last layer should contain the rain drop.

33.5   Apply the scripting concepts introduced in this chapter to create a scroll box. Include a text box and two buttons in the movie. Use the buttons to control the scrolling of the text in the text box. [*Hint*: Create a movie with two layers. In the one layer, place the text box and the two buttons. One of the buttons should increase the value of the variable *your-textbox-name*.**scroll** by 1 each time it is pressed and the other should decrease its value by 1 when it is pressed. The variable *your-textbox-name* should be changed according to the name you gave to your text box. In other words, if the text box was named **box** the buttons would alter the variable named **box.scroll**.

> **Set Variable:** "*your-textbox-name*.**scroll**" = "1"
>
> **Set Variable:** "*your-textbox-name*" = "**This text will be disp-played in the scrolling textbox**"

33.6   Construct a grade point average (GPA) calculator using some of the techniques you learned in Section 33.5.6. The calculator should include text fields to accept classes and grades, to display a running list of up to seven classes and to output the calculated overall GPA. When information is entered into the input fields it should be placed in the next available output row. The form should accept grades in letter form and convert them into numeric form for calculation and output purposes. This movie should use two buttons, one to add the inputted class and grade information and another to calculate the overall GPA.

WORKS CITED

1.   "Macromedia   tightens   integration   of   Macromedia   Flash   in   Microsoft   Internet Explorer,"<www.macromedia.com/macromedia/proom/pr/2000/index_internet_explorer.fhtml> 14 July 2000.

34

Accessibility

Objectives

- To introduce the World Wide Web Consortium's Web Content Accessibility Guidelines 1.0 (WCAG 1.0).
- To use the **ALT** attribute of the **<IMG>** tag to describe images to blind and vision impaired people, to mobile Web device users, to search engines, etc.
- To make tables more accessible to page readers by using the **HEADERS** attribute in HTML 4.01.
- To verify that HTML tags are used properly and to ensure that Web pages are viewable on any type of display or reader.
- To better understand how VoiceXML™ will change the way people with disabilities access information on the Web.
- To introduce the various accessibility aids offered in Windows 2000.

I once was lost, but now am found,
Was blind, but now I see.
John Newton

'Tis the good reader that makes the good book...
Ralph Waldo Emerson

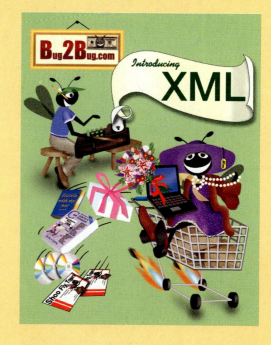

Outline

34.1 Introduction

On April 7, 1997, the World Wide Web Consortium (W3C) launched the *Web Accessibility Initiative* (WAI™). *Accessibility* refers to the level of usability of an application or Web site for people with disabilities. The vast majority of Web sites are considered inaccessible to people with visual, learning or mobility impairments. A high level of accessibility is difficult to achieve because there are many different disabilities, language barriers, hardware and software inconsistencies, etc. As greater numbers of people with disabilities begin to use the Internet, it is imperative that Web site designers increase the accessibility to their sites. The WAI is an attempt to make the Web more accessible; its mission is described at `www.w3.org/WAI`.

As a member of the World Wide Web Consortium, Deitel & Associates, Inc. is committed to supporting the WAI. This chapter discusses some of the techniques for developing accessible Web sites. The Web Content Accessibility Guidelines 1.0 (`www.w3.org/TR/WCAG10`) are divided into a three-tier structure of checkpoints according to their priority. *Priority one checkpoints* are those that must be met in order to ensure accessibility; we focus on these in this chapter. *Priority two checkpoints*, though not essential, are highly recommended. *Priority three checkpoints* slightly improve accessibility. The WAI also presents a supplemental list of *quick tips*, which contains checkpoints aimed at solving priority one problems. More information on the WAI Quick Tips can be found at `www.w3.org/WAI/References/Quicktips`.

34.2 Providing Alternatives for Multimedia Content

One important WAI requirement is to ensure that every image, movie and sound used on a Web page is accompanied by a description that clearly defines its purpose. One way of accomplishing this is to include a description of each item using the **ALT** attribute of the **<IMG>** and **<INPUT>** tags. A text equivalent for **OBJECT** elements should also be provided, because they do not have an **ALT** attribute in the HTML 4.01 specification. Figure 34.1 demonstrates using the **ALT** attribute of the **<IMG>** tag.

The lack of well-defined **ALT** elements increases the difficulty of navigating the Web for visually impaired users. Specialized *user agent*s, such as *screen readers* (programs which allow users to hear what is being displayed on their screen) and *braille displays* (devices that receive data from screen reading software and output the data as braille) allow blind and visually impaired people to access text-based information that is normally displayed on the screen. A user agent is an application that interprets Web page source code and translates it into formatted text and images. Web browsers such as Microsoft Internet Explorer and Netscape Communicator and the screen readers mentioned throughout this chapter are examples of user agents.

Web pages with large amounts of multimedia content are difficult for user agents to interpret, unless they are designed properly. Images, movies and other non-HTML objects cannot be read by screen readers. Providing multimedia-based information in a variety of ways (i.e., using the **ALT** attribute or providing inline descriptions of images) helps maximize the content's accessibility.

```
1   <!DOCTYPE HTML PUBLIC "-//W3C//DTD HTML 4.0 Transitional//EN">
2   <HTML LANG = "en">
3
4   <!-- Fig. 34.1 alttag.html                              -->
5   <!-- Using The ALT tag to Make an Image Accessible -->
6
7   <HEAD>
8   <META HTTP-EQUIV = "Content-Type"
9   CONTENT = "text/html; charset=iso-8859-1">
10
11  <TITLE>
12  How to use the "ALT" attribute
13  </TITLE>
14
15  <STYLE TYPE = "text/css">
16  BODY { background: #6666FF; color: black }
17  P { margin-top: 1em }
18  .center { text-align: center }
19  </STYLE>
20  </HEAD>
21
22  <BODY>
23  <H1>How to use the "ALT" attribute</H1>
24  <P>Below we compare two images, one with the
25  "ALT" attribute present, and one without. The
```

Fig. 34.1   Using the **ALT** attribute of the **<IMG>** tag.

```
26    "ALT" appears as a tool tip in the first
27    image, but more importantly, will help users
28    who cannot view information conveyed graphically.
29    </P>
30
31    <P CLASS = "center">
32    This image has the "ALT" attribute<BR>
33    <IMG ALT = "This is a picture of the Internet and World Wide
34    Web How To Program Text Book" SRC = "Images/iw3htpcov.jpg"
35    WIDTH = "182" HEIGHT = "238">
36    </P>
37
38    <P CLASS = "center">
39    This image does not have the "ALT" attribute<BR>
40    <!-- This markup should be changed              -->
41    <!-- becuase there is no ALT attribute          -->
42    <IMG SRC = "Images/iw3htpcov.jpg" WIDTH = "182" height="238">
43    </P>
44    </BODY>
45    </HTML>
```

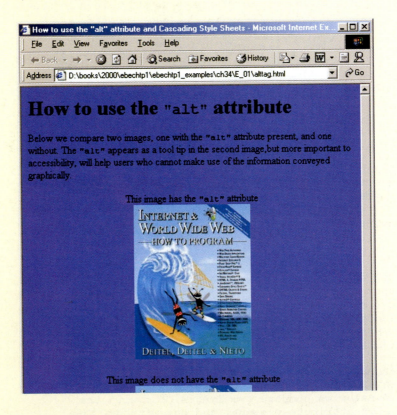

Fig. 34.1   Using the **ALT** attribute of the **<IMG>** tag.

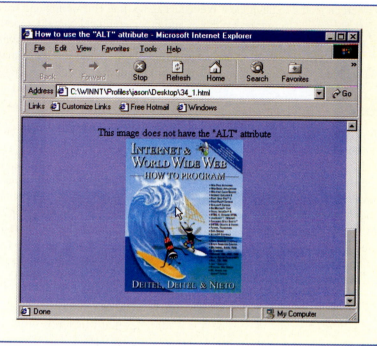

Fig. 34.1   Using the **ALT** attribute of the **<IMG>** tag.

Web designers should avoid misuse of the **ALT** attribute; it is intended to provide a short description of an HTML object which may not load properly on all user agents. For example, if the **ALT** attribute describes a sales growth chart, it should not describe chart data. Instead, it should specify the chart's title. The chart's data should be included in the Web site's text or by using the **LONGDESC** attribute, which is intended to augment the **ALT**'s description. The value of the **LONGDESC** attribute is a text-based URL which is linked to a Web page that describes the image. [*Note:* If an image is used as a hyperlink and the **LONGDESC** attribute is also used, there is no set standard as to which page is loaded when the image is clicked.]

*Server-side image maps (*images stored on a Web server with areas designated as hyperlinks*)* are another troublesome technology for some Web users—particularly those who cannot use a mouse. Server-side image maps require clicks to initiate their actions.User agent technology is unable to make server-side image maps accessible to blind people or to others who cannot use a mouse. If equivalent text links are not provided when a server-side image map is used, some users will be unable to navigate the site. User agent manufacturers will provide accessibility to server-side image maps, in the future. Until then, if image maps are used, we recommend using *client-side image maps* (image maps whose links are designated in the Web page's source and thus can be understood by non-graphical user agents). For more information regarding the use of image maps, visit **www.w3.org/TR/REC-html40/struct/objects.html#h-13.6**.

Good Programming Practice 34.1

Always provide generous descriptions and corresponding text links to all image maps.

Using a screen reader to navigate a Web site can be time consuming and frustrating as screen readers are unable to interpret pictures and other graphical content. One method of combatting this problem is to include a link at the top of each of Web page that provides easy access to the page's content. Users can use the link to bypass an image map or other inaccessible element, by jumping to another part of the page or to a different page.

34.3 Maximizing Readability by Focusing on Structure

Many Web sites use tags for aesthetic purposes rather than the purpose for which they were intended. For example, one might use the header tag, `<H1>`, to make text large and bold. This may achieve the desired visual effect, but it creates a problem for screen readers. When the screen reader software encounters text tagged as `<H1>`, it may verbally inform the user that they have reached a new section; this can confuse the user. Only use tags such as `<H1>` in accordance with their HTML specification. The `<H1>` tags are intended for use only as headings to introduce important sections of a document. Instead of using `<H1>`, the `<B>` (bold) tag should be used to achieve the same visual effect. Please use the Web Content Accessibility Guidelines 1.0 at `www.w3.org/TR/WCAG` for further examples. [*Note:* the `<STRONG>` tag may also be used to make text bold, however the inflection in which that text is spoken by screen readers may be affected.]

Another accessibility issue is *readability*. When creating a Web page intended for the general public, it is important to consider the reading level at which it is written. Web site designers can make their site more readable through the use of smaller words, as some users may have difficulty reading large words. Users from other countries may have difficulty understanding slang and other non-traditional language, so these should also be avoided.

The *Web Content Accessibility Guidelines 1.0* suggest using a paragraph's first sentence to convey its subject. Immediately stating the point makes finding crucial information much easier and allows those unable to comprehend large amounts of text to bypass unwanted material.

A good way to evaluate a Web site's readability is by using the *Gunning Fog Index*. The Gunning Fog Index is a formula which produces a readability grade when applied to a text sample. For more information on the Gunning Fog Index see `www.w3.org/TR/WAI-WEBCONTENT-TECHS`.

34.4 Accessibility in HTML Tables

Complex Web pages often contain tables and screen readers are incapable of translating tables in an understandable manner, unless they are designed properly. For example, the *CAST eReader*, a screen reader developed by the Center for Applied Special Technology (`www.cast.org`), starts at the top-left-hand cell and reads left to right and top to bottom. This is known as reading a table in a *linearized* manner. A screen reader reads the table in Fig. 34.2 as follows:

```
Price of Fruit Fruit Price Apple $0.25 Orange $0.50 Banana
$1.00 Pineapple $2.00
```

HTML does not provide any capabilities for dealing with this problem. The Web Content Accessibility Guidelines 1.0 recommend using *Cascading Style Sheets* (discussed in Chapter 19) instead of tables unless the content, in your table, linearizes in an understandable way.

```
1   <HTML>
2   <!-- Fig. 34.2 noheaders.html -->
3
4   <HEAD>
5   <TITLE>EXAMPLE WITHOUT HEADERS</TITLE>
6
7   </HEAD>
8
9   <BODY BGCOLOR = "#7E0810" TEXT = "#ffffff">
10
11  <CENTER><B> Price of Fruit </B></CENTER>
12  <TABLE WIDTH = "47%" BORDER = "1" ALIGN = "CENTER">
13     <TR>
14        <TD>Fruit</TD>
15        <TD>Price</TD>
16     </TR>
17     <TR>
18        <TD>Apple</TD>
19        <TD>$0.25</TD>
20     </TR>
21     <TR>
22        <TD>Orange</TD>
23        <TD>$0.50</TD>
24     </TR>
25     <TR>
26        <TD>Banana</TD>
27        <TD>$1.00</TD>
28     </TR>
29     <TR>
30        <TD>Pineapple</TD>
31        <TD>$2.00</TD>
32     </TR>
33  </TABLE>
34  </BODY>
35  </HTML>
```

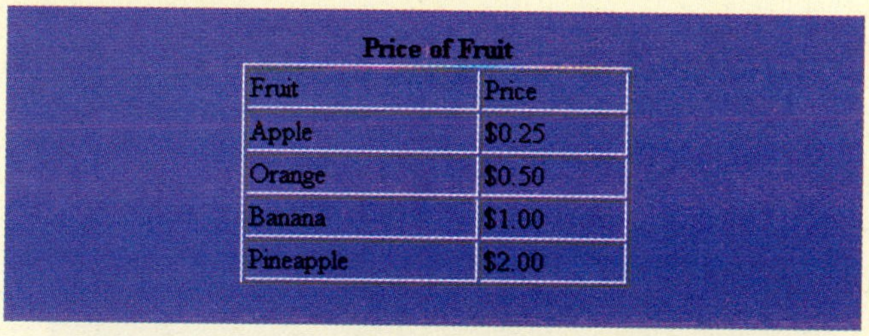

Fig. 34.2   HTML table without accessibility modifications.

If this were a large table, the output would be confusing for the person using the screen reader. By modifying the **<TD>** tag with the **HEADERS** attribute and modifying *header cells* (cells specified by the **<TH>** tag) with the **ID** attribute, you can ensure that a table is read as intended. Figure 34.3 demonstrates how these modifications change the way a table is interpreted.

```
1    <HTML>
2    <!-- Fig. 34.3 headers.html -->
3
4    <HEAD>
5    <TITLE>HEADERS EXAMPLE</TITLE>
6
7    </HEAD>
8
9    <BODY BGCOLOR = "#7E0810" TEXT = "#ffffff">
10
11   <!-- This table uses the ID and HEADERS attributes            -->
12   <!-- Using them ensures readability by text-based browsers -->
13   <!-- It also uses a SUMMARY attribute -->
14   <!-- SUMMARY explains the table to a screen reader            -->
15
16   <TABLE SUMMARY = "This table uses TH elements and ID and HEADER
17    attributes to make the table readable by screen readers"
18   WIDTH = "47%" BORDER = "1" ALIGN = "CENTER">
19   <CAPTION><B>Price of Fruit
20   </B></CAPTION>
21     <TR>
22       <TH ID = "fruit">Fruit</TH>
23       <TH ID = "price">Price</TH>
24     </TR>
25     <TR>
26       <TD HEADERS = "fruit">Apple</TD>
27       <TD HEADERS = "price">$0.25</TD>
28     </TR>
29     <TR>
30       <TD HEADERS = "fruit">Orange</TD>
31       <TD HEADERS = "price">$0.50</TD>
32     </TR>
33     <TR>
34       <TD HEADERS = "fruit">Banana</TD>
35       <TD HEADERS = "price">$1.00</TD>
36     </TR>
37     <TR>
38       <TD HEADERS = "fruit">Pineapple</TD>
39       <TD HEADERS = "price">$2.00</TD>
40     </TR>
41   </TABLE>
42   </BODY>
43   </HTML>
```

Price of Fruit	
Fruit	Price
Apple	$0.25
Orange	$0.50
Banana	$1.00
Pineapple	$2.00

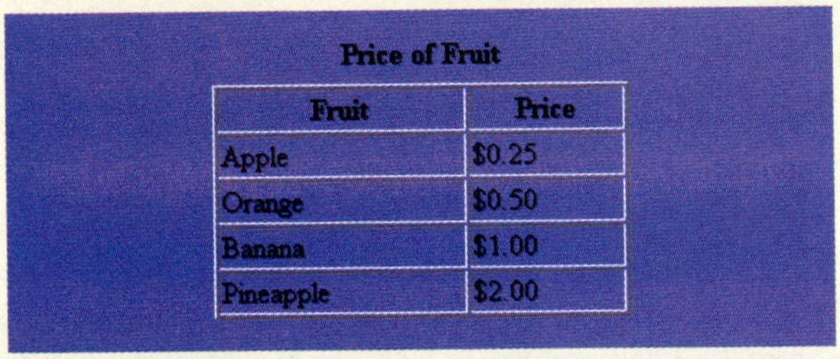

Fig. 34.3   HTML table optimized for screen reading using the **HEADERS** attribute.

This table does not appear to be different from a standard HTML table. However, to a person using a screen reader, this table is entirely different. Instead of reading the table from left to right and top to bottom, the table is now read in a more intelligent manner. A screen reader would vocalize the data from the table in Fig. 34.3 as follows:

```
Caption: Price of Fruit
Summary: This table uses TH and the ID and HEADERS attributes
to make the table readable by screen readers.
Fruit: Apple, Price: $0.25
Fruit: Orange, Price: $0.50
Fruit: Banana, Price: $1.00
Fruit: Pineapple, Price: $2.00
```

Every cell in the table is preceded its corresponding header, when read by the screen reader. This helps the listener understand the table. The **HEADERS** attribute is specifically intended for tables which hold large amounts of data. In practice, a table the size of the one in our example would probably not warrant the need for the **HEADERS** attribute. Most small tables linearize fairly well as long as the **<TH>** tag. It also helps to use the **SUMMARY** and **CAPTION** attributes are used to describe them.

For more examples demonstrating how to make tables more accessible, visit **www.w3.org/TR/WCAG**.

34.5 Accessibility in HTML Frames

Frames are a technique Web designers use to display more than one HTML file at a time and are a convenient way to ensure that certain content is always on screen. Unfortunately, frame often lack a proper description. This prevents users with text-based browsers, or users who lack sight, from navigating the Web site.

The most important part of documenting a site with frames is making sure that all of the frames are given a meaningful description within the **<TITLE>** tag. Examples of good titles might be: "*Graphical Navigation Frame*" or "*Main Content Frame.*" Users with text-based browsers such as Lynx, a UNIX-based Web browser, must choose which frame they want to open, and the use of descriptive titles can make this choice much simpler for them. However, giving frames titles does not solve all frame navigation problems.

The **<NOFRAMES>** tag allows the designer to offer alternative content to user's whose browsers do not support frames. For an example of how to use the **<NOFRAMES>** tag see Chapter 10.

Good Programming Practice 34.2

Always give a text equivalent for frames to ensure that user agents, which do not support frames, are given an alternative.

Good Programming Practice 34.3

Include a description of the each frame's contents within the **<NOFRAMES>** *tag.*

The Web Content Accessibility Guidelines 1.0 suggest using Cascading Style Sheets as an alternative to frames because they can provide similar results and are highly customizible. Unfortunately, the ability to display multiple HTML documents at a time requires the second generation of Cascading Style Sheets (CSS2), which is **not** yet fully supported by many user agents. The advantage of Cascading Style Sheets is that a user who has a text-based user agent can turn off style sheets and still have access to important content.

34.6 Using Voice Synthesis and Recognition with VoiceXML™

A joint effort by AT&T, IBM®, Lucent and Motorola has created an XML application which uses *speech synthesis* to enable the computer to speak to the user. This technology, called *VoiceXML*, has tremendous implications for visually impaired people and for the illiterate. Not only does VoiceXML read Web pages to the user, but it also includes *speech recognition* technology—a technology which enables computers to understand words spoken into the microphone—enabling it to interact with users. An example of a speech recognition tool is IBM's *ViaVoice* (`www-4.ibm.com/software/speech`).

VoiceXML is processed by a VoiceXML interpreter or VoiceXML browser; Web browsers might incorporate these interpreters in the future. Because VoiceXML is derived from XML it is platform independent. When a VoiceXML document is loaded, a *voice server* sends a message to the VoiceXML browser and begins a conversation between the user and the computer.

Voice Server SDK, which was developed by IBM, is a free beta version of a VoiceXML interpreter and can be used for desktop testing of VoiceXML documents. Visit `www.alphaworks.ibm.com` for hardware and software specifications and for more information on Voice Server SDK. Instructions on how to run VoiceXML documents can be obtained along with the software.

Figure 34.4 is an example of a VoiceXML document. The document's text is spoken to the user and the text embedded within the VoiceXML tags will allow for interactivity between the user and their browser. The output included in Fig. 34.4 demonstrates a conversation that might take place between the user and the computer when this document is loaded:

```
1   <?xml version = "1.0"?>
2   <vxml version = "1.0">
3
4   <!-- Fig. 34.4: main.vxml -->
5   <!-- Voice page            -->
6
7   <link next = "#home">
8      <grammar>home</grammar>
9   </link>
10
11  <link next = "#end">
12     <grammar>exit</grammar>
13  </link>
14
15  <var name = "currentOption" expr = "'home'"/>
16
17  <form>
18     <block>
19        <emp>Welcome</emp> to the voice page of Deitel and
20        Associates. To exit any time say exit.
21        To go to home page any time say home.
```

Fig. 34.4   A home page written in VoiceXML.

```
22        </block>
23        <subdialog src = "#home"/>
24    </form>
25
26    <menu id = "home">
27        <prompt count = "1" timeout = "10s">
28            You have just entered the Deitel home page.
29            Please make a selection by speaking one the
30            following options:
31            <break msecs = "1000 "/>
32            <enumerate/>
33        </prompt>
34
35        <prompt count = "2">
36            Please say one of the following.
37            <break msecs = "1000 "/>
38            <enumerate/>
39        </prompt>
40
41        <choice next = "#about">About us</choice>
42        <choice next = "#directions">Driving directions</choice>
43        <choice next = "publications.vxml">Publications</choice>
44    </menu>
45
46    <form id = "about">
47        <block>
48          About Deitel and Associates, Inc.
49          Deitel and Associates, Inc. is an internationally
50        recognized corporate training and publishing organization,
51          specializing in programming languages, Internet and World
52          Wide Web technology and object technology education.
53          Deitel and Associates, Inc. is a member of the World Wide
54          Web Consortium. The company provides courses on Java, C++,
55          Visual Basic, C, Internet and World Wide Web programming
56          and Object Technology.
57          <assign name = "currentOption" expr = "'about'"/>
58          <goto next = "#repeat"/>
59        </block>
60    </form>
61
62    <form id = "directions">
63      <block>
64          Directions to Deitel and Associates, Inc.
65          We are located on Route 20 in Sudbury,
66          Massachusetts, equidistant from route
67        <sayas class = "digits">128</sayas> and route
68        <sayas class = "digits">495</sayas>.
69        <assign name = "currentOption" expr = "'directions'"/>
70        <goto next = "#repeat"/>
71      </block>
72    </form>
73
```

Fig. 34.4   A home page written in VoiceXML.

```
74    <form id = "repeat">
75       <field name = "confirm" type = "boolean">
76          <prompt>
77             To repeat say yes. To go back to home, say no.
78          </prompt>
79
80          <filled>
81             <if cond = "confirm==true">
82                <goto expr = "'#' + currentOption"/>
83             <else/>
84                <goto next = "#home"/>
85             </if>
86          </filled>
87
88       </field>
89    </form>
90
91    <form id = "end">
92       <block>
93          Thank you for visiting Deitel and Associates voice page.
94          Have a nice day.
95          <exit/>
96       </block>
97    </form>
98
99    </vxml>
```

Computer:
**Welcome to the voice page of Deitel and Associates. To exit any time
say exit. To go to the home page any time say home.**

User:
Home

Computer:
**You have just entered the Deitel home page. Please make a selection
by speaking one of the following options: About us, Driving directions, Publications.**

User:
Driving directions

Computer:
**Directions to Deitel and Associates, Inc.
We are located on Route 20 in Sudbury,
Massachusetts, equidistant from route 128
and route 495.
To repeat say yes. To go back to home, say no.**

Fig. 34.4   A home page written in VoiceXML.

A VoiceXML document is made up of a series of dialogs and sub-dialogs, which result
in speech induced interaction between the user and the computer. The highest-level tags

which implement the dialogs are the **<form>** and **<menu>** tags. A **form** element presents information and gathers data from the user pertaining to a set of *field* variables. A **menu** element provides different options to the user and transfers control to other dialogs in the document based on the user's selections. The **menu** element on line 26 enables the user to select, verbally, the page to which they would like to link. The **<choice>** tag, which is always an element of either a **menu** or a **form**, presents these options to the user. Its attribute, **next**, indicates the page which is loaded after the user makes their selection, by speaking the words in the **<choice>** tag into a microphone. In this example, the first and second **choice** elements on lines 41 and 42 transfer control to a *local dialog* (i.e., a location within the same document) when they are selected. The third **choice** element transfers the user to the document **publications.vxml**

Figure 34.5 provides an explanation of each of the VoiceXML tags used in the previous example.

VoiceXML Tag	Explanation
<assign>	Assigns a value to a variable.
<block>	Presents information to the user without any interaction between user and computer (i.e., the computer does not expect any input from the user).
<break>	Instructs the computer to pause its speech output for a specified period of time.
<choice>	Specifies an option in a **menu** element.
<enumerate>	Lists all the available options to the user.
<exit>	Exits the program.
<filled>	Contains elements to be executed when the computer receives input for a **form** element from the user.
<form>	Gathers information from the user for a set of variables.
<goto>	Transfers control from one dialog to another.
<grammar>	Specifies grammar for the expected input from the user.
<if>, <else>, <elseif>	Control statements used for making logic decisions.
<link>	A transfer of control similar to the **goto** statement, but a **link** can be executed at any time during the program's execution.
<menu>	Provides user options and transfers control to other dialogs based on the selected option.
<prompt>	Specifies text to be read to the user when a decision must be made.
<subdialog>	Calls another dialog. Control is transferred back to the calling dialog after the subdialog is executed.
<var>	Declares a variable.
<vxml>	The top-level tag which specifies the document should be processed by a VoiceXML interpreter.

Fig. 34.5   Elements in VoiceXML.

34.7 Accessibility in Microsoft® Windows® 2000

Beginning with Microsoft Windows 95, Microsoft has included accessibility features in its operating systems and many of its applications, including Office 97, Office 2000 and Netmeeting. In Microsoft Windows 2000, the accessibility features have been significantly enhanced. All of the accessibility options provided by Windows 2000 are available through the **Accessibility Wizard**, which guides a user through all of the Windows 2000 accessibility features and configures their computer according to the chosen specifications. This section guides the user through the configuration of their Windows 2000 accessibility options using the **Accessibility Wizard**.

To access the **Accessibility Wizard**, you must be using Microsoft Windows 2000. Click the **Start** button and select **Programs** followed by **Accessories**, **Accessibility** and **Accessibility Wizard**. When the wizard starts, the **Welcome** screen is displayed. Click **Next >**. The next dialog (Fig. 34.6) asks the user to select a font size. Click **Next >**.

Figure 34.7 shows the next dialog displayed. This dialog allows the user to activate the font size settings chosen in the previous window, change the screen resolution, enable the *Microsoft Magnifier* (a program that displays an enlarged section of the screen in a separate window) and disable personalized menus (a feature which hides rarely used programs from the start menu), which can be a hindrance to disabled users. Make selections and click **Next >**.

The next dialog (Fig. 34.8) displayed asks questions about the user's disabilities, which allows the **Accessibility Wizard** to customize Windows to better suit their needs. We selected everything for demonstration purposes. Click **Next >** to continue.

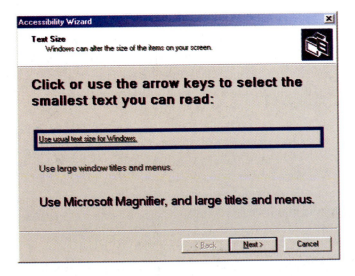

Fig. 34.6   Font Size dialog.

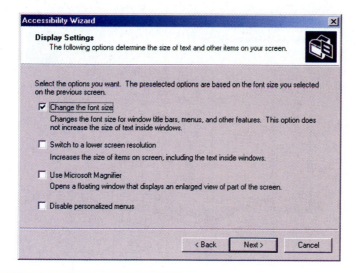

Fig. 34.7　**Display Settings** dialog.

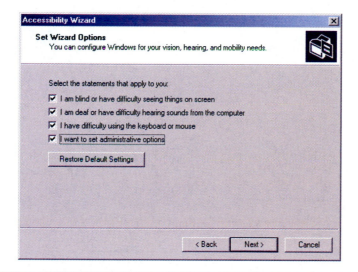

Fig. 34.8　**Accessibility Wizard** initialization options.

34.7.1 Tools for Visually Impaired People

Because we checked all of the options, in Fig. 34.8, the wizard begins by configuring Windows for visually impaired people. As shown in Fig. 34.9, this dialog box allows the user to resize the scroll bars and window borders to increase their visibility. Click **Next >** to proceed to the next dialog.

　　Figure 34.10's dialog allows the user to resize icons. Users with poor vision, as well as users who have trouble reading benefit from large icons.

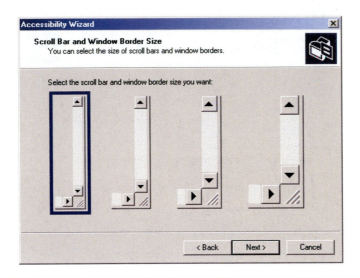

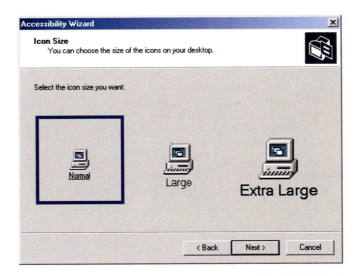

Clicking **Next >** displays the **Display Color Settings** dialog (Fig. 34.11). These settings allow the user to change Windows' color scheme and to resize various screen elements. Click **Next >** to view the dialog (Fig. 34.12) for customizing the mouse cursor.

Anyone who has ever used a laptop computer knows how difficult it is to see the mouse cursor. This is also a problem for visually impaired people. To help solve this problem the wizard offers the user the choice of using larger cursors, black cursors and cursors that invert the colors of objects underneath them. Click **Next >**.

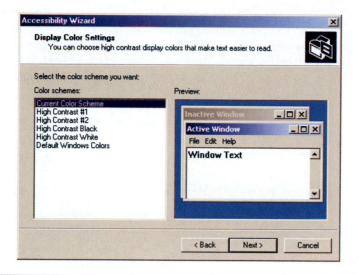

Fig. 34.11   **Display Color Settings** options.

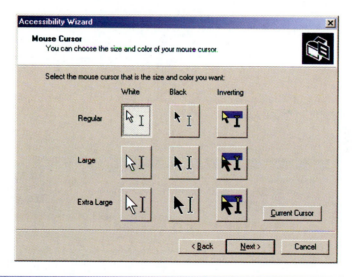

Fig. 34.12   **Accessibility Wizard** mouse cursor adjustment tool.

34.7.2 Tools for Hearing-Impaired People

This section, which focuses on accessibility for deaf and hearing-impaired people, begins with the **SoundSentry** window (Fig. 34.13). **SoundSentry** is a tool which creates visual signals when system events occur. For example, since hearing-impaired people are unable to hear the beeps, which normally warn users, **SoundSentry** flashes the screen when a beep occurs. To continue on to the next dialog click **Next >**.

The next window is the **ShowSounds** window (Fig. 34.14). **ShowSounds** adds captions to spoken text and other sounds produced by today's multimedia-rich software. For **ShowSounds** to work, software developers must specifically provide the captions and spoken text within their software. Make selections and click **Next >**.

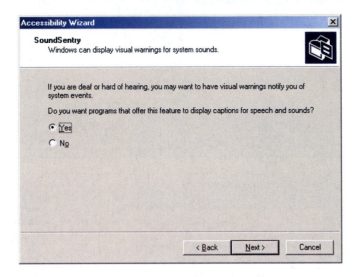

Fig. 34.13   SoundSentry dialog.

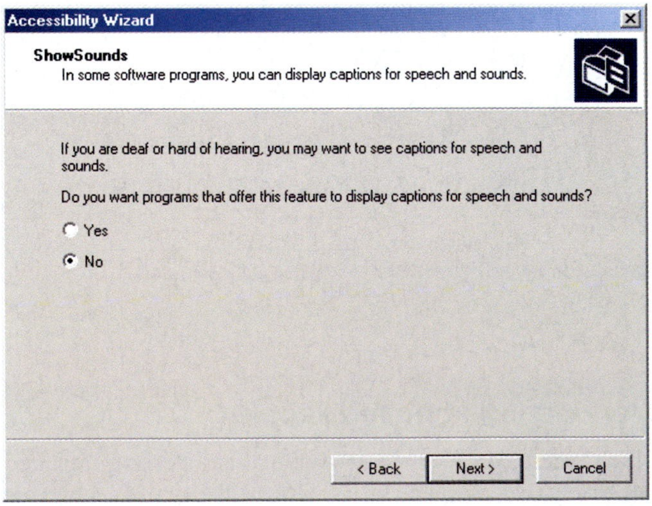

Fig. 34.14   Show Sounds dialog.

34.7.3 Tools for Users Who Have Difficulty Using the Keyboard

The next dialog is **StickyKeys** (Fig. 34.15). **StickyKeys** is a program that helps users who have difficulty pressing multiple keys at the same time. Many important computer commands can only be invoked by pressing specific key combinations. For example, the reboot command requires pressing *Ctrl+Alt+Delete simultaneously*. **StickyKeys** allows the user to press key combinations in sequence rather than at the same time. Click **Next >** to continue to the **BounceKeys** dialog (Fig. 34.16).

Another common problem for certain users with disabilities is accidentally pressing the same key more than once. This problem is typically caused by holding a key down too long. **BounceKeys** forces the computer to ignore repeated keystrokes. Click **Next >**.

ToggleKeys (Fig. 34.17) alerts the user that they have pressed one of the lock keys (i.e., *Caps Lock*, *Num Lock* and *Scroll Lock*), by sounding an audible beep. Make selections and click **Next >**.

Next, the **Extra Keyboard Help** dialog (Fig. 34.18) is displayed. This section is used to activate a tool which displays information such as keyboard shortcuts and tool tips when they are available. Like ShowSounds, this tool requires that software developers provide the content to be displayed. Clicking **Next >** will load the **MouseKeys** (Fig. 34.19) customization window.

MouseKeys is a tool which uses the keyboard to emulate mouse movements. The arrow keys direct the mouse, while the *5* key sends a single click. To double click, the user must press the *+* key, and to simulate holding down the mouse button, the user must press the *Ins* (Insert) key. To release the mouse button, the user must press the *Del* (Delete) key. To continue to the next screen in the **Accessibility Wizard**, click **Next >**.

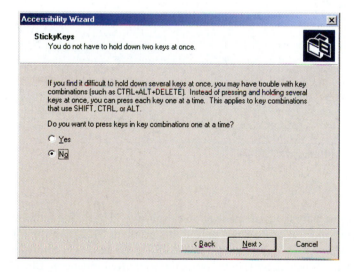

Fig. 34.15 StickyKeys window.

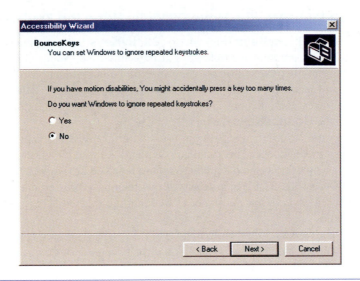

Fig. 34.16   BounceKeys dialog.

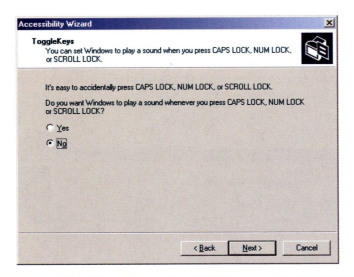

Fig. 34.17   ToggleKeys window.

Today's computer tools are made almost exclusively for right-handed users, including most computer mice. Microsoft recognized this problem by adding the **Mouse Button Settings** window (Fig. 34.20) to the **Accessibility Wizard**. This tool allows the user to create a virtual left-handed mouse, by swapping the button functions. Click **Next >**.

Mouse speed is adjusted using the **MouseSpeed** (Fig. 34.21) section of the **Accessibility Wizard**. Dragging the scroll bar changes the speed. Clicking the **Next** button sets the speed and displays the wizard's **Set Automatic Timeouts** window (Fig. 34.22).

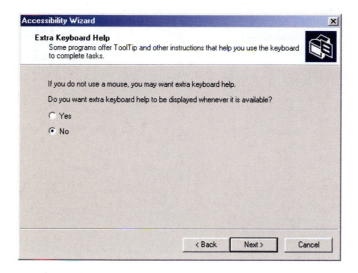

Fig. 34.18   Extra Keyboard Help dialog.

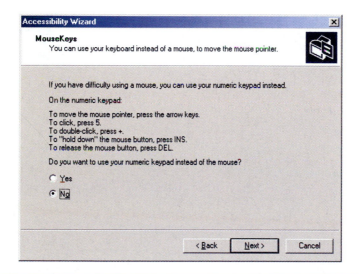

Fig. 34.19   MouseKeys window.

Although accessibility tools are important to users with disabilities, they can be a hindrance to users who do not need them. In situations where there are varying accessibility needs, it is important that the user be able to turn the accessibility tools off and on as necessary. The **Set Automatic Timeouts** window specifies a *timeout* period for the tools. A timeout either enables or disables a certain action after the computer has idled for a specified amount of time. A screen saver is a common example of a program with a timeout period. Here, a timeout is set to toggle the accessibility tools.

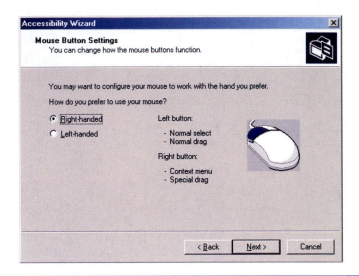

Fig. 34.20   Mouse Button Settings window.

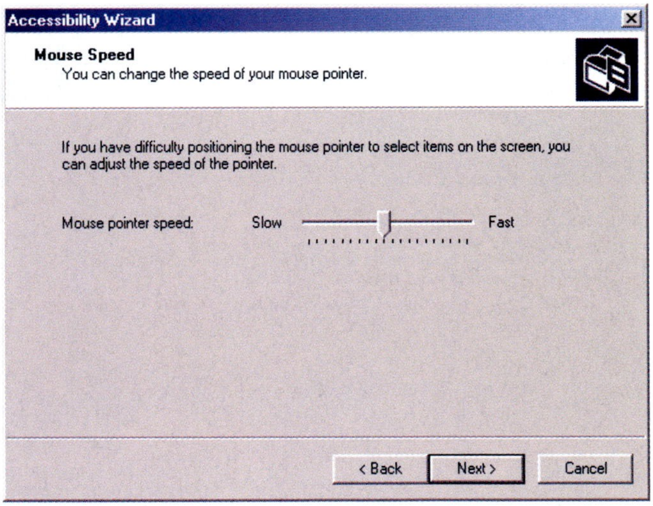

Fig. 34.21   Mouse Speed dialog.

After clicking **Next >** you will brought to the **Save Settings to File** dialog (34.23). This dialog determines whether the accessibility settings should be used as the *default settings*, which are loaded when the computer is rebooted or after a timeout. Set the accessibility settings as the default if the majority of users need them. You can also save the accessibility settings. The user can create an **.acw** file, which, when clicked, automatically activates the saved accessibility settings on any Windows 2000 computer.

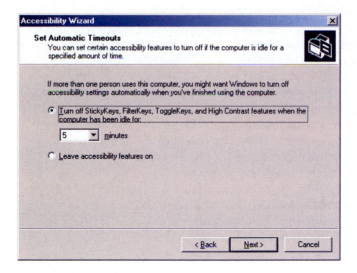

Fig. 34.22   Set Automatic Timeouts.

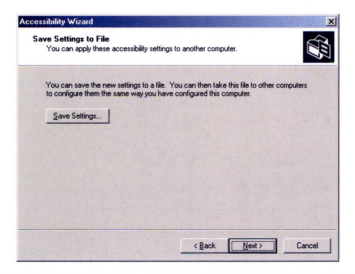

Fig. 34.23   Saving new accessibility settings.

34.7.4 Microsoft Narrator

Microsoft **Narrator** *is a* *text-to-speech* program for visually impaired people. It reads text, describes the current desktop environment and alerts the user when certain Windows events occur. **Narrator** is intended to aid in configuring Microsoft Windows. It is a screen reader that works with Internet Explorer, Wordpad, Notepad and most programs in the **Control Panel**. Though it is limited outside these applications, **Narrator** is excellent at navigating the Windows environment.

To get an idea of what **Narrator** does, we will explain how to use it with various Windows applications. Click the **Start** button and select **Programs** followed by **Accessories**, **Accessibility** and **Narrator**. Once **Narrator** is open, it describes the current foreground window. Then it reads the text inside the window aloud to the user. Clicking **OK** displays Fig. 34.24's dialog.

Checking the first option instructs **Narrator** to describe menus and new windows when they are opened. The second option instructs **Narrator** to speak the characters you are typing as you type them. The third option automatically moves the mouse cursor to the region that is being read by **Narrator**. Clicking the **Voice...** button enables the user to change the pitch, volume and speed of the narrator voice.

With **Narrator** running, open **Notepad** and click the **File** menu. **Narrator** announces the opening of the program and begins to describe the items in the **File** menu. When scrolling down the list, **Narrator** reads the current item to which the mouse is pointing. Type some text and press *Ctrl-Shift-Enter* to hear **Narrator** read it (Fig. 34.25). If the **Read typed characters** option is checked, **Narrator** reads each character as it is typed. The direction arrows on the keyboard can be used to make **Narrator** read. The up and down arrows cause **Narrator** to speak the lines adjacent to the current mouse position and the left and right arrows cause **Narrator** to speak the characters adjacent to the current mouse position.

Fig. 34.24   Narrator window.

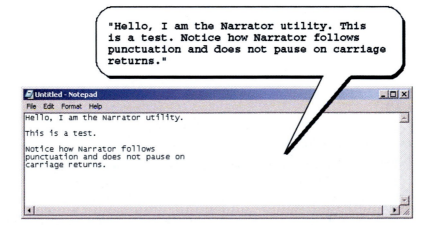

Fig. 34.25   Narrator reading **Notepad** text.

34.7.5 Microsoft On-Screen Keyboard

Some computer users lack the ability to use a keyboard, but have the ability to use a pointing device such as a mouse. For these users, the *On-Screen Keyboard* is helpful. To access the On-Screen Keyboard, click the **Start** button and select **Programs** followed by **Accessories**, **Accessibility** and **On-Screen Keyboard**. Figure 34.26 shows the layout of the Microsoft On-Screen Keyboard.

Users who still have difficulty using the On-Screen Keyboard should purchase more sophisticated products, such as *Clicker 4* by Inclusive Technology. Clicker 4 was developed as an aid for people who cannot effectively use a keyboard. Its best feature is its ability to be customized. Keys can have letters, numbers, entire words or even pictures on them. For more information regarding Clicker 4 visit **www.inclusive.co.uk/catalog/ clicker.htm**.

34.7.6 Accessibility Features in Microsoft Internet Explorer 5.0

Internet Explorer 5.0 offers a variety of options to improve usability. To access Internet Explorer 5.0's accessibility features, launch the program, click the **Tools** menu and select **Internet Options...**. From the **Internet Options** menu, press the button labeled **Accessibility...** to open the accessibility options (Fig. 34.27).

The accessibility options, in Microsoft Internet Explorer 5.0, augment the user's Web browsing. Users are able to ignore Web colors, Web fonts and font size tags. This eliminates problems that arise from poor Web page design and allows the user to customize their Web browsing. Users can even specify a *style sheet* which formats every Web site the user visits, according to their personal preferences.

These are not the only accessibility options offered in Internet Explorer 5.0. In the **Internet Options** dialog click the **Advanced** tab. This opens the dialog shown in Fig. 34.28. The first option that can be set is labeled **Always expand ALT text for images**. By default, Internet Explorer 5.0 hides some of the **<ALT>** text, if it exceeds the size of the image it describes. This option forces all of the text to be shown. The second option reads: **Move system caret with focus/selection changes**. This option is intended to make screen reading more effective. Some screen readers use the *system caret* (the blinking vertical bar associated with editing text) to decide what is read. If this option is not activated, screen readers may not read Web pages correctly.

Fig. 34.26 Microsoft **On-Screen Keyboard**.

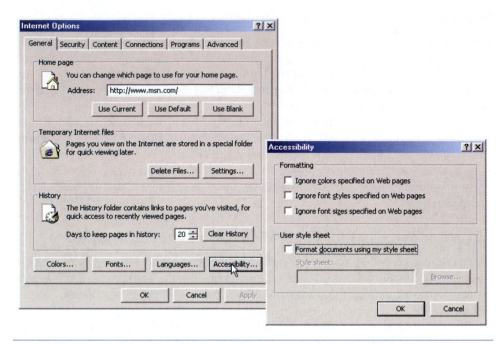

Fig. 34.27   Microsoft Internet Explorer 5.0's accessibility options.

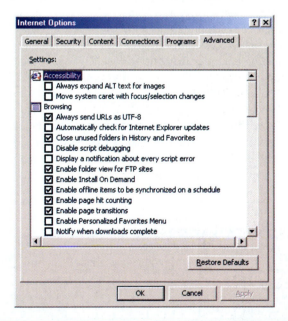

Fig. 34.28   Advanced accessibility settings in Microsoft Internet Explorer 5.0.

Web designers often forget to take accessibility into account when creating Web sites and use fonts that are too small. Many user agents have addressed this problem, by allowing for the user to adjust the text size. Click the **View** menu and select **Text Size** to change the font size using Internet Explorer 5.0. Figure 34.29 shows the resulting sub-menu. By default, the text size is set to **Medium**.

34.8 JAWS® for Windows

JAWS (Job Access With Sound) is one of the leading screen readers on the market today. It was created by Henter-Joyce a division of Freedom Scientific™, a company that tries to help visually impaired people to use technology.

To download a demonstration version of JAWS, visit **www.hj.com/JAWS/ JAWS35DemoOp.htm** and click the **JAWS 3.5 FREE Demo** link. This demo will run for 40 minutes, after which it will terminate. The computer must be rebooted before another 40 minute session can be started.

The JAWS demo is fully functional and includes an extensive help menu that is highly customizible. The user can select which voice to utilize, the rate at which text is spoken and create keyboard shortcuts. Although the demo is in English, the full version of JAWS 3.5 allows the user to choose one of several supported languages.

JAWS also includes special key commands for popular programs, such as Microsoft Internet Explorer and Microsoft Word. For example, when browsing in Internet Explorer, JAWS' capabilities extend beyond just reading the content on the screen. If JAWS is enabled, pressing *Insert + F7*, in Internet Explorer, opens a **Links List** dialog, which displays all the Web page links. For more information about JAWS and the other products offered by Henter-Joyce, visit **www.hj.com**.

34.9 Other Accessibility Tools

Most of the accessibility products offered today are aimed at helping hearing and visually impaired people. However, software does exist to help those with other types of disabilities. This section describes some other accessibility products we have not yet discussed.

One such product is the *braille keyboard*. A braille keyboard is similar to a standard keyboard except that in addition to having the letters written on every key it has the equivalent braille symbol. Most often, braille keyboards are combined with a speech synthesizer or a braille display, so the user is able to interact with the computer and verify that their typing is correct.

Fig. 34.29 Accessing the **Text Size** menu in Microsoft Internet Explorer 5.0.

In fact, speech synthesis is another area of research being done to help people with disabilities. Speech synthesizers are not new to the computer world. They have been used to aid those who are unable to verbally communicate for many years. However, the growing popularity of the Web has prompted a great deal of work in the field of speech synthesis and speech recognition. These technologies are allowing the handicapped to utilize computers more than ever before. The development of speech synthesizers is also enabling other technologies to improve such as VoiceXML and *AuralCSS* (**www.w3.org/TR/REC-CSS2/aural.html**). These tools allow visually impaired people and those who cannot read to access Web sites.

Visually impaired people are not the only beneficiaries of the effort being made to improve *markup languages*—languages such as HTML, designed to layout and link text files. The deaf also have a great number of tools to help them interpret auditory information delivered over the Web. Hearing-impaired Web users will soon benefit from what is called *Synchronized Multimedia Integration Language* (SMIL™). This markup language is designed to add extra *tracks*—layers of content found within a single audio or video file. The additional tracks can contain data such as closed captioning.

Products are also being designed to help severely handicapped persons, such as those with quadriplegia, a form of paralysis which effects the body from the neck down. One such product, *EagleEyes*, developed by researchers at Boston College, (**www.cs.bc.edu/~eagleeye**) is a system that translates eye movements into mouse movements. The user moves the mouse cursor by moving their eyes or head, through the use of electrodes.

These are just a few of the accessibility projects and technologies that currently exist. For more information on Web and general computer accessibility, see the following section entitled Internet and World Wide Web Resources.

34.10 Internet and World Wide Web Resources

There are many accessibility resources on the Internet and World Wide Web and this section lists a variety of them.

www.w3.org/WAI
The World Wide Web Consortium's *Web Accessibility Initiative (WAI)* site promotes design of universally accessible Web sites. This site will help you keep up-to-date with current guidelines and forthcoming standards for Web accessibility.

www.w3.org/TR/WCAG10
This page is a note published by the WCAG working group. It discusses techniques that can be used to comply with the WAI. This is a great resource and can be used to find additional information on many of the topics covered in this chapter.

deafness.about.com/health/deafness/msubmenu6.htm
This is the home page of **deafness.about.com**. It is an excellent resource to find information pertaining to deafness.

www.cast.org
CAST stands for the Center for Applied Special Technology. They offer software intended to help individuals with disabilities use a computer, including a valuable accessibility checker—free of charge. The accessibility checker is a Web based program used to validate the accessibility of Web sites.

www.trainingpost.org/3-2-inst.htm
This site presents a tutorial on the Gunning Fog Index. The Gunning Fog Index is a method of grading text on its readability.

www.w3.org/TR/REC-CSS2/aural.html
This page discusses Aural Style Sheets, outlining the purpose and uses of this new technology.

laurence.canlearn.ca/English/learn/newaccessguide/indie
INDIE is an acronym which stands for "Integrated Network of Disability Information and Education." This site is home to a powerful search engine which help users find out information about disabilities.

java.sun.com/products/java-media/speech/forDevelopers/JSML
This site outlines the specifications for JSML, Sun Microsystem's Java Speech Markup Language. This language, like VoiceXML, could drastically improve accessibility for visually impaired people.

www.slcc.edu/webguide/lynxit.html
Lynxit is a development tool that allows users to view any Web site just as a text-only browser would. The site's form allows you to enter a URL and returns the Web site in text-only format.

www.trill-home.com/lynx/public_lynx.html
This site allows you to use browse the Web using a Lynx browser. Doing so will allow you to see how your page will load for users without the most current technologies.

www.wgbh.org/wgbh/pages/ncam/accesslinks.html
This site provides links to other accessibility pages across the Web.

ocfo.ed.gov/coninfo/clibrary/software.htm
This is the U.S. Department of Education's Web site for software accessibility requirements. It is aimed at helping developers produce accessible products.

www.alphaworks.ibm.com
This is the home page for IBM Alphaworks. It provides information on VoiceXML and offers a download of the beta version of Voice Server SDK.

www-3.ibm.com/able/access.html
This is the homepage of IBM's accessibility site. It provides information on IBM products and their accessibility and also discusses hardware, software and Web accessibility.

www.microsoft.com/enable/dev/guidelines/software.htm
This Web site presents Microsoft's guidelines to designing accessible software.

www.w3.org/TR/voice-tts-reqs
This page explains the speech synthesis markup requirements for voice markup languages.

deafness.about.com/health/deafness/msubvib.htm
This site provides information on deafness; it outlines vibrotactile devices. These devices allow deaf people to experience audio in the form of vibrations.

web.ukonline.co.uk/ddmc/software.html
This site provides links to software for people with disabilities.

www.hj.com
Henter-Joyce a division of Freedom Scientific provides software for the blind and visually impaired people. It is the home of JAWS.

www.abledata.com/text2/icg_hear.htm
This page contains a consumer guide that discusses technologies for hearing-impaired people.

www.washington.edu/doit
The University of Washington's DO-IT (Disabilities, Opportunities, Internetworking and Technology) site provides information and Web development resources for creating universally accessible Web sites.

www.webable.com
The WebABLE site contains links to many disability-related Internet resources and is geared towards those looking to develop technologies for people with disabilities.

`www.speech.cs.cmu.edu/comp.speech/SpeechLinks.html`
The Speech Technology Hyperlinks page has over 500 links to sites related to computer-based speech and speech recognition tools.

`www.islandnet.com/~tslemko`
The Micro Consulting Limited site contains shareware speech synthesis software.

`www.chantinc.com/technology`
This is the Chant Web site, which discusses speech technology and how it works. Chant also provides speech synthesis and speech recognition software.

SUMMARY

- Accessibility, the level of usability for people with disabilities, is difficult to maintain because of disabilities, language barriers, hardware and software inconsistencies and other variables.

- One important WAI requirement is to ensure that every image, movie and sound used on a Web page is accompanied by a description that clearly defines its purpose. One way of accomplishing this is to include a description of each item using the **ALT** attribute of the **<IMG>** and **<INPUT>** tags.

- A text equivalent for **OBJECT** elements should also be provided, because they do not have an **ALT** attribute in the HTML 4.01 specification.

- Specialized *user agents*, such as *screen readers* (programs which allow users to hear what is being displayed on their screen) and *braille displays* (devices that receive data from screen reading software and output the data as braille) allow blind and visually impaired people to access text-based information that is normally displayed on the screen.

- A user agent is an application that interprets Web page source code and translates it into formatted text and images. Web browsers such as Microsoft Internet Explorer and Netscape Communicator and the screen readers mentioned throughout this chapter are examples of user agents.

- Images, movies and other non-HTML objects cannot be read by screen readers. Providing multimedia-based information in a variety of ways (i.e., using the **ALT** attribute or providing inline descriptions of images) helps maximize the content's accessibility.

- The **LONGDESC** attribute is intended to augment the description provided by the **ALT** attribute. The value of the **LONGDESC** attribute hold be a text-based URL, which describes the image.

- If you use image maps, we recommend using client-side image maps (image maps which have links that can be understood by non-graphical user agents), providing generous descriptions and providing corresponding text links to all image maps.

- Many Web sites use tags for aesthetic purposes rather than the purpose for which they were intended. For example, one might use the header tag, **<H1>**, to make text in the middle of a paragraph large and bold.

- Another accessibility issue is *readability*. When creating a Web page intended for the general public, it is important to consider the reading level at which it is written.

- The *Web Content Accessibility Guidelines 1.0* suggest using a paragraph's first sentence to convey its subject. Immediately stating the point makes finding crucial information much easier and allows those unable to comprehend large amounts of text to bypass unwanted material.

- A good way to evaluate the readability of your Web site is by using the Gunning Fog Index. The Gunning Fog Index is a formula which produces a readability grade when applied to a Web site.

- Complex Web pages often contain tables and screen readers are incapable of translating tables in an understandable manner, unless they are designed properly.

- Screen readers start at the top-left-hand cell and read left to right and top to bottom. This is known as reading a table in a *linearized* manner.

- By modifying the **<TD>** tag with the **HEADERS** attribute and modifying header cells (cells specified by the **<TH>** tag) with the **ID** attribute, you can ensure that a table will be read as intended.

- The most important part of documenting a site with frames is making sure that all of the pages in a frameset are given a meaningful description within the **<TITLE>** tag. Users with text-based browsers such as Lynx, a UNIX-based Web browser, must choose which frame they want to open, and the use of descriptive titles can make this choice much simpler for them.

- Always give a text equivalent for a frameset to ensure that user agents that do not support frames are given an alternative. To do so, use the **<NOFRAMES>** tag.

- The **<NOFRAMES>** tag explains that the user's browser does not support frames and provides the user with a link to another page (which you need to provide) where they can view the material without frames.

- The Web Content Accessibility Guidelines 1.0 suggest using Cascading Style Sheets as an alternative to frames because they provide similar results and are highly customizible.

- VoiceXML reads Web pages to the user using speech synthesis software and also includes speech recognition technology—a technology which enables computers to understand words spoken into the microphone—enabling it to interact with users.

- The text of a VoiceXML document will be spoken to the user and the code embedded within special VoiceXML tags will allow for interactivity between the user and his or her browser.

- A **form** element, in VoiceXML, presents information and gathers data from the user pertaining to a set of field variables.

- A **menu** element, in VoiceXML, provides different options to the user and transfers control to other dialogs in the document based on the user's selections.

- The **<choice>** tag, which is always an element of either a **menu** or a **form**, presents VoiceXML options to the user. Its attribute, **next**, indicates the page which is to be loaded after the user makes his or her selection. A selection is made by repeating the words in the **<choice>** tag into your microphone.

- All of the accessibility options provided by Windows 2000 are available through the **Accessibility Wizard**. The **Accessibility Wizard** takes a user step by step through all of the Windows accessibility features and configures his or her computer according to the chosen specifications.

- Microsoft Magnifier enlarges the section of your screen surrounding the mouse cursor.

- To solve problems seeing the mouse cursor Microsoft offers the ability to use larger cursors, black cursors and cursors that invert objects underneath them.

- SoundSentry is a tool which creates visual signals when system events occur.

- ShowSounds adds captions to spoken text and other sounds produced by today's multimedia-rich software.

- StickyKeys is a program that was developed to help users who have difficulty pressing multiple keys at the same time.

- BounceKeys forces the computer to ignore repeated keystrokes, solving the problem of accidentally pressing the same key more than once.

- ToggleKeys causes an audible beep to alert the user that he or she has pressed one of the lock keys (i.e., *Caps Lock*, *Num Lock*, or *Scroll Lock*).

- MouseKeys is a tool which uses the keyboard to emulate mouse movements.

- The Mouse Button Settings tool allows you to create a virtual left-handed mouse, by swapping the button functions.

- A timeout either enables or disables a certain action after the computer has idled for a specified amount of time. A common example of a timeout is a screen saver.

- Default settings are loaded when the computer is rebooted.

- You can create an **.acw** file, which, when clicked, will automatically activate the saved accessibility settings on any Windows 2000 computer.

- Microsoft **Narrator** is a text-to-speech program for visually impaired people. It reads text, describes the current desktop environment and alerts the user when certain Windows events occur.

- Some computer users lack the ability to use a keyboard, but have the ability to use a mouse. For these users, the On-Screen Keyboard can be helpful. Users who still have difficulty using the On-Screen Keyboard should purchase more sophisticated products, such as Clicker 4 by Inclusive Technology.

- A style sheet formats every Web site you visit according to your own personal preferences.

- Web designers often forget to take accessibility into account when creating Web sites.

- JAWS (Job Access With Sound) is one of the leading screen readers on the market today.

- A braille keyboard is similar to a standard keyboard except that in addition to having the letters written on every key it has the equivalent braille symbol. Most often, braille keyboards are combined with a speech synthesizer (software which enables the computer to speak aloud) or a braille display, so the user is able to interact with the computer and verify that his or her typing is correct.

- markup languages are languages designed to layout and link text files; HTML is the most common example of a markup language.

- Synchronized Multimedia Integration Language (SMIL™) is a language designed to add extra tracks, which contain data such as closed captioning, to multimedia content.

- EagleEyes, developed by researchers at Boston College is a system that translates eye movements into mouse movements. It allows the user to move the mouse cursor by moving his or her eyes or head, through the use of electrodes.

TERMINOLOGY

.acw file
ALT attribute
<assign> tag in VoiceXML
accessibility
accessibility options in Internet Explorer 5.0
Accessibility Wizard
Accessibility Wizard: Display Color Settings
Accessibility Wizard: Icon Size
Accessibility Wizard: Mouse Cursor
Accessibility Wizard: Scroll Bar and Window Border Size
AuralCSS
<B> tag (bold)
<block> tag in VoiceXML
BounceKeys
braille keyboard
braille display
<break> tag in VoiceXML
<CAPTION>
Cascading Style Sheets (CSS)
<choice> tag in VoiceXML
client-side image map

Clicker 4 by Inclusive Technology
CSS2
default settings
EagleEyes
<enumerate> tag in VoiceXML
<exit> tag in VoiceXML
field variable
frames
<filled> tag in VoiceXML
<form> tag in VoiceXML
<goto> tag in VoiceXML
<grammar> tag in VoiceXML
Gunning Fog Index
<H1>
header cells
HEADERS attribute of **<TD>** tag
IBM ViaVoice
ID attribute
<if>, **<else>**, **<elseif>** tags in VoiceXML
<IMG> tag
JAWS (Job Access With Sound by Henter-Joyce a division of Freedom Scientific
linearized reading of a table

SELF-REVIEW EXERCISES

34.1   Expand the following acronyms:

     a)   W3C

     b)   WAI

     c)   JAWS

     d)   SMIL

     e)   CSS

34.2   Fill in the blanks in each of the following.

     a)   The highest priority of the Web Accessibility Initiative is to ensure that each _____, _____ and _____ is accompanied by a description which clearly defines its purpose.

     b)   Although they can be used as a great layout tool, _____ are difficult for screen readers to interpret and convey clearly to a user.

     c)   In order to make your framesets accessible to the handicapped, it is important to include _____ tags on your page.

     d)   To make its features more accessible, Windows 2000 features a(n) _____ that helps the user customize the computer's accessibility settings.

     e)   The Microsoft _____ is a text-to-_____ program for visually impaired people.

     f)   Blind people using computers are often assisted by_____ and _____.

34.3   State whether each of the following is *true* or *false*. If the statement is *false*, explain why.

     a)   Screen readers have no problem reading and translating images.

     b)   Image maps are no problem for screen readers to translate so long as the programmer has made changes to his code to improve accessibility.

c) When writing pages for the general public, it is important to consider the reading difficulty level of the text you are writing.

d) The Windows 2000 **Accessibility Wizard** can, among other things, help you modify the appearance of your system by changing colors, fonts, sizes, etc.

e) Left-handed people have been helped by the improvements made in speech-recognition technology more than any other group.

f) The Windows **Accessibility Wizard** has a feature that changes the on-screen appearance and speed of the mouse.

ANSWERS TO SELF-REVIEW EXERCISES

34.1   a) World Wide Web Consortium. b) Web Accessibility Initiative. c) Job Access With Sound. d) Synchronized Multimedia Integration Language. e) Cascading Style Sheets.

34.2   a) Image, Movie, Sound. b) Tables. c) **<NOFRAMES>**. d) **Accessibility Wizard**. e) **Narrator**, Speech. f) Braille displays, braille keyboards.

34.3   a) False. Screen readers have no way of telling a user what is shown in an image. If the programmer includes an **ALT** attribute inside the **<IMG>** tag, the screen reader will read this to the user. b) False. Screen readers have no way of translating image maps, no matter what programming changes are made. The solution to this problem is to include text-based links alongside all image maps. c) True. d) True. e) False. Although left-handed people can utilize speech-recognition technology like everyone else, speech-recognition technology has the largest impact on the blind and those who have trouble typing. f) True.

EXERCISES

34.4   Create a set of accessibility options for yourself using the Windows **Accessibility Wizard** and save them to a floppy disk. Use these new settings for half an hour and describe how they affect your computer usage.

34.5   Insert code into the following examples to make them handicapped accessible. The contents of images and frames should be apparent from the context and filenames:

a)
```
<IMG SRC = "dogs.jpg" WIDTH = 300 HEIGHT = 250>
```

b)
```
<TABLE BORDER = 1 WIDTH = 75% ALIGN = "Center">
<TR><TH>LANGUAGE</TH><TH>VERSION</TH></TR>
<TR><TD>HTML</TD><TD>4.0</TD></TR>
<TR><TD>PERL</TD><TD>5.0</TD></TR>
<TR><TD>WINDOWS</TD><TD>2000</TD></TR>1
</TABLE>
```

c)
```
<HTML>
<HEAD><TITLE>Antfarms 'R Us</TITLE></HEAD>

<BODY>
<MAP NAME = "links">
<AREA HREF = "index.html" SHAPE = "rect" COORDS = "50, 120,
80, 150">
<AREA HREF = "catalog.html" SHAPE = "circle" COORDS = "220,
30">
</MAP>

<IMG SRC = "antlinks.gif" WIDTH = 300 HEIGHT = 200 USEMAP =
"#links">
</BODY>
</HTML>
```

HTML Special
Characters

The table of A.1 shows many commonly used HTML special characters—called *character entity references* by the World Wide Web Consortium. For a complete list of character entity references, see the site

`http://www.w3.org/TR/REC-html40/sgml/entities.html`

Character	HTML encoding	Character	HTML encoding
non-breaking space	` `	ê	`&#234;`
§	`&#167;`	ì	`&#236;`
©	`&#169;`	í	`&#237;`
®	`&#174;`	î	`&#238;`
π	`&#188;`	ñ	`&#241;`
∫	`&#189;`	ò	`&#242;`
Ω	`&#190;`	ó	`&#243;`
à	`&#224;`	ô	`&#244;`
á	`&#225;`	õ	`&#245;`
â	`&#226;`	÷	`&#247;`
ã	`&#227;`	ù	`&#249;`
å	`&#229;`	ú	`&#250;`
ç	`&#231;`	û	`&#251;`
è	`&#232;`	•	`&#8226;`
é	`&#233;`	™	`&#8482;`

Fig. A.1 HTML special characters.

HTML Colors

Colors may be specified by using a standard name (such as **aqua**) or a hexadecimal RGB value (such as **#00FFFF** for aqua). Of the six hexadecimal digits in an RGB value, the first two represent the amount of red in the color, the middle two represent the amount of green in the color, and the last two represent the amount of blue in the color. For example, **black** is the absence of color and is defined by **#000000**, whereas **white** is the maximum amount of red, green and blue and is defined by **#FFFFFF**. Pure **red** is **#FF0000**, pure green (which the standard calls **lime**) is **#00FF00** and pure **blue** is **#00FFFF**. Note that **green** in the standard is defined as **#008000**. Figure B.1 contains the HTML standard color set. Figure B.2 contains the HTML extended color set.

Color name	Value	Color name	Value
aqua	#00FFFF	navy	#000080
black	#000000	olive	#808000
blue	#0000FF	purple	#800080
fuchsia	#FF00FF	red	#FF0000
gray	#808080	silver	#C0C0C0
green	#008000	teal	#008080
lime	#00FF00	yellow	#FFFF00
maroon	#800000	white	#FFFFFF

Fig. B.1   HTML standard colors and hexadecimal RGB values.

Color name	Value	Color name	Value
aliceblue	#F0F8FF	dodgerblue	#1E90FF
antiquewhite	#FAEBD7	firebrick	#B22222
aquamarine	#7FFFD4	floralwhite	#FFFAF0
azure	#F0FFFF	forestgreen	#228B22
beige	#F5F5DC	gainsboro	#DCDCDC
bisque	#FFE4C4	ghostwhite	#F8F8FF
blanchedalmond	#FFEBCD	gold	#FFD700
blueviolet	#8A2BE2	goldenrod	#DAA520
brown	#A52A2A	greenyellow	#ADFF2F
burlywood	#DEB887	honeydew	#F0FFF0
cadetblue	#5F9EA0	hotpink	#FF69B4
chartreuse	#7FFF00	indianred	#CD5C5C
chocolate	#D2691E	indigo	#4B0082
coral	#FF7F50	ivory	#FFFFF0
cornflowerblue	#6495ED	khaki	#F0E68C
cornsilk	#FFF8DC	lavender	#E6E6FA
crimson	#DC1436	lavenderblush	#FFF0F5
cyan	#00FFFF	lawngreen	#7CFC00
darkblue	#00008B	lemonchiffon	#FFFACD
darkcyan	#008B8B	lightblue	#ADD8E6
darkgoldenrod	#B8860B	lightcoral	#F08080
darkgray	#A9A9A9	lightcyan	#E0FFFF
darkgreen	#006400	lightgoldenrodyellow	#FAFAD2
darkkhaki	#BDB76B	lightgreen	#90EE90
darkmagenta	#8B008B	lightgrey	#D3D3D3
darkolivegreen	#556B2F	lightpink	#FFB6C1
darkorange	#FF8C00	lightsalmon	#FFA07A
darkorchid	#9932CC	lightseagreen	#20B2AA
darkred	#8B0000	lightskyblue	#87CEFA
darksalmon	#E9967A	lightslategray	#778899
darkseagreen	#8FBC8F	lightsteelblue	#B0C4DE
darkslateblue	#483D8B	lightyellow	#FFFFE0
darkslategray	#2F4F4F	limegreen	#32CD32
darkturquoise	#00CED1	linen	#FAF0E6
darkviolet	#9400D3	magenta	#FF00FF

Fig. B.2   HTML extended colors and hexadecimal RGB values (part 1 of 2).

Color name	Value	Color name	Value
deeppink	#FF1493	mediumaquamarine	#66CDAA
deepskyblue	#00BFFF	mediumblue	#0000CD
dimgray	#696969	mediumorchid	#BA55D3
mediumpurple	#9370DB	plum	#DDA0DD
mediumseagreen	#3CB371	powderblue	#B0E0E6
mediumslateblue	#7B68EE	rosybrown	#BC8F8F
mediumspringgreen	#00FA9A	royalblue	#4169E1
mediumturquoise	#48D1CC	saddlebrown	#8B4513
mediumvioletred	#C71585	salmon	#FA8072
midnightblue	#191970	sandybrown	#F4A460
mintcream	#F5FFFA	seagreen	#2E8B57
mistyrose	#FFE4E1	seashell	#FFF5EE
moccasin	#FFE4B5	sienna	#A0522D
navajowhite	#FFDEAD	skyblue	#87CEEB
oldlace	#FDF5E6	slateblue	#6A5ACD
olivedrab	#6B8E23	slategray	#708090
orange	#FFA500	snow	#FFFAFA
orangered	#FF4500	springgreen	#00FF7F
orchid	#DA70D6	steelblue	#4682B4
palegoldenrod	#EEE8AA	tan	#D2B48C
palegreen	#98FB98	thistle	#D8BFD8
paleturquoise	#AFEEEE	tomato	#FF6347
palevioletred	#DB7093	turquoise	#40E0D0
papayawhip	#FFEFD5	violet	#EE82EE
peachpuff	#FFDAB9	wheat	#F5DEB3
peru	#CD853F	whitesmoke	#F5F5F5
pink	#FFC0CB	yellowgreen	#9ACD32

Fig. B.2   HTML extended colors and hexadecimal RGB values (part 2 of 2).

ASCII Character Set

ASCII character set

	0	1	2	3	4	5	6	7	8	9
0	nul	soh	stx	etx	eot	enq	ack	bel	bs	ht
1	nl	vt	ff	cr	so	si	dle	dc1	dc2	dc3
2	dc4	nak	syn	etb	can	em	sub	esc	fs	gs
3	rs	us	sp	!	"	#	$	%	&	'
4	(	)	*	+	,	-	.	/	0	1
5	2	3	4	5	6	7	8	9	:	;
6	<	=	>	?	@	A	B	C	D	E
7	F	G	H	I	J	K	L	M	N	O
8	P	Q	R	S	T	U	V	W	X	Y
9	Z	[	\	]	^	_	'	a	b	c
10	d	e	f	g	h	i	j	k	l	m
11	n	o	p	q	r	s	t	u	v	w
12	x	y	z	{	|	}	~	del		

Fig. C.1 ASCII Character Set.

The digits at the left of the table are the left digits of the decimal equivalent (0-127) of the character code, and the digits at the top of the table are the right digits of the character code. For example, the character code for "**F**" is 70, and the character code for "**&**" is 38. *Note:* Most users of this book are interested in the ASCII character set used to represent English characters on many computers. The ASCII character set is a subset of the Unicode character set used by Java to represent characters from most of the world's languages. For more information on the Unicode character set, visit the World Wide Web site **http://unicode.org/**.

Operator Precedence Charts

This appendix contains the operator precedence charts for JavaScript/JScript/ECMAScript (Fig. B.1), VBScript (Fig. B.2) and Perl (Fig. B.3). In each figure, the operators are shown in decreasing order of precedence from top to bottom.

Operator	Type	Associativity
.	member access	left to right
[]	array indexing	
()	function calls	
++	increment	right to left
--	decrement	
-	unary minus	
~	bitwise complement	
!	logical NOT	
delete	delete an array element or object property	
new	create a new object	
typeof	returns the data type of its argument	
void	prevents an expression from returning a value	
*	multiplication	left to right
/	division	
%	modulus	
+	addition	left to right
-	subtraction	
+	string concatenation	

Fig. D.1 JavaScript/JScript/ECMAScript operator precedence and associativity (part 1 of 2).

Operator	Type	Associativity
`<<`	left shift	left to right
`>>`	right shift with sign extension	
`>>>`	right shift with zero extension	
`<`	less than	left to right
`<=`	less than or equal	
`>`	greater than	
`>=`	greater than or equal	
`instanceof`	type comparison	
`==`	equality	left to right
`!=`	inequality	
`===`	identity	
`!==`	nonidentity	
`&`	bitwise AND	left to right
`^`	bitwise XOR	left to right
`|`	bitwise OR	left to right
`&&`	logical AND	left to right
`||`	logical OR	left to right
`?:`	conditional	left to right
`=`	assignment	right to left
`+=`	addition assignment	
`-=`	subtraction assignment	
`*=`	multiplication assignment	
`/=`	division assignment	
`%=`	modulus assignment	
`&=`	bitwise AND assignment	
`^=`	bitwise exclusive OR assignment	
`|=`	bitwise inclusive OR assignment	
`<<=`	bitwise left shift assignment	
`>>=`	bitwise right shift with sign extension assignment	
`>>>=`	bitwise right shift with zero extension assignment	

Fig. D.1   JavaScript/JScript/ECMAScript operator precedence and associativity (part 2 of 2).

Operator	Type	Associativity
()	parentheses	left to right
^	exponentiation	left to right
-	unary minus	left to right
* / \	multiplication division integer division	left to right
Mod	modulus	left to right
+ -	addition subtraction	left to right
&	string concatenation	left to right
= <> < <= > >= Is	equality inequality less than less than or equal greater than greater than or equal object equivalence	left to right
Not	logical NOT	left to right
And	logical AND	left to right
Or	logical OR	left to right
Xor	logical exclusive OR	left to right
Eqv	logical equivalence	left to right
Imp	logical implication	left to right

Fig. D.2   VBScript operator precedence chart .

Operator	Type	Associativity
terms and list operators	**print @array** or **sort (4, 2, 7)**	left to right
->	member access	left to right
++ --	increment decrement	none
**	exponentiation	right to left
! ~ \ + -	logical NOT bitwise one's complement reference unary plus unary minus	right to left
=~ !~	matching negated match	left to right
* / % x	multiplication division modulus repetition	left to right
+ - .	addition subtraction string concatenation	left to right
<< >>	left shift right shift	left to right
named unary operators	unary operators, e.g. **-e** (filetest)	none
< > <= >= lt gt le ge	numerical less than numerical greater than numerical less than or equal numerical greater than or equal string less than string greater than string less than or equal string greater than or equal	none
== != <=> eq ne cmp	numerical equality numerical inequality numerical comparison (returns -1, 0 or 1) string equality string inequality string comparison (returns -1, 0 or 1)	none
&	bitwise AND	left to right

Fig. D.3   Perl operator precedence chart (part 1 of 2).

Operator	Type	Associativity
|	bitwise inclusive OR	left to right
^	bitwise exclusive OR	
&&	logical AND	left to right
||	logical OR	left to right
..	range operator	none
?:	conditional operator	right to left
=	assignment	right to left
+=	addition assignment	
-=	subtraction assignment	
*=	multplication assignment	
/=	division assignment	
%=	modulus assignment	
**=	exponentiation assignment	
.=	string concatenation assignment	
x=	repetition assignment [***]	
&=	bitwise AND assignment	
|=	bitwise inclusive OR assignment	
^=	bitwise exclusive OR assignment	
<<=	left shift assignment	
>>=	right shift assignment	
&&=	logical AND assignment	
||=	logical OR assignment	
,	expression separator; returns value of last expression	left to right
=>	expression separator; groups two expressions	
not	logical NOT	right to left
and	logical AND	left to right
or	logical OR	left to right
xor	logical exclusive OR	

Fig. D.3   Perl operator precedence chart (part 2 of 2).

Bibliography

Alexander, S. "Wireless Web Access." *ComputerWorld* 5 June 2000: 84.

Allen, D. W., *Microsoft Internet Explorer 5 at a Glance,* Redmond, WA: Microsoft Press, 1999

Amor, D. *The E-business (R)Evolution.* New Jersey: Prentice Hall, 2000.

Angel, J., "Video Servers Revisited," *Network Magazine,* September 1999, pp. 56-62

Armstrong, L. "Changing the Cyber House Rules, No-fee access is making the old profit models obsolete." *Business Week* 7 Feb 2000: 46.

Basic Books, Inc. vs. Kinko's Graphics Corp., 758 F. Supp. 1522 (S.D.N.Y. 1991).

Batcheldor, B. "Auction Site Offers New Consumer Electronics." *InformationWeek* 31 January 2000: 82.

Behr, A., "Dazzle 'Em Create your Own Digital Video For The Web," *InternetWeek,* August 2, 1999, pg. 36

Berinato, S. "Feds Sign Off on e-Signatures." *eWeek* 29 May 2000: 20-21.

Bickel, B., "Anatomy of an XML Server," *Web Techniques,* June 1999, pp. 59-64

Blumenthal vs. Drudge, 992 F. Supp. 44 at _ (1998).

Bond, J. "Marketers, Your Stock Has Never Been Higher." *Revolution* March 2000: 55-59.

Booker, E. "Webcams Help Sites Provide Real-time Views of Inventory." *Internet Week* 10 Jan 2000: 15.

Booker, E., "Databases Expand in to E-commerce," *InternetWeek,* April 12, 1999, pg. 9

Borella, M. "Protocol helps stretch IPv4 addresses." *Network World* 17 Jan 2000: 43.

Bouthillier, L., "Synchronized Multimedia on the Web," Web Techniques, September 1998, pp. 53-57

Braginski, L. and M. Powell, *Running Microsoft Internet Information Server,* Redmond, WA: Microsoft Press, 1998

Brust, A. J., "ADO 2.5 Embraces the Web," *Visual Basic Programmers Journal,* November 1999, pp. 105-110

Burns, J., *JavaScript Goodies,* Indianapolis, IN: Macmillan Publishing, 1999.

Campbell, B. and R. Darnell, *Teach Yourself Dynamic HTML In a Week,* Indianapolis, IN: Sams.net Publishing, 1999.

Carr, D. F., "Web Architecture Without the Browser," *Internet World,* April 5, 1999 pg. 15

Catalano, C., "Networking Hardware," *ComputerWorld,* July 12, 1999, Pg. 66

Cauley, L. "A Speed Bump to the Wire Web." *The Wall Street Journal* 17 Feb 2000: B1+.

Child Online Protection Act of 1998 (COPA).

Children's Online Privacy Protection Act of 2000 (COPPA).

Coffee, Peter "XML Removes Last Bars To Online Data Archives," PC Week, January 25, 1999, pg. 38

Cohn, M., "An E-commerce E-primer For The E-perplexed," *ComputerWorld,* October 4, 1999, pg. 34

Cole-Gomolosky, B. "E-commerce education brings IT, Business Together in Classroom." *Computer-World* 2 Aug 1999: 32.

Communications Decency Act of 1996 (CDA).

Compuserve vs. Cyber Promotions, 962 F. Supp. 1015 at _ (S.D. Ohio 1997).

Copage, E. "Web Sites Clamor for Teens Attention." *The New York Times* 13 April 2000: E10.

Cox, J., T. Cox and E. Heydrick, *Quick Course in Microsoft Explorer 5,* Redmond, WA: Microsoft Press, 1999

Craig, R., "The Role of XML," *ENT,* May 5, 1999, pp. 38-40

Cubby vs. Compuserve, 776 F. Supp. 135 at _ (1991).

Cunningham, L. "Marketing: Only Performance Counts." *Inter@ctive Week* 1 May 2000: 116.

Cusumano, M., "Mozilla Gambit Reveals Risks of Open Sourcing," *ComputerWorld,* October 18, 1999, pg. 34

Cyber Promotions Inc. vs. America Online, 948 F. Supp. 436 at _ (Ed. Pa. 1996).

David, M., "SQL-Based XML Structure Data Access," *Web Techniques,* June 1999, pp. 67-72

Dawson, F., "Internet Video Getting Up to Speed," *Inter@ctive Video,* September 6, 1999, pp. 44-48

De Soto, R., "Creating an Active Internet Presence: A New Alternative," *Telecommunications,* December 1998, pp. 73-75

Deckmyn, D. "Wireless Web Access will be Vital." *ComputerWorld* 10 Jan 2000: 81.

Deitel, H. *An Introduction to Operating System*s. Second Edition, Reading, MA: Addison Wesley, 1990.

Dell, T., *Dynamic HTML for Webmasters,* San Diego, CA: Academic Press, 1999.

DiDio, L. "Private-key Nets Unlock e-Commerce." *Computerworld* 16 March 1998: 49-50.

Digital Millenium Copyright Act (DMCA).

Disbrow, S., "Your Own Private Idaho," *Java Report,* April 1999, pp.66-69

Dragan, R. "Microsoft Site Server 3.0 Commerce Edition." *PC Magazine* 14 December 1998: `<www.zdnet.com/filters/printerfriendly/0,6061,374713-3,00.html>`.

Duncan, A., "All The World's an Auction," *Business Week,* February 8, 1999, pp. 120-123

Duvall, M. "E-Marketplaces Getting Connected" *Inter@ctive Week* 10 Jan 2000: 40-46.

Eddy, S. E., *XML in Plain English,* Foster City, CA: IDG Books Worldwide, Inc., 1998

Encyclopedia Britannica Educational Corp. vs. Crooks, 542 F. Supp. 1156 (W.D.N.Y. 1982).

Estabrook, A. "Drive Customers To Your Web Site." *e-Business Advisor* November 1999: 22-25.

"Everything you always wanted to know about connecting to the Internet but were afraid to ask." *The Boston Globe* 20 Jan 2000: D5.

Fan, M., J. Stallaert, and B. Whinston, "Creating Electronic Markets," *Dr. Dobb's Journal,* November 1998, pp. 52-56

FCC vs. Pacifica Foundation, 438 U.S. 726 at 748-751 (1978).

Flanagan, D., *JavaScipt The Definitive Guide,* Sebastopol, CA: O'Reilly & Associates, Inc., 1998

Fletcher, J. "The Great E-Mortgage Bake-Off." *The Wall Street Journal* 2 June 2000: 12.

Floyd, M., "Extreme Markup," *Web Techniques,* July 1998, pp. 38-41

Fomichev, M., "HTML Help in Distributed Environments," *Dr. Dobb's Journal,* October 1998, pg. 102

Ford, W., and M. Baum. *Secure Electronic Commerce: Building the Infrastructure for Digital Signatures and Encryption.* Upper Saddle River, NJ: Prentice Hall, 1997.

Fuchs, M., "Why is XML Meant For Java," *Web Techniques,* June 1999, pp. 42-48

Furchgott, R. "Web to go—Sort of. Today's Net phones are OK for email, but surfing is a chore." *Business Week* 14 Feb 2000: 144.

Garfinkel, S. and Spafford, G. *Web Security and Commerce.* Cambridge, MA: O'Reilly, 1997.

Gaskin, J., "XML: user-Friendly Office Format," *Inter@ctive Week,* January 11, 1999

Gerber, C., "Transaction Servers," *ComputerWorld,* May 17, 1999, pg. 90

"German Compuserve Judgment," <**www.qlinks.net/comdocs/somm.html**>.

Ghosh, A. *E-Commerce Security: Weak Links, Best Defenses.* New York, NY: Wiley Computer Publishing, 1998.

Gibbs, M., "Getting a Handle on RIFF Audio and Video Formats," *Network World,* August 2, 1999, pg. 32

Gibbs, M., "Making Your Web Pages Active," *Network World,* April 12, 1999, pg. 36

Ginsberg vs. New York, 390 U.S. 629 at _ (1968).

Girishankar, S. "Customer Service For Business Partners." *Informationweek* 17 April 2000: 65+.

Goldfarb, C. F. and P. Prescod, *The XML handbook, Upper Saddle River, NJ: Prentice Hall, 1998.*

Goncalves, M. "Consortium Aims for Standards for E-Business." *Mass High Tech* 28 August 1999: 17.

Goncalves, M. *Firewalls: A Complete Guide.*New York, NY: McGraw-Hill, 2000.

Goodman, D., *Dynamic HTML,* Sebastopol, CA: O'Reilly & Associates, Inc., 1998

Goodman, D., *JavaScript Bible*, Foster City, CA: IDG Books Worldwide, Inc., 1998

Graham, I. S., *HTML Sourcebook a Complete Guide to HTML 4.0,* New York, NY: John Wiley and Sons, Inc., 1998.

Gray, D. *The Complete Guide To Associate and Affiliate Programs on the Net: Turning Clicks into Cash.* New York: McGraw-Hill, 2000.

Greene, T. "Voice-Over-DSL turns heads at ComNet." *Network World* 31 Jan 2000: 8.

Guthrie, B. "When Trouble Strikes." PC Novice 11 May 2000: 17.

Hall, M., *CORE Web Programming, Upper Saddle River, NJ: Prentice Hall, 1998.*

Harper and Row Publishers, Inc. v. Nation Enterprises, 471 U.S. 539 (1985).

Hayes, F., "Common Gateway Interface," *ComputerWorld,* July 19, 1999, pg. 74

Hayes, F., "Distributed Component Object Model," *ComputerWorld,* February 12, 1999, pg. 73

Hendrickson, D. "All aboard the e-commerce express" *Mass Tech High* 7-13 Feb 2000: 15.

Hoffman, R., and R. Patt-Corner, "Control Freaks and Java junkies," *Network Computing,* May 17, 1999, pp. 124-126

Holzner, S., *XML Complete,* New York, NY: McGraw-Hill, 1998

Howe, P.J. "Setting Net on its ear. Analysts: Wireless Web is the next big thing, and speech recognition is key." *Boston Globe* 14 Feb 2000:

Hunter J. and W. Crawford., *Java Servlet Programming,* Sebastopol, CA: O'Reilly & Associates, Inc., 1998

Intermatic vs. Toeppen (N.D. Ill. 1996).

Internet Tax Freedom Act.

Jelliffe, R., *The XML & SGML Cookbook, Upper Saddle River, NJ: Prentice Hall, 1998.*

Keen, P.G. "E-commerce: Chapter 2." *ComputerWorld* 13 Sep 1999: 48.

Kepka, A., "Agent Secrets", *ComputerWorld,* January 4, 1999, pg. 23

King, J. "How to B2B." *ComputerWorld* 28 February 2000.

Kippenhahn, R. *Code Breaking.* New York, NY: The Overlook Press, 1999.

Kosiur, D. *Understanding Electronic Commerce.* Redmond, WA: Microsoft Press, 1997.

Kosiur, D. *Understanding Electronic Commerce.* Redmond, WA: Microsoft Press, 1997.

Kuehl, C. "E-mail Marketing, Spam's Good Twin." *Internet World* 1 May 2000: 31-38.

Kwon, R. "Delivering Medical Records, Securely." *Internet World* 10 August 1998: 23.

Laurie B. and P. Laurie., *Apache The Definitive Guide,* Sebastopol, CA: O'Reilly & Associates, Inc., 1999

Leventhal, M., D. Lewis and M. Fuchs, *Designing XML Internet Applications, Upper Saddle River, NJ: Prentice Hall, 1998*

Lindquist, C., "Personalization," *ComputerWorld,* March 22, 1999, pp. 74-75

Majer, A. and M. Dover., "License to Bill," *New Media,* January 1999, pg. 11

Mann-Craik, F. "The Power of Advertising Your Internet Firm." *Tornado-Insider* February 2000: 92-94, 96.

Mansfield, R. and D. Revette, *Visual Interdev Bible,* Foster City, CA: IDG Books Wordwide, Inc., 1998

Marsland, R. "Hidden Cost of Technology." *Financial Times* 2 June 2 2000: 5.

McCormick, G., "The Boston TV Party," *Mass High Tech Journal,* September 6-12, 1999, pp. 1, 20

McFadden, M., "Internet Explorer 5.0: Trading Glitz for a Better UI," *ENT,* May 19, 1999, pg. 42

McGarvey, J. "E-Commerce Drives Bandwidth Needs." *Inter@ctive Week* 8 Nov 1999: 16.

McGrath, S., *XML by Example, Upper Saddle River, NJ: Prentice Hall, 1998*

McKendrick, J., "XML Promises to Enrich the Data Experience," *ENT,* October 7, 1998

McNamara, P. "Emerging Electronic Commerce Standard Passes First Big Test." *Network World* 6 October 1997: 55.

Meade, J., Crowder D. and R. Crowder, *Microsoft Dynamic HTML,* Scottsdale, AZ: The Coriolis Group, Inc., 1998

Megginson, D., *Structuring XML Documents, Upper Saddle River, NJ: Prentice Hall, 1998*

Mellen, S., "It's Future: Web, Web, More Web," *Mass High Tech Journal,* April 19-25, 1999 pg. 27

Methvin, D. W. "How to Succeed in E-Business." *Windows Magazine* August 1999: 98–108.

Miller vs. California, 413 U.S. 15 at 24-25 (1973).

Moody, J., "Scripting Your Way to Better Web Pages," *IT/IS BackOffice,* March 1998, pg. 68

Morgan, C., "MP3," *ComputerWorld,* May 10, 1999, pg. 76

Morganthal, J. P., "Enterprise Messaging with XML," *Component Strategies,* May 1999, pp.54-70

Morris, M. E. S. and J. E. Simpson, *HTML for Fun and Profit,* SunSoft Press, Upper Saddle River, NJ: Prentice Hall, 1998

Moskowitz, R., "The Byways of Digital Certificates," *Network Computing,* May 17 1999, pp. 117-118

Mossberg, W. "A simple little gadget lets you go online without using a PC." *The Wall Street Journal* 27 Jan 2000: B1.

MTV vs. Curry (S.D. N.Y. 1994).

Murphy, K., "Legislation Seeks to Spell Out Legality of Digital Signatures," *Internet World,* April 12, 1999, pp. 23-25

Murry, W. H. and C. H. Pappas, *JavaScript and HTML 4.0, Upper Saddle River, NJ: Prentice Hall, 1999.*

Musciano, C. and B. Kennedy, *HTML The Definitive Guide,* Sebastopol, CA: O'Reilly & Associates, Inc., 1998

Nemzow, M. *Building CyberStores.* New York: McGraw-Hill, 1997.

Orenstein, D., "Active Server Pages Freed From Platform," *ComputerWorld,* May 24, 1999, pg. 64

Ouellette, T., "Digital Wrappers," *ComputerWorld,* April 26, 1999, pg. 79

Ouellette, T., "Spam," *ComputerWorld,* April 5, 1999, pg. 70

Papa, J., M. Brown, C. Caison, P. Debatta and E. Wilson, *Professional ADO RDS Programming with ASP,* Birmingham, UK: Wrox Press Ltd., 1999

Peppers, D., et al. *The One To One Field Book: The Complete Toolkit for Implementing a 1 to 1 Marketing Program.* New York: Bantam Doubleday Dell Publishing Group, Inc., 1999.

Pfaffenberger, B. and A. D. Gutzman, *HTML 4 Bible,* Foster City, CA: IDG Books Wordwide, Inc., 1998

Pfleeger, C. *Security in Computing: Second Edition.* Upper Saddle River, NJ: Prentice Hall, 1997.

Playboy Enterprises, Inc. vs. Frena, 839 F. Supp. 1552 at _ (1993).

Ploskina, B., "XML Builds Bridge for Object Developers," *ENT,* January 20, 1999, pg. 14

Powell, T. and D. Whitworth, *HTML Programmers Reference,* Berkley, CA: Osborn/McGraw-Hill, 1998

Powell, T., L. Jones and D. Cutts, *Web Site Engineering, Upper Saddle River, NJ: Prentice Hall, 1998.*

Powers, S., *Developing ASP Components,* Sebastopol, CA: O'Reilly & Associates, Inc., 1999

Price, D.L. *Online Auctions at* eBay*: Bid with Confidence, Sell with Success.* Rocklin, CA: PRIMA TECH a Division of PRIMA Publishing 1999.

Ranjay G. and Garino J. "Bricks to Clicks." *Siliconindia* June 2000: 75-78.

Reno vs. American Civil Liberties Union, 117 S Ct. 2329 at _ (1997).

Rewick, J.L. "Online Ads Turn to Hand-held Devices." *The Wall Street Journal* 4 Feb 2000: B6.

Riggs, B. "Convergence Culture Shock." *Information Week* 13 Dec 1999: 143.

Rothman, M., "Public-Key Encryption for Dummies," *Network World,* May 17,1999, pg. 35

RSA Laboratories. *"RSA Laboratories' Frequently Asked Questions About Today's Cryptography, Version 4.1."* <**www.rsasecurity.com/rsalabs/faq**> RSA Security Inc., 2000.

RTC vs. Netcom, 907 F. Supp. 1361 at _ (N.D. Cal. 1995).

Rule, J, *Dynamic HTML the HTML Developer's Guide,* Reading, MA: Addison Wesley Longman, Inc., 1999

Sable Communications vs. FCC, 492 U.S. 115 at _ (1989).

Sager, I. "Cyber Crime." *Business Week* 21 February 2000: 37-42.

Sahu, M., "XML Development in Java," *Web Techniques,* June 1999, p. 51-55

Schneier, B. *Applied Cryptography: Protocols, Algorithms and Source Code in C.* New York, NY: John Wiley & Sons, Inc., 1996.

Schwartz, R., "Making a Cookie Jar," *Web Techniques*, December 1998, pp. 28-31

Section 230 of the Telecommunications Act.

Sega Enterprises Ltd. vs. MAPHIA, 857 F. Supp. 679 at _ (N.D. Cal. 1994).

Seybold, P. and R. Marshak. *Customers.com: How To Create A Profitable Business Strategy For The Internet and Beyond.* New York: Random House, Inc., 1998.

Sherif, M. *Protocols for Secure Electronic Commerce.* New York, NY: CRC Press, 2000.

Shmuller, J., *Dynamic HTML Master The Essentials,* Alameda, CA: Sybex Press, 1998

Siebel, T. and P. House. *Cyber Rules: Strategies for Excelling At E-Business.* New York: Random House, Inc., 1999.

Sliwa, C., "Secure Sockets Layer," *ComputerWorld,* May 31, 1999, pg. 69

Smith, R. *Internet Cryptography.* Reading, MA: Addison Wesley, 1997.

Smyth v. Pillsbury Co., 914 F. Supp. 97 at _ (Ed. Pa. 1996).

Spangler, T. "Home Is Where The Hack Is." *Inter@ctive Week* 10 April 2000: 28-34.

Spangler, T. "Wireless Web: Wait a Second." *Inter@ctive Week* 24 Jan 2000: 66.

Spangler, T., "Racing Toward the Always On Internet," *Inter@ctive Week,* September 6, 1999, Pp. 7-12

"Special Report: CRM e-volves." *Global Technology Business* May 2000: 48+.

"Special Report: Online Marketing: Customer Conundrum." *Upside* April 2000: 145+.

Stedman, C. "Moving to Web Applications? Don't Forget Bandwidth." *ComputerWorld* 31 Jan 2000: 59.

Steve Jackson Games, Inc. v. U.S. Secret Service (5th Cir. 1994).

Stratton Oakmont vs. Prodigy, 23 Media L. Rep. 1794 at _ (1995).

Sullivan, K., "Digital Certificates Grow Up," *PC Week*, March 1, 1999, pg. 143

Symoens, J. "Site Server is a fine set of tools for Web site building." *InfoWorld* 26 January 1998: <**www.infoworld.com**>.

Taylor, S., "Ready, Set, Script," *Application Development Trends,* January 1999, pp. 57-59

Teague, S., *DHTML for the World Wide Web, Berkeley,* CA: Peachpit Press, 1998

Tiernan, B. *E-tailing.* Chicago: Dearborn Financial Publishing, Inc., 2000.

Toub, S., "How to Design a Table of Contents," *Web Techniques,* February 1999, pp.16-21

Tucker, A., "Using Internet Explorer's HTML Parser," *Dr. Dobbs Journal,* August 1999, Pg. 82

U.S. vs. LaMachiaa, 871 F. Supp. 535 at _ (D. Mass. 1994).

United States Constitution.

United States v. Thomas, 74 F3d 701 at _, cert.denied, 117 S Ct. 74 (1996).

Viajayan, J. "Wireless Markup Language." *ComputerWorld* 24 Jan 2000: 62.

Vonder Harr, S., "Music On the Web is About to Go Live," *Inter@ctive Week,* July 26 1999, pg. 37

Wagner, M. "Google Bets Farm on Linux." *InternetWeek* 5 June 2000: 1, 84.

Walker, R. "Get Big Fast." *PC Novice* 11 May: 210-212.

Wallace, B. "The Internet Unplugged, Wireless Net Access is Creating New Opportunities." *InformationWeek* 13 Dec 1999: 22.

Walsh, B. "Building A Business Plan For An E-Commerce Project." *Network Computing* 15 September 1998: 69-71+.

Waters, J. "Getting Personal On The Web." *Application Development Trends* May 2000: 25-32.

Weber, J. "Clicks and Mortar." *The Industry Standard 2* August 1999: 5.

Weinman, L., "Fireworks vs. ImageReady," *Web Techniques,* September 1998, pp. 14-18

Weissinger, A. K., *ASP in a Nutshell,* Sebastopol, CA: O'Reilly & Associates, Inc., 1999

Whyman, B. "Crossing the Fault Line." *The Industry Standard* 21 Feb 2000: 129.

Williams, A., Barber, K. and P. Newkirk., *Active Server Pages Black Book,* Scottsdale, AZ: The Coriolis Group, Inc., 1998

Wilson, T. "Up Next: An Exchange Of Exchanges." *Internet Week* 10 April 2000: 25.

"Wireless Emerges as Remote Access Option." *InternetWeek* 1/10/2000, pg 12, author: C. Moozakis.

Witherspoon, C., *Microsoft Internet Explorer 5 Fast & Easy,* Rockilin,CA: Prima Tech Publishing, 1999

Wrixon, F. *Codes, Ciphers & Other Cryptic & Clandestine Communication* New York, NY: Black Dog & Leventhal Publishers, 1998.

Zeichick, A. and L. O'Brien, "Are You Being Web Served?," *Internet Week,* April 12, 1999, pp. 36-42

Zeichick, A., "Lesson 124: XML and XSL" *Network Magazine,* November 1998, pp. 23-24

Zeran vs. America Online, Inc., 129 F. 3d 327 at _ (1997).

Zimmerman, C. "Akamai's Intervu Deal Bolsters Content-Delivery Capabilities" *Internet Week* 14 Feb. 2000: 8.American Civil Liberties Union of Georgia v. Miller, 1:96-cv-2475-MHS (N.D. Ga. 1997).

Zippo Mfg. Co. vs. Zippo Dot Com, Inc. (W. Pa. 1997).

Index

The DEITEL & DEITEL Suite of Products...

BOOKS

e-Business & e-Commerce How to Program

BOOK / CD-ROM

©2000, 1200 pp., paper bound w/CD-ROM (0-13-028419-X)

This innovative new book in the *How to Program* series explores programming technologies for developing Web-based e-business and e-commerce solutions, and covers e-business and e-commerce models and business issues. Readers learn a full range of options, from "build-your-own" to turnkey solutions. The book examines a significant number of the top "dot-com" businesses (such as Amazon, eBay, Priceline.com, etc.), explaining the technical details about how to build successful e-business and e-commerce sites and their underlying business premises. Learn how to implement the dominant e-commerce models—shopping carts, auctions, naming-your-own-price, comparison shopping and bots/intelligent agents—by using the markup languages, scripting languages and database, security, and online payment technologies explained in the text.

Internet & World Wide Web How to Program

BOOK / CD-ROM

©2000, 1200 pp., paper bound w/CD-ROM (0-13-016143-8)

The World Wide Web is exploding, and with it is arriving a new breed of multi-tiered, Web-based applications. This innovative new book in the Deitels' *How to Program* series presents traditional introductory programming concepts using the new scripting and markup languages of the Web. Now you can learn programming fundamentals "wrapped in the metaphor of the Web." Employing the Deitels' signature "live-code" approach, the book covers markup languages (HTML, Dynamic HTML), client-side scripting (JavaScript) and server-side scripting (VBScript, Active Server Pages). Advanced topics include XML and developing e-commerce applications. Updates are regularly posted to **www.deitel.com** and the book includes a CD-ROM with software tools, source code, and live links.

Java How to Program Third Edition

BOOK / CD-ROM

©2000, 1200 pp., paper bound w/CD-ROM (0-13-012507-5)

This edition of the world's best-selling Java textbook incorporates Sun Microsystems' latest version of Java, the Java 2 Software Development Kit (J2SDK). The introduction of new functionality in this upgrade has made Java a friendlier and more accessible programming language. Reviewers of the book were unanimous in praising the Deitels for making the best use of these enhancements and writing the introductory chapters in a very engaging and accessible style. Designed for beginning through intermediate readers, it uses the Deitels' proven "live-code" approach with hundreds of complete working programs, valuable programming tips, more than 16,000 lines of code and over 1400 interesting and challenging exercises. The graphical user interface examples use Sun's new Swing GUI components. The authors have added significant coverage of JDBC, JavaBeans, RMI, Servlets, Java 2D, Java Media Framework, Collections, Serialization, Inner Classes and other topics. Includes several examples and projects on multi-tier, client/server systems development. The CD-ROM contains a complete Java Integrated Development Environment, source code for all examples in the text, and hyperlinks to valuable Java demos and resources on the Internet.

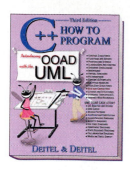

C++ How to Program
Third Edition

BOOK / CD-ROM

©2001, 1230 pp., paper
(0-13-089571-7)

The world's best-selling C++ text teaches programming by emphasizing structured and object-oriented programming, software reuse and component-oriented software construction. This comprehensive book uses the Deitels' signature "live-code" approach, presenting every concept in the context of a complete, working C++ program followed by a screen capture showing the program's output. It also includes a rich collection of exercises and valuable insights into common programming errors, software engineering observations, portability tips and debugging hints. The Third Edition includes a new case study that focuses on object-oriented analysis and design with the UML and illustrates the entire process of object-oriented analysis and design from conception to implementation. In addition, it adheres to the latest ANSI/ISO C++ standards. The accompanying CD-ROM contains Microsoft® Visual C++ 6.0 Introductory Edition software, source code for all examples in the text and hyperlinks to C++ demos and Internet resources.

Getting Started with Microsoft® Visual C++™ 6 with an Introduction to MFC

©2000, 200 pp., paper (0-13-016147-0)

This exciting new book is intended to be a companion to the ANSI/ISO standard C++ best-selling book, *C++ How to Program, Second Edition*. Learn how to use Microsoft's Visual Studio 6 integrated development environment (IDE) and Visual C++ 6 to create Windows programs using the Microsoft Foundation Classes (MFC). The book includes 17 "live-code" Visual C++/MFC programs with screen captures, dozens of tips, recommended practices and cautions and exercises accompanying every chapter. It includes coverage of Win32 and console applications, online documentation and Web resources, GUI controls, dialog boxes, graphics, message handling, the resource definition language and the debugger.

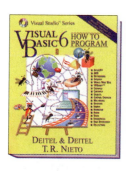

Visual Basic® 6 How to Program

BOOK / CD-ROM

©1999, 1015 pp., paper
bound w/CD-ROM
(0-13-456955-5)

Visual Basic 6 is revolutionizing software development for conventional and Internet/Intranet-based applications. This text explains Visual Basic 6's extraordinary capabilities. Part of the Deitels' *Visual Studio* series, this book uses the Deitels' "live-code" approach to cover Internet/Intranet, World Wide Web, VBScript, ActiveX, ADO, multimedia, animation, audio, video, files, database, networking, graphics, strings, data structures, collections, GUI and control creation. The accompanying CD-ROM contains Microsoft's *Visual Basic 6 Working Model Edition* software, source code and hyperlinks to valuable Visual Basic resources.

C How to Program
Third Edition

©2001, 1200 pp., paper
(0-13-089572-5)

Highly practical in approach, the Third Edition of the world's best-selling C text introduces the fundamentals of structured programming and software engineering and gets up to speed quickly. This comprehensive book not only covers the full C language, but also reviews library functions and introduces object-based and object-oriented programming in C++ and Java, as well as event-driven GUI programming in Java. The Third Edition includes a new 250-page introduction to Java 2 and the basics of GUIs, and the introduction to C++ has been condensed to approximately 250 pages and updated to be consistent with the most current ANSI/ISO C++ standards. Plus, icons throughout the book point out valuable programming tips such as Common Programming Errors, Portability Tips and Testing and Debugging Tips.

BOOK/MULTIMEDIA PACKAGES

These complete packages include books and interactive multimedia CD-ROMs, and are perfect for anyone interested in learning Java, C++, Visual Basic, Internet/World Wide Web and e-commerce programming. They are exceptional and affordable resources for college students and professionals learning programming for the first time or reinforcing their knowledge.

The Complete Internet & World Wide Web Programming Training Course

BOXED SET

©2000, boxed book and software
(0-13-085611-8)

Includes the book *Internet & World Wide Web How To Program* and the fully interactive browser-based *Internet & World Wide Web Programming Multimedia Cyber Classroom* CD-ROM that features:

- Hundreds of programs that can be run inside a browser
- Over 12 hours of audio explaining key Internet programming concepts
- Hundreds of exercises—many solved
- An integrated course completion and assessment summary feature to help you monitor your progress
- Full-text searching, hyperlinking and more
- Hundreds of tips, terms and hints
- Master client- and server-side Programming, including JavaScript, VBScript, ActiveX, ASP, SQL, XML, database and more!

Runs on Windows 95, 98, NT and Windows 2000

The Complete e-Business & e-Commerce Programming Training Course

BOXED SET

©2000, boxed book and software
(0-13-089549-0)

Includes the book *e-Business & e-Commerce How To Program* and the fully interactive *e-Business & e-Commerce Programming Multimedia Cyber Classroom* CD-ROM that features:

- Over 13 hours of detailed audio descriptions of more than 15,000 lines of fully tested "live code"
- Hundreds of example programs that readers can run with the click of a mouse button
- Practice exams with over 300 test questions
- Hundreds of self-review questions, all with answers
- Hundreds of programming exercises, half with answers
- Hundreds of tips, marked with icons, that show how to write code that is portable, reusable and optimized for performance
- An intuitive browser-based interface that includes full-text searching and hyperlinking

Runs on Windows 95, 98, NT and Windows 2000

The Complete C++ Training Course Third Edition

BOXED SET

©2001, boxed book and software
(0-13-089564-4)

The *Complete C++ Training Course* features the complete, best-selling introductory book *C++ How to Program, Third Edition* and the fully interactive *C++ Multimedia Cyber Classroom* CD-ROM that features:

- 248 complete C++ programs that readers can run with a mouse click
- Over 13 hours of detailed, expert audio descriptions of more than 13,000 lines of fully tested "live code"
- Hundreds of programming exercises, half with answers
- Practice exams with over 300 test questions
- Hundreds of self-review questions, all with answers
- Hundreds of tips, marked with icons, that show how to write C++ code that is portable, reusable and optimized for performance
- Intuitive browser-based interface with full-text searching and hyperlinking

Runs on Windows 95, 98, NT and Windows 2000

The Complete Java 2 Training Course Third Edition

BOXED SET

©2000, boxed set (0-13-085247-3)

This set includes the book *Java How to Program, Third Edition*, a complete Java Integrated development environment, and the fully interactive *Java 2 Multimedia Cyber Classroom* CD-ROM that features:

- 200+ complete Java 2 programs with approximately 12,000 lines of fully tested "live code"
- 1100+ questions and exercises, over half of them with answers
- 400+ helpful hints and tips, marked with icons
- Over 10 hours of audio describing key Java concepts and programming techniques
- A browser-based display engine

Runs on Windows 95, 98, NT and Windows 2000

The Complete Visual Basic 6 Training Course

BOXED SET

©1999, boxed set (0-13-082929-3)

You get the world's number-one VB6 interactive *Multimedia Cyber Classroom* CD-ROM plus a worldwide best-selling VB6 book and Microsoft's *VB6 Working Model Software*—ideal for experienced VB5, C/C++ and Java programmers as well as for new programmers interested in VB6's latest features.

- Over six hours of audio explaining key VB6 concepts
- Hundreds of VB6 programs with thousands of lines of fully tested code
- Hundreds of interactive programming exercises
- Master ActiveX, objects, TCP/IP networking, VBScript, multimedia, GUIs, data structures, control creation and more!

Runs on Windows 95, 98, NT and Windows 2000

Prentice Hall offers Multimedia Cyber Classroom CD-ROMs to accompany *Java How to Program, Third Edition; C++ How to Program, Third Edition; e-Business & e-Commerce How to Program; Internet & World Wide Web How To Program;* and *Visual Basic 6 How to Program.* If you have already purchased one of these books and would like to purchase a stand-alone copy of the corresponding *Multimedia Cyber Classroom* please call:

1-800-811-0912

For **Java Multimedia Cyber Classroom, 3/E**, ask for product number 0-13-014494-0

For **C++ Multimedia Cyber Classroom, 3/E**, ask for product number 0-13-089562-8

For **e-Business & e-Commerce Cyber Classroom**, ask for product number 0-13-089540-7

For **Internet & World Wide Web Cyber Classroom**, ask for product number 0-13-016842-4

For **Visual Basic 6 Multimedia Cyber Classroom**, ask for product number 0-13-083116-6

International Customers: Please contact your local Prentice Hall office to order.

Coming Fall 2000, the award-winning Deitel & Deitel Cyber Classroom Series will be available from Prentice Hall over the World Wide Web. This is an ideal solution for students and programming professionals who prefer the convenience of Internet delivery to CD-ROM delivery, and who work on platforms not supported by the CD-ROM version of the Cyber Classrooms.

The Web-based Cyber Classrooms will run on any computer that supports version 4 of either Netscape Navigator or Internet Explorer and the free Real Networks RealPlayer version 7 or higher. The Web-based version will require a 56K modem or higher connection to the Internet.

The Web-based Cyber Classrooms will contain all of the features of the CD-ROM versions, including the Deitels' signature "live code" approach to teaching programming languages. All of the audio will be available through the Web, as will the sample program code, programming tips, exercises and so forth.

We are excited to announce enhanced Web-based versions of the Deitel & Deitel Cyber Classroom Series coming in 2001. The enhanced versions will attempt to recreate the experience of being in a live programming seminar. They will contain substantially more media than the current Cyber Classrooms, including extensive use of both audio and video. The enhanced versions will also include synchronous and asynchronous communications tools to support sophisticated instructor-to-student and student-to-student communication.

For more information, please visit **http://www.phptr.com/phptrinteractive**.

Turn back one page for details on the Cyber Classroom CD-ROMs and Complete Training Courses!

For those interested in
Internet/World Wide Web

Internet & World Wide Web How to Program: Open Source Version is a non-Microsoft® specific text that emphasizes Web-based applications development with Apache, Linux, Perl/CGI, PHP, mySQL and DBI.
(0-13-032368-3)

For those interested in
e-Business and e-Commerce

e-Business & e-Commerce for Managers is an upper-level undergraduate/graduate-level business school textbook for nonprogrammers that contains an optional appendix with an extensive introduction to programming.
(0-13-032364-0)

For those interested in
Perl and CGI

Perl is one of the most widely used server-side scripting languages for building Web-based applications. *Perl/CGI How to Program* covers key topics such as Common Gateway Interface (CGI), references, strings and regular expressions, networking, object-oriented programming and the Apache Web Server. *Perl/CGI How to Program* also includes introductory chapters on two other popular scripting languages: PHP and Python.
(0-13-028418-1)

For those interested in
XML

XML is revolutionizing application development. XML is believed by many to be the key technology for e-business and e-commerce. *XML How to Program* covers key XML-related technologies such as: Simple API for XML (SAX), Document Object Model (DOM), Document Type Definition (DTD) files, Schema files, Cascading Style Sheets (CSS), Extensible Style Language (XSL), XPointer, XLink, Extensible Query Language (XQL) and XPath. *XML How to Program* also includes extensive e-commerce-related case studies.
(0-13-028417-3)

For those interested in
Java

Advanced Java How to Program is designed to be used in upper-division courses. The key focus of this book will be Enterprise Java and will include in-depth coverage of JDBC, the Web, Java Security, Java XML, Java Commerce and more.
(0-13-089560-1)

For those interested in
Microsoft® Visual Basic

Visual Basic 7 How to Program features enhanced treatment of database, Internet, Web, e-Business/e-Commerce, XML, BizTalk™, SOAP and DNA strategies. It is designed to accompany Microsoft's *Visual Studio 7.*
(0-13-029363-6)

For those interested in
Microsoft® Visual C++

Getting Started with Microsoft Visual C++ 7 with an Introduction to MFC is designed to accompany Microsoft's *Visual Studio 7*, and is available as a stand-alone publication and in an attractively priced Value Pack wrapped with *C++ How to Program, Third Edition*.
(0-13-032876-6)

Turn the page to find out more about Deitel & Associates!

License Agreement and Limited Warranty

The software is distributed on an "AS IS" basis, without warranty. Neither the authors, the software developers, nor Prentice Hall make any representation, or warranty, either express or implied, with respect to the software programs, their quality, accuracy, or fitness for a specific purpose. Therefore, neither the authors, the software developers, nor Prentice Hall shall have any liability to you or any other person or entity with respect to any liability, loss, or damage caused or alleged to have been caused directly or indirectly by the programs contained on the media. This includes, but is not limited to, interruption of service, loss of data, loss of classroom time, loss of consulting or anticipatory profits, or consequential damages from the use of these programs. If the media itself is defective, you may return it for a replacement. Use of this software is subject to the Binary Code License terms and conditions at the back of this book. Read the licenses carefully. By opening this package, you are agreeing to be bound by the terms and conditions of these licenses. If you do not agree, do not open the package.
Please refer to end-user license agreements on the CD-ROM for further details.

Using the CD-ROM

The contents of this CD are designed to be accessed through the interface provided in the file **AUTORUN.EXE**. If a startup screen does not pop up automatically when you insert the CD into your computer, double click on the icon for **AUTORUN.EXE** to launch the program or refer to the file **README.TXT** on the CD.

Contents of the CD-ROM

- Microsoft® Internet Explorer 5
- Microsoft® Agent 2.0
- Megalux Ultimate Paint v1.9 Freeware
- W3C® Amaya 3.2.1
- CUESoft EXml Editor
- Jumbo v0.1
- AspTear 1.0
- ActiveState ActivePerl™ 5.6
- Adobe® Acrobat® Reader 4
- Live links to websites mentioned in the book *e-Business and -Commerce How to Program*
- Live code examples from the book *e-Business and -Commerce How to Program*

Software and Hardware System Requirements

- Intel Pentium 133 MHz or faster processor (200 MHz recommended)
- Microsoft Windows 95 or later, or
- Microsoft Windows NT 4.0 (or later)
- 24 Mb RAM for Windows 95 or later (48 MB recommended)
- 32 Mb for Windows NT 4.0 or later (48 MB recommended)
- CD-ROM drive
- Internet connection